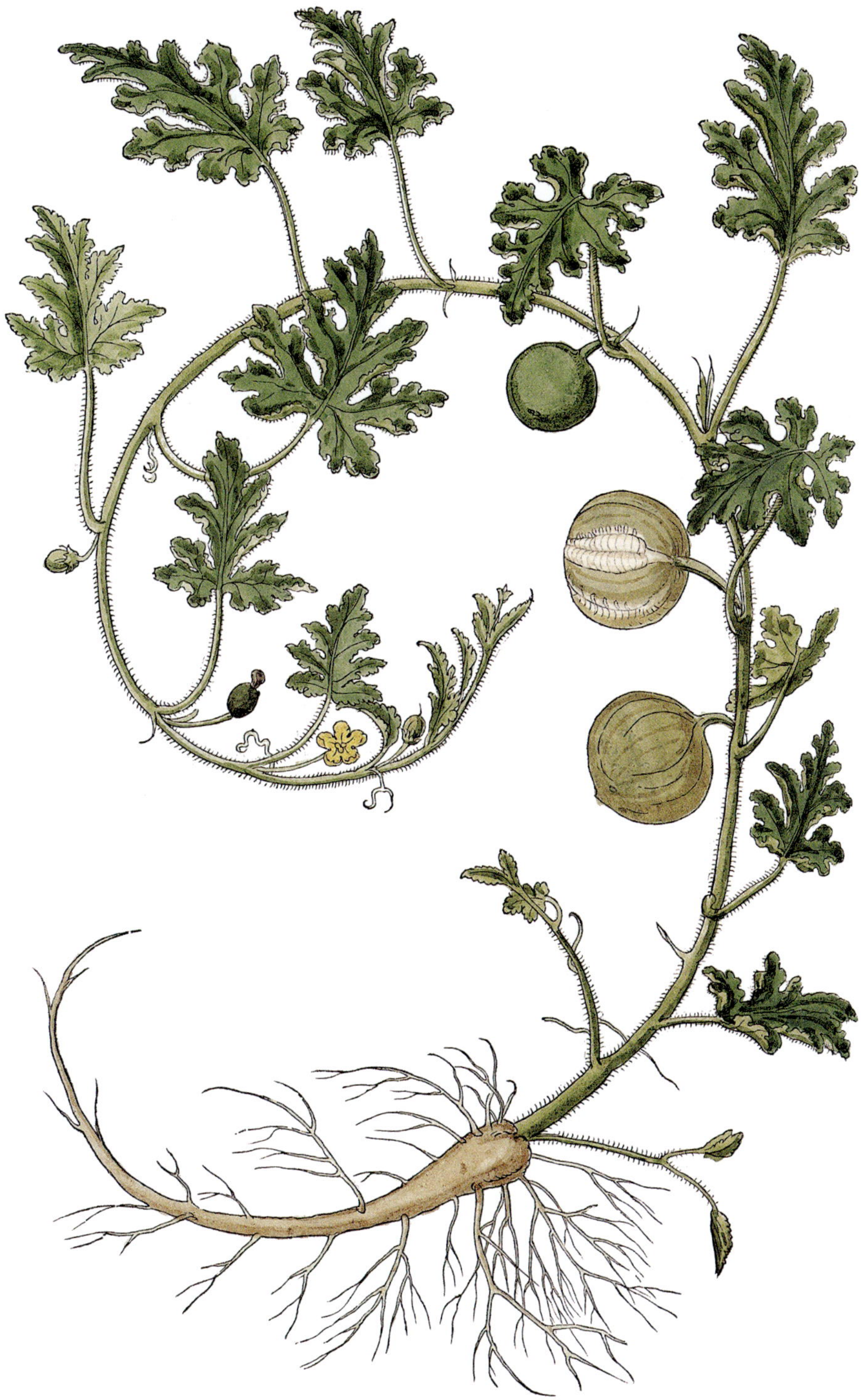

D. Leonhart Fuchs/seins alters im XLII. Jar.

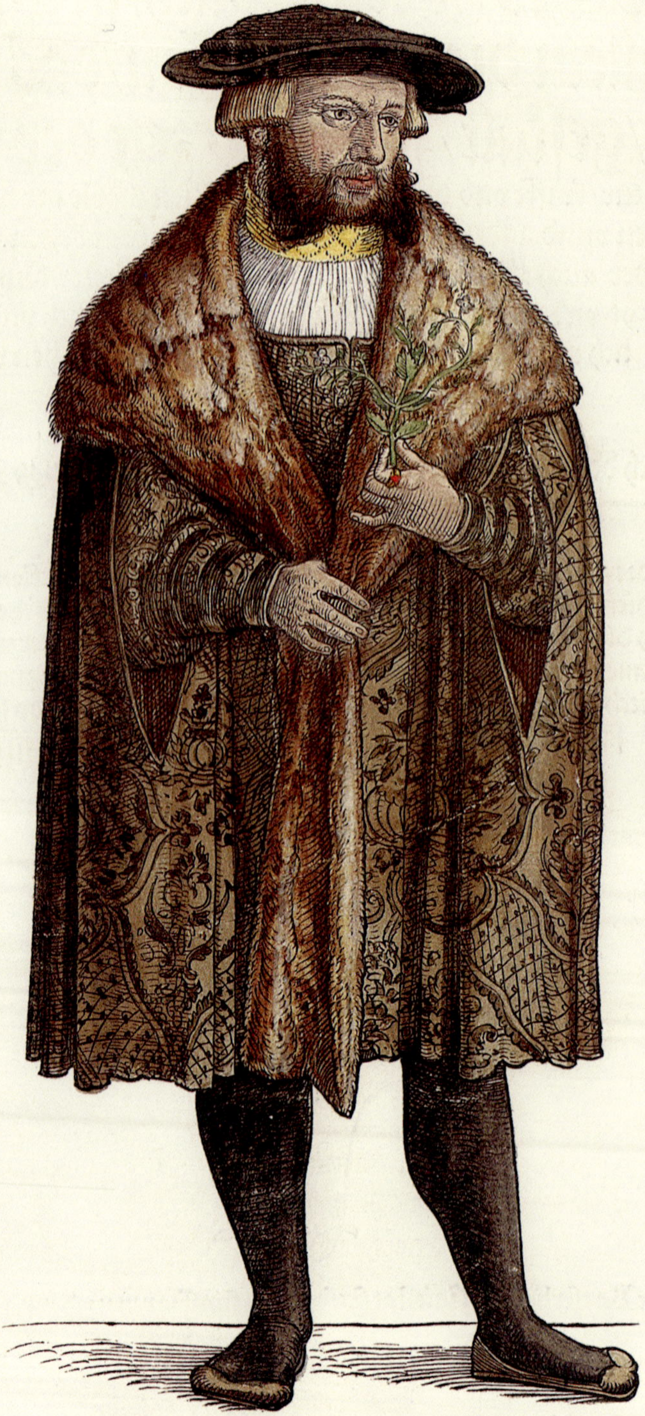

LEONHART FUCHS

The NEW HERBAL

DAS *NEW KREÜTERBUCH*
LE NOUVEL HERBIER

THE
COLOURED EDITION
OF 1543

Essay
KLAUS DOBAT

Description of Plants
WERNER DRESSENDÖRFER

This volume is based on the copy of the
STADTBIBLIOTHEK ULM

TASCHEN

New Kreüterbůch/ in welchem nit allein die gantz histori/ das ist/ namen/ gestalt/ statt vnd zeit der wach-

sung/ natur/ krafft vnd würckung/ des meysten theyls der Kreüter so in
Teütschen vnnd andern Landen wachsen/ mit dem besten vleiß beschri/
ben/ sonder auch aller derselben wurtzel/ stengel/ bletter/ blůmen/ samen/
frücht/ vnd in summa die gantze gestalt/ allso artlich vnd kunst/
lich abgebildet vnd contrafayt ist/ das deßgleichen vor/
mals nie gesehen/ noch an tag kom̃en.

Durch den hochgelerten Leonhart Fuchsen der artzney Doctorn/
vnnd derselbigen zů Tübingen Lesern.

Mit dreyen nützlichen Registern/ auß welchen die zwey ersten/ aller kreüter
daruon hierin̄ gehandlet/ Teütsche/ Lateinische vnnd Griechische namen/ auch
deren sich die Apotecker gebrauchen/ begreiffen. Im dritten aber mag man zů al
len kranckheyten vnd gebresten so dem menschen/ vnd auch zum teyl dem
viech/ mögen zůfallen/ vilfeltig artzney vnnd radt eilends finden/
sampt ettlichen andern stucken zur haußhaltung treffen-
lich nütz vnd dienstlich.

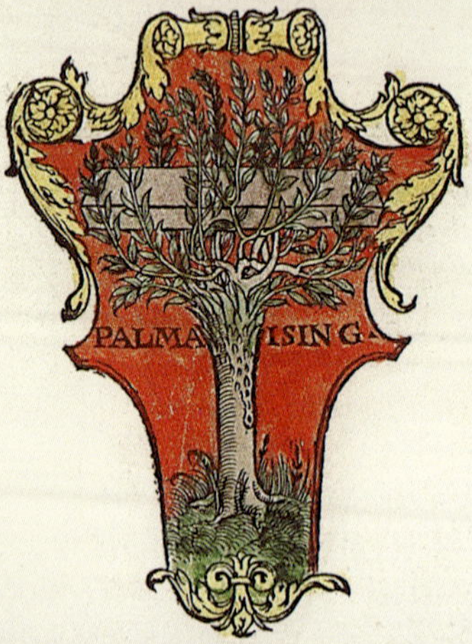

Mit Keyserlicher Maiestat freiheyt/ in fünff jaren weder nach zů tru-
cken/ noch durch ein außzug zů bekürtzen/ bey der peen so die
form/ gleich auffs Register volgend/ außweißt.

Getruckt zů Basell/
durch Michael Ysingrin/ 1 5 4 3.

CONTENTS

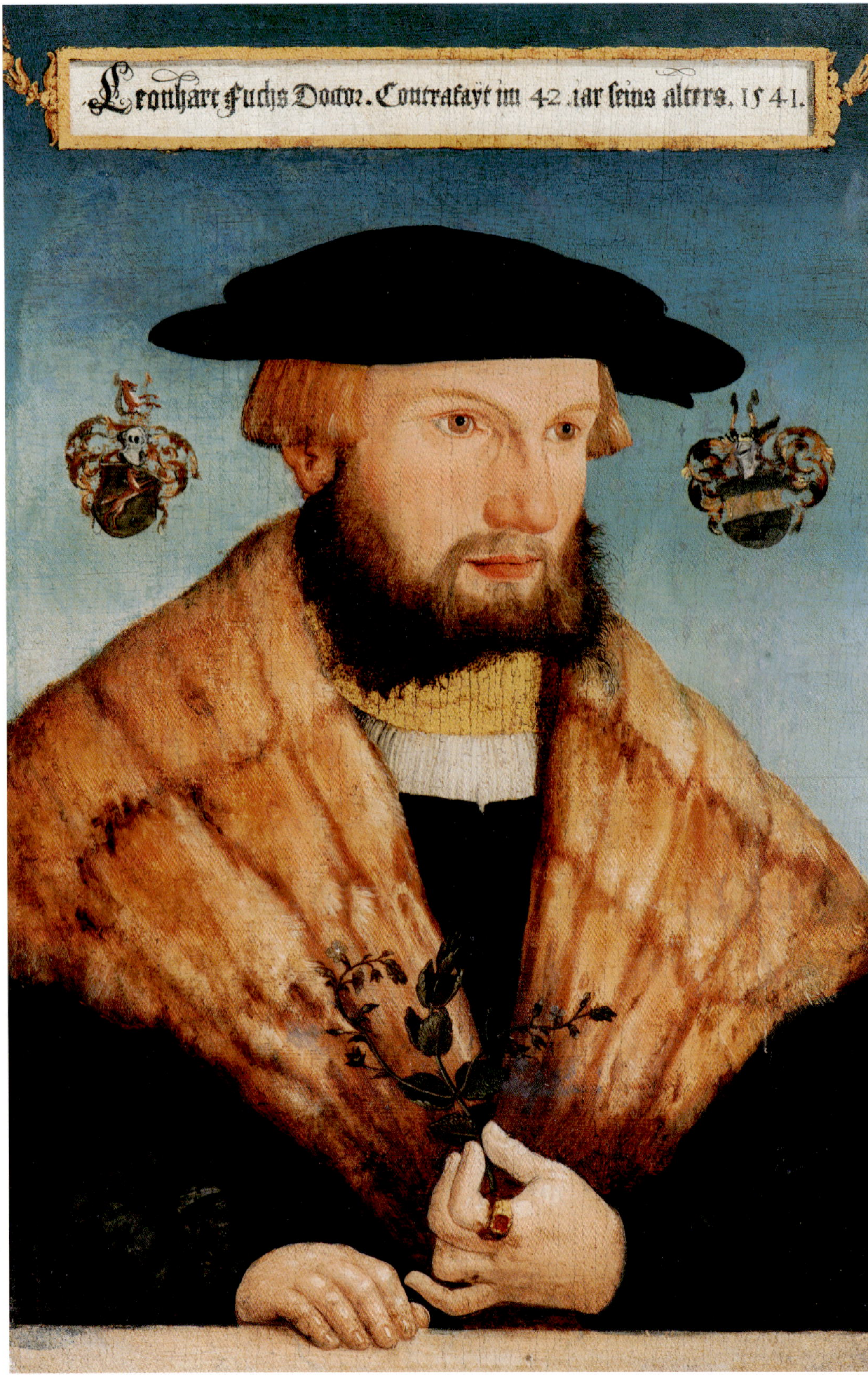
Leonhart Fuchs Doctor. Contrafayt im 42. iar seins alters. 1541.

KLAUS DOBAT

Leonhart Fuchs

Physician and Pioneer of Modern Botany

Leonhart Fuchs (1501–1566) was born in Wemding, an attractive Bavarian town east of the former free imperial city of Nördlingen. He was the youngest son of Johann Fuchs, burgomaster of the town, and his wife, Anna. The precise date of the boy's birth is unknown; there is in fact documentary evidence neither for the often-cited 17 January, nor for 1 January or 17 February, according to Meyer et al. (1999, p. 819).

After the premature death of his father in 1506, young Leonhart received his early education from his mother and grandfather, who had also served as burgomaster of Wemding. As early as 1511, the family sent the clever boy to the grammar school in Heilbronn, where his teacher Conrad soon recognized the boy's unusual talent and zeal. Thus, the following year he entered St. Mary's School (Marienschule) at Erfurt in Thuringia. The school offered an intensive programme in Latin and Greek to prepare the pupils for entrance to the university in Erfurt, at the time one of the most highly respected universities in Germany. In the autumn of 1515, Fuchs matriculated in the Faculty of Arts, and by the winter semester of 1516/1517 had completed his studies as a Baccalaureus artium, a title that qualified him as a teacher. At the age of 17, Fuchs opened a private school in Wemding, but in 1519 he decided instead to continue his studies, this time at the University of Ingolstadt. After passing his master's examination (1521) and receiving the title of Medicinae Doctor in 1524, Fuchs practised medicine for two years in Munich. Here he married Anna Friedberger, a councillor's daughter, who was considered a "well brought-up, honourable girl of respectable family" (Roth 1898, p. 162). Ten children were born to the marriage (four sons and six daughters), two of whom died before being baptized.

From Doctor to University Professor: A Problematic Career

In 1526, Fuchs was offered the chair of medicine at Ingolstadt. Although the university was considered a bastion of Catholicism, Fuchs accepted the distinguished nomination despite the fact that he had already begun to feel drawn to the ideas of Martin Luther. Aside from economic considerations, the decisive motives in accepting the appointment probably lay in the opportunities it offered for teaching and research. As it turned out, however, the young scholar found himself in a milieu of intellectual and religious narrow-mindedness – a

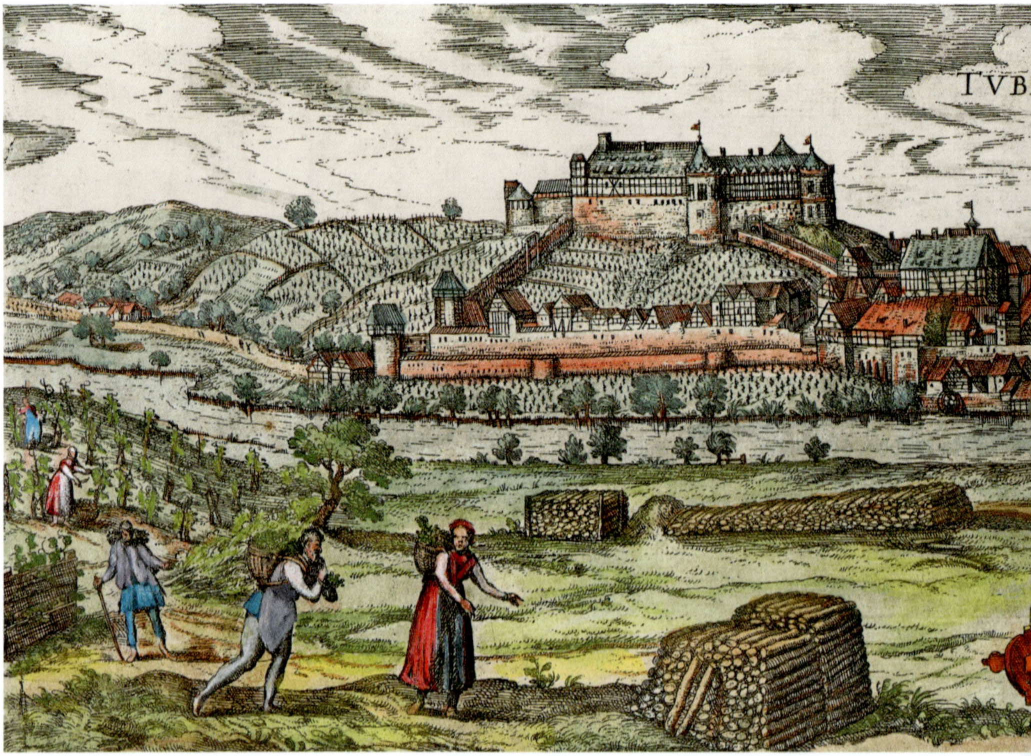

university which spied upon and regulated the religious opinions of its professors. For this reason, two years later Fuchs accepted the position of personal physician at the court of the Protestant Prince Georg, margrave of Brandenburg, in Ansbach (then known as Onoltzbach). Here the future held promise of a professorship at the planned university, and in the meantime, as a respected medical doctor, Fuchs could freely pursue his scientific and literary interests.

Among the various medical publications emerging from these years, Fuchs's *Errata recentiorum medicorum* (Errors of modern doctors) attracted particular attention. With this first work, published in 1530, Fuchs entered into an academic controversy, whose roots reached back to the late 14th century and which had split the medical profession into two camps. On one hand, the so-called "Arabist" physicians based their practice on the traditions of Arab medical teaching; their opponents on the other hand followed the tenets of Greek medicine. With youthful zeal, Fuchs vehemently and rigorously defended the sole

View of/Ansicht von/Vue de Tübingen
Coloured etching from: Georg Braun and Franz Hogenberg, *Beschreibung und Contrafactur der vornembster Stät der Welt,* 6 vols., Cologne 1574–1618, vol. 4, 1594, plate 40

PAGE 6
HEINRICH FÜLLMAURER, *Portrait of/Porträt von/Portrait de Leonhart Fuchs,* 1541
Oil on fir wood, 35.7 × 24.3 cm (14 × 9 5/8 in.), Stuttgart, Landesmuseum Württemberg

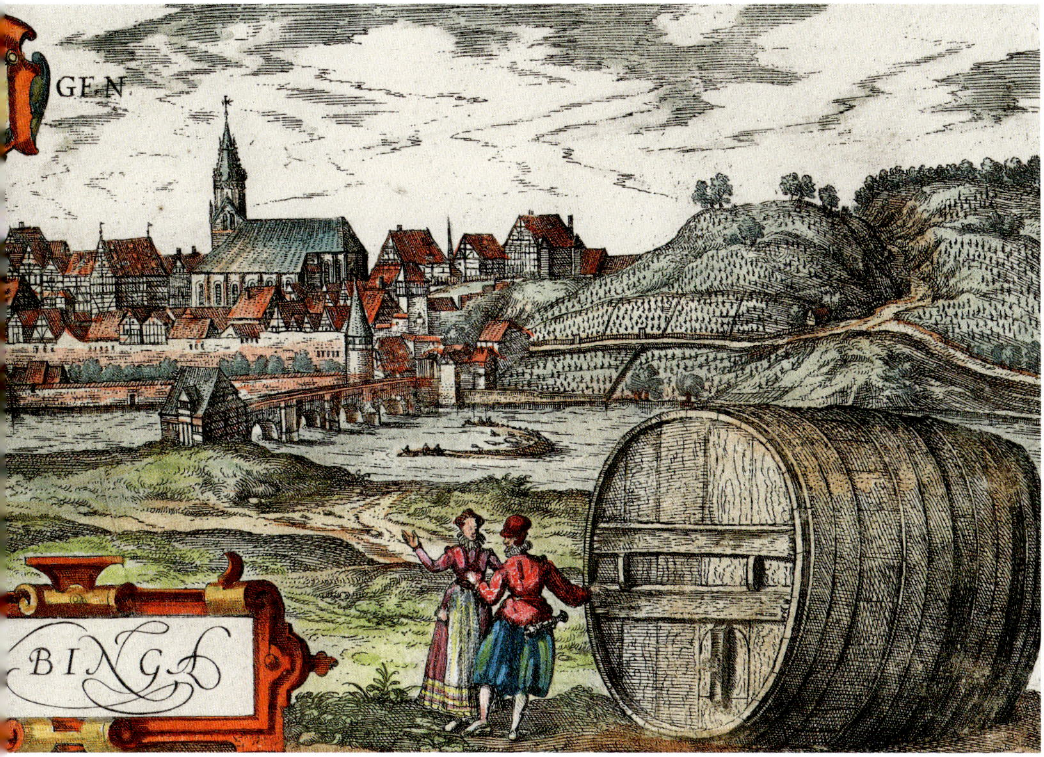

validity of Greek medicine – a position in which his humanistic education and comprehensive knowledge of literature proved of great benefit to him. Armed with numerous quotations, he exposed the contradictions between the two doctrines. In his criticism, however, he often went too far, rejecting even the uncontested merits of Arab medicine or passing over them in silence. On the other hand, Fuchs properly pointed out the false nomenclature of many medicinal plants and the confusion of certain herbal medicines with others, which were therefore unable to produce the medical effects attributed to them. The young scholar's pharmacological-botanical discourses found particular favour with Otto Brunfels (1488–1534), who printed them almost without change in the second volume of his own herbal (*Novi herbarii Tomus II*, 1531). Fuchs also took a challenging stand on controversial therapeutic and anatomical questions. Completely convinced of the correctness of his own opinions, he clearly desired to shake up and reform the system. Fuchs would have been well aware that, in addition to winning the acclaim he desired, his work would inevitably be vehemently rejected by his Arabist-oriented colleagues. In any case, Fuchs quickly made a name for himself.

Among other works, Fuchs completed his first compendium of medicine (*Compendiaria... in medendi artem...*, 1531) in Ansbach. This work, which became one of the most popular medical textbooks, was continually revised and expanded by him over the next two decades. The compendium contributed to his growing fame, as did his translation and commentary to a Greek edition of Hippocrates on epidemic diseases (*Hippocratis medicorum omnium longe principis Epidemiorum liber sextus...*, 1532).

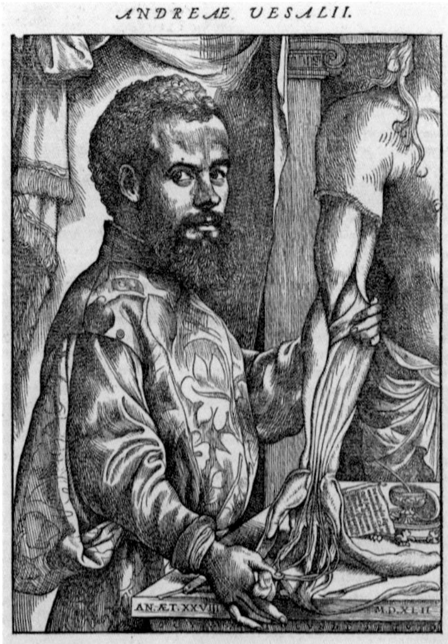

In spite of his success as an author and the recognition he received from the prince, Fuchs nonetheless felt himself increasingly drawn to academic teaching. It was impossible to fulfil this vocation in Ansbach, because the founding of the intended university had been postponed ever further into the future. In spring 1533, Fuchs therefore accepted a second invitation to Ingolstadt. Contrary to his hopes, however, the situation there had hardly changed, and hostilities began anew. When Fuchs, as an uncompromising Protestant, was even forbidden to give lectures (cf. Prantl 1872, p. 197), he resigned his appointment, and in August of the same year returned to his former position in Ansbach at the invitation of Prince Georg. Filled with gratitude that he had thus been rescued "from the jaws of the Ingolstadt sophists" ("ex Ingolstadiensium Sophistarum faucibus"), Fuchs dedicated the second revision of his above-mentioned medical compendium to the margrave in 1535. Although Fuchs remained in as high esteem as ever at the court, when, in the summer of 1534, the plans for founding a university at Ansbach ultimately fell through, he began negotiating an appointment at the University of Tübingen. In this, he received support from the famous Humanist and reformer Philipp Melanchthon (1497–1560), who knew Fuchs from his student days in Ingolstadt.

A New Start in Tübingen

Appointed as "a special scholarly doctor in languages" (Roth 1877, p. 183), Fuchs was specifically commissioned to reorganize the university along humanistic lines by the ruling Duke Ulrich of Württemberg (1487–1550). With Fuchs's appointment to the chair of medicine in Tübingen on 14 August 1535, the doctor had entered a state shaken by the Reformation and assumed a position at a university with a strong Catholic tradition. The revolutionary mood of those years has been impressively described by Decker-Hauff & Setzler (1977). Not only did "Ulrich [mount] a strong attack on the assets of the Church" (p. 69), but at the same time he introduced an inexorable reform of the university, promulgated by the Duke Ulrich Order of 30 January 1535. The decree "recommended all university teachers either to accept the new faith or to leave. On 7 March 1535 the Mass was abolished in Tübingen, and on 9 March the command to convert or leave was repeated" (p. 64).

Fuchs had never in his life been a opportunist; now, with extraordinary diligence, the 34-year-old professor threw himself energetically and self-confidently into the work of reforming both religious and medical traditions. Appropriately timed, as it were, for his

ANDREAS VESALIUS, Frontispiece from / Frontispiz aus / Frontispice de:
De humani corporis fabrica libri septem, Basel, 1534

LEONHART FUCHS

Title pages from / Titelblätter von / Pages de titre de:

Apologia Leonardi Fvchsii Contra Hieremiam Thriuerum Brachelium, Medicum Louaniensem, Hagenau, 1534

Operum Leonharti Fuchsii Medici et Philosophi Excellentissimi, Frankfurt, 1566

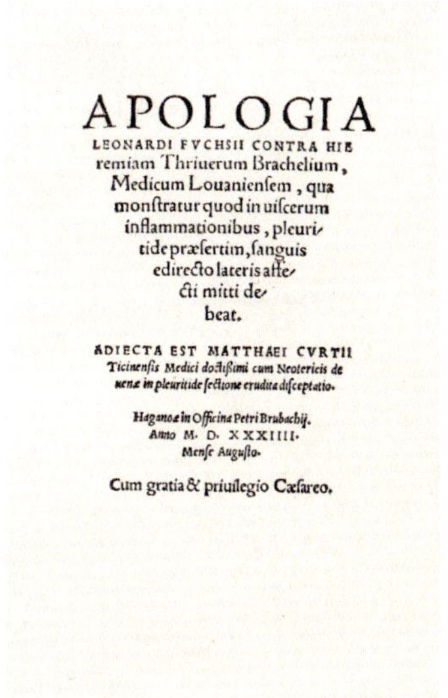

APOLOGIA
LEONARDI FVCHSII CONTRA HIE
remiam Thriuerum Brachelium,
Medicum Louanienſem, qua
monſtratur quod in uiſcerum
inflammationibus, pleuri-
tide præſertim, ſanguis
e directo lateris affe-
cti mitti de-
beat.

ADIECTA EST MATTHAEI CVRTII
Ticinenſis Medici doctiſsimi cum Neotericis de
uenæ in pleuritide ſectione erudita diſceptatio.

Haganoæ in Officina Petri Brubachij.
Anno M. D. XXXIIII.
Menſe Auguſto.

Cum gratia & priuilegio Cæſareo.

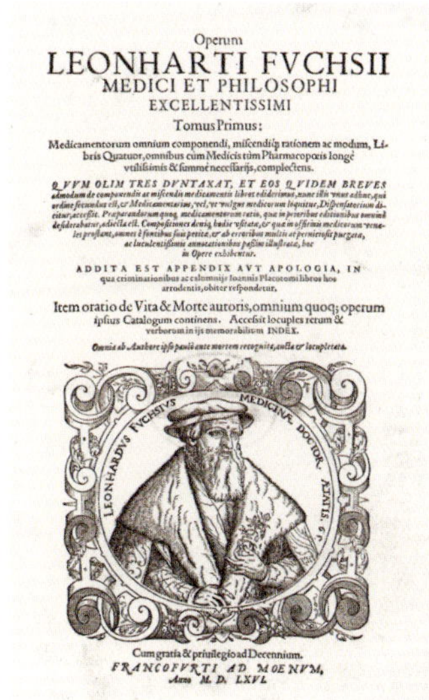

Operum
LEONHARTI FVCHSII
MEDICI ET PHILOSOPHI
EXCELLENTISSIMI
Tomus Primus:
Medicamentorum omnium componendi, miſcendiq́ rationem ac modum, Libris Quatuor, omnibus cùm Medicis tùm Pharmacopœis longè vtiliſsimis & ſummè neceſſarijs, complectens.

QVVM OLIM TRES DVNTAXAT, ET EOS QVIDEM BREVES admodum de componendis ac miſcendis medicamentis libros ediderimus, nunc illis vnus adhuc, qui ordine ſecundus eſt, & Medicamentarius, vel, vt vulgus medicorum loquitur, Diſpenſatorium dicitur, acceſsit. Præparandorum quoq; medicamentorum ratio, quæ in prioribus editionibus omninò deſiderabatur, adiecta eſt. Compoſitiones deniq; hodie vſitatæ, & quæ in officinis medicorum venales proſtant, omnes è fontibus ſuis petitæ, & ab erroribus multis ac pernicioſis purgatæ, ac luculentiſsimis annotationibus paſsim illuſtratæ, hoc in Opere exhibentur.

ADDITA EST APPENDIX AVT APOLOGIA, IN qua criminationibus ac calumnijs Ioannis Placotomi libros hos arrodentis, obiter reſpondetur.

Item oratio de Vita & Morte autoris, omnium quoq; operum ipſius Catalogum continens. Acceſsit locuples rerum & verborum in ijs memorabilium INDEX.

Omnia ab Authore ipſo paulò ante mortem recognita, aucta & locupletata.

Cum gratia & priuilegio ad Decennium.
FRANCOFVRTI AD MOENVM,
Anno M. D. LXVI.

assumption of duties in Tübingen, the expanded version of the *Errata* appeared under the title *Paradoxorum medicinae libri tres*, a work which provided a clear outline of his views. Today, it is hardly possible to imagine the bitterness and prejudice with which Fuchs once again took a stand against Arab medicine. His claim that the Greek authors alone were worthy of credence has an almost poetic ring to it: “Let us therefore return to the sources, and from them draw the pure and unclouded water of medical knowledge.” (Sprengel 1827, p. 151). In this treatise dedicated to the duke, Fuchs even accused Ibn Sina (Lat. Avicenna, 980–1037 AD), one of the most outstanding exponents of Arabic medicine and science, of largely copying from the Greeks. Those of Fuchs’s colleagues who still adhered to the old faith at least knew what lay in store for them.

Already in October 1535 Fuchs was appointed dean, only to observe with grim regret: “Just how carelessly the business of the medical faculty has been administered up to now can best be seen by the fact that my predecessors have not left behind a single word from which posterity might learn of what they have done” (Haller 1927, pp. 133 f.). Between 1536 and 1565, Fuchs served seven terms as rector of the university, and from this position, he was able to put many of his ideas into effect. Together with the like-minded Joachim Camerarius (1500–1574), who had studied with him in Erfurt and remained a lifelong friend, Fuchs formulated the new university statutes of 1538. Within the medical school, they also effected a revolutionary change that clearly bears Fuchs’s signature. Astronomy, which had until then been a required subject, was struck off the curriculum. Furthermore, Arabic writings were “to be drawn upon only extremely sparingly” in comparison to the favoured Greek literature (Fichtner 1967, p. 4). According to the old statutes dating from 1497, “the dissection of a human body should be undertaken at least every three or four years, and during the proceedings [a selection] from the writings of Mundinus should be read aloud.” Fuchs altered the statutes to require at least one dissection per year, which students were now obliged to attend. Furthermore, because the previously required text book by Mundinus (that is, his *Anathomia* of 1316) was “full of

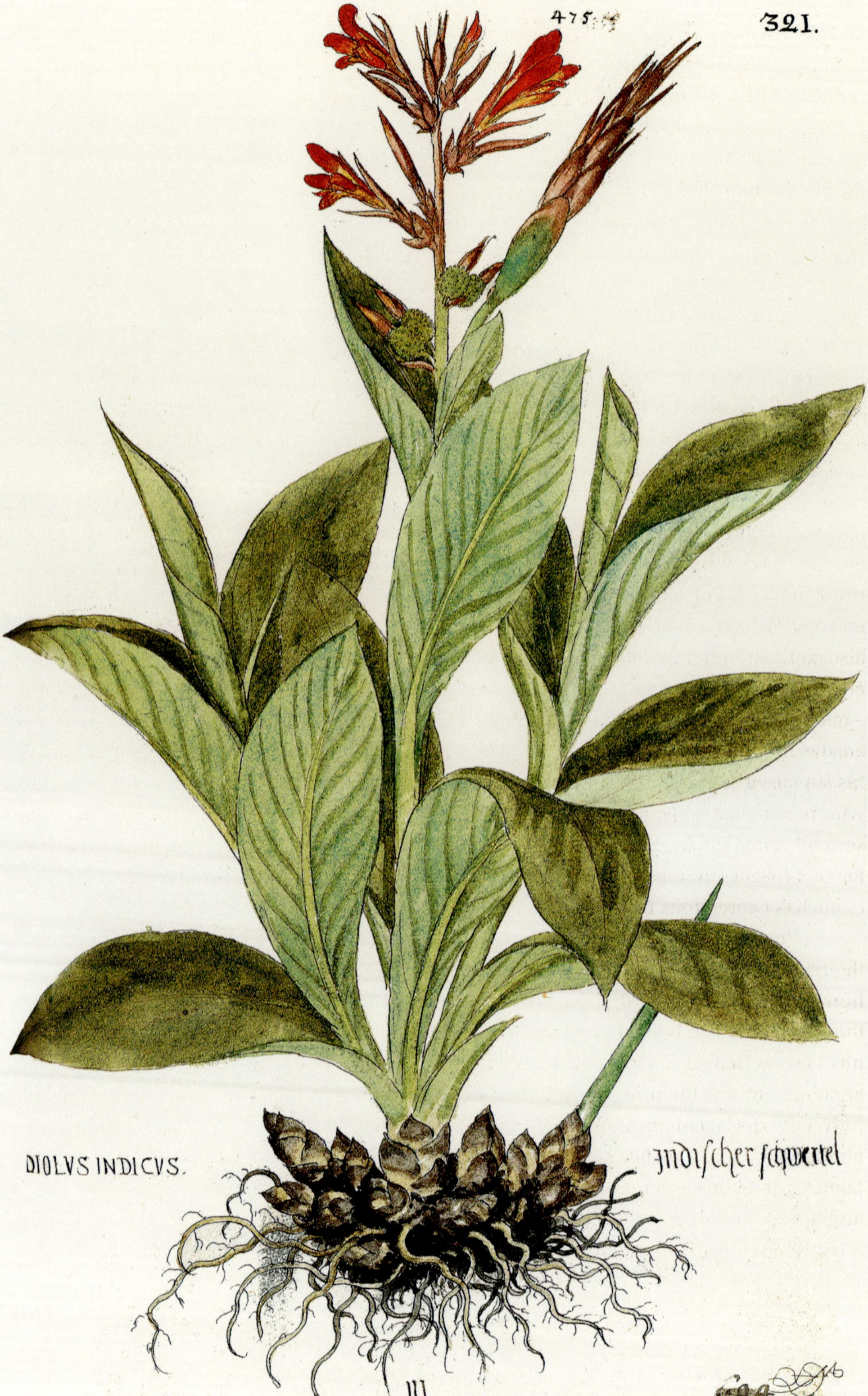

DIOLVS INDICVS.

Indischer schwertel

III.

694

mistakes and errors, one should do without it and instead read the appropriate chapter from Galen during the dissection" (Froriep 1811, pp. 1, 3 f.). Fuchs also lent new impulse to medical research and teaching at our university [Tübingen] through the introduction of *De humani corporis fabrica* by Andreas Vesal (1515–1564). Published in 1543, the work represented the first complete text book on human anatomy in history (p. 10). Likewise, the acquisition of the first human skeleton in 1546/47 no doubt caused a great stir. Acting upon a proposal from Fuchs, Duke Ulrich gave instructions for the purchase of a "man of bones" (at the high price of 30 gulden), to enable the students to learn with their own eyes "how the frame of a human being is formed and [the bones] set one upon another and arranged" (Froriep 1902, p. VI). Not least, Fuchs himself promoted medical education through his numerous scientific publications and his well-attended lectures, which were "famous for their clear organization and their generally understandable, and yet classical, presentation" (Moll 1852, p. 357).

It is obvious that Fuchs had to fight hard to influence the course of these important and forward-looking reforms, and that he therefore found himself in a maelstrom of praise and disapproval. According to Stübler (1928, p. 175), "his stubborn adherence to what he held to be right, together with his chronic fits of intolerance against those who thought differently, had earned him much enmity, even within the university itself." On top of these internal faculty quarrels there were also constant altercations with the court bureaucracy of Duke Ulrich, as a result of which Fuchs's friend and colleague Joachim Camerarius transferred to Leipzig at the end of 1541. Fuchs, who was a committed Lutheran and by no means an ivory-tower scientist, also suffered under the ongoing political and religious turmoil. How much time must these quarrels with scholars outside the university – at times justified, at timed provoked by jealousy – must have cost him. The quarrel with the physician Janus Cornarius (1500–1558) provides a good example. Although both were proponents of Greek medicine, each begrudged the other his supposed or actual success and, over the course of twelve years, they reviled one another with increasing vehemence in their publications. Cornarius accused his opponent of mere scribbling and intellectual theft; Fuchs proclaimed that his rival's works were at most suitable for cockroaches and moths – and these observations were "harmless" in comparison to some of Fuchs's expressions that are not to be found in even the thickest of Latin dictionaries.

Fuchs was furthermore dissatisfied with his material situation in Tübingen, even though, from 1537 onwards, he received a respectable annual income of 200 gulden, making him one of the most highly paid professors at the university. Repeatedly Fuchs entertained thoughts of leaving both city and duchy. As early as 1537/38, he would have had an opportunity to go to Denmark as personal physician at the court of King Christian III. Attached to this appointment was the prospect of becoming professor of medicine at the planned Protestant university in Copenhagen. After his experience in Ansbach, however, Fuchs had grown cautious. In addition, the offer was in fact "miserly," and did not match up to his financial expectations. Citing this as a reason, along with his wife's pregnancy, his large number of children and books, as well as his position and professional duties in Tübingen, Fuchs declined the offer. He even rejected a still more honourable and, in the material sense, highly attractive

LEONHART FUCHS, *Codex Fuchs*, Tübingen, *c.* 1536–1566
Vienna, Österreichische Nationalbibliothek, HAN: Cod. 11117–11125 (9 vols.)
Canna indica (L.) – Indian Shot / Westindisches Blumenrohr / Conflore, Cod. 11122, p. 321

nomination in 1544. Duke Cosimo de' Medici of Florence had offered Fuchs, as the leading German scholar, the directorship of the Botanical Garden at Pisa, which had been founded in 1543 and thus represents the oldest such garden in the world. Rejecting this offer did not come easy to Fuchs, as we learn from a letter to Camerarius dated 1 November 1544; in the end, it was probably religious reservations that tipped the scale (for more details see Stübler 1928, pp. 172 ff.; Fichtner 1968, p. 69; Krafft 1998, p. 137; Meyer et al. 1999, pp. 37 f.).

In spite of this professional and private turbulence, Fuchs still managed to produce an amount of work unimaginable to us today. In addition to his duties as rector; his efforts towards university reform; his theological and political activity; his lectures on anatomy, practical medicine and pharmacology; and, in particular, his own medical practice, Fuchs was also extremely active as an author in his Tübingen years. Among his various works was a five-volume edition of Galen, composed together with Camerarius and other authors (1538). This was succeeded by his own textbooks, translations, commentaries, and polemic treatises (p. 11), all of which are contained in the valuable monograph by Meyer et al. (1999, pp. 633 ff.). In addition, Fuchs dedicated himself with increasing intensity to botanical-pharmaceutical studies.

Commited to Medicine and Botany

Leonhart Fuchs had already openly voiced his support for improvement of botanical instruction in the faculty statutes of 1538. Various of his office-bound colleagues could not have been pleased with the order: "Ultimately in the summer, he [the teacher] should often visit the fields and mountains with the medical students, and in the process observe the appearance of the plants and convey their living aspect, and not, as many have done until now, leave the knowledge of medicinal plants to the apothecaries, those uneducated men, and stupid little women." ("Aestatis denique tempore cum medicinae studiosis rura montesque saepius petat ac plantarum uultum diligenter obseruet illisque uiuas eorundem imagines demonstret, neque ut hactenus consueuere multi, simplicium notitiam seplasiariis illis hominibus rudibus et stultis mulierculis committat," Roth 1877, p. 312).

Supporting his own "recommendations" by good example, he was the first professor of the university to conduct botanical excursions. In Ingolstadt, Fuchs had already recognized the importance of excursions of this sort, which were an ideal complement to academic instruction. That Fuchs placed particular emphasis on maintaining this practice in Tübingen, and moreover diligently pursued his botanical interest on his own hikes, is beyond doubt. He needed a large number of extremely fresh plants not only for his lectures, but in particular for the sake of describing and illustrating them in his two books on medicinal plants. These, far more than his purely medical publications, form the foundation of Fuchs's enduring fame.

Two Superior Works on Medicinal Plants: *De historia stirpium* (1542) and *New Kreüterbuch* (1543)

Fuchs had already begun the manuscript of *Historia*, a history of medicinal plants intended for the academic world, during his days in Ansbach. It may be that the publication of the first volume of Brunfels's *Herbarum vivae eicones* (pp. 38–39) in 1530 spurred Fuchs to quick action in realizing, as soon as possible, plans that he may have already been nursing for quite a while. Whether it was Brunfels's "glaring errors," as maintained by Meyer et al. (1999,

p. 48), or rather the circumstance that there had "not yet been as clean a sweep of Arabic and Arabist authors as [Fuchs] deemed desirable" (Stübler 1928, p. 231), in any case, Fuchs wanted to do the job "better." His book – in addition to providing a thorough evaluation and commentary on the writings of Galen, Dioscorides (pp. 28–29), Hippocrates, Theophrastus, Pliny and other classical authors – was also to include the new plant species that Fuchs had collected. His slow progress with the work is explained by the turbulence of his life during these years: "I have now completed a herbarium, but it has not yet been printed. In it, more than three hundred and fifty herbs are illustrated with their roots, stems, leaves, seeds and flowers – [it] will be a merry book to look at. Have brought it to completion, praise God, with great cost and work," Fuchs wrote in 1538 to Duke Albrecht of Prussia (Voigt 1841, p. 269). Fuchs's claim was a little premature, as it turned out, for the author repeatedly became acquainted with further plants, or encountered others in the area around Tübingen; furthermore, the most recent publications had to be taken into account, such as the *New Kreütter Buch* by Hieronymus Bock (1498–1554; pp. 22–23) published in 1539 or the *Contrafayt Kreüterbuch* by Brunfels dating from 1532–1537 (pp. 25, 32). Thus four more years were to pass before the publication in 1542 of *Historia*, with its more than 900 pages and a total of 511 excellent plant illustrations (p. 41).

The *New Kreüterbuch*, which Fuchs published in 1543, presents us again with the same woodcuts, to which six new plates have been added. For centuries, up to the present day, his herbal has served as a model of botanical book illustration, and the plates in the present edition are also impressive in their high scientific and artistic quality. Despite the astoundingly short preparation time, the German *Kreüterbuch* is in every way the equal of *Historia*. Since *New Kreüterbuch* was intended for a broad readership, it was not simply a question of translating *Historia*. Instead, Fuchs had to undertake a major revision of the text and strive for comprehensibility. In his introduction, which is very much worth reading, he stated that the work should be primarily "useful and appropriate for the general reader seeking to extend his knowledge of herbs" and also rather wickedly pointed out that reading the book would do physicians no harm, either. In accordance with this aim, the scholarly exposition on the knowledge of the ancient doctors is greatly abbreviated, and in return, the botanical plant descriptions are more comprehensive, thus facilitating the recognition and finding of the plants. In addition, Fuchs provides practical hints on soil and location for the sake of cultivating medicinal herbs. It was "good and useful," he opined, "that the herbs should now and again be diligently planted and cultivated in gardens not only by physicians, but also by lay persons and commoners, in order that this same knowledge may daily grow and increase in German lands to such an extent that it may never fall into oblivion." At the same time, Fuchs called attention to the dangers of self-treatment: "even if a person already knows many a herb, this by no means makes him a doctor."

As in *Historia*, so also in *New Kreüterbuch*, the plants were arranged alphabetically according to their Greek names. For almost every species, Fuchs organized the text clearly and methodically into seven sections: "Names," "Kinds," "Form," "Habitat," "Time," "Nature and Temperament," and "Power and Effect." The first section presents the various Greek, Latin and German names, along with the terms usual to the apothecaries. (It should be remarked in passing that Fuchs coined the genera *Campanula*, *Digitalis* and *Ophioglossum*, and that these names, along with many of the scientific plant names introduced by him – *Allium ursinum*,

Angelica sylvestris, Digitalis purpurea, Hordeum distichon, Iris germanica, Origanum vulgare and others – are still in use today.) The second section deals not with the female or male sexual characteristics of the plant, for these were fully unknown at the time, but rather with the relationships between the plants. Usually this included a reference to systems of closely related species or genera or, rarely, to kinds of plants or cultivated forms (see Cap. CXVIII [118], CCLXXXI [281], CCCXX [320]). Understandably, errors also occurred (see Cap. XXX [30], XXXI [31]).

In both books, the third, fourth and fifth sections are of particular interest to the botanist. As was typical of the age, Fuchs naturally drew heavily from the old literature, especially from the *De materia medica* by Dioscorides. The close reliance on this book, a work that Fuchs considered unsurpassed, explains many an inconsistency in Fuchs's own texts, and also the brevity and incompleteness of many plant descriptions. It is quite clear that Fuchs also recognized this deficiency; indeed, in the Foreword to *Historia*, he emphasized that an illustration conveys the image of a plant better than words. *New Kreüterbuch* justly drew criticism – although often in the form of exaggerated carping. Many critics, in concentrating on a scholarly comparison of the texts, undervalued or overlooked Fuchs's own independent achievement, presented in the description of his "new discoveries," i. e. of the various kinds of plants that he failed to find in the Greek writings. In these cases, his familiarity with the given variety is evident, and his own observation provides the basis for the often detailed descriptions of the development and appearance of the plant, data relating to its structural arrangement, and the form and colour of leaves, blossoms or fruit. Fuchs was the first to observe the colour change in the flowers of *Echium vulgare* as the plant ages (see for example Cap. CLV [155]). Similarly, he identified the season when flowers unfold and fruit ripens, pointed to the plant's sensitivity to frost, or its ability to tolerate sun or shade. Also with his astounding breadth of precise information on location and habitat, he treated important ecological aspects of the plants. Moreover, above and beyond his actual "programme," Fuchs did not evaluate the plants exclusively in terms of their suitability for medicine, that is, according to their "nature and complexion" or "power and effect" (see the observations of W. Dressendörfer on this topic, pp. 33 ff.). Instead, he admitted many species into his work, knowledge of whose medicinal value was scanty or entirely lacking, as with the *Tagetes patula* (plate XXVII [27]) for example, *Solanum melongena* (plate CCC [300]) or *Digitalis purpurea* (plate CCCCCXIII [513]). In the case of *Quercus robur* Fuchs directed attention to the Oak Gall (plate CXXIX [129]) caused by the Gall Wasp (*Cynips quercusfolii* L.), and for *Rosa gallica* (plate CCCLXXIIII [374]), he illustrated – presumably for the first time – the galls of the Rose Wasp (*Diplolepis rosae* L.). In chapter CXCVIII [198] on *Morus nigra*, with great enthusiasm he also depicted the development of the silk worm (*Bombyx mori* L.) from the egg, through the pupa to the emerging butterfly. For all his faith in authority, Fuchs, more than any other herbalist before him, succeeded in taking a very broad approach to the observation of the plant organism. Precisely this combination of botanical-medicinal knowledge drawn from the Greeks with the wealth of his own perceptions illustrates the greatness of Fuchs's forward-looking and masterly work.

LEONHART FUCHS, *Codex Fuchs*, Tübingen, *c.* 1536–1566
Vienna, Österreichische Nationalbibliothek, HAN: Cod. 11117–11125 (9 vols.)
Hemerocallis lilioasphodelus (L.) – Lemon Daylily / Gelbe Taglilie / Hémérocalle jaune, Cod. 11118, p. 109

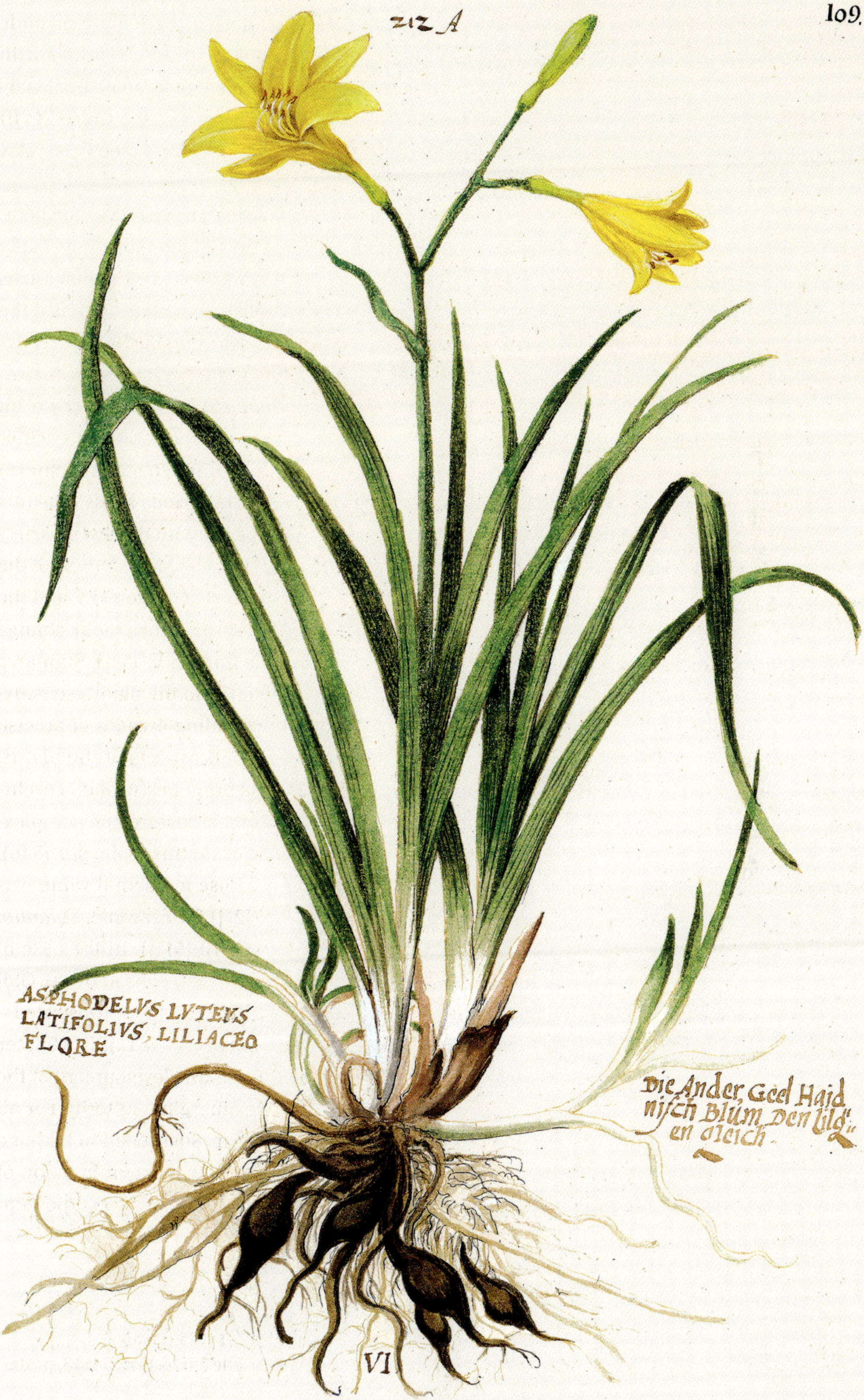
212 A
ASPHODELVS LVTEVS
LATIFOLIVS, LILIACEO
FLORE
Die Ander Geel Haid
nisch Blum Den lilg'"
en gleich
VI

His work moreover considerably enlarged the range of plant species known at the time. Calculating roundly, among the more than 500 types of plants illustrated, approximately 400 are native "wild plants" of the European flora, of which around 330 are indigenous to Germany. The 100 remaining plant varieties, largely of foreign origin, can be classified under the heading of "cultigens." The plants that were reckoned as medicinally useful par excellence included not only these cultigens, but also most of the garden flowers, herbs, vegetables, fruits and other useful plants of garden and field. For approximately 100 of these "wild" and "cultivated" plants, Fuchs was either the first to describe and register them botanically, or at least to illustrate them (see Sprague & Nelmes 1931, p. 565; Marzell 1938, pp. 15 ff.; Meyer et al. 1999, pp. 143 ff.). These statistics alone suffice to document the importance of his contribution.

Fuchs had already encountered many of these plants in the vicinity of Erfurt, Ingolstadt, Onoltzbach (Ansbach), as well as Bayreuth, Kulmbach and Nuremberg. Later, from 1535/36 onwards, he discovered further species that were as yet unknown to him on his excursions in and around Tübingen (Spitzberg, Österberg, Lustnau, Bebenhausen and Farrenberg), as well as on his walking tours through the Neckar valley into neighbouring Rottenburg, or his journeys to Nürtingen and Bad Cannstatt. Of these discoveries, many subsequently proved to be completely new to science (such as *Dactylorhiza maculata*, *Muscari botryoides*, *Paris quadrifolia*, *Scilla bifolia* and *Senecio ovatus*); others were illustrated for the first time in the history of botany (*Antennaria dioica*, *Digitalis purpurea*, *Orchis mascula*, *O. militaris*, *O. morio*, *Platanthera bifolia*, etc.); still others serve as important first evidence of a particular plant's growth in south-west Germany (see Künkele 1987; Sebald et al. 1992–1998; Seybold 1983, 1986, 1994).

The variety of "cultigens" that had been domesticated more than 450 years ago is also noteworthy, for in those days, far more than today, the population had to provide for themselves (see Vogellehner 1966, pp. 158 f.; Dobat 2000 b, pp. 10 f.). But the Tübingen professor certainly cannot have gathered all his plant varieties from the fields or private gardens, especially not the "exotics" that were still largely unknown at the time. A mere 50 years after the discovery of America, Fuchs's work offers us the first European illustrations of plants that are today essential to the economy throughout the world, such as *Zea mays* (plate CCCCLXXIII [473]), *Phaselous vulgaris* (plate CCCCIIII) [404]), *Cucurbita pepo* (plate CCCXCIX [399], CCCC [400]) and *Capsicum annuum* (plate CCCCXVIII–CCCCXX [418–420]). Further specialities originating in Africa and Asia include *Solanum melongena* (plate CCC [300]), *Momordica balsamina* (plate CV [105]) and *Impatiens balsamina* (plate CVI [106]). Without a doubt, Fuchs must have cultivated these and other rarities himself.

The Garden next to the Nonnenhaus: One of the World's Oldest University Gardens

After a decree issued by Duke Ulrich in 1536 had dissolved the Beguine religious communities in Württemberg, the Nonnenhaus ("nuns' house") in Tübingen, together with the land belonging to it, became state property (p. 35). The house is not documented as the assigned official residence of Leonhart Fuchs and his family until its entry in the so-called "servants' book" of 1549, however (see Dobat & Mägdefrau 1975, p. 12). The document makes clear that the house and garden came under the administration of the university; that is, they were not the private possession of the scholar, as had long been supposed.

Fuchs however must have had access to nearby grounds suitable for cultivation considerably earlier than 1549. Where else but in the Nonnenhaus garden could he have protected such rare varieties of plants and observed and gathered them at the proper moment? Several chapters in *Historia* and *New Kreüterbuch* provide indirect evidence of the existence of this garden (see for example Cap. XL [40], CLXXII [172]). Particularly convincing in this respect are his data on the larch (*Larix decidua*, see Cap. CLXXXIX [189]): from Ansbach, Margrave Georg had "sent one to Tübingen" for Fuchs, and the scholar would surely have planted this valuable specimen, received from the hand of his former lord, immediately, probably in late autumn 1541, for the Foreword to *Historia* stems from March 1542. Confirmation of this time frame exists also in the scholar's surviving manuscripts, in which he reports of *Veratrum album*, that "two roots that I entrusted to the earth in 1542 already bloomed and bore fruit the following year" (see Seybold 1990, p. 241). Thus, Fuchs must have been using the Nonnenhaus garden for scientific purposes not merely since 1549, but from as far back as 1542. Conrad Gesner (1516–1565) also sent him seeds of *Nicotiana tabacum*, as already noted by Ganzinger (1959, p. 223). Without a doubt, in the Nonnenhaus garden, Fuchs raised many additional plants that he had received from botanist friends or from his son Friderich (1532–1604), who was studying in Italy. Indeed, if one describes Fuchs's garden as the "first botanical garden in Tübingen," as Meyer et al. (1999, p. 124) respectfully designates it, then one must add that the garden would be one of the oldest botanical gardens in the world.

"... Which Are all Artfully Painted/ and Described with Great Diligence...": The Synthesis of Art and Science

There can be no question that the exemplary plant illustrations contribute significantly to the scientific interest of *Historia* and *New Kreüterbuch* and the high respect they still garner today. The illustrations were done by three unquestionably talented artists working in demonstrably close collaboration with Fuchs, who – insofar as one can tell – won them for the project only after his arrival in Tübingen and paid for their services at his own cost. The presence of the artists' portraits in both herbals testifies to the high level of respect Fuchs accorded their achievement as artists. Although we first meet the artists only at the very end of the two works, equivalent to a "glorious conclusion," their appearance nonetheless signifies a most unusual, and even unique, procedure for the age. The scholar thus raised an enduring memorial to the artists; at the same time the illustration conveys a true-to-life understanding of their activity.

Albrecht Meyer is painting an almost finished watercolour, which would subsequently serve as a pattern to be transferred to the wood block later used for printing. Heinrich Füllmaurer is holding such a plate in his hand, together with the plant illustration painted on parchment, which had served as a pattern. Copying this drawing onto the smooth, finely sanded surface of the wood was done with great care, as the 23 remaining "herbal plates" in Tübingen show (see Dobat 1983, 2000 a). The third member of the this group of artists was Veyt Rudolff Speckle, one of the most important relief engravers of the age. His task was to work out the illustration with all its details in relief on the wood block. The wood carver, who lived in Strasbourg, used many instruments in his work. The entire free surface of the block had to be removed, until in the end only the individual lines of

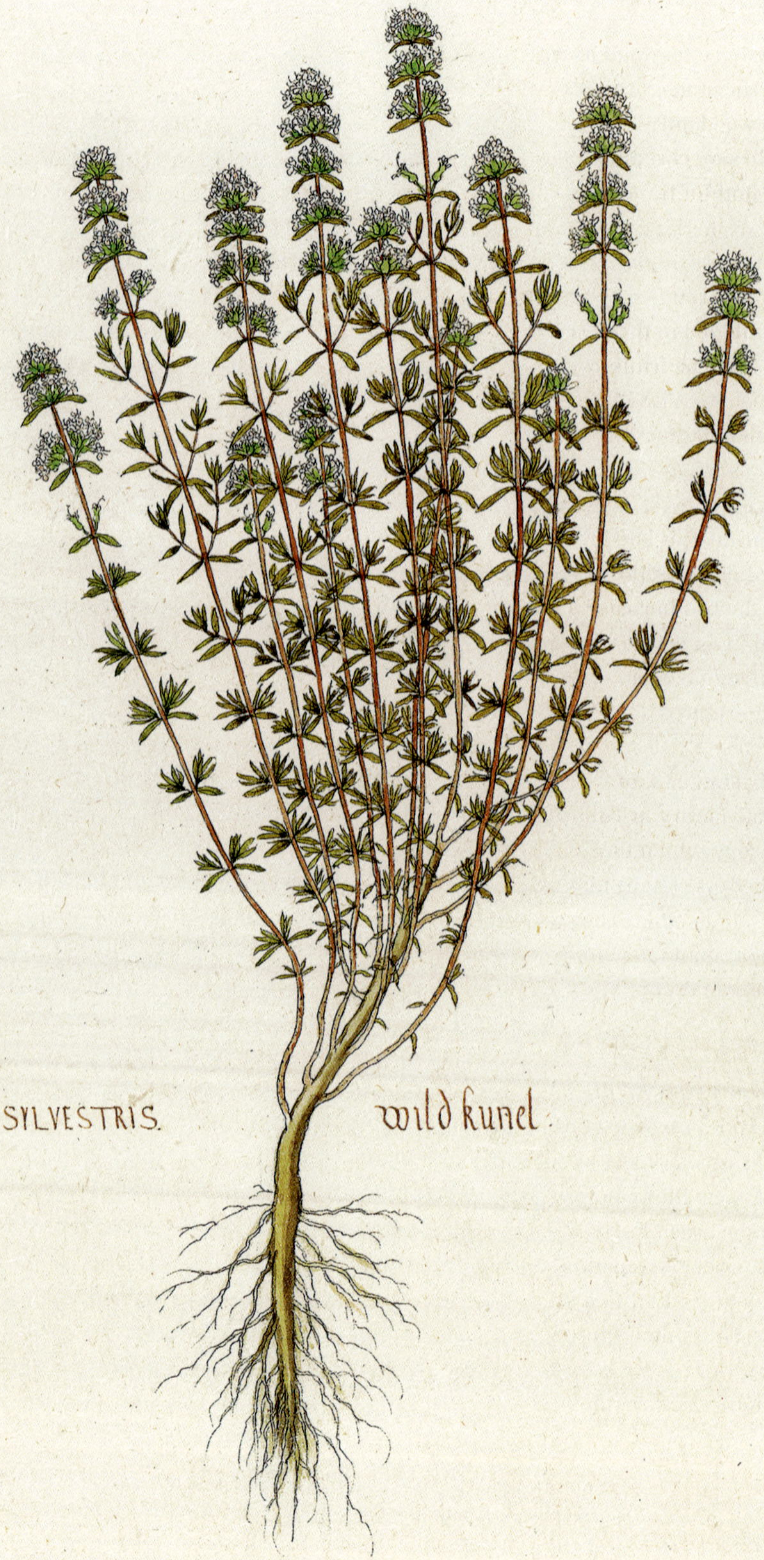

THYMBRA SYLVESTRIS. wild kunel

the drawing remained as narrow raised ridges. After inking, these raised areas resulted in a mirror image of the original drawing. How many days would Speckle have needed for a single woodcut?

To save cost and space, Fuchs occasionally presented related species in a single illustration. Both of the roses (see plate CCCLXXIIII [374]), for example, "spring" from a single root, as do the three different species of *Lamium* (see plate CCLXIIII [264]). Beautifully blooming garden plants (see plates CC [200], CCLXXXVII [287]), as well as individual varieties of important cultivars (see plates XLVI [46], CCXXXIX [239], CCCCLXXIII [473]) have been combined in this fashion. Similarly, the simultaneous depiction of freshly opened flowers and overripe fruits, as found here in the Peach Tree (see plate CCCXLI [341]) or redcurrants (plate CCCLXXVII [377]), was probably undertaken at the scholar's behest. For many of the wild plants, Fuchs alone was familiar with blossoming and fruiting seasons; his co-workers then added the individual stages of development, with which Fuchs presented them, forming an impressive collective illustration of the given species. Many an illustration begun in the spring thus had to wait for the autumn or winter for completion.

Afterwards, the hand-colouring of the print also required a great deal of time. For this reason, the two herbals were offered for sale both in an inexpensive "black-and-white" edition and in an elaborately coloured "luxury" edition. In a letter written in November 1542, Fuchs mentioned a high price of 15 gulden for a coloured copy of *Historia*. The cost thus corresponded almost exactly with his own monthly income, and he was thus unable to give a book even to his closest friends (Fichtner 1967, 1968). The situation with *New Kreüterbuch* was probably similar, and it is almost a miracle that Fuchs's hand-coloured personal copy from his private library in Tübingen has survived the passage of time. The present reprint is based on this copy, which today resides in Ulm. This volume is the most authoritative copy of the herbal because Fuchs himself would have followed and checked the colouring of this copy of his work, if no other. The plants illustrated so carefully and painstakingly created by Fuchs's team more than four hundred years ago appear to us today as if they had just been brought back from an excursion, or obtained fresh from the garden.

The Last two Decades

Historia and *New Kreüterbuch* carried Fuchs's name throughout the world; nonetheless, by 1543 he was embarking on a continuation of his history of plants. The first part of this manuscript was completed by 1550 at the latest (see Stübler 1928, p. 99), and by July 1551, more than 300 new illustrations had been prepared for it (see Seybold 1986, p. 12). An exchange of letters between Fuchs and his friend Camerarius tells us a great deal about their gradual progress over the ensuing years. In 1557, Fuchs finished a second volume with 400 additional pictures, and this was ultimately followed by the manuscript for a third volume in 1563/64. Thus, after approximately 20 years of diligent labour and commitment, the entire project was largely complete. Fuchs apparently identified himself ever more strongly with this work; it had become a part of him – only so can one explain his immense achievement.

LEONHART FUCHS, *Codex Fuchs*, Tübingen, *c.* 1536–1566
Vienna, Österreichische Nationalbibliothek, HAN: Cod. 11117–11125 (9 vols.)
Satureja cf. montana (L.) – Winter Savory / Winter-Bohnenkraut / Sarriette vivace, Cod. 11120, p. 51

It is also understandable when Fichtner (1968, p. 75) remarks: "On the whole, the longer he worked, the less his medical practice seems to have featured in Fuchs's life." Even harsh reversals failed to shake his perseverance, for in the course of the two decades, his search to find a sponsor to print the work was futile. Anyone else probably would have given up; Fuchs however remained steadfastly at work, and had the drawings, wood blocks, and specimen prints of the newly added plants finished at his own expense (see Rytz 1933). Around 1550, Fuchs even employed another extraordinarily talented and assiduous painter in the person of Jerg Ziegler. He was to be the last of Fuchs's artistic collaborators. A number of the 440 watercolours signed by Ziegler in the manuscript can be more precisely dated, because they were completed after the herbal of the Augsburg physician and traveller Leonhard Rauwolff (1535–1596). He may have visited Fuchs in 1563 and made his herbarium available to him (see Ganzinger 1963, p. 28; Seybold 1986, p. 20, 1990, pp. 251 ff.; Meyer et al. 1999, pp. 185 ff.). Furthermore, among the uncut herbal plates remaining in Tübingen, eight are based on these models and bear Ziegler's monogram. As ever, Fuchs therefore strove to expand his knowledge of plants, to complete his manuscript and to obtain support from foreign botanists. These goals he pursued until his very last years, which were overshadowed by the death of his wife Anna in February 1563. The following year, he married Afra Graeter, a pastor's widow from Schwäbisch Hall, but Fuchs's strength was dwindling. Further desperate attempts to obtain money from various princes and imperial cities for the printing of his "life's work" ended in failure. None of his hopes had come to fruition. Deeply disappointed, stricken by illness and plagued by increasing loss of eyesight, Leonhart Fuchs died in Tübingen on 10 May 1566. He was buried at the side of his first wife in the cemetery located along on the river Ammer, whose grounds were incorporated into the Old Botanical Garden in 1835/36. An arboretum was planted above his grave, and some of the old trees are standing yet. Somewhere beneath, both are laid to rest at an unknown spot.

Fuchs's eldest son Friderich (1532–1604), who served as city physician in Ulm, was also unable to bring about the printing of the manuscript, despite great efforts. After the son's death, the manuscript was sold, and was presumed lost for more than 200 years. Fortunately, since 1756 it has been peacefully resting in a safe haven: the Austrian National Library (Österreichische Nationalbibliothek) in Vienna. On the occasion of an exhibition in 1954, someone remembered the manuscript, which was finally unearthed by Ganzinger (1959). This three-volume *Codex Vindobonensis Palatinus*, divided into nine volumes with innumerable closely written folio pages and more than 1500 illustrations, is a further enduring legacy of the Tübingen scholar, who has properly entered history as "one of the German fathers of botany" (pp. 12, 17, 20, 23, 43, 50, 53, 62, 66, 70).

LEONHART FUCHS, *Codex Fuchs*, Tübingen, *c.* 1536–1566
Vienna, Österreichische Nationalbibliothek, HAN: Cod. 11117–11125 (9 vols.)
Dryas octopetala (L.) – Mountain Avens / Silberwurz / Dryade à huit pétales, Cod. 11125, p. 323

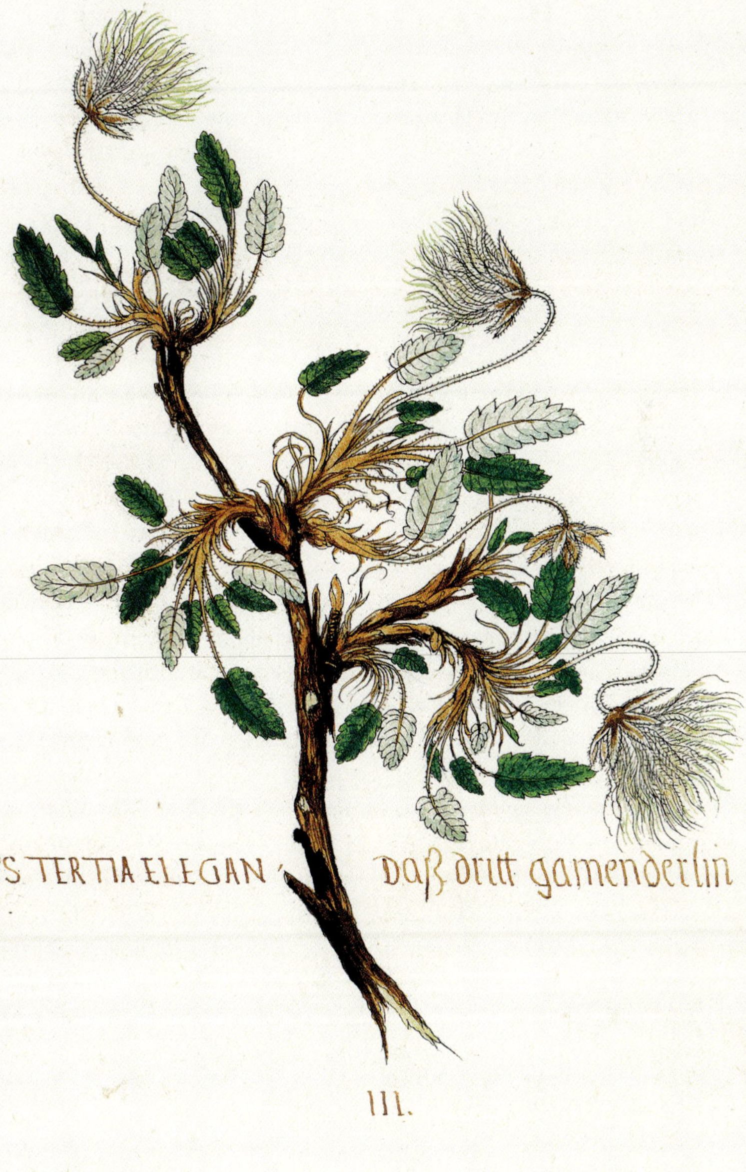

CHAMAEDRYS TERTIA ELEGAN-
TISSIMA.

Daß dritt gamenderlin

III.

Klaus Dobat

Leonhart Fuchs

Arzt und Pionier der modernen Botanik

Leonhart Fuchs (1501–1566) wurde im bayerischen Wemding, einem reizvollen Ort östlich der einstigen Reichsstadt Nördlingen, als jüngster Sohn des Bürgermeisters Johann Fuchs und dessen Ehefrau Anna geboren. Der genaue Tag seiner Geburt ist nicht bekannt. Weder für den am häufigsten genannten 17. Januar noch für den 1. Januar oder 17. Februar gibt es nach Meyer et al. (1999, S. 819) einen urkundlichen Beleg.

Ersten Unterricht erhielt er nach dem frühen Tod seines Vaters im Jahre 1506 durch die Mutter und den Großvater, der ebenfalls Wemdinger Bürgermeister gewesen war. Bereits 1511 schickte die Familie den aufgeweckten Knaben an die Lateinschule in Heilbronn, wo sein Lehrer Conrad bald die außergewöhnliche Begabung und Strebsamkeit des Jungen bemerkte. Daher kam er im darauffolgenden Jahr an die Marienschule nach Erfurt in Thüringen, deren Schüler durch intensives Latein- und Griechischstudium zur Aufnahme in die dortige Universität – damals eine der renommiertesten in Deutschland – vorbereitet wurden. Im Herbst 1515 wurde Fuchs an der Artistenfakultät immatrikuliert und beendete schon im Wintersemester 1516/17 seine Ausbildung als *Baccalaureus artium*, ein Titel, der ihn zum Lehrberuf berechtigte. In Wemding eröffnete er im Alter von 17 Jahren eine Privatschule, entschloss sich dann aber 1519 zur Fortsetzung des Studiums an der Universität Ingolstadt. Nach der Magisterprüfung (1521) und der 1524 erfolgten Promotion zum *Medicinae Doctor* praktizierte Fuchs zwei Jahre lang in München. Hier heiratete er die Ratsherrentochter Anna Friedberger, ein, wie es heißt, „wohlerzogenes, ehrbares Mädchen aus achtbarer Familie" (Roth 1898, S. 162). Insgesamt zehn Kinder (vier Söhne und sechs Töchter) sollten aus dieser Ehe hervorgehen, von denen zwei noch vor der Taufe starben.

Vom Medicus zum Universitätsprofessor – eine Karriere mit Hindernissen

1526 erreichte ihn das Angebot aus Ingolstadt, als Professor den Lehrstuhl für Medizin zu übernehmen. Obwohl diese Universität als eine der Hochburgen des Katholizismus galt und sich Fuchs schon frühzeitig zu den Ideen Martin Luthers hingezogen fühlte, folgte er dem ehrenvollen Ruf. Ausschlaggebend waren neben wirtschaftlichen Überlegungen vor allem wohl die sich bietenden Lehr- und Forschungsmöglichkeiten. Doch er kam an einen Ort

Contrafayt

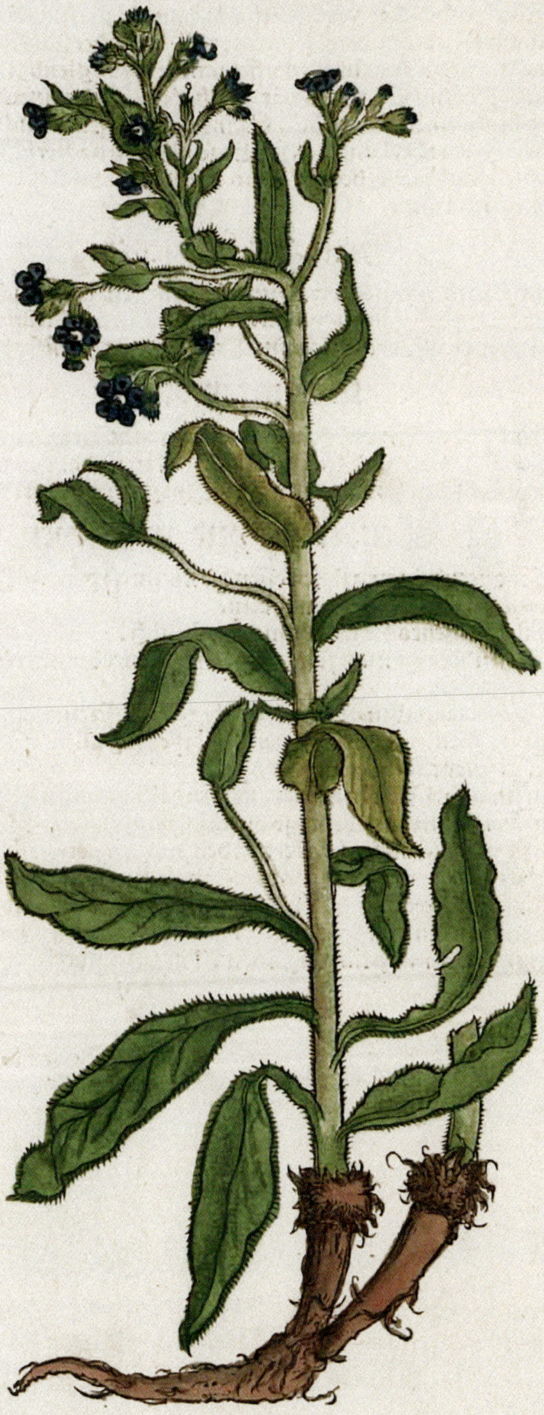

Ochssenzung.

anchusa officinalis class. 5.

geistiger und geistlicher Enge, an eine Hochschule, die die religiöse Einstellung ihrer Professoren bespitzelte und maßregelte. Daher übernahm er zwei Jahre später die Stelle des Leibarztes am Hofe des protestantischen Markgrafen Georg von Brandenburg in Ansbach (dem damaligen Onoltzbach). Eine Professur an der dort geplanten Universität stand in Aussicht, außerdem konnte Fuchs frei von Glaubenszwängen als angesehener Mediziner seine wissenschaftlich-literarischen Interessen verfolgen.

Unter den verschiedenen medizinischen Publikationen, die in jener Zeit entstanden, erregten vor allem die *Errata recentiorum medicorum* („Irrtümer der neueren Ärzte") beachtliches Aufsehen. Mit diesem 1530 gedruckten Erstlingswerk schaltete sich Fuchs ein in den bis ins 14. Jahrhundert zurückreichenden medizinischen Lehrstreit, der die damalige Ärzteschaft in zwei Lager spaltete: Während die sogenannten „arabistischen" Mediziner nach den Überlieferungen der arabischen Arzneilehre praktizierten, vertraten ihre Gegner die Erkenntnisse der griechischen Heilkunde. Mit jugendlichem Eifer, vehement und unnachsichtig plädierte Fuchs für die Alleingültigkeit der griechischen Medizin, wobei ihm seine humanistische Bildung und die umfassenden Literaturkenntnisse sehr zugutekamen. Anhand zahlreicher Zitate belegte er Widersprüche zwischen den beiden Lehrmeinungen, schoss mit seiner Kritik allerdings oft über das Ziel hinaus, indem er selbst unbestreitbare Verdienste der arabischen Heilkunde entweder nicht akzeptierte oder sie mit Stillschweigen überging. Andererseits wies er zu Recht auf die falsche Benennung vieler Heilpflanzen und die Verwechslung pflanzlicher Arzneimittel hin, die in der medizinischen Anwendung deshalb nicht die ihnen zugeschriebene Wirkung zeigten. Besondere Würdigung fanden diese ersten pharmakologisch-botanischen Ausführungen des jungen Gelehrten bei Otto Brunfels (1488–1534), der sie nahezu unverändert im zweiten Band (*Novi herbarii Tomus II*, 1531) seines eigenen Kräuterbuches abdrucken ließ. Auch zu umstrittenen therapeutischen und anatomischen Fragen nahm Fuchs herausfordernd Stellung. Zweifellos wollte er – von der Richtigkeit seiner Auffassungen völlig überzeugt – aufrütteln und bewegen. Dass neben der erhofften Zustimmung auch die heftigste Ablehnung durch seine arabistisch orientierten Kollegen zu erwarten war, wird er bewusst einkalkuliert haben. Auf jeden Fall wurde er rasch bekannt!

In Ansbach beendete Fuchs unter anderem auch sein erstes Kompendium der Medizin (*Compendiaria … in medendi artem …*, 1531), das zu einem äußerst beliebten Lehrbuch werden sollte und von ihm in den nächsten zwei Jahrzehnten laufend überarbeitet und erweitert wurde. Es trug ebenso zu seiner wachsenden Berühmtheit bei wie die Übersetzung und Kommentierung einer griechischen Hippokrates-Ausgabe über epidemische Krankheiten (*Hippocratis medicorum omnium longe principis Epidemiorum liber sextus …*, 1532).

Trotz des schriftstellerischen Erfolgs und der großen Wertschätzung von Seiten des Fürsten fühlte sich Fuchs jedoch immer stärker zur akademischen Lehre berufen. Diese feste Überzeugung konnte er in Ansbach nicht verwirklichen, zumal sich die beabsichtigte Universitätsgründung immer weiter hinausschob. Im Frühjahr 1533 folgte er daher zum zweiten Mal einem Ruf nach Ingolstadt. Entgegen seiner Hoffnung hatte sich dort allerdings

PAGE 25
OTTO BRUNFELS, *Contrafayt Kreüterbuch*
Straßburg 1532, München, Bayerische Staatsbibliothek, Rar. 2264-1/2#1
Anchusa officinalis (L.) – German Bugloss, Alkanet/
Ochsenzung, Wilde Ochsenzung/Buglosse officinale, p. 40

nicht viel geändert, die Anfeindungen begannen erneut. Als ihm, dem kompromisslosen Protestanten, sogar das Abhalten von Vorlesungen verboten wurde (vgl. Prantl 1872, S. 197), resignierte Fuchs und kehrte auf Einladung Markgraf Georgs im August des gleichen Jahres in seine alte Ansbacher Stellung zurück. Voller Dank, dass dieser ihn „aus dem Rachen der Ingolstädter Sophisten" („ex Ingolstadiensium Sophistarum faucibus") gerettet habe, widmete er ihm 1535 die zweite Bearbeitung des schon erwähnten Kompendiums. Obwohl am Hofe nach wie vor hoch angesehen, trat Fuchs, als die Hochschulgründung in Ansbach endgültig scheiterte, noch im Sommer 1534 in Berufungsverhandlungen mit der Universität Tübingen. Gefördert wurde er dabei von dem berühmten Humanisten und Reformator Philipp Melanchthon (1497–1560), der ihn bereits von seiner Ingolstädter Studienzeit her kannte.

Der Neubeginn in Tübingen

Als „ain sonder gelerter Artzat in sprachen" (Roth 1877, S. 183) berufen und von Herzog Ulrich von Württemberg (1487–1550), dem damaligen Landesherrn, ausdrücklich mit der humanistischen Neuordnung der Universität beauftragt, übernahm Leonhart Fuchs am 14. August 1535 den Lehrstuhl für Medizin in Tübingen. Er betrat damit ein von der Reformation erschüttertes Land, eine noch stark katholisch geprägte Hochschule. Eindrucksvoll haben Decker-Hauff & Setzler (1977) die Umbruchsstimmung jener Jahre geschildert, in denen nicht nur „Ulrichs harter Zugriff zum reichen Kirchenvermögen" (S. 69) erfolgte, sondern zugleich eine unerbittliche Universitätsreform eingeleitet wurde: Die sogenannte Herzog Ulrichs Ordnung, am 30. Januar 1535 in Kraft getreten, „empfahl allen Hochschullehrern, entweder den neuen Glauben anzunehmen oder auszuwandern. Am 7. März 1535 wurde die Messe in Tübingen abgeschafft, am 9. schon der Befehl, zu konvertieren oder auszuwandern, wiederholt" (S. 64).

Wie in seinem bisherigen Leben zu keinerlei Opportunismus bereit, stürzte sich der 34-jährige Professor mit ungewöhnlichem Fleiß, energisch und selbstbewusst in die reformatorische Arbeit – gegen kirchliche wie gegen medizinische Traditionen. „Termingerecht" zu seinem Tübinger Amtsantritt war unter dem Titel *Paradoxorum medicinae libri tres* die erweiterte Überarbeitung der *Errata* erschienen, die seine Ansichten klar umriss. Mit welcher Verbitterung und Voreingenommenheit Fuchs erneut gegen die arabische Medizin Stellung nahm, ist heute kaum mehr nachvollziehbar. Ausschließlich griechische Autoren ließ er gelten und geradezu poetisch klingt seine Forderung: „Gehen wir daher zu den Quellen zurück, und schöpfen wir aus ihnen das reine und ungetrübte Wasser der medicinischen Kenntnisse!" (Sprengel 1827, S. 151). Sogar Ibn Sina (lat. Avicenna, 980–1037 n. Chr.), einem der überragendsten Vertreter der arabischen Medizin und Wissenschaft, unterstellte er in dieser dem Herzog gewidmeten Schrift weitgehende Abschreiberei von den Griechen. Seine noch der alten Lehre anhängenden Amtskollegen jedenfalls wussten, was sie zu erwarten hatten.

Schon im Oktober 1535 wurde Fuchs Dekan und stellte mit grimmigem Bedauern fest: „Wie nachlässig bisher die Geschäfte der medizinischen Fakultät verwaltet worden sind, kann man bestens daraus ersehen, daß meine Vorgänger auch nicht ein Wort hinterlassen haben, woraus die Nachwelt erfahren könnte, was sie getan haben" (Haller 1927, S. 133 f.). Zwischen 1536 und 1565 war Fuchs insgesamt siebenmal Rektor der Universität und konnte in dieser Position manche seiner Vorstellungen realisieren. Gemeinsam mit dem gleichgesinnten Joachim Camerarius (1500–1574), der mit ihm in Erfurt studiert hatte und mit dem

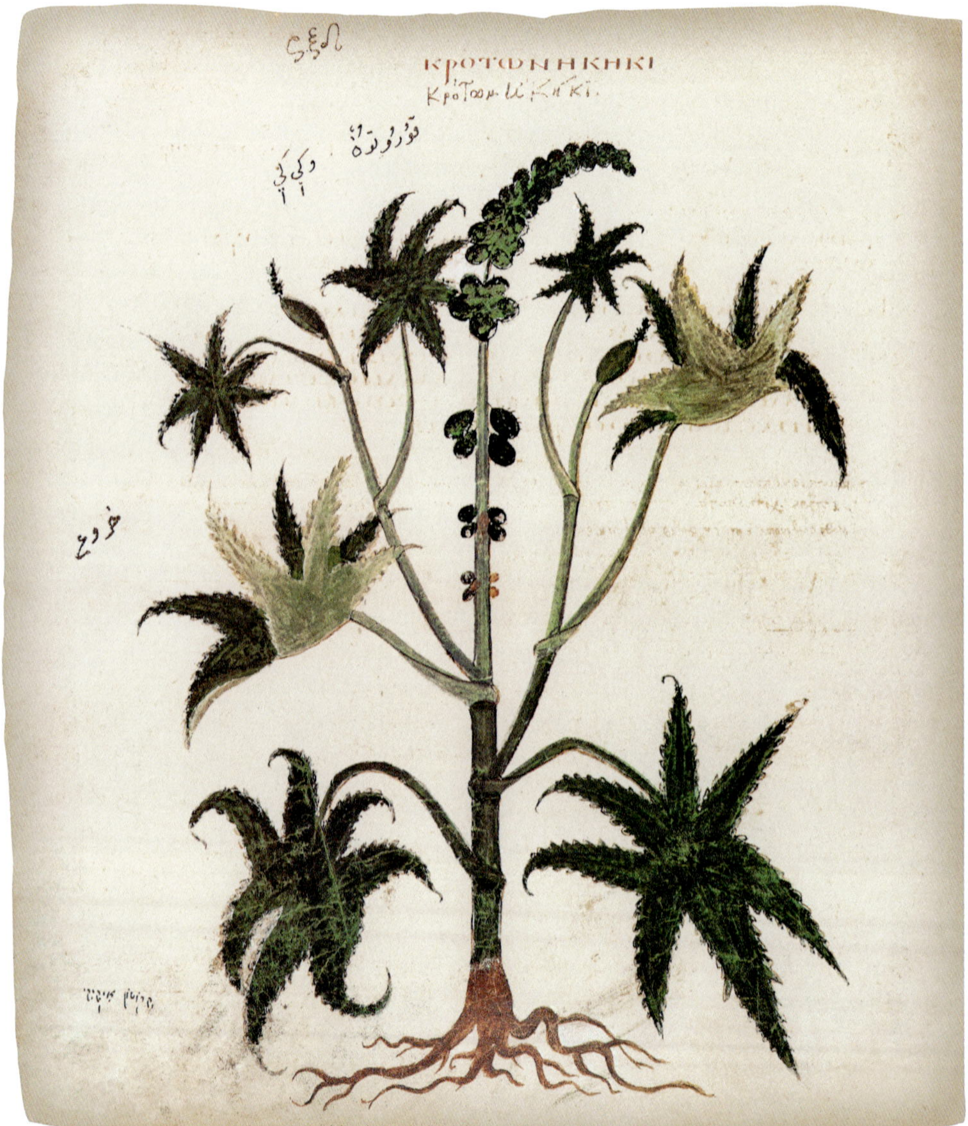

Vienna Dioscorides or *Codex Aniciae Julianae*, Byzantium, before 512
Vienna, Österreichische Nationalbibliothek, HAN: Cod. Med. gr. 1

Physalis alkekengi (L.) – Chinese Lantern / Wilde Blasenkirsche / Alkekengi
Folio 359 verso

Ricinus communis (L.) – Castor Oil Plant / Rizinus / Ricin commun
Folio 170 verso

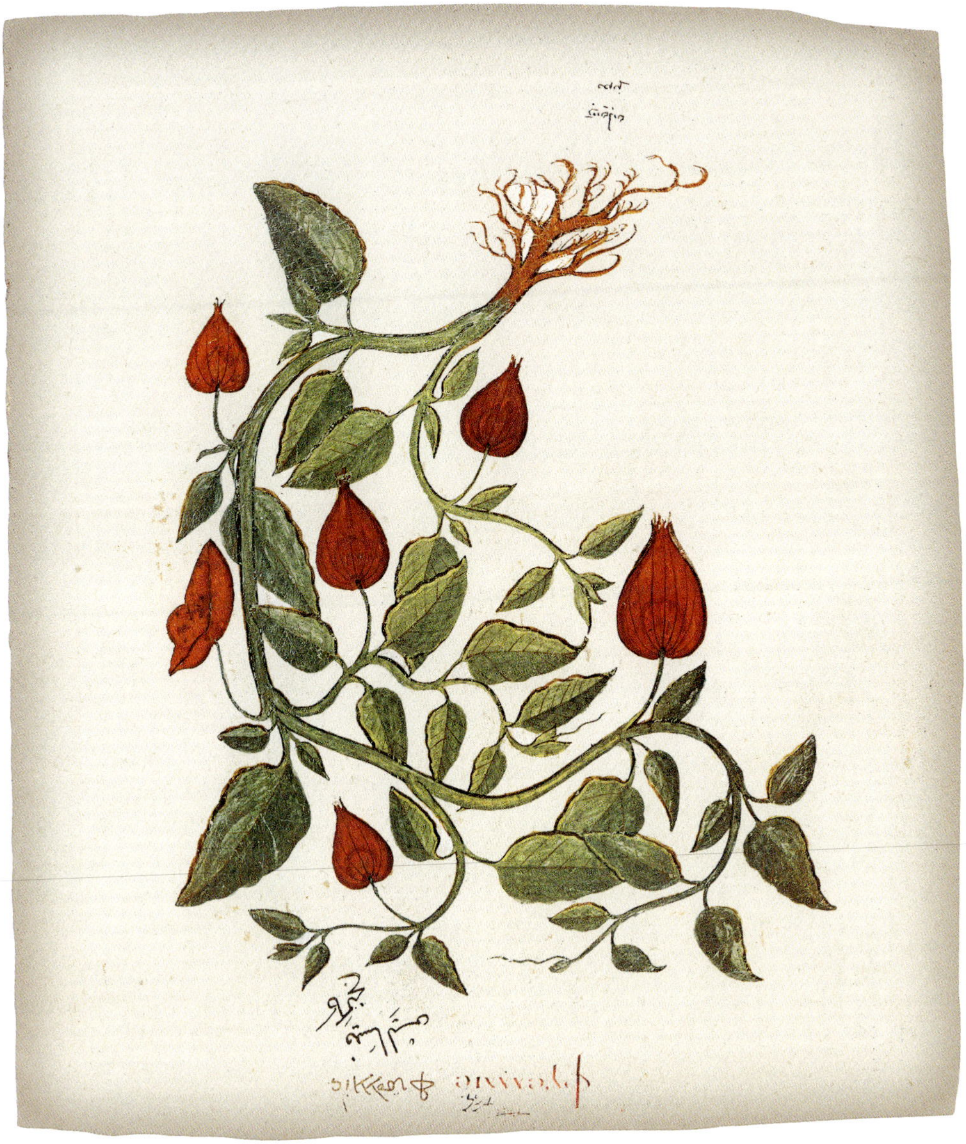

ihn eine lebenslange Freundschaft verband, erarbeitete er die neuen Statuten der Universität Tübingen des Jahres 1538. Sie bewirkten auch innerhalb der medizinischen Fakultät einen revolutionären Wandel, der unverkennbar Fuchs' Handschrift trägt: Das bislang pflichtgemäße Studium der Astronomie wurde gestrichen, arabische Literatur zu Gunsten der griechischen „nur sparsamst zur Lehre herangezogen" (Fichtner 1967, S. 4). Während nach den alten Statuten von 1497 „wenigstens alle drei bis vier Jahre eine Zergliederung eines menschlichen Körpers vorgenommen und dabey aus der Schrift des Mundinus vorgelesen werden sollte", regte Fuchs an, dass in jedem Jahr mindestens eine Sektion durchgeführt werden sollte, an deren Teilnahme die Studenten verpflichtet waren. Da das früher vorgeschriebene Lehrbuch von Mundinus (gemeint ist dessen *Anathomia* von 1316) „voller Fehler und

Irrthümer sey, so solle man es weglassen und lieber während der Zergliederung das passende Capitel aus dem Galen vorlesen" (Froriep 1811, S. 1, 3 f.).

Auch durch die Einführung des 1543 erschienenen Werkes *De humani corporis fabrica* (S. 10) von Andreas Vesal (1515–1564) – das erste vollständige Lehrbuch der menschlichen Anatomie in der Geschichte – verlieh Fuchs der medizinischen Forschung und Lehre an unserer Universität neue Impulse. Für großes Aufsehen dürfte in diesem Zusammenhang 1546/47 der Ankauf des ersten menschlichen Skeletts gesorgt haben: Auf seinen Vorschlag hin hatte Herzog Ulrich angewiesen, einen ‚bainin man' für den hohen Preis von 30 Gulden zu erwerben, damit die Studierenden durch eigenen Augenschein lernen könnten, „wie die gebain im Menschen geartet und ains uf das ander sazet oder gericht ist" (Froriep 1902, S. VI). Nicht zuletzt förderte er selbst die Ausbildung der Mediziner durch seine zahlreichen Fachpublikationen und durch seine gut besuchten Vorlesungen, die wegen „der lichtvollen Ordnung und des gemein verständlichen und dabei klassischen Vortrags sehr gerühmt" wurden (Moll 1852, S. 357).

Es liegt auf der Hand, dass Fuchs seine Einflussnahme auf diese wichtigen und zukunftsträchtigen Reformen hart erkämpfen musste und in ein „Wechselbad" von Anerkennung und Ablehnung geriet. „Sein starres Festhalten an dem von ihm als richtig Erkannten und seine immer wieder an den Tag tretende Unduldsamkeit anders Denkenden gegenüber hat ihm auch innerhalb des Universitätskörpers manche Feindschaft eingetragen", schreibt dazu Stübler (1928, S. 175). Zu diesen fakultätsinternen Zwistigkeiten kamen die laufenden Auseinandersetzungen mit der Hofbürokratie Herzog Ulrichs, welche Ende 1541 seinen Kollegen und Freund Joachim Camerarius zum Wechsel nach Leipzig veranlassten. Schwer litt der keineswegs weltfremde Wissenschaftler und überzeugte Lutheraner ebenfalls unter den andauernden politisch-religiösen Konflikten im Land. Wieviel Zeit müssen ihn des Weiteren die – oft berechtigten, oft von Neid diktierten – Streitigkeiten auch mit auswärtigen Gelehrten gekostet haben! Beispielhaft sind seine Auseinandersetzungen mit dem Arzt Janus Cornarius (1500–1558), der wie er für die griechische Medizin eintrat. Trotzdem missgönnten beide einander vermeintliche oder tatsächliche Erfolge und beschimpften sich in ihren Veröffentlichungen über zwölf Jahre hinweg mit zunehmender Heftigkeit. Während Cornarius seinem Kontrahenten Vielschreiberei und geistigen Diebstahl vorwarf, bescheinigte Fuchs seinem Gegner, dass dessen Werke höchstens für Schaben und Motten geeignet seien – noch „harmlose" Äußerungen im Vergleich zu anderen, die man selbst im dicksten Lateinwörterbuch vergebens sucht.

Auch mit seiner materiellen Lage war Fuchs unzufrieden, obwohl er ab 1537 mit einem ansehnlichen Jahresgehalt von 200 Gulden zu den am besten bezahlten Professoren der Universität gehörte. Mehrfach trug er sich daher mit dem Gedanken, Stadt und Land zu verlassen. Bereits 1537/38 hätte er die Gelegenheit gehabt, als Leibarzt an den Hof König Christians III. von Dänemark zu gehen. Damit verbunden war zugleich die Aussicht auf die Professur für Medizin an der geplanten protestantischen Universität in Kopenhagen. Nach seinen Erfahrungen in Ansbach war Fuchs allerdings vorsichtig geworden, zudem entsprach das – in der Tat „knauserige" – Angebot nicht seinen finanziellen Vorstellungen. Unter Hinweis darauf, aber auch auf die Schwangerschaft seiner Frau, die große Zahl seiner Kinder und Bücher sowie auf seine Position und beruflichen Aufgaben in Tübingen, lehnte er ab. Selbst einen noch ehrenvolleren und in materieller Hinsicht höchst verlockenden Ruf im Jahr 1544 nahm Fuchs nicht an. Herzog Cosimo Medici von Florenz hatte ihm als ersten deutschen Gelehrten die Direktorenstelle am 1543 gegründeten Botanischen Garten in Pisa angetragen, der als der älteste der Welt gilt. Die Absage fiel ihm sehr schwer, wie wir aus einem Brief vom 1. November 1544 an Camerarius wissen; letztendlich waren vor allem wohl religiöse Bedenken ausschlaggebend (Näheres siehe Stübler 1928, S. 172 ff.; Fichtner 1968, S. 69; Krafft 1998, S. 137; Meyer et al. 1999, S. 37 f.).

Trotz der angedeuteten beruflichen und privaten Turbulenzen bewältigte Fuchs ein heute unvorstellbares Arbeitspensum! Neben den Verpflichtungen als Rektor, der Beteiligung am reformatorischen, theologischen und politischen Geschehen, seinen Vorlesungen in Anatomie, praktischer Medizin und Arzneikunde sowie nicht zuletzt neben seiner ärztlichen Praxis war er in Tübingen nach wie vor auch literarisch ungemein aktiv. Unter anderem verfasste er mit Camerarius und weiteren Autoren eine fünfbändige Galen-Ausgabe (1538), eigene Lehrbücher, Übersetzungen, Kommentierungen und Streitschriften folgten (S. 11), die sämtlich in der verdienstvollen Monografie von Meyer et al. (1999, S. 633 ff.) zusammengestellt sind. Mit zunehmender Intensität wandte sich Fuchs darüber hinaus botanisch-arzneikundlichen Studien zu.

Der Medizin und der Botanik verpflichtet

Leonhart Fuchs war bereits in den Fakultäts-Statuten von 1538 offenen Wortes für eine Verbesserung des botanischen Unterrichts eingetreten. Sicherlich nicht zur Freude des einen oder anderen stubenhockenden Kollegen lautete die Anweisung: „Er soll schließlich zur Sommerszeit mit den Medizinstudenten die Felder und Berge öfters besuchen und dabei das Aussehen der Pflanzen beobachten und ihnen ihre lebendige Anschauung vermitteln und nicht, wie es bisher viele zu tun pflegten, die Kenntnis der Heilpflanzen den Arzneikrämern, jenen ungebildeten Menschen, und den einfältigen Kräuterweibern überlassen" („Aestatis denique tempore cum medicinae studiosis rura montesque saepius petat ac plantarum uultum diligenter obseruet illisque uiuas eorundem imagines demonstret, neque ut hactenus consueuere multi, simplicium notitiam seplasiariis illis hominibus rudibus et stultis mulierculis committat", Roth 1877, S. 312). Seinen eigenen „Empfehlungen" mit gutem Beispiel vorangehend, führte er als erster Professor der Universität botanische Exkursionen durch. Schon in Ingolstadt hatte Fuchs die Bedeutung derartiger Lehrausflüge erkannt, die den akademischen Unterricht in idealer Weise ergänzten. Dass er diese Tradition in Tübingen mit besonderem Nachdruck fortsetzte und daneben auf privaten Wanderungen fleißig botanisierte, steht außer Zweifel. Denn nicht nur für die Vorlesungen benötigte er eine Vielzahl möglichst frischer Pflanzen, sondern vor allem auch für die Beschreibung und Darstellung in seinen beiden Arzneipflanzenbüchern, die weit mehr als alle rein medizinischen Veröffentlichungen den Nachruhm des Gelehrten begründeten.

Zwei Arzneipflanzenwerke von Weltrang: *De historia stirpium* (1542) und *New Kreüterbuch* (1543)

Mit dem Manuskript zur *Historia*, einer für die akademische Welt bestimmten „Geschichte der Heilpflanzen", begann Fuchs noch während seiner Ansbacher Zeit. Ausschlaggebend dafür, eventuell schon länger gehegte Pläne möglichst rasch in die Tat umzusetzen, könnte die Veröffentlichung des ersten Bandes von O. Brunfels' *Herbarum vivae eicones* (S. 38–39) im Jahre 1530 gewesen sein. Ob es nun die darin enthaltenen „glaring errors" [ins Auge

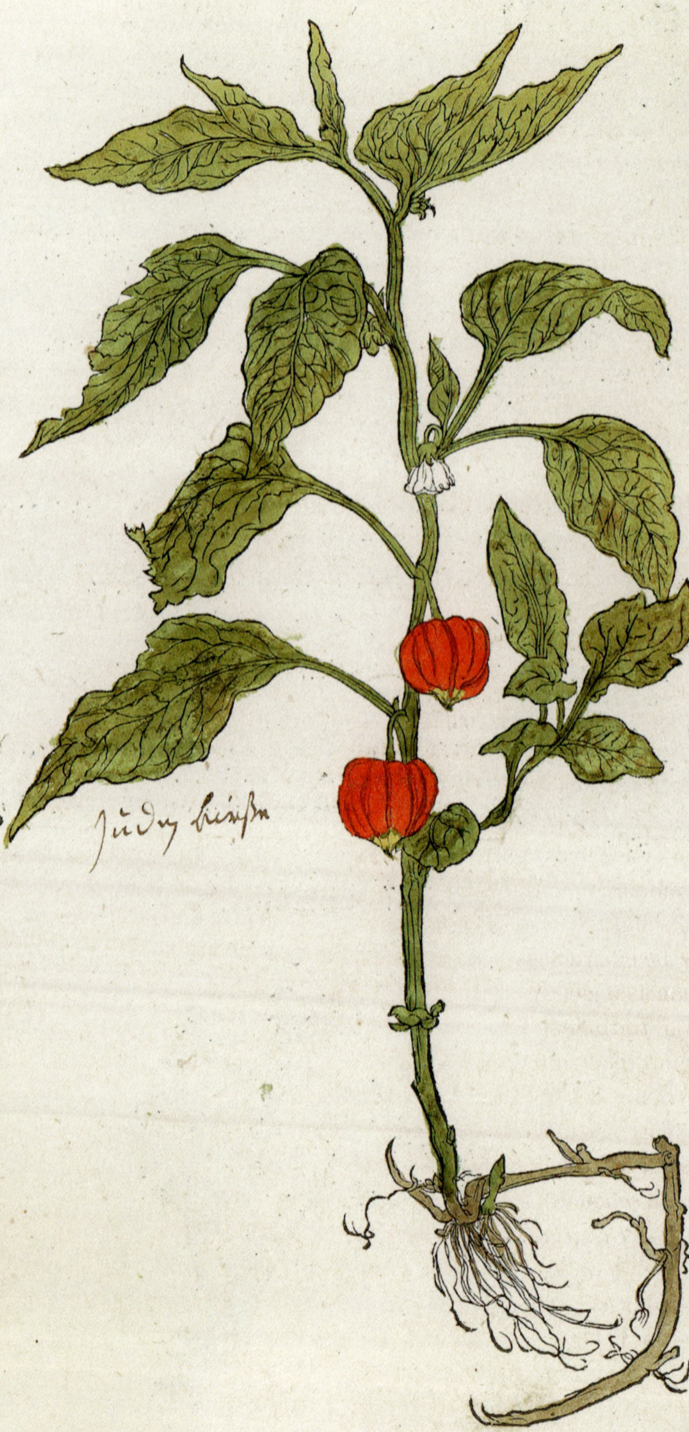

Schlutten.

Juden kirssen

X

springenden Fehler] waren, wie Meyer et al. (1999, S. 48) annehmen, oder eher der Umstand, dass „noch nicht in dem Maß mit den arabischen und arabistischen Autoren aufgeräumt war, wie er es für wünschenswert hielt" (Stübler 1928, S. 231): Fuchs wollte es auf jeden Fall „besser" machen. Neben einer gründlichen Auswertung und Kommentierung der Schriften von Galen, Dioskurides (S. 28–29), Hippokrates, Theophrastos, Plinius und anderer Klassiker sollten auch die von ihm neu gefundenen Pflanzenarten berücksichtigt werden. Sein bewegtes Leben in jenen Jahren erklärt den nur langsamen Fortschritt der Arbeit: „Ich habe jetzund ein Herbarium verfertigt; es ist aber noch nicht im Druck; darin sind mehr als vierthalbhundert [350] Kräuter abconterfeit mit ihren Wurzeln, Stengeln, Blättern, Saamen und Blumen, wird ein lustig Buch zu sehen. Hab's mit großer Kost und Arbeit, Gott habe Lob, ans Ende gebracht", schreibt er 1538 an Herzog Albrecht von Preußen (Voigt 1841, S. 269). Etwas voreilig, wie sich zeigen sollte. Denn immer weitere Pflanzen wurden ihm bekannt oder kamen aus der Umgebung Tübingens hinzu, die neueste Literatur musste berücksichtigt werden, wie zum Beispiel das *Contrafayt Kreüterbuch* von O. Brunfels aus den Jahren 1532–1537 (S. 25, 32) oder das 1539 gedruckte *New Kreütter Buch* von Hieronymus Bock (1498–1554; S. 22–23). So sollten noch vier weitere Jahre ins Land gehen, bevor 1542 die *Historia* mit ihren über 900 Seiten und insgesamt 511 großartigen Pflanzenabbildungen erschien (S. 41).

Im *New Kreüterbuch*, das Fuchs bereits 1543 herausgab, begegnen uns sämtliche Holzschnitte wieder, zudem um sechs neue Bildtafeln ergänzt. Über Jahrhunderte hinweg bis heute Vorbild der botanischen Buchillustration, begeistern sie auch im vorliegenden Nachdruck durch ihre hohe wissenschaftliche und künstlerische Qualität. Trotz der erstaunlich kurzen Bearbeitungszeit steht dieses deutschsprachige Werk an Bedeutung der *Historia* keineswegs nach. Da das *New Kreüterbuch* für einen breiten Leserkreis gedacht war, kam eine reine Übersetzung nicht infrage. Fuchs musste eine weitgehende Überarbeitung des Textes vornehmen, sich um Verständlichkeit bemühen. Zwar deutet er in der sehr lesenswerten Einleitung recht boshaft an, dass auch den Medizinern eine Lektüre nicht schaden könne, doch sollte es vor allem „dem gemeinen mann zu der erkantnuß der kreüter … nützlich und fueglich sein". Dementsprechend sind die gelehrten Ausführungen über das Wissen der antiken Ärzte stark gekürzt, dafür die Pflanzenbeschreibungen ausführlicher, um ihr Erkennen und Auffinden zu erleichtern. Daneben gibt Fuchs praktische Hinweise zur Arzneipflanzenkultur, etwa im Hinblick auf Substratverhältnisse und Standortsansprüche. Es sei „gut und nützlich", meint er, „das die kreüter nit allein von den aertzten/sonder auch von den Leyen und dem gemeinen mann in gaerten hin und wider vleissig gepflantzt und aufferzogen werden/darmit derselben erkantnuß in Teütschen landen dermassen taeglich wachs und zuneme/das sie nimmer in vergessung moege gestelt werden." Ebenfalls auf die Gefahren einer Selbstbehandlung macht er aufmerksam: „ob schon einer vil kreüter kent/so würdt er dannest noch lang kein artzt sein".

Wie in der *Historia* erfolgt auch im *New Kreüterbuch* die Anordnung der Pflanzen nach dem Alphabet ihrer griechischen Namen. Methodisch und übersichtlich gliederte Fuchs den Text für jede Art in meist sieben Abschnitte: „Namen", „Geschlecht", „Gestalt", „Statt irer wachsung", „Zeit", „Die natur und complexion" und „Krafft und würckung".

OTTO BRUNFELS, *Contrafayt Kreüterbuch*
Strasbourg, 1532, Munich, Bayerische Staatsbibliothek, Rar. 2264-1/2#1
Physalis alkekengi (L.) – Chinese Lantern / Wilde Blasenkirsche / Alkekengi, p. 241

Zuerst werden die verschiedenen griechischen, lateinischen und deutschen sowie die bei den Apothekern gebräuchlichen Bezeichnungen aufgeführt. Dass Fuchs die Gattungsbezeichnungen *Campanula, Digitalis* und *Ophioglossum* geprägt hat, dass sie wie manche der von ihm eingeführten wissenschaftlichen Pflanzennamen – *Allium ursinum, Angelica sylvestris, Digitalis purpurea, Hordeum distichon, Iris germanica, Origanum vulgare* und andere – noch heute gültig sind, sei nur am Rande vermerkt. Im zweiten Abschnitt werden nicht etwa die seinerzeit noch völlig unbekannten weiblichen oder männlichen Geschlechtsmerkmale der Pflanze angesprochen, sondern die Verwandtschaftsverhältnisse. Dabei wird meistens auf systematisch nahestehende Arten oder Gattungen hingewiesen, seltener auf Sorten oder Kulturformen (vgl. Cap. CXVIII [118], CCLXXXI [281], CCCXX [320]); dass es auch zu einigen Irrtümern kam (vgl. Cap. XXX [30], XXXI [31]), ist verständlich.

Von besonderem Interesse für den Botaniker sind in beiden Büchern die Abschnitte drei bis fünf. Natürlich hat Fuchs darin vieles – wie damals allgemein üblich – aus der Literatur „geschöpft", vor allem aus der *De materia medica* von Dioskurides. Die enge Anlehnung an dieses Werk, das er für unübertroffen hielt, erklärt manche Ungereimtheit und spiegelt sich auch in der Kürze und Unvollständigkeit zahlreicher Pflanzenbeschreibungen wider. Ganz offenbar hat Fuchs diesen Mangel selbst erkannt, betont er doch im Vorwort der *Historia*, dass eine Abbildung besser als Worte eine Pflanze wiedergebe. Die berechtigte, nicht selten allerdings mit übertriebener „Beckmesserei" vorgenommene Kritik blieb nicht aus. Vor lauter philologischen Textvergleichen unterschätzten oder übersahen manche Autoren die selbständige Leistung von Fuchs, die in der Beschreibung seiner „Neuentdeckungen" zutage tritt, bei jenen Arten also, die er in den griechischen Schriften vergebens suchte. Hier zeigt sich seine Vertrautheit mit der jeweiligen Art, beruhen doch die oft detaillierten Schilderungen ihrer Entwicklung und ihres Aussehens, die Angaben über Anordnung, Form und Farbe ihrer Blätter, Blüten oder Früchte auf eigener Erfahrung. Er beobachtet als Erster den altersbedingten Farbwechsel bei den Blüten von *Echium vulgare* (vgl. z. B. Cap. CLV [155]), nennt bei vielen Pflanzen den Zeitpunkt der Blütenentfaltung und der Fruchtreife, weist auf Frostempfindlichkeit, Sonnen- oder Schattenverträglichkeit hin. Auch mit seinen vielfach erstaunlich genauen Angaben über Standort und Lebensraum spricht er wichtige ökologische Gesichtspunkte an. Über sein eigentliches „Programm" hinausgehend, bewertet Fuchs die Pflanze nicht ausschließlich nach ihrer medizinischen Eignung, nach ihrer „Natur und complexion" oder „Krafft und würckung" (vergleiche hierzu den Beitrag von W. Dressendörfer, S. 33 ff.). Er nimmt viele Arten in sein Werk auf, über deren Heilwirkung ihm wenig oder nichts bekannt war, wie zum Beispiel *Tagetes patula* (Taf. XXVII [27]), *Solanum melongena* (Taf. CCC [300]) oder *Digitalis purpurea* (Taf. CCCCCXIII [513]). Bei *Quercus robur* lenkt er den Blick auf die von der Eichengallwespe (*Cynips quercusfolii* L.) hervorgerufenen Galläpfel (Taf. CXXIX [129]), und bei *Rosa gallica* (Taf. CCCLXXIIII [374]) stellt er – vermutlich erstmals – die sogenannten „Schlafäpfel" dar, die Gallen der Rosengallwespe (*Diplolepis rosae* L.). Mit großer Begeisterung schließlich schildert er im Kapitel CXCVIII [198] über *Morus nigra* die Entwicklung des Seidenspinners (*Bombyx mori* L.) vom Ei über die Verpuppung bis zum schlüpfenden Schmetterling. Trotz aller Autoritätsgläubigkeit gelangt Fuchs insgesamt, wie kaum ein anderer vor ihm, zu einer sehr weitreichenden Betrachtungsweise des pflanzlichen Organismus. Gerade in der Verknüpfung des botanisch-arzneikundlichen Wissens der Griechen mit der Fülle eigener Erkenntnisse zeigt sich die große, in die Zukunft gerichtete Meisterschaft.

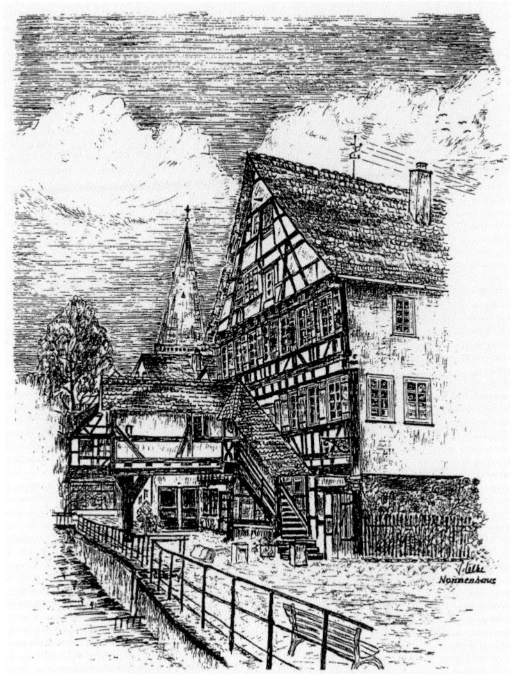

Durch sein Werk wurde darüber hinaus das Spektrum der damals bekannten Pflanzenarten erheblich erweitert. Großzügig gerechnet, gehören unter den über 500 abgebildeten Arten etwa 400 als „Wildpflanzen" zur europäischen Flora, rund 330 davon sind in Deutschland beheimatet. Die übrigen 100 Arten sind vorwiegend fremder Herkunft und lassen sich unter dem Überbegriff „Kulturpflanzen" vereinen: Medizinisch genutzt wurden ja nicht nur die eingeführten Arzneipflanzen „par excellence", sondern ebenfalls die meisten Zierstauden, Gewürzkräuter, Gemüse-, Obst- und sonstigen Nutzpflanzen der Gärten und Felder. Von diesen „Wild-" und „Kulturpflanzen" hat Fuchs insgesamt etwa 100 Arten entweder als Erster überhaupt beschrieben und in die Botanik eingeführt oder sie zumindest erstmals abgebildet (vgl. Sprague & Nelmes 1931, S. 565; Marzell 1938, S. 15 ff.; Meyer et al. 1999, S. 143 ff.). Allein diese Zahlen dokumentieren seine großen Verdienste.

Viele Pflanzen hatte er bereits bei Erfurt, Ingolstadt, Onoltzbach (Ansbach), aber auch Bayreuth, Kulmbach oder Nürnberg gesehen. Ab 1535/36 begegneten ihm dann auf jeder Exkursion in und um Tübingen (Spitzberg, Österberg, Lustnau, Bebenhausen oder Farrenberg), bei Wanderungen durchs Neckartal ins benachbarte Rottenburg oder auf Reisen nach Nürtingen oder Bad Cannstatt weitere, ihm noch unbekannte Arten. Manche erwiesen sich später als völlig neu für die Wissenschaft (wie *Dactylorhiza maculata, Muscari botryoides, Paris quadrifolia, Scilla bifolia* oder *Senecio ovatus*), viele wurden zum ersten Mal in der Geschichte der Botanik im Bild dargestellt (*Antennaria dioica, Digitalis purpurea, Orchis mascula, O. militaris, O. morio, Platanthera bifolia* etc.), andere sind wichtige Erstnachweise für Südwestdeutschland (vgl. Künkele 1987; Sebald et al. 1992–1998; Seybold 1983, 1986, 1994).

Beachtlich ist ebenfalls die Vielfalt der vor mehr als 450 Jahren angebauten „Kulturpflanzen", denn weit mehr als heute war die Bevölkerung auf Selbstversorgung angewiesen (vgl. Vogellehner 1966, S. 158 f.; Dobat 2000 b, S. 10 f.). Doch längst nicht alle Arten kann der Tübinger Professor auf den Feldern gesammelt oder aus Privatgärten erhalten haben, vor allem nicht die damals noch weithin unbekannten „Exoten". Nur 50 Jahre nach der Entdeckung Amerikas finden wir in seinem Werk die ersten europäischen Abbildungen von heute unverzichtbaren Weltwirtschaftpflanzen, wie *Zea mays* (Taf. CCCCLXXIII [473]), *Phaseolus*

SIEGFRIED LELKE, *The "Nonnenhaus" in Tübingen / Das Nonnenhaus in Tübingen / La «Nonnenhaus» à Tübingen.* 1990s, Print

vulgaris (Taf. CCCCIIII [404]), *Cucurbita pepo* (Taf. CCCXCIX [399], CCCC [400]) oder *Capsicum annuum* (Taf. CCCCXVIII–CCCCXX [418–420]). Aus Afrika und Asien stammen mit *Solanum melongena* (Taf. CCC [300]), *Momordica balsamina* (Taf. CV [105]) oder *Impatiens balsamina* (Taf. CVI [106]) weitere Besonderheiten. Kein Zweifel: Fuchs muss diese und andere Raritäten selbst herangezogen haben!

Der Garten beim Nonnenhaus – einer der ältesten Universitätsgärten der Welt

Als 1536 ein Erlass Herzog Ulrichs die Beginengemeinschaften in Württemberg aufhob, gelangte auch das Nonnenhaus in Tübingen mit den dazugehörigen Ländereien in Staatsbesitz (S. 35). Urkundlich als Dienstwohnung von Leonhart Fuchs und seiner Familie nachgewiesen ist das Gebäude allerdings erst im sogenannten „Dienerbuch“ von 1549 (vgl. Dobat & Mägdefrau 1975, S. 12). Aus dem dortigen Text wird ersichtlich, dass Haus und Garten der Verwaltung der Universität unterstanden, also nicht Privatbesitz des Gelehrten waren, wie lange angenommen wurde.

Fuchs muss jedoch aus naheliegenden Gründen schon bedeutend früher ein geeignetes Kulturgelände zur Verfügung gestanden haben. Wo sonst auch hätte er gerade die seltenen Arten besser schützen, beobachten und zum geeigneten Zeitpunkt einsammeln können? Indirekte Hinweise auf die Existenz dieses Gartens findet man in einigen Kapiteln der *Historia* und des *New Kreüterbuchs* (vgl. z. B. Cap. XL [40], CLXXII [172]). Besonders aufschlussreich erscheinen in diesem Zusammenhang seine Angaben über den „Loerchenbaum“ (*Larix decidua*, vgl. Cap. CLXXXIX [189]): Markgraf Georg hatte ihm aus Ansbach „einen gen Tübingen geschickt“. Fuchs wird das für ihn wertvolle Exemplar aus der Hand seines einstigen Dienstherrn bestimmt sofort eingepflanzt haben, vermutlich spätestens im Herbst 1541, da das Vorwort zur *Historia* vom März 1542 stammt. Eine Bestätigung dieses Zeitraums findet sich im hinterlassenen Manuskript des Gelehrten, in dem er über *Veratrum album* mitteilt, dass „zwei Wurzeln, die ich im Jahre 1542 der Erde anvertraut hatte, schon im folgenden Jahr Blüten und Früchte“ hervorbrachten (vgl. Seybold 1990, S. 241). Nicht erst seit 1549, sondern mindestens ab 1542 nutzte er demnach diesen Garten für wissenschaftliche Zwecke! Auch Conrad Gesner (1516–1565) schickte ihm Samen von *Nicotiana tabacum*, worauf schon Ganzinger (1959, S. 223) hinweist. Viele weitere Pflanzen, die er von befreundeten Botanikern oder von seinem in Italien studierenden Sohn Friderich (1532–1604) erhielt, zog Fuchs zweifellos im Garten am Nonnenhaus heran. Ob man ihn allerdings als „first botanical garden in Tübingen“ bezeichnen kann, wie ihn Meyer et al. (1999, S. 124) ehrenvoll nennen, sei dahingestellt: Dann wäre er einer der ältesten Botanischen Gärten der Welt!

„… auff das aller künstlichst abgemalt/ unnd mit hohem grossen vleiss beschriben …“: Die Synthese von Kunst und Wissenschaft

Ohne Frage haben die vorzüglichen Pflanzenabbildungen in ganz erheblichem Maße zur wissenschaftlichen Bedeutung und bis heute andauernden Wertschätzung der *Historia* und des *New Kreüterbuchs* beigetragen. In nachweisbar sehr enger Zusammenarbeit mit Fuchs wurden sie von drei geradezu begnadeten Künstlern geschaffen, die er – soweit bekannt – erst nach seiner Ankunft in Tübingen für die Mitarbeit gewann und auf eigene Kosten in Dienst stellte. Die hohe Anerkennung, die er ihrer künstlerischen Leistung zumaß, belegen ihre Porträts in beiden Werken. Wenn wir ihnen dort auch erst ganz am Ende begegnen, gleichsam als „krönender Abschluss“, so war dies doch ein für die damalige Zeit ganz außergewöhnlicher und einmaliger Vorgang. Der Gelehrte setzte ihnen damit ein bleibendes Denkmal, wobei uns die Abbildung zugleich eine lebensnahe Vorstellung ihrer Tätigkeit vermittelt.

Albrecht Meyer aquarelliert gerade eine nahezu fertige Zeichnung, die dann als Vorlage für die Übertragung auf den Holzstock, die spätere Druckplatte, diente. Heinrich Füllmaurer hält eine solche Holztafel in der Hand, außerdem die als Vorbild dienende Pflanzendarstellung auf dem Pergament. Ihre Umzeichnung auf die glatte, feingeschliffene Holzoberfläche wurde mit großer Sorgfalt durchgeführt, wie die 23 noch in Tübingen vorhandenen „Kräuterbuchtafeln“ zeigen (vgl. Dobat 1983, 2000 a). Der Dritte im „Künstlerbunde“ war Veyt Rudolff Speckle, einer der bedeutendsten Formschneider der Zeit. Seine Aufgabe bestand darin, die Abbildung auf dem Holzstock mit ihren sämtlichen Details erhaben herauszuarbeiten. Dazu dienten dem in Straßburg lebenden Holzschneider verschiedene Instrumente. Alle freien Flächen mussten eingetieft werden, bis schließlich jede einzelne Linie der Zeichnung als erhöhter, schmaler Grat zurückblieb. Nach der Einfärbung ergab diese reliefartige Erhöhung beim Abdruck eine seitenverkehrte Wiedergabe der ursprünglichen Originalzeichnung. Wie viele Tage Speckle wohl für einen einzigen Holzschnitt benötigte?

Um Kosten und Platz zu sparen, ließ Fuchs gelegentlich miteinander verwandte Arten in einem Bild vereinen. Einer gemeinsamen Wurzel zum Beispiel „entspringen“ die beiden Rosen (vgl. Taf. CCCLXXIIII [374]) oder die drei verschiedenen *Lamium*-Arten (vgl. Taf. CCLXIIII [264]). Auch schönblühende Gartenformen (vgl. Taf. CC [200], CCLXXXVII [287]) oder einzelne Sorten wichtiger Kulturpflanzen (vgl. Taf. XLVI [46], CCXXXIX [239], CCCCLXXIII [473]) sind auf diese Weise „zusammengesetzt“. Ebenso wird die gleichzeitige Darstellung von frisch entfalteten Blüten und überreifen Früchten, um hier nur den Pfirsichbaum (vgl. Taf. CCCXLI [341]) oder die Johannisbeere (vgl. Taf. CCCLXXVII [377]) zu nennen, wohl auf Anweisung des Gelehrten vorgenommen worden sein. Bei vielen Wildpflanzen kannte nur Fuchs den Zeitpunkt ihres Blühens und Fruchtens; seine Mitarbeiter fügten dann die einzelnen Entwicklungsstadien, die er ihnen vorlegte, zu einem einprägsamen Gesamtbild der jeweiligen Art zusammen. Manche im Frühjahr begonnene Zeichnung konnte somit erst im Herbst beendet und im Winter weiter bearbeitet werden.

Sehr viel Zeit erforderte ebenfalls die anschließende Handkolorierung des Drucks. Beide Werke gelangten daher sowohl in einer preiswerteren „Schwarzweiß-Ausgabe“, als auch in einer aufwendig kolorierten „Prachtedition“ in den Handel. Den hohen Preis von 15 Gulden für ein derartiges Exemplar der *Historia* nennt Fuchs in einem Brief vom November 1542. Er entsprach somit fast seinem eigenen Monatsgehalt, und nicht einmal seinen engsten Freunden konnte er ein Buch schenken (Fichtner 1967, 1968). Ähnlich dürfte es beim *New Kreüterbuch* gewesen sein, und fast an ein Wunder grenzt die Tatsache, dass davon ausgerechnet das persönliche Handexemplar aus seiner einstigen Privatbibliothek in Tübingen die Zeiten überstand. Heute in Ulm aufbewahrt, wurde nach ihm der vorliegende Nachdruck angefertigt. Fuchs wird die Kolorierung gerade auch dieses Bandes selbst verfolgt und überprüft haben, sodass größtmögliche Authentizität gegeben ist. Wie soeben von einer Exkursion mitgebracht oder frisch aus dem Garten geholt, erscheinen uns die vor über vier Jahrhunderten in sorgfältiger und mühevoller Gemeinschaftsarbeit entstandenen Pflanzenbilder.

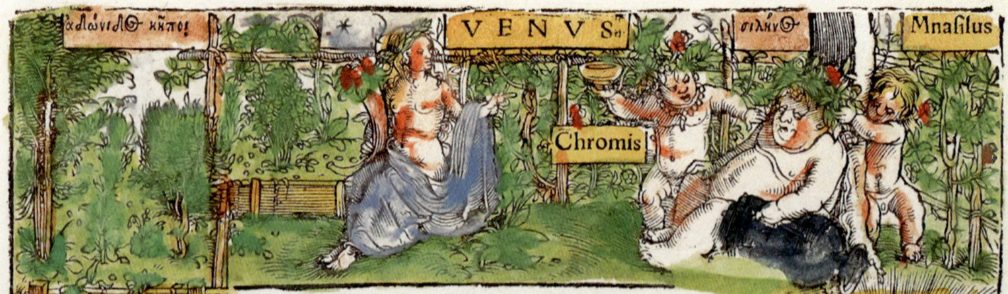

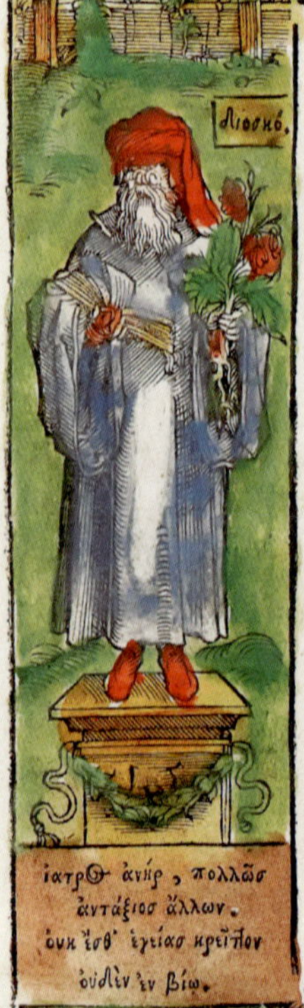

HERBARVM VIVAE EICONES

ad naturæ imitationem, sũma cum diligentia & artificio effigiatæ, una cum EFFECTIBVS earundem, in gratiam ueteris illius, & iamiam renascentis Herbariæ Medicinæ,

PER OTH. BRVNF. recens editæ. M. D. XXXII.

¶ Quibus adiecta ad calcem, APPENDIX isagogica de usu & administratione SIMPLICIVM.

Item Index Contentorum singulorum.

Argentorati apud Ioannem Schottũ, cum Cæs. Maiest. Priuilegio ad Sexennium.

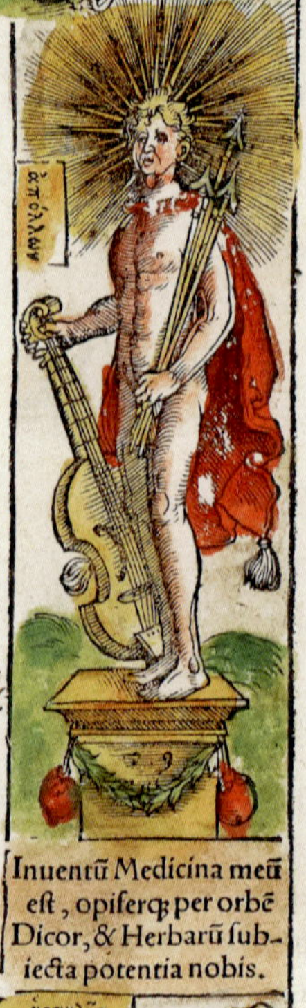

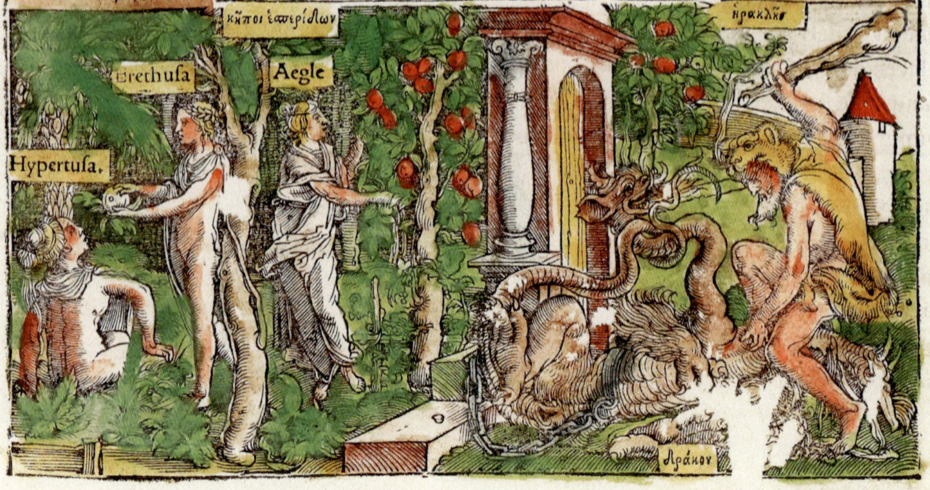

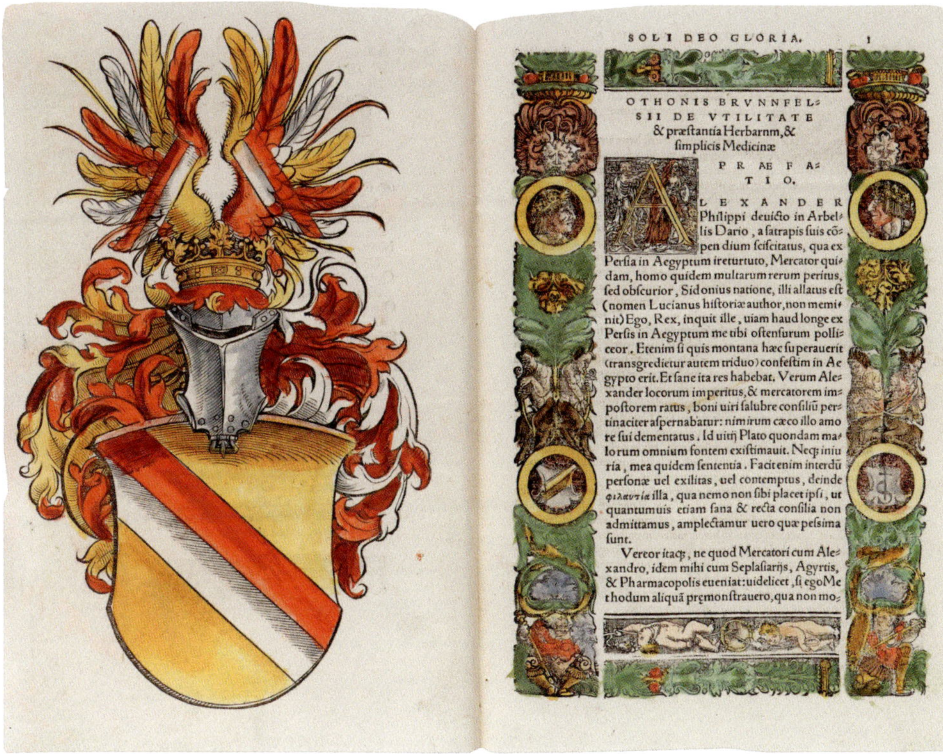

Die letzten zwei Jahrzehnte

Historia und *New Kreüterbuch* trugen Fuchs' Namen hinaus in alle Welt – und dennoch begann er schon 1543 mit der Fortsetzung seiner Pflanzengeschichte. Spätestens 1550 lag der erste Teil dieser Handschrift fertig vor (vgl. Stübler 1928, S. 99), bis zum Juli 1551 waren über 300 neue Abbildungen hinzugekommen (vgl. Seybold 1986, S. 12). Anhand des Briefwechsels mit seinem Freund Camerarius sind wir über den allmählichen Fortgang während der nächsten Jahre recht gut unterrichtet: 1557 war ein zweiter Band mit 400 weiteren Bildern abgeschlossen, dem 1563/64 schließlich das Manuskript eines dritten Bandes folgte. Damit war nach rund 20-jährigem Fleiß und Einsatz das Gesamtwerk weitgehend vollendet. Immer stärker hat sich der Gelehrte offenbar mit dieser Arbeit identifiziert, sich geradezu in sie „verbissen" – anders ist diese immense Leistung wohl kaum zu erklären. Verständlich auch, wenn Fichtner (1968, S. 75) anmerkt: „Insgesamt scheint die Praxis je länger je weniger eine Rolle im Leben von Fuchs gespielt zu haben." Selbst herbe Rückschläge konnten seine Beharrlichkeit nicht ins Wanken bringen, denn mehrfach hatte er in diesen zwei Jahrzehnten vergeblich versucht, einen Geldgeber für den Druck zu finden. Jeder andere hätte wohl resigniert, doch er blieb unentwegt tätig und ließ auf eigene Kosten Zeichnungen, Holzstöcke und Probedrucke von den neu aufgenommenen Pflanzen anfertigen (vgl. Rytz 1933). Mit

OTTO BRUNFELS, *Herbarum vivae eicones,* Strasbourg, 1532
Title page, coat of arms, preface / Titelblatt, Wappen, Vorwort / Page de titre, blason, préface
Private collection

Jerg Ziegler stellte er um 1550 sogar einen weiteren außerordentlich befähigten und tüchtigen Maler ein. Er sollte der letzte künstlerische Mitarbeiter von Fuchs werden. Einige der 440 von ihm signierten Aquarelle im Manuskript lassen sich genauer datieren, da sie nach dem Herbar des Augsburger Arztes und Reisenden Leonhard Rauwolff (1535–1596) angefertigt wurden. Er dürfte Fuchs 1563 besucht haben und stellte ihm seine Pflanzensammlung zur Verfügung (vgl. Ganzinger 1963, S. 28; Seybold 1986, S. 20, 1990, S. 251 ff.; Meyer et al. 1999, S. 185 ff.). Auch acht der in Tübingen verbliebenen und noch ungeschnittenen Kräuterbuchtafeln gehen auf diese Vorlagen zurück und tragen Zieglers Monogramm. Nach wie vor bemühte sich Fuchs also um eine Erweiterung seiner Pflanzenkenntnisse, um die Vervollständigung der Handschrift und um die Unterstützung durch auswärtige Botaniker, dies bis in seine letzten Lebensjahre hinein, die vom Tod seiner Frau Anna im Februar 1563 überschattet waren. Im darauf folgenden Jahr heiratete er Afra Graeter, die Witwe eines Pfarrers aus Schwäbisch Hall, doch seine Kräfte ließen allmählich nach. Weitere verzweifelte Versuche, von verschiedenen Fürsten und Reichsstädten Gelder für den Druck seines „Lebenswerkes" zu erhalten, scheiterten. Keine seiner Hoffnungen erfüllte sich. Tief enttäuscht, von Krankheiten gezeichnet und von zunehmender Sehschwäche geplagt, starb Leonhart Fuchs am 10. Mai 1566 in Tübingen. Beerdigt wurde er an der Seite seiner ersten Frau auf dem einstigen Friedhof bei der Ammer, dessen Gelände man 1835/36 in den Alten Botanischen Garten eingliederte. Ein Arboretum wurde darauf angelegt, und noch immer stehen dort einige der alten Bäume. Unter ihnen ruhen beide an ungewisser Stelle.

Auch Fuchs' ältester Sohn Friderich (1532–1604), der Stadtarzt in Ulm war, konnte trotz großer Bemühungen die Drucklegung der Handschrift nicht verwirklichen. Nach seinem Tod gelangte das Manuskript in den Handel. Über 200 Jahre galt es als verschollen – und schlummerte zum Glück doch seit 1756 an einem sicheren Ort: in der Österreichischen Nationalbibliothek in Wien. Dort erinnerte man sich 1954 anlässlich einer Ausstellung an die Handschrift, die schließlich durch Ganzinger (1959) aus ihrem „Dornröschenschlaf" erweckt wurde. Dieser dreibändige *Codex Vindobonensis Palatinus*, gegliedert in neun Teilbände mit zahllosen eng beschriebenen Folioseiten und über 1500 Abbildungen, ist ein weiteres bleibendes Vermächtnis des Tübinger Gelehrten, der mit Recht als einer der „deutschen Väter der Pflanzenkunde" in die Geschichte einging (S. 12, 17, 20, 23, 43, 50, 53, 62, 66, 70).

LEONHART FUCHS, Title page from / Titelblatt von / Page de titre de: *De historia stirpium*, Basel 1542
Pittsburgh, Hunt Institute for Botanical Documentation, HI call no. + CA F951h

DE HISTORIA STIRPIUM COMMENTARII INSIGNES, MAXIMIS IMPENSIS ET VIGILIIS ELABORATI, ADIECTIS EARUNDEM VIVIS PLUSQUAM quingentis imaginibus, nunquam antea ad naturæ imitationem artificiosius effictis & expresſis, LEONHARTO FUCHSIO medico hac nostra ætate longè clariſsimo, autore.

Regiones peregrinas pleriq;, alij alias, ſumptu ingenti, ſtudio indefeſſo, nec ſine diſcrimine uitæ nonnunquam, adierunt, ut ſimplicium materiæ cognoſcendæ facultatem compararent ſibi: eam tibi materiam uniuerſam ſummo & impenſarum & temporis compendio, procul diſcrimine omni, tanquam in uiuo iucundiſsimoq; uiridario, magna cum uoluptate, hinc cognoſcere licebit.

Acceſsit ijs ſuccincta admodum uocum difficilium & obſcurarum paſsim in hoc opere occurrentium explicatio.

Unà cum quadruplici Indice, quorum primus quidem ſtirpium nomenclaturas græcas, alter latinas, tertius officinis ſeplaſiariorum & herbarijs uſitatas, quartus germanicas continebit.

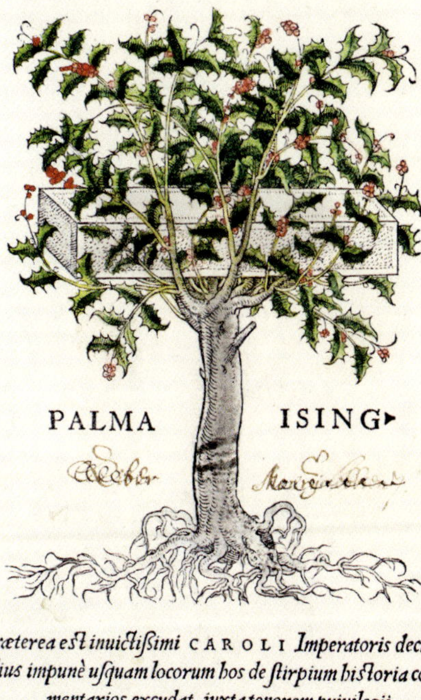

Cautum præterea eſt inuictiſsimi CAROLI *Imperatoris decreto, ne quis alius impunè uſquam locorum hos de ſtirpium hiſtoria commentarios excudat, iuxta tenorem priuilegij antè à nobis euulgati.*

BASILEÆ, IN OFFICINA ISINGRINIANA,
ANNO CHRISTI M. D. XLII.

KLAUS DOBAT

Leonhart Fuchs

Médecin et pionnier de la botanique moderne

Leonhart Fuchs (1501–1566) est né à Wemding, une charmante localité bavaroise située à l'est de la ville impériale de Nördlingen. Il est le fils cadet du bourgmestre Johann Fuchs et de sa femme Anna. On ne connaît pas le jour exact de sa naissance : peut-être est-ce le 17 janvier ou le 1er janvier, voire le 17 février. Mais d'après Meyer et al. (1999, p. 819), il n'existe aucun document corroborant l'une ou l'autre de ces dates.

Après la mort précoce de son père, il reçoit un premier enseignement de sa mère et de son grand-père, lui-même ancien bourgmestre de Wemding. C'est un enfant vif et intelligent que sa famille envoie dès 1511 à l'école de latin de Heilbronn, où il se fait bientôt remarquer de son professeur Conrad pour ses dons et son application. L'année suivante, il fréquente la Marienschule, une école d'Erfurt en Thuringe, qui prépare par une étude intensive du latin et du grec à l'admission à l'université de la ville, l'un des établissements les plus renommés de son temps. Inscrit à l'automne 1515 à la faculté des arts, il termine ses études dès le semestre d'hiver 1516/1517 avec le titre de *Baccalaureus artium* (bachelier ès arts), lequel l'habilite à enseigner. Revenu à Wemding, Fuchs y ouvre à l'âge de 17 ans une école privée, puis il décide en 1519 de poursuivre ses études à l'université d'Ingolstadt. Après son magistère ès arts (1521) et son doctorat en médecine (1524), il exerce pendant deux ans la médecine à Munich, où il épouse la fille d'un conseiller municipal de la ville, Anna Friedberger, « jeune fille respectable et bien éduquée, issue d'une famille honorable » (Roth 1898, p. 162). Dix enfants (quatre fils et six filles) naîtront de ce mariage, dont deux qui décèdent avant leur baptême.

De la pratique médicale au professorat d'université – une carrière semée d'embûches

En 1526, Fuchs se voit proposer la chaire de médecine à l'université d'Ingolstadt et accepte cet honneur, bien que l'établissement soit considéré comme un des bastions du catholicisme et qu'il ait embrassé depuis longtemps les idées de Martin Luther. Outre les considérations financières, ce sont la perspective de pouvoir faire de la recherche et son goût pour l'enseignement qui le décident. Mais il se retrouve dans une ville où règne l'étroitesse d'esprit, une université qui surveille et sanctionne les idées religieuses de ses professeurs.

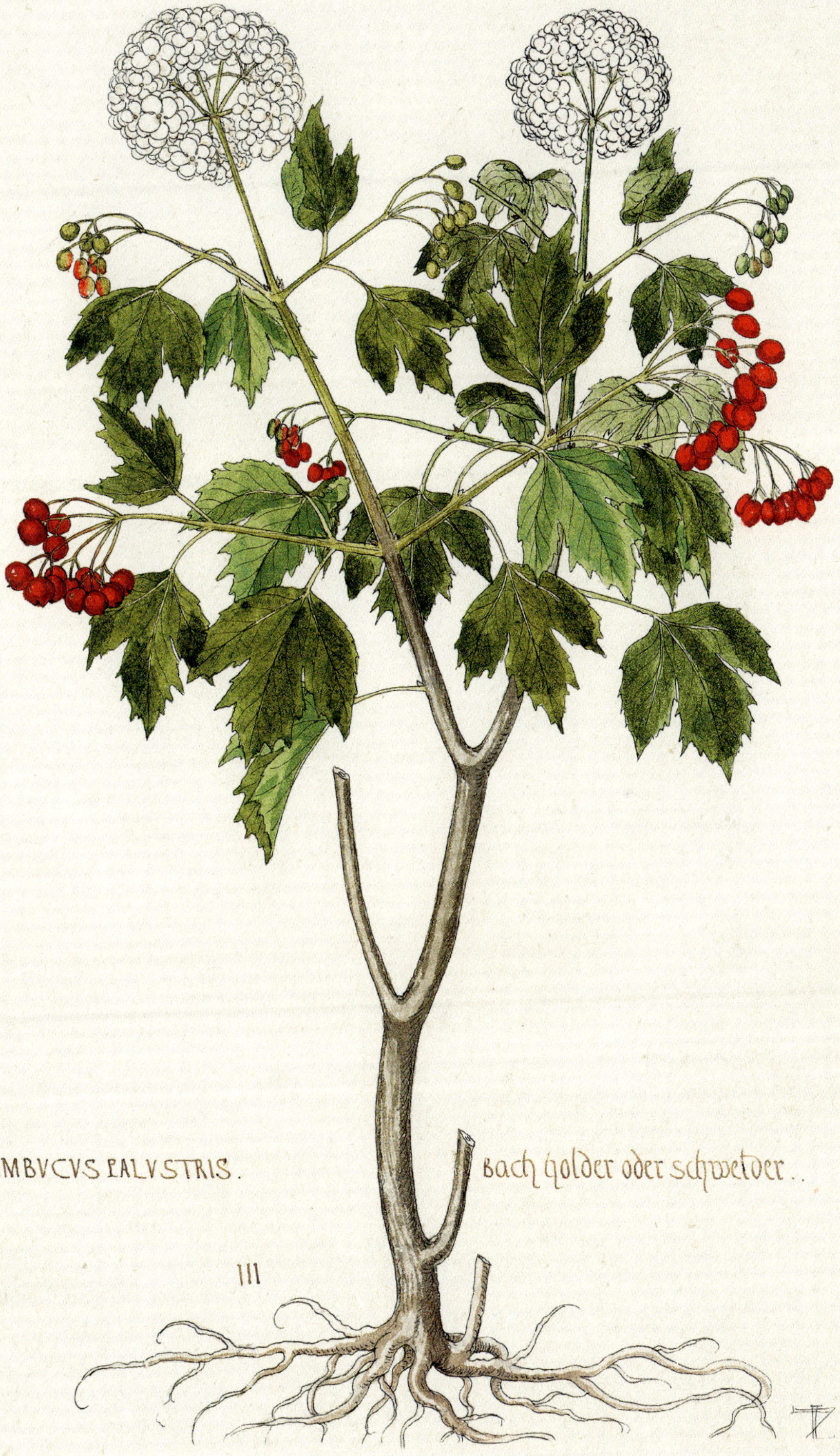

SAMBVCVS PALVSTRIS.

bach holder oder schwelder..

III

Aussi quitte-t-il Ingolstadt deux ans plus tard pour devenir premier médecin du margrave Georg von Brandenburg à Ansbach (l'ancienne Onoltzbach). Non seulement Fuchs a en vue une place de professeur à l'université qui doit y être fondée, mais comme médecin renommé, il peut également s'adonner en toute liberté à ses études scientifiques et littéraires.

Parmi les ouvrages médicaux parus en ce temps-là, l'un en particulier, *Errata recentiorum medicorum* (Erreurs des médecins modernes), fait grand bruit. À la suite de sa publication en 1530, Fuchs intervient dans une polémique remontant au XIVe siècle et qui divise le corps médical en deux camps : d'un côté, les «arabistes» qui exercent selon les préceptes de l'école arabe, de l'autre, les tenants de la médecine grecque. Avec la fougue de la jeunesse et un esprit impitoyable, Fuchs plaide en faveur de la médecine grecque, d'une validité absolue à ses yeux. Servi par une solide formation humaniste et une grande connaissance des textes anciens, il s'appuie sur de nombreuses citations pour démontrer les antinomies existant entre les deux écoles, mais il va souvent trop loin dans ses critiques, soit en rejetant certains mérites incontestables de la médecine arabe, soit en les passant sous silence. De plus, il signale à juste titre les erreurs de nomenclature botanique et la confusion entre certaines plantes médicinales, lesquelles ne montrent pas, et pour cause, l'effet qu'on leur a prêté. Les premiers exposés botaniques et pharmacologiques du jeune savant sont particulièrement appréciés d'Otto Brunfels (1488–1534) puisque celui-ci les reprend presque tels quels dans le second volume de son herbier (*Novi herbarii Tomus II*; 1531). Fuchs adopte aussi une position provocatrice sur des questions controversées de thérapeutique et d'anatomie. Convaincu de la justesse de ses idées, il veut incontestablement secouer et faire évoluer le monde médical de son temps. S'il espère être applaudi, il s'attend également, car il est conscient des remous qu'il va provoquer, à récolter de violentes critiques de la part de ses collègues arabistes. En tout cas, il se fait vite un nom !

À Ansbach, Fuchs achève, entre autres, son premier compendium de la médecine (*Compendiaria … in medendi artem …*, 1531), un ouvrage qui va remporter un vif succès et qu'il remaniera constamment au cours des deux décennies suivantes. Sa réputation, Fuchs la doit à cette publication, ainsi qu'à la traduction commentée d'un traité d'Hippocrate sur les maladies épidémiques (*Hippocratis medicorum omnium longe principis Epidemiorum liber sexus …*, 1532).

Malgré ses succès littéraires et la grande considération que lui montre le prince, Fuchs est plus que jamais convaincu que sa vocation est d'enseigner. Ce n'est pourtant pas à Ansbach qu'il peut le faire, d'autant plus que le projet d'université est sans cesse reporté. C'est pourquoi, rappelé à l'université d'Ingolstadt, il quitte Ansbach au printemps 1533. Mais contre tout espoir, rien n'y a changé, et les hostilités reprennent. Lui, le protestant intransigeant, se voit même interdit de cours magistraux (Prantl 1872, p. 197). Fuchs, résigné, reprend sa place de premier médecin du margrave à l'été de la même année. Pour montrer sa reconnaissance envers le prince qui l'a sauvé «du gouffre des sophistes

PAGE 43
LEONHART FUCHS, *Codex Fuchs*, Tübingen, *c.* 1536–1566
Vienna, Österreichische Nationalbibliothek, HAN: Cod. 11117–11125 (9 vols.)
Viburnum opulus (L.) – Guelder Rose / Gewöhnlicher Schneeball / Viorne obier, Cod. 11117, p. 239

d'Ingolstadt» («ex Ingolstadiensium Sophistarum faucibus»), il lui dédie la seconde mise à jour de son compendium en 1535. Fuchs, cependant, bien que toujours très estimé à la cour, entre en pourparlers avec l'université de Tübingen dès l'été 1534, encouragé par le célèbre humaniste luthérien Philipp Melanchthon (1497–1560) qui le connaît depuis ses études à l'université d'Ingolstadt.

Une nouvelle vie à Tübingen

Appelé à Tübingen en tant que «médecin particulièrement érudit en langues» (Roth 1877, p. 183), et chargé par le duc Ulrich von Württemberg (1487–1550) de réorganiser les études d'humanités, Leonhart Fuchs obtient la chaire de médecine de l'université le 14 août 1535. Mais il s'installe dans un pays secoué par la Réforme et une université encore fortement imprégnée de catholicisme. Decker-Hauff et Setzler (1977) ont relaté de façon saisissante l'atmosphère de bouleversements qui règne alors car, outre «la mainmise brutale d'Ulrich sur les biens de l'Église» (p. 69), celui-ci engage une réforme impitoyable de l'université : «l'ordre du duc Ulrich», ainsi qu'on l'appelle, entre en vigueur le 30 janvier 1535 et «enjoint à tous les professeurs d'embrasser la nouvelle foi ou d'émigrer.» Le 7 mars 1535, la messe est interdite à Tübingen, et le 9 est renouvelé l'ordre de «se convertir ou d'émigrer» (p. 64).

Âgé seulement de 34 ans, mais sûr de lui et plein d'énergie, Fuchs se jette dans sa tâche réformatrice – contre les traditions de l'Église et de la médecine – avec un zèle particulier, car il est toujours aussi peu enclin à l'opportunisme. À peine investi dans ses fonctions, il publie sous le titre *Paradoxorum medicinae libri tres* une mise à jour de ses *Errata* qui donne une idée précise de ses opinions. Il est difficile aujourd'hui de comprendre pourquoi Fuchs montre autant d'âpreté et de partialité à pourfendre la médecine arabe. Il ne voit que par les auteurs grecs, devenant même poétique quand il écrit : «Pour cette raison, revenons à la source et puisons en elle l'eau pure et inaltérée des connaissances médicales !» (Sprengel 1827, p. 151). Même Avicenne (l'Arabe Ibn Sīnā, 980–1037), l'un des plus éminents représentants de la médecine et de la science arabes, ne trouve pas grâce à ses yeux, car il l'accuse dans son ouvrage dédié au duc d'avoir largement copié les auteurs grecs. Ses collègues adeptes de la science ancienne savent en tout cas à quoi s'attendre.

Fuchs est nommé dès octobre 1535 doyen de la faculté et constate avec une déception mêlée de courroux : «Que mes prédécesseurs n'aient laissé aucun écrit permettant à la postérité d'apprendre ce qu'ils ont fait montre avec quelle négligence les affaires de la faculté de médecine ont été conduites» (Haller 1927, p. 133 et s.). Entre 1536 et 1565, Fuchs sera désigné six fois comme président de l'université et peut grâce à cette position réaliser certaines de ses idées. Il élabore en 1538, conjointement avec Joachim Camerarius (1500–1574), rencontré durant leurs études à Erfurt et qui restera un ami jusqu'à la fin de sa vie, les nouveaux statuts de l'université de Tübingen. Ils procèdent aussi à des changements révolutionnaires au sein même de la faculté de médecine, lesquels portent indubitablement l'empreinte de Fuchs : l'étude de l'astronomie, jusque-là obligatoire, est supprimée, et la littérature arabe ne doit «être étudiée qu'avec parcimonie» au profit de la littérature grecque (Fichtner 1967, p. 4). Par ailleurs, Fuchs suggère d'effectuer au moins une dissection par an, avec la participation obligatoire des étudiants, alors que les anciens statuts de 1497 prévoyaient de «disséquer un corps humain au moins tous les trois ou quatre ans et de l'analyser selon l'ouvrage de Mondino». Étant donné que le livre d'anatomie de Mondino (il est question de l'*Anathomia*

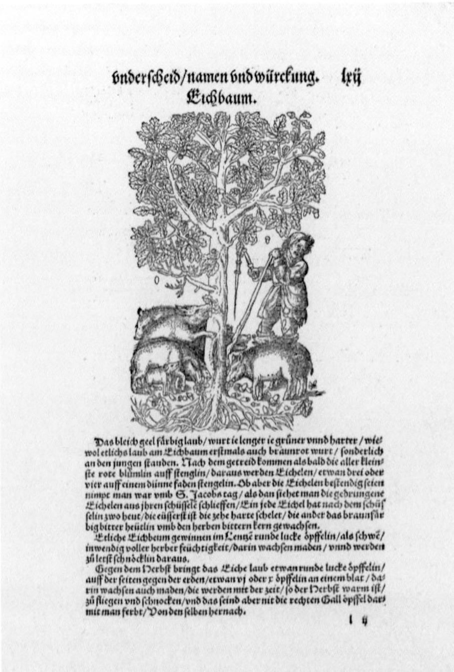

vnderscheid/namen vnd würckung. lxij
Eichbaum.

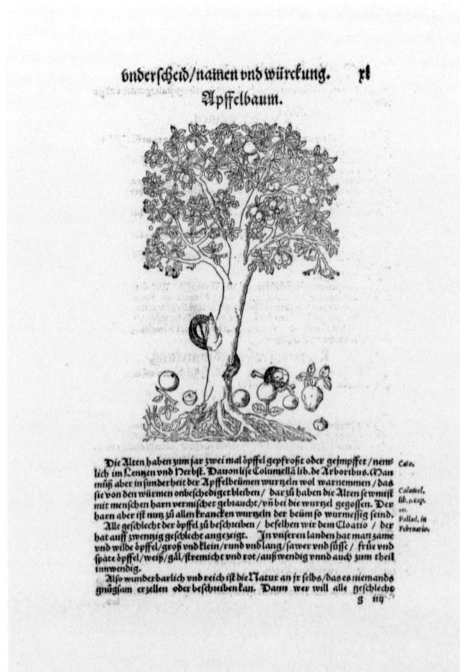

vnderscheid/namen vnd würckung. xl
Apffelbaum.

HIERONYMUS BOCK, *Kreuterbuch*, Strasbourg, 1546
2nd ed. of the *New Kreütter Buch* from 1539
Vienna, Österreichische Nationalbibliothek, SIAWD 79.A.27

Quercus robur (L.) – English Oak / Stiel-Eiche / Chêne pédonculé
Vol. 3, folio 62 recto

Malus domestica (Borkh.) – Apple / Kulturapfel / Pommier cultivé
Vol. 3, folio 50 recto

Vitis vinifera (L.) – Grape / Weinrebe / Vigne
Vol. 3, folio 45 recto

parue en 1316) est selon lui « plein de défauts et d'erreurs, il vaudrait mieux l'abandonner et lire pendant la dissection le chapitre correspondant de Galien » (Froriep 1811, p. 1, 3 et s.). Mais Fuchs donne aussi de nouvelles impulsions à la recherche et l'enseignement médicaux de l'université en introduisant le traité d'anatomie humaine d'André Vésale (1515–1564), *De humani corporis fabrica* (p. 10), premier ouvrage complet sur cette science publié en 1534.

Pour rester dans le sujet, mentionnons une autre initiative de Fuchs qui a dû faire grand bruit en 1546/1547 : l'achat du premier squelette humain. Le duc Ulrich, sur la proposition de Fuchs, acquiert pour le prix de 30 florins un « homme décharné » pour permettre aux étudiants d'observer « comment sont faits l'ossature humaine et l'assemblage des os » (Froriep 1902, p. VI). Enfin, il assure la formation des médecins par ses nombreuses publications et ses cours, toujours beaucoup fréquentés et « très réputés en raison de la méthode claire et de l'exposé, compréhensible et classique à la fois » (Moll 1852, p. 357).

Weinreben.

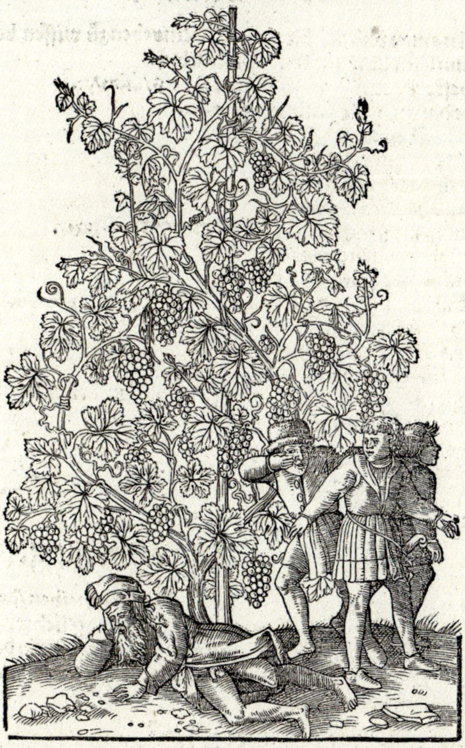

men Edel oder Lautertrauben / Rißling wachsen an der Mosel/Rhein/ vnd im Wormser gawe/Hinsch trauben seind die aller gemeinste beinahe in allen weinländern. Drutsch vnd Albich traubē/wachsen am gebirg vmb die statt Landaw. Genßfüssel vmb die Newenstatt. Harthinsch vmb Thürckeim vñ Wachenheim. Früschwartz oder Kleber bei Weissenburg. Desgleichen das Grünfrenckisch. Schwartz Lamperß drauben/ zielt man vast in dem Cleburger ampt bei Weissenburg.

Wer will aber alle geschlecht so an einem jeden ort wachsen/erzellen? als Osterreicher drauben/Frenckisch drauben/vnd deren vil ꝛc.

Der alt Theophrastus sagt von einem Rebstock der hab draubē on laub bracht/lib. ij. cap. iiij. die vrsach will ich nicht ausfechten.

Wie nun die reben auffwachsen vnd gepflantzet werden / ist offenbar/ Doch so hat ein jedes land sein eigen brauch / also das nichts gewiß dauon zů schreiben ist / wer aber solchs zů wissen begert / der lese vnder anderen Columellam lib. iiij. durch aus/vnd Palladium lib. iij. vnd iiij. vnd xj.

Rißling.
Hynsch.
Trutsch.
Albich.
Gensfůssel.
Harthinisch.
Kleber oder Frůschwartz.
Grůnfrenckisch.
Läpersch.

Il est évident que Fuchs doit se battre pour imposer ces réformes importantes et prometteuses, et faire face alternativement à l'approbation et au rejet. « Sa propension à ne pas démordre de ce qu'il considère comme exact et sa fréquente intolérance envers ceux qui n'ont pas les mêmes idées lui ont valu aussi certaines hostilités au sein même du corps enseignant de l'université », écrit Stübler (1928, p. 175). À ces dissensions internes s'ajoutent les démêlés continuels avec la bureaucratie de la cour du duc Ulrich, lesquels amèneront aussi son collègue et ami Joachim Camerarius à quitter Tübingen pour Leipzig. De plus, luthérien convaincu et scientifique réaliste, Fuchs souffre beaucoup des conflits politico-religieux qui agitent le pays. Enfin, que de temps précieux les querelles qui l'opposent à d'autres savants, justifiées ou dictées par la jalousie, ne lui coûtent-elles pas ! Un bon exemple nous en est donné par la dispute qui l'oppose au médecin Janus Cornarius (1500–1558), un adepte comme lui de la médecine grecque. Malgré ce point commun, Fuchs et Cornarius se jalousent l'un l'autre pour des succès réels ou supposés, et pendant douze ans ils s'injurient dans leurs publications avec une véhémence croissante. Cornarius accuse Fuchs de vol intellectuel et le traite de plumitif ; celui-ci écrit de son côté que les œuvres de Cornarius sont tout juste bonnes pour les cafards et les mites – des déclarations bien inoffensives comparées à d'autres, que l'on désespérerait de trouver dans les plus gros dictionnaires de latin.

Fuchs n'est guère satisfait non plus sur le plan financier, bien qu'avec un salaire confortable de 200 florins par an il compte parmi les professeurs les mieux rétribués de l'université. Aussi, à plusieurs reprises, a-t-il l'intention de quitter la ville et le pays. En 1537/1538, il aurait pu devenir premier médecin à la cour du roi Christian III du Danemark et obtenir en plus la chaire de médecine à l'université protestante de Copenhague qui était alors en projet. Toutefois, les mauvaises expériences qu'il a faites à Ansbach l'ont rendu prudent. En outre, les émoluments qu'on lui propose sont effectivement loin de correspondre à ce qu'il souhaite toucher, si loin même que cela relève de la pingrerie pure et simple.

Dans ces conditions, il décline l'offre, surtout que d'autres raisons viennent se greffer là-dessus : sa femme se trouve une nouvelle fois enceinte, et il a une famille nombreuse ; de plus, il a déjà beaucoup publié, et ses tâches comme sa position à l'université sont intéressantes. Fuchs refuse même en 1544 une autre proposition plus honorable encore, et particulièrement avantageuse sur le plan matériel, que lui fait Cosme de Médicis. Il est, en effet, le premier savant allemand à qui le duc offre de diriger le jardin botanique fondé à Pise en 1543 et considéré comme le plus vieux jardin botanique du monde. Devoir refuser un tel honneur lui coûte beaucoup, ainsi qu'il l'écrit dans une lettre du 1er novembre 1544 à Camerarius. Mais finalement, ce sont avant tout des considérations religieuses qui motivent sa décision (Stübler 1928, p. 172 et s. ; Fichtner 1968, p. 69 ; Krafft 1998, p. 137 ; Meyer et al. 1999, p. 37 et s.).

Malgré une vie professionnelle et privée mouvementée à Tübingen, Fuchs accomplit un immense travail, difficile à imaginer aujourd'hui ! En dehors de ses obligations de président de l'université, de sa participation aux événements politiques, théologiques et réformateurs de son temps, de ses cours d'anatomie, de médecine générale et de pharmacologie, et bien sûr de son cabinet médical, il reste un auteur extrêmement prolifique. Ainsi il publie en collaboration avec Camerarius et d'autres auteurs un ouvrage en cinq volumes sur Galien (1538) ; seul, il rédige des manuels, des traductions, des commentaires et des écrits polémiques (p. 11), tous compilés dans la précieuse monographie de Meyer et al. (1999, p. 633 et s.). Enfin, Fuchs se tourne de plus en plus vers l'étude pharmacologique des plantes.

Au nom de la médecine et de la botanique

Dans les statuts de l'université de 1538, Leonhart Fuchs préconisait déjà une amélioration de l'étude de la botanique. Les directives suivantes n'ont sûrement pas mis en joie l'un ou l'autre de ses collègues casaniers : « Et enfin, il doit durant l'été se rendre souvent avec les étudiants en médecine dans les champs et les montagnes, observer attentivement l'aspect des plantes et leur en présenter une image vivante, et non, comme beaucoup avaient coutume de le faire jusqu'à maintenant, laisser la connaissance des plantes médicinales aux épiciers, aux hommes frustes et aux bonnes femmes » (« Aestatis denique tempore cum medicinae studiosis rura montesque saepius petat ac plantarun uultum diligenter obseruet illisque uiuas eorundem imagines demonstret, neque ut hactenus consueuere multi, simplicium notitiam seplasiariis illis hominibus rudibus et stultis mulierculis committat », Roth 1877, p. 312).

Donnant lui-même l'exemple, il est le premier professeur de l'université à faire des excursions botaniques ! Fuchs a découvert durant sa vie à Ingolstadt combien est importante l'observation dans la nature, pour lui un complément idéal à l'enseignement académique. Nul doute qu'il n'ait poursuivi cette tradition à Tübingen avec une belle persévérance et n'ait fait aussi de la botanique lors de promenades privées. Car il a grand besoin de plantes fraîches non seulement pour ses cours, mais surtout pour les décrire minutieusement et les représenter dans ses deux célèbres herbiers. Ce sont eux qui, bien plus que toutes les simples publications médicales dont il est l'auteur, assureront au savant une gloire posthume !

Deux herbiers de réputation mondiale : *De historia stirpium* (1542) et *New Kreüterbuch* (1543)

Fuchs entreprend la rédaction d'*Historia*, une « histoire des plantes médicinales » destinée aux universitaires, dès son séjour à Ansbach. Il est possible que la publication en 1530 du premier tome de l'*Herbarum vivae eicones* de Brunfels (p. 38–39) l'ait incité à réaliser un projet depuis longtemps caressé. Étaient-ce les « glaring errors », les erreurs sautant aux yeux, commises par Brunfels qui ont été déterminantes, comme le présument Meyer et al. (1999, p. 48), ou le fait qu'« on n'en eût pas encore fini avec les auteurs arabes et arabistes autant qu'il le souhaitait » (Stübler 1928, p. 231) ? Toujours est-il que Fuchs veut faire « mieux ». Son dessein est de présenter, outre une évaluation approfondie et commentée des œuvres de Galien, Dioscoride (p. 28–29), Hippocrate, Théophraste, Pline et d'autres auteurs, toutes les espèces végétales qu'il a rassemblées jusqu'alors. La vie agitée qu'il mène en ce temps-là explique la lenteur de son travail : « J'ai fait un herbier, mais il n'est pas encore imprimé. Il comprend plus de trois-cent cinquante plantes avec leurs racines, tiges, feuilles, graines et fleurs ; ce sera un livre plaisant à voir. Je l'ai achevé – Dieu soit loué – après beaucoup de travail et de dépenses », écrit-il en 1538 au duc Albrecht von Preußen (Voigt 1841, p. 269). Mais c'est un peu prématuré comme il s'avère. Car il découvre ou fait venir des environs de Tübingen toujours plus de plantes ; en outre, il doit tenir compte d'ouvrages récents comme le *New Kreütter Buch* de Jérôme Bock (1498–1554 ; p. 22–23), imprimé en 1539, ou le *Contrafayt Kreüterbuch* d'Otto Brunfels paru dans les années 1532–1537 (p. 25, 32). C'est ainsi que quatre longues années s'écoulent avant que l'*Historia*, avec ses 900 pages et ses 511 illustrations magnifiques, ne voit enfin le jour en 1542 (p. 41).

On retrouve dans le *New Kreüterbuch*, que Fuchs publie dès 1543, les mêmes gravures sur bois, plus six nouvelles planches. Cet herbier est resté jusqu'à nos jours un modèle de

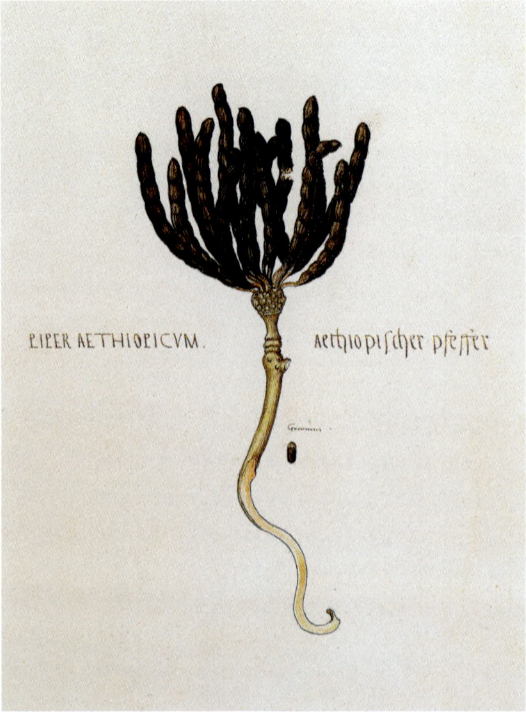

l'illustration de livre botanique et enthousiasme encore dans la présente réédition par sa grande qualité scientifique et artistique. Malgré le peu de temps qu'a mis Fuchs pour l'achever, l'importance de cet ouvrage écrit en allemand ne cède en rien à celle de l'*Historia*. Étant donné que le *New Kreüterbuch* s'adresse à un large public, il n'est pas question pour Fuchs d'en faire une simple traduction. Il doit donc le remanier complètement pour le rendre intelligible à tous.

Certes, dans son introduction qui mérite d'être lue, il laisse entendre, non sans méchanceté, qu'une lecture ne pourrait faire de mal aux médecins, mais il précise aussi que l'ouvrage doit avant tout « être utile à l'homme commun et lui servir à connaître les plantes ». C'est pourquoi les savants exposés sur le savoir des Anciens sont très abrégés et les descriptions de plantes plus détaillées pour permettre de mieux les identifier et les récolter. En plus de cela, Fuchs donne des renseignements pratiques sur la culture des plantes médicinales, évoquant les conditions essentielles au développement, par exemple la nature du terrain ou l'emplacement adéquat. Il serait « bon et utile », écrit-il, « que les plantes ne soient pas plantées et entretenues dans les jardins uniquement par les médecins, mais encore par les néophytes et l'homme commun afin que, dans les pays allemands, leur connaissance s'accroisse journellement au point de ne jamais tomber dans l'oubli ». Il veille par ailleurs à mettre le lecteur en garde contre les dangers d'une automédication : « Même celui qui connaît bien les plantes ne fera jamais un médecin. »

Comme dans *Historia*, les plantes du *New Kreüterbuch* sont classées selon l'ordre alphabétique de leurs appellations grecques. Pour chaque plante, Fuchs structure son texte de façon méthodique et claire, généralement en sept paragraphes : « Noms », « Genres », « Forme », « Lieu de croissance », « Temps », « Nature et complexion » et « Puissance et effet ».

Il énumère tout d'abord les différentes dénominations, grecques, latines et allemandes, ainsi que les noms courants employés par les apothicaires. Notons en passant que Fuchs a marqué de son empreinte les noms génériques de *Campanula*, *Digitalis* et *Ophioglossum*, et que ceux-ci sont toujours en vigueur aujourd'hui, comme d'ailleurs les noms scientifiques

LEONHART FUCHS, *Codex Fuchs*, Tübingen, *c.* 1536–1566
Vienna, Österreichische Nationalbibliothek, HAN: Cod. 11117–11125 (9 vols.)
Xylopia aethiopica (Dun.) Rich. – Guinea Pepper / Guineapfeffer / Poivre de Guinée, Cod. 11123, p. 135

d'espèces qu'il a introduits – *Allium ursinum, Angelica sylvestris, Digitalis purpurea, Hordeum distichon, Iris germanica, Origanum vulgare,* pour n'en citer que quelques-uns.

Le second paragraphe est consacré aux liens de parenté botanique, et non aux caractères féminins et masculins puisque la sexualité des plantes est encore inconnue à cette époque. Du reste, Fuchs se limite généralement à signaler les genres ou les espèces proches, plus rarement les variétés ou les formes horticoles (v. Cap. CXVIII [118], CCLXXXI [281], CCCXX [320]). Qu'il ait commis également de temps à autre quelques erreurs (v. Cap. XXX [30], XXXI [31]) est pour le moins compréhensible.

Dans les deux livres, les paragraphes trois, quatre et cinq sont particulièrement intéressants pour les botanistes. Bien entendu, comme beaucoup d'autres savants de son temps, Fuchs a puisé dans les textes anciens, en particulier dans *De materia medica* de Dioscoride. Le fait même qu'il s'inspire de cette œuvre, inégalée à ses yeux, explique certaines absurdités ainsi que la brièveté et l'insuffisance de nombreuses descriptions de plantes. Conscient de cela, Fuchs souligne dans la préface d'*Historia* qu'une illustration rend beaucoup mieux que les mots. Les critiques justifiées, mais souvent aussi vétilleuses à l'excès, ne manquent pas. Devant tant de comparaisons philologiques, certains auteurs sous-estiment ou ne voient pas le travail indépendant accompli par Fuchs, qui se révèle dans la description de ses «découvertes», c'est-à-dire les espèces qu'il a vainement cherchées dans les traités grecs. C'est là qu'il montre combien il est familiarisé avec chaque plante et que son étude repose sur l'expérience personnelle : les descriptions du développement et de l'aspect sont souvent détaillées, et les indications sur la classification, la forme et le coloris des feuilles, des fleurs ou des fruits précises. Il est le premier à observer le changement de couleur des fleurs de l'*Echium vulgare* au cours de sa maturation (v. par ex. Cap. CLV [155]) ; il mentionne chez de nombreux spécimens le moment de l'éclosion des fleurs et de la maturité des fruits, signale leur sensibilité au gel, leur résistance au soleil ou à l'ombre. Il aborde aussi des questions écologiques importantes lorsqu'il indique, avec une précision souvent étonnante, le lieu de croissance et l'habitat. Fuchs déborde même du cadre qu'il s'est fixé quand il juge les plantes sans se limiter à leur valeur médicinale, à leur «nature et complexion» ou à leur «puissance et effet» (voir la contribution de W. Dressendörfer, p. 33 et s.). Il intègre dans son herbier bon nombre d'espèces dont il connaît mal ou pas du tout les effets curatifs, par exemple *Tagetes patula* (pl. XXVII [27]), *Solanum melongena* (pl. CCC [300]) ou *Digitalis purpurea* (pl. CCCCCXIII [513]). Dans le cas de *Quercus robur*, il attire l'attention sur les noix de galle (pl. CXXIX [129]) occasionnées par le cynips (*Cynips quercusfolii* L.), et dans celui de *Rosa gallica* (pl. CCCLXXIIII [374]), il représente, vraisemblablement pour la première fois en botanique, les bédégars, ou galles formées par le cynips gallicole (*Diplolepis rosae* L.). Enfin, au chapitre *Morus nigra* (CXCVIII [198]), il relate avec enthousiasme la métamorphose du ver à soie (*Bombyx mori* L.), depuis l'œuf jusqu'à l'éclosion du papillon en passant par le cocon.

Même si Fuchs croit fermement en l'autorité des naturalistes grecs, personne avant lui n'a réussi à donner une vue aussi étendue de l'organisme végétal. Et c'est précisément dans la synthèse entre le savoir des médecins grecs en ce qui concerne les vertus thérapeutiques des plantes et le nombre de ses propres découvertes que se révèle la grandeur novatrice de Fuchs.

De plus, grâce à son œuvre, l'éventail des espèces végétales connues en ce temps-là s'est considérablement enrichi. Disons grosso modo que, parmi les 500 plantes représentées,

400 environ sont des «plantes sauvages» appartenant à la flore européenne, dont 330 espèces croissant en Allemagne. Les 100 espèces restantes sont originaires de pays étrangers et présentées avec d'autres sous le vocable «plantes cultivées» : en médecine, on utilise non seulement les grandes plantes médicinales à proprement parler, introduites en Europe, mais encore la plupart des herbacées ornementales, des plantes aromatiques et légumières ainsi qu'un grand nombre d'arbres fruitiers et autres plantes utiles des jardins et des prés. Une centaine environ de ces plantes «sauvages» et «cultivées» ont été soit décrites pour la première fois par Fuchs et introduites en botanique, soit représentées également pour la première fois (v. Sprague & Nelmes 1931, p. 565 ; Marzell 1938, p. 15 et s. ; Meyer et al. 1999, p. 143 et s.). Ces chiffres prouvent à eux seuls les grands mérites de Fuchs.

Parmi les plantes qu'il a répertoriées, il en avait déjà vu beaucoup dans les environs d'Erfurt, d'Ingolstadt, d'Onoltzbach (Ansbach), mais aussi à Bayreuth, Kulmbach ou Nuremberg. À partir de 1535/1536, il découvre d'autres espèces inconnues de lui au cours de ses excursions à Tübingen et dans les alentours (Spitzberg, Österberg, Lustnau, Bebenhausen ou Farrenberg) ou lors de promenades jusqu'à Rottenbourg par la vallée du Neckar, ou encore pendant ses voyages à Nürtingen et Bad Cannstatt. Certaines d'entre elles sont entièrement nouvelles en science botanique (par ex. *Dactylorhiza maculata*, *Muscari botryoides*, *Paris quadrifolia*, *Scilla bifolia* ou *Senecio ovatus*) ; beaucoup sont représentées pour la première fois dans l'histoire de la botanique (*Antennaria dioica*, *Digitalis purpurea*, *Orchis mascula*, *O. militaris*, *O. morio*, *Platanthera bifolia* etc.) ; d'autres plantes enfin apportent la preuve de leur existence dans le sud-ouest de l'Allemagne (v. Künkele 1987 ; Sebald et al. 1992–1998 ; Seybold 1983, 1986, 1994).

La diversité des «plantes cultivées», que l'on fait pousser depuis plus de 450 ans puisque la population doit bien plus qu'aujourd'hui subvenir elle-même à ses besoins, est également considérable (v. Vogellehner 1966, p. 158 et s. ; Dobat 2000 b, p. 10 et s.). Cependant, le professeur de Tübingen n'a pu récolter dans la nature ou recevoir de jardins privés toutes les espèces étudiées, et surtout pas les plantes «exotiques» qui ne sont encore que des curiosités botaniques. Cinquante ans seulement après la découverte de l'Amérique, on trouve dans son œuvre les premières illustrations de grandes plantes de l'économie mondiale, ainsi le maïs (*Zea mays*, pl. CCCCLXXIII [473]), le haricot commun (*Phaseolus vulgaris*, pl. CCCCIIII [404]), la citrouille (*Cucurbita pepo*, pl. CCCXCIX [399], CCCC [400]) ou le poivron (*Capsicum annuum*, pl. CCCCXVIII–CCCCXX [418–420]). D'autres curiosités originaires d'Afrique et d'Asie y sont également représentées, comme *Solanum melongena* (pl. CCC [300]), *Momordica balsamina* (pl. CV [105]) ou *Impatiens balsamina* (pl. CVI [106]). Aucun doute sur ce point : Fuchs a fait pousser lui-même ces raretés botaniques et certainement d'autres !

LEONHART FUCHS, *Codex Fuchs*, Tübingen, *c.* 1536–1566
Vienna, Österreichische Nationalbibliothek, HAN: Cod. 11117–11125 (9 vols.)
Cucurbita pepo (L.) – Vegetable Marrow / Gemüse-Kürbis / Courge, Cod. 11124, p. 119

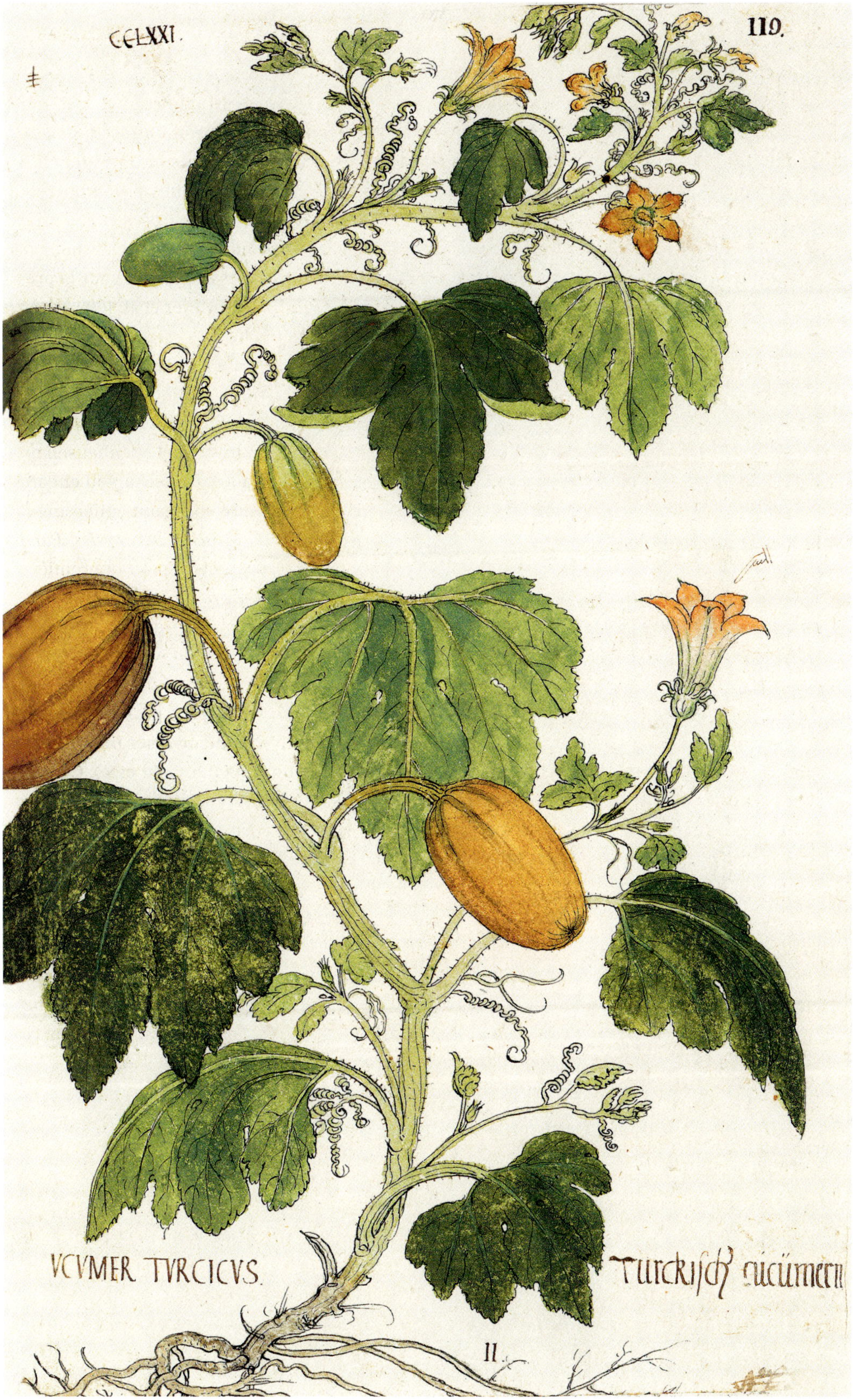

VCVMER TVRCICVS. Turckisch cucümeren

Un des plus anciens jardins universitaires du monde : le jardin des béguines

Lorsqu'en 1536 une ordonnance d'Ulrich abolit le béguinage du Wurtemberg, la maison de Tübingen ainsi que les terres appartenant à la communauté deviennent propriété du duché (p. 35). La maison sert de logement de fonction à Leonhart Fuchs et à sa famille (v. Dobat & Mägdefrau 1975, p. 12), ce qui n'apparaît que dans un document officiel de 1549, le «Dienerbuch» (Registre des serviteurs de l'Etat). Il ressort effectivement de ce document que la maison et le jardin étaient administrés par l'université et n'étaient donc pas la propriété privée du savant comme on l'a longtemps supposé.

Toutefois, pour des raisons évidentes, Fuchs a dû disposer bien plus tôt d'un terrain cultivable. Sinon, comment aurait-il pu planter des espèces rares, les observer et les récolter au bon moment ? Nous trouvons d'ailleurs une preuve indirecte de l'existence de ce jardin dans quelques chapitres d'*Historia* et du *New Kreüterbuch* (v. par ex. Cap. XL [40], CLXXII [172]). A ce propos, les indications qu'il donne sur le mélèze d'Europe (*Larix decidua*, v. Cap. CLXXXIX [189]) sont très révélatrices : le margrave Georg lui en a «envoyé un à Tübingen» depuis Ansbach. Fuchs n'a certainement pas attendu pour replanter ce précieux spécimen, en tout cas pas après l'automne 1541, vu que la préface d'*Historia* date de mars 1542. Le manuscrit que nous a laissé le savant confirme ce laps de temps. Il écrit en effet au sujet de *Veratrum album* que «deux souches que j'avais confiées à la terre en 1542 [ont donné] l'année suivante des fleurs et des fruits» (v. Seybold 1990, p. 241). Par conséquent, ce n'est pas depuis 1549, mais bien à partir de 1542, si ce n'est avant, qu'il utilise le jardin à des fins scientifiques ! Conrad Gesner (1516–1565) lui a envoyé aussi des graines de tabac (*Nicotiana tabacum*), ce que signale déjà Ganzinger (1959, p. 223). Par ailleurs, il est hors de doute que Fuchs n'ait fait pousser dans le jardin des béguines beaucoup d'autres plantes, que des amis botanistes ou son fils Friderich (1532–1604), qui étudie à l'époque en Italie, lui font parvenir. Peut-on pour cette raison qualifier le jardin de «first botanical garden in Tübingen», comme le font Meyer et al. (1999, p. 124) avec vénération ? Ce serait ainsi l'un des plus vieux jardins botaniques du monde ! Mais laissons la question en suspens.

« ... Peintes de la manière la plus artistique/ et décrites avec beaucoup d'application ... » : la synthèse de l'art et de la science.

Sans nul doute, l'importance scientifique et la valeur, encore reconnue de nos jours, de l'*Historia* et du *New Kreüterbuch* proviennent en grande partie de la qualité des illustrations. Elles sont dues assurément à trois artistes hors pair qui ont travaillé en étroite collaboration avec Fuchs. D'après ce que l'on sait, le savant réussit à se les adjoindre comme collaborateurs après son arrivée à Tübingen et les payait personnellement de sa poche. Fuchs reconnaît si bien leurs mérites et leur travail artistique qu'il publie leur portrait dans les deux œuvres. Certes, nous ne les trouvons qu'en fin d'ouvrage – le bouquet final, pourrait-on dire –, il n'en reste pas moins que le simple fait de les représenter est absolument exceptionnel pour l'époque. Ainsi Fuchs immortalise-t-il les trois artistes tout en nous donnant une image vivante de leur travail.

Albrecht Meyer est en train de passer à l'aquarelle un dessin presque achevé, lequel servira de modèle pour la planche à graver. Heinrich Füllmaurer tient dans la main gauche l'une de ces planches et la représentation sur parchemin, et de la main droite dessine le modèle sur la surface finement polie du bois, avec un soin méticuleux comme l'attestent les 23 planches de l'herbier conservées à Tübingen (v. Dobat 1983, 2000 a). Le troisième artiste est Veyt Rudolff Speckle, l'un des plus grands graveurs de son temps. Sa tâche est de rendre en relief, et dans tous ses détails, la représentation de la plante. Pour ce faire, le graveur sur bois travaillant à Strasbourg utilise de multiples outils. Pour graver, il recourt à la taille d'épargne, une technique qui consiste à creuser les parties libres de la planche pour mettre en relief chaque ligne du dessin. Les traits sont ensuite passés à l'encre et apparaissent à l'envers après impression. Combien de journées Speckle n'a-t-il consacrées à une seule gravure ?

Pour économiser place et argent, Fuchs regroupe parfois des espèces voisines sur une même planche. D'une souche commune par exemple naissent deux roses (v. pl. CCCLXXIIII [374]), ou trois espèces différentes de *Lamium* (v. pl. CCLXIIII [264]) sont figurées ensemble. Il en est de même pour des plantes de jardin dont la floraison est particulièrement belle (v. pl. CC [200], CCLXXXVII [287]) ou pour diverses variétés de plantes cultivées importantes (v. pl. XLVI [46], CCXXXIX [239], CCCCLXXIII [473]). Les artistes représentent aussi sur une même plante, à l'initiative du savant bien entendu, des fleurs fraîchement écloses et des fruits très mûrs, comme c'est le cas pour le pêcher (v. pl. CCCXLI [341]) ou le groseillier (v. pl. CCCLXXVII [377]), pour ne citer que ceux-là. En ce qui concerne les plantes sauvages, Fuchs est souvent le seul à connaître leur période de floraison et de fructification ; ses collaborateurs ajoutent alors, sur ses indications, les différents stades de développement afin de donner une image complète et marquante de ces plantes. Combien de dessins ont-ils ainsi commencé à ébaucher au printemps pour ne les terminer qu'à l'automne et continuer à les élaborer durant les mois d'hiver ?

La mise en couleurs de la planche exigeait également beaucoup de temps. C'est pourquoi les deux ouvrages furent publiés dans une édition noir et blanc bon marché et une édition de luxe coloriée. Dans une lettre de novembre 1542, Fuchs mentionne le prix de 15 florins pour l'édition de luxe de l'*Historia*. Une somme importante en ce temps-là, qui correspond presque à son salaire mensuel. Aussi même à ses amis les plus proches ne peut-il faire cadeau d'un exemplaire de l'ouvrage (Fichtner 1967, 1968). Il en était probablement de même pour le *New Kreüterbuch*, et cela tient du miracle si c'est précisément l'exemplaire de sa bibliothèque privée de Tübingen qui a survécu au temps !

Le présent ouvrage est la reproduction de ce spécimen, conservé à Ulm. Fuchs a certainement aussi supervisé la mise en couleurs du *New Kreüterbuch* pour lui donner autant d'authenticité que possible. Nées d'un travail commun minutieux et pénible, les illustrations de cet herbier, qui a traversé plus de quatre siècles avant d'arriver jusqu'à nous, font découvrir des plantes que l'on croirait sorties tout droit du jardin ou fraîchement cueillies lors d'une excursion !

Les vingt dernières années de sa vie

Grâce à ses deux livres, *Historia* et *New Kreüterbuch*, son nom est maintenant connu dans le monde entier. Et pourtant, dès 1543, Fuchs entreprend la suite de son histoire des plantes. La première partie de cette œuvre est prête au plus tard en 1550 (v. Stübler 1928, p. 99) ; jusqu'au mois de juillet 1551 s'y ajoutent 300 nouvelles illustrations (v. Seybold 1986, p. 12). Par sa correspondance avec son ami Camerarius, on est bien informé sur l'évolution du projet au cours des années qui suivent : en 1557, il achève un second volume comprenant 400 nouvelles illustrations, suivi en 1563/1564 du manuscrit d'un troisième volume. Ainsi, après une vingtaine d'années de labeur et d'engagement personnel, l'œuvre de Fuchs est-il quasiment achevé. À l'évidence, il s'est identifié chaque jour un peu plus à cette tâche, s'est «acharné» sur elle, pourrait-on dire – sinon comment décrire le travail immense qu'il a accompli ? La remarque suivante de Fichtner (1968, p. 75) se comprend ainsi aisément : «Dans l'ensemble, plus le temps passe, moins la pratique semble avoir joué un rôle dans la vie de Fuchs.» Même les échecs cuisants ne peuvent ébranler son opiniâtreté car, à plusieurs reprises au cours de ces vingt années, il cherchera vainement une aide financière pour l'impression.

Tout autre que lui se serait résigné. Fuchs, imperturbable, persévère et fait exécuter à ses frais dessins, planches de bois et épreuves pour les nouvelles plantes (v. Rytz 1933). C'est même un autre peintre talentueux et qualifié qu'il engage en 1550 en la personne de Jerg Ziegler. Certaines des 440 aquarelles portant sa signature peuvent se dater avec plus de précision, car elles ont été exécutées d'après l'herbier de Léonard Rauwolff (1535–1596), médecin et grand voyageur d'Augsbourg, qui a dû rendre visite à Fuchs en 1563 et mettre à sa disposition sa collection de plantes (v. Ganzinger 1963, p. 28 ; Seybold 1986, p. 20, 1990, p. 251 et s. ; Meyer et al. 1999, p. 185 et s.). Huit des planches non gravées, restées à Tübingen, ont été réalisées d'après cet herbier et portent le monogramme de Ziegler.

Ainsi Fuchs, sans relâche, s'efforce encore d'enrichir ses connaissances botaniques, d'achever son manuscrit et de se faire aider par d'autres botanistes, et ce jusque dans les dernières années de sa vie, assombries par le décès de sa femme Anna au mois de février 1563. L'année suivante, il épouse Afra Graeter, la veuve d'un pasteur du Jura souabe, mais ses forces déclinent. Fuchs fait encore des démarches désespérées auprès de divers princes et villes impériales pour financer «l'œuvre de sa vie», mais sans succès. Aucun de ses espoirs ne se réalise. Profondément déçu, affaibli par les maladies et perdant la vue, Leonhart Fuchs meurt le 10 mai 1566 à Tübingen. Il est enterré aux côtés de sa première femme dans l'ancien cimetière d'Ammer, qui sera rattaché en 1835/1836 à l'Ancien Jardin Botanique. Un arboretum y a été planté, et on peut voir encore quelques-uns des anciens arbres. Et quelque part sous la terre reposent Fuchs et sa femme.

Mais pas plus que lui, son fils aîné Friderich, médecin de la ville d'Ulm, ne réussira malgré tous ses efforts à faire imprimer le manuscrit. Après sa mort, celui-ci sera vendu et considéré comme disparu pendant deux siècles. Heureusement, il «dormait» depuis 1756 à un endroit sûr : la Bibliothèque Nationale Autrichienne à Vienne ! Puis, en 1954, à l'occasion d'une exposition, on se souvient du manuscrit, que Ganzinger tire enfin de sa «léthargie» en 1959. Ce *Codex Vindobonensis Palatinus* en trois volumes se compose de neuf tomes comprenant d'innombrables folios à l'écriture serrée et 1500 illustrations. Le savant de Tübingen nous a ainsi légué une autre œuvre impérissable, méritant bien son nom de «père de la botanique allemande» (p. 12, 17, 20, 23, 43, 50, 53, 62, 66, 70).

LEONHART FUCHS, *De historia stirpium commentarii insignes*, Basel, 1542
Vienna, Österreichische Nationalbibliothek, POR: 8414
Portrait of / Porträt von / Portrait de Veit Rudolf Speckle, p. 897

SCVLPTOR

Vitus Rodolph. Speckle.

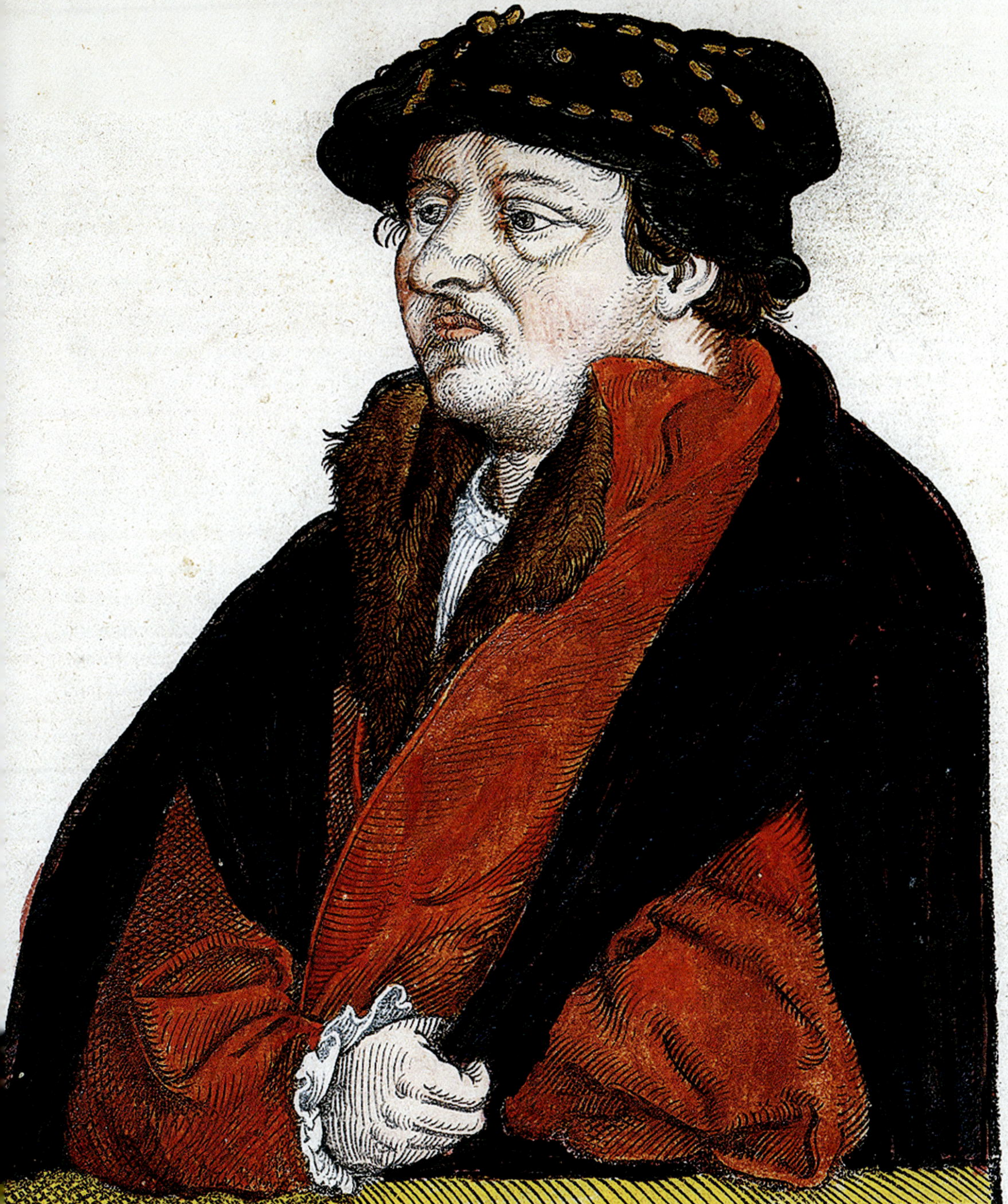

KLAUS DOBAT

Glossary

Explanation of Commonly Used Terms

This reprint of Leonhart Fuchs's herbal offers not only an excellent opportunity to study the beautiful engravings of the original, but also to peruse the text. There, the interested and discerning reader will find many items of historical significance while some statements may seem quite foreign to our present understanding. It is only natural that, to begin with, the language and the inconsistent spelling will appear strange. In many cases, these problems can be overcome by reading the text aloud – and by using a little imagination. The following short explanatory list will clarify the most important of the difficult medical terms that recur throughout the text.

Glossar
Zum besseren Verständnis ungewohnter Ausdrücke

Die vorliegende vollständige Wiedergabe des Fuchs'schen Kräuterbuchs bietet die sehr empfehlenswerte Möglichkeit, nicht nur die schönen Bilder zu betrachten, sondern sich auch in den Text einzulesen. Der interessierte und aufmerksame Leser wird dabei viel historisch Bedeutsames, aber auch aus unserer heutigen Sicht Kurioses finden. Natürlich werden am Anfang die Sprache und die uneinheitliche Schreibweise sehr ungewohnt sein. In vielen Fällen helfen aber lautes Lesen und ein wenig Sprachfantasie. Die wichtigsten medizinischen Fachausdrücke, die häufiger wiederkehren und schwer verständlich sind, werden im Folgenden kurz erläutert.

Glossaire
Pour une meilleure compréhension

La présente réédition intégrale du *New Kreüterbuch* n'est pas seulement une invite à contempler de belles illustrations, elle offre aussi la possibilité de découvrir un texte qui mérite d'être lu. Le lecteur intéressé et attentif y trouvera, outre des aspects importants sur le plan historique, diverses choses paraissant insolites aujourd'hui. Si la langue et l'orthographe, qui varie parfois pour un même mot, demandent au début quelques efforts de compréhension, une lecture à haute voix et un peu d'imagination permettent généralement de surmonter les difficultés. Cependant, pour rendre le texte original plus intelligible, il nous a paru judicieux de traduire les termes médicaux récurrents les plus importants.

ander grad
The second degree of strength according to the theory of fluids
Der zweite Stärke-Grad in der Säftelehre
Second degré d'intensité dans la théorie des humeurs

apostema
Abscess, ulcer / Abszess, Geschwür / Apostème (abcès, tumeur purulente)

bauchfluß
Diarrhoea, dysentery / Durchfall, Ruhr
Diarrhée, dysenterie

bläst
Flatulence / Blähung / Ballonnement

blöd
Malfunctioning, unusable (upset stomach, disturbed eyesight)
In der normalen Funktion gestört, untauglich (blöder magen, blöde augen)
Caractérisé par le dysfonctionnement (blöder magen = estomac dérangé, blöde augen = troubles de la vue)

blödigkeit der frawen
Menstruation / Menstruation / Menstruation

blödigkeit, bringt den frawen ihre b.
Fostering menstruation
Menstruationsfördernd
Qui provoque la menstruation

blust
Climax, peak / Blüte / Fleur

breyte würm
Tapeworm / Bandwurm / Ténia

bürdlin
Afterbirth / Nachgeburt / Arrière-faix

denen die mu(t)ter über sich steigt
Womb, in the sense of an animal (toad) that wanders within the body
Gebärmutter als Tier (Kröte) gedacht, das im Körper wandert
Utérus, imaginé comme un animal (crapaud) se déplaçant dans le corps

dewung (= däuung)
Digestion / Verdauung / Digestion

fallender siechtag
Epilepsy / Epilepsie / Épilepsie

fell der augen
A growth on the conjunctiva
Bindegewebswucherung
Tumeur du tissu conjonctif

flachßader
Tendon / Sehne / Tendon

freysch, freischlin
Tetany, muscle spasms in children
Fraissen, Krampfanfälle bei Kindern
Éclampsie

gemecht
Male genital organ
Männliches Geschlechtsteil
Appareil génital mâle

gleych, das
Joint / Gelenk / Articulation

gleychen, das
Podagra, gout / Podagra, „gleychsichtig" /
Podagre, goutte articulaire

grawlecht
Grey / Grau / Gris

gulden ader
Haemorrhoids / Hämorrhoiden / Hémorroïdes

hauptfluß
Catarrh, cold, runny nose, sinus headache
Katarrh, Schnupfen, Schmerzen im Kopf
Catarrhe, rhume, douleurs de la tête

hexgen
Hiccups / Schluckauf / Hoquet

heymliche orte
Genital region / Genitalbereich / Parties génitales

knöpff
Knot, node / Knoten / Nodosité

knöpff am hindern
Condyloma / Feigwarzen / Condylome

leibfarb
Flesh-coloured / Fleischfarben / Couleur de chair

lendenstein
Kidney stone / Nierenstein / Calcul rénal

luck
Loose, light / Locker / Lâche, mou

mut(t)er
Womb (see also: womb as animal)
Gebärmutter (s. a. *denen die mutter* …)
Utérus (voir précédemment «denen die mutter …»)

ohrmützel
Mumps / Mumps / Oreillons

raess
Sharp, acute / Scharf / Fort, épicé

roßmucken
Freckles / Sommersprossen / Taches de rousseur

row
Raw / Roh / Cru, brut

üchse
Armpit / Achselhöhle / Creux de l'aisselle

undewen
To vomit / Erbrechen / Vomir, rendre

zasel
Fibre / Faser / Fibre

zilen
To cultivate, raise plants
Pflanzen ziehen, anbauen
Cultiver

zwagen
To wash / Waschen / Laver

Roman Numerals

Equivalents I = 1 V = 5 X = 10 L = 50 C = 100

The value of a number is determined by adding the values of the individual numerals, reading from right to left, for example: XI = 11; XVI = 16; XX = 20; CV = 105; CCLXXVII = 100+100+50+10+10+5+1+1 = 277.

When a numeral representing a lower value precedes one of a higher value, then the lower value must be subtracted from the higher, for example: IX = 10-1 = 9; CCXC = 100+100+(100-10) = 290; XCIIII = (100-10)+1+1+1+1 = 94

Contrary to the usual practice, for the number four (IV), Fuchs used the numeral IIII; similarly for five hundred (D), he used CCCCC. We have retained his original numeration.

Römische Zahlzeichen

Zeichenwert: I = 1 V = 5 X = 10 L = 50 C = 100

Der Zahlenwert ergibt sich durch Zusammenzählen des Werts der einzelnen Zeichen, soweit dieser von links nach rechts fallend ist, z. B. XI = 11; XVI = 16; XX = 20; CV = 105; CCLXXVII = 100+100+50+10+10+5+1+1 = 277.

Steht ein niedrigerwertiges Zeichen vor einem höherwertigen, ist sein Wert von diesem abzuziehen, z. B. IX = 10-1 = 9; CCXC = 100+100+(100-10) = 290; XCIIII = (100-10)+1+1+1+1 = 94

Statt des üblichen „D“ für 500 verwendet Fuchs „CCCCC“ und statt „IV“ für 4 „IIII“. Diese originale Nummerierung haben wir beibehalten.

Chiffres romains

Équivalence en chiffres arabes : I = 1 V = 5 X = 10 L = 50 C = 100

La valeur numérale s'obtient de la manière suivante : chaque lettre placée à la droite d'une autre ajoute à celle-ci. Par exemple, XI correspond à 11 ; XVI à 16 ; XX à 20 ; CV à 105 ; CCLXXVII, c'est-à-dire 100 + 100 + 50 + 10 + 10 + 5 + 1 + 1, à 277.

Au contraire, on retranche de la lettre supérieure en valeur nominale celle de moindre valeur quand celle-ci est placée à sa gauche. Ainsi 9, c'est-à-dire 10 – 1, s'écrit IX ; 290 ou 100 + 100 + (100 – 10), CCXC ; 94 ou (100 – 10) + 1 + 1 + 1 + 1, XCIIII.

À la différence du système romain, Leonhart Fuchs a employé les lettres numérales IIII au lieu de IV pour le chiffre 4 et CCCCC au lieu de D pour 500. Nous avons conservé cette numération originale.

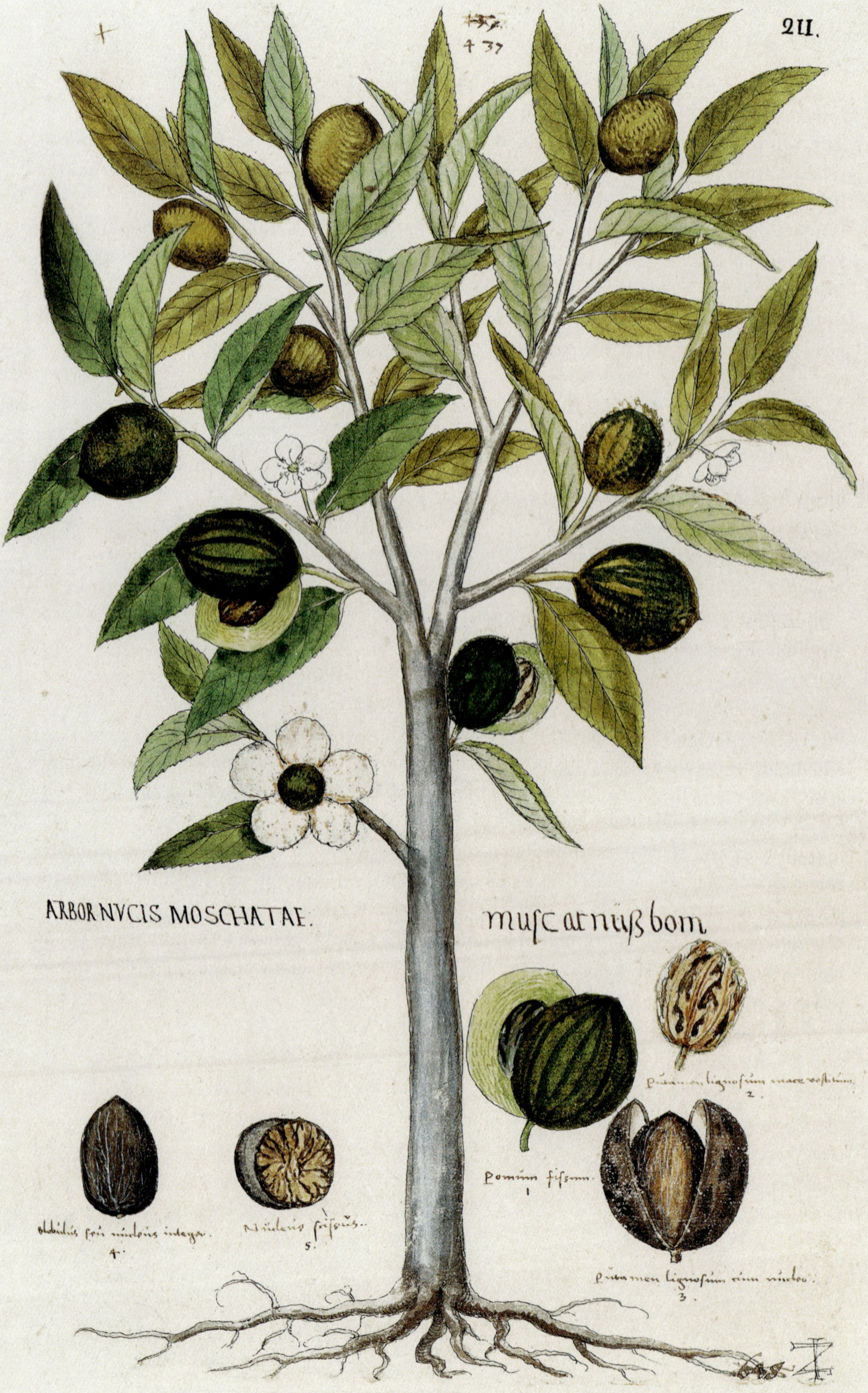
ARBOR NVCIS MOSCHATAE.
muſcat nüß bom
Pomum fissum. 1
Putamen lignosum mace vestitum. 2.
Putamen lignosum cum nucleo. 3.
Globulus seu nucleus integer. 4.
Nucleus fissus. 5.

WERNER DRESSENDÖRFER

"Beggar's Lice" and "Miracle Tree"

On the Plants of the New Kreüterbuch

In 1543, three scientific books were published which pioneered new territory in their respective fields. In Nuremberg, Nicolaus Copernicus published his *De Revolutionibus Orbium Coelestium Libri VI* (On the revolution of the planets), in which he removed the earth – and therefore mankind – from the centre of the universe; instead, all now revolved around the sun. In Basle, Oporinus brought out Andreas Vesal's *De Humani Corporis Fabrica*, a monumental inventory of the construction of the human body. In revealing the errors of the ancient classical doctors, the work thus laid the foundation for the development of modern anatomy. Also in Basle, the apothecary Michael Isingrin brought out the *New Kreüterbuch* by the Tübingen doctor Leonhart Fuchs. The artistic illustrations of the *Kreüterbuch* represent a high point of botanical book illustration, still worthy of admiration today, and the text foreshadows the course of botany over the coming decades.

Fuchs had set himself an ambitious goal, announced at great length on the title page: nothing less than a compilation of all herbal knowledge, "the like of which has never been seen before, nor yet been done." The word "before" here probably refers primarily to comparable works by Otto Brunfels and Hieronymus Bock which had appeared in 1532 and 1539 respectively – that is, only a few years before the *Kreüterbuch.* These works represented the continuation of a fairly new tradition that had begun in 1484 with the first such illustrated work, printed in Mainz. The *Hortus sanitatis* (Garden of health) had been composed in Latin and was therefore directed towards physicians and apothecaries. But already in the following year, a much more comprehensive work appeared, *Gart der Gesundheit*, this time written in the vernacular German and comprehensible to the general public. Although the woodcuts of the plants tended to be coarse and schematic, the dictionary-like arrangement of the written text along with an identifying picture stirred popular interest to such an extent that this new type of book, the "herbal," became a best-seller in the 15th and 16th centuries, and remains so today, for new versions are always appearing.

LEONHART FUCHS, *Codex Fuchs*, Tübingen, c. 1536–1566
Vienna, Österreichische Nationalbibliothek, HAN: Cod. 11117–11125 (9 vols.)
Myristica fragrans (Houtt.) – Nutmeg / Muskatnuss / Muscadier, Cod. 11122, p. 211

In the organization of his texts, Leonart Fuchs adhered strictly to a scheme: immediately after the heading and chapter number came a paragraph devoted to "Names," in which the German, Latin and Greek names appear, at times accompanied by an explanation of their meanings. Where necessary, Fuchs also noted other common names, particularly those typically used by apothecaries – but, as a medical doctor, he was at times unable to resist ridiculing them. Thus, for example in Chapter V, he notes of the apothecaries that they "always like to put in something special."

Under the heading "Kind" comes botanical information distinguishing the various types of plants within the same group from one another. This is especially clear in Chapter LVII in the case of crowfoot, for example, where the text "There are… many kinds of crowfoot" is accompanied by seven different illustrations. The designations "mennlin" (masculine) and "weiblin" (feminine) occur frequently. These terms do not designate sexually dimorphous plants, however, but rather varieties that differ in some other characteristic, as for example in the colour of the blossoms or the size of growth.

Parallel to the illustration, the section entitled "Form" describes the external appearance of the plant, including its various stages of development, for example, from the bud to the open blossom to the fruit. "Habitat" suggests typical locations where the plant is to be found. On numerous occasions Fuchs also mentions the occurrence of the plant in the area around Tübingen and other places known to him. In the section titled "Time," he gives the time of blooming and often also mentions the period during which the given medicinal plant should be gathered.

For modern readers, the information offered under "Nature and Temperament" seems incomprehensible, for here, when the text uses the expressions "warm," "cold," "moist," "dry," or similar terms, or speaks of the taste of the plant, we find ourselves confronted with the ancient classical understanding of pharmacology. According to this scheme, all things of animate or inanimate nature were composed of a combination of four "elements": fire, water, air and earth. Each of these elements was associated with two properties, or "qualities," each of which was derived from opposing pairs of characteristics: "cold – warm" and "moist – dry" respectively. In the realm of medicine, the elements were furthermore equivalent to the bodily fluids, which in turn indirectly determined a person's given temperament. One can present this "pathology of humours" (Lat. humor, juice), or "doctrine of fluids" briefly as follows:

Element	Property	Taste	Bodily fluid	Temperament
fire	dry and warm	bitter	yellow bile	choleric
water	moist and cold	salty	phlegm	phlegmatic
air	moist and warm	sweet	blood	sanguine
earth	dry and cold	sour	black bile	melancholy

Each individual was presumed to possess a personal mixture of these four fluids for the course of a lifetime. As long as the mixture remained in balance, the person remained healthy; but if the combination was disturbed, sickness resulted. In examining a patient, the task of the doctor was therefore to determine which of these fluids was present in excess or in deficiency in the body of the sick person. This analysis determined the qualities that had to be strengthened or reduced in order to return the patient's fluids again to a state of balance and thus restore him or her to health. For this reason, all healing herbs were classified according to this scheme and correspondingly used as medicines.

The next section, "Power and Effect," logically concerned itself with medical indications, that is, the applications of the healing plants. Many descriptions also included a short reference to the method of preparation. In these statements, however, a decisive role was played by a magical perspective known as the theory of "signatures." According to this "art of the signatum," as Paracelsus called it, the human body is viewed as a microcosm which stands in direct correspondence to the macrocosmic order of the universe. The internal relationships between the two – the so-called "sympathies" – were supposedly reflected through external correspondences, or "signatures." Traits such as shared colours or forms, or similar characteristics, allowed the correspondences to be identified. Thus a plant's yellow sap or yellow petals suggested an effect on the yellowish-green bile of the gall bladder, just as the colour red suggested use for haemorrhages, or the heart-shaped leaves of garden balm indicated an effect on heart problems.

All of this not only clearly illustrates the thought processes of mediaeval medicine, but also that the claims made by the old herbals should not be read uncritically today as valid recommendations for self-healing: Rather, in the best of cases, they serve as references to a long history of experience, whose value and justification deserves investigation by modern scientific methods, so that on the one hand nothing valuable is lost but, on the other hand, useless or dangerous information no longer indiscriminately retains the reputation of tried-and-true tradition. Both kinds of information are to be found in Leonhart Fuchs's herbal.

It would be well to finish this short review with the closing words of Leonhart Fuchs at the end of his book:

Therefore we hereby bring the first part of this herbal to a close, and in time,
if God be willing, the other part, which we have already begun,
will also be printed for the use of many. Praise be to our dear Lord and God,
honour and praise and glory for ever and ever, Amen.

The hopes of the botanist-physician remained unfulfilled. Although another 23 years of life were granted to Fuchs, this was not long enough to publish the planned sequel. Almost four hundred years passed before the manuscript and the drawings were again discovered by chance. The first volume alone was enough, however, to make Leonhart Fuchs immortal.

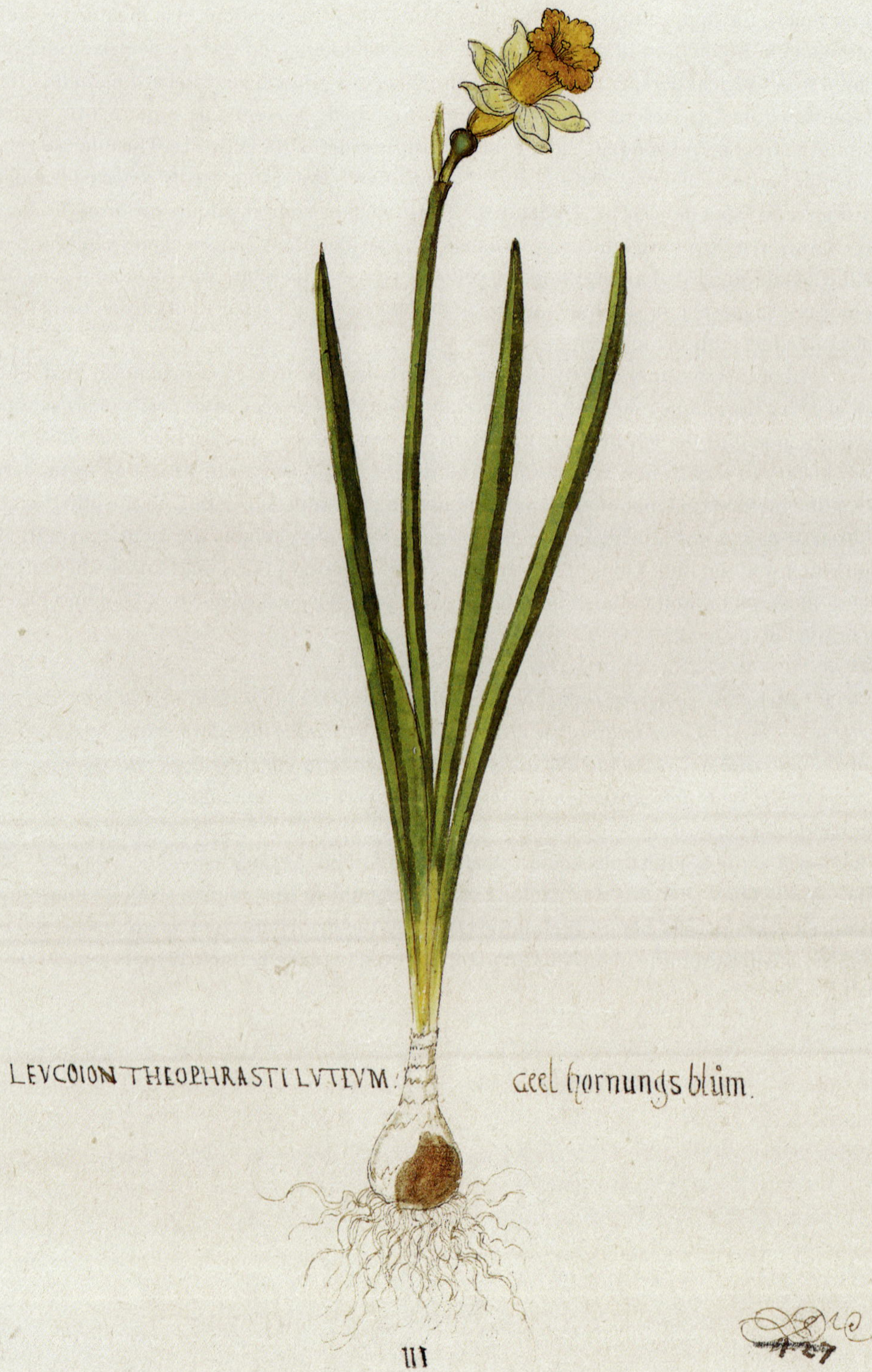
LEVCOION THEOPHRASTI LVTEVM:
Geel hornungs blům.
111

WERNER DRESSENDÖRFER

„Bettlersleuss“ und „Wunderbaum“

Zu den Pflanzen des New Kreüterbuch

Im Laufe des Jahres 1543 erschienen drei wissenschaftliche Bücher, die, jedes auf seinem Fachgebiet, in weitgehendes Neuland führten. Nikolaus Kopernikus veröffentlichte in Nürnberg sein *De Revolutionibus Orbium Coelestium Libri VI*, in dem er die Erde und damit auch den Menschen aus dem Zentrum der Welt rückt und die Sonne in den Mittelpunkt des Universums stellt. In Basel bei Oporinus erschien Andreas Vesals *De Humani Corporis Fabrica*, eine monumentale Bestandsaufnahme vom Bau des menschlichen Körpers, die die Irrtümer der antiken Ärzte offenbarte und damit das Fundament für die Entwicklung hin zur modernen Anatomie legte. Ebenfalls in Basel, aber in der Offizin Michael Isingrins, kam das *New Kreüterbuch* des Tübinger Mediziners Leonhart Fuchs heraus, dessen kunstvolle Abbildungen einen bis heute bewunderten Höhepunkt der botanischen Buchillustration darstellen und dessen Text bereits ahnen lässt, wie sich die Botanik in den kommenden Jahrzehnten weiter entwickeln wird.

Fuchs hatte sich, wie er auf dem Titelblatt weitschweifig verkündet, das ehrgeizige Ziel gesetzt, alles Wissen über die Kräuter in einem Umfang darzulegen, „deßgleichen vormals nie gesehen, noch an den Tag kommen“. Das „vormals“ bezieht sich dabei in erster Linie wohl auf die vergleichbaren Werke von Otto Brunfels und Hieronymus Bock, die 1532 bzw. 1539, also nur wenige Jahre zuvor, erschienen waren und eine noch recht junge Tradition fortsetzten, die 1484 mit dem ersten derartigen bebilderten Druck in Mainz begonnen hatte. Dieser *Hortus sanitatis* war noch in lateinischer Sprache abgefasst, richtete sich also an die Ärzte und Apotheker. Aber schon im folgenden Jahr erschien mit deutlich größerem Umfang der deutschsprachige *Gart der Gesundheit*, der nun auch für Laien verständlich war. Obwohl die Holzschnitte der Pflanzen anfangs noch sehr grob und schematisch ausfielen, entsprach die wörterbuchartige Verbindung von beschreibendem Text und identifizierendem Bild doch so sehr dem Interesse der Menschen, dass dieser neue Buchtyp, das *Kräuterbuch*,

LEONHART FUCHS, *Codex Fuchs*, Tübingen, c. 1536–1566
Vienna, Österreichische Nationalbibliothek, HAN: Cod. 11117–11125 (9 vols.)
Narcissus pseudonarcissus (L.) – Wild Daffodil / Osterglocke / Narcisse jaune, Cod. 11121, p. 317

zu einem Bestseller nicht nur des 15. und 16. Jahrhunderts wurde, sondern bis in die Gegenwart immer wieder neue Ausgaben erlebte.

Leonhart Fuchs gliedert seine Texte nach einem streng durchgehaltenen Schema: der Überschrift samt Kapitelnummer folgt der Abschnitt „Namen", in dem er die deutschen, lateinischen und griechischen Bezeichnungen nennt und teilweise auch von ihrem Wortsinn her erklärt. Andere übliche Namen werden bei Bedarf vermerkt, insbesondere die in den Apotheken gebräuchlichen, wobei es sich der Arzt nicht verkneifen kann, diese pharmazeutische Nomenklatur hin und wider etwas spöttisch zu kritisieren, so wenn er z. B. im Kapitel V die Apotheker betreffend anfügt: „haben allwegen gern etwas besunders."

Unter der Überschrift „Geschlecht" folgen botanische Angaben, durch die verschiedene Arten der gleichen Gattung unterschieden werden. Dies wird z. B. im Kapitel LVII deutlich, wo vom Hahnenfuß die Rede ist und sieben verschiedene Abbildungen die Aussage „Es seind ... vil geschlecht der Hanenfuß" anschaulich bestätigen. Häufig finden sich hier, wie z. B. beim Gauchheil, Kapitel VI, auch „mennlin" und „weiblin" genannt, worunter jedoch keineswegs eingeschlechtliche Pflanzen zu verstehen sind, sondern verschiedene Arten oder Varietäten, die sich bei sonstiger Ähnlichkeit z. B. durch die Blütenfärbung oder ihre Wuchsgröße unterscheiden.

Der Abschnitt „Gestalt" beschreibt parallel zur Abbildung das äußere Erscheinungsbild der Pflanze, wobei auch die verschiedenen Reifestadien, z. B. von der Knospe über die geöffnete Blüte zur Frucht, Berücksichtigung finden. „Statt irer wachsung" nennt Fuchs typische Standorte, an denen die Pflanze zu finden ist. Hier erwähnt er mehrfach auch Vorkommen in der Umgebung Tübingens und an anderen, ihm bekannten Orten. Im Abschnitt „Zeit" gibt er die Blütezeit an und nennt häufig auch den Zeitraum, in dem die jeweilige Arzneipflanze gesammelt werden soll.

Für uns heute unverständlich sind die Angaben, die sich unter „Die natur und complexion" finden, denn wenn darin von „werme", „kelte", „feucht", „trucken" oder ähnlichen Begriffen, aber auch vom Geschmack die Rede ist, werden wir mit der Grundlage der antiken Vorstellungen von der Materie konfrontiert. Danach sollten alle Dinge der belebten und unbelebten Natur aus einer Mischung der vier „Elemente" Feuer, Wasser, Luft und Erde bestehen. Diesen Elementen sprach man je zwei Eigenschaften, auch Qualitäten genannt, zu, von denen je eine aus den beiden Gegensatzpaaren „kalt – warm" und „feucht – trocken" stammte. In der Medizin setzte man darüber hinaus die Elemente mit Körpersäften gleich, die indirekt auch das jeweilige Temperament der Person regierten, sodass man diese „Humoralpathologie" (lat. humor = Saft) oder „Säftelehre" in folgendem Schema kurz darstellen kann:

Element	**Eigenschaft**	**Geschmack**	**Körpersaft**	**Temperament**
Feuer	trocken & warm	bitter	gelbe Galle	Choleriker
Wasser	feucht & kalt	salzig	Schleim	Phlegmatiker
Luft	feucht & warm	süß	Blut	Sanguiniker
Erde	trocken & kalt	sauer	schwarze Galle	Melancholiker

Für jeden Menschen sollte lebenslang ein individuelles Mischungsverhältnis dieser vier Säfte gelten. Solange es erhalten blieb, war der Mensch gesund, wurde es jedoch gestört, entstand daraus eine Erkrankung. Aufgabe des Arztes war es dann, durch die Untersuchung des Patienten festzustellen, an welchem Saft im Körper des Kranken Überschuss oder Mangel bestand. Daraus ergaben sich jene Qualitäten, die entweder verringert oder verstärkt werden mussten, um die Säfte des Kranken wieder in das Stadium des Gleichgewichts und ihn selbst wieder zur Gesundheit zu bringen. Deshalb wurden alle Heilpflanzen ebenfalls nach diesen Qualitäten klassifiziert und dementsprechend als Medikament eingesetzt. Auf die Säftelehre beziehen sich auch Begriffe wie „ausleitend“, „ableitend“ oder „ausführend“, mit denen die erwünschte Verringerung der überschüssigen Körpersäfte vor allem durch Anregung von Blase und Darm bezeichnet wird. Hatten sich diese Säfte an bestimmten Stellen im Körper angesammelt, was sich z. B. durch Schwellungen oder Verhärtungen zeigen konnte, mussten sie „zerteilt“, sozusagen also zum „Auseinanderlaufen“ gebracht werden.

Folgerichtig beschäftigt sich der nächste Abschnitt „Die krafft und würckung“ mit den Indikationen, also den Anwendungsgebieten der Heilpflanzen, wobei oft auch ein kurzer Hinweis auf die Art der Arzneizubereitung gegeben wird. Für diese Aussagen spielt allerdings recht häufig eine magische Anschauung die entscheidende Rolle: die „Signaturenlehre“. Diese „Kunst Signatum“, wie sie Paracelsus nennt, ist eine Vorstellung, die den menschlichen Körper als Mikrokosmos begreift, der in direkter Beziehung zur Ordnung des universalen Makrokosmos steht. Innere Verwandtschaften zwischen beiden, sogenannte „Sympathien“, sollten durch äußerliche Ähnlichkeiten, die „Signaturen“, wie z. B. übereinstimmende Farben oder Formen und sonstige Auffälligkeiten bezeichnet werden und sich so erkennen lassen. So schienen gelber Milchsaft oder gelbe Blüte einer Pflanze deren Wirkung auf die gelblich-grüne Galle ebenso anzuzeigen, wie Rot auf die Anwendung bei Blutungen oder die herzförmigen Blätter der Melisse auf deren Wirksamkeit bei Herzbeschwerden schließen ließen.

Aus alledem werden nicht nur Denkweisen der mittelalterlichen Medizin deutlich, ebenso klar wird, dass Aussagen, die sich in den alten Kräuterbüchern finden, durchaus nicht unkritisch als heute noch gültige Empfehlungen für die Selbstbehandlung zu verstehen sind, sondern bestenfalls als Hinweise auf lange Erfahrung, deren Wert und Berechtigung mit modernen wissenschaftlichen Methoden untersucht werden sollte, damit Wertvolles nicht verloren geht, Nutzloses oder Gefährliches aber nicht länger unberechtigt den Ruf des Altbewährten behält. Beides findet sich auch im Kräuterbuch des Leonhart Fuchs.

Am Ende dieser kurzen Übersicht mögen jene Worte stehen, mit denen Leonhart Fuchs selbst sein Buch beschließt:

> *Allso wöllen wir disen ersten theyl diß Kreüterbuchs hie beschliessen unnd mit der zeit, wills Gott, den andern theyl, so wir schon haben angefangen, auchmeniglichem zu nutz im truck lassen aušgeen. Demselbigen unserm lieben Herrn und Gott sey lob, ehr unnd breiß inewigkeyt. Amen.*

Diese Hoffnung des Botaniker-Arztes hat sich nicht erfüllt. Es blieben ihm zwar noch 23 Jahre bis zu seinem Tod, doch reichte diese Zeit nicht mehr aus, die geplante Fortsetzung erscheinen zu lassen. Fast vierhundert Jahre vergehen, bis sein Manuskript und die Zeichnungen durch Zufall wiederentdeckt werden. Der erste Band aber hat ausgereicht, um Leonhart Fuchs unsterblich zu machen.

Et primo tomo

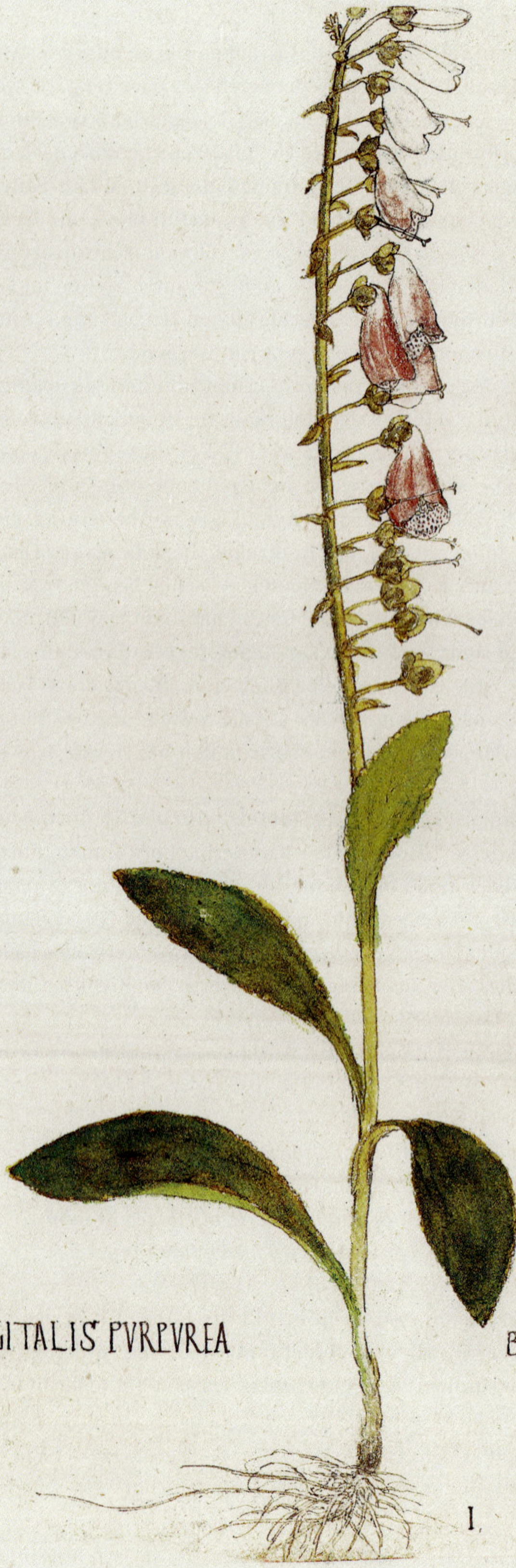

DIGITALIS PVRPVREA

Braúner fingerhůt.

I.

WERNER DRESSENDÖRFER

«Pou à mendiant» et «arbre merveilleux»

Les plantes du New Kreüterbuch

L'année 1543 voit la parution de trois ouvrages qui, chacun à sa manière, ouvrent de nouvelles voies à la science. Nicolas Copernic publie son *De Revolutionibus Orbium Cœlestium Libri VI* dans lequel il permute le lieu, et la fonction, de la Terre – par conséquent de l'homme – en plaçant le Soleil au centre de l'Univers. À Bâle, André Vésale fait imprimer chez Jean Oporin un traité d'anatomie monumental, *De Humani Corporis Fabrica*, qui s'attaque aux théories médicales des Anciens, posant ainsi les bases de l'anatomie moderne. C'est à Bâle également, dans l'officine de Michel Isingrin, que le médecin de Tübingen Leonhart Fuchs publie son *New Kreüterbuch*. Les planches de cet herbier représentent par leur beauté un sommet de l'illustration de livres botaniques, encore admiré de nos jours, et le texte laisse déjà entrevoir l'évolution de la botanique au cours des décennies suivantes.

L'ambition de Fuchs, ainsi qu'il l'annonce avec prolixité sur la page de titre, est de faire une synthèse des connaissances botaniques «comme on en a jamais vu ni conçu auparavant». «Auparavant» se rapporte en premier lieu aux ouvrages similaires d'Otto Brunfels et de Jérôme Bock, publiés respectivement en 1532 et 1539, et qui entérinent une tradition encore jeune, née à Mayence en 1484 avec la publication d'un recueil illustré. Rédigé encore en latin, cet *Hortus sanitatis* s'adressait aux médecins et aux apothicaires. Mais, dès l'année suivante, paraissait un plus gros ouvrage intitulé *Der Gart der Gesundheit* (Le jardin de la santé), qui était accessible cette fois aux néophytes parce que rédigé en langue allemande. Bien que les gravures des plantes en soient encore grossières et schématiques, ce nouveau genre de livre qui réunissait sous forme de lexique textes et illustrations correspondantes répondait si bien à l'intérêt des gens qu'il devient non seulement un best-seller aux XVe et XVIe siècles, mais ne cessera de paraître jusqu'à nos jours.

Leonhart Fuchs adopte un plan strict pour structurer son ouvrage : vient d'abord le titre correspondant à une espèce, suivi du numéro du chapitre, puis le paragraphe «Noms», dans lequel il mentionne les dénominations allemandes, latines et grecques et qu'il explique

LEONHART FUCHS, *Codex Fuchs*, Tübingen, c. 1536–1566
Vienna, Österreichische Nationalbibliothek, HAN: Cod. 11117–11125 (9 vols.)
Digitalis purpurea (L.) – Foxglove / Roter Fingerhut / Digitale pourpre; Cod. 11119, p. 115

en partie par leur sens. Il indique aussi, si nécessaire, les noms courants, ceux en particulier utilisés par les pharmaciens, ce qui est l'occasion pour lui, médecin, de brocarder cette nomenclature pharmaceutique. Ainsi ce commentaire de Fuchs sur les apothicaires au chapitre V : «Ils aiment bien de toute façon se faire remarquer.»

Le paragraphe «Genres» est consacré aux descriptions botaniques par lesquelles Fuchs différencie les variétés de la même plante. Par exemple, au chapitre LVII où il est question de la renoncule, sept illustrations explicitent la remarque suivante : «Ce sont ... les nombreux genres de la renoncule.» On trouve souvent, comme c'est le cas pour le mouron (chapitre VI), les qualificatifs de «mâle» et de «femelle». Il ne s'agit pas de plantes unisexuées, mais de diverses espèces ou sous-espèces qui ne se distinguent que par la teinte ou la taille.

Le paragraphe «Forme» décrit, parallèlement à l'illustration, les détails anatomiques de la plante, tout en précisant les stades de maturation, par exemple du bouton à la fleur épanouie, jusqu'au fruit.

Fuchs nomme «Lieu de croissance» la distribution géographique de la plante. À plusieurs reprises, il signale même l'existence de certaines espèces dans les environs de Tübingen ou des endroits qu'il connaît. Au paragraphe «Temps», il donne la période de floraison et le meilleur moment pour récolter la plante.

Il est difficile à notre époque de suivre les explications données à «Nature et complexion». En effet, lorsqu'il est question de «chaud», «froid», «humide», «sec», mais aussi de bien d'autres notions comme le goût par exemple, c'est au cœur même des conceptions antiques de la matière que nous nous trouvons. Pour les Anciens, toutes les choses de la nature animée et inanimée sont faites d'un mélange des quatre éléments, Feu, Eau, Air et Terre. De leur côté, ces éléments présentent des qualités physiques constituées chacune de l'une des deux oppositions «froid – chaud» et «humide – sec». En médecine, on met en outre sur le même plan les quatre éléments et les humeurs, qui régissent indirectement aussi le tempérament de l'individu. La théorie des humeurs peut par conséquent se résumer de la manière suivante :

Élément	**Qualité**	**Goût**	**Humeur**	**Tempérament**
Feu	sec + chaud	amer	bile jaune	colérique
Eau	humide + froid	salé	flegme	flegmatique
Air	humide + chaud	sucré	sang	sanguin
Terre	sec + froid	acide	bile noire	mélancolique

La proportion des humeurs est propre à chacun et l'accompagne sa vie durant. L'individu est en bonne santé tant que l'équilibre des humeurs est assuré, et tout dérèglement du jeu humoral conduit à la maladie. La tâche du médecin consiste alors à déterminer par l'examen du patient laquelle des humeurs est excessive ou insuffisante. Les qualités qui en résultent doivent être soit réduites, soit augmentées pour rétablir l'équilibre humoral et parvenir à la guérison. Pour cette raison, toutes les plantes médicinales étaient classifiées, et employées, en fonction de ces qualités.

Le paragraphe suivant, «Puissance et effet», est donc dédié aux indications thérapeutiques, accompagnées, le cas échéant, d'une brève mention du mode d'utilisation. À vrai dire, ce répertoire pharmacologique est souvent empreint d'une vision magique du monde, en l'occurrence, la théorie des signatures. Selon « l'art du signatum », comme le nommait Paracelse, le corps humain est un microcosme qui est en rapport direct avec l'ordre du macrocosme universel. Il existe entre les deux entités ce qu'il appelle des « sympathies intérieures ». Selon lui, elles peuvent se reconnaître par des ressemblances extérieures, les « signatures », c'est-à-dire des formes ou des couleurs correspondantes ou toute autre particularité. Ainsi, les plantes à suc ou à fleur jaune auraient un effet sur la bile, jaune verdâtre ; les rouges sur les hémorragies. De même, les feuilles de la mélisse seraient efficaces contre les affections cardiaques à cause de leur forme cordée.

Si ces explications permettent d'éclairer la pensée du Moyen Âge, elles montrent aussi que ce qui est mentionné dans les anciens herbiers ne peut plus se prendre au pied de la lettre et servir aujourd'hui de base à une automédication. Au mieux peut-on y voir l'indication d'une longue expérience, dont la valeur et le bien-fondé devraient être analysés par des méthodes scientifiques modernes non seulement pour conserver un savoir précieux, mais pour ne plus considérer comme avéré ce qui est inutile ou dangereux. C'est ce qui ressort aussi de l'ouvrage de Leonhart Fuchs.

Nous aimerions pour clore ce bref exposé citer les derniers mots du livre de Fuchs :

« Ainsi s'achève la première partie de cet herbier qui, si Dieu le veut,
sera suivie d'une seconde, que nous avons déjà commencée et qui sera
imprimée pour l'utilité de certains. Notre Seigneur et Dieu soit loué,
honoré et glorifié pour l'éternité. Amen. »

L'espoir du médecin botaniste n'a pu toutefois se réaliser. Les 23 années qui lui restent à vivre ne lui permettront pas de publier le second ouvrage. Près de quatre siècles s'écouleront avant que son manuscrit et ses dessins ne soient découverts par hasard. Mais ce premier volume a suffi pour immortaliser Leonhart Fuchs.

PAGES 74/75
LEONHART FUCHS, *De historia stirpium commentarii insignes*, Basel, 1542
Vienna, Österreichische Nationalbibliothek, POR: 8414
Portraits of / Porträts von / Portraits de Heinrich Füllmaurer & Albrecht Meyer, p. 897

PICTORE

Heinricus Füllmaurer.

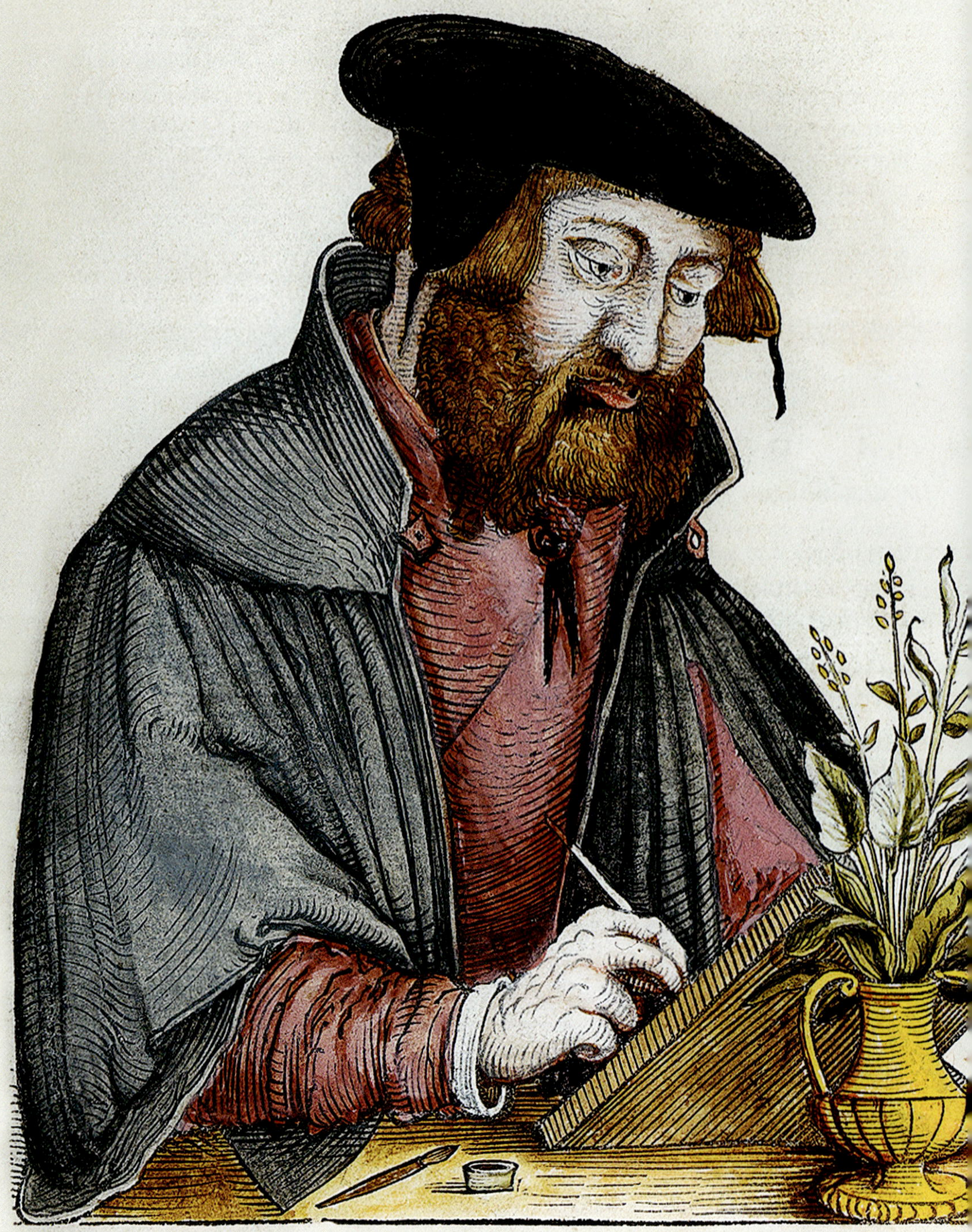

PERIS,

Albertus Meyer.

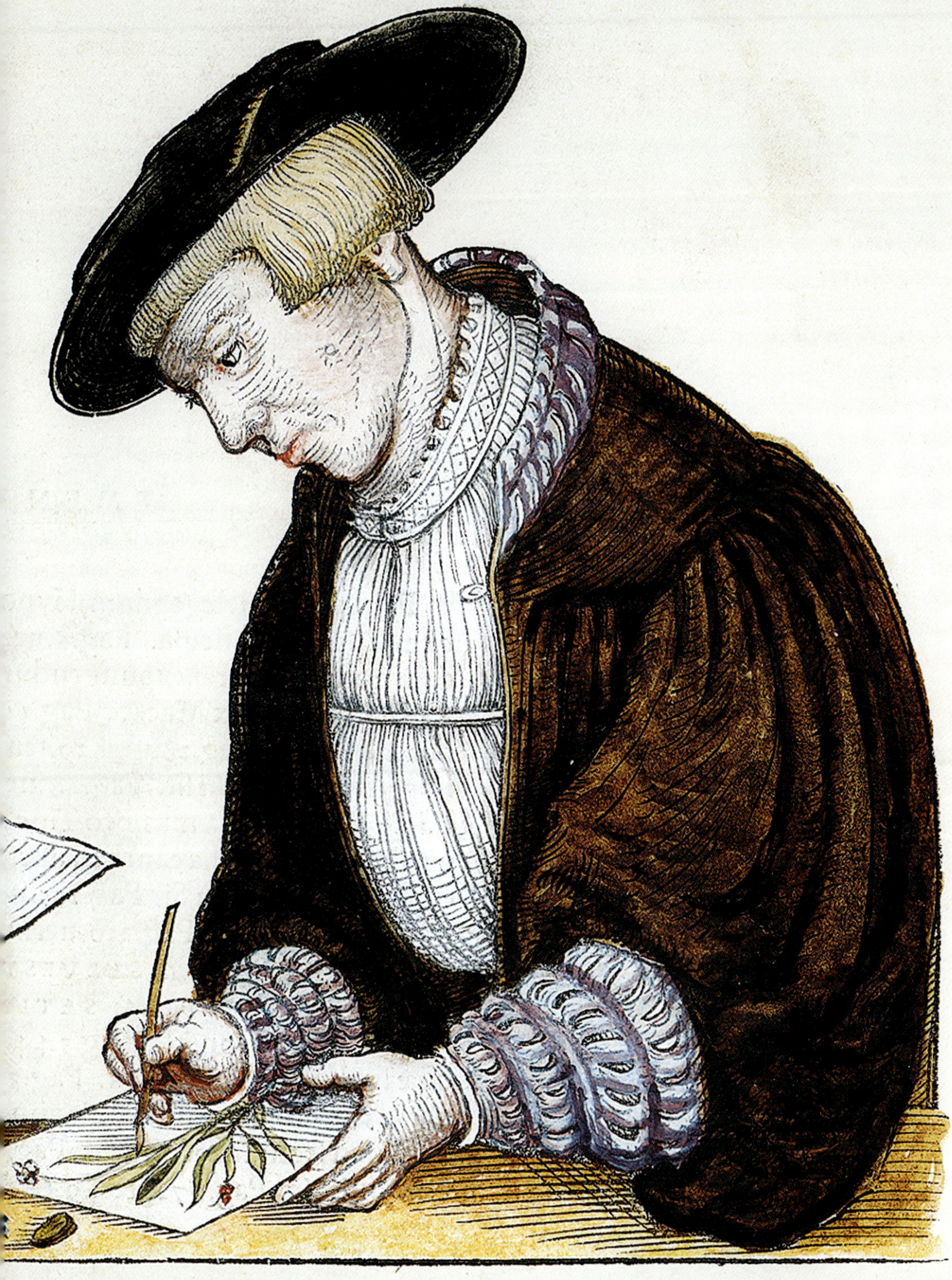

WORMWOOD

The first of the long series of chapters begins with WORMWOOD (I*). The plant's unusual name in fact derives from an Old English root wermod, closely related to the plant's German name "Wermut," whose origin remains uncertain to this day. Fuchs derived a bold etymology from the herb's bitter taste, which "defends against, or drives away, joy and courage." In terms of application, the herb's effect on the stomach and digestive tract is still recognized today, but the broad spectrum of further recommendations gives the reader a hint of the Baroque diversity of indications to follow.

WERMUT

Der WERMUT (Cap. I*) eröffnet die lange Reihe der 346 Kapitel. Seinen ungewöhnlichen, bis heute nicht völlig geklärten Namen leitet Fuchs in kühner Etymologie vom bitteren Geschmack des Krautes ab, der alle „freud und mut weret und vertreibt". Was die Anwendung betrifft, wird man die Wirkung auf Magen und Verdauungstrakt auch heute noch anerkennen, das ganze Spektrum der weiteren Empfehlungen lässt aber bereits ahnen, mit welch barocker „Indikationslyrik" der Leser in den folgenden Kapiteln konfrontiert werden wird.

ABSINTHE

Le premier des 346 chapitres que compte l'herbier s'ouvre sur l'ABSINTHE (I*). Son nom allemand, «Wermut», est singulier, et on n'en connaît toujours pas l'origine exacte. Selon l'étymologie audacieuse de Fuchs, le nom s'expliquerait par le goût amer de la plante, laquelle selon lui «entrave et chasse toute la joie et la bonne humeur» (le suffixe «Mut» signifie «humeur» en ancien allemand). Si l'on reconnaît encore aujourd'hui ses vertus apéritives, la pléthore des usages thérapeutiques laisse déjà entrevoir au lecteur qu'il sera confronté au «lyrisme des indications» aux chapitres suivants.

* Roman numerals denote the chapter. In case of illustrations, the numeral is preceded by the word "plate."
Die römischen Ziffern beziehen sich auf die Kapitel. Bei Illustrationen steht ihnen die Abkürzung „Taf." voran.
Les chiffres romains désignent les numéros des chapitres, lorsqu'il s'agit d'illustrations, les chiffres romains sont précédés de l'abbréviation «pl.».

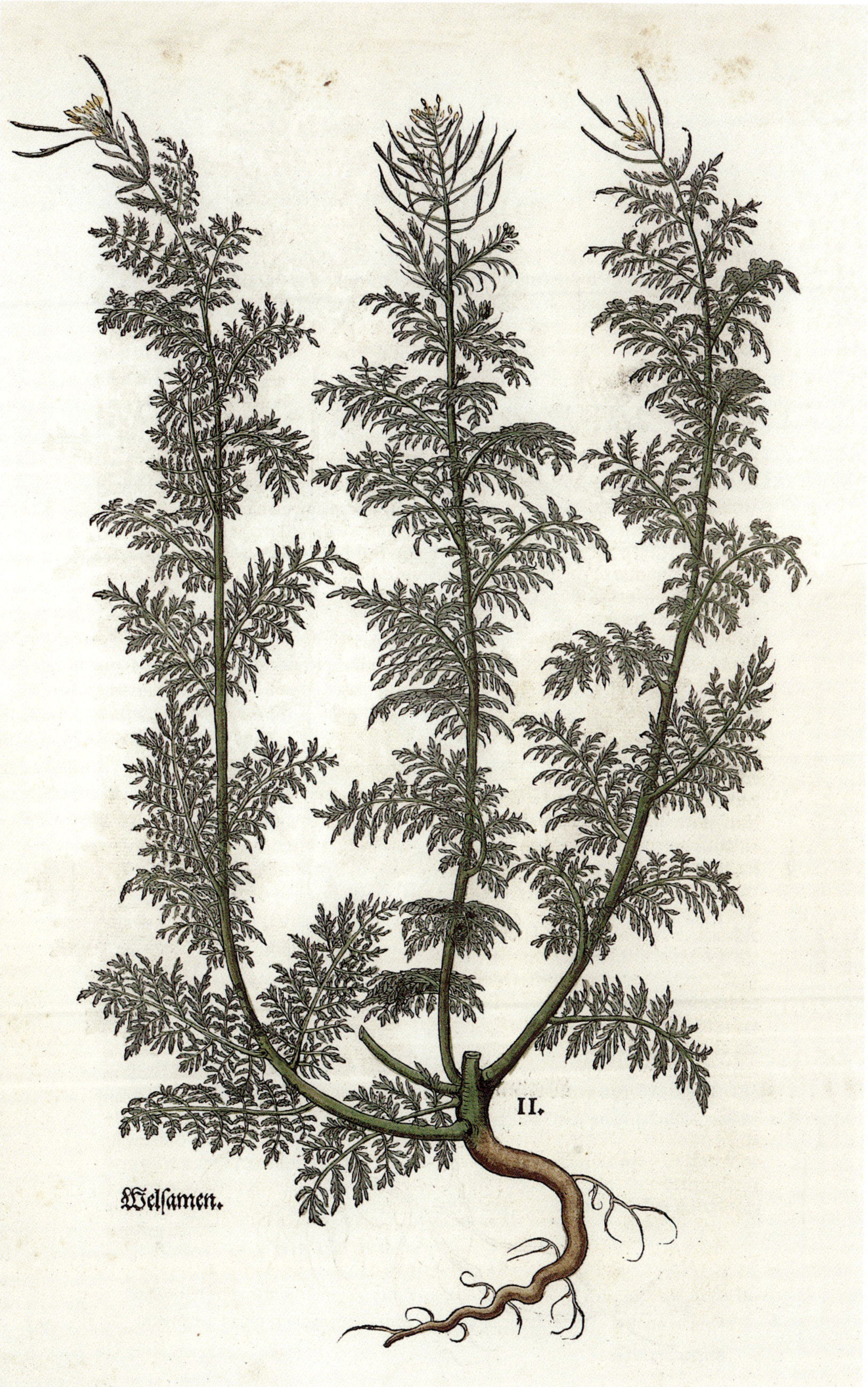
II.
Welſamen.

SOUTHERNWOOD

The next chapter (II) includes two close botanical relations to wormwood which are used only occasionally as herbs: SOUTHERNWOOD or Old Man, and Roman wormwood.

„STAUBWURTZ“

Die „STAUBWURTZ“ (Cap. II), botanisch eng mit dem Wermut verwandt, wird heute als Eberraute bezeichnet und nur noch gelegentlich als Gewürz verwendet.

ARMOISE CITRONNELLE

L'ARMOISE CITRONNELLE (II), parente de l'absinthe, n'est plus aujourd'hui qu'un condiment, employé de temps à autre en cuisine.

PAGE 80

ASARABACCA

Neither does ASARABACCA (III), any longer play a significant role as a medicinal plant. Also known as Hazelwort, it is used occasionally for respiratory problems. Earlier, it appeared as an ingredient of sneezing powder.

HASELWURZ

Auch die HASELWURZ (Cap. III) spielt als Heilpflanze keine nennenswerte Rolle mehr und wird nur noch vereinzelt bei Atemwegserkrankungen eingesetzt, sie fand sich früher auch in Niespulvern.

ASARET D'EUROPE

La médecine moderne a délaissé aussi l'ASARET D'EUROPE (III), sauf usage sporadique dans les maladies des voies respiratoires. Il entrait autrefois dans la composition de poudres à éternuer.

PAGE 81

YELLOW FLAG

YELLOW FLAG (IIII), also known as Water Iris or Jacob's Sword, appears under the designation “dragon root” in Fuchs, where it is recommended as an astringent.

„DRACHENWURTZ“ (SUMPF-SCHWERTLILIE)

Die gelbblühende Sumpf-Schwertlilie erscheint unter der Bezeichnung „DRACHENWURTZ“ (Cap. IIII) und wird als zusammenziehendes Mittel empfohlen.

IRIS DES MARAIS

L'IRIS DES MARAIS (IIII), de couleur jaune, est mentionné sous le nom de «Drachenwurtz» (racine à dragon) et préconisé comme remède astringent.

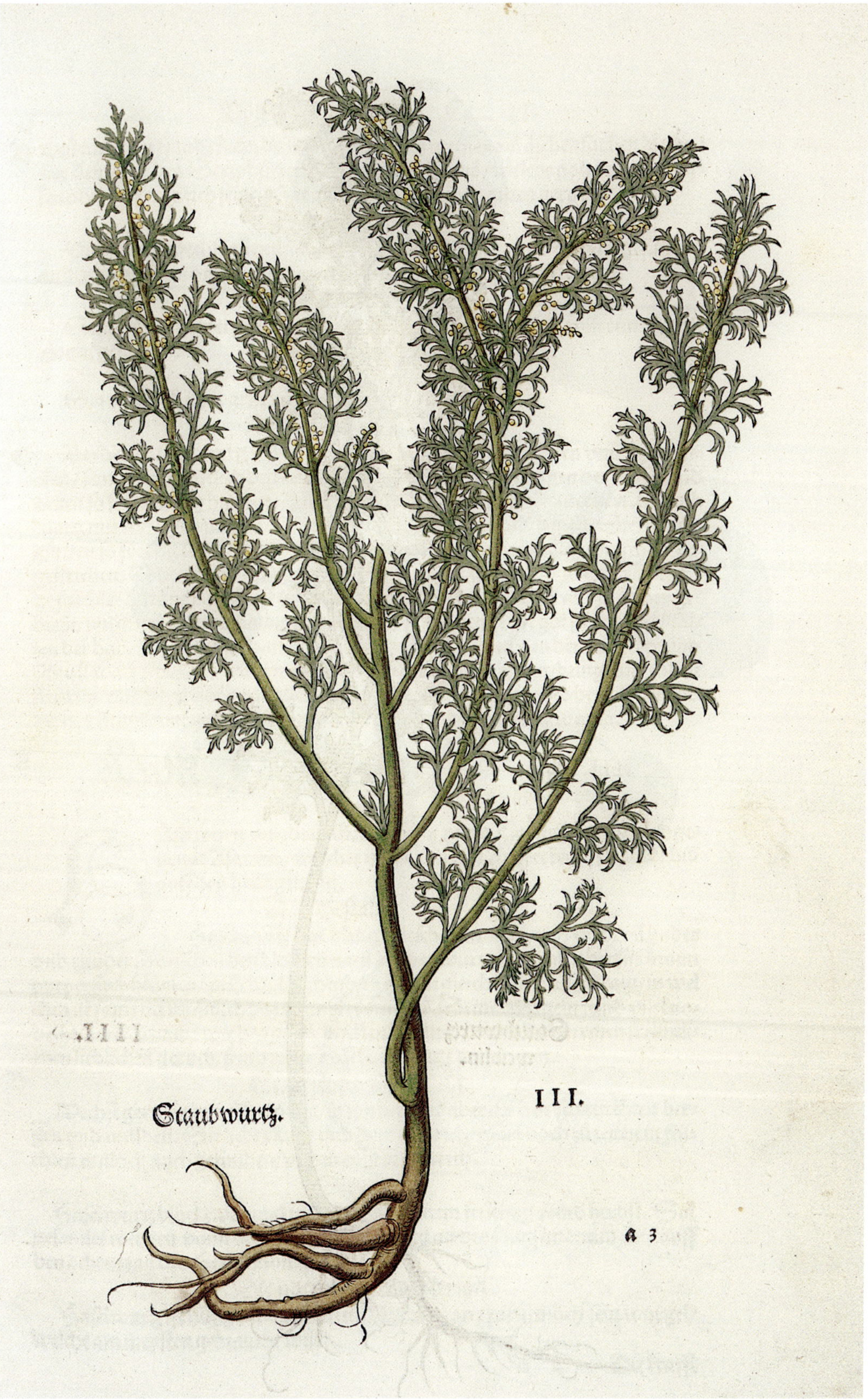
Staubwurtz.
III.
a 3

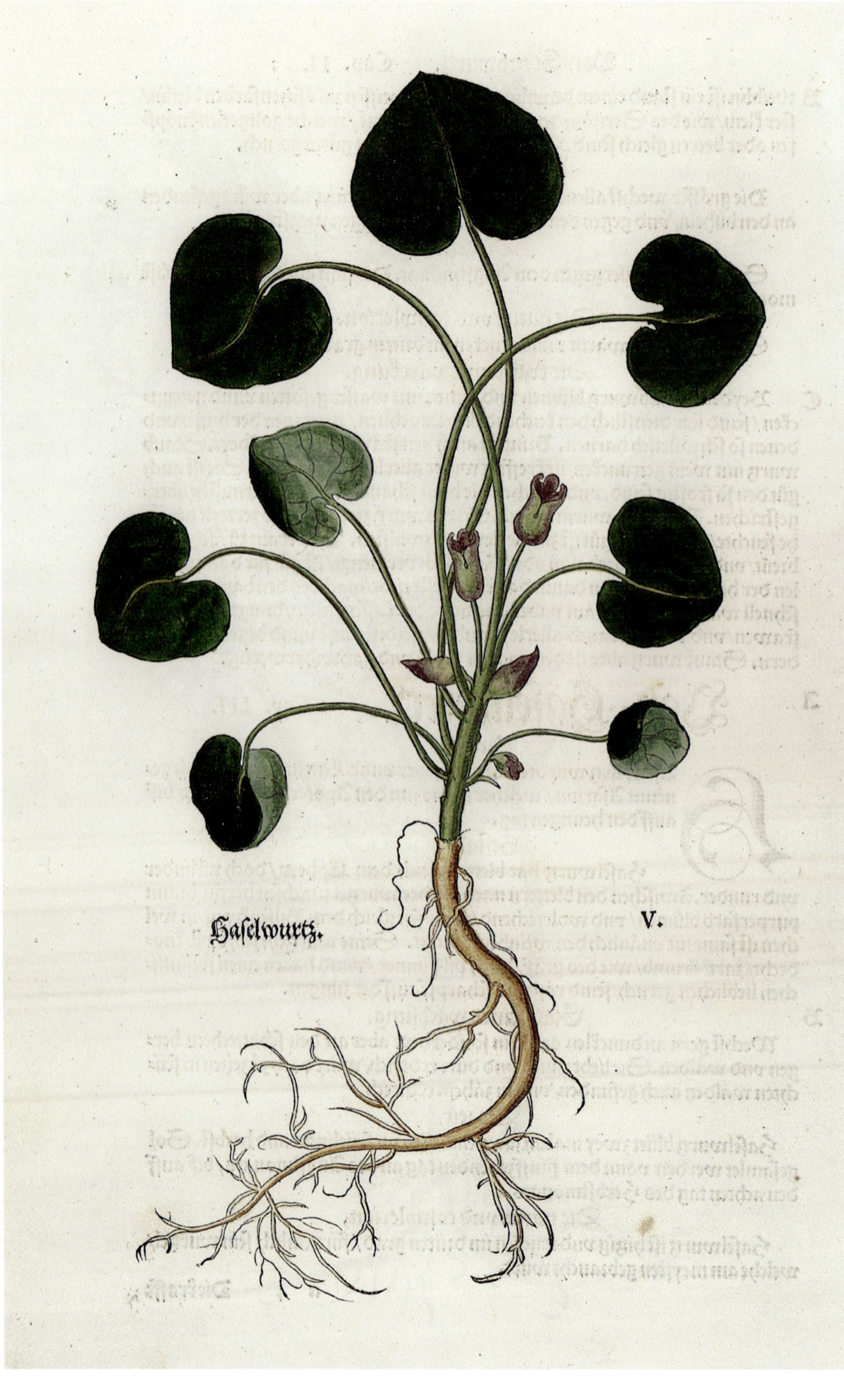
Haselwurtz.
V.

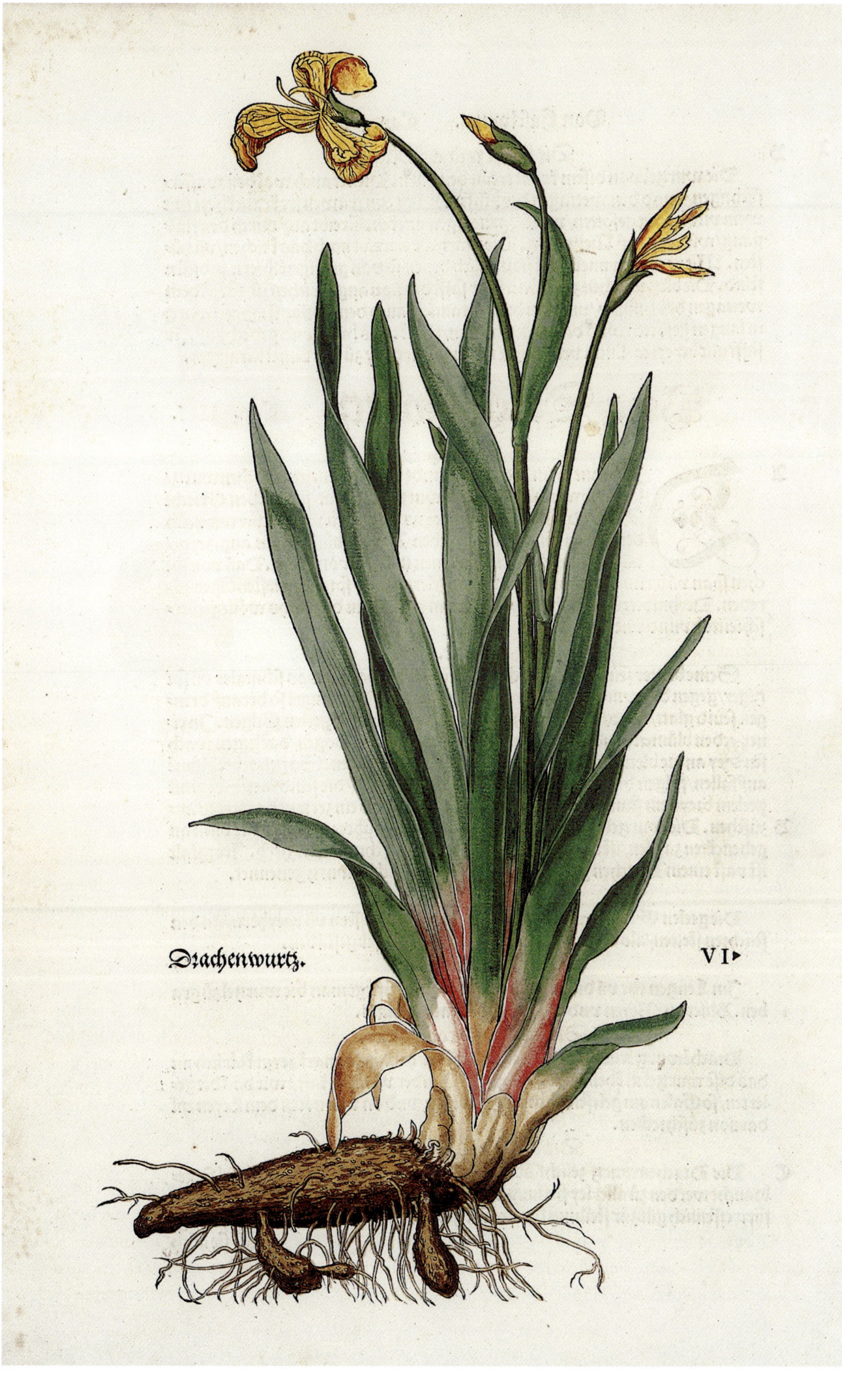
Drachenwurtz.
VI

MARSH MALLOW

With MARSH MALLOW (V), an important medicinal plant again makes an appearance in the herbal, although the application of the plant is only partly covered by Fuchs's reference to the palliative and emollient effect of the mucilage, which the plant does in fact possess. Today, the use of the plant for the expulsion of afterbirths and "other superfluities that remain in the womb after the birth," as well as its action against the bite of poisonous animals, are of merely historic interest.

EIBISCH

Mit dem EIBISCH (Cap. V) erscheint wieder eine der wichtigen Heilpflanzen, allerdings ist ihre Anwendung nur teilweise vom tatsächlich vorhandenen Schleimgehalt und seiner lindernden und erweichenden Wirkung geprägt. Die erwähnte Verwendung zur Austreibung der Nachgeburt und „andere überflüssikeyt so nach der geburt ist in muter leib beliben" besitzt ebenso wie der Einsatz gegen den Biss giftiger Tiere nur historische Bedeutung.

GUIMAUVE OFFICINALE

Avec la GUIMAUVE OFFICINALE (V), c'est une autre plante médicinale majeure qui est évoquée ici. Son application n'est toutefois pas très marquée parce que dépendant de sa teneur effective en mucilage et de son effet émollient. En revanche, son utilisation pour expulser l'arrière-faix et « autre liquide subsistant dans les entrailles de la mère après la naissance » ainsi que son emploi contre la morsure d'animaux venimeux n'ont plus qu'un intérêt historique.

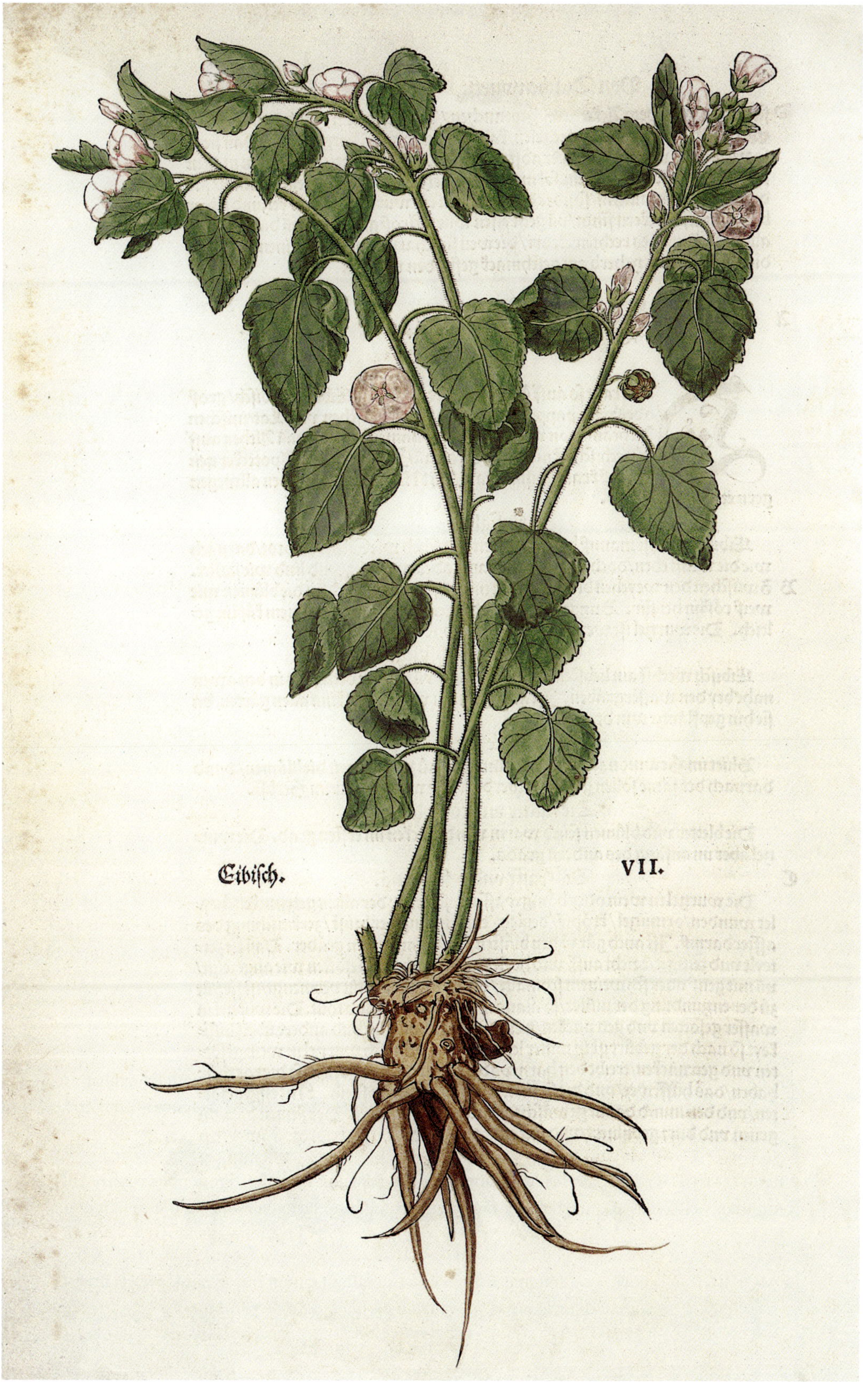
Eibisch.
VII.

PIMPERNEL

The German name of PIMPERNEL (VI), gauchheil, is interesting in that gauch formerly designated a burdensome ne'er-do-well, whereas heil implied the cure.

GAUCHHEIL

Beim GAUCHHEIL (Cap. VI) ist besonders die Erklärung des Pflanzennamens reizvoll, wenn man weiß, dass „Gauch" früher einen Tunichtgut und lästigen Menschen bezeichnete.

MOURON

Le MOURON (VI) porte en allemand le nom de « Gauchheil », nom intéressant, car « Gauch » désignait dans le passé un vaurien ou quelqu'un de pénible.

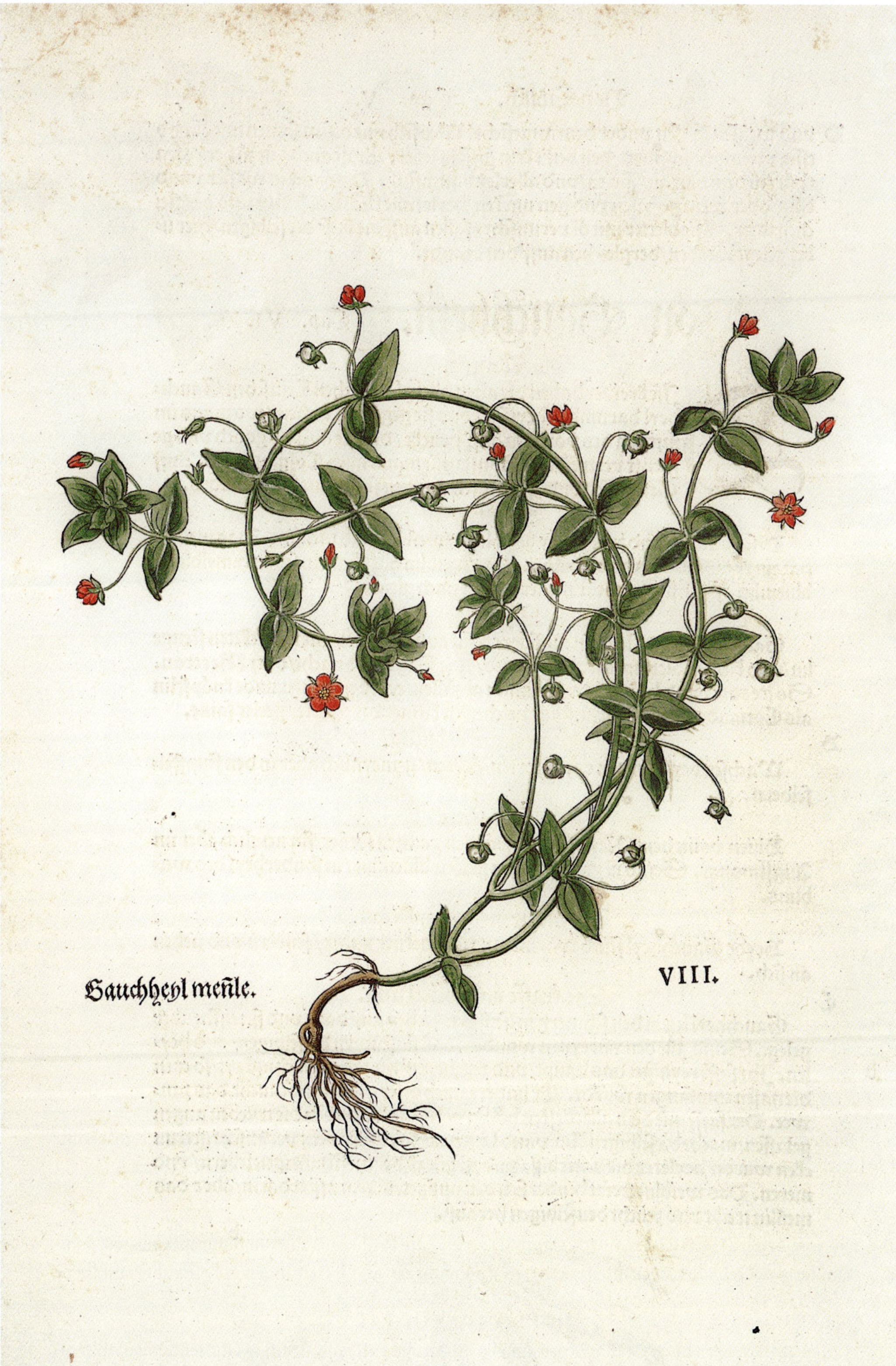

PIMPERNEL | GAUCHHEIL | MOURON

CHICKWEED

The four varieties of CHICKWEED (VII) demonstrate the problems still confronting 16th-century botanists in distinguishing between various species and closely related genera.

„HÜNERDÄRM"

Die vier Arten „HÜNERDÄRM" (Cap. VII) zeigen die Probleme, die die Botaniker des 16. Jahrhunderts noch hatten, verschiedene Arten und nah verwandte Gattungen auseinanderzuhalten.

MOURON DES OISEAUX

Les quatre espèces de MOURON présentées ensemble (VII) montrent les difficultés qu'avaient encore au XVIe siècle les botanistes pour distinguer des espèces différentes et des genres proches.

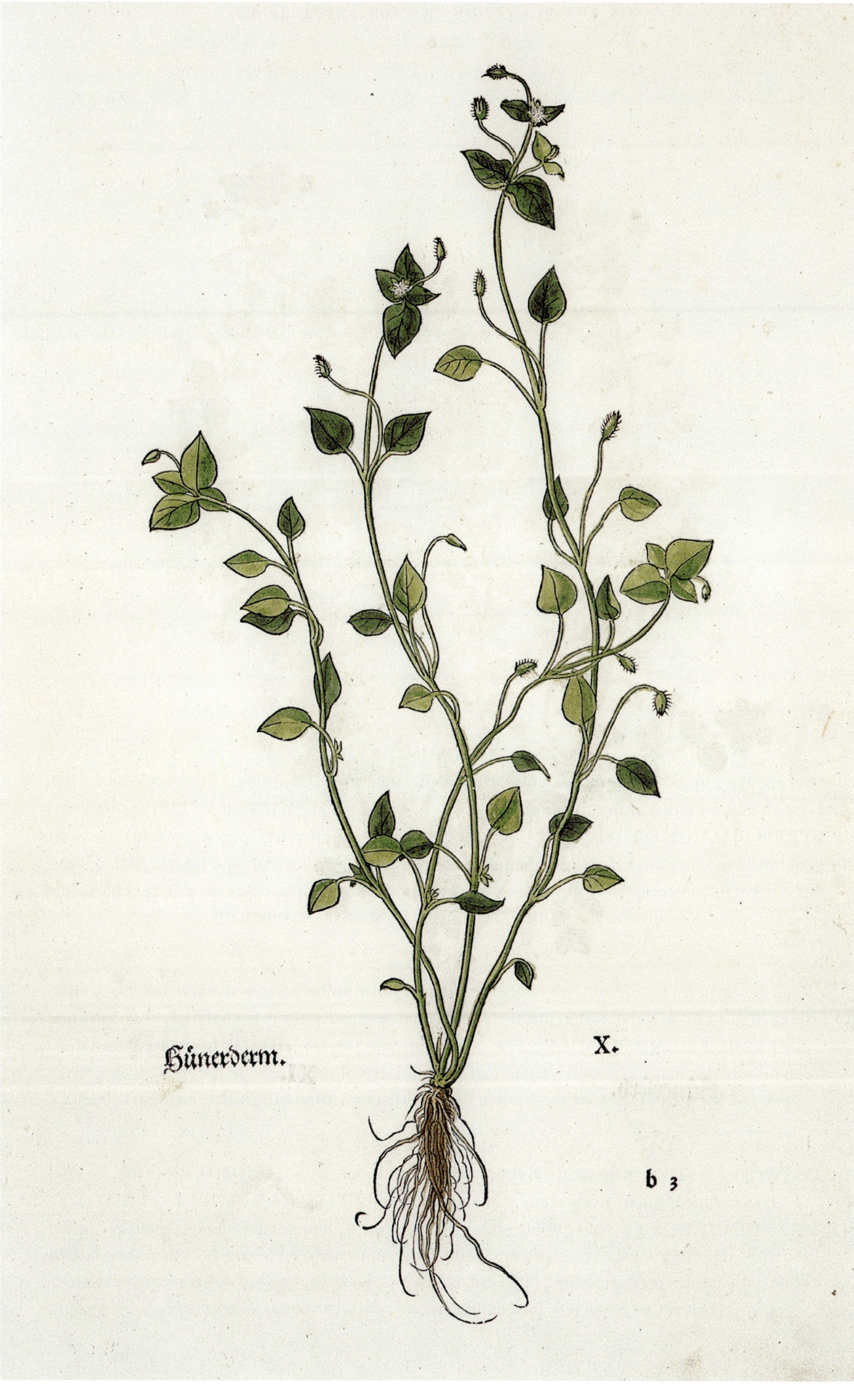
Hünerderm.
X.
b 3

CHAMOMILE

Surprisingly, the well-known CHAMOMILE (VIII) illustrates the problem of identification even more clearly. Included under the name are not only wild CHAMOMILE (plate XIII) and yellow, or DYER'S CHAMOMILE (plate XIIII) – which are similar in appearance, even down to the colours of the blossoms – but also field larkspur. Presented as a "third variety" of CHAMOMILE, the latter is not only a completely unrelated plant botanically, but also has entirely different blossoms; furthermore, it can be dangerous when taken internally.

KAMILLE

Noch deutlicher wird dies überraschenderweise bei der wohlbekannten KAMILLE (Cap. VIII), wo nicht nur die bis auf die Blütenfarbe ähnlich aussehende ECHTE KAMILLE (Taf. XIII) und die FÄRBER-HUNDSKAMILLE (Taf. XIIII) darunter verstanden werden, sondern auch der botanisch überhaupt nicht verwandte und völlig andere Blüten tragende Rittersporn als „dritt geschlecht" angeführt wird, das zudem bei innerlicher Anwendung nicht ungefährlich ist.

CAMOMILLE

Ceci est encore plus évident, et surprenant aussi, dans le cas de la CAMOMILLE (VIII). En effet, non seulement Fuchs range dans le même genre la PETITE CAMOMILLE (pl. XIII) et L'ANTHÉMIS DES TEINTURIERS (pl. XIIII), à cause de leur ressemblance (seule la couleur des fleurs diffère), mais il leur ajoute une plante qui n'appartient en aucun cas à la même famille et ne porte pas les mêmes fleurs : le pied-d'alouette. Celui-ci est qualifié de « troisième variété », ce qui ne serait pas sans danger si on l'administrait par voie interne.

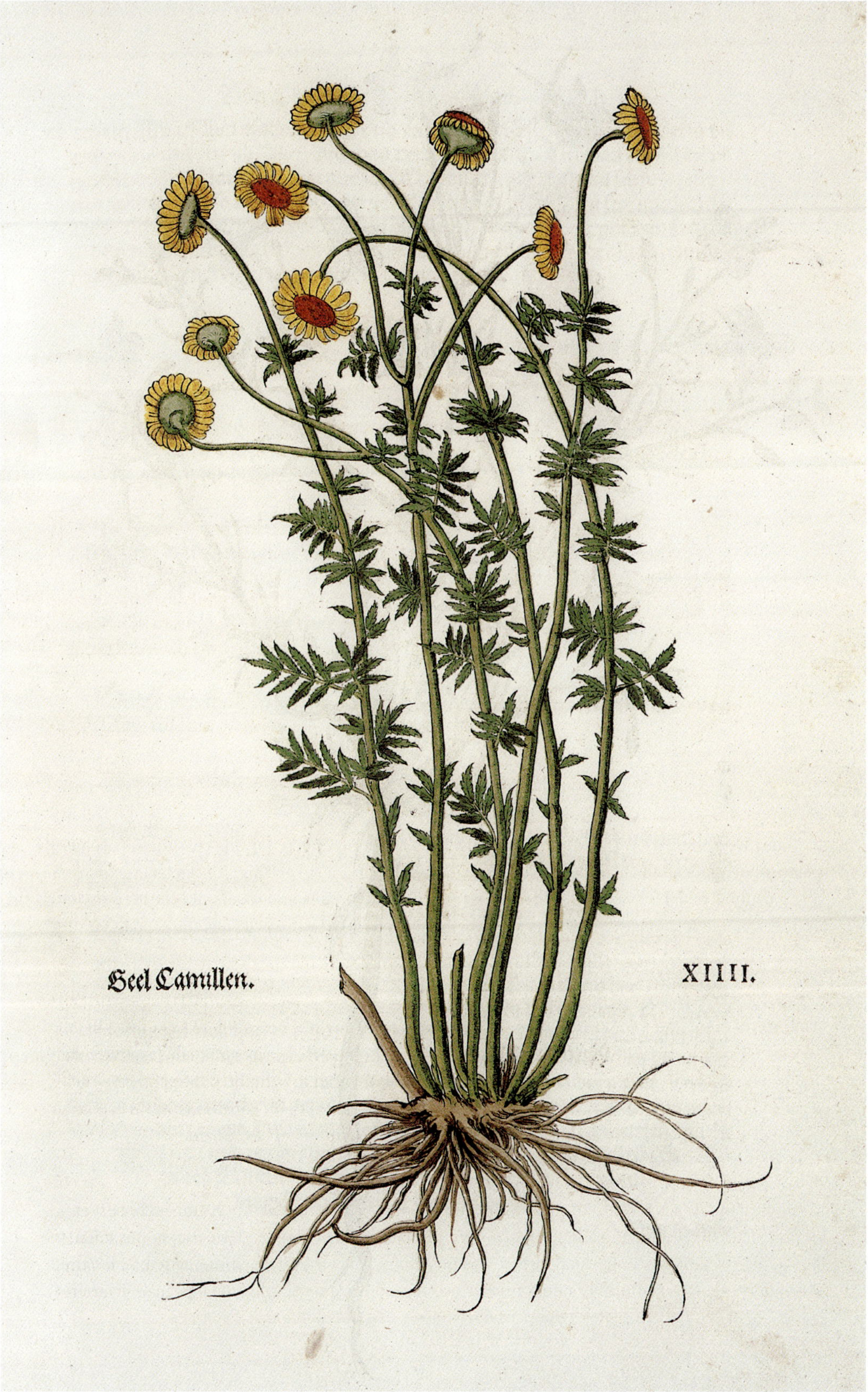
Seel Camillen.
XIIII.

DILL

Today we know DILL (IX) almost exclusively as a culinary herb; for this reason, the broad spectrum of applications ascribed to it by Fuchs is all the more surprising: it is lactogenic, diuretic and carminative; effective against hiccups as well as condylomas and ulcers; it relieves pain and induces sleep. But undesirable effects are also ascribed to DILL; thus "it robs the seed of vitality," and "makes the eyes dark and shadowy."

DILL

Den DILL (Cap. IX) kennen wir heute fast nur noch als Gewürz; umso überraschender ist das breite Anwendungsspektrum, das Fuchs ihm zuschreibt: milch-, harn- und blähungstreibend, gegen Schluckauf, Feigwarzen und Geschwüre wirksam, zudem schmerzstillend und schlaffördernd. Aber auch negative Wirkungen werden ihm zugeschrieben. So „tilgt er aus den samen der geburt dienstlich" und „macht die augen dunckel und finster".

ANETH ODORANT

Aujourd'hui, L'ANETH ODORANT (IX) est surtout un condiment. Fuchs lui attribue bien des propriétés : lactifère, diurétique, actif contre les flatuosités, le hoquet, les condylomes ainsi que les ulcères ; il serait en outre analgésique et soporifique. Mais il évoque en même temps les effets secondaires en cas d'administration prolongée : « Il rend les yeux sombres et obscurs » et « détruit les semences nécessaires à la naissance ».

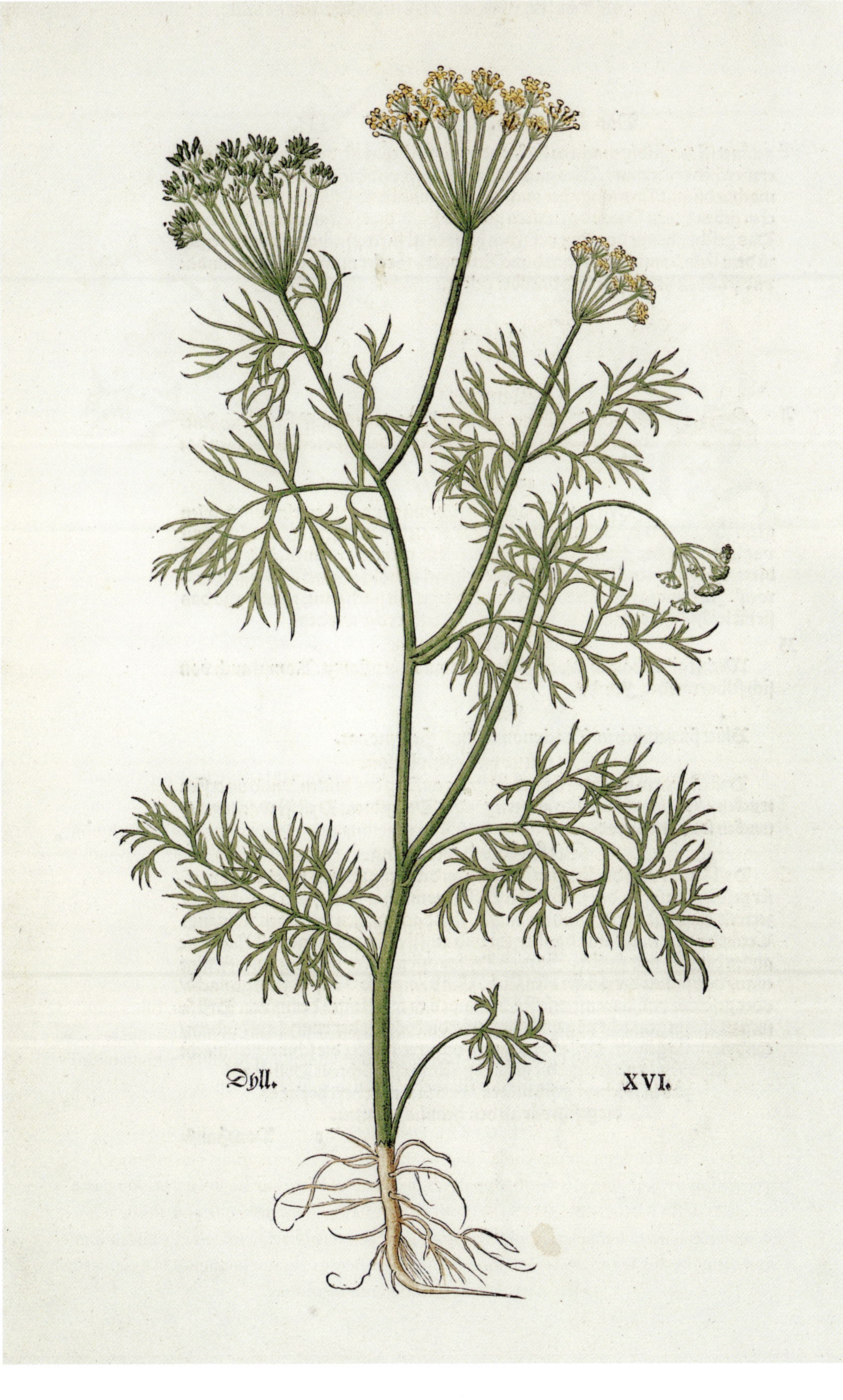
Dyll.
XVI.

HOUSELEEK

Every child used to recognize the thick-leaved plant known as HOUSELEEK (X), also known as "welcome home husband however drunk you be," which often grew on the roofs of houses and was reputed to have the power of repelling lightning and storms. Medicinally, it was supposed to help cure erysipelas, infections and boils. The juice was moreover effective against dysentery, diarrhea and worms.

„HAUSSWURTZ"

Als „Donnerbart" kannte früher jedes Kind die dickblättrige Pflanze, die oft auf Hausdächern wuchs und deshalb „HAUSSWURTZ" (Cap. X) genannt wurde. Dieser Bewuchs war keineswegs unerwünscht, denn man sprach der Pflanze die Fähigkeit zu, Blitze und Sturm abzuhalten. Auch ihre medizinische Wirkung wurde gelobt, denn sie sollte bei Rotlauf, Entzündungen und Geschwüren helfen, der Saft zudem bei Ruhr, Durchfällen und Wurmerkrankungen dienlich sein.

JOUBARBE DES TOITS

Autrefois, tout enfant connaissait la « herbe du tonnerre » (« Donnerbart » en allemand, barbe à tonnerre), plante aux feuilles épaisses poussant souvent sur les toits, d'où son autre nom de JOUBARBE DES TOITS (X). Loin de déranger, on lui prêtait le pouvoir de tenir à distance éclairs et tempêtes. Appréciée aussi pour ses vertus médicinales, elle aurait une action salutaire sur le rouget, les inflammations et les ulcères ; le suc soignerait la dysenterie et les diarrhées, et serait même vermifuge.

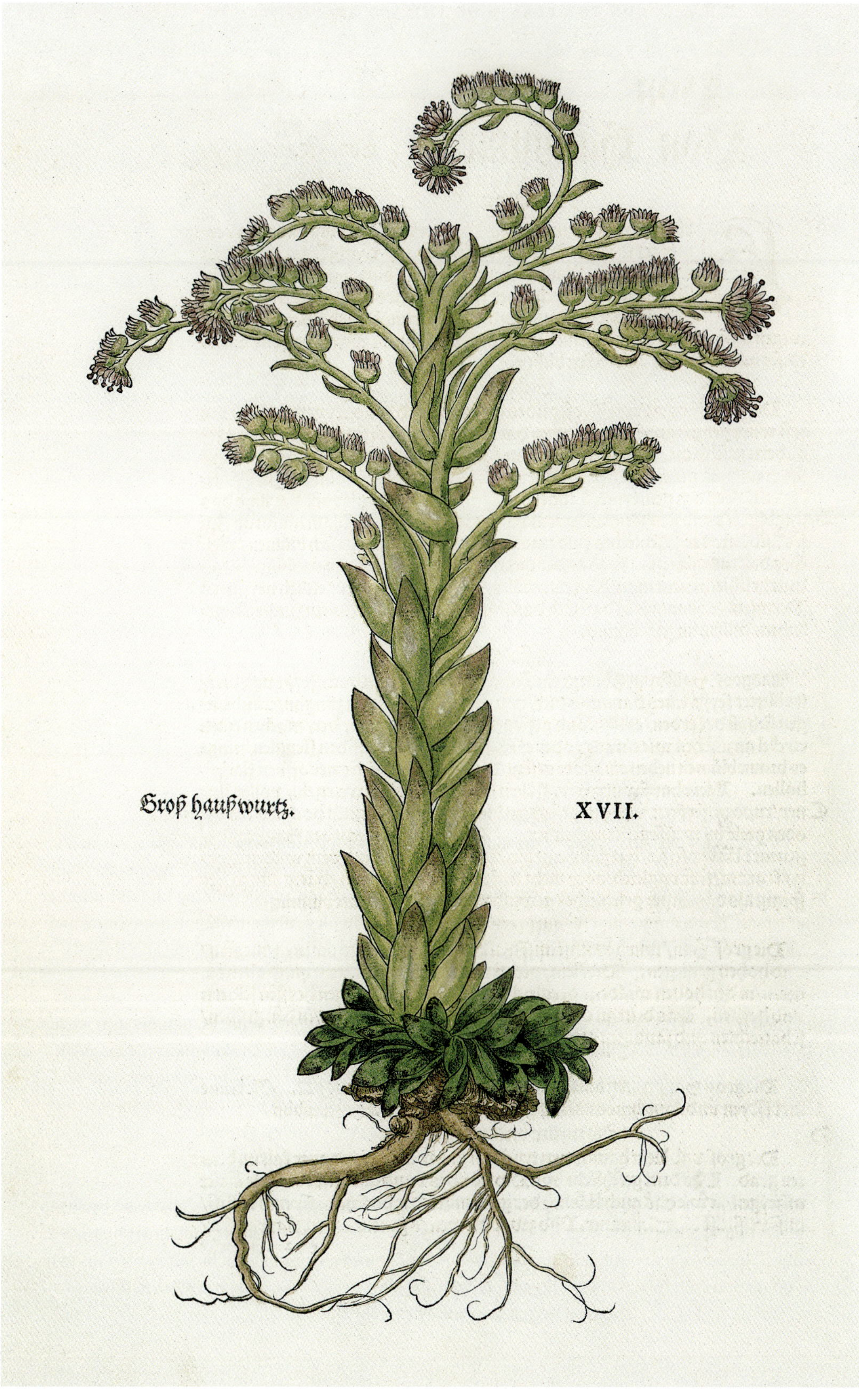
Groß haußwurtz.
XVII.

PLANTAIN

PLANTAIN (XI), too, is one of the older companions of the human race. Its leaves, whose appearance caused the plant to be known as "sheep's tongue," were frequently used as oracle plants: By tearing out the midrib of the leaf, the bundles of veins stood out, and depending on their number and length, deductions could be made either magically or in play. Medicinally, the desiccating and astringent power of the plant was used for example against oozing skin eruptions and wounds.

WEGERICH

Auch der WEGERICH (Cap. XI) ist ein alter Begleiter des Menschen. Seine Blätter, die ihm wegen ihres Aussehens den Namen „Schafszunge" einbrachten, wurden als Orakelpflanze verwendet, weil beim Durchreißen aus den Blattrippen die Leitbündel herausragen und aus ihrer Zahl und Länge magisch oder spielerisch gefolgert wer-den konnte. Medizinisch wurde die austrocknende Kraft z. B. bei nässenden Ausschlägen und Wunden genutzt.

PLANTAIN

Le PLANTAIN (XI) a des feuilles, dont l'aspect lui a valu le nom courant de «langue de brebis» et qui servait souvent d'oracle. En effet, lorsqu'on les déchire, les nervures font apparaître les paquets de vaisseaux, variables en nombre et en longueur, avec lesquels on faisait par jeu ou non des prédictions. En médecine, on l'appliquait sur les plaies et les éruptions cutanées suintantes en raison de son pouvoir astringent et dessicatif.

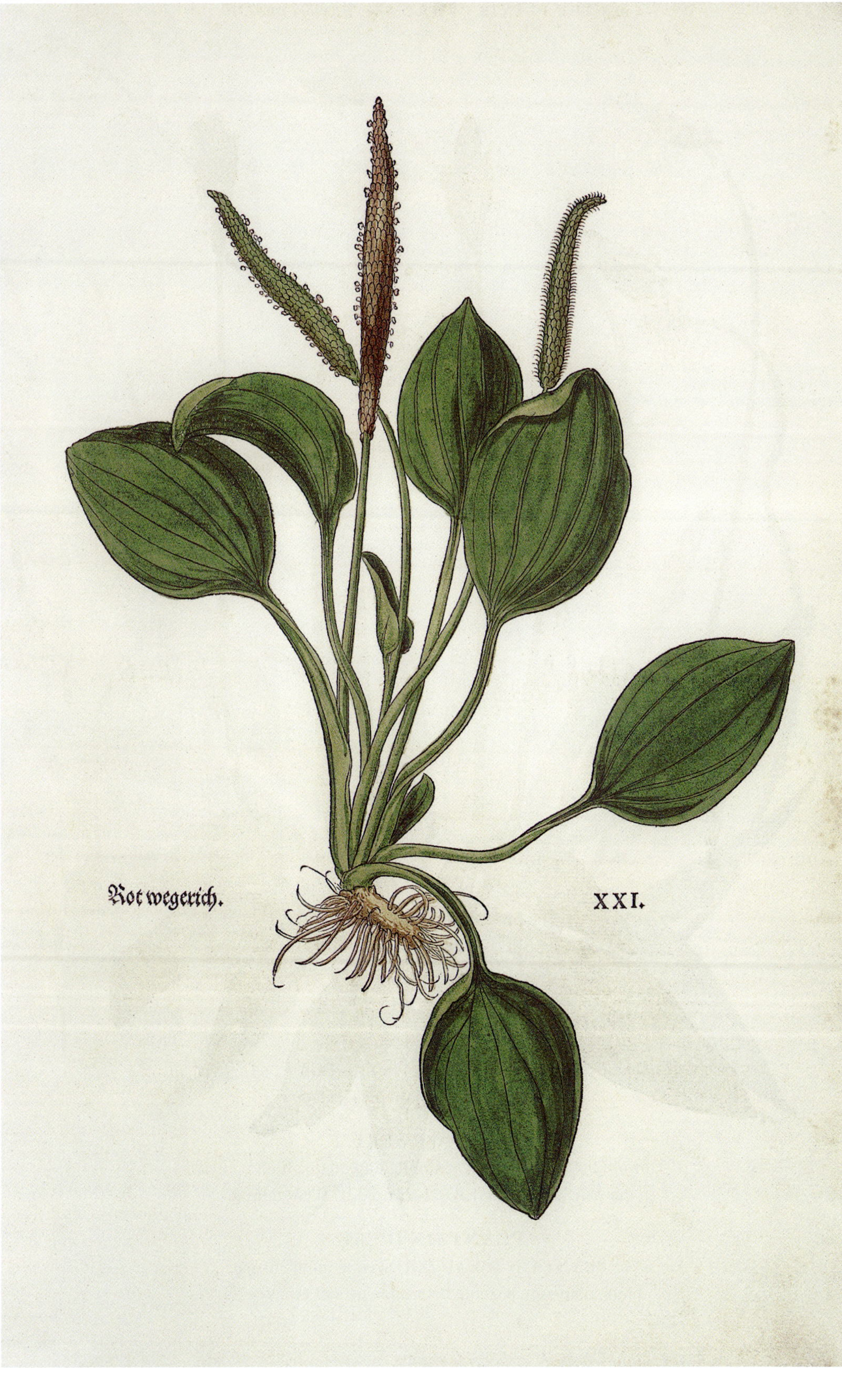
Rot wegerich.
XXI.

WATER PLANTAIN

Analogous uses were ascribed to WATER PLANTAIN (XII), although there is no botanical relation.

WASSERWEGERICH

Obwohl botanisch nicht verwandt, fand analog hierzu auch der WASSERWEGERICH (Cap. XII) Verwendung.

PLANTAIN D'EAU

Le PLANTAIN D'EAU (XII) avait le même usage, bien qu'aucune parenté botanique ne soit évoquée ici.

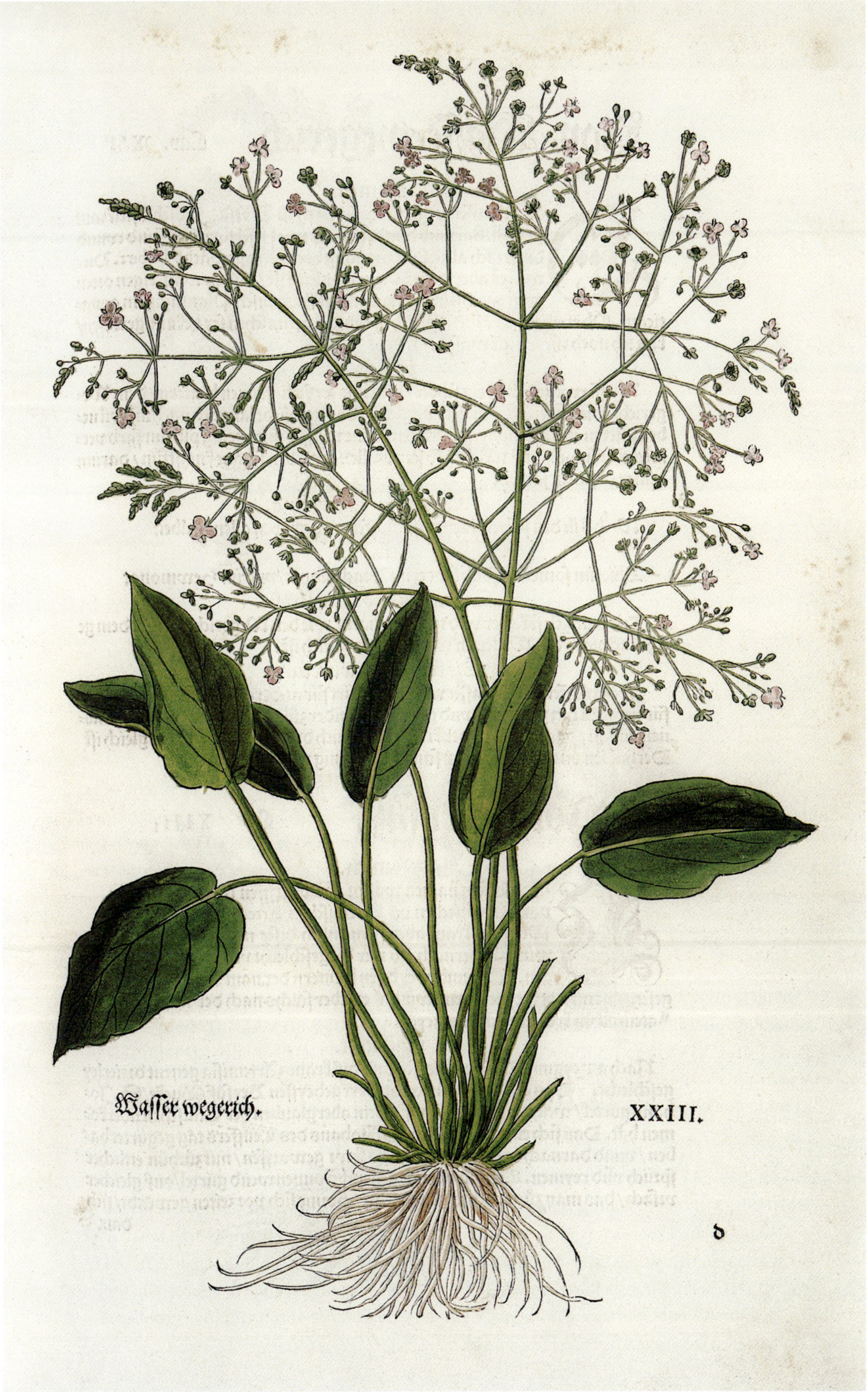
Waſſer wegerich.
XXIII.
d

MUGWORT

With the MUGWORT (artemisia) group (XIII), we once again come upon the name of an important medicinal plant, although the chapter brings four very different kinds of plant together: COMMON MUGWORT (plate XXIIII), FEVERFEW (plate XXV), COMMON TANSY (plate XXVI) and FRENCH MARIGOLD (plate XXVII). According to Fuchs, they were useful for female disorders, bladder, kidney or gallstones, etc., and against poisonous animals; the common tansy was particularly recommended against worms.

BEIFUSS

Mit dem BEIFUSS (Cap. XIII) begegnet uns wieder der Name einer wichtigen Heilpflanze, unter dem allerdings mit dem GEWÖHNLICHEN BEIFUSS (Taf. XXIIII), dem MUTTERKRAUT (Taf. XXV), dem RAINFARN (Taf. XXVI) und der STUDENTENBLUME (Taf. XXVII) vier sehr unterschiedliche Pflanzen zusammengefasst werden. Sie finden nach Fuchs bei Frauenkrankheiten ebenso Einsatz wie bei Steinerkrankungen und gegen giftige Tiere, der Rainfarn insbesondere auch bei Wurmerkrankungen.

ARMOISE

L'ARMOISE (XIII) est une autre plante médicinale majeure, sous le nom de laquelle Fuchs associe cependant quatre espèces fort différentes : l'ARMOISE COMMUNE (pl. XXIII), la GRANDE CAMOMILLE (pl. XXV), la TANAISIE VULGAIRE (pl. XXVI) et l'ŒILLET D'INDE (pl. XXVII). Selon Fuchs, elles s'emploient toutes dans les maladies particulières à la femme, les calculs et la morsure d'animaux venimeux ; la tanaisie serait en plus vermifuge.

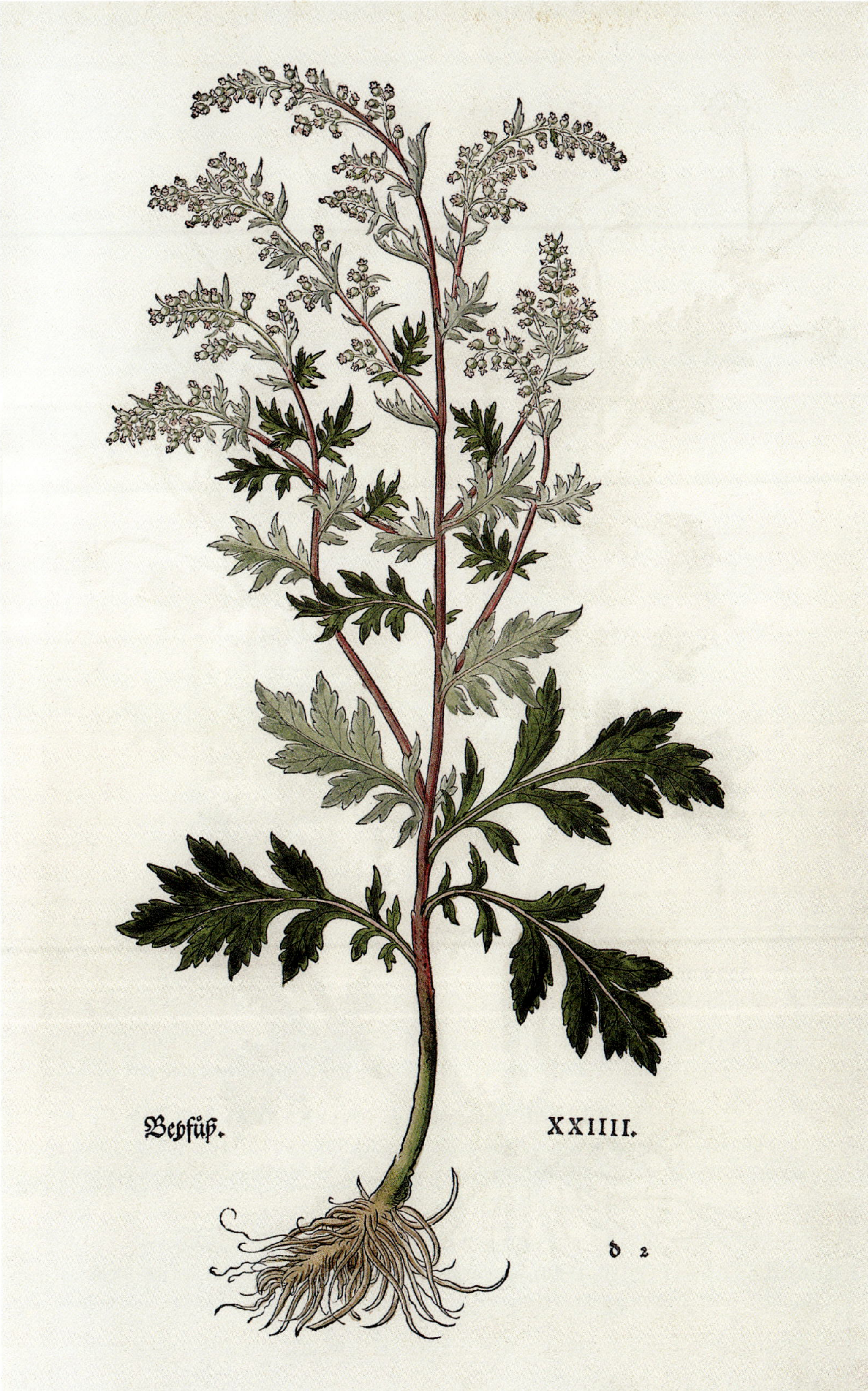
Beyfůß.
XXIIII.
d 2

BEDSTRAW

BEDSTRAW (XIIII), also known as Cleavers or Goosegrass, was supposed to help not only against the bite of poisonous animals, but also against earache and goitres.

„KLEBKRAUT" (KLETTEN-LABKRAUT)

Das Kletten-Labkraut, Fuchs nennt es anschaulich „KLEBKRAUT" (XIIII), soll ebenfalls gegen den Biss giftiger Tiere helfen, daneben auch gegen Ohrenschmerzen, und außerdem gegen Kröpfe wirken.

GAILLET GRATTERON

Le GAILLET GRATTERON (XIIII), pour lequel Fuchs utilise le nom très imagé de « Klebkraut » (plante à colle), serait également efficace contre la morsure d'animaux venimeux ainsi que les maux d'oreilles et les goitres.

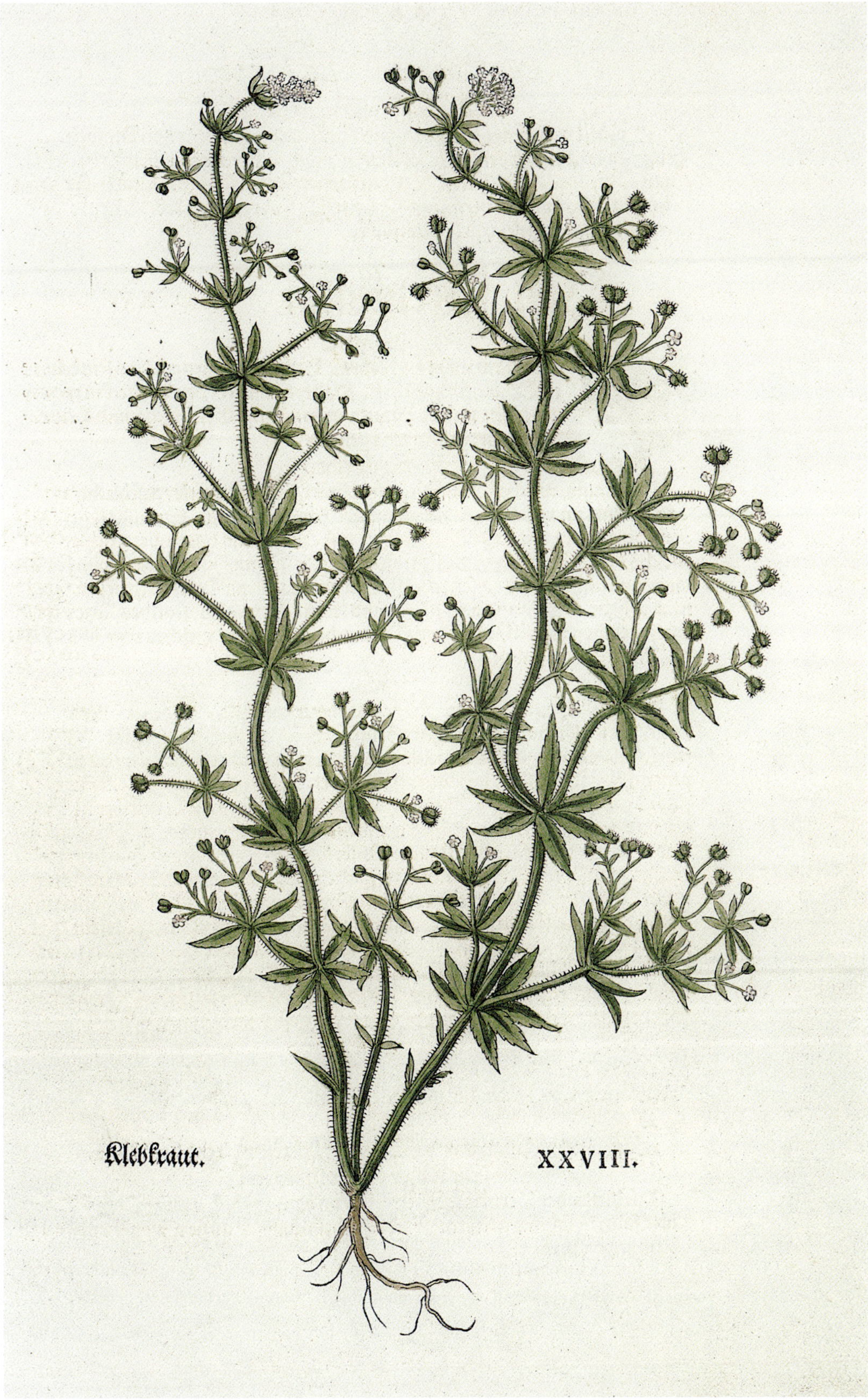
Klebkraut.
XXVIII.

ACANTHUS

Under the heading ACANTHUS (XV) appear not only BEAR'S BREECH (XXIX) – the ACANTHUS whose leaves have made it well known in art – but also Cow Parsnip, or HOGWEED (plate XXX). The plants are judged to have different effects. They were used for dislocated joints.

„BERNKLAW"

Unter „BERNKLAW" (Cap. XV) wird der wegen seiner Blätter aus der Kunst bekannte Akanthus, der ECHTE BÄRENKLAU (Taf. XXIX), vorgestellt, aber auch der WIESEN-BÄRENKLAU (Taf. XXX). Die Wirkungen werden unterschiedlich beurteilt, wobei der Ausdruck „die gleych verruckt" ein ausgekugeltes Gelenk meint.

ACANTHE

Sous le nom de «Bernklaw» (griffe d'ours; XV), Fuchs présente deux plantes différentes : l'ACANTHE (pl. XXIX), célèbre pour ses feuilles décoratives et motif récurrent en architecture, et la PATTE-D'OURS (pl. XXX), ou BERCE DES PRÉS, qu'il appelle «griffe d'ours allemande». Il en juge diversement les effets et parle d'une luxation lorsqu'il évoque «l'articulation déplacée» («die gleych verruckt»).

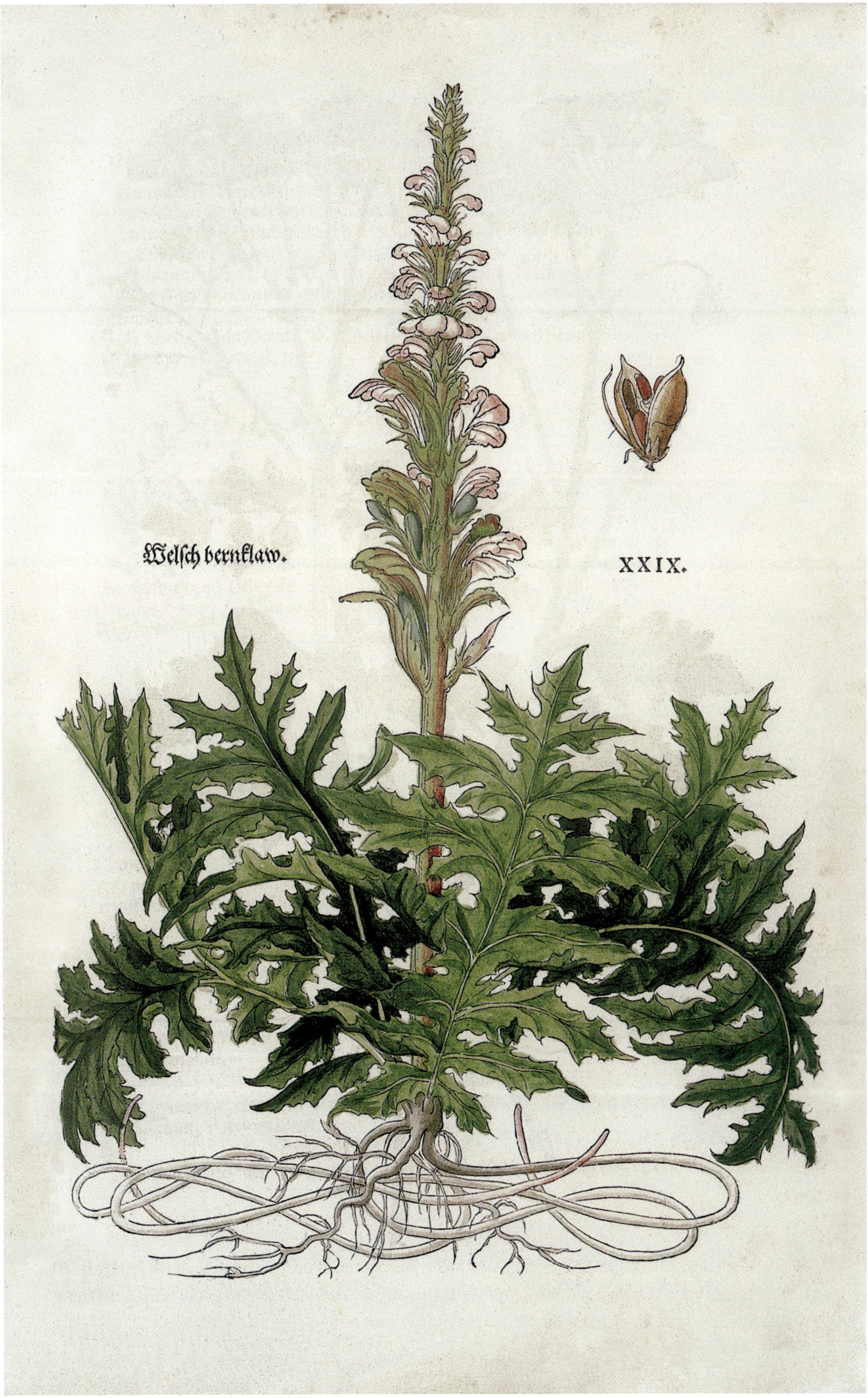
Welsch bernklaw.
XXIX.

WHITE THISTLE

Under WHITE THISTLE (XVI), Fuchs includes the MILK or HOLY THISTLE (plate XXXI) earlier praised by Hildegard of Bingen as "Mary's thistle"; the German designation of "white" referred to the plant's striking white-speckled leaves, which also holds true for the silvery-white cast of the giant, or SCOTCH THISTLE (plate XXXII).

„WEISS DISTEL"

„WEISS DISTEL" (Cap. XVI) bezeichnet bei Fuchs die schon von Hildegard von Bingen gelobte MARIEN-DISTEL (Taf. XXXI), für deren auffällig weißgefleckten Blätter der Name durchaus zutreffend ist, was allerdings ebenso für die weiß-silbrig überlaufene ESELSDISTEL (Taf. XXXII) gilt.

CHARDON MARIE

Le CHARDON MARIE (pl. XXXI), déjà tant prisé par Hildegarde von Bingen, et l'ONOPORDE ACANTHE (pl. XXXII) sont qualifiés de « Weiß Distel », ou CHARDON BLANC (XVI), un nom qui convient bien car leurs feuilles sont panachées de blanc.

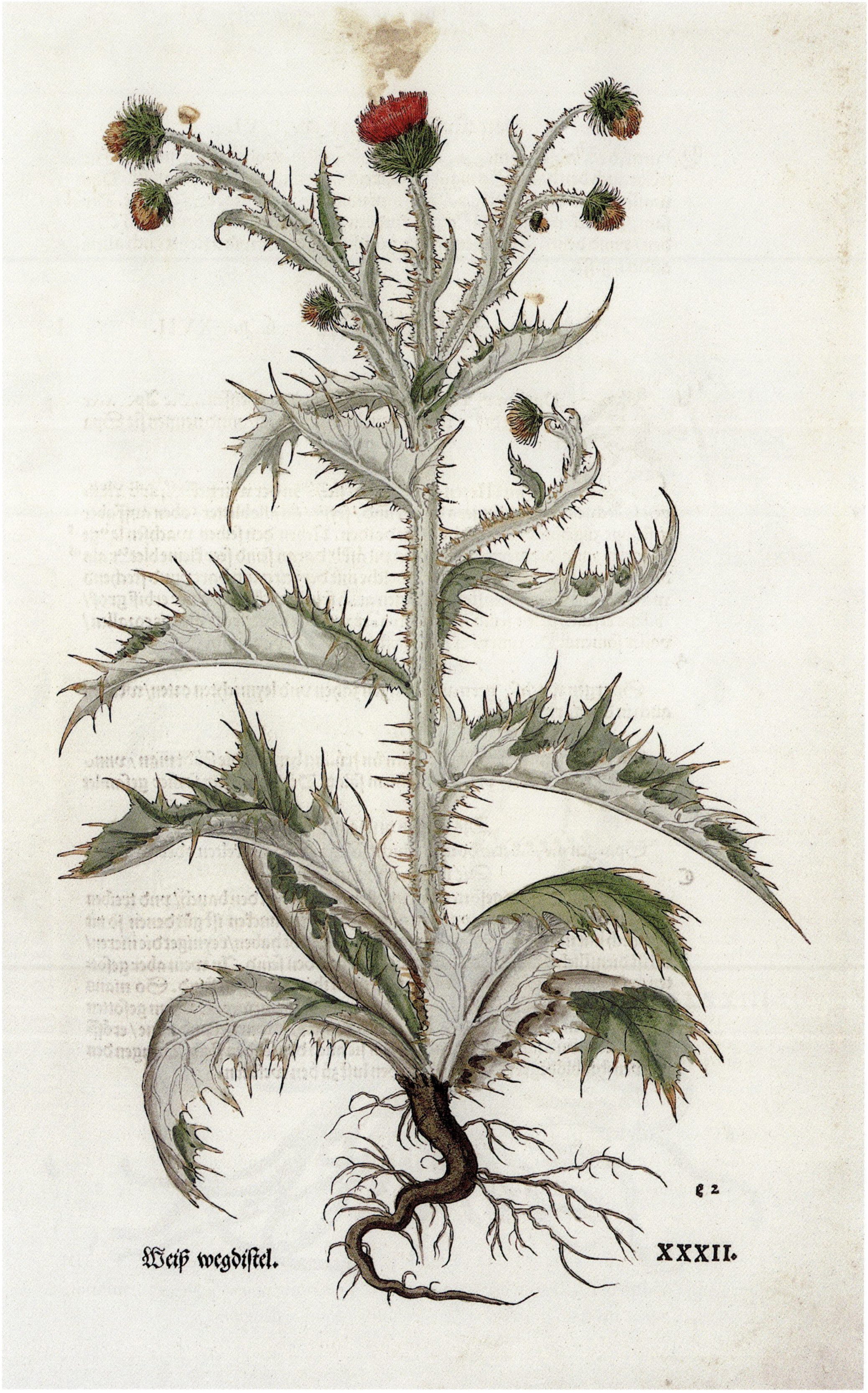
e 2
Weiß wegdistel.
XXXII.

COMMON ASPARAGUS

COMMON ASPARAGUS (XVII), too, is not only reserved for today's gourmets, but is still applied medicinally as a diuretic; the same is true for SPINY RESTHARROW (XVIII), the origin of whose name draws Fuchs into long reflections.

SPARGEL

Der SPARGEL (Cap. XVII) ist auch heute nicht nur den Feinschmeckern vorbehalten, sondern wegen seiner harntreibenden Wirkung immer noch in medizinischem Gebrauch, ebenso wie der HAUHECHEL (Cap. XVIII), über dessen Namensherkunft Fuchs ausführliche Überlegungen anstellt.

ASPERGE

Aujourd'hui, l'ASPERGE (XVII) n'est pas seulement un légume apprécié des gourmets, mais aussi un diurétique, encore utilisé en pharmacopée.

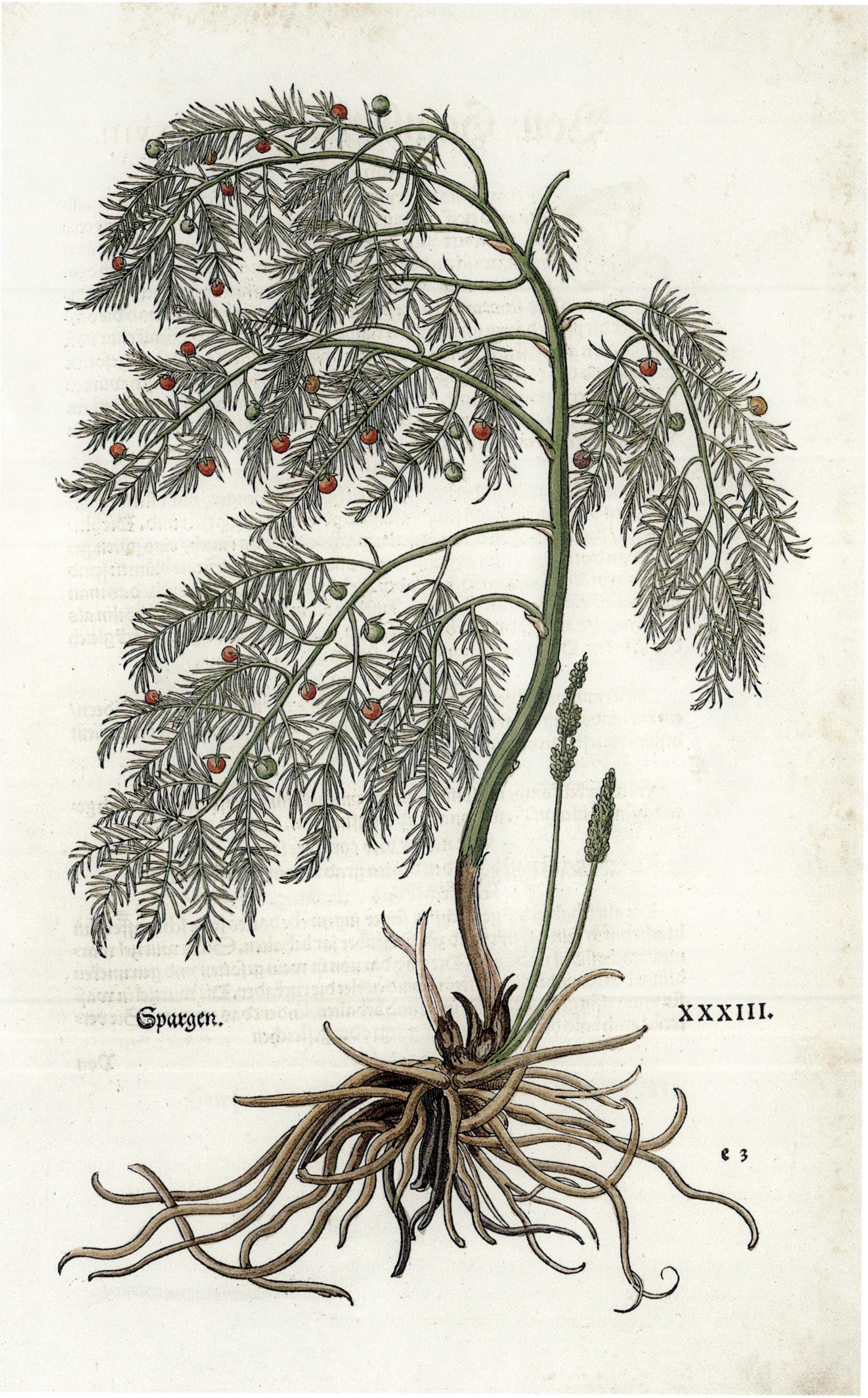
Spargen.
XXXIII.
e 3

ANISE

Both as a spice and a medicinal herb, ANISE (XIX) has long been valued as a seed and as an aromatic oil. When combined with Fennel and Caraway, for example, it constitutes an excellent carminative, and is also useful in cough remedies.

ANIS

Als Gewürz und Heilpflanze wird auch der ANIS (Cap. XIX) in Form seiner Früchte und seines aromatischen Öls nach wie vor geschätzt, weil er z. B. in der Mischung mit Fenchel und Kümmel ein hervorragendes blähungstreibendes Mittel ergibt und auch in Hustenmitteln einsetzbar ist.

ANIS

Les fruits et l'huile aromatique de l'ANIS (XIX) sont toujours aussi appréciés comme condiment et médication. L'anis est un excellent remède contre les flatuosités en combinaison avec l'aneth et le cumin, et un composant de remèdes antitussifs.

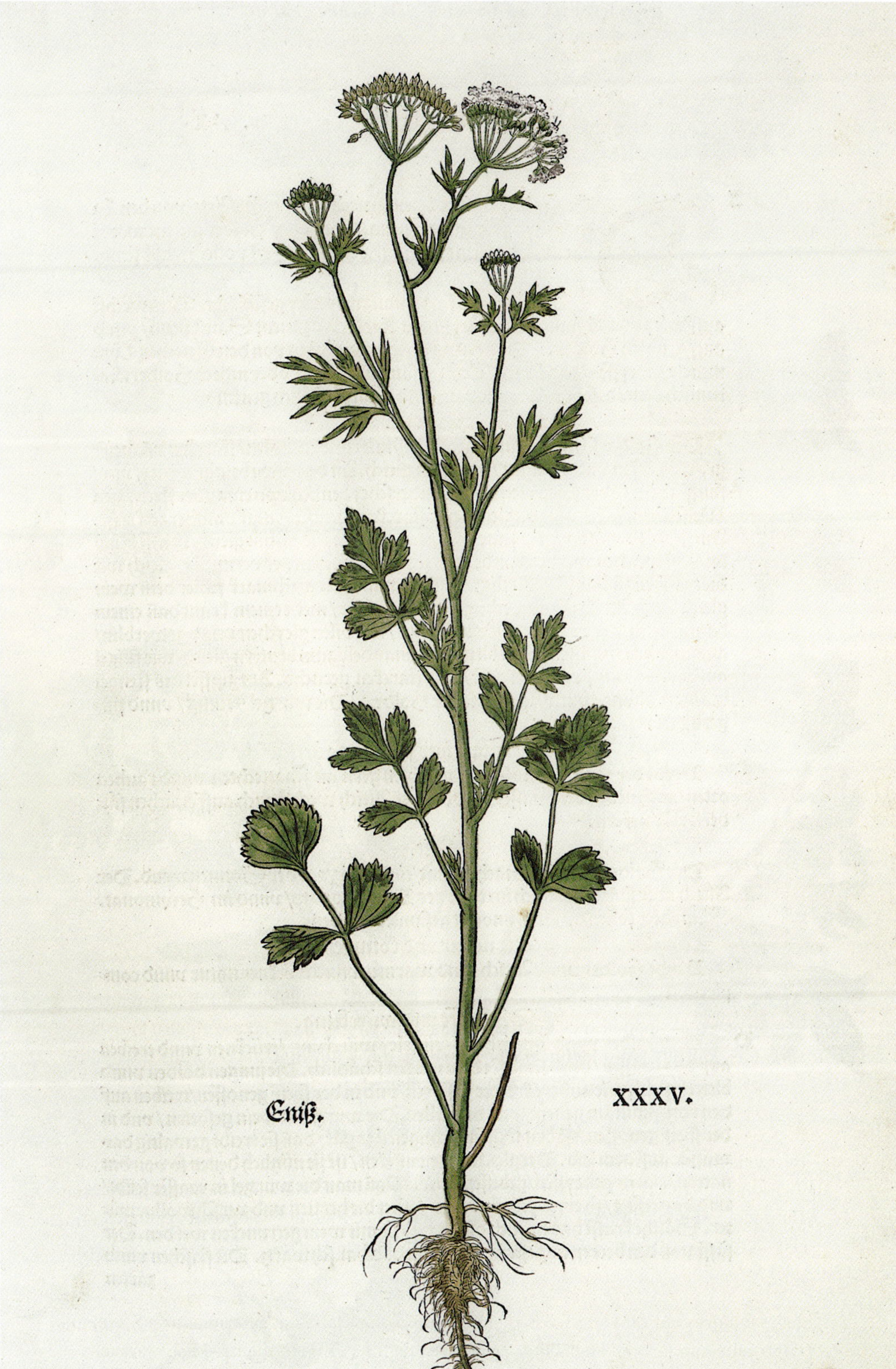
Eniß.
XXXV.

ELDER

Among the laity, the healing powers of ELDER (XX) brought the plant the German appellation of "God's apothecary." Fuchs illustrates black elder and Danewort, also known as Dwarf elder, and attributes identical effects to both; today, however, his recommendations are no longer followed.

HOLDER (HOLUNDER)

Herrgotts-Apotheke heißt der HOLUNDER oder HOLDER (Cap. XX) wegen seiner Heilwirkung im Volk. Fuchs bildet den Schwarzen Holunder und den Attich, auch Zwerg-Holunder genannt, ab und spricht beiden übereinstimmende Wirkungen zu, denen wir jedoch heute nicht mehr folgen werden.

SUREAU

Ses effets salutaires ont valu au SUREAU (XX) le nom populaire de «pharmacie du Seigneur» («Herrgotts-Apotheke»). Fuchs illustre le sureau noir et l'hièble, dit aussi petit sureau, et leur attribue des vertus similaires qu'on ne reconnaît plus aujourd'hui.

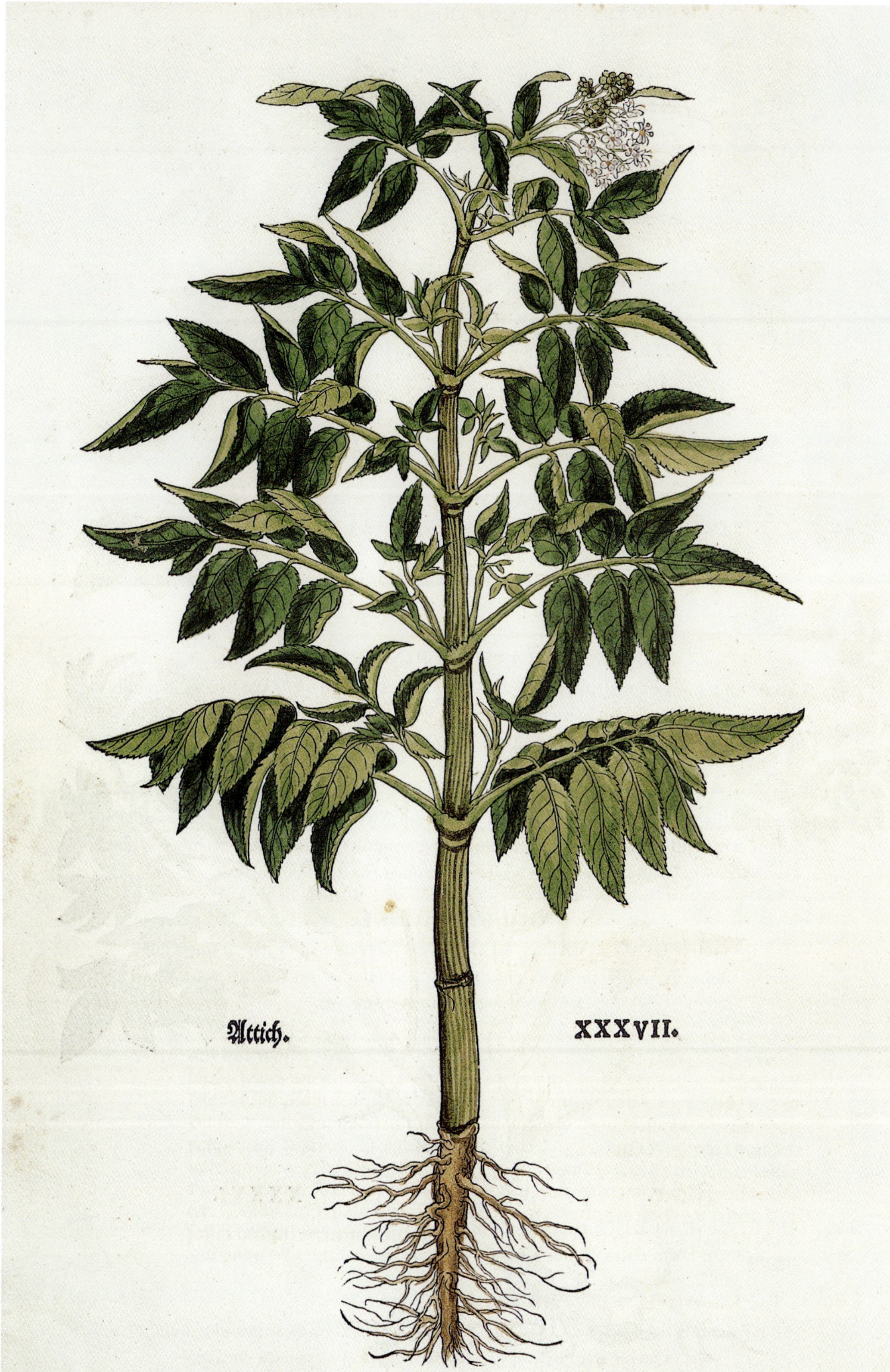
Attich.
XXXVII.

FALSE BISHOP'S WEED

FALSE BISHOP'S WEED (XXI) is no longer used medicinally.

„AMMEY" (KNORPELMÖHRE)

Die Knorpelmöhre, der „AMMEY" bei Fuchs (Cap. XXI), wird heute nicht mehr arzneilich verwendet.

AMMI ÉLEVÉ

L'AMMI ÉLEVÉ (XXI) n'est plus usité de nos jours en médecine.

PAGE 114

CUCKOO PINT

The striking flower construction of CUCKOO PINT (XXII), or Wake Robin, inevitably earns attention. The plant is recommended for cleansing wounds; moreover, the leaves remove maggots from over-ripe cheese.

ARONSTAB

Der auffällige Blütenbau des ARONSTABS (Cap. XXII) musste das Interesse auf sich ziehen. Arzneilich wird er zur Wundsanierung empfohlen, die Blätter darüber hinaus bei überreifem Käse zur Entfernung der Maden.

GOUET MACULÉ

Très tôt, le GOUET MACULÉ (XXII) s'est fait remarquer par sa floraison spectaculaire. Il est préconisé ici pour traiter les plaies, et ses feuilles pour éliminer les vers sur le fromage trop fait.

PAGE 115

GREAT BURDOCK

Today, in the form of an oleaginous extract, the folk-medicinal use of GREAT BURDOCK (XXIII) is almost exclusively restricted to promoting hair growth.

GROSSE KLETTE

Die GROSSE KLETTE (Cap. XXIII) findet heute praktisch nur noch volkstümlich in Form eines öligen Auszugs als Haarwuchsmittel Verwendung.

GRANDE BARDANE

La GRANDE BARDANE (XXIII) n'a plus sa place que dans la pratique populaire sous la forme d'un extrait huileux activant la pousse des cheveux.

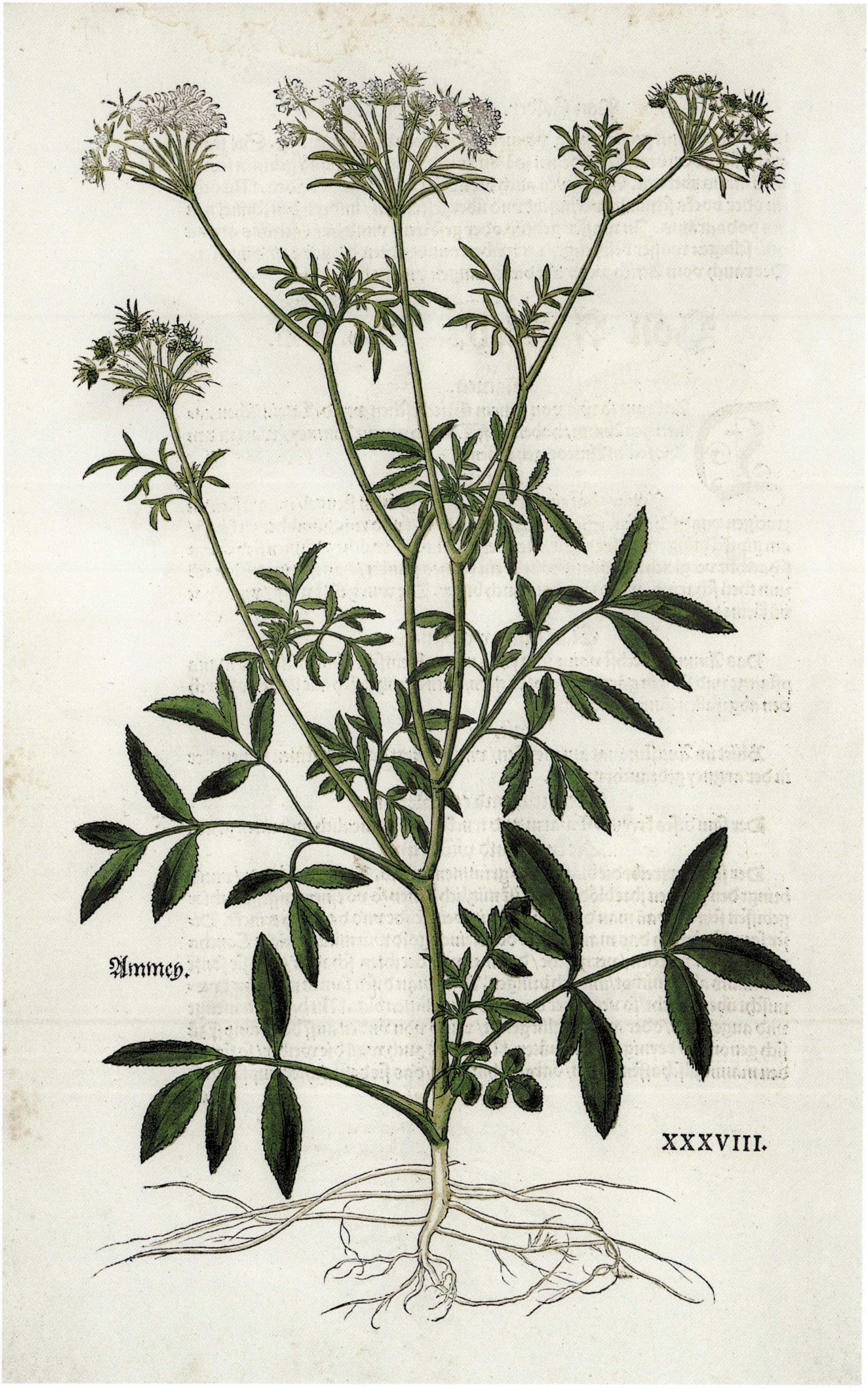
Ammey.
XXXVIII.

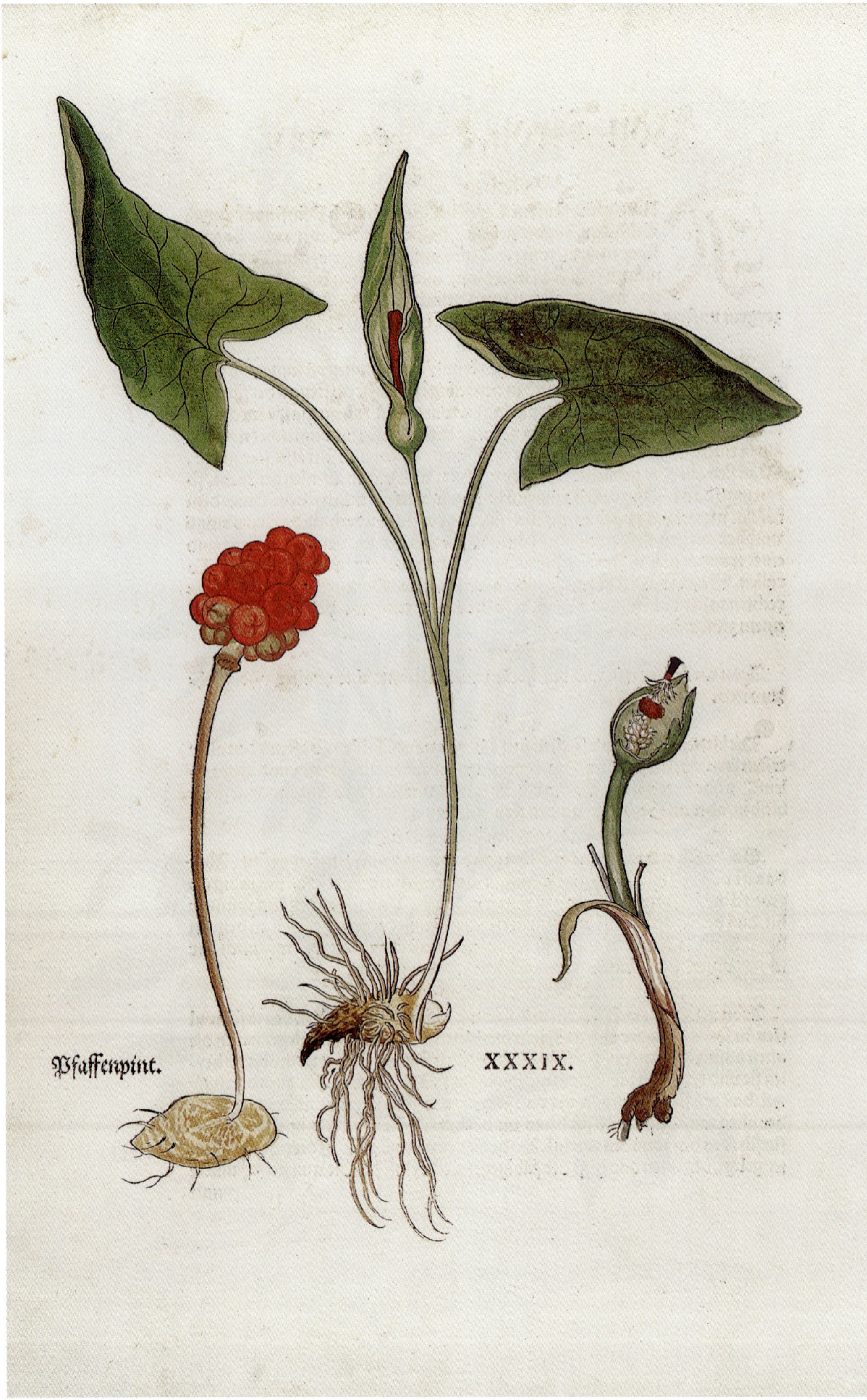
Pfaffenpint.
XXXIX.

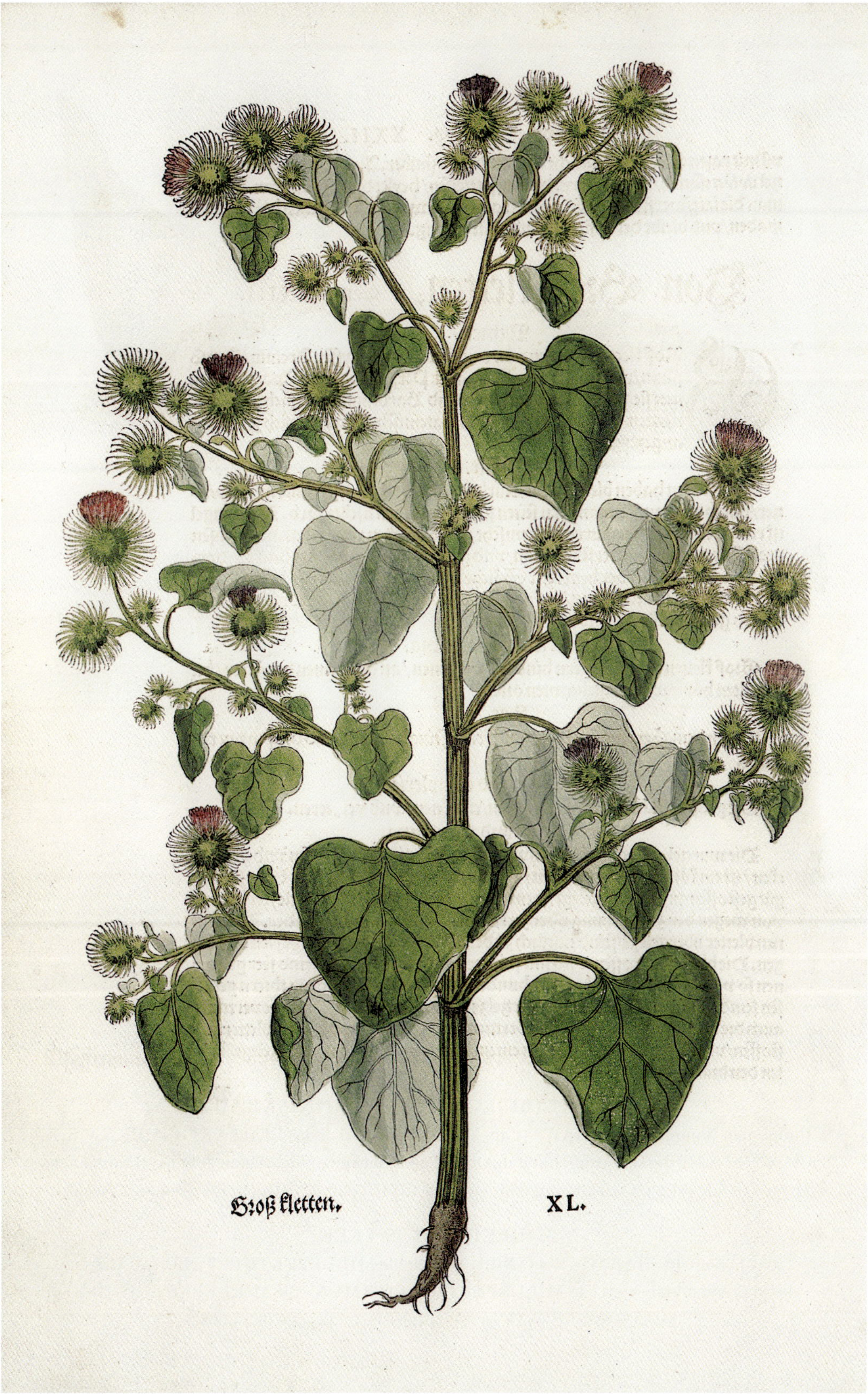

GREAT BURDOCK | GROSSE KLETTE | GRANDE BARDANE

HAIRY ST. JOHN'S WORT

Fuchs rightly recognized the similarity between HAIRY ST. JOHN'S WORT (XXIIII; plate XLI) and MOUNTAIN ST. JOHN'S WORT (XXV).

„HARTHAW" (BEHAARTES JOHANNISKRAUT)

Hinter dem Namen „HARTHAW" (Cap. XXIIII) verbirgt sich das BEHAARTE JOHANNISKRAUT (Taf. XLI), dessen Ähnlichkeit mit dem Tüpfelhartheu, dem Echten Johanniskraut, Fuchs ebenso richtig erkennt wie die mit dem „KUNRATH" (Cap. XXV), dem Berg-Johanniskraut.

MILLEPERTUIS VELU

Sous le nom de «HARTHAW» (XXIIII) se cache le MILLEPERTUIS VELU (pl. XLI), dont la ressemblance avec le MILLEPERTUIS COMMUN et le MILLEPERTUIS DES MONTAGNES (XXV) n'est pas passée inaperçue de Fuchs.

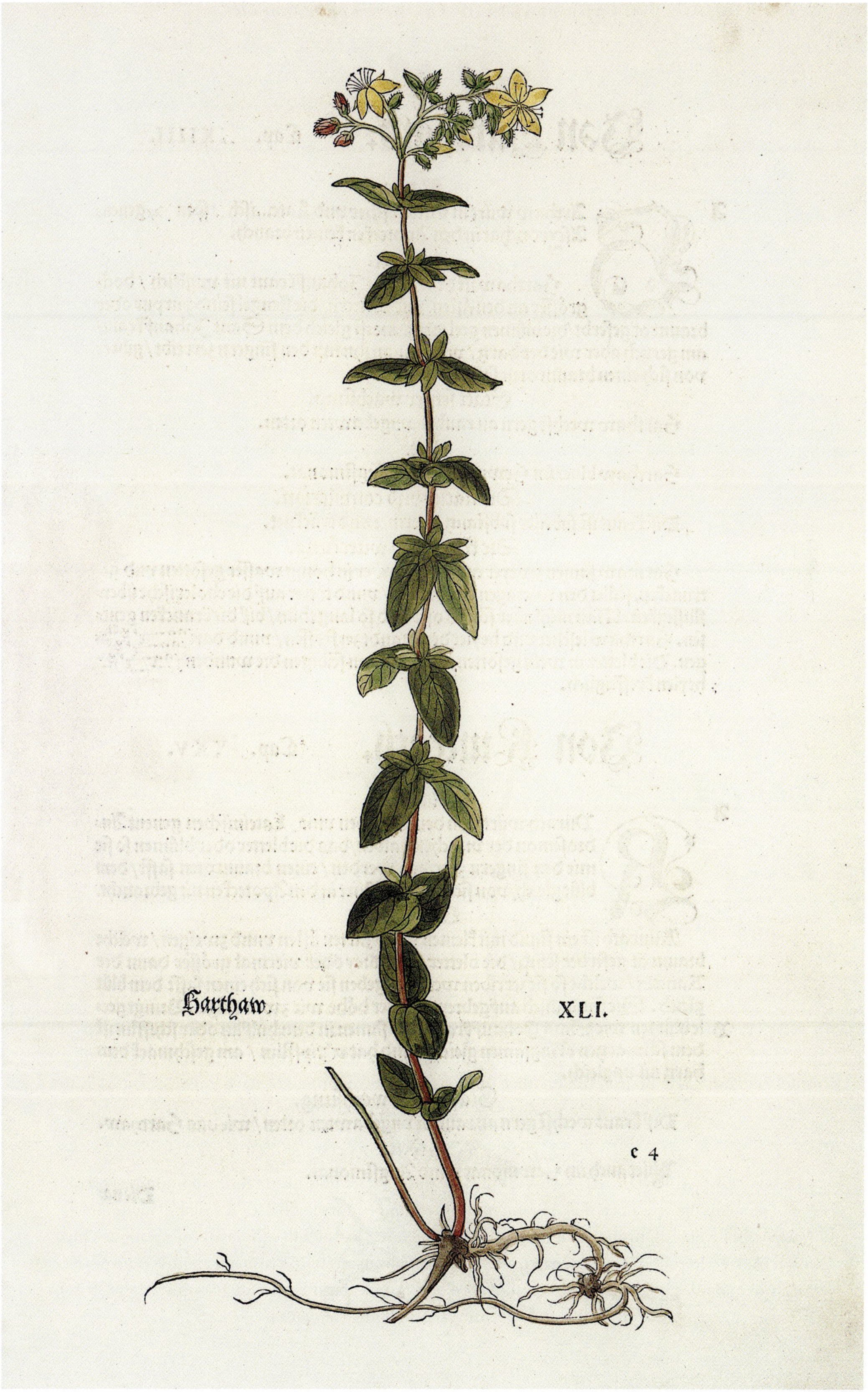
Harthaw
XLI.
c 4

COMMON JUNIPER

Although the wood of COMMON JUNIPER (XXVI) is no longer used as a fumigant against the plague, its berries still find application as a powerful desiccant. Juniper oil occurs as a muscle-relaxing component in bath oils.

WACHOLDER

Der WACHOLDER (Cap. XXVI) war früher neben vielen anderen Bezeichnungen auch als Machandel und Kranewitt bekannt. Heute benötigen wir sein Holz nicht mehr als Räuchermittel bei Pest, seine Beeren finden aber immer noch Anwendung als stark entwässerndes Mittel und sein Öl als Zusatz zu muskelentspannenden Bädern.

GENÉVRIER COMMUN

Le GENÉVRIER COMMUN (XXVI) portait autrefois de nombreux noms populaires, ainsi on l'appelait dans le nord de l'Allemagne «Machandel», forme dérivée du mot «Wacholder» (approximativement, branches à tresser), et en Bavière «Kranewitt» (bois à grue). Aujourd'hui, on n'utilise plus son bois contre la peste (les émanations du bois brûlé auraient le pouvoir de guérir la maladie), mais ses baies sont encore employées comme remède très diurétique, et son huile comme adjuvant de bains relaxants.

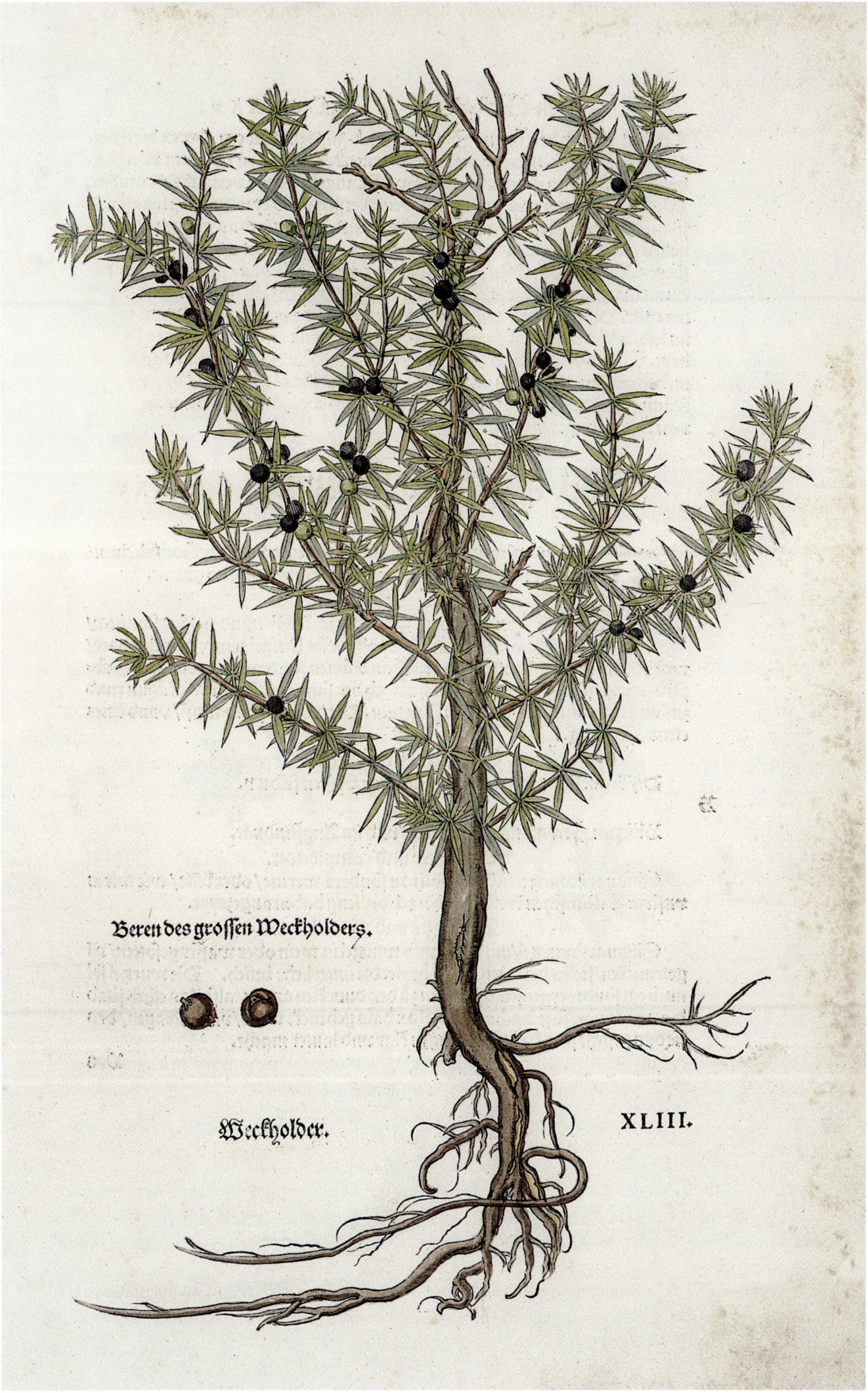
Beren des grossen Weckholders.
Weckholder.
XLIII.

CUT-LEAVED MALLOW

CUT-LEAVED MALLOW (XXVII), also known as Hollyhock Mallow or Vervain Mallow, is an unmistakable member of its family; merely hanging the root around one's neck was supposed to improve the eyesight.

SIGMARSKRAUT

Unverkennbar zu den Malvengewächsen gehört das SIGMARSKRAUT (Cap. XXVII), das sogar durch das bloße Umhängen der Wurzel die Sehkraft stärken sollte.

MAUVE ALCÉE

La MAUVE ALCÉE (XXVII) a manifestement tous les caractères de la Malvacée. Selon la croyance populaire, le simple fait de porter la racine autour du cou aurait fortifié la vue.

PAGE 122

MEDITERRANEAN MAIDENHAIR FERN

The delicate MEDITERRANEAN MAIDENHAIR FERN (XXVIII) is now only rarely applied in folk medicine as a remedy for bronchial problems.

VENUS- ODER FRAUENHAAR

Das VENUS- ODER FRAUENHAAR (Cap. XXVIII), ein zierlicher Farn des Mittelmeergebiets, dient in der Volksmedizin nur noch sehr selten als Bronchialmittel.

CAPILLAIRE DE MONTPELLIER

Très estimée dans le passé, la CAPILLAIRE DE MONTPELLIER (XXVIII), ou cheveux-de-Vénus, gracile fougère des régions méditerranéennes, n'est plus que très rarement employée aujourd'hui contre les bronchites.

PAGE 123

WINE GRAPE

Today, the European or WINE GRAPE (XXIX) plays a role only as a source of sweet grapes and the wine that is made from them – although wine enjoyed in moderation is often considered to promote good health.

WEINSTOCK

Der WEINSTOCK (Cap. XXIX) spielt für uns heute nur noch als Lieferant süßer Trauben und des daraus hergestellten Weins eine Rolle, wobei mäßigem Weingenuss nicht selten auch eine gesundheitsfördernde Wirkung zugebilligt wird.

VIGNE

La VIGNE (XXIX) est pour nous encore un précieux fournisseur de raisin et de vin. Depuis quelques années, on prétend même que la consommation modérée de vin est bonne pour la santé.

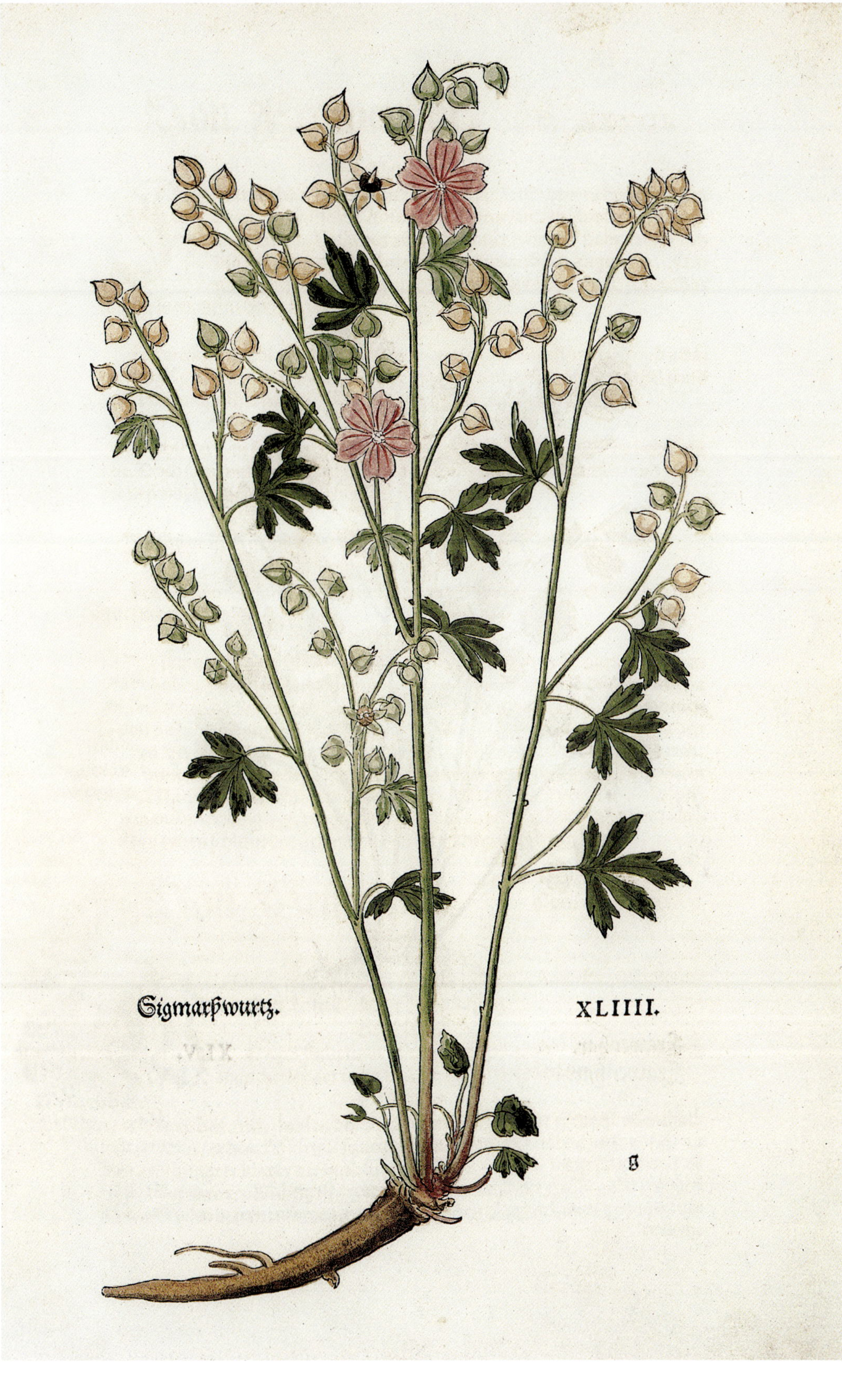
Sigmarßwurtz.
XLIIII.

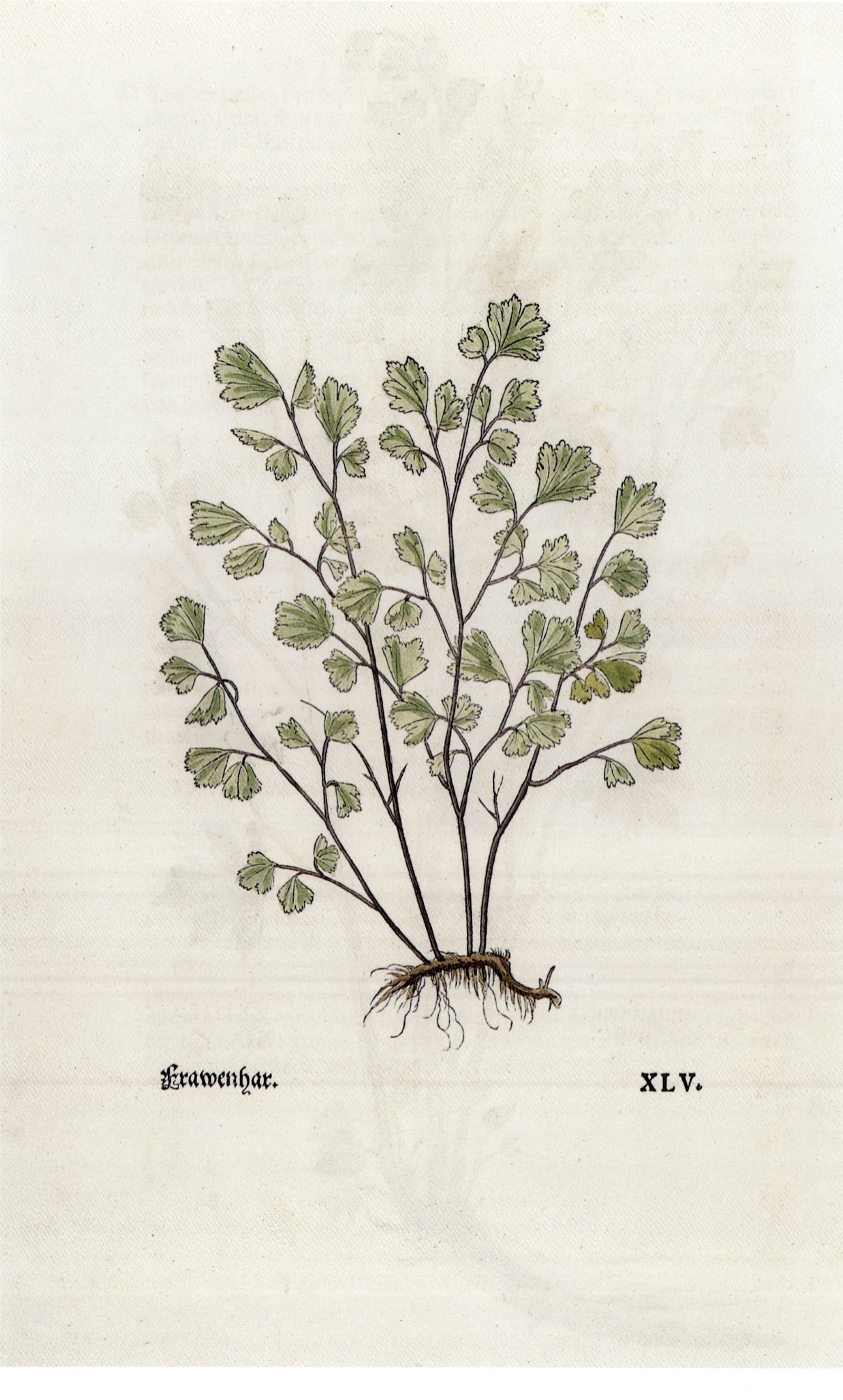
Frawenhar.
XLV.

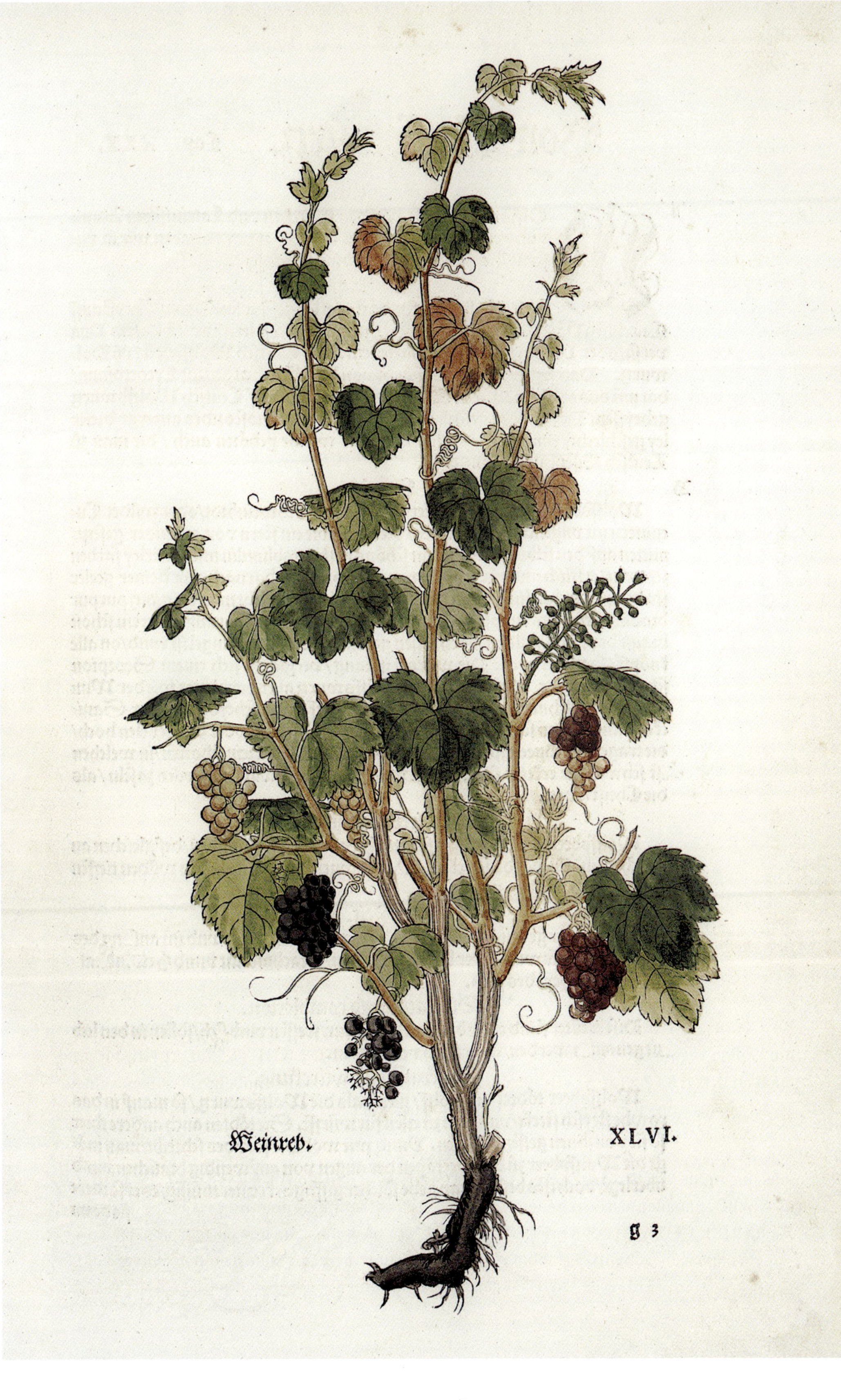
Weinreb.
XLVI.
g 3

WOLFSBANE

The name "WOLFSBANE" (XXX) – in former days the plant was used as bait to kill wolves – points to the poisonous nature of MONKSHOOD (plate XLVIII). Similarly, the German name of the unrelated herb PARIS (plate XLVII) suggests that poisonous effects have been observed. Fuchs explicitly warned against internal use.

„WOLFFSWURTZ"

Der Name „WOLFFSWURTZ" (Cap. XXX) – die Pflanze wurde früher als Köder zum Töten von Wölfen verwendet – weist bereits auf die Giftigkeit des EISENHUTS (Taf. XLVIII) hin und auch DOLWURTZ (Taf. XLVII) für die botanisch nicht verwandte Einbeere lässt beobachtete Vergiftungen erahnen. Fuchs warnt ausdrücklich vor innerlicher Anwendung.

RACINE À LOUP

Sous le nom de «Wolffswurtz» (XXX), ou RACINE À LOUP, apparaît l'ACONIT TUE-LOUP (pl. XLVIII), une plante très vénéneuse que l'on utilisait autrefois pour tuer les loups. De même, la PARISETTE À QUATRE FEUILLES (pl. XLVII), qui n'a aucune parenté avec l'aconit, a été baptisée «Dolwurtz» (racine violente), probablement par suite d'empoisonnements. Du reste, Fuchs en déconseille fortement l'usage interne.

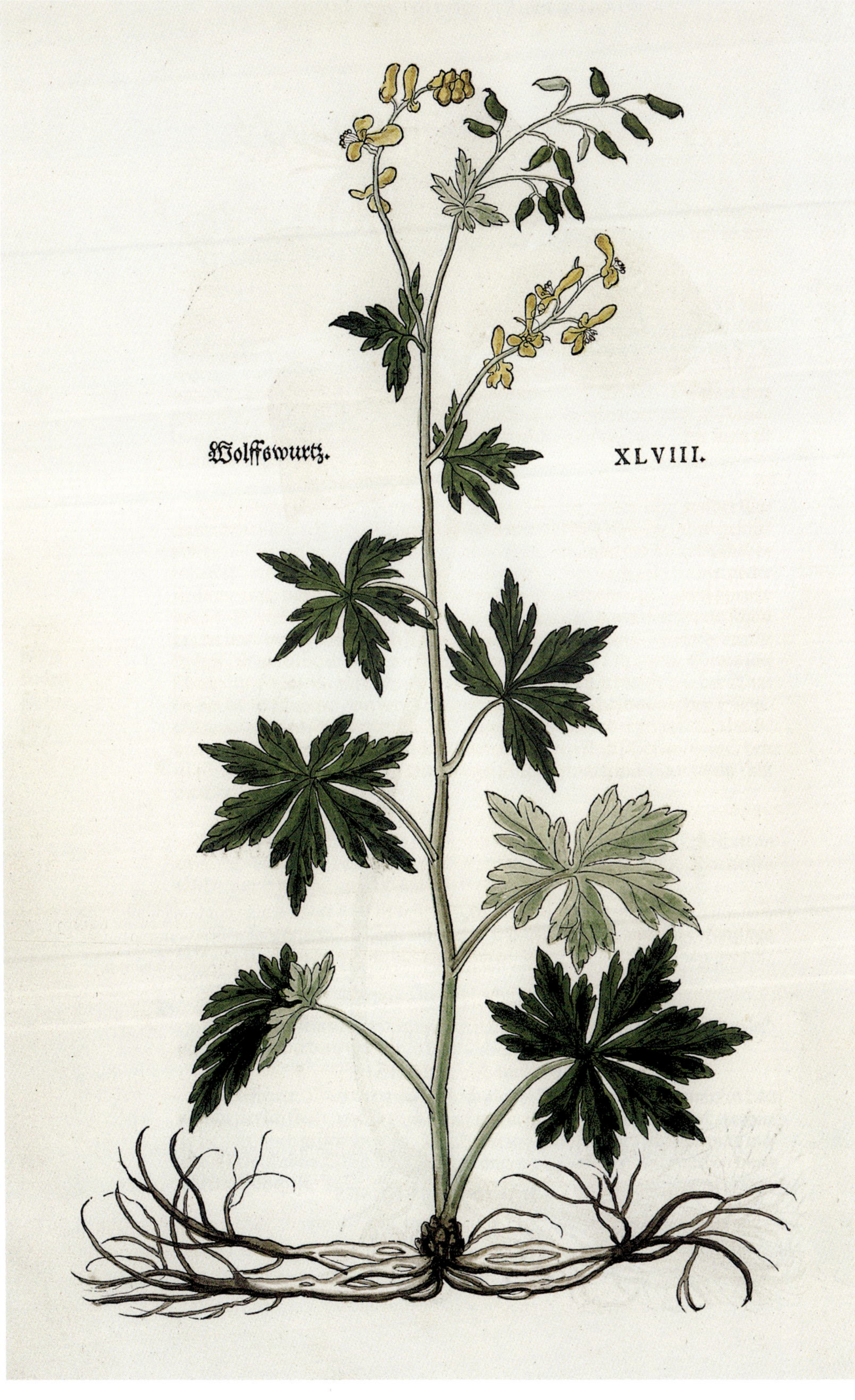
Wolffswurtz.
XLVIII.

WOLFSBANE

The chapter (XXXI) including BIRTHWORT and FUMEWORT also contains botanically different plants. The possibility of serious side effects caused by BIRTHWORT (plate XLIX) has led to its removal from the medicine chest; FUMEWORT (plate L) is today occasionally used as a sedative.

„HOLWURTZ“

Auch im Kapitel „HOLWURTZ“ (Cap. XXXI) werden unterschiedliche Pflanzen zusammengefasst. Die „LANG HOLWURTZ“ (Taf. XLIX), die Osterluzei, wurde wegen ihrer möglichen schweren Nebenwirkungen inzwischen aus dem Arzneischatz genommen, die „RUNDE HOLWURTZ“ (Taf. L) wird vereinzelt als Beruhigungsmittel verwendet.

RACINES CREUSES

Au chapitre « RACINES CREUSES » (« Holwurtz » en allemand, XXXI), ce sont également des plantes très différentes qu’illustre Fuchs. La SARRAZINE (pl. XLIX) a été rayée de la pharmacopée en raison de ses graves effets secondaires ; le CORYDALE À TUBERCULE CREUX (pl. L) est encore employé quelquefois comme calmant.

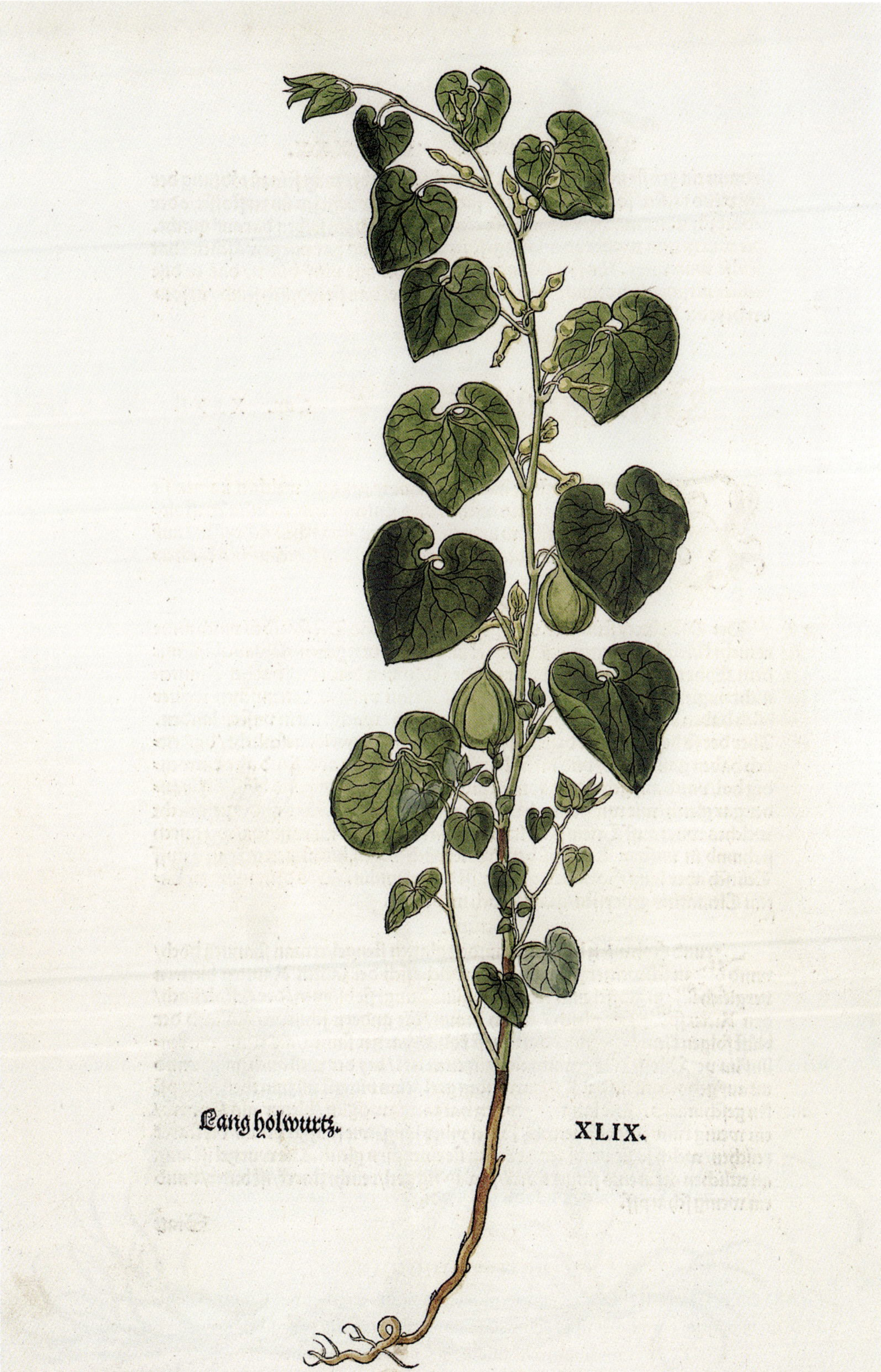
Lang holwurtz.
XLIX.

RED BRYONY

RED BRYONY (XXXII) was recommended against the painful disease of gout; preparations made from the root, however, act as a violent purgative.

„STICKWURTZ" (GICHTWURZ)

Die „STICKWURTZ" (Cap. XXXII) wurde auch Gichtwurz genannt, weil sie gegen diese schmerzhafte Krankheit empfohlen wurde, Zubereitungen aus der Wurzel dienten als drastische Abführmittel.

BRYONE DIOÏQUE

La BRYONE DIOÏQUE (XXXII) porte plusieurs noms en allemand, dont « Gichtwurtz » ou racine de la goutte, car elle était préconisée pour cette maladie très douloureuse ; on préparait aussi avec sa souche des purgatifs violents.

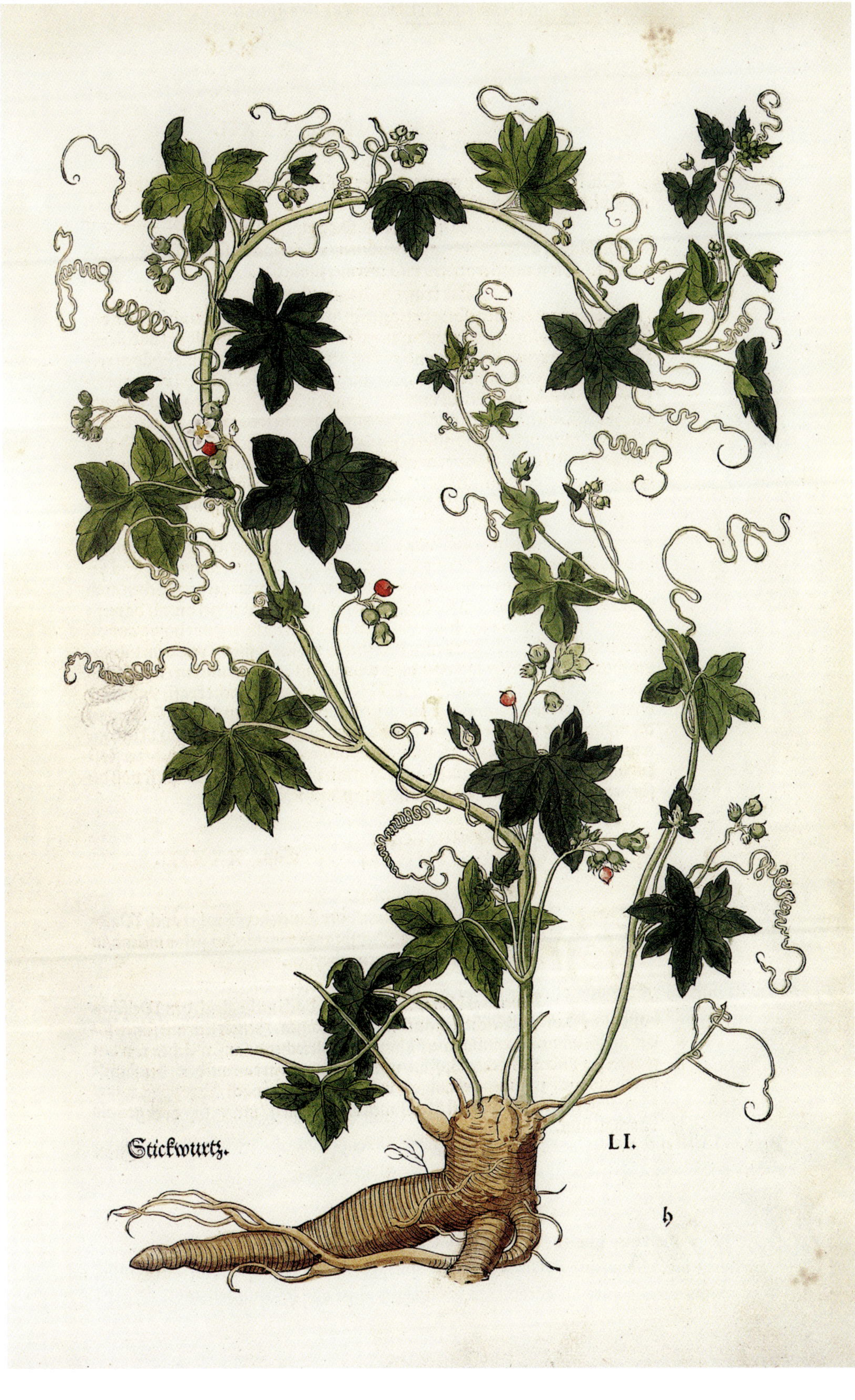
Stickwurtz.
LI.
h

OLD MAN'S BEARD

Fuchs introduces another climber under the name of OLD MAN'S BEARD (XXXIII), also known as Traveller's Joy, a member of the clematis family. In earlier times it was used against eczema and boils as well as rheumatism.

„LYNEN" (WALDREBE)

Als weitere rankende Pflanze führt Fuchs unter der Bezeichnung „LYNEN" (Cap. XXXIII) die Waldrebe an, die früher gegen Ekzeme und Geschwüre, aber auch bei Rheumatismus eingesetzt wurde.

CLÉMATITE BLANCHE

Voici une autre plante grimpante, la CLÉMATITE BLANCHE (XXXIII), ou herbe aux gueux, que Fuchs représente sous le nom de «Lynen». On l'employait autrefois contre les eczémas et les ulcères ainsi que les rhumatismes.

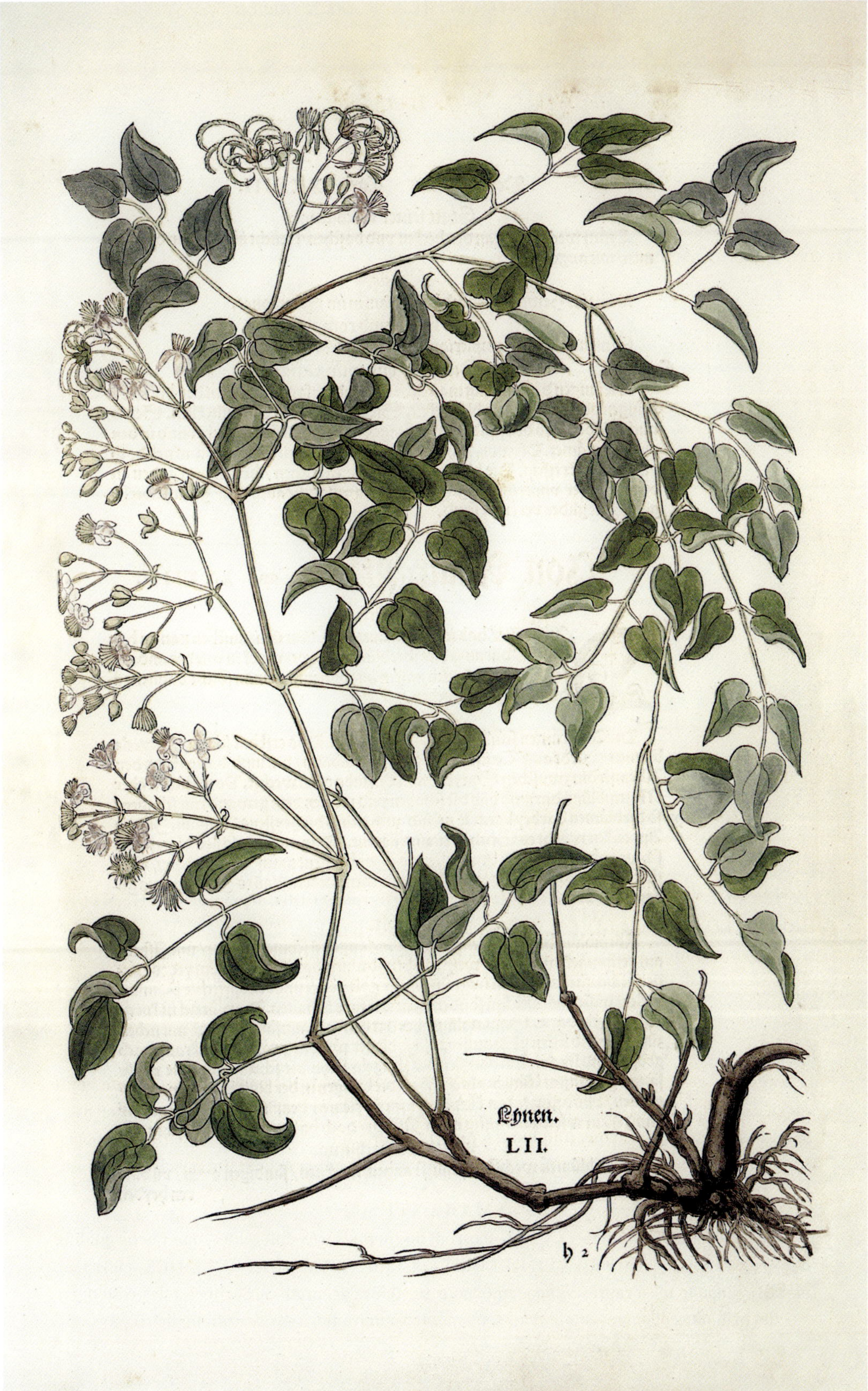
Lynen.
LII.
h 2

AMARANTH

The chapter entitled AMARANTH (XXXIIII) once more presents two completely different plants as "two kinds" of the same species: WOOL FLOWER (plate LIIII), also known as GENTLE PURPLE FLOWER, and LIVE-EVER (plate LIII), or Yellow Everlasting Daisy. Designated here as "sand strawflowers," they were included only because their brightly coloured dried blossoms fit the literal meaning of the word "amaranth," that is, unfading.

„AMARANT"

Im Kapitel „AMARANT" (Cap. XXXIIII) werden wieder zwei völlig unterschiedliche Pflanzen als „zweyerley geschlecht" geführt: die „SAMATBLUM" (Taf. LIIII) heißt botanisch auch heute noch Amaranth oder Garten-Fuchsschwanz, die „RHEINBLUMEN" (Taf. LIII) werden als Sandstrohblumen bezeichnet und fanden hier nur Aufnahme, weil ihre auch getrocknet noch leuchtenden Blüten dem Wortsinn von „Amaranth" entsprechen: unverwelklich.

AMARANTES

Au chapitre « AMARANTES » (XXXIIII) figurent des plantes très différentes, que Fuchs qualifie de « deux genres » : l'AMARANTE CÉLOSIE (pl. LIIII) et l'IMMORTELLE DES SABLES (pl. LIII), laquelle n'est représentée ici que pour ses fleurs décoratives. Séchées, elles restent en effet brillantes et correspondent au sens même d'amarante, à savoir « qui ne flétrit pas ».

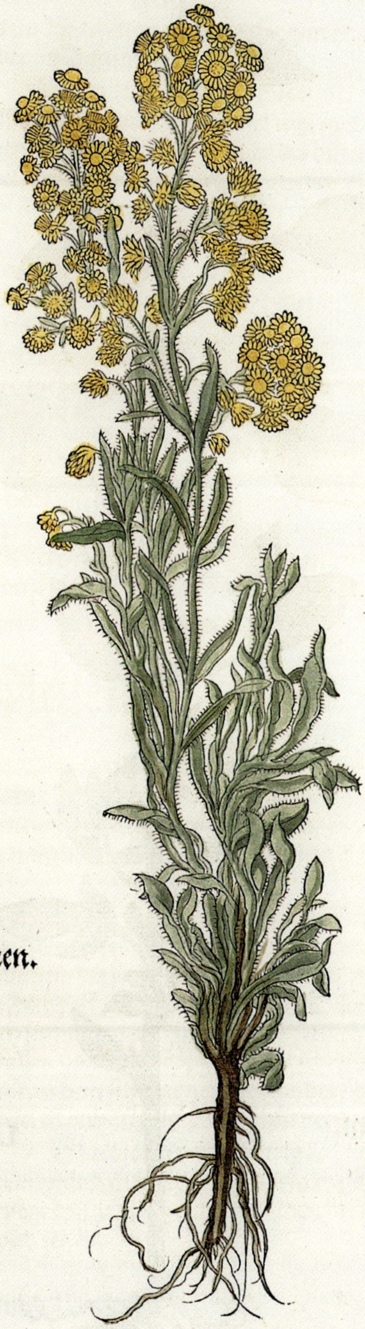

Rheinblůmen. LIII.

h 3

COLUMBINE

COLUMBINE (XXXV) is used today only in homeopathic medicine, and Fuchs already warned against fabricated indications.

„AGLEY“

Die Akelei, „AGLEY“ (Cap. XXXV) wird nur noch in der Homöopathie verwendet und schon Fuchs warnt vor erdichteten Indikationen.

ANCOLIE COMMUNE

L'ANCOLIE COMMUNE (XXXV) n'est plus utilisée qu'en homéopathie, et Fuchs avertit déjà le lecteur des dangers d'indications fantaisistes.

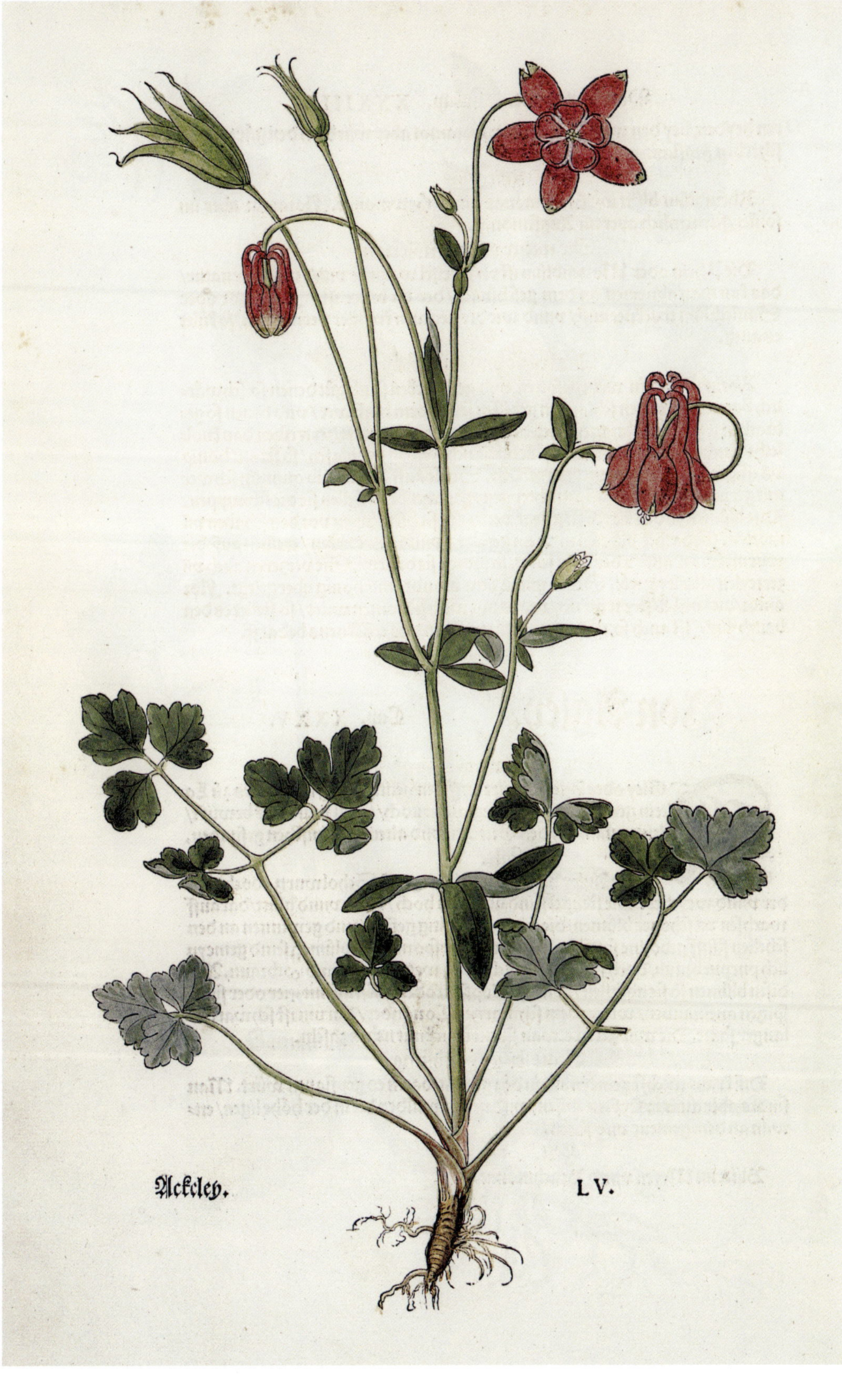

COLUMBINE | „AGLEY“ | ANCOLIE COMMUNE

HEDGE GARLIC | KNOBLAUCHSRAUKE | ALLIAIRE OFFICINALE

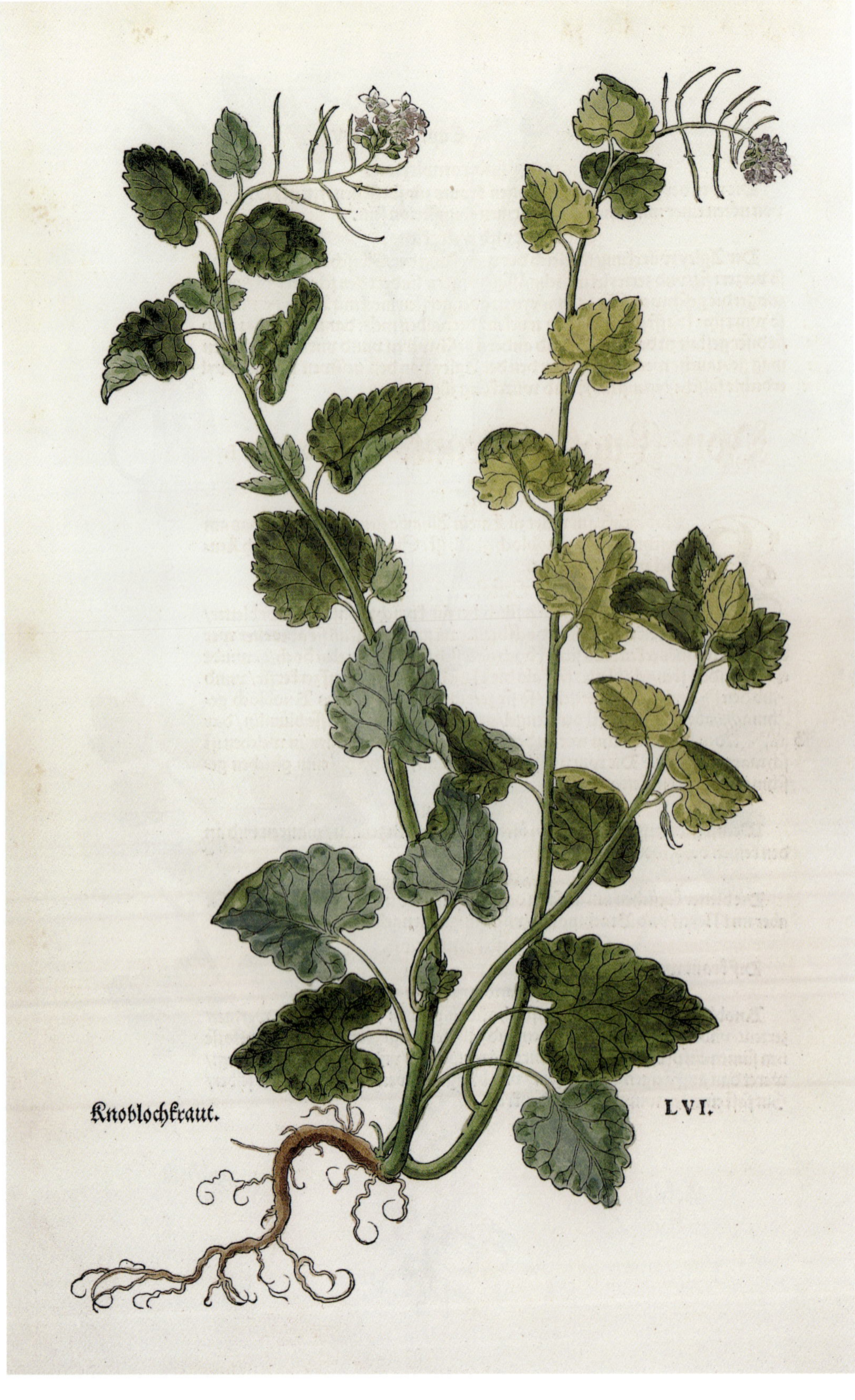

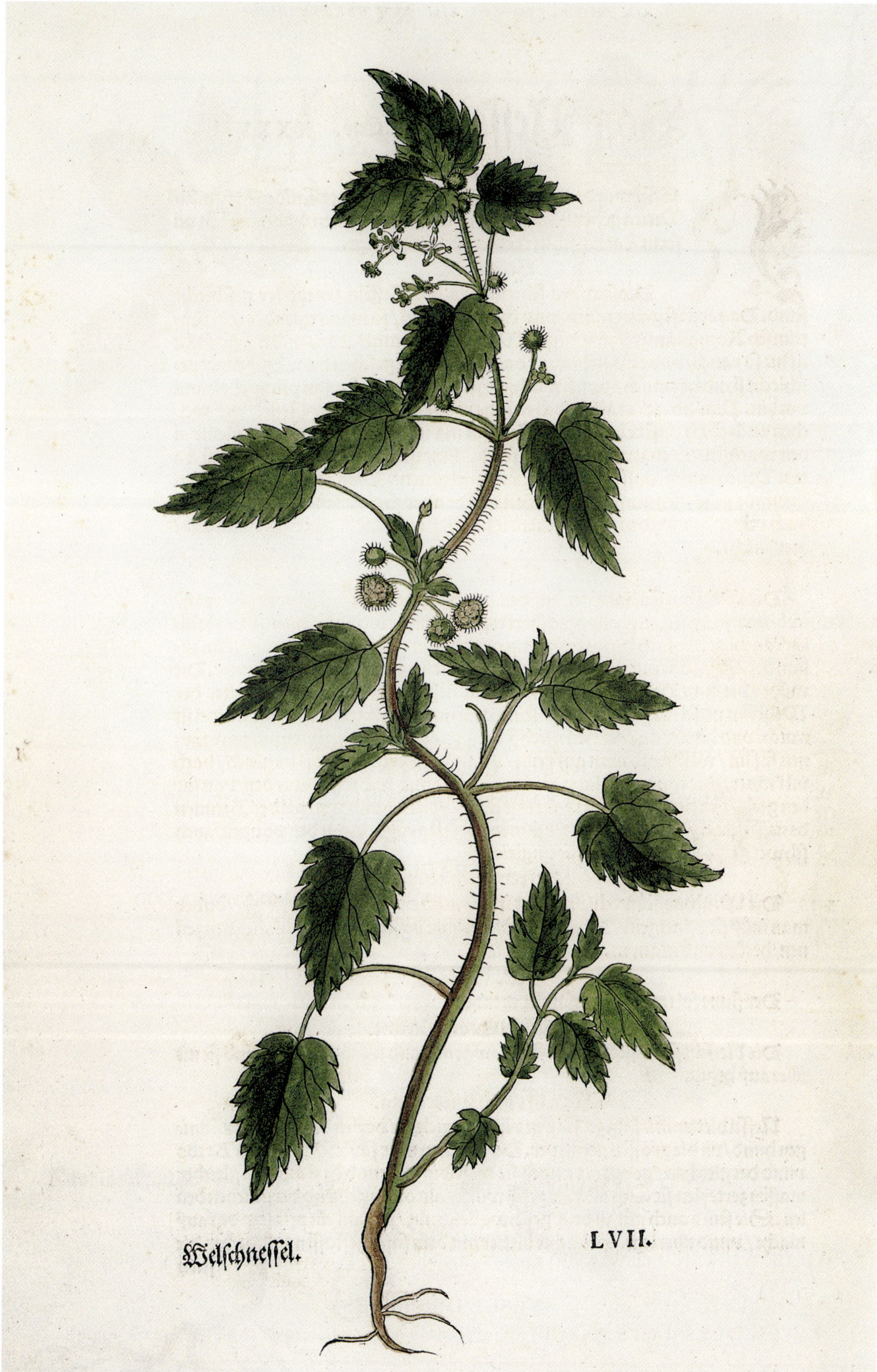
Welschnessel.
LVII.

PAGES 136, 137

HEDGE GARLIC / NETTLE

HEDGE GARLIC, or GARLIC MUSTARD (XXXVI), is followed by three varieties of NETTLE (XXXVII).

KNOBLAUCHSRAUKE / NESSELN

Der KNOBLAUCHSRAUKE (Cap. XXXVI) folgen die NESSELN (XXXVII) mit drei verschiedenen Arten.

ALLIAIRE OFFICINALE / ORTIE

L'ALLIAIRE OFFICINALE (XXXVI) est suivie de trois variétés d'ORTIE (XXXVII) : l'ortie à pilules, la grande ortie et la petite ortie.

BUSH VETCH

BUSH VETCH (XXXVIII) is recommended for diarrhoea as well as heartburn.

WILDE WICKEN

WILDE WICKEN (Cap. XXXVIII) werden empfohlen bei Durchfall, aber auch bei Sodbrennen.

VESCE DES HAIES

La VESCE DES HAIES (XXXVIII) est préconisée pour la diarrhée et les aigreurs d'estomac.

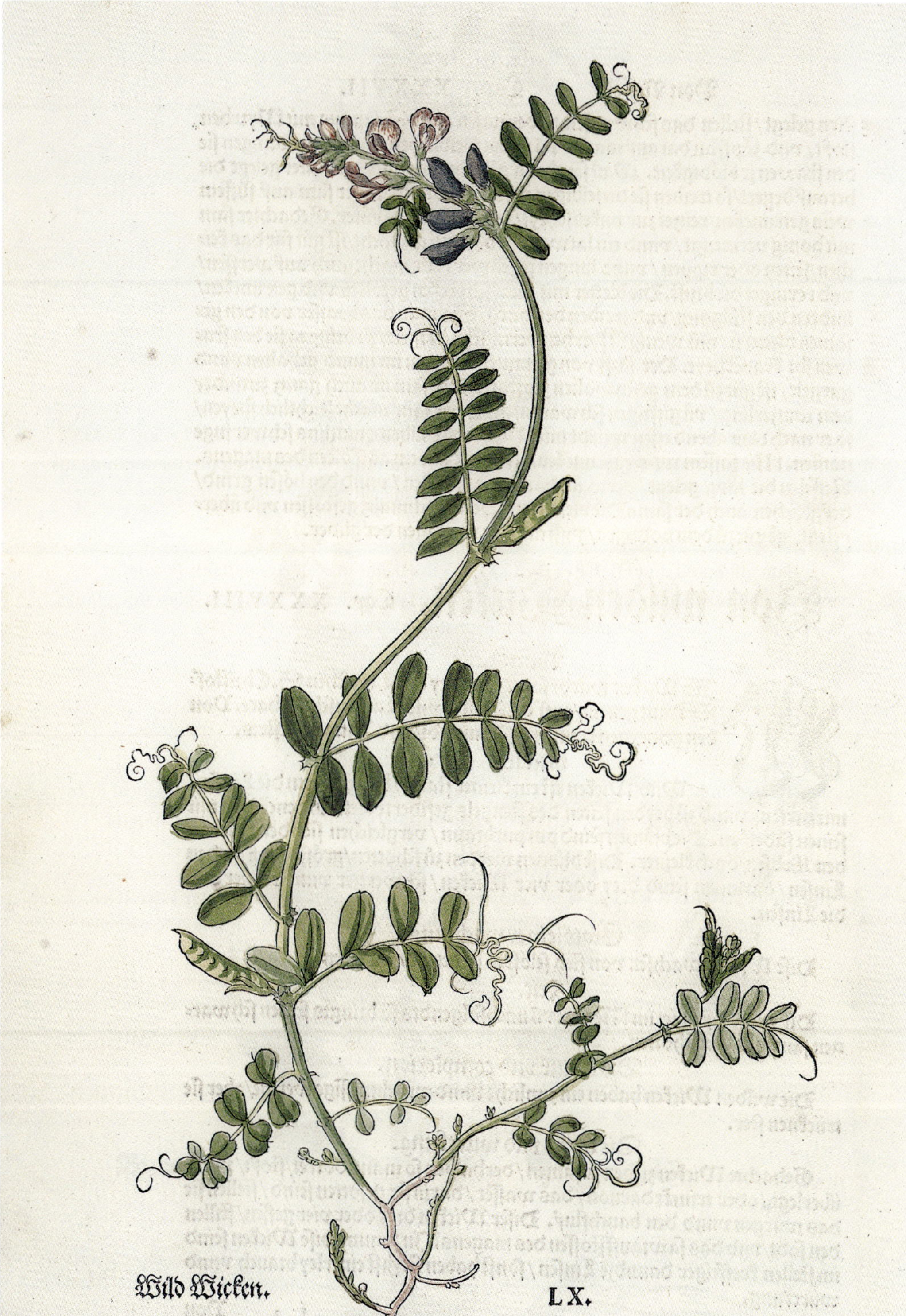

BUSH VETCH | WILDE WICKEN | VESCE DES HAIES

PURSLANE

PURSLANE (XXXIX) derives from the Latin word *portulaca*. The comprehensive list of applications includes use of the plant as a vegetable, and the buds as a substitute for capers.

„BURTZELKRAUT“

Aus dem lateinischen *Portulaca* bildete sich das deutsche „BURTZELKRAUT“ (Cap. XXXIX), für das eine umfangreiche Liste der Anwendungen genannt wird, wozu auch die Verwendung als Gemüse und der Knospen als Kapernersatz gehört.

POURPIER

Le nom allemand du POURPIER (XXXIX), «Burtzelkraut», dérive du latin *Portulaca*. Le pourpier a trouvé de très nombreuses applications en médecine, mais c'est aussi une plante potagère et un substitut des câpres.

PAGE 142

MARTAGON LILY

In the chapter on MARTAGON LILY (XL), Fuchs demonstrates his knowledge of local flora when he notes that the plant "grows in great numbers on the Österberg in Tübingen."

„GOLDWURTZ“

Im Kapitel „GOLDWURTZ“ (Cap. XL) erweist sich Fuchs als Kenner seiner Lokalflora, wenn er vermerkt, dass der Türkenbund „zu Tübingen am Österberg … mit hauffen wechst“.

RACINES DORÉES

Au chapitre «Goldwurtz» (XL), ou RACINES DORÉES, Fuchs s'affirme comme un connaisseur de la flore locale puisqu'il fait remarquer que le lis martagon «croît abondamment… à Tübingen-sur-l'Österberg».

PAGE 143

ORACHE

ORACHE (XLI) was recommended for digestive and liver problems, as well as for abscesses.

„MOLTEN“

Die „MOLTEN“ (Cap. XLI), heute sprechen wir von Melde, werden bei Verdauungsbeschwerden und Leberproblemen, aber auch bei Abszessen empfohlen.

ARROCHE DES JARDINS

L'ARROCHE DES JARDINS (XLI) est préconisée pour les troubles digestifs et hépatiques ainsi que les abcès.

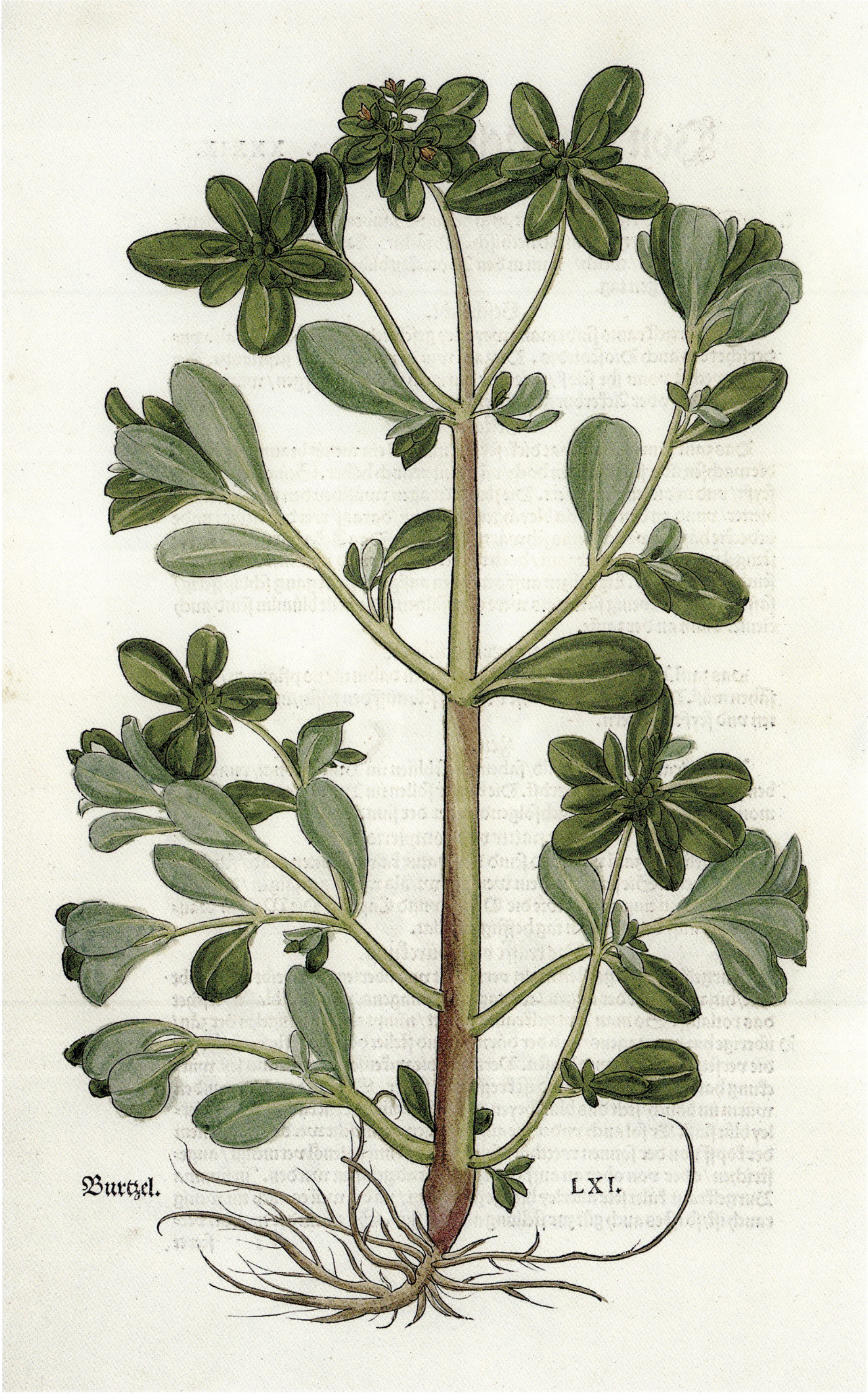
Burtzel.
LXI.

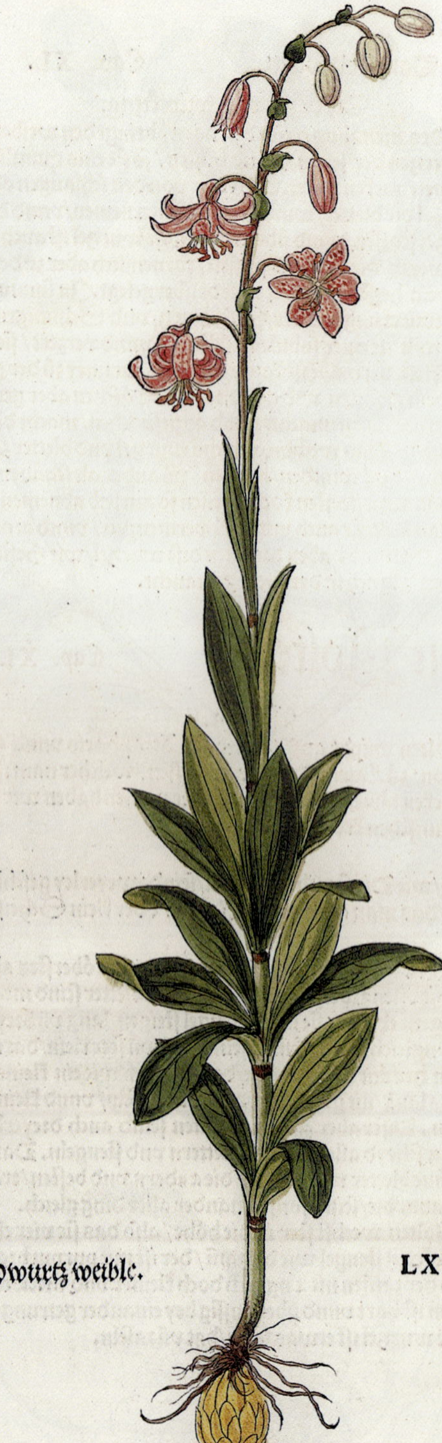

Goldwurtz weible. LXIII.

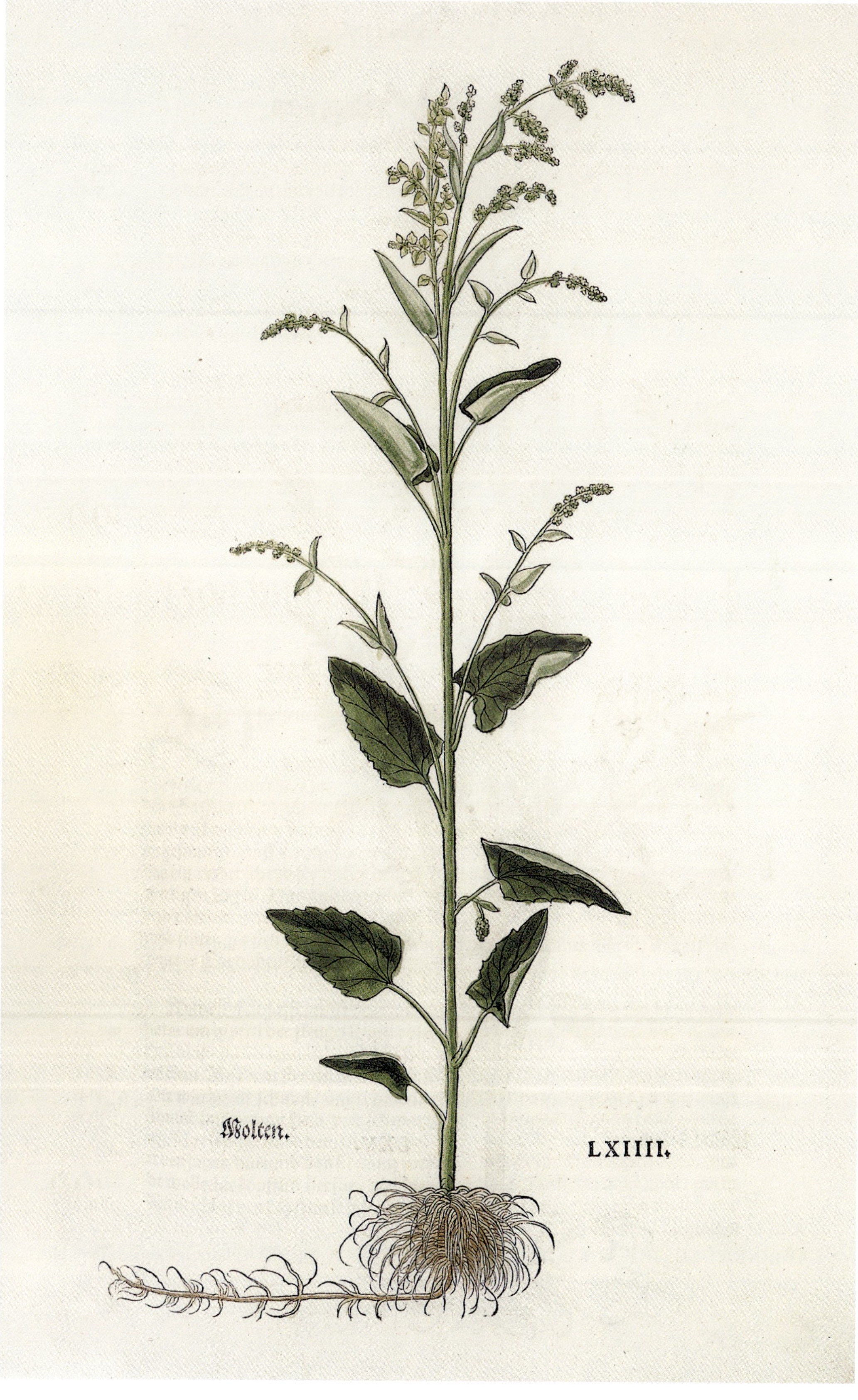

ORACHE | „MOLTEN“ | ARROCHE DES JARDINS

CROCUS

Anyone expecting to see the autumn CROCUS for the plant termed by Fuchs in German "Wild Field Saffron" (XLII) is instead confronted with the CARLINE THISTLE (plate LXVI) and the BLESSED THISTLE (plate LXVII). The latter name explains why the plant was often used.

„WILDER FELDSAFFRAN“

Wer beim „WILDEN FELDSAFFRAN“ (Cap. XLII) den Safrankrokus erwartet, sieht sich unvermittelt der KLEINEN EBERWURZ (Taf. LXVI) und dem BENEDIKTENKRAUT (Taf. LXVII) gegenüber, wobei letzterer Name im Volk als „gesegnetes Kraut“ übersetzt wurde und so die häufige Verwendung der Pflanze erklärt.

SAFRAN DES PRÉS

Sous le nom de «SAFRAN DES PRÉS» (XLII), on imagine le crocus. En fait, il s'agit ici de la CARLINE VULGAIRE (pl. LXVI) et du CHARDON BÉNIT (pl. LXVII) dont les gens du peuple avaient traduit le nom «Benediktenkraut» (herbe des Bénédictins) par «herbe bénie», ce qui explique sa fréquente utilisation.

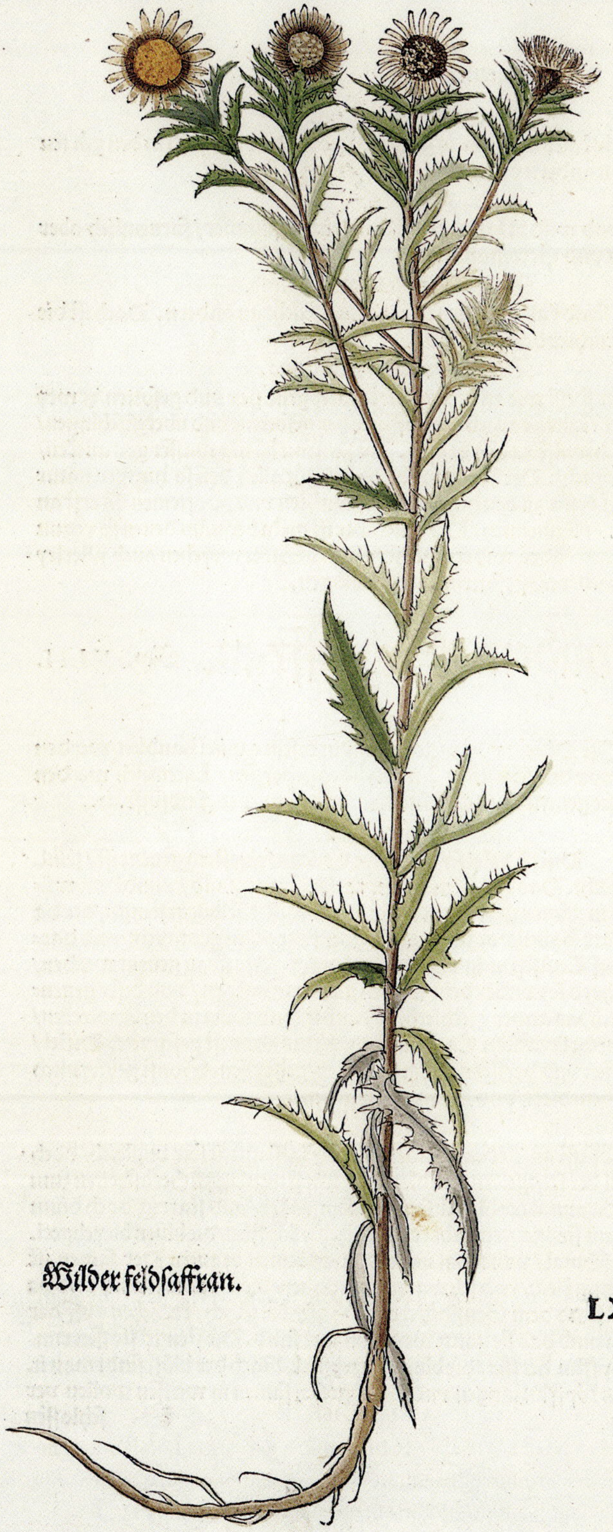

Wilder feldsaffran.

LXVI.

ANGELICA

The name ANGELICA (XLIII) also conveys a sense of the respect awarded to the strongly smelling plant, whose essential oil is still an ingredient in some stomach remedies.

„ANGELICK“

Auch der Name Engelwurz, „ANGELICK“ (Cap. XLIII), lässt die Achtung spüren, die man der stark riechenden Pflanze entgegenbrachte, deren ätherisches Öl noch heute in manchen Magenmitteln enthalten ist.

ANGÉLIQUE

Son nom d'«ANGÉLIQUE» (XLIII) montre le respect qu'on avait envers cette plante très aromatique et dont l'huile essentielle entre encore dans la composition de certains remèdes stomachiques.

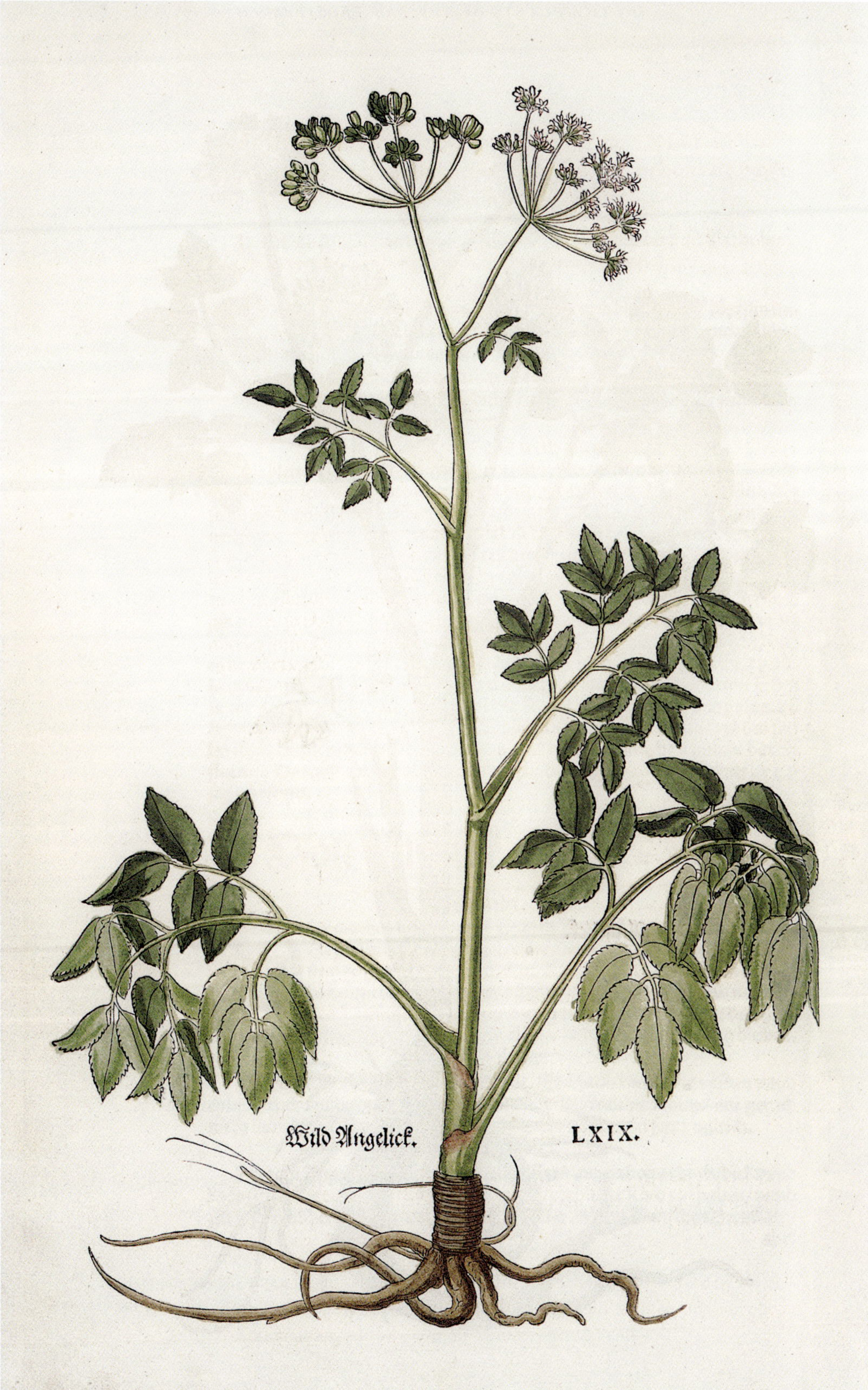
Wild Angelick.
LXIX.

CORN COCKLE

CORN COCKLE (XLIIII) is a pretty but feared field weed, which has now been almost eradicated. Earlier, however, it was valued as a medicinal herb.

KORNRADE

Die KORNRADE (Cap. XLIIII) ist ein schönes, aber gefürchtetes Ackerunkraut, das heute praktisch ausgerottet ist, früher jedoch auch als Heilpflanze geschätzt wurde.

NIELLE DES BLÉS

La NIELLE DES BLÉS (XLIIII) est une belle plante qui a quasiment disparu de nos campagnes. Bien que redoutée comme adventice des champs de céréales, elle était très estimée pour ses vertus médicinales.

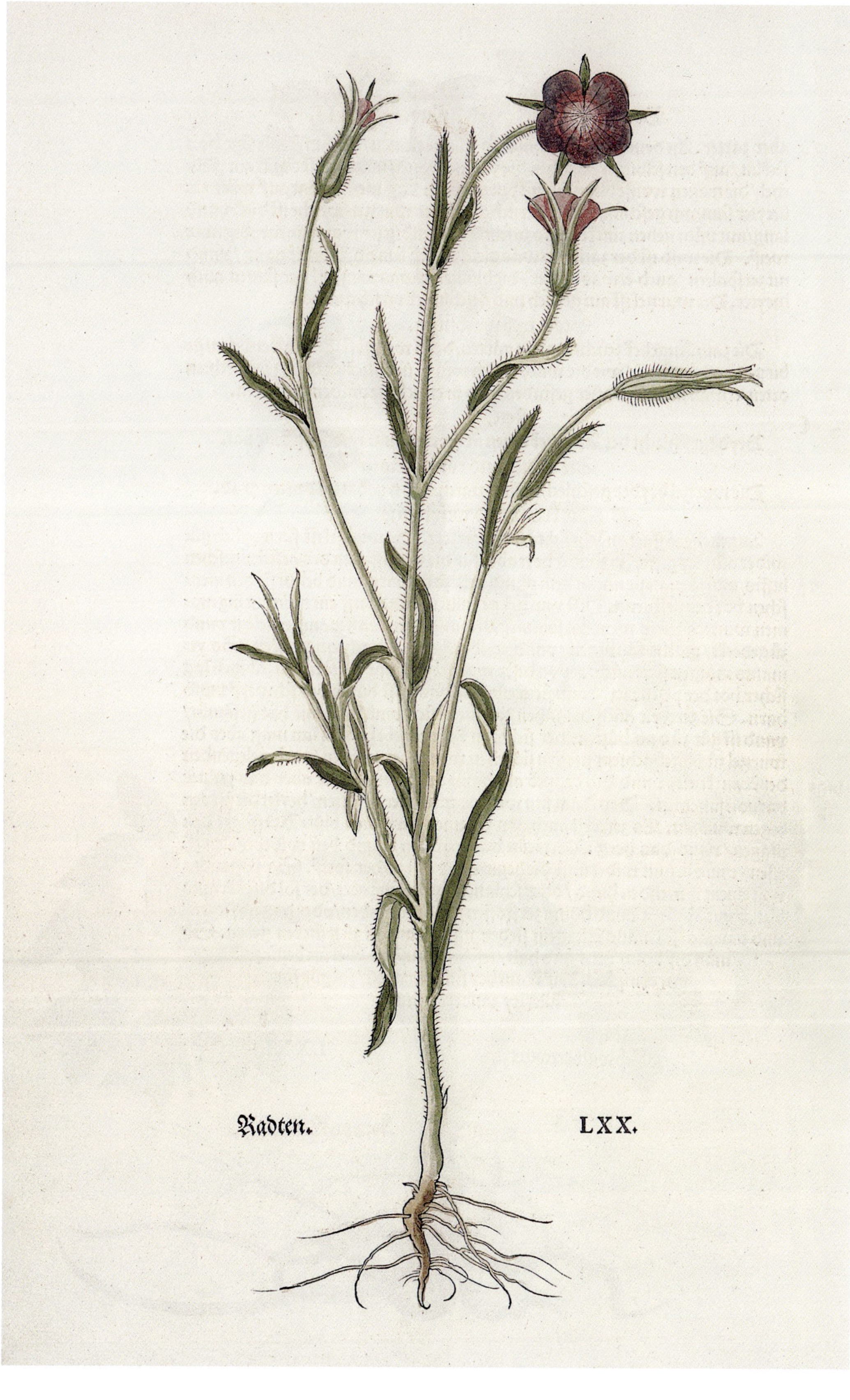
Radten.
LXX.

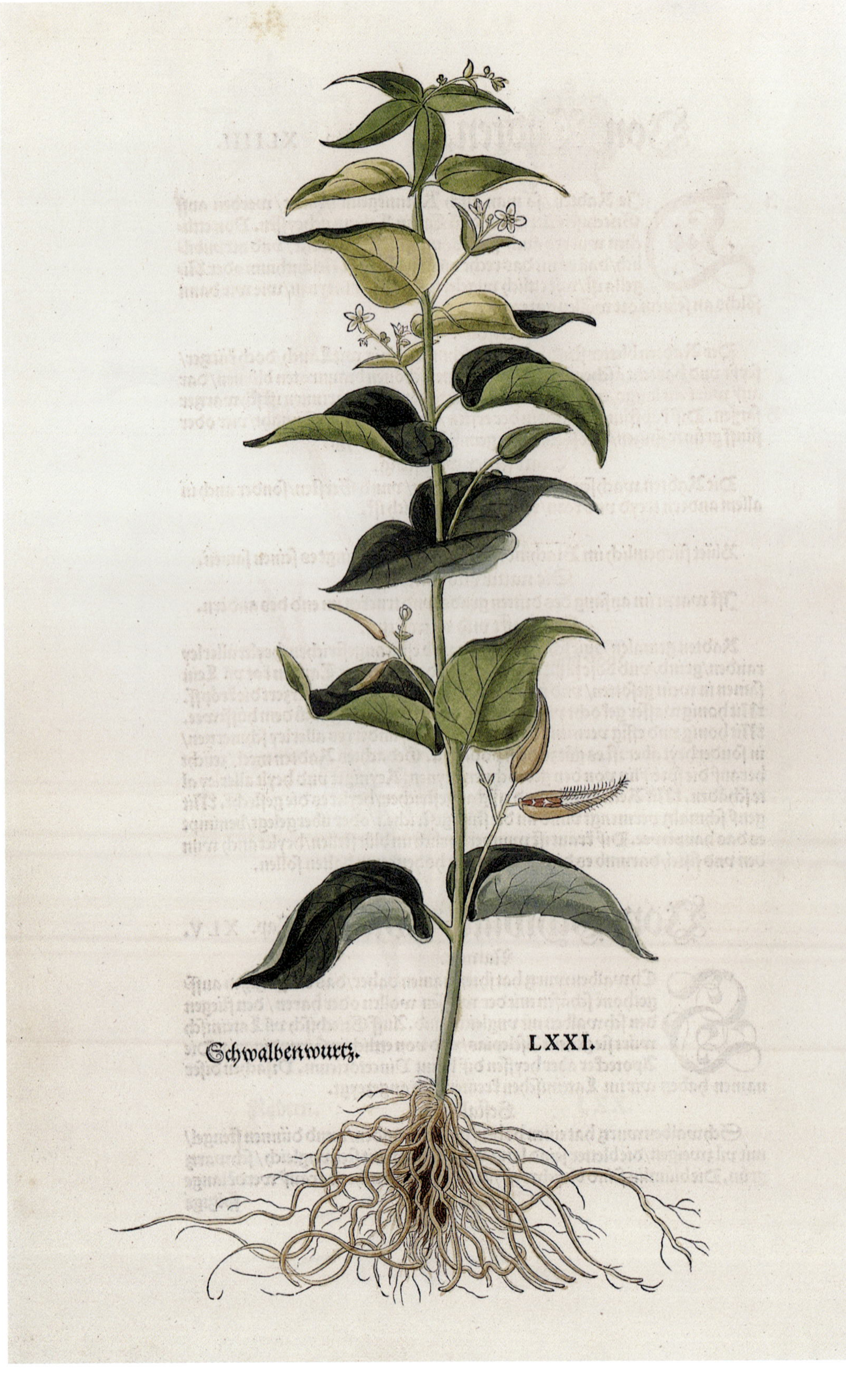
Schwalbenwurtz.
LXXI.

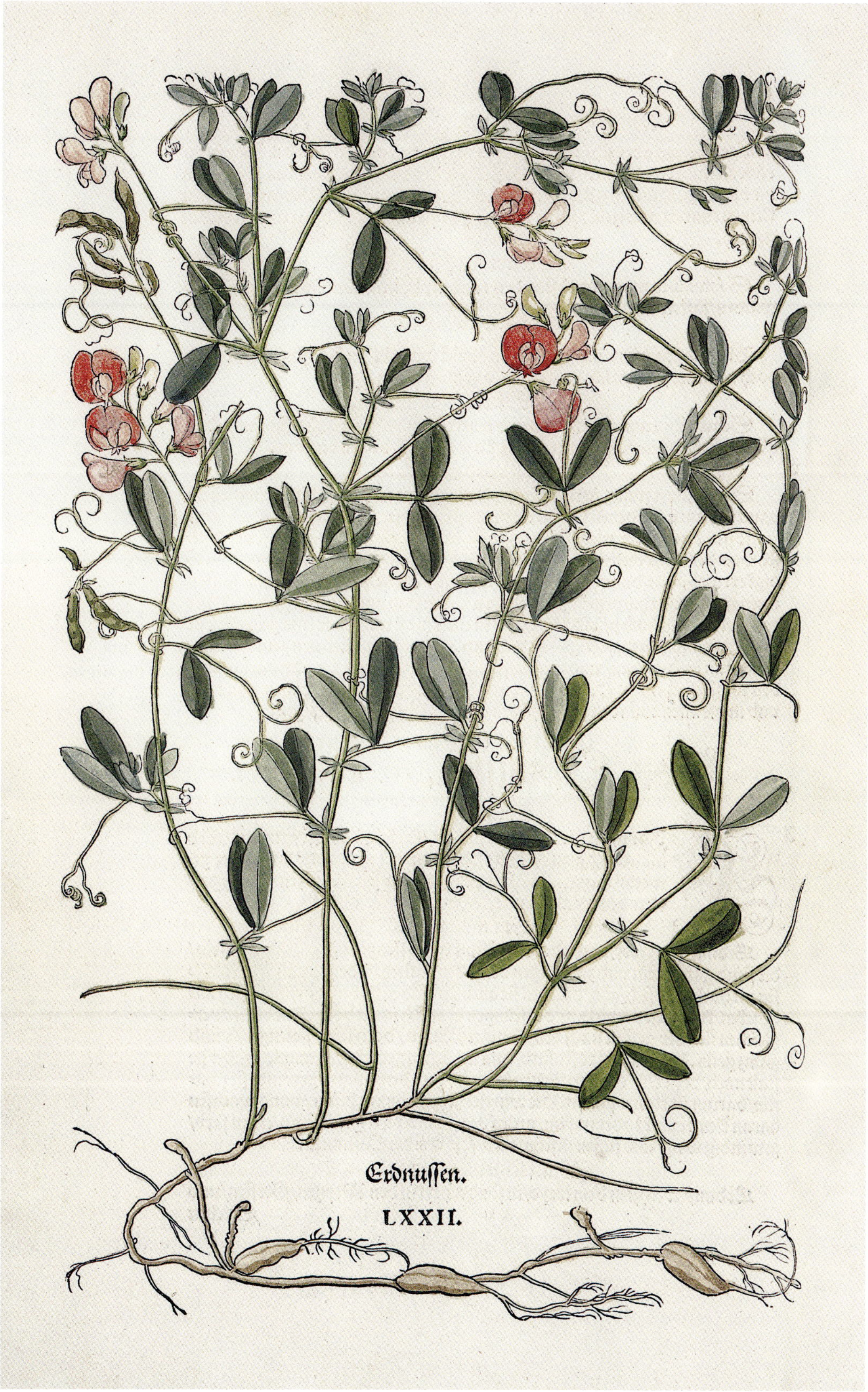
Erdnussen.
LXXII.

PAGES 150, 151

SWALLOW-WORT / EARTHNUT PEA

The seldom-used SWALLOW-WORT, or COMMON VINCETOXICUM (XLV), is followed by TUBEROUS PEA, or EARTHNUT PEA (XLVI). The latter is not, however, the Ground Nut, or Peanut, which originally stemmed from America and today is found throughout the world, providing a valuable oil, but rather a native European tuberous Meadow Pea.

„SCHWALBENWURTZ" / „ERDNUSS"

Der selten verwendeten „SCHWALBENWURTZ" (Cap. XLV) folgt die „ERDNUSS" (Cap. XLVI), bei der es sich jedoch nicht um die ursprünglich aus Amerika stammende, heute weltweit verbreitete Frucht handelt, aus der auch ein wertvolles Öl gewonnen wird, sondern um die einheimische Knollen-Platterbse.

DOMPTE-VENIN / NOIX DE TERRE

Le DOMPTE-VENIN (XLV), plante très rarement utilisée, est suivi de la «NOIX DE TERRE» (en allemand «Erdnuss», qui est aussi le nom moderne de la cacahuète). Il ne s'agit pas du fruit de l'arachide, plante tropicale native de l'Amérique, dont on extrait une huile, mais de la GESSE TUBÉREUSE (XLVI), dite aussi gland de terre, qui est originaire de nos régions.

ITALIAN ASTER

ITALIAN ASTER, or ITALIAN STARWORT (XLVII), also known as European Michaelmas Daisy, was recommended by Fuchs for abdominal ailments.

STERNKRAUT

Das STERNKRAUT (Cap. XLVII) wird bei Erkrankungen des Unterleibs empfohlen.

STELLAIRE HOLOSTÉE

Fuchs préconise la STELLAIRE HOLOSTÉE (XLVII) pour les maladies de l'abdomen.

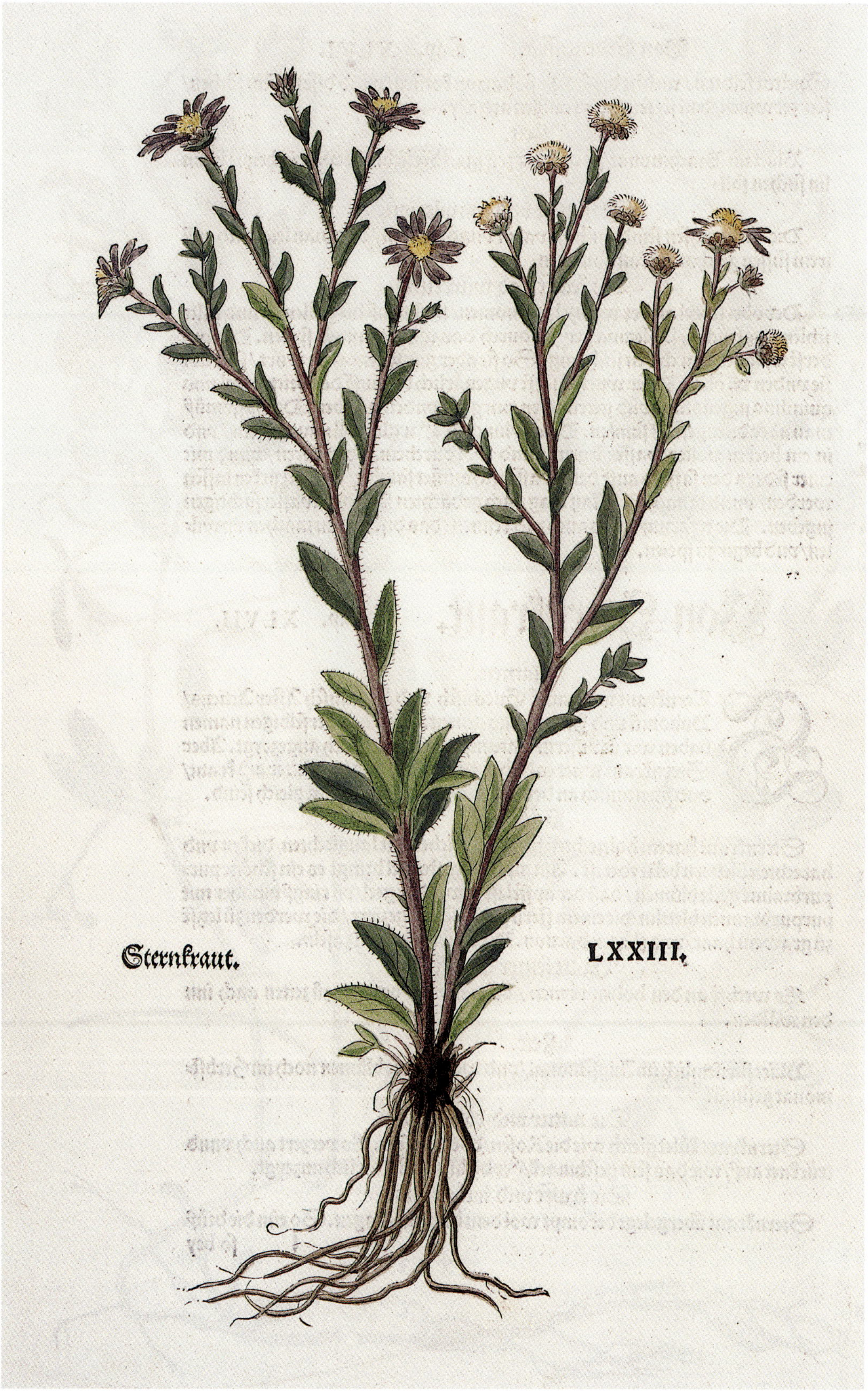

ITALIAN ASTER | STERNKRAUT | STELLAIRE HOLOSTÉE

SATIN FLOWER

In the case of Greater Stitchwort, or SATIN FLOWER (XLVIII), it may seem surprising that a herbal also includes grass, but we must recall that Hayseed is often used medicinally even today.

GRAS

Es mag vielleicht überraschen, dass sich in einem Kräuterbuch auch ein Kapitel über GRAS (Cap. XLVIII) findet, doch wollen wir nicht vergessen, dass noch heute Heublumen relativ häufig medizinisch verwendet werden.

HERBES

Trouver ici un chapitre sur les «HERBES» (XLVIII) pourrait surprendre, mais n'oublions pas que l'emploi des fleurs du foin est encore aujourd'hui assez fréquent.

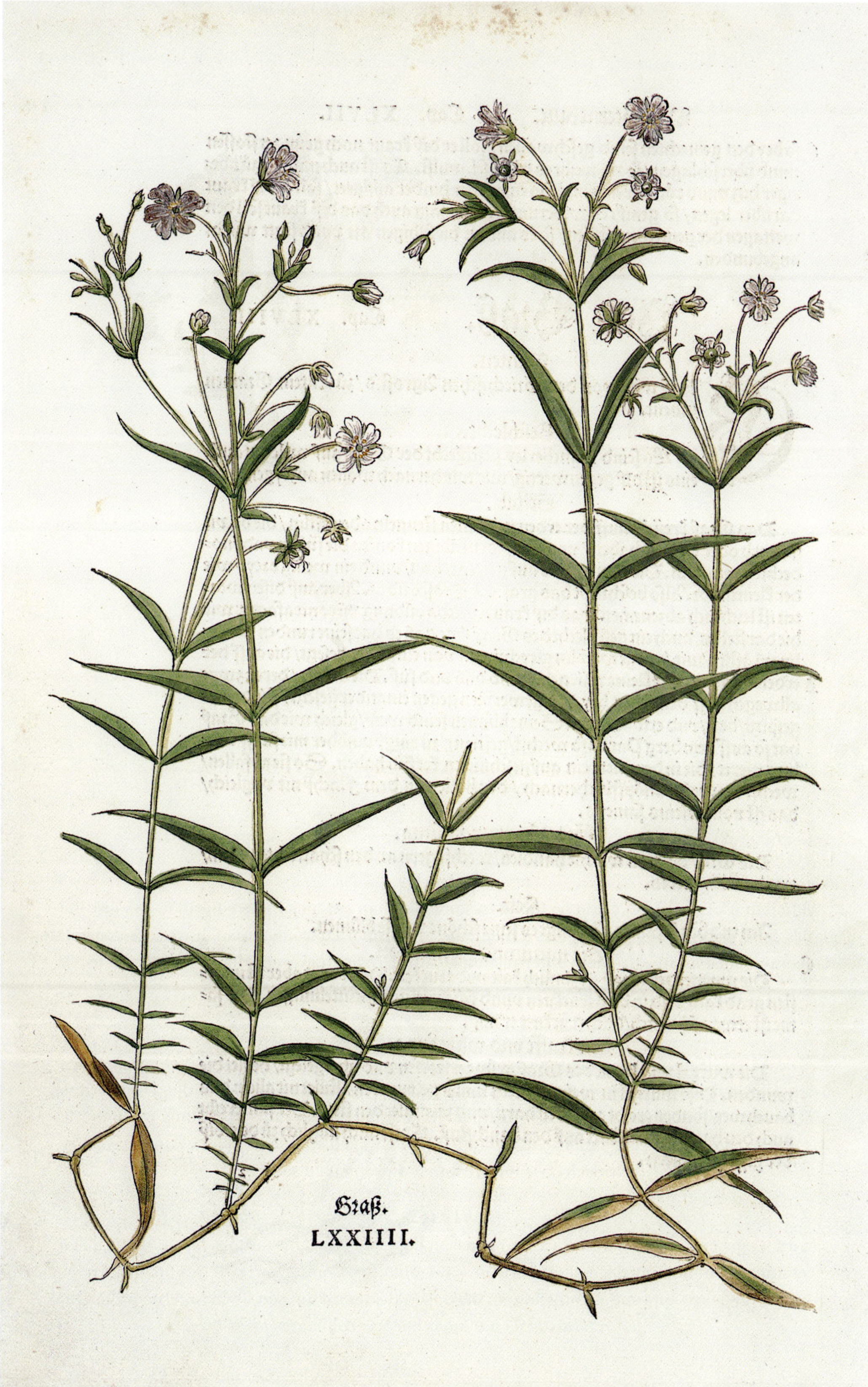
Graß.
LXXIIII.

ALOE

Although ALOE (XLIX) could be found in some German gardens in Leonhart Fuchs's day, the plant's dried juice, which was used as a medicine, was imported from abroad. It was then correctly recommended as an extremely bitter-tasting laxative. Today, however, long-term internal use is discouraged because of a number of side effects.

ALOE

Die ALOE (Cap. XLIX) wuchs zu Zeiten Leonhart Fuchs' zwar schon in manchen Gärten, den getrockneten Saft, der als Arznei gebraucht wurde, bezog man aber über den Fernhandel. Als extrem bitter schmeckendes Abführmittel fand er angemessene Verwendung, wenngleich der länger andauernde innerliche Gebrauch heute wegen einiger Nebenwirkungen sehr kritisch gesehen wird und unterbleiben sollte.

ALOÈS

Si, du temps de Fuchs, l'ALOÈS (XLIX) poussait déjà dans certains jardins, le suc, durci à l'air et utilisé comme remède, était importé de pays lointains. Comme purgatif très amer, il avait trouvé un usage approprié. Toutefois, on déconseille aujourd'hui son usage interne prolongé en raison de quelques effets secondaires.

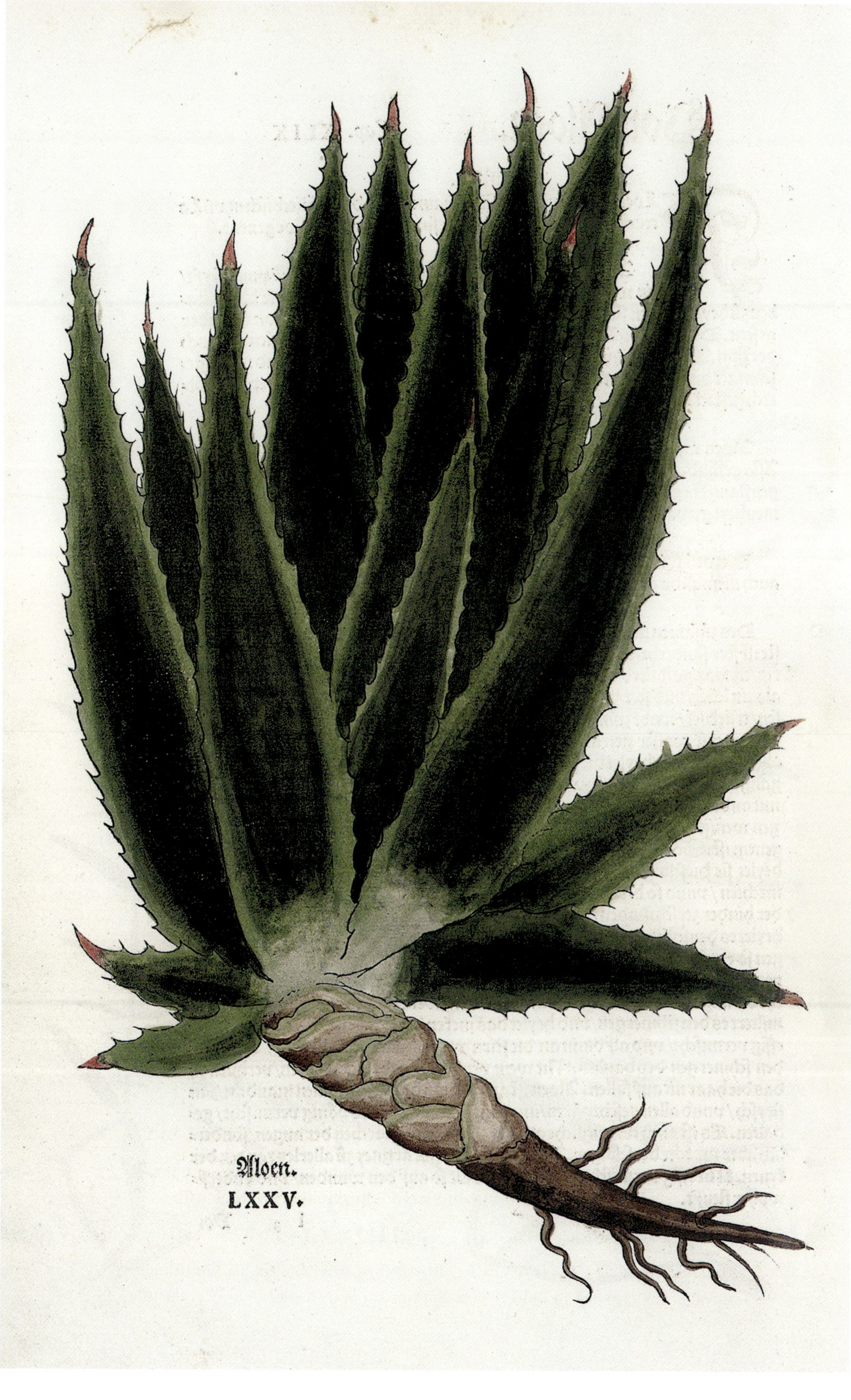
Aloen.
LXXV.

COLTSFOOT

With COLTSFOOT (L) Fuchs describes a plant whose smoke was to be inhaled through a tube to ease coughs and asthma.

„ROSSHUB"

Unter „ROSSHUB" (Cap. L) beschreibt Fuchs den Huflattich, dessen Rauch u. a. bei Husten und Asthma durch ein Rohr inhaliert werden sollte.

PAS-D'ÂNE

Fuchs nomme le PAS-D'ÂNE (L) «Rosshub» (sabot de cheval). On inhalait autrefois ses vapeurs au moyen d'un chalumeau pour traiter la toux et l'asthme.

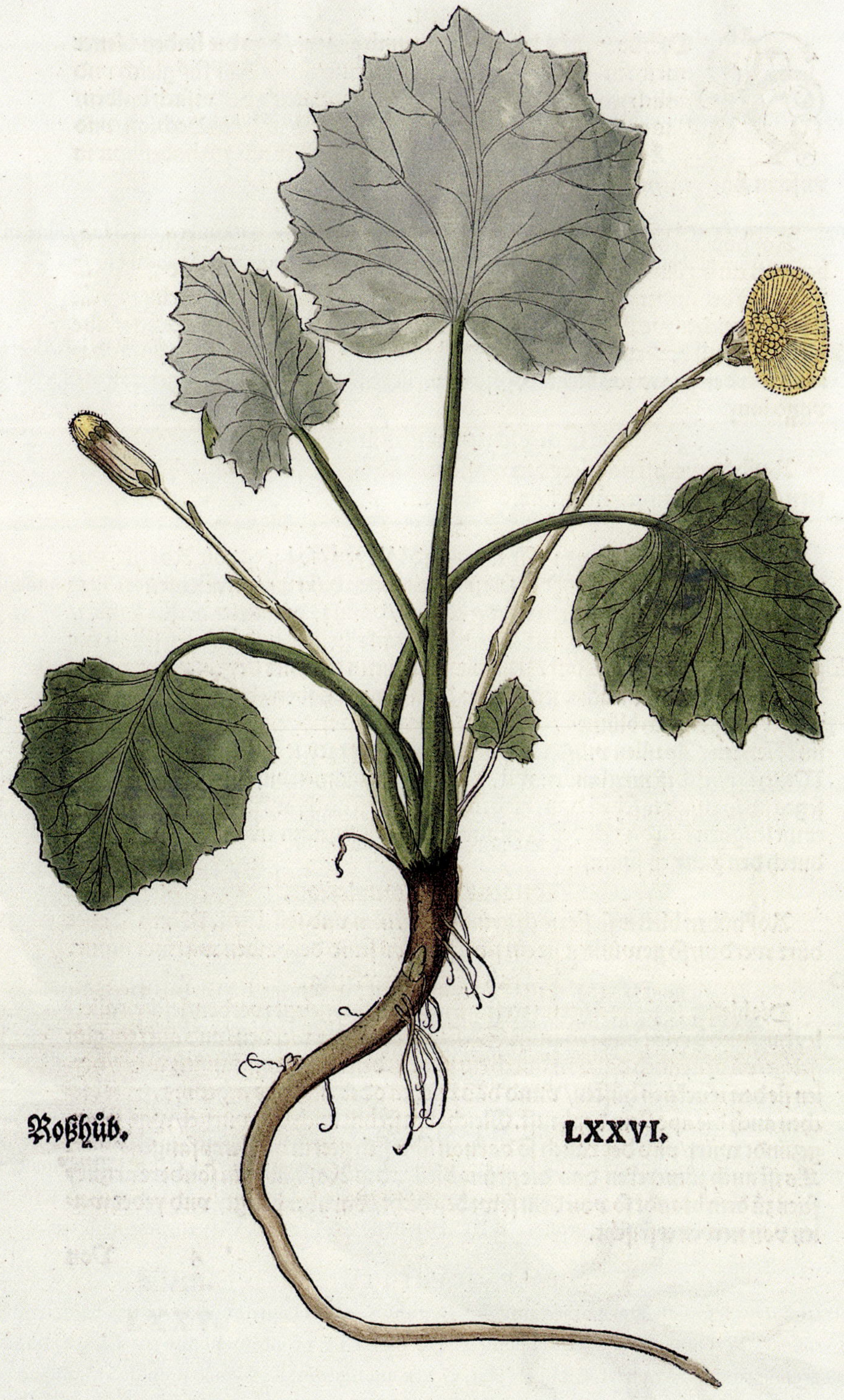

Roßhůb. LXXVI.

BORAGE

Fuchs ascribed psychological effects to BORAGE (LI): steeped in wine, its flowers were supposed to make a person cheerful and drive away sorrow.

„BURRETSCH“

Dem „BURRETSCH“ (Cap. LI) billigt Fuchs auch psychoaktive Wirkungen zu, denn seine in Wein gelegten Blüten sollen fröhlich machen und Traurigkeit vertreiben.

BOURRACHE OFFICINALE

Ce sont, entre autres, des effets salutaires sur le psychisme que Fuchs prête à la BOURRACHE OFFICINALE (LI) : ses fleurs macérées dans du vin rendraient joyeux et chasseraient la tristesse.

PAGE 162

SCENTLESS MAYWEED

SCENTLESS SHAMOMILE, or SCENTLESS MAYWEED (LII), is a stronger form of Chamomile.

„RINDSSAUG“

Die Falsche Kamille, wegen ihrer typischen Blüten „RINDSSAUG“ (Cap. LII), wegen der zerteilten Blätter auch Kuhdill genannt, gilt als schärfere Art der Kamille.

CAMOMILLE INODORE

La CAMOMILLE INODORE (LII), appelée aussi «œil-de-vache» («Rindssaug») ou encore «aneth à vache» («Kuhdill») à cause de ses feuilles très découpées, est considérée ici comme une variété plus forte de camomille.

PAGE 163

DAISY

Under the designation DAISY (LIII) Fuchs included the delicate ENGLISH DAISY (plates LXXIX, LXXX) along with the larger MARGUERITE (plate LXXXI), which is also known as the Moon or Ox-eye Daisy. He termed the yellow base of the blossom the “apple” and the white crown of petals the “wheel.”

„MASSLIEBEN“

„Apffel“ nennt Fuchs den gelben Blütenboden und „Rädle“ den Kranz der weißen Blütenblätter bei „MASSLIEBEN“ (Cap. LIII), worunter er das zierliche GÄNSEBLÜMCHEN (Taf. LXXIX, LXXX) und die deutlich größere WUCHERBLUME (Taf. LXXXI) zusammenfasst.

PÂQUERETTE

Pour Fuchs, leurs disques jaunes sont des «pommes» et les couronnes de ligules blanches, des «roues». C'est ainsi qu'il décrit la petite PÂQUERETTE proprement dite (pl. LXXIX, LXXX) et sa grande sœur, la MARGUERITE (pl. LXXXI), qui figurent ici sous le nom de «Maßlieben», ou «CHÈRES À MARIE» (LIII).

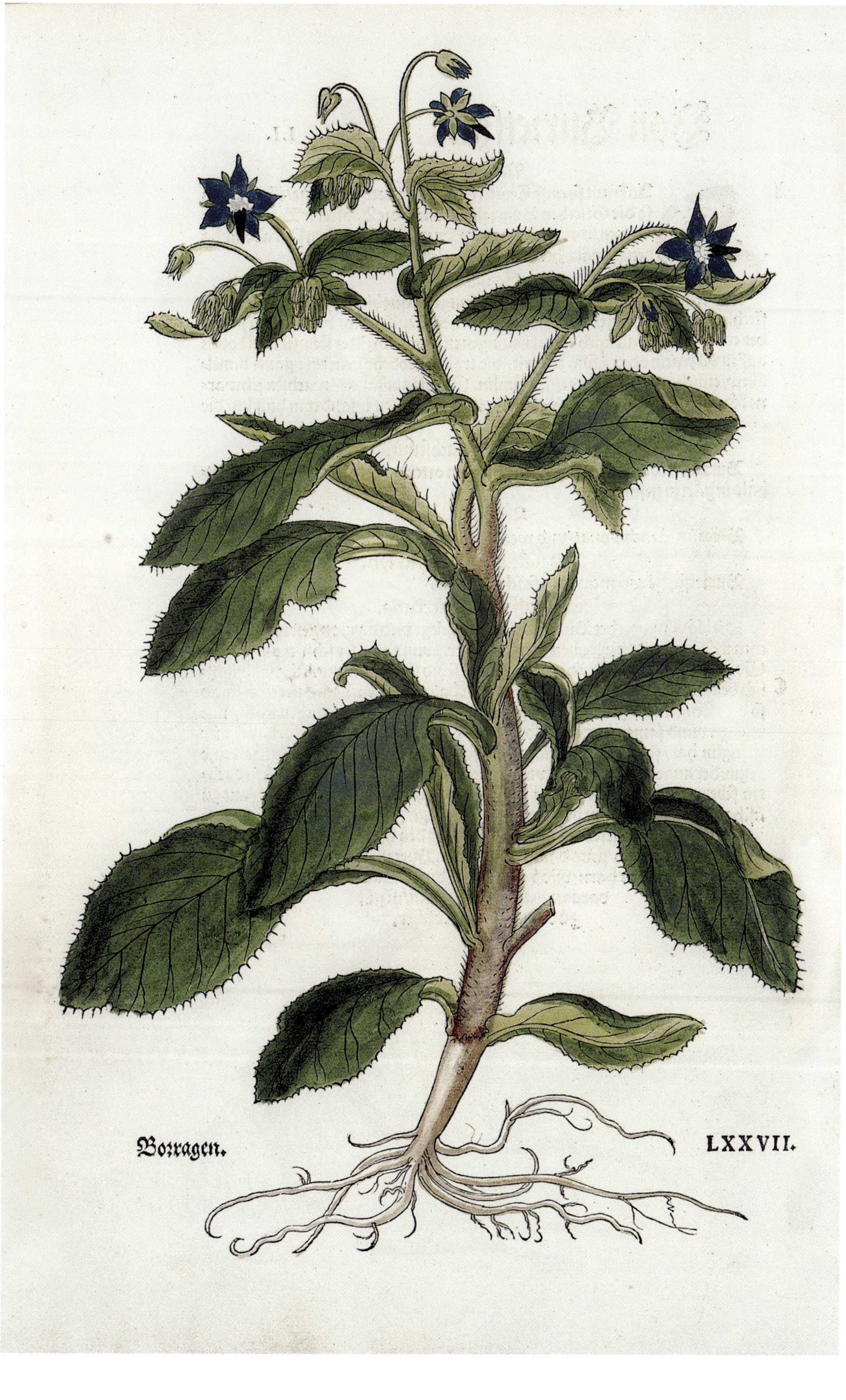
Borragen.
LXXVII.

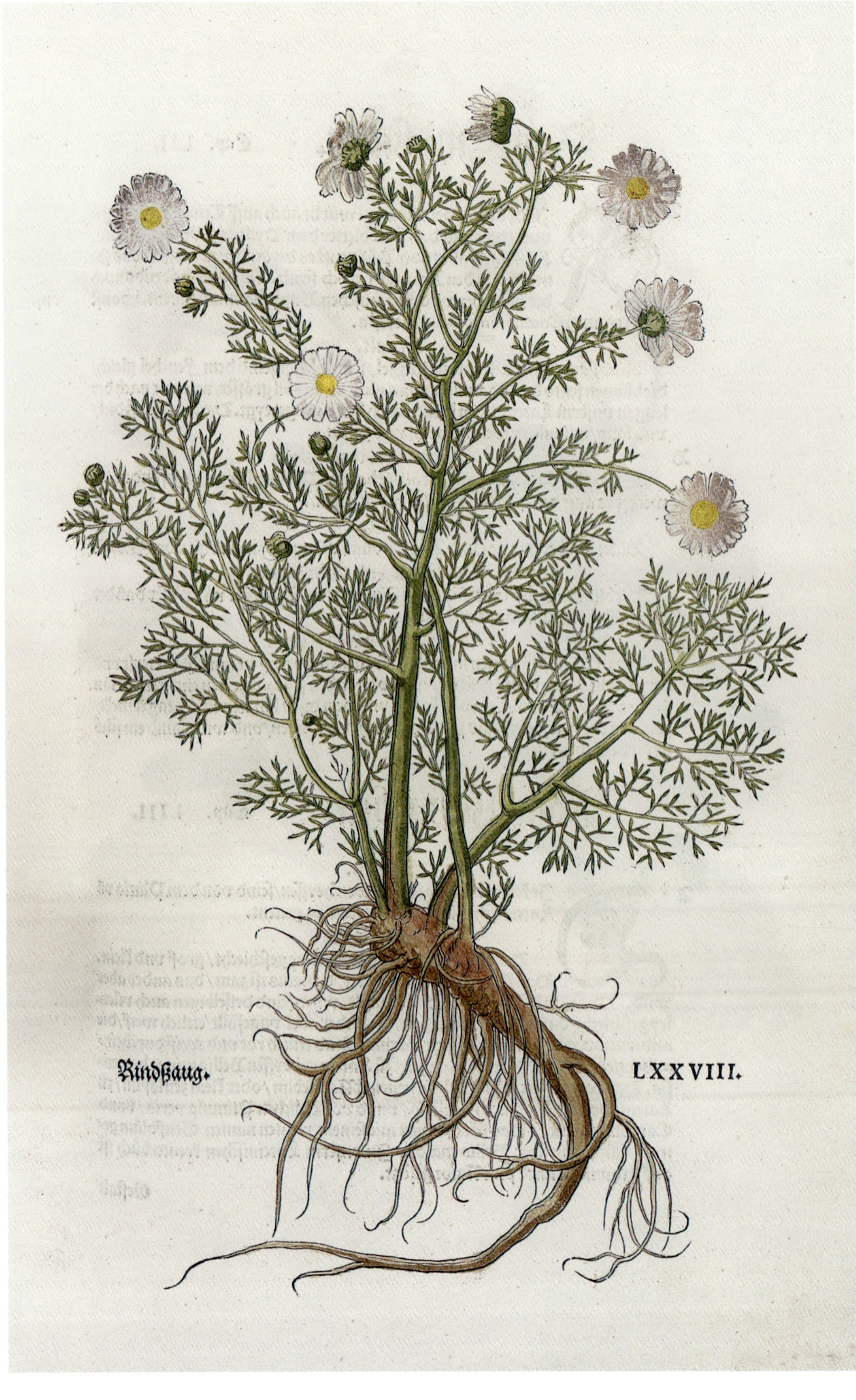
Rindßaug.
LXXVIII.

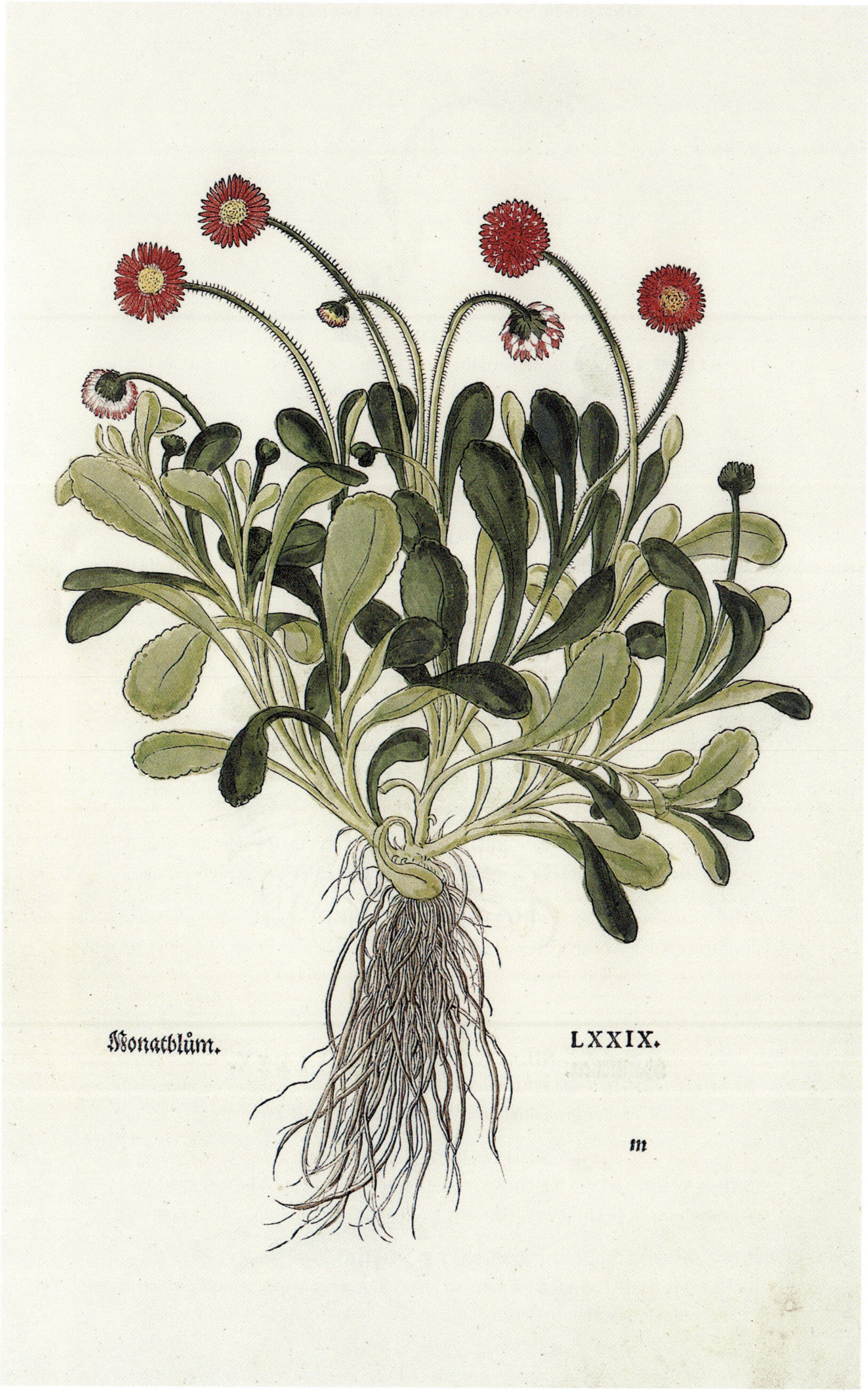
Monatblům.
LXXIX.
m

SABINE

SABINE (LIIII), a member of the Juniper family, was often used as an abortifacient in earlier days.

„SEVENBAUM"

Der „SEVENBAUM" (Cap. LIIII), eine Wacholderart, wurde früher oftmals als Abtreibungsmittel verwendet.

GENÉVRIER SABINE

Le GENÉVRIER SABINE (LIIII) est, comme son nom l'indique, une variété de genévrier, que l'on utilisait souvent à tort comme abortif.

PAGE 166

BLACKBERRY

In the case of BLACKBERRY (LV), Fuchs had both "kinds" illustrated on one and the same plant in order to clarify the differences in size.

„BROMBEER"

Die beiden „geschlecht" der „BROMBEER" (Cap. LV) lässt Fuchs an ein und derselben Pflanze abbilden, um die Größenunterschiede zu verdeutlichen.

RONCE COMMUNE

Fuchs illustre les deux «genres» de la RONCE COMMUNE (LV) sur une même plante pour en faire ressortir la différence de taille.

PAGE 167

BLACK HOREHOUND

BLACK HOREHOUND (LVI) finds use today in folk medicine as an ingredient in teas for bronchial disorders and gall bladder problems.

„SCHWARTZ ANDORN"

Der „SCHWARTZ ANDORN" (Cap. LVI) wird heute noch volkstümlich in Teemischungen bei Bronchialerkrankungen und Gallenbeschwerden eingesetzt.

BALLOTE NOIRE

La BALLOTE NOIRE (LVI) a toujours sa place en pharmacopée populaire sous forme d'infusions mixtes contre les maladies des bronches et de la vésicule biliaire.

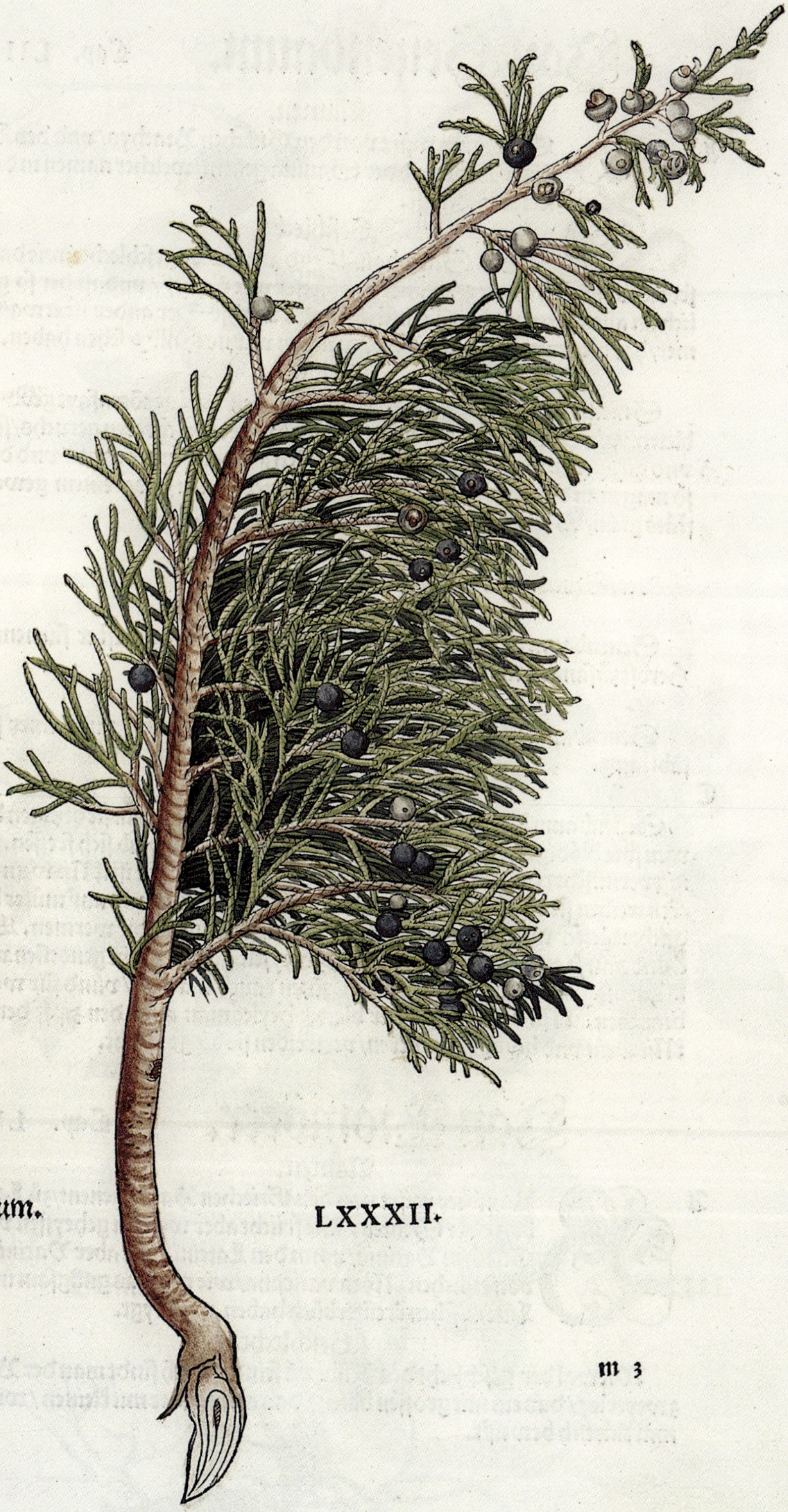

Seuenbaum. LXXXII.

m 3

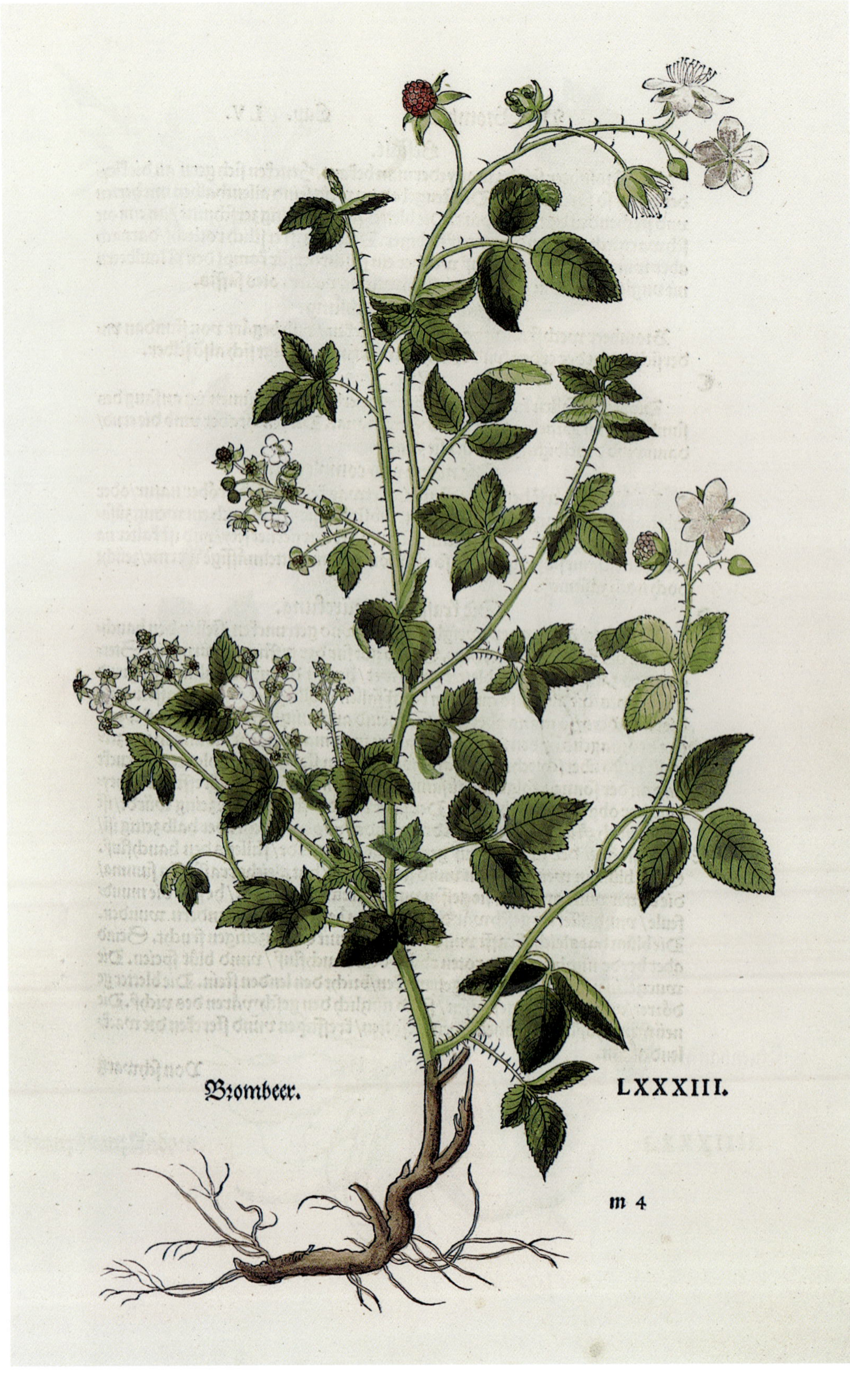
Brombeer.
LXXXIII.
m 4

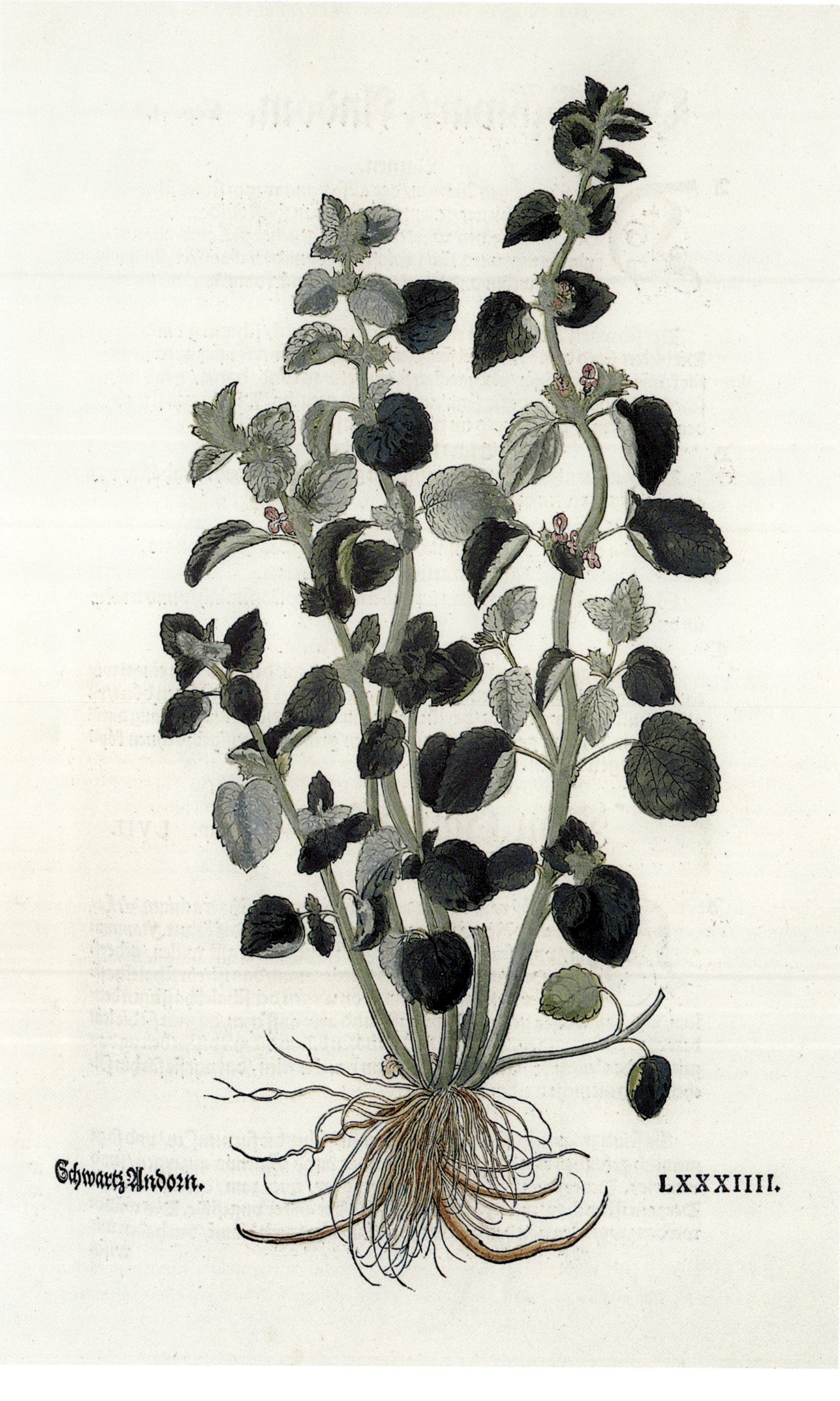

BLACK HOREHOUND | „SCHWARTZ ANDORN" | BALLOTE NOIRE

CROWFOOT

Today, owing to their irritant effect on the skin, the various kinds of CROWFOOT included in this chapter (LVII) find application only rarely against warts, gout and rheumatism.

HAHNENFUSS

Die verschiedenen HAHNENFUSS-Arten (Cap. LVII) werden nur noch selten wegen ihrer hautreizenden Wirkung volksmedizinisch gegen Warzen, aber auch bei Gicht und Rheumatismus angewendet.

RENONCULE

Les différentes espèces de RENONCULE (LVII) ne sont plus guère employées de nos jours à cause de leur effet irritant sur la peau. Leur usage était fréquent dans le passé pour enlever les verrues, mais aussi pour soigner la goutte et les rhumatismes.

PAGE 170

COMMON HOP

Because of its bitter taste, COMMON HOP (LVIII) is used today to stimulate the appetite, and also in tranquillizing preparations. The hop is furthermore essential for the proper brewing of beer.

„HOPFFEN“

„HOPFFEN“ (Cap. LVIII) wird heute wegen seines bitteren Geschmacks zur Appetitanregung gebraucht, insbesondere aber als Bestandteil beruhigender Präparate. Unverzichtbar ist er bei nach dem Reinheitsgebot gebrautem Bier.

HOUBLON COMMUN

Le HOUBLON COMMUN (LVIII), excellent tonique et apéritif par ses principes amers, est toujours employé de nos jours. Il entre également dans la composition de remèdes contre la nervosité et est un aromate indispensable de la bière brassée conformément à la loi de pureté allemande.

PAGE 171

COMMON SPEEDWELL

In the case of COMMON SPEEDWELL (LIX), one of its German designations, Grundheil, supposedly expresses the plant's fundamentally wholesome effect.

EHRENPREIS

Der EHRENPREIS (Cap. LIX) wurde auch Grundheil genannt, worin seine von Grund auf heilsame Wirkung zum Ausdruck kommt.

VÉRONIQUE OFFICINALE

La VÉRONIQUE OFFICINALE (LIX) portait aussi le nom de «Grundheil» une expression imagée qui signifie «celle qui guérit à la source» et qui indique très bien ses effets salutaires.

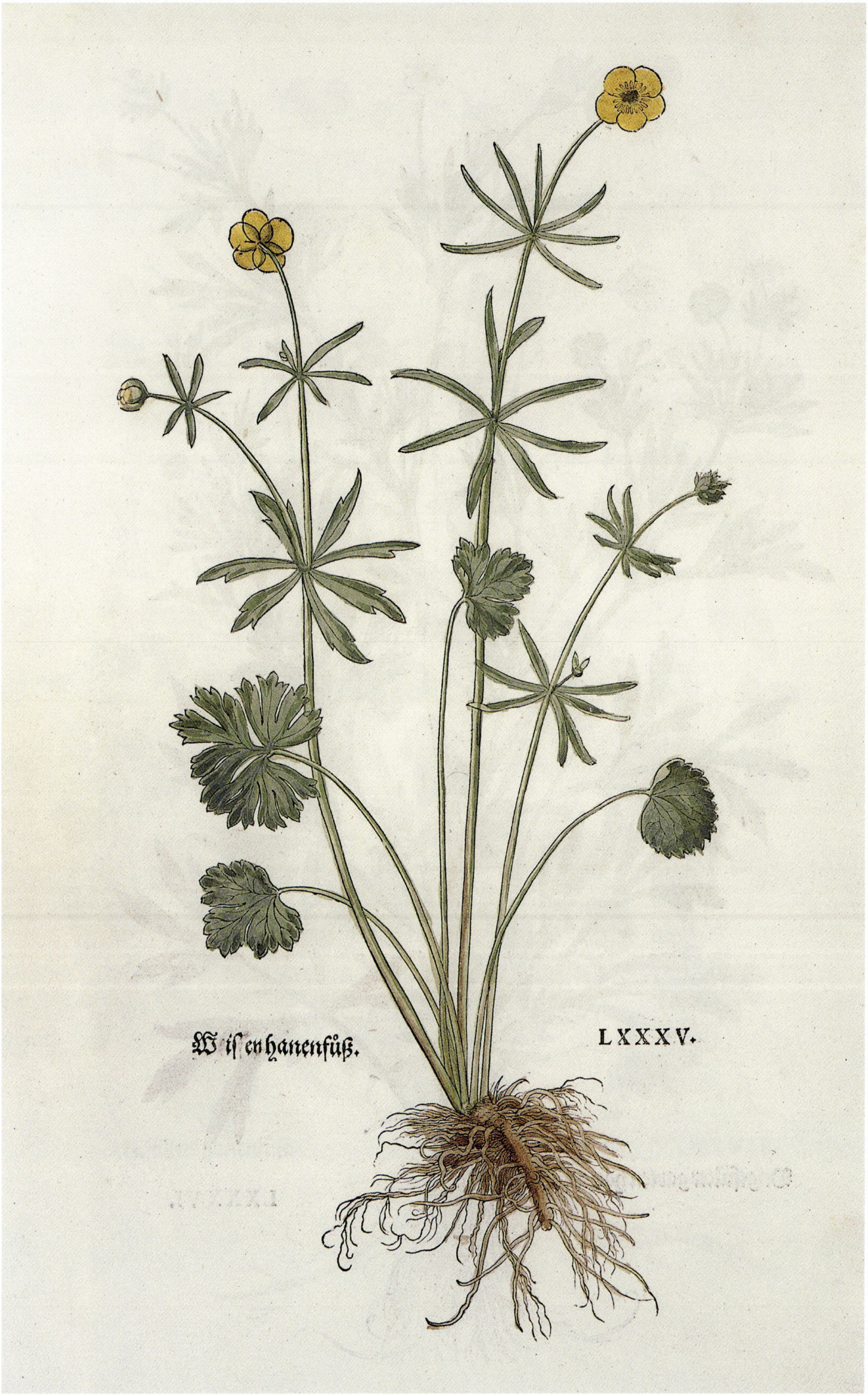
Wisen hanenfüß.
LXXXV.

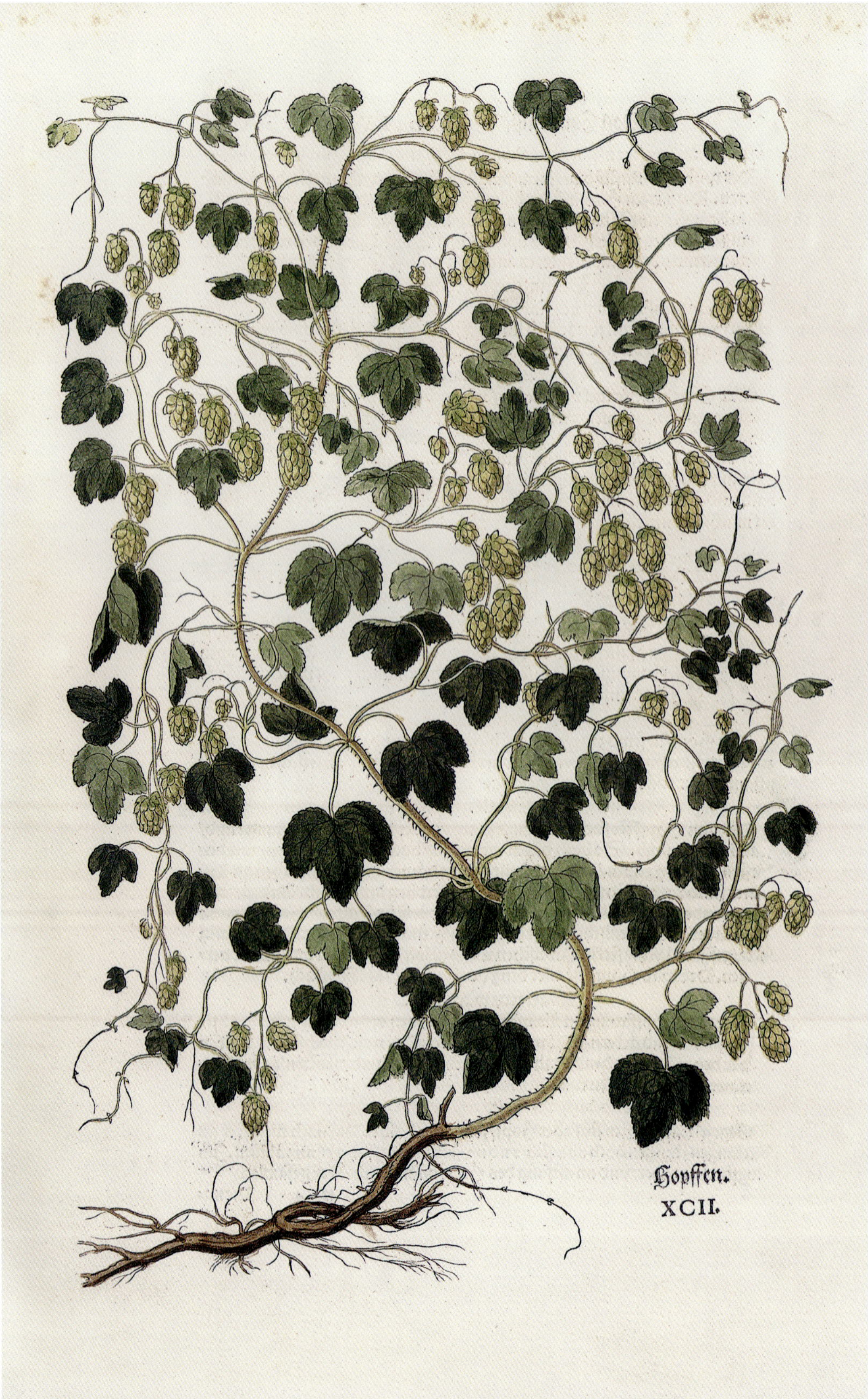
Hopffen.
XCII.

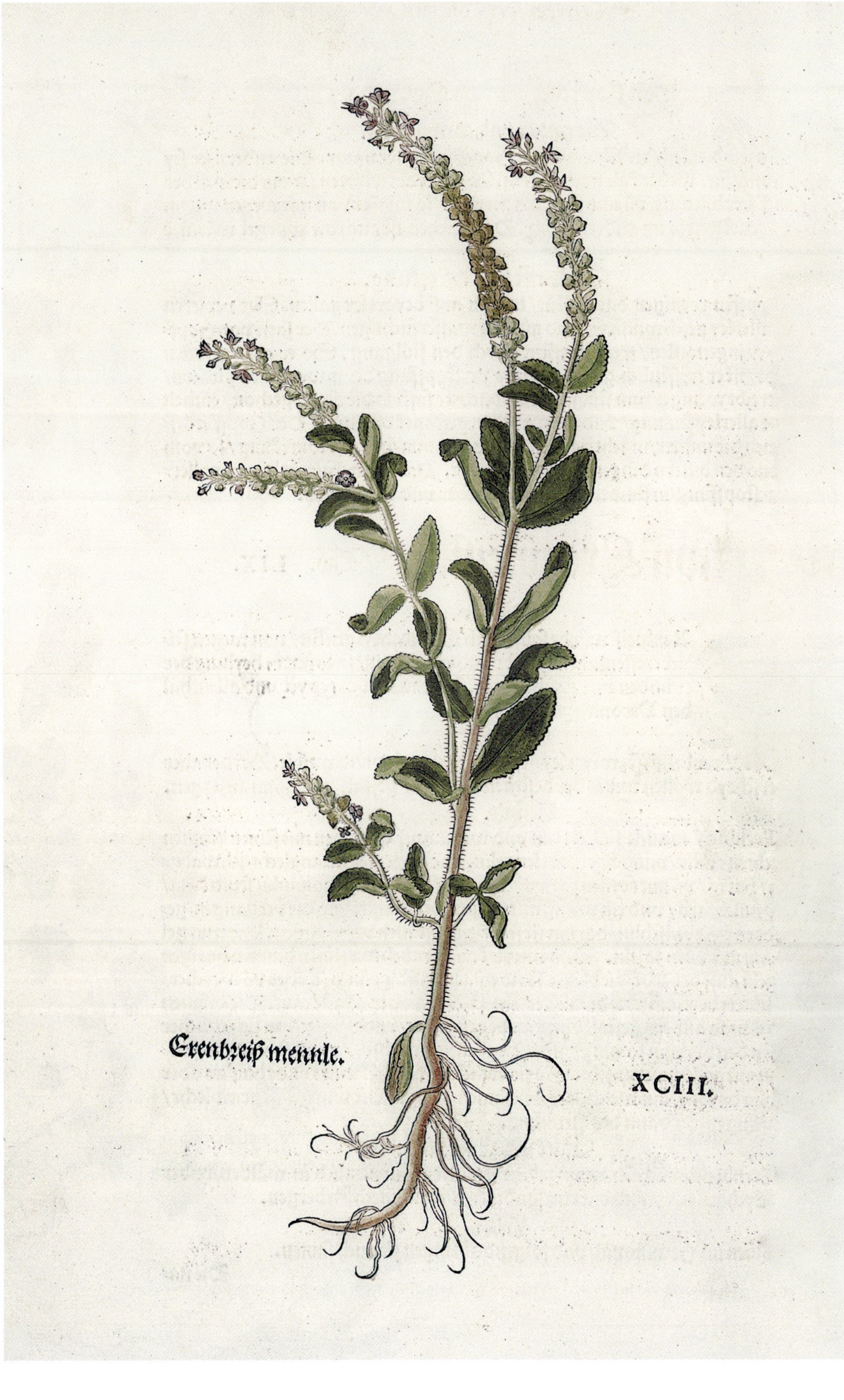
Erenbreiß mennle.
XCIII.

YELLOW STAR-OF-BETHLEHEM

Under the traditional German name of "Fildzwibel," or "Field Onion," we find the YELLOW STAR-OF-BETHLEHEM (LX; plate XCV), which was probably used only very rarely.

„FELDZWIBEL“

Hinter dem Namen „FELDZWIBEL“ (Cap. LX) verbirgt sich der zierliche WALD-GELBSTERN (Taf. XCV), der wohl nur sehr selten tatsächlich arzneilich verwendet wurde.

OIGNON DES CHAMPS

Sous le nom de «Feldzwibel» ou «OIGNON DES CHAMPS» (LX) se cache la gracile GAGÉE JAUNE (pl. XCV) dont l'usage thérapeutique était très rare.

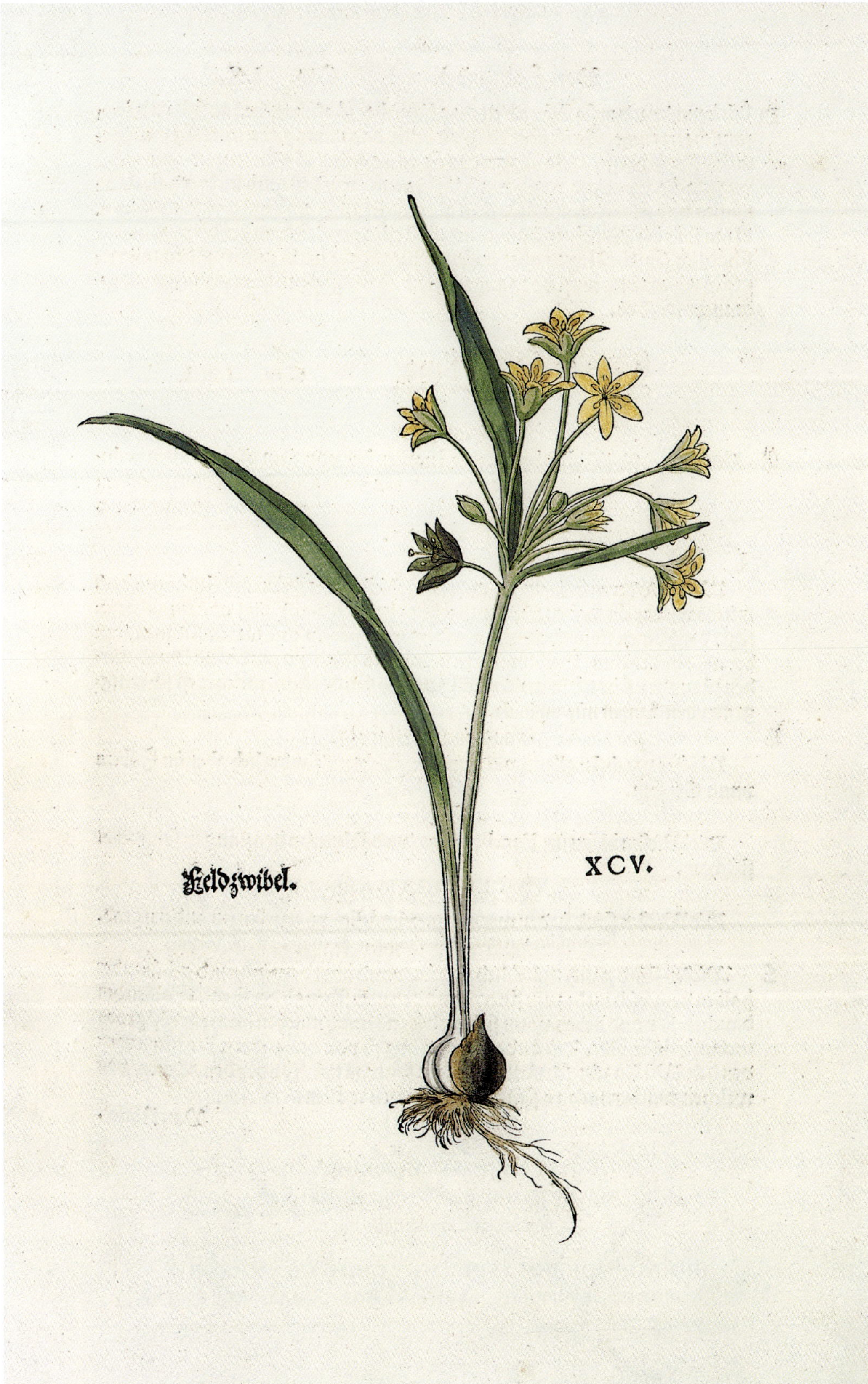

YELLOW STAR-OF-BETHLEHEM | „FELDZWIBEL“ | OIGNON DES CHAMPS

VETCHES

Fuchs apparently included VETCHES (LXI) only out of botanical interest, for they lack medical significance.

WICKEN

Die WICKEN (LXI) werden offenbar aus botanischem Interesse berücksichtigt, medizinische Gründe finden sich nicht.

VESCES CULTIVÉES

Les VESCES CULTIVÉES (LXI) sont présentées à l'évidence pour leur intérêt botanique puisqu'elles n'ont pas d'emploi en médecine.

PAGES 176, 177

ALL-SEED / TURNIP

Similarly, neither ALL-SEED (LXII) nor TURNIPS (LXIII) play a medicinal role.

„MAIER" / STECKRÜBE

Auch der „MAIER" (LXII) und die STECKRÜBEN (Cap. LXIII) spielen keine arzneiliche Rolle.

CHÉNOPODE POLYSPERME / CHOU CHAMPÊTRE

Le CHÉNOPODE POLYSPERME (LXII) et les CHOUX CHAMPÊTRES (LXIII) – navet rond et rave longue – ne jouent également aucun rôle en médecine.

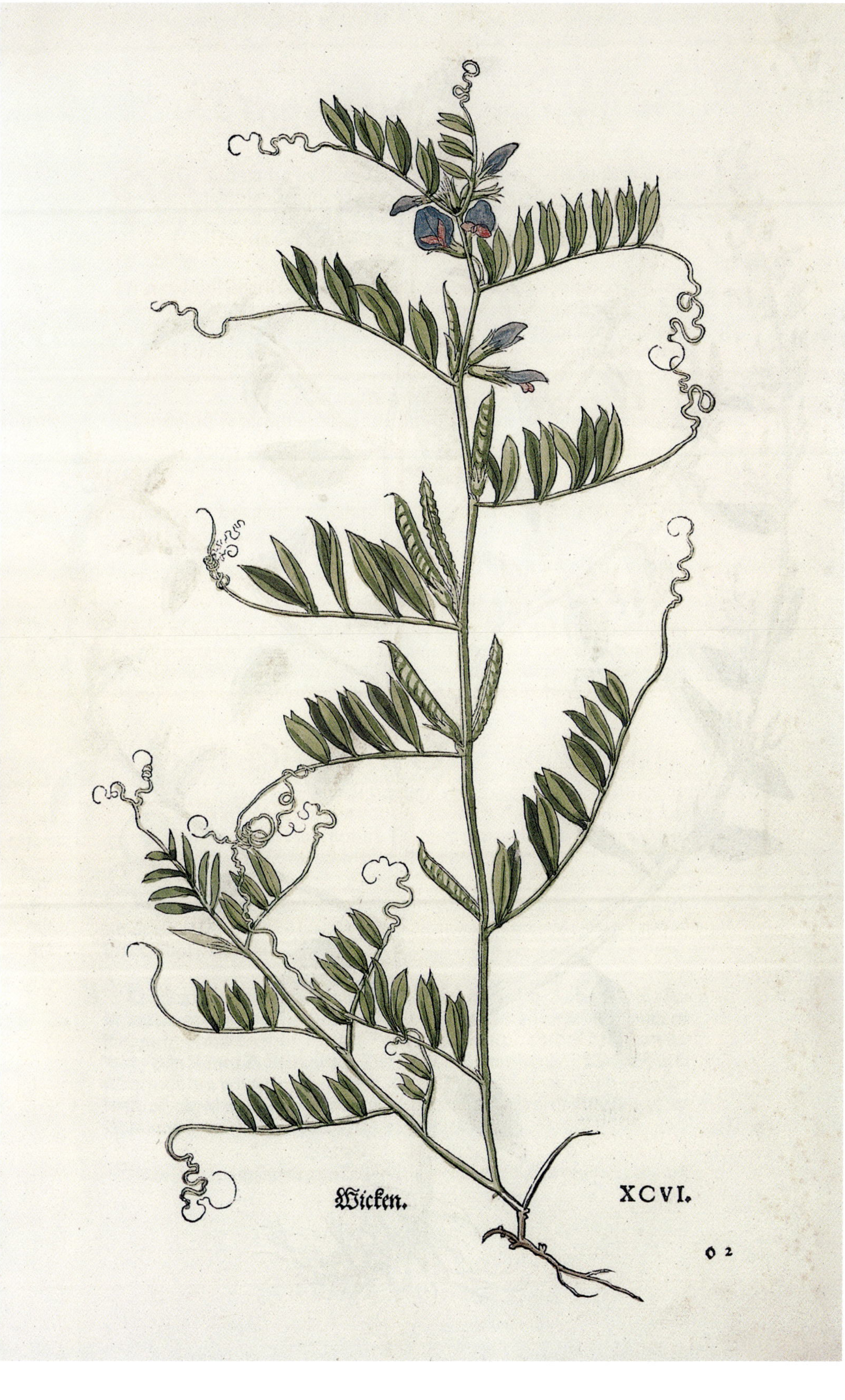
Wicken.
XCVI.
O 2

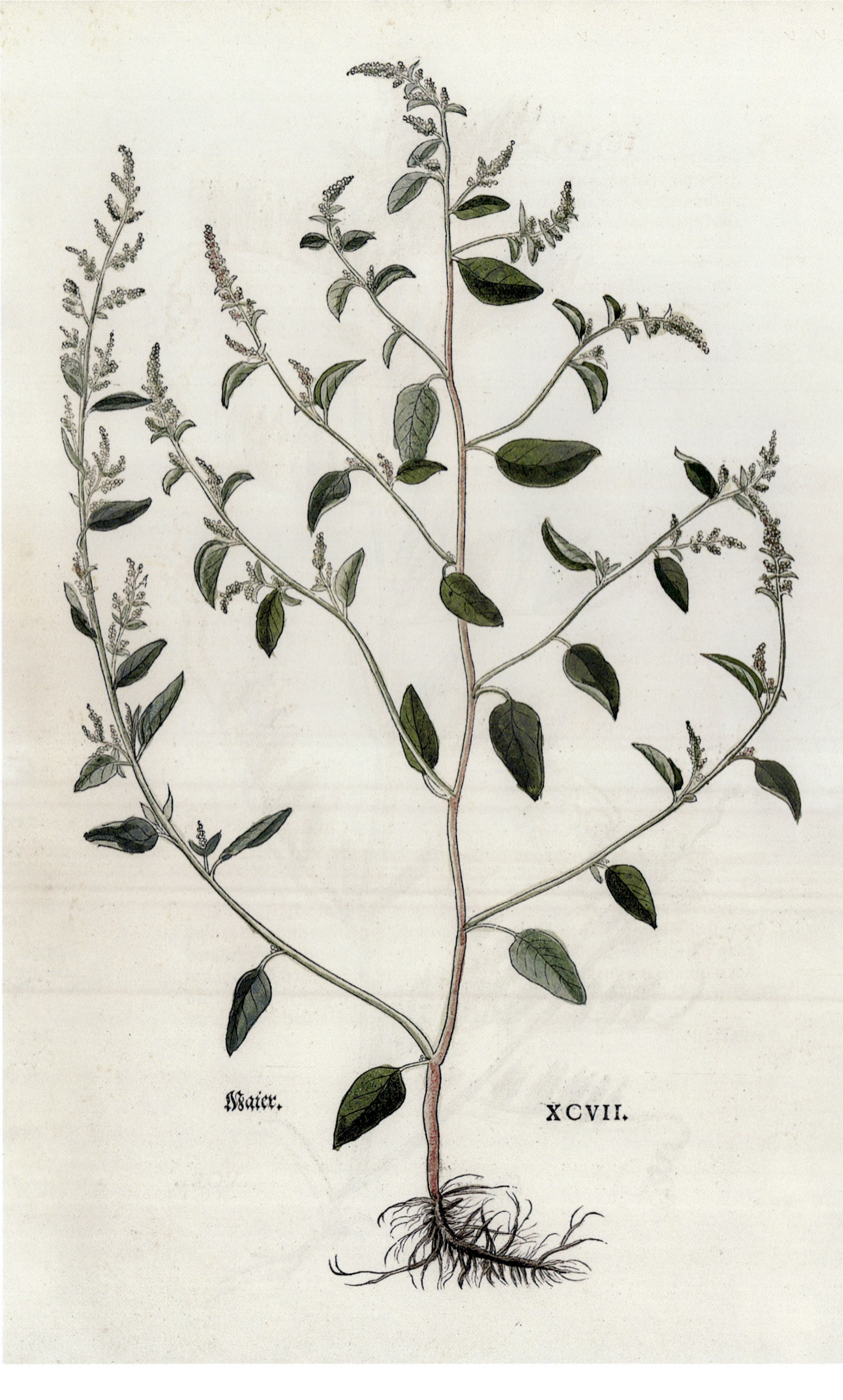
Maier.
XCVII.

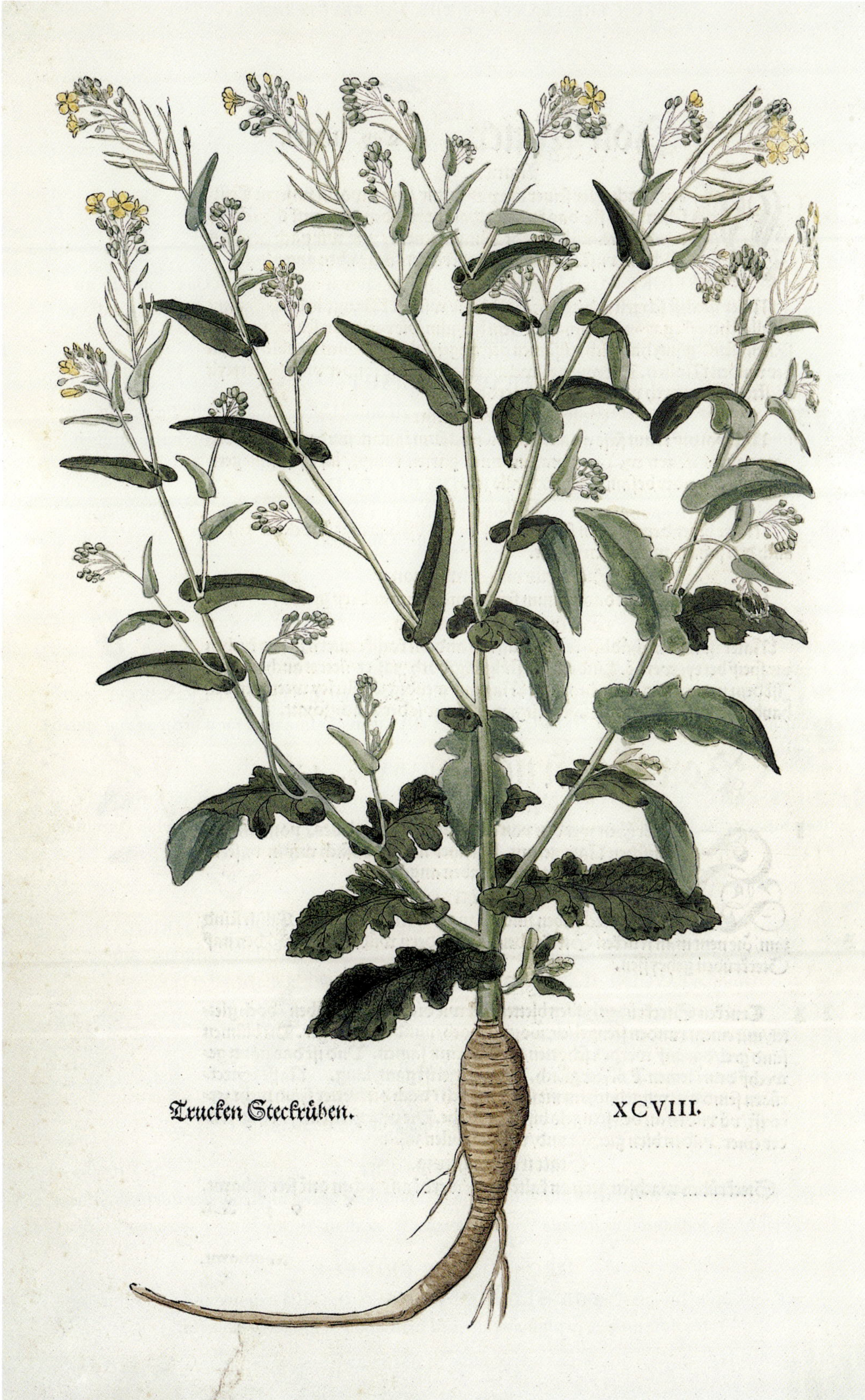

TURNIP | STECKRÜBE | CHOU CHAMPÊTRE

STICKY GOOSEFOOT

The entry for STICKY GOOSEFOOT (LXIIII), also known as Jerusalem Oak, contains an irregularity: as the herbal was being printed, the illustration of the plant was omitted, and was therefore added at the end of the book.

TRAUBENKRAUT

Beim TRAUBENKRAUT (Cap. LXIIII) kommt es zu einer Unregelmäßigkeit: die zugehörige Abbildung wurde beim Druck vergessen und findet sich am Ende des Bandes nachgetragen.

CHÉNOPODE BOTRYDE

La planche correspondant au CHÉNOPODE BOTRYDE (LXIIII), oubliée à l'impression, a été reportée en fin d'ouvrage.

PAGE 180

GOAT'S-BEARD

Owing to their bitter taste, both GOAT'S-BEARD (LXV) and MOTH MULLEIN (LXVI) were described as medicinal plants; COMMON OAT (LXVII) was recommended for diarrhoea and coughs.

„GEYSSBART"

„GEYSSBART" (Cap. LXV) und SCHABENKRAUT (Cap. LXVI) werden wegen ihres bitteren Geschmacks als Heilpflanzen beschrieben, HAFER (Cap. LXVII) zur Anwendung bei Durchfall und Husten empfohlen.

ARONCE DIOÏQUE

L'ARONCE DIOÏQUE (LXV), ou barbe-de-bouc, et la MOLÈNE BLATTAIRE (LXVI) sont décrites comme des plantes médicinales, car elles contiennent des principes amers. Quant à l'AVOINE (LXVII), elle est recommandée pour la diarrhée et la toux.

PAGE 181

GOOSEBERRY

Fuchs refers to the supposed power of GOOSEBERRY (LXVIII) to ward off danger, and for this reason, it was grown on fences.

„KRÜSELBEER"

Als „KRÜSELBEER" (Cap. LXVIII) wird die Stachelbeere bezeichnet, bei der Fuchs auf ihre vermeintlich schadenabwehrende Wirkung verweist, weshalb sie an Zäunen gezogen werde.

GROSEILLIER ÉPINEUX

Fuchs prête lui aussi au GROSEILLIER ÉPINEUX (LXVIII) le pouvoir de prévenir les dommages, expliquant ainsi sa plantation le long des clôtures.

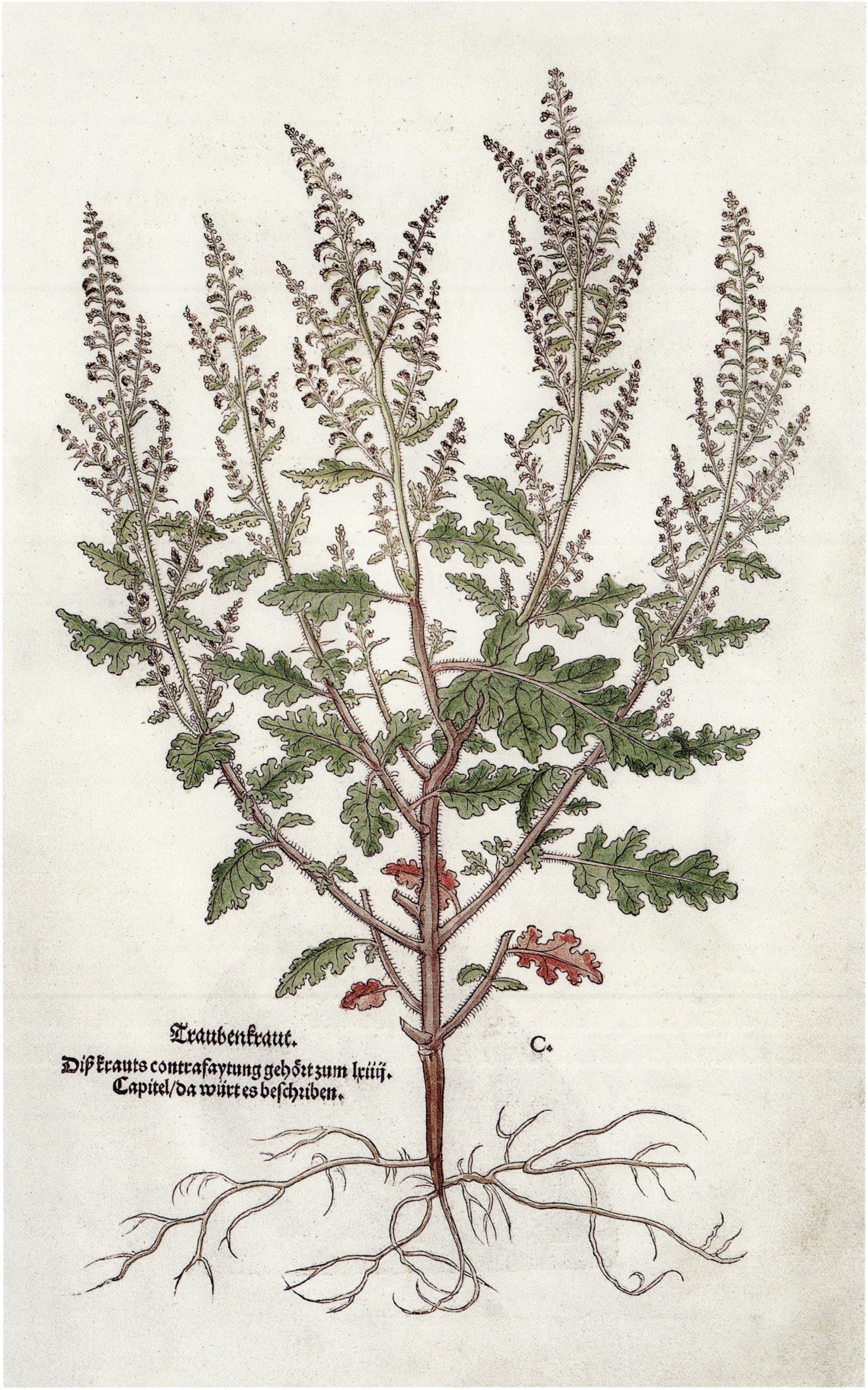
Traubenkraut.
Diß krauts contrafaytung gehört zum lxiiij.
Capitel/da würt es beschriben.
C.

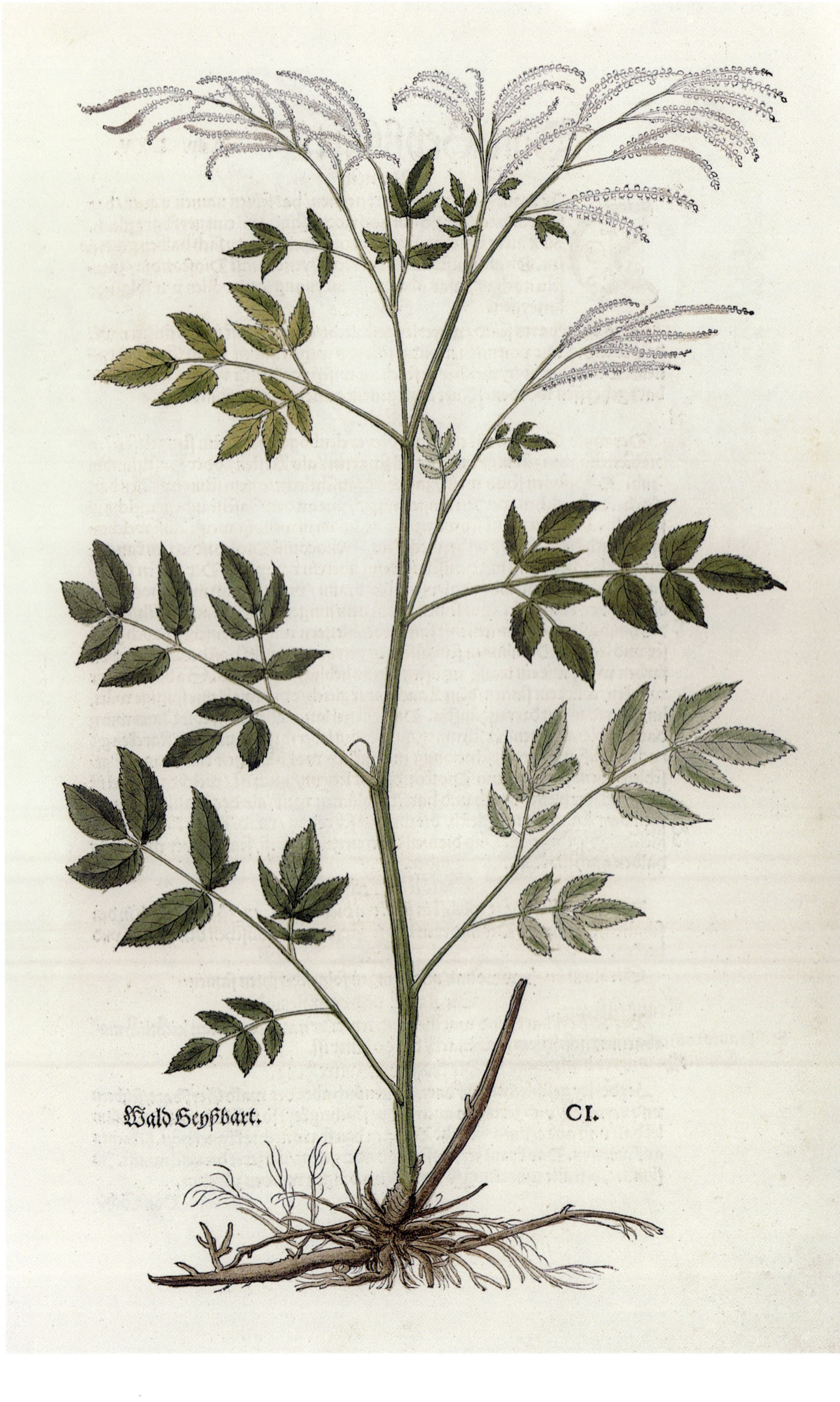
Wald Geyßbart.
CI.

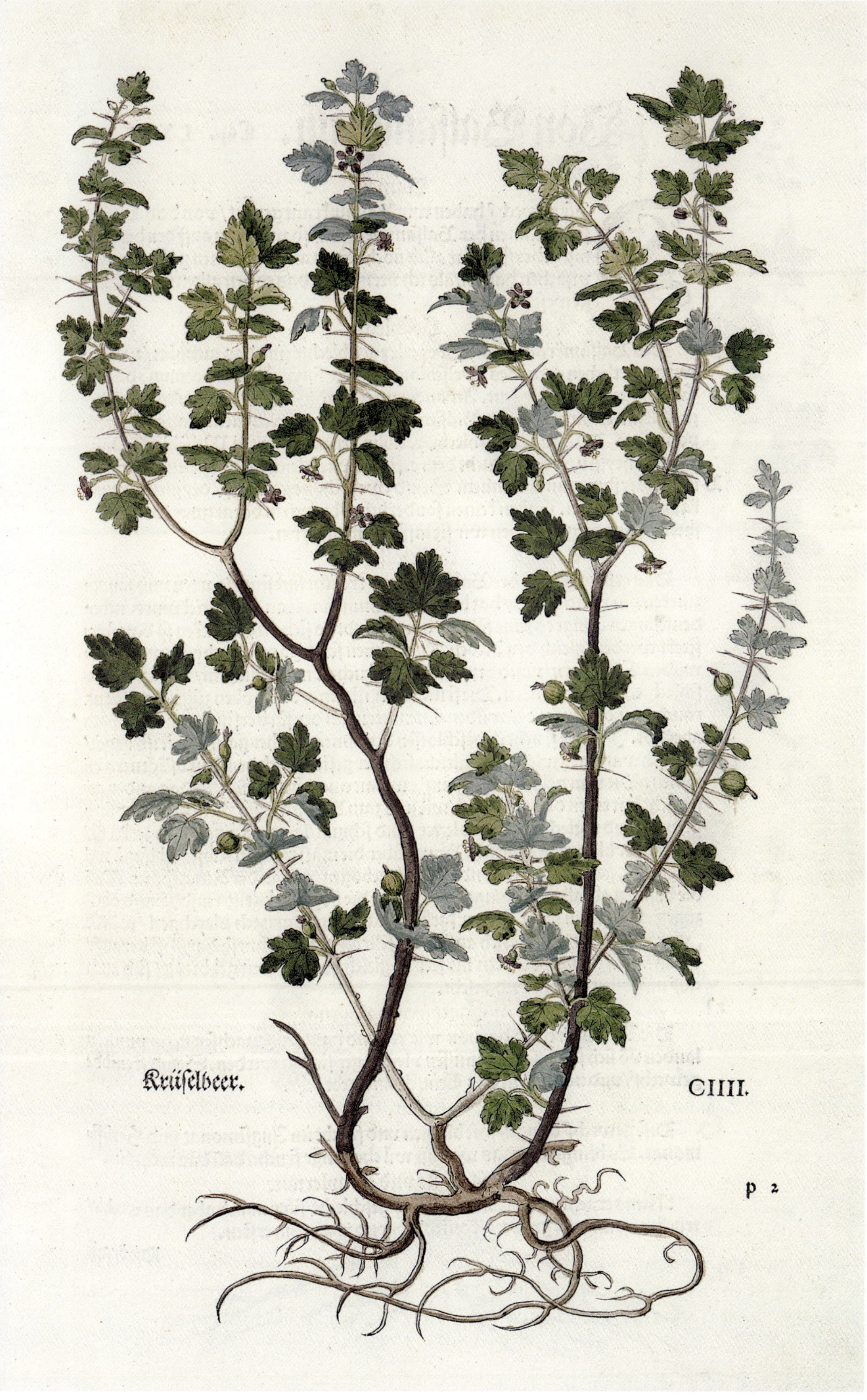

GOOSEBERRY | „KRÜSELBEER“ | GROSEILLIER ÉPINEUX

BALSAMS

Under the BALSAMS (LXIX), Fuchs combined two plants that had been only "recently brought to Germany" from Asia, and whose application was therefore still uncertain. The "male" Balsam Apple (MOMORDICA BALSAMINA; plate CV) is a form of gourd, whereas the "female" Garden Balsam, or Jewelweed (IMPATIENS BALSAMINA; plate CVI) is a member of the Balsam family.

BALSAMKRAUT

Unter der Bezeichnung BALSAMKRAUT (Cap. LXIX) vereint Fuchs zwei Pflanzen, die aus Asien erst „newlich in das Teutschland gebracht" wurden und deren Anwendung deshalb noch nicht gesichert ist. Beim „mennle" handelt es sich um MOMORDICA BALSAMINA (Taf. CV), ein Kürbisgewächs, beim „weible" um IMPATIENS BALSAMINA (Taf. CVI), aus der Familie der Balsaminengewächse.

BALSAMINES

Sous la dénomination de «BALSAMINES» (LXIX) Fuchs associe deux plantes originaires d'Asie, récemment introduites en Allemagne («newlich in das Teutschland gebracht») et dont l'emploi, évidemment, n'est pas encore bien défini. La première, «masculine», est la POMME DE MERVEILLE (pl. CV), une Cucurbitacée comestible, et la seconde, «féminine», est la BALSAMINE DES JARDINS (pl. CVI), de la famille des Balsaminacées.

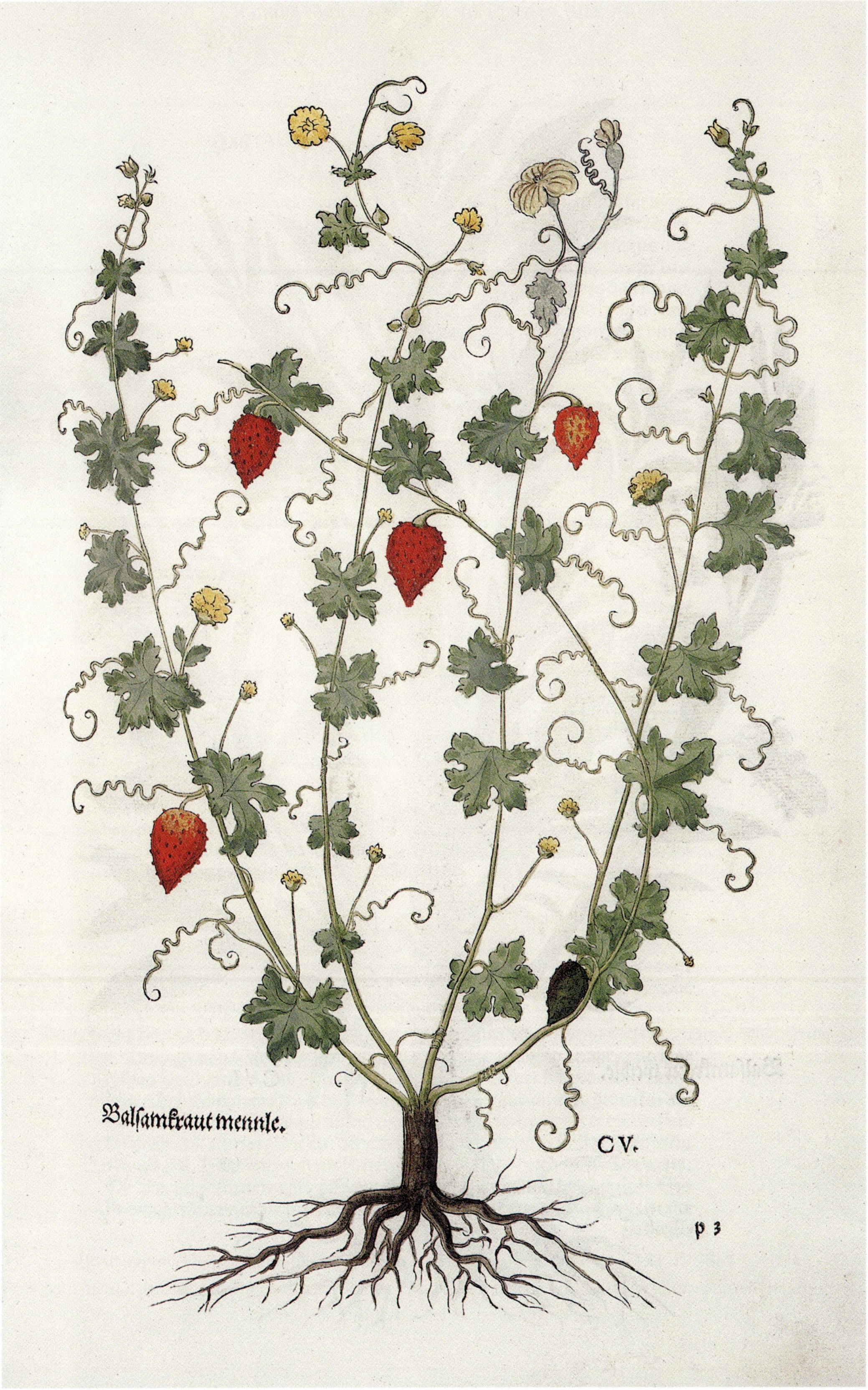
Balſamkraut mennle.
CV.
p 3

LICORICE

LICORICE (LXX) or Sweet root, garnered high praise – the variety grown in Bamberg being particularly famous. Preparations made from the root were quite properly used against hoarseness and inflammations of the mucous lining of the stomach, for example.

„SÜESSHOLTZ“

Mit großem Lob wird das „SÜESSHOLTZ“ (Cap. LXX) erwähnt, von dem besonders das aus Bamberg stammende berühmt war. Zubereitungen aus der Wurzel wurden z. B. bei Heiserkeit und Magenschleimhautentzündung zu Recht eingesetzt.

RÉGLISSE

La RÉGLISSE (LXX) est louée ici pour ses vertus curatives ; celle de Bamberg, en particulier, jouissait d’une grande réputation. Les préparations à base de rhizome étaient utilisées à juste titre pour l’enrouement et les irritations d’estomac.

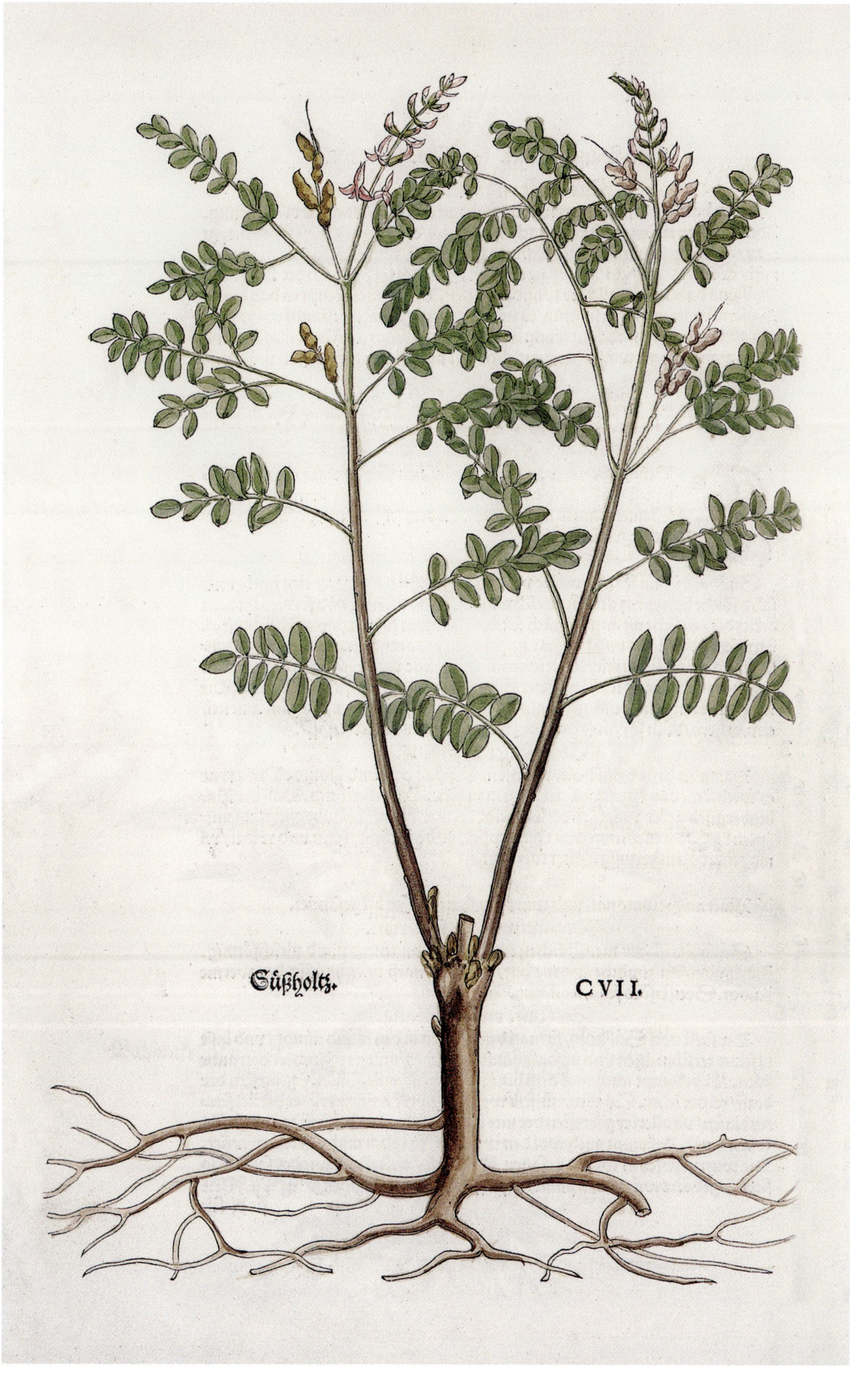
Süßholtz.
CVII.

WATER BETONY

WATER BETONY (LXXI), or Water figwort, was chiefly applied externally, but could also act internally against worms.

„BRAUNWURTZ“

„BRAUNWURTZ“ (Cap. LXXI) wurde überwiegend äußerlich angewendet, konnte aber auch bei der Einnahme als Wurmmittel wirken.

SCROPHULAIRE AURICULÉE

La SCROPHULAIRE AURICULÉE (LXXI), était employée surtout en usage externe, mais elle pouvait s'administrer aussi comme vermifuge.

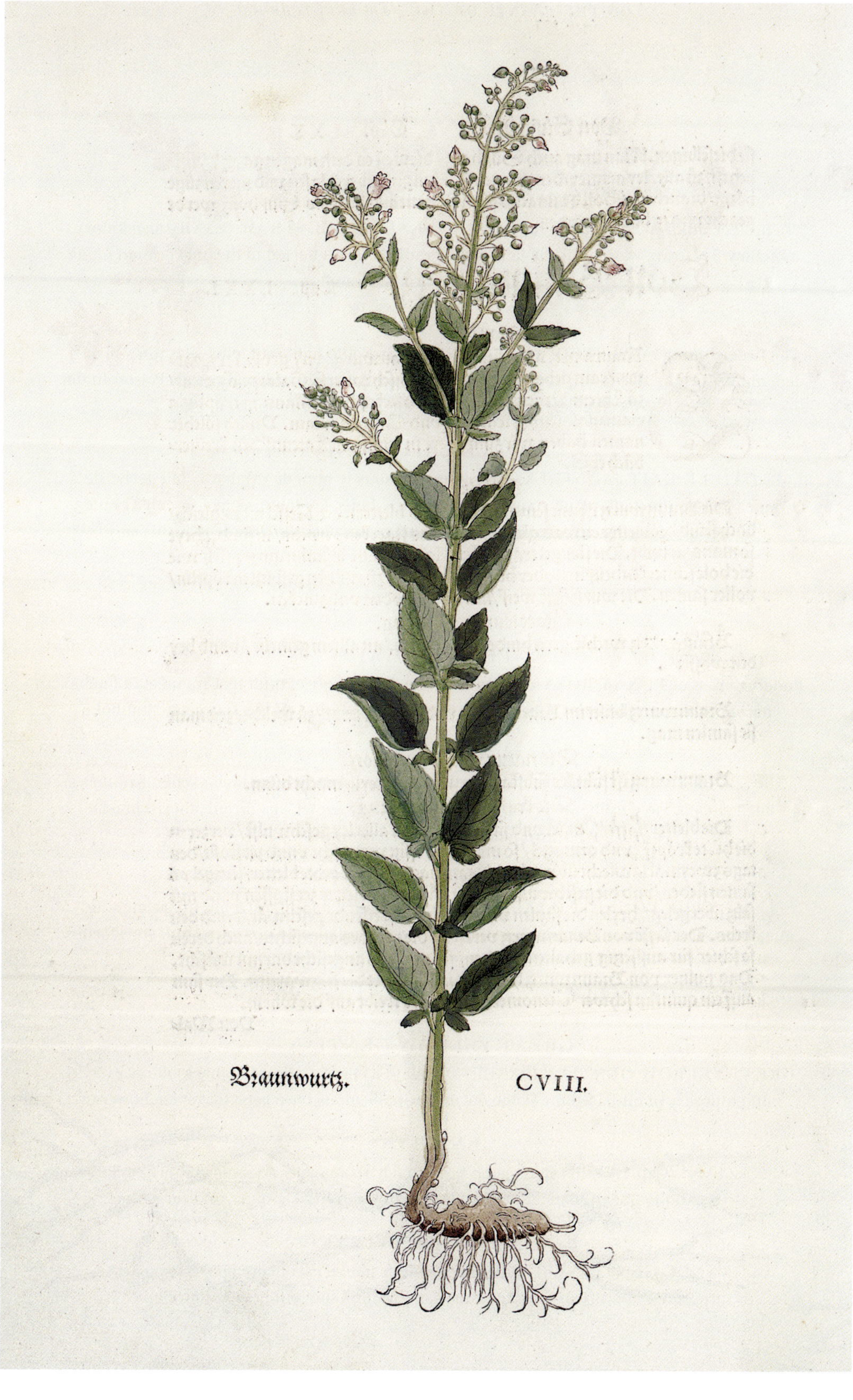
Braunwurtz.
CVIII.

DRIED LADY'S BEDSTRAW

To protect children against witchcraft DRIED LADY'S BEDSTRAW (LXXII), also known as Yellow Bedstraw, was popularly laid in the cradle, a use reflected in the old German name for the plant "Cradle straw."

„WALSTRO"

Die Bezeichnung „WALSTRO" (Cap. LXXII) für das Echte Labkraut leitet sich von „Wagel", dem alten Wort für Wiege, ab, denn die getrockneten Pflanzen wurden gerne als Polster in die Wiegen gelegt, um die Kinder vor Zauberei zu schützen.

CAILLE-LAIT JAUNE

Le CAILLE-LAIT JAUNE (LXXII) apparaît ici sous le nom de « Walstro » qui dérive de « Wagel », ancien mot allemand signifiant « berceau ». Jadis, la plante séchée servait à confectionner des coussins qu'on plaçait dans les berceaux pour éloigner le mauvais sort.

PAGE 190

PENNY-ROYAL

Pudding grass or PENNY-ROYAL (LXXIII), is the first variety of mint that we meet in Fuchs's herbal. Although the plant is hardly used today, its essential oil is a source of Menthol.

„POLEY"

Die „POLEY" (Cap. LXXIII) ist die erste Minzenart, auf die wir im Fuchs'schen Kräuterbuch stoßen. Sie wird heute praktisch nicht mehr verwendet, aus ihrem ätherischen Öl wird jedoch Menthol gewonnen.

MENTHE POULIOT

La MENTHE POULIOT (LXXIII), ou herbe de Saint-Laurent, est la première menthe que nous trouvons dans l'herbier. Elle n'est plus guère utilisée de nos jours, sauf sous forme de menthol, extrait de son huile essentielle.

PAGE 191

GREAT YELLOW GENTIAN

GREAT YELLOW GENTIAN (LXXIIII) still plays a certain role as stomach bitters even in contemporary plant-based medicine; its other applications have been forgotten, however.

„ENTZIAN"

„ENTZIAN" (Cap. LXXIIII) spielt auch heute noch als magenwirksames Bittermittel eine gewisse Rolle in der Pflanzenheilkunde, die anderen Indikationen sind vergessen.

GRANDE GENTIANE

La GRANDE GENTIANE (LXXIIII), de couleur jaune, est encore appréciée pour ses propriétés apéritives, mais ses autres indications sont oubliées aujourd'hui.

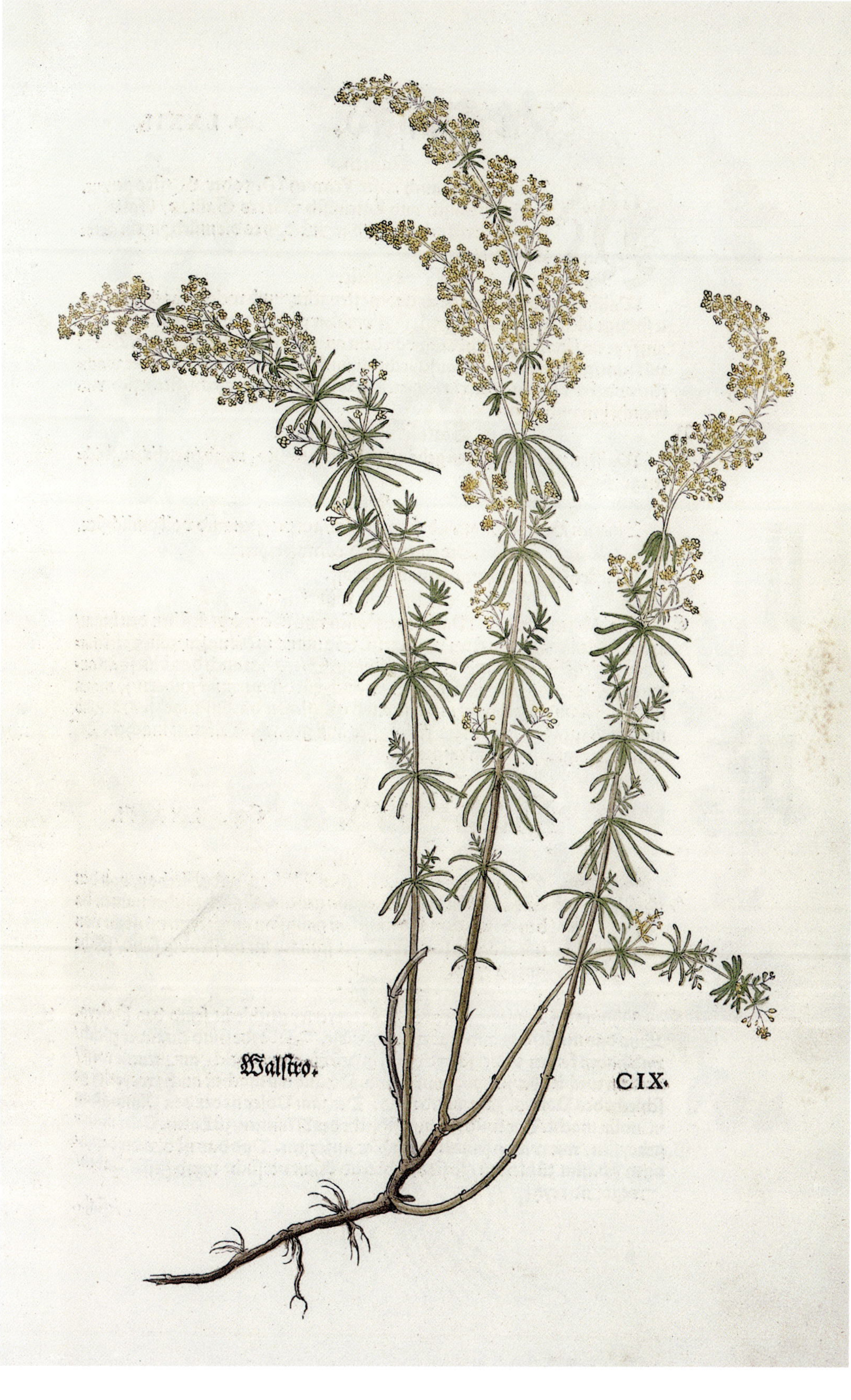
Walstro.
CIX.

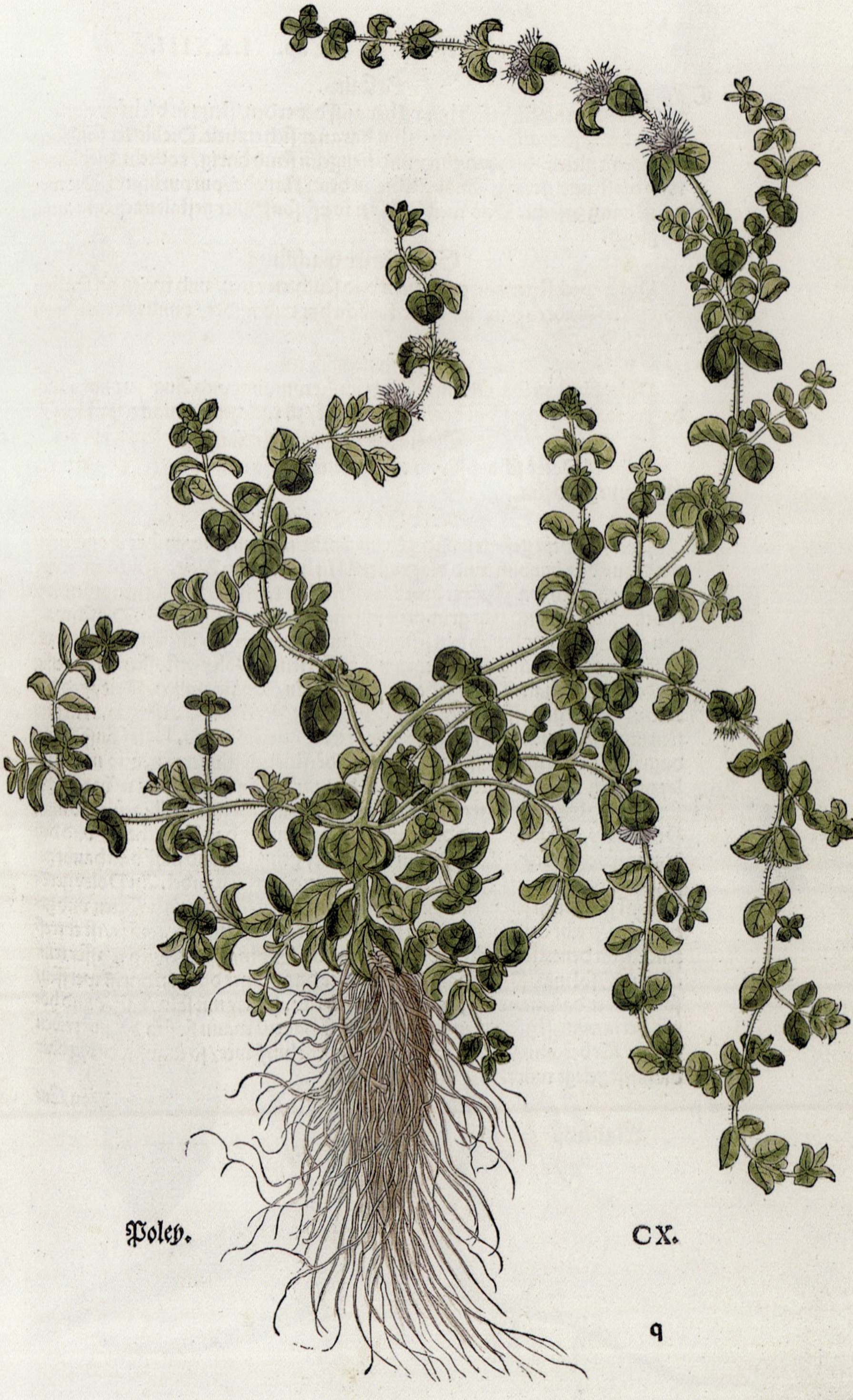

Poley. CX.

q

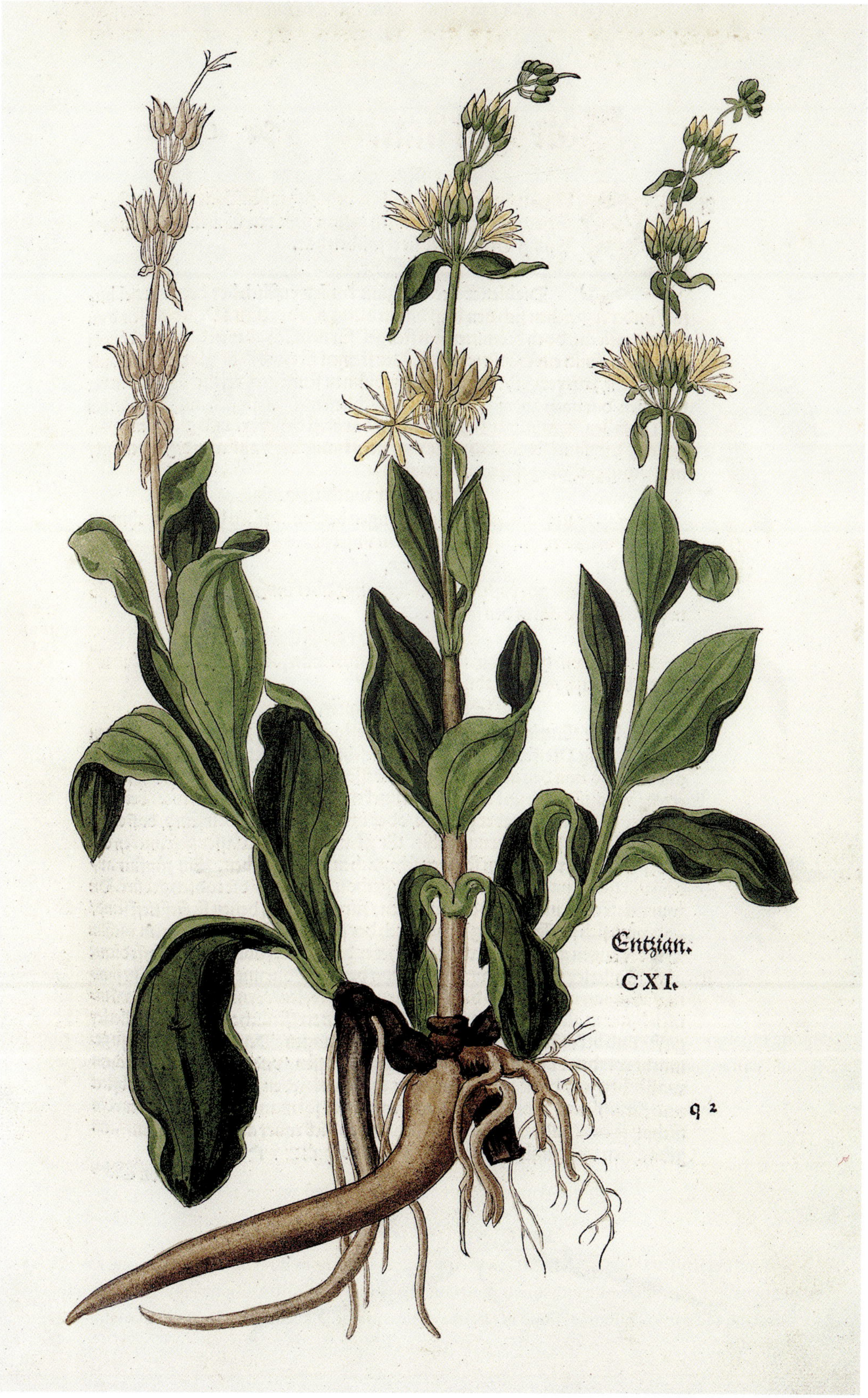
Entzian.
CXI.
q 2

COTTAGE PEONY

Among the uses of common or COTTAGE PEONY (LXXV) was its supposed effect against spastic and painful paralysis of the limbs, for which the root was bound around the patient's neck.

„GICHTWURTZ“

Die Pfingstrose erscheint unter dem Namen „GICHTWURTZ“ (Cap. LXXV), weil sie neben anderen Anwendungen auch gegen das Gegicht, epilepsieartige Krampfanfälle, wirken sollte und dazu die Wurzel um den Hals gebunden wurde.

PIVOINE OFFICINALE

La PIVOINE OFFICINALE (LXXV) apparaît sous le nom de «racine de la goutte» («Gichtwurtz»). Ses tubercules n'étaient pourtant pas seulement utilisés pour cette maladie, mais aussi, pendus autour du cou, pour l'éclampsie, une maladie accompagnée de convulsions.

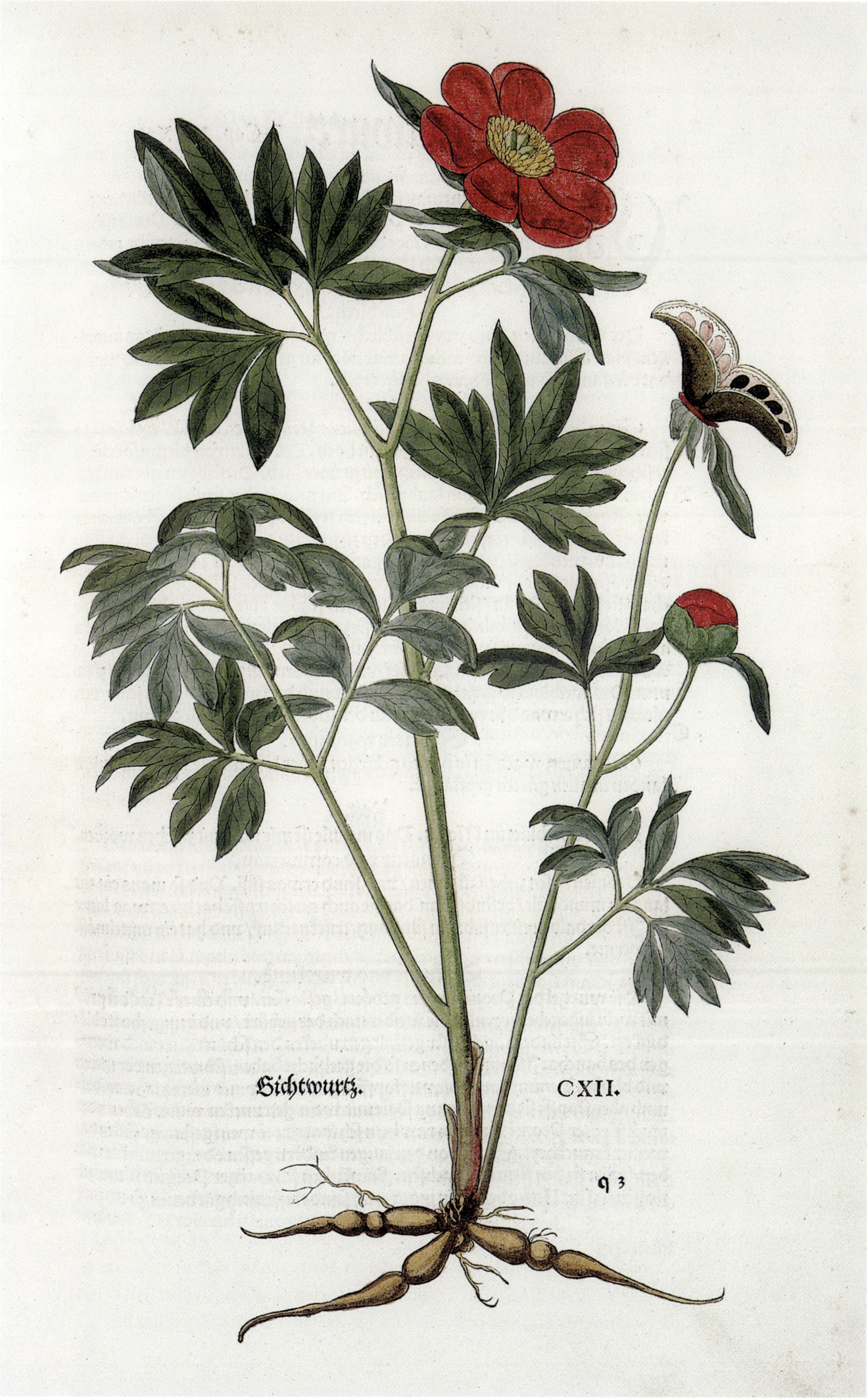
Gichtwurtz.
CXII.
q 3

CRANESBILL

Six varieties of CRANESBILL, STORKSBILL, and HERB ROBERT (LXXVI) are illustrated in this chapter, which also provides descriptions of their various effects.

STORCHSCHNABEL

Sechs Arten der Gattung STORCHSCHNABEL (Cap. LXXVI) werden im Bild vorgestellt und ihre unterschiedlichen Wirkungen besprochen.

GÉRANIUM

Fuchs présente six espèces de GÉRANIUM (LXXVI) en indiquant leurs effets respectifs.

PAGES 196, 197

RUTABAGA / CHERVIL

The chapter on RUTABAGA and RED BEET (LXXVII; plate CXIX), which also includes Bellflower, or RAMPION (plate CXXI) as a "wild kind," once again presents a food that is also used for medical purposes. In the case of CHERVIL (LXXVIII), Fuchs describes a well-known herb that is "more a medicine than a food."

RÜBEN / KERBEL

Mit den RÜBEN (Cap. LXXVII; Taf. CXIX), zu denen auch die „RAPUNTZEL" (Taf. CXXI) als „wild geschlecht" gerechnet wird, begegnet uns wieder ein Nahrungsmittel, das auch medizinischen Einsatz finden kann und mit dem KERBEL (Cap. LXXVIII) ein bekanntes Gewürz, das „mehr ein artzney dann ein speys" ist.

BETTERAVES / CERFEUIL

Voici d'autres plantes comestibles et médicinales présentées sous le nom de « Rüben » (LXXVII ; pl. CXIX) ou BETTERAVES : le rutabaga et la betterave rouge, auxquels Fuchs ajoute la CAMPANULE RAIPONCE (pl. CXXI), qu'il qualifie de « variété sauvage », et le CERFEUIL (LXXVIII), un condiment connu qui est « plus un remède qu'un aliment » selon lui.

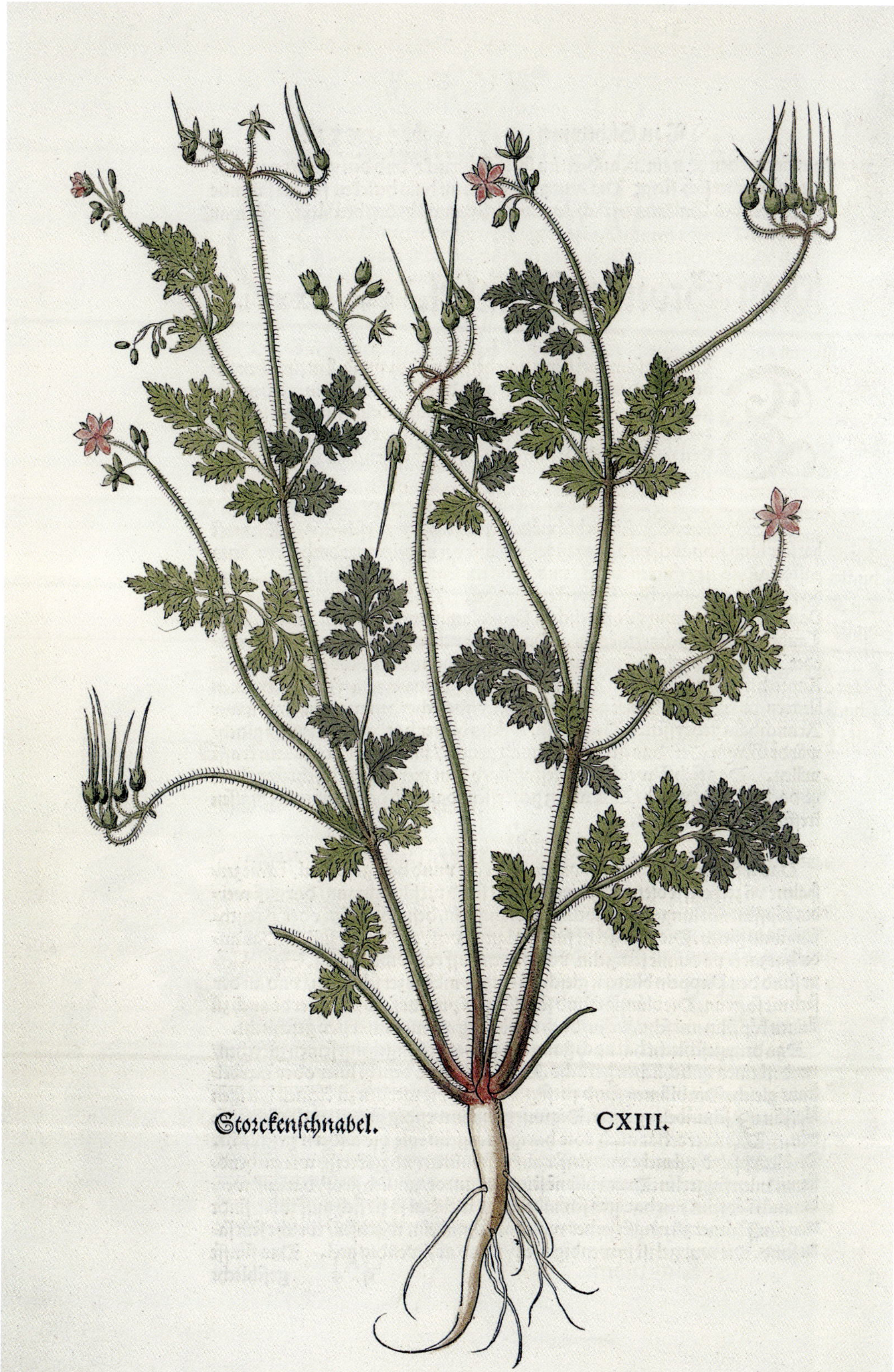

Storckenschnabel. CXIII.

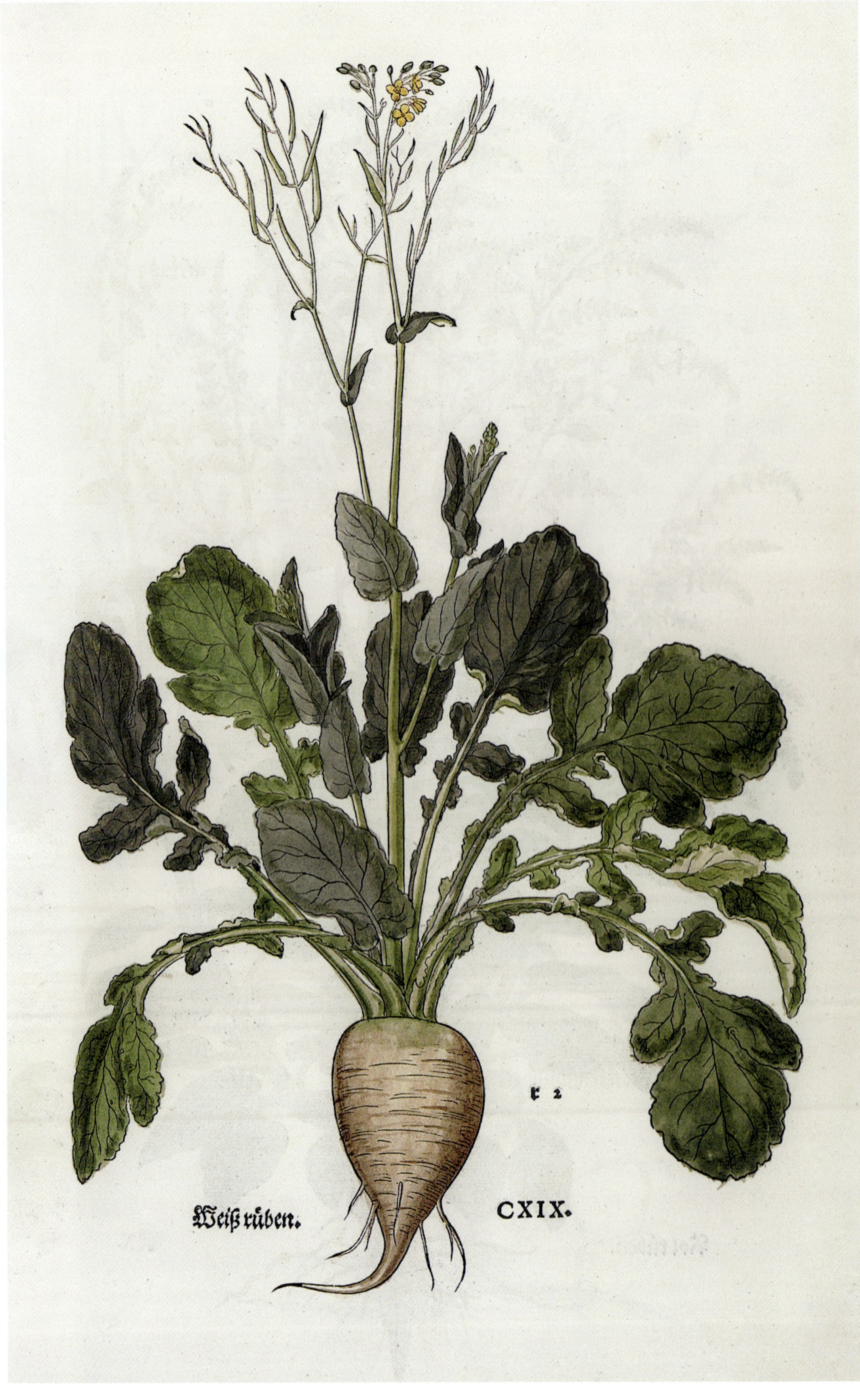
k 2
Weiß rüben.
CXIX.

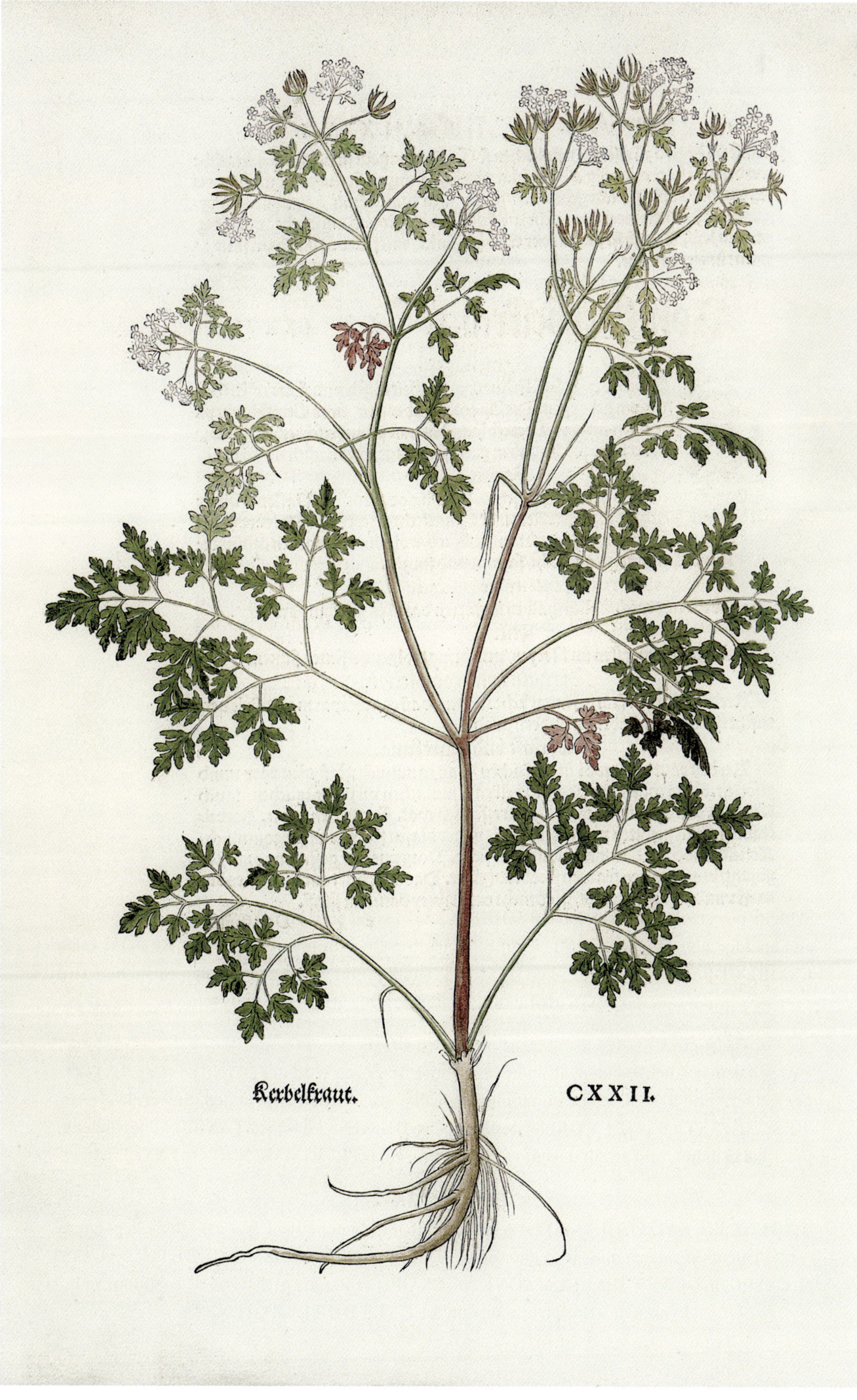
Kerbelkraut.
CXXII.

BROOM

With its powerful purgative effect, BROOM (LXXIX) is recommended not only against podagra and bladder stones, but also against goitre. In contrast to common or SCOTCH BROOM (plate CXXIII), GERMAN BROOM (plate CXXIIII) is smaller and grows closer to the earth, hence its German name "Erdtpfrimmen" (LXXX).

„GINST"

Wegen seiner ausführenden, also entwässernden Wirkung wird der „GINST" (Cap. LXXIX) bei Podagra und Blasensteinen empfohlen, soll aber auch beim Kropf helfen. Im Vergleich zum BESENGINSTER (Taf. CXXIII) ist der DEUTSCHE GINSTER (Taf. CXXIIII) kleinwüchsig, erdnäher, und erhält deshalb den Namen „ERDTPFRIMMEN" (Cap. LXXX).

GENÊT À BALAIS

Le GENÊT À BALAIS (LXXIX) est recommandé pour son pouvoir évacuant dans la podagre et les calculs vésicaux, mais il soignerait aussi le goitre. Plus petit que le GENÊT À BALAIS (pl. CXXIII), le GENÊT D'ALLEMAGNE (pl. CXXIIII) croît plus près de terre, ce qui lui vaut ici le nom de « Erdtpfrimmen » ou ALÊNES DE TERRE (LXXX).

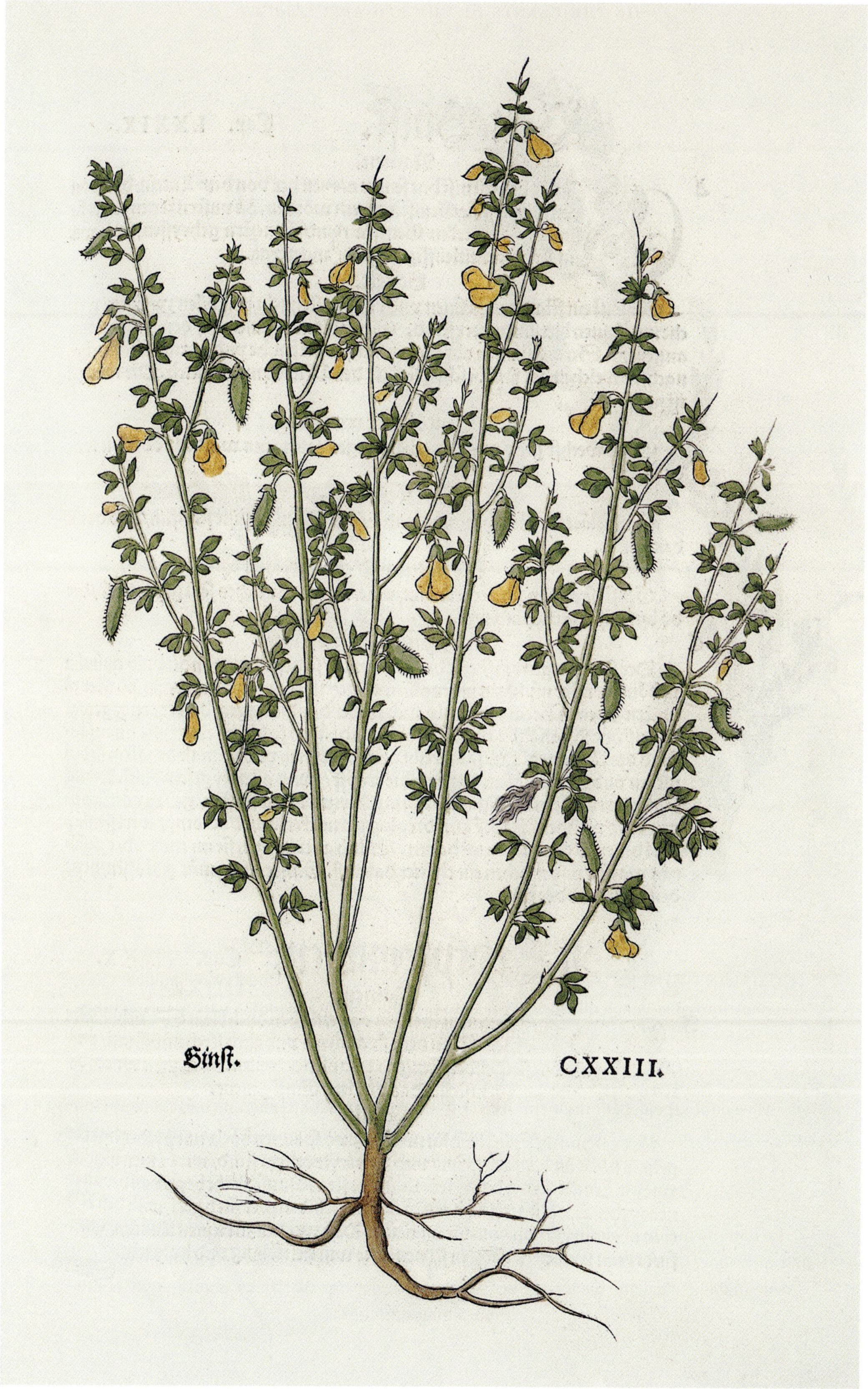
Ginst.
CXXIII.

COMMON CUDWEED

COMMON CUDWEED (LXXXI), also known as Cottonrose or Cuddleweed, appears as a remedy for red stomach discharge (the colour is the result of blood), a bacterial dysentery accompanied by strong cramps.

RUHRKRAUT

Das Anwendungsgebiet kommt beim RUHRKRAUT (Cap. LXXXI) bereits im Pflanzennamen zum Ausdruck, denn es galt als Medizin beim roten, weil blutigen Bauchfluss, einer von starken Krämpfen begleiteten bakteriellen Dysenterie.

COTONNIÈRE VULGAIRE

Le nom même de la plante, «Ruhrkraut» ou herbe de la dysenterie, indique son emploi thérapeutique. La COTONNIÈRE VULGAIRE (LXXXI) était en effet employée pour soigner cette maladie d'origine bactérielle se caractérisant par une diarrhée sanguinolente et des coliques abdominales.

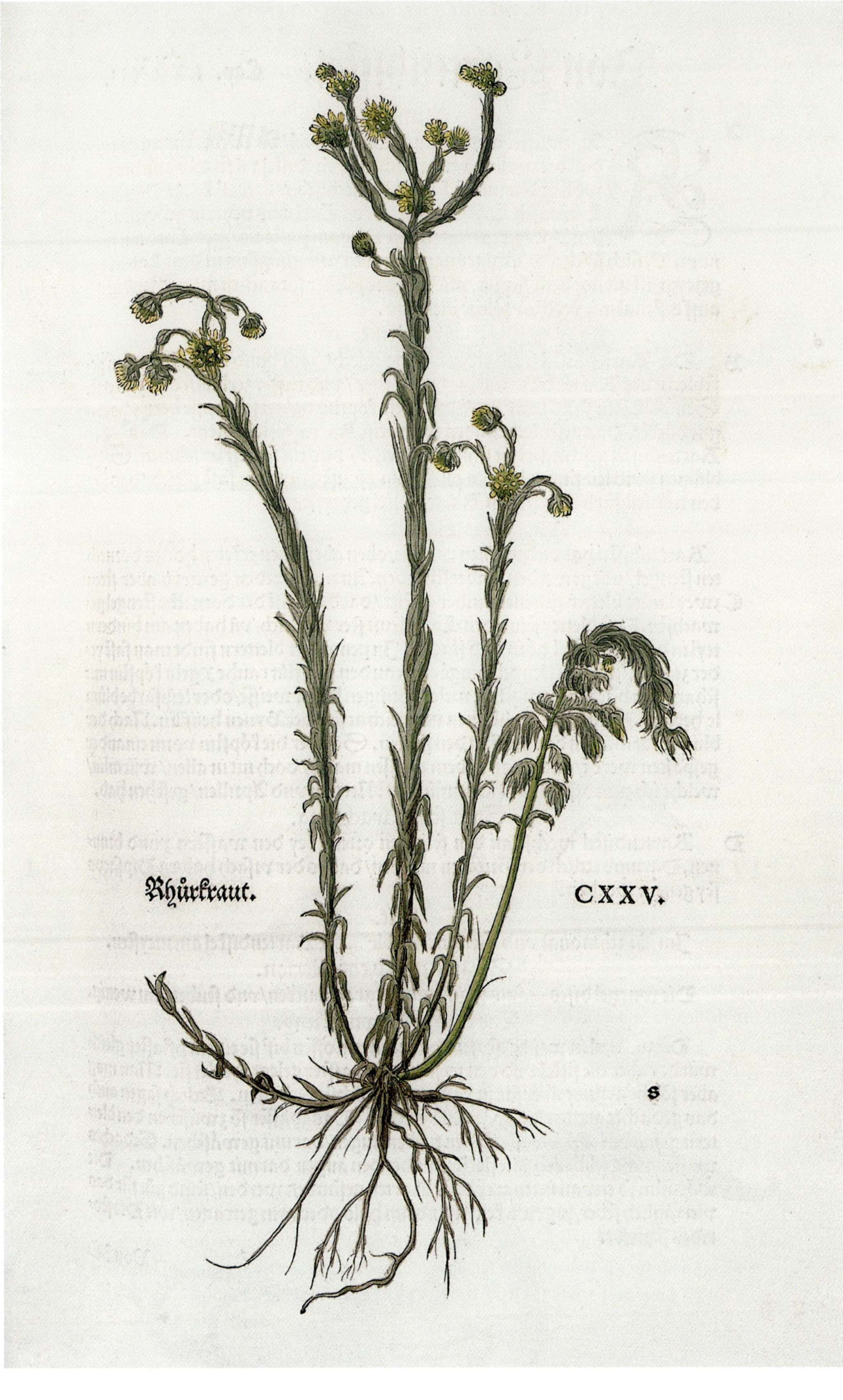
Rhůrkraut.
CXXV.
s

FULLER'S TEASEL

Today we can only wonder that medical power was ever attributed to the water gathered in the leaves and even the "little worm" in the stalk of FULLER'S TEASEL and COMMON TEASEL (LXXXII).

WEBERDISTEL / KARDENDISTEL

Bei der WEBER- oder KARDENDISTEL (Cap. LXXXII) wundern wir uns heute, dass dem in den Blättern gesammelten Wasser und sogar den „würmlin" im Stängel Arzneikraft zugeschrieben wurde.

CARDÈRE

On s'étonne aujourd'hui que l'eau retenue par les feuilles en forme de tube corolle et même le «petit ver» («Würmlin» = ici, parasite) qui loge sur sa tige aient suffi autrefois pour prêter à la CARDÈRE (LXXXII) des vertus médicinales.

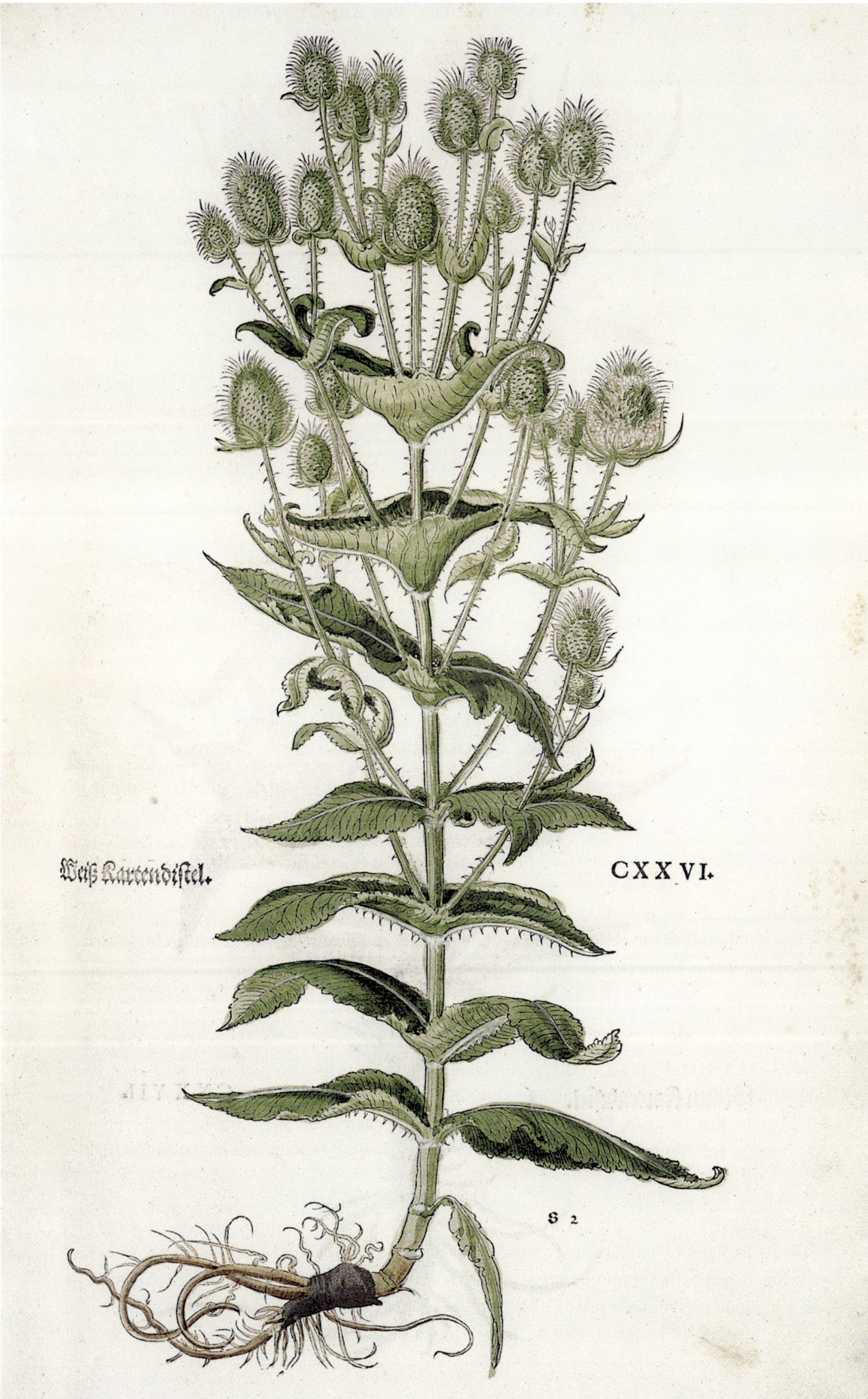

FULLER'S TEASEL | WEBERDISTEL | CARDÈRE

MEZEREON

Today, the highly poisonous nature of MEZEREON (LXXXIII), or Paradise Plant, is well known; therefore the claims made by Fuchs for its application are all the more surprising, especially his claim that 15 "grains" (fruits? seeds?) "purge thoroughly" – for swallowing even ten of the seeds can be lethal.

„ZEILAND"

Als „ZEILAND" (Cap. LXXXIII) ist der Seidelbast heute sicherlich nicht mehr bekannt, umso mehr aber als sehr giftige Pflanze, und deshalb überraschen die Angaben, die Fuchs zur Anwendung macht, insbesondere die Behauptung, dass 15 „Körner" (Früchte, Samen?) „volkommenlich purgieren", denn beim Verschlucken von zehn Früchten besteht bereits Lebensgefahr.

DAPHNÉ

Le DAPHNÉ (LXXXIII), dit aussi BOIS-GENTIL, est plus connu de nos jours comme plante hautement toxique que comme «liber des dieux» («Zeiland» en allemand). Aussi les vertus thérapeutiques mentionnées par Fuchs ne peuvent-elles que surprendre, en particulier lorsqu'il préconise la prise de 15 «grains» (fruits, graines ?) pour «purger parfaitement», alors que l'ingestion de 10 fruits seulement peut être mortelle.

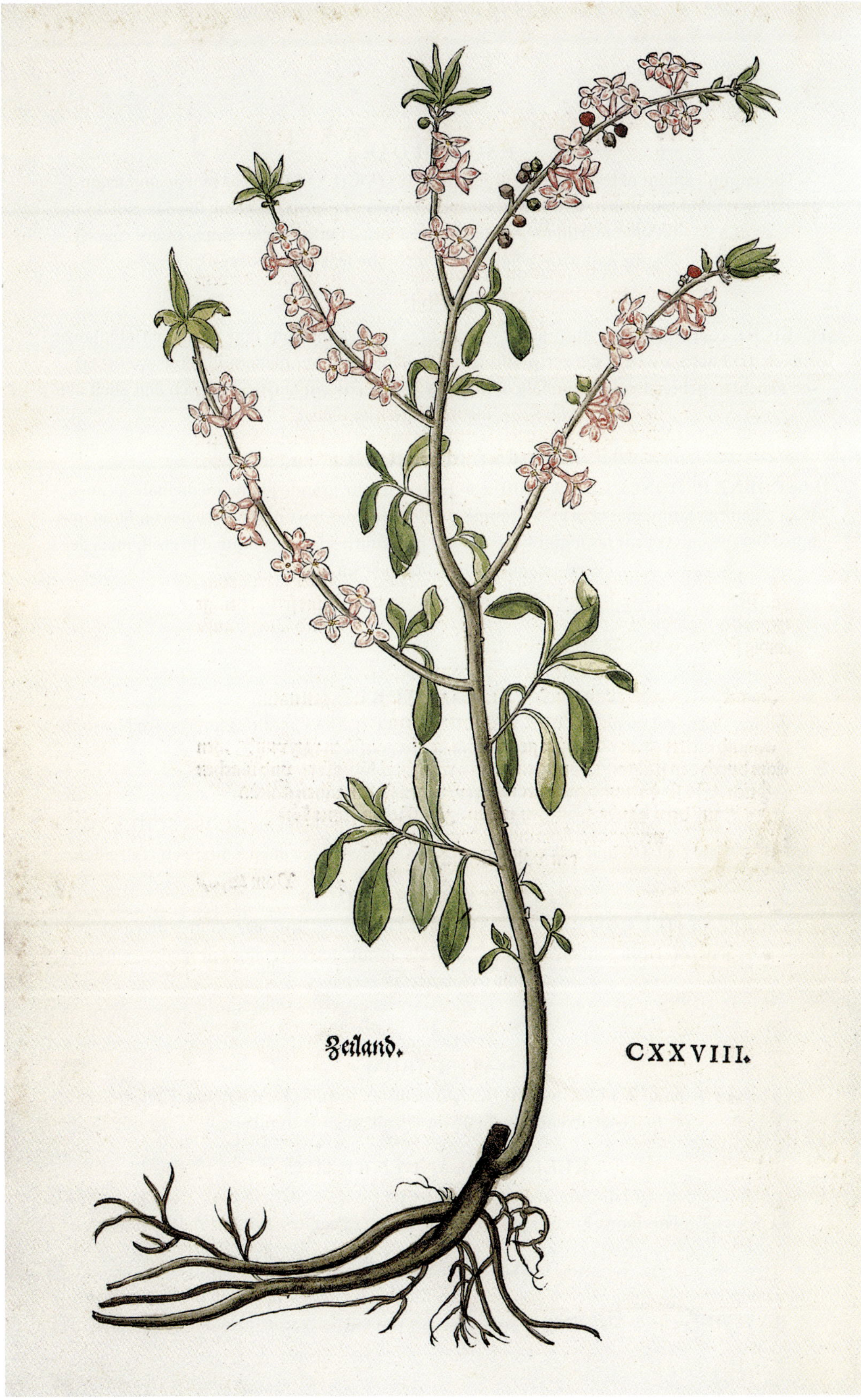
Zeiland.
CXXVIII.

ENGLISH OAK

The tannin content of Pedunculate, or ENGLISH OAK (LXXXIIII) makes it as important a medicinal plant today as it was earlier. Fuchs is however in error in seeing the oak-gall on the leaves as a second kind of fruit in addition to the acorns, for these excrescences are caused by the gall wasp when it punctures the leaf to lay its eggs.

EICHE

Die EICHE (Cap. LXXXIIII) war und ist wegen ihres Gerbstoffgehalts eine wichtige Heilpflanze, doch irrt Fuchs, wenn er die gerbstoffreichen Galläpfel auf den Blättern für eine zweite Art von Früchten neben den Eicheln hält, denn diese Wucherungen entstehen durch den Stich der Gallwespe, die dort ihre Eier ablegt.

CHÊNE PÉDONCULÉ

Le CHÊNE PÉDONCULÉ (LXXXIIII) a toujours été une grande plante médicinale à cause de sa teneur en tanin, mais Fuchs se trompe sur l'origine des noix de galle, riches en tanin, qui apparaissent souvent sur les feuilles : ce ne sont pas d'autres fruits comme il le croit, mais des excroissances provoquées par un cynips.

PAGE 208

DRAGONWORT

In addition to several medicinal uses, DRAGONWORT (LXXXV) with its impressive blossoms was also supposed to drive away snakes.

GROSS SCHLANGENKRAUT

Die Gemeine Drachenwurz mit ihrer imponierenden Blüte erscheint als GROSS SCHLANGENKRAUT (Cap. LXXXV) und soll neben mancher Arzneiwirkung auch Schlangen vertreiben.

SERPENTAIRE COMMUNE

La SERPENTAIRE COMMUNE (LXXXV), à la fleur imposante, est qualifiée de «grande herbe à serpents» («Groß Schlangenkraut»), car elle aurait, outre certaines propriétés curatives, le pouvoir d'éloigner les serpents.

PAGE 209

WATER ARUM

In his description of WATER ARUM (LXXXVI), also known as Wild Dragon, Fuchs refers to its occurrence on the River Pegnitz near Nuremberg.

„KLEIN SCHLANGENKRAUT“

Davon unterschieden wird die Sumpf-Calla als „KLEIN SCHLANGENKRAUT“ (Cap. LXXXVI), bei dessen Beschreibung Fuchs auf Vorkommen an der Pegnitz nahe Nürnberg hinweist.

CALLA DES MARAIS

Voici maintenant la «petite herbe à serpents» («Klein Schlangenkraut») qui n'est autre que la (LXXXVI). Fuchs en signale la présence sur les rives de la Pegnitz près de Nuremberg.

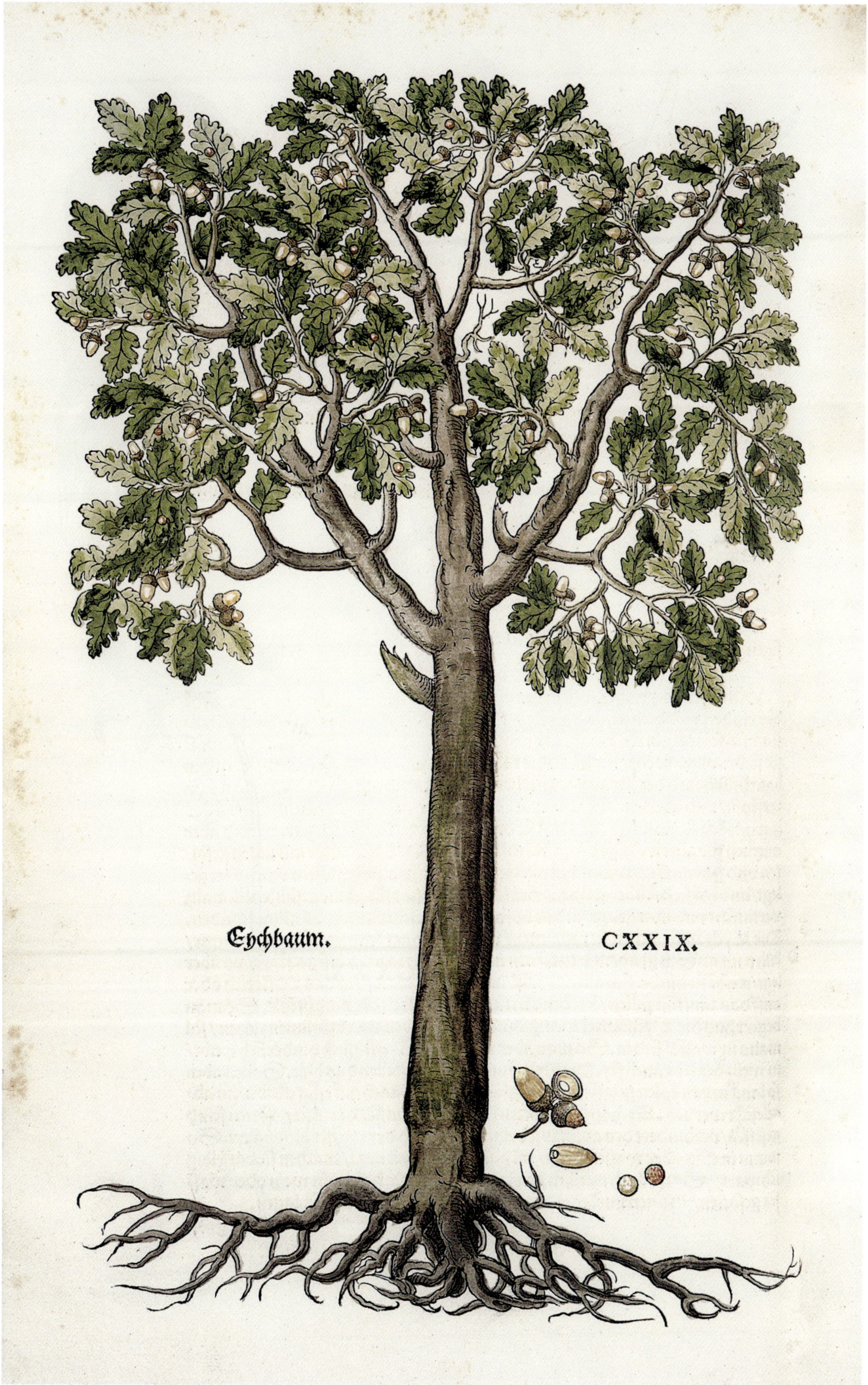

ENGLISH OAK | EICHE | CHÊNE PÉDONCULÉ

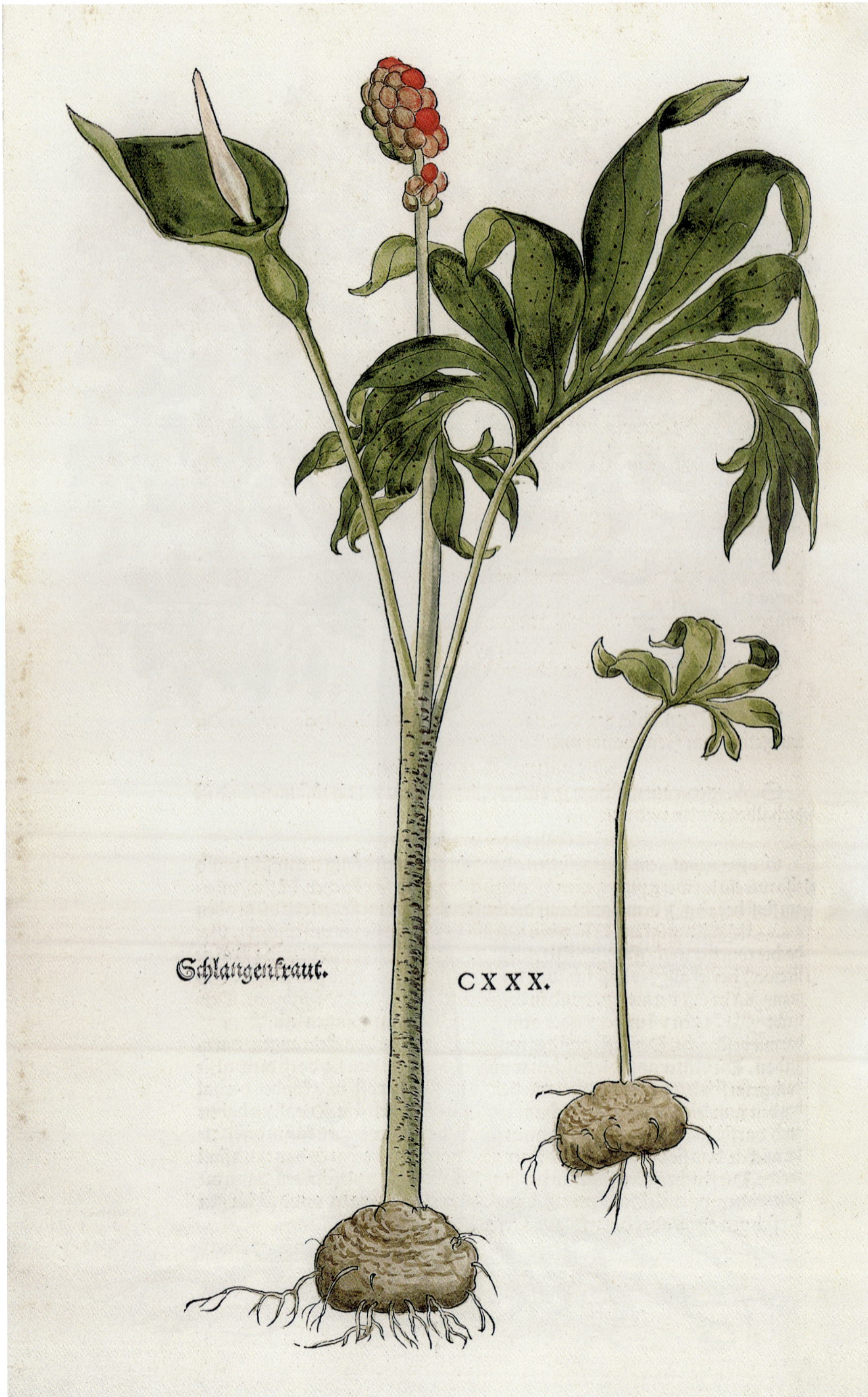
Schlangenkraut.
CXXX.

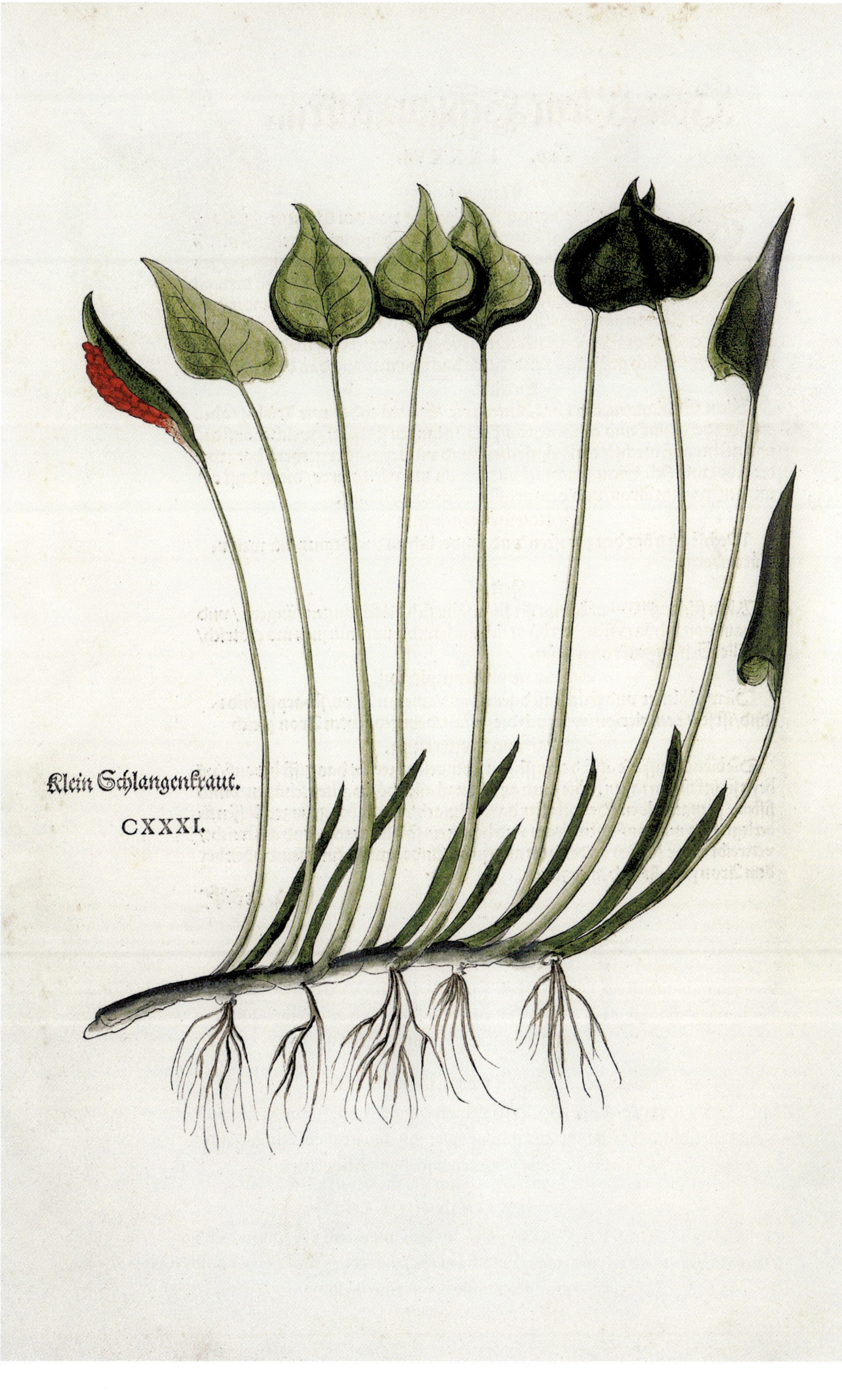
Klein Schlangenkraut.
CXXXI.

ALEXANDER'S LAUREL

The German name of ALEXANDER'S LAUREL (LXXXVII), also known as Double Tongue, refers to the strikingly high sepals that surround the fruit and which together with the tongue-shaped leaves are reminiscent of the uvula.

„ZÄPFFLINKRAUT"

„ZÄPFFLINKRAUT" (Cap. LXXXVII) erhielt seinen Namen wegen des auffälligen Hochblatts, das die Frucht umgibt und im Zusammenspiel mit den großen, zungen-ähnlichen Blättern an das Gaumenzäpfchen erinnert.

FRAGON PIQUANT

Le FRAGON PIQUANT (LXXXVII) doit son nom allemand «Zäpfflinkraut» ou herbe à luette à la particularité de ses bractées : entourant les fruits, elles font penser à des luettes sur les grandes feuilles en forme de langue.

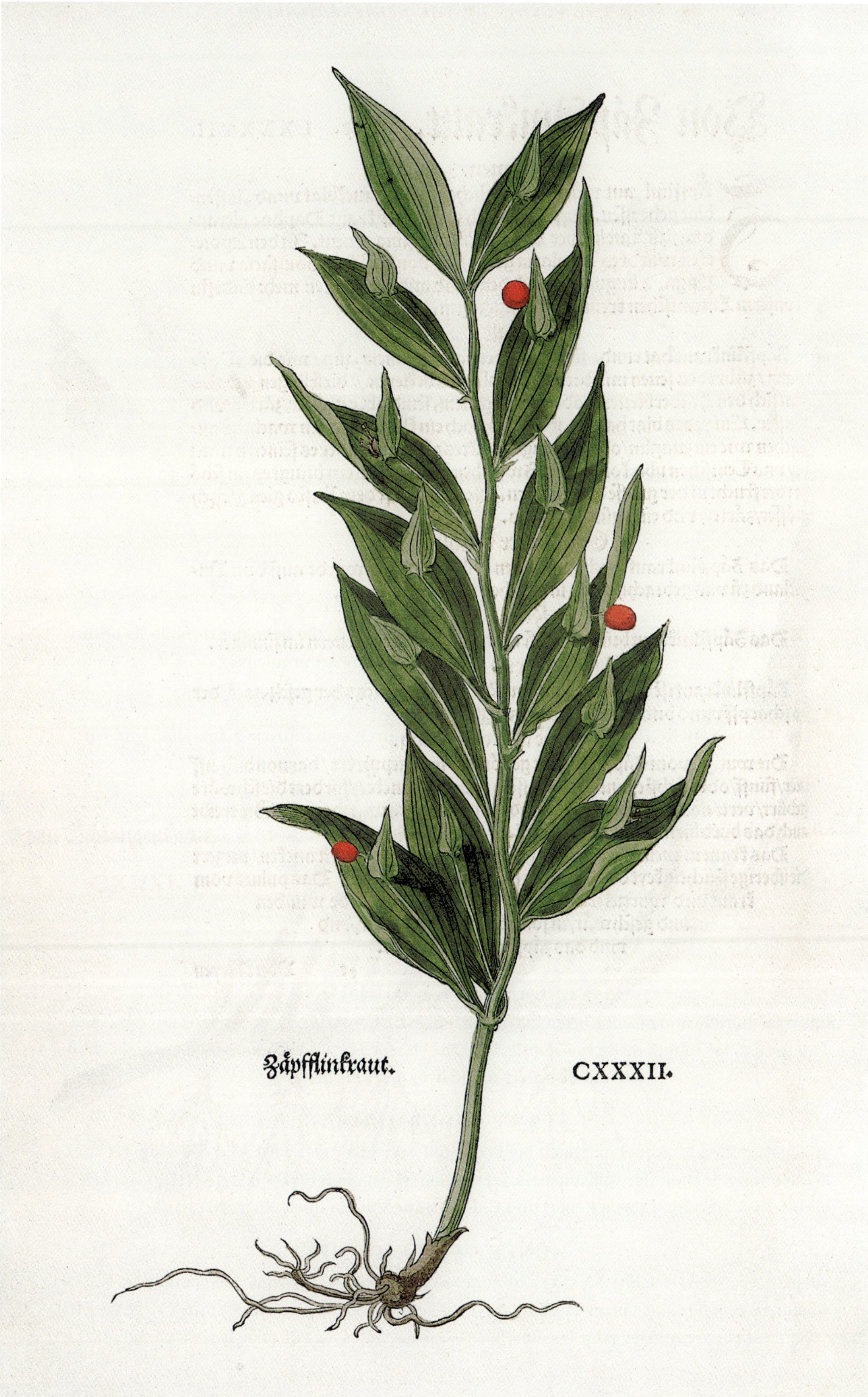
Zäpfflinkraut.
CXXXII.

LILY-OF-THE-VALLEY

LILY-OF-THE-VALLEY (LXXXVIII) not only brings joy to the beholder through its beauty but remains an effective remedy for heart problems.

MAIGLÖCKCHEN

Das MAIGLÖCKCHEN (Cap. LXXXVIII) erfreut durch sein hübsches Aussehen und wird immer noch als wirksames Herzmittel verwendet.

MUGUET

Le MUGUET (LXXXVIII) est toujours un plaisir pour les yeux. C'est aussi un puissant tonicardiaque encore utilisé de nos jours.

PAGES 214, 215

ELECAMPANE / AGRIMONY

Both as a diuretic and also for bronchial disorders, ELECAMPANE, or SCABWORT (LXXXIX), is still used today in folk medicine; similarly AGRIMONY (XC) is recommended against diarrhoea and disorders of the liver and gall-bladder.

ALANT / ODERMENNIG

Als harntreibendes Mittel und auch bei Bronchial-erkrankungen wird ALANT (Cap. LXXXIX) heute immer noch in der Volksmedizin verwendet, wie auch der ODERMENNIG (Cap. XC) bei Durchfall sowie Leber- und Gallenerkrankungen noch eingesetzt wird.

AUNÉE / AIGREMOINE

La GRANDE AUNÉE (LXXXIX) a toujours sa place dans la pharmacopée populaire, car sa souche fournit des substances diurétiques et expectorantes, tout comme l'AIGREMOINE (XC), qui est encore utilisée pour les diarrhées et les maladies du foie et de la vésicule biliaire.

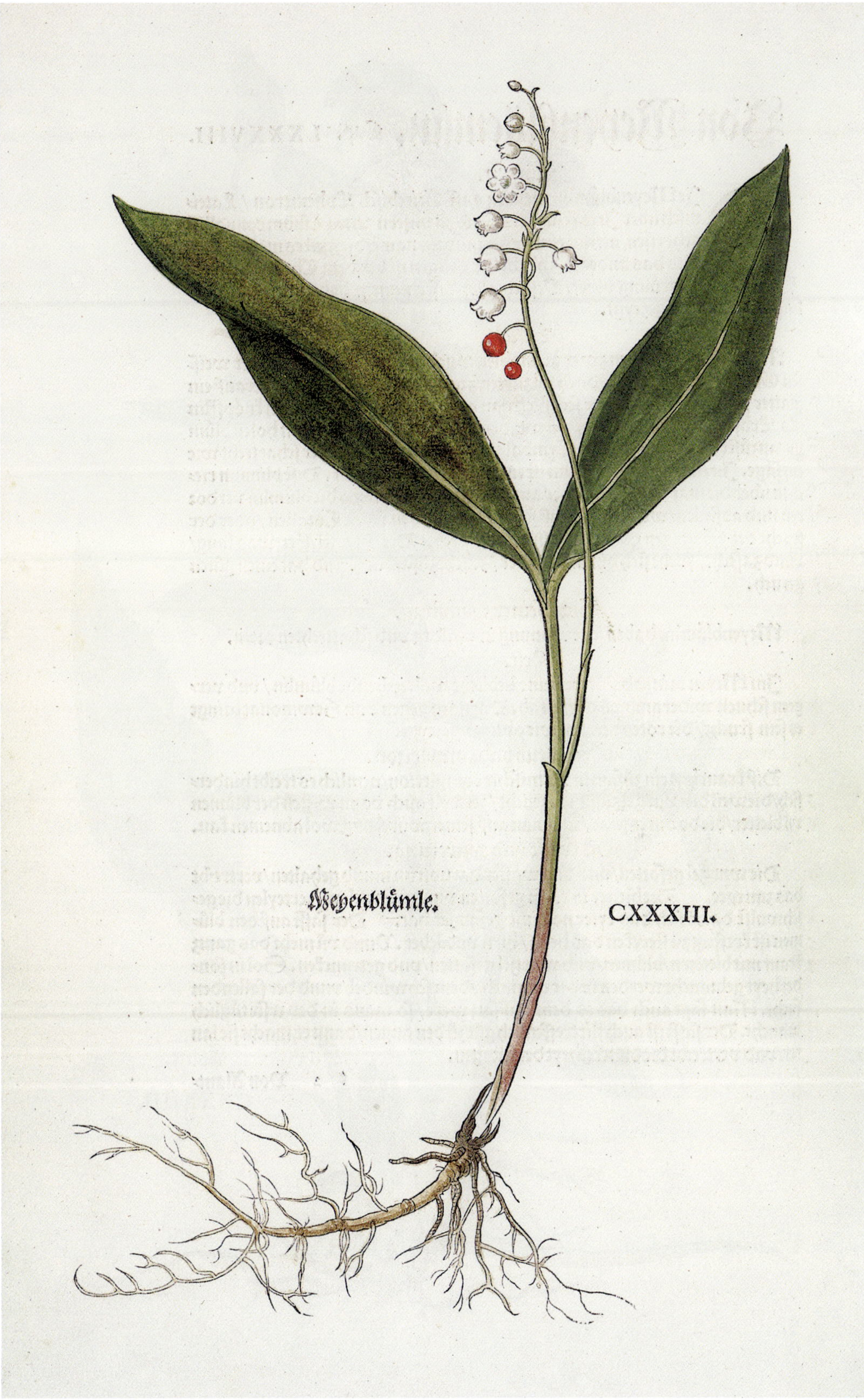
Meyenblůmle.
CXXXIII.

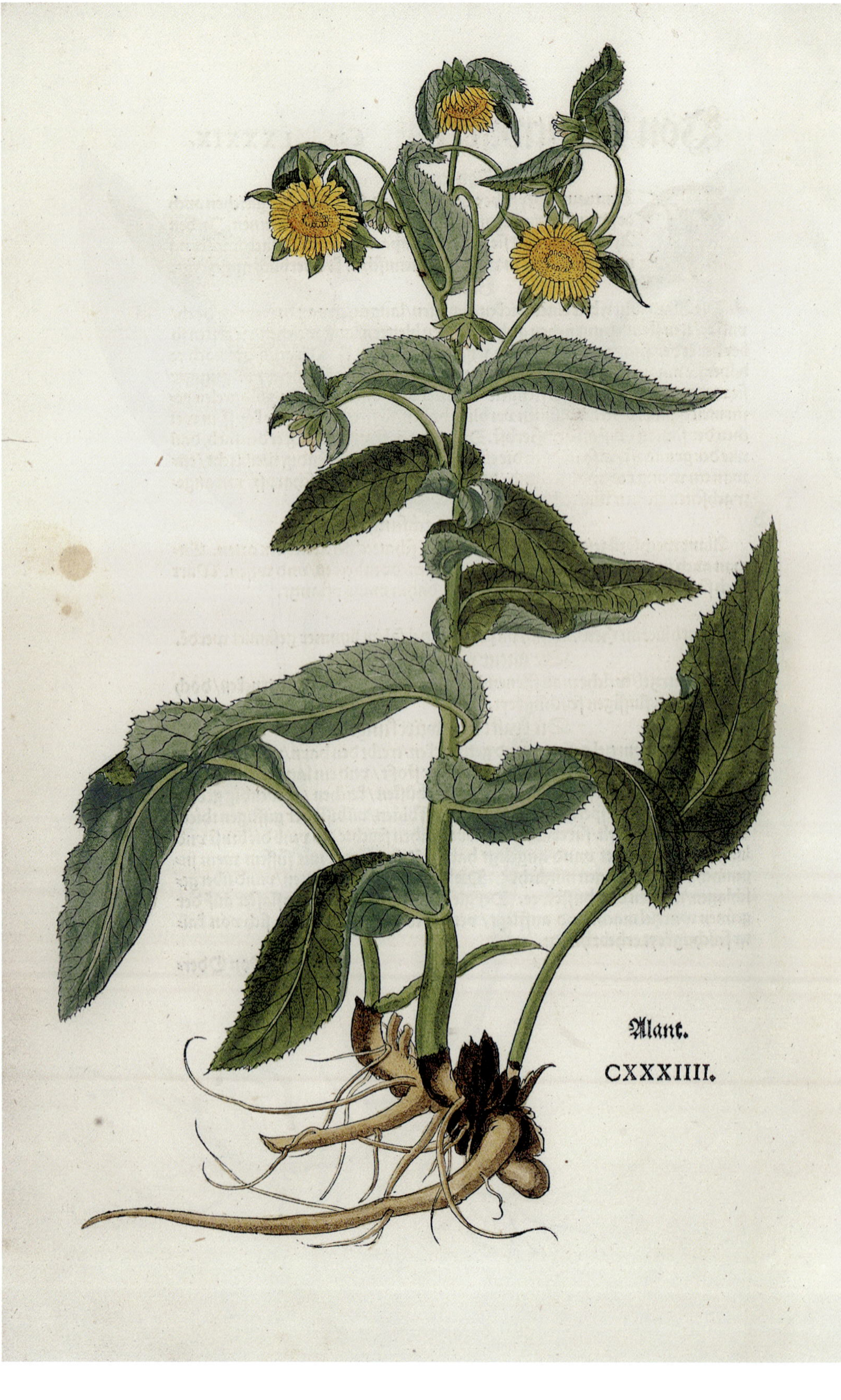
Alant.
CXXXIIII.

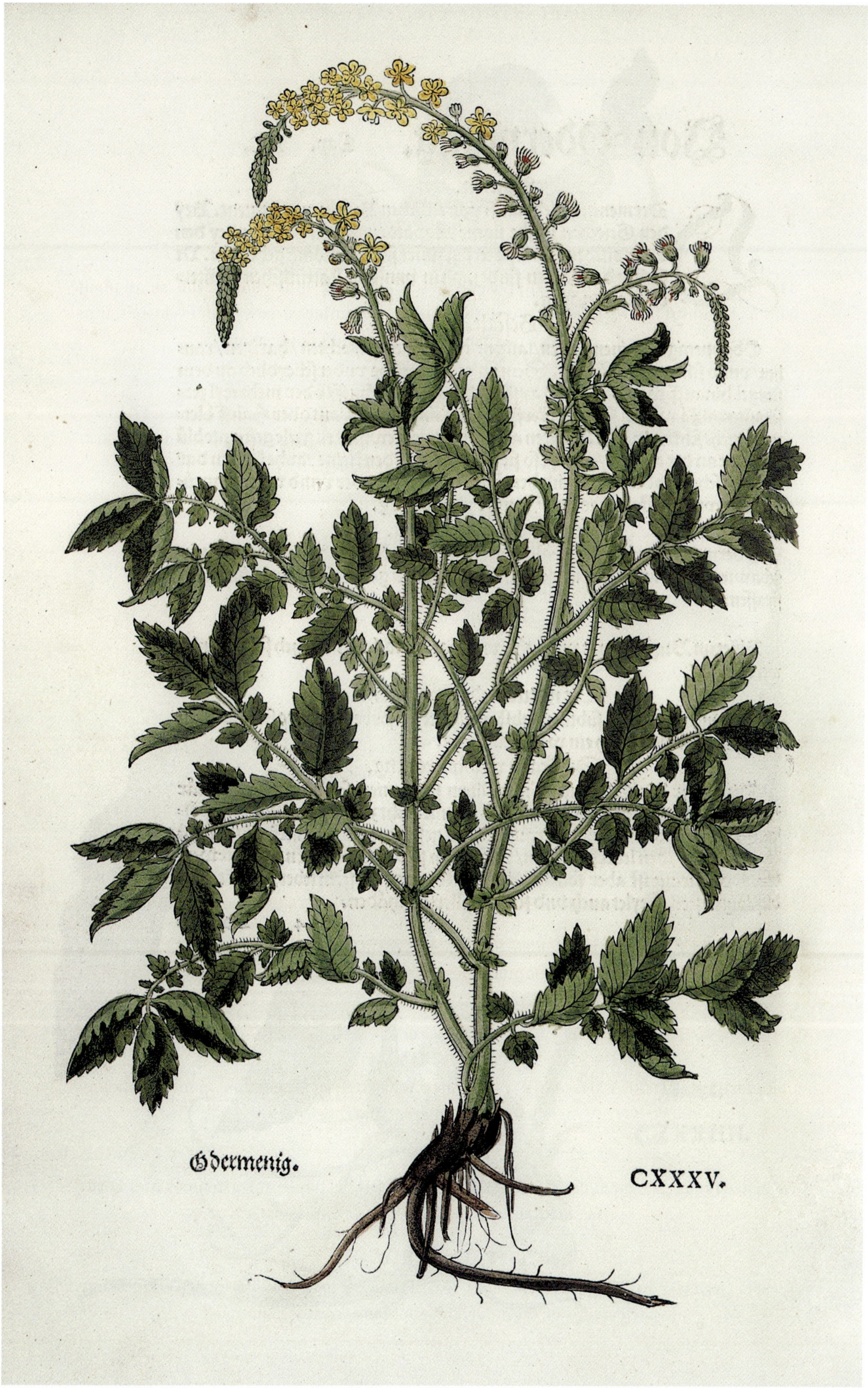

AGRIMONY | ODERMENNIG | AIGREMOINE

EYEBRIGHT

The name EYEBRIGHT (XCI) supposedly described the healing effect of this small plant with its beautiful flower. The interior of the blossom resembles an eye with eyelashes, thus creating a clear "signature" for the plant's application.

AUGENTROST

Der Name AUGENTROST (Cap. XCI) beschreibt die Heilwirkung der kleinen Pflanze mit der schönen Blüte, deren Inneres an ein bewimpertes Auge erinnert und deshalb die eindeutige Signatur erhielt.

EUPHRAISE

Le nom de casse-lunettes, « Augentrost » en allemand, ou réconfort des yeux donné à l'EUPHRAISE (XCI), à cause de ses petites fleurs dont la gorge ressemble à des cils, décrit bien son emploi thérapeutique.

PAGE 218

SAGE

Beyond a doubt, SAGE (XCII) numbers among the most valuable medicinal plants; its earlier applications exploited its disinfectant action.

SALBEI

Zu den wertvollsten Arzneipflanzen gehört ohne Zweifel der SALBEI (Cap. XCII), bei dessen früherer Anwendung man sich mehrfach die desinfizierende Wirkung zunutze machte.

SAUGE

La SAUGE (XCII) est sans conteste l'une de nos plantes médicinales les plus précieuses. Ses applications étaient nombreuses en raison de son pouvoir désinfectant.

PAGE 219

WILD THYME

Similarly, WILD THYME (XCIII) is still used today in teas for coughs; in folk medicine it is used to counteract diarrhoea.

QUENDEL

Ebenso findet sich auch der QUENDEL (Cap. XCIII) bis heute in Hustentees und wird volksmedizinisch bei Durchfällen eingesetzt.

THYM SERPOLET

C'est le cas aussi du THYM SERPOLET (XCIII), qui est toujours administré en infusions expectorantes et, en médecine populaire, contre la diarrhée.

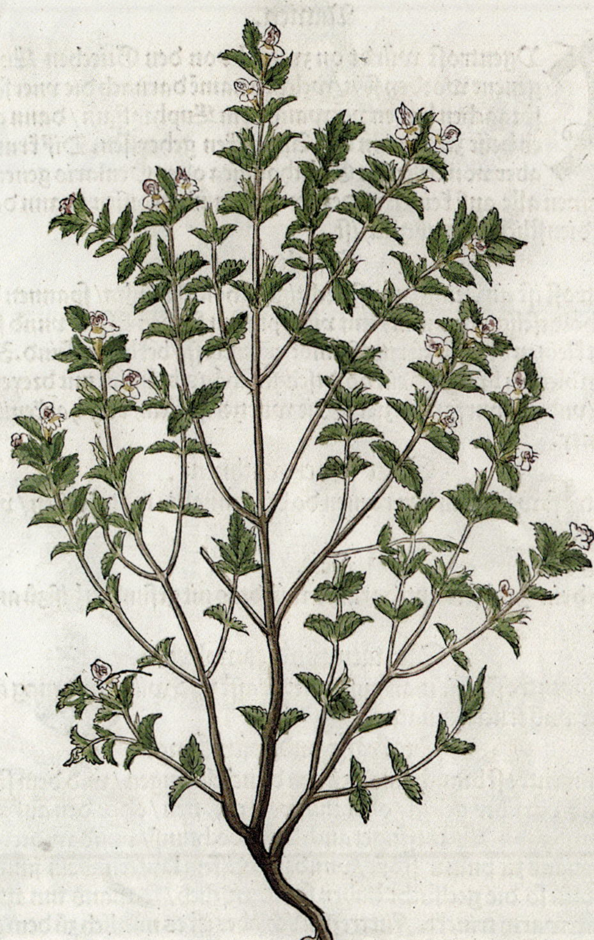

Augentrost. CXXXVI.

EYEBRIGHT | AUGENTROST | EUPHRAISE

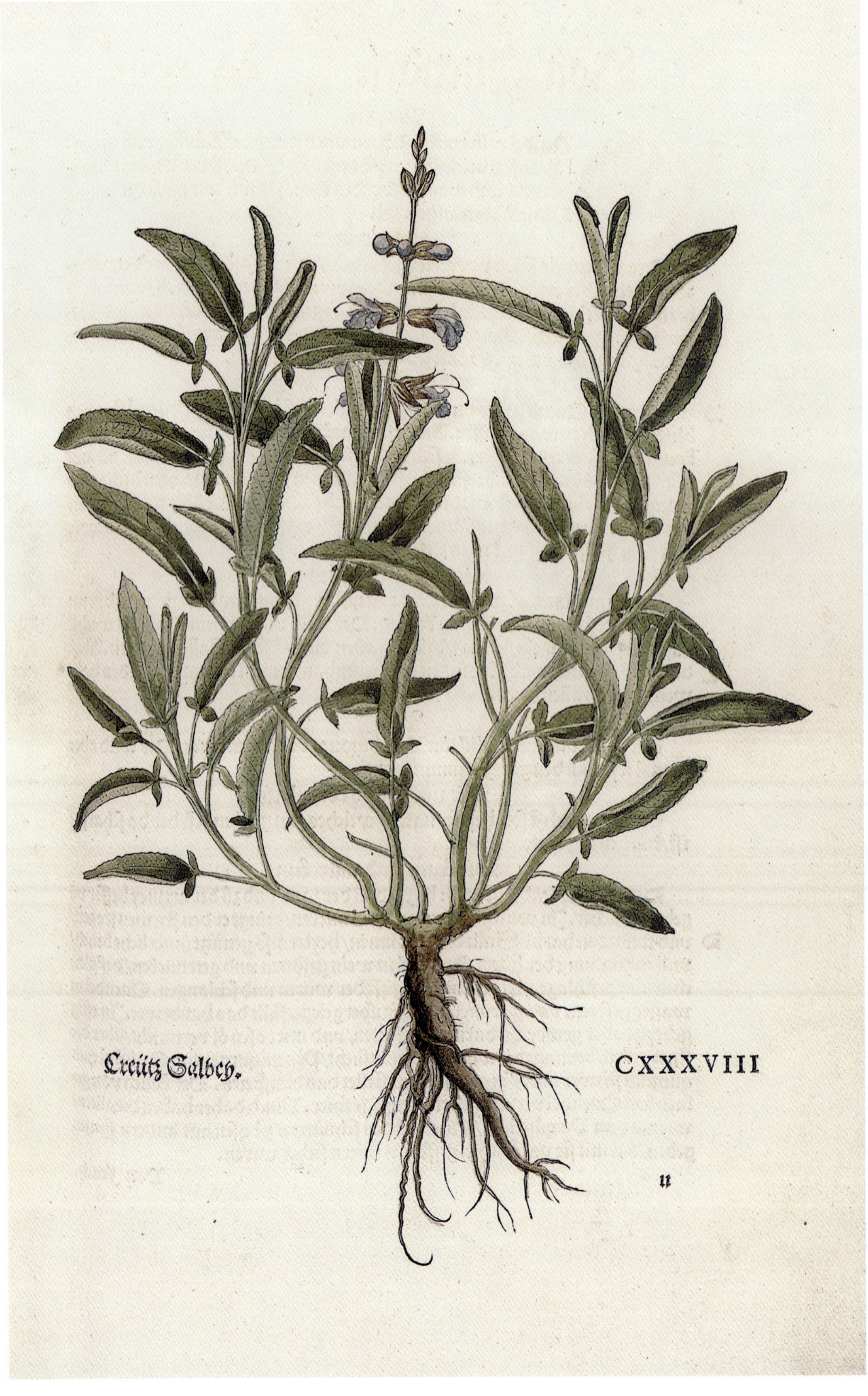
Creütz Salbey.
CXXXVIII
u

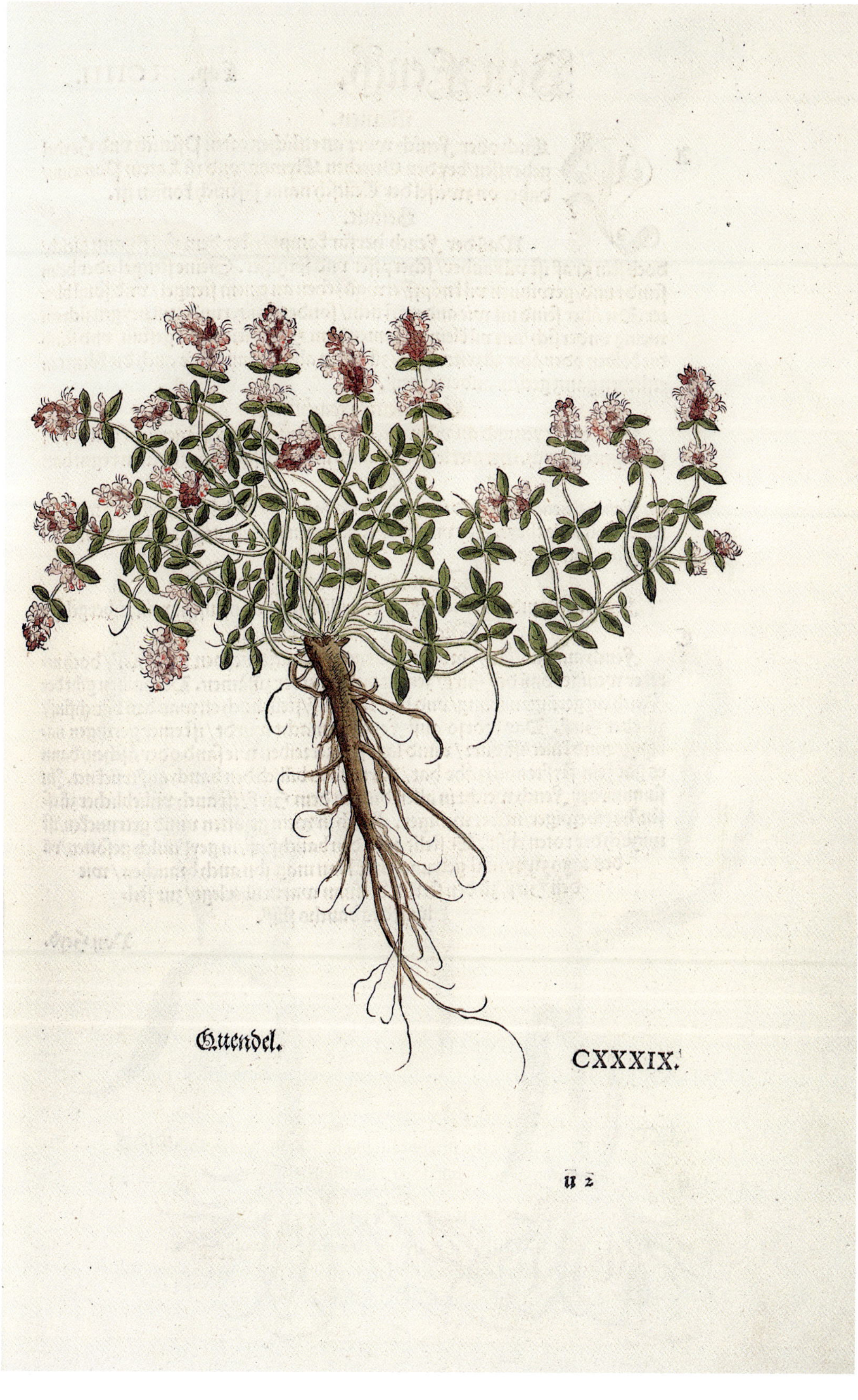

WILD THYME | QUENDEL | THYM SERPOLET

FOXTAIL MILLET

ITALIAN or FOXTAIL MILLET (XCIIII) is less highly regarded than millet.

„FENCH“

„FENCH“ (Cap. XCIIII) ist der heute ungebräuchliche Name für die Kolbenhirse, die weniger geschätzt wird als die Hirse.

SÉTAIRE D’ITALIE

La SÉTAIRE D’ITALIE (XCIIII), ou millet des oiseaux, est moins estimée que le millet. Le millet s’appelait jadis «Fench», mais ce nom a été remplacé dans un passé plus récent par celui de «Kolbenhirse» (mil à épis).

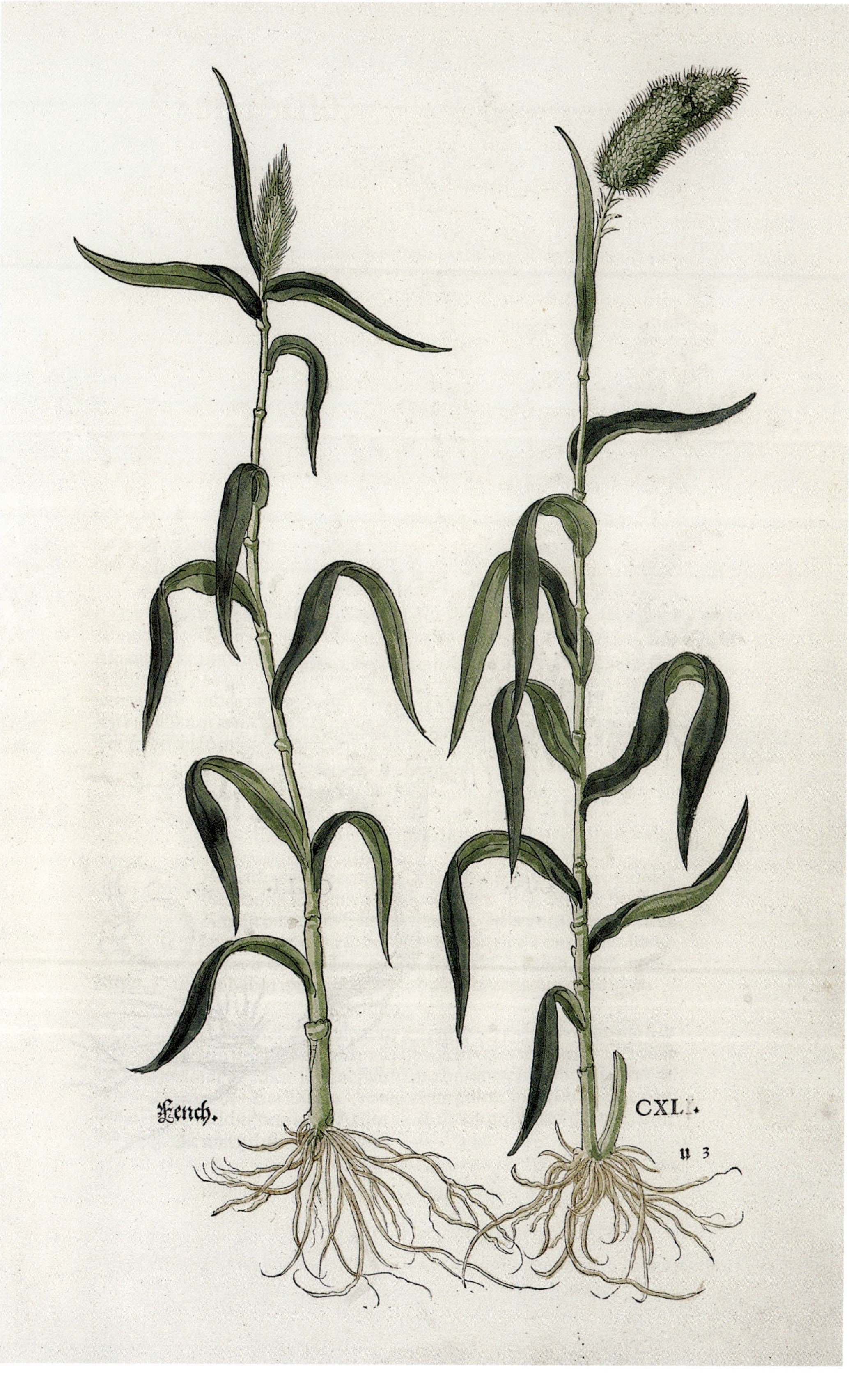
Fench.
CXLI.
n 3

PAGES 223, 224

LING / CHARLOCK

According to Fuchs, HEATHER, or LING (XCV) was "not used at all by the apothecaries" of the time, and the same held true for Field Mustard, or CHARLOCK (XCVI). Nonetheless, he surprisingly lists a complete series of medicinal effects for both.

„HEYD" / HEDERICH

Obwohl die „HEYD" (Cap. XCV) laut Fuchs „bey den Apoteckern in keinen brauch" steht und dies auch für den HEDERICH (Cap. XCVI) gelten soll, nennt er überraschenderweise für beide eine ganze Reihe medizinischer Wirkungen.

FAUSSE BRUYÈRE / MOUTARDE DES CHAMPS

D'après Fuchs, la FAUSSE BRUYÈRE (XCV) et la MOUTARDE DES CHAMPS (XCVI) ne sont pas «en usage chez les apothicaires». Contre toute attente cependant, il énumère un grand nombre d'indications.

PAGE 225

FIELD BINDWEED

The name of the widespread cornbine, or FIELD BINDWEED (XCVII) clearly points to its habitat.

„MITTELWIND"

„MITTELWIND" (Cap. XCVII) bedeutet „mittlere Winde" und bezeichnet die weit verbreitete Acker-winde.

LISERON DES CHAMPS

«Mittelwind» ou «liseron moyen» est l'ancien nom allemand du LISERON DES CHAMPS (XCVII), très répandu dans nos régions.

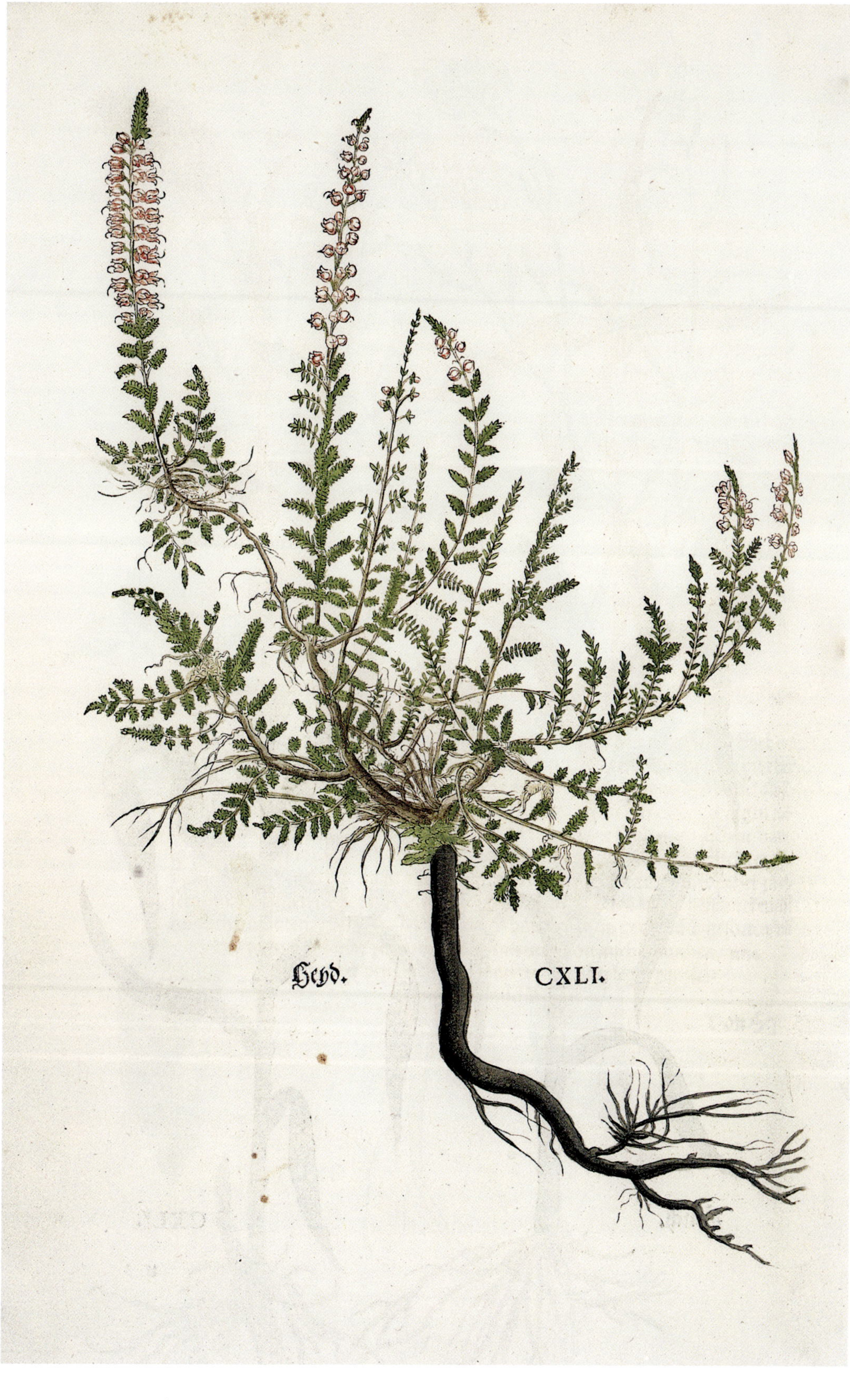
Heyd.
CXLI.

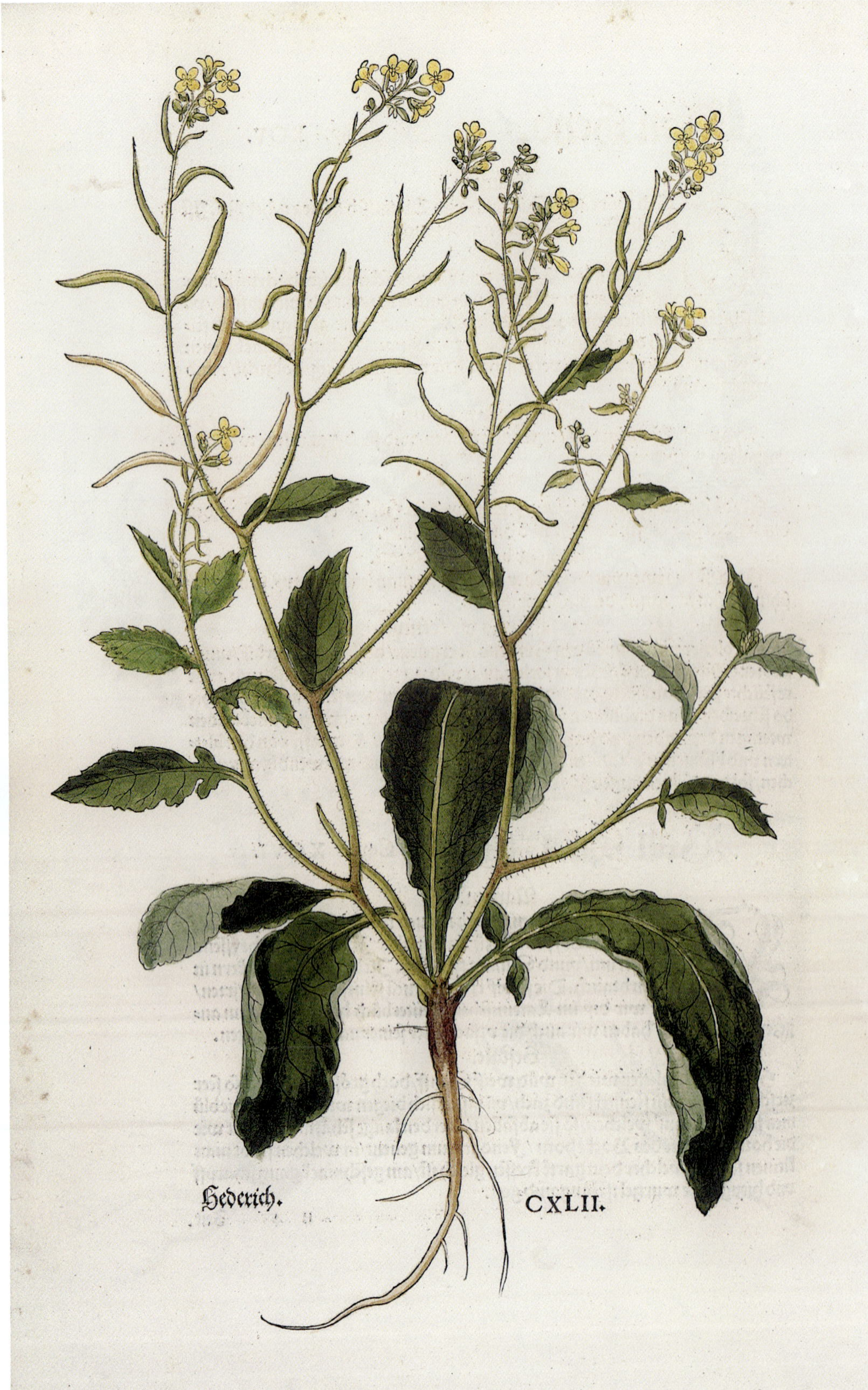
Hederich.
CXLII.

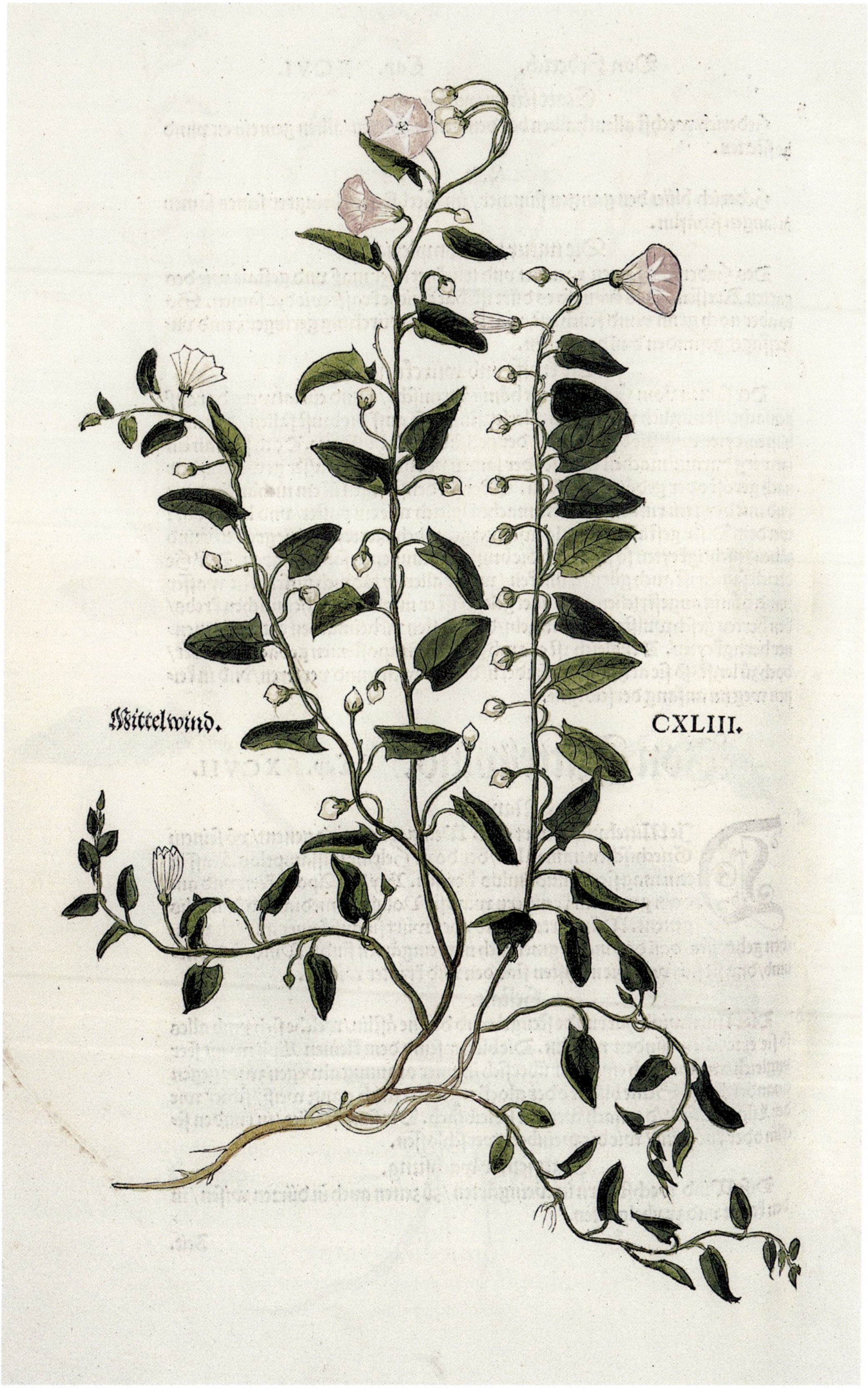

FIELD BINDWEED | „MITTELWIND“ | LISERON DES CHAMPS

COMMON TORMENTIL

COMMON TORMENTIL (XCVIII) provides an ideal example of the theory of signatures, because the milky red sap that emerges when the root is broken apart seemed to indicate a connection with blood. Since this colouration is produced by tannin, the sap can serve to staunch the flow of blood in small wounds and for diarrhoea.

TORMENTILL

TORMENTILL (Cap. XCVIII) ist ein Musterbeispiel für die Signaturenlehre, weil sein aus der zerbrochenen Wurzel austretender roter Milchsaft die Verbindung zum Blut anzuzeigen scheint. Da diese Färbung durch Gerbstoffe hervorgerufen wird, kann der Saft tatsächlich zur Blutstillung bei kleinen Wunden, aber auch bei Durchfall verwendet werden.

TORMENTILLE

La TORMENTILLE (XCVIII) est l'illustration type de la théorie des signatures. De son rhizome coupé coule un suc rouge dont la couleur est due au tanin qu'il contient. Ce fut interprété comme l'indice d'effets salutaires sur le sang, et il est de fait qu'appliqué sur des plaies le suc peut arrêter les petites hémorragies. Il peut s'employer également contre les diarrhées.

PAGE 228

ROCKET

ROCKET (XCIX) helped in digestive problems and the removal of spots on the skin; in addition Fuchs mentions it as a spice.

„WEISS SENFF"

Der „WEISS SENFF" (Cap. XCIX) dient bei Verdauungsproblemen ebenso wie zur Beseitigung von Hautflecken, aber auch als Gewürz wird er erwähnt.

DIPLOTAXIS À FEUILLES TÉNUES

Fuchs présente le DIPLOTAXIS À FEUILLES TÉNUES et le CRESSON DES FORÊTS sous le nom de « moutarde blanche » (« weiß Senf », XCIX). Ils s'utilisent pour les troubles digestifs et les taches cutanées, mais aussi comme condiment.

PAGE 229

HEMP AGRIMONY

HEMP AGRIMONY (C) was efficacious against poison and served as a vulnerary as well.

KUNIGUNDENKRAUT

Giftwidrige und ausführende Wirkung, aber auch der Einsatz als Wundkraut wird dem KUNIGUNDENKRAUT (Cap. C) zugeschrieben.

EUPATOIRE CHANVRINE

L'EUPATOIRE CHANVRINE (C) aurait des propriétés antitoxiques et dépuratives et serait cicatrisante.

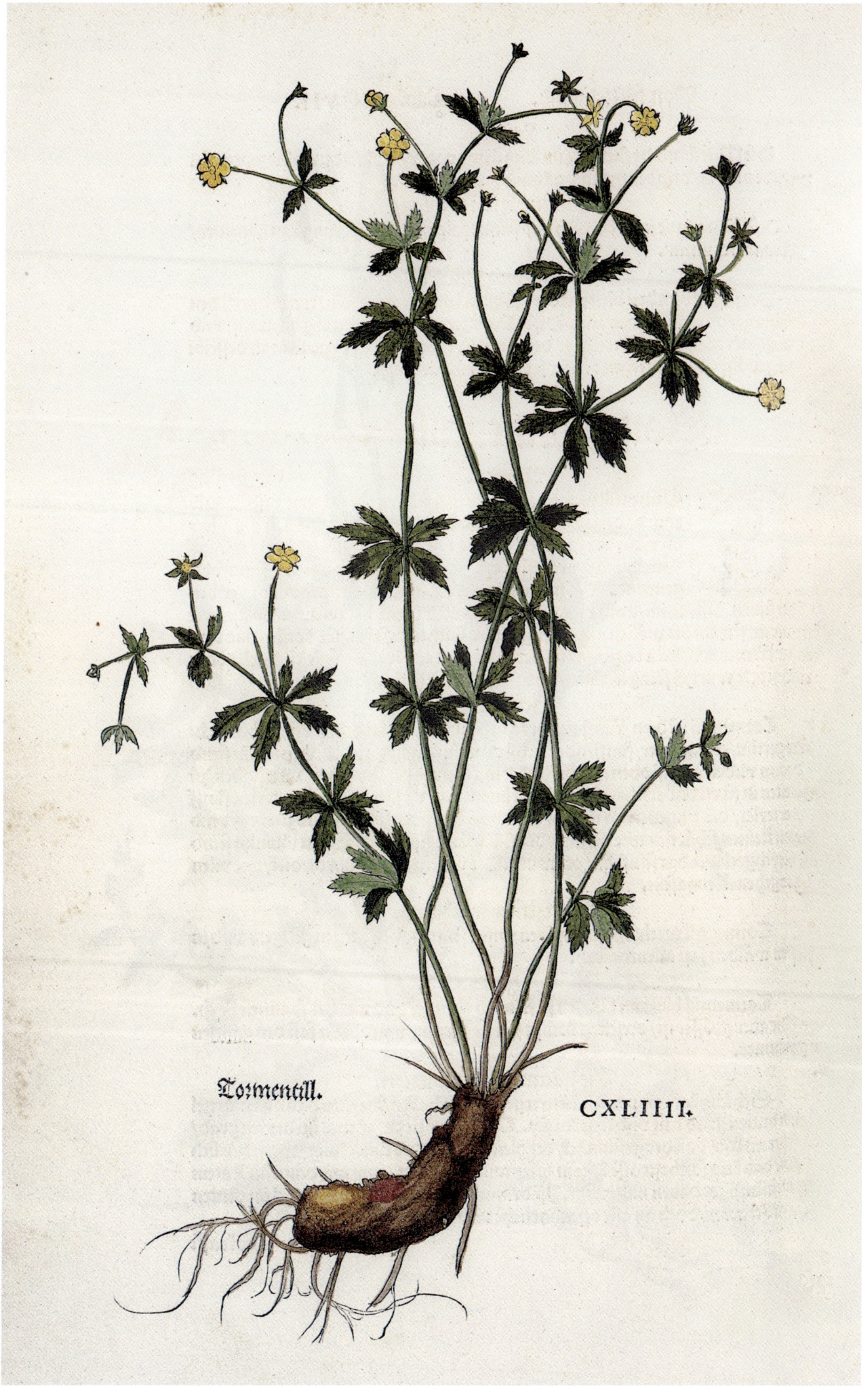
Tormentill.
CXLIIII.

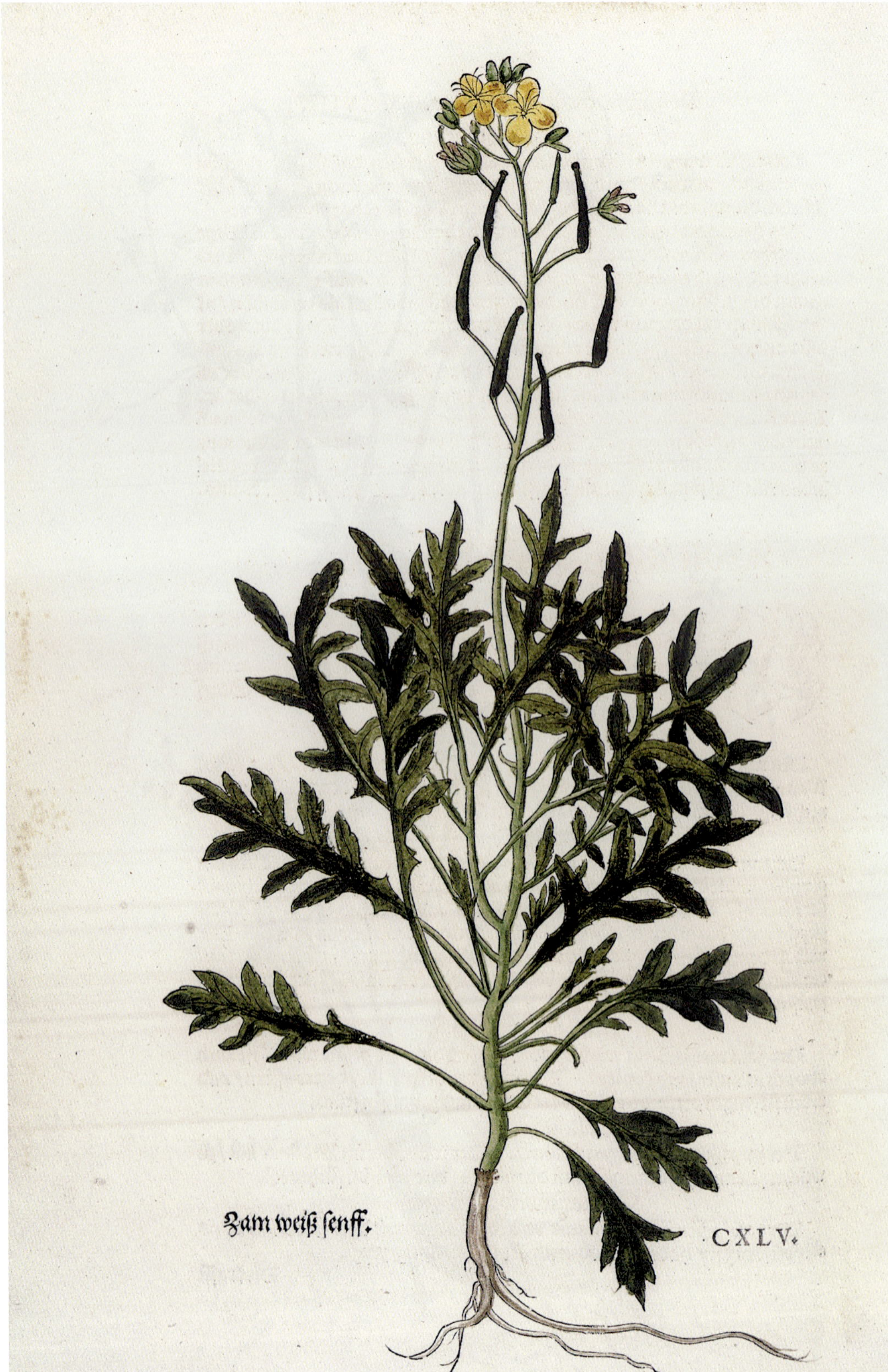
Zam weiß senff.
CXLV.

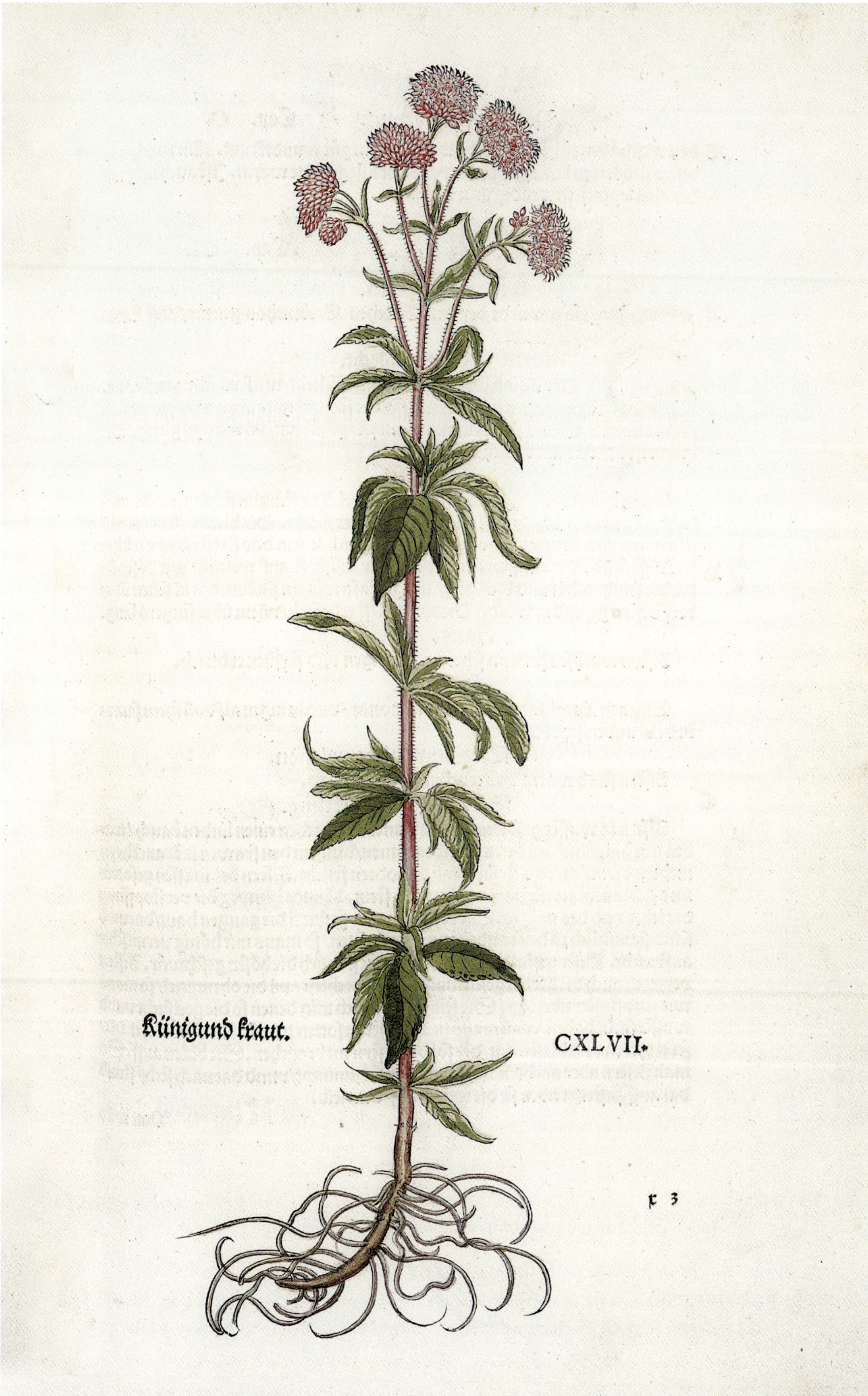

HEMP AGRIMONY | KUNIGUNDENKRAUT | EUPATOIRE CHANVRINE

CHICKPEA

In addition to being a staple food in many regions, CHICKPEA (CI), also known as Garbanzo, has many medicinal applications, particularly purgative.

„ZISER“ (KICHERERBSE)

Die Kichererbse, nach ihrem lateinischen Namen „ZISER“ (Cap. CI) genannt, erhält, obwohl sie in vielen Gegenden als Nahrungsmittel dient, auch zahlreiche arzneiliche Anwendungen, insbesondere ausführende, zugesprochen.

POIS CHICHE

Le POIS CHICHE (CI), appelé ici «Ziser», de son nom latin CICER, est non seulement un légume consommé dans de nombreuses régions, mais aussi une plante médicinale qui serait, entre autres, dépurative.

PAGE 232

FIELD BUGLOSS

FIELD BUGLOSS (CII), supposedly efficacious against poison, indicates once more that Fuchs was well acquainted with the local flora, for he names Rottenburg on the Neckar as a habitat.

WILDE OCHSENZUNGE

Bei der WILDEN OCHSENZUNGE (Cap. CII) erweist sich Fuchs wieder als Kenner der lokalen Flora, denn er erwähnt Rottenburg am Neckar als Wuchsort der vermeintlich giftwidrigen Pflanze.

BUGLOSSE DES CHAMPS

Fuchs se montre à nouveau connaisseur de la flore locale lorsqu'il mentionne l'existence du BUGLOSSE DES CHAMPS (CII), ou langue-de-bœuf, que l'on pensait toxique, à Rottembourg-sur-le-Neckar.

PAGE 233

NARROW-LEAVED PARSNIP

For NARROW-LEAVED PARSNIP also known as WATER PARSNIP (CIII, plate CL), Fuchs refers to the chapter on BLACK LOVAGE (CXXIII).

„WASSEREPFF“

Als „WASSEREPFF“ (Cap. CIII) bildet Fuchs den SCHMALBLÄTTRIGEN MERK (Taf. CL) ab und verweist ansonsten auf das Kapitel zum Garteneppich (Cap. CXXIII).

BERLE DRESSÉE

La BERLE DRESSÉE (pl. CL) est présentée ici sous le nom de «Wasserepff», CÉLERI D'EAU (CIII) ; pour le reste, Fuchs renvoie au chapitre sur les berles cultivées (CXXIII).

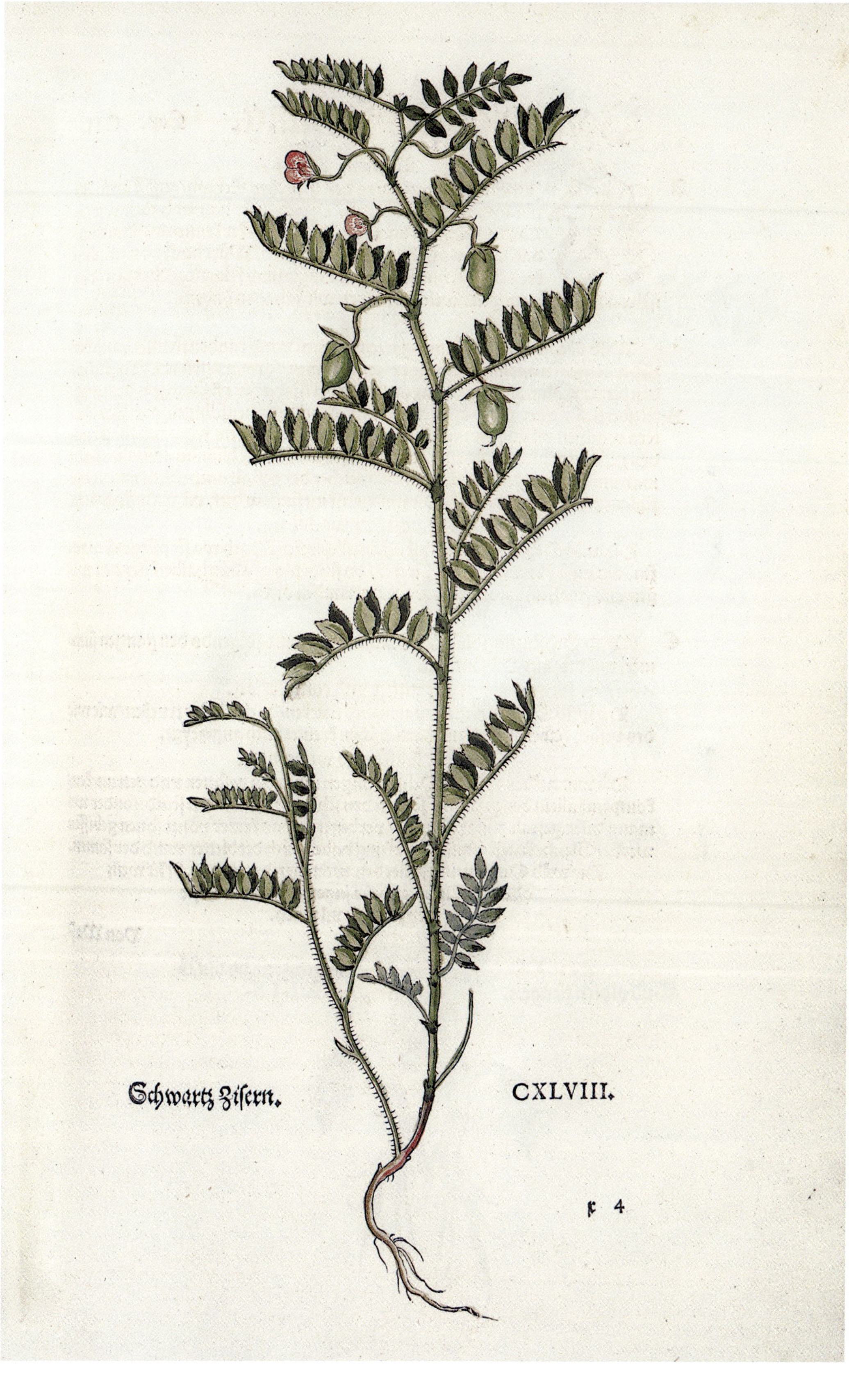
Schwartz Zisern.
CXLVIII.
k 4

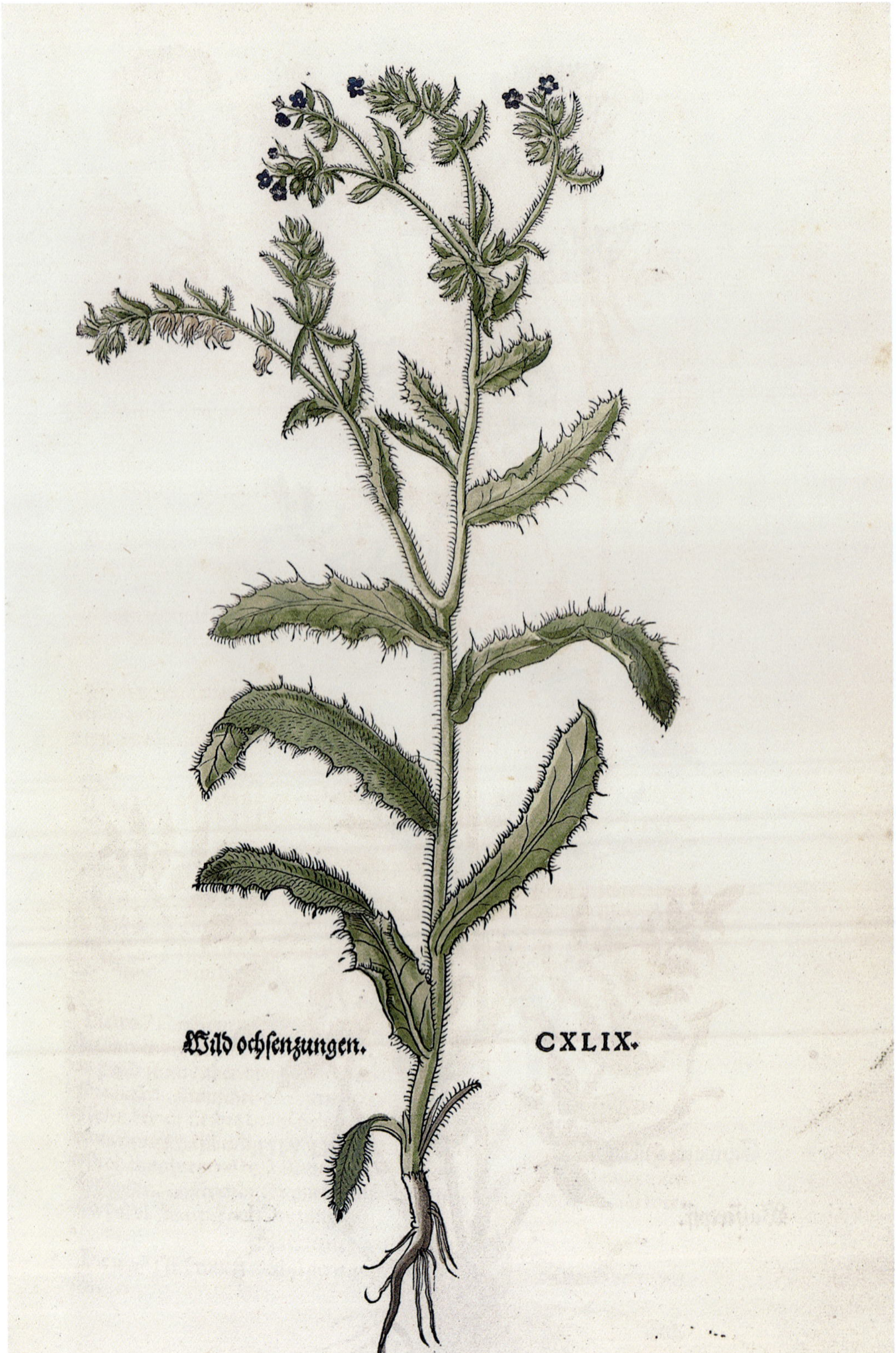
Wild ochsenzungen.
CXLIX.

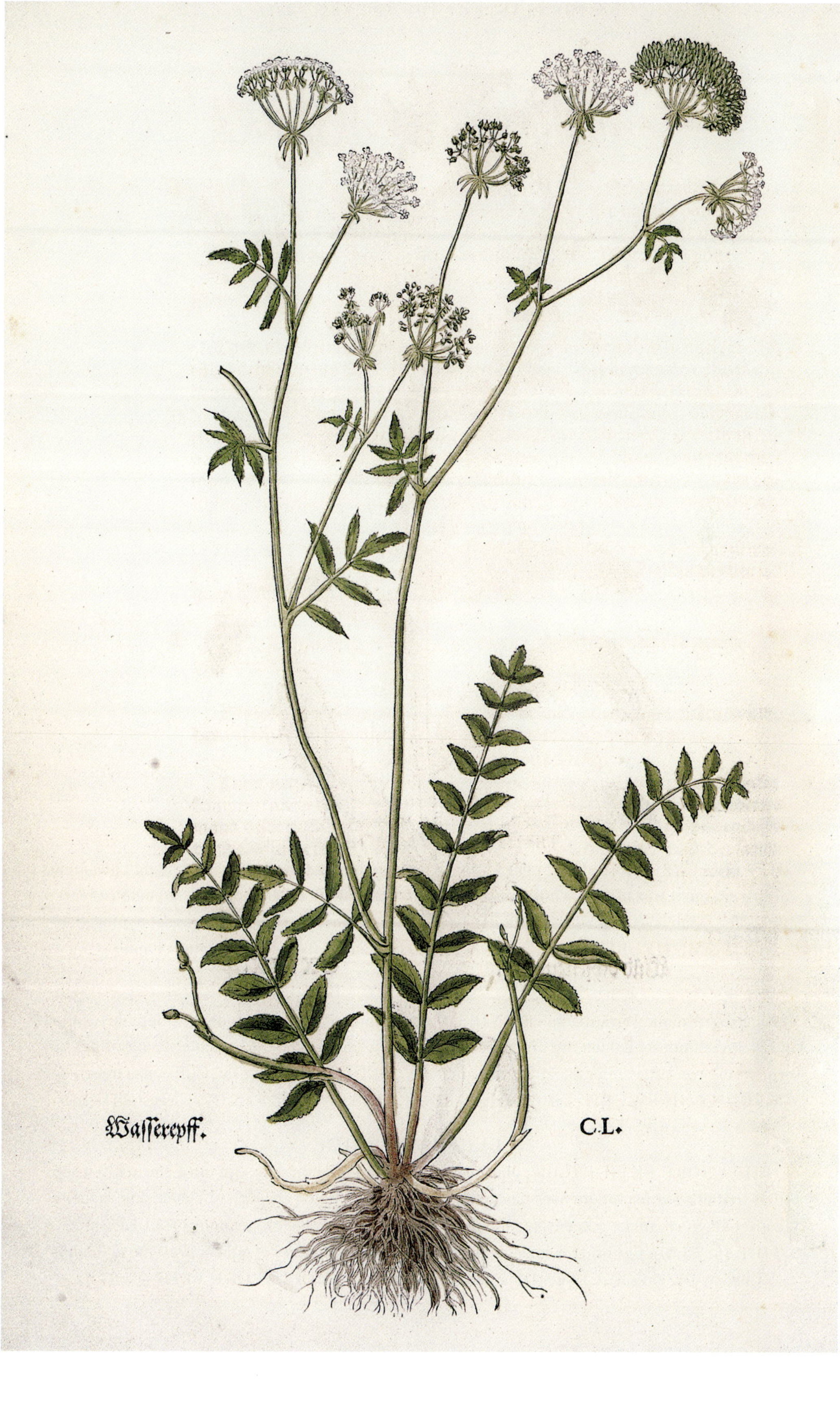

NARROW-LEAVED PARSNIP | „WASSEREPFF“ | BERLE DRESSÉE

WHITE HELLEBORINE

WHITE HELLEBORINE (CIIII; plate CLI) is a nasal irritant and is furthermore highly poisonous. For this reason it was almost wholly unsuited for internal application, but was used against insect pests. The same is true of STINKING HELLEBORE (plate CLIII), which is presented together with GREEN HELLEBORE, or BEAR'S FOOT (plate CLII) in the following chapter (CV).

NIESWURZ

Ihre nasenreizende Wirkung gab der NIESWURZ (Cap. CIIII; Taf. CLI) den Namen, ihre hohe Giftigkeit verhinderte jedoch die innerliche Anwendung wei-testgehend, machte sie allerdings zur Vernichtung von Ungeziefer geeignet, wie auch das „LEUSSKRAUT“ (Taf. CLIII), das neben der GRÜNEN NIESWURZ (Taf. CLII) im Kapitel CHRISTWURZ (Cap. CV) vorgestellt wird.

HELLÉBORE FÉTIDE

L'HELLÉBORE FÉTIDE (CIIII ; pl. CLI) doit son nom allemand de «racine à éternuer» à ses effets irritants sur les muqueuses nasales. Si sa haute toxicité en empêchait l'usage interne, elle convenait en revanche à la destruction des parasites. Il en est de même pour l'HELLÉBORE FÉTIDE (pl. CLIII), figurant ici sous le qualificatif d'«herbe à poux» et qui est présenté au chapitre «Christwurz» ou «RACINES DU CHRIST» (CV) avec l'HELLÉBORE VERT (pl. CLII).

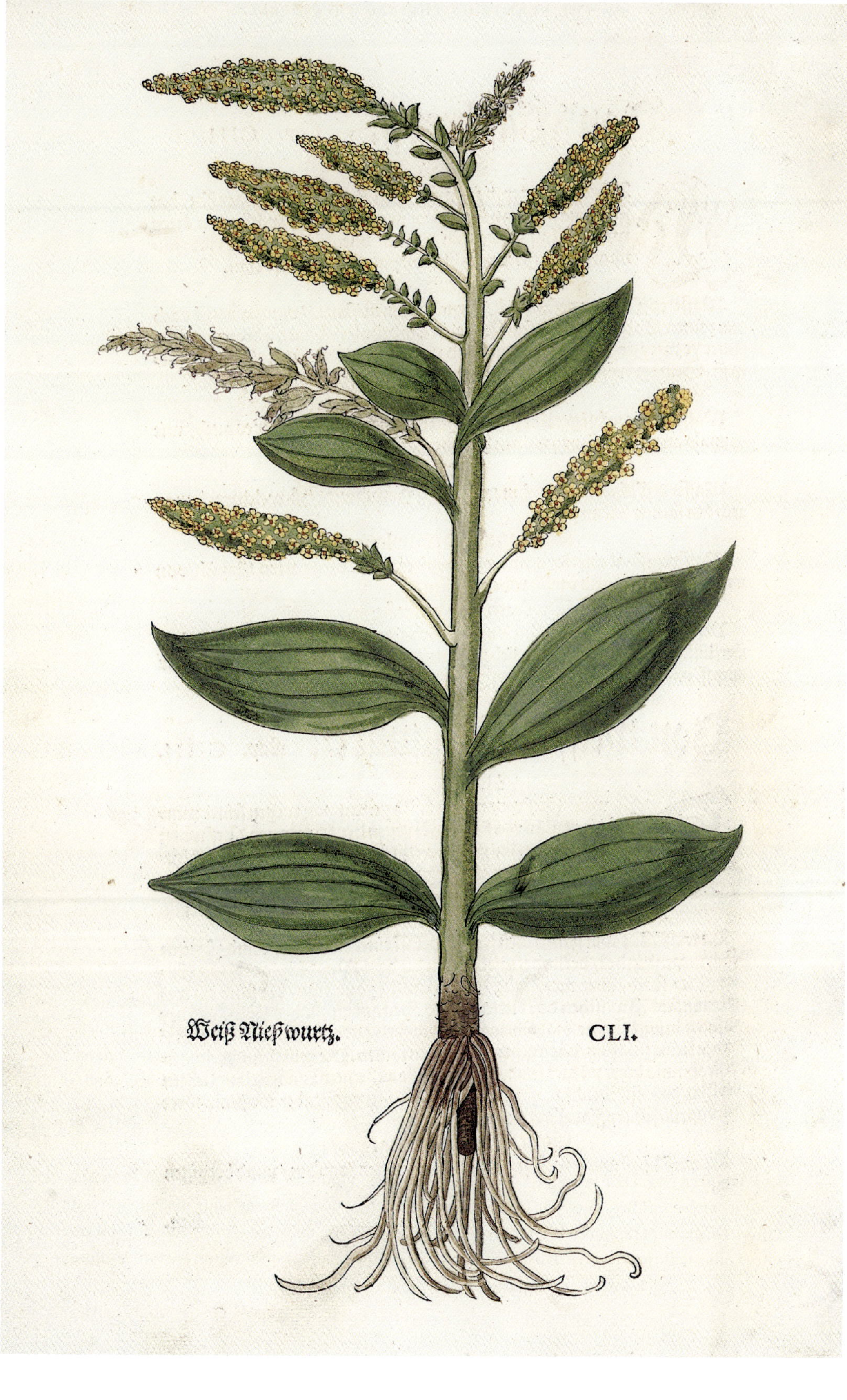
Weiß Nieswurtz.
CLI.

PELLITORY-OF-THE-WALL

The leaves of PELLITORY-OF-THE-WALL (CVI) appear to have transparent dots, giving a mottled day-and-night effect. The plant's ashes were earlier used for cleaning glass. Both references are reflected in the German names of the plant. Medicinally, the plant was chiefly applied externally for ulcers and skin diseases.

„TAG UND NACHT"

„TAG UND NACHT" (Cap. CVI) nannte man das Glaskraut wohl, weil seine Blätter durchscheinend punktiert aussehen und somit Hell neben Dunkel steht, während der heute noch gebräuchliche Name Glaskraut auf die frühere Verwendung seiner Asche zum Glasreinigen anspielt. Medizinisch wird vor allem auf die äußerliche Anwendung bei Geschwüren und Hautkrankheiten hingewiesen.

PARIÉTAIRE OFFICINALE

La PARIÉTAIRE OFFICINALE (CVI) porte le nom populaire de «jour et nuit» («Tag und Nacht»), car ses feuilles, vues par transparence, semblent panachées de clair-obscur. Son autre nom, «Glaskraut» ou herbe à verre, toujours usité, rappelle qu'on se servait autrefois de ses cendres pour nettoyer le verre. Parmi ses applications médicales, Fuchs relève surtout son usage interne contre les ulcères et les maladies de la peau.

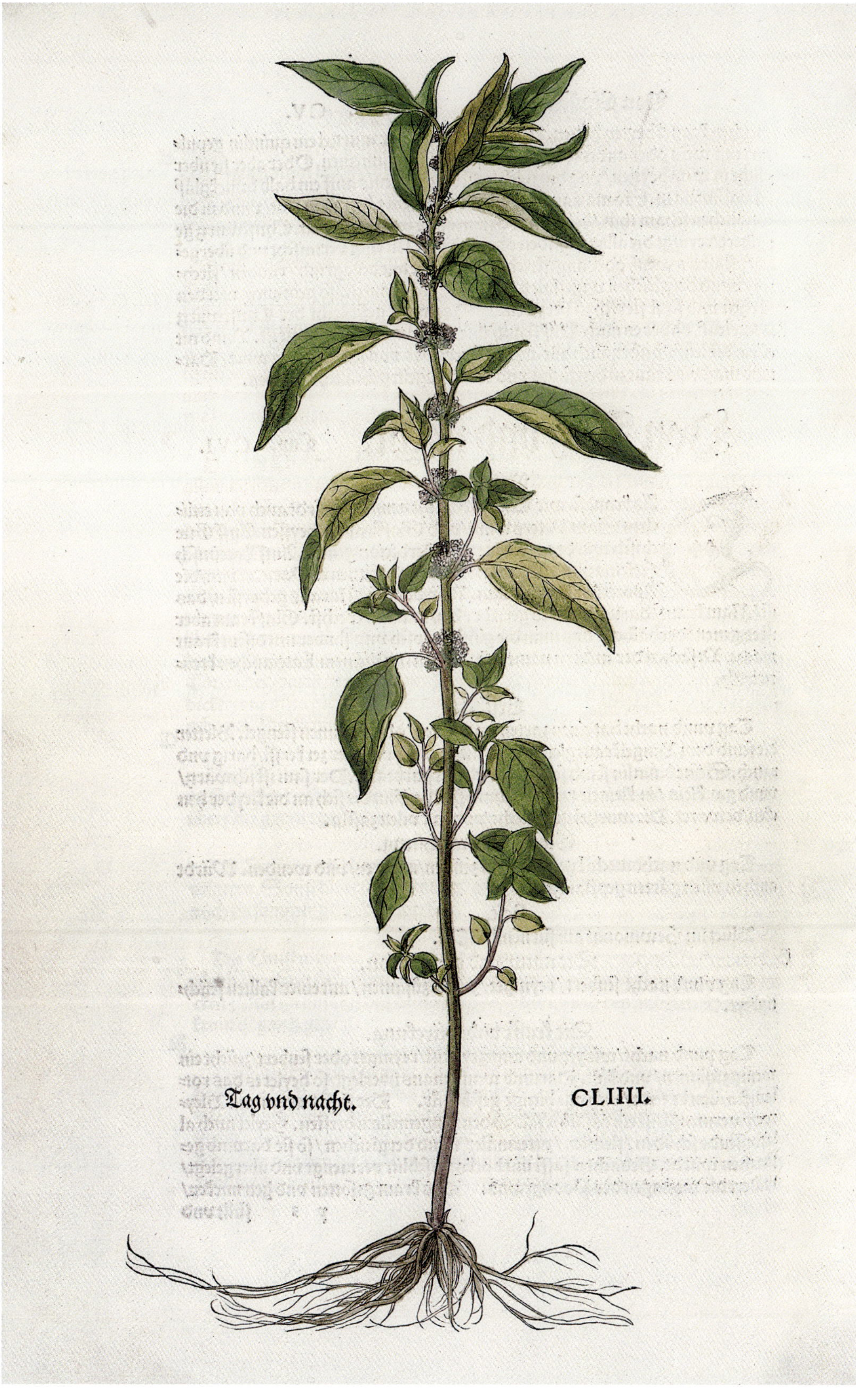
Tag vnd nacht.
CLIIII.

DYER'S MADDER

In this chapter (CVII), Fuchs included the actual DYER'S MADDER (plate CLV), which served as an important colouring agent, and GREAT HEDGE BEDSTRAW (plate CLVI), an only distantly related plant whose applications are not further specified.

„RÖDTE“

Im Kapitel „RÖDTE“ (Cap. CVII) erfasst Fuchs die eigentliche FÄRBERRÖTE (Taf. CLV), die als Krapp eine wichtige Färberpflanze war, und ebenso das botanisch nicht sehr eng verwandte WIESEN-LABKRAUT (Taf. CLVI), deren Wirkung nicht weiter unterschieden wird.

ROUGES

Au chapitre «ROUGES» (CVII) se trouvent réunis la GARANCE proprement dite (pl. CLV), plante tinctoriale de première importance autrefois, et le CAILLE-LAIT BLANC (pl. CLVI), ou gaillet mollugine, qui n'est pas, botaniquement, proche de la première. Fuchs n'en différencie pas les effets respectifs.

PAGE 240

DINKEL WHEAT

DINKEL WHEAT or SPELT (CVIII), designates the ancient form of wheat which played a great role in the work of Hildegard of Bingen. ONE-GRAINED WHEAT (plates CLVIII, CLVIII), on the other hand, is only rarely cultivated today.

„SPELTZ“

Als „SPELTZ“ (Cap. CVIII) oder Dinkel wird die uralte Weizenart heute noch bezeichnet, die bei Hildegard von Bingen eine große Rolle spielt, während das EINKORN (Taf. CLVII, CLVIII) heute nur noch vereinzelt kultiviert wird.

ÉPEAUTRE

L'ÉPEAUTRE (CVIII) a conservé son vieux nom de «Stelz» (glume). Cette très ancienne céréale, tant estimée d'Hildegarde von Bingen, est encore cultivée. Il en est de même pour le PETIT ÉPEAUTRE (pl. CLVII, CLVIII), appelé aussi ENGRAIN.

PAGE 241

COMMON GROUNDSEL

COMMON GROUNDSEL (CIX) supposedly not only helped to heal scab-forming skin disorders, but also was a remedy for bloody vomit and coughs.

GRINDKRAUT

GRINDKRAUT (Cap. CIX) sollte nicht nur bei krustenbildenden Hautkrankheiten helfen, sondern auch bei Blutspeien und Husten gute Dienste leisten.

SÉNEÇON COMMUN

Le SÉNEÇON COMMUN (CIX) serait efficace non seulement contre les affections cutanées accompagnées de croûtes, mais aussi contre la toux et l'hémoptysie.

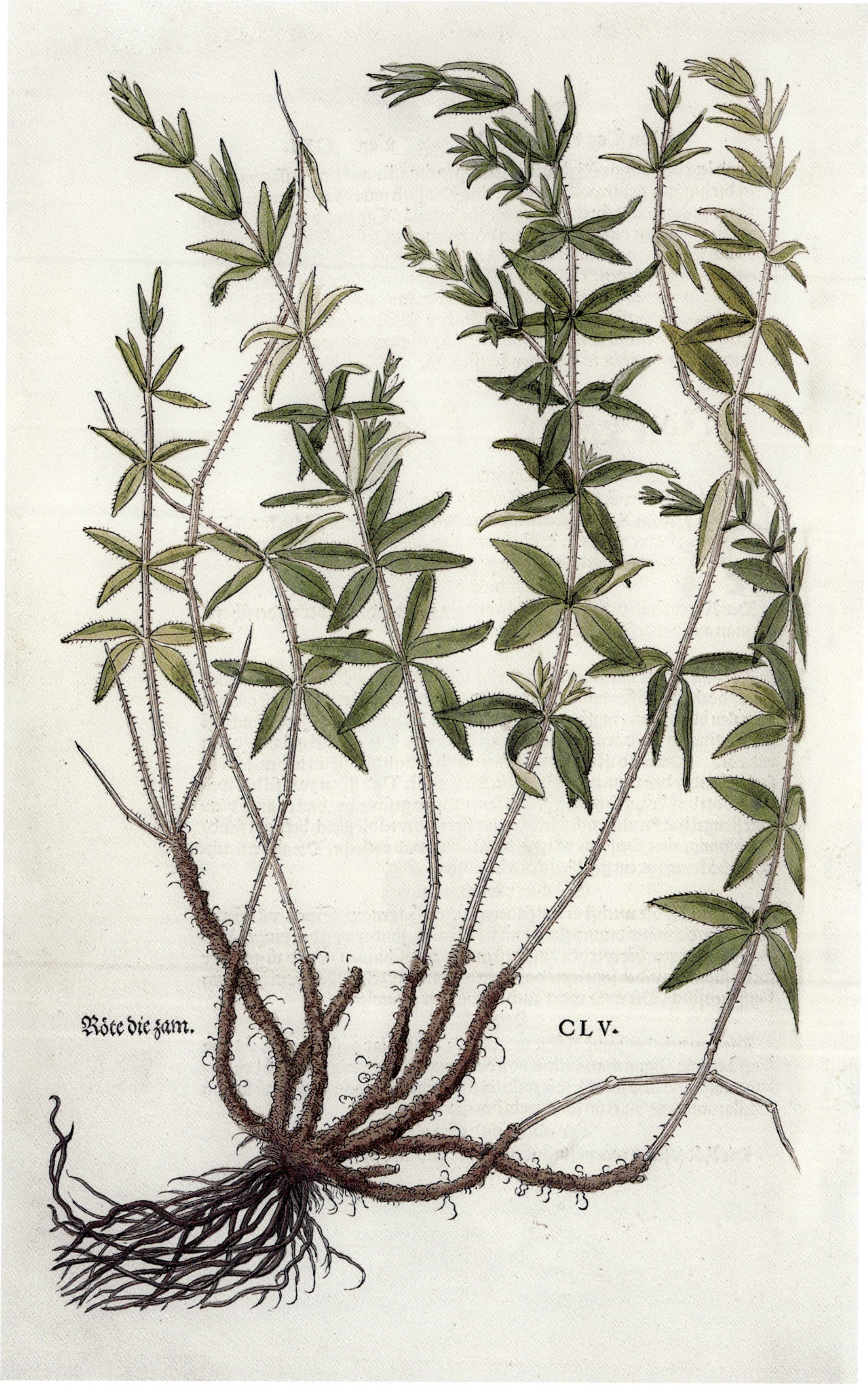
Rôte die zam.
CLV.

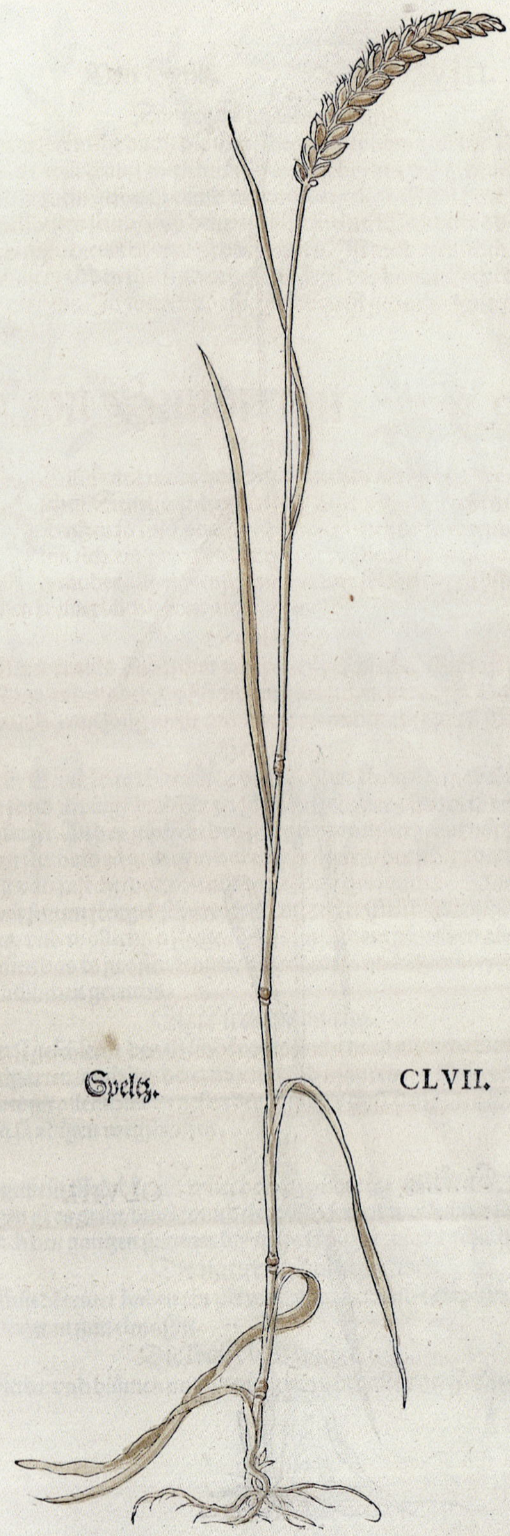

Speltz. CLVII.

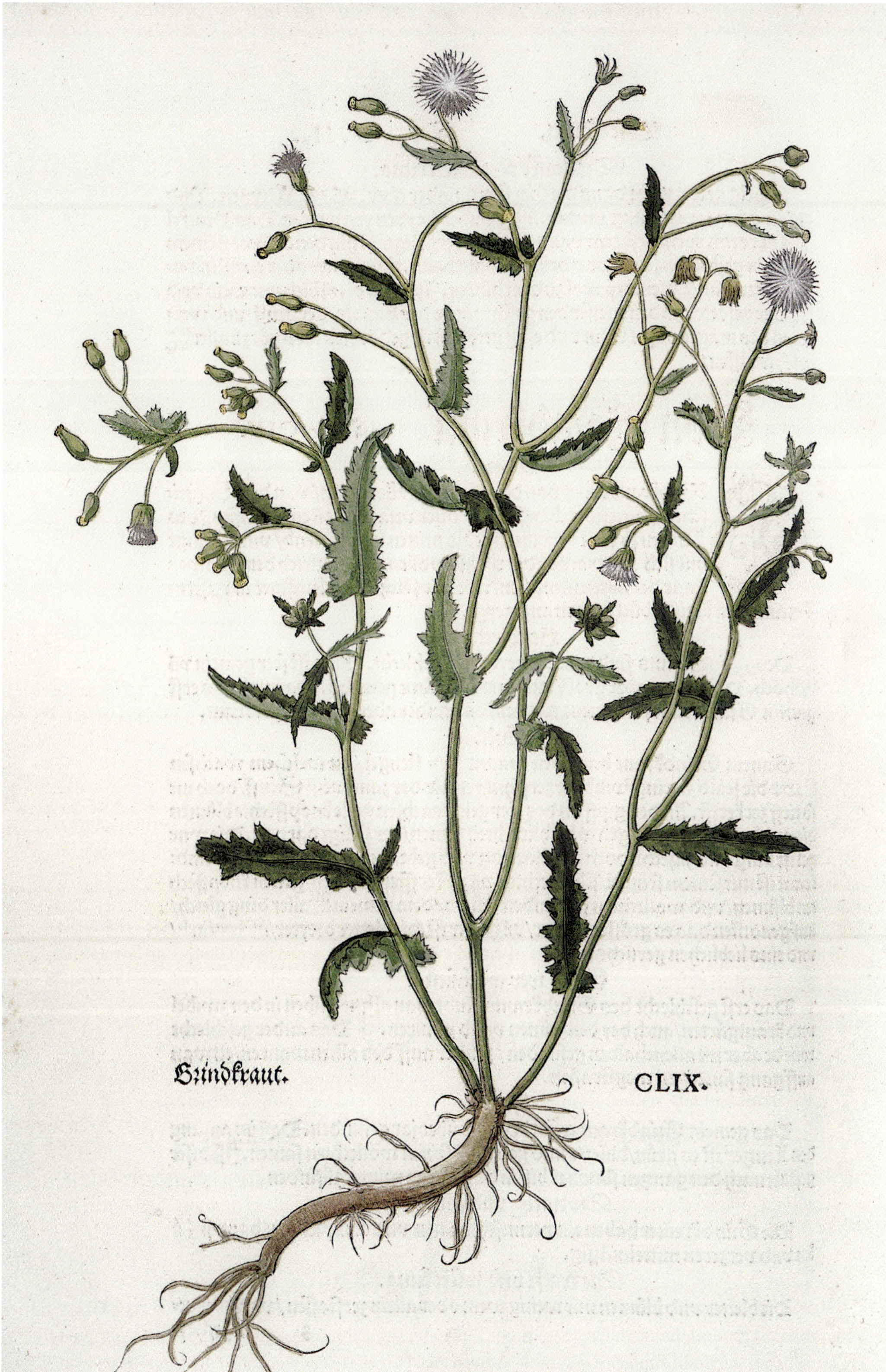
Grindkraut.
CLIX.

MINT

This chapter presents five illustrations from the MINT group (CX). Peppermint, which first springs to mind today, was not yet known in Fuchs's time.

„MÜNTZEN"

Die „MÜNTZEN" (Cap. CX) werden durch fünf Abbildungen von Vertretern der Gattung Mentha, Minze, vorgestellt. Die Pfefferminze, die wir heute in erster Linie darunter verstehen, war allerdings zur Zeit von Fuchs noch nicht bekannt.

MENTHA

Le genre MENTHA (CX) est représenté avec cinq espèces différentes. La menthe telle que nous l'entendons aujourd'hui n'était pas encore connue à l'époque.

PAGE 244

HART'S TONGUE

The lines of brown spores on the underside of the leaves make it clear that HART'S TONGUE (CXI), which was used for spleen ailments, is a fern.

HIRSCHZUNGE

Dass die bei Milzerkrankungen eingesetzte HIRSCHZUNGE (Cap. CXI) zu den Farnen gehört, darauf weisen höchstens die strichförmigen braunen Sporenhaufen auf der Unterseite der Blätter hin.

SCOLOPENDRE

Seuls les alignements de spores bruns au revers des feuilles nous révèlent que la SCOLOPENDRE (CXI), dite aussi langue-de-cerf, est une fougère, employée contre les maladies de la rate.

PAGE 245

FIELD ERYNGO

In the case of FIELD ERYNGO (CXII), none of the applications mentioned by Fuchs suggest that the plant had any real effect on male potency although its German name suggests that.

„MANSSTREW"

Die Herkunft des Namens „MANSSTREW" (Cap. CXII) ist nicht sicher zu belegen; jedenfalls lassen die bei Fuchs erwähnten Heilanzeigen nichts davon vermuten, dass man ihr eine treue, also sichere Wirkung auf die männliche Potenz nachsagte.

PANICAUT CHAMPÊTRE

Il est difficile d'expliquer l'origine du nom allemand du PANICAUT CHAMPÊTRE (CXII), «Mannstrew» (littéralement, fidèle à l'homme). Les indications thérapeutiques mentionnées par Fuchs ne laissent aucunement supposer que cette plante a aussi un effet «fidèle», donc éprouvé, sur la virilité.

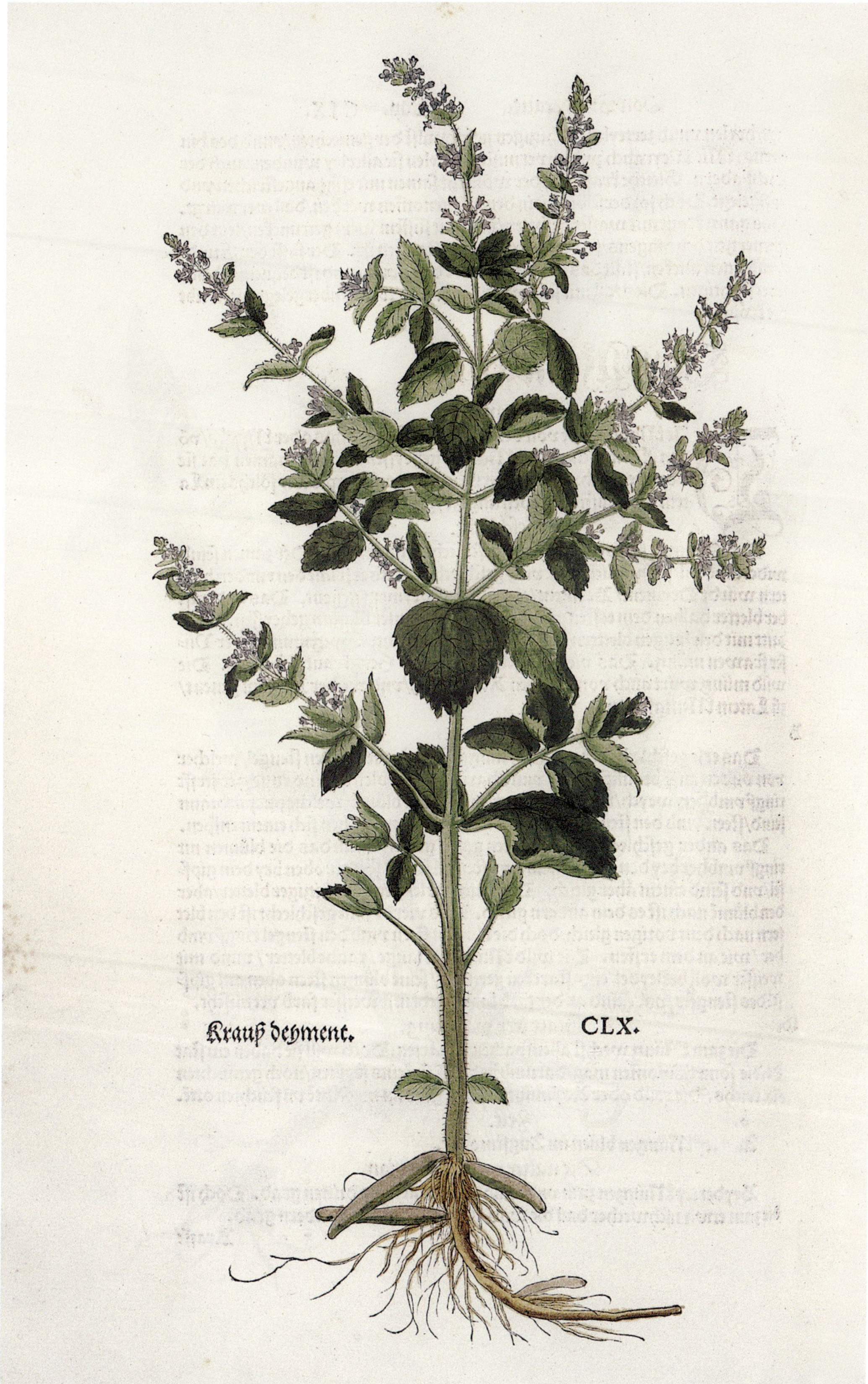

Krauß deyment. CLX.

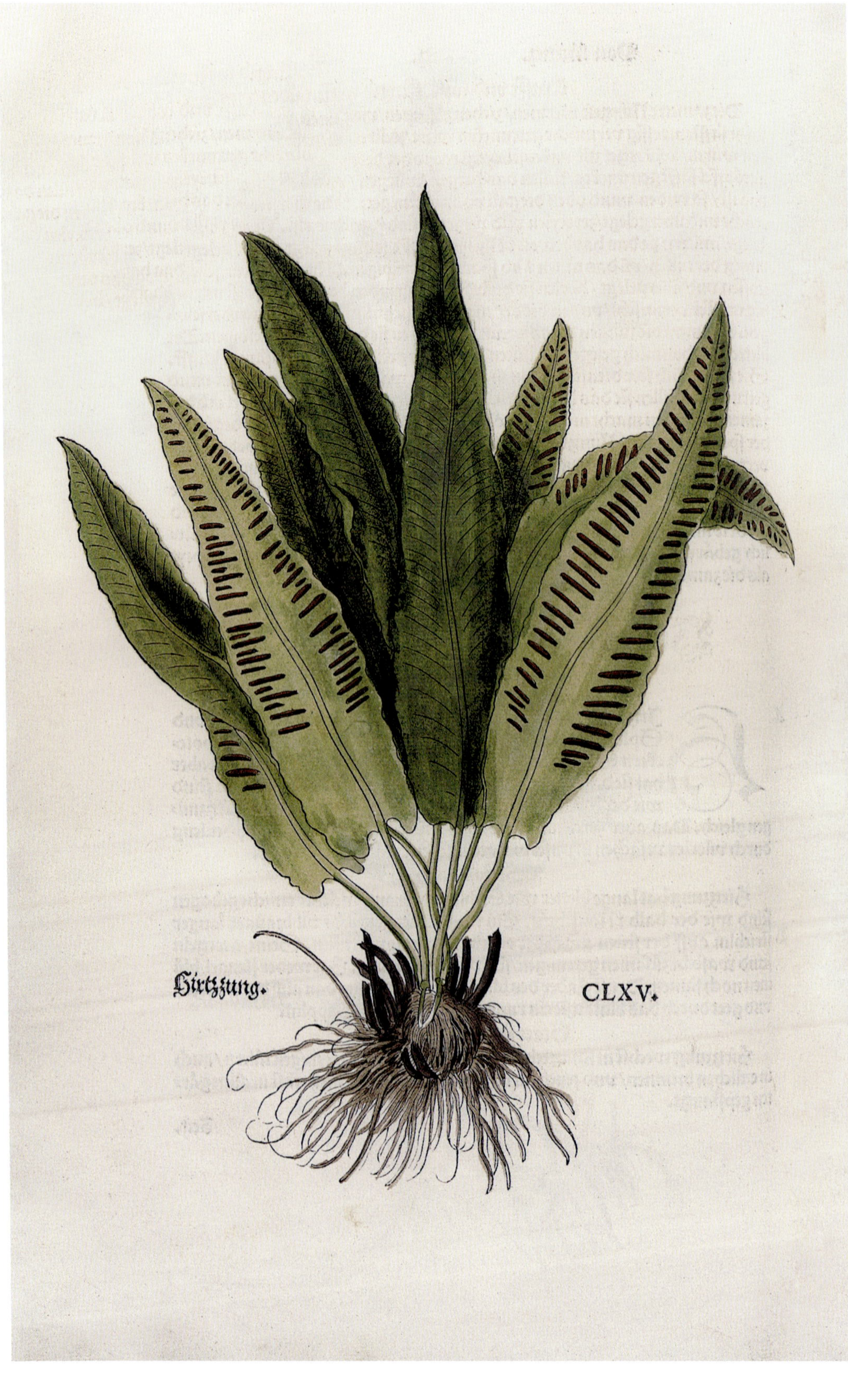
Hirtzzung.
CLXV.

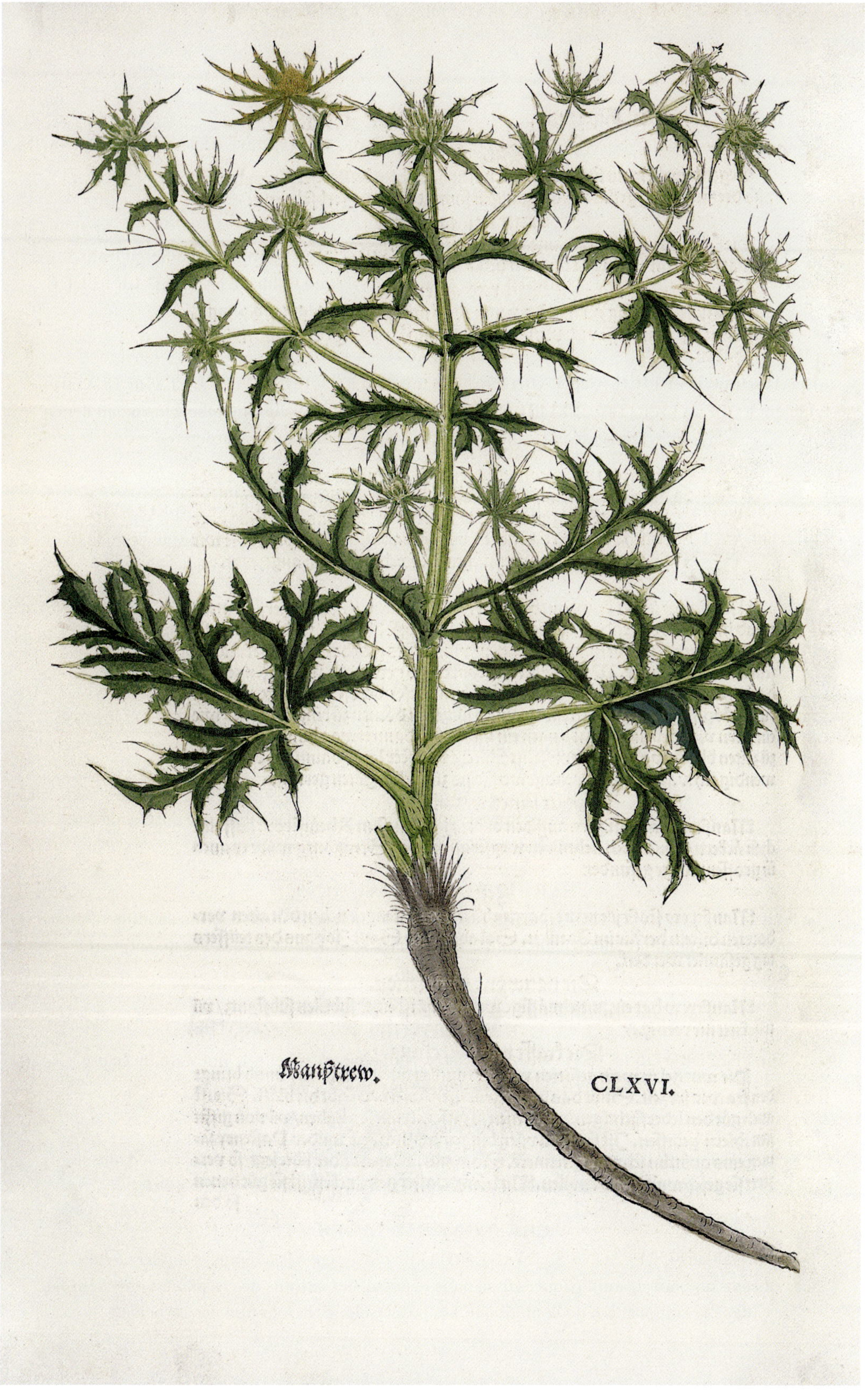
Manſtrew.
CLXVI.

LETTUCE

The illustrations in this chapter on LETTUCE (CXIII) clearly show how it differed from today's cultigens: Curly or LEAF LETTUCE (plate CLXVII) and Cabbage or HEAD LETTUCE (plate CLXVIII), both of which are still common food plants.

LATTICH

Der Abschnitt LATTICH (Cap. CXIII) führt uns mit dem RÖMISCHEN SALAT (Taf. CLXVII) und dem KOPFSALAT (Taf. CLXVIII) zwei noch heute gebräuchliche Nutzpflanzen vor, an denen die Unterschiede zur heutigen Kulturform gut sichtbar werden.

LAITUES

Au chapitre «LAITUES» (CXIII), nous découvrons la LAITUE FRISÉE (pl. CLXVII) et la LAITUE POMMÉE (pl. CLXVIII), bien différentes, comme on peut le voir, des deux plantes cultivées de nos jours.

PAGE 248

SUMMER SAVORY

SUMMER SAVORY (CXIIII) was not only indicated as a culinary herb, but was also described as having similar medicinal properties to Wild Thyme.

„SATURON"

„SATURON" (Cap. CXIIII), das Bohnenkraut, ist nicht nur als Gewürz angezeigt, sondern auch ähnlich dem Quendel arzneilich verwendbar.

SARRIETTE DES JARDINS

La SARRIETTE DES JARDINS (CXIIII) est figurée ici non seulement comme condiment mais aussi comme plante médicinale, dont les propriétés sont analogues à celles du serpolet.

PAGE 249

PEPPERWORTS

The PEPPERWORTS (CXV) were associated with a purgative effect, and were therefore considered suitable as theriac or cure-alls for poisons.

„WILDE KRESSEN"

Den „WILDEN KRESSEN" (Cap. CXV) wird ausführende Wirkung zugeschrieben, die sie sogar für den vermeintlich giftwidrigen Theriak geeignet erscheinen ließ.

CRESSONS SAUVAGES

On prêtait aux CRESSONS SAUVAGES (CXV) – passerage des champs et passerage des décombres – un pouvoir antitoxique. Aussi, dans le passé, des extraits de ces plantes entraient-ils dans la composition de la thériaque, supposée soigner la morsure des serpents.

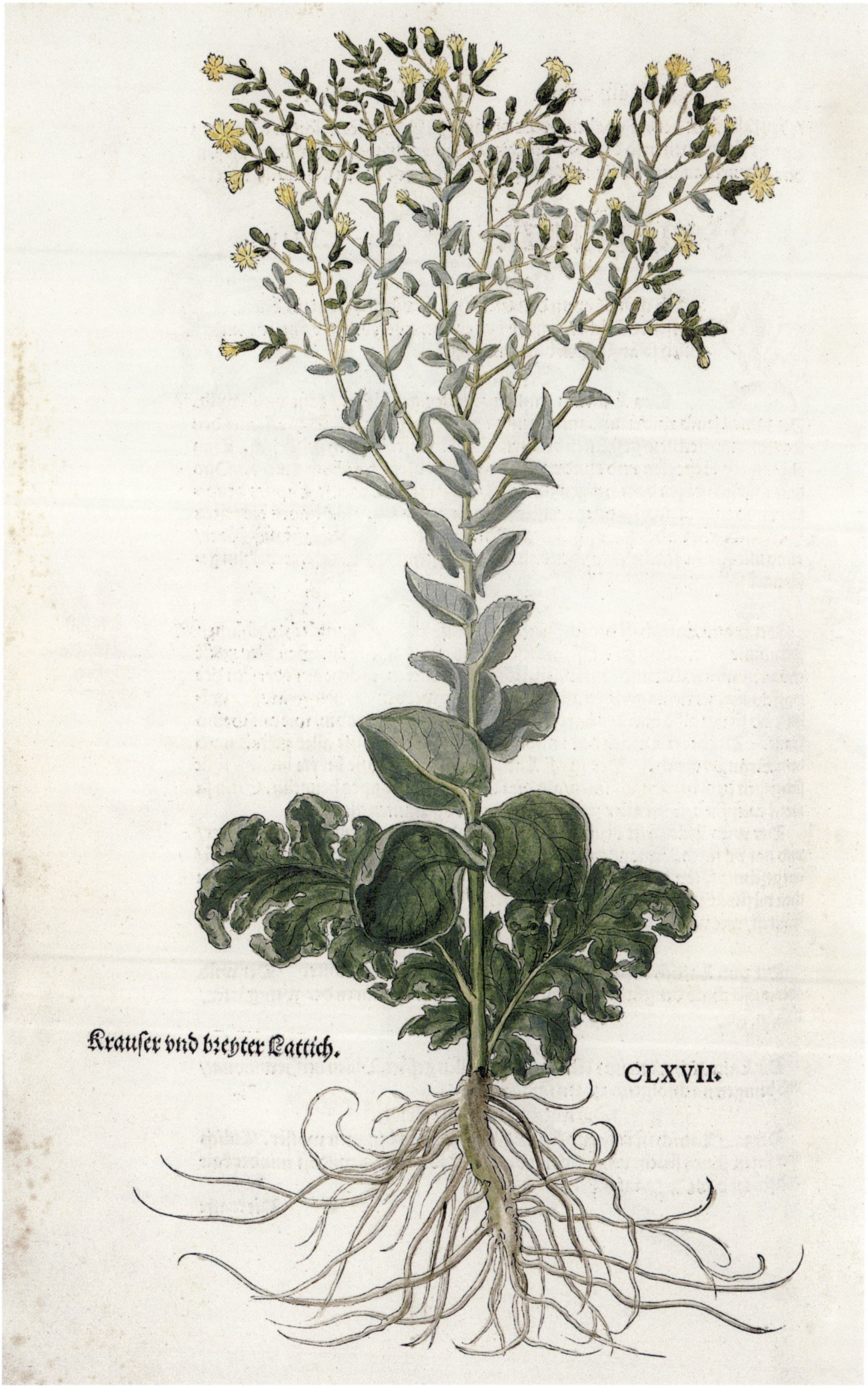
Krauser vnd breyter Lattich.
CLXVII.

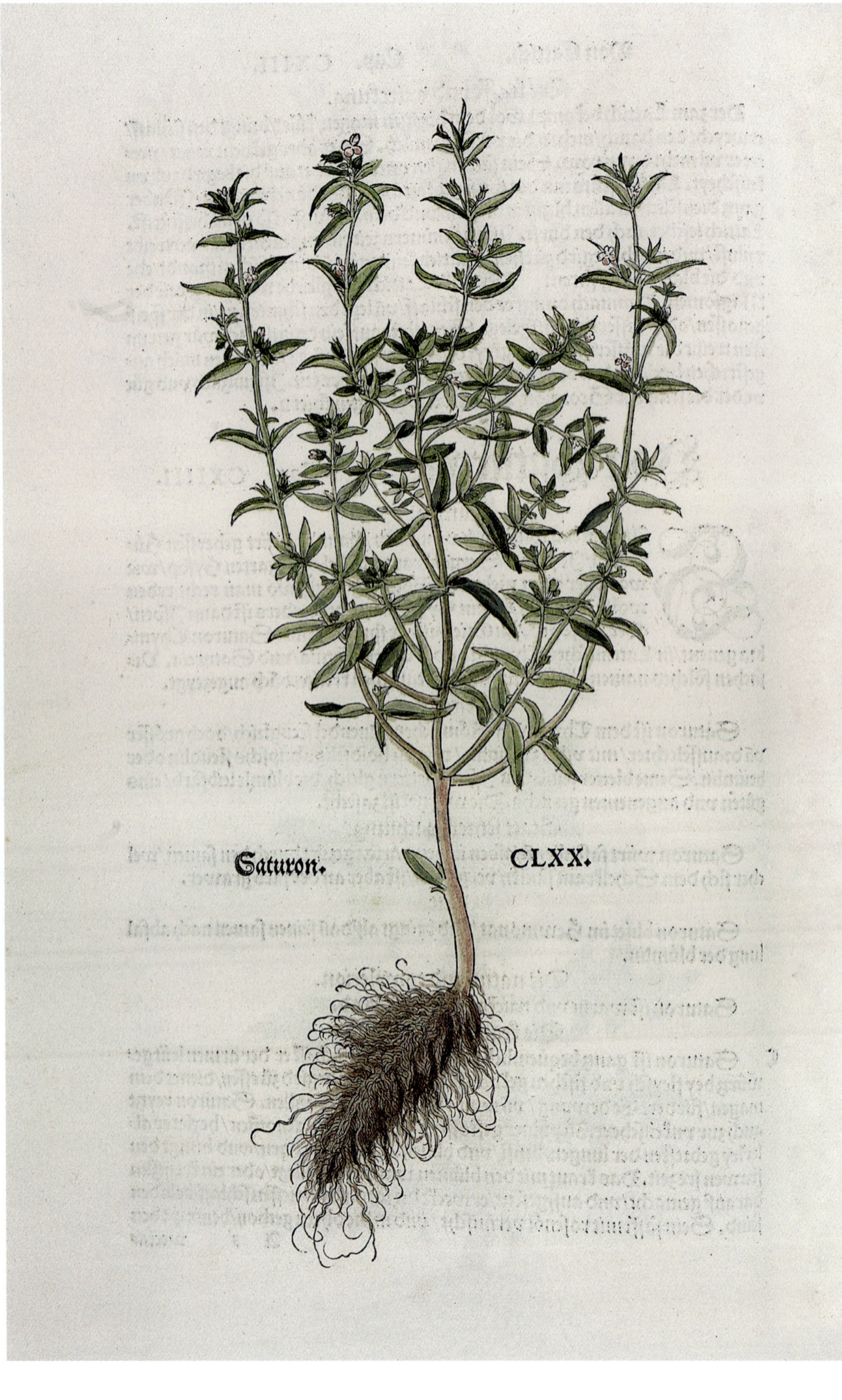
Saturon.
CLXX.

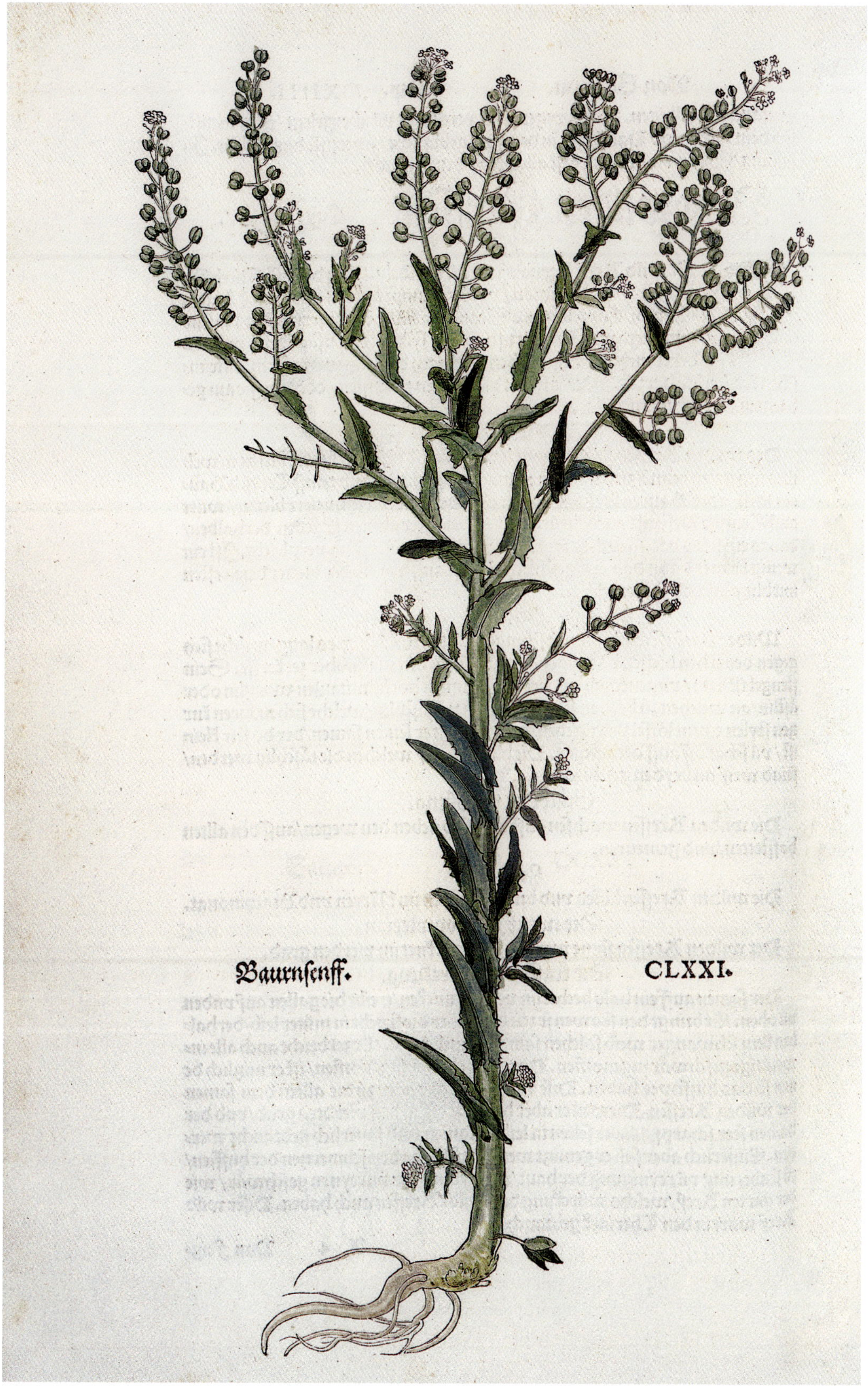
Baurnſenff.
CLXXI.

BITTER-TASTING WHITE LUPIN

In addition to its role as a worm medicine, or vermifuge, the (CXVI) BITTER-TASTING WHITE LUPIN was also considered an effective remedy for disorders ranging from diseases of the liver and spleen to skin eruptions in cattle.

„FEIGBONEN“

Den bitter schmeckenden „FEIGBONEN“ (Cap. CXVI), die wir heute Lupinen nennen, wurde neben ihrer Rolle als Wurmmittel auch heilende Wirkung bei Leber- und Milzerkrankungen bis hin zu Hautausschlägen des Viehs zugeschrieben.

LUPIN BLANC

Le LUPIN BLANC (CXVI) avait une réputation de vermifuge à cause de son goût amer. On croyait également qu'il avait des effets salutaires sur les maladies du foie et de la rate, et même sur les éruptions cutanées du bétail.

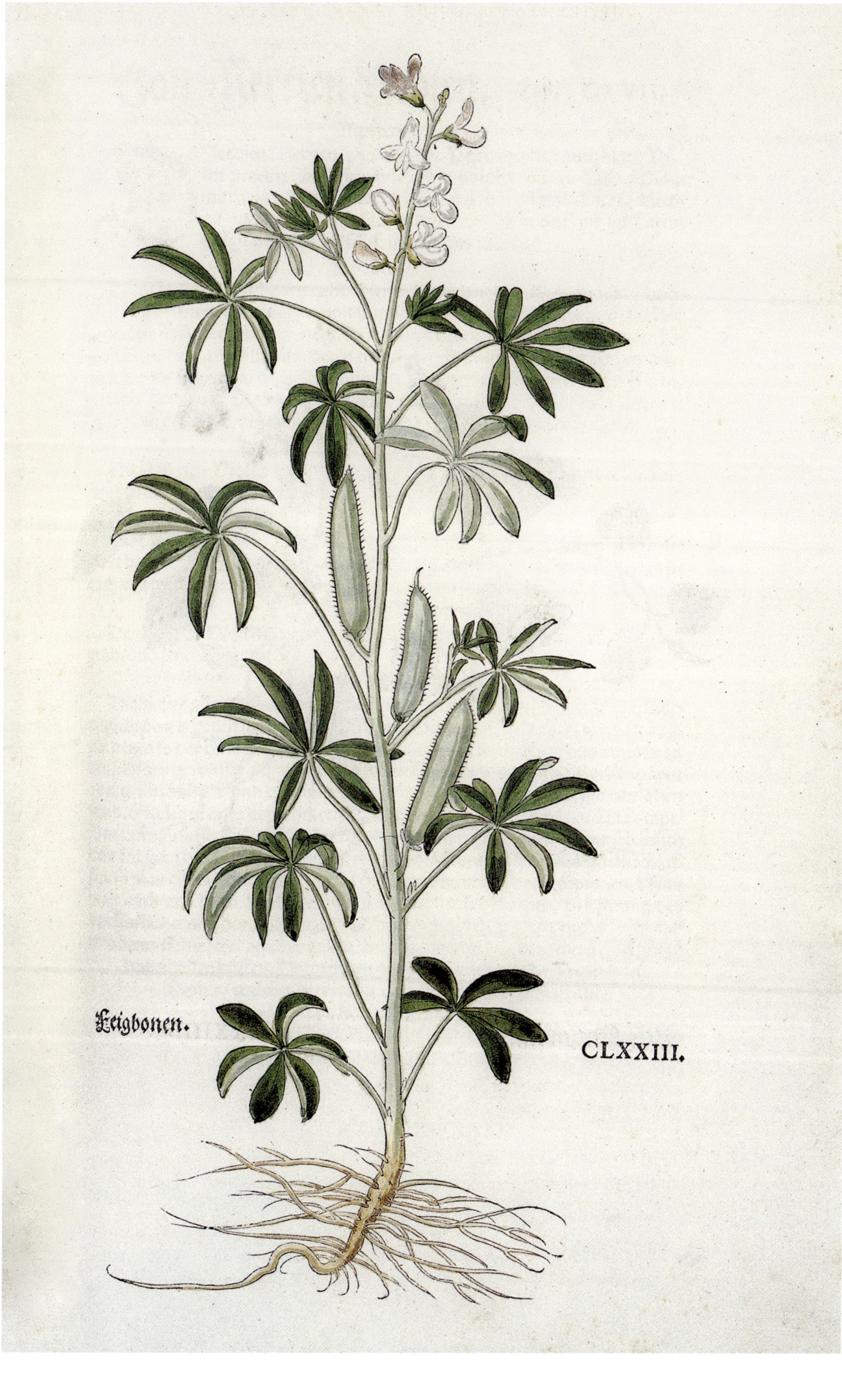
Feigbonen.
CLXXIII.

SWEET VIOLET

SWEET VIOLET (CXVII) is not only a beautiful harbinger of spring, but also long served as a medicinal plant, although it is hardly used today.

MÄRZVEILCHEN

MÄRZVEILCHEN (Cap. CXVII) sind nicht nur schöne Frühlingsboten, als Heilpflanze werden sie seit Langem eingesetzt, heute allerdings kaum mehr gebraucht.

VIOLETTE ODORANTE

La VIOLETTE ODORANTE (CXVII) n'est pas seulement une jolie fleur annonçant le printemps, elle possède aussi des propriétés dont on s'est servi pendant longtemps.

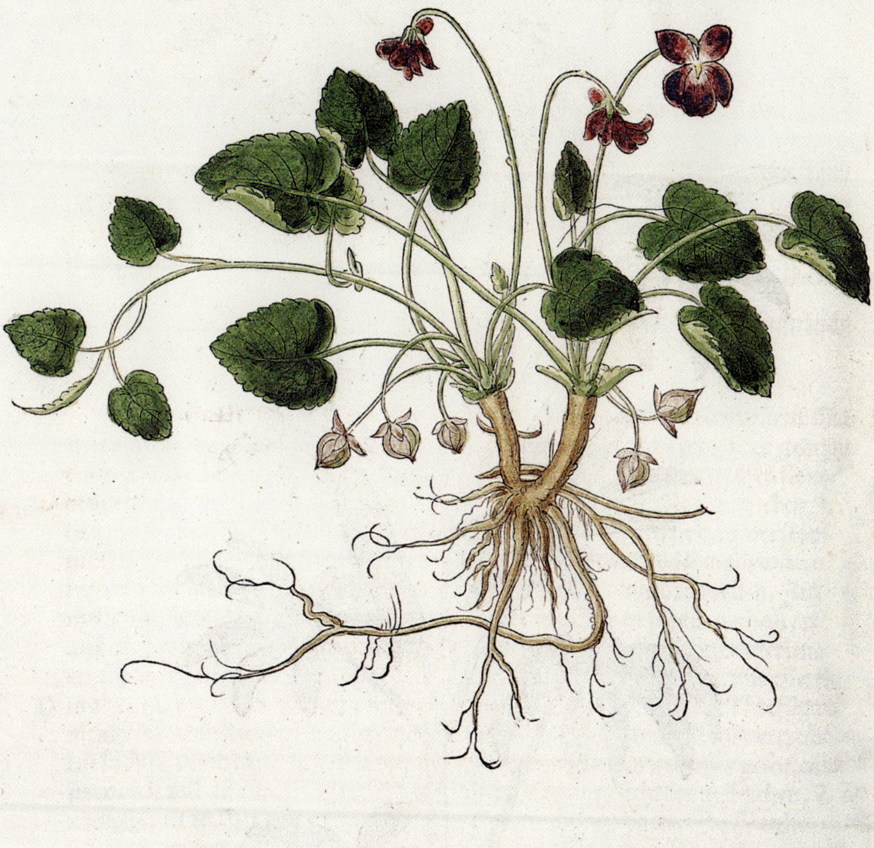

Mertzen veiel. CLXXIIII.

SWEET VIOLET | MÄRZVEILCHEN | VIOLETTE ODORANTE

DAME'S VIOLET

STOCK, or DAME'S VIOLET (CXVIII), is a hardy annual. Fuchs provides three specimens with various coloured flowers.

WINTER-VIOLE

Ihre Frostbeständigkeit brachte der Nachtviole den Namen WINTER-VIOLE (Cap. CXVIII) ein. Fuchs bildet von ihr drei Exemplare in unterschiedlicher Blütenfärbung ab.

GIROFLÉE

La GIROFLÉE (CXVIII) doit son nom de «violier d'hiver» («Winter-Viole») à sa résistance particulière au gel. Fuchs en présente trois exemplaires aux coloris différents.

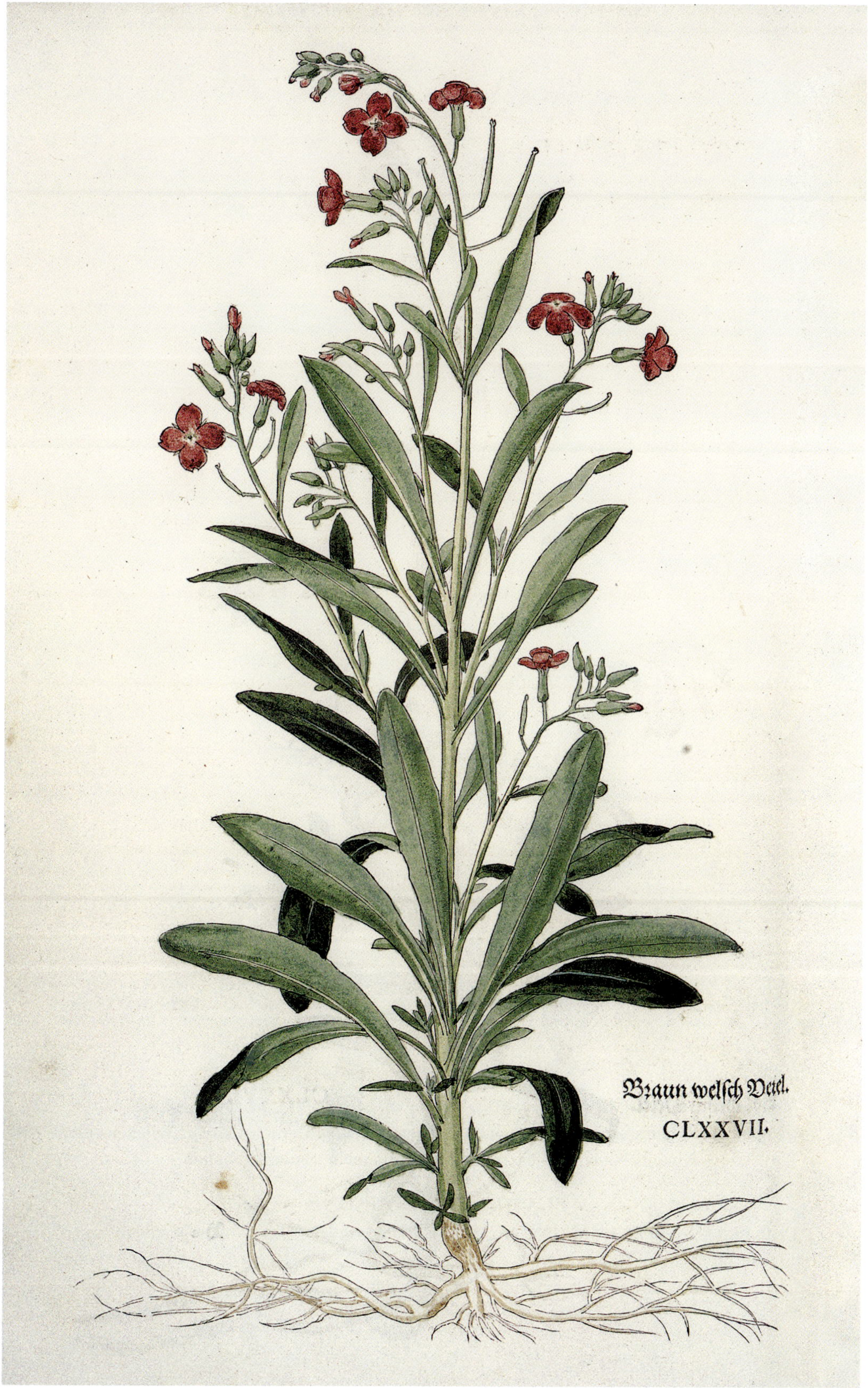
Braun welsch Veiel.
CLXXVII.

IRIS

With its violet-like scent, the rhizome of the blue GERMAN, or COMMON, IRIS (CXIX) was used for many years as an analgesic for teething children.

„GILGEN“

Von der blauen „GILGEN“ (Cap. CXIX), der Blauen Schwertlilie, hat sich am längsten die Anwendung ihres Wurzelstocks – wegen des veilchenähnlichen Geruchs wird er Veilchenwurzel genannt – zur Schmerzstillung bei zahnenden Kindern gehalten.

FLAMBE D'ALLEMAGNE

De la FLAMBE D'ALLEMAGNE (CXIX), un iris de couleur bleue, c'est essentiellement le rhizome qui a connu la plus longue application médicale : sous forme de «racine de violette», appelée ainsi à cause de son odeur agréable, on la donnait à mâcher aux enfants pour faire leurs dents et soulager leurs douleurs.

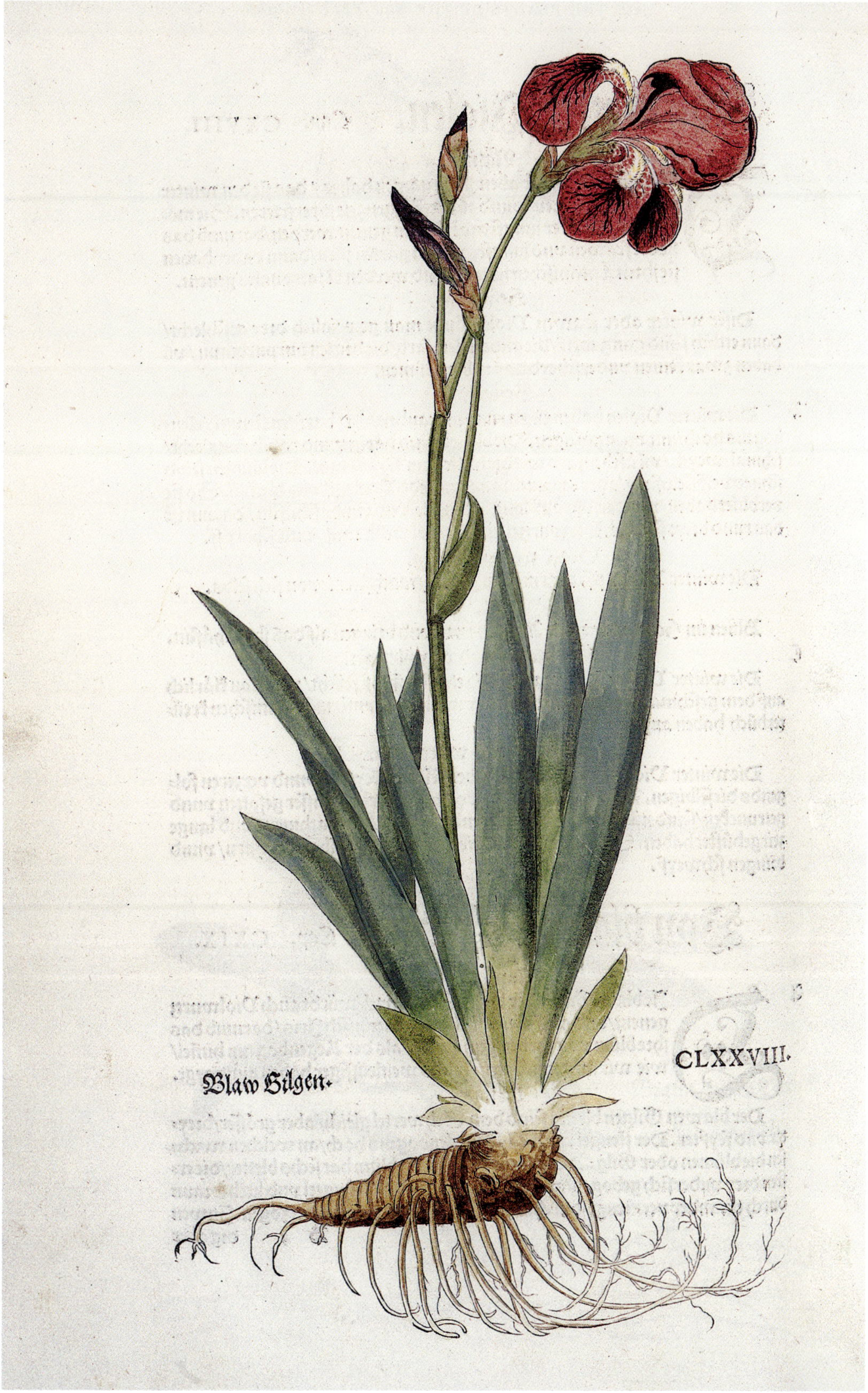
Blaw Gilgen.
CLXXVIII.

HAWKWEEDS

Fuchs illustrates the chapter on HAWKWEEDS (CXX) with SOW THISTLE (plate CLXXIX), also known as Field Milk Thistle, and HAWKS-BEARD (plate CLXXX).

„HABICHKRAUT"

„HABICHKRAUT" (Cap. CXX) wird durch die ACKER-GÄNSEDISTEL (Taf. CLXXIX) und den DACH-PIPPAU (Taf. CLXXX) repräsentiert.

LAITERON DES CHAMPS

Le LAITERON DES CHAMPS (pl. CLXXIX) et la CRÉPIDE DES TOITS (pl. CLXXX) représentent ici les «ÉPERVIÈRES» (CXX).

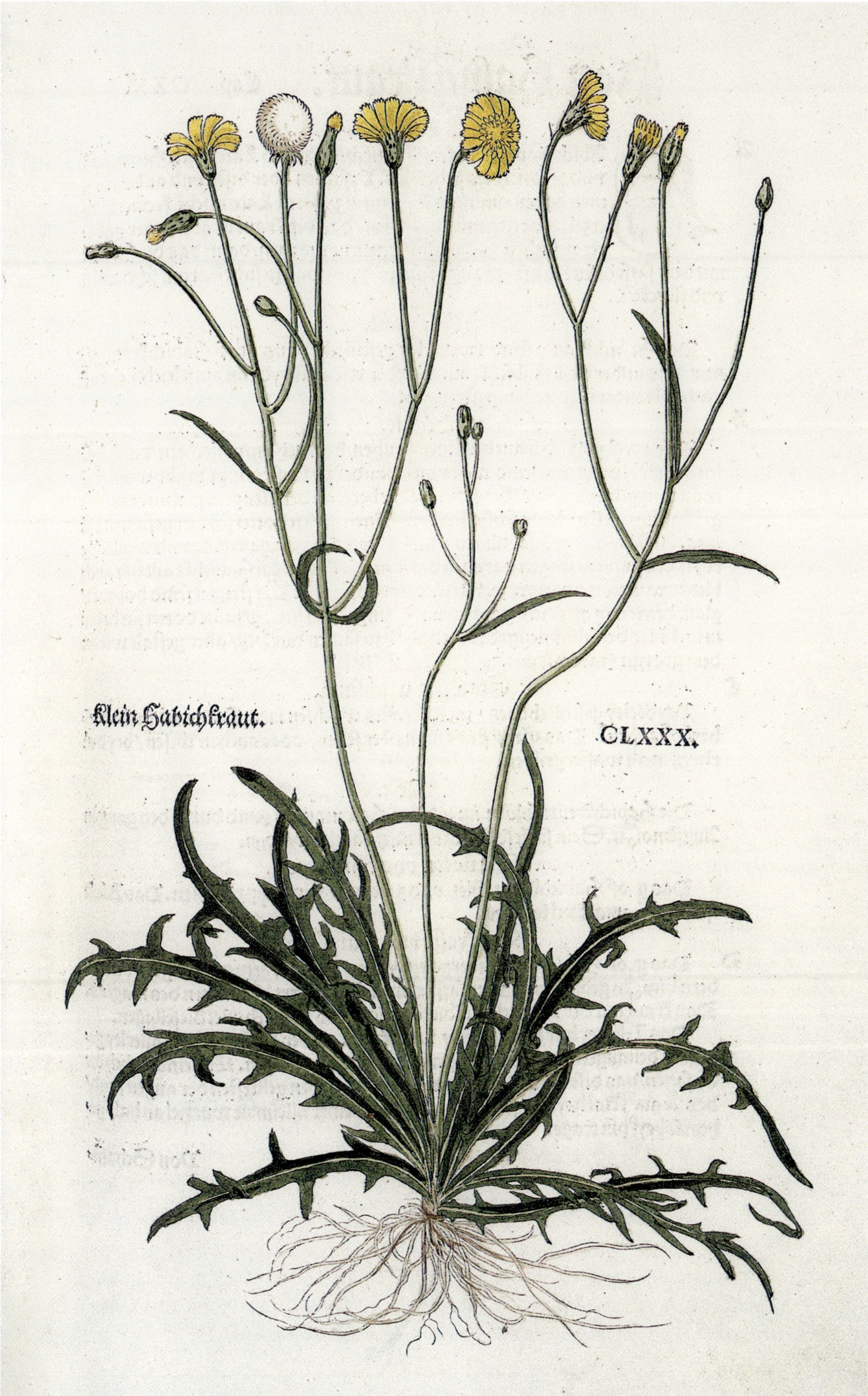
Klein Habichkraut.
CLXXX.

HORSETAIL

Here Fuchs depicts two species of HORSETAIL (CXXI): the poisonous MARSH HORSETAIL (plate CLXXXI) and COMMON HORSETAIL (plate CLXXXII). To both Fuchs attributes diuretic and vulnerary powers.

„SCHAFFTHEW“

Zu dem Kapitel „SCHAFFTHEW“ (Cap. CXXI) bildet Fuchs zwei Arten ab, den giftigen SUMPF-SCHACHTELHALM (Taf. CLXXXI) und den ACKER-SCHACHTELHALM (Taf. CLXXXII), für die er vor allem harntreibende und wundheilungsfördernde Wirkungen beschreibt.

FOIN À HAMPE

Au chapitre «Schaffthew» ou FOIN À HAMPE (CXXI), Fuchs illustre deux plantes, la PRÊLE DES MARAIS (pl. CLXXXI) et la PRÊLE DES CHAMPS (pl. CLXXXII), dont il souligne les effets diurétiques et cicatrisants.

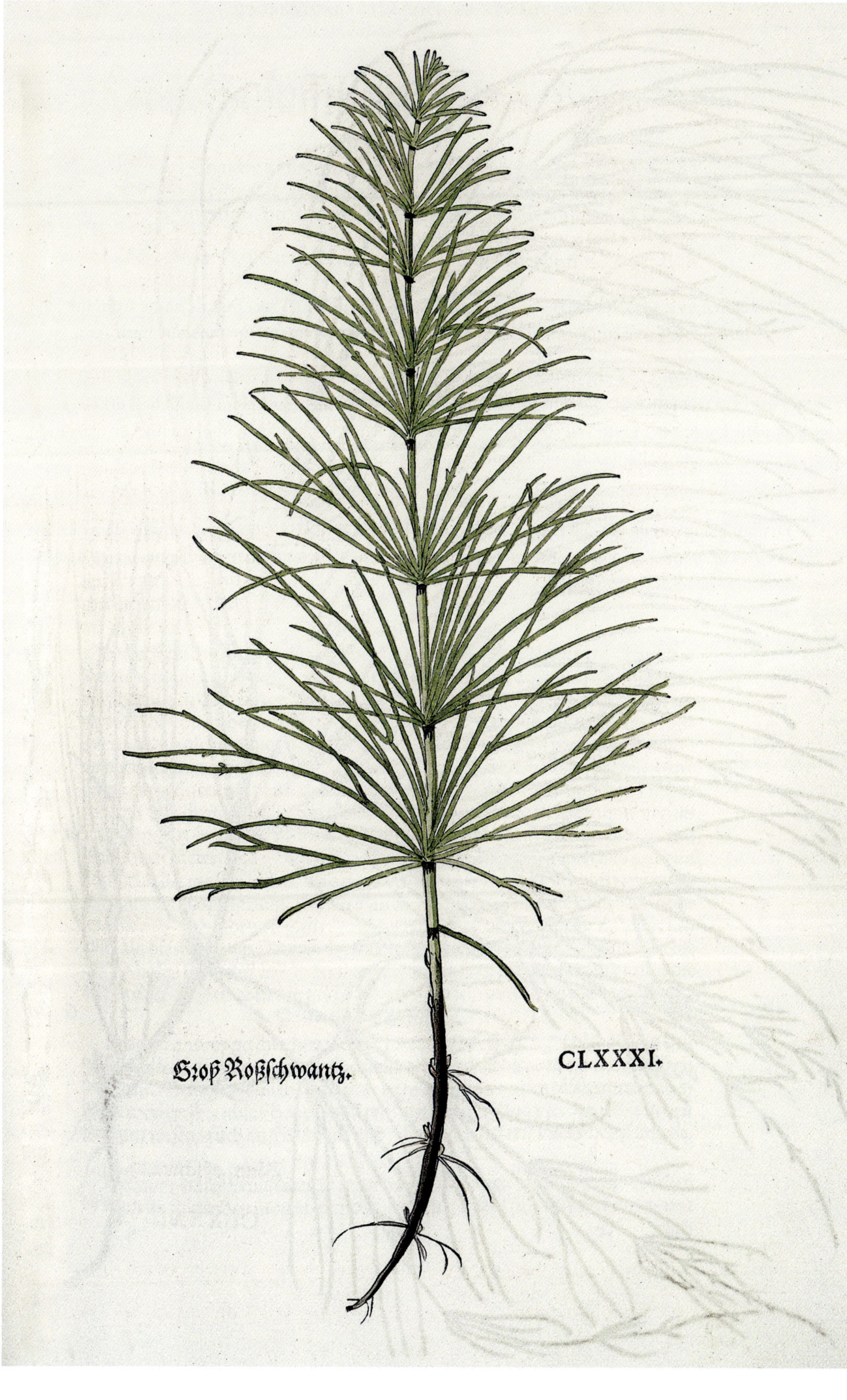
Groß Roßschwantz.
CLXXXI.

LADY'S SMOCK

Also known as LADY'S SMOCK, CUCKOO FLOWER (CXXII) received its name from the bird, which was supposed to have caused the drops of foam on the meadow herb.

„GAUCHBLUM"

Bei der „GAUCHBLUM" (Cap. CXXII) lässt sich der Name nicht wie beim Gauchheil erklären, vielmehr kommt der erste Teil vom Guckgauch, dem Kuckuck, von dem man meinte, er würde die Schaumklümpchen auf dem Wiesenschaumkraut verursachen.

CARDAMINE DES PRÉS

Le nom allemand de la CARDAMINE DES PRÉS (CXXII), «Gauchblum», signifie «fleur à coucou», car on pensait que cet oiseau déposait la mousse blanchâtre maculant souvent ses tiges.

PAGE 264

BLACK LOVAGE

BLACK LOVAGE (CXXIII), or Alexanders, was recommended not only as a culinary herb, but also as a remedy for rabies.

„GROSS EPPICH"

Der „GROSS EPPICH" (Cap. CXXIII) fand nicht nur als Gewürz Verwendung, er sollte sogar gegen Tollwut helfen.

MACERON

Le MACERON (CXXIII) n'était pas seulement un condiment, mais aussi une plante médicinale qui aurait soigné la rage.

PAGE 265

EVERGREEN MISTLETOE

Fuchs had already mentioned EVERGREEN MISTLETOE (CXXIIII) in connection with Oak; here it appears with its own, albeit short, description of its ability to drain and disperse.

IMMERGRÜNE MISTEL

Die IMMERGRÜNE MISTEL (Cap. CXXIIII), bereits im Zusammenhang mit der Eiche erwähnt, erscheint hier mit einer eigenen, wenn auch kurzen Beschreibung ihrer ableitenden und zerteilenden Kraft.

GUI

Le GUI (CXXIIII), déjà évoqué avec le chêne, figure ici accompagné d'une brève description de son pouvoir évacuant et résolutif.

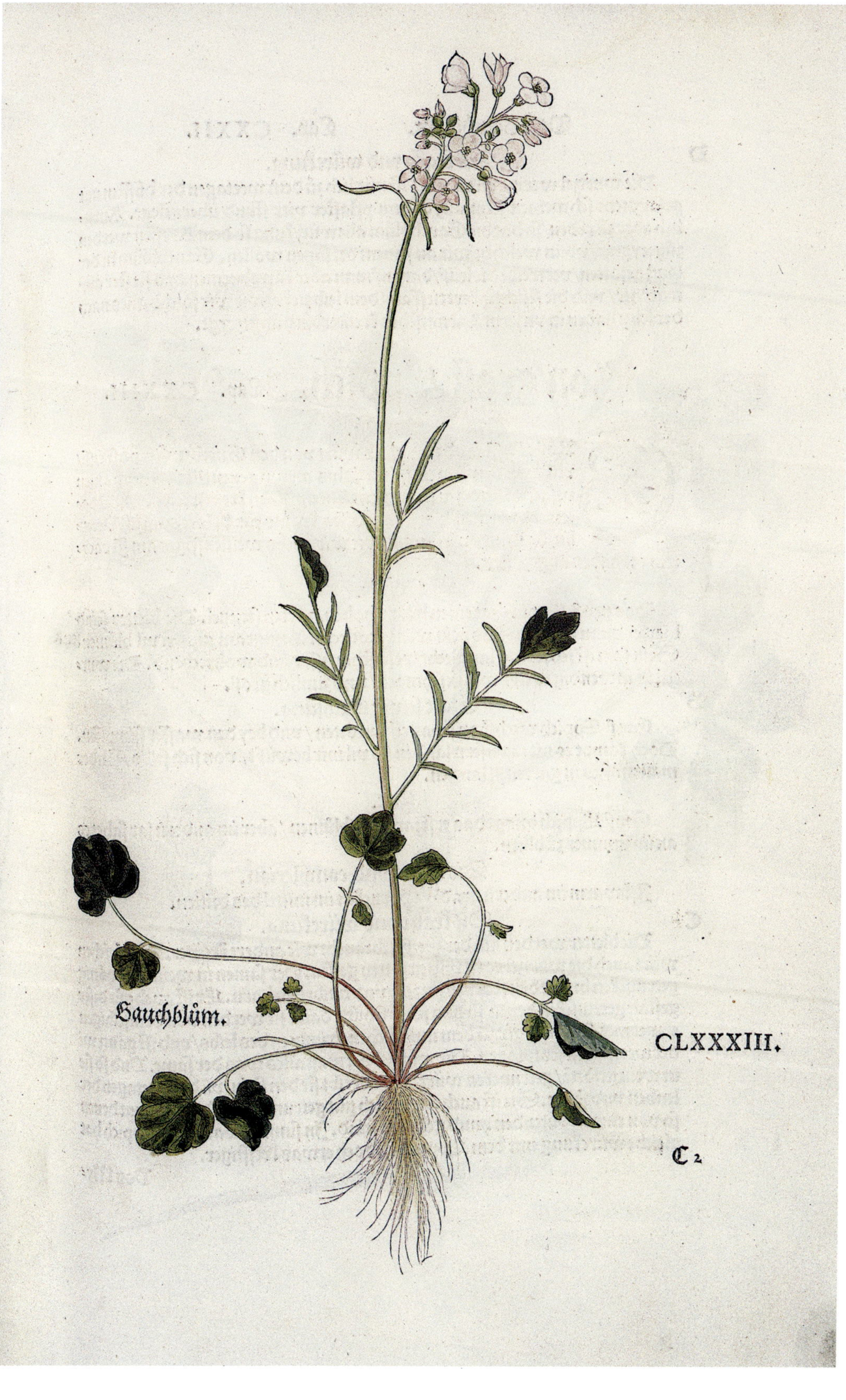

LADY'S SMOCK | „GAUCHBLUM“ | CARDAMINE DES PRÉS

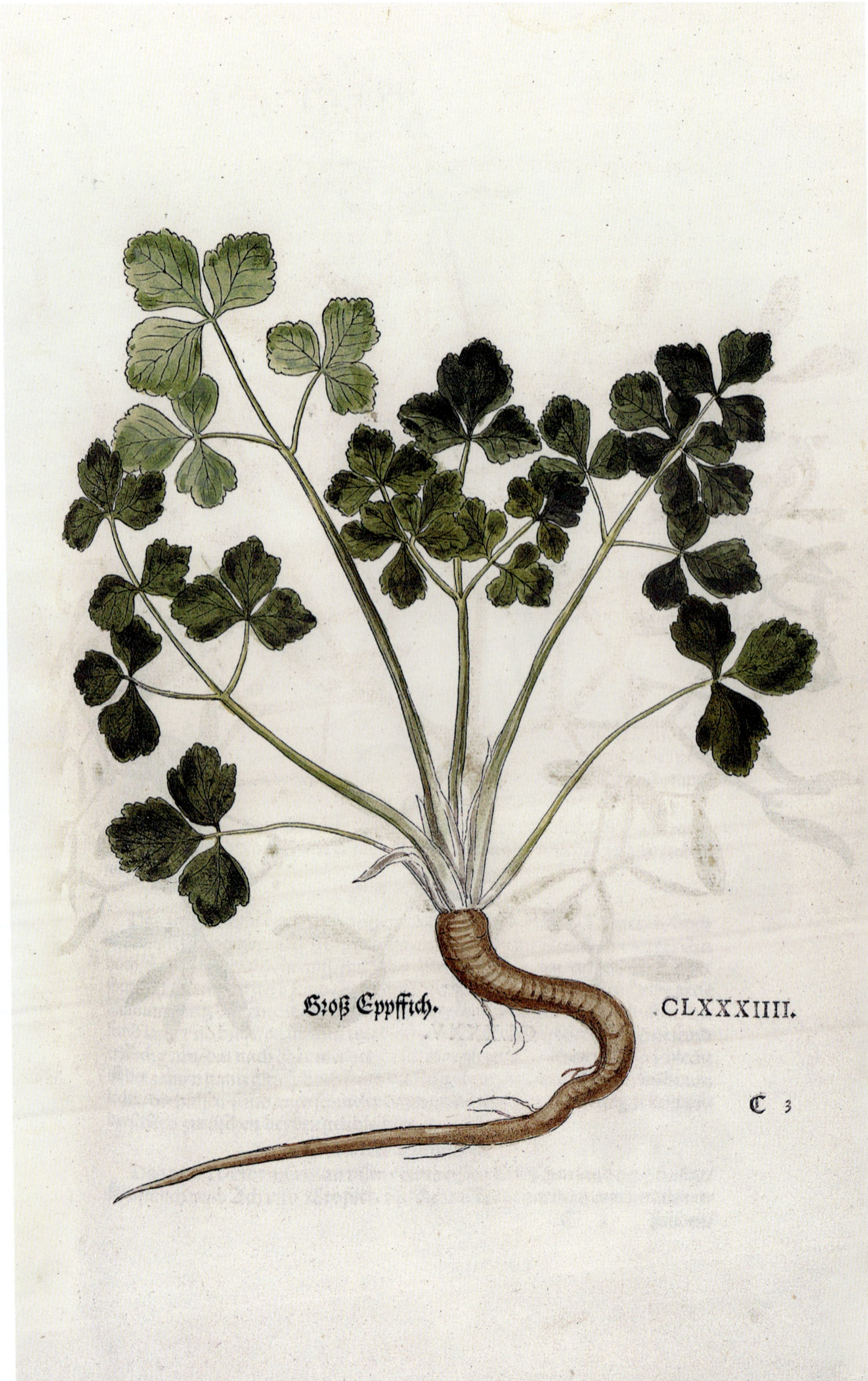
Groß Eppfich.
.CLXXXIIII.
C 3

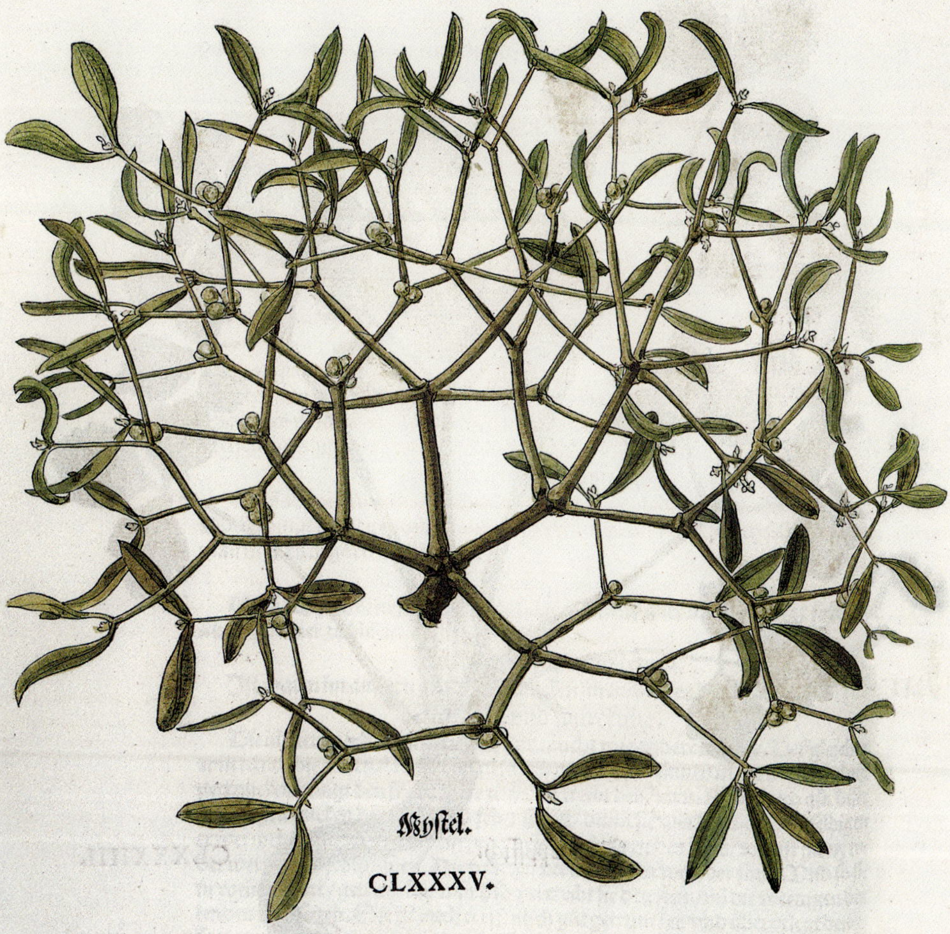

Myſtel.

CLXXXV.

WOAD

The two varieties of WOAD (CXXV) illustrated are of very different habit. Fuchs records Aachen and Erfurt (Thuringia) as sites where the important domesticated WOAD was raised for dye; for Wild Woad, he mentions his own city of Tübingen as a place where the plant was to be found.

WAID

Beim WAID (Cap. CXXV), Fuchs schreibt „Weydt", werden zwei Varietäten abgebildet, die sich im Habitus deutlich unterscheiden. Für den wichtigen Färberwaid nennt er Aachen und das thüringische Erfurt als Anbauorte, für den Wilden Waid führt er das heimatliche Tübingen als Standortbeispiel an.

PASTEL DES TEINTURIERS

Fuchs présente le PASTEL DES TEINTURIERS (CXXV) sous deux formes nettement distinctes, en précisant leur distribution géographique. La première est cultivée dans les régions d'Aix-la-Chapelle et d'Erfurt, en Thuringe, tandis que le pastel sauvage se rencontre par exemple à Tübingen, où vit Fuchs.

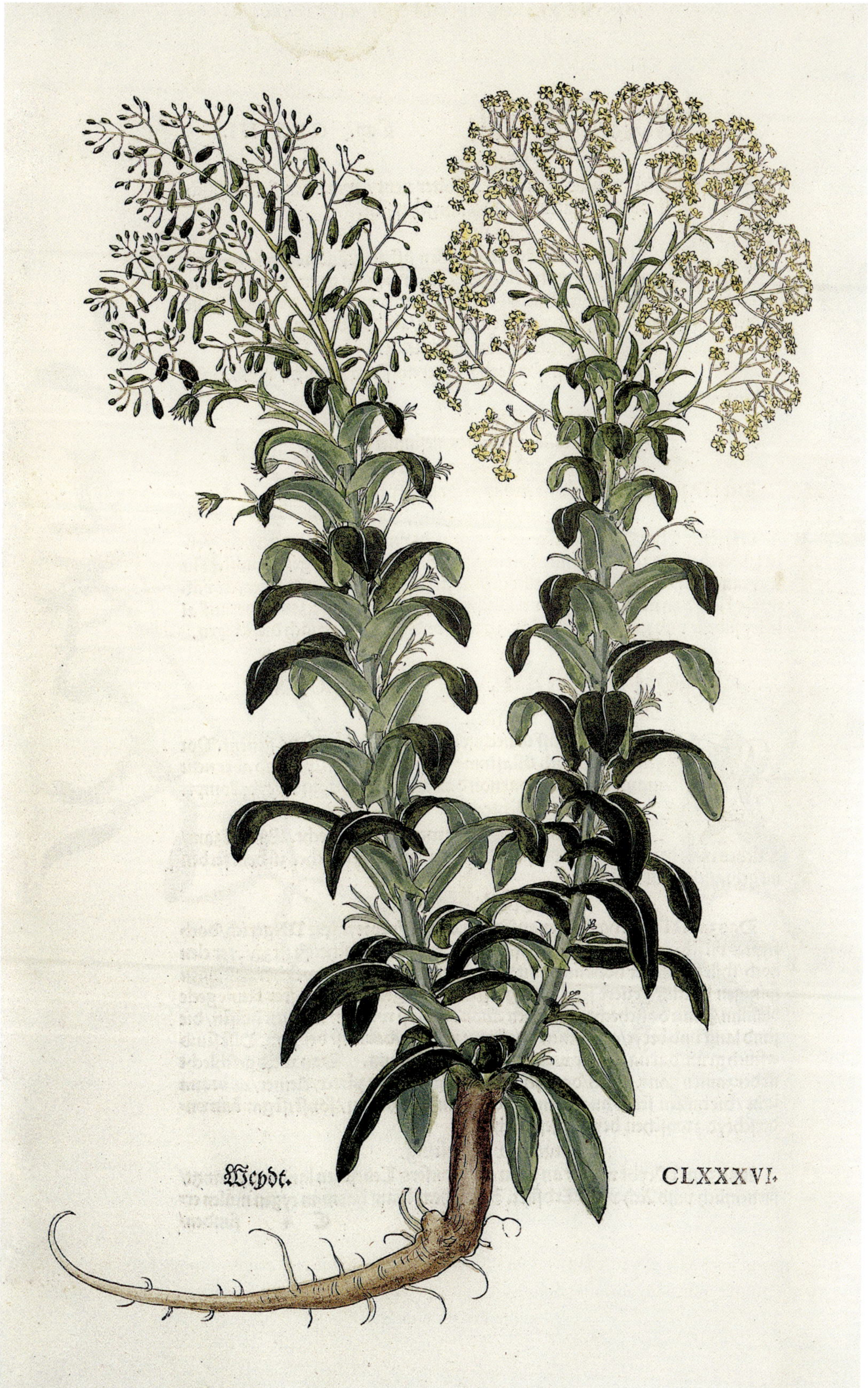
Weydt.
CLXXXVI.

WILLOWS

In the case of the WILLOWS (CXXVI), the suggested application for podagra reflects their actual pain-relieving effect; similarly, the observation that a WILLOW broth loosens dandruff refers to the plant's keratolytic effect.

WEIDEN

Die WEIDEN (Cap. CXXVI) schließen sich an und hier deuten die Anwendung gegen Podagra auf die tatsächlich schmerzstillende Wirkung und die Beobachtung, dass der Sud Schuppen auf dem Kopf löst, auf die keratolytische Wirkung hin.

SAULES

Suivent les SAULES (CXXVI) et leurs indications thérapeutiques. Fuchs évoque la podagre, ce qui prouve leur pouvoir antalgique, ainsi que l'effet salutaire du suc, observé à l'époque, sur les pellicules du cuir chevelu.

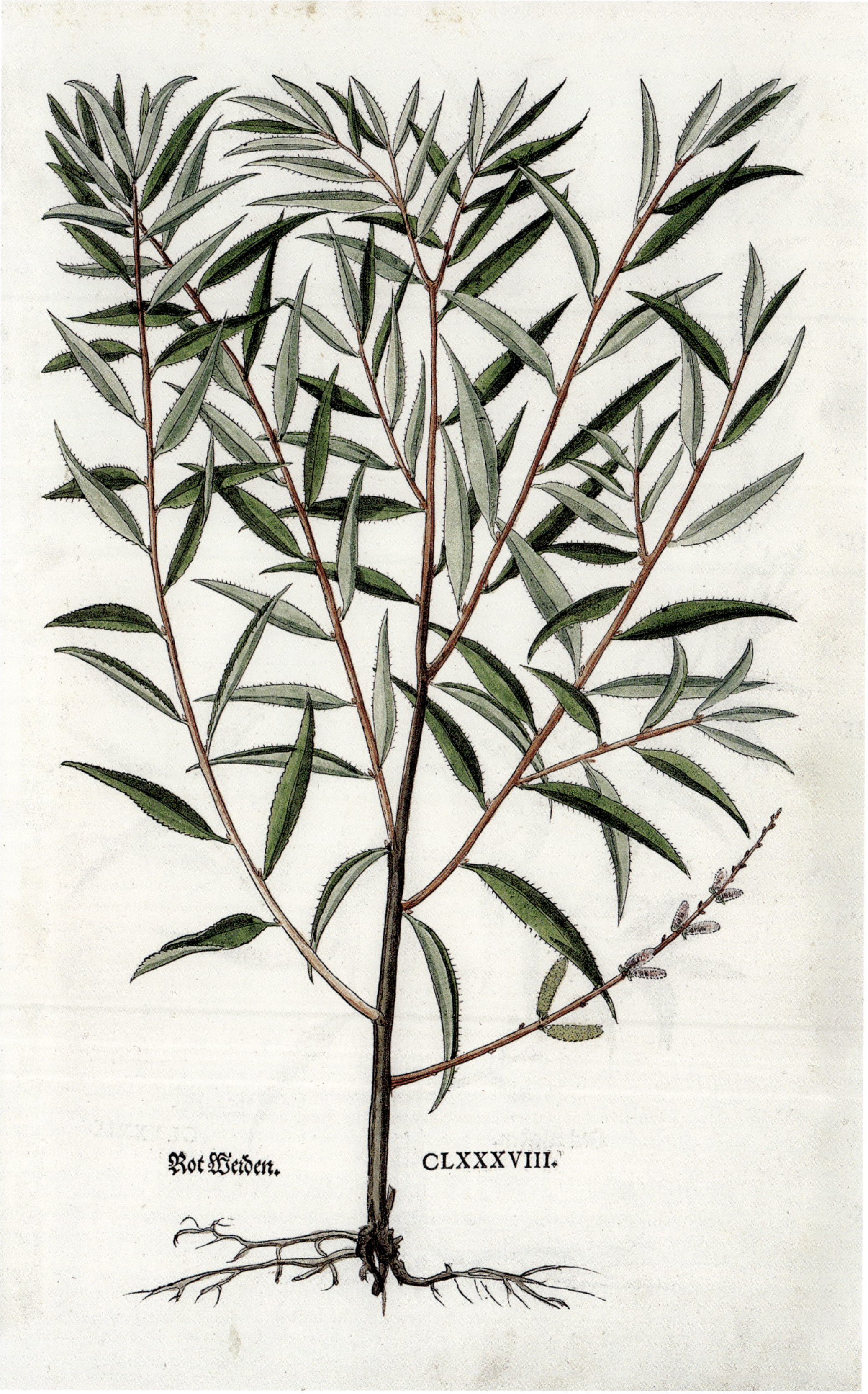
Rot Weiden.
CLXXXVIII.

COMMON FUMITORY

Also numbered among the old medicinal plants is COMMON FUMITORY (CXXVII), which is today used for gall ailments, as described above.

„ERDTRAUCH"

Zu den alten Heilpflanzen gehört der „ERDTRAUCH" (Cap. CXXVII), der noch heute als gallenwirksames Mittel eingesetzt wird, wie dies schon Fuchs beschrieb.

FUMETERRE OFFICINALE

La FUMETERRE OFFICINALE (CXXVII) est l'une de nos plus anciennes plantes médicinales. Elle est encore utilisée de nos jours comme cholagogue, une indication que Fuchs signale déjà.

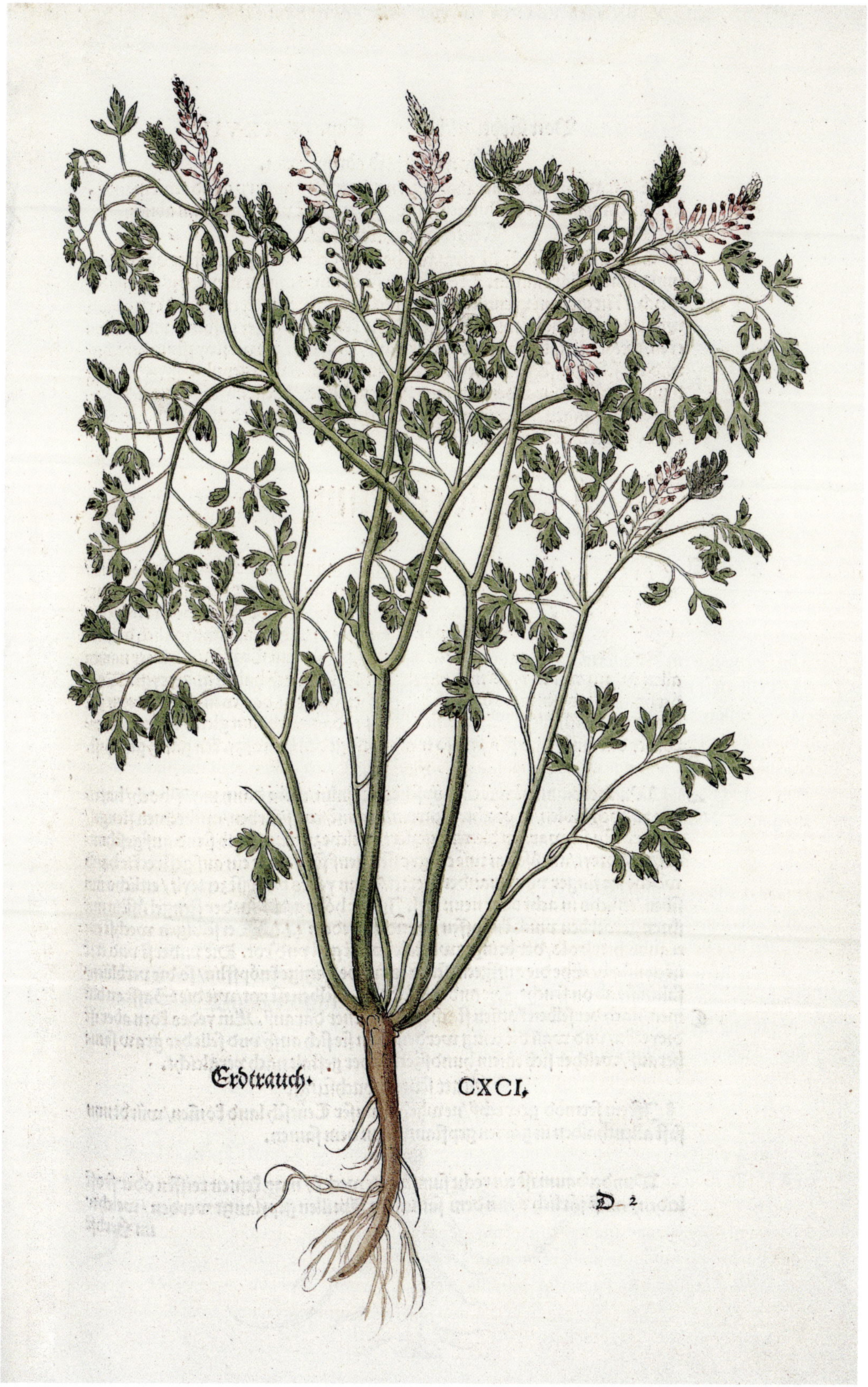
Erdtrauch.
CXCI.
D 2

CASTOR OIL PLANT

The German term Wunderbaum ("miracle tree") does not necessarily lead one to think of the CASTOR OIL PLANT (CXXVIII), also known as Castor Bean, which had only "recently arrived in our Germany." Its striking blossoms had already caused it to be "planted everywhere in gardens" in Fuchs's day. His recommendation that a preparation made of 30 grains of the unusually shaped seeds should be taken as a laxative is incomprehensible, since such a dosage of the highly poisonous seeds would be fatal for an adult. At least he remarks that "such a purgation [would be] rough and strenuous" – for the described effects already constitute life-threatening symptoms of poisoning.

WUNDERBAUM

Hinter der Bezeichnung WUNDERBAUM (Cap. CXXVIII) erwartet man nicht unbedingt den Rizinus, der erst „newlich in unser Teutschland kommen" ist und wegen seiner auffälligen Blüten zu Fuchs' Zeiten schon „allent-halben in gärten gepflantzt" wird. Die Samen werden wegen ihres Aussehens Zeckenkörner genannt und die Einnahme einer Zubereitung aus 30 Körnern empfiehlt Fuchs unverständlicherweise als Abführmittel, denn eine derartige Dosis der hochgiftigen Samen wäre für einen Erwachsenen tödlich. Wenigstens vermerkt er, dass eine „sölche purgation unlieblich und müeselig" sei, denn die beschriebenen Wirkungen sind bereits Symptome einer lebensgefährlichen Vergiftung.

RICIN

Nous découvrons avec surprise que le «arbre merveilleux» dont parle Fuchs est le RICIN (CXXVIII). Bien qu'«arrivé depuis peu dans notre Allemagne», il est déjà «planté partout dans les jardins» à cause de ses fleurs inhabituelles. Les graines sont appelées «graines de tiques» («Zeckenkörner»), par analogie de forme avec la tique du chien, ou ricin. Il est étonnant aussi que Fuchs recommande une préparation à base de 30 graines comme purgatif, car une telle dose, vu leur grande toxicité, serait mortelle. «Une purge pareille serait désagréable et pénible», remarque-t-il, car les effets qu'il décrit sont déjà les symptômes d'un empoisonnement.

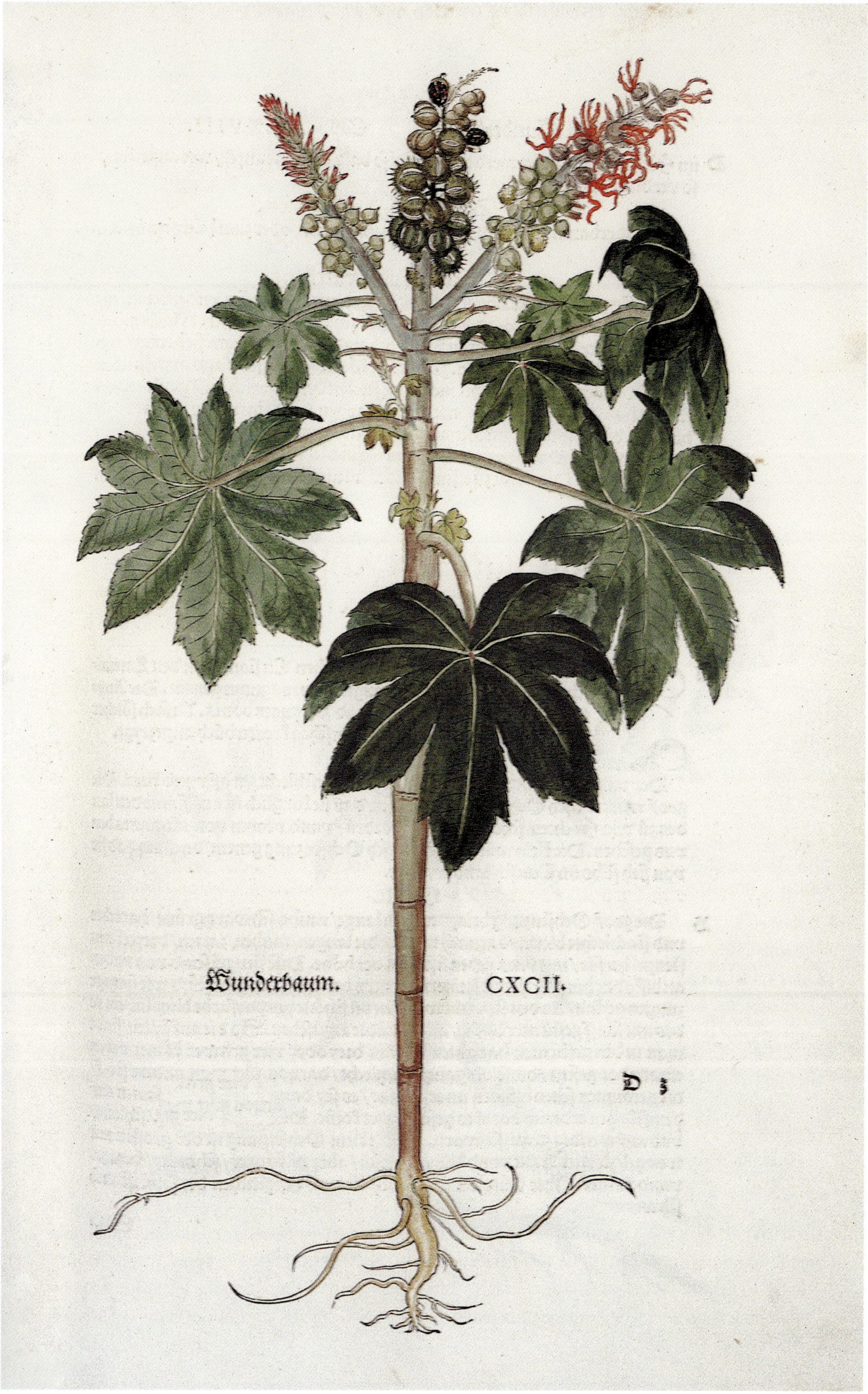
Wunderbaum.
CXCII.
D 3

ALKANET

For the seeds of the bugloss, or ALKANET (CXXIX), whose effect is similar to that of borage, Fuchs distinguishes between what he terms the true, GERMAN BUGLOSS (plate CXCIII) and the "alien" ITALIAN BUGLOSS, or LARGE BLUE ALKANEt (plate CXCIIII), which was becoming popular in gardens. For the smaller species, he notes its occurrence near Nuremberg and Tübingen.

„ZAME OCHSENZUNGEN"

Bei den „ZAMEN OCHSENZUNGEN" (Cap. CXXIX), deren Wirkung dem Borretsch gleichkommt, unterscheidet Fuchs die DEUTSCHE, ECHTE OCHSENZUNGE (Taf. CXCIII) und die „WELSCHE", ITALIENISCHE OCHSENZUNGE (Taf. CXCIIII), die besonders gerne in Gärten gezogen wurde. Für die kleinere Art erwähnt er Vorkommen bei Nürnberg und Tübingen.

BUGLOSSES

Les BUGLOSSES (CXXIX), ou langues-de-bœuf, dont l'action est comparable à celle de la bourrache, apparaissent ici sous deux formes distinctes : la BUGLOSSE OFFICINALE (pl. CXCIII) et la BUGLOSSE « ÉTRANGÈRE » ou D'ITALIE (pl. CXCIIII), cultivée dans les jardins. Fuchs mentionne la présence de l'espèce plus petite dans les environs de Nuremberg et de Tübingen.

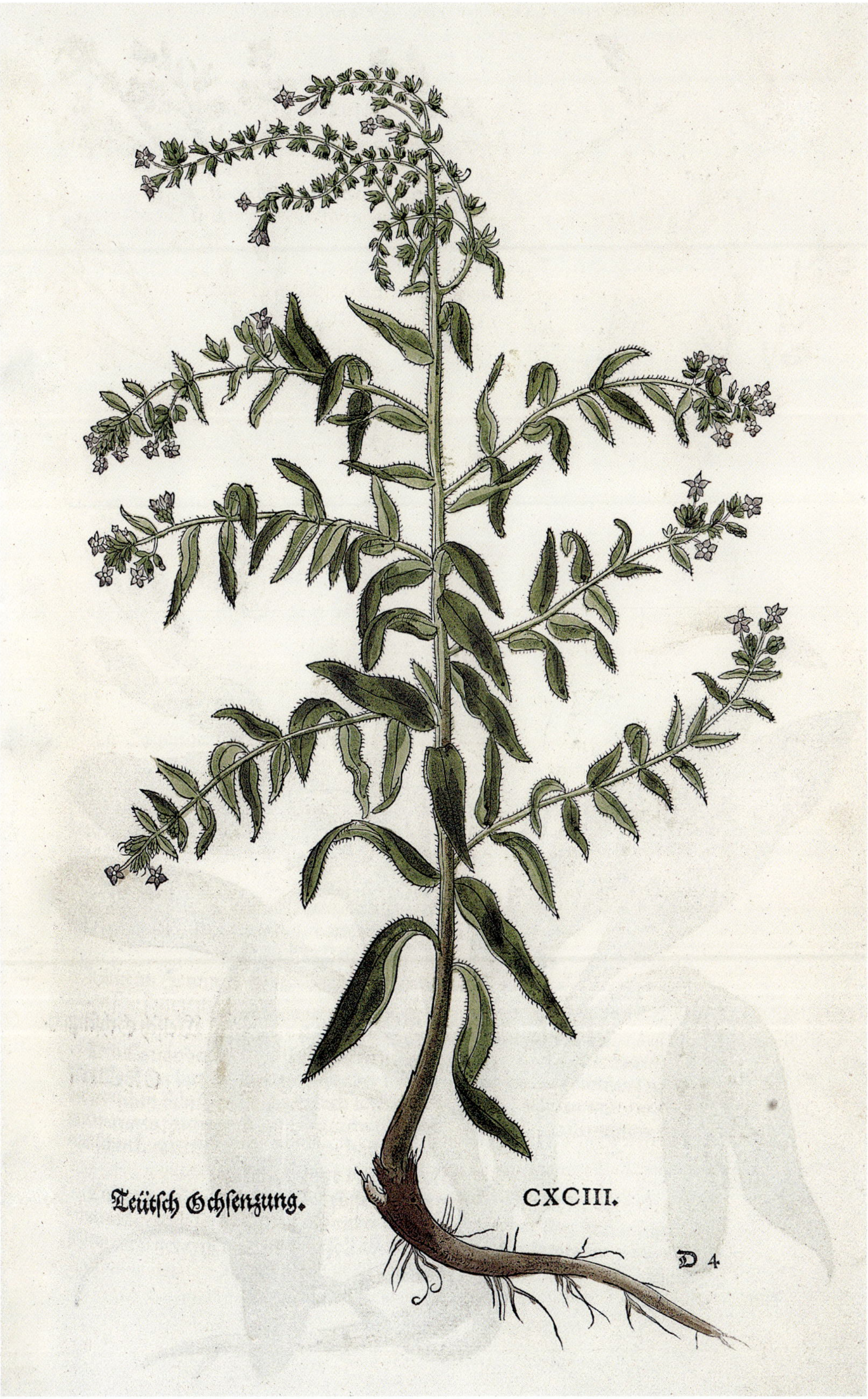
Teütsch Ochsenzung.
CXCIII.
D 4

CORIANDER

CORIANDER (CXXX) does not receive a favourable description, for Fuchs emphasizes that "no vermin can smell as terrible as green coriander" and reinforces this by claiming that its leaves "stink like wall lice."

KORIANDER

Der KORIANDER (Cap. CXXX) kommt bei der Beschreibung nicht gut davon, denn Fuchs betont, dass „kein wantz kann nit so übel stincken als der grün Coriander", seine Blätter „stincken wie die wandleuß".

CORIANDRE

Fuchs ne semble guère estimer la CORIANDRE (CXXX) car, selon lui, « aucune punaise n'empeste autant que, la coriandre verte » ; il renchérit même en écrivant que ses feuilles « puent comme le pou des murs ».

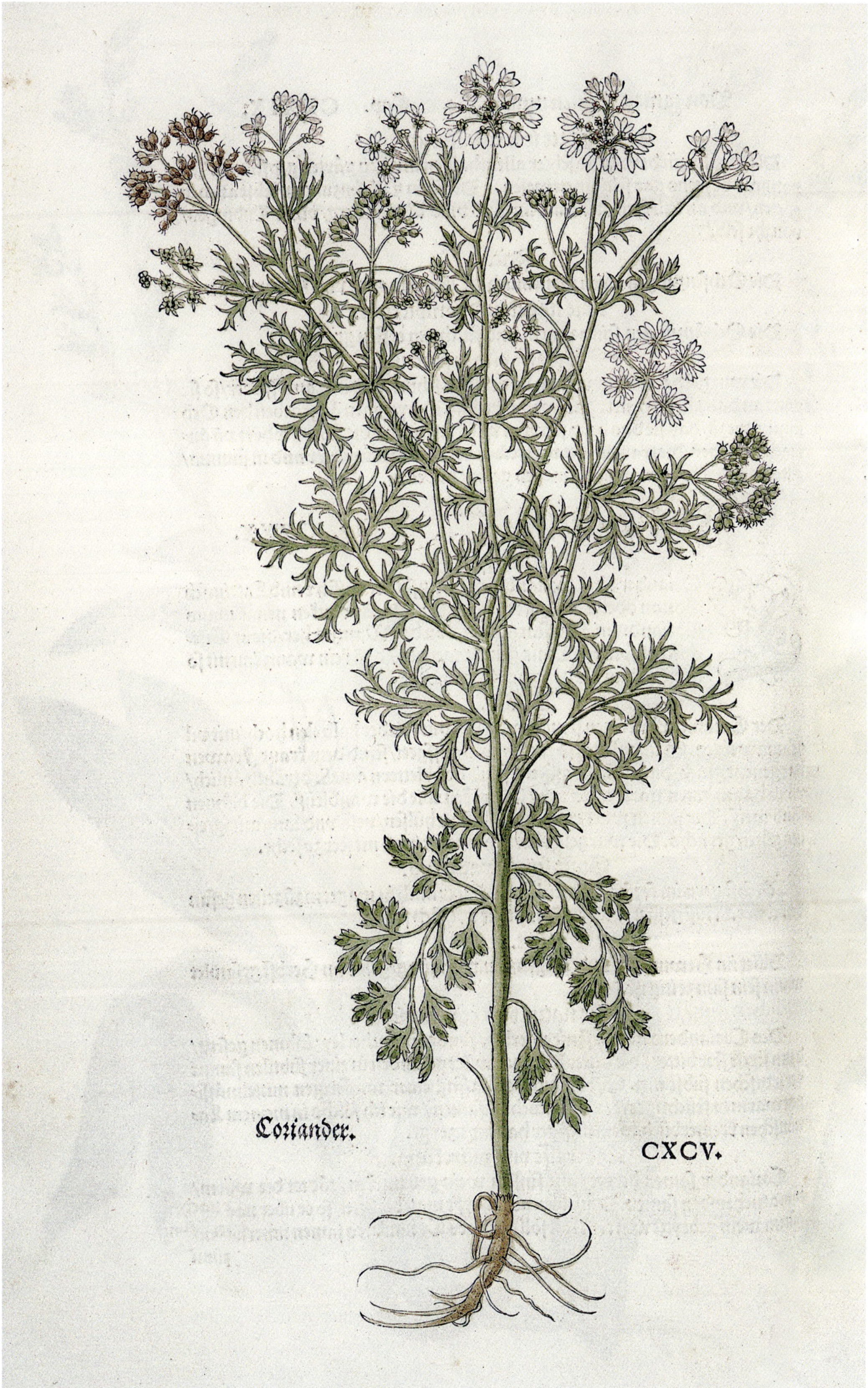
Coriander.
CXCV.

FLAX DODDER

FLAX DODDER (CXXXI), a parasite of FLAX, is no longer used medicinally today, although earlier it was considered most efficacious for the liver.

FILZKRAUT

Das auf dem Lein schmarotzende FILZKRAUT (Cap. CXXXI), die Flachsseide, ist heute nicht mehr im medizinischen Gebrauch, auch wenn sie früher als sehr leberwirksam galt.

CUSCUTE

La CUSCUTE (CXXXI), parasite du lin, n'est plus utilisée de nos jours en médecine, même si dans le passé on lui prêtait de grandes vertus hépatiques.

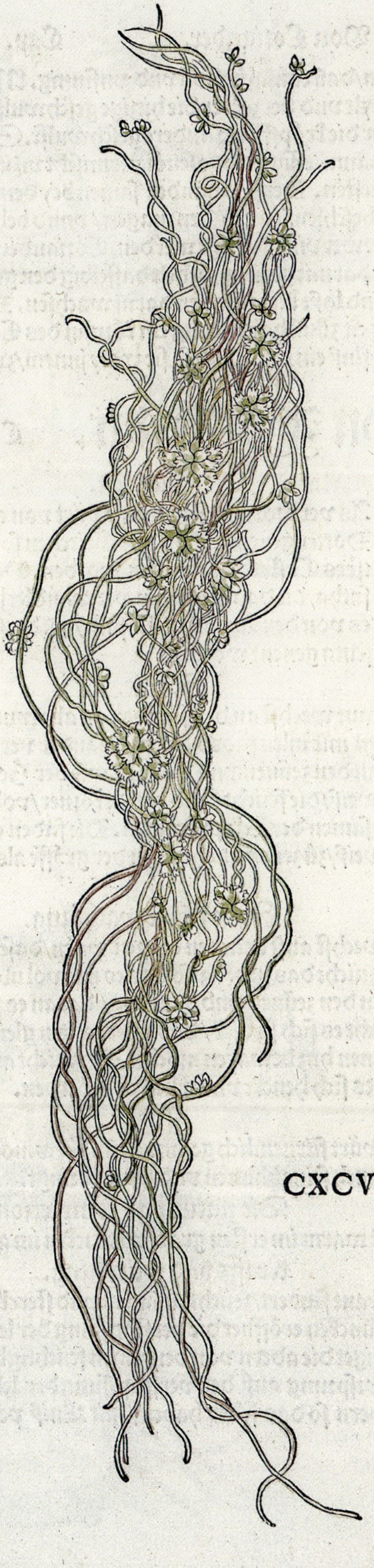

Flachß seiden. CXCVI.

BETONY

The same is true for BETONY (CXXXII), which even in Antiquity had inspired entire treatises and had “a large application in medicine,” but is today used only in folk medicine.

„BETONICK“

Ähnliches gilt für die „BETONICK“ (Cap. CXXXII), der bereits in der Antike ganze Traktate gewidmet wurden und die „einen grossen brauch in der artzney“ hatte, heute jedoch nur noch in der Volksheilkunde verwendet wird.

BÉTOINE

Il en est de même pour la BÉTOINE (CXXXII), dite aussi ÉPIAIRE OFFICINALE. Si les médecins de l’Antiquité lui consacraient des traités entiers et qu’elle «est très usitée en pharmacopée» d’après Fuchs, elle n’a plus de place aujourd’hui qu’en pharmacopée populaire.

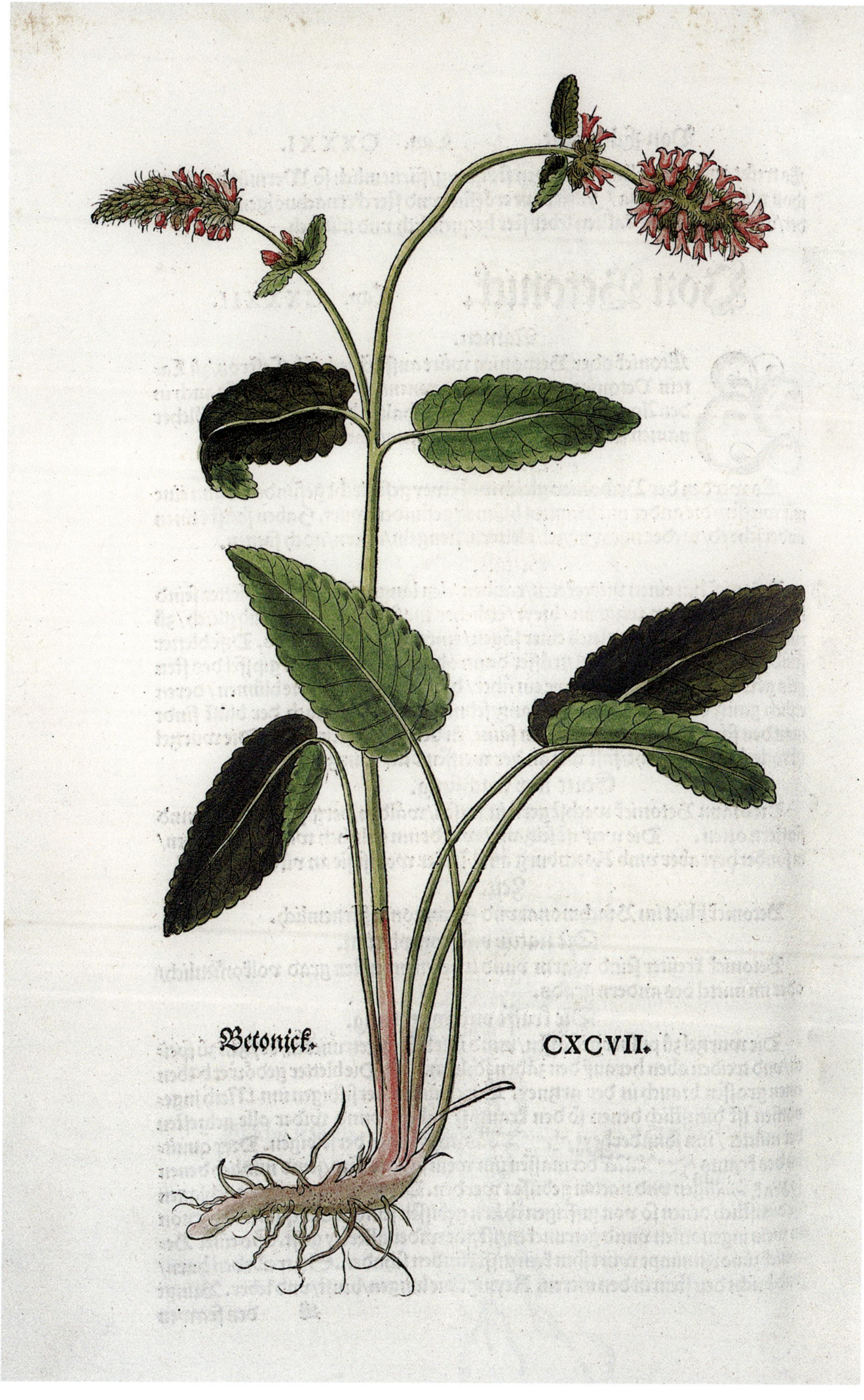
Betonick.
CXCVII.

CARNATIONS

Today we value CARNATIONS (CXXXIII) for their beauty and therefore seek them in the garden rather than the pharmacy. Fuchs however reports an entire series of important medicinal applications, all of which have been forgotten today.

„NEGELBLUMEN“

Die „NEGELBLUMEN“ (Cap. CXXXIII) bezeichnen wir heute als Nelken, schätzen sie wegen ihrer Schönheit und suchen sie deshalb im Garten und nicht in der Apotheke. Fuchs berichtet jedoch über eine ganze Reihe wichtiger medizinischer Einsatzgebiete, die heute allesamt vergessen sind.

ŒILLETS

Les «fleurs à clou» («Negelblumen») ne sont autres que les ŒILLETS (CXXXIII), ici l'œillet des Chartreux et l'œillet superbe. Nous les aimons pour leur beauté et les recherchons plutôt pour la décoration des jardins que pour leurs propriétés curatives. Fuchs signale cependant de très nombreuses applications thérapeutiques, toutes oubliées de nos jours.

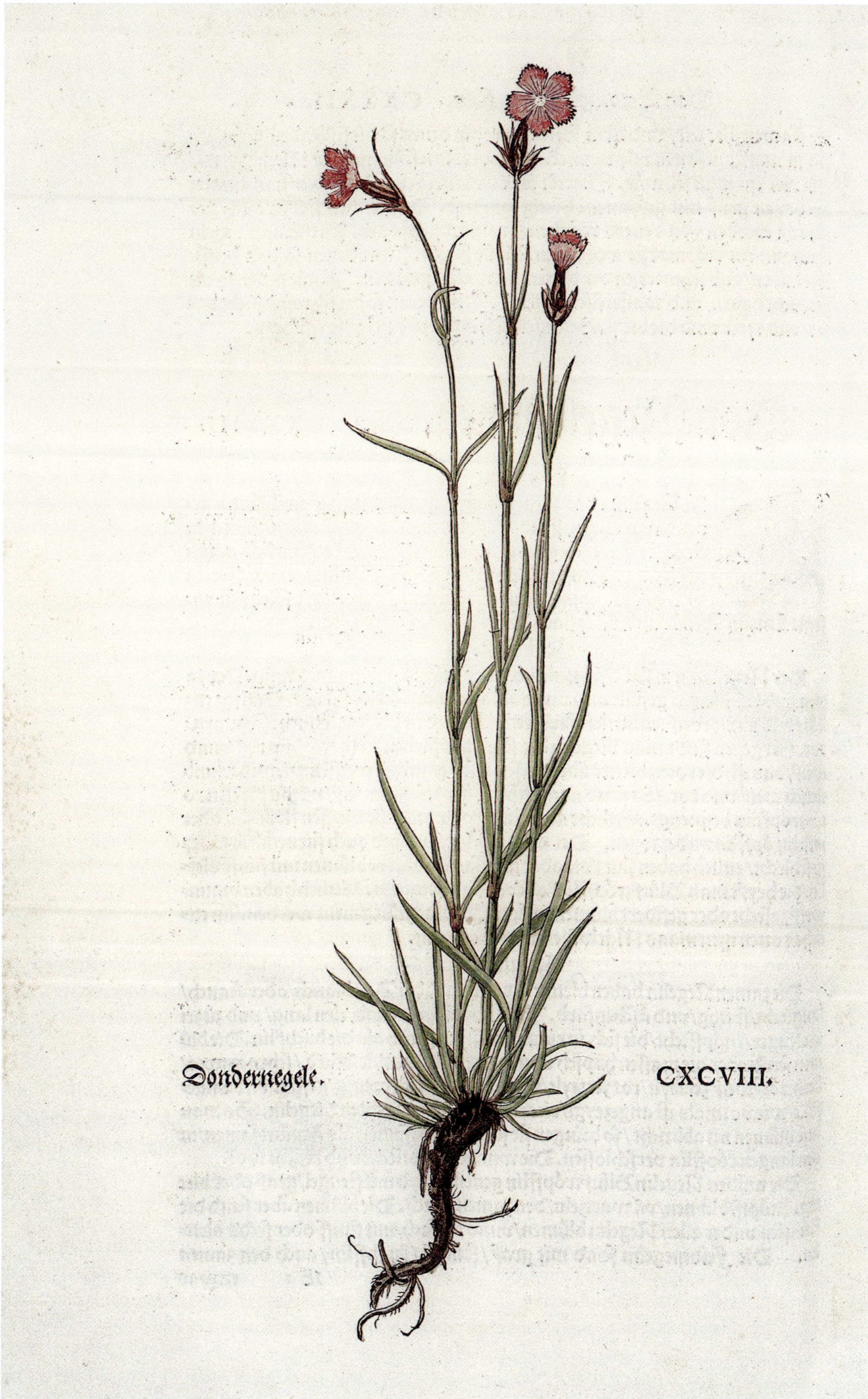
Dondernegele.
CXCVIII.

MEADOW SAFFRON

In the case of MEADOW SAFFRON (CXXXIIII), or Autumn Crocus, which was ubiquitous in Germany at the time, Fuchs expressly warned against the danger of poisoning, especially from the root, and also offered directions for treating such poisoning. Today the effective ingredients have been isolated and are successfully and safely applied in the treatment of acute gout.

ZEITLOSE

Vor der Giftigkeit der in Deutschland damals weitverbreiteten ZEITLOSEN (Cap. CXXXIIII), insbesondere der Wurzel, warnt Fuchs ausdrücklich und gibt sogar Anweisungen zur Behandlung einer Vergiftung. Heute wird der isolierte Inhaltsstoff zur Behandlung akuter Gichtanfälle erfolgreich und sicher eingesetzt.

COLCHIQUE D'AUTOMNE

Fuchs met en garde contre la haute toxicité du COLCHIQUE D'AUTOMNE (CXXXIIII), très répandu en Allemagne en ce temps-là. C'est surtout des dangers de la souche vénéneuse qu'il avertit, et il indique même comment traiter les empoisonnements. On l'emploie aujourd'hui avec succès contre la goutte aiguë depuis qu'on a isolé son alcaloïde toxique, la colchicine.

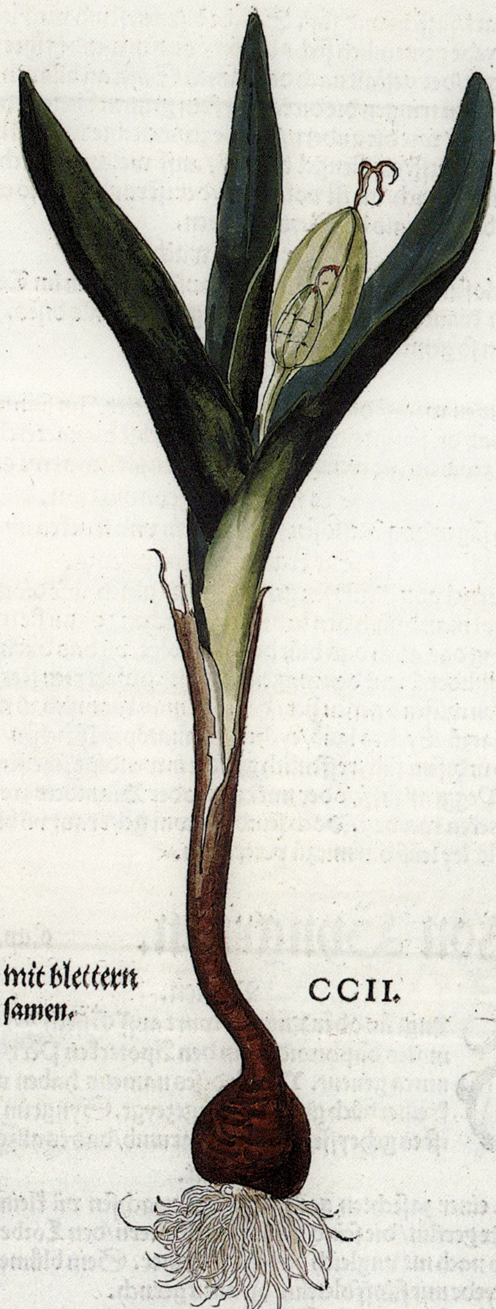

Zeitlosen mit blettern vnd samen.

CCII.

MEADOW SAFFRON | ZEITLOSE | COLCHIQUE D'AUTOMNE

COMMON PERIWINKLE

The german name for COMMON PERIWINKLE (CXXXV), or Trailing myrtle, means "Evergreen," an apt description, for its components still play an important role in modern phytotherapy by improving circulation and metabolic exchange in the brain.

„SYNGRÜEN" (IMMERGRÜN)

Das Immergrün, früher „SYNGRÜEN" (Cap. CXXXV) genannt, ist in der Tat ein „Evergreen", denn in der modernen Phytotherapie spielen seine Wirkstoffe bei der Verbesserung der Hirndurchblutung und des Hirnstoffwechsels eine wichtige Rolle.

PETITE PERVENCHE

La PETITE PERVENCHE (CXXXV) est appelée en allemand « Immergrün » (toujours verte). Ce nom lui convient bien car c'est effectivement une « Evergreen » de la phytothérapie. Ses principes actifs sont employés de nos jours pour améliorer la circulation sanguine et le métabolisme du cerveau.

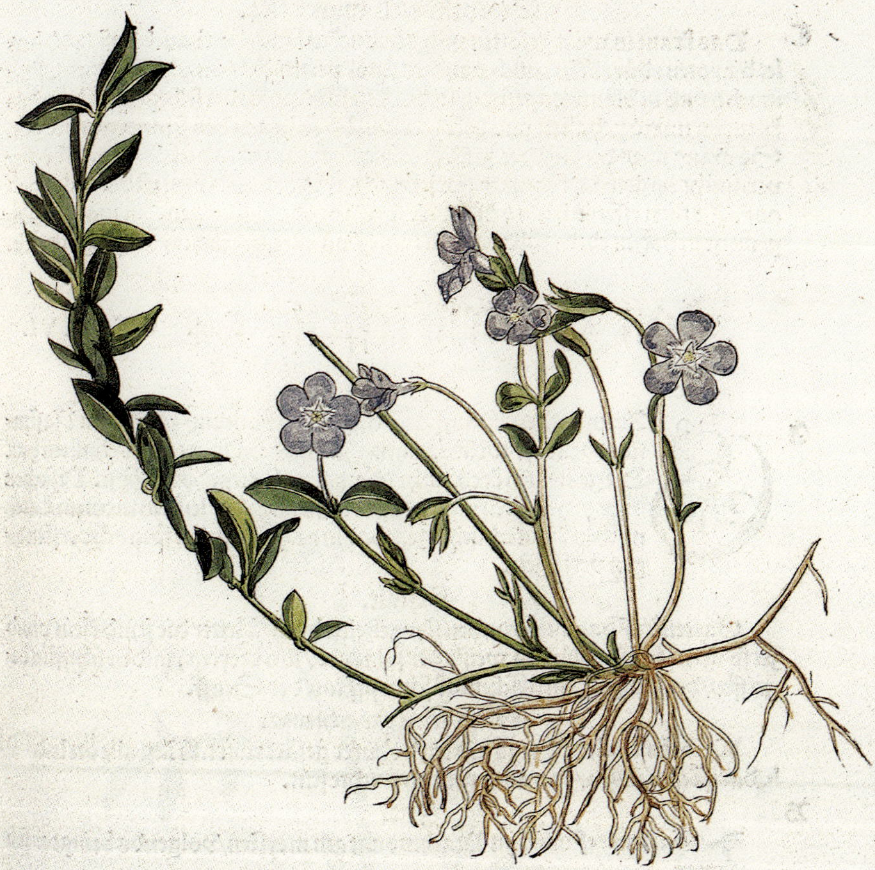

Syngrün. CCIII.

COMMON PERIWINKLE | „SYNGRÜEN“ | PETITE PERVENCHE

GARDEN CRESS

GARDEN CRESS (CXXXVI) earns a long series of indications, in part similar to those attributed to Mustard.

GARTENKRESSE

Der GARTENKRESSE (Cap. CXXXVI) wird eine lange Reihe von Indikationen zugestanden, die teilweise denen des Senfs entsprechen.

CRESSON ALÉNOIS

Les indications du CRESSON ALÉNOIS (CXXXVI), ici très nombreuses, recoupent celles de la moutarde.

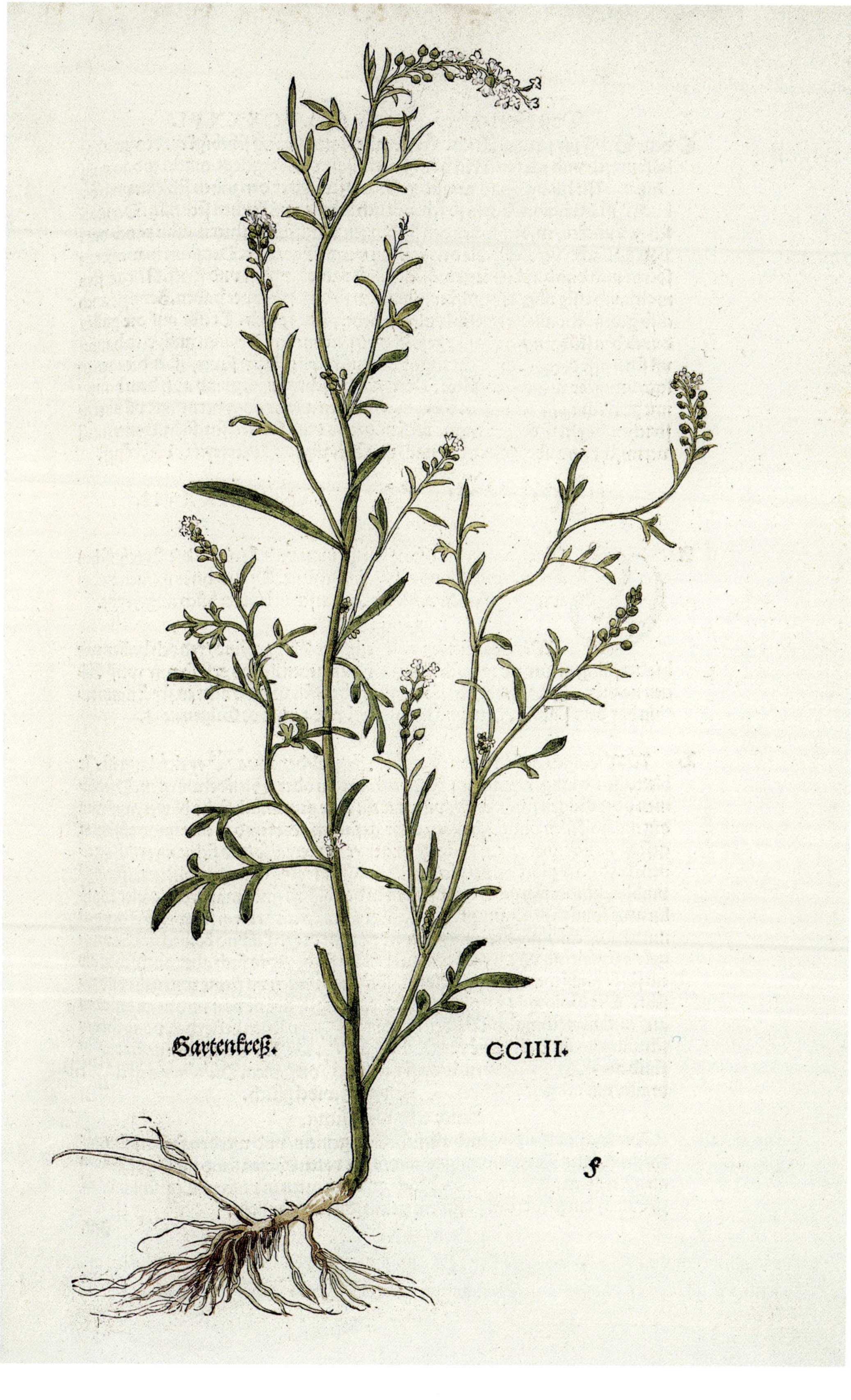
Gartenkreß.
CCIIII.
f

MADONNA LILY

In this chapter (CXXXVII), Fuchs lists a broad spectrum of medicinal uses for the individual parts of MADONNA LILY, or WHITE LILY (plate CCV), and orange or FIRE LILY (plate CCVI).

„GILGEN"

Die MADONNENLILIE (Taf. CCV) und die FEUERLILIE (Taf. CCVI) erfasst Fuchs im Kapitel von „GILGEN" (Cap. CXXXVII) und nennt für die einzelnen Pflanzenteile ein breites Spektrum ihrer medizinischen Verwendung.

LIS BLANC

Le chapitre CXXXVII est consacré aux LIS : LIS BLANC (pl. CCV), ou lis de la Madone, et LIS SAFRANÉ (pl. CCVI). Fuchs recense les nombreuses utilisations de chaque partie de la plante.

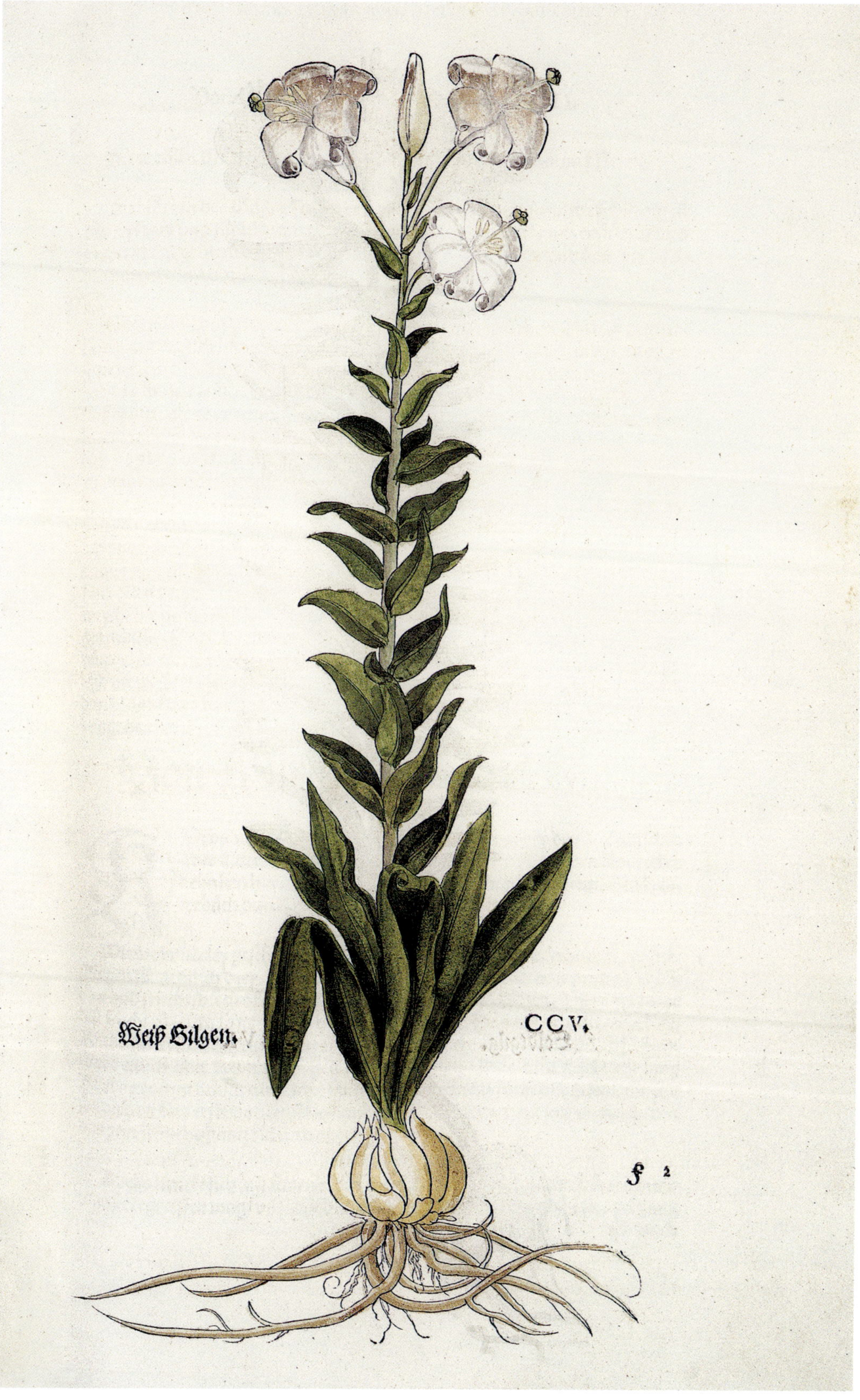
Weiß Gilgen.
CCV.
f 2

BOTTLE GOURD

A wide range of applications also appears for BOTTLE GOURD (CXXXVIII), three species of which Fuchs presented. The juice of the GOURD occurred in many medicines, but Fuchs warned against eating the raw flesh.

KÜRBIS

Dies gilt auch für den KÜRBIS (Cap. CXXXVIII), der in dreierlei Arten vorgestellt wird. Sein Saft dient zu vielfältiger Arznei, während vor dem Genuss von rohem Kürbis gewarnt wird.

CALEBASSIER

Un chapitre entier est également dédié au CALEBASSIER (CXXXVIII), figuré ici par trois spécimens. Son suc sert sous de multiples formes, mais Fuchs met en garde contre l'ingestion de calebasse crue.

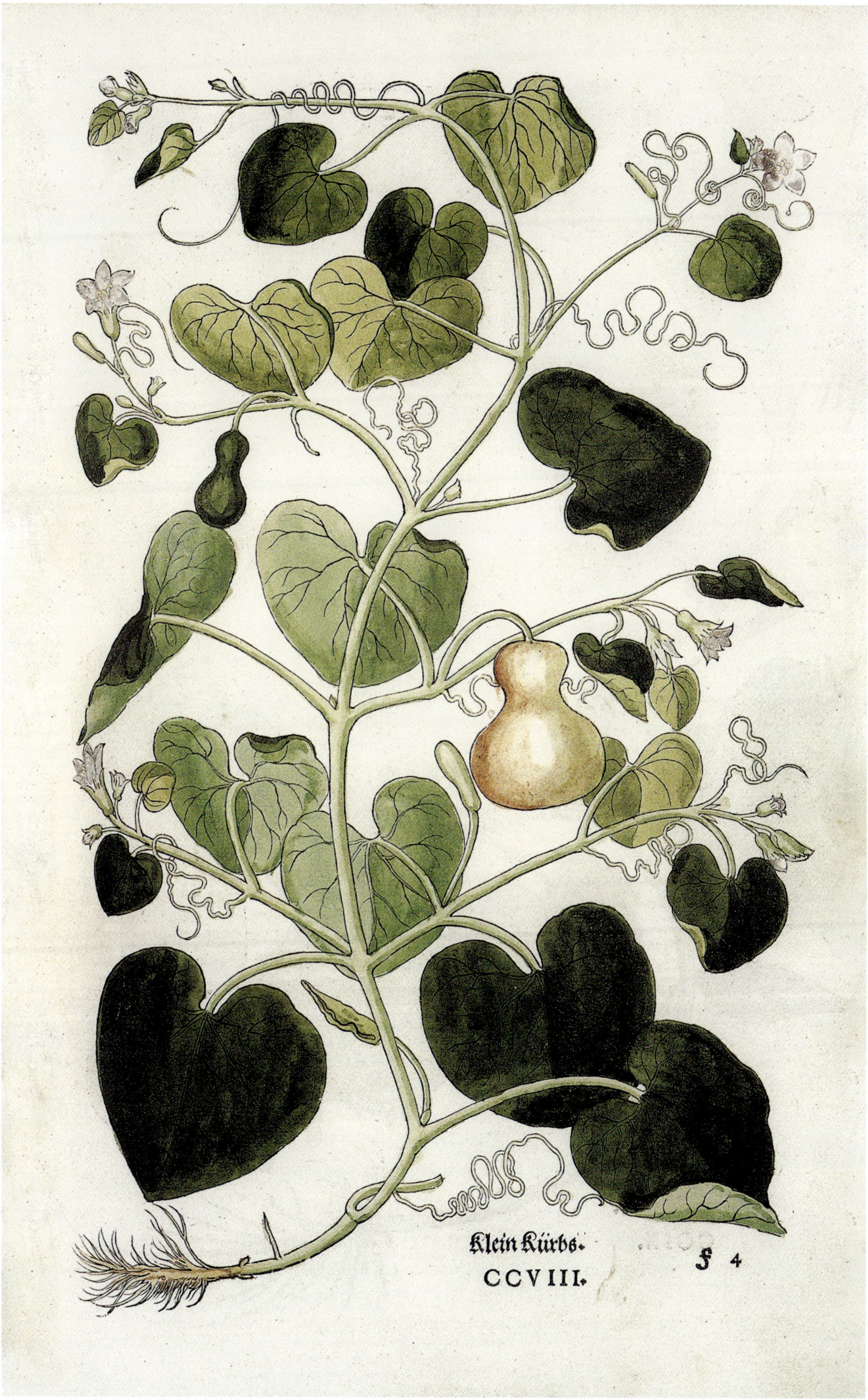
Klein Kürbs.
CCVIII.
f 4

COLOCYNTH

After the gourds comes the botanically closely related COLOCYNTH (CXXXIX), also known as Bitter or Sodom's Apple, which was used as a drastic laxative. Its sudden and powerful effect meant that all kinds of charlatans offered the drug, behind the backs of physicians and apothecaries. Fuchs exposed the resulting danger in passionate language and warned against inappropriate use of the potentially poisonous fruit.

KOLOQUINTHE

Die botanisch eng verwandte KOLOQUINTHE (Cap. CXXXIX) schließt sich an. Sie wurde als drastisches Abführmittel eingesetzt und, wegen ihrer durchschlagenden Wirkung, von allerlei Scharlatanen an Arzt und Apotheker vorbei angeboten. Die daraus entstehende Gefahr prangert Fuchs mit leidenschaftlichen Worten an, um vor Schäden durch unsachgemäßen Umgang mit den nicht ungiftigen Früchten zu warnen.

COLOQUINTE COMMUNE

Suit la COLOQUINTE COMMUNE (CXXXIX), botaniquement proche de la calebasse. Elle était utilisée comme purgatif drastique et vendue pour sa soi-disant efficacité par toutes sortes de charlatans aux médecins et aux apothicaires. Fuchs met en garde avec véhémence contre le danger que représente l'utilisation abusive de ses graines assez toxiques.

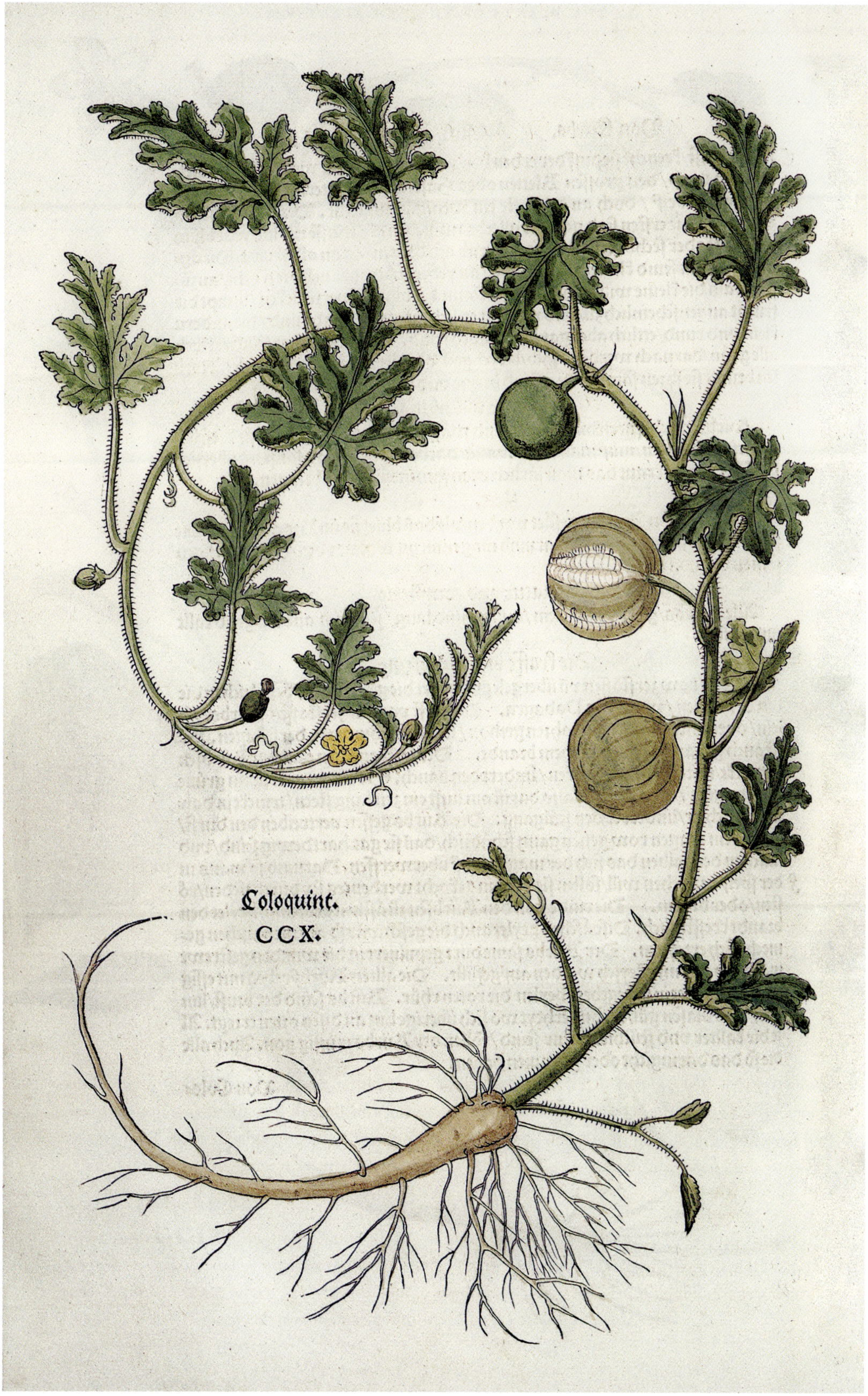
Coloquint.
CCX.

COMMON QUINCE

COMMON QUINCE (CXL) has become rare in Germany, and the fruit is largely used for preserves and jelly. Fuchs still knew of medicinal applications and also mentioned its positive effect on the unborn child, which would become "intelligent and skilful" if the mother often ate QUINCES.

QUITTEN

Die QUITTEN (Cap. CXL) sind heute in Deutschland selten geworden und ihre Früchte dienen überwiegend zur Konfekt- oder Geleeherstellung. Fuchs kennt noch ihre medizinische Anwendung und erwähnt auch ihre vermeintlich positiven Wirkungen auf das ungeborene Kind, das „sinnreich und geschickt" werden soll, falls die schwangeren Mütter häufig Quitten essen.

COGNASSIER

Les fruits du COGNASSIER (CXL), devenu rare en Allemagne, sont employés essentiellement dans l'industrie alimentaire (confiserie et gelées). Fuchs connaît encore leurs vertus thérapeutiques et signale en outre leurs effets bénéfiques, ou supposés tels, sur le fœtus : l'enfant sera «ingénieux et habile» si sa mère mange beaucoup de coings.

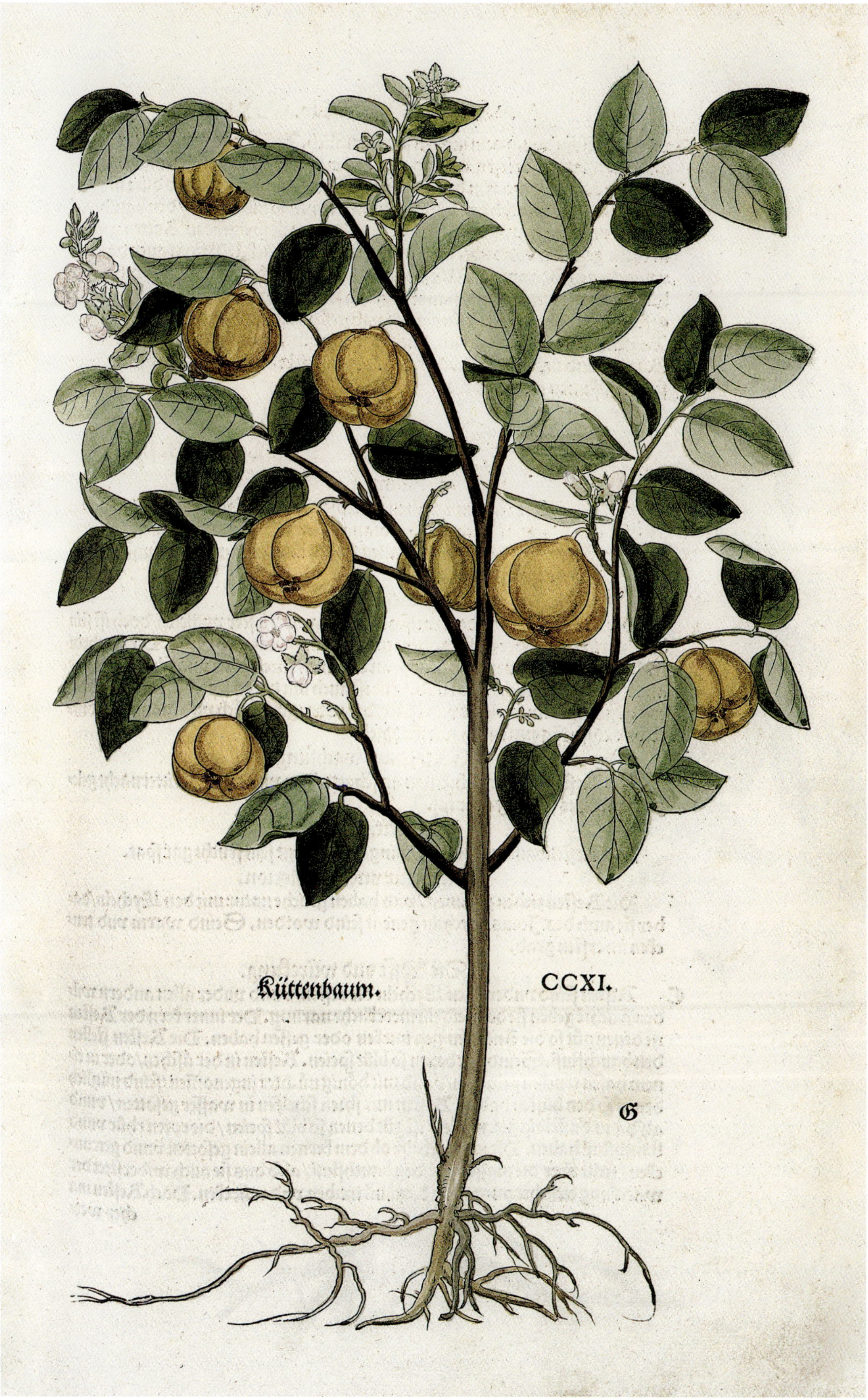
Küttenbaum.
CCXI.
G

EUROPEAN CHESTNUT

The edible EUROPEAN CHESTNUT (CXLI) is roasted in winter. Considered as a kind of acorn, the CHESTNUT was supposed not only to have had an astringent effect but also to provide "considerable nourishment."

„KESTEN“ (KASTANIEN)

„KESTEN“ (Cap. CXLI) ist das alte Wort für Kastanien und bezeichnet die essbaren, die im Winter als Maroni geröstet werden. Als eine Art Eicheln betrachtet, wird ihnen zusammenziehende Wirkung, aber auch „merckliche narung“ zugeschrieben.

CHÂTAIGNIER

«Kesten» (du latin CASTANEA), ancien nom allemand de la châtaigne, désigne les fruits comestibles du CHÂTAIGNIER (CXLI) que l'on mange grillés l'hiver. Considérés comme une sorte de glands, ils ont la réputation d'avoir une action astringente et une haute valeur nutritive.

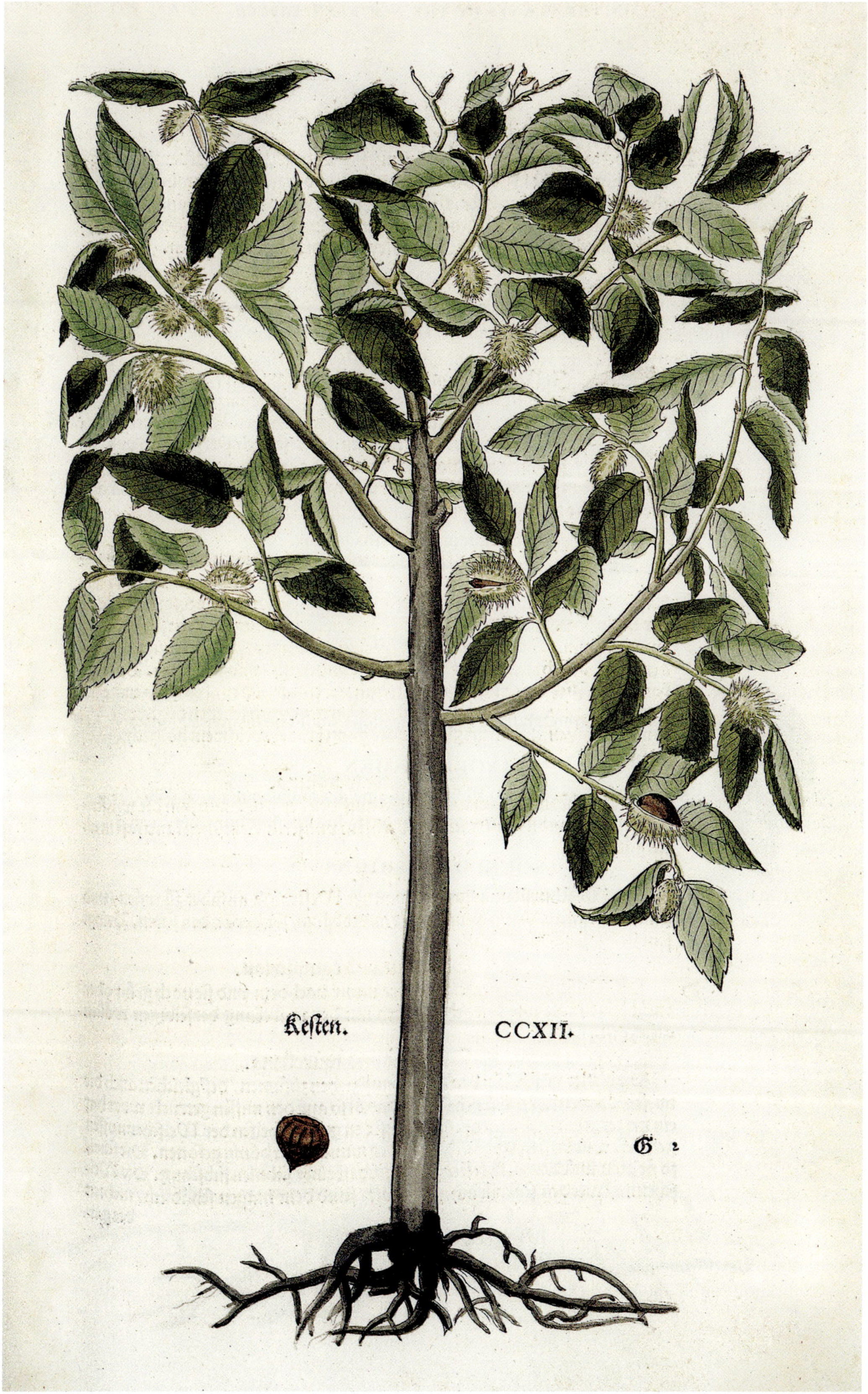
Kesten.
CCXII.
G 2

ENGLISH WALNUT

Persian, or ENGLISH WALNUT (CXLII) closes the chapters on fruits for the time being. The WALNUT was designated in Germany as "foreign," to distinguish it clearly from the native Hazelnut. The many applications lead one to suspect the presence of tannin – which the WALNUT in fact possesses.

„WELSCHNUSS"

Als vorerst letzte Frucht schließt sich die „WELSCHNUSS" (Cap. CXLII) an, die wir heute als Walnuss kennen. Ihr erster Namensbestandteil „Welsch" deutet auf die fremdartige Herkunft hin und soll sie klar von der einheimischen Nuss, der Haselnuss, unterscheiden. Manche Anwendungen lassen die Wirkung des tatsächlich vorhandenen Gerbstoffs erahnen.

NOIX

La NOIX (CXLII) clôt momentanément les illustrations sur les fruits. Elle figure ici sous le nom de «noix étrangère» («Welschnuß») pour la différencier de la noisette autochtone («Haselnuß» en allemand). A certains emplois thérapeutiques signalés par Fuchs se devine l'effet du tanin présent dans la noix.

PAGE 302

CALENDULA

With CALENDULA, or POT MARIGOLD (CXLIII), Fuchs presented one of today's favourite medicinal plants, although the older applications would be dismissed today.

RINGELBLUMEN

Mit den RINGELBLUMEN (Cap. CXLIII) stellt Fuchs eine der auch heute noch beliebtesten Heilpflanzen vor, wenngleich die damalige Anwendung heute keine Zustimmung mehr erhalten wird.

SOUCI DES JARDINS

Le SOUCI DES JARDINS (CXLIII) est l'une de nos plantes médicinales préférées, encore que maintenant on ne puisse plus souscrire à l'usage qu'on en faisait dans le passé.

PAGE 303

AVENS

The clove-like odour of its rhizome is a distinguishing feature of AVENS (CXLIIII). The plant was frequently used as a sachet in the linen-chest, but also in medicines.

BENEDIKTENWURZ

Die BENEDIKTENWURZ (Cap. CXLIIII) macht durch den nelkenähnlichen Geruch des Wurzelstocks auf sich aufmerksam, erhielt deshalb den Namen Nelkenwurz, wurde gerne zwischen die Wäsche gelegt, fand aber auch in Arzneien Verwendung.

BENOÎTE COMMUNE

La BENOÎTE COMMUNE (CXLIIII), ou herbe de Saint-Benoît, se remarque par l'odeur de girofle émanant de son rhizome, d'où son autre nom de «Nelkenwurz» (racine giroflée). Outre son emploi en médecine, on en parfumait volontiers le linge.

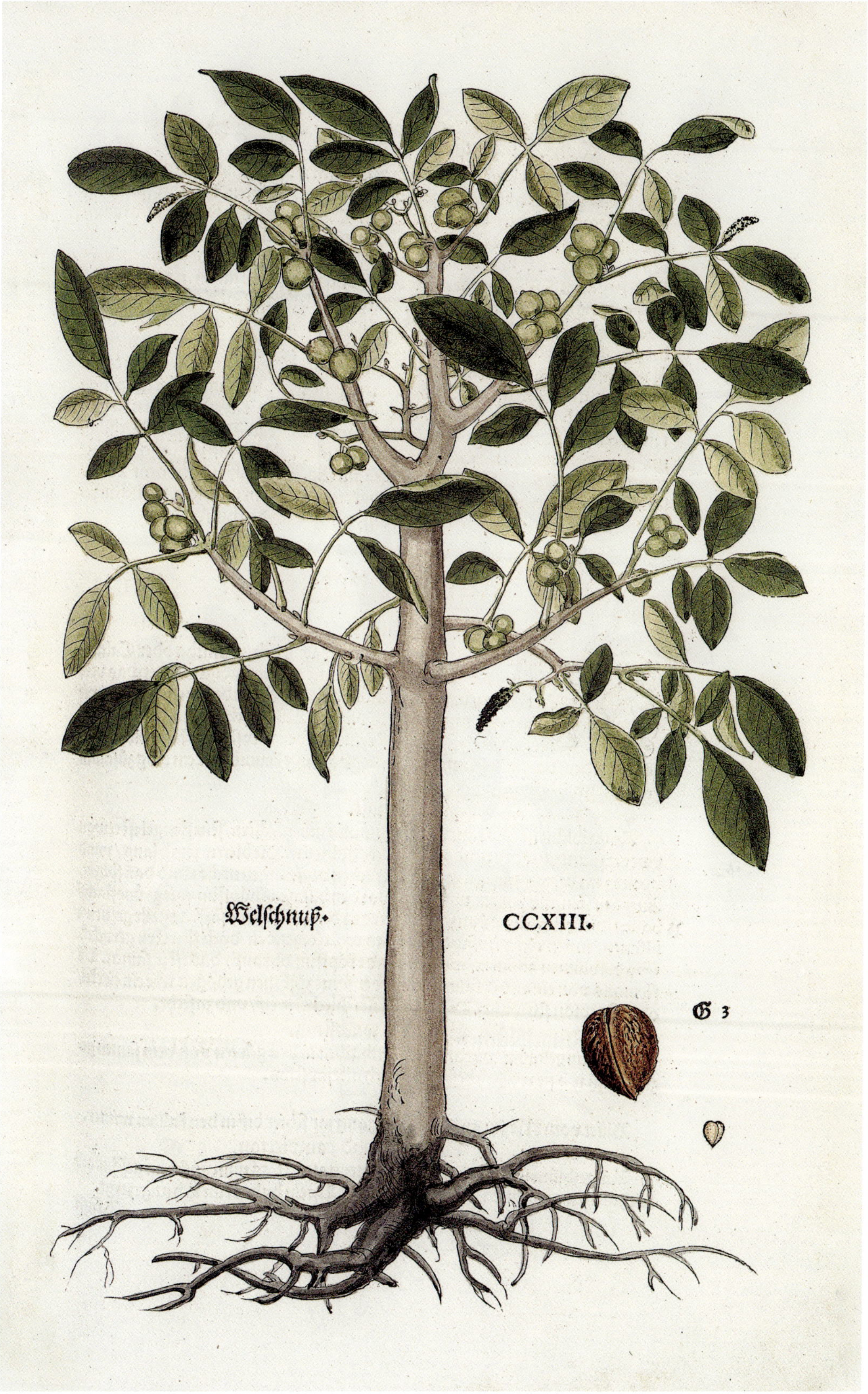
Welschnuß.
CCXIII.
G 3

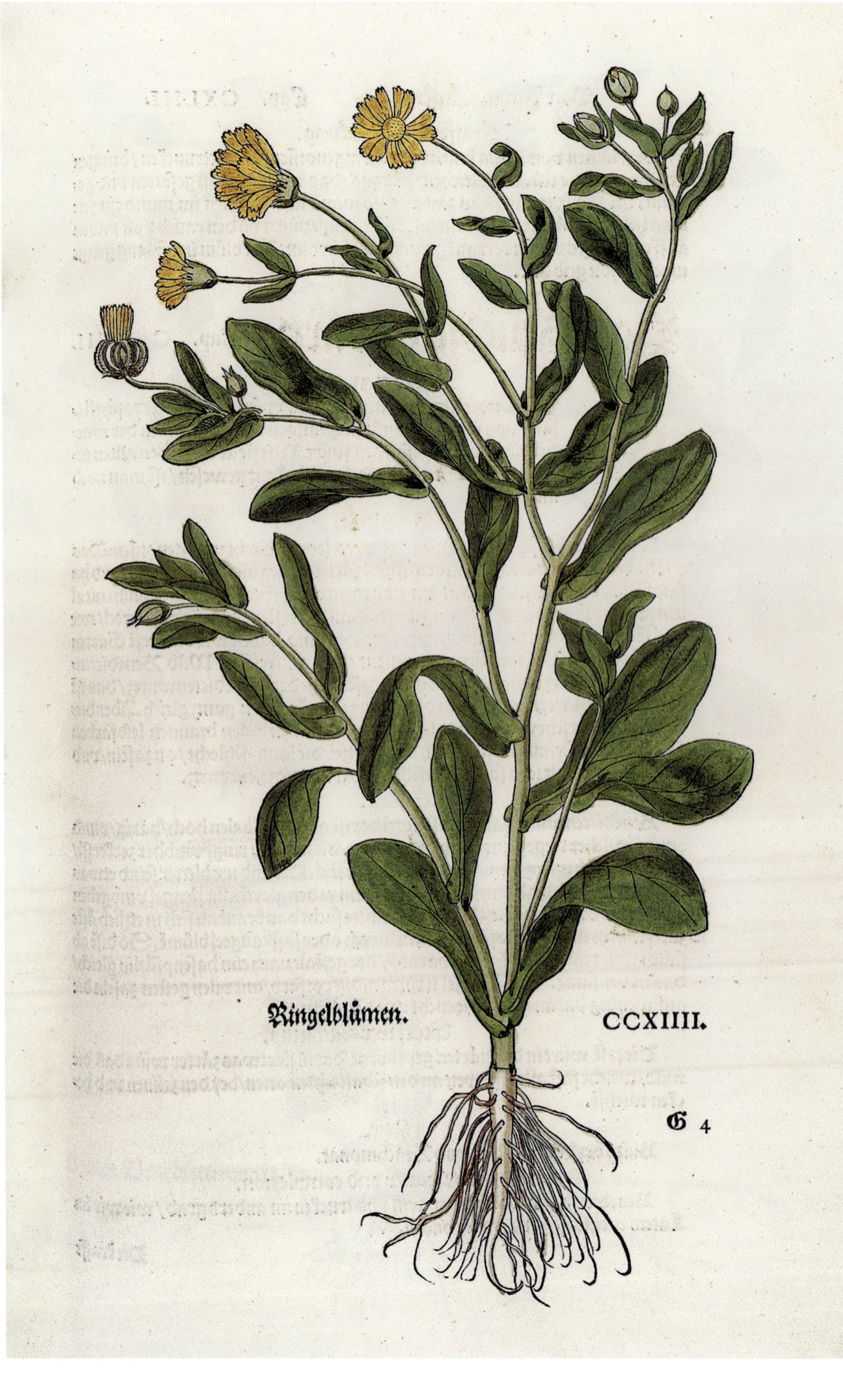
Ringelblůmen.
CCXIIII.
G 4

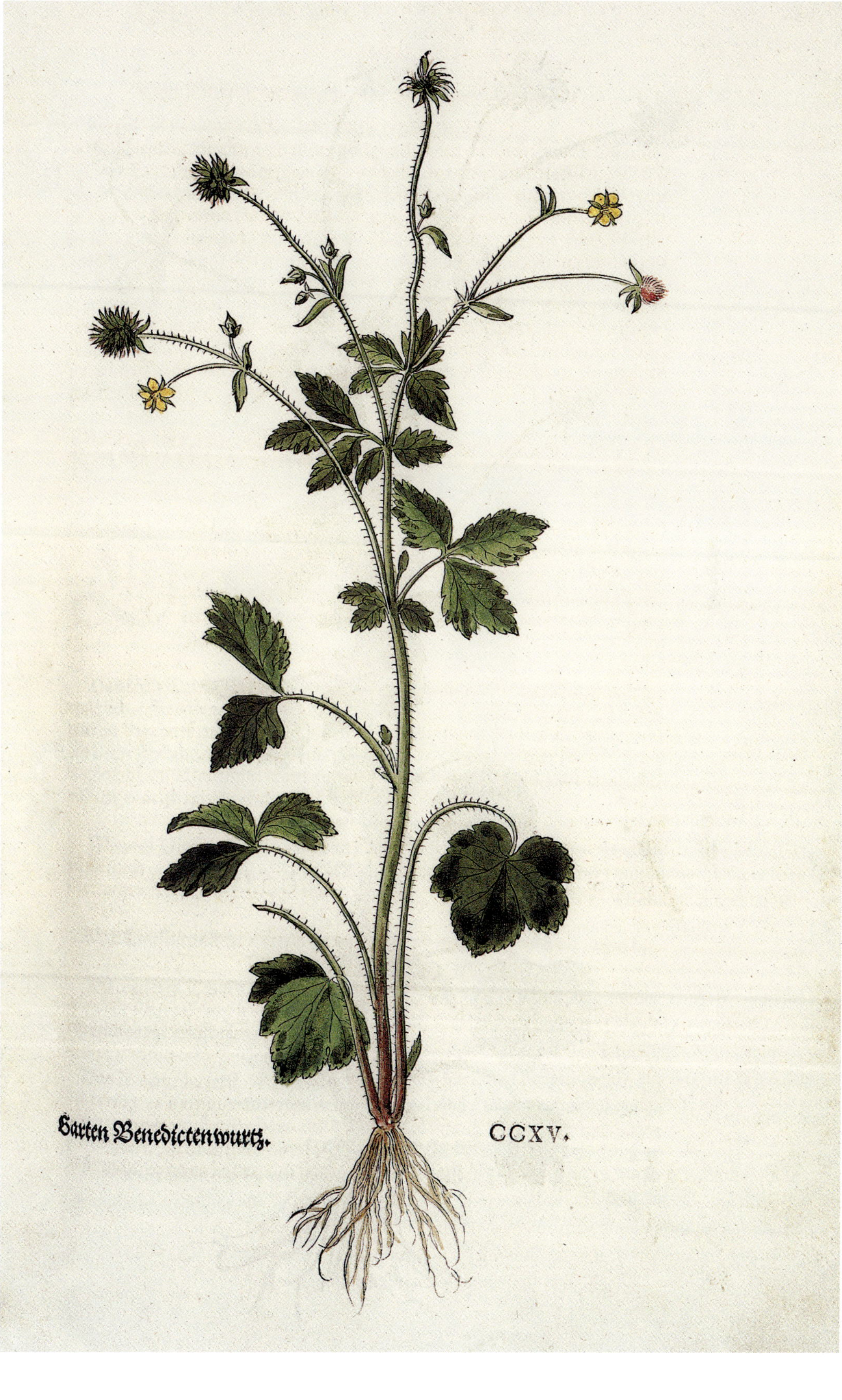
Garten Benedictenwurtz.
CCXV.

COMMON CENTAURY

It was not its odour, but rather its strikingly bitter taste that recommended COMMON CENTAURY (CXLV) as a medicinal herb for fever and digestive problems. However, it was also used to heal wounds and even for disorders of vision. For these ailments as well as an entire array of other applications, Fuchs also recommended FAVA BEAN (CXLVI), or Broad Bean, but he strongly warned against their flatulent effect and their burden on the stomach.

TAUSENDGÜLDENKRAUT

Nicht der Geruch, sondern der auffallend bittere Geschmack empfahl das TAUSENDGÜLDENKRAUT (Cap. CXLV) als Heilpflanze bei Fieber und Verdauungsbeschwerden; es wurde allerdings auch zur Wundheilung und sogar bei Sehbeschwerden eingenommen. Hierzu und zu einer ganzen Reihe anderer Anwendungen empfiehlt Fuchs auch die BOHNEN (Cap. CXLVI), auf deren blähende und magenbelastende Wirkung er ausdrücklich hinweist.

PETITE CENTAURÉE

La réputation de la PETITE CENTAURÉE (CXLV) ne venait pas de son odeur, mais de son goût amer. Préconisée contre la fièvre et les douleurs digestives, elle s'utilisait aussi pour traiter les plaies et même les troubles de la vue. Ici Fuchs recommande également les haricots, dont la FÈVE (CXLVI), et en mentionne les nombreuses indications, sans omettre de rappeler explicitement leurs effets flatulents.

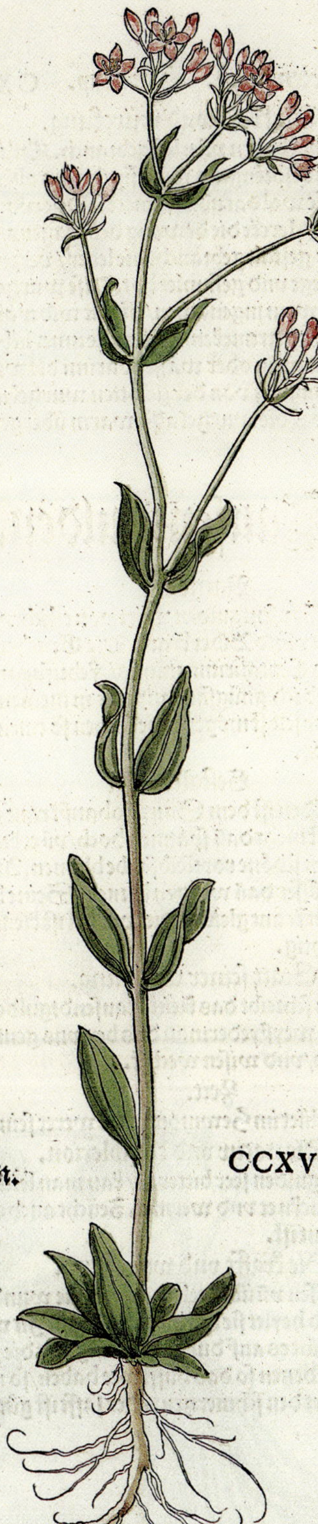

Klein Tausendtgulden. CCXVII.

COMMON CENTAURY | TAUSENDGÜLDENKRAUT | PETITE CENTAURÉE

COMMON BUGLE

COMMON BUGLE (CXLVII) was highly valued as a vulnerary; in Germany, it earned the appellation consolida, a reference to its ability to draw the wound back together.

„GULDEN GUNTZEL“

Der „GULDEN GUNTZEL“ (Cap. CXLVII) war zur Wundheilung sehr geschätzt, weshalb er Consolida genannt wurde, da er die Wunden wieder „zusammenfügte“.

BUGLE RAMPANTE

La BUGLE RAMPANTE (CXLVII), très estimée pour son pouvoir cicatrisant, était appelée CONSOLIDA, celle qui « ressoude » les plaies.

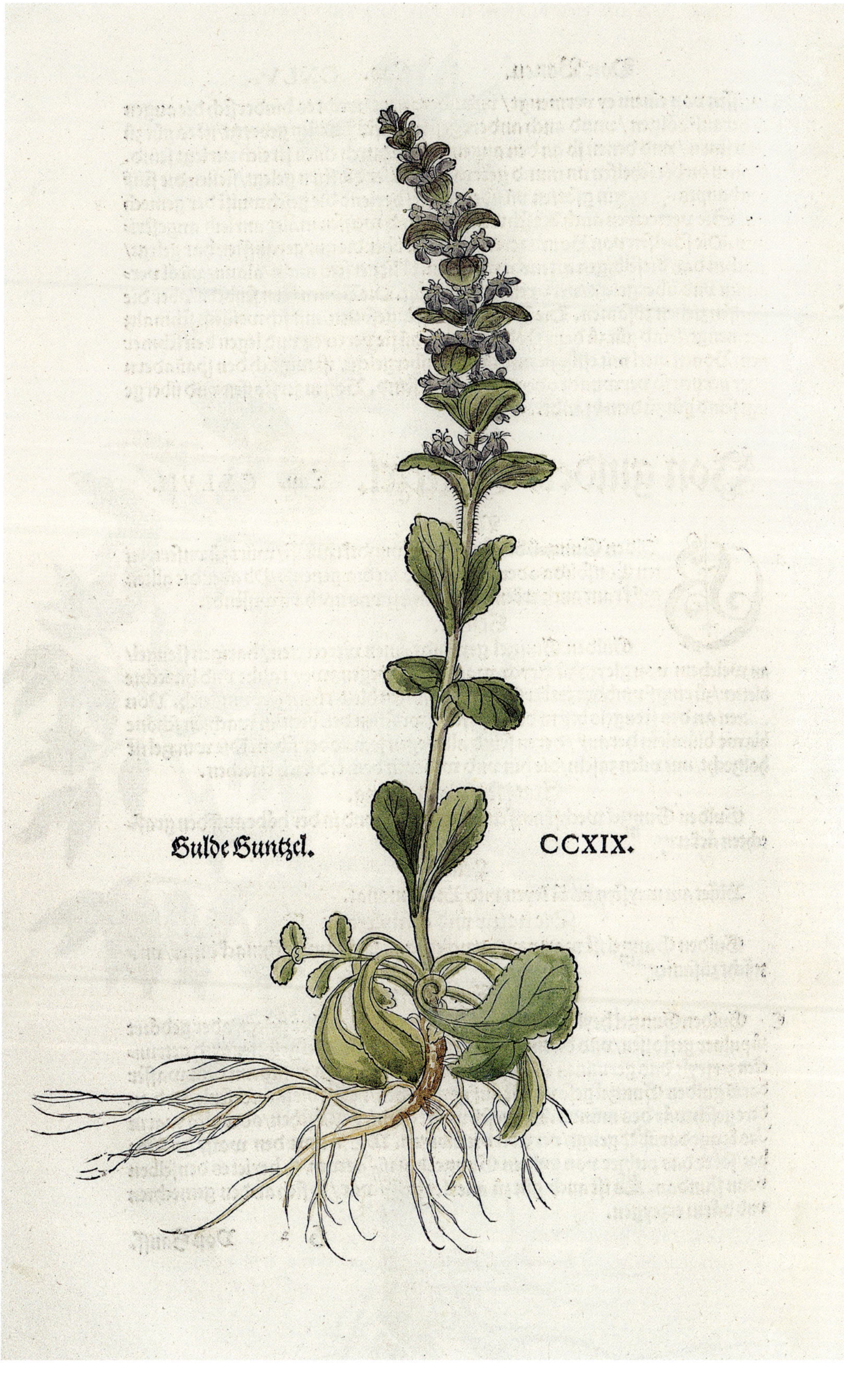
Gulde Guntzel.
CCXIX.

HEMP

Owing to frequent misuse, HEMP (CXLVIII) is no longer part of the pharmacopia, although earlier it was even consumed as food.

HANF

Wegen des häufigen Missbrauchs gehört der HANF (Cap. CXLVIII) heute nicht mehr zum offiziellen Arzneischatz, war früher jedoch sogar als Nahrungsmittel gebräuchlich.

CHANVRE

Le CHANVRE (CXLVIII) ne fait plus partie aujourd'hui de la pharmacopée officielle en raison des usages abusifs qui en ont été faits. Il fut même cultivé autrefois comme plante alimentaire.

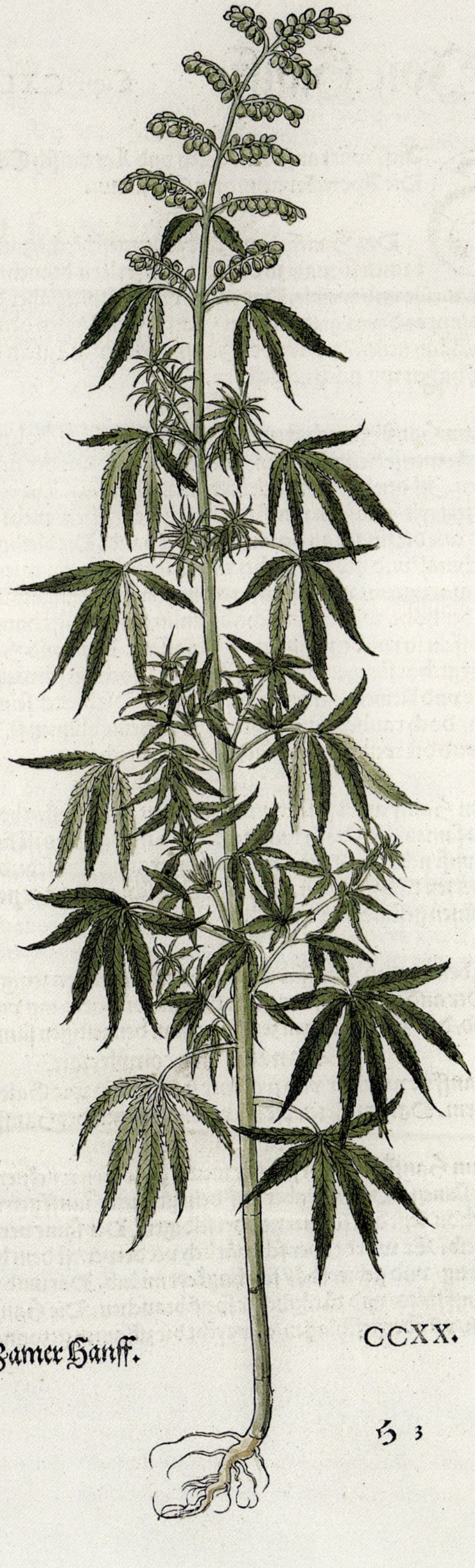

Zamer Hanff.

CCXX.

H 3

HEMP | HANF | CHANVRE

MOTHERWORT

MOTHERWORT (CXLXIX), which served primarily for nervous disorders of the heart, is still at times used to the same end today.

„HERTZGESPANN" (LÖWENSCHWANZ)

„HERTZGESPANN" (Cap. CXLIX), auch Löwenschwanz genannt, diente in erster Linie als Medikament bei nervösen Herzbeschwerden und wird auch heute teilweise noch so eingesetzt.

AGRIPAUME CARDIAQUE

L'AGRIPAUME CARDIAQUE (CXLIX), une variété de faux marrube, s'utilisait, et s'utilise encore maintenant, pour les troubles cardiaques d'origine nerveuse.

PAGE 312

CARAWAY

The essential oils of CARAWAY (CL) make it an ideal spice and carminative.

KÜMMEL

Der KÜMMEL (Cap. CL) eignet sich wegen seiner ätherischen Öle hervorragend als Gewürz und als blähungstreibendes Mittel.

CUMIN DES PRÉS

Grâce à son huile essentielle, le CUMIN DES PRÉS (CL) est un excellent condiment et un remède contre le météorisme.

PAGE 313

HAZELNUT

For its effects, HAZELNUT (CLI) was given preference over the foreign walnut, but no useful information is given about its medical applications.

HASELNUSS

Die HASELNUSS (Cap. CLI) wird in ihrer Wirkung der fremdländischen Walnuss vorgezogen, doch finden sich keine sinnvollen Angaben zur medizinischen Anwendung.

NOISETTE

Fuchs juge les effets de la NOISETTE (CLI) supérieurs à ceux de la noix, d'origine étrangère, sans donner pour autant le moindre renseignement judicieux sur ses applications médicales.

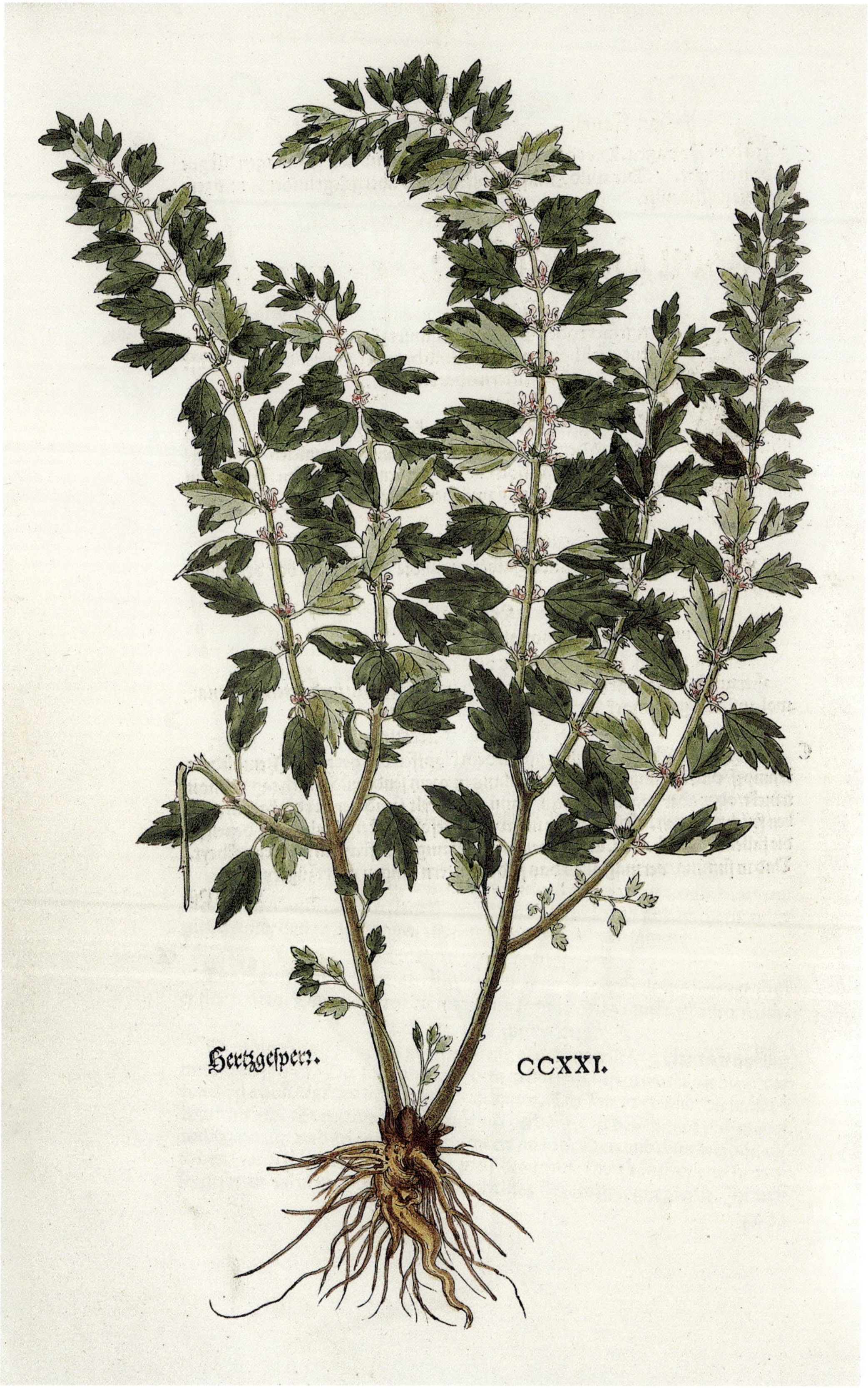
Hertzgespen.
CCXXI.

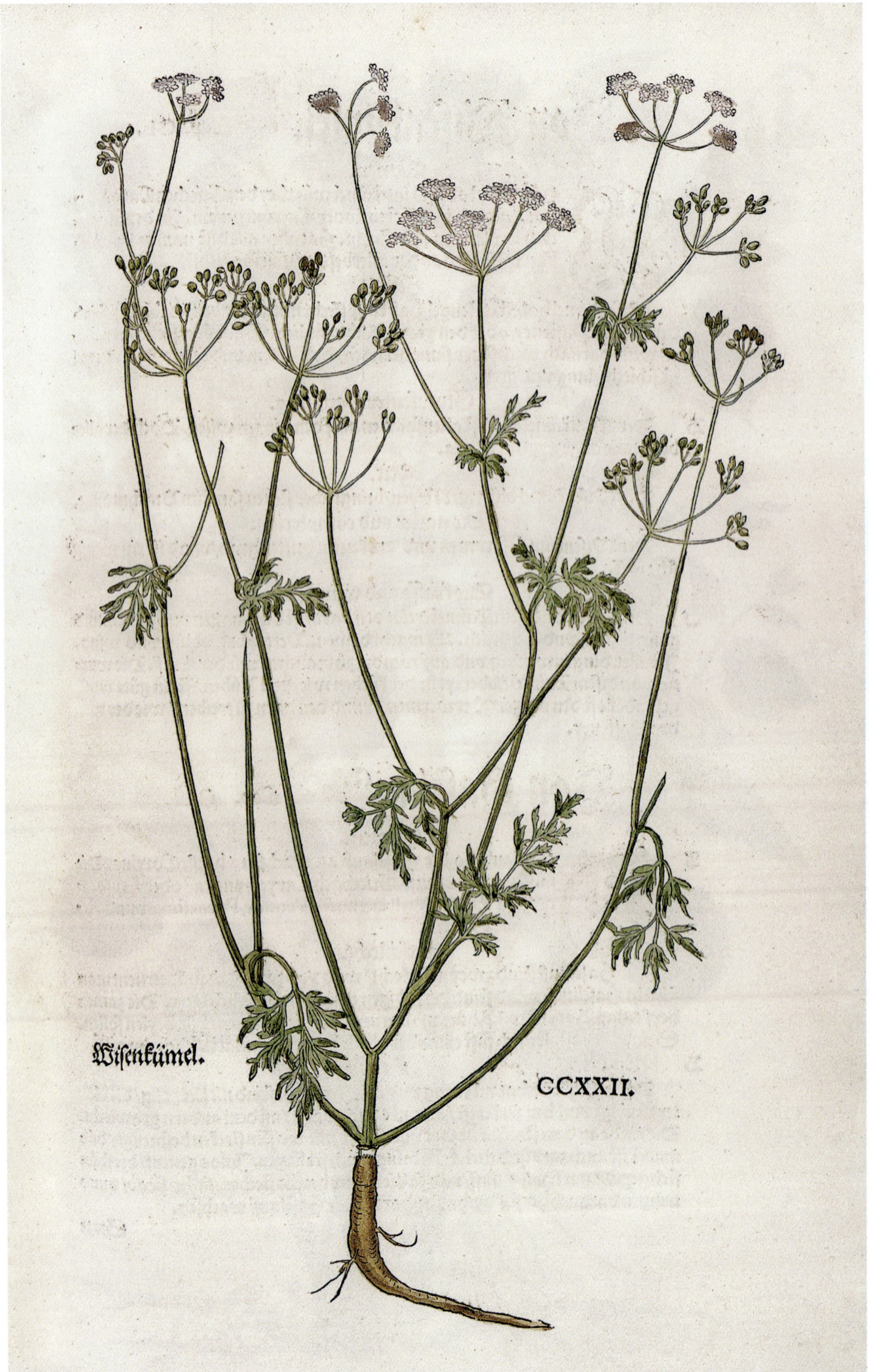
Wiſenkümel.
CCXXII.

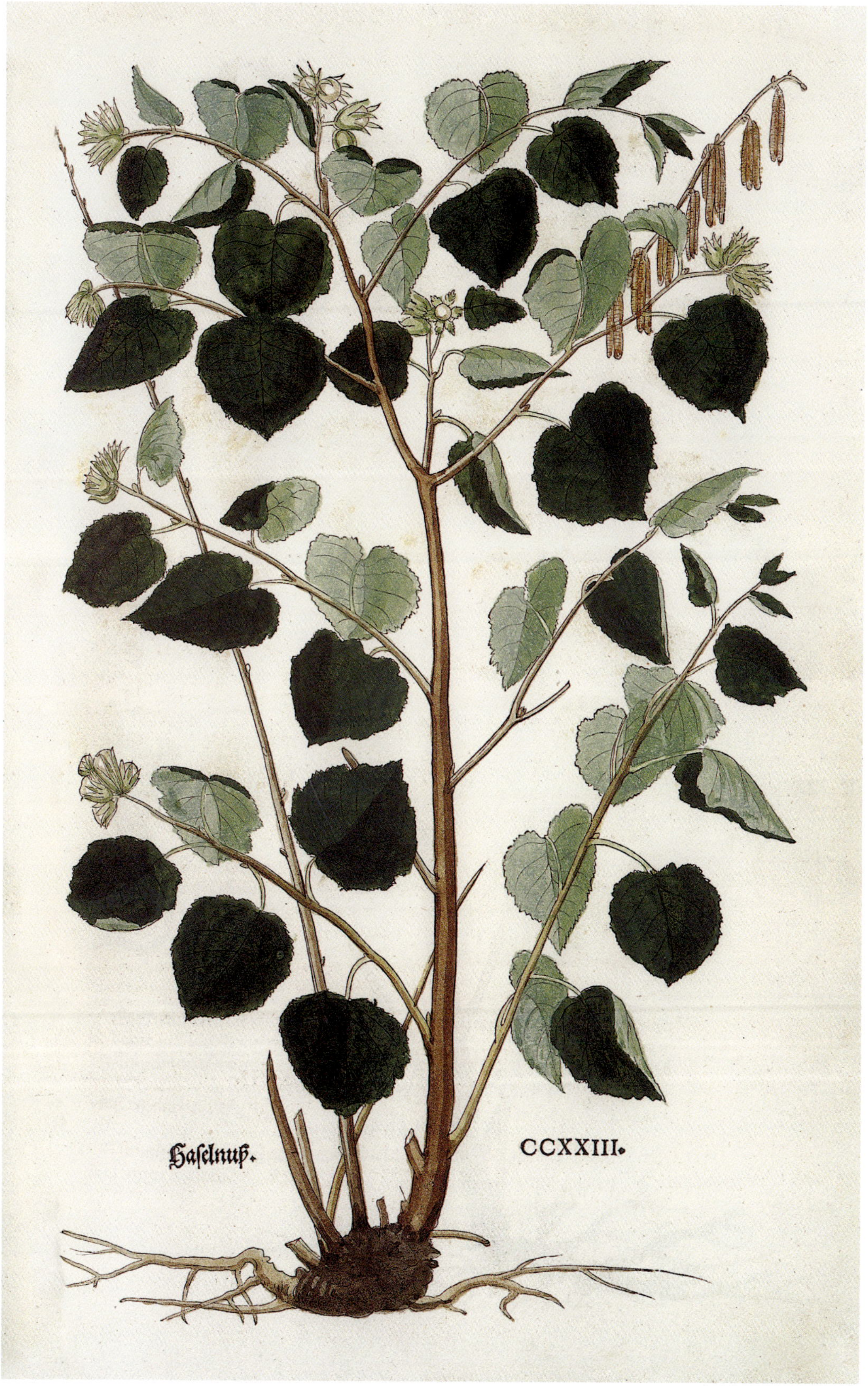
Haſelnuß.
CCXXIII.

CREEPING JENNY

Moneywort, or CREEPING JENNY (CLII), was at one time valued for the healing of internal and external wounds.

EGELKRAUT

Das EGELKRAUT (Cap. CLII), das wir heute Pfennigkraut nennen, war früher ein geschätztes Mittel bei äußerlichen und innerlichen Verletzungen.

NUMMULAIRE

La NUMMULAIRE (CLII), ou herbe aux écus, appelée ici «Egelkraut» (herbe à sangsues, car elle aime l'eau), était utilisée pour les blessures internes et externes.

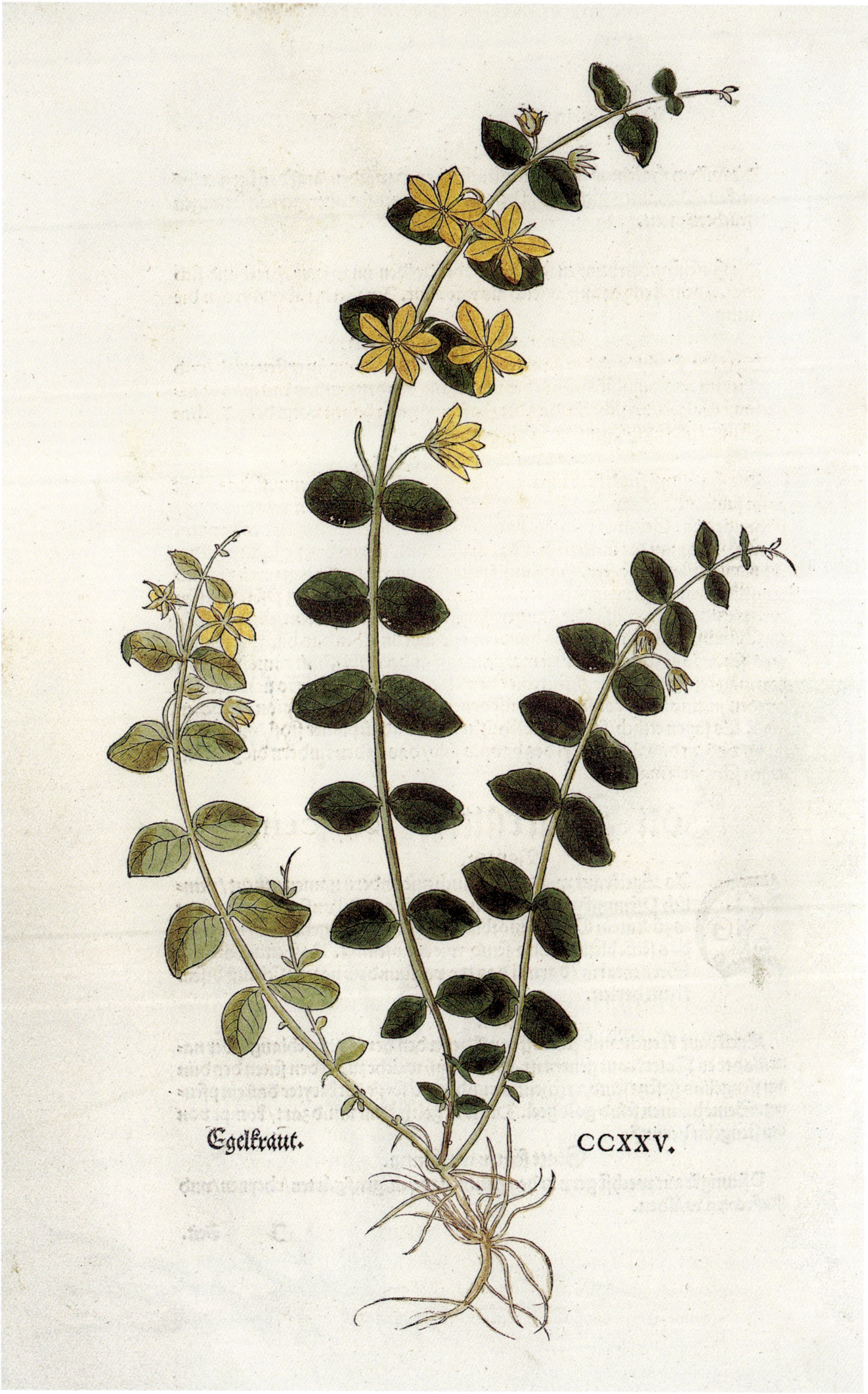
Egelkraut.
CCXXV.

PLUMS

Among the PLUMS (CLIII), Fuchs illustrated the PLUM (plate CCXXVI) as the "tame kind" and the BLACKTHORN, or SLOE (plate CCXXVII) as the wild form; neither, however, had much significance as medicines.

PFLAUMEN

Zu den PFLAUMEN (Cap. CLIII) bildet Fuchs als „zam geschlecht" die GARTEN-PFLAUME (Taf. CCXXVI) und als wilde Form die SCHLEHE (Cap. CCXXVII) ab, die aber beide keine sehr große Bedeutung als Arznei besaßen.

PRUNIER

Au chapitre «PRUNIERS» (CLIII), Fuchs présente le PRUNIER proprement dit (pl. CCXXVI), qu'il qualifie de «genre domestiqué», et sa forme sauvage, le PRUNELLIER (pl. CCXXVII). Aucun d'eux cependant n'avait une importance médicale particulière.

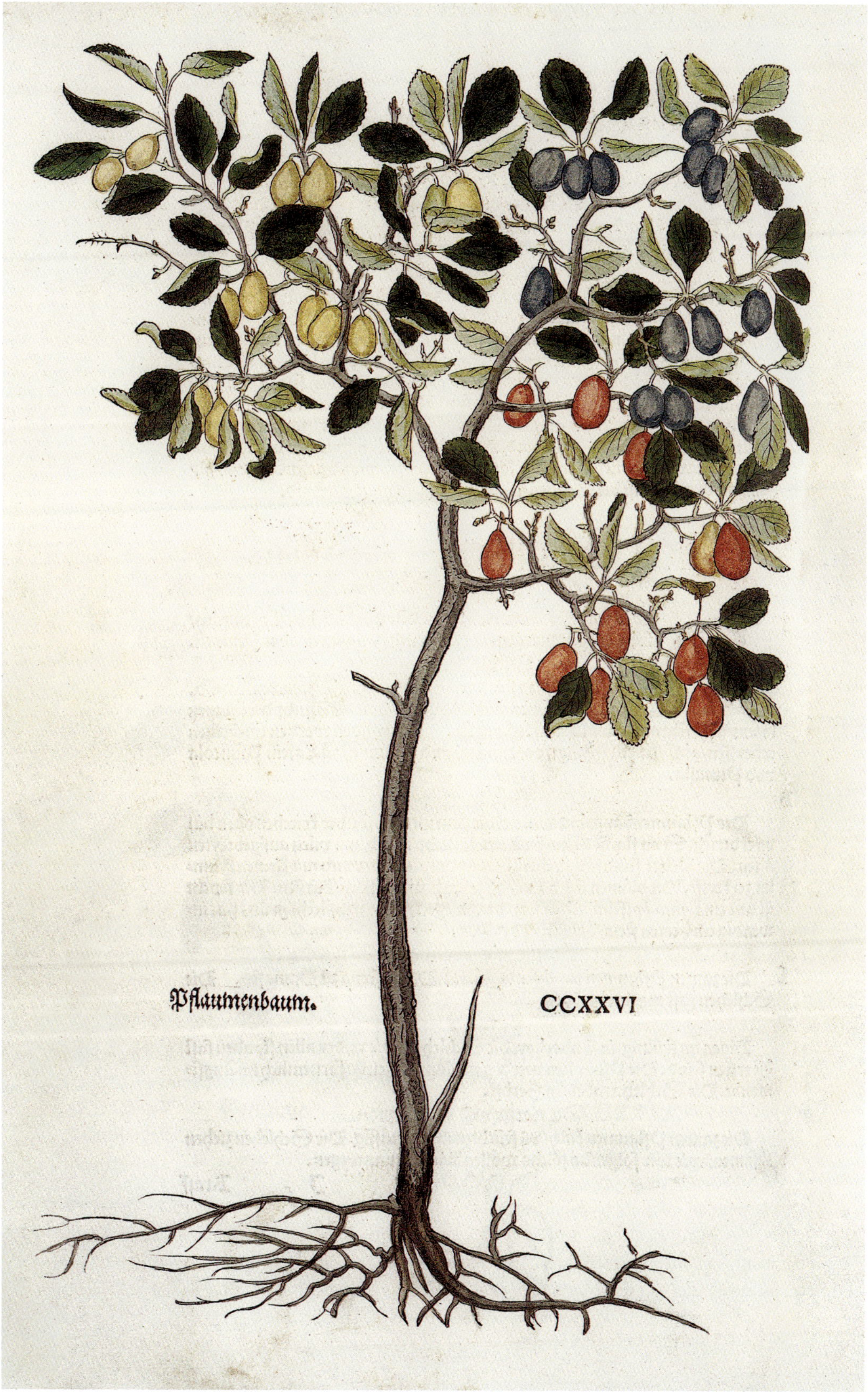
Pflaumenbaum.
CCXXVI

HEMLOCK

The juice of the highly toxic HEMLOCK (CLIIII) is well known for having cost Socrates his life. Fuchs also warned against its application and referred to the danger of accidental poisoning. Unfortunately, his advice on administering a good wine as an antidote is useless.

WÜTERICH

Hinter dem Namen WÜTERICH (Cap. CLIIII) verbirgt sich der hochgiftige Schierling, dessen Saft bekanntlicherweise schon Sokrates das Leben gekostet hat. Fuchs warnt denn auch vor der Anwendung und weist auf die Gefahr versehentlicher Vergiftung hin, wobei sein Ratschlag, zur Hilfe guten Wein zu verabreichen, allerdings im Notfall leider wirkungslos bleiben dürfte.

GRANDE CIGUË

Sous le nom de «Wüterich» (approximativement, celle qui est furieuse) se cache la GRANDE CIGUË (CLIIII). L'extrême toxicité de son suc est connue depuis l'Antiquité puisque Socrate fut condamné à boire la ciguë. Fuchs met en garde contre son usage et les dangers d'un empoisonnement accidentel. Qu'il recommande cependant le bon vin comme antidote ne devrait pas être d'une grande efficacité dans les cas urgents !

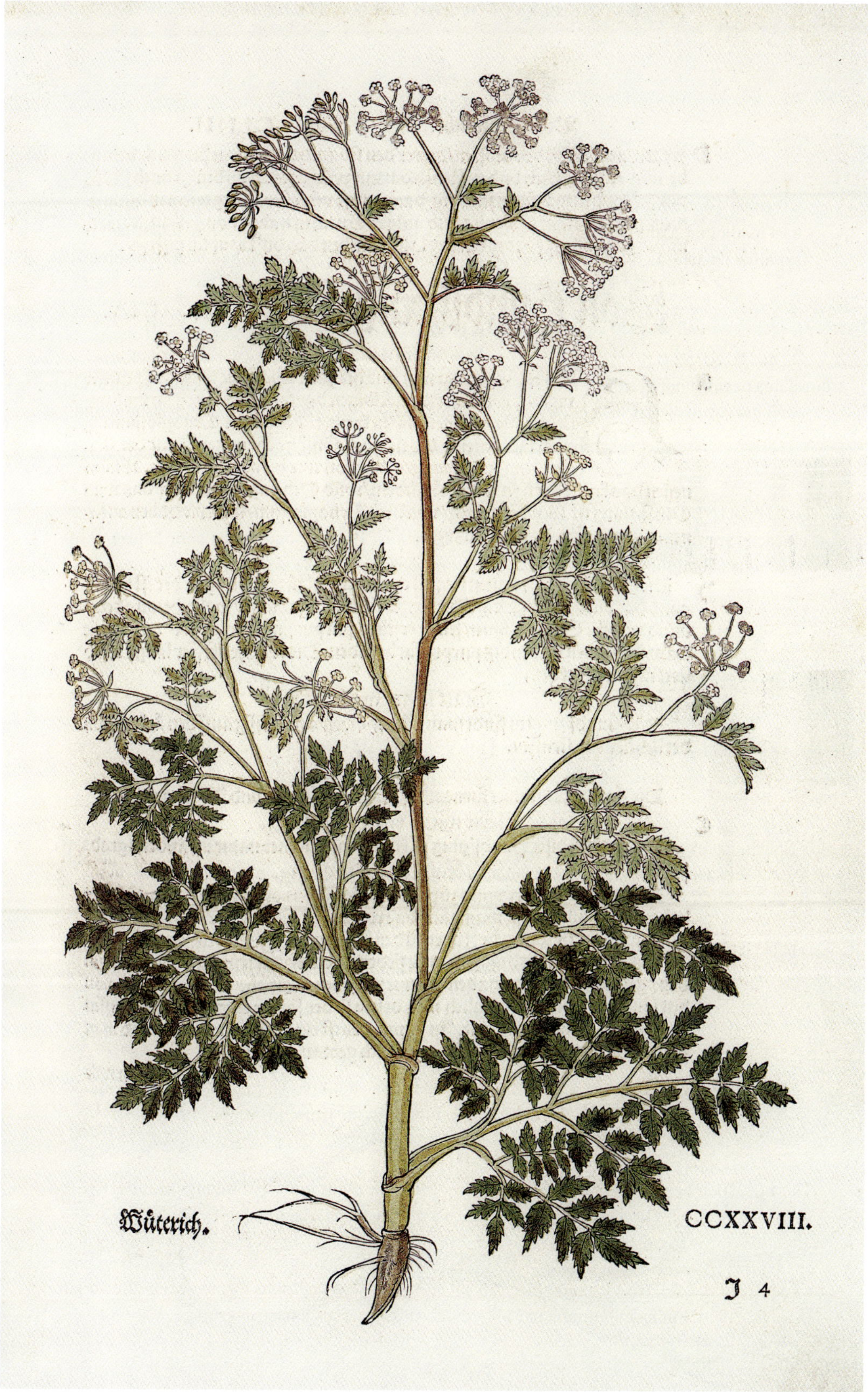
Wüterich.
CCXXVIII.
J 4

VIPER'S BUGLOSS

Termed "superfluous in the fields," VIPER'S BUGLOSS (CLV) was nonetheless valued as a medicinal plant for dysentery and wounds. In his reference to "the French disease" or syphilis, Fuchs was the first expressly to mention this scourge, which had begun to spread throughout Germany at the end of the 15th century.

HUNDSZUNGE

Die HUNDSZUNGE (Cap. CLV) ist „überflüssig auf den äckern", aber als Heilpflanze durchaus begehrt bei der Ruhr und zur Wundheilung. Erstmals erwähnt Fuchs hier ausdrücklich auch die „frantzosen", wie in Deutschland die seit dem Ende des 15. Jahrhunderts neu und verbreitet auftretende Syphilis genannt wurde.

VIPÉRINE COMMUNE

La VIPÉRINE COMMUNE (CLV), «abondante dans les champs», est très estimée pour son efficacité sur la dysenterie et la cicatrisation des plaies. Fuchs évoque aussi pour la première fois, sous le qualificatif de «française», une nouvelle maladie, la syphilis, qui s'est répandue en Allemagne depuis la fin du XVe siècle.

PAGE 322

SAFFLOWER

SAFFLOWER (CLVI), also known as Dyer's Saffron, was used as food colouring, while the seeds were occasionally used in medicine.

„WILDER GARTEN SAFFRAN"

Als Nahrungsfärbemittel wurden die Blüten des „WILDEN GARTEN SAFFRAN" (Cap. CLVI), des Färber-Saflor, in den Küchen gebraucht, der Same vereinzelt zur Arznei.

SAFRAN BÂTARD

Les pétales pressés du SAFRAN BÂTARD (CLVI), appelé «Saflor» (fleur de safran) dans le texte, donnaient un pigment jaune utilisé en cuisine ; les graines étaient parfois employées en médecine.

PAGE 323

COMMON MILLET

The primary use of COMMON MILLET (CLVII) was doubtless as a milk-based porridge, but Fuchs also mentions poultices made from the grain.

HIRSE

Der mit Milch bereitete Hirsebrei war sicherlich früher die Hauptverwendung für die HIRSE (Cap. CLVII), daneben erwähnt Fuchs auch Umschläge mit den Früchten.

PANIC MILLET

Le PANIC MILLET (CLVII), ou mil, s'utilisait surtout en cuisine, sous forme de bouillie au lait ; Fuchs mentionne par ailleurs des cataplasmes à base de fruits.

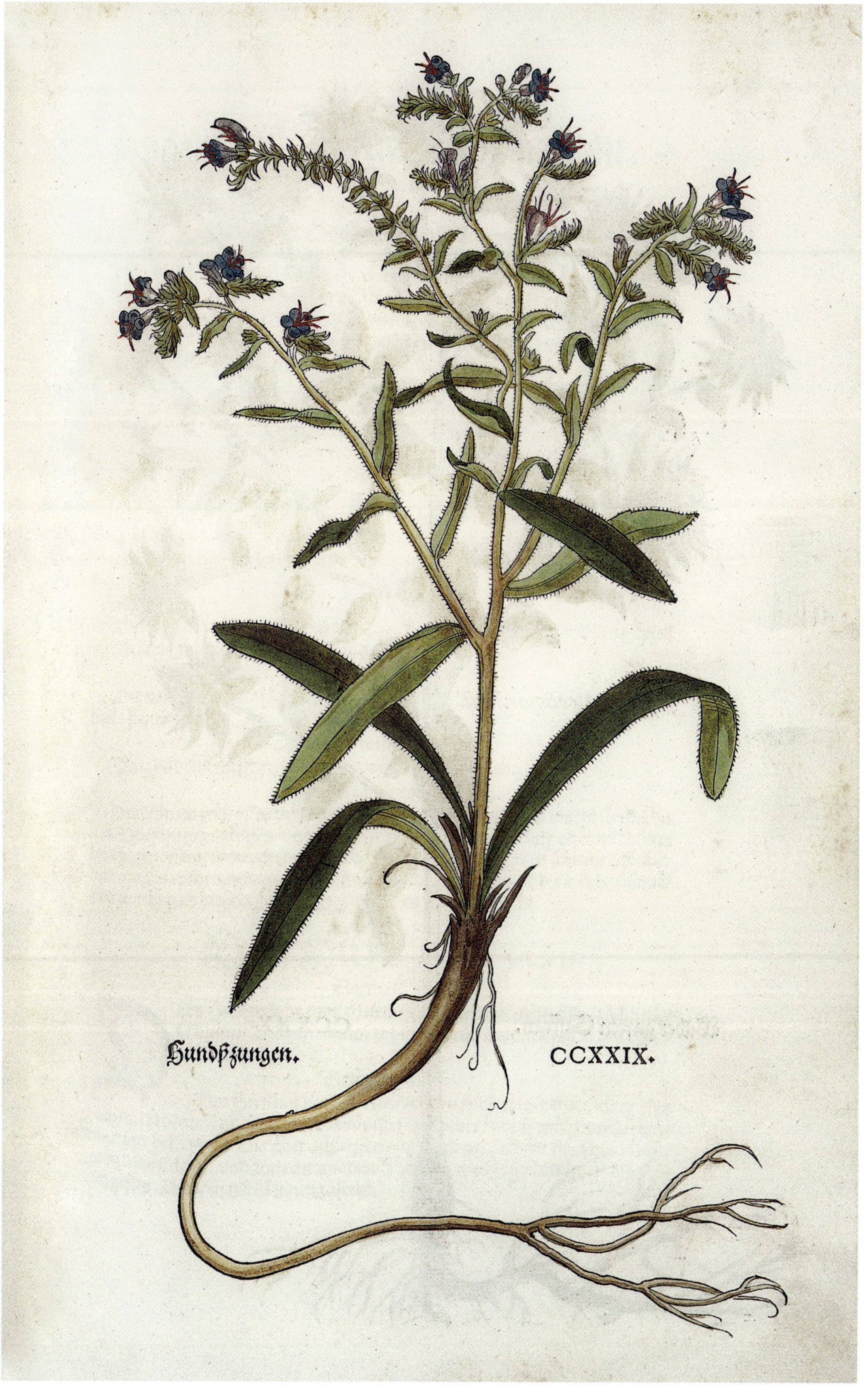

VIPER'S BUGLOSS | HUNDSZUNGE | VIPÉRINE COMMUNE

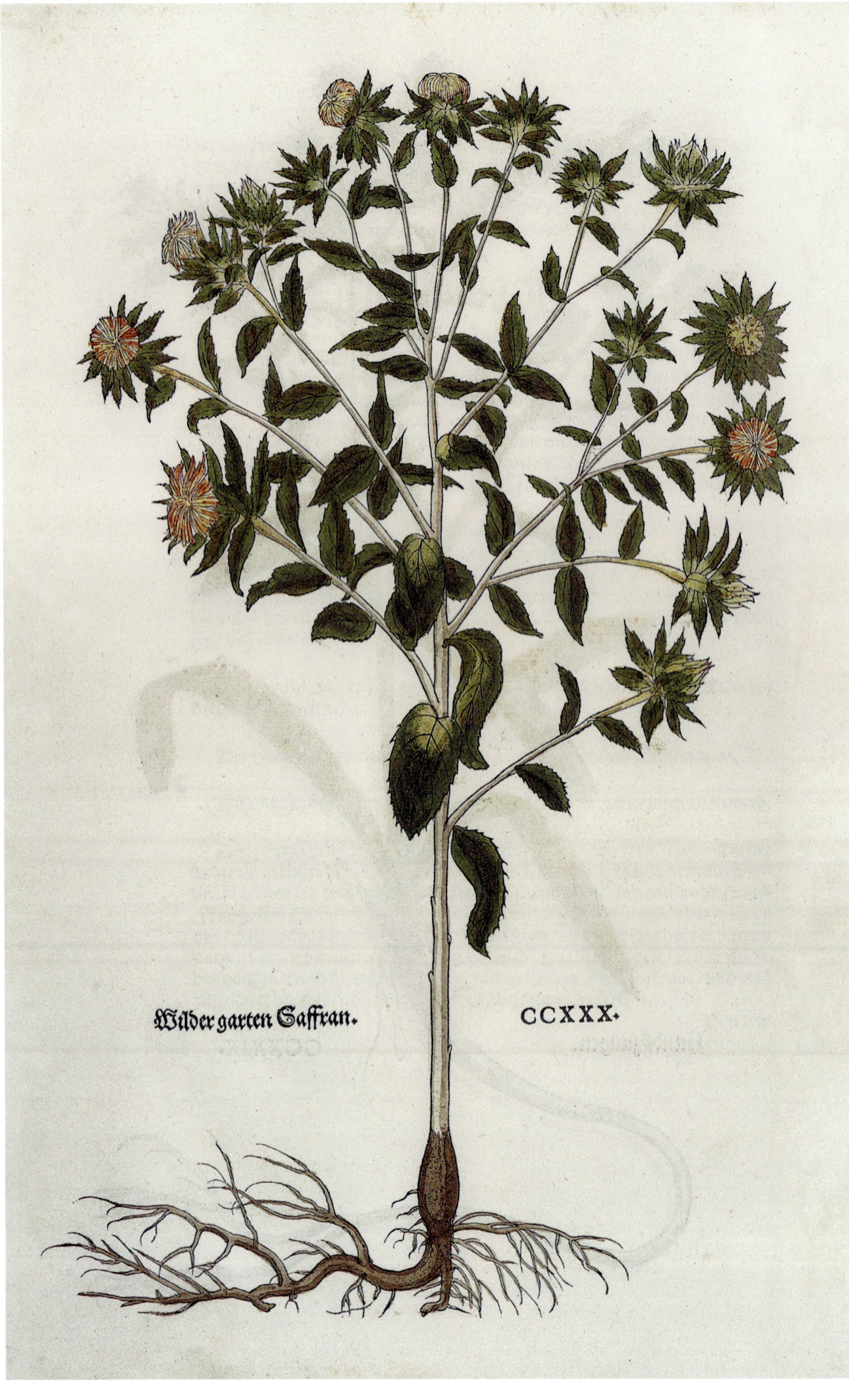
Wilder garten Saffran.
CCXXX.

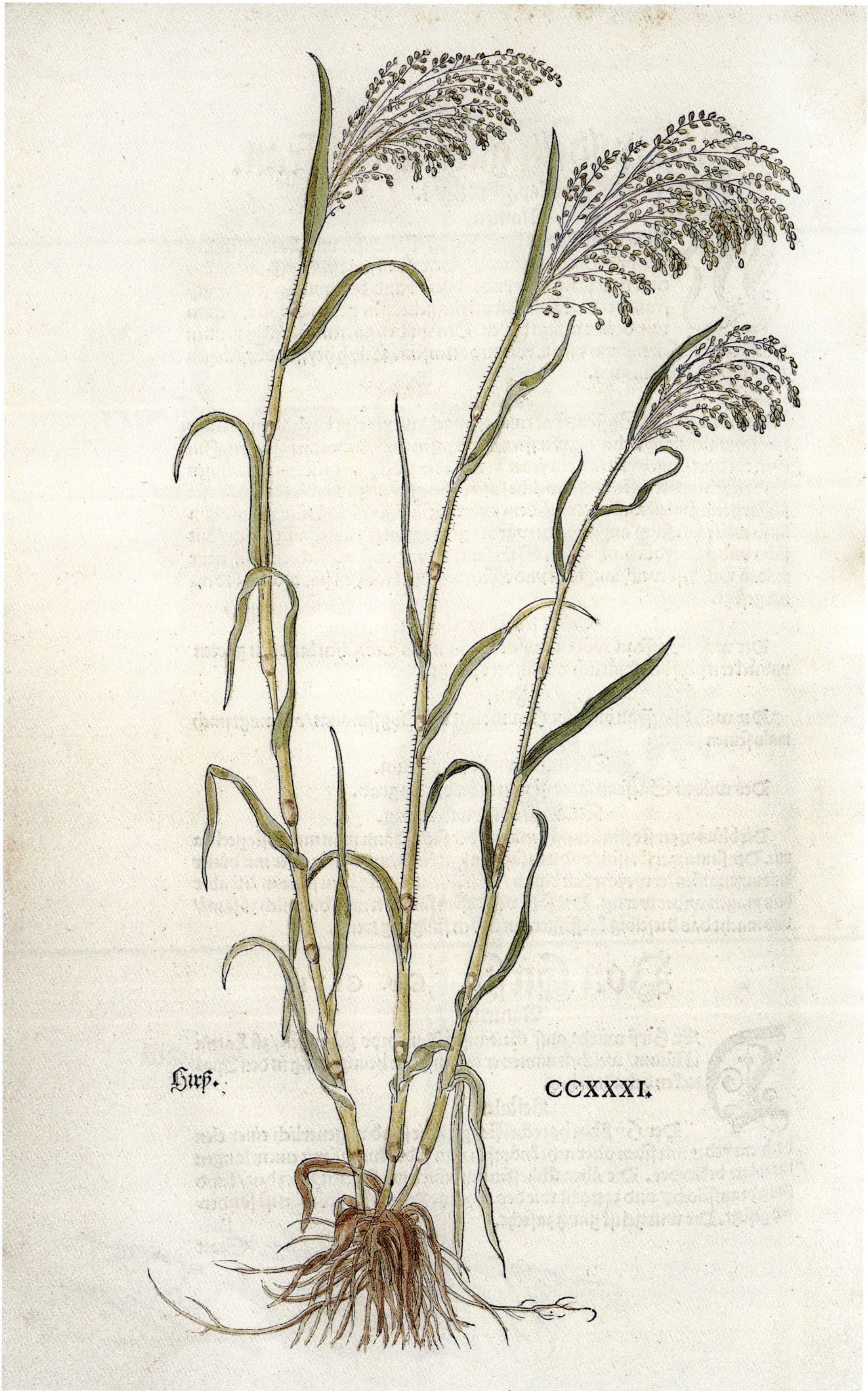
Hirs.
CCXXXI.

KALE

Fuchs presents five different species of KALE and CABBAGE (CLVIII) without distinguishing their uses. He speaks of their effect as fibre for stimulating bowel movements, but also mentions the flatulence often associated with the plant. He even recommends the leaves of the CABBAGE against loss of hair and the juice against haematoma.

KOHL

Gleich fünf verschieden Arten stellt Fuchs beim KOHL (Cap. CLVIII) vor, unterscheidet ihre Wirkung jedoch nicht weiter. Neben der Anregung der Verdauung durch ihre Ballaststofffunktion erwähnt er auch die häufigen Blähungen und empfiehlt sogar Kohlblätter gegen Haarausfall und den Saft gegen Blutergüsse.

CHOU

Fuchs présente le CHOU (CLVIII) avec cinq espèces, mais sans différencier leurs effets respectifs. Il évoque le pouvoir tonique de leurs fibres sur la digestion, tout en signalant les fréquentes fermentations intestinales qu'ils occasionnent, et recommande même les feuilles contre la chute des cheveux et le suc contre les hématomes.

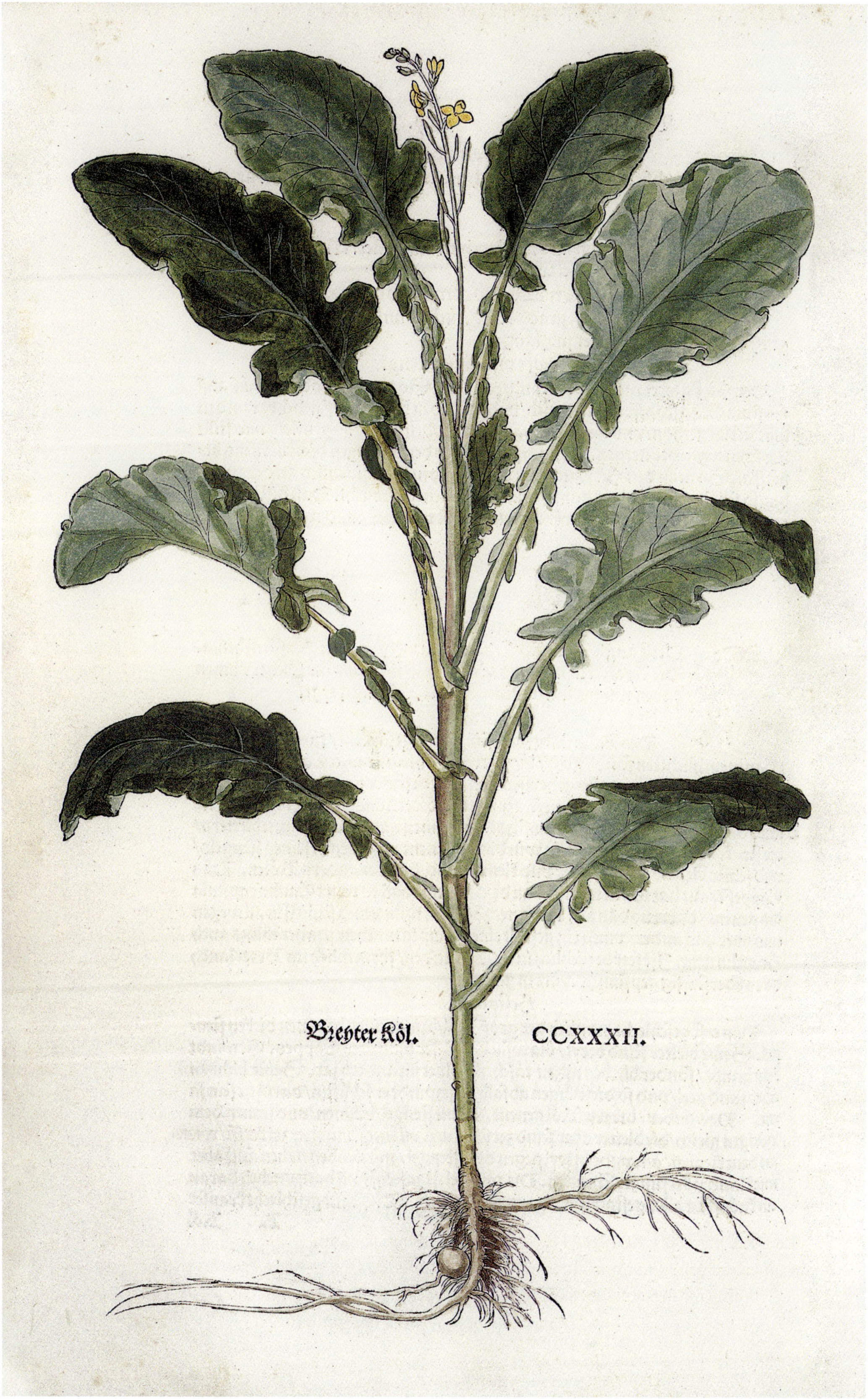
Breyter Köl.
CCXXXII.

CROSS GENTIAN

Since the rhizome of CROSS GENTIAN (CLIX) appeared to be slashed, it was recommended as a vulnerary. Neither this nor its application in stimulating the digestion is recognized today.

„MADELGEER" (KREUZ-ENZIAN)

Der Name „MADELGEER" (Cap. CLIX) für den Kreuz-Enzian ist uns heute nicht mehr geläufig, ebenso wie dessen Anwendung zur Wundheilung, wegen des zerstochen aussehenden Wurzelstockes, und zur Anregung der Verdauung.

GENTIANE CROISETTE

La GENTIANE CROISETTE (CLIX) a perdu non seulement son ancien nom allemand «Madelgeer» (on la nomme aujourd'hui «Kreuz-Enzian», ou gentiane à croix), mais aussi son usage comme cicatrisant – l'aspect piqué de sa racine semblait l'indice de vertus particulières – et comme tonique de la digestion.

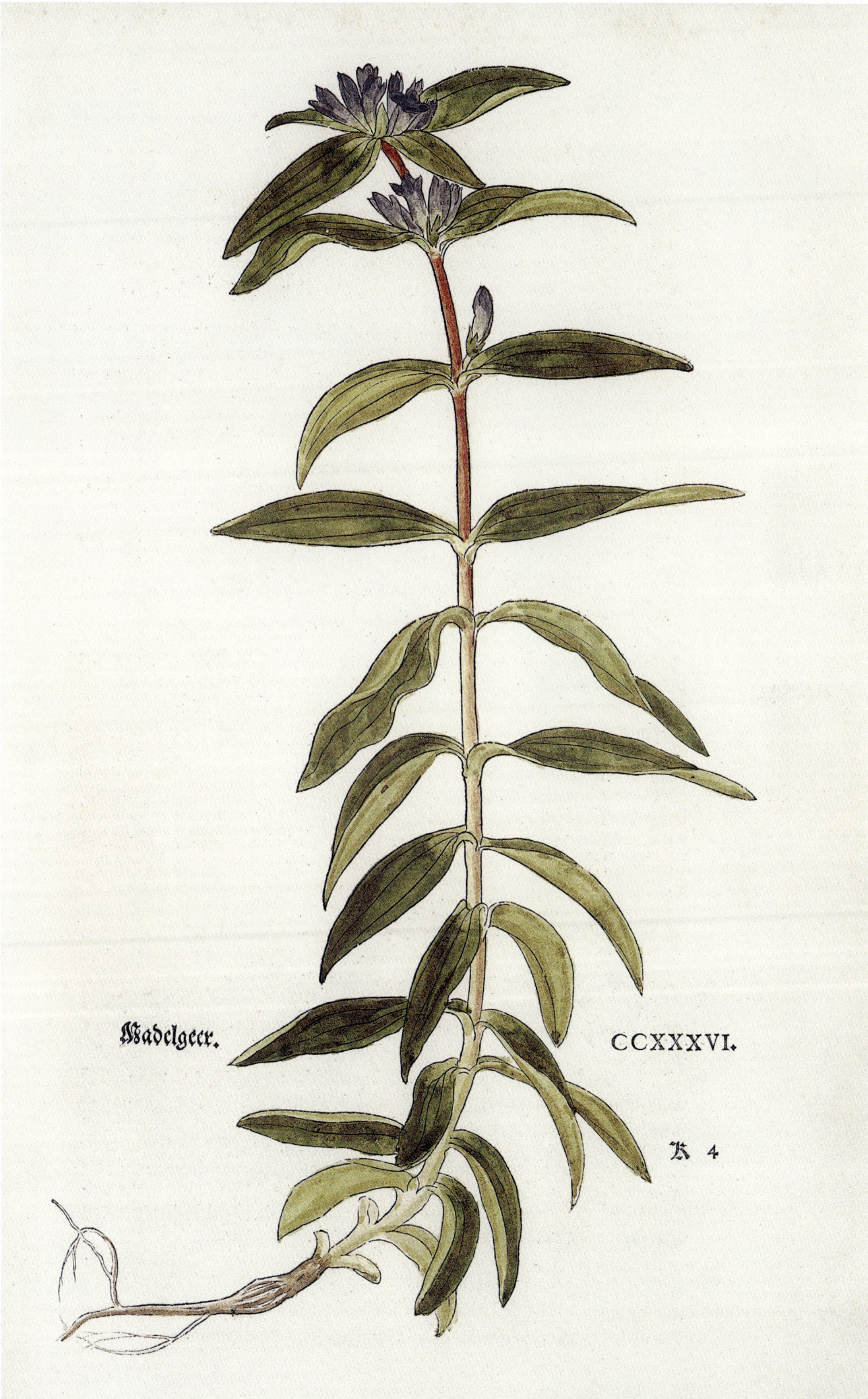
Madelgeer.
CCXXXVI.
K 4

IVY

As an effective cough medicine, preparations made from IVY (CLX) are very popular today, although this application is absent from the long list of uses mentioned here.

EFEU

Als wirksames Hustenmittel sind Zubereitungen aus dem EFEU (Cap. CLX) heute sehr beliebt, werden aber trotz langer Aufzählung hier nicht genannt.

LIERRE

Les préparations expectorantes à base de LIERRE (CLX) sont très prisées aujourd'hui, alors que Fuchs ne les évoque même pas dans sa longue liste d'indications.

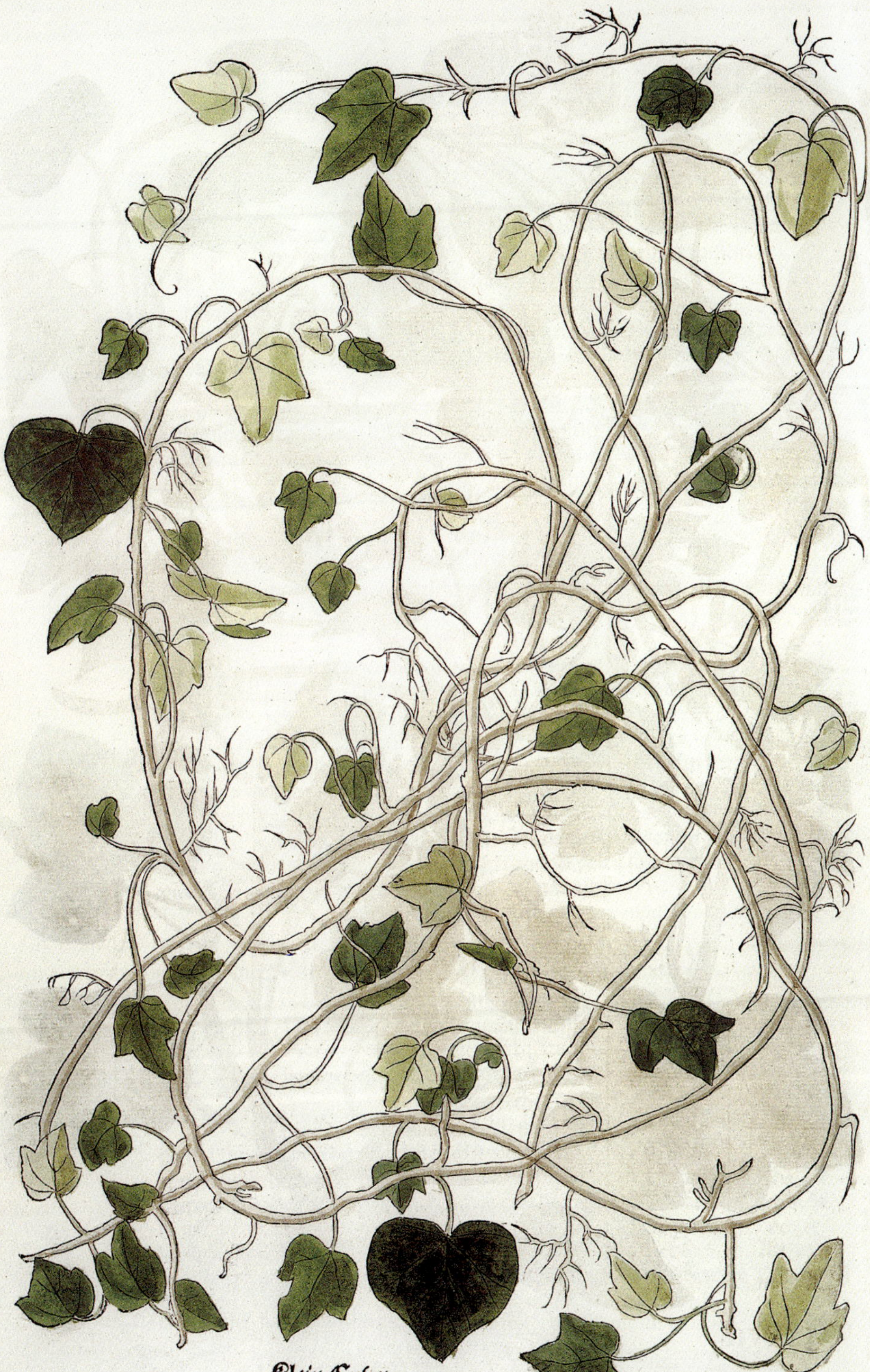

Klein Ephew.

CCXXXVIII.

CHERRY

The sleight-of-hand Fuchs used to present the three “kinds” of CHERRY (CLXI) in a single illustration becomes clear only in the coloured editions. The lighter coloured CHERRY of the amarelle group is clearly distinct from the Dark Morelle and also from the smaller fruits of the Bird or Sweet Cherry. The recommendation that the fruit, still wet with dew, should be swallowed together with the stone to stimulate bowel movements is beyond explanation.

KIRSCHEN

Der Kunstgriff, den Fuchs anwenden ließ, um die drei „geschlecht“ der KIRSCHEN (Cap. CLXI) in einer einzigen Abbildung darzustellen, wird erst in der kolorierten Ausgabe deutlich, wenn sich die hellere Amarelle oder Glaskirsche neben der dunklen Morelle oder Süßweichsel deutlich abhebt und auch die kleineren Früchte der Vogelkirsche erkennbar sind. Verblüffend ist die Anweisung, die noch taufeuchten Früchte mitsamt dem Stein zu schlucken, um den Stuhlgang anzuregen.

CERISE

Pour représenter sur une même illustration les trois «genres» de la CERISE (CLXI), Fuchs recourt à un artifice que seule l’édition coloriée fait découvrir : la cerise amarelle se détache nettement sur la cerise morello plus sombre, tandis que la merise des oiseaux se remarque par sa taille plus petite. D’après Fuchs, l’ingestion de cerises entières couvertes de rosée stimule la digestion, une affirmation qui ne laisse pas de surprendre.

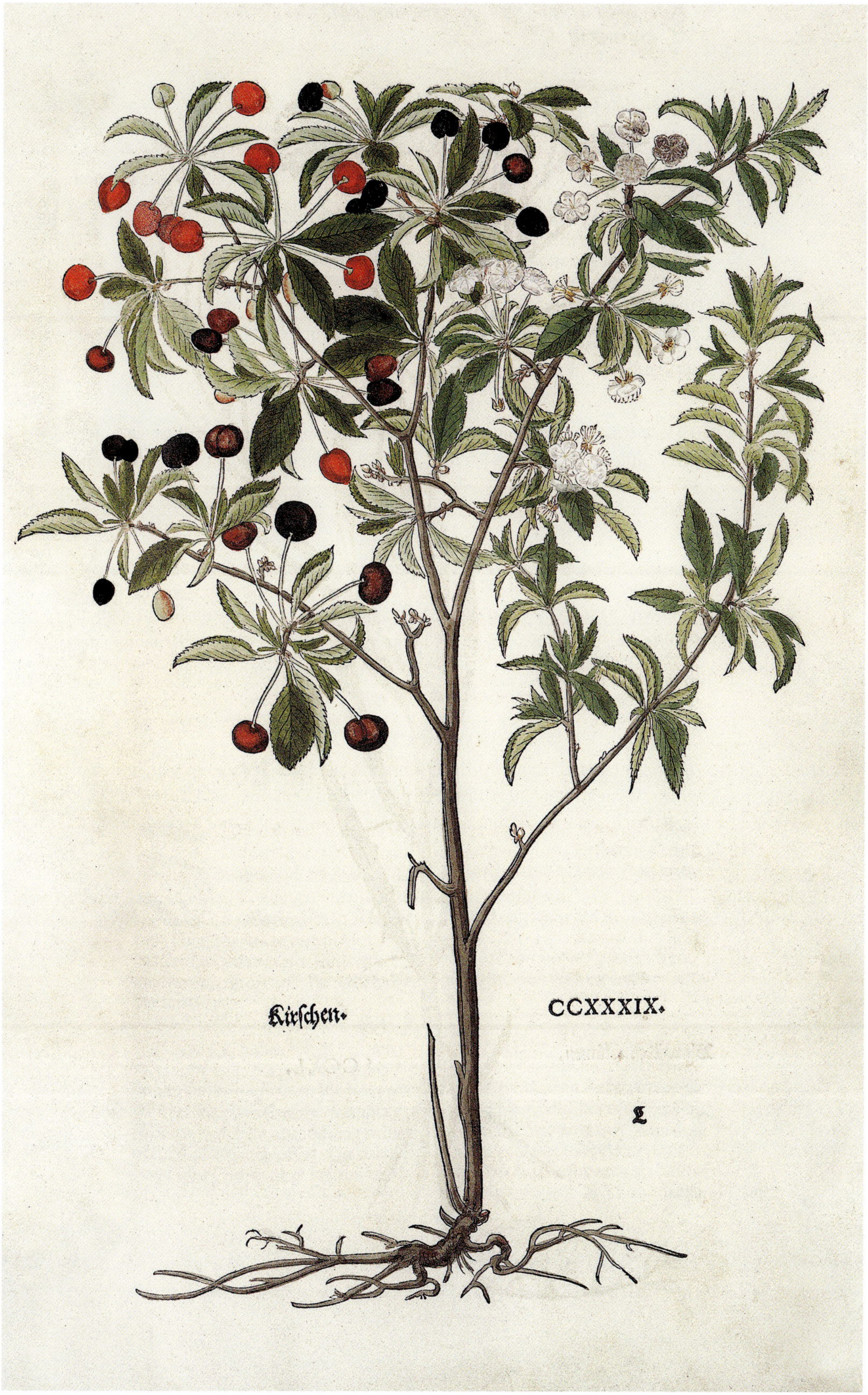
Kirschen.
CCXXXIX.
L

CORNFLOWER

CORNFLOWER, or BACHELOR'S BUTTON (CLXII), today a beautiful and uncommon blue field weed, was recommended for the healing of wounds and inflammations, but, in fact, no particular effect can be expected from the plant.

KORNBLUME

Auch die KORNBLUME (Cap. CLXII), das heute selten gewordene schöne blaue Ackerunkraut, wird bei der Wundheilung und bei Entzündungen empfohlen, wobei allerdings keine spezifische Wirkung zu erwarten sein dürfte.

BLEUET

Le beau BLEUET (CLXII), autrefois abondant dans les moissons, est préconisé comme cicatrisant et anti-inflammatoire, alors qu'il ne faudrait en attendre aucun effet spécifique.

PAGE 334

COMMON ONION

With the well known COMMON ONION (CLXIII), the herbal once again presents a plant that is equally useful as a food and a medicine. Fuchs mentions the ONION's irritating effect on the eye and nose, and recommends its use for example as a haemorrhoidal suppository, a remedy for rabies and an aid against loss of hair.

ZWIEBEL

Mit der altbekannten ZWIEBEL (Cap. CLXIII) erscheint wieder eine Pflanze, die gleichermaßen als Nahrungs- wie als Arzneimittel dient. Ihre reizende Wirkung auf Auge und Nase wird ebenso erwähnt wie z. B. der Einsatz als Hämorrhoidalzäpfchen, bei Tollwut und bei Haarausfall.

OIGNON

Avec l'OIGNON (CLXIII), c'est une autre plante utile et bien connue tant sur le plan alimentaire que thérapeutique que nous rencontrons ici. Sont mentionnés par exemple ses effets irritants sur les yeux et le nez, son usage en suppositoires pour les hémorroïdes ainsi que son emploi contre la rage et la chute des cheveux.

PAGE 335

BATS-IN-THE-BELFRY

BATS-IN-THE-BELFRY (CLXIIII) was supposed to relieve sore throat and complaints in the mouth.

HALSKRAUT

Halsschmerzen und Beschwerden im Mundbereich sollten durch das HALSKRAUT (Cap. CLXIIII) gelindert werden.

CAMPANULE GANTELÉE

La CAMPANULE GANTELÉE (CLXIIII) serait efficace contre les maux de gorge et de la bouche.

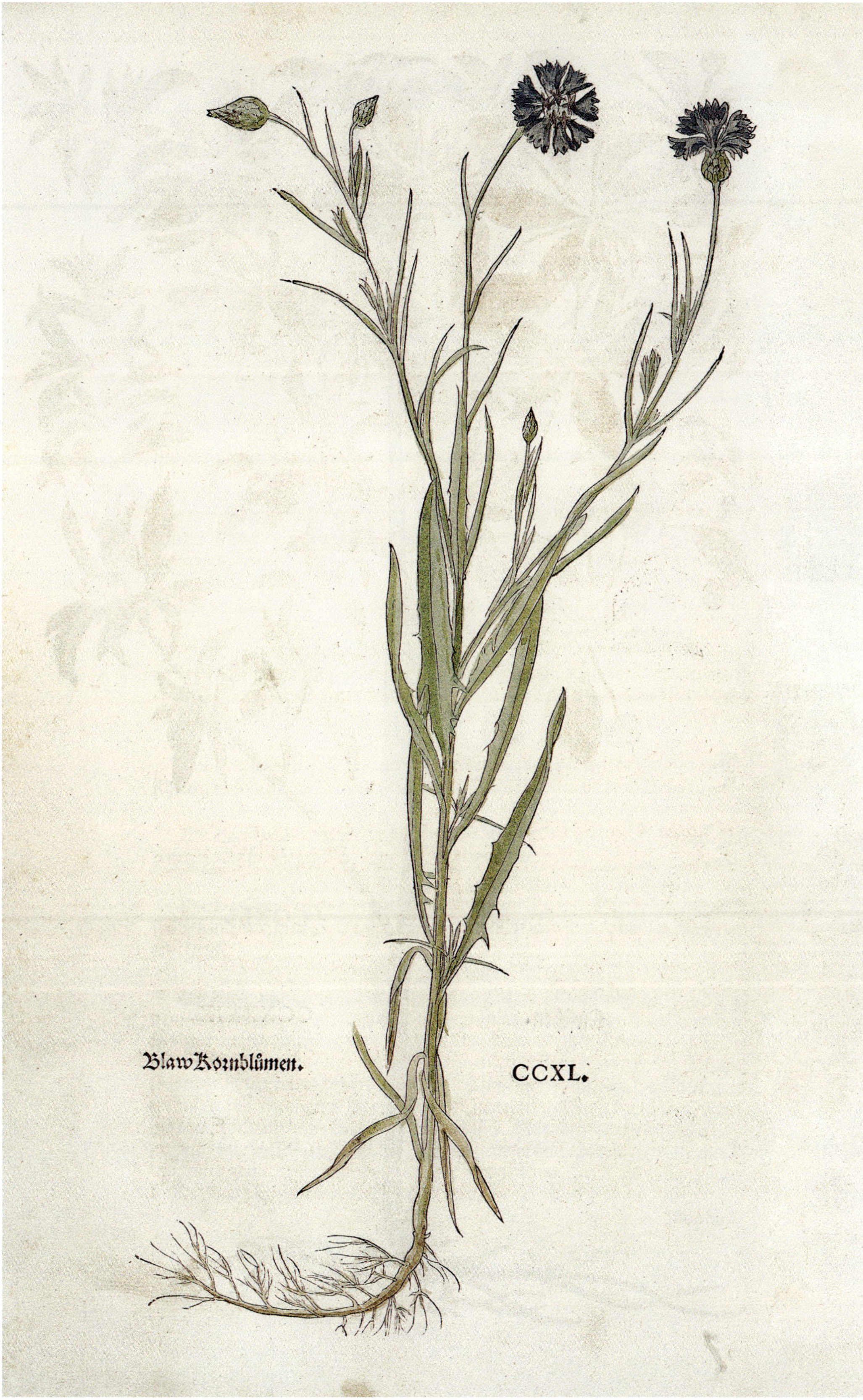
Blaw Kornblůmen.
CCXL.

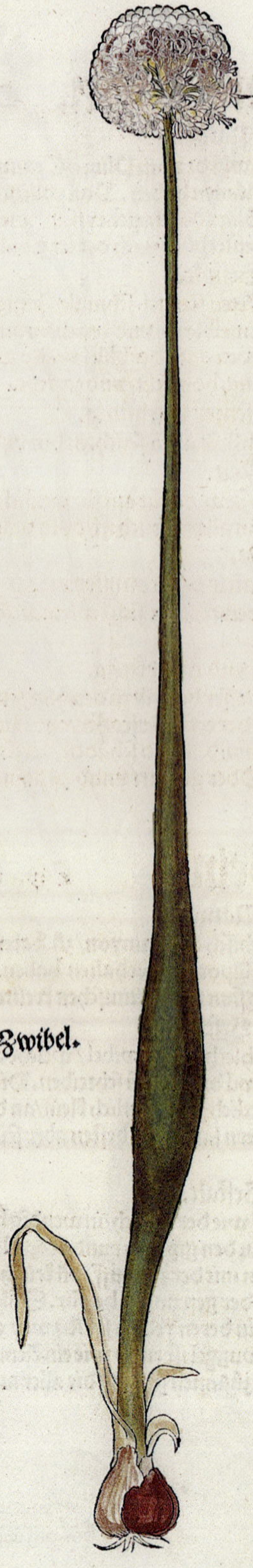

Zwibel. CCXLI.

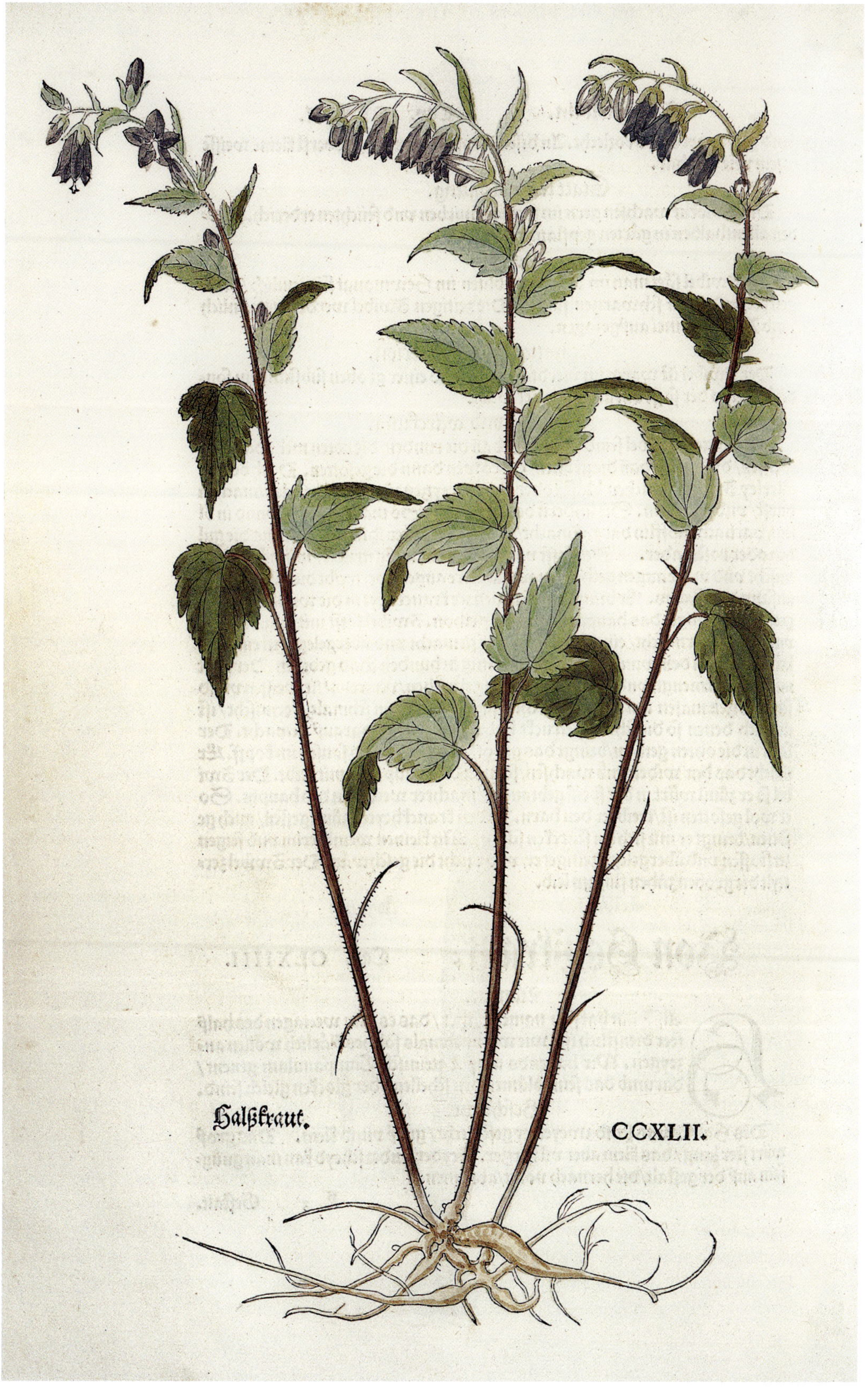
Halßkraut.
CCXLII.

CAT-MINT

The illustration of CAT-MINT (CLXV), also known as CATNIP, clearly reveals the uncertainty of botanists in the age before Linneas. Following CAT-MINT and Corn Mint as the supposedly third "kind" of Mint comes greater Fleabane, which is not a labiated flower at all, but a composite, and thus botanically unrelated.

„CALAMINTHEN"

Bei den Abbildungen zum Kapitel „CALAMINTHEN" (Cap. CLXV) zeigt sich deutlich die Unsicherheit der Botaniker in der vorlinéeschen Zeit, denn die vermeintlich dritte Minzen-Art nach der Katzenminze und der Acker-Minze, das Ruhr-Flohkraut, ist keineswegs auch ein Lippenblütler, sondern ein Korbblütler und damit botanisch überhaupt nicht verwandt.

CALAMINTHES

La chapitre sur les «CALAMINTHES» (CLXV) montre bien la difficulté qu'avaient les botanistes de l'époque prélinéenne à classer les plantes selon leur genre. Ainsi la pulicaire dysentérique, ou herbe de Saint-Roch, considérée ici comme une menthe, au même titre que l'herbe aux chats et la menthe des champs, n'est pas une Lamiacée mais une Composée, et n'a de ce fait aucune parenté avec les deux autres.

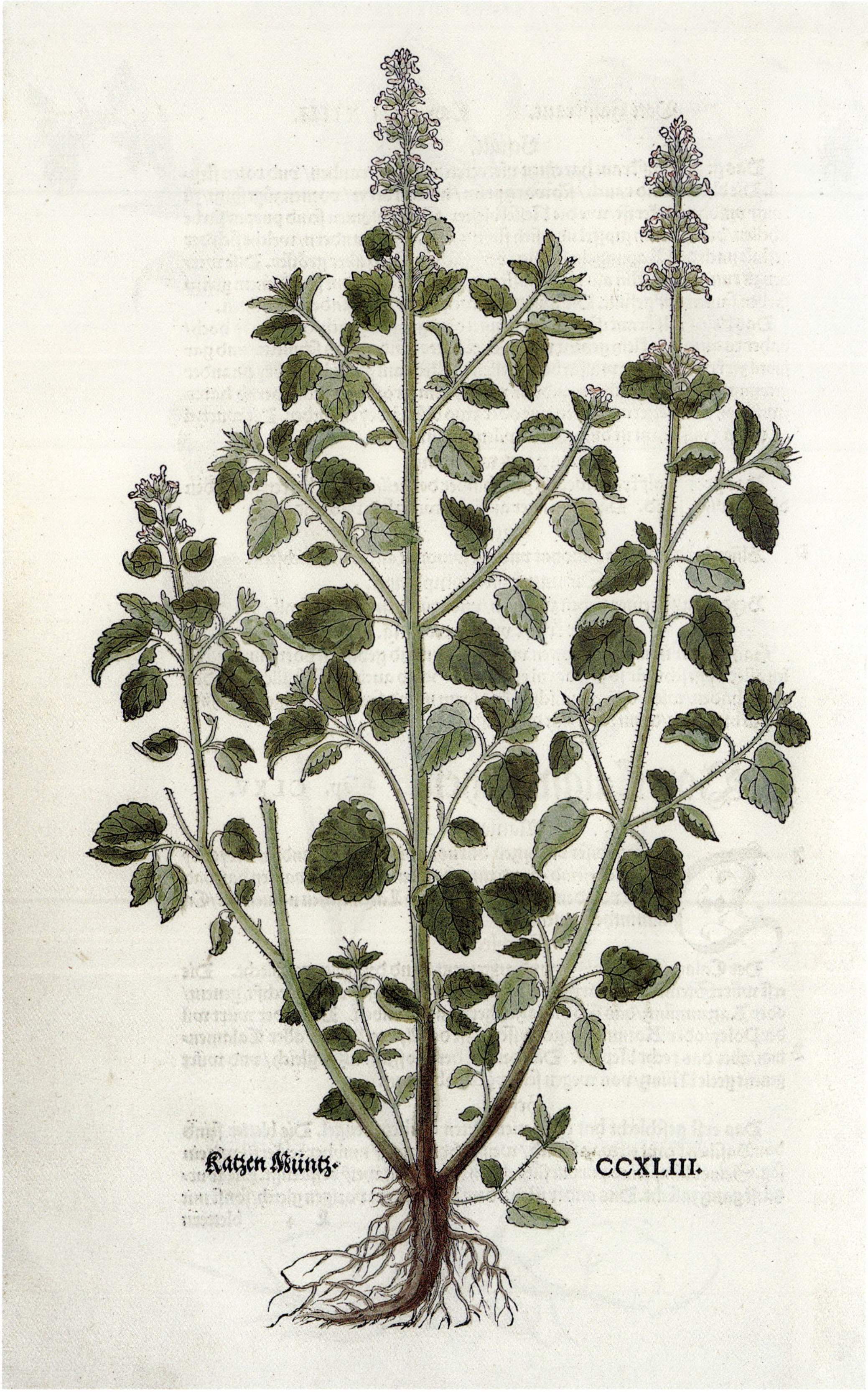
Katzen Müntz.
CCXLIII.

BARLEY

The medicinal applications of the flour ground from BARLEY (CLXVI) were chiefly external.

GERSTE

Überwiegend äußerlich angewendet wird das Mehl der GERSTE (Cap. CLXVI).

FARINE D'ORGE

C'est surtout à l'extérieur qu'est employée la FARINE D'ORGE (CLXVI).

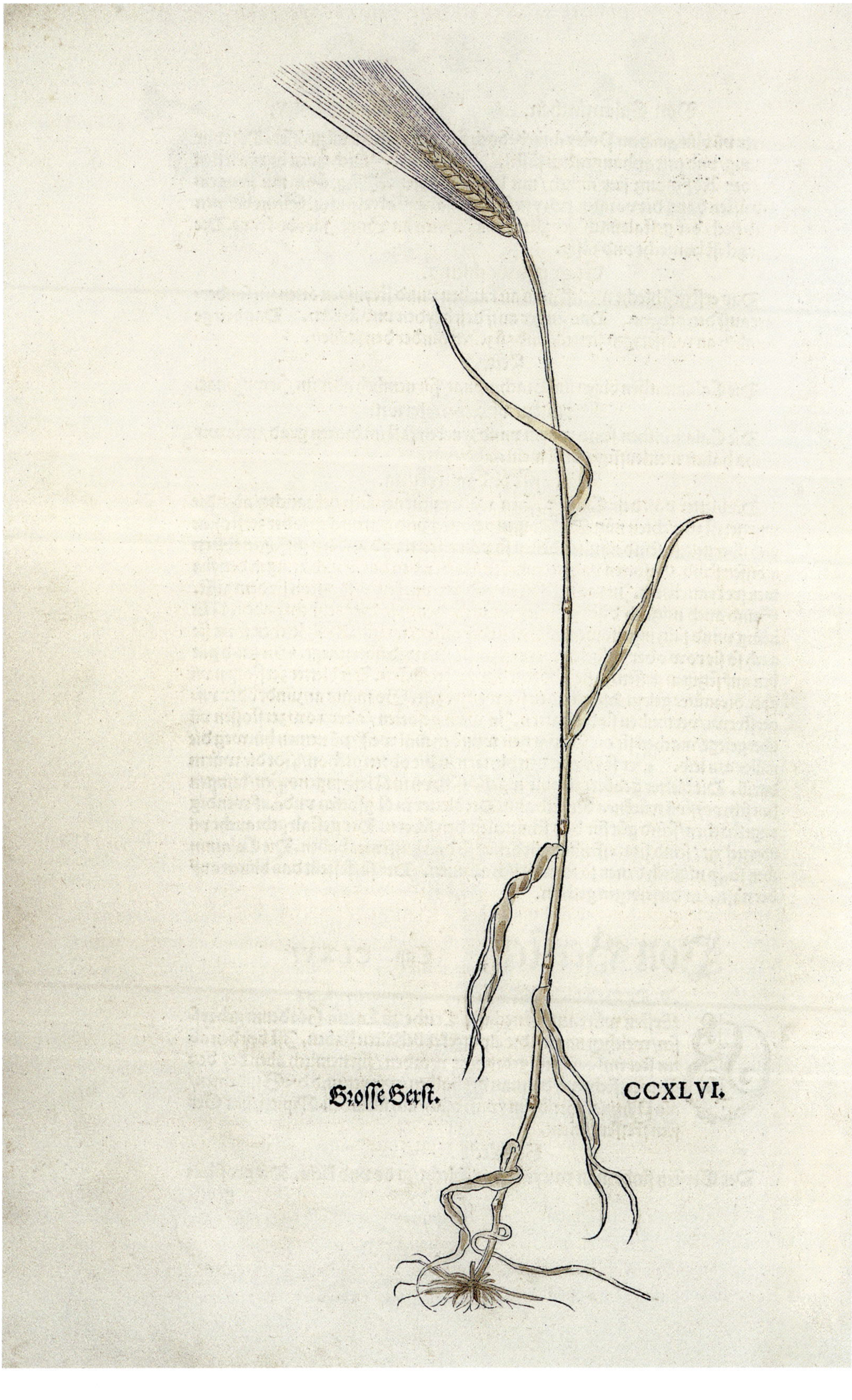
Groſſe Gerſt.
CCXLVI.

SAFFRON

Among the most expensive of the spices is SAFFRON (CLXVII), whose stigmas are the source of the much sought-after powder with which food can be coloured an intense yellow. Medicinally Saffron was chiefly used for its diuretic effect, although the poisonous nature of the plant, which could be used for abortions, was also known.

SAFRAN

Zu den teuersten Gewürzen zählt der SAFRAN (Cap. CLXVII), dessen Narbenschenkel das begehrte Pulver liefern, mit dem die Speise intensiv gelb gefärbt werden kann. In der Medizin nutzte man in erster Linie die harntreibende Wirkung, obwohl man um die Giftigkeit der Pflanze wusste, die teilweise auch zu Abtreibungen verwendet wurde.

SAFRAN

Le SAFRAN (CLXVII) compte parmi les plantes aromatiques les plus chères qui soient. La poudre, tant recherchée, provient des stigmates et colore les plats en jaune. En médecine, c’est surtout son pouvoir diurétique qui était employé, bien que la toxicité de la plante ait été déjà connue. Dans le passé, on l’utilisait aussi abusivement comme abortif.

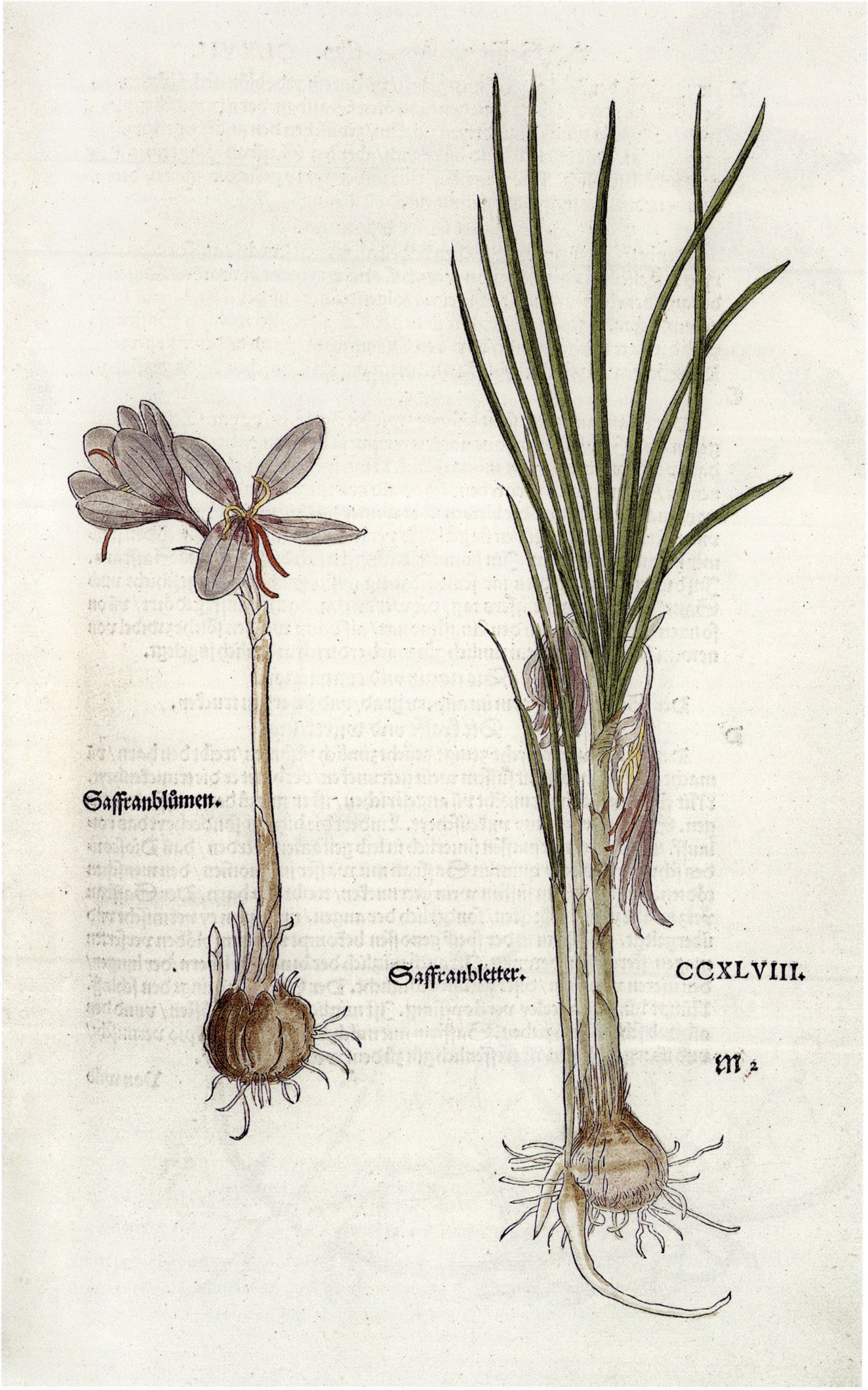

SAFFRON | SAFRAN | SAFRAN

DOG'S MERCURY

DOG'S MERCURY (CLXVIII) was probably mentioned because of its common occurrence and stimulating effect on the digestion.

BINGELKRAUT

Das BINGELKRAUT (Cap. CLXVIII) findet wohl wegen seines häufigen Vorkommens Erwähnung und wird zur Anregung der Verdauung eingenommen.

MERCURIALE VIVACE

La MERCURIALE VIVACE (CLXVIII), communément appelée aremberge, figure ici parce qu'elle est très répandue. C'est un tonique de la digestion.

PAGE 344

BLADDER SENNA

Only the markedly balloon-like pods of BLADDER SENNA (plate CCL) and ALEPPO or ITALIAN SENNA (plate CCLI) led to their inclusion together in the same chapter (CLXIX) and to their classification a laxatives – a claim which is in fact as correct for Senegal Senna.

„WELSCH LINSEN" (BLASENSTRAUCH)

Nur die auffällig blasigen Hülsenfrüchte führten offensichtlich dazu, dass der Blasenstrauch als „WELSCH LINSEN" (Taf. CCL) und die SENNA (Taf. CCLI) im Kapitel „SENET" (Cap. CLXIX) zusammen aufgeführt und – für Senna berechtigterweise – als Abführmittel empfohlen werden.

BAGUENAUDIER COMMUN

Le chapitre «SENET» (CLXIX) associe le BAGUENAUDIER COMMUN (pl. CCL) avec le SÉNÉ (pl. CCLI), à cause de la ressemblance de leurs gousses formant des vésicules très enflées. Les deux plantes sont préconisées – à juste titre pour le séné – comme laxatif.

PAGE 345

BUCK'S-HORN PLANTAIN

In the case of BUCK'S-HORN PLANTAIN (CLXX), Fuchs's concern was apparently more to register this plant, whose preferred habitat is on the coast, than to provide information on its medicinal application, which was in any case "unknown to apothecaries."

KRÄHENFUSS

Beim KRÄHENFUSS (Cap. CLXX), einer Wegerich-Art, geht es offenbar mehr um die Erfassung der bevorzugt an Küsten wachsenden Pflanze als um deren medizinische Anwendung, zumal sie „den Apoteckern unbekant" ist.

PLANTAIN CORNU

Dans le cas du PLANTAIN CORNU (CLXX), qui habite les régions maritimes, pour Fuchs, manifestement, il s'agit plus de répertorier la plante elle-même que d'indiquer son usage médical, d'autant plus qu'il est «inconnu des apothicaires».

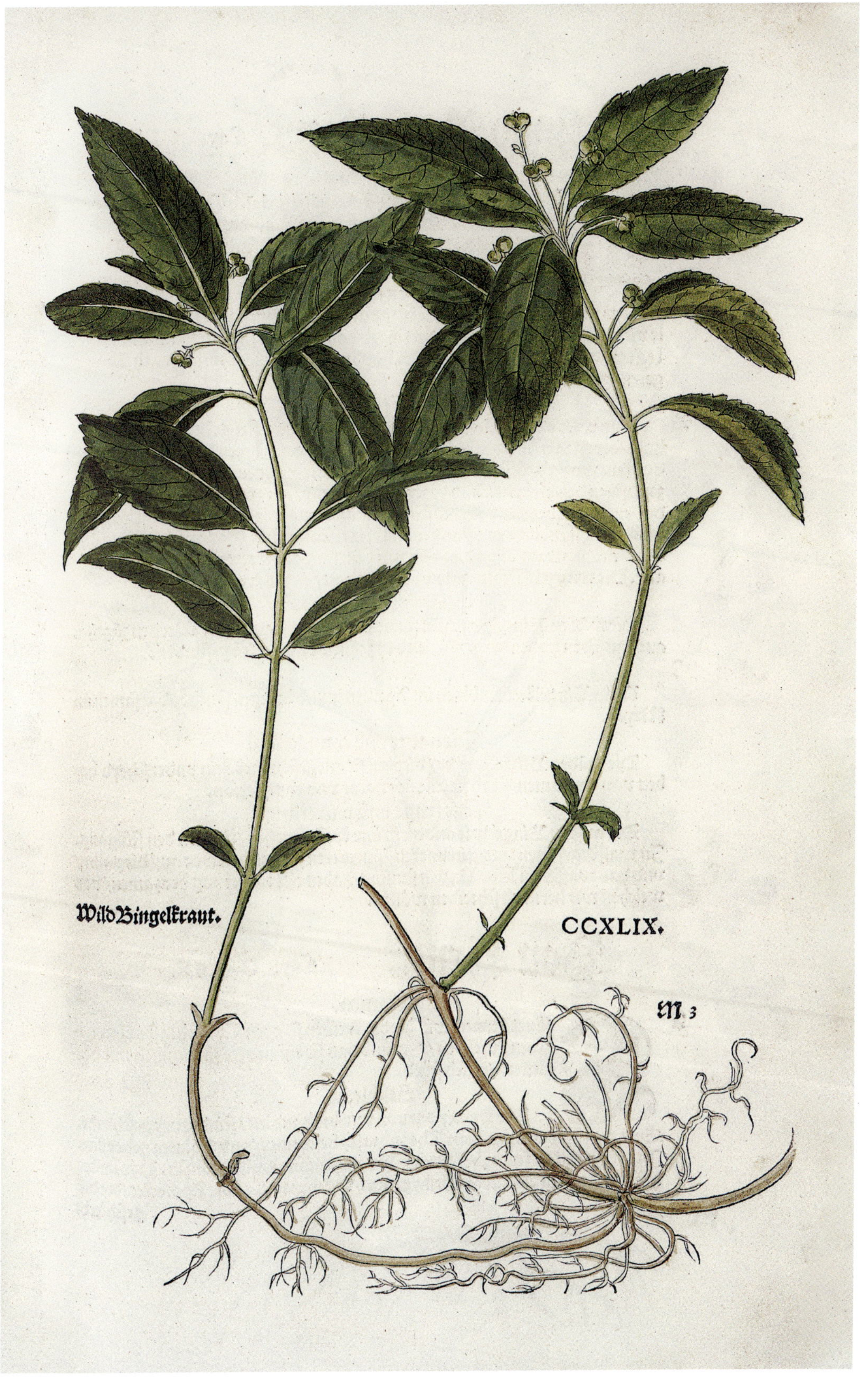
Wild Bingelkraut.
CCXLIX.
M 3

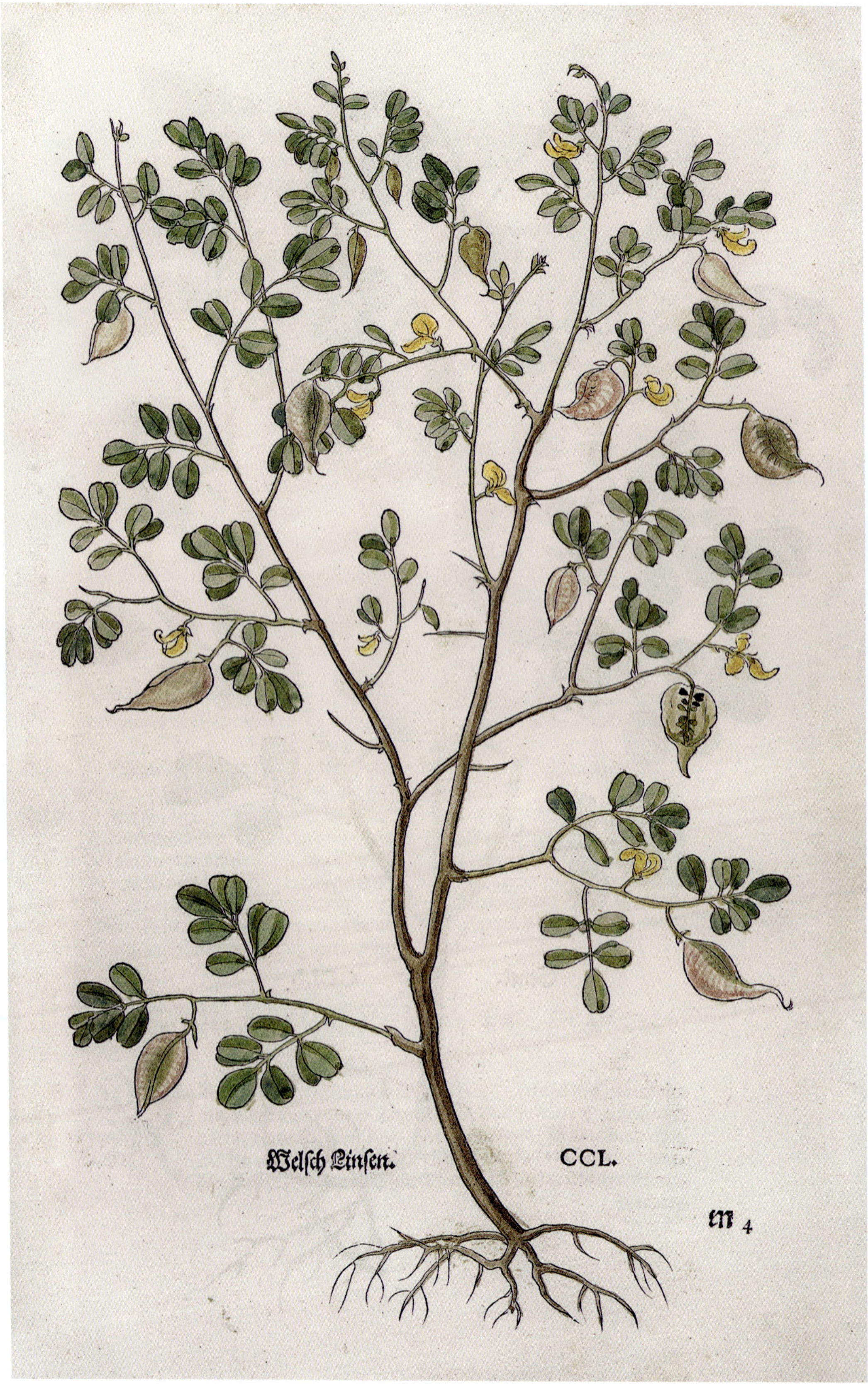
Welsch Linsen.
CCL.
M 4

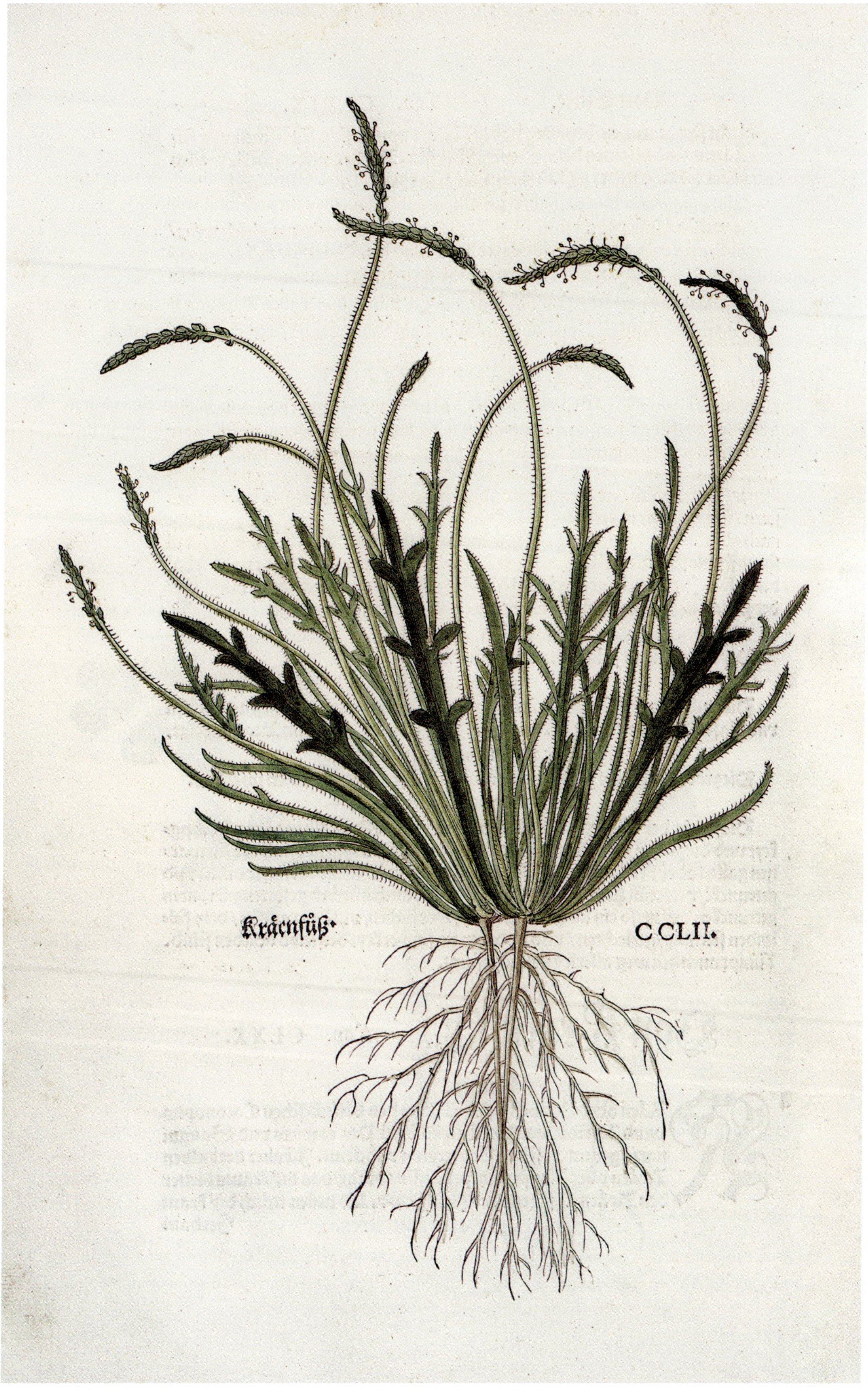
Kräcnfüß·
CCLII.

SOW-BREAD

Also known as SOW-BREAD, COMMON CYCLAMEN (CLXXI) was presented for its purging and analgesic effects, and for its supposedly fatal effect on pregnant women.

„SCHWEINBROT" (ALPENVEILCHEN)

Unter der Bezeichnung „SCHWEINBROT" (Cap. CLXXI) würden wir wohl kaum das Alpenveilchen erwarten, das hier wegen seiner purgierenden und lindernden Wirkung besprochen wird und dem vermeintlich fatale Auswirkungen auf Schwangere zugeschrieben werden.

CYCLAMEN D'EUROPE

Trouver le CYCLAMEN D'EUROPE (CLXXI), de couleur pourpre, sous le nom de «pain à pourceau» («Schweinbrot») est inattendu. Fuchs lui prête un effet purgatif et apaisant, et des propriétés qui seraient fatales aux femmes enceintes.

PAGE 348

GERMAN GALINGALE

For Fuchs, it was the native GERMAN GALINGALE (CLXXII), rather than the Asian variety, which served as diuretic, healed wounds and helped with female disorders.

WILDER GALGANT

Nicht der asiatische Galgant, sondern der WILDE GALGANT (Cap. CLXXII), der in Deutschland angebaut werden kann, erscheint bei Fuchs als harntreibend, wundheilungsfördernd und wirksam bei Frauenkrankheiten.

SOUCHET LONG

L'illustration suivante ne représente pas le galanga de Chine, mais le SOUCHET LONG (CLXXII) que l'on peut cultiver en Allemagne. Fuchs indique son pouvoir diurétique et cicatrisant ainsi que son efficacité sur les maladies particulières à la femme.

PAGE 349

CAPER SPURGE

CAPER SPURGE (CLXXIII), a Mediterranean variety that had been introduced into Germany, was considered to be strongly purgative. Furthermore, its juice could be applied externally for skin tumours, warts and spots.

SPRINGKRAUT

Als stark abführend wurde das SPRINGKRAUT (Cap. CLXXIII), eine mittelmeerische, in Deutschland eingebürgerte Wolfsmilchart, eingeschätzt, deren Saft äußerlich angewendet Hautwucherungen, Warzen und Flechten beseitigen sollte.

GRANDE ÉPURGE

En usage interne, la GRANDE ÉPURGE (CLXXIII), plante originaire du Bassin méditerranéen, mais acclimatée en Allemagne, est très purgative et, en usage externe, son suc soignerait les excroissances cutanées, les verrues et les dartres.

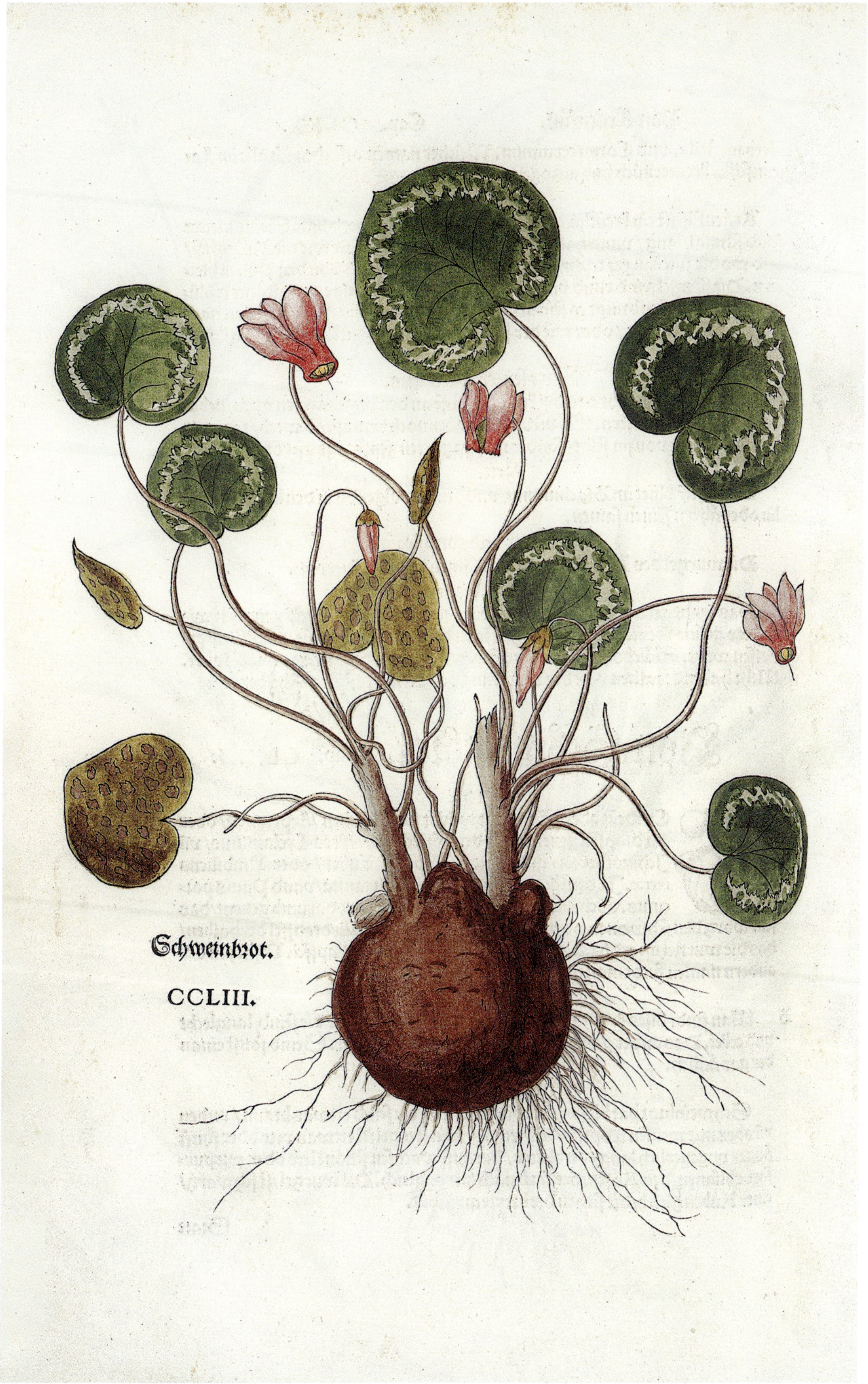
Schweinbrot.
CCLIII.

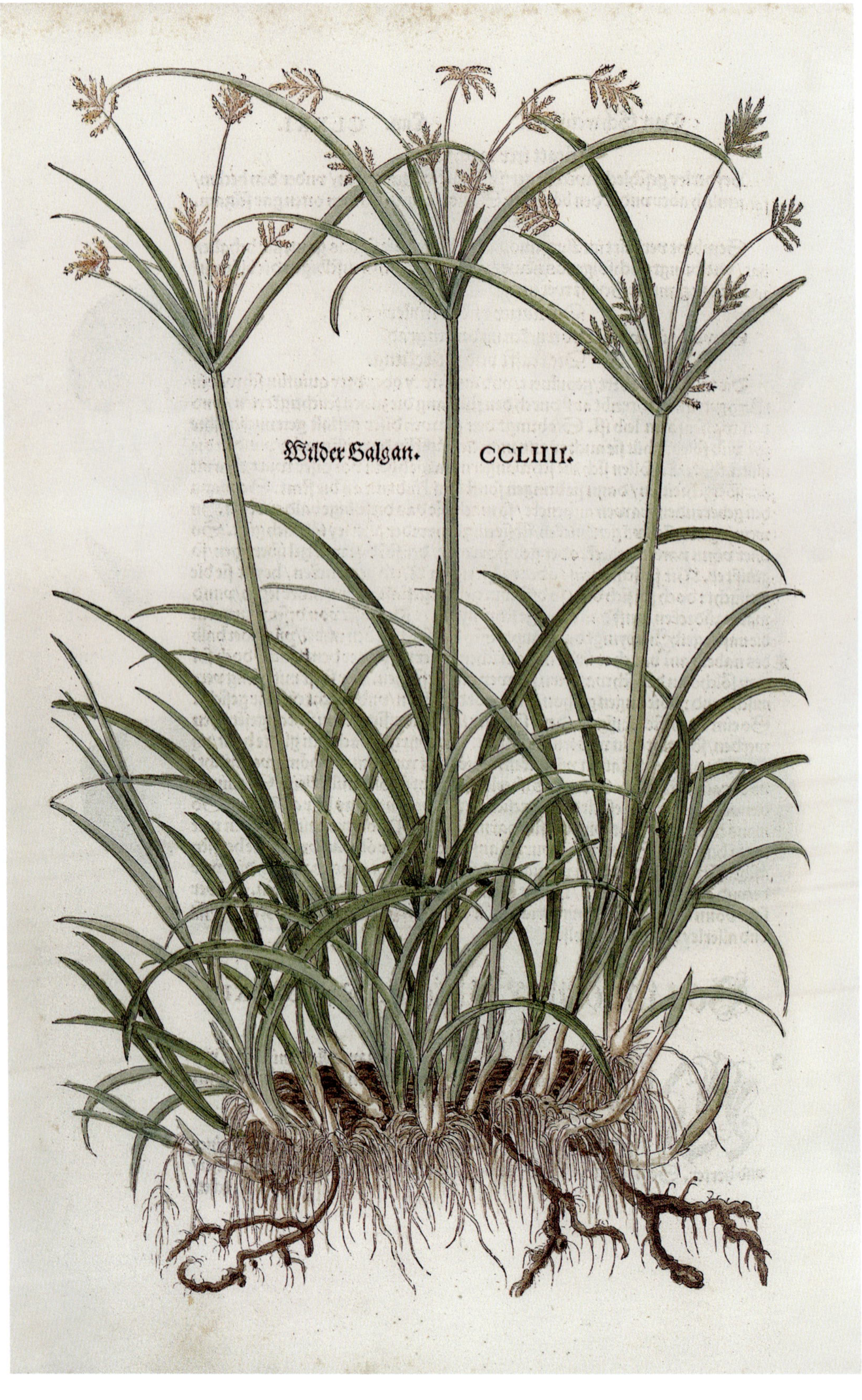
Wilder Galgan.
CCLIIII.

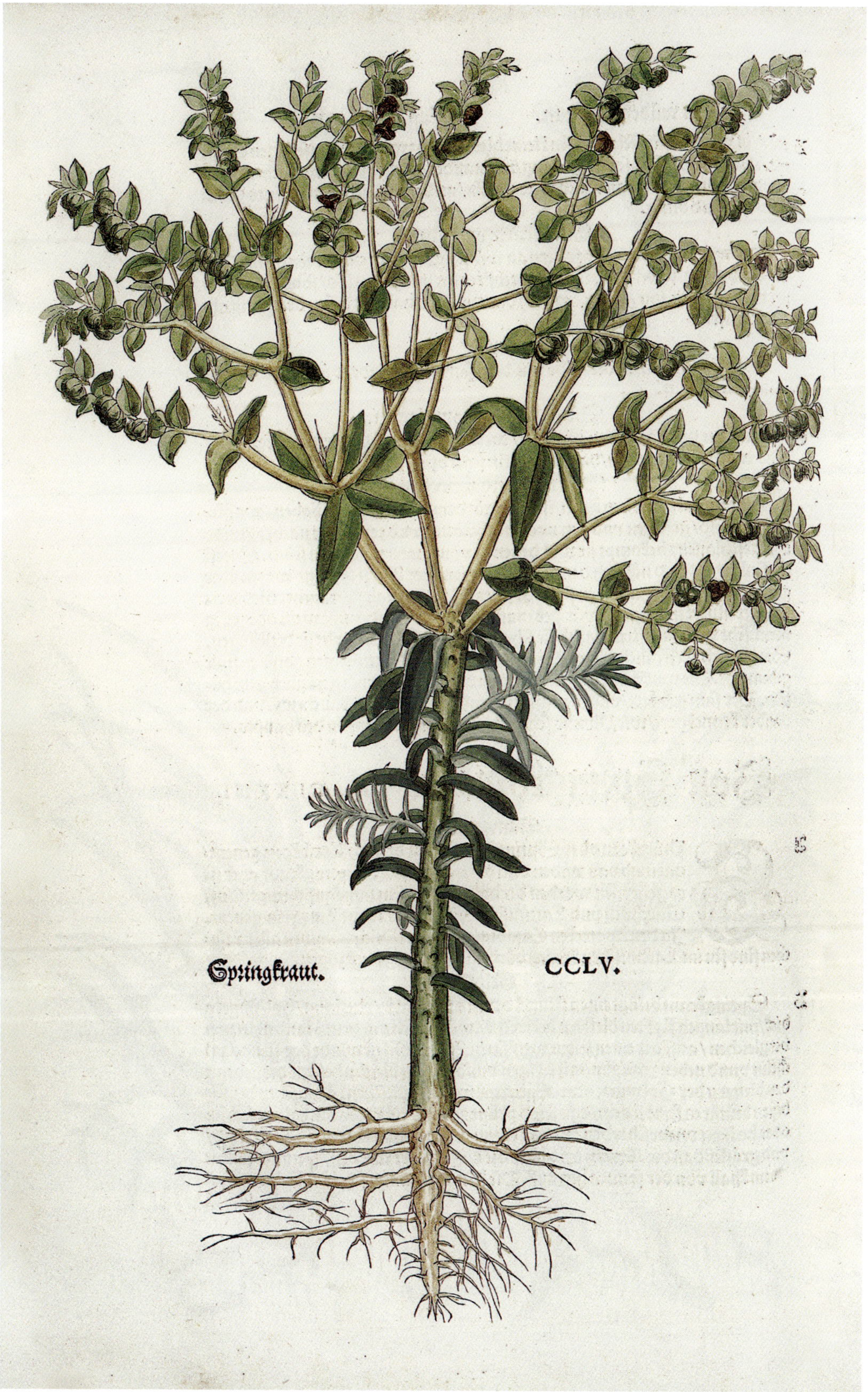
Spꝛingkraut.
CCLV.

VIOLET

The term VIOLET used to be applied to numerous flowers. This chapter (CLXXIIII) thus includes two different plants, WALLFLOWER (plate CCLVI) and DAME'S VIOLET, also known as VESPER FLOWER (white: plate CCLVII; violet: plate CCLVIII).

„VEIEL“ (VEILCHEN)

Die Bezeichnung „VEIEL“, Veilchen, wurde früher auf viele Blumen angewendet. So finden sich auch im Kapitel CLXXIIII zwei unterschiedliche Pflanzen, der GOLDLACK (Taf. CCLVI) und die NACHTVIOLE (weiß: Taf. CCLVII; violett: Taf. CCLVIII), gemeinsam aufgeführt.

VIOLETTE

Le nom de «Veiel», ou VIOLETTE, désignait dans le passé bon nombre de fleurs. Ainsi, au chapitre CLXXIIII, sont réunies deux plantes différentes : la GIROFLÉE (pl. CCLVI) et la JULIENNE DES DAMES (blanche : pl. CCLVII ; pourpre : pl. CCLVIII).

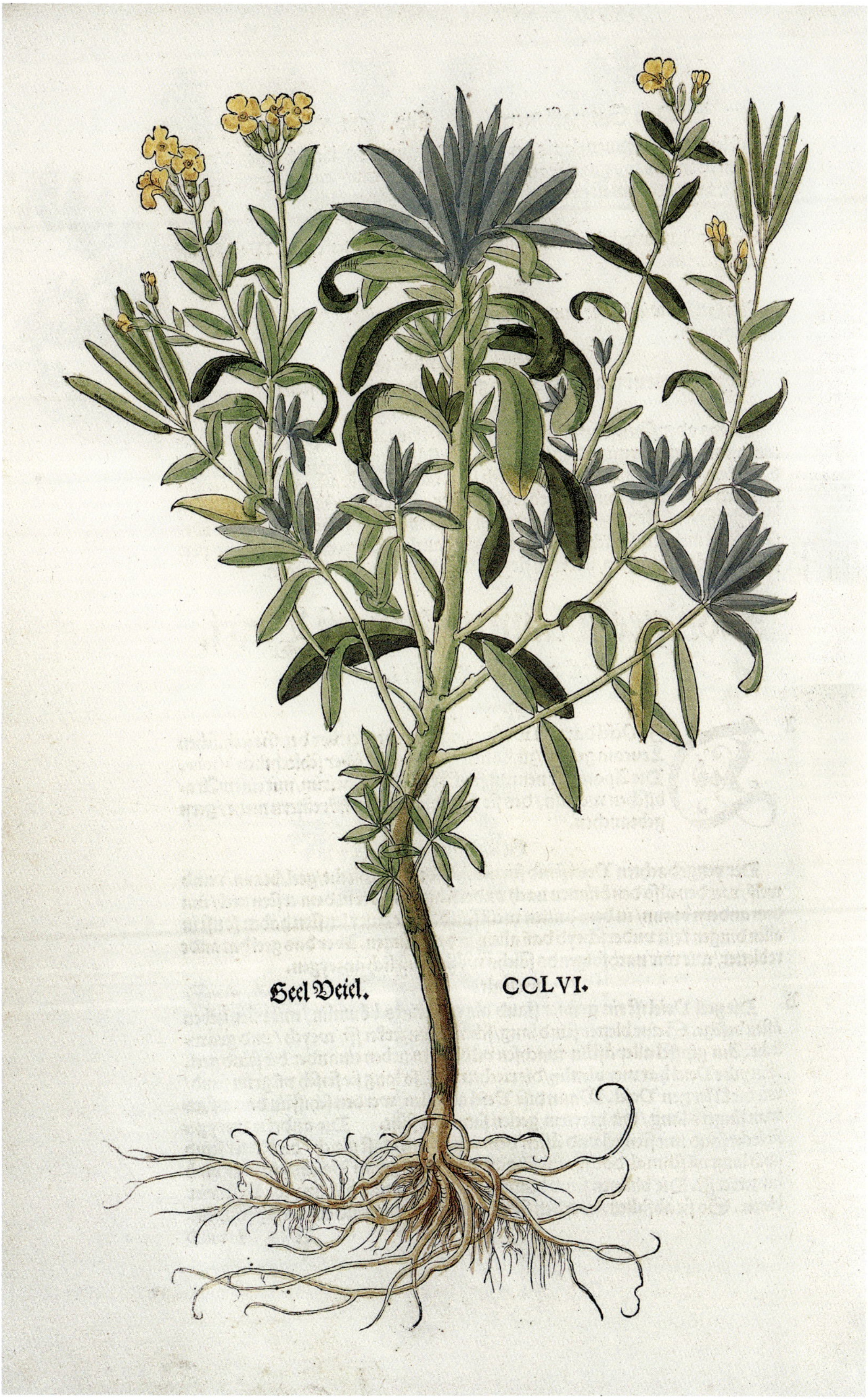
Geel Veiel.
CCLVI.

BROAD-LEAVED DOCK

Fuchs here not only describes BROAD-LEAVED DOCK, or PALE PERSICANA (CLXXV; plate CCLIX), and two other types of SORREL (plates CCLX, CCLXII), but also presents the traditional GOOD KING HENRY, also known as ALL-GOOD or MERCURY (plate CCLXI), as yet another "kind." For each, he lists the individual medicinal effects.

„MENGELWURTZ" (AMPFER-KNÖTERICH)

Als „MENGELWURTZ" (CLXXV) bezeichnet Fuchs den AMPFER-KNÖTERICH (Taf. CCLIX) und fügt noch zwei AMPFERARTEN (Taf. CCLX, CCLXII) und den altbekannten GUTEN HEINRICH (Taf. CCLXI) als weitere Geschlechter an, für die er die einzelnen arzneilichen Wirkungen auflistet.

RENOUÉE À FEUILLES DE PATIENCE

Fuchs appelle la RENOUÉE À FEUILLES DE PATIENCE (pl. CCLIX) «Mengelwurtz», ce qui pourrait se traduire par «RACINE POUR LA FAIBLESSE» (CLXXV). Il lui ajoute deux autres espèces de RUMEX (pl. CCLX, CCLXII) et une plante bien connue, l'ÉPINARD SAUVAGE (pl. CCLXI), ou ansérine Bon-Henri, dont il recense les effets respectifs.

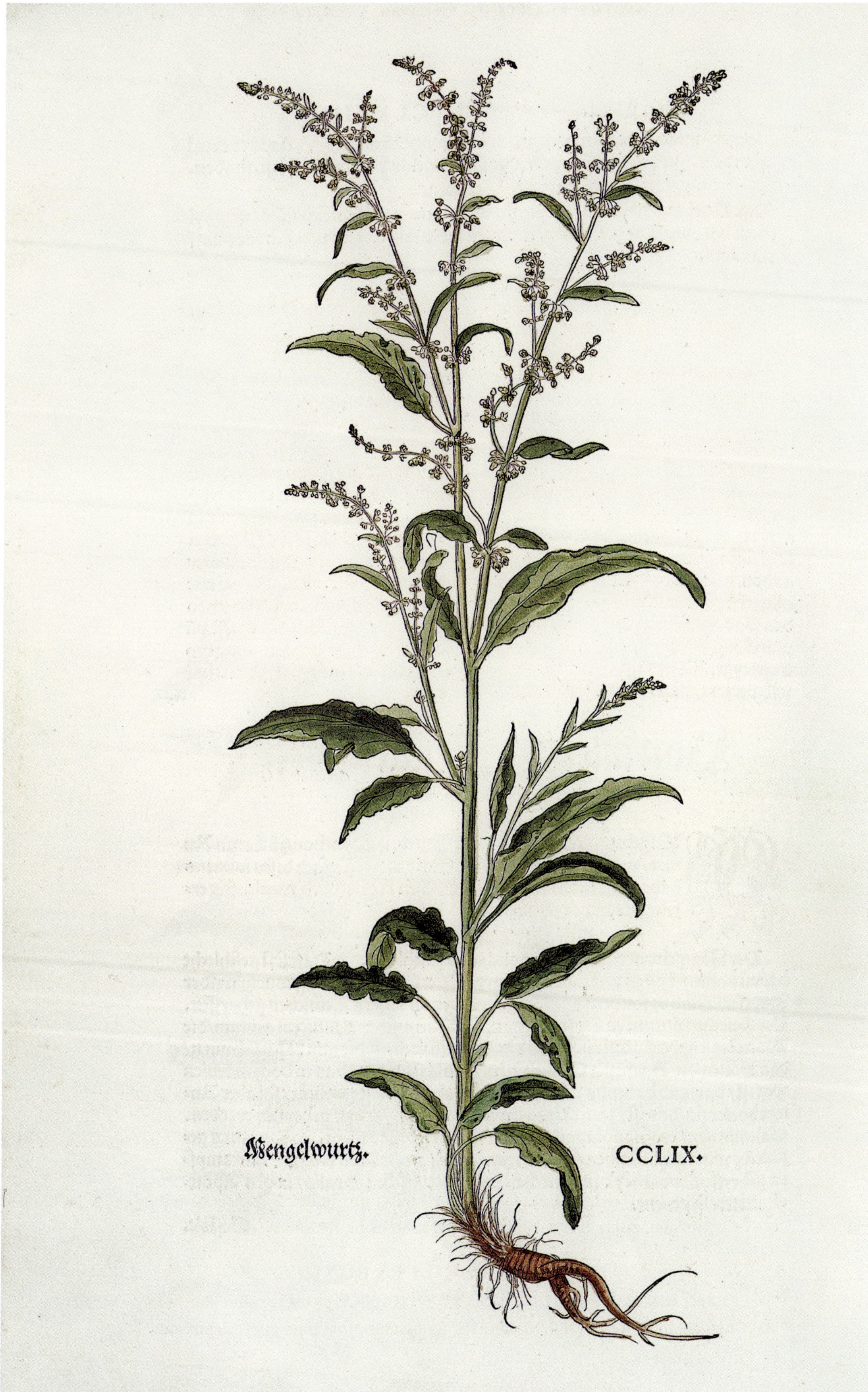
Mengelwurtz.
CCLIX.

WINTERGREEN

Round-leaved, or larger, WINTERGREEN (CLXXVI) has not only become rare in the wild, but is also hardly used in today's medicine.

WINTERGRÜN

Das WINTERGRÜN (Cap. CLXXVI) ist nicht nur in der Natur recht selten geworden, auch in der Medizin wird man es heute kaum mehr finden.

PYROLE À FEUILLES RONDES

La PYROLE À FEUILLES RONDES (CLXXVI) s'est raréfiée dans la nature, mais aussi en médecine où on ne l'emploie plus guère à présent.

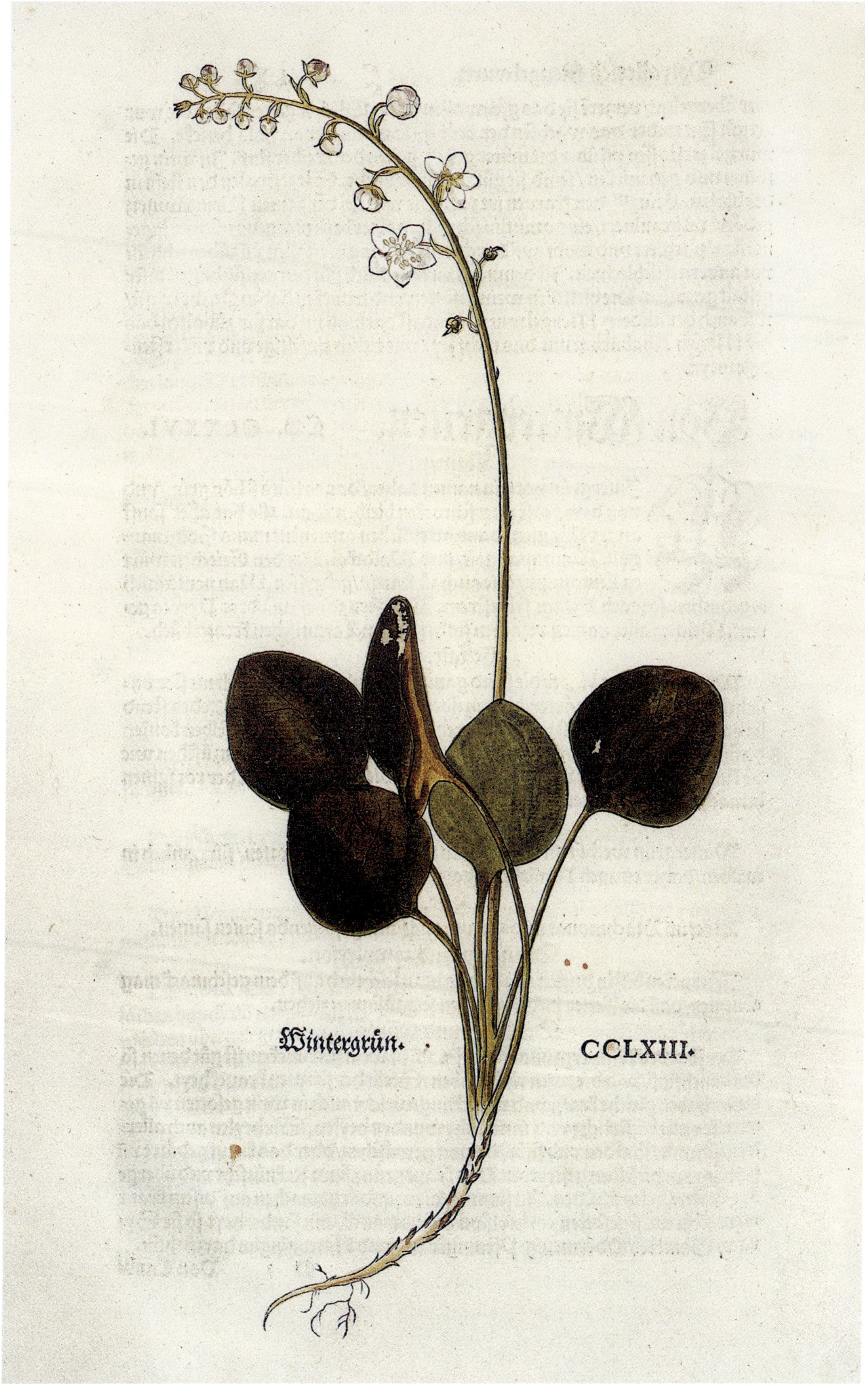
Wintergrün.
CCLXIII.

DEADNETTLE

In the illustration of DEADNETTLE (CLXXVII; plate CCLXIIII), Fuchs once again combines three kinds of plant: Yellow Archangel, Spotted Deadnettle and White deadnettle. His text, however, makes the distinctions clear.

TAUBNESSEL

Bei der Abbildung der TAUBNESSEL (Cap. CLXXVII; Taf. CCLXIIII) vereinigt Fuchs wieder die drei Arten Goldnessel, Gefleckte Taubnessel und Weiße Taubnessel in einer Pflanze, weist im Text jedoch ausdrücklich darauf hin.

LAMIER

Fuchs présente à nouveau une seule plante, en le signalant clairement, pour figurer cette fois trois variétés de LAMIER (CLXXVII ; pl. CCLXIIII) : le lamier jaune, le lamier tacheté et le lamier blanc.

PAGE 358

CULTIVATED FLAX

CULTIVATED FLAX (CLXXVIII) represents one of the most important commercial plants. Today the oil-bearing seeds, known as linseeds, are still used as a laxative.

FLACHS

Mit dem FLACHS (Cap. CLXXVIII) erscheint eine der wichtigsten Nutzpflanzen überhaupt, von der die ölhaltigen Samen, bekannt als Leinsamen, früher wie heute als Abführmittel gebraucht wurden.

LIN CULTIVÉ

Le LIN CULTIVÉ (CLXXVIII) est l'une de nos plantes utiles les plus importantes. Ses graines oléagineuses, appelées linettes, sont utilisées depuis longtemps comme remède laxatif.

PAGE 359

COMMON LIVERWORT

In discussing COMMON LIVERWORT (CLXXIX), Fuchs referred to a plant primarily used for external applications.

BRUNNENLEBERKRAUT

Auch wenn Fuchs von einem Kraut, dem BRUNNENLEBERKRAUT (Cap. CLXXIX), spricht, handelt es sich botanisch um ein Lebermoos, das überwiegend äußerlich angewendet wurde.

HÉPATIQUE DES FONTAINES

Même si Fuchs en parle comme d'une plante herbacée, l'HÉPATIQUE DES FONTAINES (CLXXIX) est une mousse, usitée, comme son nom l'indique, pour ses propriétés hépatiques.

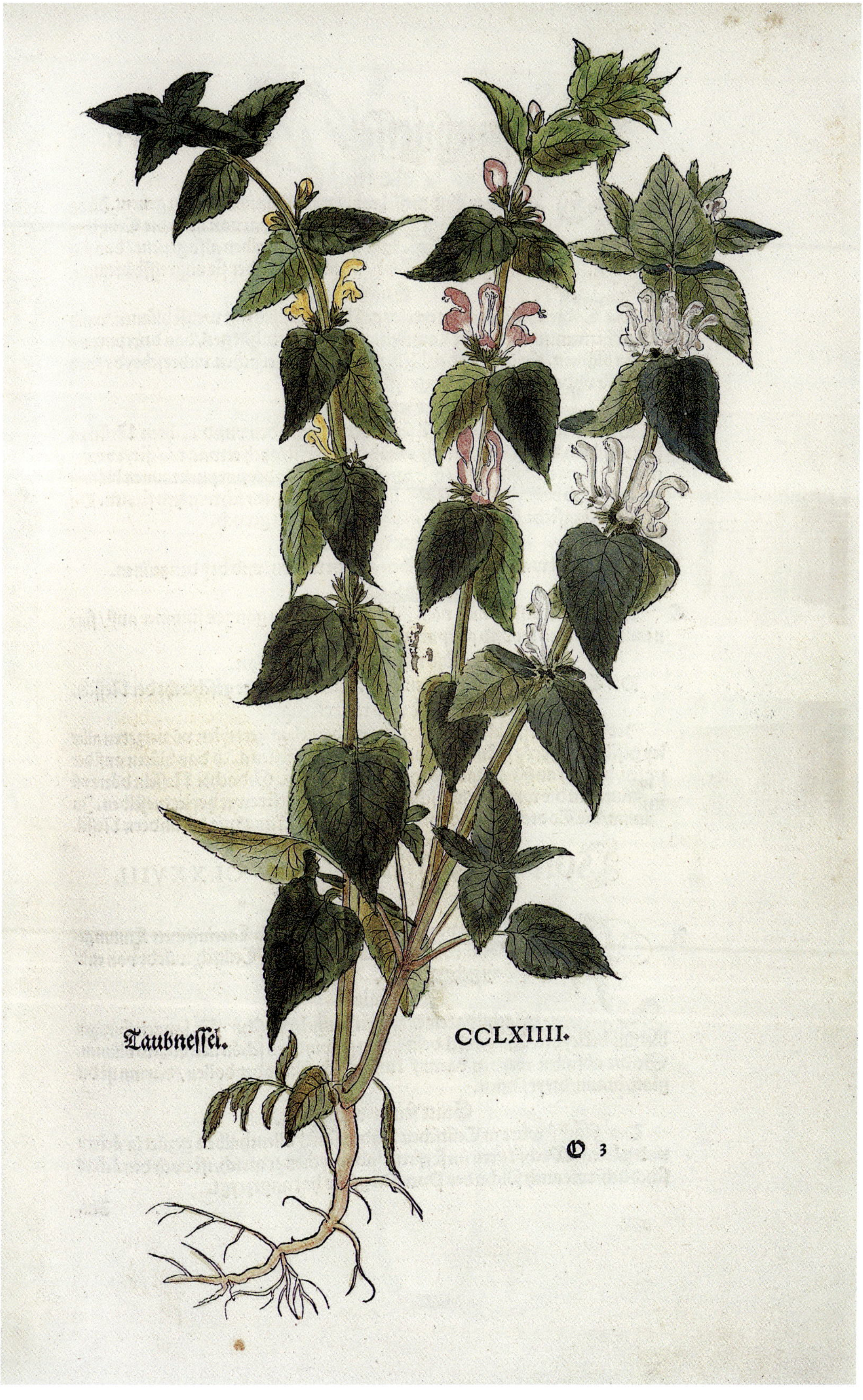
Taubneſſel.
CCLXIIII.
O 3

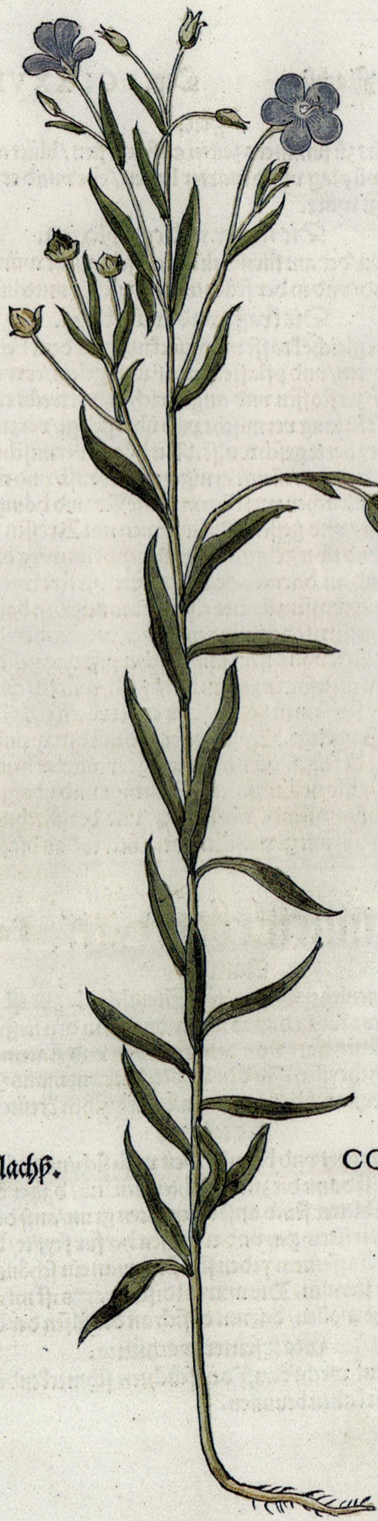

Flachß.

CCLXV.

O 4

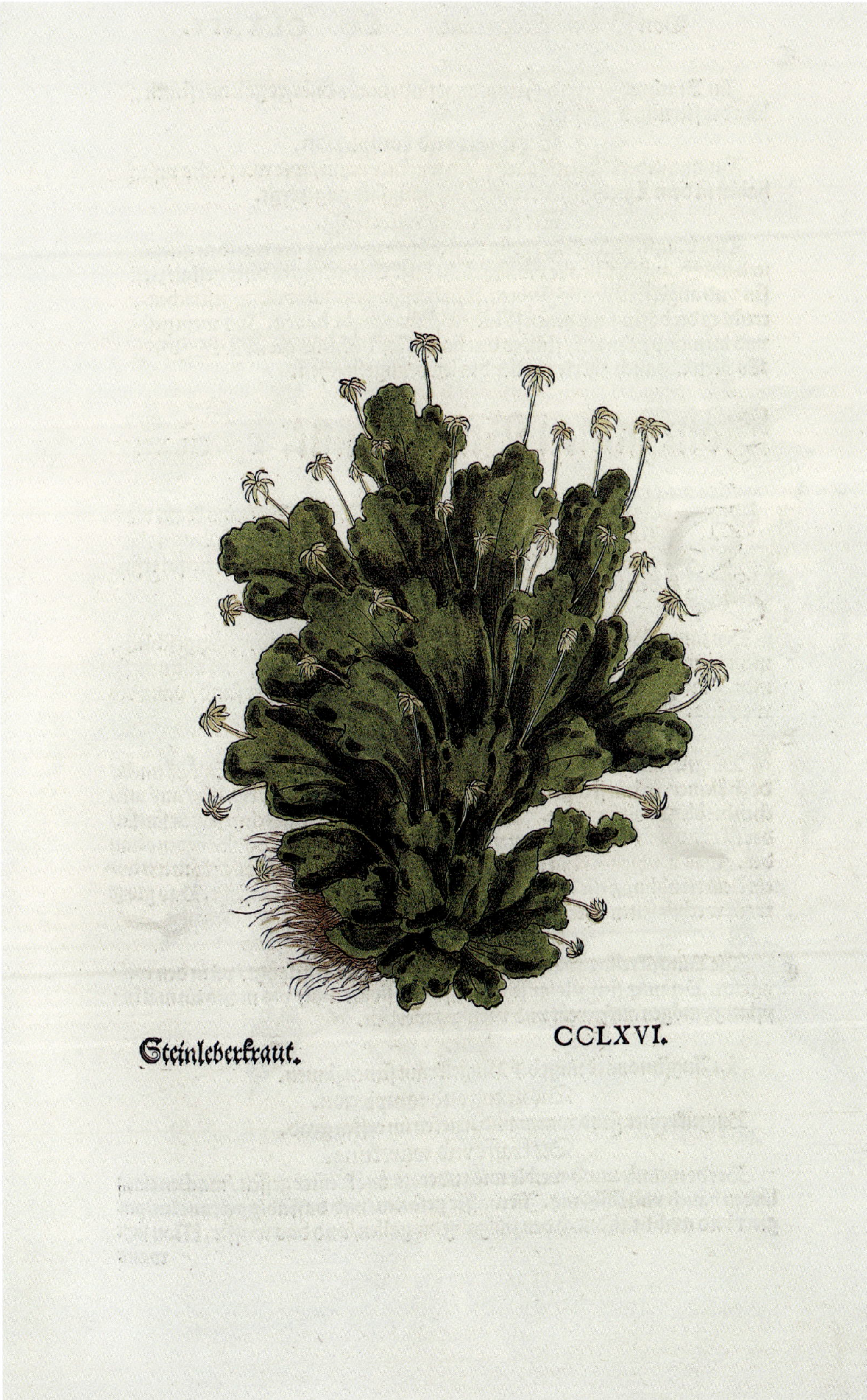
Steinleberkraut.
CCLXVI.

ANNUAL MERCURY

ANNUAL MERCURY (CLXXX) occurs in a male and female form, because the plant is dioecious, that is, male and female blossoms appear on different plants. However, because Fuchs proceeded from the external form of the plant, and did not recognize the blossoms as the sexual organs, he placed them in the wrong categories.

BINGELKRAUT

Beim BINGELKRAUT (Cap. CLXXX) gibt es tatsächlich ein „mennle" und ein „weible", weil die Pflanze zweihäusig ist, also männliche und weibliche Blüten an jeweils getrennten Pflanzen auftreten. Da Fuchs jedoch vom Habitus ausgeht und die Blüte noch nicht als Sexualorgan der Pflanze erkennen kann, trifft er genau die falsche Zuordnung.

MERCURIALE ANNUELLE

La MERCURIALE ANNUELLE (CLXXX) a ceci de particulier que les fleurs mâles et femelles sont séparées sur des plantes différentes. Il existe donc bien une « mâle » (« mennle ») et une « femelle » (« weible »), ce qui cependant n'empêche pas Fuchs de mal les classer, étant donné qu'il se base sur l'aspect extérieur de la plante et ignore encore que la fleur en est l'organe sexuel.

PAGE 362

ROSEMARY

ROSEMARY (CLXXXI) is still essential today as a medicinal plant. It is no longer taken internally, however, but is used externally in salves and for baths.

ROSMARIN

Auch heute noch ist der ROSMARIN (Cap. CLXXXI) als Heilpflanze unverzichtbar, wird jedoch nicht mehr innerlich, sondern äußerlich für Einreibungen und Bäder verwendet.

ROMARIN

Le ROMARIN (CLXXXI) reste une plante médicinale de première importance. Il ne s'utilise plus par voie interne, mais en traitement externe sous forme de frictions ou de bains.

PAGE 363

COMMON PRIVET

In contrast, COMMON PRIVET (CLXXXII) remains as useless as ever to herbal medicine.

„BEINHÖLTZLEIN"

Das „BEINHÖLTZLEIN" (Cap. CLXXXII) dagegen ist nach wie vor in der Pflanzenheilkunde ungebräuchlich.

TROÈNE COMMUN

En revanche, le TROÈNE COMMUN (CLXXXII), appelé par Fuchs « petit bois-os » (« Beinholtzlein »), n'a jamais eu la moindre application médicale.

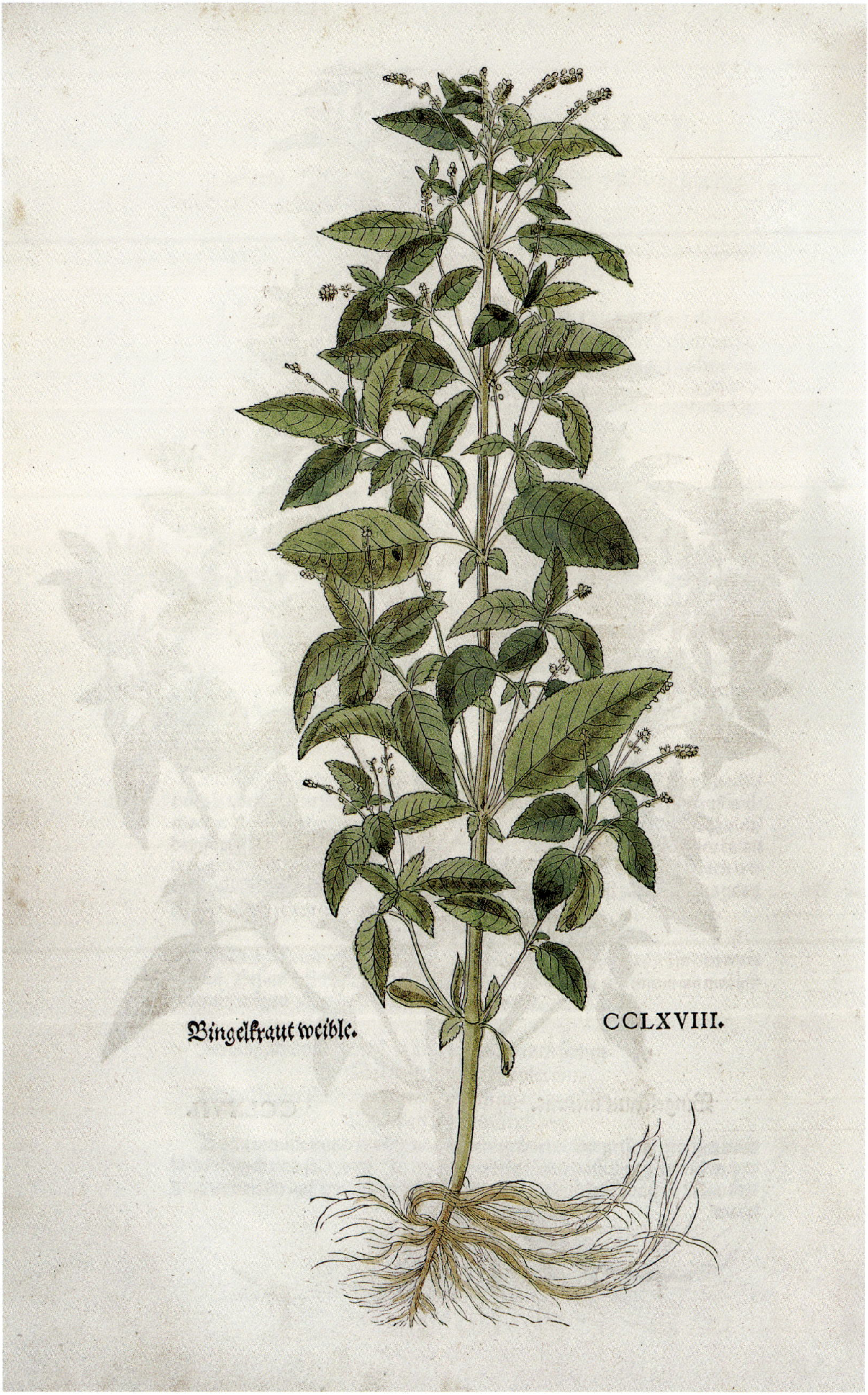
Bingelkraut weible.
CCLXVIII.

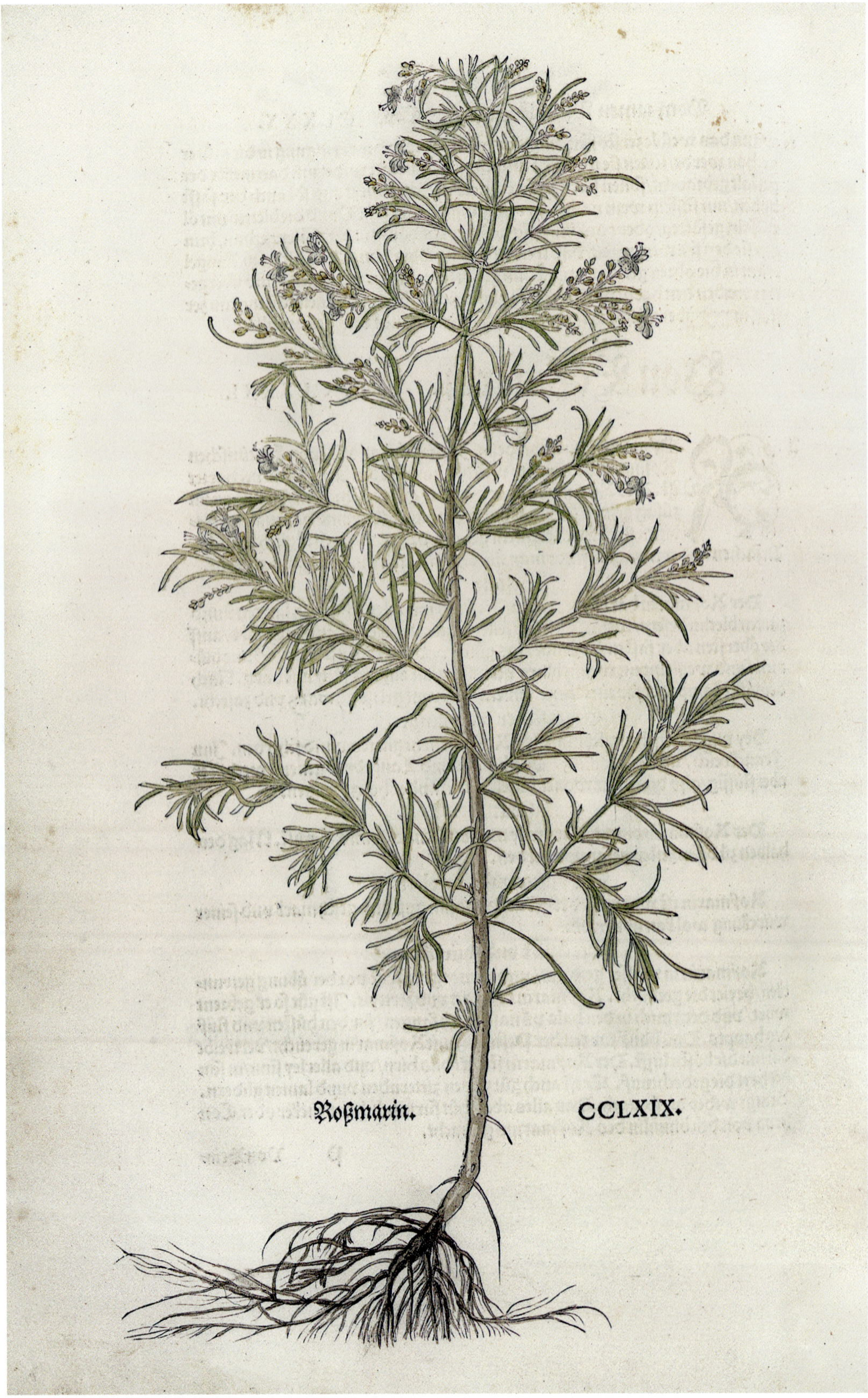
Roßmarin.
CCLXIX.

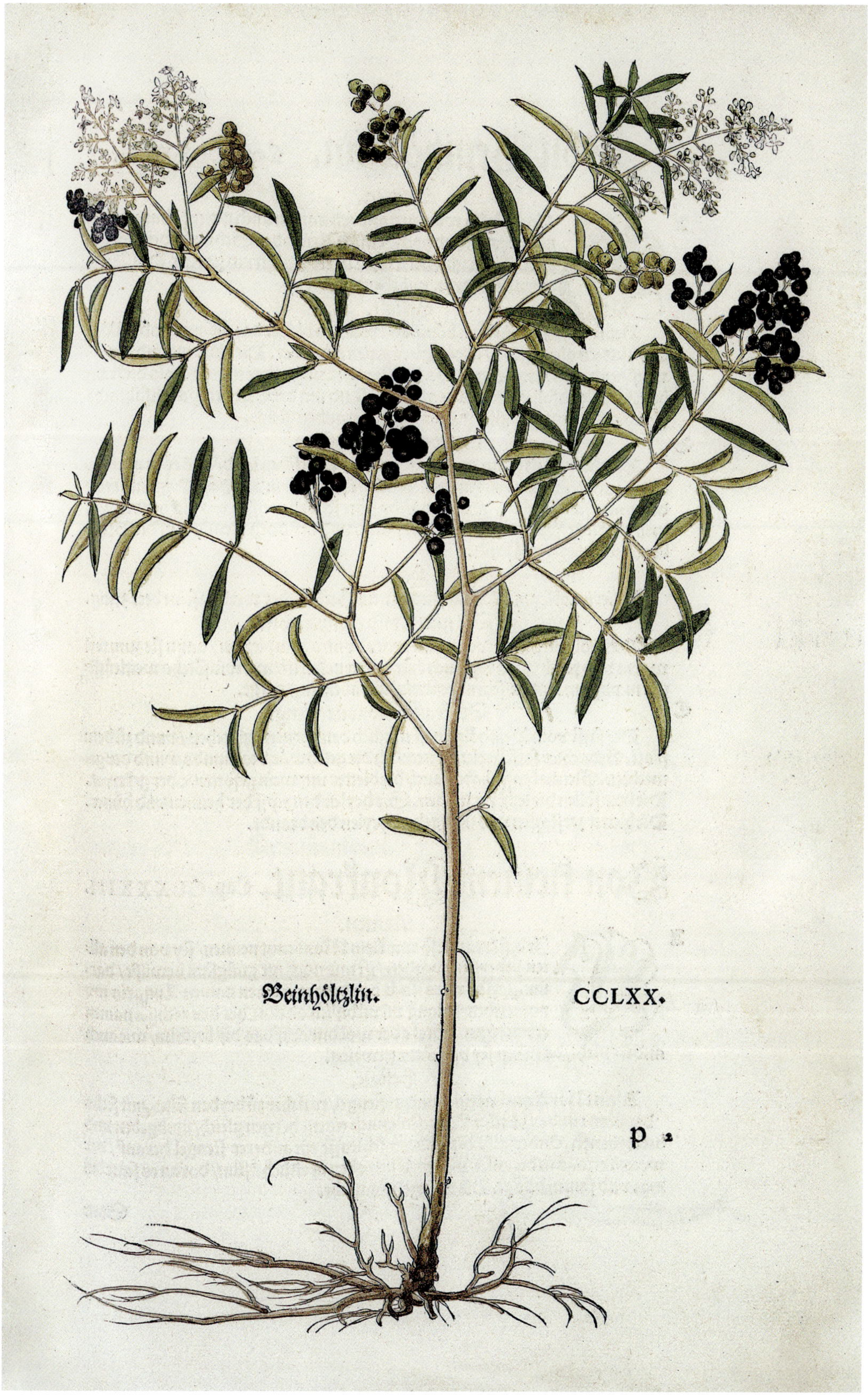
Beinhöltzlin.
CCLXX.
p 2

MOONWORT

MOONWORT (CLXXXIII) apparently attracted Fuchs's attention because of its occurrence "around Tübingen on the Österberg," and he remarks that alchemists pursue "their adventurous experiments with this herb."

„MONKRAUT" (MONDRAUTE)

Das „MONKRAUT" (Cap. CLXXXIII) – heute nennen wir es Mondraute – erregte offenbar wegen seines Vorkommens „umb Tübingen am Österberg" die Aufmerksamkeit von Fuchs, der auch anmerkt, die Alchemisten trieben „mit disem kraut auch ihr abentheur".

BOTRYCHE LUNAIRE

C'est par sa présence « dans les environs de Tübingen-sur-l'Österberg » que le BOTRYCHE LUNAIRE (CLXXXIII), dit aussi PETITE LUNAIRE, s'est fait remarquer de Fuchs. Celui-ci note en outre que les alchimistes emploient « cette herbe pour mener leurs expériences aventureuses ».

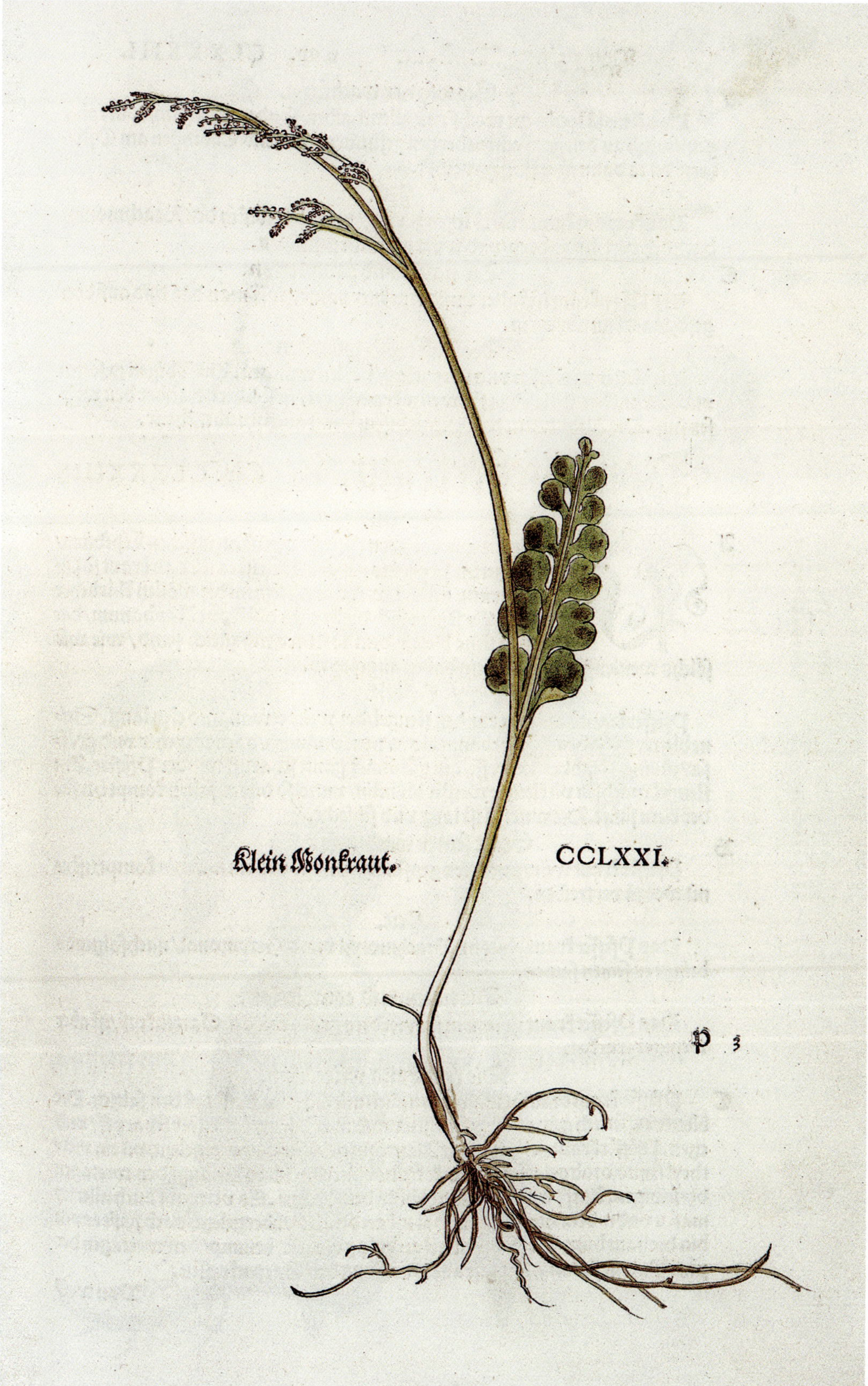

MOONWORT | „MONKRAUT" | BOTRYCHE LUNAIRE

BROAD-LEAVED PEPPERWORT

The broad-leaved cress known as BROAD-LEAVED PEPPERWORT (CLXXXIIII) or DITTANDER, has an acrid taste and was used earlier as a flavouring.

PFEFFERKRAUT

Der scharfe Geschmack hat zu dem noch heute geläufigen Namen PFEFFERKRAUT (Cap. CLXXXIIII) für die Breitblättrige Kresse geführt, die früher auch als Gewürz verwendet wurde.

PASSERAGE À LARGES FEUILLES

Le PASSERAGE À LARGES FEUILLES (CLXXXIIII) doit son nom allemand de «Pfefferkraut» (herbe poivrée) à son goût très fort. Il était du reste utilisé comme épice avant la découverte du poivre.

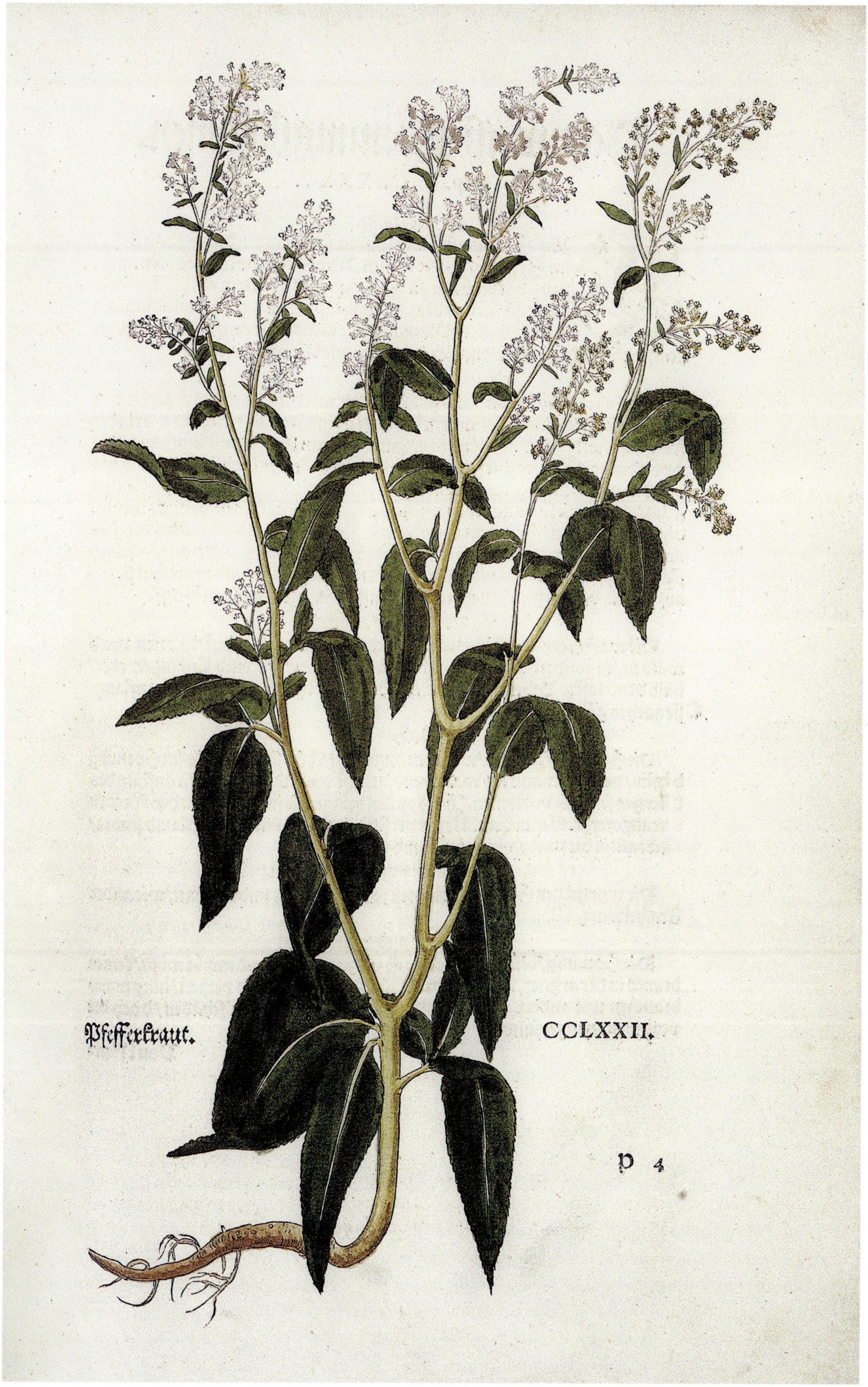
Pfefferkraut.
CCLXXII.
p 4

SNOWFLAKE

One can only describe the illustration of SNOWFLAKE (CLXXXV; plate CCLXXIII) as a chimera, for the artists have here created a plant that on the left possesses the characteristics of the spring snowflake, but on the right is clearly a common snowdrop. Fuchs included the SNOWFLAKE because it grows in the vicinity of the monastery at Bebenhausen near Tübingen, not because it had any medicinal properties.

„HORNUNGSBLUM“

Als Chimäre müssten wir die Abbildung der „HORNUNGSBLUM“ (Cap. CLXXXV; Taf. CCLXXIII) bezeichnen, denn hier haben die Künstler eine Pflanze geschaffen, die links die Blütenmerkmale der Frühlingsknotenblume zeigt, rechts aber deutlich eine Schneeglöckchenblüte erkennen lässt. Weil die Märzenbecher beim Kloster Bebenhausen in der Nähe Tübingens wachsen, hat Fuchs die Pflanze aufgenommen, obwohl sie medizinisch keine Rolle spielte.

NIVÉOLE DU PRINTEMPS

L'illustration suivante (CLXXXV ; pl. CCLXXIII)) fait songer à une chimère car, ici, les artistes ont créé une plante qui présente, à gauche, les caractéristiques florales de la NIVÉOLE DU PRINTEMPS, à droite, une fleur qui ne peut être que celle du PERCE-NEIGE. Fuchs choisit de représenter la nivéole, qui ne joue pourtant aucun rôle médicinal, parce qu'elle se rencontre au monastère de Bebenhausen, situé près de Tübingen.

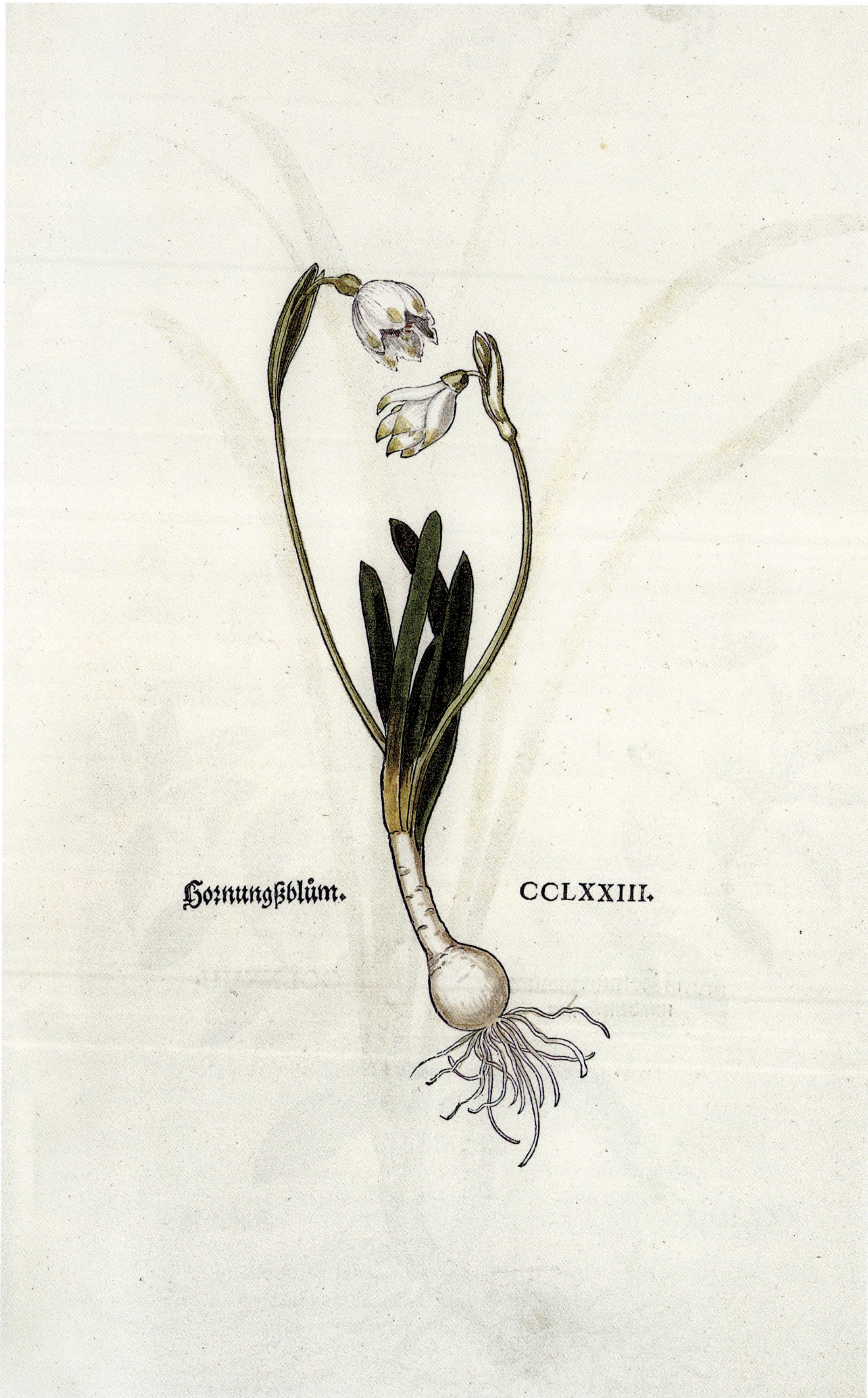

SNOWFLAKE | „HORNUNGSBLUM“ | NIVÉOLE DU PRINTEMPS

GROMWELL

GROMWELL (CLXXXVI), also known as COMMON ALKANET, was used to dissolve stones (calculi) and as a diuretic.

„MEERHIRSS“

Die „MEERHIRSS“ (Cap. CLXXXVI), auch Steinsame genannt, war als steinbrechendes und entwässerndes Mittel begehrt.

GRÉMIL OFFICINAL

Le GRÉMIL OFFICINAL (CLXXXVI), dit aussi HERBE AUX PERLES, était très recherché comme diurétique et comme antilithique, d'où son nom allemand de «Steinsame» ou graine à calcul.

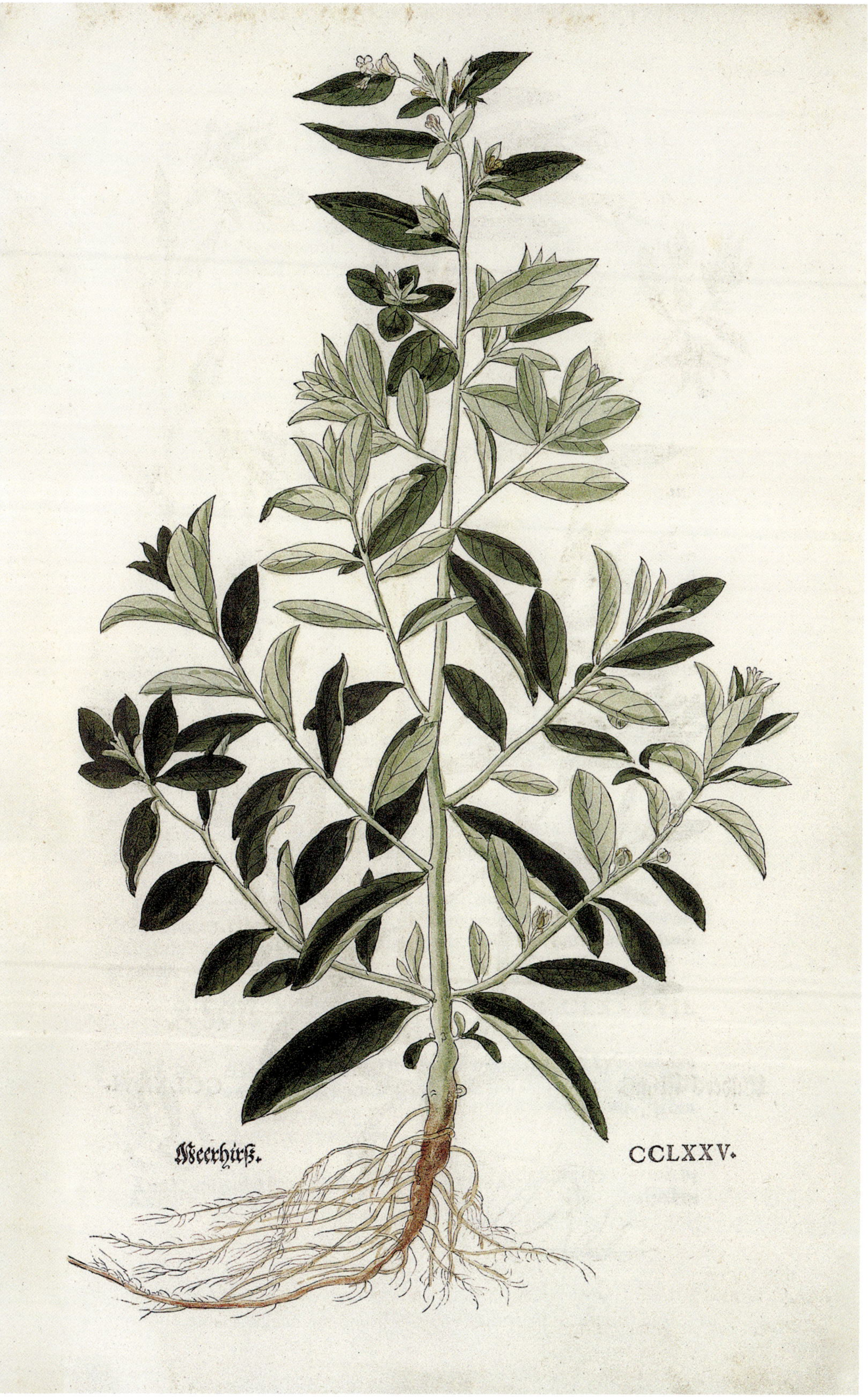
Meerhirß.
CCLXXV.

CODLINS AND CREAM

In this chapter (CLXXXVII), Fuchs combines GREAT HAIRY WILLOW HERB, also known as CODLINS AND CREAM, with YELLOW LOOSESTRIFE. To both, he ascribes a haemostatic effect, which he claims was unknown to the apothecaries.

WEIDERICH

Beim WEIDERICH (Cap. CLXXXVII), laut Fuchs den Apothekern unbekannt, werden die blutstillenden Eigenschaften erwähnt.

LYSIMAQUE COMMUNE

La LYSIMAQUE COMMUNE (CLXXXVII), ou chasse-bosse, inconnue des apothicaires selon Fuchs, est figurée ici pour ses propriétés hémostatiques.

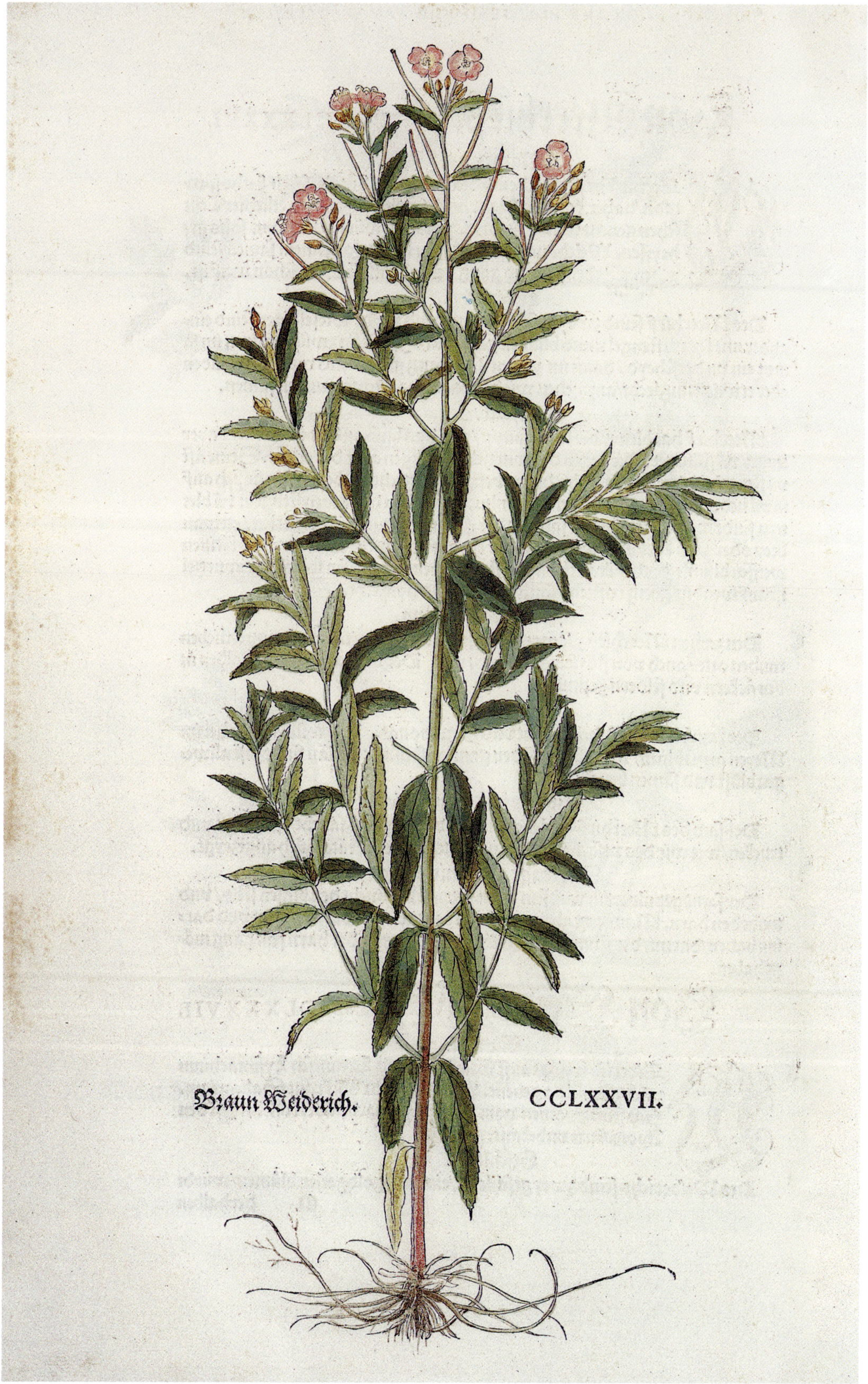
Braun Weiderich.
CCLXXVII.

HARE'S-FOOT

Fever is one of the indications noted for HARE'S-FOOT (CLXXXVIII), also known as TREFOIL or WHITE CLOVER.

KATZENKLEE

Fieber ist eine der Indikationen für den KATZENKLEE (Cap. CLXXXVIII).

TRÈFLE DES CHAMPS

La fièvre est l'une des indications du TRÈFLE DES CHAMPS (CLXXXVIII), appelé aussi pied-de-lièvre.

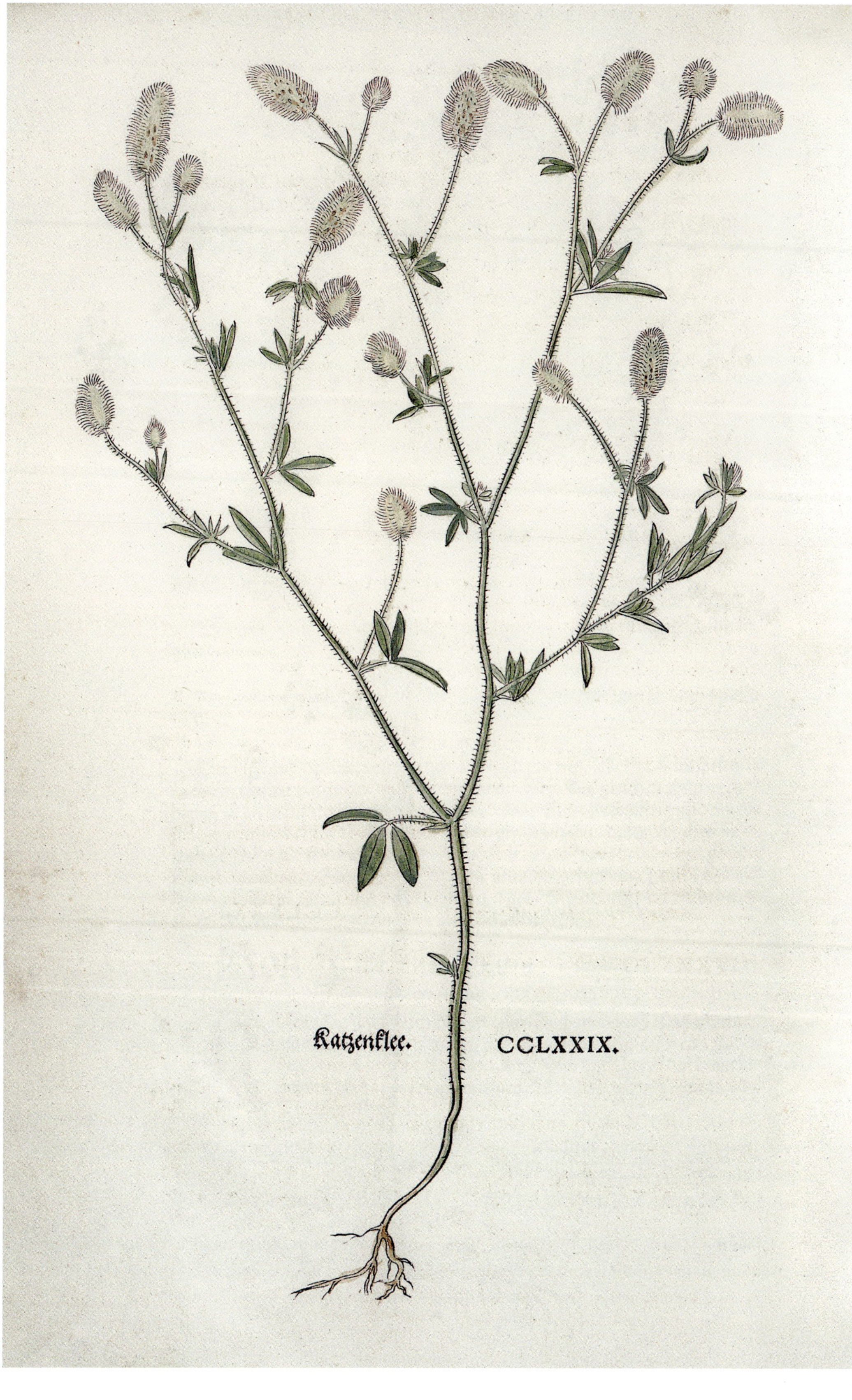
Katzenklee.
CCLXXIX.

EUROPEAN LARCH

With EUROPEAN LARCH (CLXXXIX), Fuchs recalled his Ansbach period, when his "gracious lord" had LARCHES planted and also had one dispatched to his former personal physician, now in Tübingen. The bark, the needles and the resin all find medicinal use.

LÄRCHE

Bei der LÄRCHE (Cap. CLXXXIX) erinnert sich Fuchs an seine Zeit in Ansbach, wo sein „gnediger Herr" Lärchen anpflanzen und seinem früheren Leibarzt auch eine nach Tübingen schicken ließ. Medizinische Verwendung finden die Rinde, die Nadeln und das Harz.

MÉLÈZE

En évoquant le MÉLÈZE (CLXXXIX), Fuchs se souvient du temps qu'il a passé à Ansbach, où son « bienveillant maître », dont il était le premier médecin, plantait des mélèzes et lui en avait fait livrer un à Tübingen. L'écorce, les aiguilles et la résine sont employées en médecine.

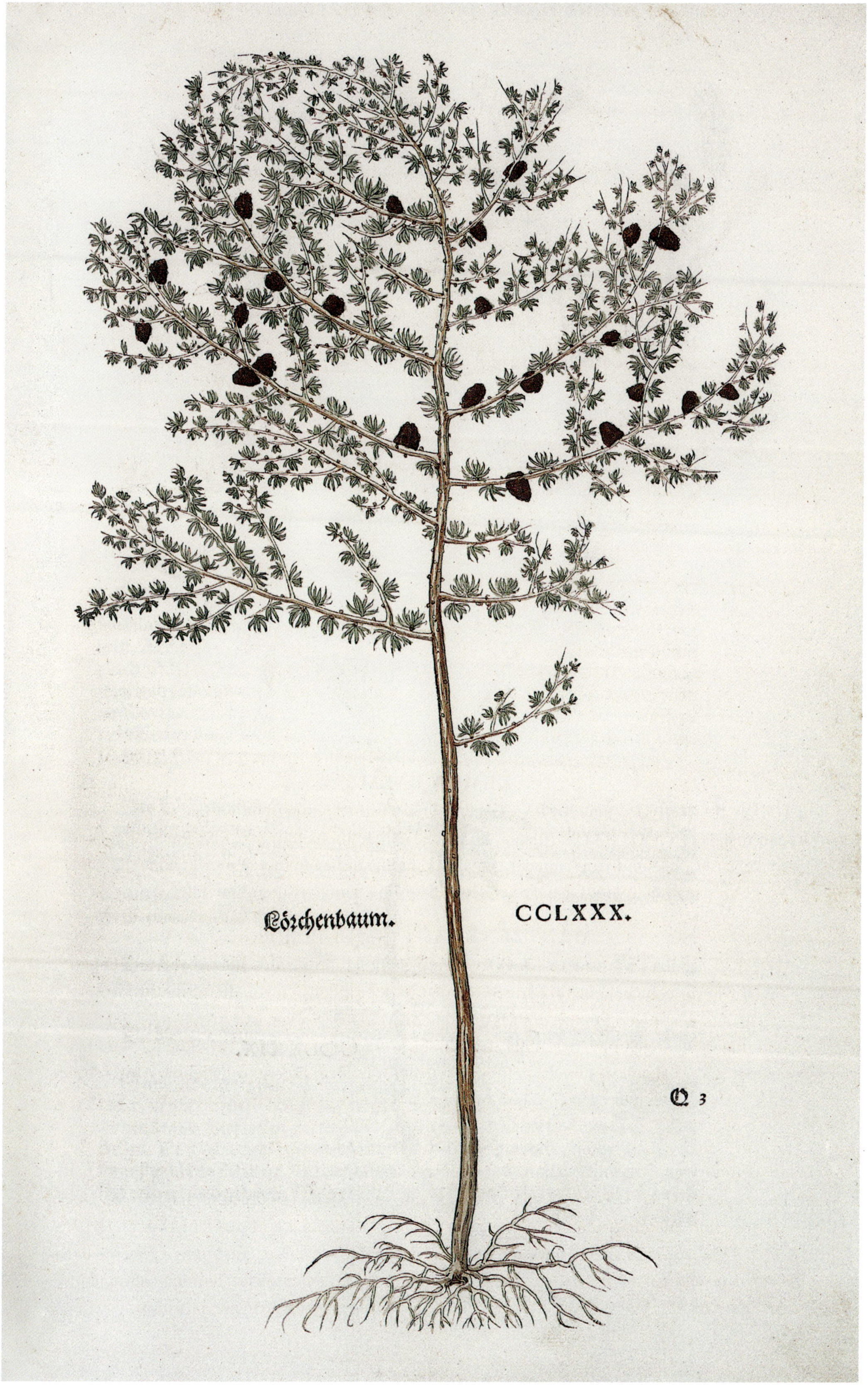
Lörchenbaum.
CCLXXX.
Q 3

LEMON BALM

LEMON BALM (CXC, plate CCLXXXII) develops a rather pungent odour late in the season. In contrast, BASTARD BALM (plate CCLXXXI), which Fuchs found growing near Ingolstadt and Ansbach, "has an extraordinarily pleasant smell, similar to that of citronella." The later use of the plant for nervous heart disorders is not yet mentioned here.

„WANTZENKRAUT“ (MELISSE)

„WANTZENKRAUT“ (Taf. CCLXXXII) ist kein sehr schöner Name für die als Heilpflanze nach wie vor sehr beliebte MELISSE (Cap. CXC); er leitet sich von der etwas strengen Geruchsnote der späten Pflanze ab. Als angebliche MELISSE (Taf. CCLXXXI) wird dagegen das Immenblatt abgebildet, das „über die massen wol reucht, wie die Citrinatöpffel“ und bei Ingolstadt und Ansbach von Fuchs gefunden wurde. Von der später sehr beliebten Anwendung bei nervösen Herzbeschwerden findet sich hier noch nichts.

MÉLISSE OFFICINALE

On ne peut dire que «herbe à punaises» («Wantzenkraut», pl. CCLXXXII) soit un joli nom pour désigner la MÉLISSE OFFICINALE (CXC), plante médicinale encore appréciée de nos jours. Elle doit ce nom à l'odeur un peu forte qu'elle exhale à maturité. La MÉLITTE À FEUILLES DE MÉLISSE (pl. CCLXXXI), qui «sent très fort comme le citron» et que Fuchs a trouvée dans les environs d'Ingolstadt et d'Ansbach, est confondue ici avec la mélisse. Son indication pour les troubles cardiaques d'origine nerveuse ne sera découverte que plus tard.

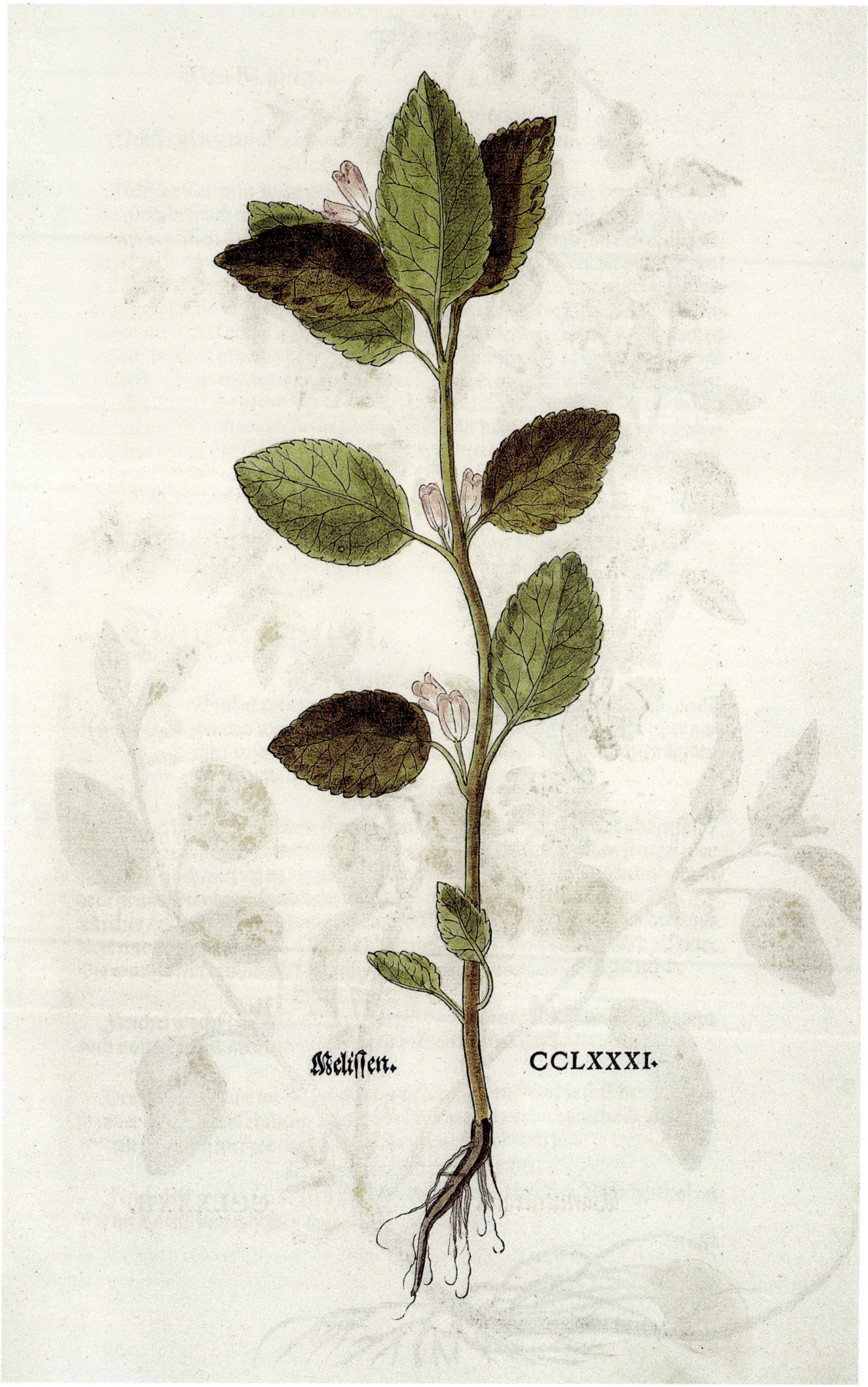
Melissen.
CCLXXXI.

FENNEL

For hundreds of years, FENNEL (CXCI) has retained its significance in plant medicine – although not to the exaggerated extent claimed for it in the 16th century. Today it is used primarily for bronchial disorders and flatulence.

FENCHEL

Auch der FENCHEL (Cap. CXCI) hat über die Jahrhunderte seine Bedeutung in der Phytotherapie behalten, allerdings nicht in dem ausufernden Umfang des 16. Jahrhunderts, sondern in erster Linie bei Bronchialerkrankungen und gegen Blähungen.

FENOUIL COMMUN

L'importance du FENOUIL COMMUN (CXCI) en phytothérapie ne s'est jamais démentie, même si le nombre des indications a diminué depuis le XVIe siècle, se limitant aujourd'hui aux affections bronchiques et aux ballonnements.

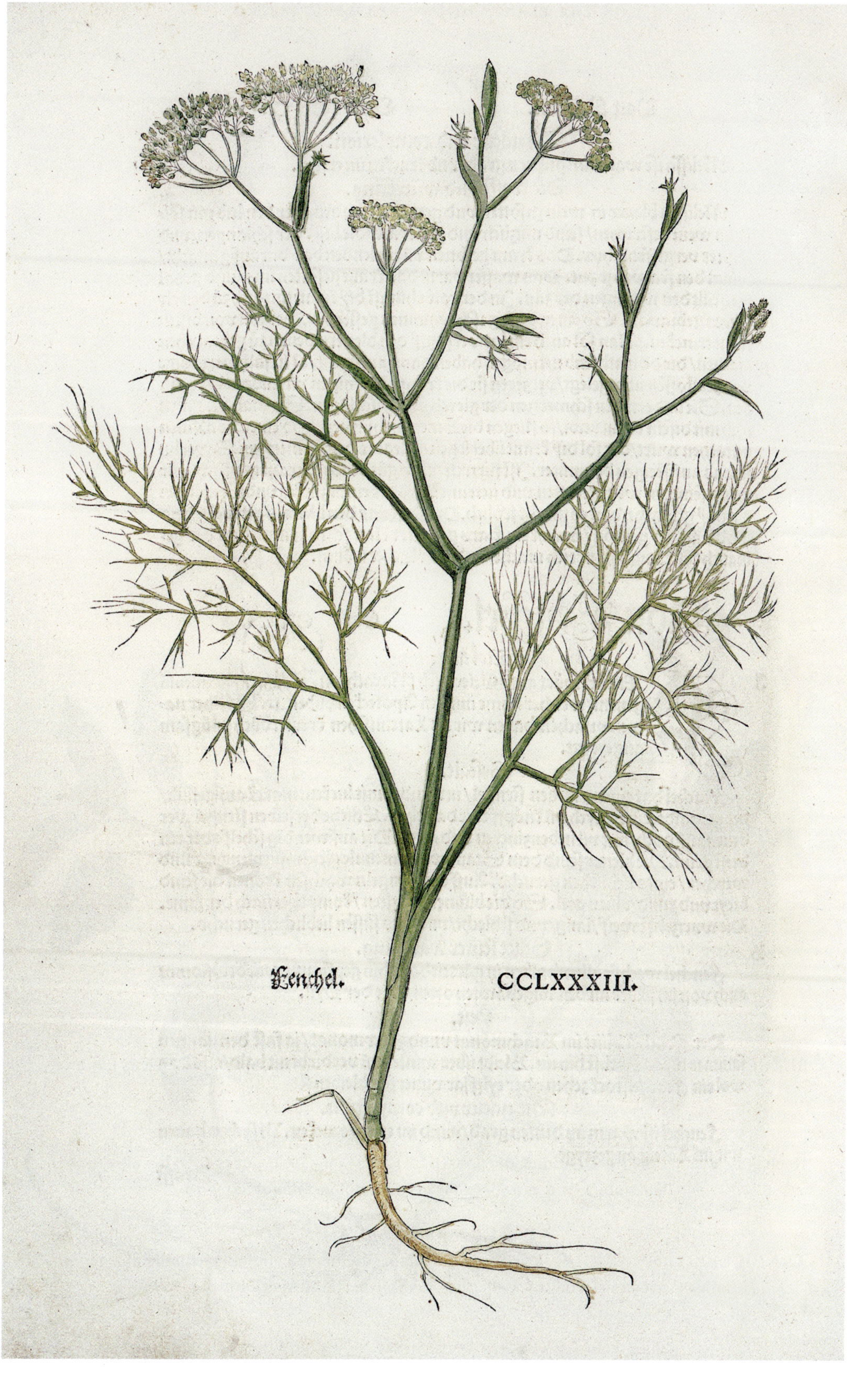
Fenchel.
CCLXXXIII.

BLACK CUMIN

BLACK CUMIN (CXCII), whose oil is recommended against allergic reactions such as hay fever, is of great interest today.

„NIGELLEN“ (SCHWARZKÜMMEL)

Hochaktuell ist der Schwarzkümmel, die „NIGELLEN“ (Cap. CXCII), dessen Öl bei allergischen Reaktionen, wie zum Beispiel Heuschnupfen, empfohlen wird.

NIGELLE AROMATIQUE

La NIGELLE AROMATIQUE (CXCII) est une plante médicinale toujours actuelle puisque son huile est préconisée pour les allergies, comme le rhume des foins par exemple.

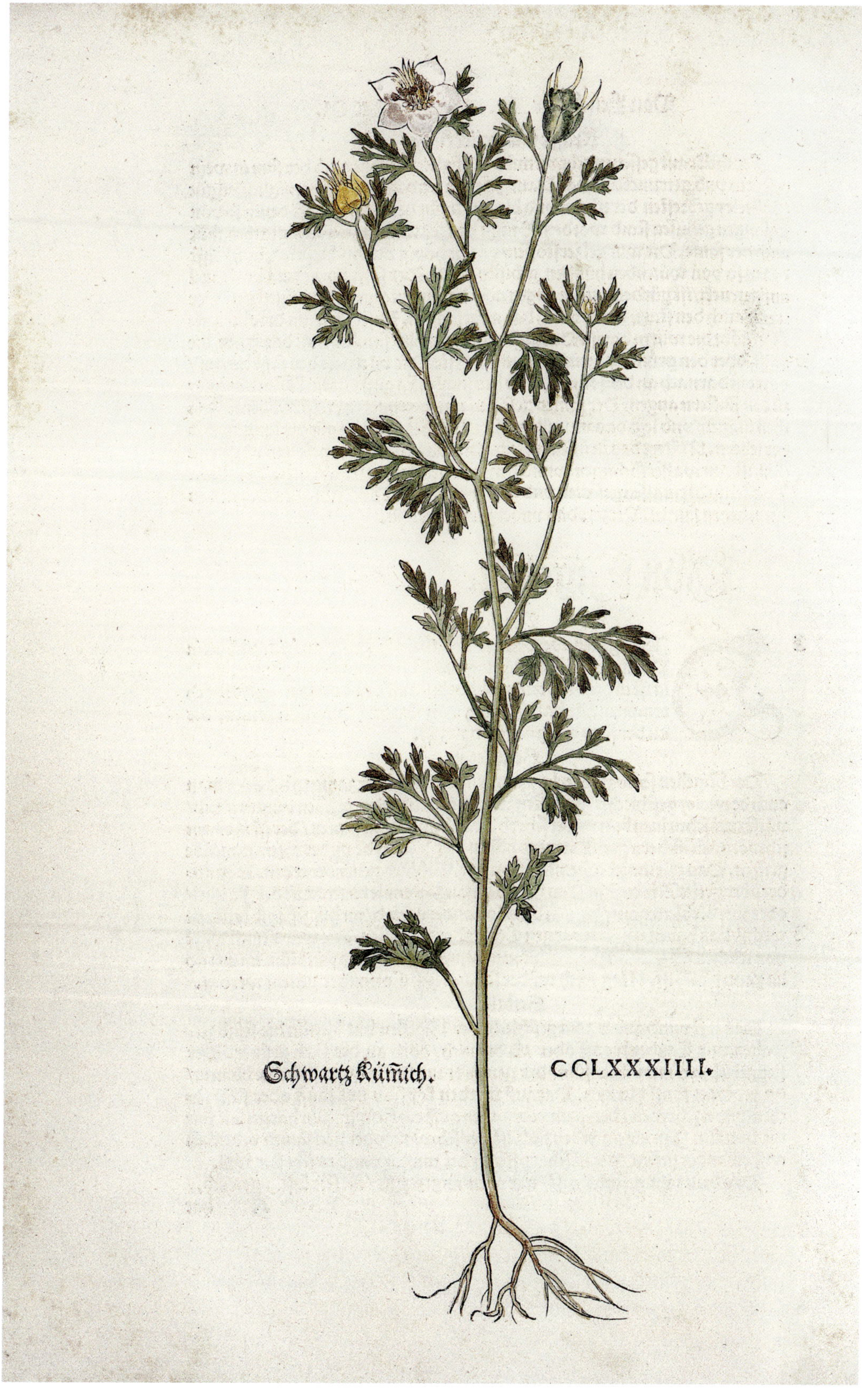
Schwartz Kümich.
CCLXXXIIII.

MALLOW

MALLOW (CXCIII) includes HOLLYHOCK, or GARDEN MALLOW (plate CCLXXXVII), DWARF MALLOW (plate CCLXXXVIII) and common or HIGH MALLOW (plate CCLXXXVIIII). Owing to their high mucilage content, these plants were used for example in bronchial disorders.

PAPPEL

Der alte Ausdruck PAPPEL (Cap. CXCIII) bezeichnet nicht den gleichnamigen Baum, sondern krautige Malvengewächse wie die STOCKROSE (Taf. CCLXXXVII), die WEG-MALVE (Taf. CCLXXXVIII) und die WILDE MALVE (Taf. CCLXXXVIIII), die auch heute noch Käsepappel heißt. Wegen ihres Gehalts an pflanzlichem Schleim werden sie z. B. bei Bronchialerkrankungen eingesetzt.

MAUVES HERBACÉES

Le mot «Pappel» (CXCIII) ne désigne pas l'arbre du même nom – en allemand moderne, «Pappel» est le peuplier –, mais les MAUVES HERBACÉES telles que la ROSE TRÉMIÈRE (pl. CCLXXXVII), la PETITE MAUVE (pl. CCLXXXVIII) et la MAUVE SYLVESTRE (pl. CCLXXXVIIII), qu'en Allemagne on appelle encore aujourd'hui «mauve à fromage» («Käsepappel»). Le pouvoir émollient du mucilage est apprécié dans les affections bronchiques.

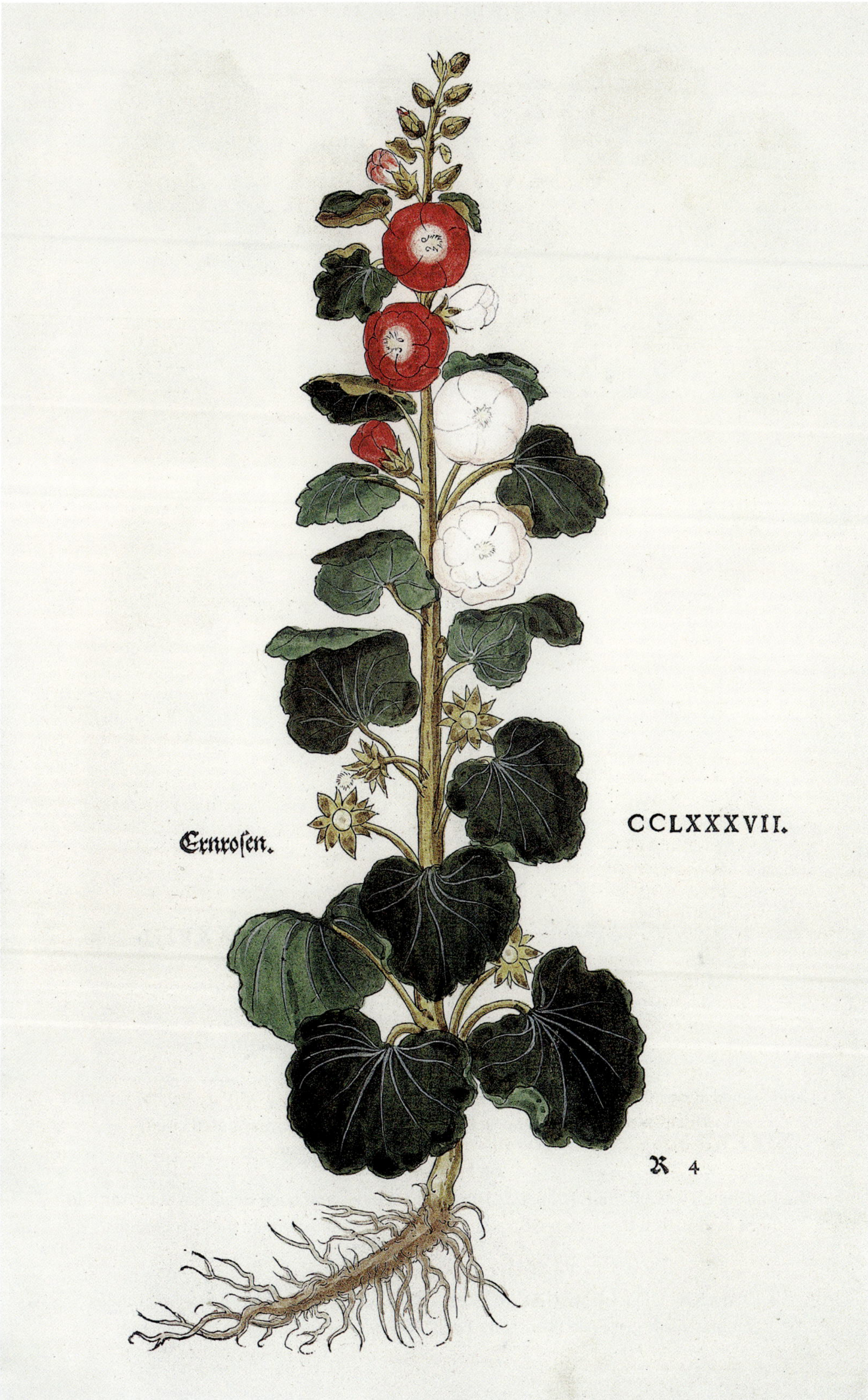
Ernrosen.
CCLXXXVII.
R 4

SHRUB

Large stands of German, or SHRUB, TAMARISK (CXCIIII; plate CCXC) are still found today along the Isar and Lech rivers, but the plants are no longer used medicinally.

TAMARISKE

Die Deutsche TAMARISKE (Cap. CXCIIII; Taf. CCXC) kommt auch heute noch an Isar und Lech in größeren Beständen wild vor, wird aber medizinisch nicht mehr verwendet.

TAMARIN D'ALLEMAGNE

Le TAMARIN D'ALLEMAGNE (CXCIIII ; pl. CCXC) se rencontre encore en grandes colonies sur les rives de l'Isar et du Lech, mais n'est plus employé en médecine.

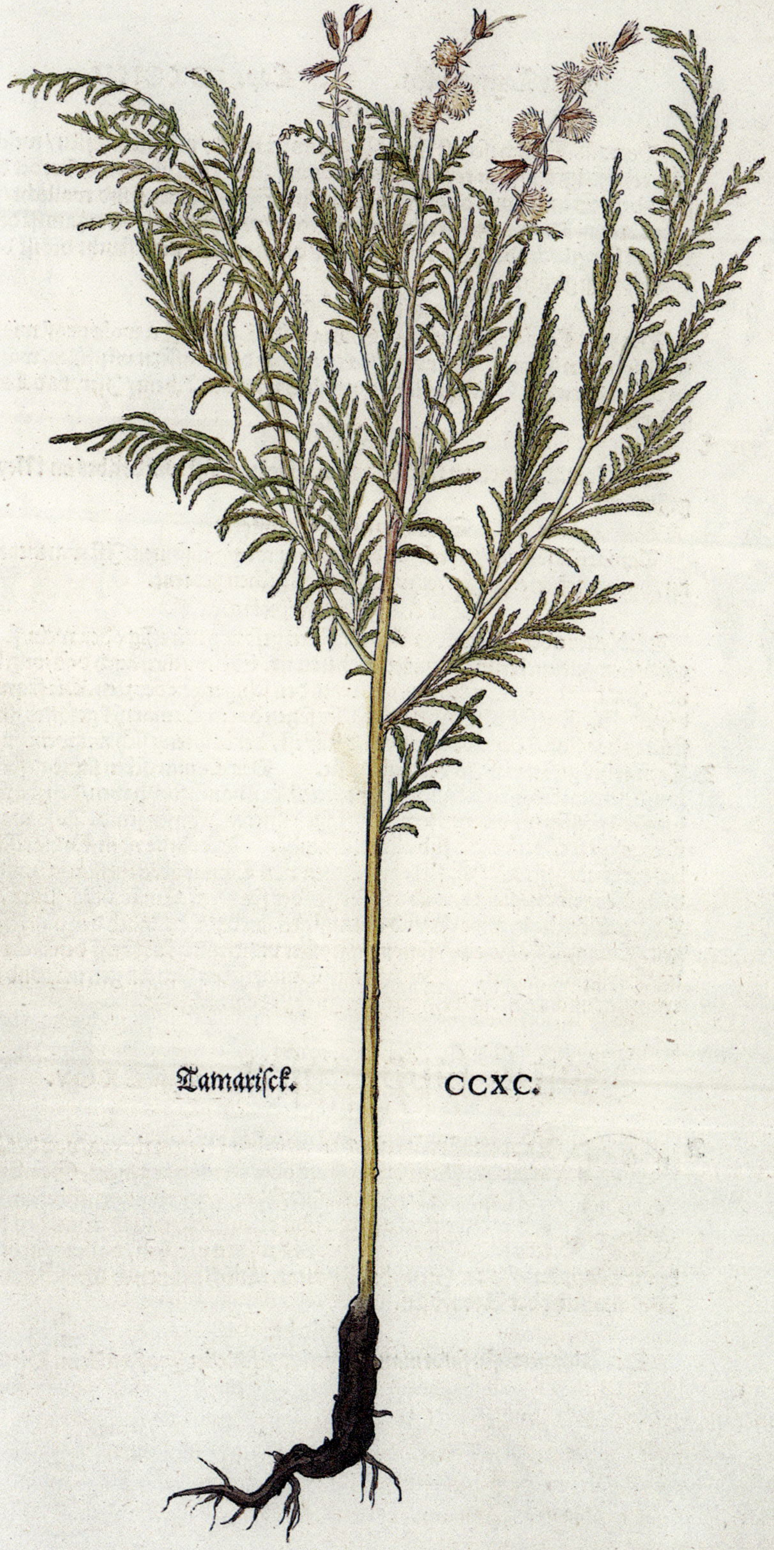

Tamarisck. CCXC.

CORN POPPY

CORN POPPY (CXCV), also known as Field Poppy, together with GIANT or OPIUM POPPY (CXCVI), were both recommended for pain and insomnia, as well as for many other applications that are today of merely historic interest. The pain-relieving alkaloid morphium, which was isolated by the German apothecary Friedrich Sertürner in 1805, is derived from the Opium Poppy.

KLAPPERROSEN

KLAPPERROSEN (Cap. CXCV) nannte man den Klatschmohn, während der Schlafmohn als MAGSAMEN (Cap. CXCVI) bezeichnet wurde. Beide werden bei Schmerzen und zur Schlafanbahnung empfohlen, erhalten zusätzlich jedoch auch zahlreiche andere Indikationen zugeschrieben, die nur noch historische Bedeutung besitzen. Aus dem Schlafmohn wird Opium gewonnen, dessen Hauptwirkstoff, das schmerzstillende Alkaloid Morphin, der deutsche Apotheker Friedrich Sertürner 1805 daraus isolierte.

GRAND COQUELICOT

Le GRAND COQUELICOT était appelé en allemand «Klapperrosen» (approximativement, rose à crécelle, CXCV) et le PIVOT À OPIUM, «Magsamen» (graine de pavot, CXCVI). Tous deux sont recommandés comme antidouleur et somnifère. Les autres indications, très nombreuses, ne présentent plus qu'un intérêt historique. L'opium, extrait du pavot, contient un alcaloïde, la morphine, que le pharmacien allemand Friedrich Sertürner réussit à isoler en 1805.

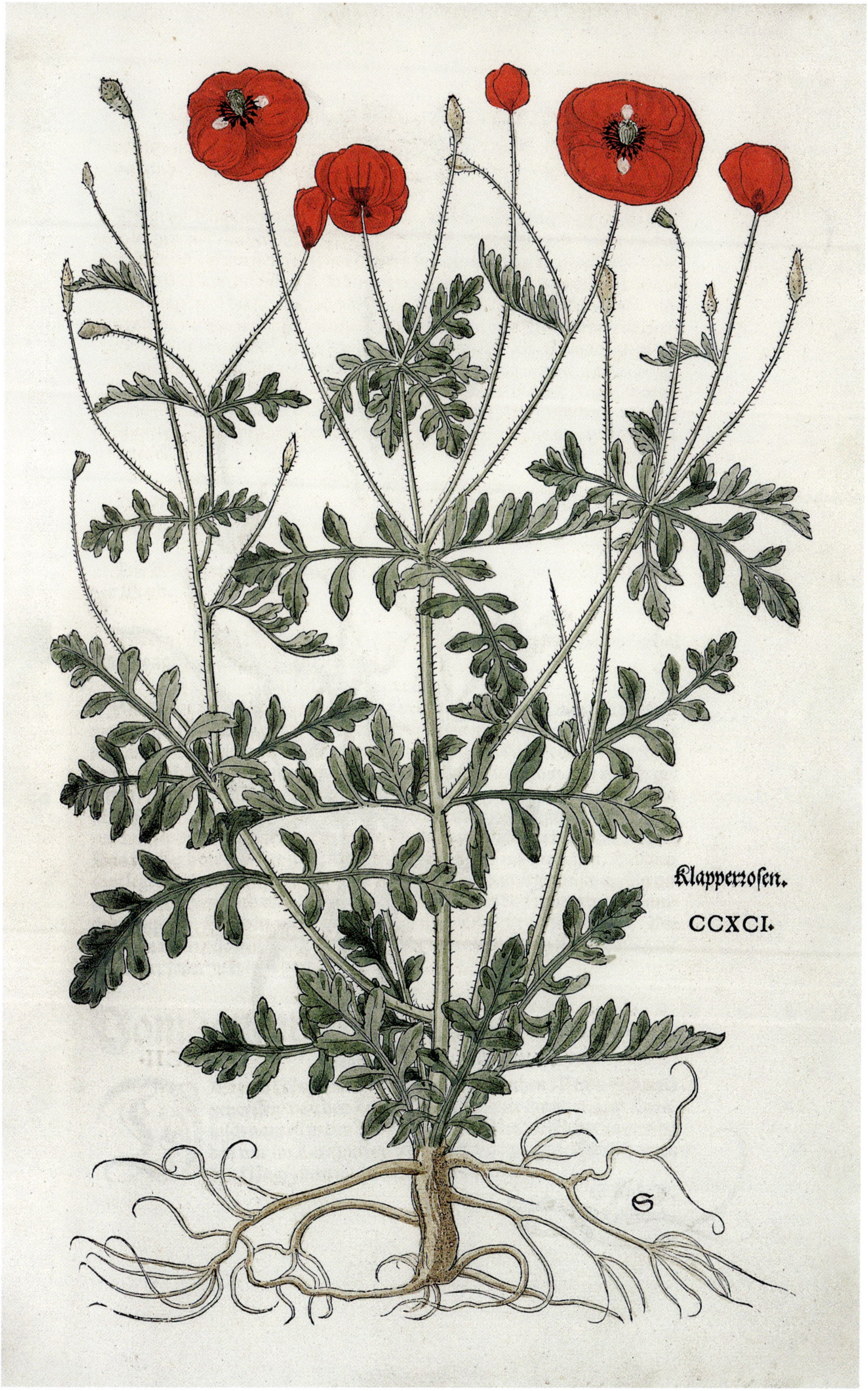
Klapperrosen.
CCXCI.

YELLOW-HORNED POPPY

An old German word for Poppy, "Mag," appears in "ölmagen," the YELLOW-HORNED POPPY (CXCVII; plate CCXCIIII).

GELBER HORNMOHN

Das alte Wort „Mag" für Mohn findet sich auch in „ÖLMAGEN" (Cap. CXCVII), worunter der GELBE HORNMOHN (Taf. CCXCIIII) verstanden wird.

PAVOT À HUILE

Le vieux mot «Mag», qui désigne le pavot, se retrouve aussi dans «Ölmagen» (CXCVII) ou PAVOT À HUILE, ancien nom allemand du PAVOT CORNU (pl. CCXCIIII).

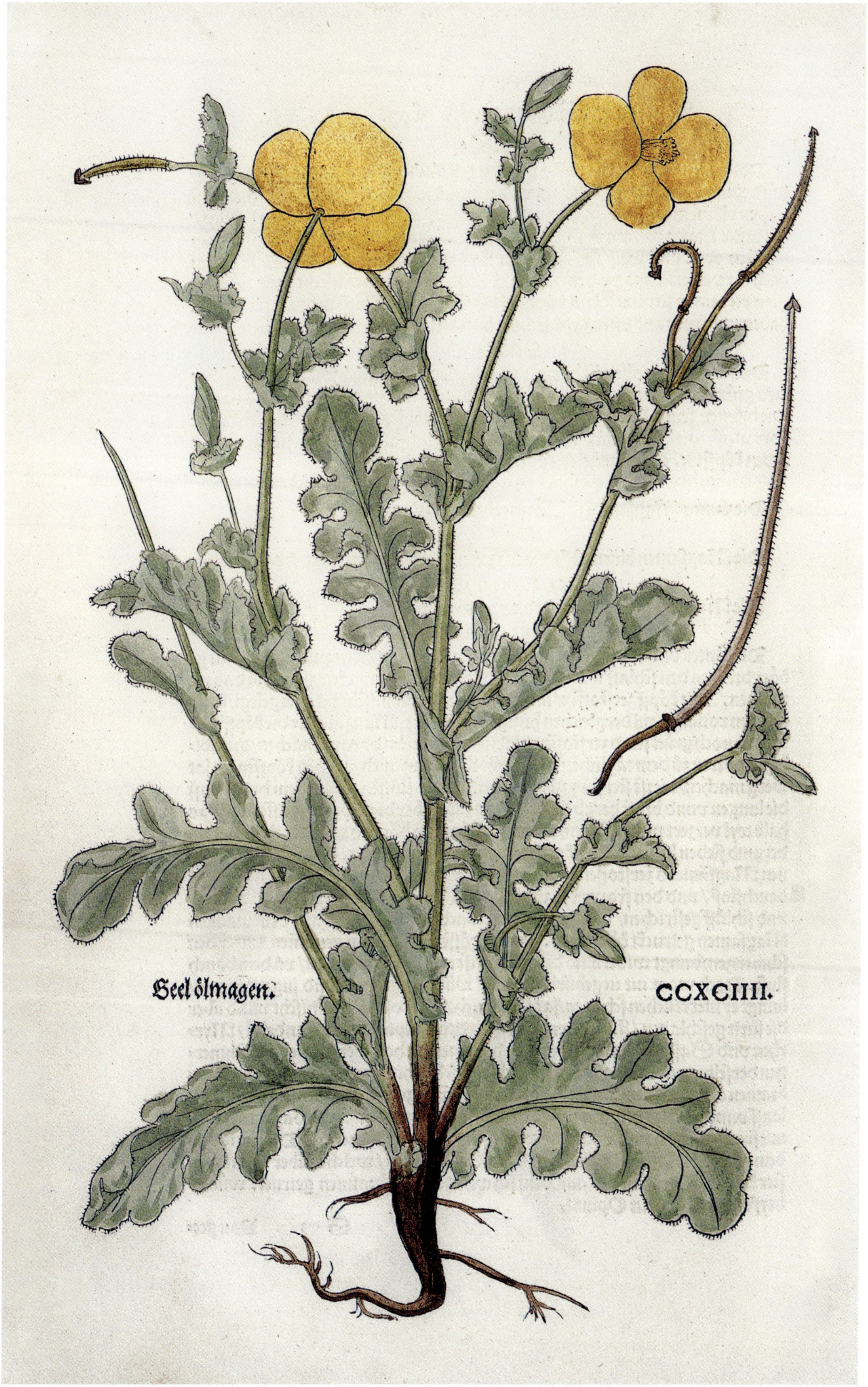
Geel ölmagen.
CCXCIIII.

MULBERRIES

Under MULBERRIES (CXCVIII), Fuchs gives extensive consideration to the raising of silk worms, for whom the leaves are an essential food. Among other medical uses of the plant, the text mentions the application of MULBERRIES as a vermifuge for tapeworms.

MAULBEEREN

Bei den MAULBEEREN (Cap. CXCVIII) geht Fuchs ausführlich auf die Seidenraupenzucht ein, zu der die Blätter als Futter benötigt werden. Medizinisch wird u. a. die Anwendung als Bandwurmmittel erwähnt.

MÛRIER NOIR

En présentant le MÛRIER NOIR (CXCVIII), Fuchs s'étend sur l'élevage du ver à soie qu'on nourrit avec les feuilles, et mentionne divers usages thérapeutiques, dont celui de vermifuge contre le ténia.

PAGE 394

CHERVIL

The text expressly mentions the great danger of confusing CHERVIL (CXCIX) with Poison Hemlock. Today, CHERVIL is no longer used medicinally.

KERBEL

Auf die große Gefahr einer Verwechslung mit dem giftigen Schierling wird beim KERBEL (Cap. CXCIX) ausdrücklich hingewiesen. Medizinisch wird er heute nicht mehr verwendet.

ANTHRISQUE SAUVAGE

Fuchs met en garde contre une possible confusion de l'ANTHRISQUE SAUVAGE (CXCIX) avec la ciguë, hautement toxique. L'anthrisque n'a plus d'emploi en médecine.

PAGE 395

BIRDSFOOT TREFOIL

BIRDSFOOT TREFOIL (CC; plate CCXCVII), also known as BACON AND EGGS, and SICKLE-FRUITED FENUGREEK (plate CCXCVIII) were combined in a single chapter and recommended as a poultice for inflamed swellings.

HORNKLEE

Der HORNKLEE (Taf. CCXCVII) und der ITALIENISCHE BOCKSHORNKLEE (Taf. CCXCVIII) werden im Kapitel STEINKLEE (Cap. CC) zusammengefasst und zur Auflage bei entzündlichen Geschwülsten empfohlen.

LOTIER CORNICULÉ

Au chapitre «MÉLILOTS» (CC) sont figurés ensemble le LOTIER CORNICULÉ (pl. CCXCVII), dit aussi PIED-DE-POULE, et la TRIGONELLE À PETITES CORNES (pl. CCXCVIII), que Fuchs préconise d'utiliser en compresses sur les tumeurs.

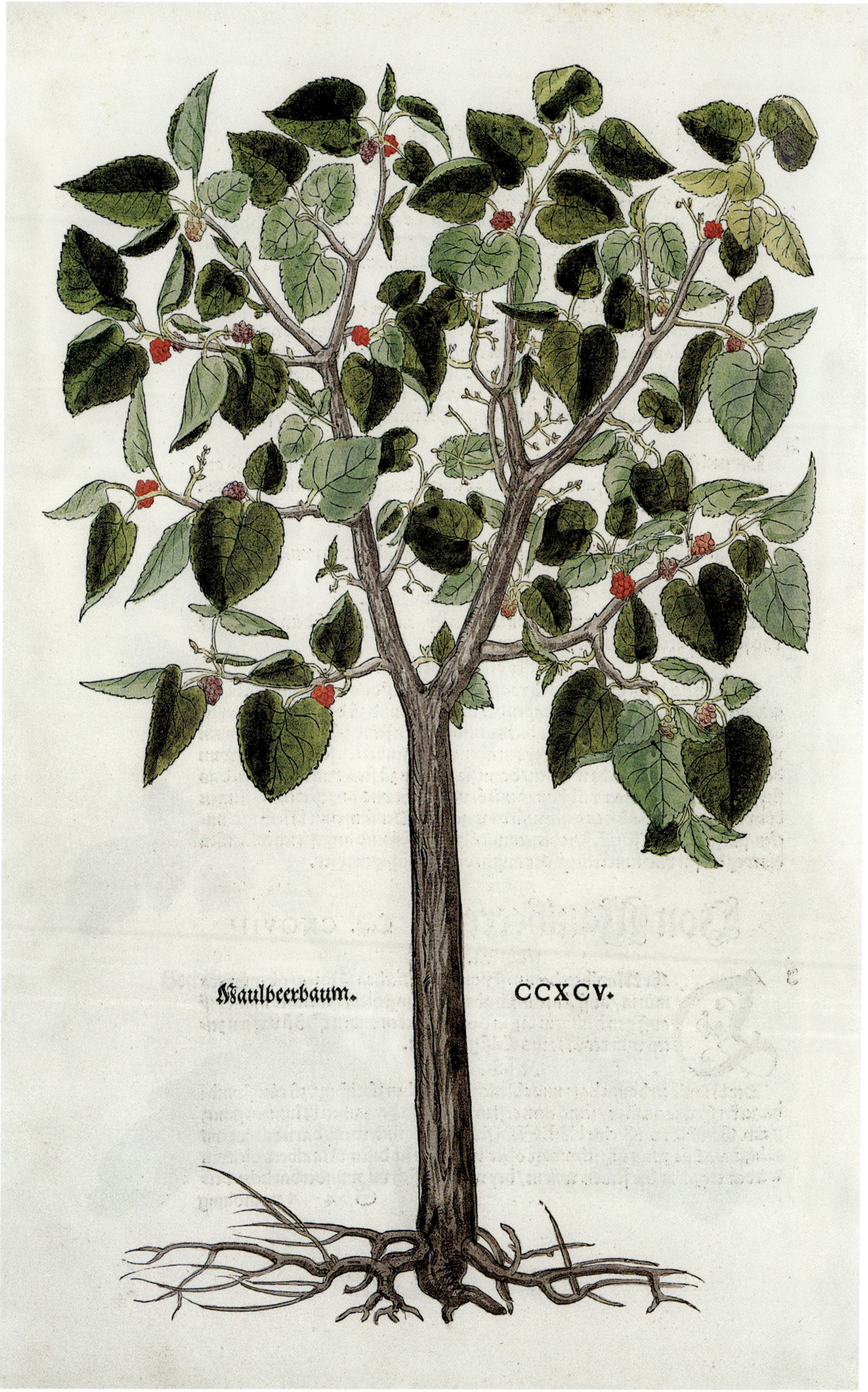
Maulbeerbaum.
CCXCV.

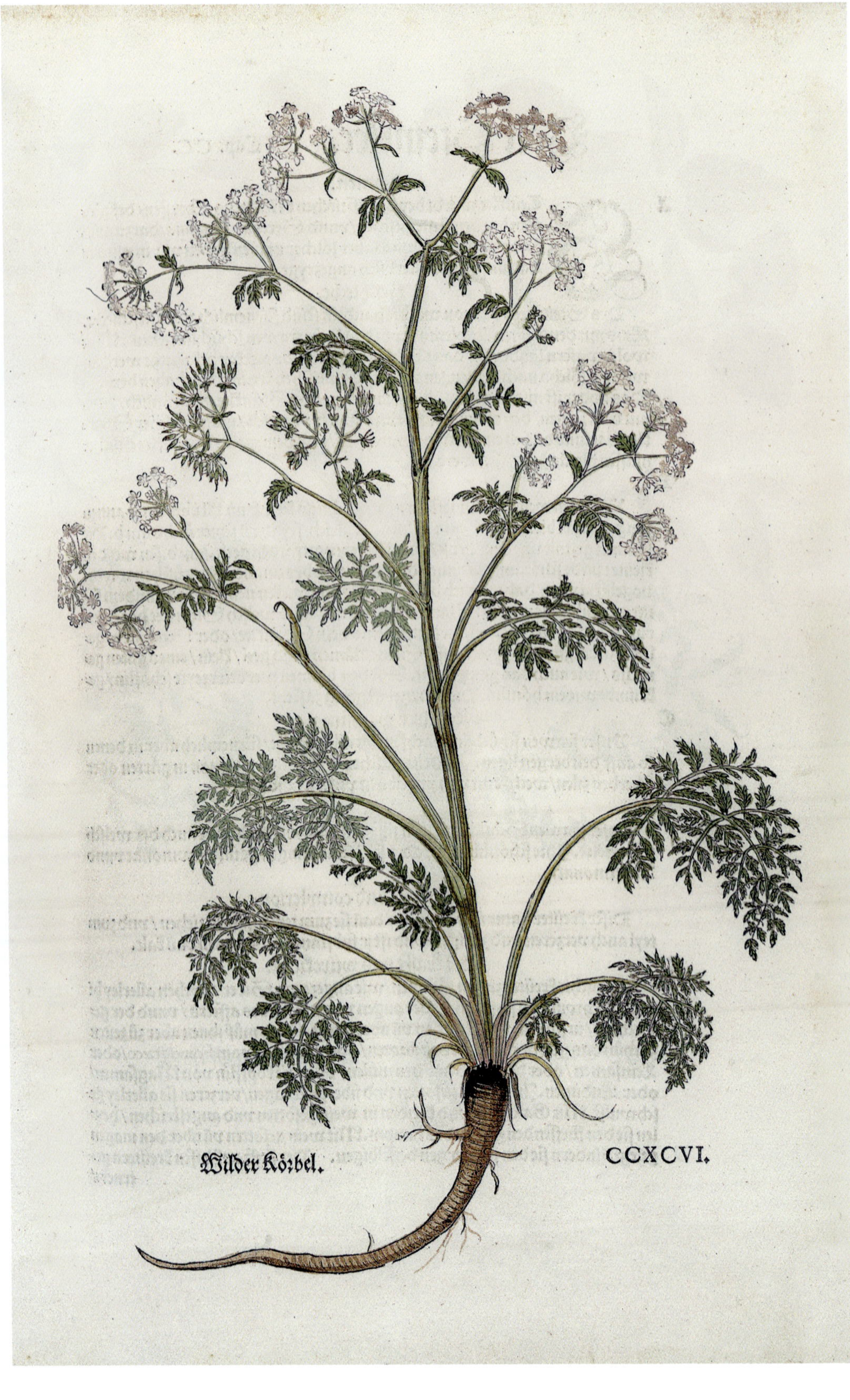
Wilder Körbel.
CCXCVI.

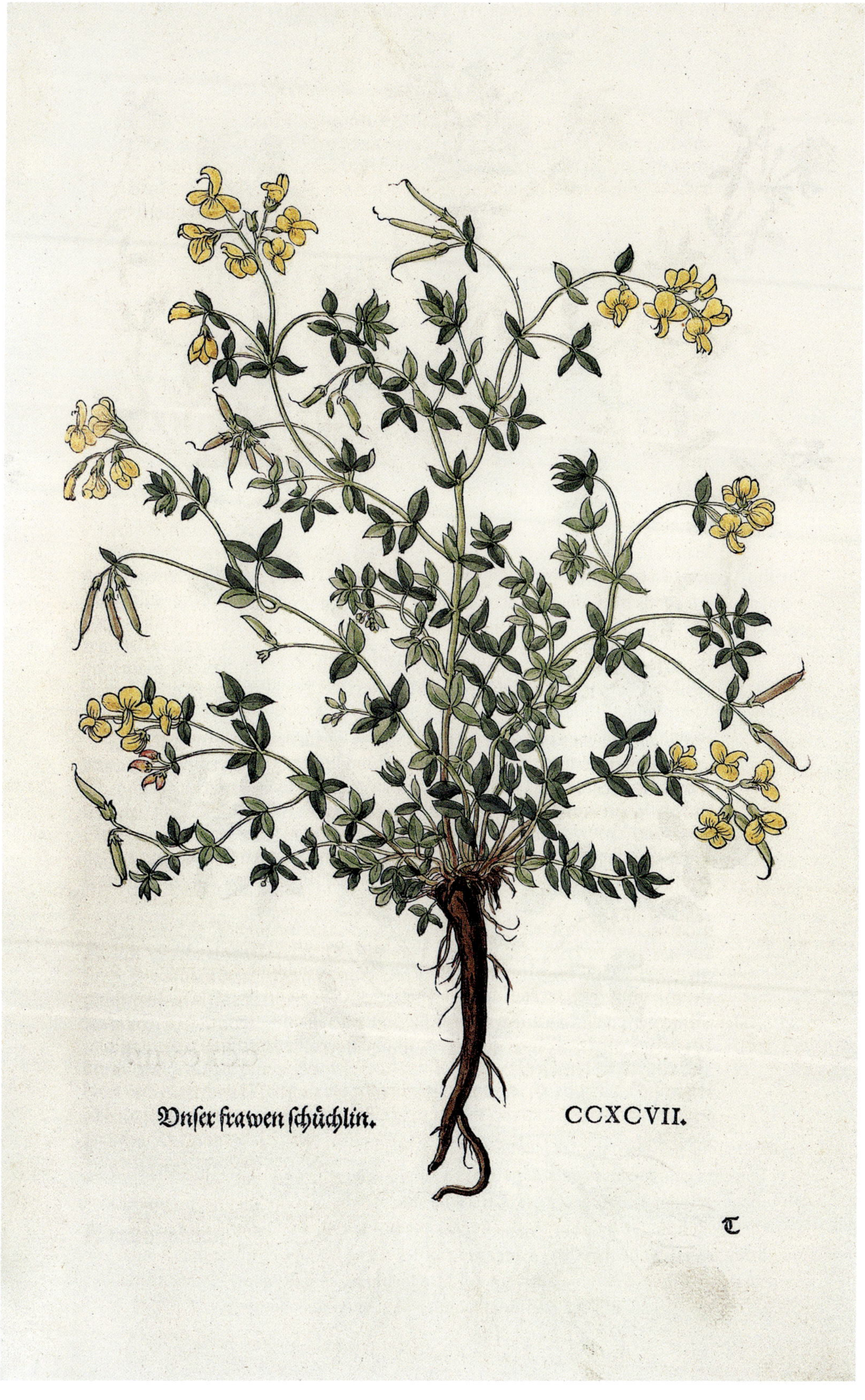
Vnser frawen schůchlin.
CCXCVII.
C

MANDRAKE

The third group of a hundred descriptions begins with MANDRAKE (CCI), which has surely accrued more legends than almost any other plant. Daemonic properties were attributed to the MANDRAKE because its root has a slight resemblance to the two-legged human body. This characteristic not only made the act of extracting the plant from the earth mortally dangerous, but also lent the plant value as a talisman against evil. Fuchs, who of course was familiar with all of these tales concerning the "little gallows man," as the MANDRAKE was nicknamed in German, explicitly opposed the deceptions associated with the plant. The poisonous juice was of particular use in relieving pain and inducing sleep, but was also applied as an anaesthetic for patients "whom one wished to cut or cauterize on sensitive parts."

ALRAUNE

Die ALRAUNE (Cap. CCI), mit der das dritte Hundert der Beschreibungen beginnt, ist die sagenumwobenste Pflanze überhaupt. Da ihre Wurzel wegen der meist gegabelten Spitze entfernt an einen menschlichen Körper erinnert, schrieb man ihr dämonische Eigenschaften zu, die nicht nur das Herausziehen zu einem lebensgefährlichen Unternehmen werden ließen, sondern sie auch als unheilabwehrenden Talisman kostbar machten. Fuchs, der all diese Erzählungen vom „Galgenmännlein" kannte, wendet sich ausdrücklich gegen die damit begangenen Betrügereien. Angewendet wurde der giftige Saft zur Schmerzstillung und Schlafförderung, aber auch zu einer Art Narkose bei Patienten, „die man on alle empfindlicheyt will schneiden oder brennen".

MANDRAGORE OFFICINALE

La MANDRAGORE OFFICINALE (CCI), qui ouvre la troisième partie de l'ouvrage, est la plante la plus marquée par les légendes et les superstitions. À cause de sa racine fusiforme et fourchue, qui faisait penser à un corps humain sans tête, on lui prêtait des caractères démoniaques. Il eût été dangereux de l'arracher du sol sans prendre de précautions et, séchée, sa racine était un talisman précieux. Fuchs, qui connaît bien entendu toutes les légendes entourant le «gibier de potence», condamne toutes les escroqueries qui sont commises avec. Le suc toxique, employé comme antidouleur et soporifique, servait même d'anesthésique sur les patients «qu'on voulait couper ou brûler sans douleurs».

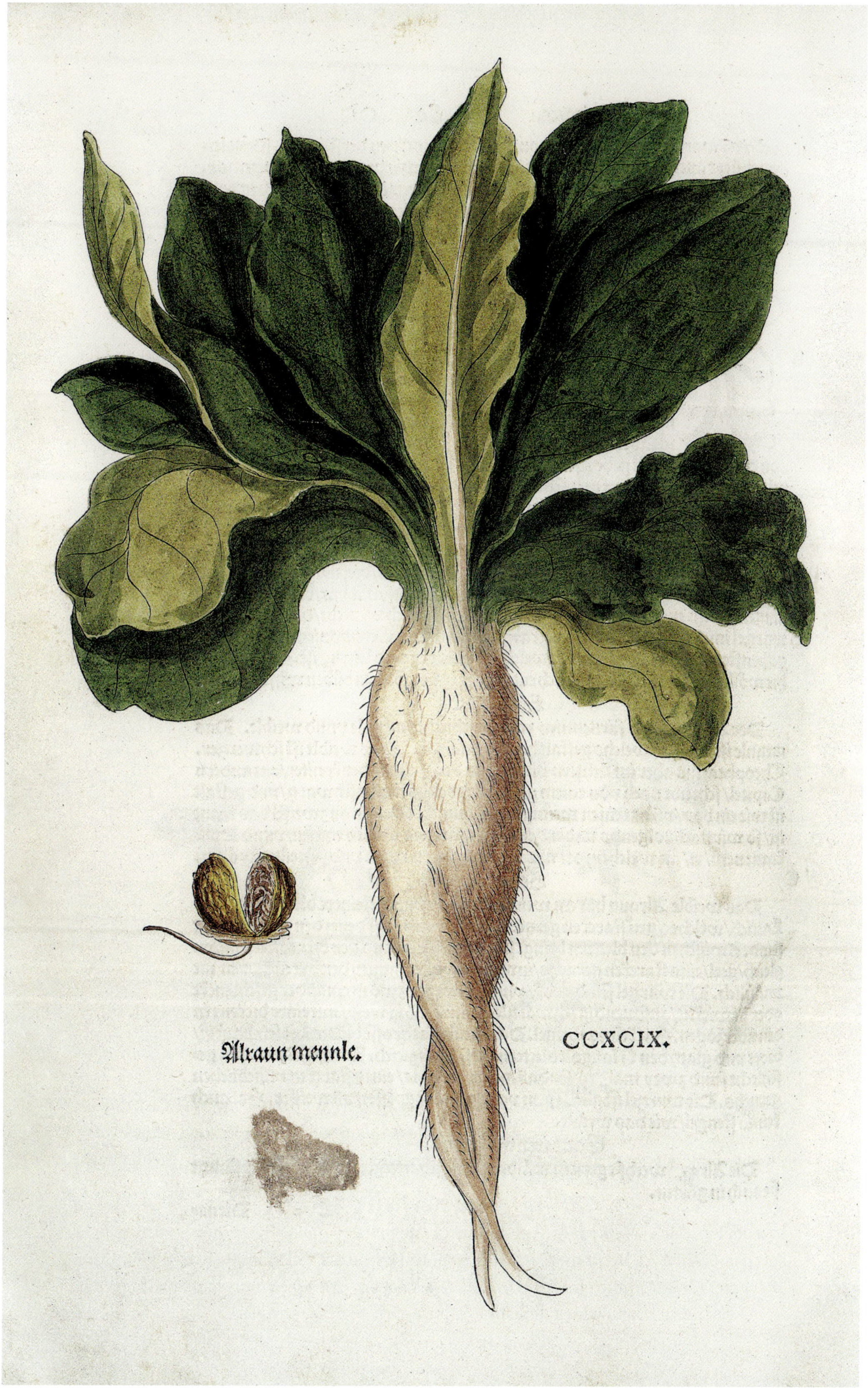
Alraun mennle.
CCXCIX.

AUBERGINE

AUBERGINE, or EGGPLANT (CCII), also belongs to the nightshade family. The plant, still very new to Europe in Fuchs's day, was not yet used medicinally, although it had already won admiration among gourmets.

„MELANZAN" (AUBERGINE)

Ebenfalls zu den Nachtschattengewächsen gehört die „MELANZAN" (Cap. CCII), die wir als Aubergine kennen. Sie war zu Zeiten von Fuchs noch sehr neu in Europa, wurde noch nicht arzneilich genutzt, hatte aber unter den Feinschmeckern schon viele Liebhaber.

AUBERGINE

La mélongène («Melanzan» dans le texte), que nous connaissons aujourd'hui sous le nom courant d'AUBERGINE (CCII), fait partie elle aussi de la famille des Solanacées. Récemment introduite en Europe, elle n'a pas encore pris place dans la pharmacopée, mais c'est déjà un légume apprécié des gourmets.

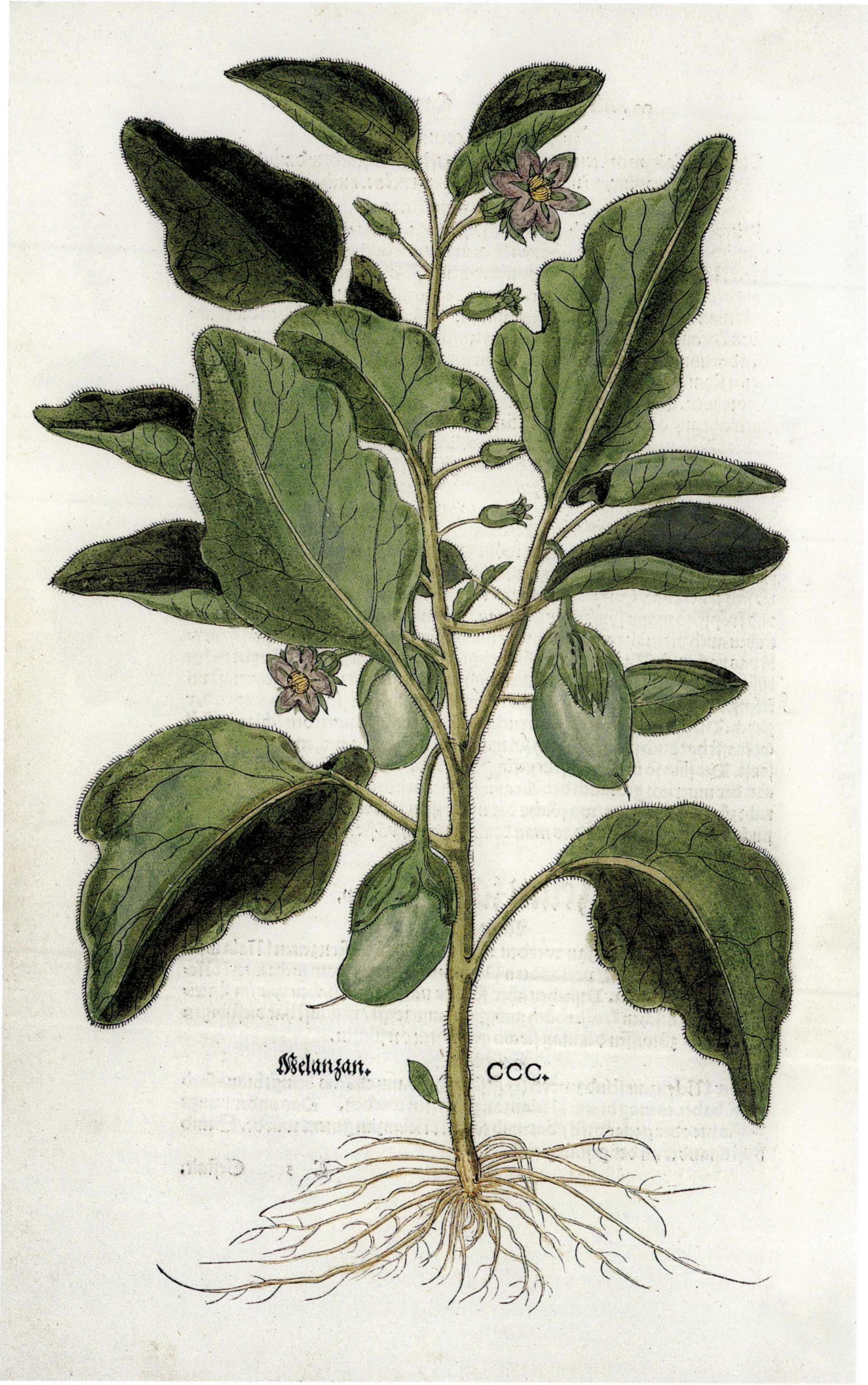
Melanzan. CCC.

WATER-LILIES

Fuchs ascribes medicinal effects also to WATER-LILIES (CCIII); he recommended WHITE WATER-LILY (plate CCCI) and YELLOW-WATER LILY (plate CCCII) particularly for the digestive tract.

SEEBLUMEN

Auch für die SEEBLUMEN (Cap. CCIII), nämlich die WEISSE SEEROSE (Taf. CCCI) und die GELBE TEICHROSE (Taf. CCCII), nennt Fuchs Arzneiwirkungen, insbesondere auf den Verdauungstrakt.

NÉNUPHAR BLANC

Fuchs mentionne les effets salutaires, surtout sur l'appareil digestif, du NÉNUPHAR BLANC (pl. CCCI) et du NÉNUPHAR JAUNE (pl. CCCII), présentés sous le nom de «Seeblumen» ou FLEURS DES LACS (CCIII).

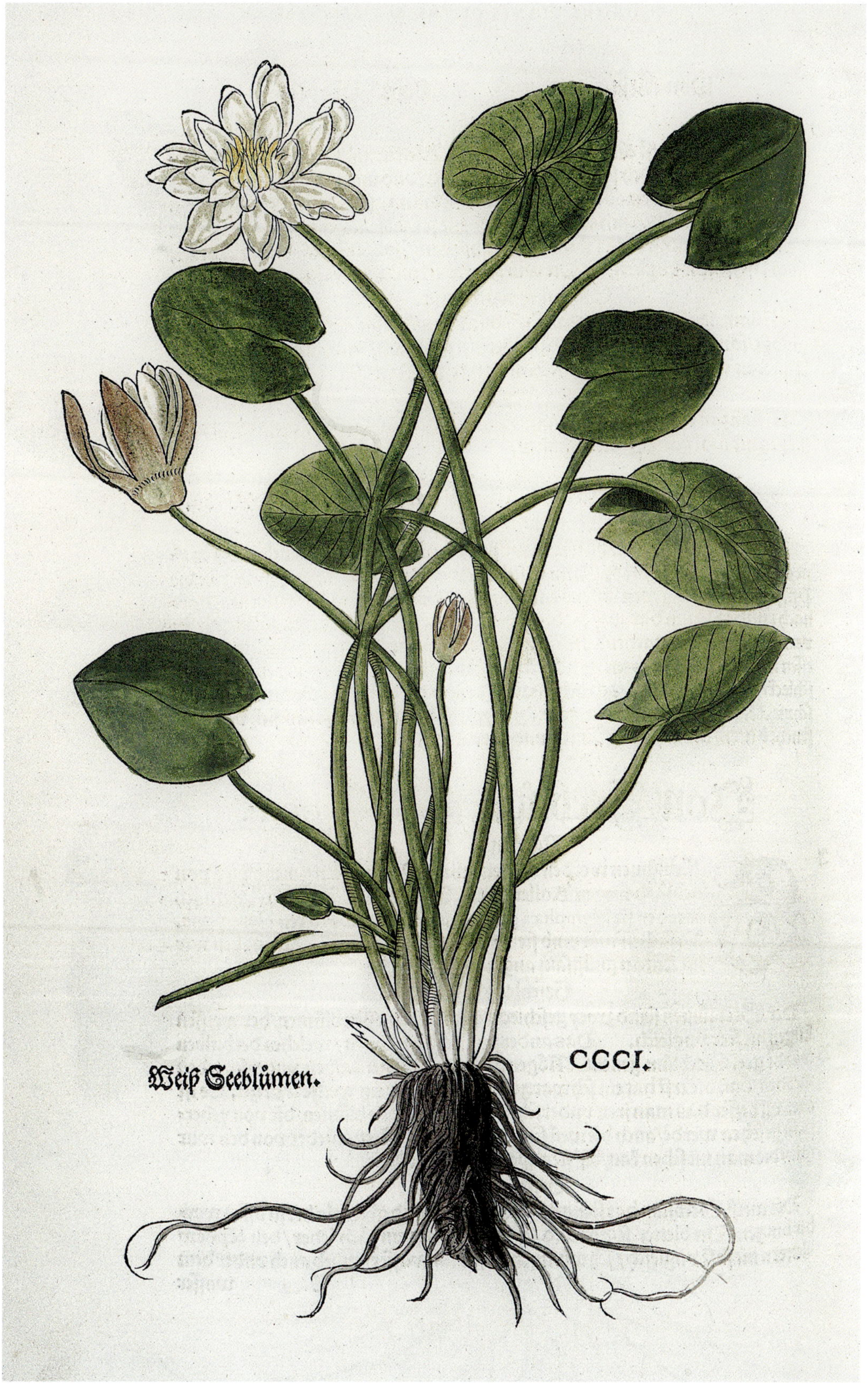
Weiß Seeblůmen.
CCCI.

SALAD ROCKET

Fuchs describes garden or SALAD ROCKET (CCIIII; plates CCCIII, CCCIIII) as “tame mustard,” which was to be taken for colds and applied externally as a poultice to stimulate blood circulation.

„ZAMEN SENFF“ (SENF-RAUKE)

Unter dem „ZAMEN SENFF“ (Cap. CCIIII) wird die SENF-RAUKE (Taf. CCCIII, CCCIIII) verstanden, die bei Erkältungen, aber auch äußerlich als durchblutungsförderndes Pflaster eingesetzt wird.

ROQUETTE CULTIVÉE

La ROQUETTE CULTIVÉE (pl. CCCIII, CCCIIII) apparaît sous le qualificatif de «MOUTARDE DOMESTIQUÉE» (CCIIII). Elle s’utilise pour les refroidissements et comme révulsif.

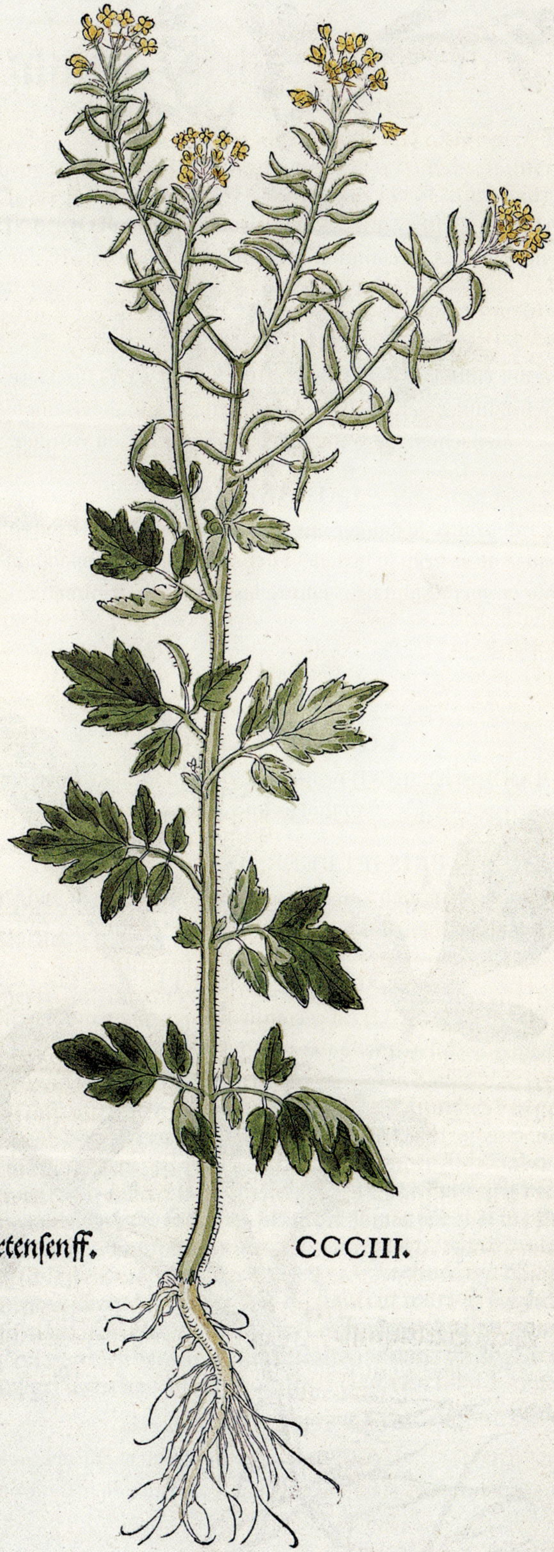

Seeler gartensenff. CCCIII.

OLEANDER

Although Fuchs explicitly warns of the poisonous effect of OLEANDER (CCV) on animals, he nonetheless re-commended it as a "healing remedy" for those suffering from poisonous animal bites.

OLEANDER

Obwohl vor der Giftigkeit des OLEANDERS (Cap. CCV) für Tiere ausdrücklich gewarnt wird, findet sich auch eine Empfehlung zur „heylsamen artzney" für Menschen, die von giftigen Tieren gebissen wurden.

LAURIER-ROSE

S'il met en garde contre le danger que représente le LAURIER-ROSE (CCV) pour le bétail à cause de sa grande toxicité, Fuchs le préconise cependant chez l'homme comme «remède salutaire» contre les morsures d'animaux venimeux.

PAGE 406

COMMON BARBERRY

COMMON BARBERRY (CCVI) proved useful both for diarrhoea and the extraction of thorns and arrows.

„PEISSELBEER" (SAUERDORN)

Bei Durchfall, aber auch zum Herausziehen von Dornen und Pfeilen wird der Sauerdorn empfohlen, der hier „PEISSELBEER" (Cap. CCVI) genannt wird.

ÉPINE-VINETTE

L'ÉPINE-VINETTE (CCVI) est recommandée comme antidiarrhéique et pour l'extraction des épines et des flèches.

PAGE 407

TOADFLAX

TOADFLAX, also known as BUTTER-AND-EGGS (CCVII), was supposed to be a diuretic and a remedy for jaundice. For the latter recommendation, the yellow colour of the flowers certainly acted as a "signature" of the plant's effect.

„LYNKRAUT"

Harntreibend soll das „LYNKRAUT" (Cap. CCVII) sein und gegen Gelbsucht wirken, wobei im letzteren Fall sicherlich die gelbe Blütenfarbe als Signatur gewertet wurde.

LINAIRE COMMUNE

La LINAIRE COMMUNE (CCVII) serait diurétique et efficace contre la jaunisse. En effet, selon la théorie des signatures, la couleur jaune de la fleur ne pouvait être que l'indice d'un pouvoir hépatique.

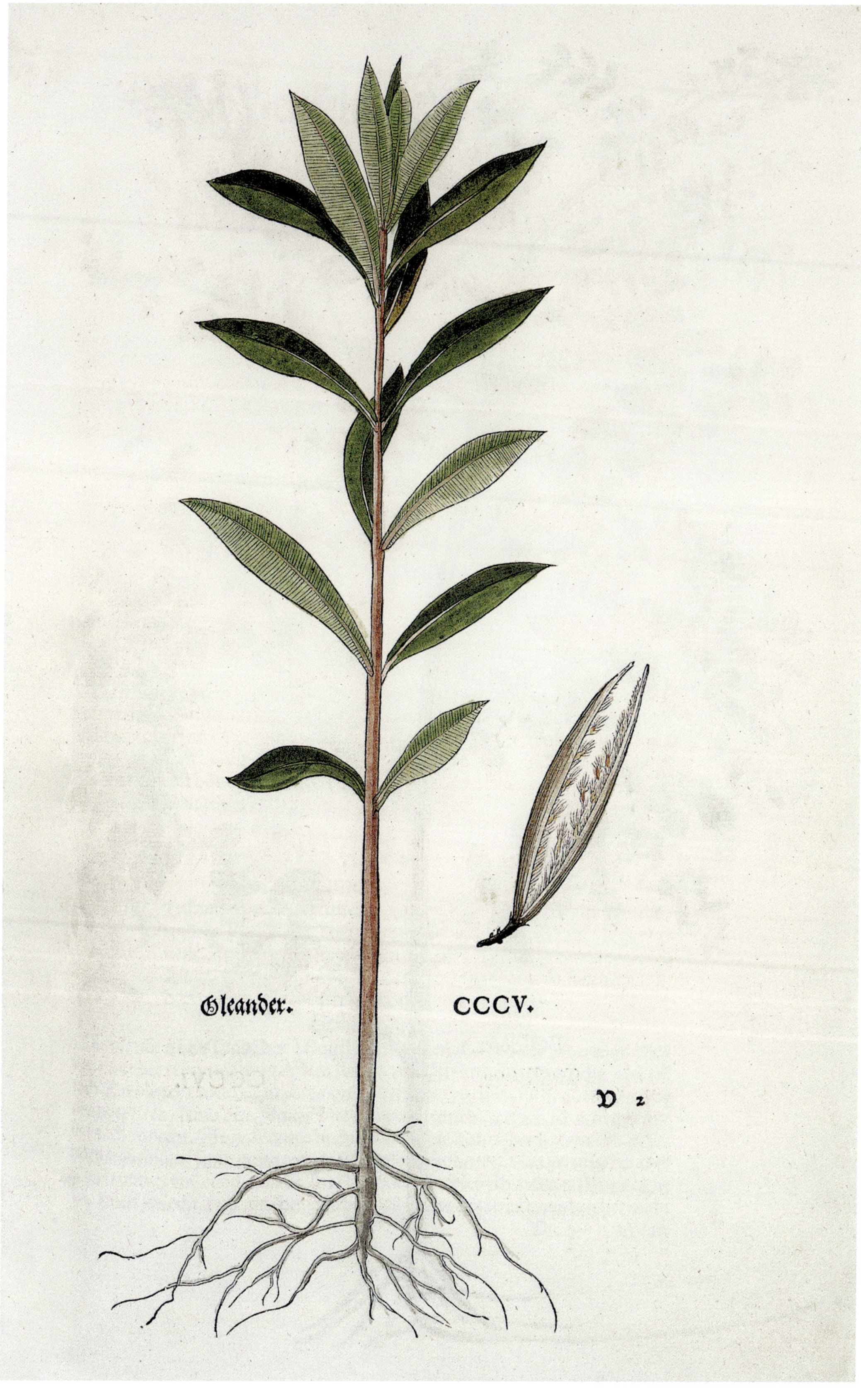

Oleander.
CCCV.
V 2

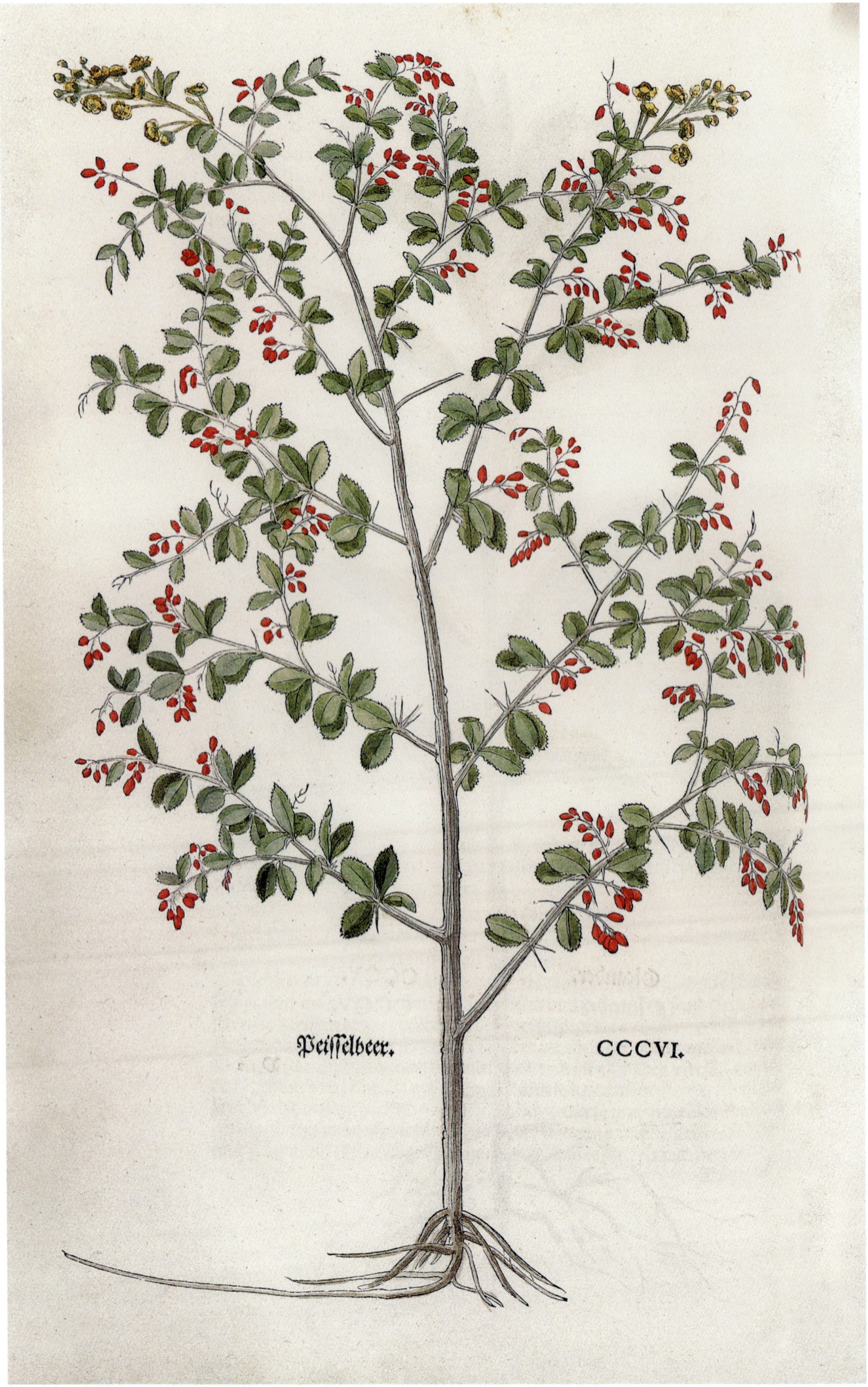
Peiſſelbeer.
CCCVI.

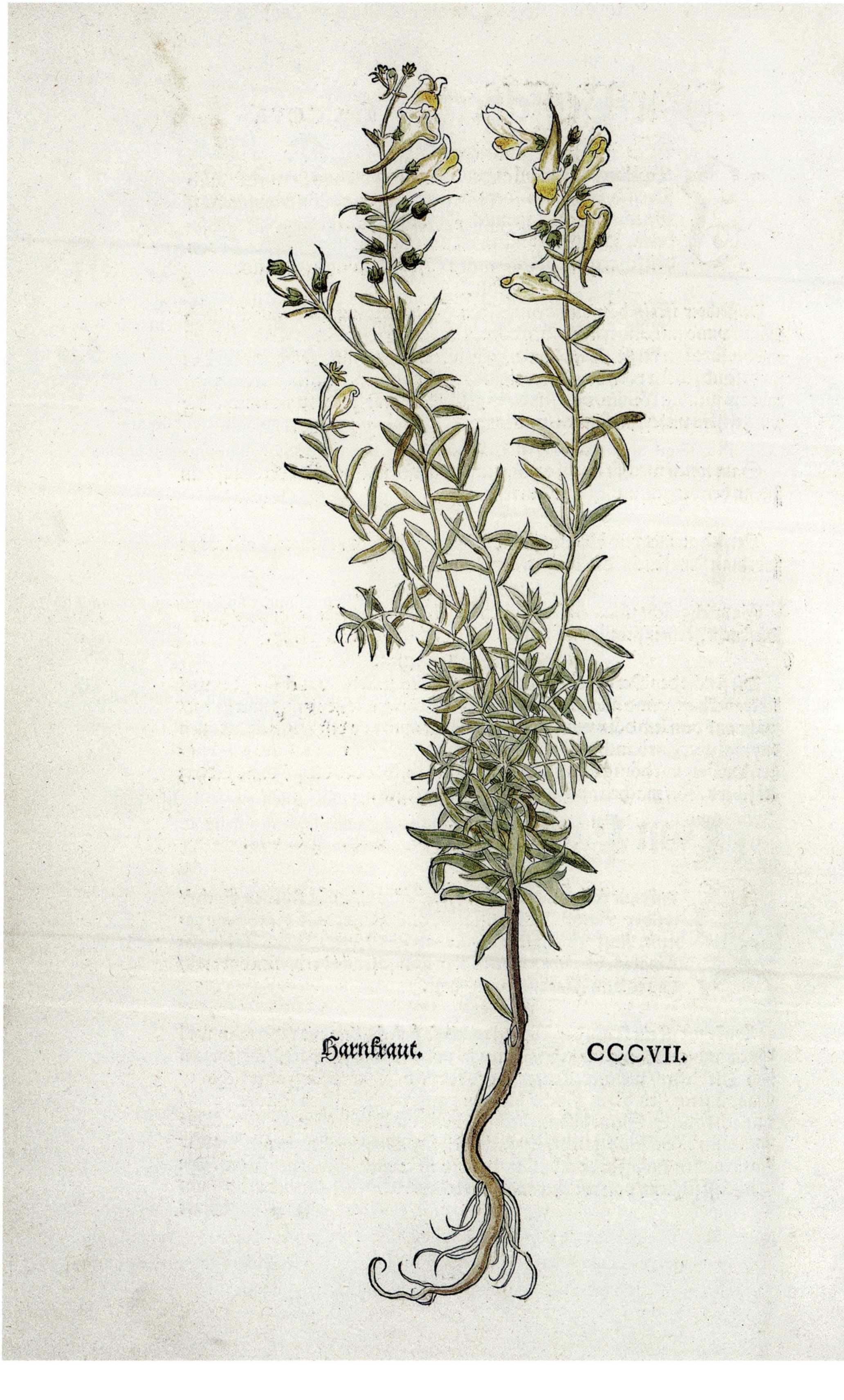
Harnkraut.
CCCVII.

BASIL

Three varieties of BASIL (CCVIII) are presented in this chapter. The name of this plant, famed through the ages, derives from the Greek word meaning "royal," and thus reflects the respect accorded to the plant at the time.

„BASILGRAM"

Drei Varietäten des Basilienkrauts werden im Kapitel „BASILGRAM" (Cap. CCVIII) vorgestellt. Im Namen dieser lange Zeit hochgerühmten Pflanze steckt das griechische Wort für „königlich" als Ausdruck der einstigen Wertschätzung.

BASILIC

Le BASILIC (CCVIII) figure sous trois formes différentes. Son nom vient du grec BASILISKOS qui signifie «petit roi», ce qui montre la haute estime dont jouissait la plante.

PAGE 410

MARJORAM

Fuchs mentions the strong odour of MARJORAM (CCIX); its many applications earned it the German name of "Wolgemut," suggesting its generally favourable effect.

„WOLGEMUT"

Studiert man die Anwendungsempfehlungen, die Fuchs für den Dost aufzählt, wundert es nicht, dass diese aromatisch riechende Pflanze den Namen „WOLGEMUT" (Cap. CCIX) erhielt.

ORIGAN

Le nom que Fuchs donne à l'ORIGAN (CCIX), «Wolgemut» (bien-être), ne surprend pas lorsqu'on lit les diverses indications de cette plante aromatique.

PAGE 411

ORCHIDS

Various ORCHIDS (CCX) – Early Purple, Green-winged, dark-winged (or burnt) and Pyramid – are included in this chapter. The testicle-shaped root was of course read as an unmistakable "signature" for the plant's effect.

KNABENKRAUT

Das Männliche, das Kleine und das Brand-Knabenkraut, aber auch die Hundswurz, eine andere Orchideenart, werden im Kapitel KNABENKRAUT (Cap. CCX) abgebildet. Der eigentümliche Name leitet sich von der hoden-ähnlich aussehenden Wurzel ab und galt natürlich als eindeutige Signatur für die Wirkung.

ORCHIDÉES

Le chapitre CCX est dédié aux ORCHIDÉES. L'orchis mâle, l'orchis bouffon et l'orchis brûlé y figurent aux côtés de l'orchis pyramidal, une autre espèce d'orchidée. Comme leur nom l'indique, ces plantes étaient censées avoir des vertus particulières à cause de leurs tubercules en forme de testicule (ORKHIS en grec).

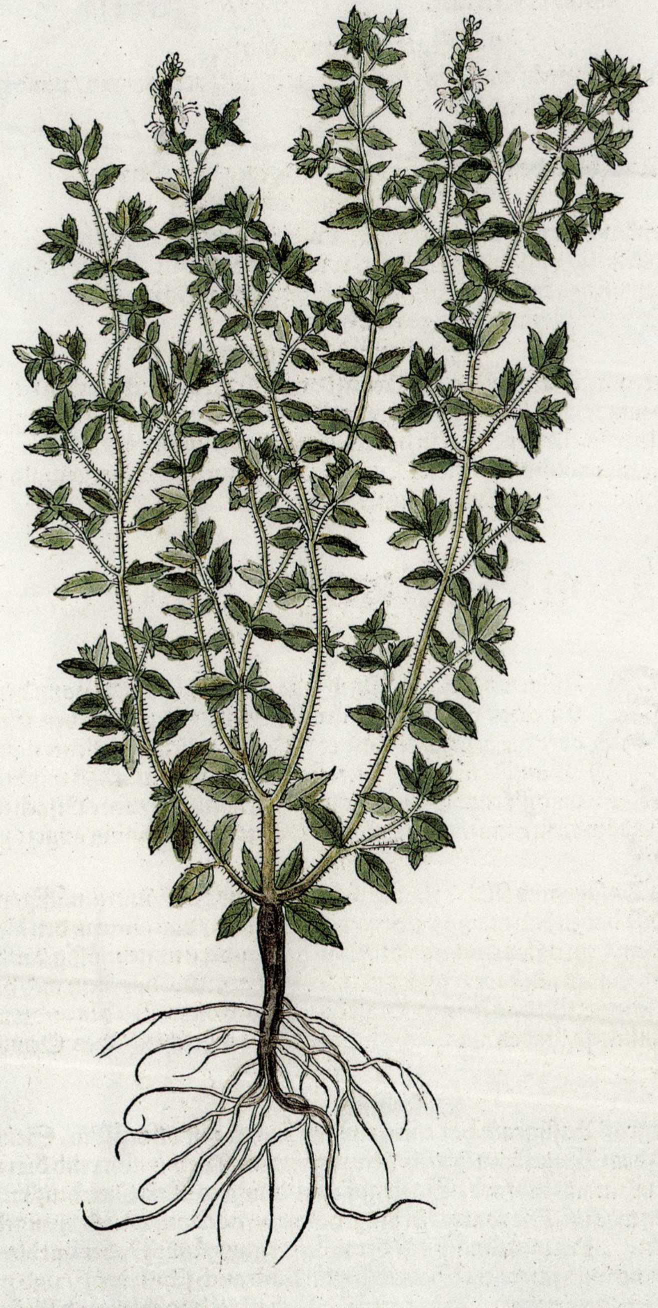

Klein Basilien. CCCVIII.

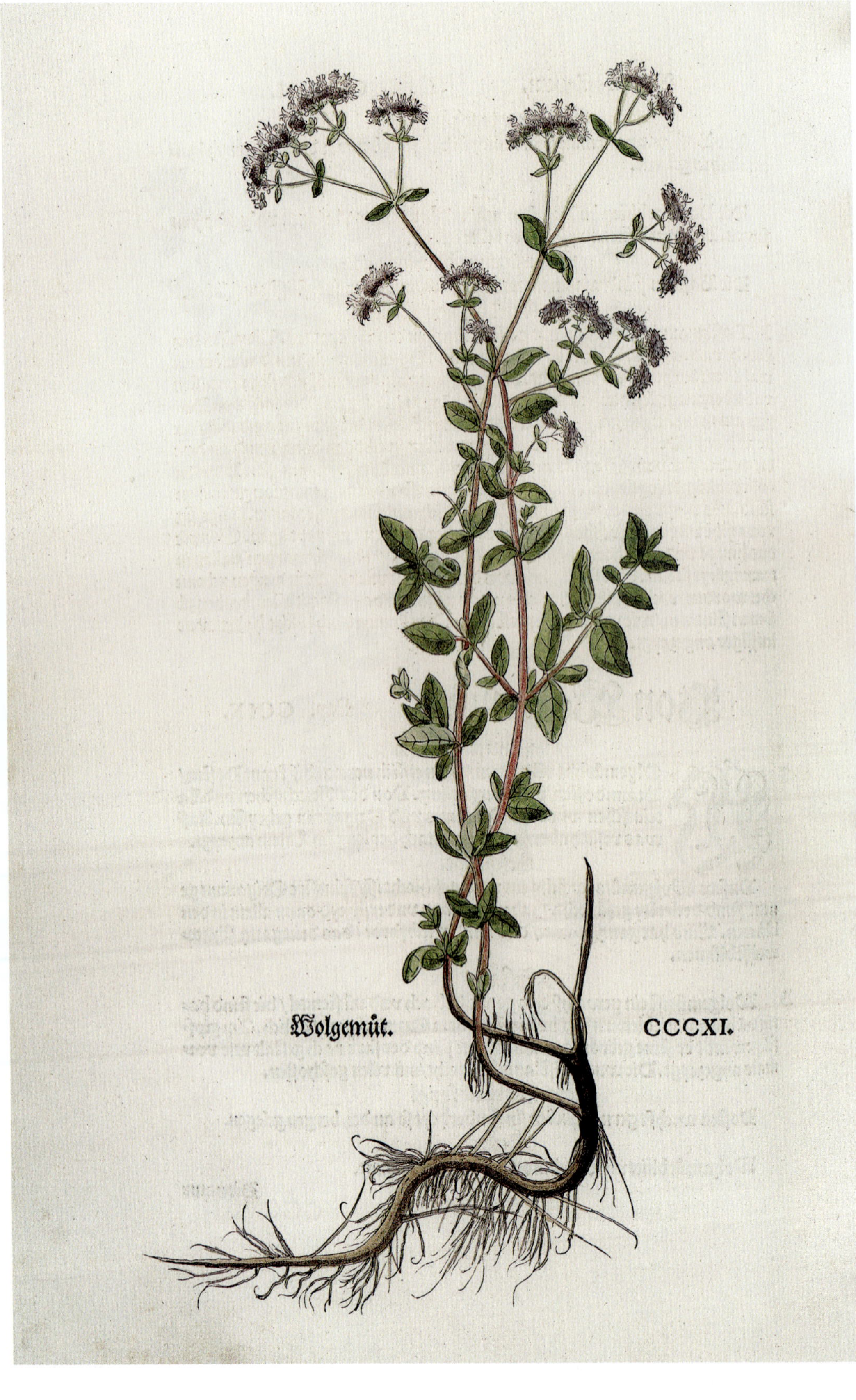
Wolgemût.
CCCXI.

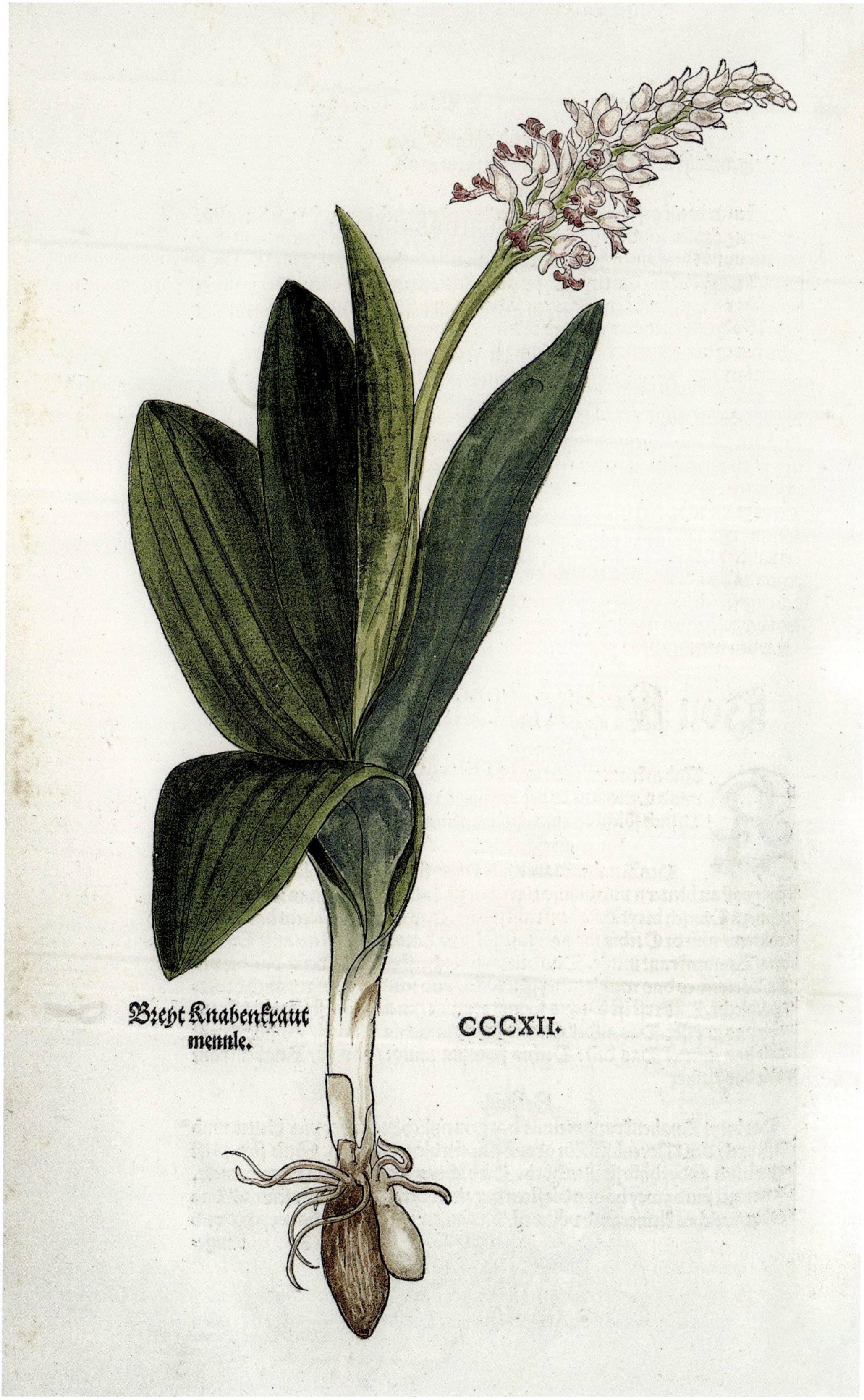
Breyt Knabenkraut
mennle.
CCCXII.

LATE SPIDER ORCHID

Other orchids include the bee and the LATE SPIDER ORCHID (CCXI). The mucilage contained in the root tubers of the GREEN-WINGED ORCHID (plate CCCXVII) is the effective component in both external and internal applications of the plant.

„RAGWURTZ“

Ebenfalls zu den Orchideen zählt die „RAGWURTZ“ (Cap. CCXI), bei deren äußerlicher und innerlicher Anwendung der in den Wurzelknollen des SALEP-KNABENKRAUTS (Taf. CCCXVII) enthaltene Pflanzenschleim zur Geltung kommt.

OPHRYS BOURDON

L'OPHRYS BOURDON (CCXI) compte aussi parmi les orchidées. Toutes sont utilisées en usage externe et interne parce qu'elles renferment divers agents actifs, dont le salep, substance mucilagineuse extraite des bulbes de l'ORCHIS BOUFFON (pl. CCCXVII).

PAGE 414

DROPWORT

According to the ancient doctors, DROPWORT (CCXII) supposedly broke up urinary stones.

STEINBRECH

Der STEINBRECH (Cap. CCXII) sollte nach Anschauung der alten Ärzte seinem Namen alle Ehre machen und auch Blasensteine zerkleinern.

FILIPENDULE VULGAIRE

La FILIPENDULE VULGAIRE (CCXII) est représentée ici sous le nom de «Steinbrech» ou casse-pierre, car, dans la médecine ancienne, on prêtait à cette plante le pouvoir de détruire les calculs.

PAGE 415

WOOD-SORREL

The somewhat toxic WOOD-SORREL (CCXIII), which in English as well as German was known under a variety of names, today finds application only in homeopathic medicine.

„BUCHAMPFFER“

Reizvoll ist es, die verschiedenen Namen des „BUCHAMPFFER“ (Cap. CCXIII) zu lesen, den wir heute Sauerklee nennen. Die nicht ungiftige Pflanze findet heute nur noch in der Homöopathie vereinzelt Anwendung.

PAIN-DE-COUCOU

C'est un plaisir de lire les noms donnés par Fuchs au PAIN-DE-COUCOU (CCXIII). Cet oxalis, appelé de nos jours «Sauerklee» (trèfle acide, à cause du goût acidulé de ses feuilles) est assez toxique et complètement inusité aujourd'hui, sauf parfois en homéopathie.

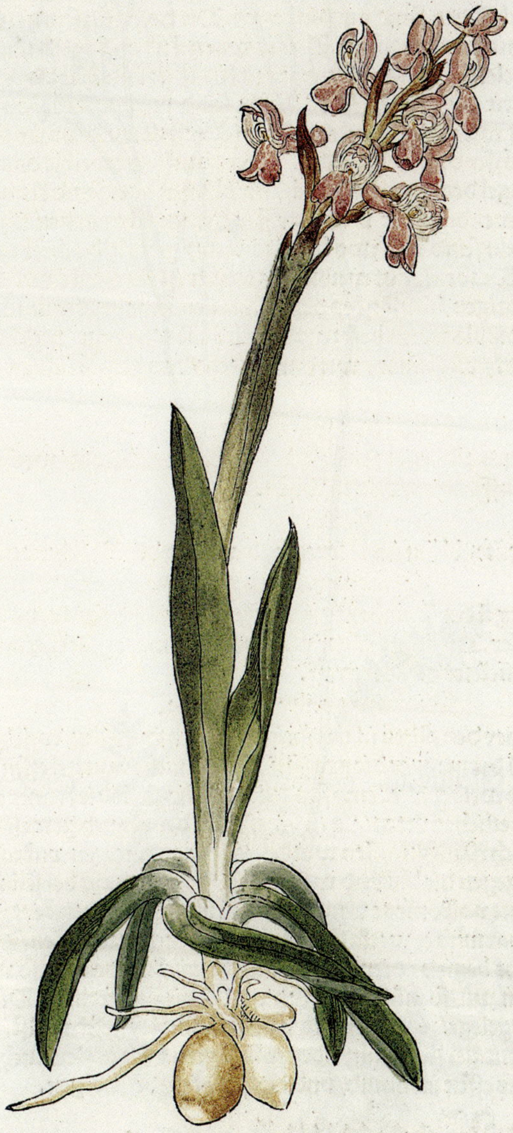

Ragwurtz mennle. CCCXVII.

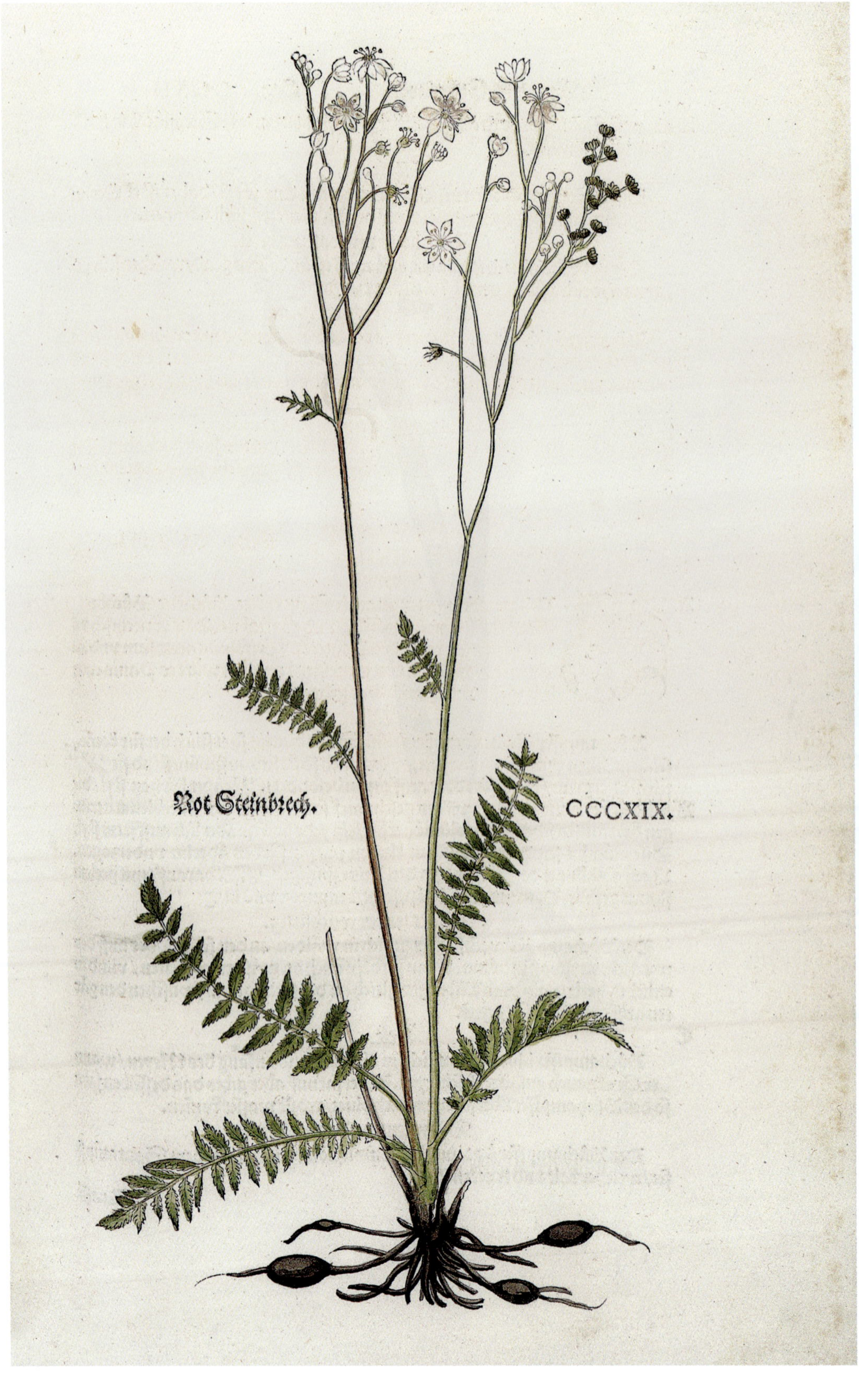
Rot Steinbrech.
CCCXIX.

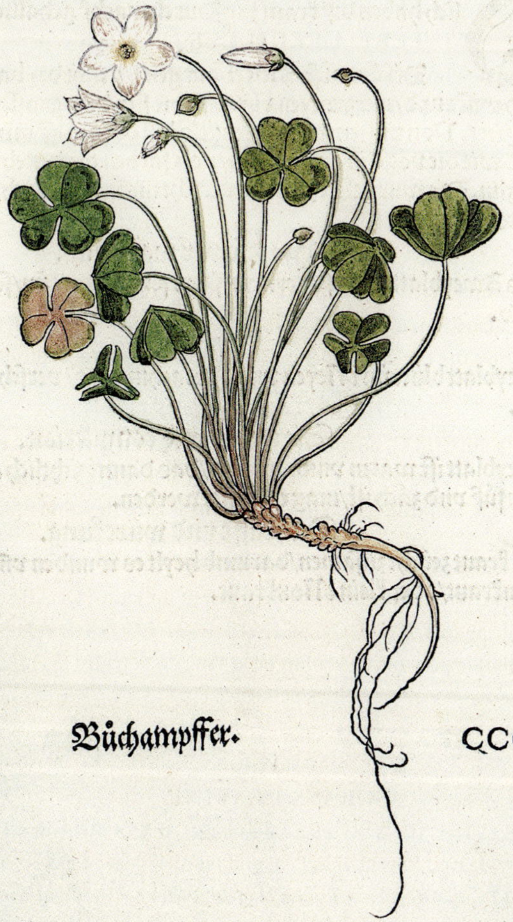

Büchampffer. CCCXX.

R

COMMON TWAYBLADE

COMMON TWAYBLADE (CCXIIII), which received short shrift from Fuchs, plays an insignificant role in medicine today.

„ZWEYBLATT"

Das „ZWEYBLATT" (Cap. CCXIIII), zu dem Fuchs nur wenig anmerkt, spielte in der Medizin keine nennenswerte Rolle.

LISTÈRE À FEUILLES OVALES

Fuchs dit très peu de choses sur la LISTÈRE À FEUILLES OVALES (CCXIIII), car elle ne jouait qu'un rôle très annexe en médecine.

PAGE 418

CLARY SAGE

In the CLARY chapter (CCXV), CLARY SAGE, or CLARY (plate CCCXXII) and MEADOW SAGE, also known as MEADOW CLARY (plate CCCXXIII) were supposed to improve the eyesight, disperse tumours and extract splinters.

SCHARLACH (SALBEI)

Als SCHARLACH (Cap. CCXV), abgeleitet vom lateinischen „sclareia", bezeichnete man verschiedene Salbei-Arten. MUSKATELLER-SALBEI (Taf. CCCXXII) und WIESEN-SALBEI (Taf. CCCXXIII) sollen die Sehkraft stärken, Geschwülste zerteilen und Splitter herausziehen.

SCLAREIA

Le terme allemand « SCHARLACH » (CCXC) provient du latin SCLAREIA et correspond à différentes variétés de sauge. LA SAUGE SCLARÉE (pl. CCCXXII) et la SAUGE DES PRÉS (pl. CCCXXIII) auraient le pouvoir de renforcer la vue, de détruire les tumeurs et d'extraire les échardes.

PAGE 419

GRASS PEAVINE

Although GRASS PEAVINE (CCXVI), also known as GRASS-PEA or CHICKLING PEA, together with Narrow-leaved Everlasting Pea, and Narrow-leaved Everlasting Pea, was still unrecognized by apothecaries, Fuchs ascribes various medical uses to them.

„ERVEN"

Obwohl die „ERVEN" (Cap. CCXVI) in den Apotheken nicht bekannt waren, gibt Fuchs für die Platterbsen verschiedene medizinische Einsatzmöglichkeiten an.

GESSES

Bien qu'inconnues dans les officines d'apothicaires, les GESSES – « Erven » dans le texte (CCXVI) – n'en ont pas moins des propriétés que Fuchs mentionne ici.

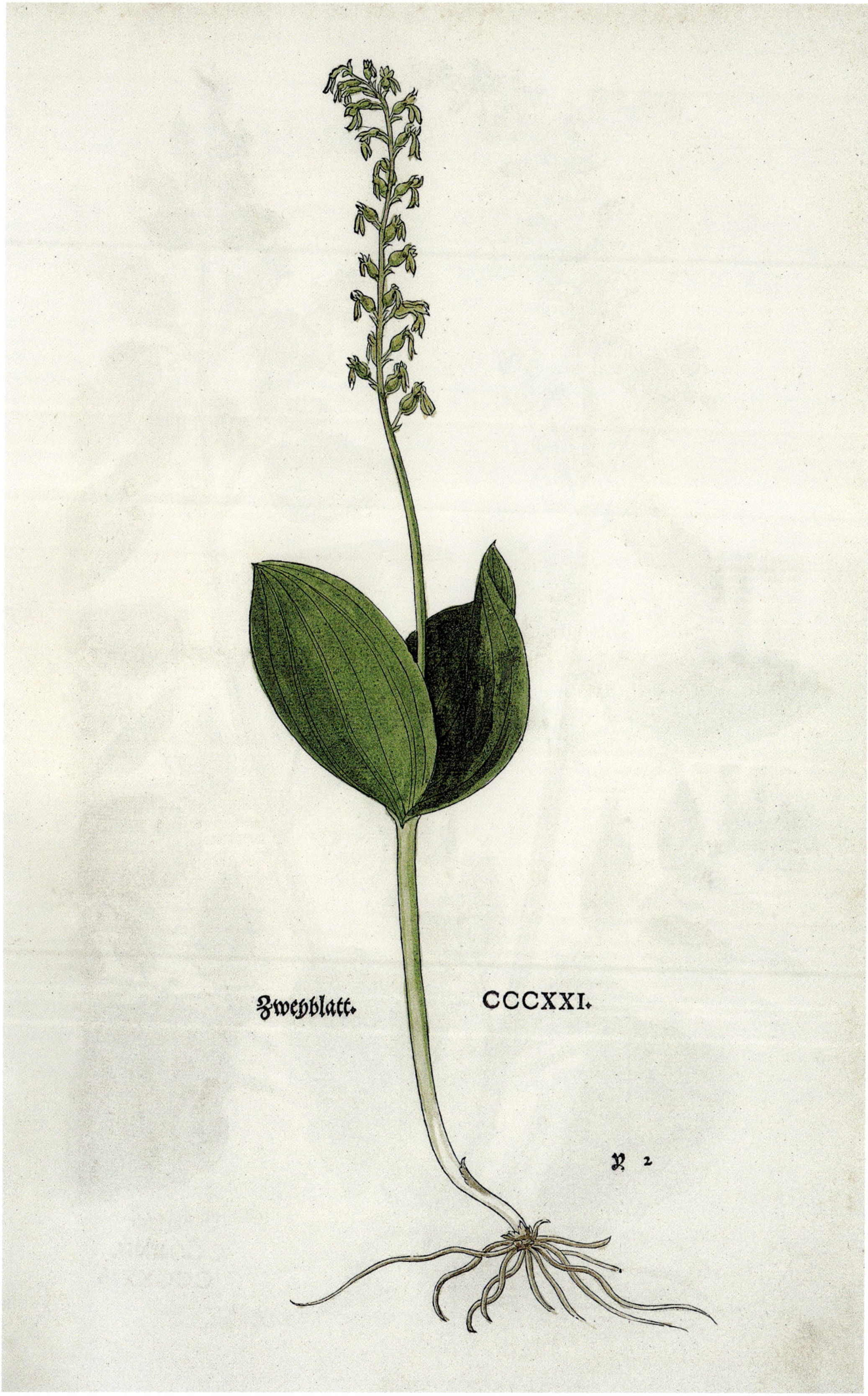
Zweyblatt.
CCCXXI.

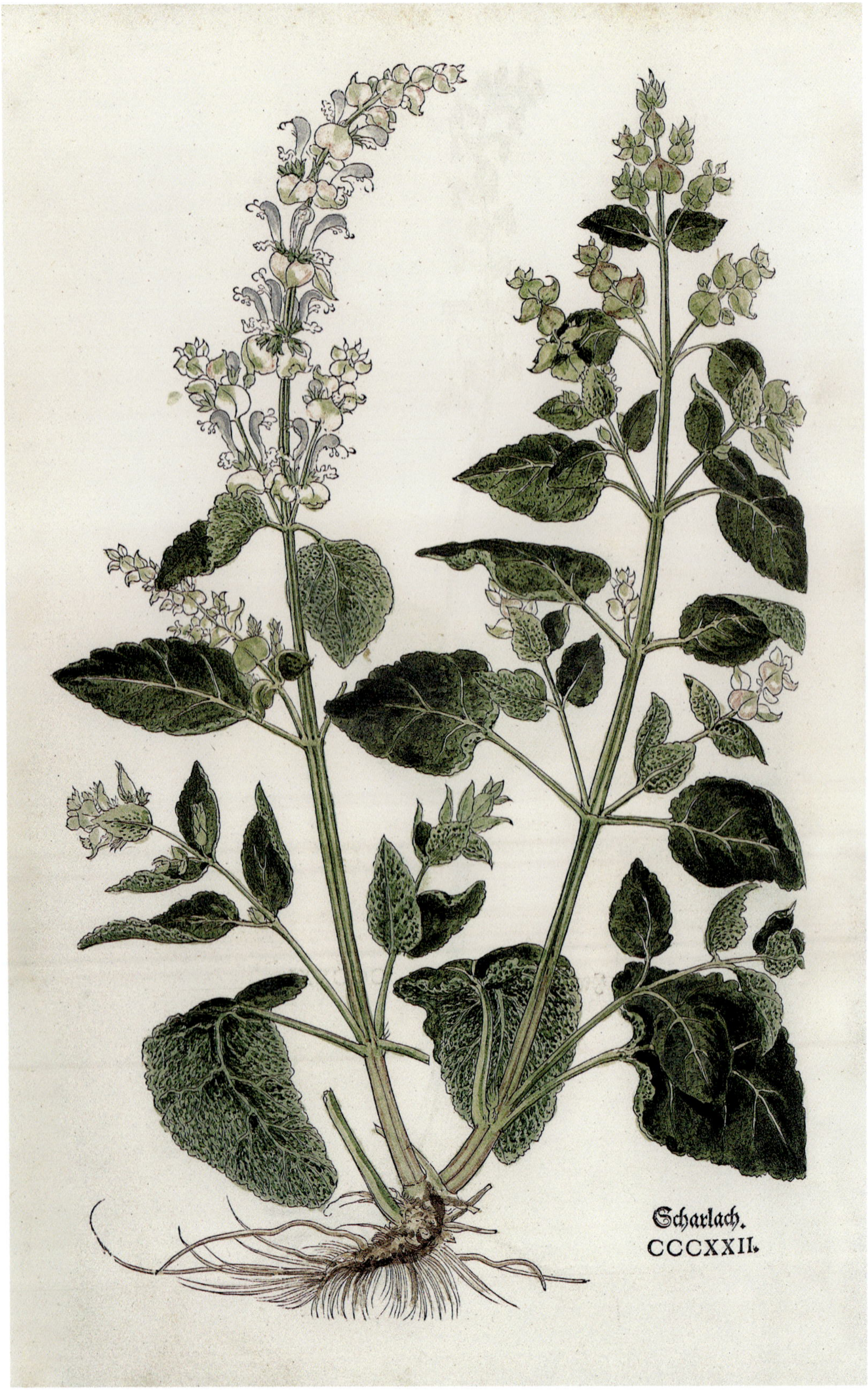
Scharlach.
CCCXXII.

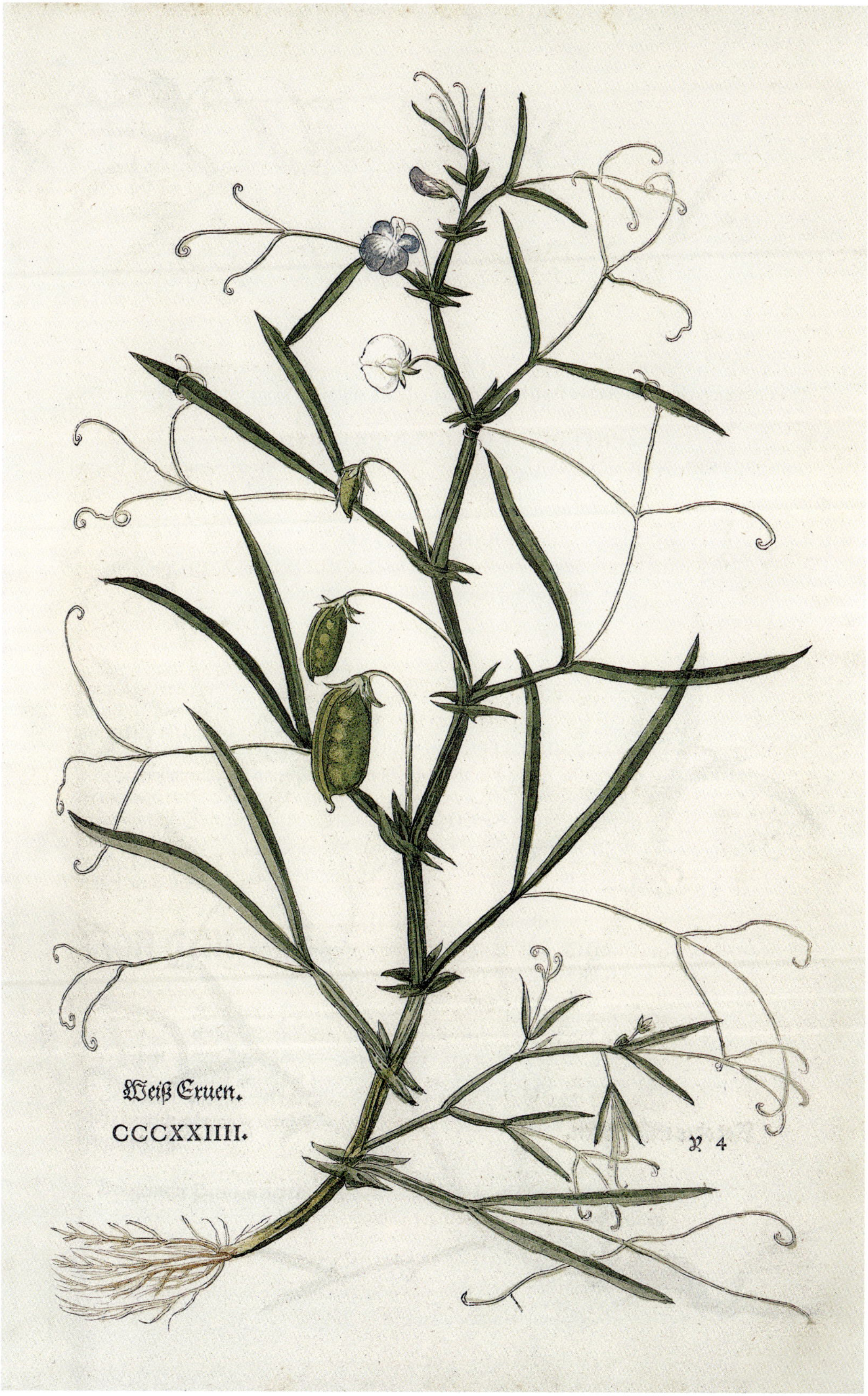
Weiß Eruen.
CCCXXIIII.
R 4

PARSLEY

The herbage, seeds and root of PARSLEY (CCXVII) are still used today for their diuretic effect.

„PETERLIN" (GARTEN-PETERSILIE)

Vom „PETERLIN" (Cap. CCXVII), der Garten-Petersilie, werden Kraut, Samen und Wurzel auch heute noch wegen ihrer entwässernden Wirkung verwendet.

PERSIL CULTIVÉ

La partie verte, les graines et la racine du PERSIL CULTIVÉ (CCXVII) s'utilisent aujourd'hui encore comme diurétique.

PAGE 422

SORB APPLE

Although the fruits of the SORB APPLE, or SERVICE TREE (CCXVIII), are edible, Fuchs sees their value instead in their medicinal application for diarrhoea.

SPEIERLING

Die Früchte des SPEIERLINGS (Cap. CCXVIII) sind zwar essbar, ihr Wert liegt für Fuchs aber in der arzneilichen Anwendung bei Durchfall.

BAIES DE CORMIER

Les BAIES DE CORMIER (CCXVIII) sont certes comestibles, mais Fuchs s'intéresse avant tout à leurs propriétés antidiarrhéiques.

PAGE 423

ADDER'S TONGUE

ADDER'S TONGUE (CCXIX) appears as a vulnerary; Fuchs also remarks that it was commonly to be found around Tübingen.

„NATERZÜNGLIN"

Als Wundkraut wird das „NATERZÜNGLIN" (Cap. CCXIX) beschrieben und sein häufiges Vorkommen bei Tübingen erwähnt.

LANGUE-DE-SERPENT

La LANGUE-DE-SERPENT (CCXIX) est décrite comme une plante cicatrisante, croissant dans les environs de Tübingen.

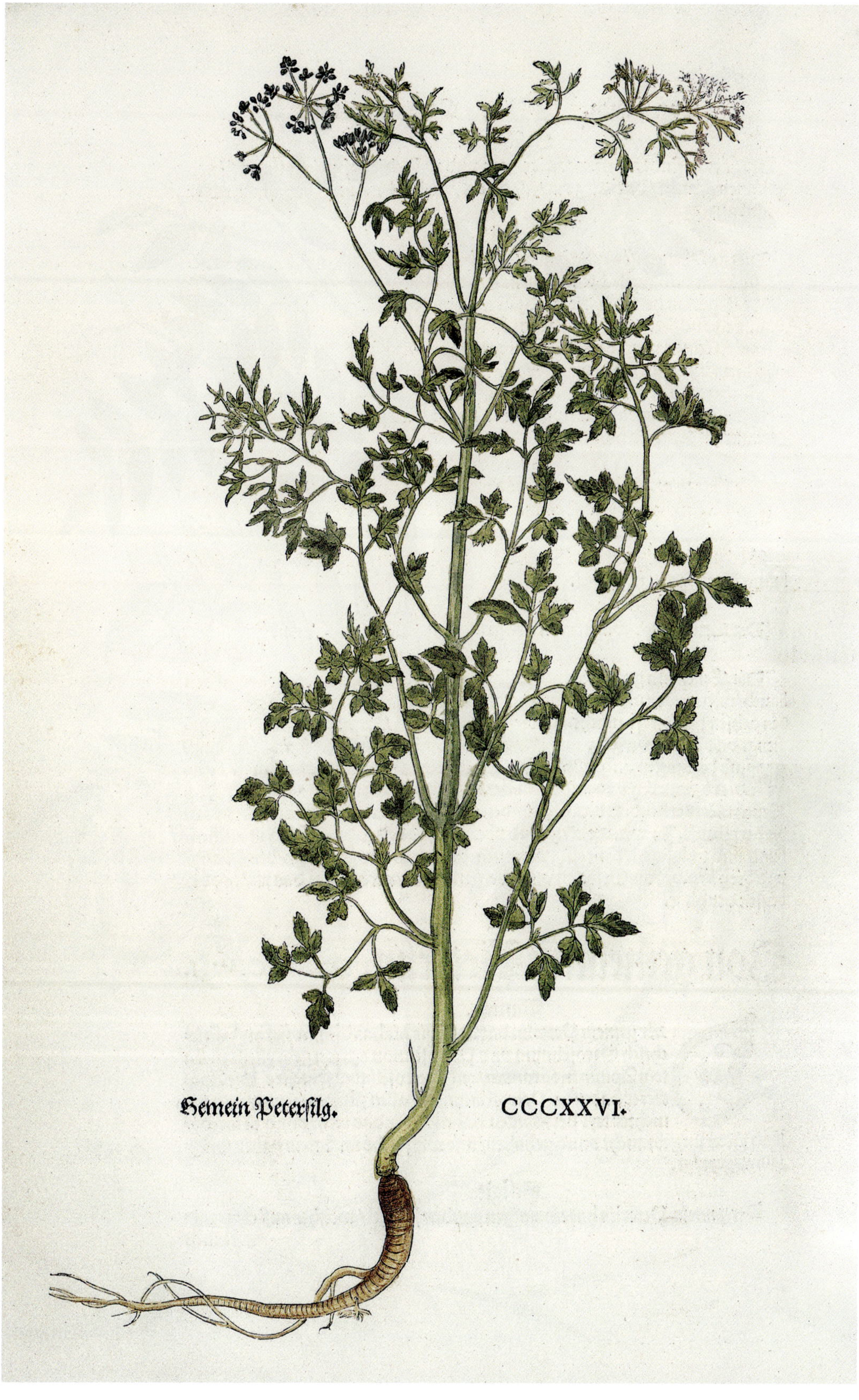

Gemein Peterſilg. CCCXXVI.

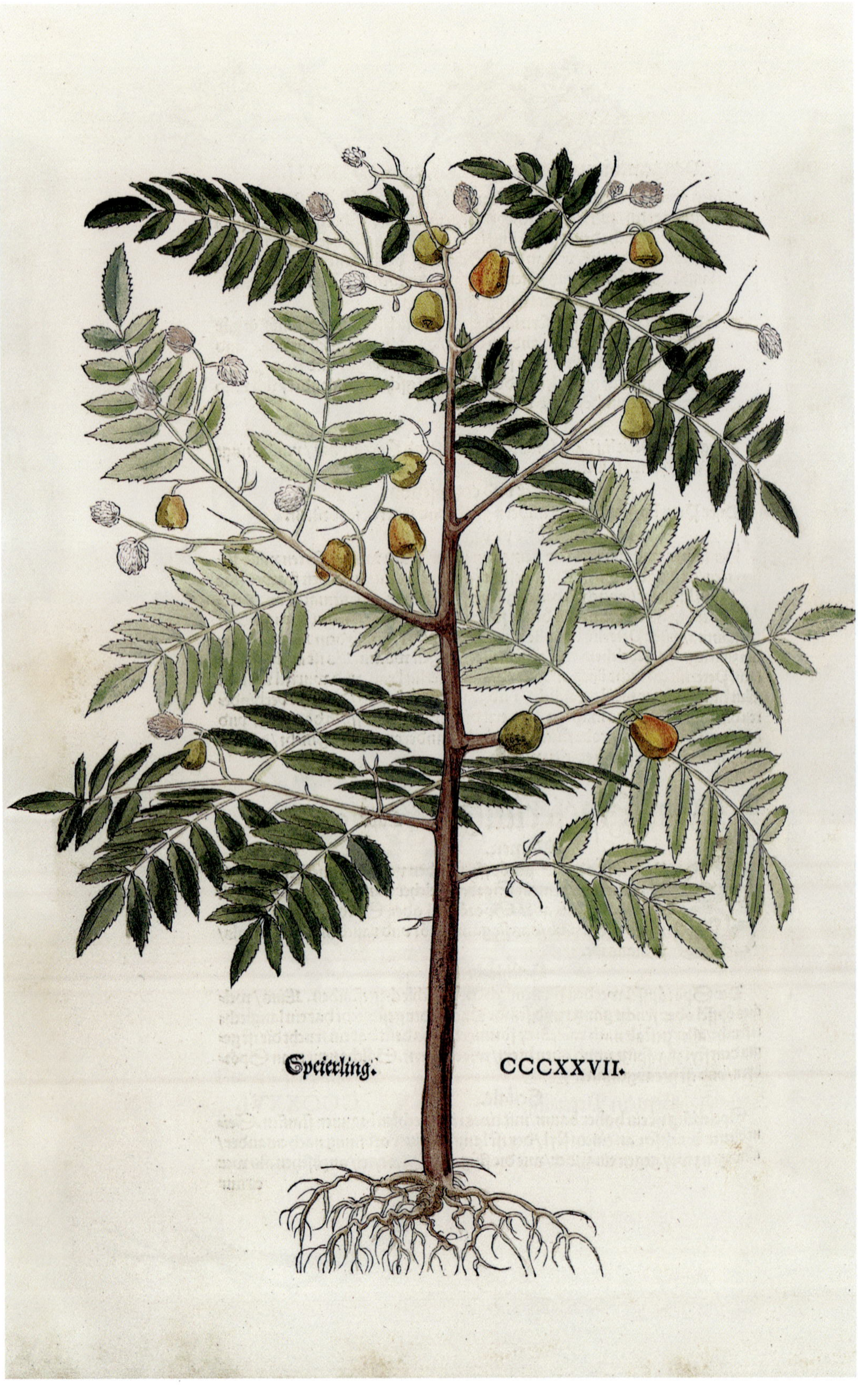
Speierling.
CCCXXVII.

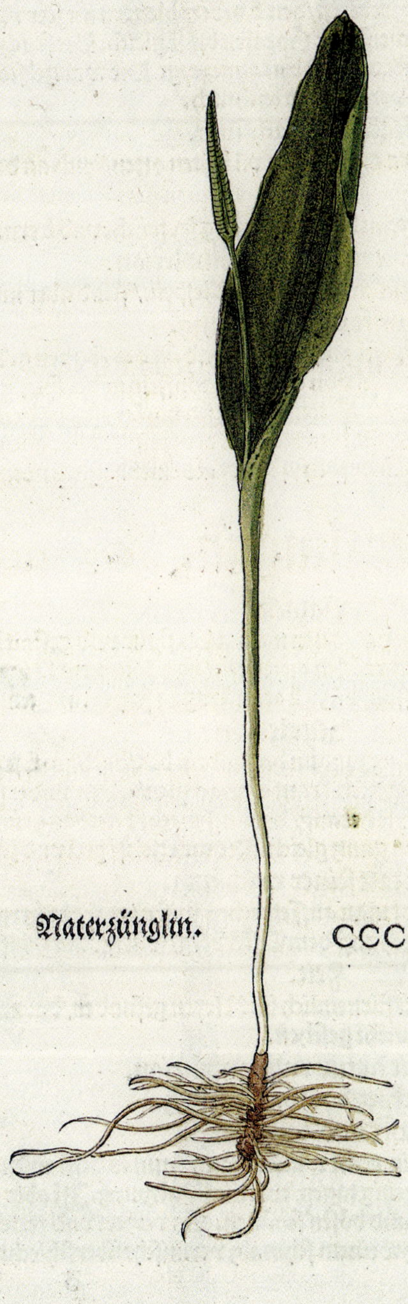

Naterzünglin. CCCXXVIII.

COCKLEBUR

The barbed fruits of COCKLEBUR (CCXX) cling to the clothing like lice to beggars – an action reflected in the plant's old German name meaning "Beggar's Lice."

„BETTLERSLEUSS"

So wie die Läuse auf den Bettlern bleiben die Klettenfrüchte der „BETTLERSLEUSS" (Cap. CCXX) an der Kleidung der Vorbeigehenden hängen.

LAMPOURDE GLOUTERON

Les fruits épineux de la LAMPOURDE GLOUTERON (CCXX) s'accrochent aux vêtements comme les poux sur les mendiants, d'où le nom de «Bettlersleuß» ou pou à mendiant donné à la plante.

PAGE 426

LEVANT COTTON

The seed hairs of common or LEVANT COTTON (CCXXI), were not yet formed into wads; instead, Fuchs recommends the leaf, seeds and seed oil as medicines.

BAUMWOLLE

Von der BAUMWOLLE (Cap. CCXXI) werden noch nicht die Samenhaare als Watte verwendet, sondern der Saft der Blätter, die Samen und das Samenöl als Arznei empfohlen.

COTONNIER

Les poils soyeux des graines du COTONNIER (CCXXI) n'ont pas encore trouvé d'application à cette époque, mais le suc des feuilles, les graines ainsi que l'huile qu'on en extrait s'utilisent en médecine.

PAGE 427

STINKING MAYWEED

In earlier times, physicians used STINKING MAYWEED (CCXXII), also known as stinking chamomile and mugwort, for the elimination of mucous and black bile.

„KROTTENDILL"

Den „KROTTENDILL" (Cap. CCXXII), den wir heute als Stinkende Hundskamille bezeichnen, setzten die Ärzte früher u. a. zum Ausführen des Schleims und der Schwarzen Galle ein.

CAMOMILLE DES CHIENS

Autrefois, les médecins recouraient à la CAMOMILLE DES CHIENS (CCXXII), appelée «Krottendill» dans le texte, pour faciliter l'excrétion des mucosités et de la bile noire.

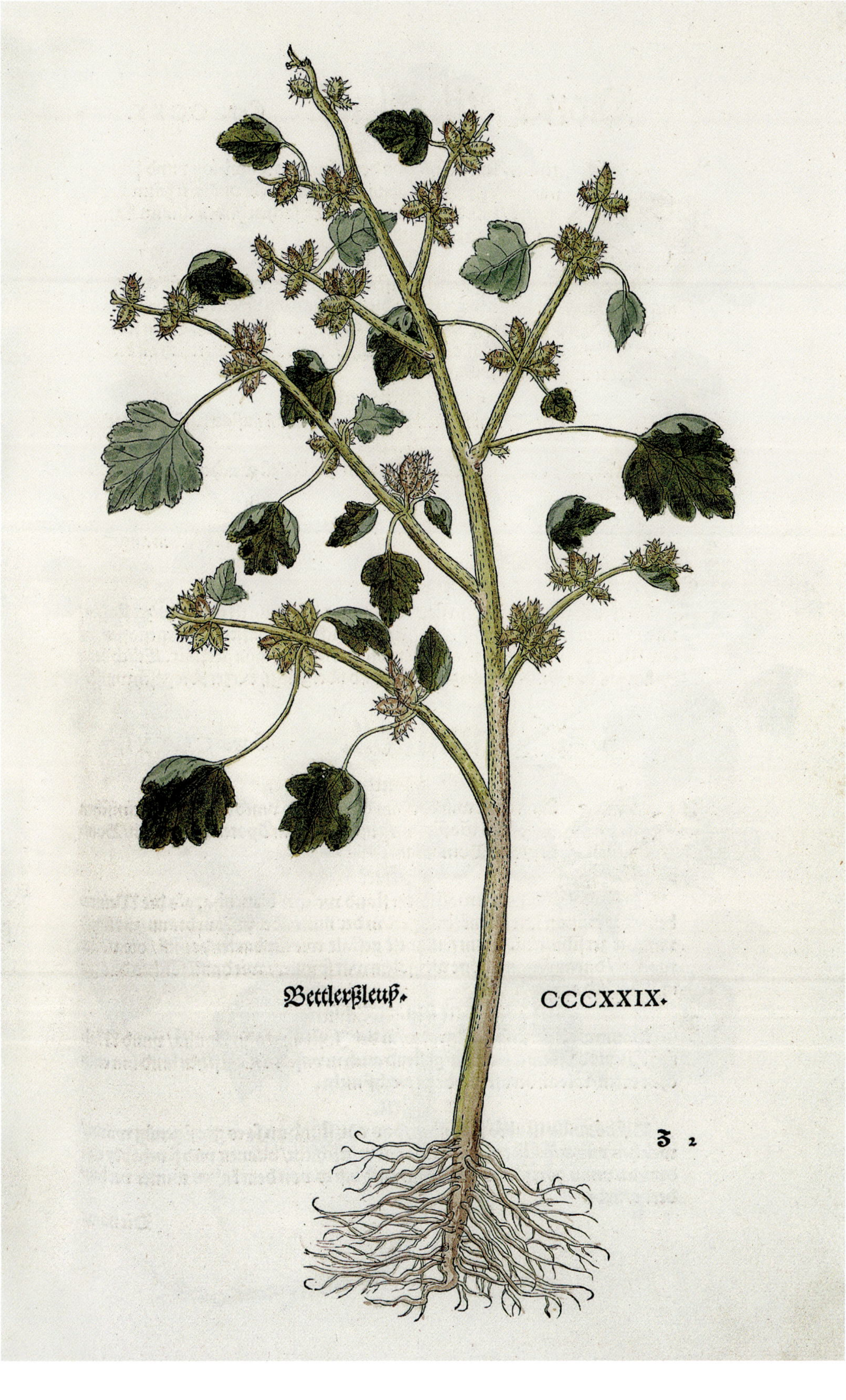
Bettlerßleuß.
CCCXXIX.
Z 2

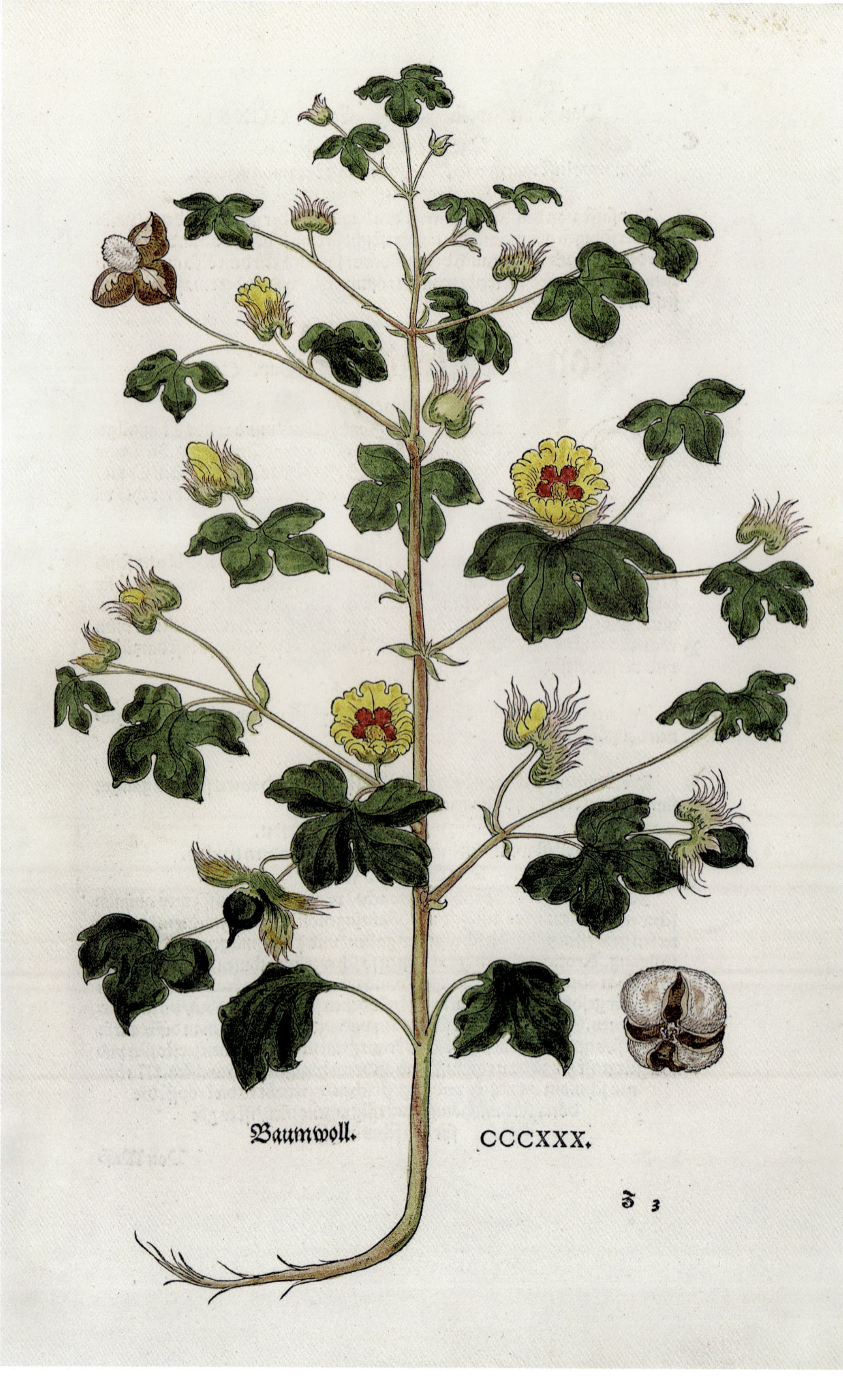
Baumwoll.
CCCXXX.
Z 3

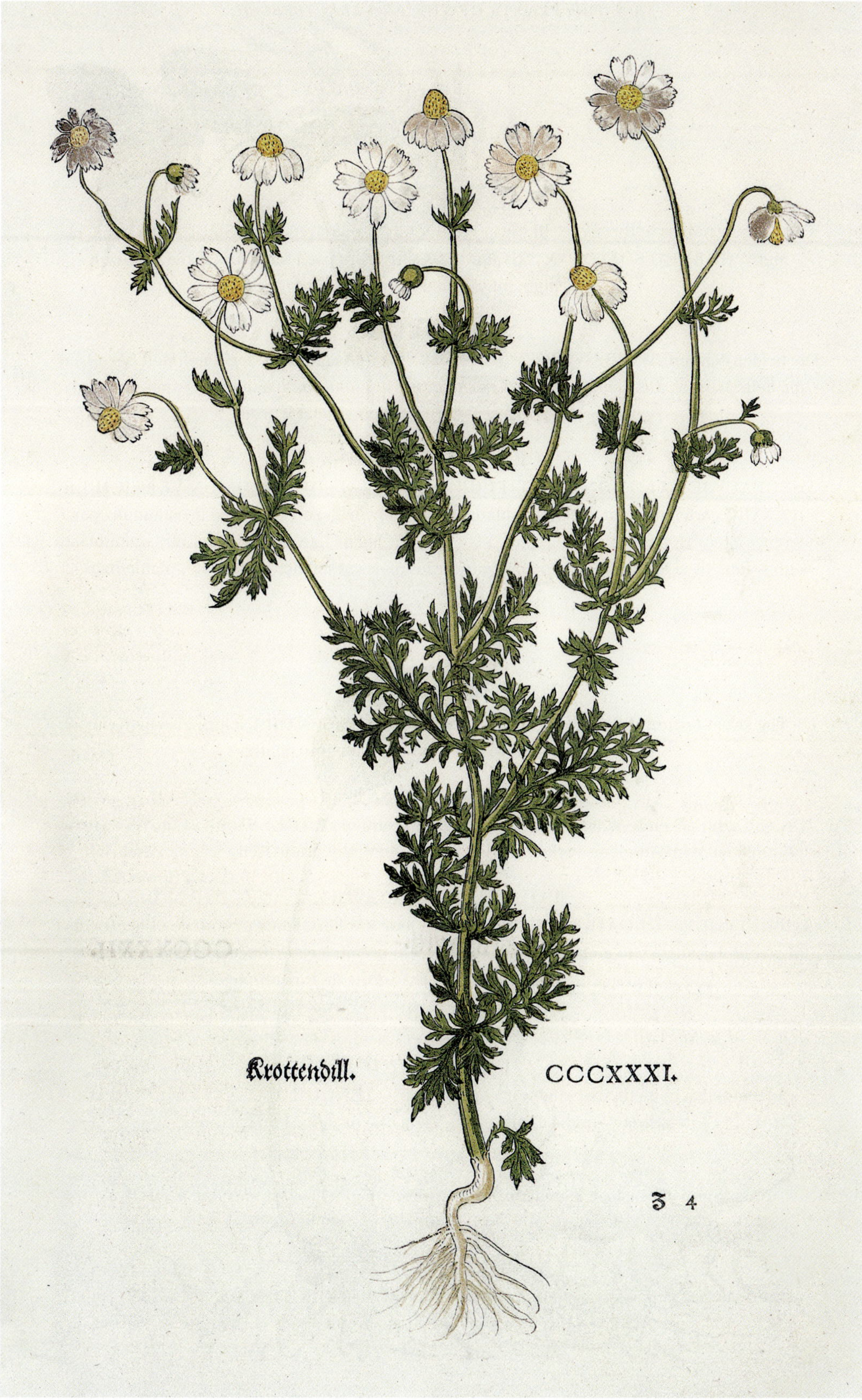
Krottendill.
CCCXXXI.
Z 4

SOLOMON'S SEAL

Owing their names to the signet-like scars in their light-coloured roots, SOLOMON'S SEAL and WHORLED SOLOMON'S SEAL (CCXXIII) were used for wounds and localized pigment disorders of the skin.

„WEISSWURTZ"

Die beiden Namen „WEISSWURTZ" (Cap. CCXXIII) und Salomonssiegel nehmen Bezug auf die helle Wurzel, die siegelähnliche Narben aufweist und deshalb auch als Wundkraut und bei fleckigen Pigmentstörungen eingesetzt wurde.

SCEAU-DE-SALOMON

Le SCEAU-DE-SALOMON MULTIFLORE et le SCEAU-DE-SALOMON VERTICILLÉ (CCXXIII) portent le nom de «racine blanche» («Weißwurtz») ou de «sceau de Salomon» par référence à leur rhizome blanchâtre qui, à la chute de chaque tige, garde une cicatrice semblable à un sceau. Aussi les utilisait-on pour cicatriser les plaies et soigner les troubles pigmentaires.

PAGE 430

COMMON POLYPODY

The sweet-tasting rhizome of COMMON POLYPODY (CCXXIIII), a fern also native to Tübingen, was said to possess great healing qualities.

„ENGELSSÜSS"

Der süß schmeckende Wurzelstock führte zu dem Namen „ENGELSÜSS" (Cap. CCXXIIII) für den auch in Tübingen vorkommenden Farn, dem man große Heilwirkung zuschrieb.

POLYPODE VULGAIRE

Le POLYPODE VULGAIRE (CCXXIIII), ou réglisse des bois, doit son nom de «Engelssüß» (douceur des anges) au goût sucré de sa racine. On prêtait à cette fougère, habitant aussi la région de Tübingen, de grandes vertus thérapeutiques.

PAGE 431

HOREHOUND

A lengthy list of medicinal effects accompanies HOREHOUND (CCXXV); nonetheless, its primary application was for bronchial problems and asthma.

ANDORN

Auch wenn die Liste der medizinischen Anwendungen lang ist, war der ANDORN (Cap. CCXXV) in erster Linie ein Heilmittel bei Bronchialleiden und Asthma.

MARRUBE COMMUN

La liste de ses indications est longue, pourtant le MARRUBE COMMUN (CCXXV) était surtout utilisé pour traiter les affections bronchiques et l'asthme.

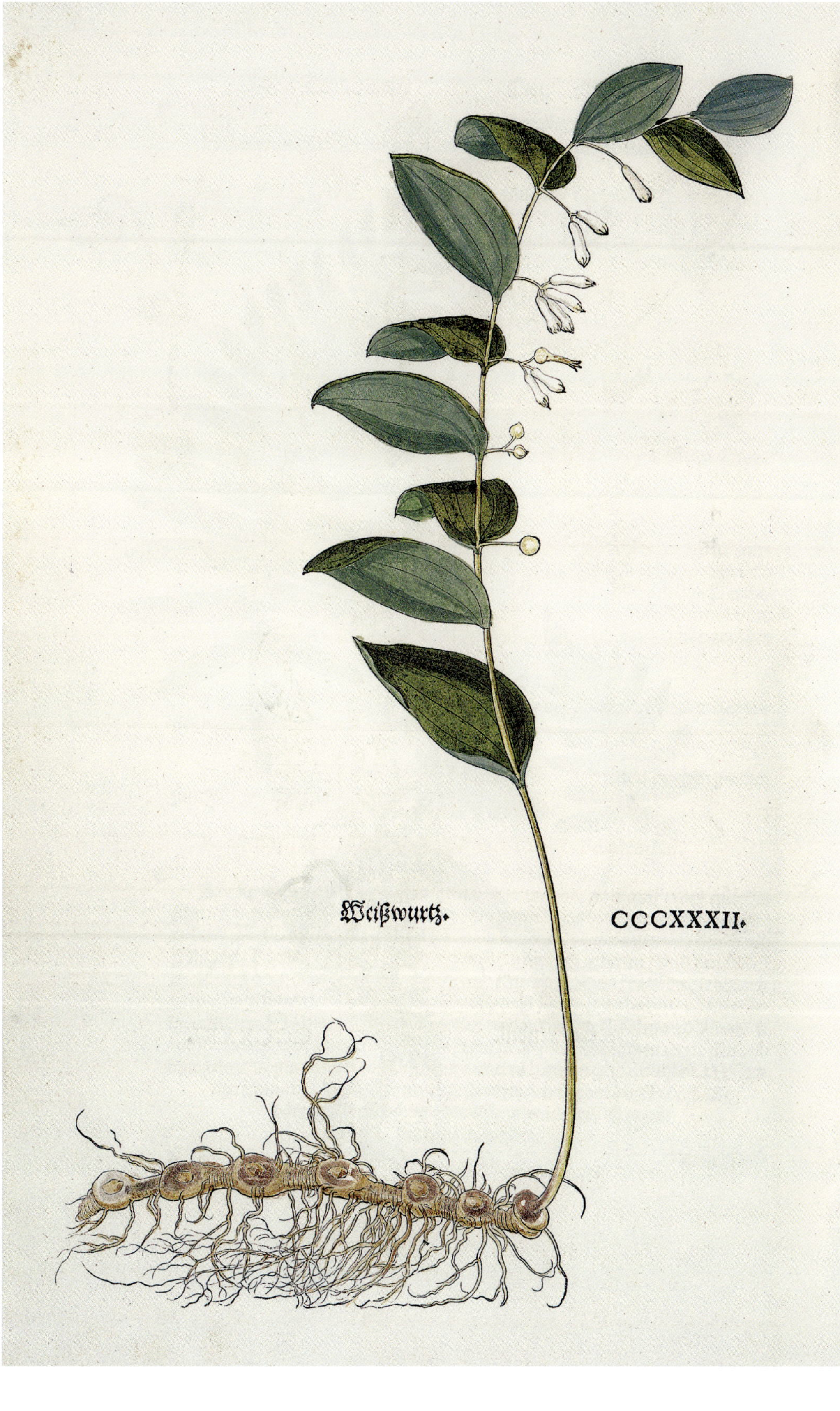
Weißwurtz.
CCCXXXII.

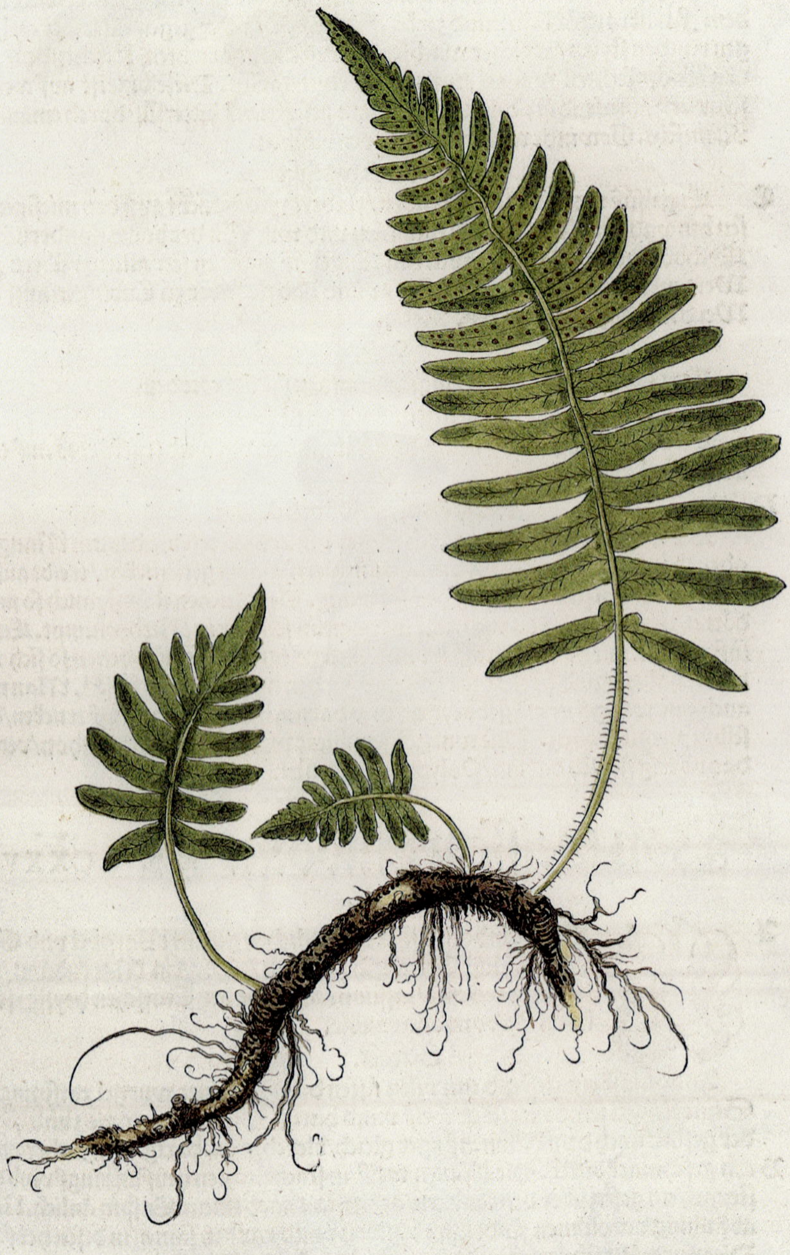

Engelſüß. CCCXXXIIII.

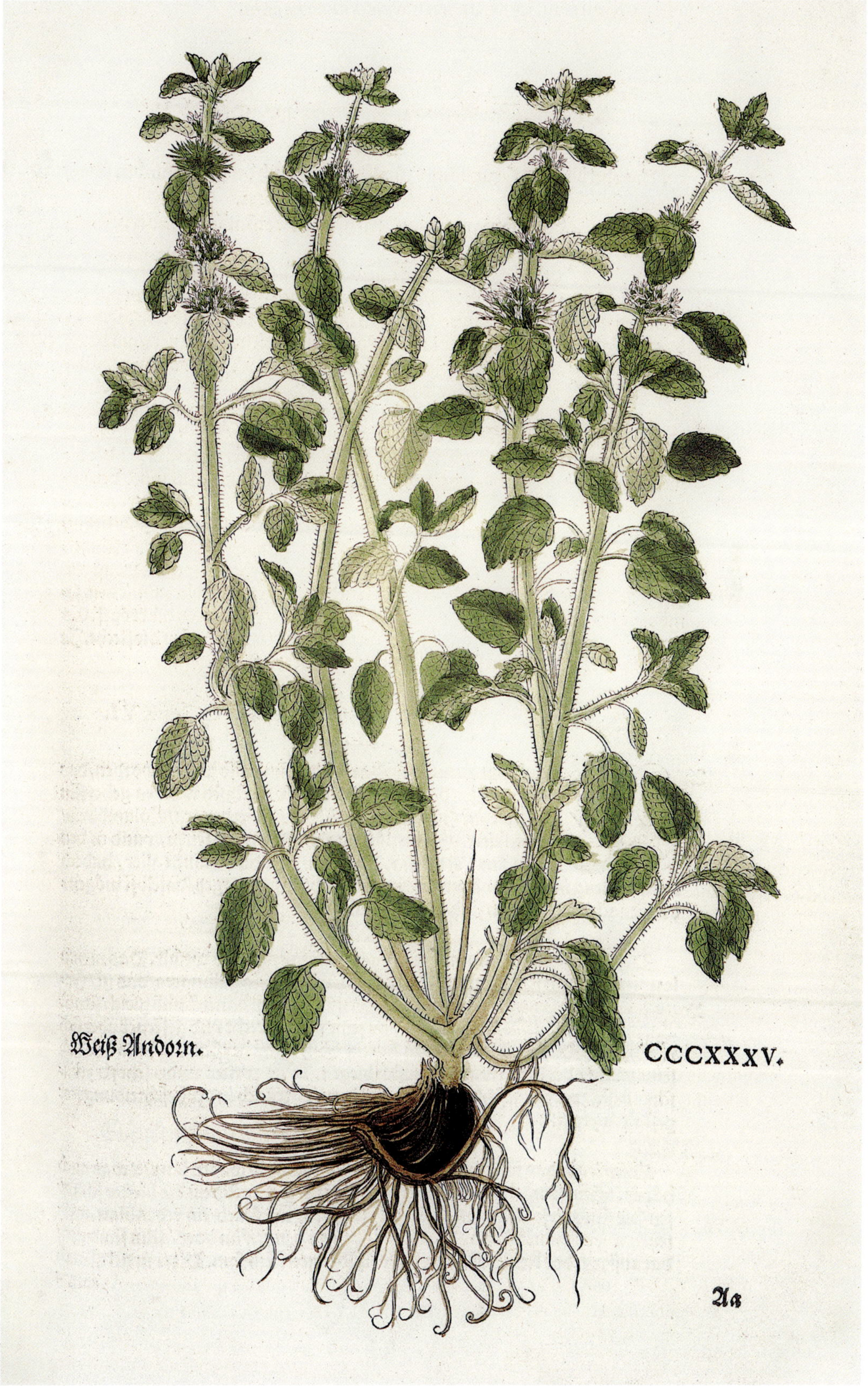
Weiß Andorn.
CCCXXXV.
Aa

VERVAIN

Possibly its hard stems or its purported use in the production of iron earned COMMON HEDGE MUSTARD and VERVAIN (CCXXVI) their German designation of "Eisenkraut" ("iron herb"). The "male" HEDGE MUSTARD (plate CCCXXXVI), however, was a widespread plant possessing only a distant resemblance to the "female" VERVAIN (plate CCCXXXVII), which was also known as herb-of-grace.

EISENKRAUT

Vielleicht waren es die harten Stängel, vielleicht seine angebliche Verwendung bei der Eisenherstellung, die der Verbena den Namen EISENKRAUT (Cap. CCXXVI) einbrachten. Beim „EISENKRAUT MENNLE" (Taf. CCCXXXVI) handelt es sich allerdings um die weitverbreitete Wegrauke, die nur entfernte Ähnlichkeit mit dem „WEIBLE" (Taf. CCCXXXVII) besitzt.

VERVEINE OFFICINALE

Voici à présent la VERVEINE OFFICINALE (CCXXVI). Son nom, «Eisenkraut» (herbe à fer), est difficile à expliquer. Peut-être vient-il de la dureté de sa tige ou de son prétendu emploi dans la fabrication du fer. Il est certain en tout cas que la «HERBE À FER MÂLE» (pl. CCCXXXVI) est le sisymbre officinal, qui n'a qu'une vague ressemblance avec la «HERBE À FER FEMELLE» (pl. CCCXXXVII).

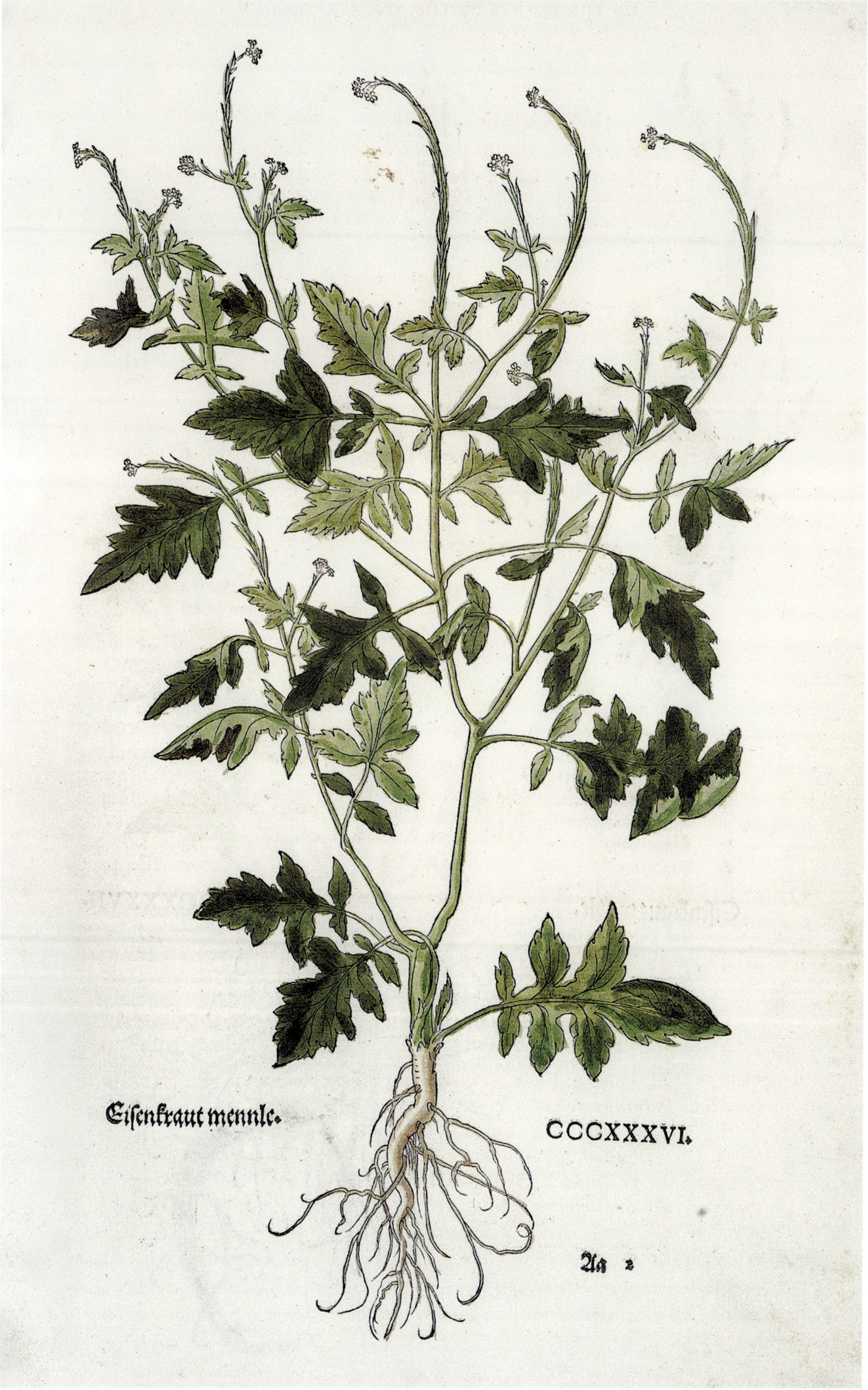
Eiſenkraut mennle.
CCCXXXVI.
Aa 2

FERN

Here (CCXXVII), as above, two different kinds of plants are presented as male and female forms of a single FERN. Male or Shield Fern and Bracken were seen as remedies for "broad" and "round" worms, that is for tapeworms as well as ell worms and pinworms. The text expressly warns pregnant women against using the plant, however.

„WALDTFARN"

Auch beim „WALDTFARN" (Cap. CCXXVII) werden unterschiedliche Farne als männliche und weibliche Art verstanden und als Medikament gegen die „breyten" und „runden Würm", also gegen Bandwürmer und Spul- bzw. Madenwürmer, empfohlen, Schwangere jedoch ausdrücklich vor der Anwendung gewarnt.

« FOUGÈRE DE BOIS »

Fuchs se trompe également sur la « FOUGÈRE DES BOIS » (« Waldtfarn »). Il présente l'une comme une forme mâle et l'autre comme une forme femelle, alors que la fougère mâle et la VERVEINE OFFICINALE (CCXXVII) sont des espèces différentes. Elles étaient utilisées comme remède contre les « vers ronds » et « larges », c'est-à-dire le ténia et l'ascaride. Toutefois, Fuchs met sérieusement en garde contre leur usage chez la femme enceinte.

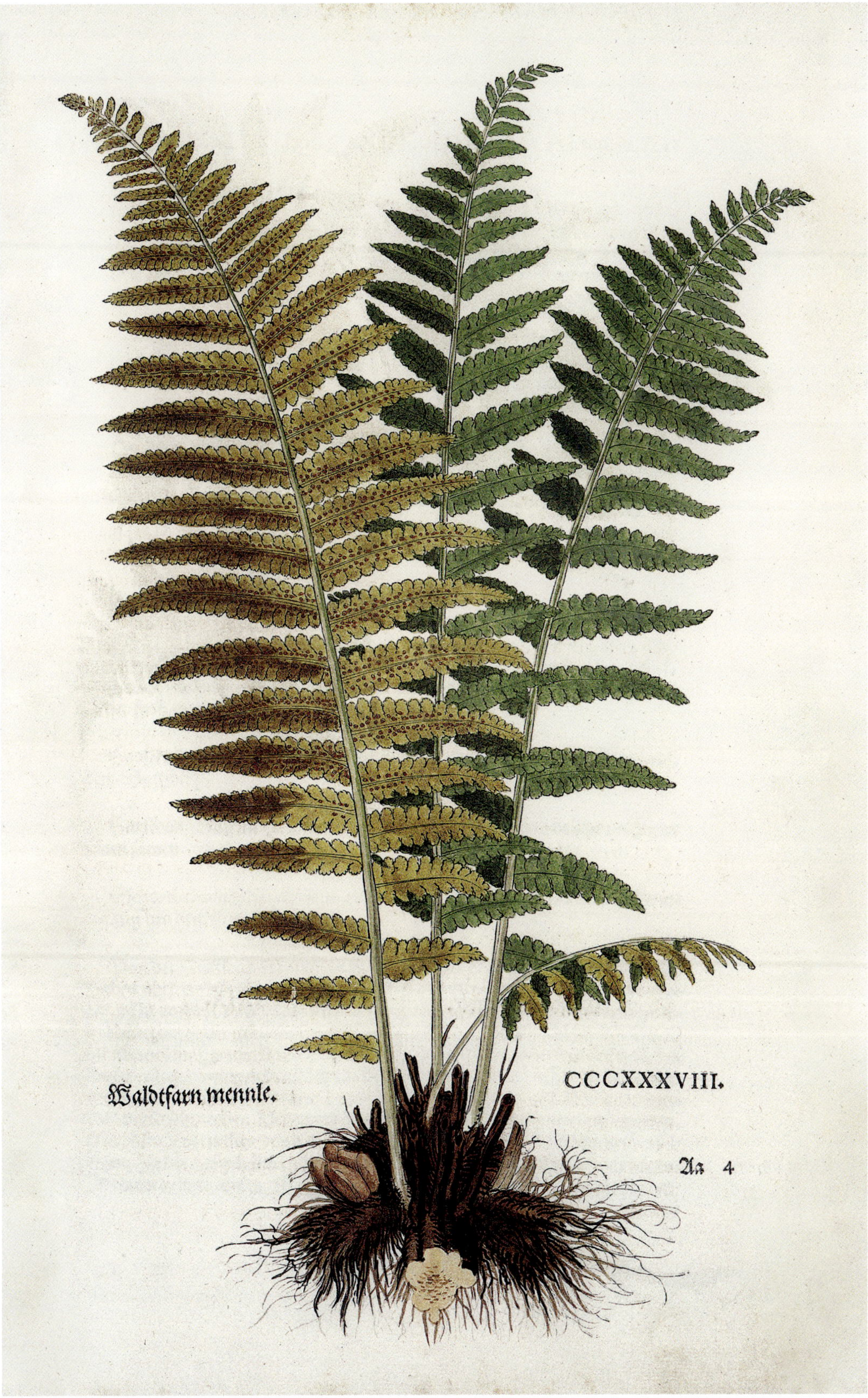

Waldtfarn mennle.
CCCXXXVIII.
Aa 4

HOG'S FENNEL

HOG'S FENNEL or SULPHUR-WEED (CCXXVIII) possesses not only root hairs, but an unpleasant-smelling root sap, similar to Sulphur Balm, characteristics which presumably contributed to its name.

„HARSTRANG"

Es waren wohl die Wurzelhärchen, die zum Namen „HARSTRANG" (Cap. CCXXVIII) führten; auf den unangenehm nach Schwefelbalsam riechenden Wurzelsaft dürfte der volkstümliche Nameå „Schwebelwurz" zurückgehen.

PEUCÉDAN OFFICINAL

Ce sont les petits poils de ses racines qui ont donné au PEUCÉDAN OFFICINAL (CCXXVIII) son nom de «Harstrang» (touffe de poils) et sa désagréable odeur de soufre celui de «Schwebelwurz» (racine soufrée).

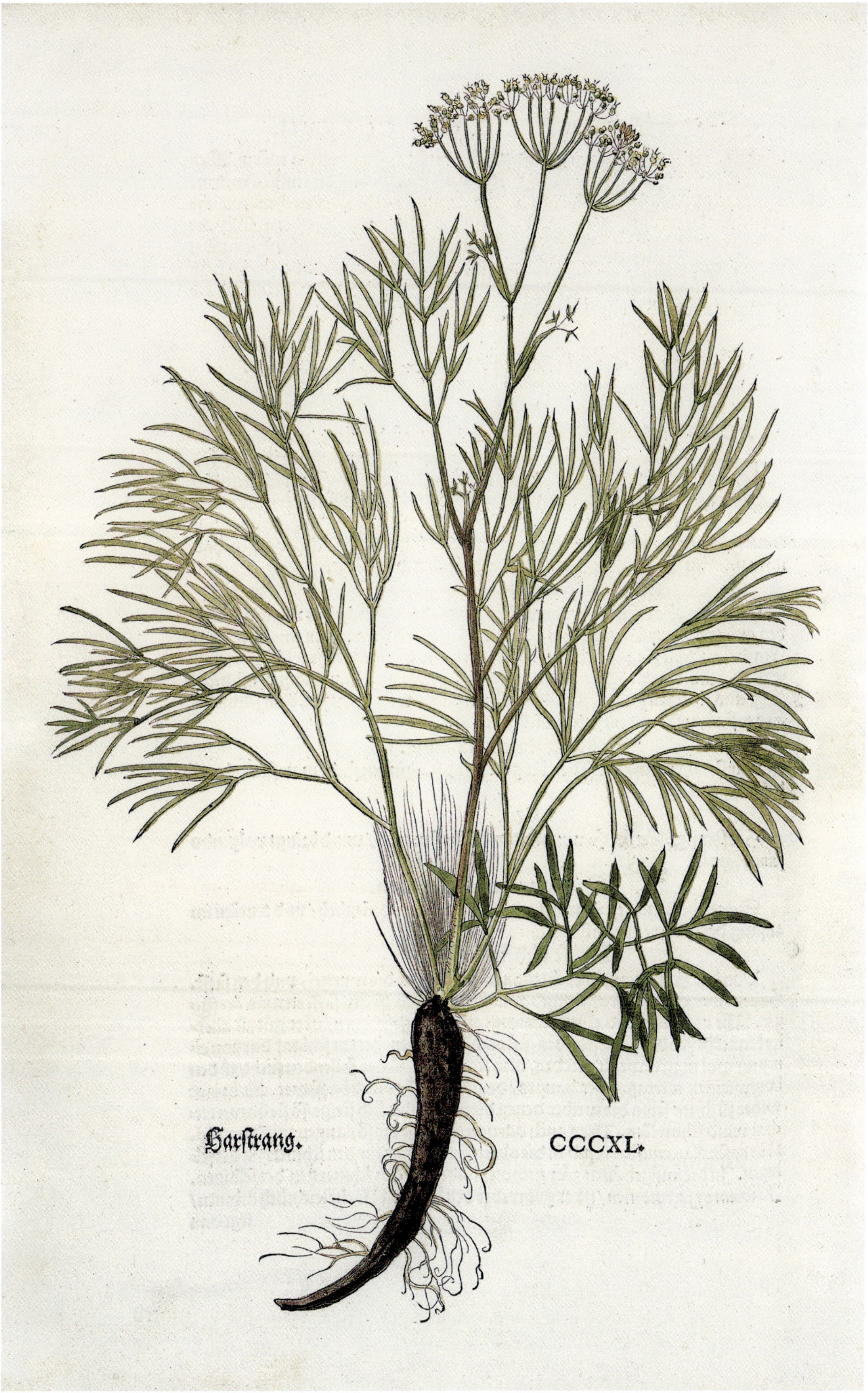

HOG'S FENNEL | „HARSTRANG" | PEUCÉDAN OFFICINAL

PEACH

PEACH (CCXXIX) is familiar to us today only as a tasty fruit; earlier, however, the leaves, stone and resin were used in medicines.

PFIRSICH

Der PFIRSICH (Cap. CCXXIX) ist uns heute nur noch als wohlschmeckende Frucht bekannt, die aber früher ebenso wie die Blätter, der Kern und der Gummi auch als Arznei verwendet wurden.

PÊCHE

Pour nous, la PÊCHE (CCXXIX) est surtout un fruit appétissant, mais les feuilles, le noyau et la gomme s'utilisaient aussi en médecine.

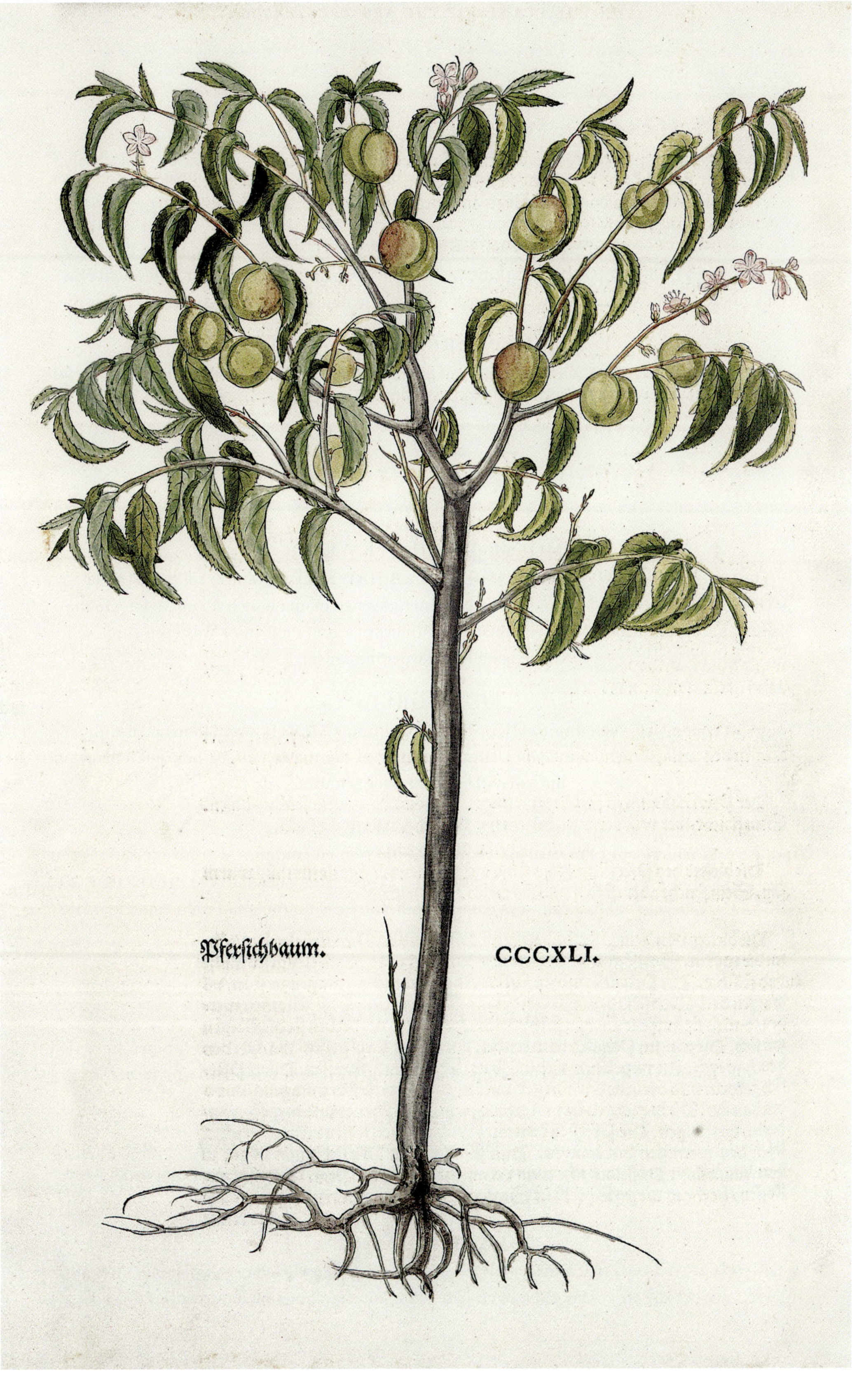
Pferſichbaum.
CCCXLI.

PETTY SPURGE

PETTY SPURGE (CCXXX) was used medicinally in former times, although like other spurges, it is in fact poisonous, as its German name "Wolfsmilch" ("Wolf's Milk") suggests.

„TEUFFELSMILCH"

Der Name „TEUFFELSMILCH" (Cap. CCXXX) lässt ebenso wie der heute gebräuchliche „Wolfsmilch" auf die Giftigkeit der Pflanze schließen, die dennoch arzneilich eingesetzt wurde.

EUPHORBE PÉPLUS

L'EUPHORBE PÉPLUS (CCXXX) s'appelle en allemand «lait de loup» («Wolfsmich») ; autrefois, elle portait même le nom de «lait du diable» («Teuffelsmilch») à cause de sa toxicité, ce qui ne l'a pas empêchée de prendre place en pharmacopée.

PAGE 442

MOUSE-EAR HAWKWEED

The chapter (CCXXXI) including MOUSE-EAR HAWKWEED and CAT'S-FOOT or MOUNTAIN EVERLASTING, once again includes two plants which do not belong to the same family botanically. Both are praised as vulneraries, and their juice was even supposed to be good for sharpening knives.

„MEUSSÖRLIN"

Wie so oft finden sich auch unter „MEUSSÖRLIN" (Cap. CCXXXI) zwei Pflanzen zusammengefasst, die botanisch nicht derselben Gattung angehören. Sie werden als Wundkraut hochgelobt, ihr Saft soll sogar Messer schärfen.

PIED-DE-CHAT

Comme c'est fréquent chez Fuchs, deux plantes n'ayant rien en commun se trouvent réunies sous le nom de «petites oreilles de souris» («Meußörlin») : l'épervière piloselle et le PIED-DE-CHAT (CCXXXI). Elles étaient très estimées comme vulnéraires, et on racontait même que leur suc pouvait aiguiser un couteau.

PAGE 443

BURNET SAXIFRAGES

Especially during the plague, the BURNET SAXI-FRAGES (CCXXXII), like Juniper, were very popular. A German proverb promised that eating this plant would stave off death.

BIBERNELL

BIBERNELL (Cap. CCXXXII) erfreute sich besonders zu Zeiten der Pest zusammen mit dem Wacholder größter Beliebtheit, als man empfahl: „Esst Kranewitt und Bibernell, dann sterbt ihr nicht so schnell!"

GRAND BOUCAGE

Le GRAND BOUCAGE (CCXXXII) était très réputé à l'époque de la peste, au même titre que le genièvre. Aussi disait-on : «Mangez du genièvre et du boucage, vous ne mourrez pas avant l'âge !»

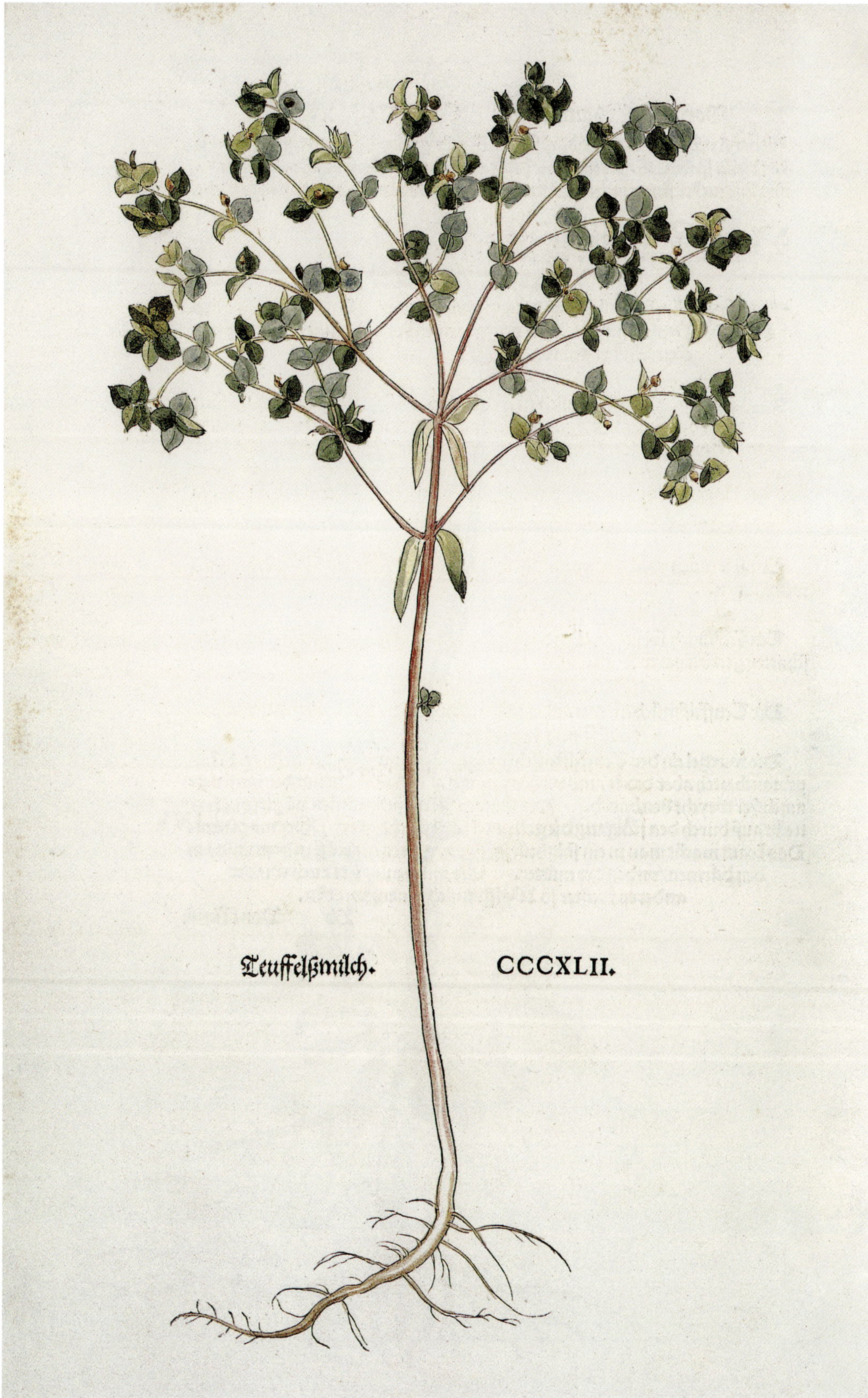
Teuffelßmilch.
CCCXLII.

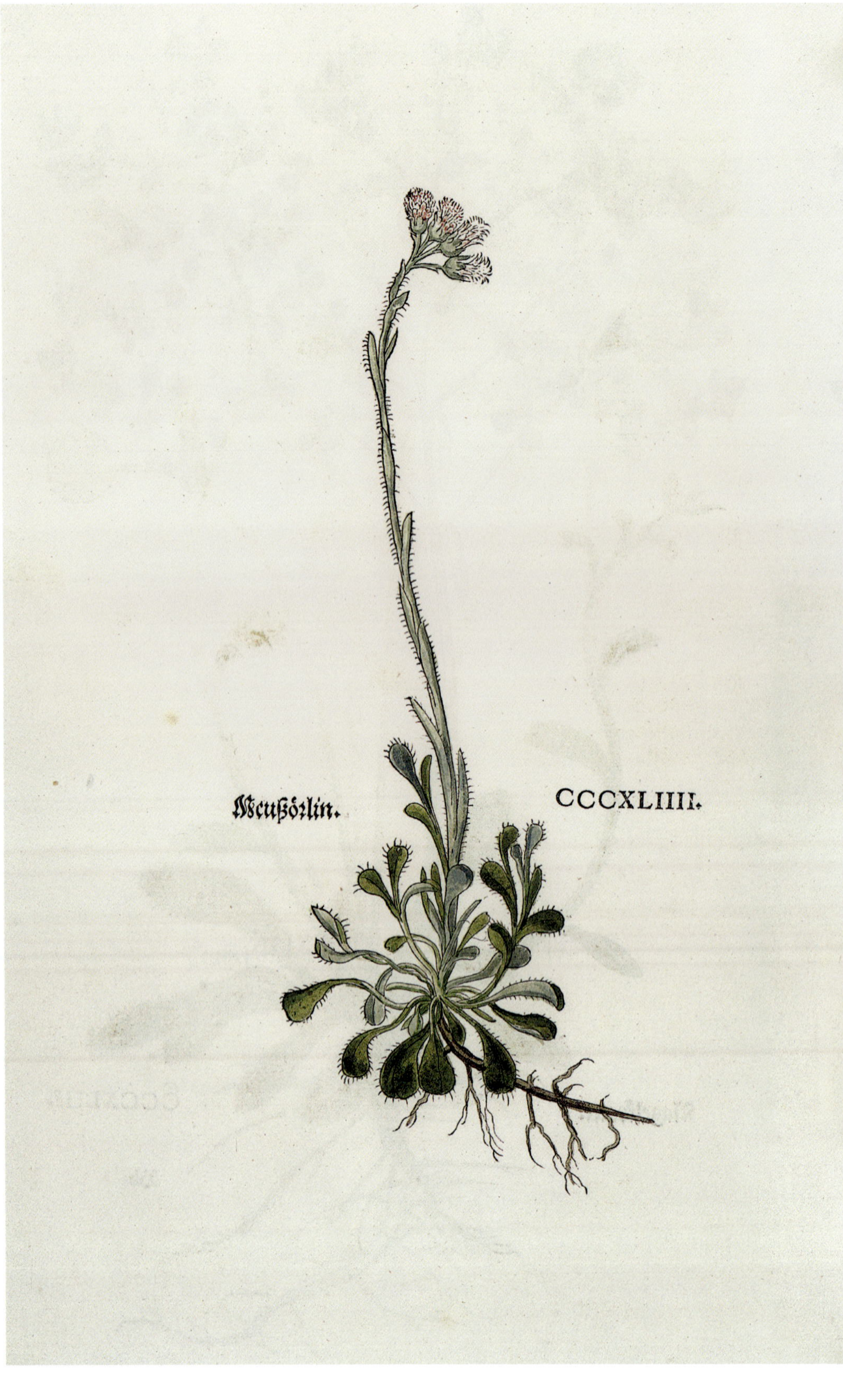
Meußörlin.
CCCXLIIII.

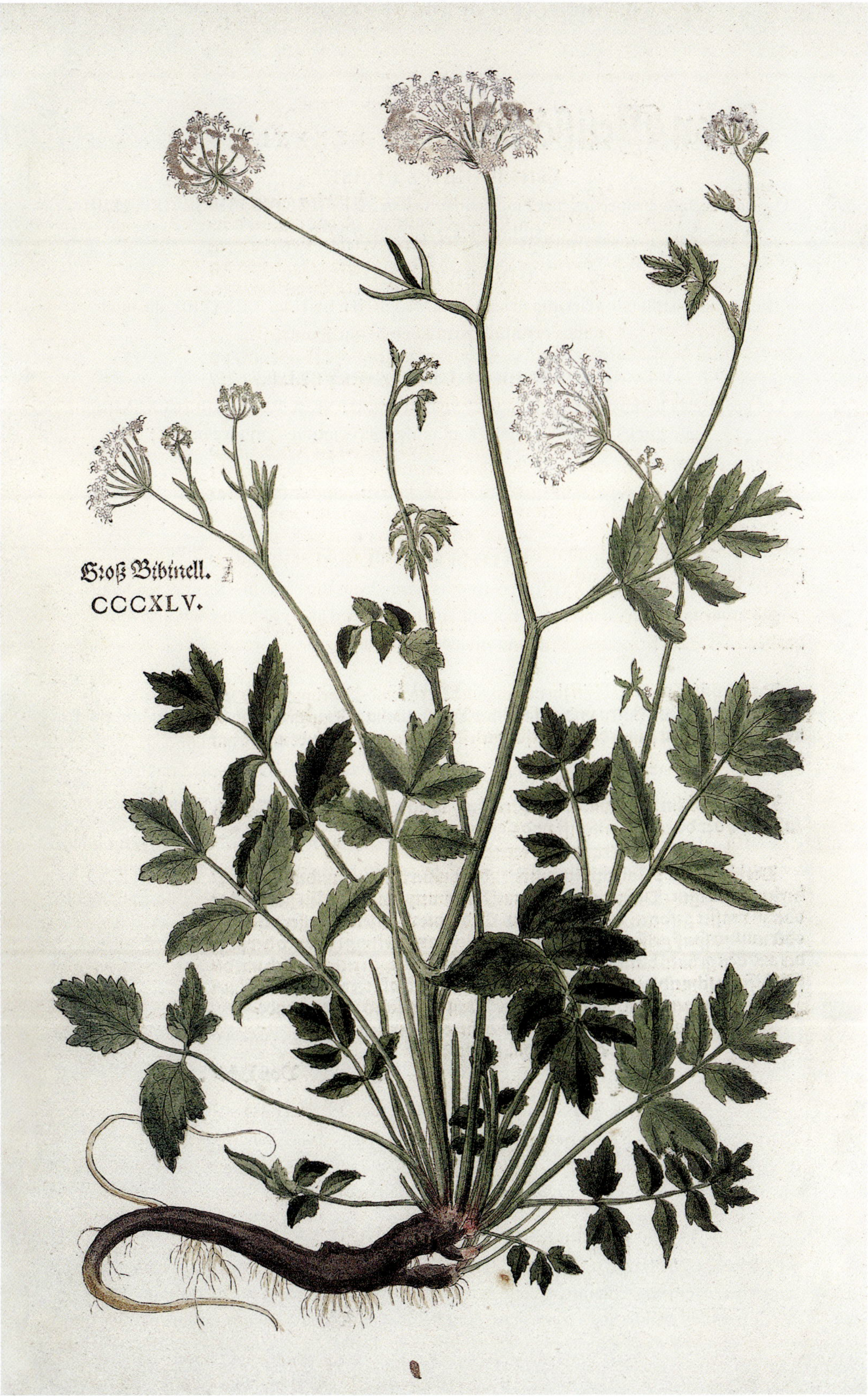
Groß Bibinell.
CCCXLV.

SHEPHERD'S PURSE

The haemostatic properties that Fuchs attributes to SHEPHERD'S PURSE (CCXXXIII) still render it useful today.

HIRTENTÄSCHEL

Die blutungsstillende Wirkung des HIRTENTÄSCHELS (Cap. CCXXXIII), die auch Fuchs erwähnt, wird noch heute genutzt.

CAPSELLE BOURSE-À-PASTEUR

Les propriétés hémostatiques de la CAPSELLE BOURSE-À-PASTEUR (CCXXXIII), que Fuchs mentionne déjà, sont toujours reconnues aujourd'hui.

PAGE 446

LADY'S MANTLE

LADY'S MANTLE (CCXXXIIII) received its name from the cape-like form of the leaves. Also known as Lion's Foot, it was not only highly praised as a vulnerary, but also found gynaecological application.

„SYNAW"

„SYNAW" (Cap. CCXXXIIII) ist die heute unverständliche Bezeichnung für den Frauenmantel, der seinen Namen wegen der einem Radmantel ähnlichen Form der Blätter erhielt und als Wundkraut hochgeschätzt war, aber auch in der Frauenheilkunde Verwendung fand.

ALCHÉMILLE VULGAIRE

L'ALCHÉMILLE VULGAIRE (CCXXXIIII) figure ici sous le vocable de «Synaw», un mot incompréhensible de nos jours. Ses feuilles plissées, qui évoquent un manteau, lui ont valu son nom courant de manteau de dame. Très estimée comme vulnéraire, elle était également utilisée comme remède gynécologique.

PAGE 447

KNOTGRASS

KNOTGRASS, or KNOTWEED (CCXXXV), commonly found alongside paths, could supposedly stop bleeding, evacuate the bladder, sink fevers, and had many other applications as well.

„WEGGRASS" (VOGEL-KNÖTERICH)

Der Vogel-Knöterich fand sich so häufig an den Wegen, dass er früher „WEGGRASS" (Cap. CCXXXV) genannt wurde. Ihm wurden blutstillende, harntreibende, fiebersenkende und viele andere Eigenschaften zugebilligt.

RENOUÉE DES OISEAUX

La RENOUÉE DES OISEAUX (CCXXXV), appelée aussi traînasse, était si répandue autrefois le long des chemins qu'elle fut baptisée «Weggraß» ou herbe de chemin. On lui prêtait de nombreuses propriétés, dont hémostatiques, diurétiques et fébrifuges.

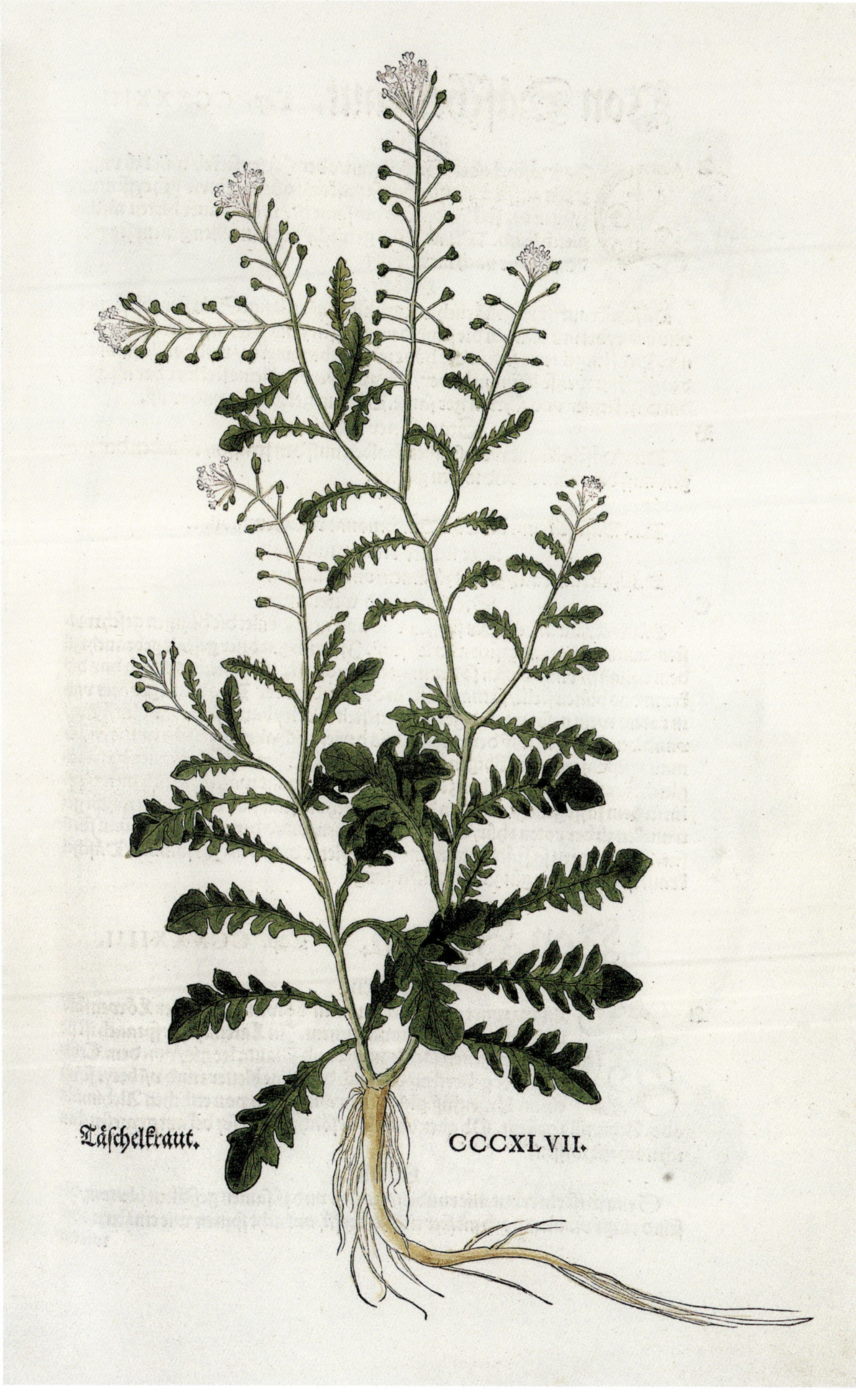
Täschelkraut.
CCCXLVII.

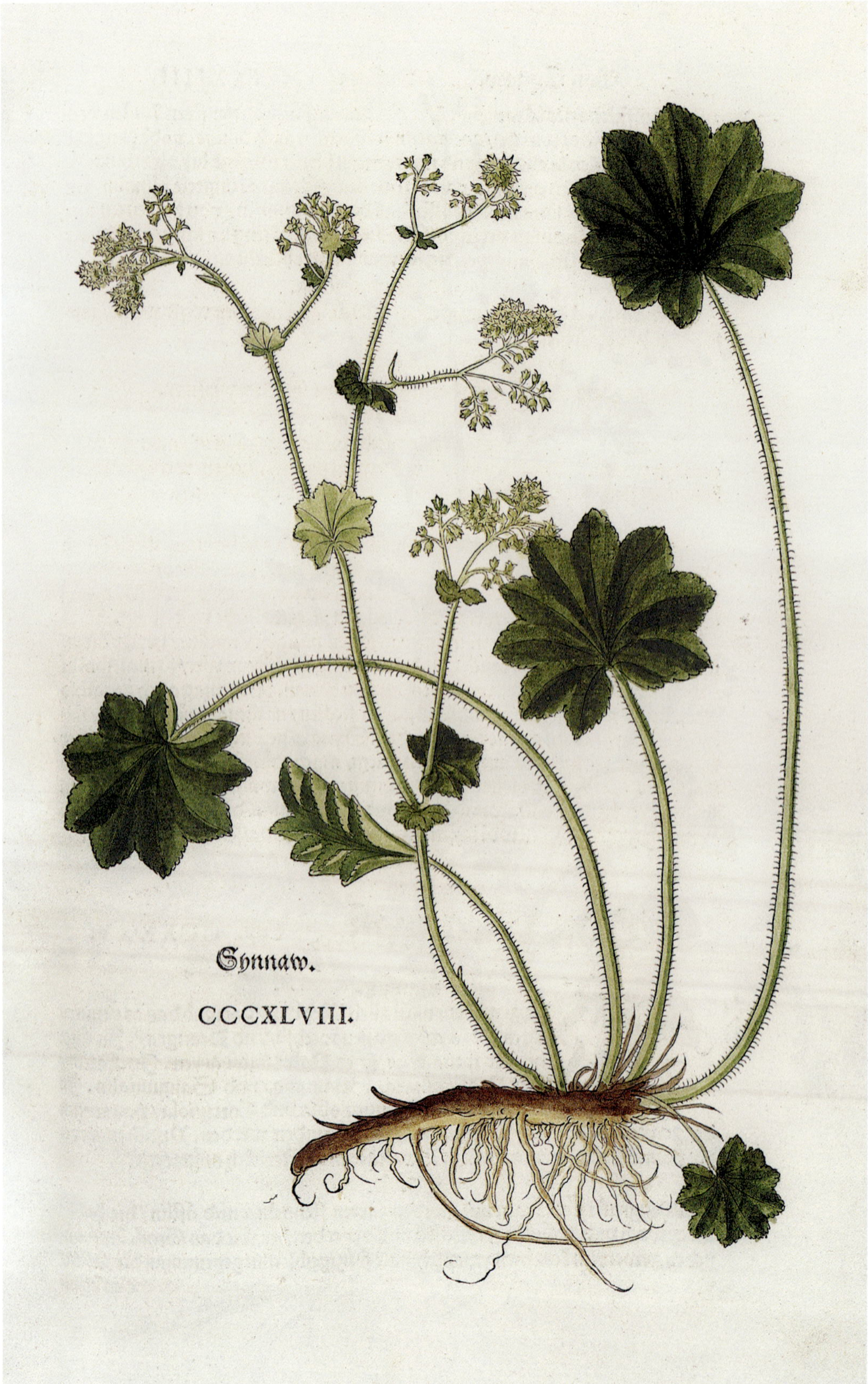
Synnaw.
CCCXLVIII.

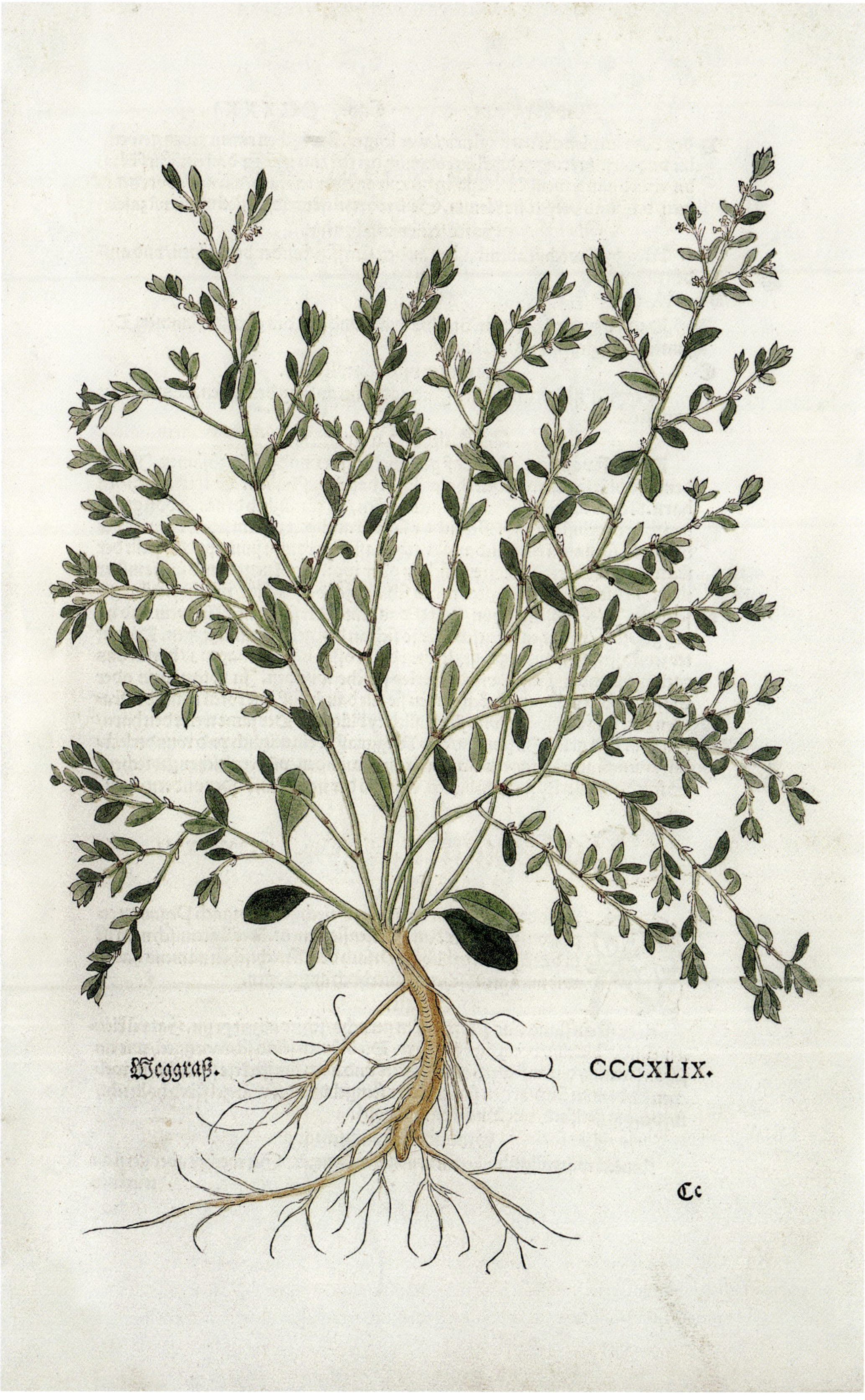
Weggraß.
CCCXLIX.
Cc

COMMON RUE

COMMON RUE (CCXXXVI), highly valued in the Middle Ages, contains rutosid, which today is used for its effect on veins.

RAUTE

Der isolierte Wirkstoff der im Mittelalter hochgeschätzten RAUTE (Cap. CCXXXVI), das venenwirksame Rutosid, findet noch heute in vielen Medikamenten Anwendung.

RUE FÉTIDE

La RUE FÉTIDE (CCXXXVI) était une plante médicinale très réputée au Moyen Âge. Son principe actif isolé, le rutoside, est encore employé aujourd'hui dans de nombreux médicaments.

PAGE 450

SILVERWEED

Fuchs compares the qualities of SILVERWEED (CCXXXVII), also known as WILD AGRIMONY, to those of WHITE CINQUEFOIL, which belongs to the same genus and is presented two chapters later.

„GENSERICH" (GÄNSEFINGERKRAUT)

Die Eigenschaften des im Kapitel CCXXXVII vorgestellten „GENSERICHS", den wir heute Gänsefingerkraut nennen, werden mit denen des Fünffingerkrauts verglichen, das zwei Kapitel später besprochen wird und botanisch derselben Gattung angehört.

ANSÉRINE

Les propriétés de l'ANSÉRINE (CCXXXVII) sont comparées avec celles de la potentille, présentée deux chapitres plus loin. Les deux plantes appartiennent au même genre botanique.

PAGE 451

SELF-HEAL

Fuchs credits SELF-HEAL, or HEAL-ALL (CCXXXVIII), with a healing effect against a certain brown-toned inflammation of the mucous membrane of the mouth.

BRAUNELLE

Unter „braun" verstand man früher einen blau-violetten Farbton, sodass die BRAUNELLE (Cap. CCXXXVIII) ihren Namen ursprünglich wohl wegen der Blütenfarbe bekommen hat, auch wenn Fuchs ihn auf die Verwendung gegen die Mundbräune zurückführt, eine Entzündung der Mundschleimhaut.

BRUNELLE

Par « brun », on entendait autrefois une couleur bleu violet, ce qui explique que la BRUNELLE (CCXXXVIII), dont les pétales sont bleu violet foncé, ait été dénommée ainsi. Par analogie de couleur également, elle s'utilisait contre l'inflammation du mucus buccal (en allemand, « Mundbräune » ou hâle de la bouche), une indication que mentionne Fuchs.

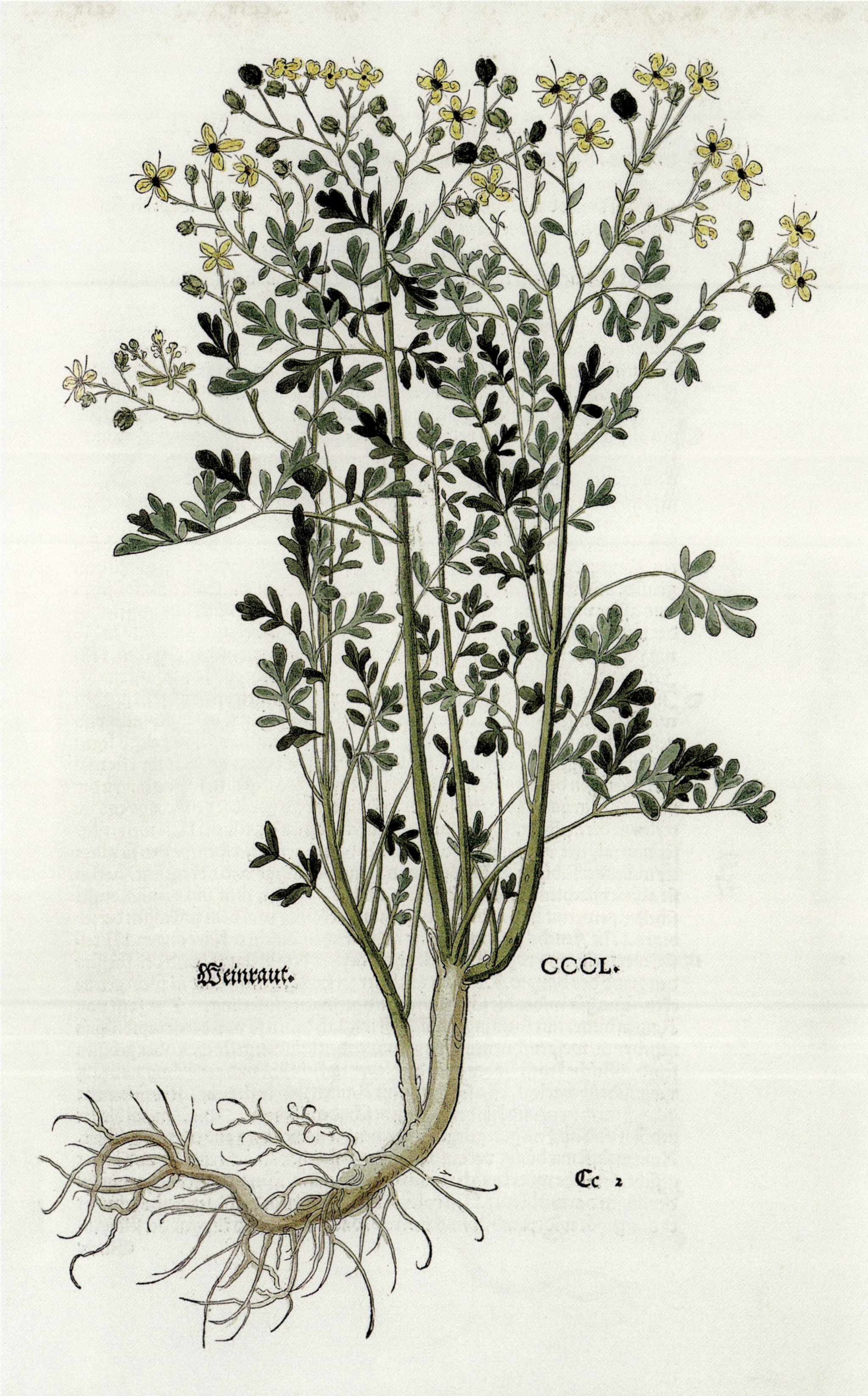
Weinraut.
CCCL.
Cc 2

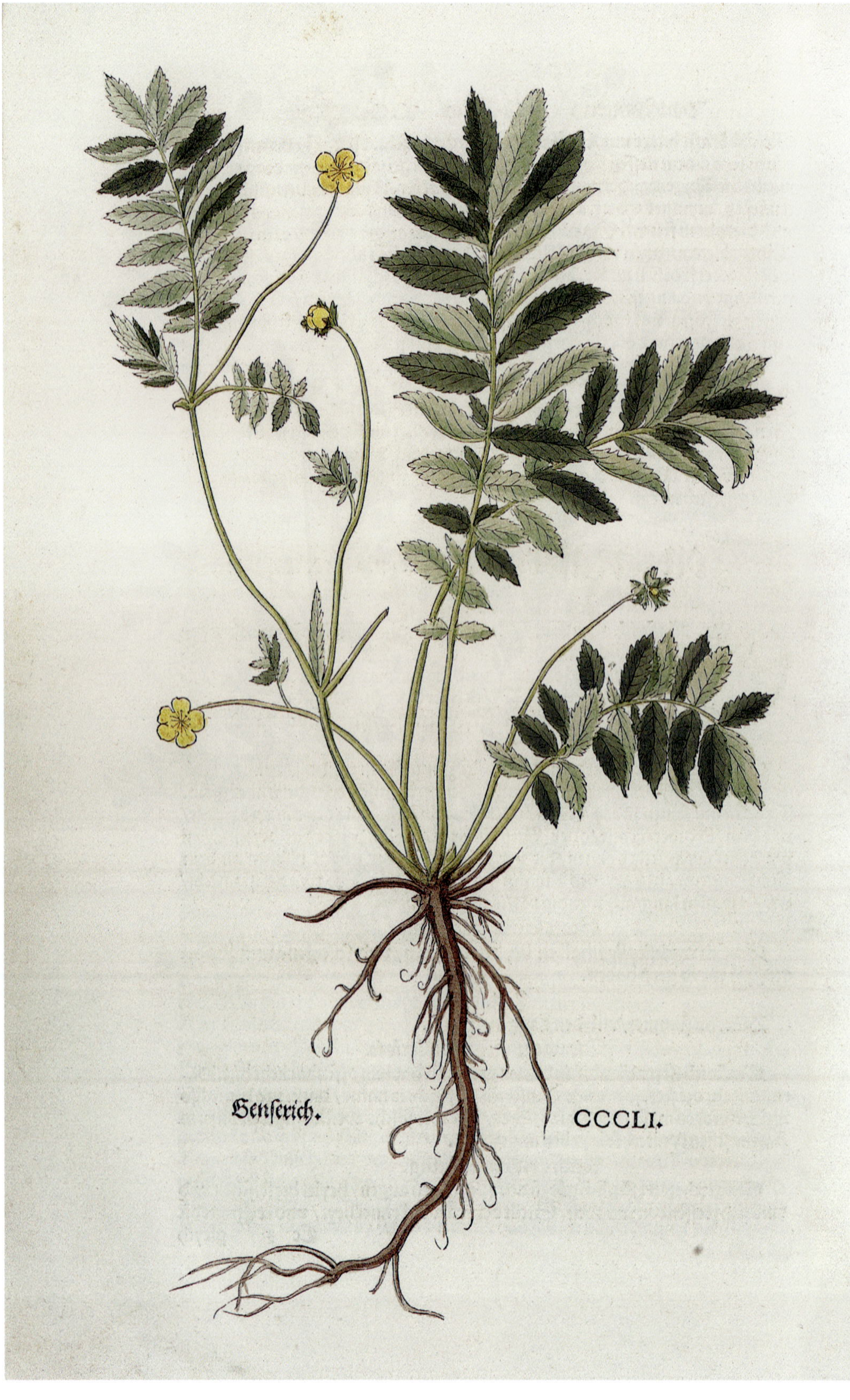
Genserich.
CCCLI.

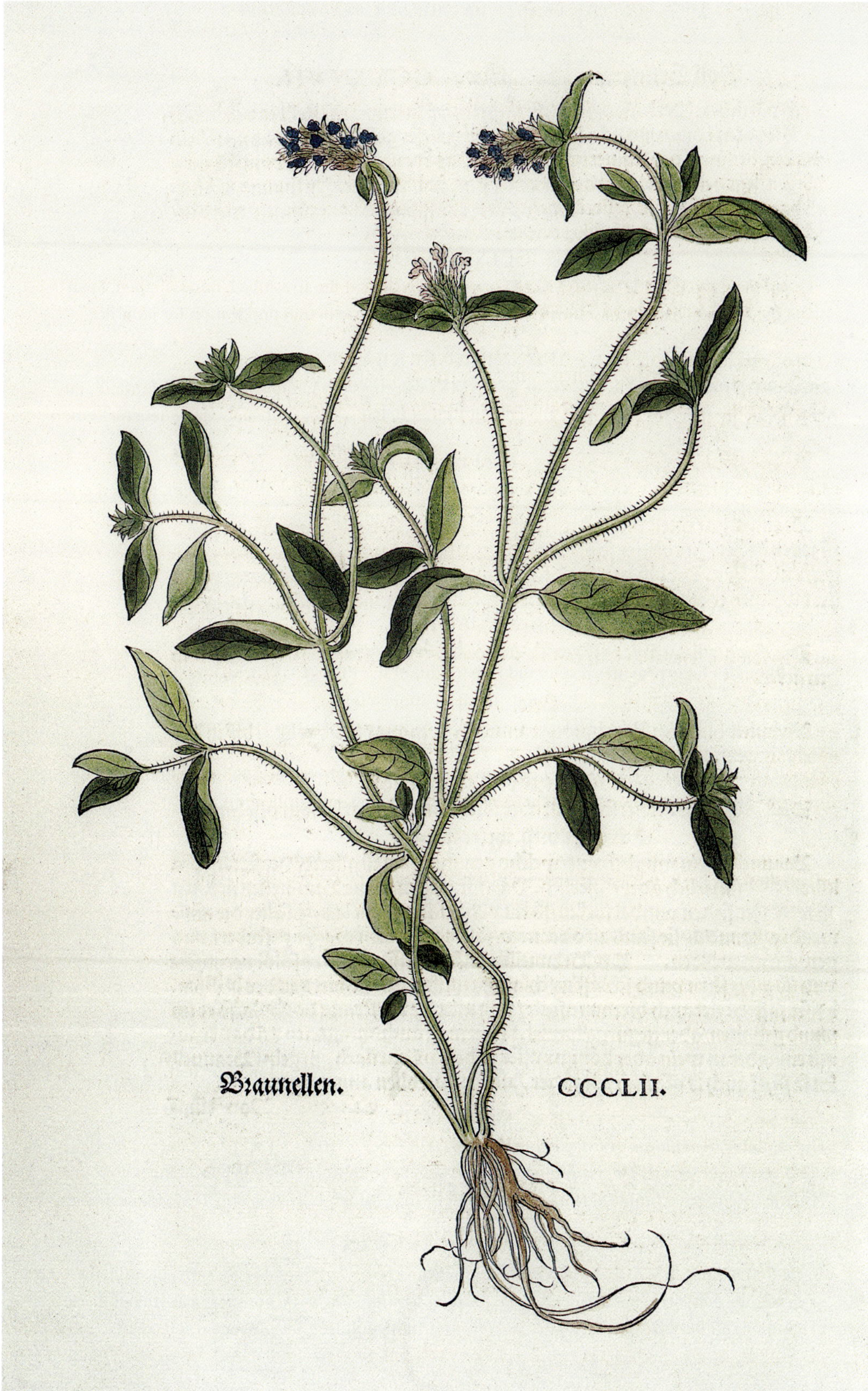
Braunellen.
CCCLII.

CINQUEFOIL

The name CINQUEFOIL (CCXXXIX) originally reflected the five-lobed, hand-shaped, form of the leaves. The plant's yellow blossoms suggested a medicinal application for jaundice.

FÜNFFINGERKRAUT

Beim FÜNFFINGERKRAUT (Cap. CCXXXIX) waren es die handförmigen bzw. fünfteiligen Blätter, die ihm den Namen gaben, die gelben Blüten ließen es bei Gelbsucht geeignet erscheinen.

POTENTILLE

La POTENTILLE (CCXXXIX) doit son nom de «Fünffingerkraut» (littéralement, herbe à cinq doigts) à ses feuilles digitées. On la croyait hépatique à cause de ses fleurs jaunes.

PAGE 454

PEA

Although Fuchs provides a splendid illustration of the PEA (CCXL), he had little to offer on its medical application.

ERBSEN

Die ERBSEN (Cap. CCXL) stellt Fuchs zwar mit einer prachtvollen Abbildung dar, bleibt bei ihrer medizinischen Verwendung jedoch sehr unbestimmt.

POIS CULTIVÉS

C'est avec une composition magnifique que Fuchs présente les POIS CULTIVÉS (CCXL), mais il reste très vague quant à leur emploi médical.

PAGE 455

HAIRCAP MOSSES

For the HAIRCAP MOSSES and CORD MOSS (CCXLI), the presence of hairs served as a "signature" for their application against loss of hair. Because the plants are very short, they were not given a full-page illustration, but instead were fitted into the text.

„WIDERTHON"

Die Signatur des Haares drängt sich beim „WIDERTHON" (Cap. CCXLI) auf, der gegen Haarausfall verordnet wurde. Wegen seiner geringen Wuchshöhe werden die beiden Pflanzen nicht mit einer ganzseitigen Abbildung vorgestellt, sondern ihre Bilder zwischen den Text eingeschoben.

POLYTRIC ÉLÉGANT

Le POLYTRIC ÉLÉGANT (CCXLI) s'employait contre la chute des cheveux, ce qui peut s'expliquer par son aspect. En raison de leur petite taille, Fuchs ne consacre pas une planche entière au polytric et à la funaire polygrométrique, mais les a représentés sous le texte.

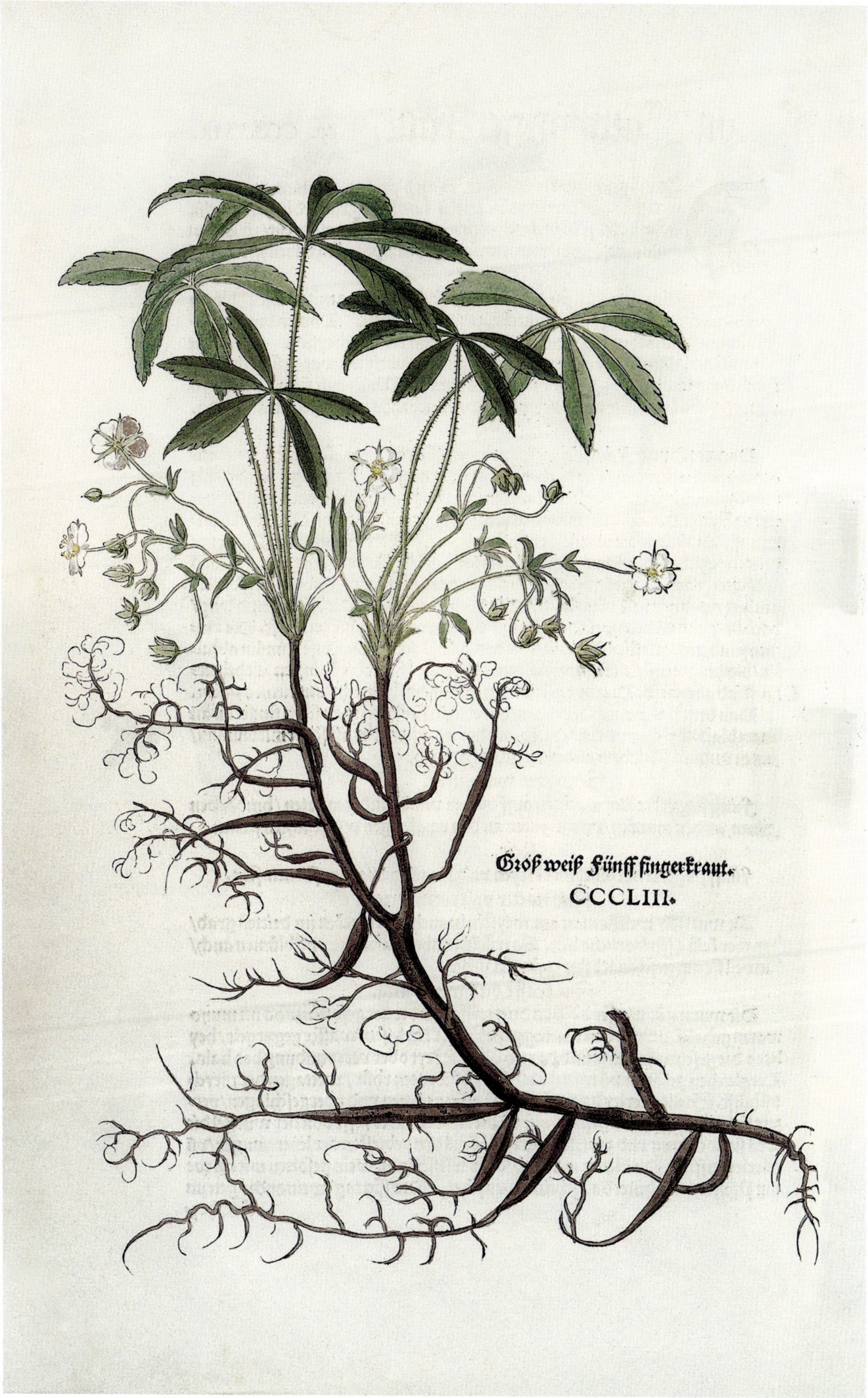
Groß weiß Fünff fingerkraut.
CCCLIII.

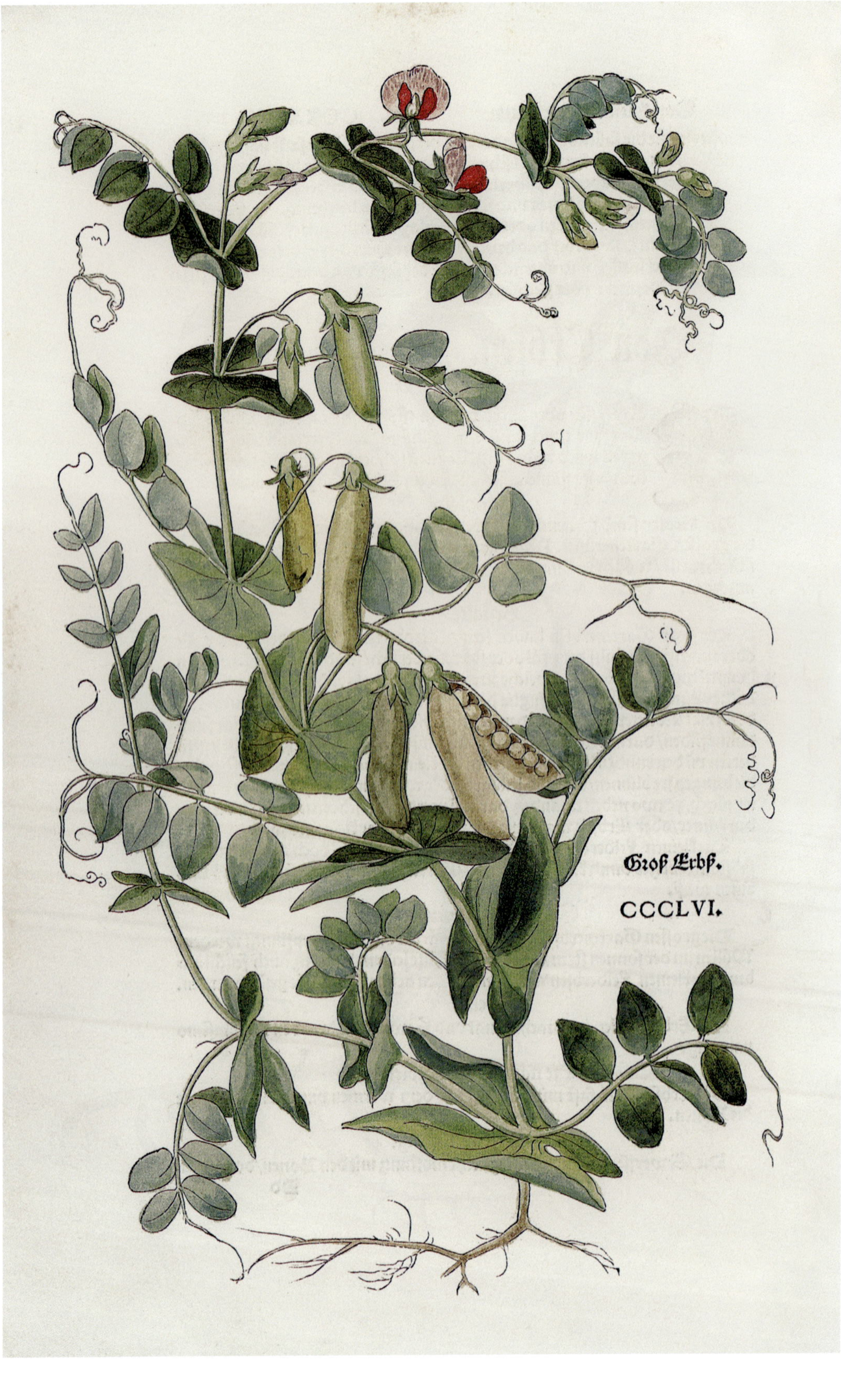
Groß Erbß.
CCCLVI.

D sie nit wie dieselbigen/seubern auch nit/darumb sie langsam vndersich tringen. So vil würckung haben die allten den Erbsen zůgeschriben vnnd nit mehr. Darumb sehen die newen ärtzt zů/die jhnen vil mehr krafft vnnd würckung zůschreiben dañ wir yetzund erzelt haben/wie sie sölches mit schrifft vertädingen vnd verantworten wöllen.

Das groß gulden Widerthon.
CCCLVII.

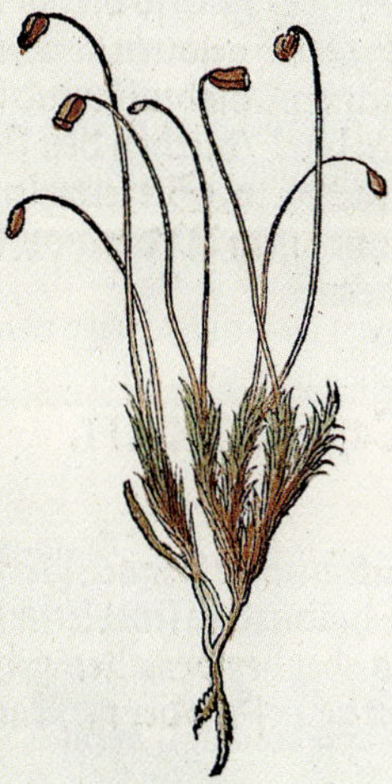

Das klein gulden Widerthon.
CCCLVIII.

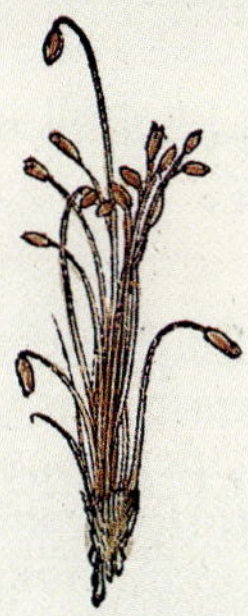

Von goldtfarbem Widerthon.

Cap. CCXLI.

Namen.

A Goldtfarber oder guldener Widerthon/oder Widertodt/ist on zweifel das Polytrichon Apuleij. Würdt inn den Apotecken nit gebraucht.

Geschlecht.

Des guldin Widerthons seind zwey geschlecht/eins groß/das ander klein/wie wir in beschreibung der gestalt weitleüffiger wöllen anzeygen.

Gestalt.

Das groß hat glatt braungeel härlin oder stengelin/ fingers lang/am gipffel derselbigen seine körnlin/welche sich den Meerlinsen oder Weytzenkorn vergleichen/einerley farb mit den stengelin/vmb welche vil kleiner blettlin als die härlin wachsen/zum teyl grůn/zum teyl auch goldtfarb. Das klein ist dem grossen gleich/aber kürtzer/vnnd mit dem öbersten sämlin oder körnlin kleiner/wie sölchs das gemäl klärlich außweißt.

Statt irer wachsung.

Das groß wechßt auff den moßechten vñ allzeit nassen wisen so in den wälden zwüschen den bergen ligen/zů zeiten auch inn den hohen wälden auß dem

Dd 2 mieß

RED SHANK

The dark-red flecks on the leaves suggested that RED SHANK (CCXLII), also known as Willow Weed or Persicaria, was an excellent vulnerary herb.

„FLÖHKRAUT“

Die dunkelroten Flecken auf den Blättern verstand man als Hinweis darauf, dass mit dem „FLÖHKRAUT“ (Cap. CCXLII) ein wertvolles Wundheilkraut vorliegt.

RENOUÉE PERSICAIRE

Les feuilles de la RENOUÉE PERSICAIRE (CCXLII), dite aussi pied rouge, portent une grosse tache d'un rouge noirâtre. On voyait dans cette particularité l'indice de grandes vertus cicatrisantes.

PAGE 458

HARE'S EAR

The leaves of HARE'S EAR, or THOROW-WAX (CCXLIII) are noticeably penetrated by the stem. For this reason, the plant was indicated for wounds and umbilical hernias.

DURCHWACHS

Die auffälligen, vom Stängel durchwachsenen Blätter gaben dem DURCHWACHS (Cap. CCXLIII) seinen Namen und ließen ihn bei Verwundungen und Nabelbrüchen angezeigt sein.

BUPLÈVRE À FEUILLES RONDES

Le BUPLÈVRE À FEUILLES RONDES (CCXLIII), ou perce-feuille, a lui aussi des feuilles particulières : dépourvues de pétiole, elles sont si engainantes qu'elles semblent percées par la tige. Aussi employait-on la plante contre l'hernie ombilicale et les blessures.

PAGE 459

LEEK

This chapter (CCXLIIII) presents the LEEK (plate CCCLXI) and CHIVES (plate CCCLXII), which like their cousin, the ONION (CLXIII) are still in use today.

PORREE

Mit dem PORREE (Taf. CCCLXI) und dem SCHNITTLAUCH (Taf. CCCLXII) erscheinen nach der ZWIEBEL (Cap. CLXIII) zwei ebenfalls noch heute gebräuchliche Arten von LAUCH (Cap. CCXLIIII).

POIREAU

Après l'OIGNON (CLXIII), deux nouvelles espèces d'AIL (CCXLIIII) font leur apparition : le POIREAU (pl. CCCLXI) et la CIBOULETTE sauvage (pl. CCCLXII).

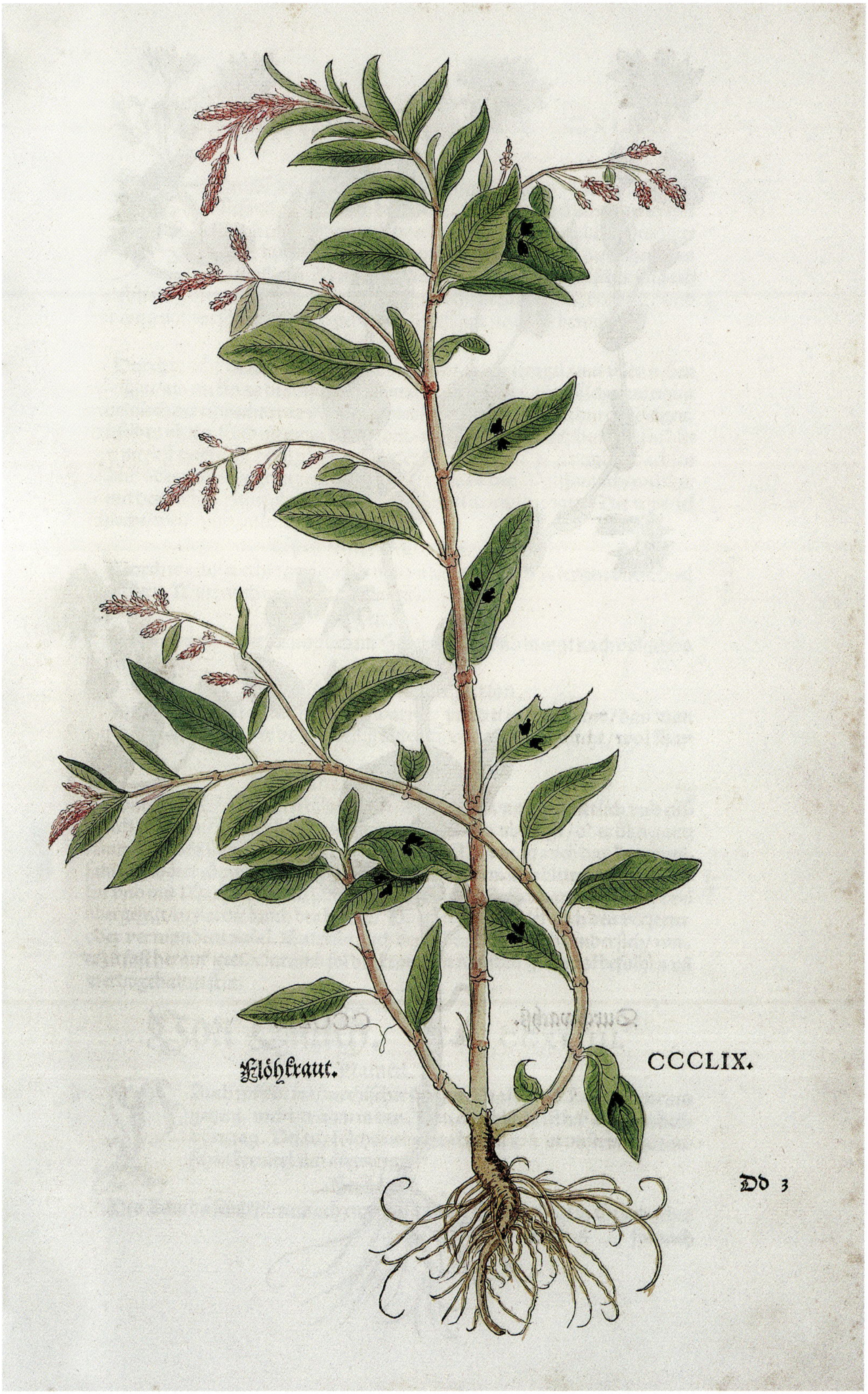
Flöhkraut.
CCCLIX.
Dd 3

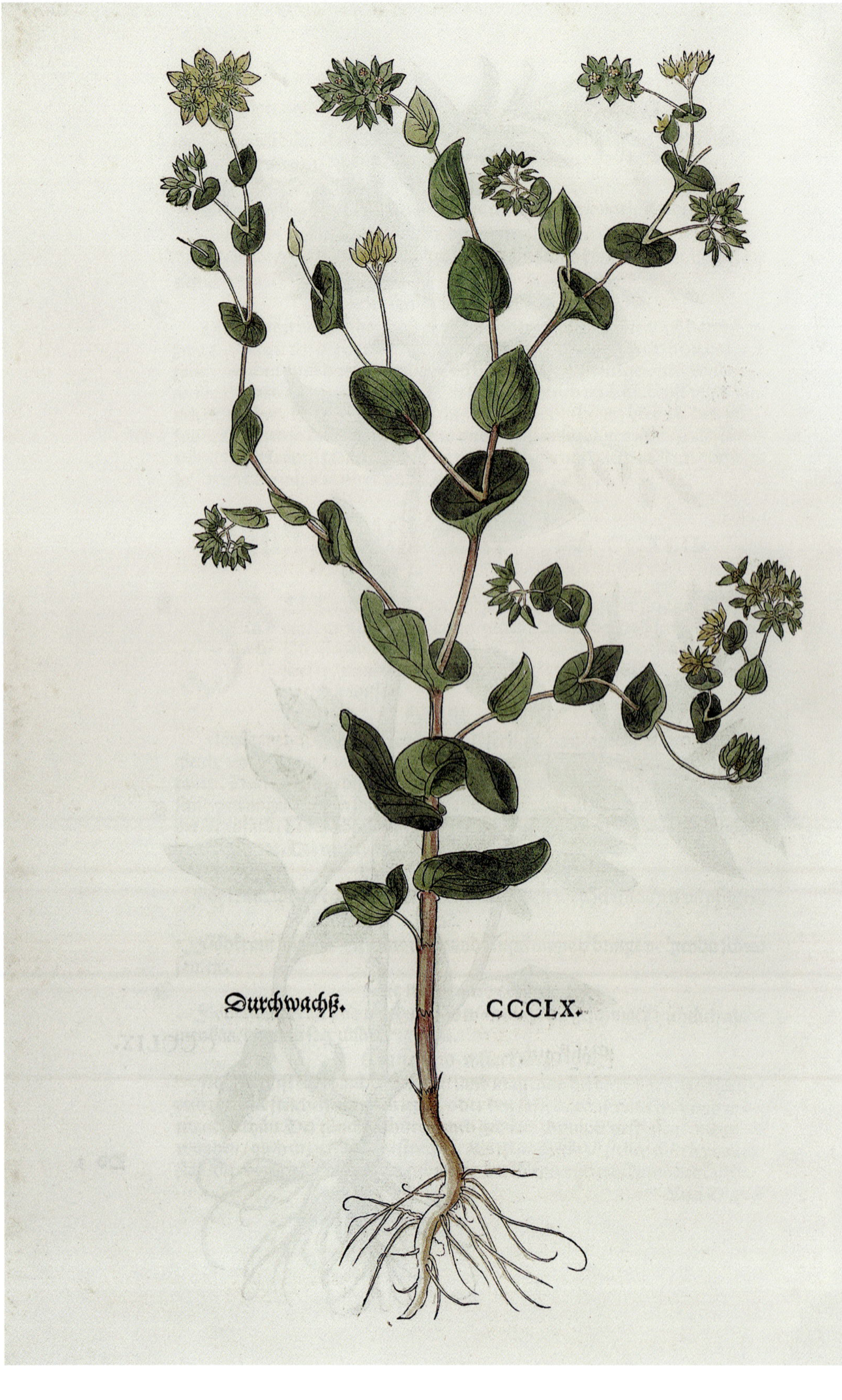
Durchwachß.
CCCLX.

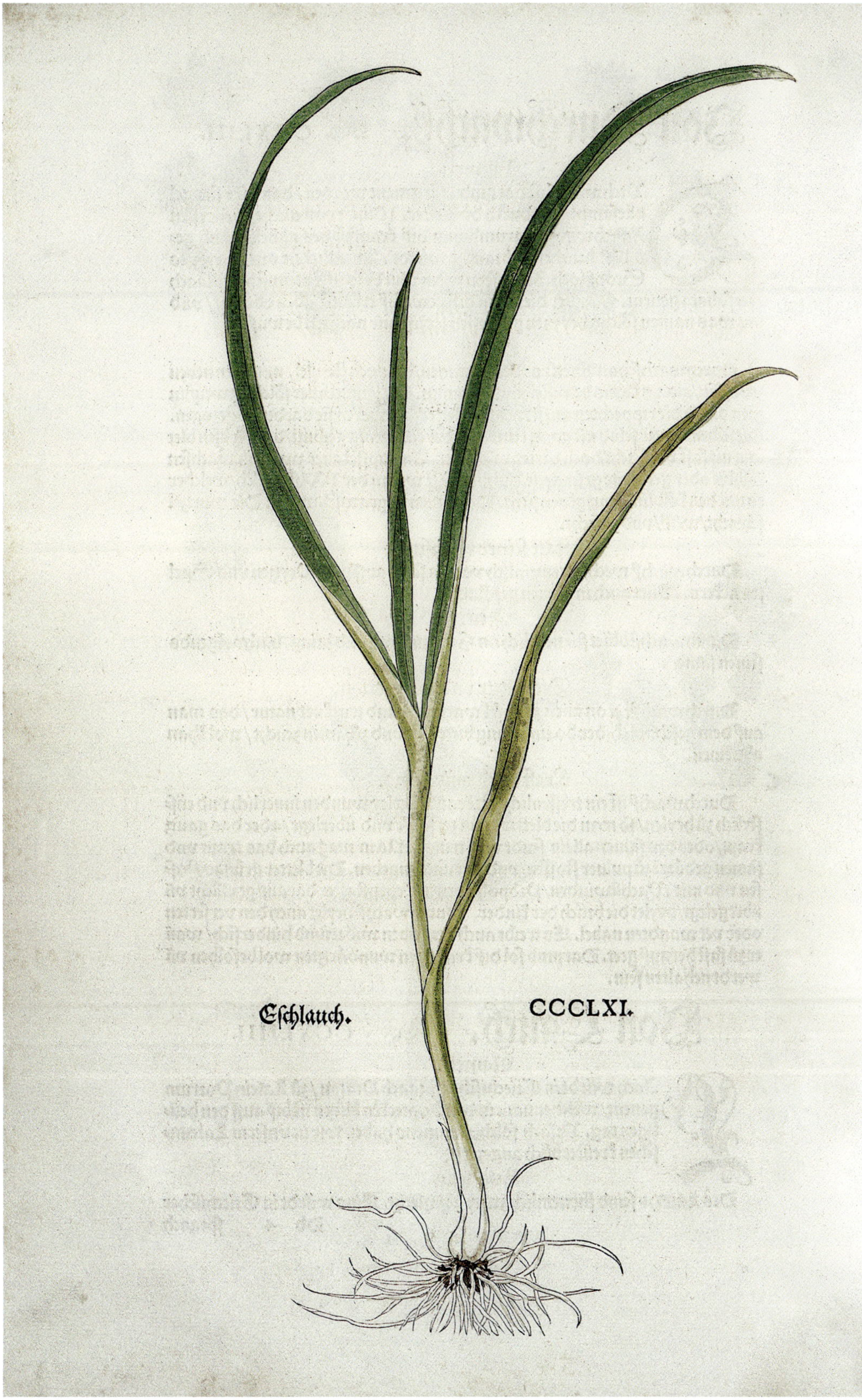

Eschlauch.
CCCLXI.

LUNGWORT

For Fuchs, both the appearance and name of LUNGWORT, or OAK LUNGS (CCXLV), determined its medicinal application. His reference to "spitting up blood" should be read as a symptom of tuberculosis.

LUNGENKRAUT

Unter LUNGENKRAUT (Cap. CCXLV) versteht Fuchs die Lungenflechte, deren Aussehen den Namen und die medizinische Anwendung bestimmt hat. Das „blut speien" ist als Symptom der Tuberkulose zu werten.

LICHEN POUMONS

Comme son nom l'indique, le LICHEN POUMONS (CCXLV), appelé ici «Lungenkraut» ou herbe à poumons, était utilisé dans les maladies pulmonaires. L'expression «blut speien» (cracher du sang) doit évidemment se comprendre comme le symptôme de la tuberculose.

PAGE 462

SNEEZEWORT

According to the theory of humours, the reaction implied by the name of SNEEZEWORT (CCXLVI) should cause the evacuation of mucous.

WILDER BERTRAM

Das Niesen, das der WILDE BERTRAM (Cap. CCXLVI) auslöst, ist im Sinne der Säftelehre als ein Abführen von Schleim zu verstehen.

PYRÈTHRE

Conformément à la théorie des humeurs, l'éternuement que provoque le PYRÈTHRE (CCXLVI) était considéré comme une expulsion de glaires. Le nom générique PYRETHRUM vient du grec PYROS, qui signifie feu.

PAGE 463

ROMAN PELLITORY

The sharp, burning taste of the root of ROMAN PELLITORY (CCXLVII), also known as Pellitory of Spain, derives from its essential oil, which also determined its medicinal uses.

BERTRAM

BERTRAM (Cap. CCXLVII) leitet sich ab vom lateinischen Pflanzennamen *Pyrethrum*, der seinerseits auf das griechische Wort „pyros", Feuer, zurückgeht und den wegen des ätherischen Öls scharf brennenden Geschmack der Wurzel bezeichnet, durch den auch die medizinische Anwendung bestimmt wird.

BERTRAM

Le nom allemand, «BERTRAM» (CCXLVII), dérive également de *Pyrethrum* et renvoie à la saveur pimentée de l'huile volatile contenue dans sa racine. Son usage médical correspondait à sa saveur.

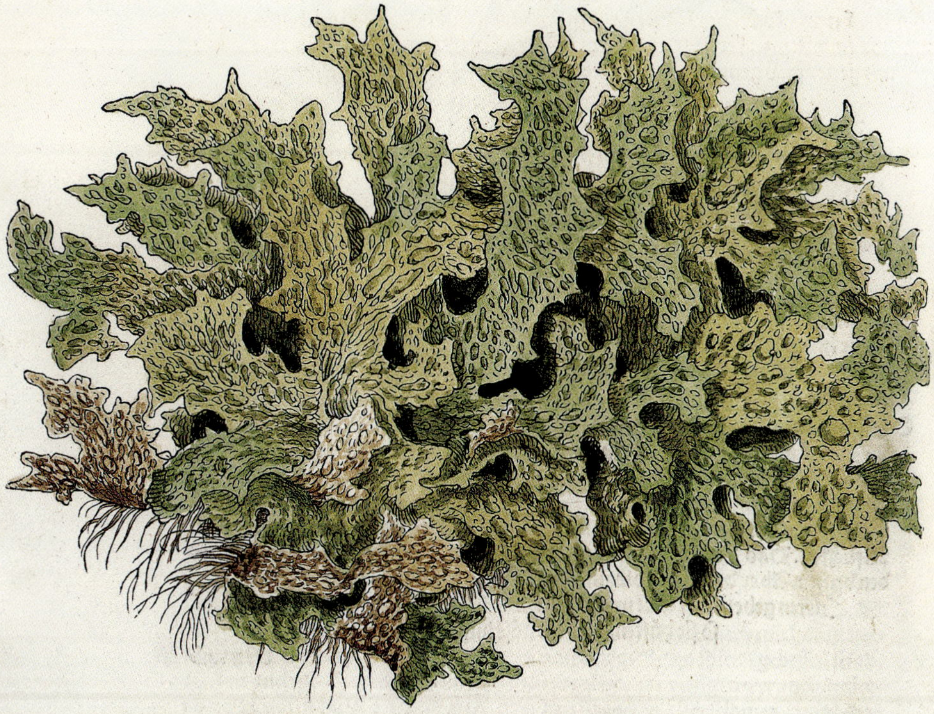

Lungenkraut. CCCLXIII.

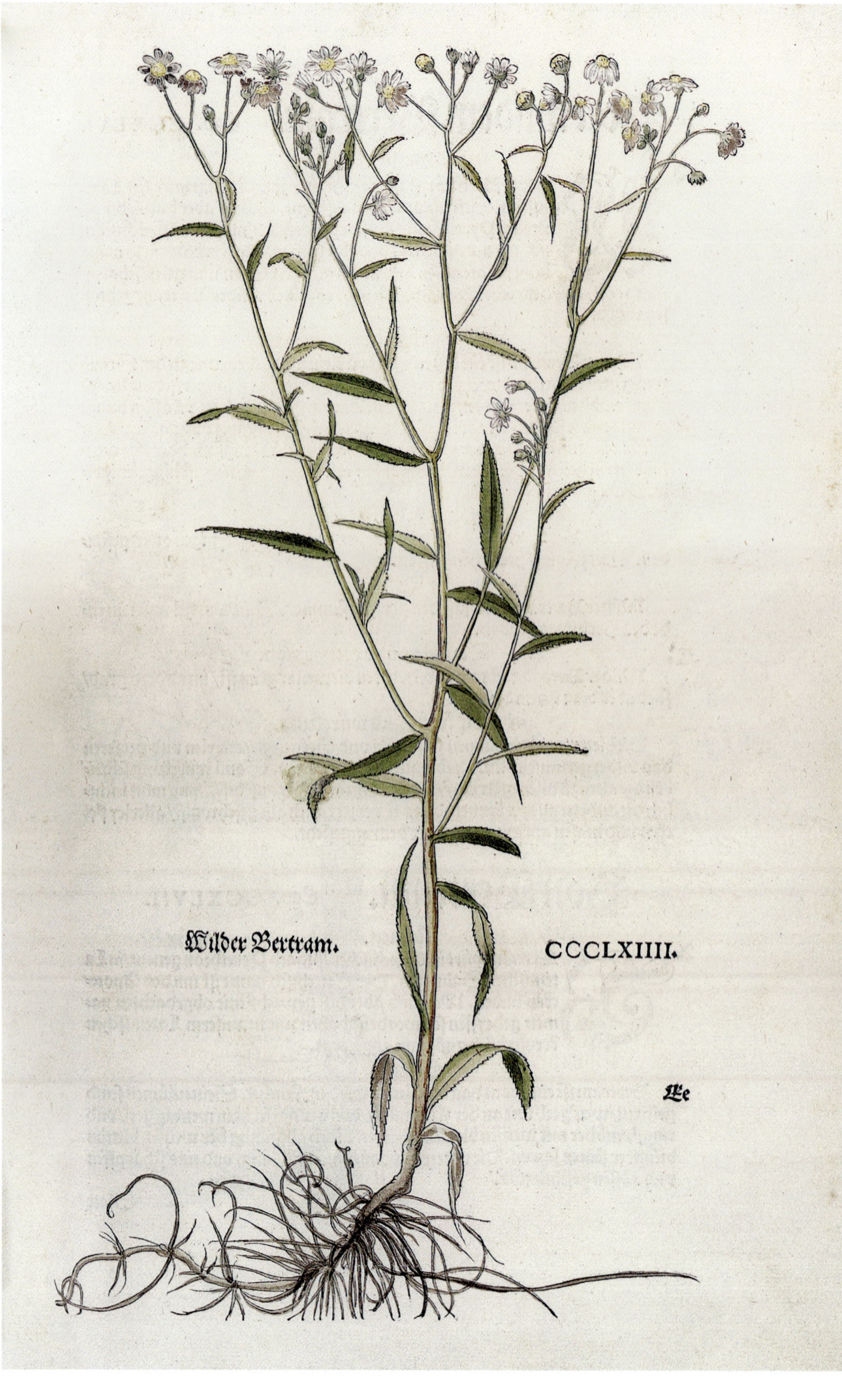
Wilder Bertram.
CCCLXIIII.

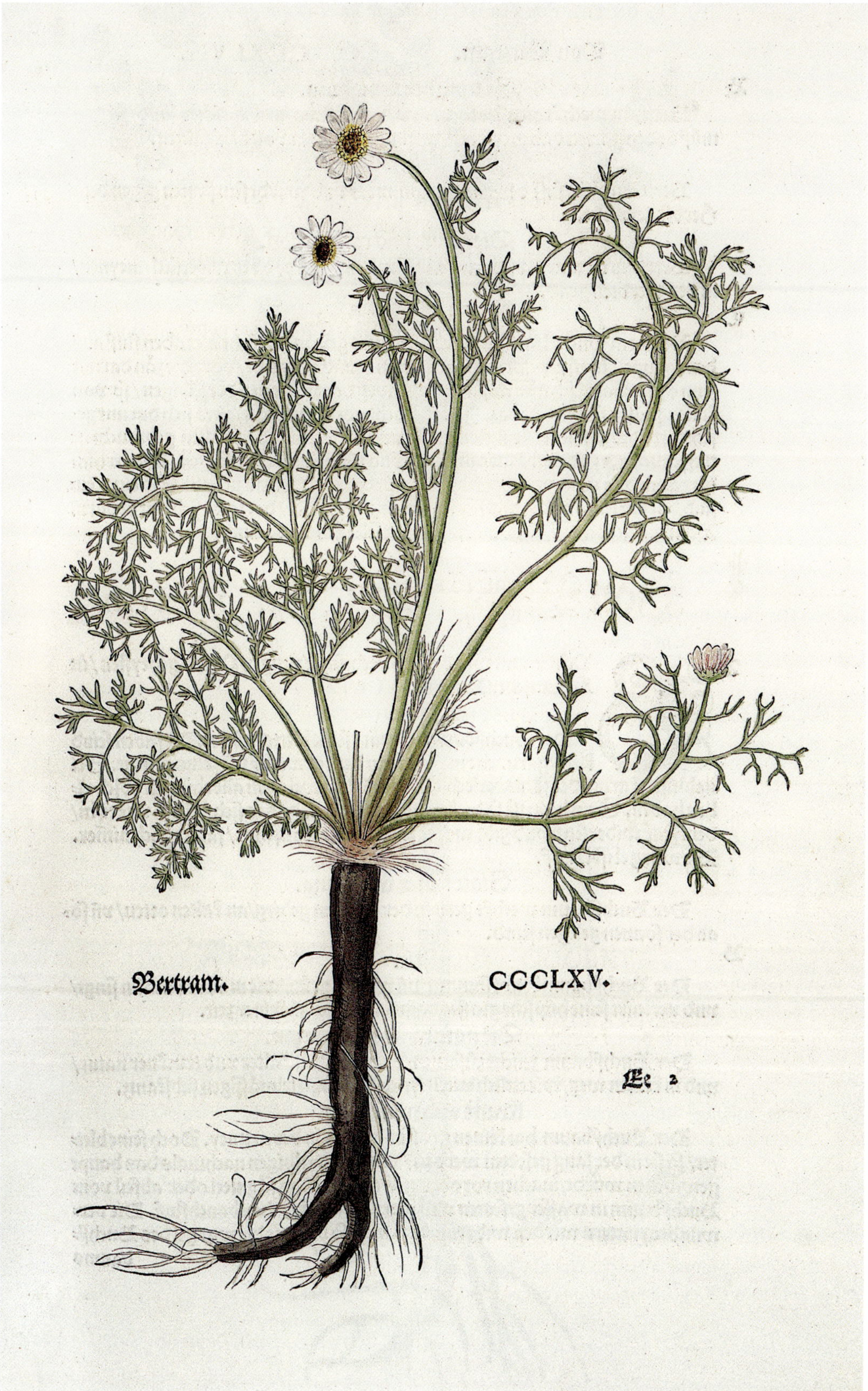
Bertram.
CCCLXV.
Ee 2

COMMON BOX

Fuchs expressly warns against sleeping under the COMMON BOX (CCXLVIII), because the plant had an antagonising effect on human beings.

BUCHSBAUM

Eindringlich warnt Fuchs davor, unter dem BUCHSBAUM (Cap. CCXLVIII) zu schlafen, weil er der Natur des Menschen zuwiderlaufe.

BUIS

Fuchs déconseille fortement de dormir sous le BUIS (CCLVIII) parce qu'il serait, selon lui, contraire à la nature humaine.

PAGE 466

BUTTERBUR

It remains unclear how BUTTERBUR (CCXLIX) could be unknown to the apothecaries, when it was such a "precious medicine… against the plague."

„PESTILENTZWURTZ"

Es bleibt unverständlich, warum die „PESTILENTZWURTZ" (Cap. CCXLIX) in den Apotheken unbekannt gewesen sein soll, wenn sie eine derart „köstlich artzney … wider die pestilentz" war.

PÉTASITE OFFICINAL

Il est difficile de comprendre pourquoi les apothicaires ne connaissaient pas la «racine à pestilence» («Pestilentzwurtz») – le PÉTASITE OFFICINAL (CCXLIX), dit aussi CHAPEAU-DU-DIABLE –, si «elle est un précieux remède […] contre la pestilence».

PAGE 467

WOODBINE

Whereas the striking flowers of WOODBINE (CCL), also known as HONEYSUCKLE, made it a desirable garden plant, the leaves and berries were also used medicinally, even if some of the effects Fuchs describes are in fact the early symptoms of poisoning.

„GEYSSBLATT"

Seine auffällige Blüte machte das „GEYSSBLATT" (Cap. CCL) in den Gärten begehrt, seine Blätter und Beeren wurden jedoch auch arzneilich verordnet, wobei einige der beschriebenen Wirkungen als Anzeichen einer beginnenden Vergiftung zu werten sind.

CHÈVREFEUILLE DES BOIS

Le CHÈVREFEUILLE DES BOIS (CCL) était très apprécié dans les jardins pour ses fleurs décoratives. Mais ce n'était pas qu'une ornementale puisqu'on utilisait ses feuilles et ses baies en médecine. Cependant certains effets que décrit Fuchs peuvent être considérés aujourd'hui comme les prémices d'un empoisonnement.

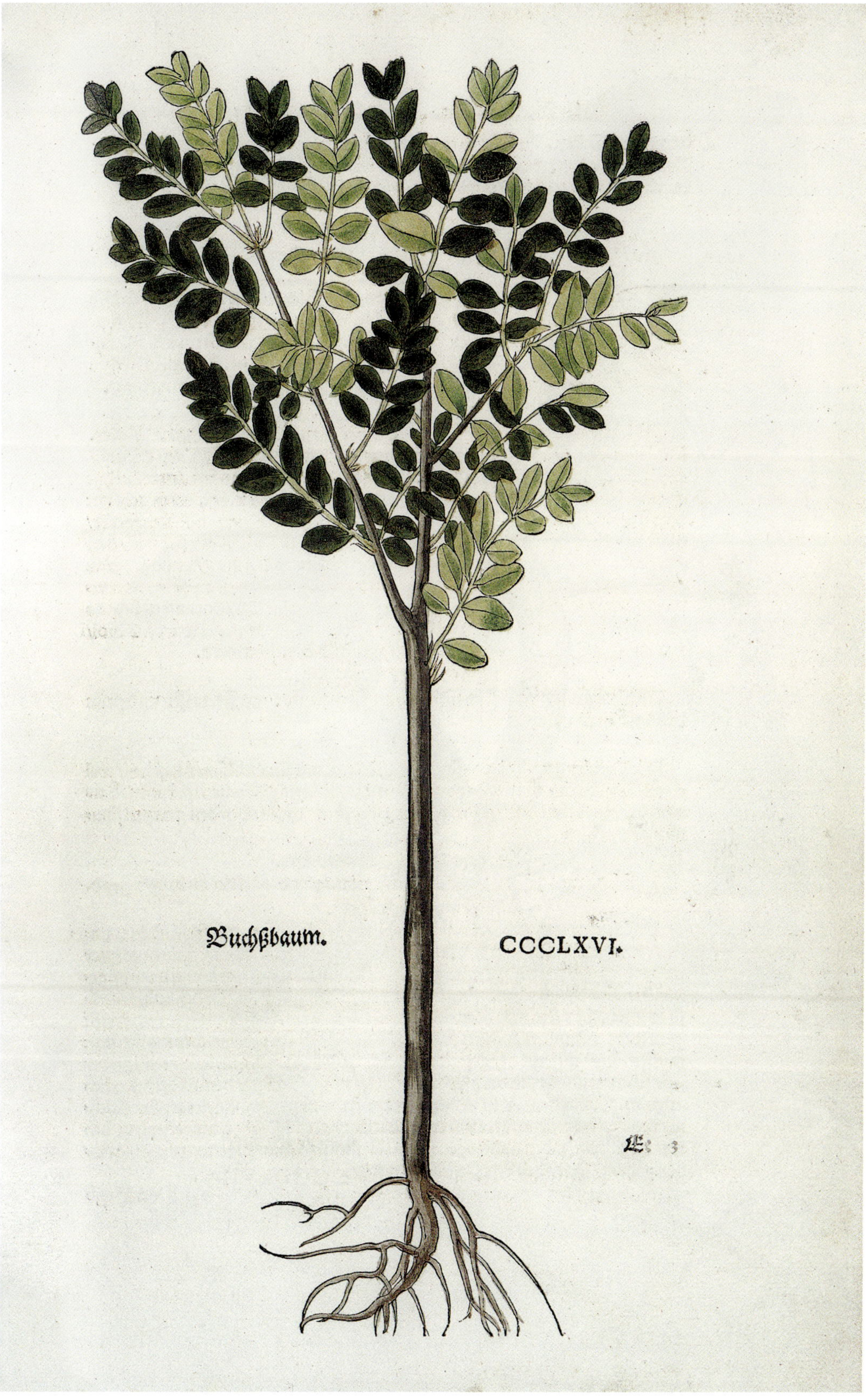
Buchßbaum.
CCCLXVI.
E 3

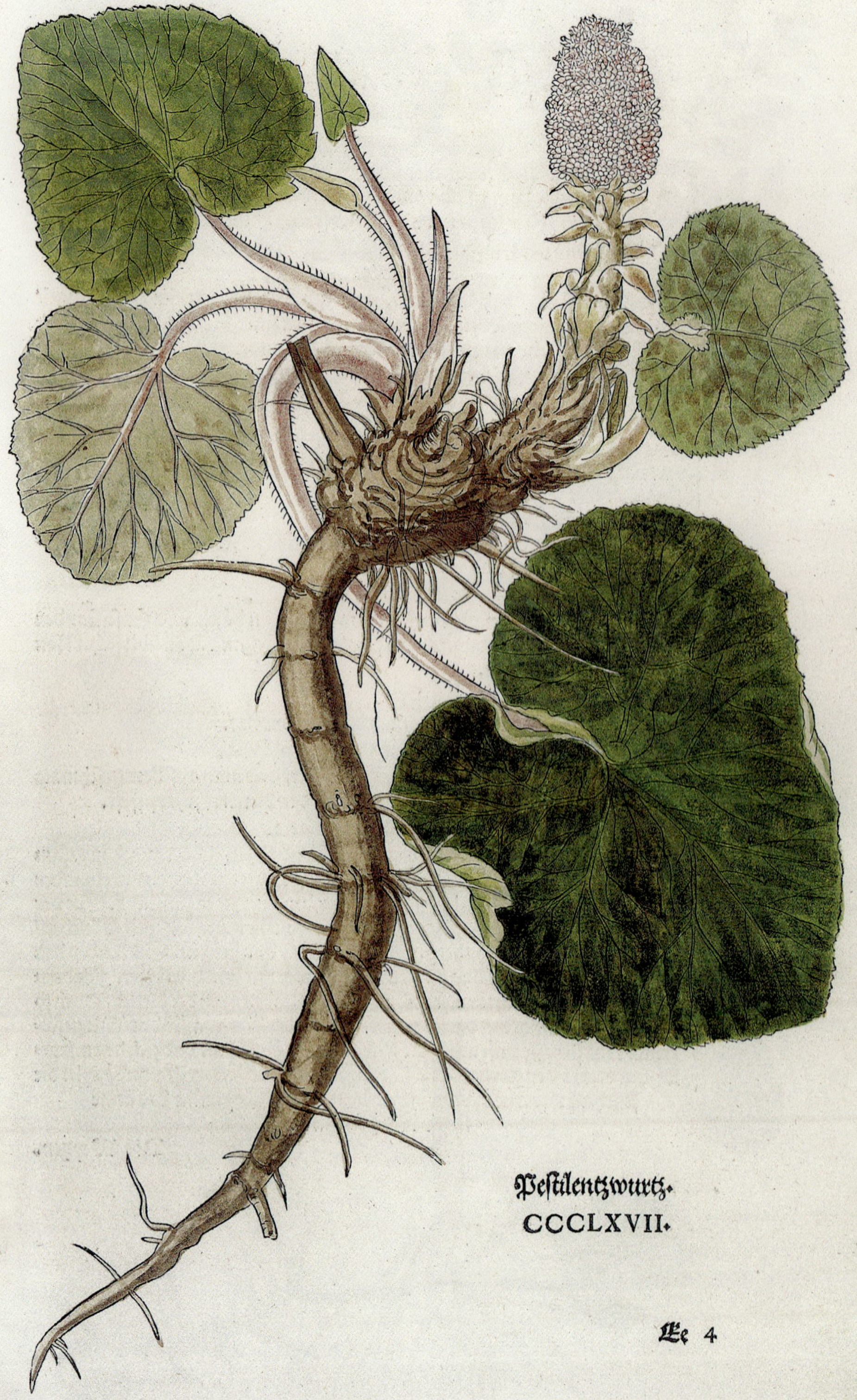

Pestilentzwurtz.
CCCLXVII.

Ee 4

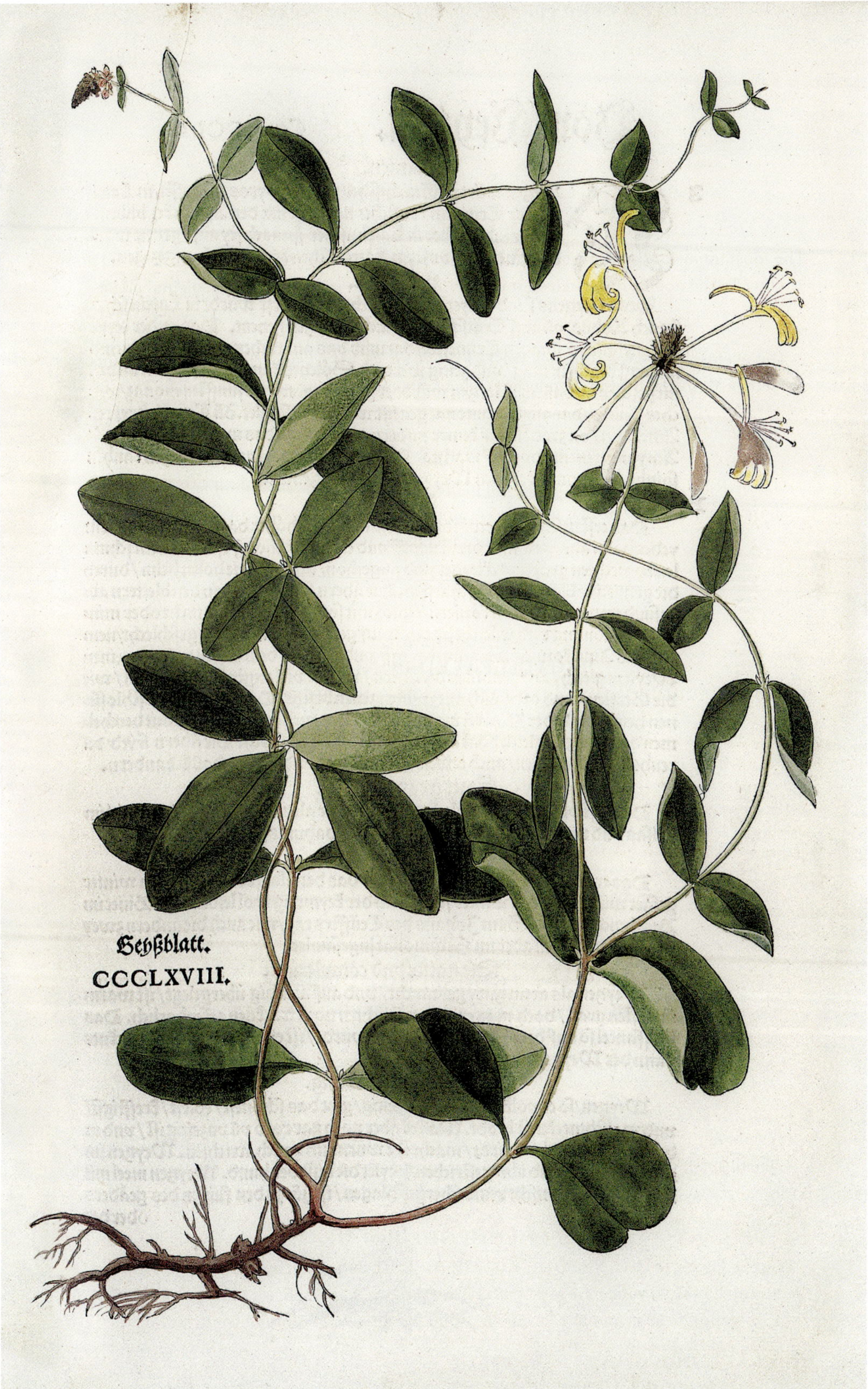
Geyßblatt.
CCCLXVIII.

WHEAT

The most important application of WHEAT (CCLI) is certainly its use as flour in bread and other baked goods; nonetheless, it is still interesting to read about its medicinal effects.

WEIZEN

Die wichtigste Verwendung des WEIZENS (Cap. CCLI) ist sicherlich die Verarbeitung seines Mehls zu Brot und anderem Gebäck; dennoch ist es reizvoll, auch den Text zu seinen medizinischen Wirkungen zu lesen.

BLÉ

Le BLÉ (CCLI) est évidemment une plante alimentaire majeure, dont la farine sert à faire le pain et les gâteaux, mais il est intéressant aussi de lire les diverses indications thérapeutiques recensées par Fuchs.

PAGE 470

BROAD-LEAVED PONDWEED

BROAD-LEAVED PONDWEED (CCLII) is a water plant that is no longer used medicinally.

„SAMKRAUT“

„SAMKRAUT“ (Cap. CCLII) kennen wir als Wasserpflanze heute unter dem Namen Laichkraut, jedoch nicht mehr aus der Pflanzenheilkunde.

POTAMOT NAGEANT

Le POTAMOT NAGEANT (CCLII) est une plante aquatique, appelée en allemand «Samkraut» (herbe à graines ou herbe à frai) et qui a disparu de la pharmacopée.

PAGE 471

GOOSEFOOT

Precisely why red GOOSEFOOT, or GOOSE HERB (CCLIII), was thought to be fatal to pigs remains unclear; perhaps the resemblance of its leaves to those of the Thorn Apple played a role, as the reference to NIGHTSHADE suggests.

„GENSSFUSS“

Warum der „GENSSFUSS“ (Cap. CCLIII) für Schweine tödlich sein soll, bleibt unklar; vielleicht spielt die Ähnlichkeit der Blätter mit jenen des Stechapfels eine Rolle, wofür auch der Vergleich mit dem Nachtschatten spricht.

CHÉNOPODE ROUGE

D’après Fuchs, le CHÉNOPODE ROUGE (CCLIII), ou patte-d’oie rouge, serait fatal aux pourceaux, mais la raison n’en est pas claire. Peut-être parce que les feuilles ressemblent à celles de la stramoine, ce que la comparaison avec la morelle confirmerait.

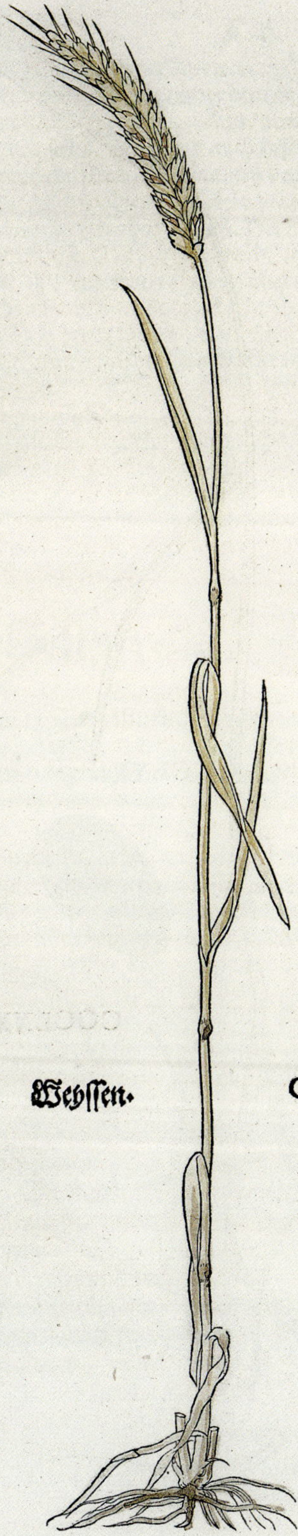

Weyssen. CCCLXIX.

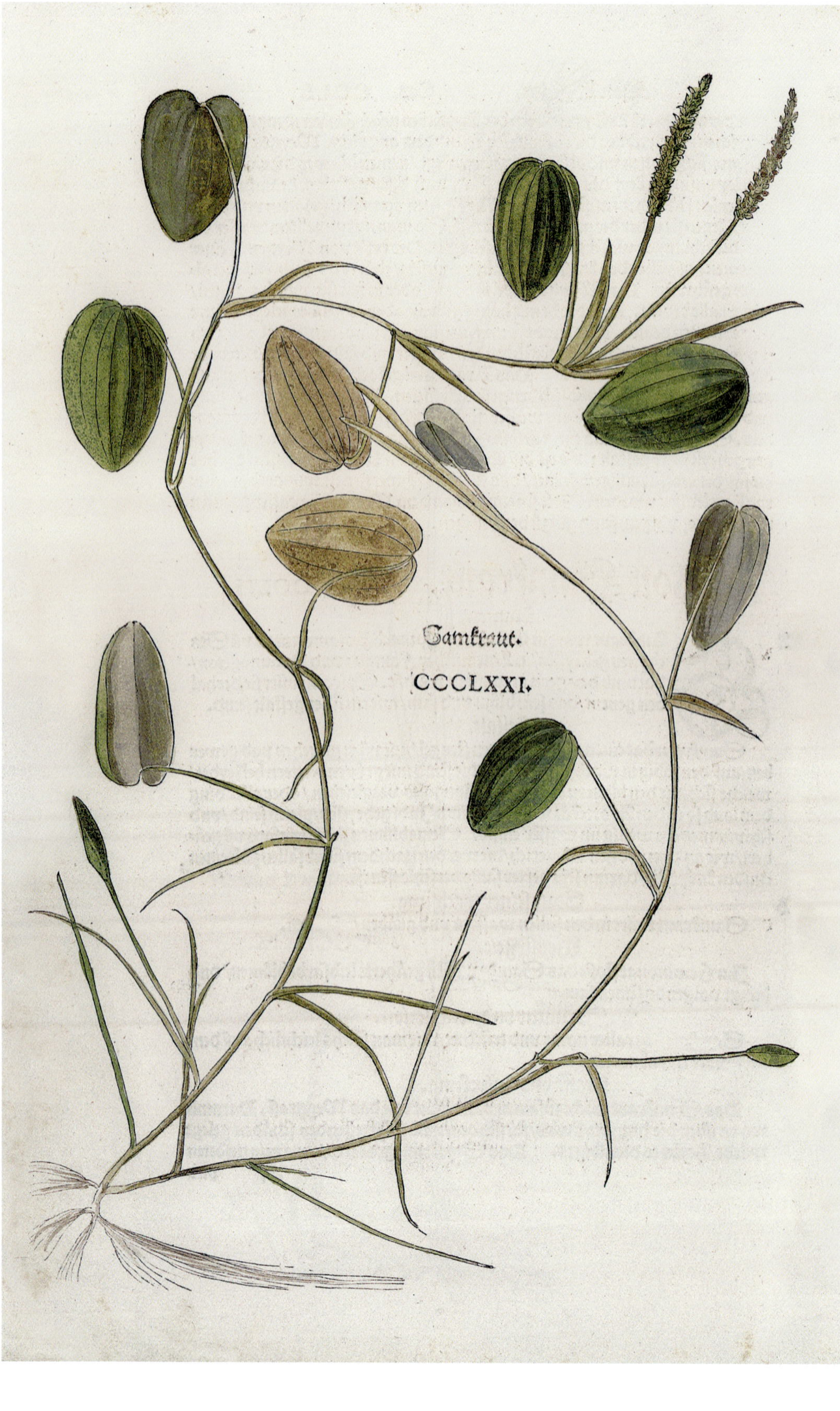
Samkraut.
CCCLXXI.

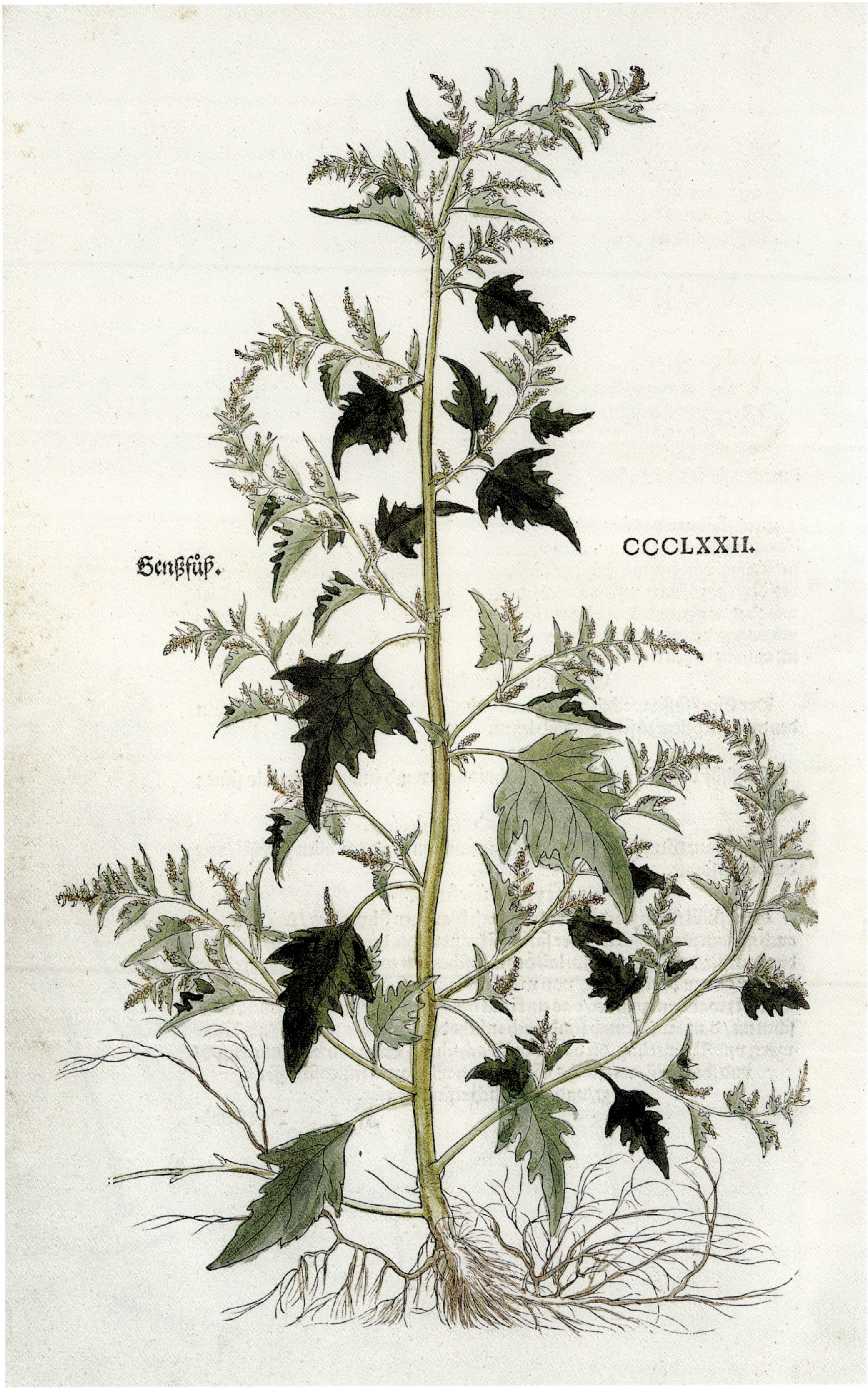
Genßfüß.
CCCLXXII.

MACEDONIAN PARSLEY

Although stone or MACEDONIAN PARSLEY (CCLIIII) is in fact not a Parsley at all, the same effects are attributed to it.

„FREMBDE PETERSILG" (GEWÜRZDOLDE)

Bei der „FREMBDEN PETERSILG" (Cap. CCLIIII) handelt es sich keineswegs um eine Petersilienart, sondern um die Gewürzdolde, der jedoch trotzdem die Wirkung der Petersilie zugeschrieben wird.

SISON AROMATIQUE

Dans le cas du «persil étranger» («frembde Petersilg» dans le texte), il ne s'agit pas d'une variété de persil, mais bien du SISON AROMATIQUE (CCLIIII), dont les effets sont comparés à ceux du persil.

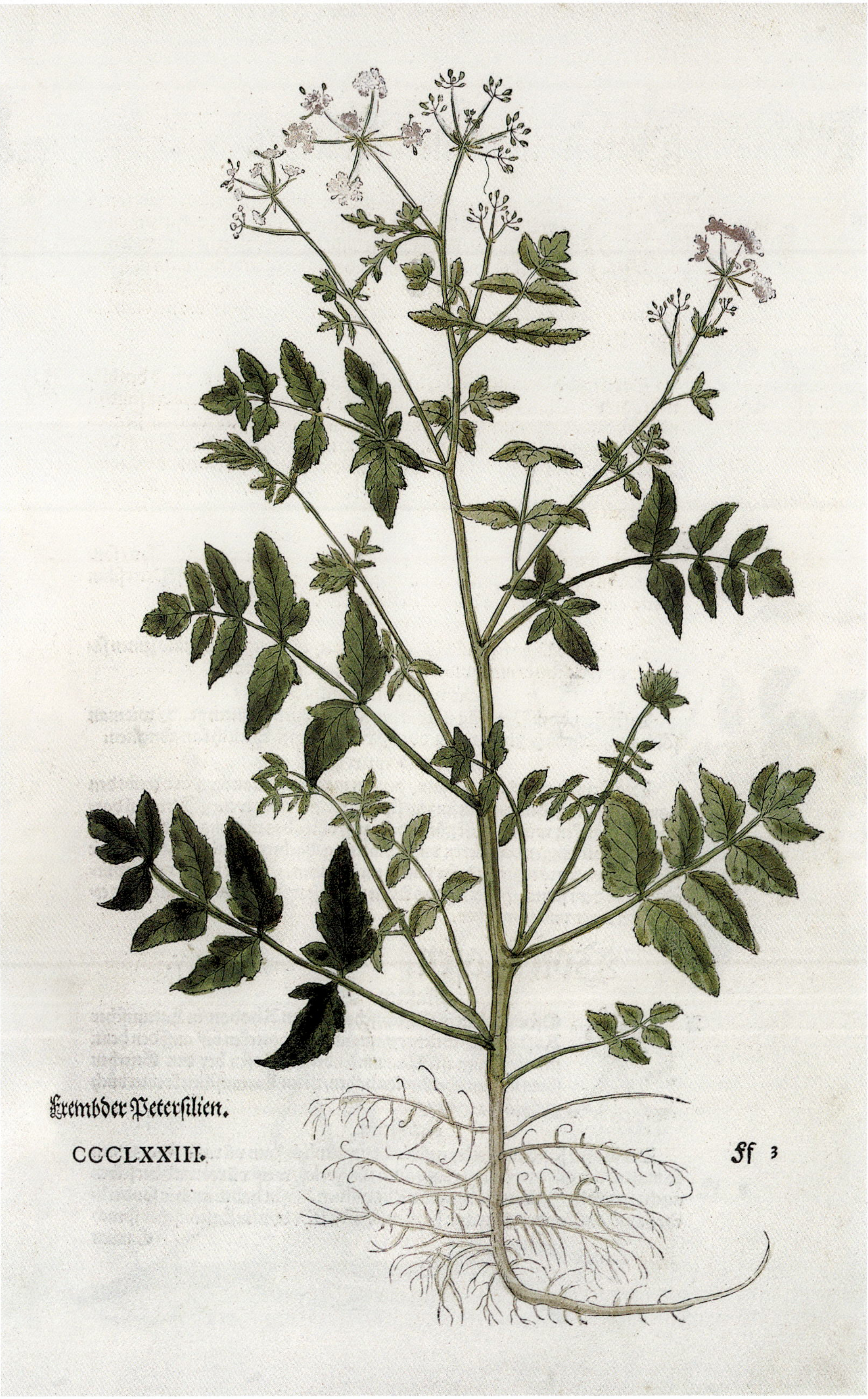
Frembder Petersilien.
CCCLXXIII.
Ff 3

ROSE

Today, we consider the ROSE (CCLV) only as a decorative plant; however, its significance and medical applications in earlier centuries can hardly be overestimated. The last remaining applications of the ROSE are in Rose Honey, used for ulcerative stomatitis, and Rose Water, which is an ingredient of marzipan and other products. Plate CCCLXXIIII presents a combination of DOG ROSE (left) and FRENCH ROSE (right).

ROSE

Auch wenn wir die ROSE (Cap. CCLV) nur noch als Zierpflanze kennen, kann für die früheren Jahrhunderte ihre Bedeutung und Verwendung in der Medizin kaum überschätzt werden. Letzte Überreste sind der Rosenhonig gegen Mundfäule und das Rosenwasser, das heute nur noch zur Marzipanherstellung gebraucht wird. Tafel CCCLXXIIII stellt eine Kombination von HUNDS-ROSE, links, und ESSIG-ROSE, rechts, dar.

ROSE

Nous connaissons avant tout la ROSE (CCLV) comme fleur ornementale, mais c'était sans conteste une plante médicinale majeure dans le passé. Il ne subsiste aujourd'hui de ses nombreuses applications que le miel rosat utilisé pour la stomatite ulcéreuse et l'eau de roses servant à la fabrication de la pâte d'amandes. La planche CCCLXXIIII réunit deux variétés de rose : l'ÉGLANTIER COMMUN (à g.), ou rosier des chiens, et le ROSIER DE FRANCE (à dr.).

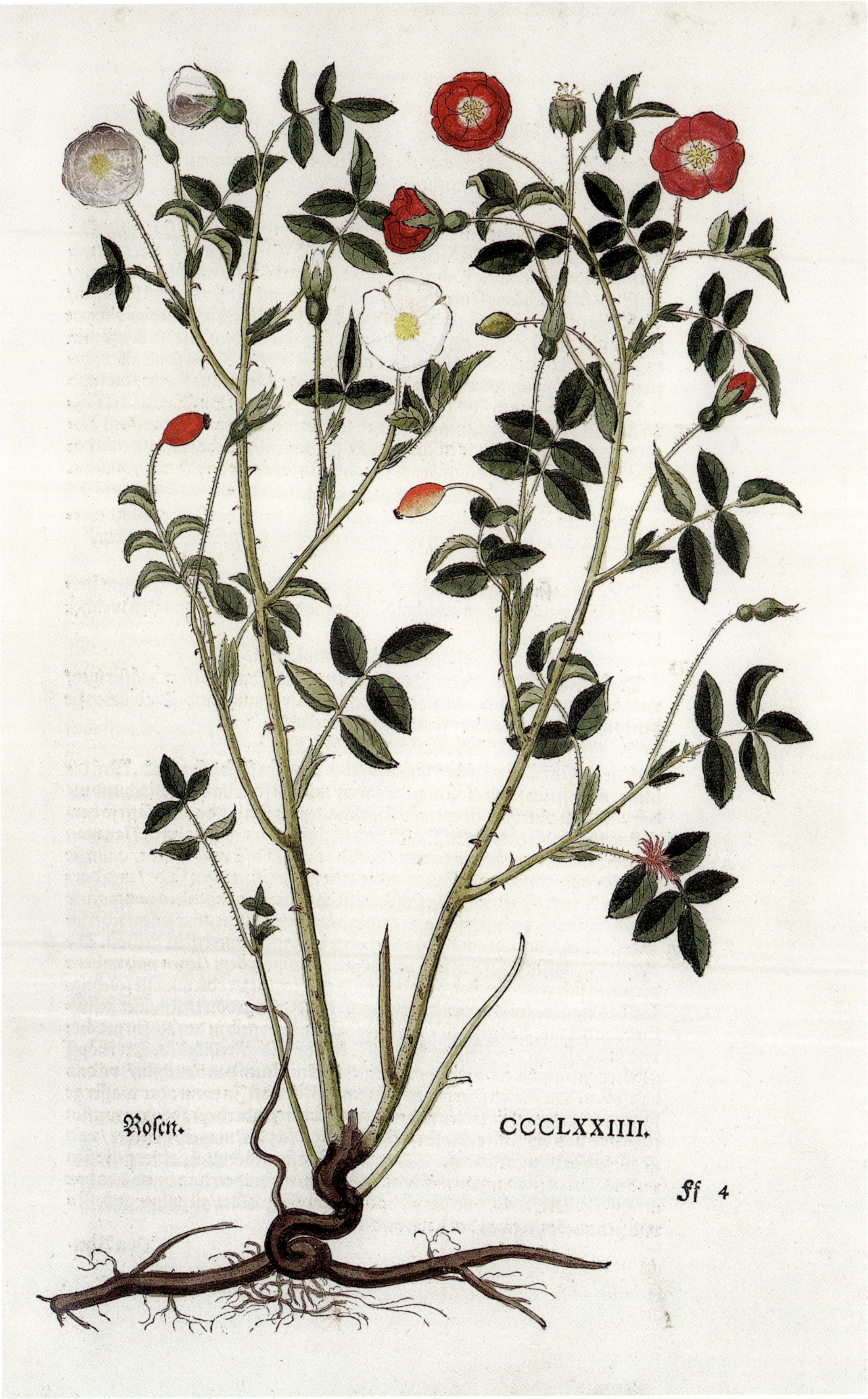
Rosen.
CCCLXXIIII.
Ff 4

RADISH

For RADISH (CCLVI), which includes Garden and Horse Radish, Fuchs speaks not only of their medicinal effects, but also of the culinary use of the hot-tasting root, for which it is also used today.

RETTICH

Neben den medizinischen Anwendungen erwähnt Fuchs beim RETTICH (Cap. CCLVI), zu dem er auch den Meerrettich zählt, ebenso die noch heute beliebten Einsatzmöglichkeiten der scharf schmeckenden Wurzel in der Küche.

RADIS CULTIVÉ

Pour le RADIS CULTIVÉ (CCLVI), auquel il rattache le raifort, Fuchs mentionne, outre ses usages thérapeutiques, les divers emplois culinaires de sa racine aromatique.

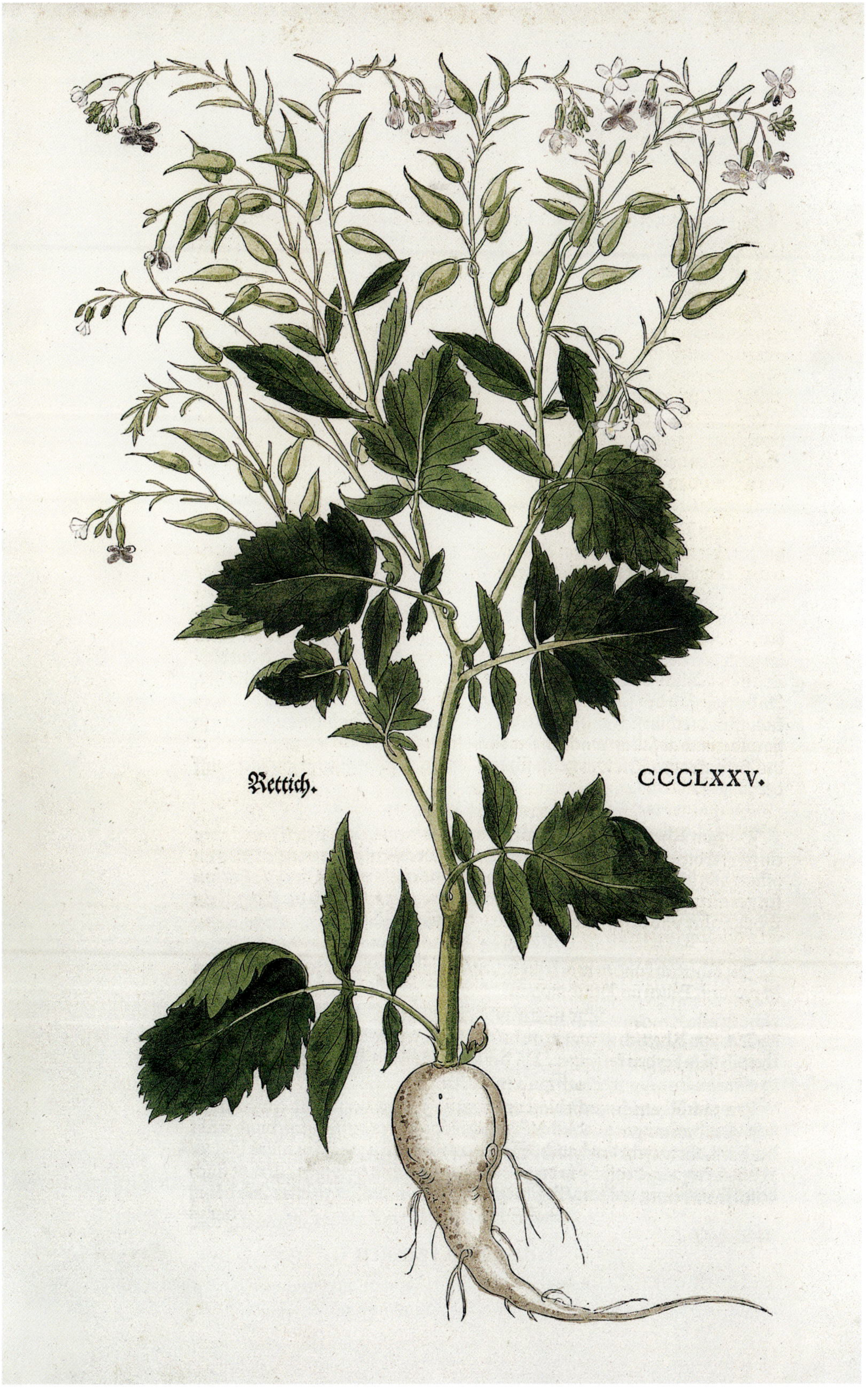
Rettich.
CCCLXXV.

REDCURRANT

Whereas the fruits of REDCURRANT (CCLVII) were supposed to strengthen the stomach and stimulate the appetite, the juice was recommended to feverish patients.

ROTE JOHANNISBEERE

Magenstärkend und appetitanregend sollten die Früchte der ROTEN JOHANNISBEERE (Cap. CCLVII) sein, der Saft wird fiebernden Patienten empfohlen.

GROSEILLIER ROUGE

Les baies du GROSEILLIER ROUGE (CCLVII) seraient un tonique de l'estomac et stimulerait l'appétit ; le jus est recommandé aux fiévreux.

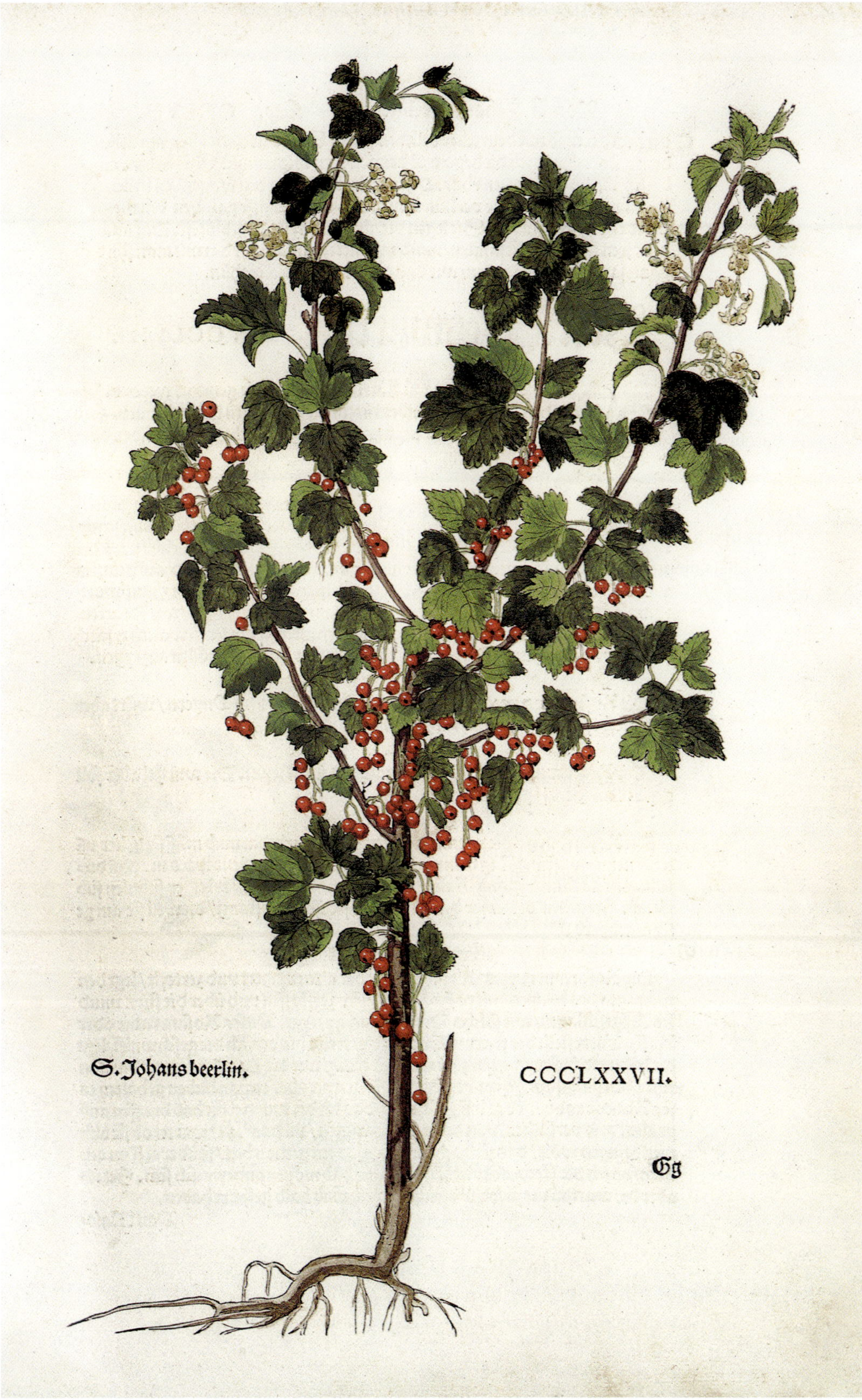
S. Johans beerlin.
CCCLXXVII.
Gg

ROSE-ROOT

The description of the effects of the thick-leaved plant known as ROSE-ROOT (CCLVIII), MIDSUMMER-MEN or KING'S CROWN illustrates the problems associated with botanical identification in former days.

„ROSENWURTZ"

Zu den Dickblattgewächsen gehört die „ROSENWURTZ" (Cap. CCLVIII), bei deren Beschreibung der Wirkung wir die früheren Probleme der botanischen Identifikation gut nachvollziehen können.

ORPIN ROSE

L'ORPIN ROSE (CCLVIII) appartient à la famille des Crassulacées. La description de ses effets thérapeutiques montre bien les difficultés que rencontraient les botanistes anciens pour identifier les plantes.

PAGE 482

SWEET MARJORAM

SWEET MARJORAM (CCLIX) was not only valued for its diuretic properties but also for its strengthening effect on the brain.

MAJORAN

Der MAJORAN (Cap. CCLIX) wird wegen seiner harntreibenden Eigenschaften geschätzt, soll aber auch das Gehirn stärken.

MARJOLAINE DES JARDINS

La MARJOLAINE DES JARDINS (CCLIX) est une plante très appréciée pour ses propriétés diurétiques ; elle aurait en outre une action fortifiante sur le cerveau.

PAGE 483

SANICLE

SANICLE or POOLROOT (CCLX), whose properties were similar to those of comfrey, was famed for its wound-healing properties.

„SANICKEL"

Der „SANICKEL" (Cap. CCLX) wird als Wundkraut gerühmt, dessen Eigenschaften denen des Beinwells entsprechen.

SANICLE D'EUROPE

La SANICLE D'EUROPE (CCLX), dont les propriétés sont analogues à celles de la grande consoude, est louée pour ses vertus cicatrisantes.

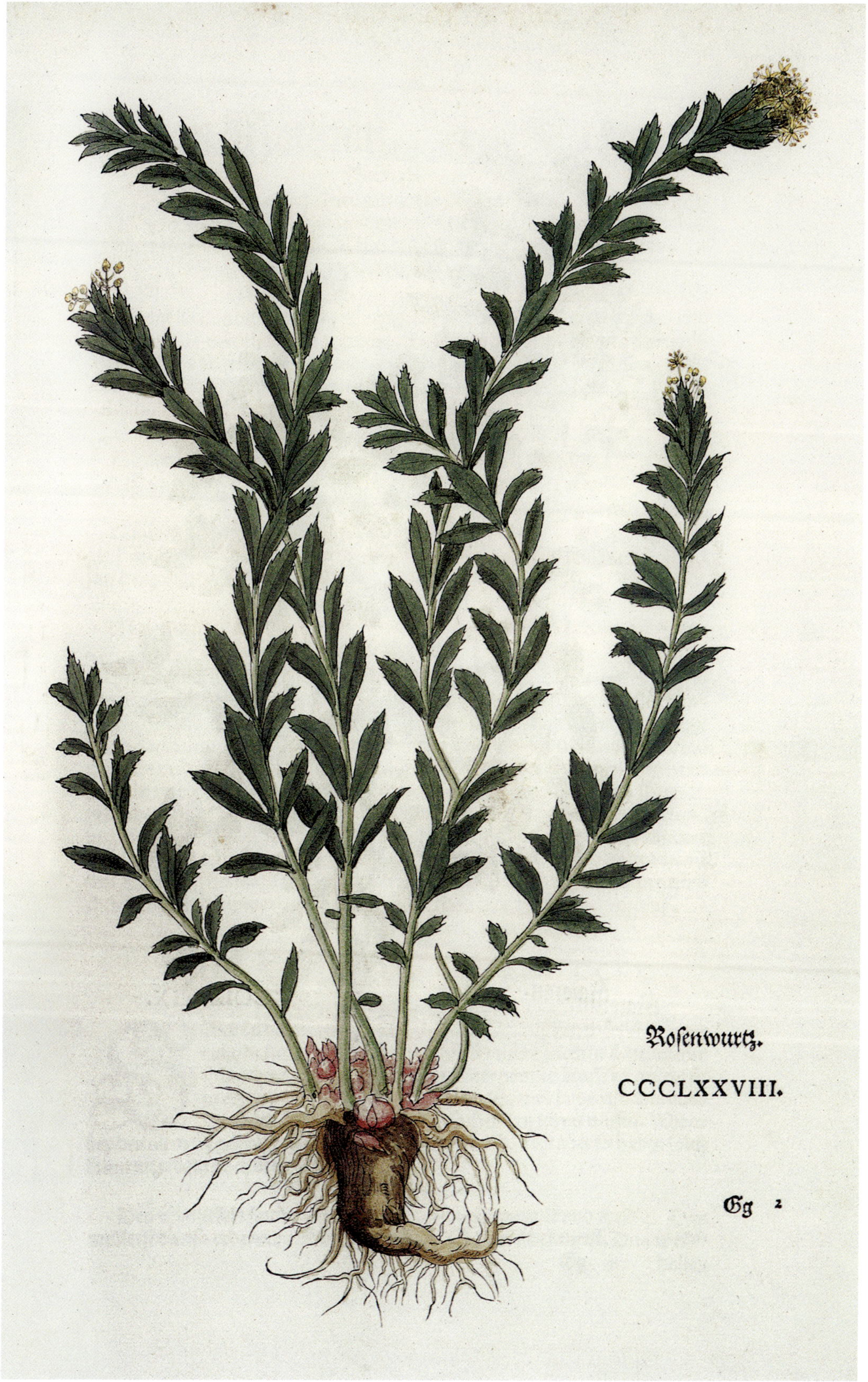
Rosenwurtz.
CCCLXXVIII.
Gg 2

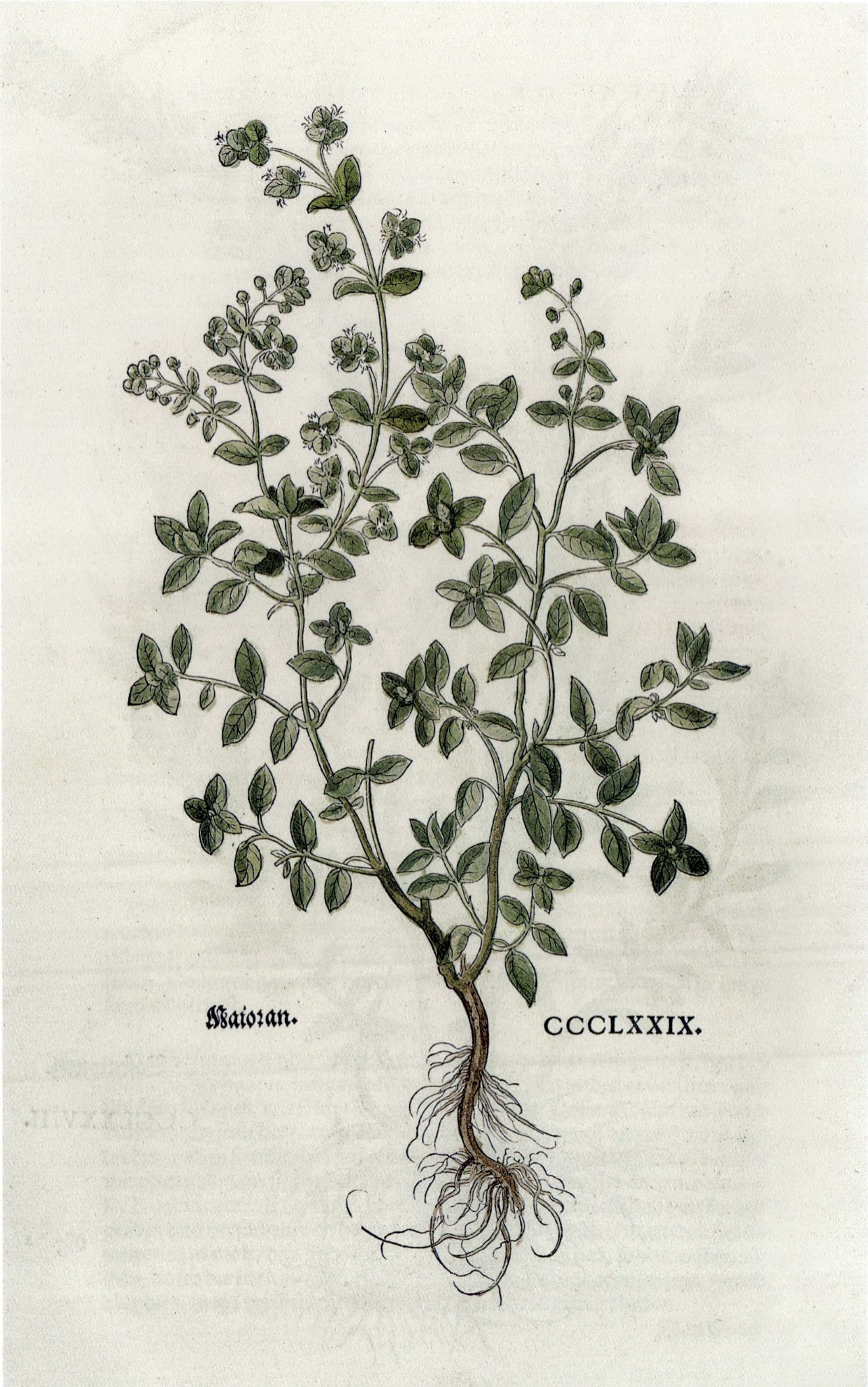
Maioran.
CCCLXXIX.

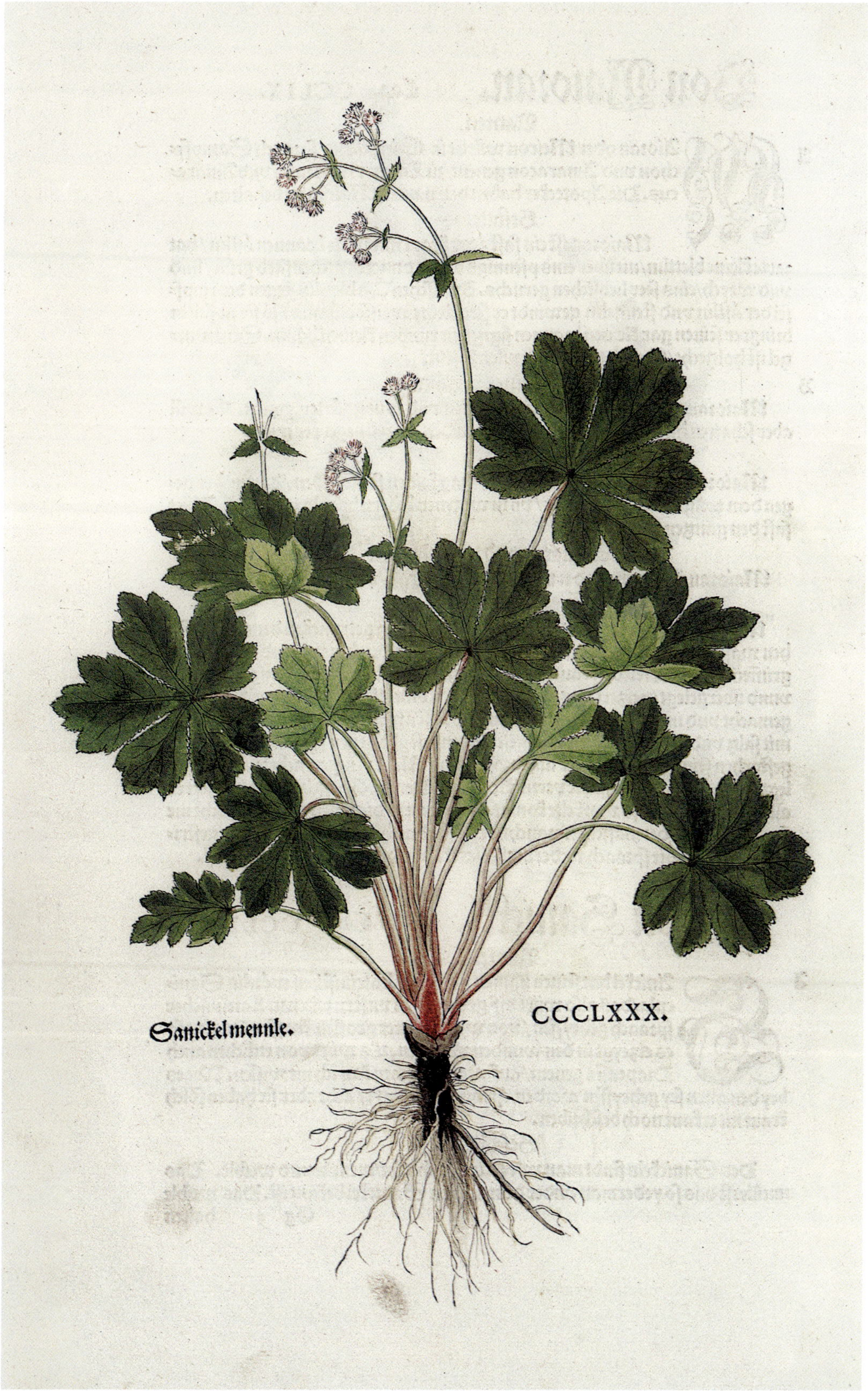
Sanickelmennle.
CCCLXXX.

SPINACH

The culinary use of SPINACH (CCLXI) clearly stands in the foreground, in spite of several references to its medicinal effect.

SPINAT

Beim SPINAT (Cap. CCLXI) steht trotz einiger Anmerkungen zur Arzneiwirkung der Küchengebrauch eindeutig im Vordergrund.

ÉPINARD

Hormis quelques remarques sur ses vertus thérapeutiques, l'ÉPINARD (CCLXI) est surtout évoqué comme plante alimentaire.

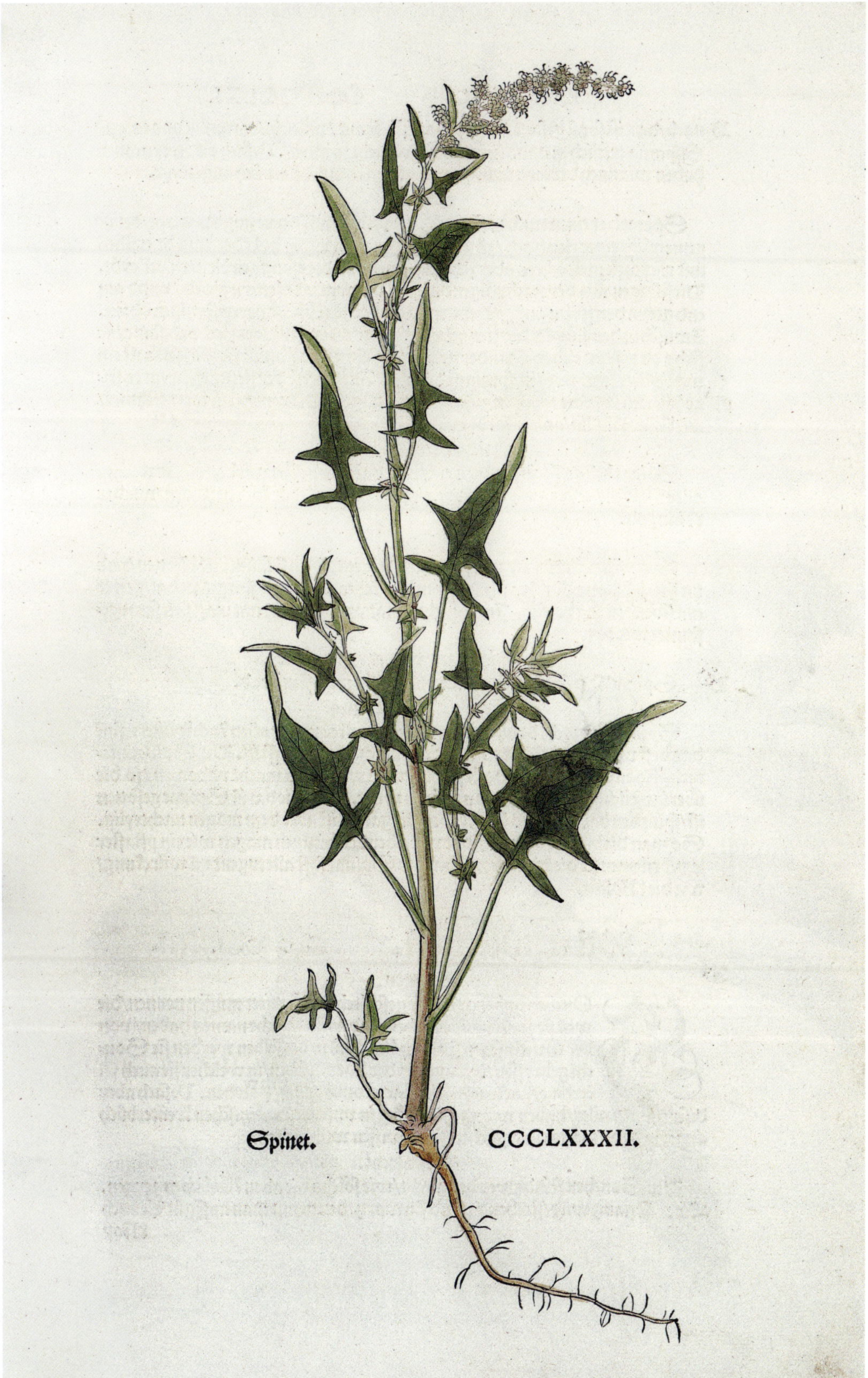
Spinet.
CCCLXXXII.

SOW THISTLES

In choosing a title for the chapter on the MILK or SOW THISTLES (CCLXII), Fuchs simply germanized the Latin name of the plants.

„SONCHEN"

Bei der Bezeichnung „SONCHEN" (Cap. CCLXII) hat Fuchs den lateinischen Pflanzennamen *Sonchus*, der noch heute gültig ist, einfach eingedeutscht.

LAITERONS

Fuchs a tout simplement germanisé le mot latin *Sonchus*, qui désigne les LAITERONS, lorsqu'il parle de «Sonchen» (CCLXII). Le nom générique SONCHUS est toujours usité de nos jours.

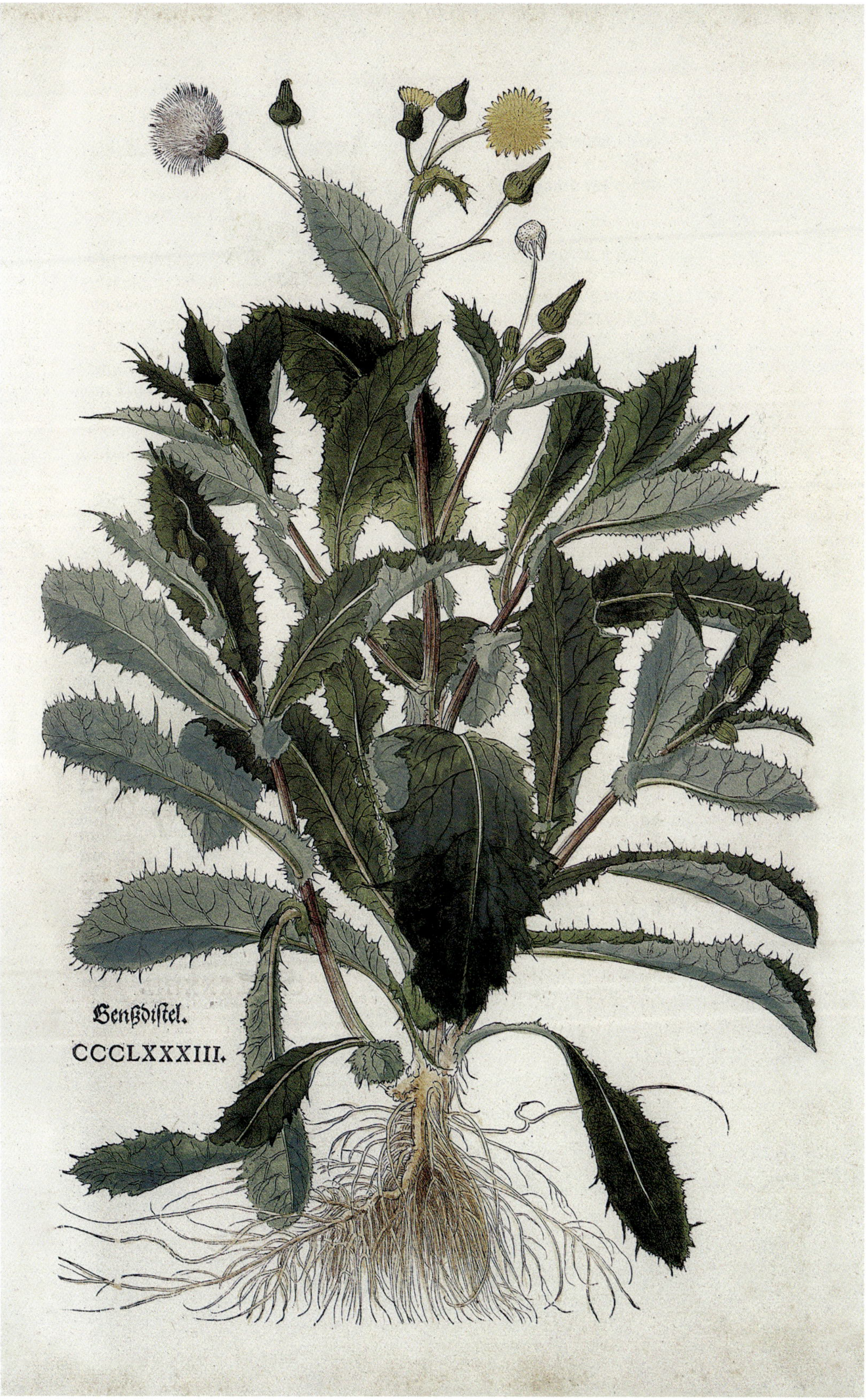
Genßdistel.
CCCLXXXIII.

WILD CHICORY

As so often in Fuchs, this chapter (CCLXIII) includes several different kinds of plants: BROAD-LEAVED ENDIVE (plate CCCLXXXV), NARROW-LEAVED ENDIVE (plate CCCLXXXVI), WILD CHICORY (plate CCCLXXXVII) and, surprisingly, COMMON DANDELION (plate CCCLXXXVIII), whose picturesque German name wittily compares the bald base of the "dandelion clock" to the tonsured head of a monk.

WEGWARTE

Wie so oft, finden sich auch bei der WEGWARTE (Cap. CCLXIII) mehrere Pflanzenarten zusammengefasst: die WINTER-ENDIVIE (Taf. CCCLXXXV), die SCHMALBLÄTTRIGE ENDIVIE (Taf. CCCLXXXVI), die eigentliche WEGWARTE (Taf. CCCLXXXVII) und überraschenderweise auch der LÖWENZAHN (Taf. CCCLXXXVIII), dessen alter Name „Pfaffenröhrlin" ebenso derb wie bildhaft ist, wenn man den teilweise kahlen Fruchtboden der Pusteblume als Kopf mit der mönchsüblichen Tonsur betrachtet.

CHICORÉE SCARIOLE

Une fois encore, Fuchs associe diverses espèces, ici sous l'appellation «CHICORÉE» (CCLXIII) : la CHICORÉE SCARIOLE (pl. CCCLXXXV), la CHICORÉE BLANCHE (pl. CCCLXXXVI), la CHICORÉE SAUVAGE (pl. CCCLXXXVII) et, ce qui est surprenant, le PISSENLIT (pl. CCCLXXXVIII). Celui-ci portait autrefois le nom populaire de «Pfaffenröhrlin» (tuyau de curé), ce qui est aussi cru qu'imagé, si l'on voit dans son capitule dégarni en partie de ses aigrettes un crâne de moine arborant la tonsure habituelle.

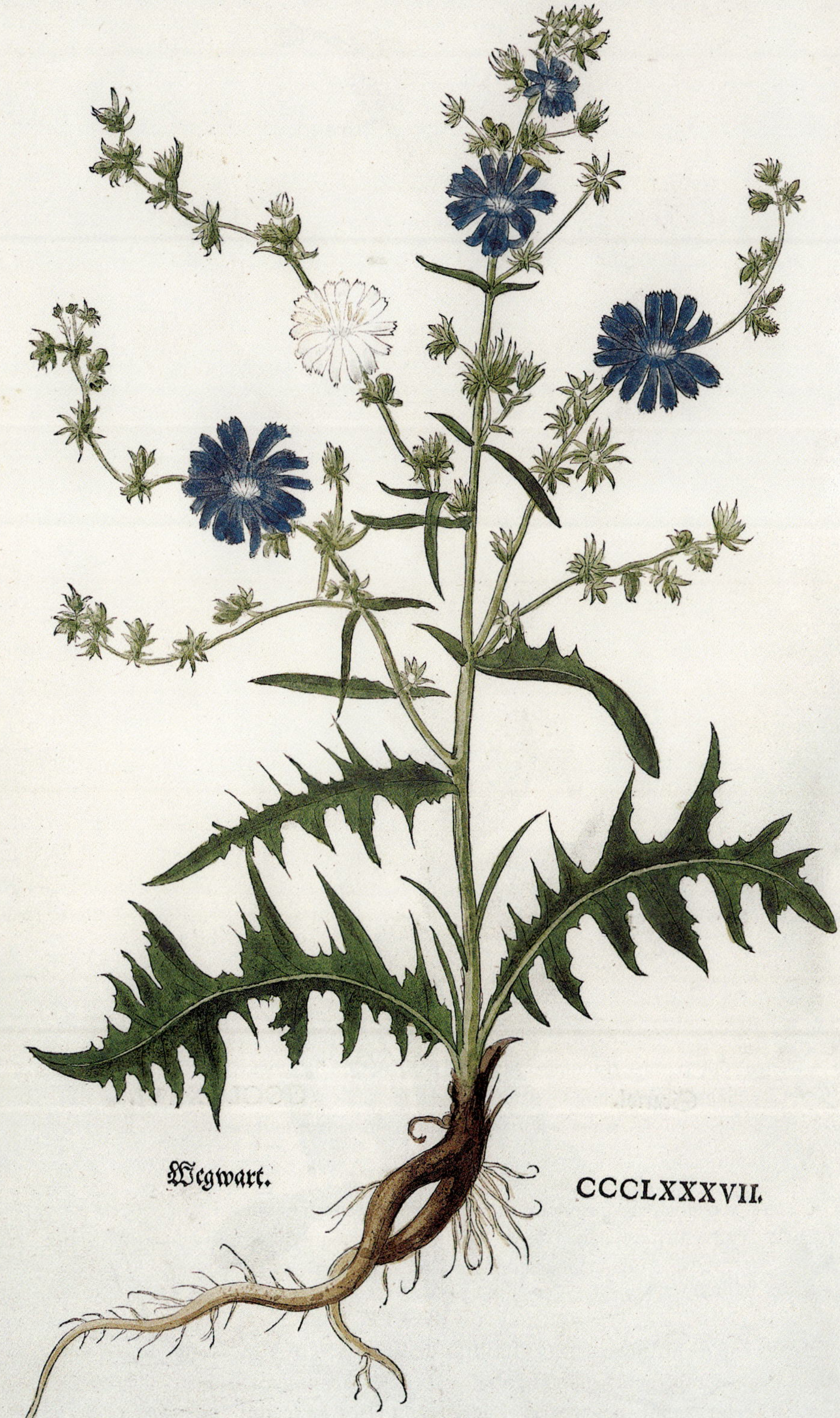
Wegwart.
CCCLXXXVII.

CARROT

Three different representatives of CARROT (CCLXIIII) make their appearance in this chapter. In addition to its medicinal effects, the yellow garden carrot was also supposed to possess aphrodisiac properties.

„PASTNACHEN“

Drei verschiedene Vertreter der Möhre erscheinen im Kapitel „PASTNACHEN“ (Cap. CCLXIIII), von denen der Gelben Rübe neben allerhand arzneilicher Wirkung auch eine aphrodisische zugeschrieben wird.

CAROTTE

Au chapitre « Pastnachen » (CCLXIIII) – du latin PASTINACA = nourriture –, sont figurées trois représentantes de la CAROTTE, dont la carotte jaune. On prêtait à celle-ci, outre des propriétés déjà nombreuses, un pouvoir aphrodisiaque.

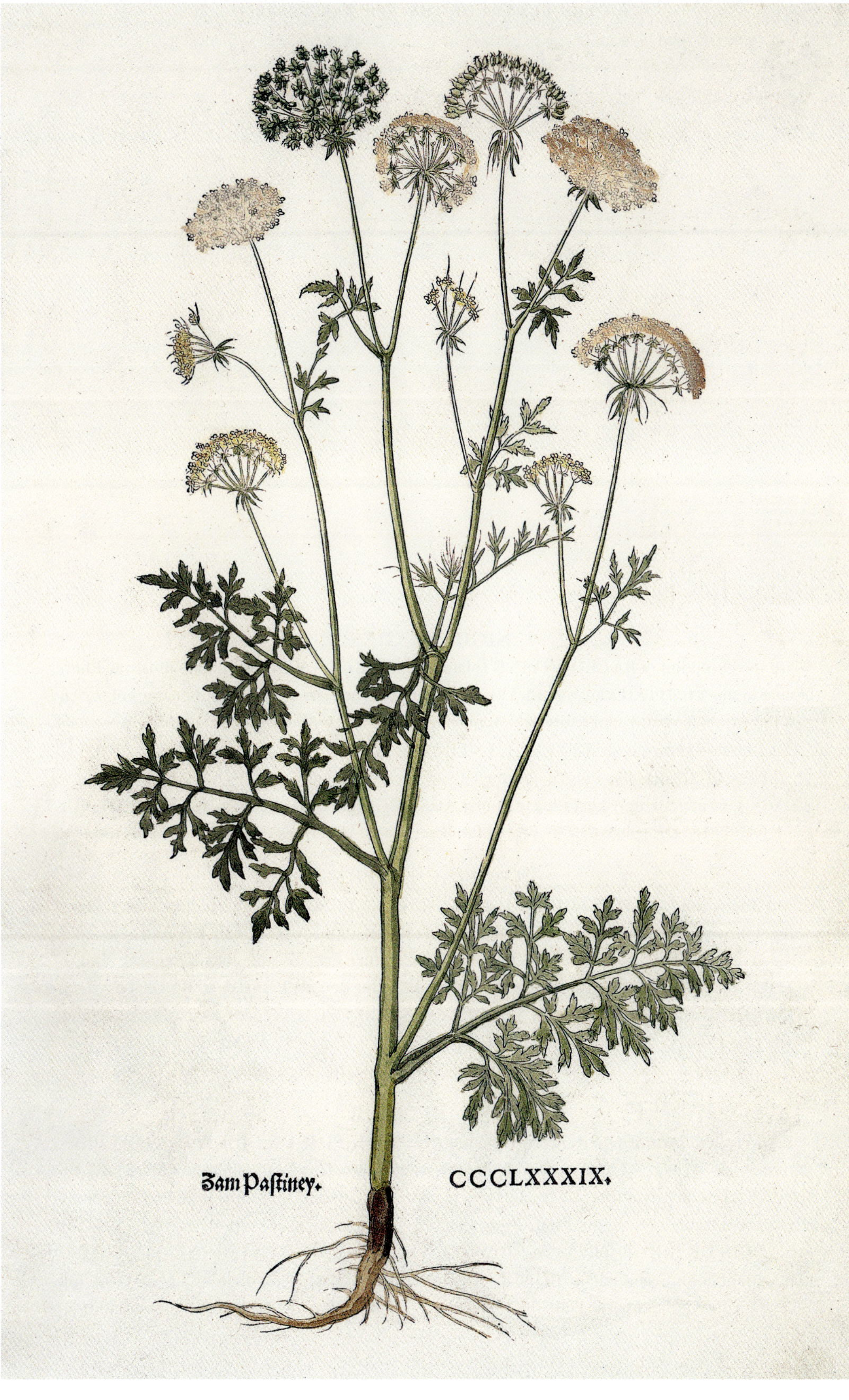
Zam Pastiney.
CCCLXXXIX.

NIGHTSHADES

With the exception of BALLOONVINE (plate CCCXCIIII), the other four plants illustrated here belong to the NIGHTSHADES (CCLXV), which are characterized by different degrees of toxicity. All the plants have unusual fruits, which may be inflated, as with CHINESE LANTERN (plate CCCXCIII), also known as JAPANESE LANTERN or WINTER CHERRY, and BALLOONVINE (plate CCCXCIIII), also known as Heart-Pea; prickly, as in downy THORN-APPLE (plate CCCXCVI); or appetizingly gleaming, as in BLACK NIGHTSHADE (plate CCCXCII) or DEADLY NIGHTSHADE (plate CCCXCV). For the latter, Fuchs described a fatal case of poisoning.

NACHTSCHATTEN

Mit Ausnahme der „WELSCH SCHLUTTEN“ (Taf. CCCXCIIII) gehören die anderen vier abgebildeten Pflanzen tatsächlich zu den NACHTSCHATTEN (Cap. CCLXV) und zeichnen sich durch ihre Giftigkeit aus. Sie fallen alle durch ihre Früchte auf, die aufgeblasen sind wie bei der JUDENKIRSCHE (Taf. CCCXCIII) oder den „WELSCH SCHLUTTEN“ (Taf. CCCXCIIII), dornig wie beim STECHAPFEL (Taf. CCCXCVI) oder appetitlich glänzend wie beim SCHWARZEN NACHTSCHATTEN (Taf. CCCXCII) oder der TOLLKIRSCHE (Taf. CCCXCV), für die Fuchs einen Fall tödlicher Vergiftung schildert.

POIS DE CŒUR

Parmi les cinq plantes figurant sur cette planche, seul le POIS DE CŒUR (pl. CCCXCIIII), nommé ici « Welsch Schlutten » ou gousse enflée étrangère, n’appartient pas aux MORELLES (CCLXV). Les quatre autres se caractérisent par une toxicité plus ou moins grande. En revanche, elles se remarquent toutes pour leur fruit, vésiculé comme celui du COQUERET (pl. CCCXCIII) ou du POIS DE CŒUR (pl. CCCXCIIII), épineux comme chez la STRAMOINE (pl. CCCXCVI), ou brillant comme celui de la MORELLE NOIRE (pl. CCCXCII) ou de la BELLADONE (pl. CCCXCV). En ce qui concerne cette dernière, Fuchs relate même un cas d’empoisonnement mortel.

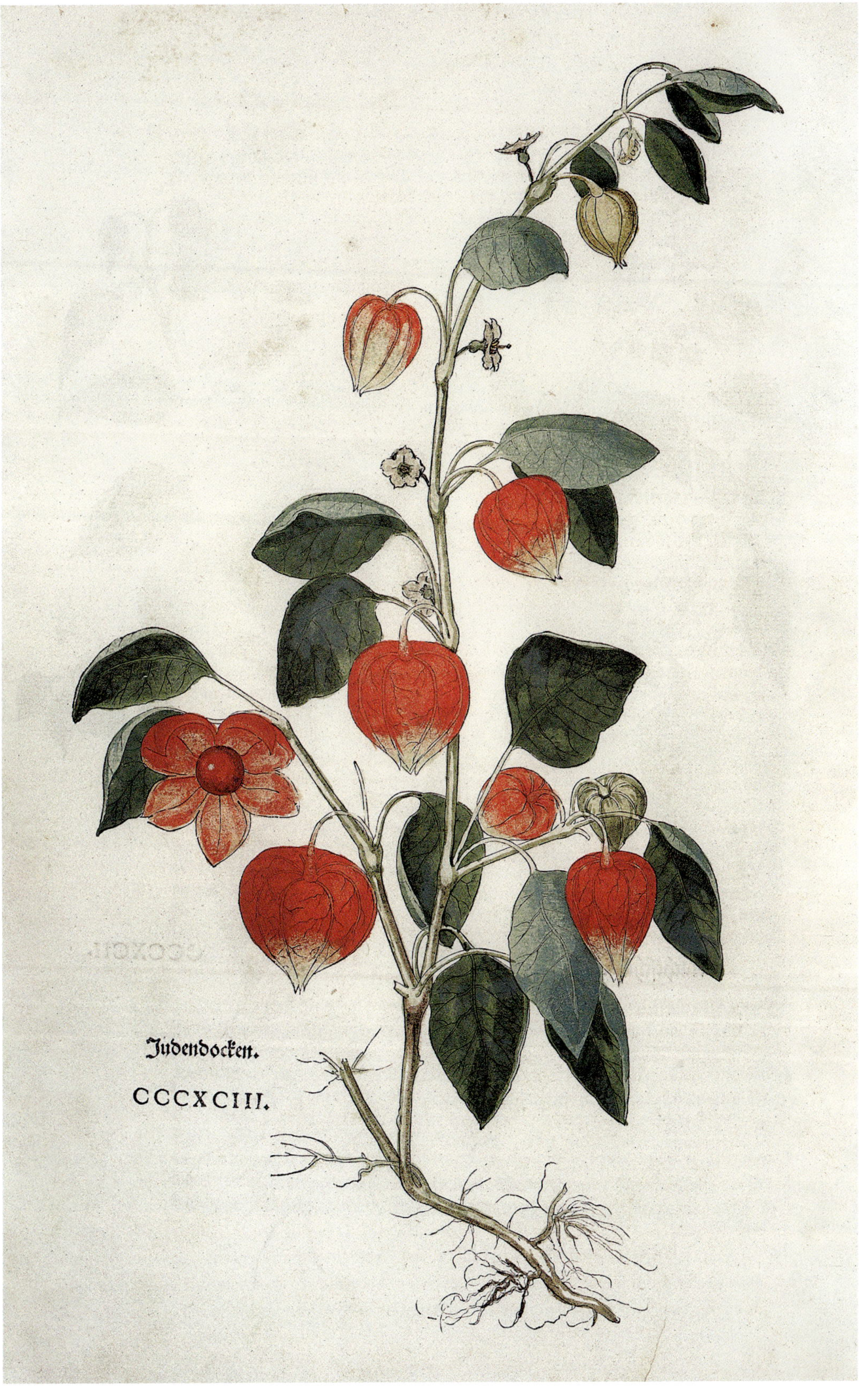
Judendocken.
CCCXCIII.

BONESET

The roots of comfrey, or BONESET (CCLXVI) were highly prized for wounds and broken bones. So strong was the plant's supposed ability to re-unite what had come apart that the herb was reputed even to make pieces of meat in the soup cauldron grow back together.

„WALWURTZ“

„WALWURTZ“ (Cap. CCLXVI) oder „Schwarzwurtz“ wurde der Beinwell genannt, dessen Wurzel als Wundmittel und bei Knochenbrüchen höchst begehrt war. Das Zusammenwachsen sollte so weit gehen, dass sogar Fleischstücke wieder zusammenwachsen würden, wenn sie im Kochtopf mit Beinwell gekocht würden.

GRANDE CONSOUDE

La GRANDE CONSOUDE (CCLXVI), qui figure ici sous le nom de «racine à os» ou «racine noire», était très recherchée pour sa souche cicatrisant les plaies et ressoudant les os. On racontait même que des lambeaux de chair se rattachaient s'ils étaient bouillis avec la souche.

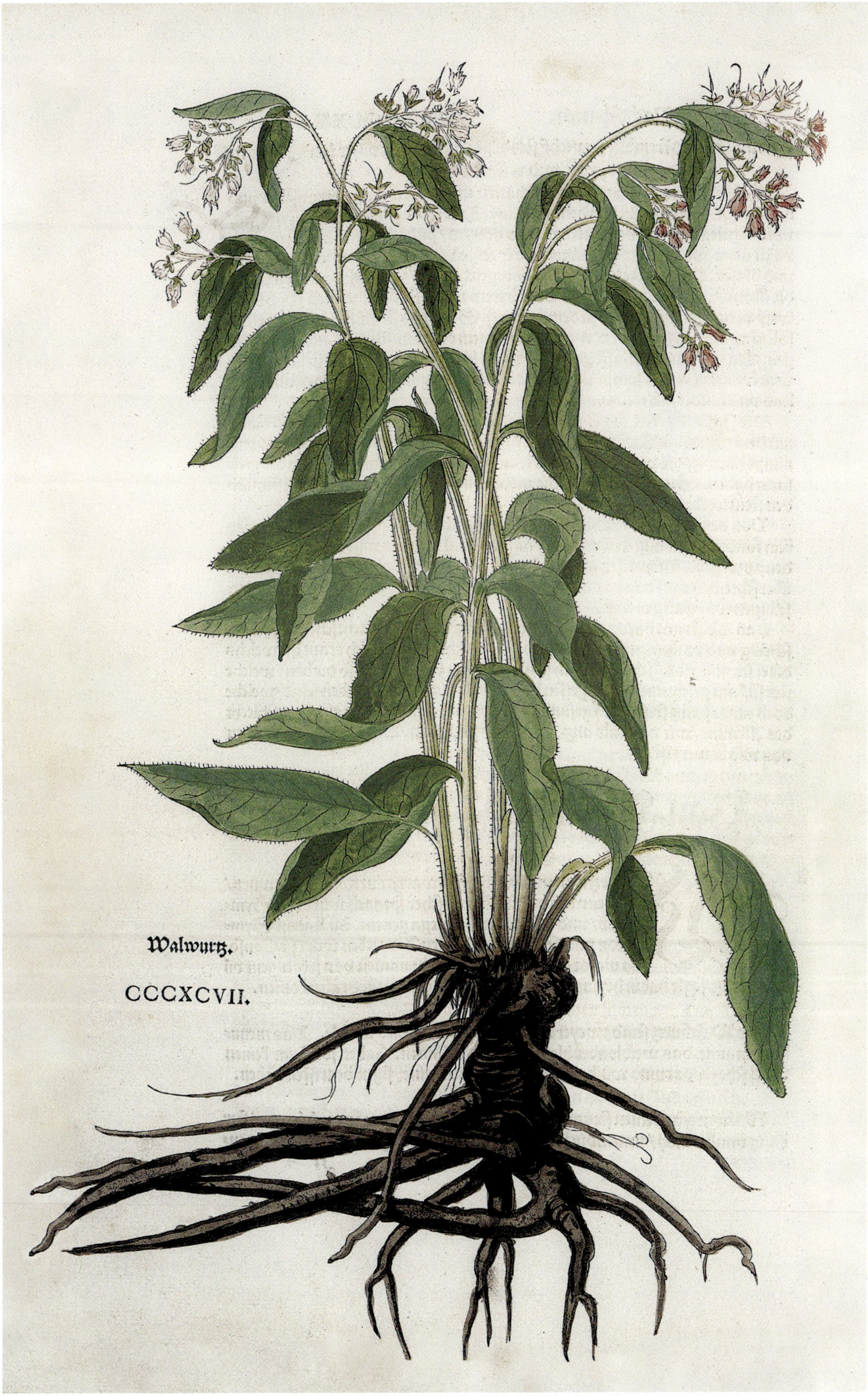
Walwurtz.
CCCXCVII.

CUCUMBERS

The chapter on CUCUMBERS (CCLXVII) combines cucumber, pumpkin, melon and cantaloupe. Among numerous other indications, the plants were helpful "when the bladder is being difficult," an application which coincides with the modern application of pumpkin seeds.

„CUCUMER"

Gurke, Kürbis und Melonen erscheinen im Kapitel „CUCUMER" (Cap. CCLXVII) angeführt. Unter den zahlreichen Indikationen findet sich auch das Problem „so die blaß schwirig ist" und dies deckt sich mit der uns heute vertrauten Anwendung der Kürbiskerne.

CONCOMBRE

« Cucumer » (CCLXVII) est consacré au CONCOMBRE, aux CITROUILLES et MELONS. Les graines de courge étaient préconisées « quand la vessie devient difficile », une utilisation encore reconnue aujourd'hui.

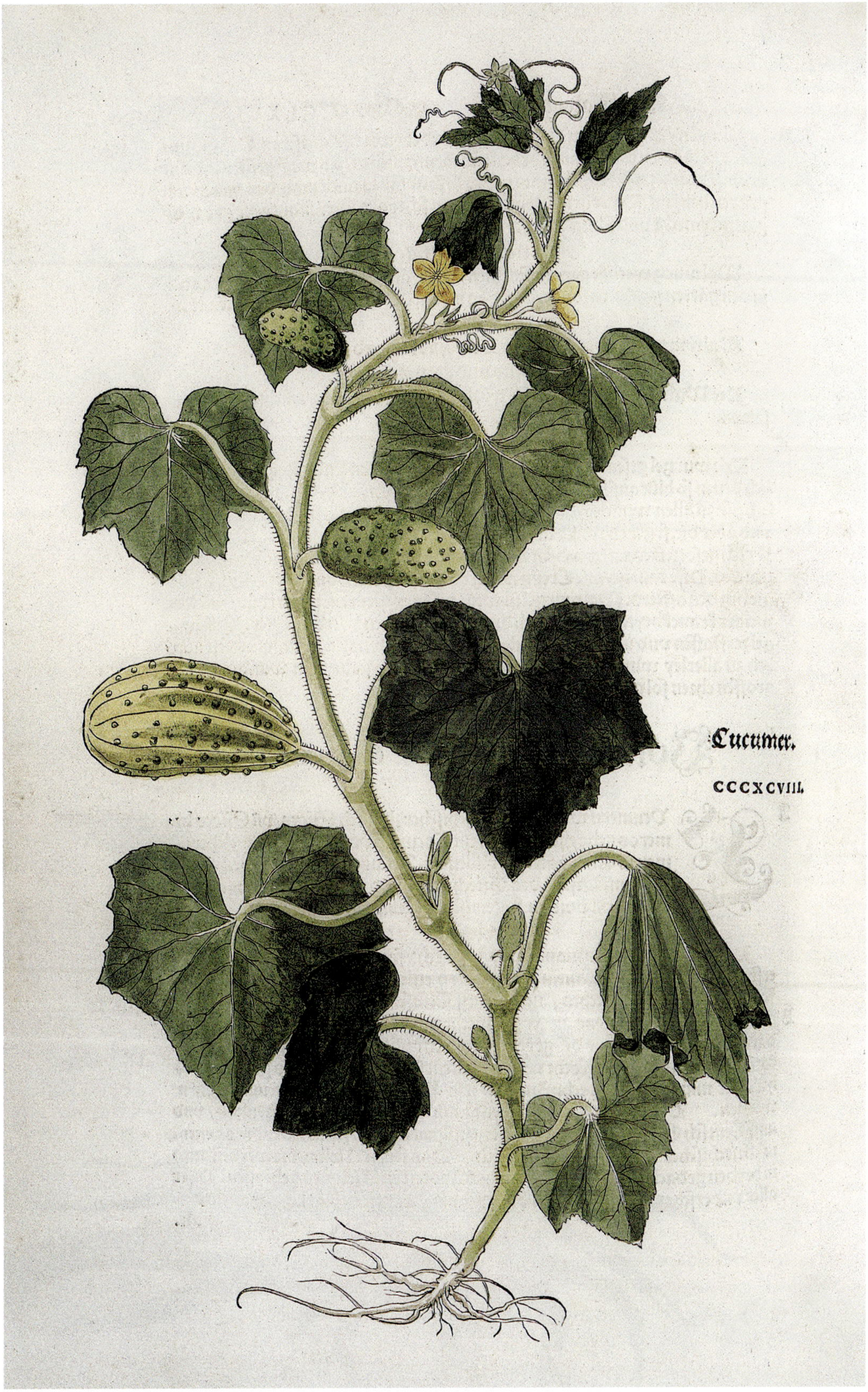
Cucumer.
CCCXCVIII.

SQUIRTING CUCUMBER

THE SQUIRTING CUCUMBER (CCLXVIII) is spectacular in that juice and seed kernels are squirted out under great pressure when the fruit is removed. Fuchs gives clear warning of the toxicity of the juice, which, among other applications, is prescribed as a laxative.

„WILDER CUCUMER“

Als „WILDER CUCUMER“ (Cap. CCLXVIII) wird die Spritzgurke vorgestellt, die dadurch Aufsehen erregt, dass beim Ablösen der Früchte Saft und Samenkerne mit großem Druck verspritzen. Auf die Giftigkeit des u. a. als Abführmittel verordneten Saftes weist Fuchs hin.

PISTOLET-DES-DAMES

Le PISTOLET-DES-DAMES (CCLXVIII), ou concombre-d’âne, est qualifié ici de « concombre sauvage » (« wilder Cucumer ») à cause de son fruit remarquable : à maturation, le suc amer contenu dans la capsule fait céder l’attache et propulse la baie en libérant les graines. Fuchs met en garde contre le suc violemment purgatif.

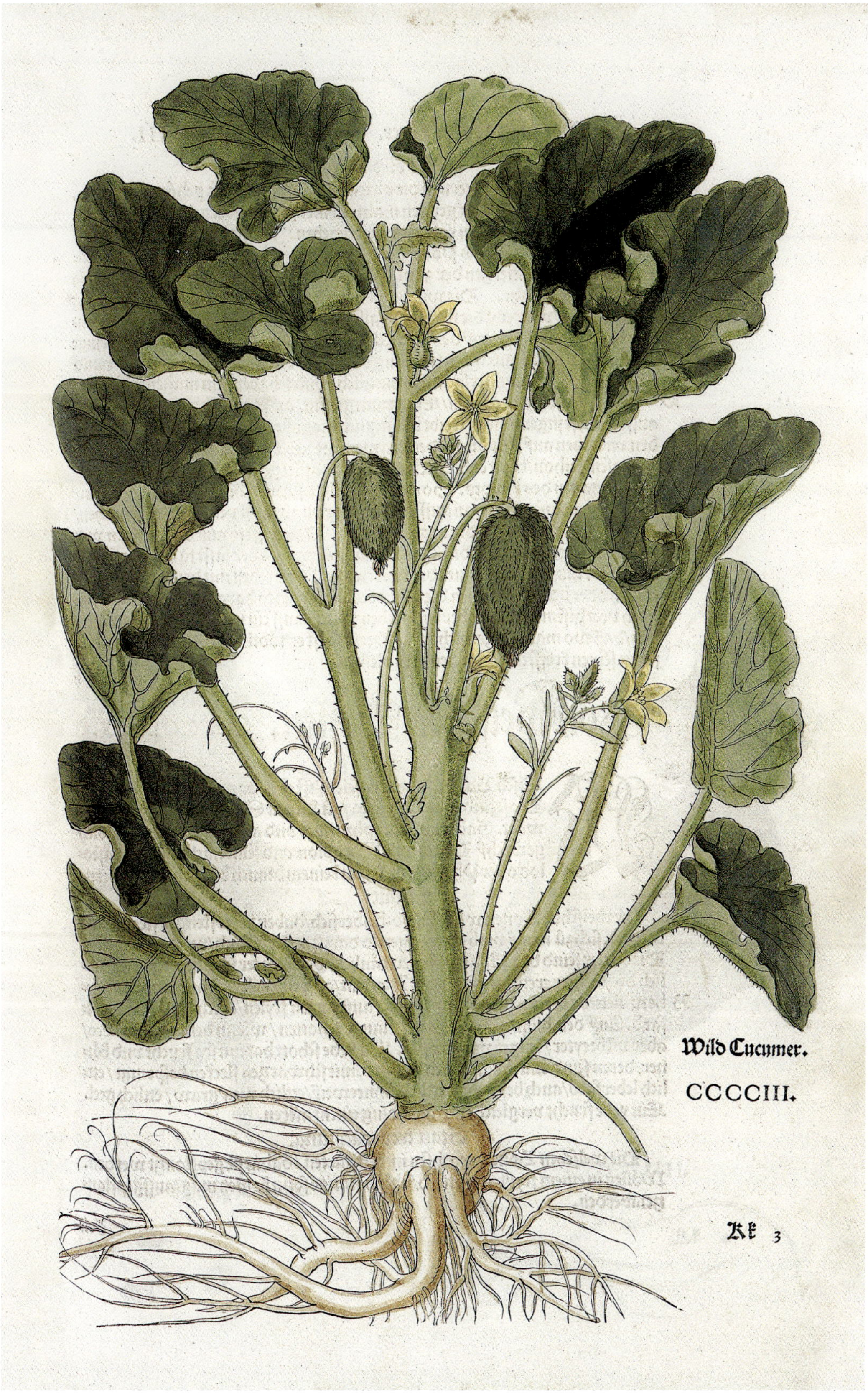
Wild Cucumer.
CCCCIII.
Kk 3

GARDEN BEAN

The GARDEN BEAN (CCLXIX), also known as the French or Kidney Bean, is another vegetable that is also used in medicine. Folk medicine had long recognized its diuretic properties, and also claimed that tea made from the bean hulls could reduce the sugar content of the blood.

„WELSCHE BOHNEN“

Mit den „WELSCHEN BOHNEN“ (Cap. CCLXIX) kommt wieder ein Gemüse vor, das auch in der Medizin eingesetzt wird. Seine harntreibende Wirkung findet sich noch lange in den Anschauungen der Volksmedizin, ebenso wie die angebliche Senkung des Zuckerspiegels durch Bohnenschalentee.

HARICOT COMMUN

Voici une autre plante potagère utilisée en médecine : le HARICOT COMMUN (CCLXIX), qualifié ici d'« étranger ». La pharmacopée populaire reconnaîtra longtemps ses effets diurétiques et prêtera même à l'infusion de gousses le pouvoir de baisser le taux de sucre.

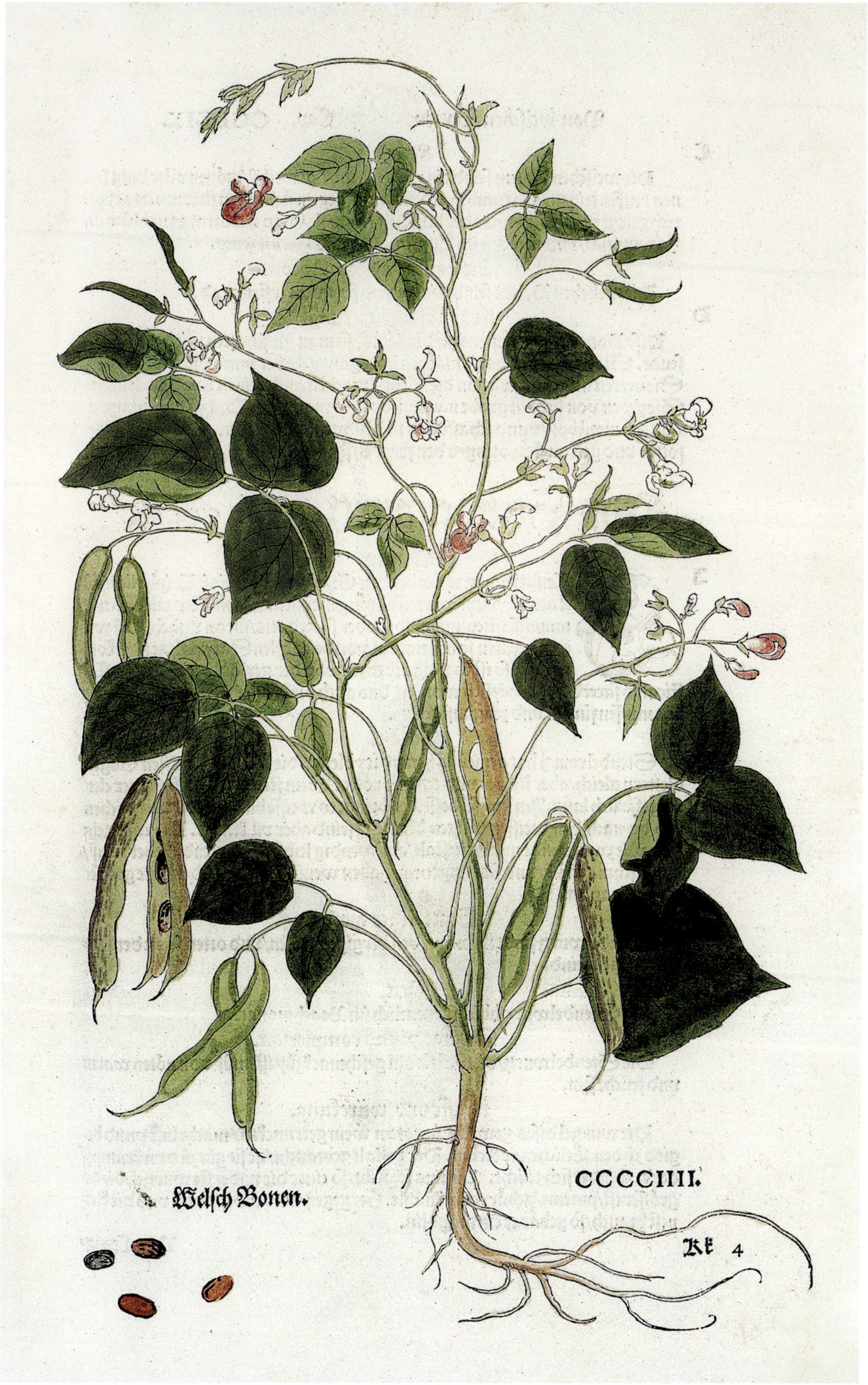
CCCCIIII.
Welsch Bonen.
Kk 4

LESSER BUTTERFLY ORCHID

The three different orchids included under LESSER BUTTERFLY ORCHID (CCLXX), FRAGRANT ORCHID and COMMON SPOTTED ORCHIDS (CCLXXI) are no longer used medicinally.

„STENDELWURTZ“

Unter „STENDELWURTZ“ (Cap. CCLXX) und „CREUTZBLUMEN“ (Cap. CCLXXI) werden drei verschiedene Orchideen verstanden, die schon lange nicht mehr im medizinischen Gebrauch sind.

RACINE ÉRIGÉE

Fuchs présente sous le nom de «Stendelwurtz» ou RACINE ÉRIGÉE (CCLXX) et de «Creutzblumen» ou FLEURS À CROIX (CCLXXI), trois ORCHIDÉES, oubliées depuis longtemps en médecine.

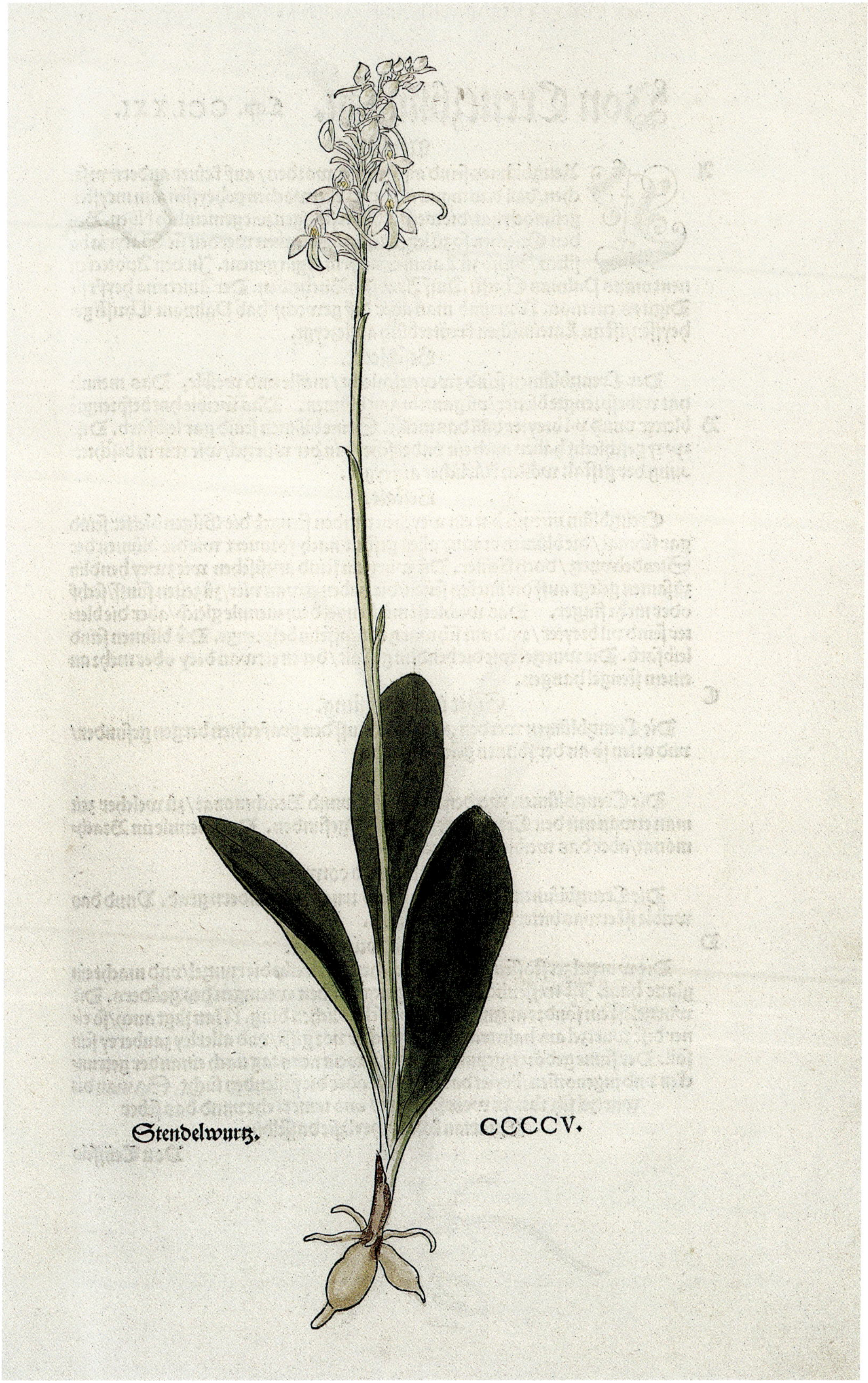

LESSER BUTTERFLY ORCHID | „STENDELWURTZ“ | RACINE ÉRIGÉE

DEVIL'S-BIT SCABIOUS

DEVIL'S-BIT SCABIOUS (CCLXXII) owes its name to the devil's alleged attempt to destroy it by biting its root. The plant was said to be useful not only in staunching the flow of blood but also against the fearsome plague.

„TEUFELS ABBISS"

Da angeblich der Teufel die Wurzel abgebissen hat, um diese wertvolle Heilpflanze zu vernichten, erhielt sie den eigenartigen Namen „TEUFELS ABBISS" (Cap. CCLXXII). Sie sollte bei Blutergüssen helfen, aber ebenso gegen die gefürchtete Pest.

SUCCISE DES PRÉS

La SUCCISE DES PRÉS (CCLXXII) doit son curieux nom de «mors du diable» («Teufels Abbiß» en allemand) à une légende : le diable, voulant détruire cette plante très précieuse, en aurait mordu la racine. On lui prêtait des effets salutaires sur les hématomes et même sur la peste, si redoutée au Moyen Age.

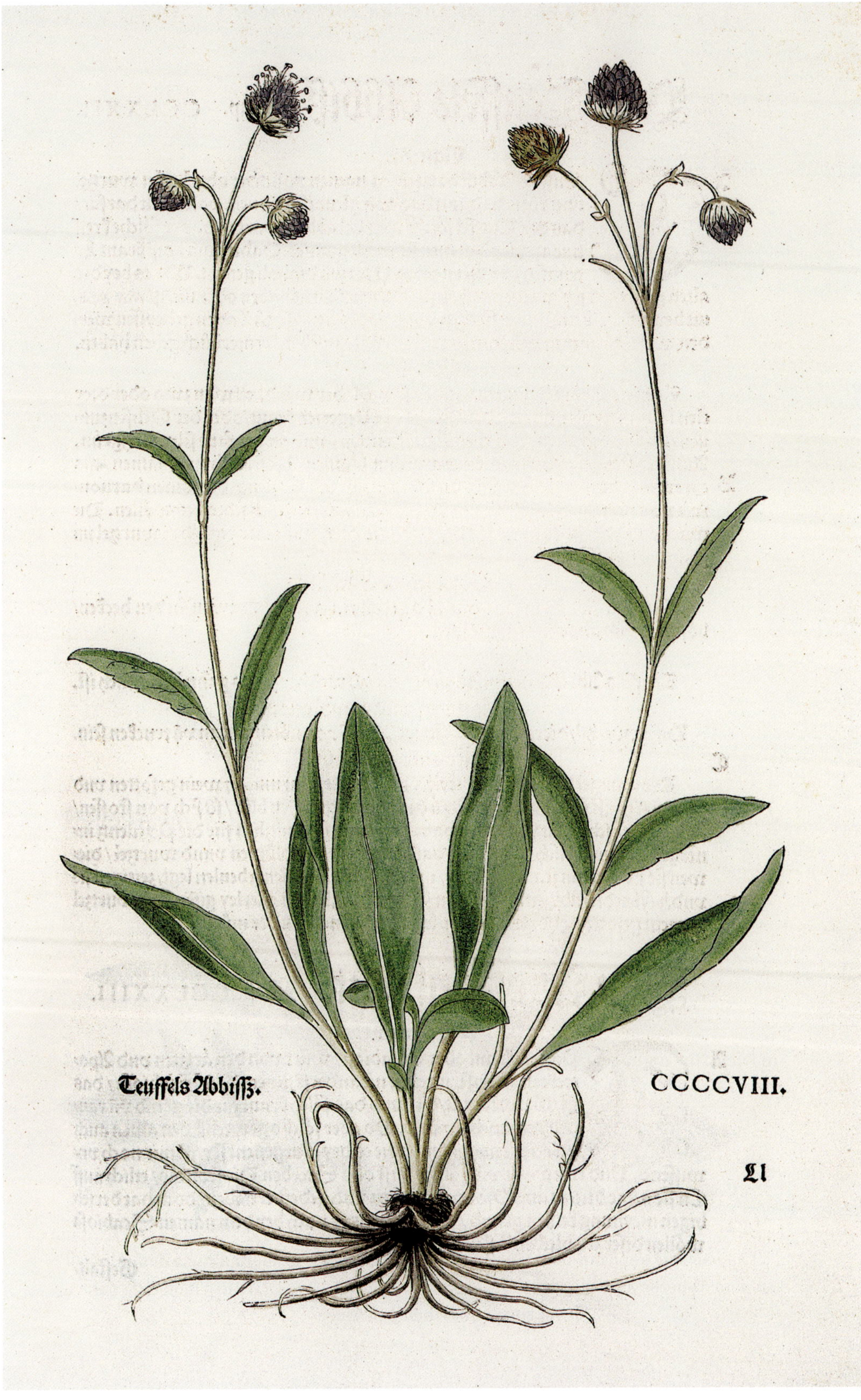
Teuffels Abbissz.
CCCCVIII.
Ll

FIELD SCABIOUS

In Fuchs, the traditional German name apostem for FIELD SCABIOUS (CCLXXIII) referred to ulcers.

APOSTEMKRAUT

Als „APOSTEM" bezeichnete man Geschwüre, weshalb der Name Apostemkraut (Cap. CCLXXIII) oder Grindkraut bereits alles über die Anwendung aussagt.

KNAUTIE DES PRÉS

La médecine ancienne appelait «apostème» une tumeur humorale, qui a donné son nom d'«herbe à apostème» à la KNAUTIE DES PRÉS (CCLXXIII), indiquant par là son emploi thérapeutique.

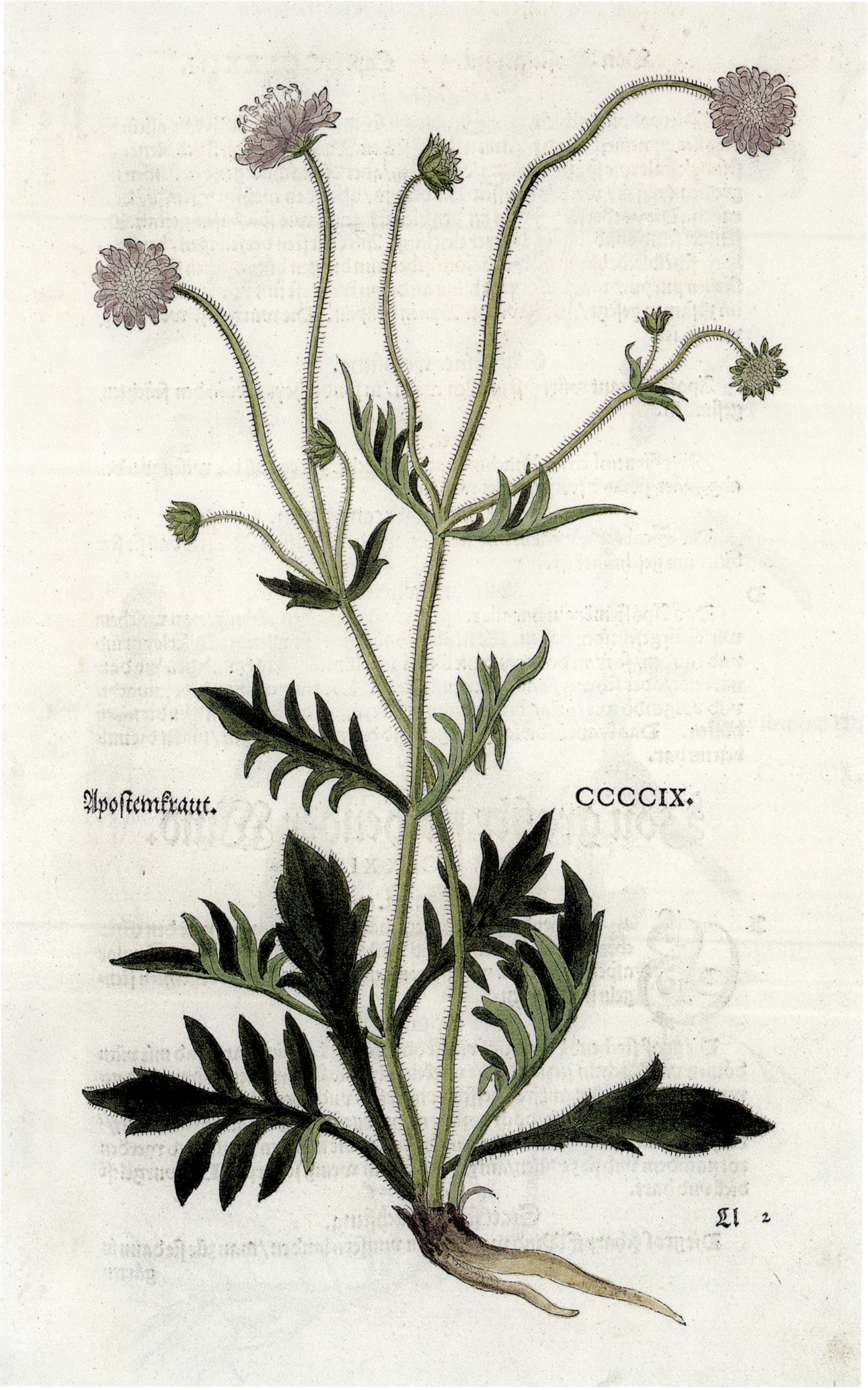

FIELD SCABIOUS | APOSTEMKRAUT | KNAUTIE DES PRÉS

BINDWEED

The next two chapters discuss two kinds of BINDWEED: ROUGH (CCLXXIIII) and HEDGE or LARGER BINDWEED (CCLXXV), which was native to Germany. The former is credited with imaginary antitoxic properties; the text for the latter, however, admits doubts about the trustworthiness of the traditional applications.

WINDEN

Die beiden folgenden Kapitel besprechen zwei Windenarten: die große „STECHENDE WIND“ (Cap. CCLXXIIII) und die einheimische große „GLATTE WIND“(Cap. CCLXXV), wobei der ersten fantastische giftwidrige Eigenschaften zugebilligt werden, bei der zweiten jedoch die Unsicherheit der Überlieferung im Text deutlich wird.

LISERON ÉPINEUX

Les deux chapitres suivants sont dédiés aux liserons : le LISERON ÉPINEUX (CCLXXIIII), ou salsepareille d'Europe, et le LISERON DES HAIES (CCLXXV). D'après la légende, le premier a un pouvoir d'antidote ; quant au second, on notera que ses propriétés restent incertaines dans la tradition …

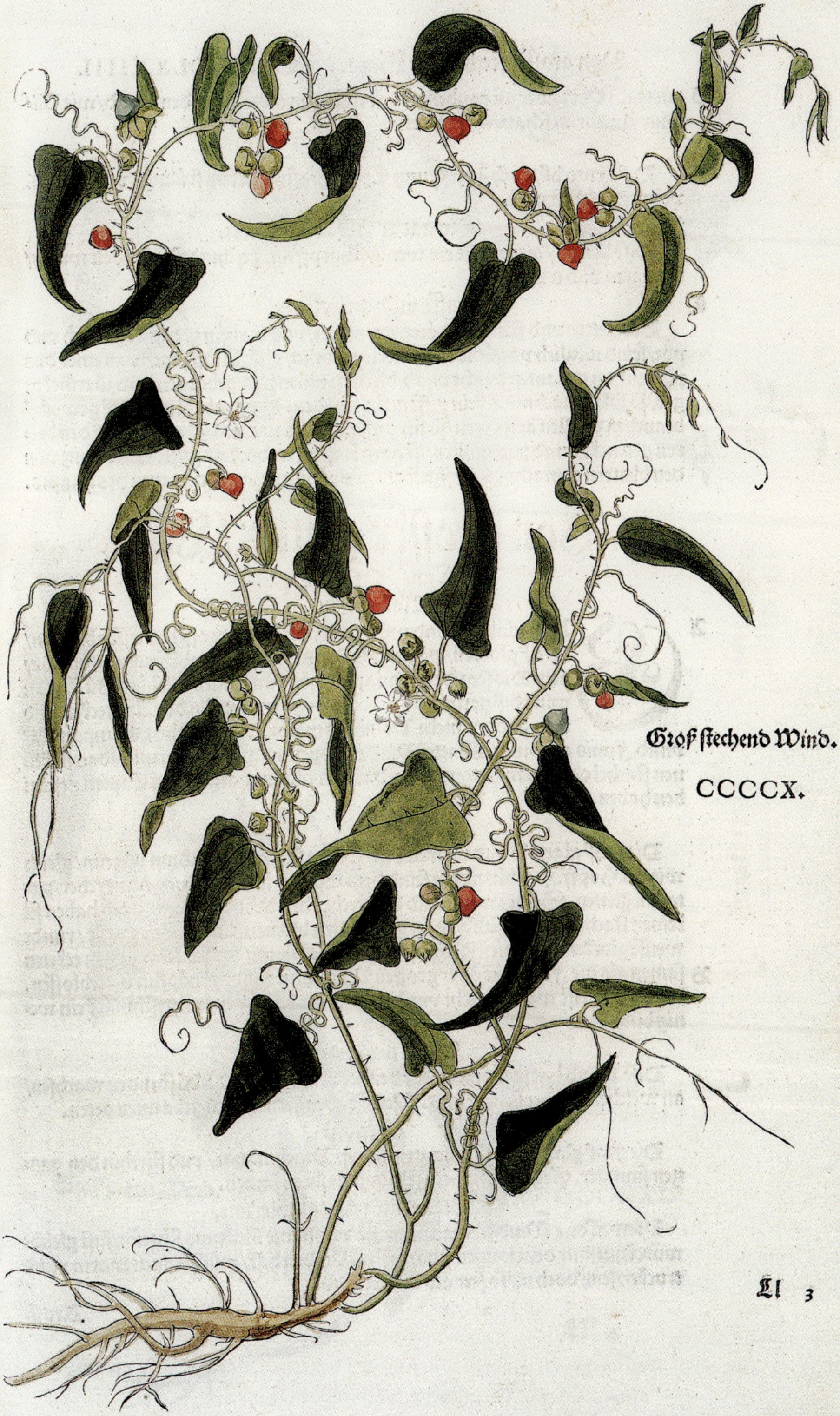

Groß stechend Wind.

CCCCX.

Ll 3

WATER MINT

Fuchs unites WATER MINT and watercress in a single chapter (CCLXXVI). It is possible that the essential oil of mint may have relieved "intestinal gripes"; certainly the administering of watercress juice with vinegar would have caused the patients to become more "awake."

„SISYMBER" (WASSER-MINZE)

Als „SISYMBER" (Cap. CCLXXVI) bezeichnet Fuchs die Wasser-Minze und die Brunnenkresse. Das ätherische Öl der Minze mag das „grimmen der därme" gelindert haben und das Einflößen von Brunnenkressesaft mit Essig hat sicherlich den Patienten „wachend" gemacht.

CRESSON DE FONTAINE

Fuchs qualifie de « sisymbres » la menthe aquatique et le CRESSON DE FONTAINE (CCLXXVI). L'huile essentielle de menthe aurait soulagé les « ires de l'intestin », et le suc de cresson mêlé à du vinaigre devait effectivement « réveiller » le patient !

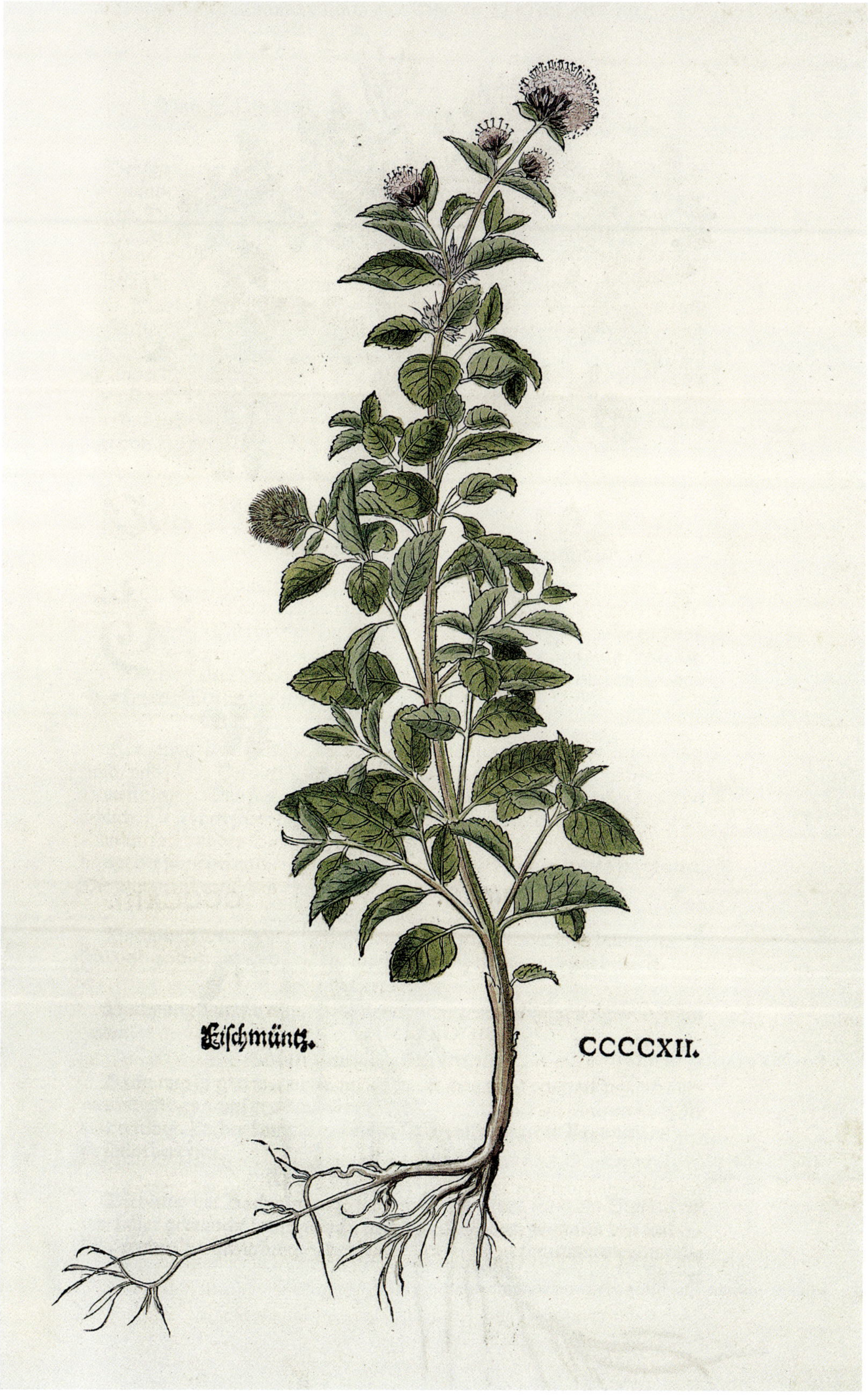
Kischmüntz.
CCCCXII.

BROOKLIME

BROOKLIME (CCLXXVII), a kind of SPEEDWELL, was prescribed particularly for its diuretic effect and its ability to break up kidney stones.

„BACHPUNGEN“

Die „BACHPUNGEN“ (Cap. CCLXXVII), eine Art des Ehrenpreis, werden insbesondere wegen ihrer harntreibenden und den Nierenstein ausführenden Wirkung beschrieben.

CRESSON DE CHEVAL

Le CRESSON DE CHEVAL (CCLXXVII), une véronique aimant les lieux humides et présentée sous le nom de «Bachpunge» (approximativement, caisse de rivière), est décrit avant tout pour ses effets diurétiques et comme remède contre les calculs rénaux.

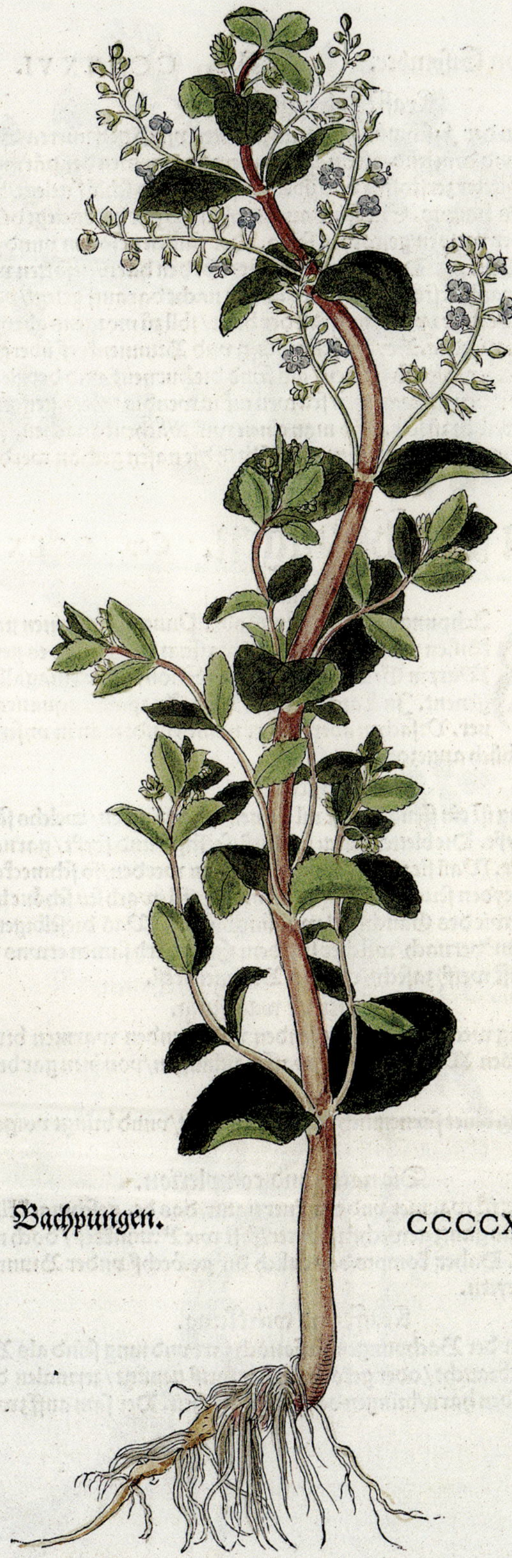

Bachpungen. CCCCXIII.

COMMON YARROW

COMMON YARROW, or MILFOIL (CCLXXVIII), is noticeable for its very finely divided leaflets, which earned the plant its botanical species name Millefolium, or “thousand-leaved.” This YARROW was a treasured vulnerary and was “for this reason used daily by surgeons.”

SCHAFGARBE

Die SCHAFGARBE (Cap. CCLXXVIII) fällt durch ihre sehr fein zerteilten Blättchen auf, die ihr den botanischen Artnamen „millefolium“, die tausendblättrige, einbrachten. Sie war ein sehr geschätztes Wundkraut und stand „derhalben bey den wundärtzten in täglichem brauch“.

ACHILLÉE MILLEFEUILLE

L'ACHILLÉE MILLEFEUILLE (CCLXXVIII), dite aussi millefeuille, doit son nom à ses fines feuilles bipennatilobées, à petits segments étroits. Cette achillée jouissait d'une grande estime pour ses vertus cicatrisantes et était « pour cette raison utilisée quotidiennement par les chirurgiens. »

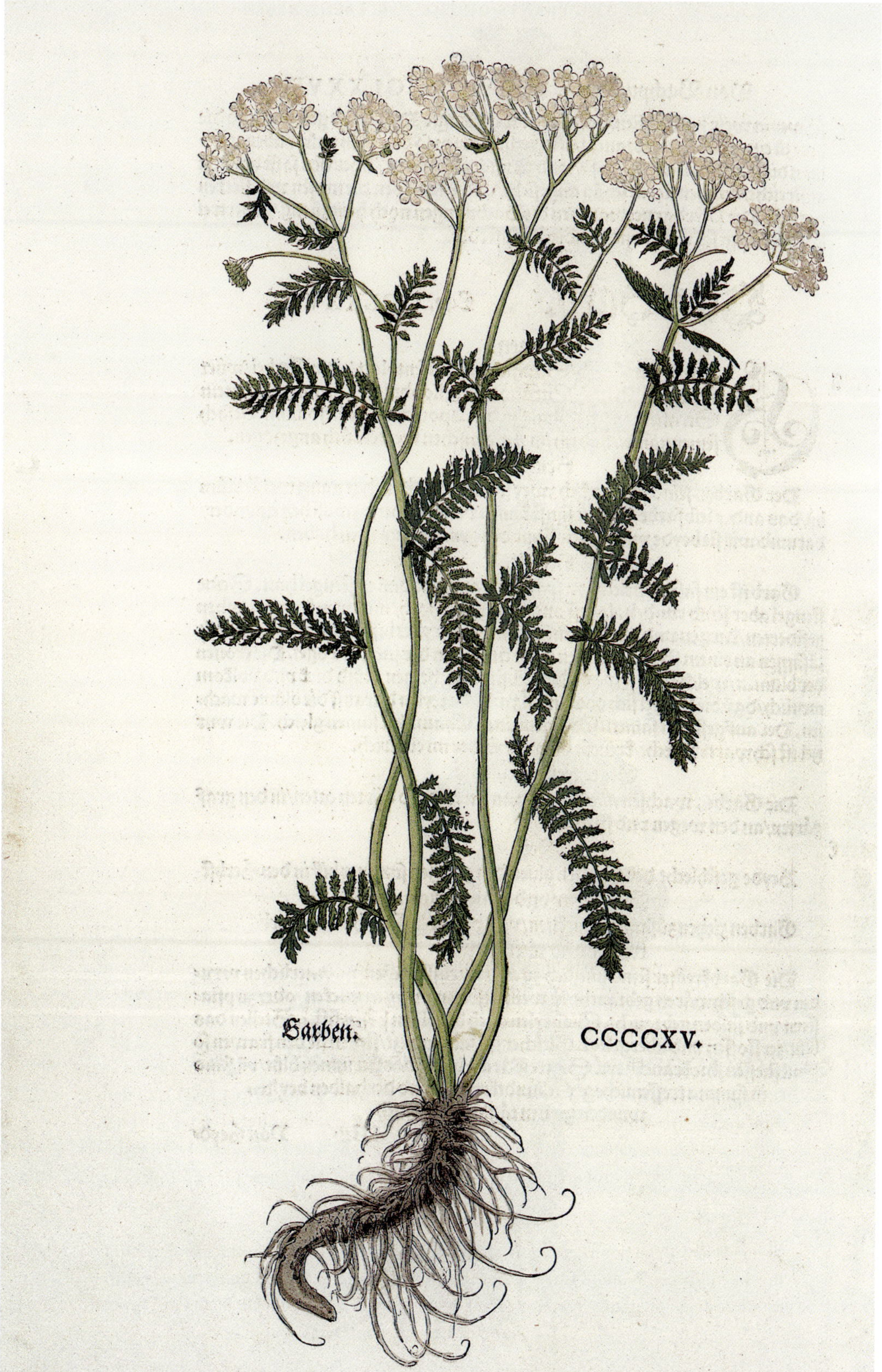
Garben.
CCCCXV.

RAGWORT

The same is true of Fuchs's RAGWORT (CCLXXIX), also known as Fuchs's groundsel. Another completely unrelated feature of the plant deserves mention here: until recently, the plant's botanical name was *Senecio fuchsii*; today, the name of the plant still commemorated the author of our herbal.

„HEYDNISCHES WUNDTKRAUT“

Das gilt auch für das „HEYDNISCHE WUNDTKRAUT“ (Cap. CCLXXIX), zu dem eine andere Besonderheit zu vermerken ist: bis vor Kurzem lautete sein botanischer Name *Senecio fuchsii*, deutsch heißt es immer noch Fuchs'sches Kreuzkraut und erinnert damit an den Verfasser unseres Kräuterbuches.

SÉNEÇON OVALE

Il en est de même pour le SÉNEÇON OVALE (CCLXXIX) figurant ici sous le nom de « heydnisches Wundtkraut » ou herbe à plaies païenne. Mentionnons ici une autre particularité de la plante : son nom scientifique était Senecio fuchsii, lequel se rapporte à l'auteur de cet herbier.

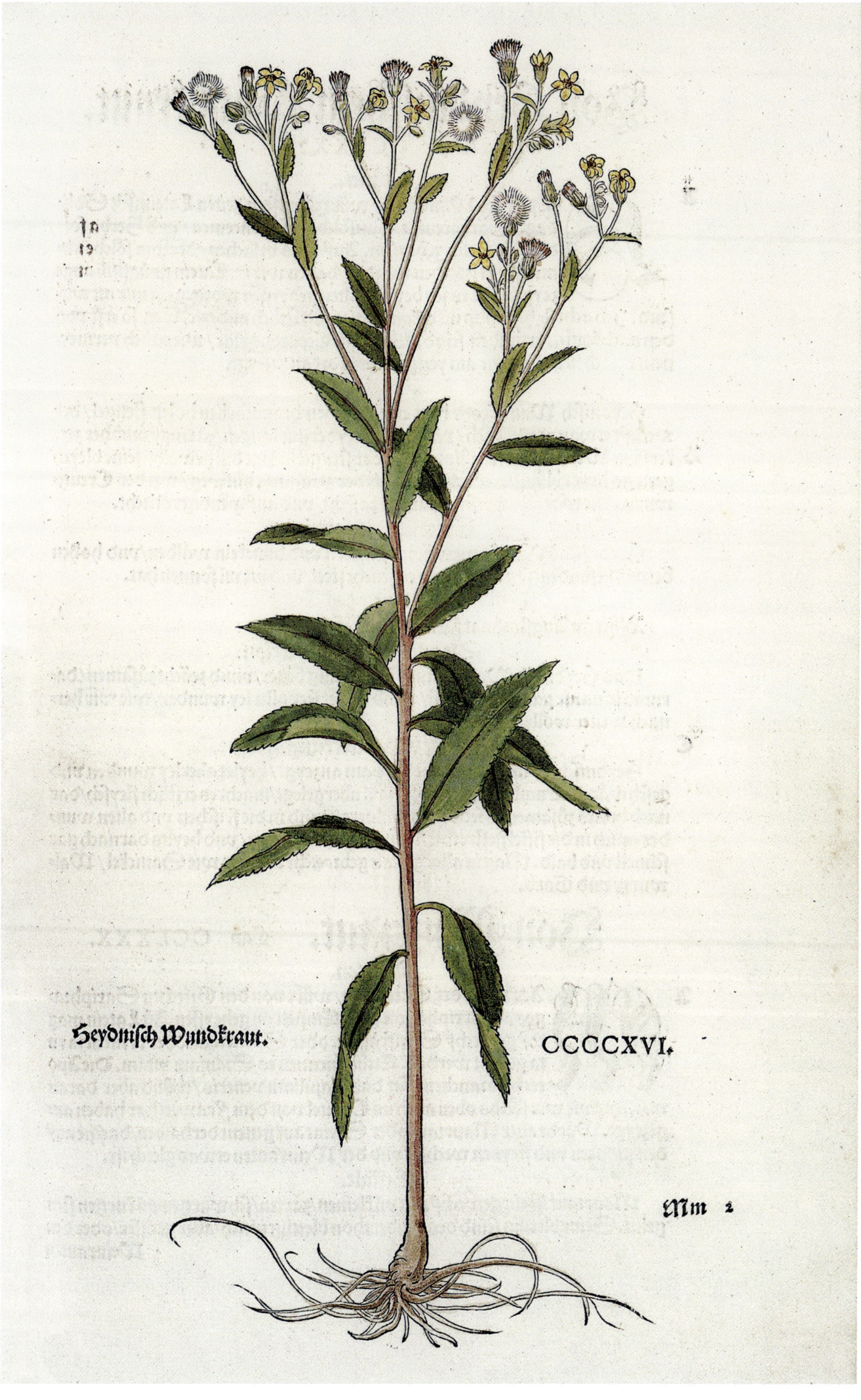
Heydnisch Wundkraut.
CCCCXVI.
Mm 2

WALL RUE

WALL RUE (CCLXXX) is a delicate, relatively common asplenium, which had a reputation as a diuretic.

MAUERRAUTE

Bei der MAUERRAUTE (Cap. CCLXXX) handelt es sich um einen relativ häufigen, zierlichen Streifenfarn, dem harntreibende Wirkung zugeschrieben wird.

RUE DES MURAILLES

La RUE DES MURAILLES (CCLXXX) est une plante cryptogramme filicinée assez courante, supposée avoir des effets diurétiques.

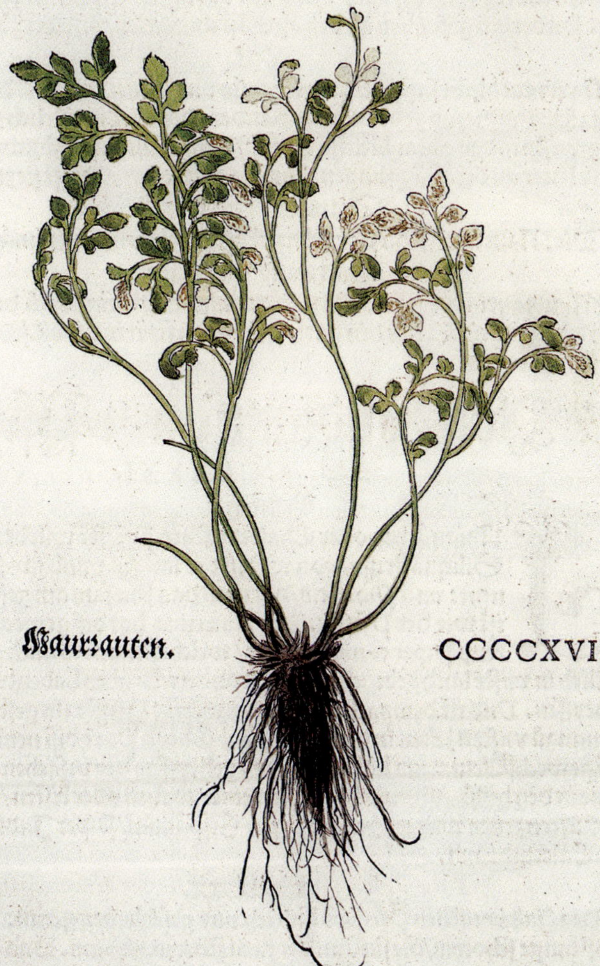

Maurrauten. CCCCXVII.

Mm 3

INDIAN PEPPER

Fuchs had three specimens of what he termed "INDIAN PEPPER" (CCLXXXI) illustrated with differently shaped fruits. His reflections upon what the classical world or Arabian doctors might have called the plant are futile, for Peppers originated in America, and thus became known in Europe only after 1492. Medicinally, "Indian" Pepper was seen as the equivalent of Hot Pepper. Although the scientific content of the fruit was not understood in those days, Fuchs's remark that Pepper provides nourishment for the gums could be a reference to the vitamin C content of the fruits, which cared scurvy, whose symptoms include the receding of bleeding gum tissue.

„INDIANISCHER PFEFFER"

Den „INDIANISCHEN PFEFFER" (Cap. CCLXXXI) kennen wir als Paprika, von dem Fuchs drei Exemplare abbilden lässt. Seine Überlegungen, wie die Pflanze in der Antike oder bei den arabischen Ärzten geheißen haben mag, bleiben müßig, denn Paprika stammt aus Amerika und wurde in Europa erst nach 1492 bekannt. Die Bemerkung, er sei dem Zahnfleisch nützlich, könnte ein Hinweis auf die Wirkung des Vitamin-C-Gehalts der Früchte sein, die den durch Vitaminmangel hervorgerufenen Skorbut heilen – und eben den mit ihm einhergehenden Rückgang des blutenden Zahnfleischs stoppen.

PIMENT

Le «poivre indien» est le PIMENT (CCLXXXI), présenté sous trois formes aux fruits différents. Fuchs a vainement cherché à savoir comment les Anciens ou les médecins arabes appelaient cette plante, mais, originaire d'Amérique, elle n'a pu être connue en Europe qu'après 1492. Ses effets thérapeutiques étaient considérés comme comparables à ceux du poivre. Fuchs remarque en passant que le piment est bon pour les gencives. Certes, on ignorait encore en ce temps-là sa teneur en vitamine C, mais on avait remarqué que la consommation de piment arrêtait les hémorragies de la gencive provoquées par le scorbut.

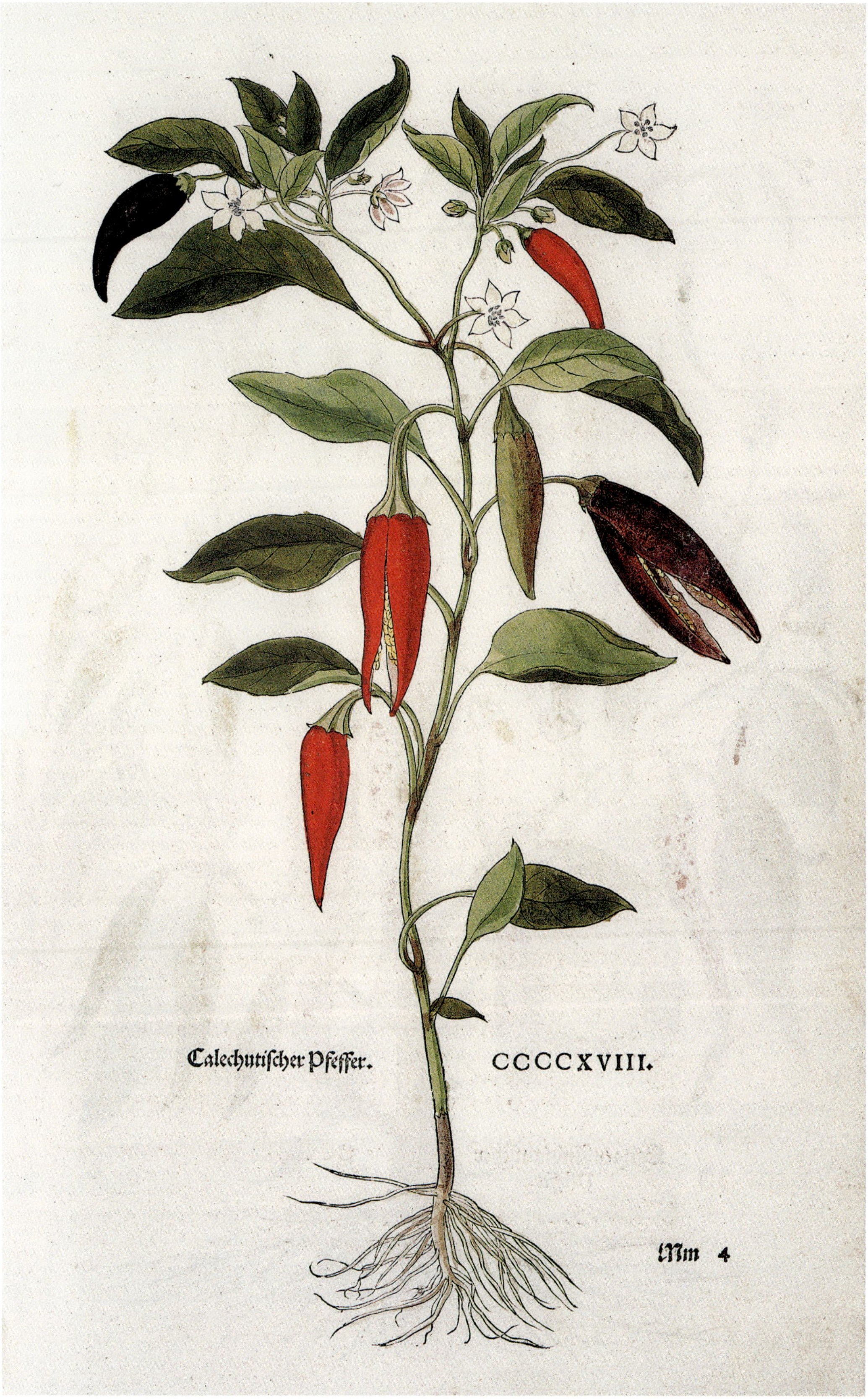
Calechutischer Pfeffer.
CCCCXVIII.
Mm 4

GARLIC

GARLIC (CCLXXXII), too, is another medicinal plant that is still respected today. It is at times substituted by Ramson's, or BEAR'S GARLIC (plate CCCCXXIIII). In contrast, no medicinal application was ascribed to CROW GARLIC or WILD GARLIC (plates CCCCXXII, CCCCXXIII). Today we would only accept a small number of the broad descriptions of the effects of GARLIC.

KNOBLAUCH

Der KNOBLAUCH (Cap. CCLXXXII) gehört zu den noch heute geschätzten Heilpflanzen; zuweilen wird er durch Bärlauch, den WALDKNOBLAUCH (Taf. CCCCXXIIII), ersetzt. WEINBERG-LAUCH und GEMÜSE-LAUCH (Taf. CCCCXXII, CCCCXXIII) finden keine arzneiliche Verwendung. Der weitläufigen Beschreibung seiner Wirkungen werden wir nur sehr bedingt folgen wollen.

AIL

L'AIL (CCLXXXII) compte encore parmi les plus estimées des plantes médicinales. Il a parfois pour substitut l'AIL DES OURS (pl. CCCCXXIIII) alors que l'AIL DES VIGNES et l'AIL DES CHAMPS (pl. CCCCXXII, CCCCXXIII) n'ont trouvé aucune application en médecine. Fuchs s'étend sur ses multiples effets, mais seul un petit nombre peut encore être reconnu aujourd'hui.

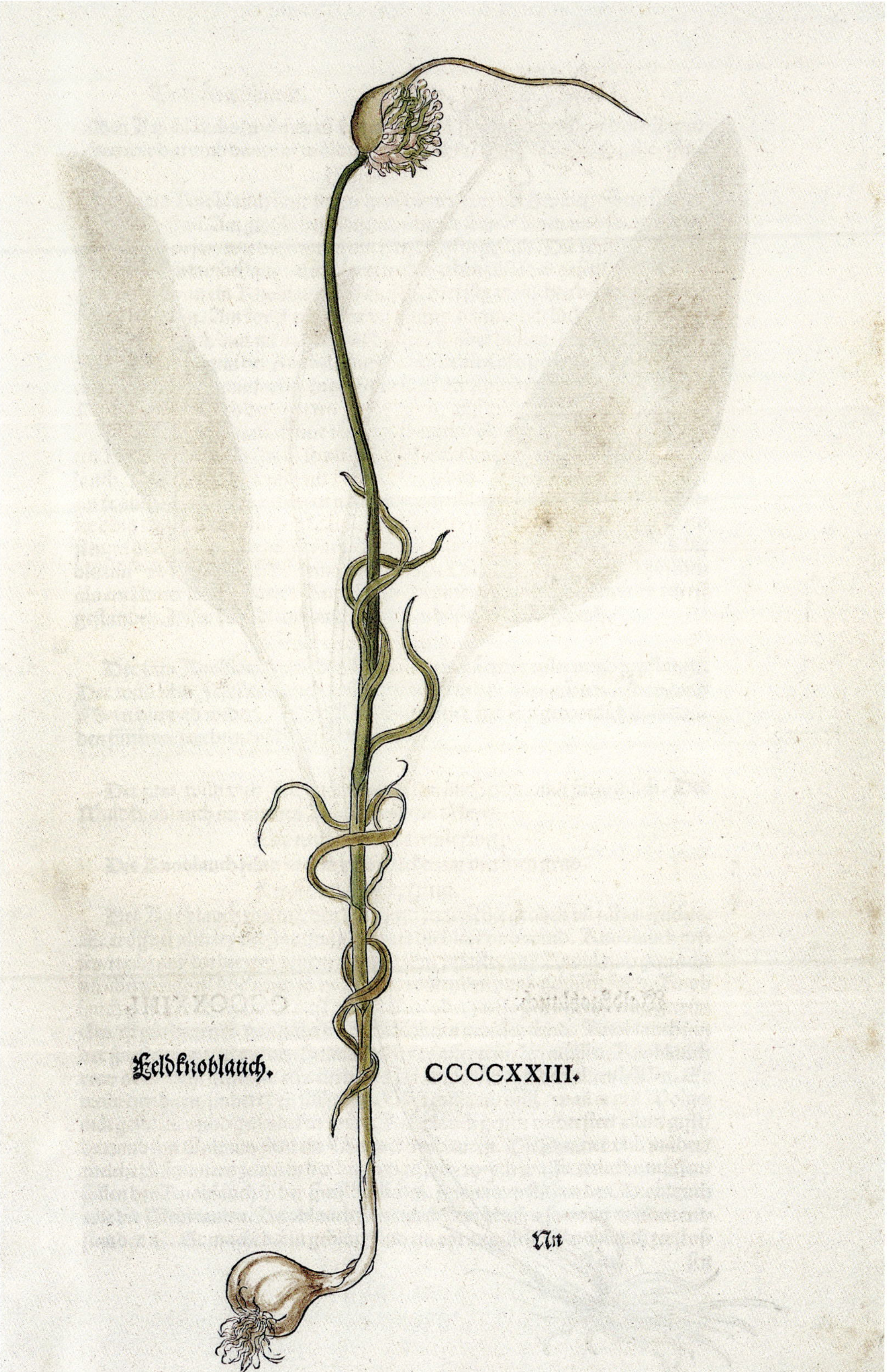
Feldknoblauch.
CCCCXXIII.
Nn

ST. JACOB'S HERB

ST. JACOB'S HERB, or COMMON RAGWORT (CCLXXXIII) is botanically close to Fuchs's GROUNDSEL (CCLXXIX) and was used accordingly.

„SANKT JACOBS BLUM"

Die „SANKT JACOBS BLUM" (Cap. CCLXXXIII) ist botanisch nahe mit dem HEIDNISCHEN WUNDKRAUT (Cap. CCLXXIX) verwandt und wird auch entsprechend eingesetzt.

ÉNEÇON JACOBÉE

La «herbe de Saint Jacob» ou SÉNEÇON JACOBÉE (CCLXXXIII) a une parenté botanique et pharmacologique avec le SÉNEÇON OVALE (CCLXXIX).

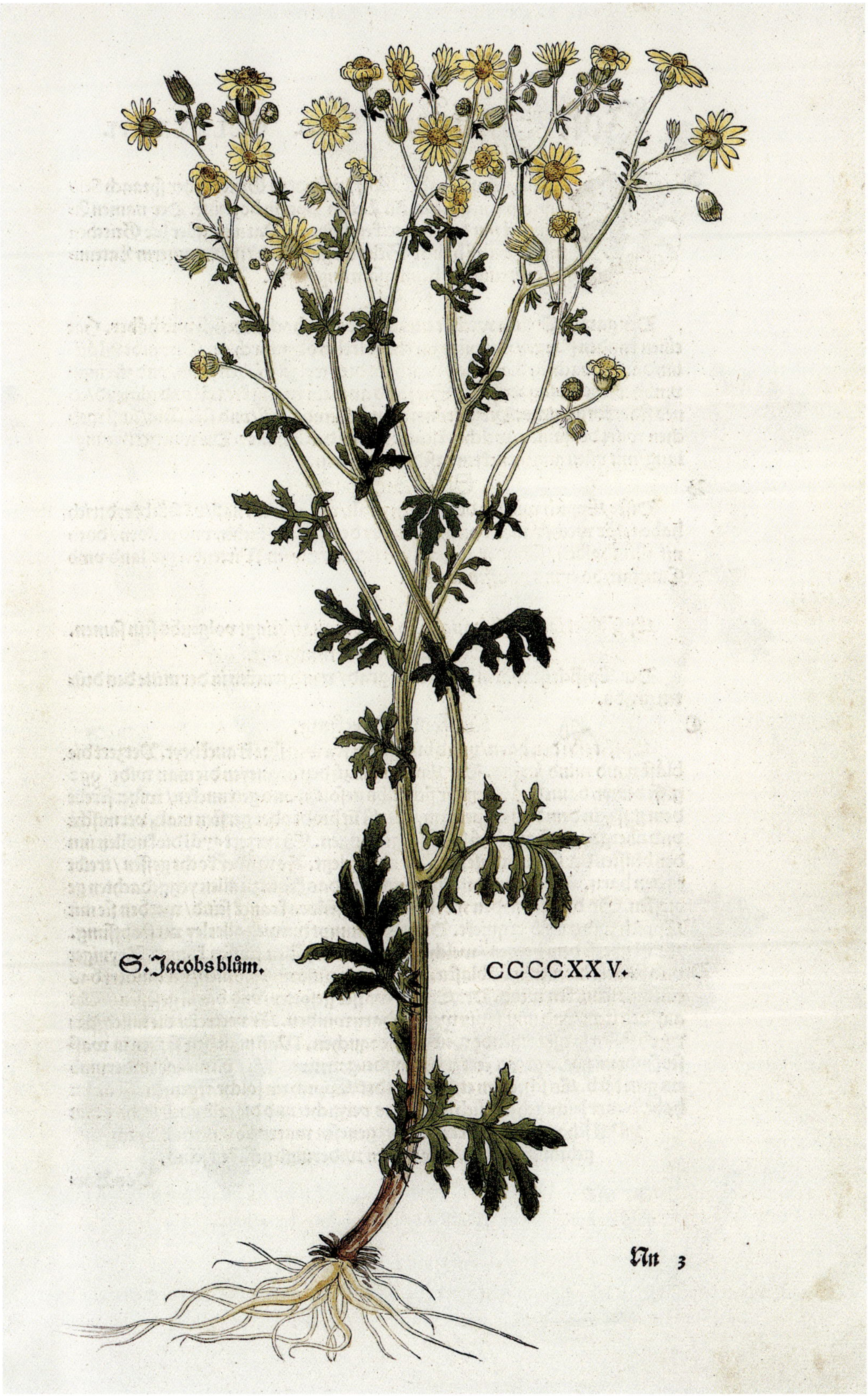
S. Jacobs blům.
CCCCXXV.
Nn 3

CELERY

Many of the claims for the effect of CELERY (CCLXXXIIII) are peculiar. Its diuretic effect is now uncontested, but the assertion that it can cause epileptic attacks remains inexplicable.

„EPPICH"

Eigenartig sind manche Angaben über die Wirkung des „EPPICH" (Cap. CCLXXXIIII), heute Sellerie genannt. Während die harntreibende Wirkung unbestritten ist, bleibt die Behauptung, dass er epileptische Anfälle auslösen könne, rätselhaft.

CÉLERI

Certains commentaires sur les effets du CÉLERI (CCLXXXIIII) sont pour le moins curieux. S'il est indiscutablement diurétique, prétendre qu'il peut provoquer des crises d'épilepsie reste une énigme.

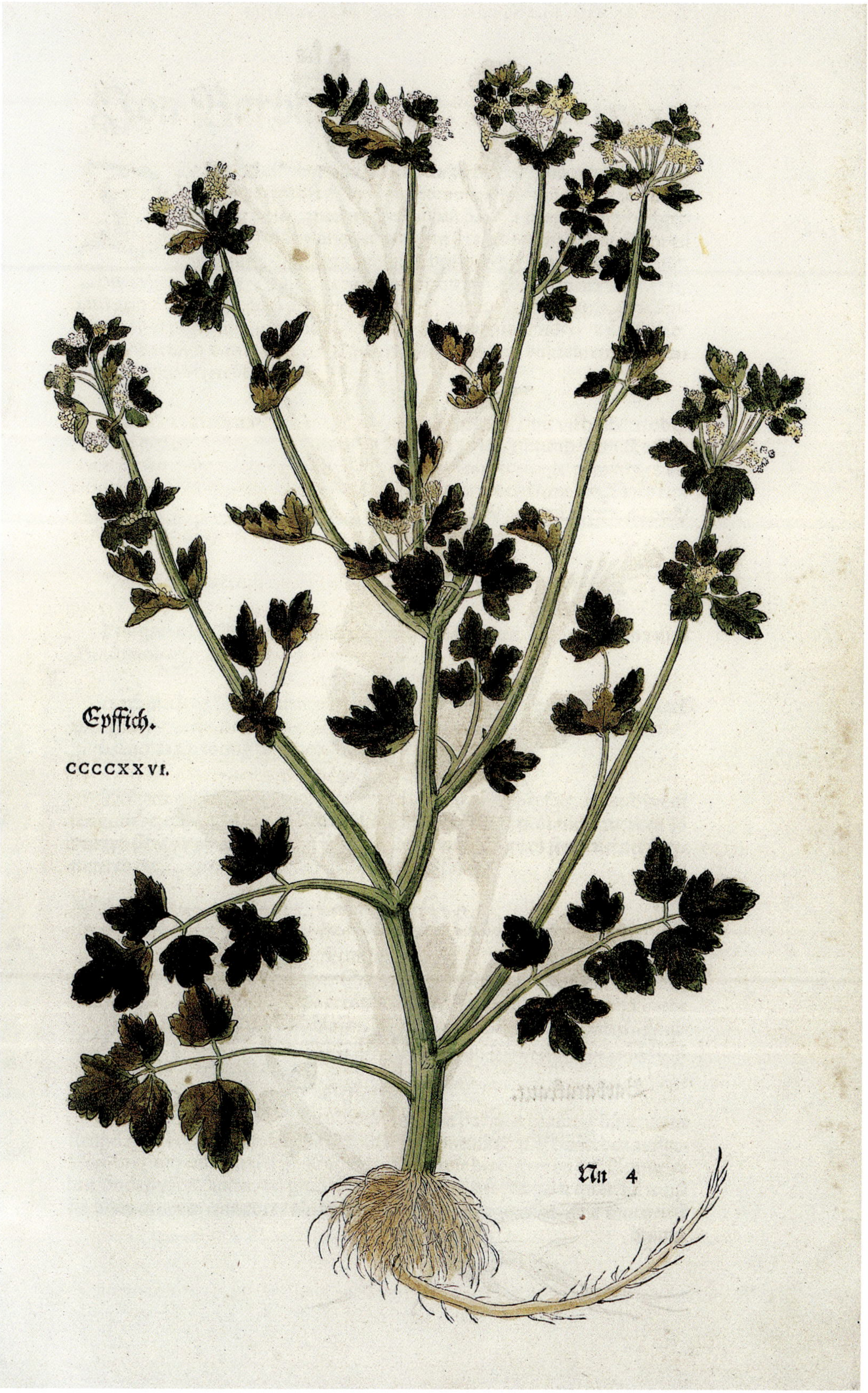
Epffich.
CCCCXXVI.
An 4

COMMON WINTER CRESS

With COMMON WINTER CRESS, or YELLOW ROCKET (CCLXXXV), it is still unclear whether Fuchs's reflections about the origin of the German name are correct. In any case, his note that the plant should be used especially for "unclean" (i. e. infected) wounds is interesting because it constitutes a reference to the effects of the mustard oil glycosides that are present in crucifers.

BARBARAKRAUT

Ob Fuchs mit seiner Herleitung des Namens BARBARAKRAUT (Cap. CCLXXXV) recht hatte, ist bis heute noch nicht geklärt, nur der Name hat sich erhalten. Interessant ist der Hinweis, dass es besonders bei „unreinen", also infizierten Wunden gebraucht werden soll, weil hier ein Bezug auf die Wirkung der in Kreuzblütlern verbreitet vorhandenen Senfölglykoside vermutet werden kann.

BARBARÉE VULGAIRE

On ignore toujours si Fuchs a eu raison sur l'origine du nom «Barbarakraut» qui désigne la BARBARÉE VULGAIRE (CCLXXXV). En tout cas, il est toujours usité. Fuchs préconise la plante pour cicatriser les plaies infectées ou «impures», ainsi qu'il écrit. Cette indication est intéressante, car elle fait penser à l'effet du sénevol contenu dans les crucifères.

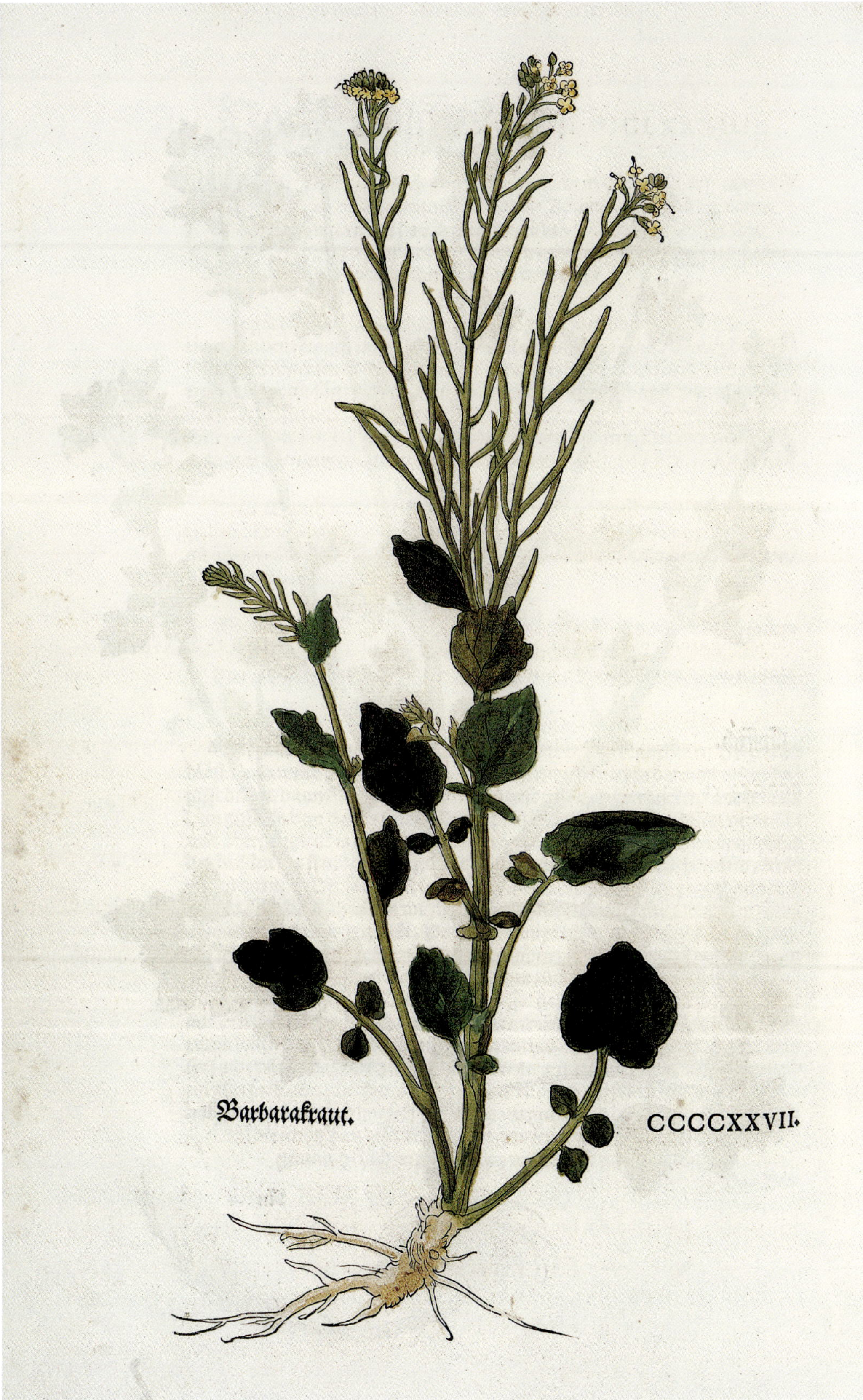
Barbarakraut.
CCCCXXVII.

MEADOW SAXIFRAGE

The German name of MEADOW SAXIFRAGE (CCLXXXVI) ("stone-breaker") refers to its powers as a diuretic and of breaking up kidney stones.

STEINBRECH

Als harntreibende und Blasen- sowie Nierensteine vermeintlich brechende Heilpflanze machte der STEINBRECH (Cap. CCLXXXVI) seinem Namen alle Ehre.

SAXIFRAGE GRANULÉE

La SAXIFRAGE GRANULÉE (CCLXXXVI) faisait honneur à son nom de «Steinbrech» (casse-pierre) comme diurétique et par son prétendu pouvoir de détruire les calculs rénaux et urinaires.

PAGE 532

BLUE FENUGREEK

The strong aroma of BLUE FENUGREEK, or SWEET TREFOIL (CCLXXXVII) alters according to the humidity level, leading to the belief that the plant changed seven times a day.

„SIEBEN GEZEIT“

Der von der Luftfeuchtigkeit abhängige, stark aromatische Geruch der Pflanze führte zu der Meinung, dass er sich siebenmal am Tag ändere und damit zum ungewöhnlichen Namen „SIEBEN GEZEIT“ (Cap. CCLXXXVII). Schabzigerklee wird er heute genannt, weil er wegen seines Aromas dem gleichnamigen Käse zugesetzt wird.

TRIGONELLE BLEUE

Le parfum de la TRIGONELLE BLEUE (CCLXXXVII), plus ou moins intense selon le taux d'humidité de l'air, a fait croire qu'il changeait sept fois dans la journée, d'où son curieux surnom de «Sieben gezeit» (sept moments). La dénomination actuelle «Schabzigerklee», ou trèfle de Schabziger, vient du fromage suisse du même nom, qu'on aromatise avec ses feuilles.

PAGE 533

COMMON MELLIOT

Since COMMON MELLIOT (CCLXXXVIII) shares almost the same complexion as Fenugreek, identical effects were therefore attributed to it.

STEINKLEE

Dem STEINKLEE (Cap. CCLXXXVIII) werden wegen der fast gleichen Complexion auch dieselben Wirkungen zugeschrieben wie dem Schabzigerklee.

MÉLILOT OFFICINAL

Le MÉLILOT OFFICINAL (CCLXXXVIII) aurait les mêmes propriétés que la trigonelle bleue, car leur complexion est presque similaire.

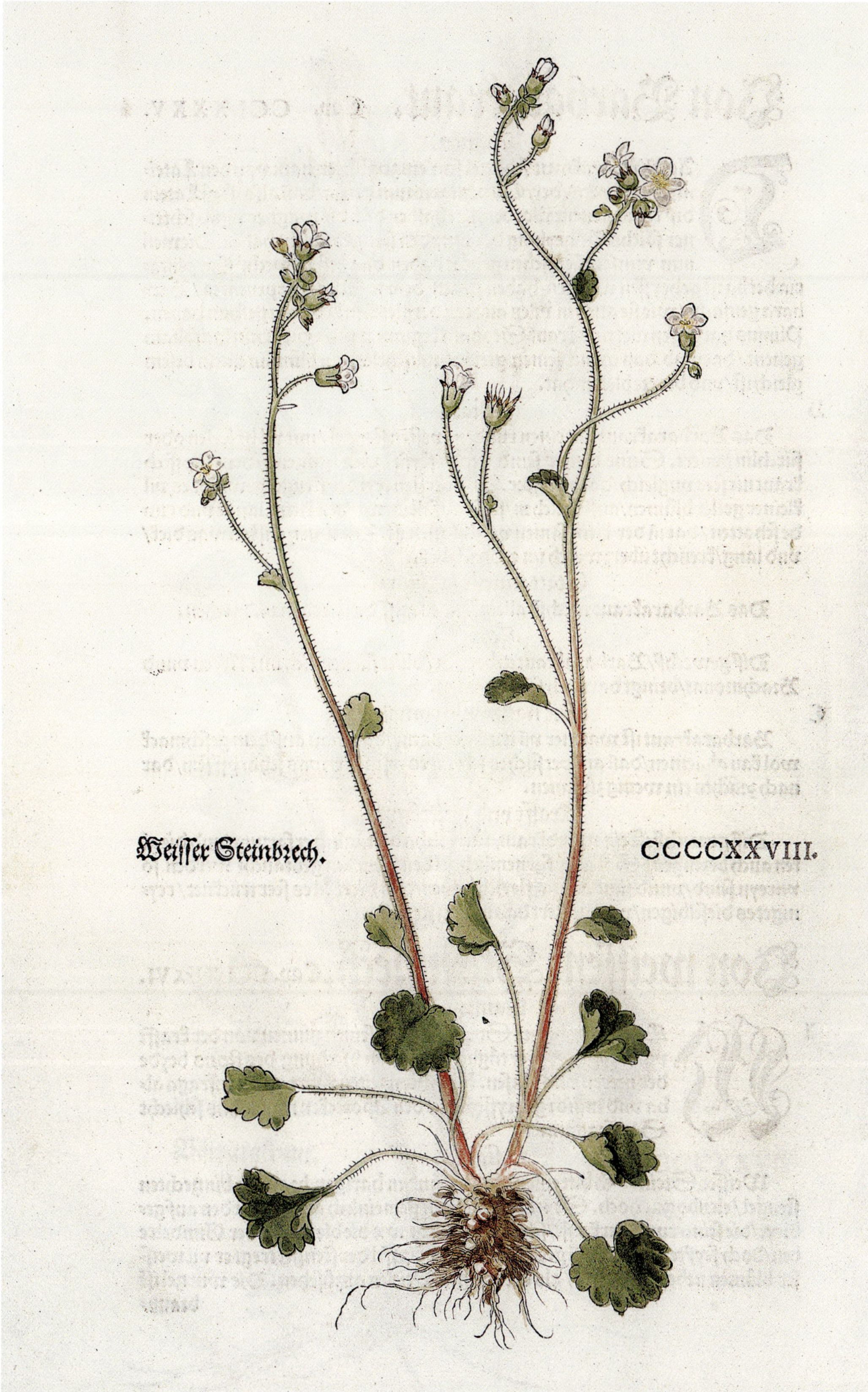
Weisser Steinbrech.
CCCCXXVIII.

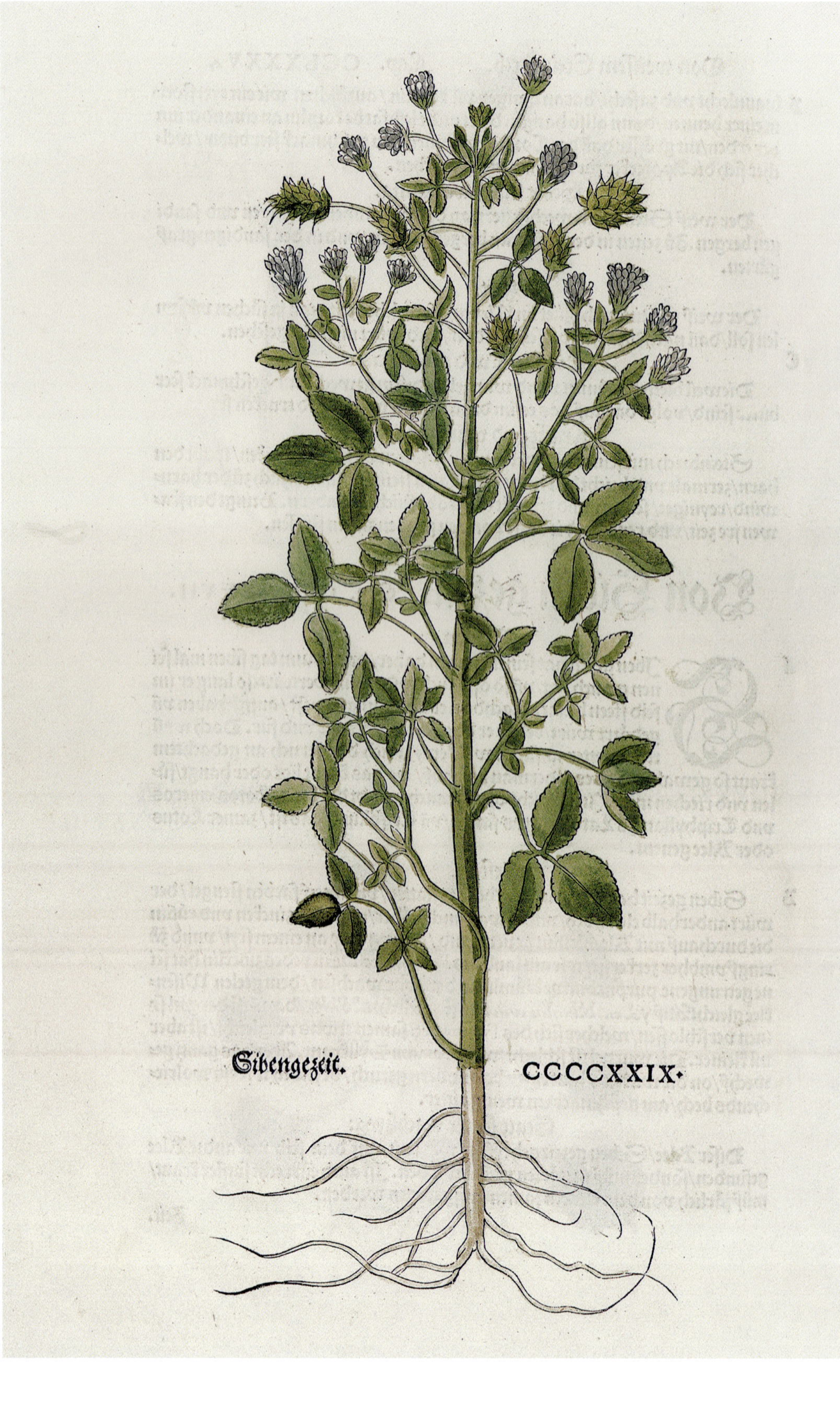
Sibengezeit.
CCCCXXIX.

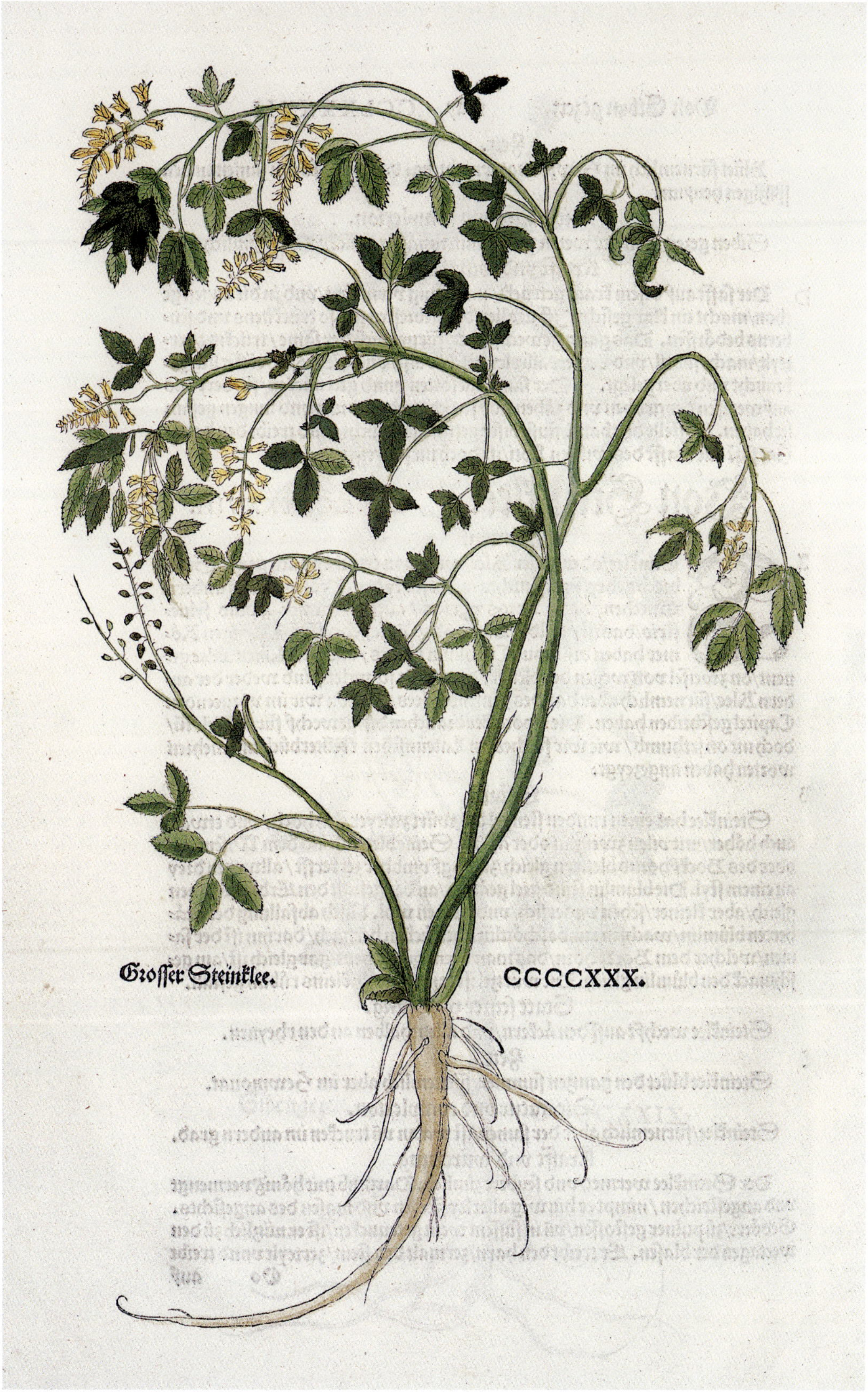
Grosser Steinklee.
CCCCXXX.

PARSNIPS

The chapter on PARSNIPS (CCLXXXIX; plates CCCCXXXI, CCCCXXXIII) also includes Skirret, or Water Parsnip (plate CCCCXXXII). They were classified as diuretics, an aid to digestion and an appetite stimulant.

„SISERN"

Der PASTINAK (Taf. CCCCXXXI, CCCCXXXIII) und die ZUCKERWURZ (Taf. CCCCXXXII) verbergen sich hinter dem „SISERN" (Cap. CCLXXXIX), der als harntreibend, verdauungsfördernd und appetitanregend eingeordnet wird.

PANAIS CULTIVÉ

Sous le nom de «SISERN» (CCLXXXIX) se cachent le PANAIS CULTIVÉ (pl. CCCCXXXI, CCCCXXXIII) et le CHERVIS (pl. CCCCXXXII), que Fuchs recommande pour les voies urinaires, la digestion et comme stimulant de l'appétit.

PAGE 536

COMMON FIG

COMMON FIG (CCXC) represents a well-known cultivated plant. When fresh, the fruits have a laxative effect; dried Figs, however, were considered harmful to the stomach, although they were nonetheless prescribed for many conditions.

FEIGENBAUM

Mit dem FEIGENBAUM (Cap. CCXC) erscheint wieder eine sehr bekannte Nutzpflanze, deren frische Früchte abführen, deren getrocknete, obwohl als magenschädlich angesehen, aber vielseitig verordnet wurden.

FIGUIER

Voici une autre plante utile très connue : le FIGUIER (CCXC). Frais, ses fruits sont laxatifs ; séchés, ils ont de multiples indications, même s'ils sont considérés ici comme nuisibles à l'estomac.

PAGE 537

SPANISH BROOM

The seeds and pressed juice of SPANISH BROOM (CCXCI) were used as a laxative.

„PFRIMMEN"

Als „PFRIMMEN" (Cap. CCXCI) bezeichnete man den Ginster, dessen Samen und ausgepresster Saft als Abführmittel gebraucht wurden.

GENÊT D'ESPAGNE

Par analogie de forme, le GENÊT D'ESPAGNE (CCXCI) portait en allemand le nom de «Pfrimmen» ou alênes. Ses graines et son suc pressé s'utilisaient comme purgatif.

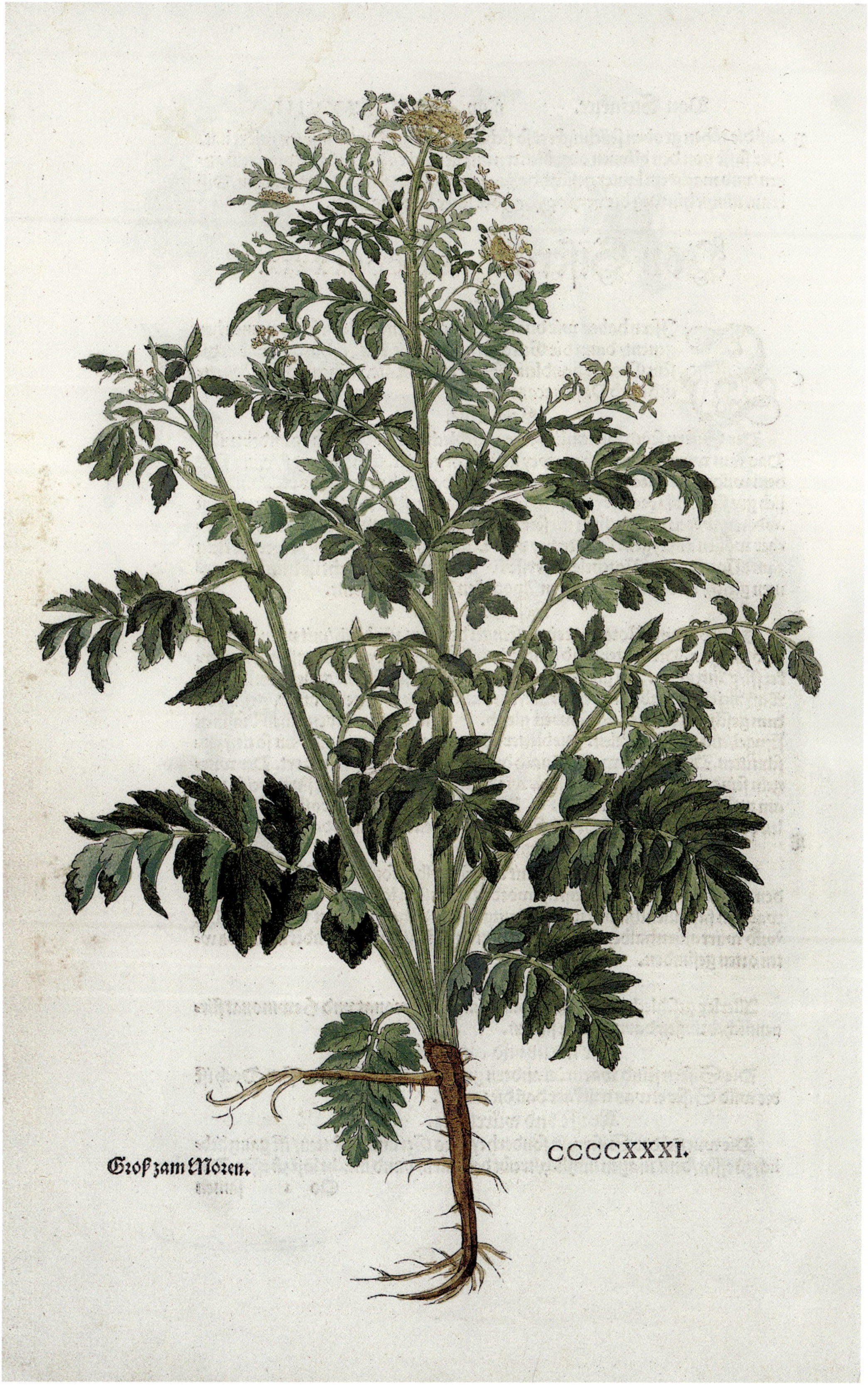
Groß zam Moren.
CCCCXXXI.

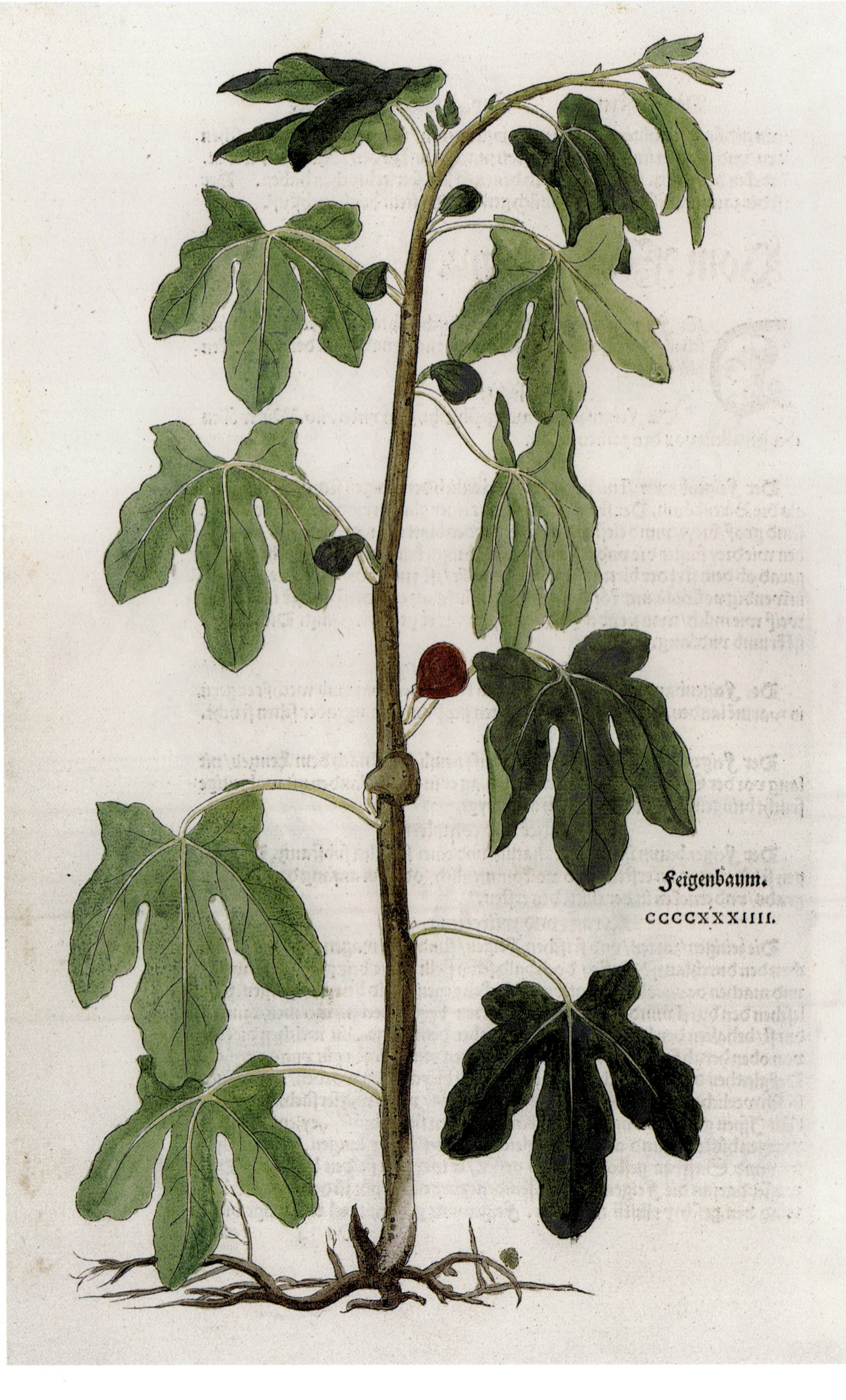
Feigenbaum.
CCCCXXXIIII.

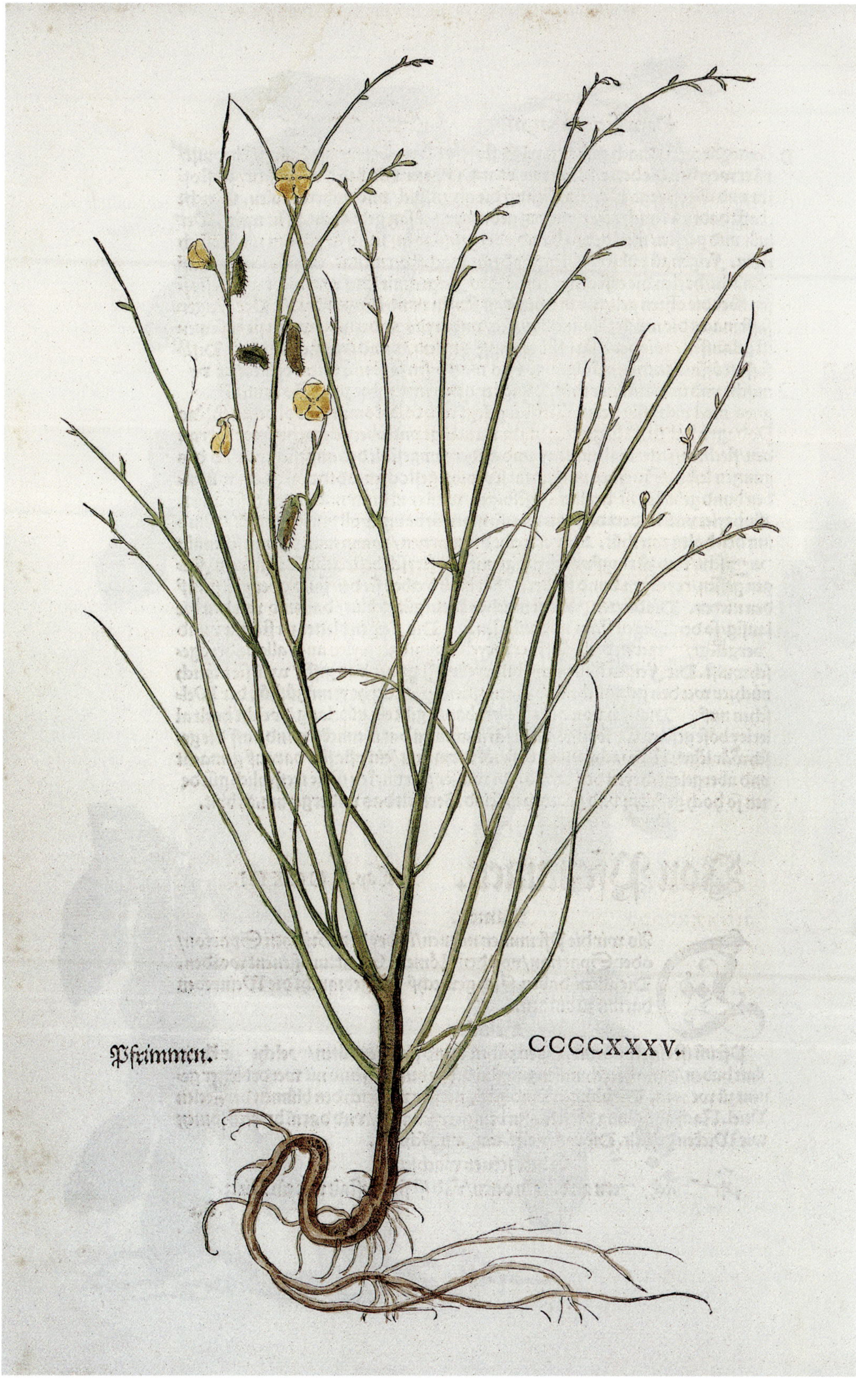
Pfrimmen.
CCCCXXXV.

LOVAGE

LOVAGE (CCXCII), which was used for its detoxifying properties, was, and is, also popular as a kitchen herb. The German and English names both derive from the Latin *levisticum*.

LIEBSTÖCKEL

Aus dem lateinischen *Levisticum* hat sich der deutsche Name LIEBSTÖCKEL (Cap. CCXCII) für die Maggi-ähnlich riechende Pflanze entwickelt, die als Gewürz ebenso beliebt war und ist wie als entwässernde Heilpflanze.

LIVÈCHE OFFICINALE

La LIVÈCHE OFFICINALE (CCXCII) est une plante aromatique, aussi appréciée comme condiment que comme diurétique.

PAGE 540

MASTERWORT

The name MASTERWORT (CCXCIII) was earned by the excellent curative effects of the root of this plant. Fuchs, presuming it to be the famous SILPHION, or TRUE ASAFOETIDA of Antiquity, describes its cleansing purgative and anti-toxic properties.

„MEISTERWURTZ“

Bereits der Name „MEISTERWURTZ“ (Cap. CCXCIII) lässt die Einschätzung ahnen, die man mit der meisterlich wirkenden Wurzel verband. Fuchs mutmaßt, dass es sich dabei um das berühmte Silphion der Antike handelt und berichtet über ausleitende und giftwidrige Eigenschaften.

PEUCÉDAN OSTRUTHIUM

Le nom courant d'impératoire donné au PEUCÉDAN OSTRUTHIUM (CCXCIII) rappelle la valeur supérieure qu'on attribuait aux propriétés de sa racine. Fuchs voit en lui le silphion, panacée des médecins grecs, et relate ses effets évacuants et de contrepoison.

PAGE 541

DOWNY WOUNDWORT

DOWNY WOUNDWORT (CCXCIIII), also known as German Stachys, is treated only briefly. Presented as a stimulant to menstrual flow, the plant was not supposed to be taken by pregnant women.

„STINCKENDER ANDORN“

Der „STINCKENDE ANDORN“ (Cap. CCXCIIII) wird nur kurz besprochen und als menstruationsfördernde Pflanze vorgestellt, vor deren Anwendung durch Schwangere gewarnt wird.

ÉPIAIRE D'ALLEMAGNE

La présentation de l'ÉPIAIRE D'ALLEMAGNE (CCXCIIII), appelée ici «marrube malodorant» («stinckende Andorn»), est brève, et Fuchs la contre-indique chez les femmes enceintes, car elle provoque les menstrues.

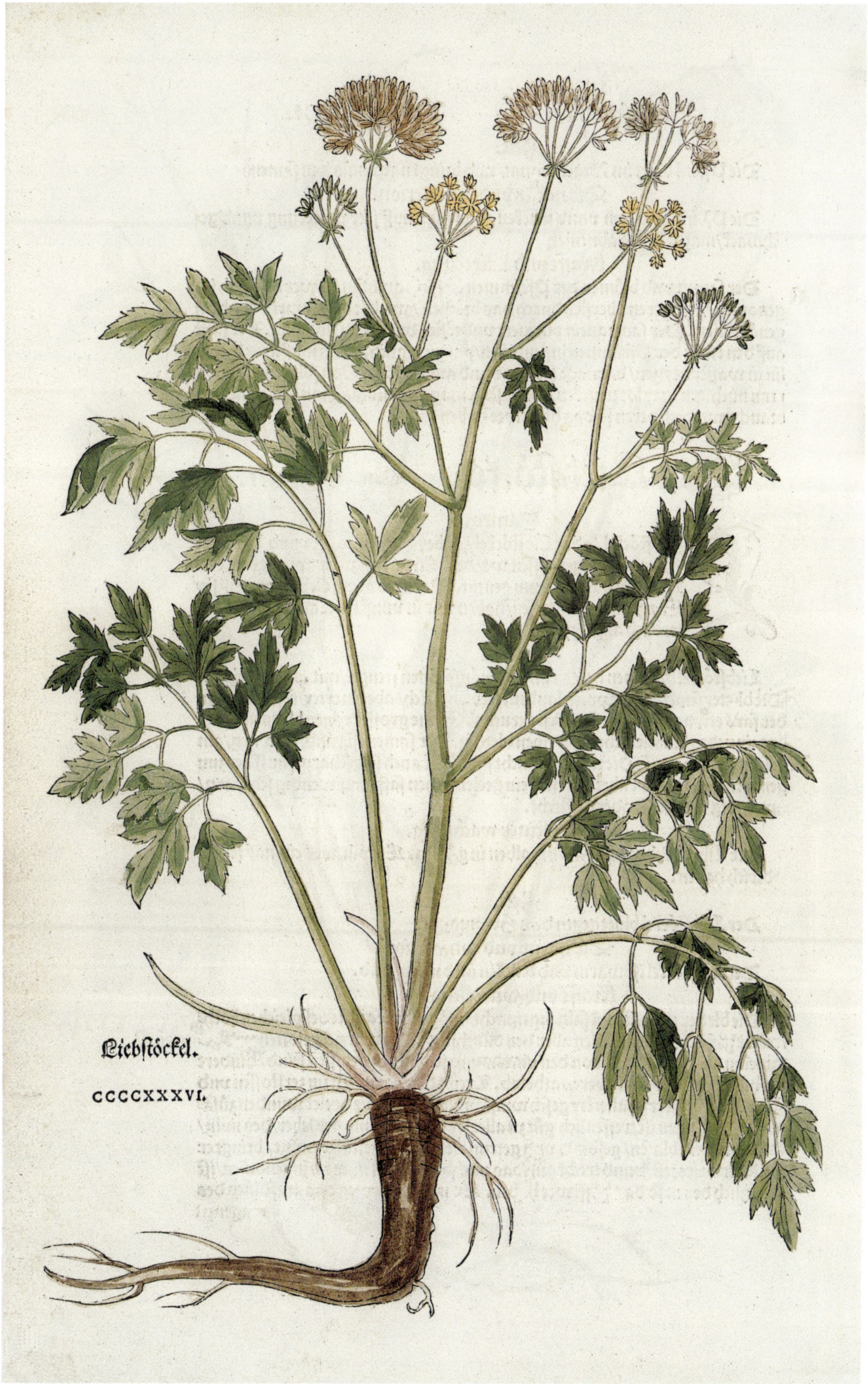

LOVAGE | LIEBSTÖCKEL | LIVÈCHE OFFICINALE

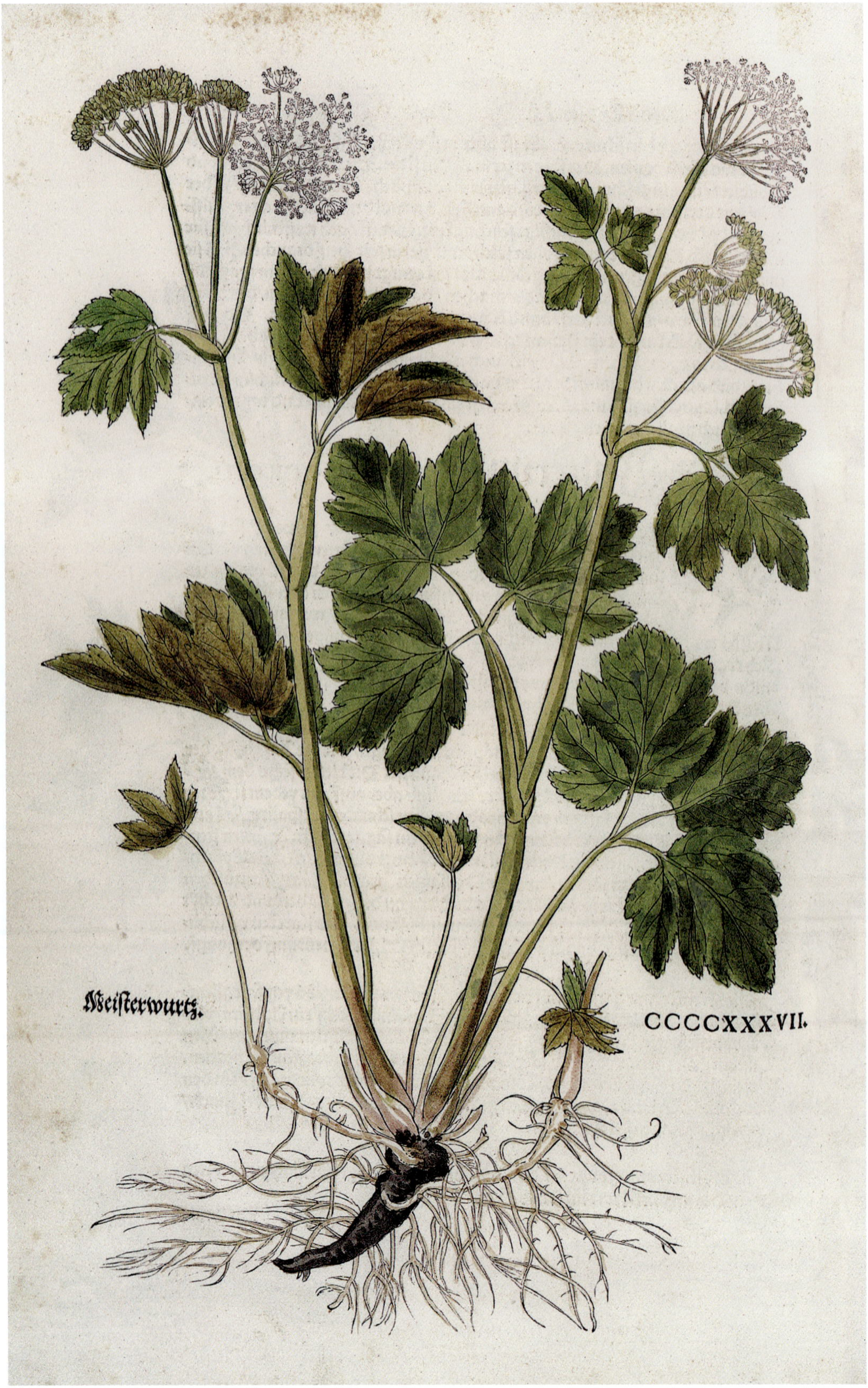
Meisterwurtz.
CCCCXXXVII.

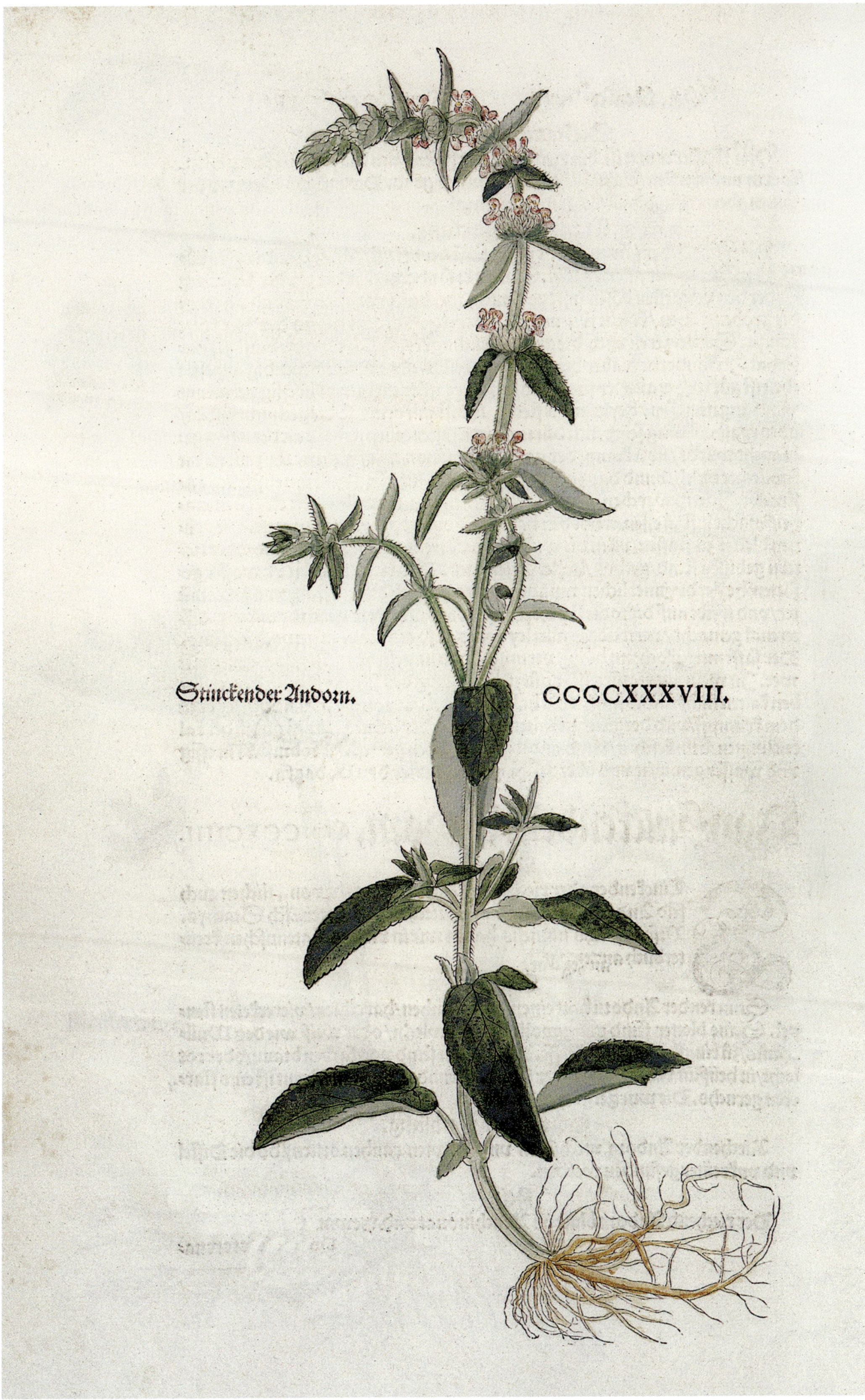
Stinckender Andorn.
CCCCXXXVIII.

RYE

The chapter on RYE (CCXCV) illustrates just how much effort Fuchs invested in harmonizing the descriptions and names from the classical world with the plants with which he was familiar. Nonetheless, he subsequently mentions the plant only as a grain for bread.

ROGGEN

Wie sehr Fuchs bemüht war, die antiken Beschreibungen und Namen mit den ihm bekannten Pflanzen in Einklang zu bringen, zeigt sich an der Diskussion des Namens für den ROGGEN (Cap. CCXCV), der dann jedoch nur als Brotgetreide erwähnt wird.

SEIGLE

Fuchs se donne beaucoup de mal pour faire correspondre les descriptions anciennes avec les noms des plantes qu'il connaît, ce qui est manifeste quand il s'agit pour lui de donner un nom au SEIGLE (CCXCV), lequel finalement n'est évoqué que comme plante alimentaire.

PAGE 544

UPRIGHT HEDGE-NETTLE

Similar to Downy Woundwort, UPRIGHT HEDGE-NETTLE (CCXCVI), a Stachys known as Perennial Yellow Woundwort, is praised for its vulnerary effects.

„GLIDKRAUT"

Auch das „GLIDKRAUT" (Cap. CCXCVI) ist wie der STINKENDE ANDORN (Cap. CCXCIIII) ein Ziest, bei dem jedoch die wundheilende Wirkung im Vordergrund steht.

ÉPIAIRE DROITE

Bien que l'ÉPIAIRE DROITE (CCXCVI), figurant ici sous le nom de «Glidkraut» (herbe pour membre blessé), soit un Stachys comme l'épiaire d'Allemagne, Fuchs met au premier plan ses effets cicatrisants.

PAGE 545

SORGHUM

SORGHUM (CCXCVII), also known as Kaffir or Guinea Corn, is the most important Millet today. Fuchs, lacking a German name for the plant, designated it "foreign" Millet. Considered similar to Italian or Foxtail Millet, the grain had no medicinal use in Fuchs's day.

„WELSCH HIRSS" (SORGHUMHIRSE)

Die SORGHUMHIRSE, die Fuchs mangels eines eigenen deutschen Namens „WELSCH HIRSS" (Cap. CCXCVII) nennt, ist heute die wichtigste Hirseart, war zu seinen Zeiten aber im medizinischen Gebrauch noch unbekannt und wird der Kolbenhirse gleich geachtet.

SORGHO COMMUN

Le SORGHO COMMUN (CCXCVII), que Fuchs, faute d'un nom allemand, nomme le «millet étranger» («welsch Hirß»), est aujourd'hui la plus importante variété de millet qui existe, mais à cette époque il est encore inconnu en médecine et considéré comme le mil à épis.

Rocken. CCCCXXXIX.

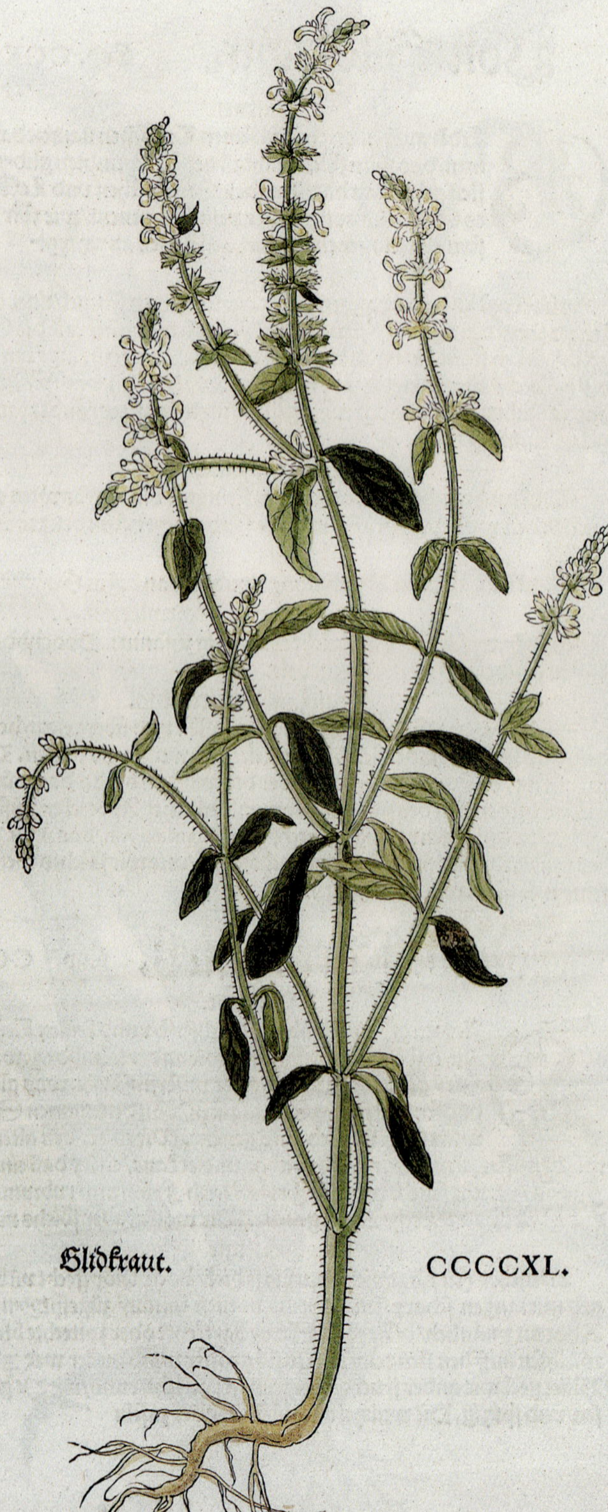

Glidkraut. CCCCXL.

Pp 4

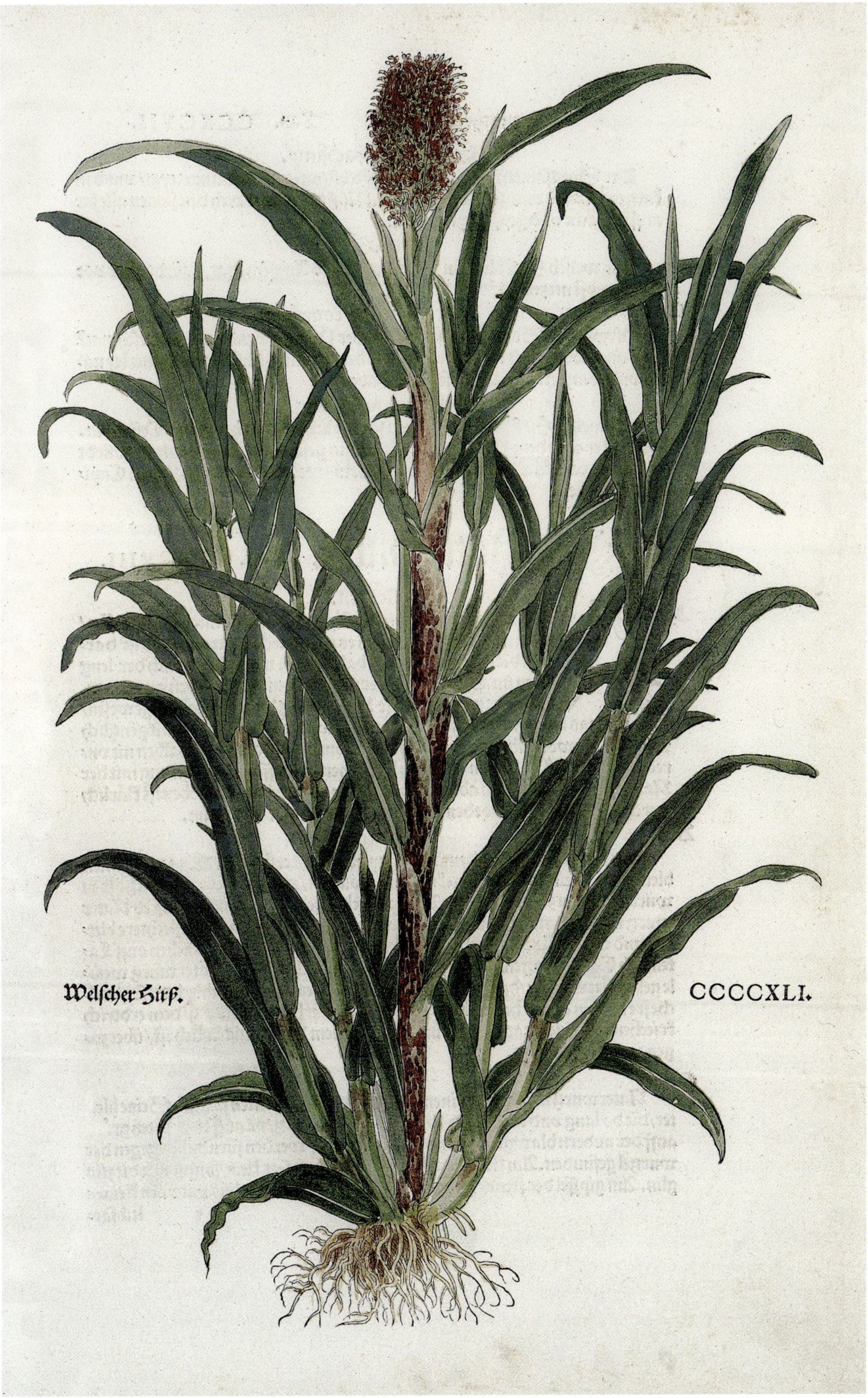

SORGHUM | „WELSCH HIRSS“ | SORGHO COMMUN

BISTORT

Fuchs describes BISTORT, or SNAKEROOT (CCXCVIII), as healing wounds, halting diarrhoea and fostering menstruation.

„NATERWURTZ"

Wundheilend, den Durchfall stoppend und menstruationsfördernd, so wird die Wirkung der „NATERWURTZ" (Cap. CCXCVIII) beschrieben.

BISTORTE

Les effets de la renouée BISTORTE (CCXCVIII), ou «racine à couleuvres» («Naterwurtz») par allusion à sa racine tordue, sont décrits comme cicatrisants, antidiarrhéiques et favorisant la venue des règles.

PAGE 548

WATER GERMANDER

Many of the attributes of the strongly smelling WATER GERMANDER (CCXCIX), much prized as a component of the universal antidote theriac, were comparable to those of garlic.

„WASSER BATHENIG"

Unter „WASSER BATHENIG" (Cap. CCXCIX) versteht Fuchs den stark riechenden Knoblauch-Gamander, der als Bestandteil des giftwidrigen Theriak begehrt war und in vielem mit dem Knoblauch verglichen wurde.

GERMANDRÉE D'EAU

Pour Fuchs, la GERMANDRÉE D'EAU (CCXCIX) est une «bétoine aquatique» («Wasser Bathenig»). Plante très odorante, elle entrait dans la composition de la thériaque et était comparée à l'ail sur de nombreux points.

PAGE 549

FRENCH LAVENDER

The illustration of FRENCH LAVENDER (CCC) wrongly appears only after the following chapter and under a false number. Its pleasant odour was supposed to "strengthen the head," just as preparations made from the plant were thought to be purgative and effective against poison.

„STICHASKRAUT"

Die Abbildung zum „STICHASKRAUT" (Cap. CCC) findet sich erst nach dem folgenden Kapitel unter falscher Nummer. Sein angenehmer Geruch sollte „das Haupt stärken", Zubereitungen der Pflanze sollten abführen und gegen Gifte wirksam sein.

LAVANDE À TOUPET

L'illustration de la LAVANDE À TOUPET (CCC) se trouve au chapitre suivant sous un numéro inexact. C'est une plante considérée comme céphalique puisque son odeur agréable aurait «fortifié la tête» ; des préparations à base de lavande seraient purgatives et efficaces contre les poisons.

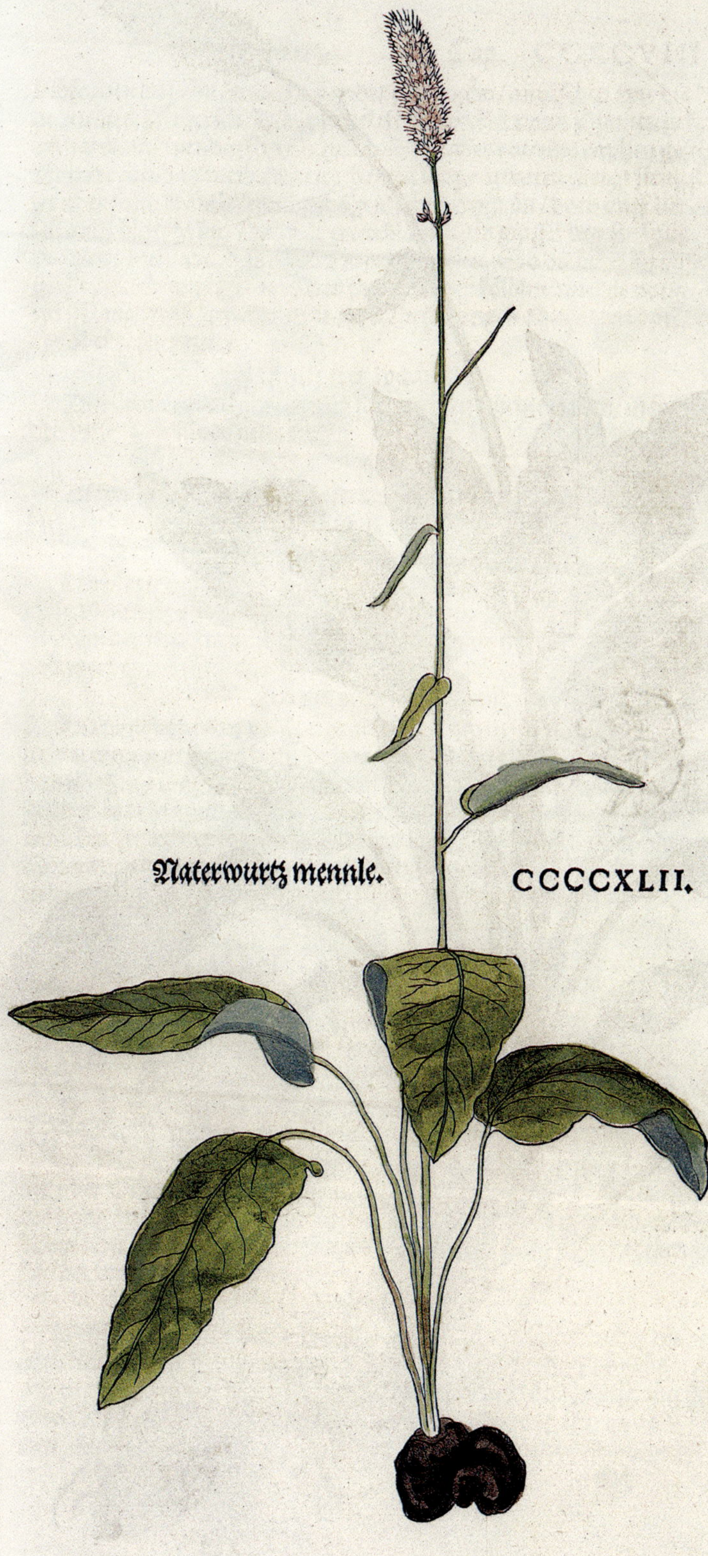

Naterwurtz mennle. CCCCXLII.

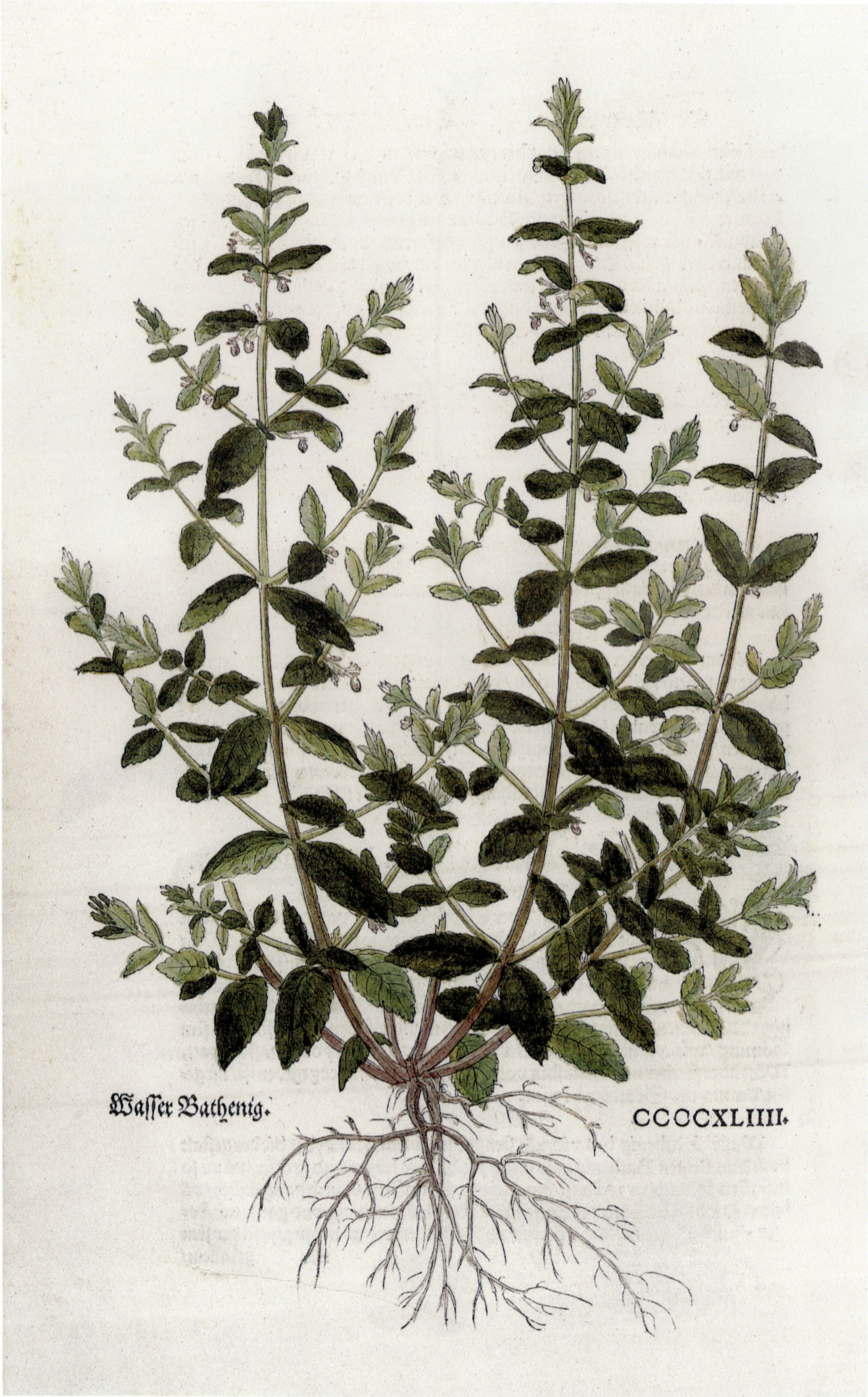
Wasser Bathenig.
CCCCXLIIII.

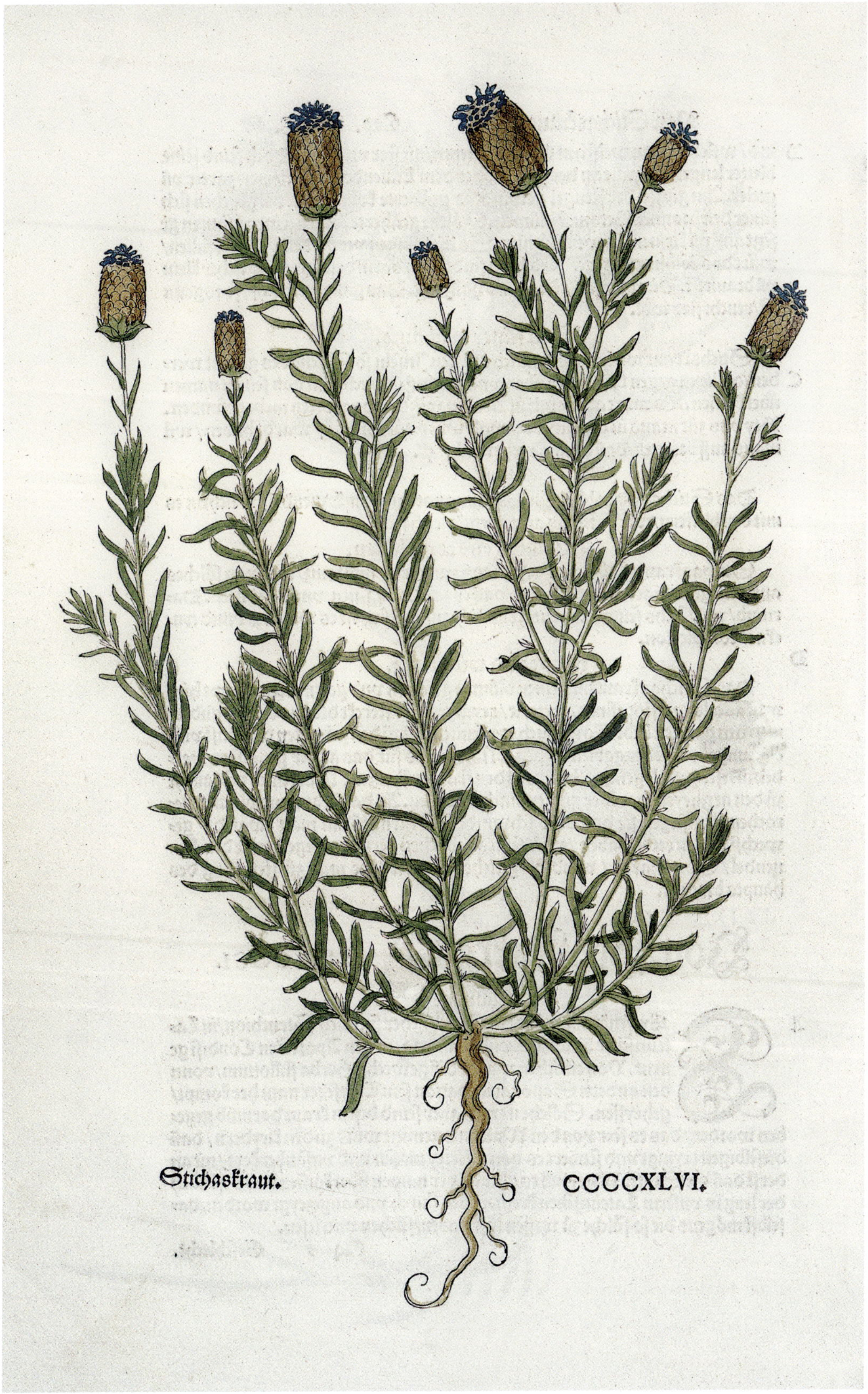
Stichaskraut.
CCCCXLVI.

SOAPWORT

SOAPWORT (CCCI) was named after the persistent foam produced by the plant when shaken with water. Also known as BOUNCING BETT, it was quite properly recognized in earlier times as a diuretic and as an expectorant cough medicine.

„SEYFFENKRAUT“

Weil die Pflanze beim Schütteln mit Wasser einen stabilen Schaum ergibt, erhielt sie den Namen „SEYFFENKRAUT“ (Cap. CCCI) und wurde zu Recht schon früher harntreibend und als schleimlösendes Hustenmittel eingesetzt.

SAPONAIRE OFFICINALE

La SAPONAIRE OFFICINALE (CCCI), ou savonnière, doit son nom à une particularité : sa tige produit une mousse stable, si on l'agite dans l'eau. Elle était employée à juste titre comme diurétique et antitussif.

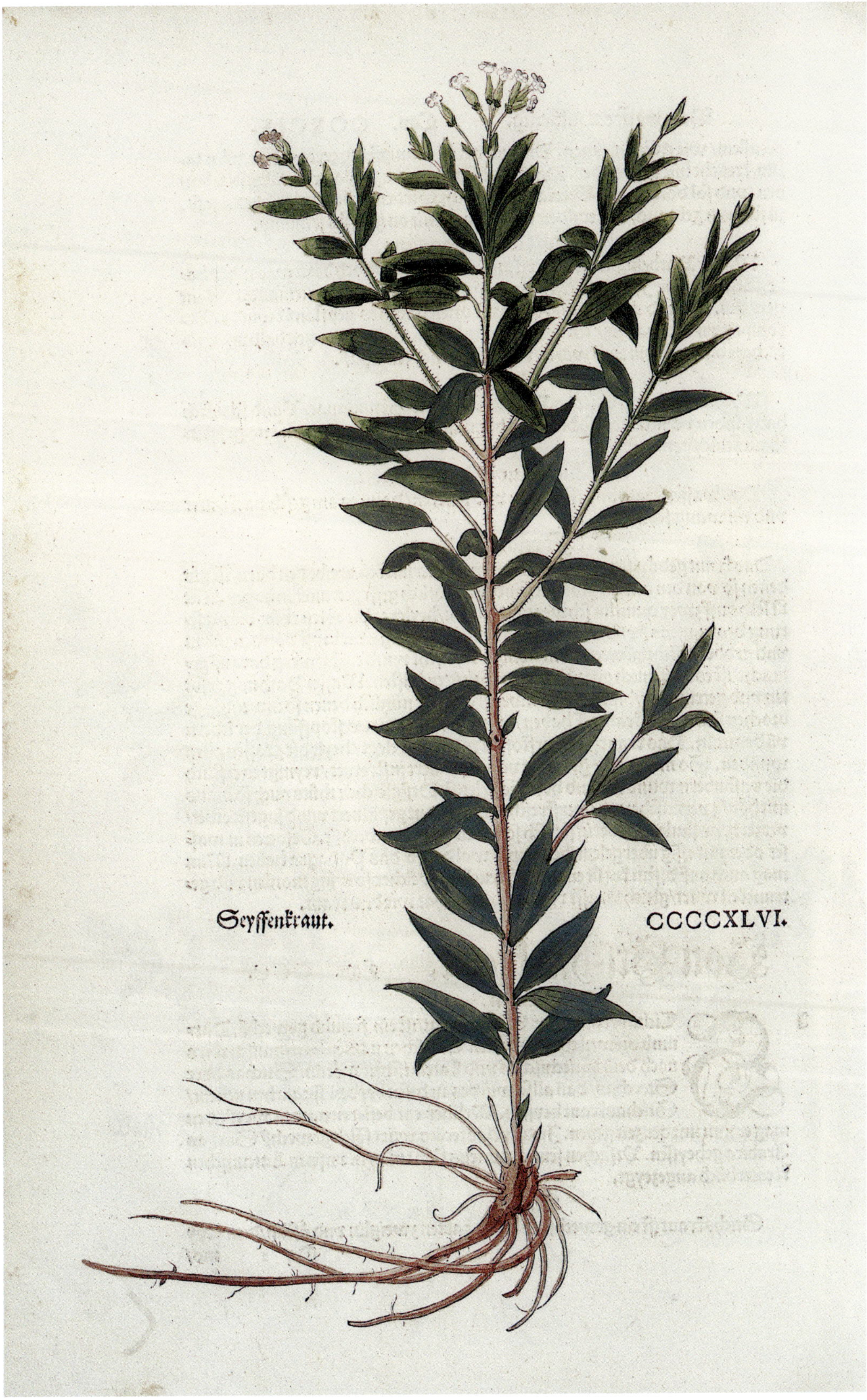

SOAPWORT | „SEYFFENKRAUT" | SAPONAIRE OFFICINALE

SEA ONION

The contents of SEA ONION (CCCII), also known as Sea or Red squill, still play a role today in heart medicine. Although Fuchs was not yet able to determine the plant's effect on the heart, he understood its strongly diuretic effect on the bladder.

MEERZWIEBEL

Die Inhaltsstoffe der MEERZWIEBEL (Cap. CCCII) spielen noch heute eine Rolle in herzwirksamen Medikamenten, bedingen jedoch auch die Giftigkeit der Pflanze. Die Wirkung aufs Herz war für Fuchs jedoch noch nicht feststellbar, sehr wohl aber die stark diuretische, harntreibende Wirkung.

SCILLE MARITIME

Les principes actifs de la SCILLE MARITIME (CCCII) s'utilisent encore aujourd'hui dans les médicaments cardiaques, mais donnent aussi une certaine toxicité à la plante. S'il ne peut encore déterminer son action cardiaque, Fuchs connaît en revanche ses effets très diurétiques.

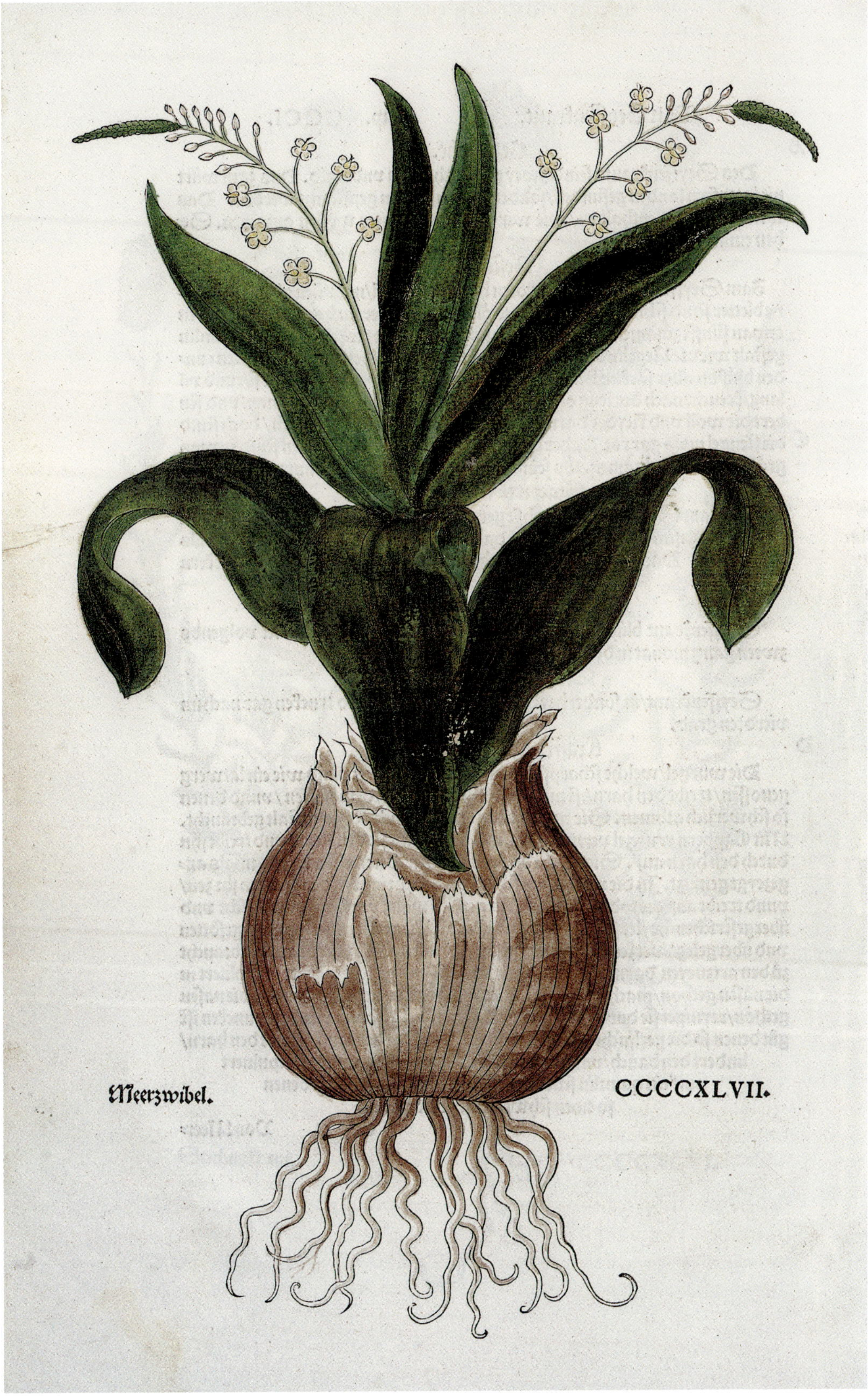
Meerzwibel.
CCCCXLVII.

STAVESACRE

The seeds of STAVESACRE, or LICEBANE (CCCIII), are very poisonous and lead to vomiting. Nonetheless, they were recommended for relieving toothache, just as a vinegar decoction of the herb was supposed to rid clothing of lice.

„BISSMÜNTZ" (LÄUSE-RITTERSPORN)

Hinter „BISSMÜNTZ" (Cap. CCCIII) verbirgt sich keine Minze, sondern der Läuse-Rittersporn, dessen sehr giftige Samen unter starken Nebenwirkungen Erbrechen auslösen, aber auch das Zahnweh lindern sollen, während ein Essigabsud des Krauts die Läuse in den Kleidern vertreibt.

DAUPHINELLE STAPHYSAIGRE

Sous le nom de «Bißmüntz» (menthe à morsure se cache non une menthe, mais la DAUPHINELLE STAPHYSAIGRE (CCCIII), ou herbe à poux. Ses graines hautement toxiques provoquent des vomissements ainsi que des effets secondaires violents. Mais elles soulageraient aussi les maux de dents, et la décoction au vinaigre de sa partie verte chasserait les poux des vêtements.

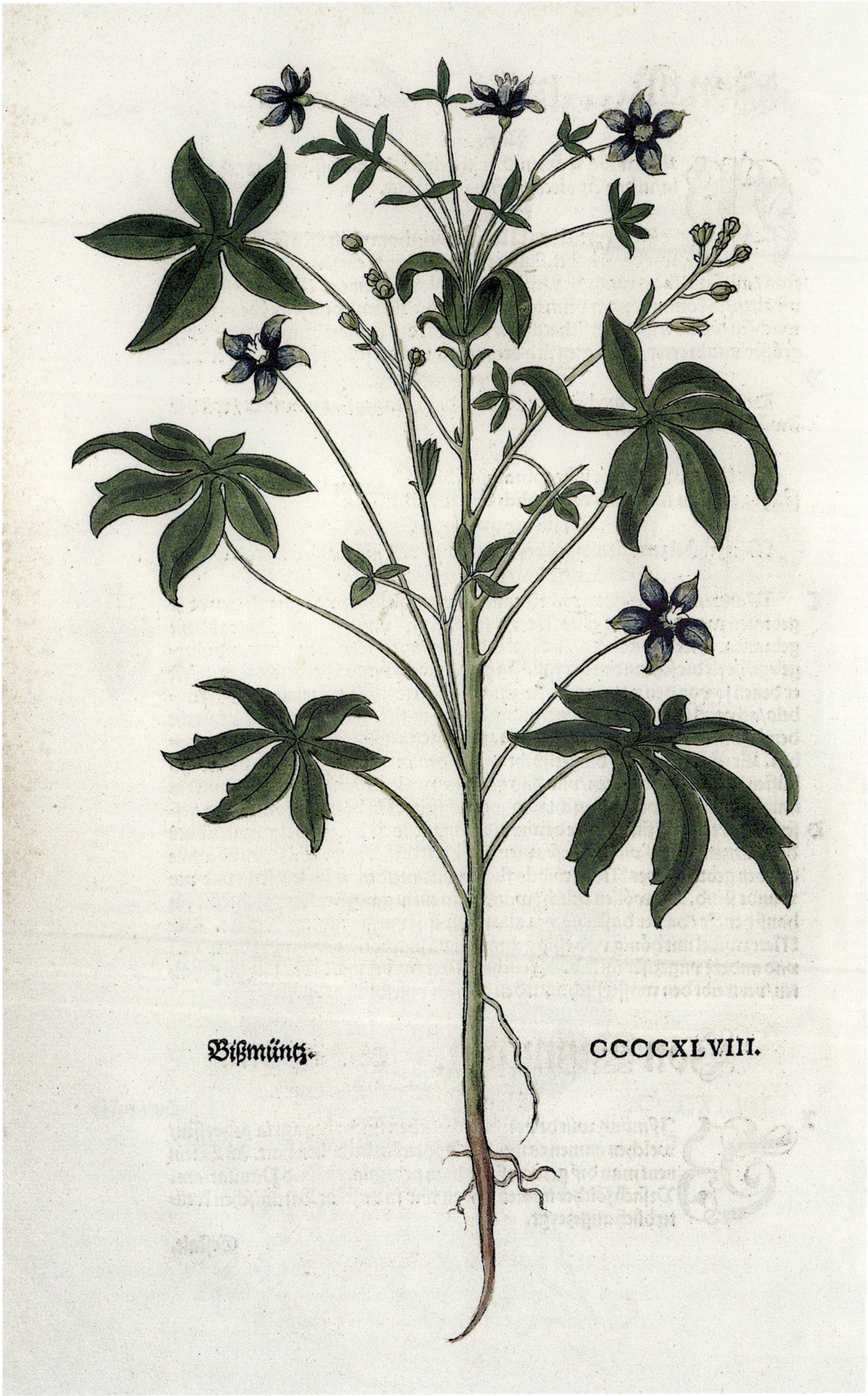
Bißmüntz.
CCCCXLVIII.

SESELI

Although Fuchs named three "kinds" of SESELI (CCCIIII), he was able to illustrate only White and Black Hog Fennel, or Milk Parsley. He had never seen the true *Siler montanum* with his own eyes, and the fact that he did not produce an imaginary illustration, as his forebears would have done, speaks for Fuchs's scientific understanding.

„SESEL"

Obwohl Fuchs drei „geschlecht" des „SESEL" (Cap. CCCIIII) nennt, kann er nur die Weiße und die Schwarze „Hirtzwurtz" abbilden lassen. Den eigentlichen *Siler montanum* hat er noch nicht mit eigenen Augen wachsen sehen können. Dass er deshalb nicht auf Fantasiebilder zurückgreift, wie dies früher sehr wahrscheinlich gewesen wäre, spricht für seine wissenschaftliche Anschauung.

LASER

Fuchs mentionne trois «genres» de LASER (CCCIIII), mais il n'a figuré que le laser blanc et sa forme noire, l'herbe aux cerfs, n'ayant pu encore observer lui-même le laser proprement dit, *Siler montanum* ou laser siler. Notons cependant que Fuchs ne recourt pas à une représentation imaginaire, comme c'était souvent le cas dans la botanique ancienne, ce qui dénote un esprit scientifique peu commun.

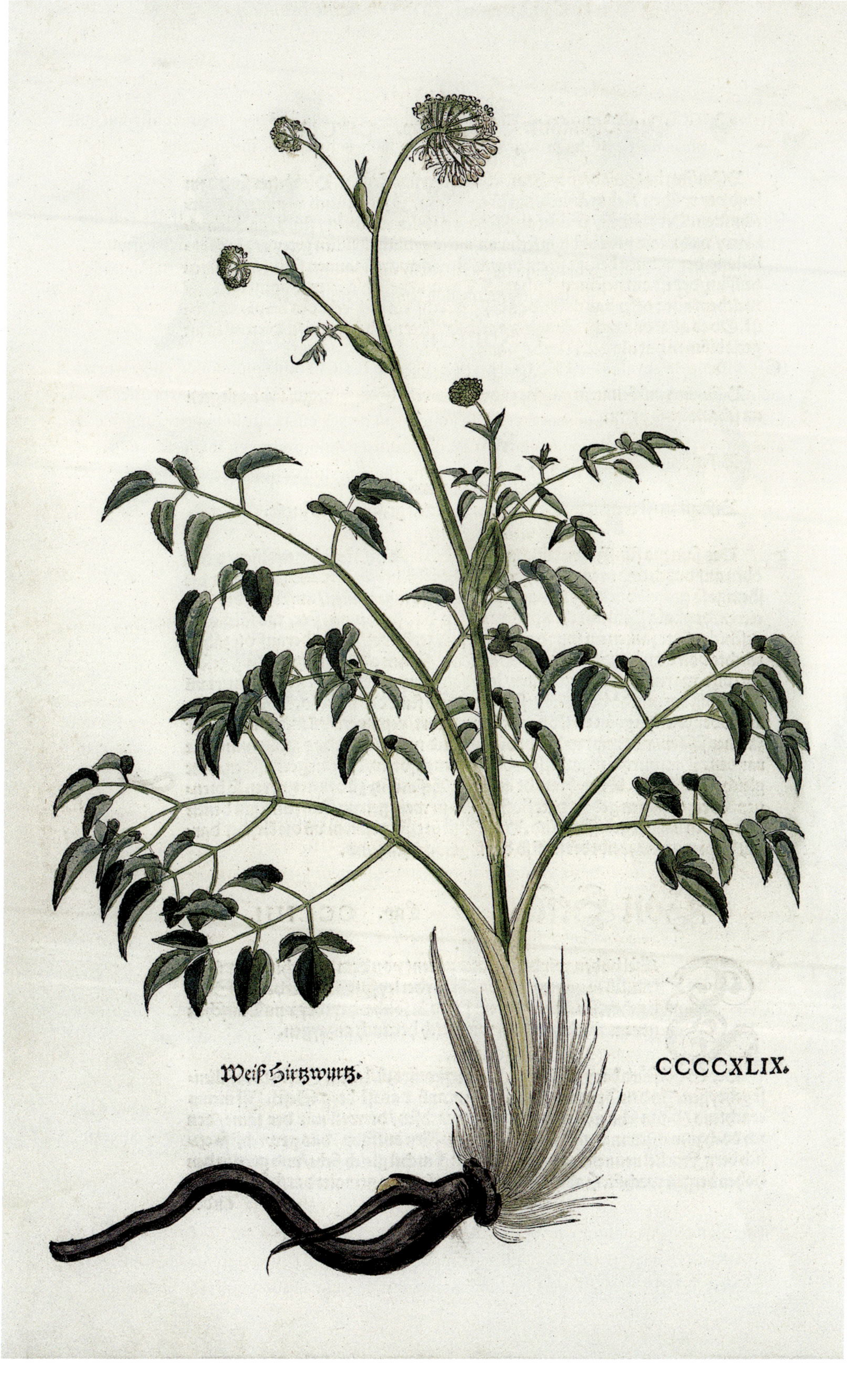
Weiß Hirtzwurtz.
CCCCXLIX.

SPIGNEL

SPIGNEL (CCCV), also known as Meu or Baldmoney, is no longer used medicinally but still plays a role in the production of an aromatic schnaps for the stomach.

„BEERWURTZ"

Ob der Name „BEERWURTZ" (Cap. CCCV) wegen der behaarten Wurzel auf das Fell der Bären zurückzuführen ist oder wegen der medizinischen Wirkung auf die Gebärmutter, ist ungeklärt. Arzneilich heute nicht mehr verwendet, dient er aber noch der Herstellung eines aromatischen Magenschnapses.

FENOUIL DES ALPES

Il est difficile de savoir si le FENOUIL DES ALPES (CCCV) doit son nom de «Beerwurtz» (racine aux ours, de «Beer» ou «Bär» = ours et «Wurtz» = racine) à l'aspect particulier de sa racine – sa pilosité ferait penser à celle de l'ours – ou de ses effets sur la matrice, appelée en allemand «Gebärmutter». Si la plante n'est plus utilisée aujourd'hui en médecine, elle sert encore à la fabrication d'une liqueur stomachique.

PAGE 560

BISNAGA

Under *Ammi visnaga* (L.) one finds BISNAGA (CCCVI), also known as lesser Bishop's-weed and Toothpick-ammi, which is still found today in several medicines.

VOGELNEST (ZAHNSTOCHER-AMMEI)

Zwar nicht mehr unter VOGELNEST (Cap. CCCVI), aber unter *Ammi visnaga* (L.) wird man den Zahnstocher-Ammei finden, der noch heute in manchen Medikamenten enthalten ist.

AMMI VISNAGA

Ce n'est plus sous le nom de «Vogelnest» (nid d'oiseau) que l'on trouve aujourd'hui *Ammi visnaga* (L.), mais celui d'HERBE AUX CURE-DENTS (CCCVI). La plante est encore un composant de certains remèdes modernes.

PAGE 561

BURNET

According to the theory of signatures, the flower heads of BURNET or BLOODWORT (CCCVII) signalled an effect on the blood. For this reason, the sanquisorba, or "blood-absorber" as Fuchs explains, was applied to staunch the flow of blood.

„KÖLBLESKRAUT"

Die roten Blütenköpfchen des „KÖLBLESKRAUTS" (Cap. CCCVII) signalisieren nach der Signaturenlehre eine Wirkung auf das Blut, weshalb die Sanguisorba, die Blutaufsaugerin, wie Fuchs erklärt, zur Blutstillung eingesetzt wurde.

PIMPRENELLE OFFICINALE

Par analogie de couleur, on voyait dans les têtes florales rouges de la PIMPRENELLE OFFICINALE (CCCVII) l'indice d'un effet sur le sang. D'où son nom générique, SANGUISORBA, que Fuchs traduit par suceuse de sang, et son emploi hémostatique.

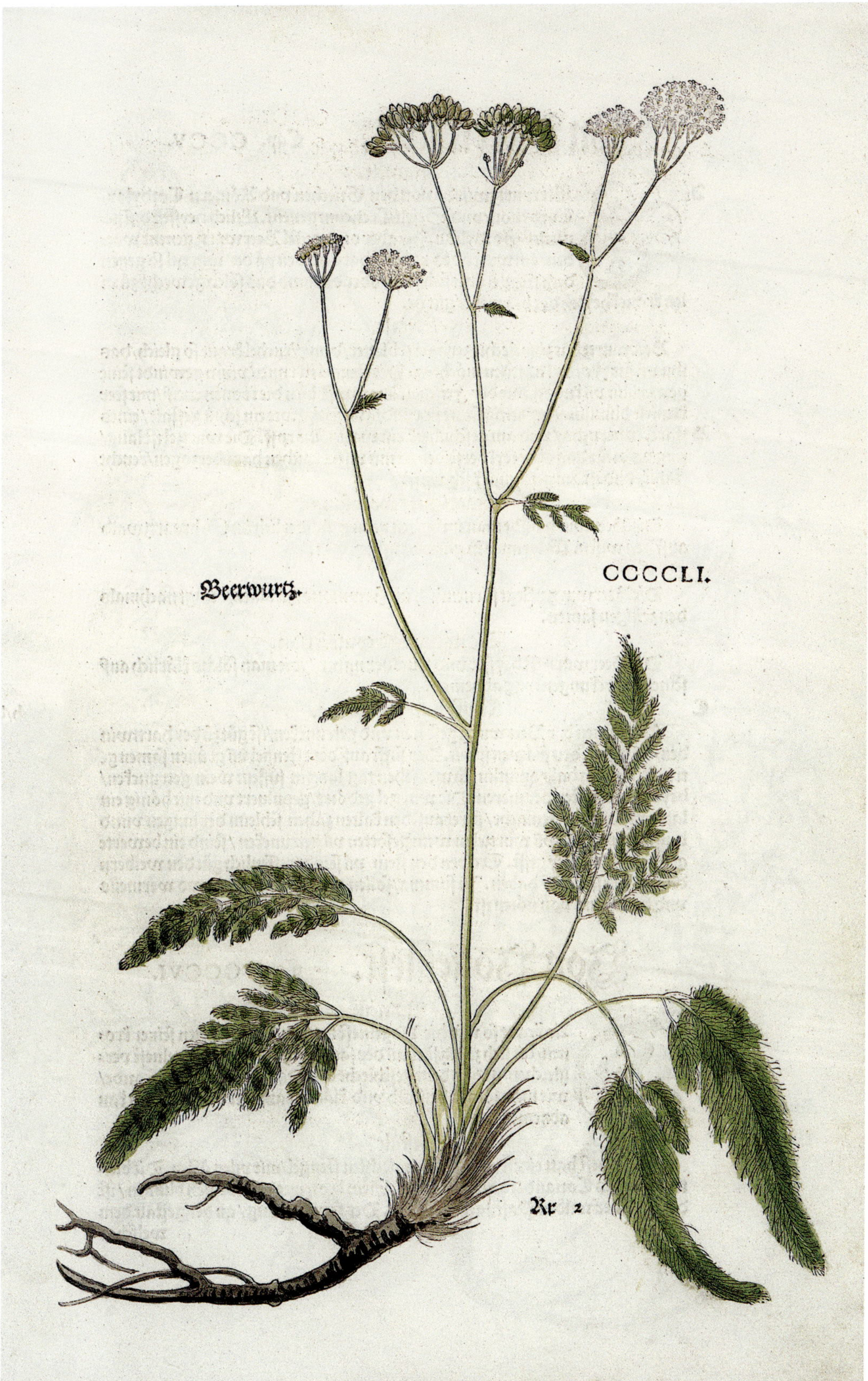
Beerwurtz.
CCCCLI.
Rr 2

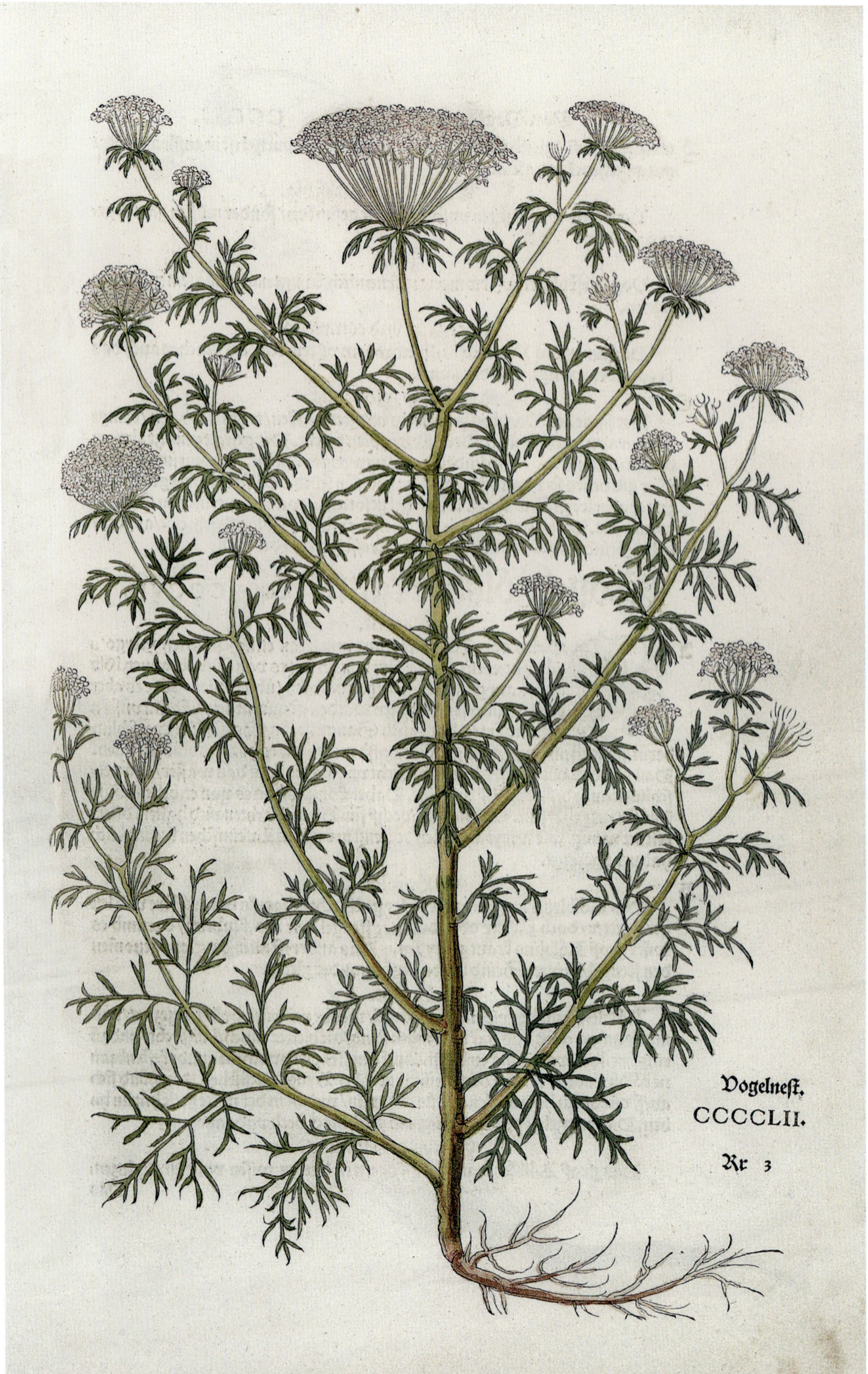
Vogelneſt.
CCCCLII.
Rr 3

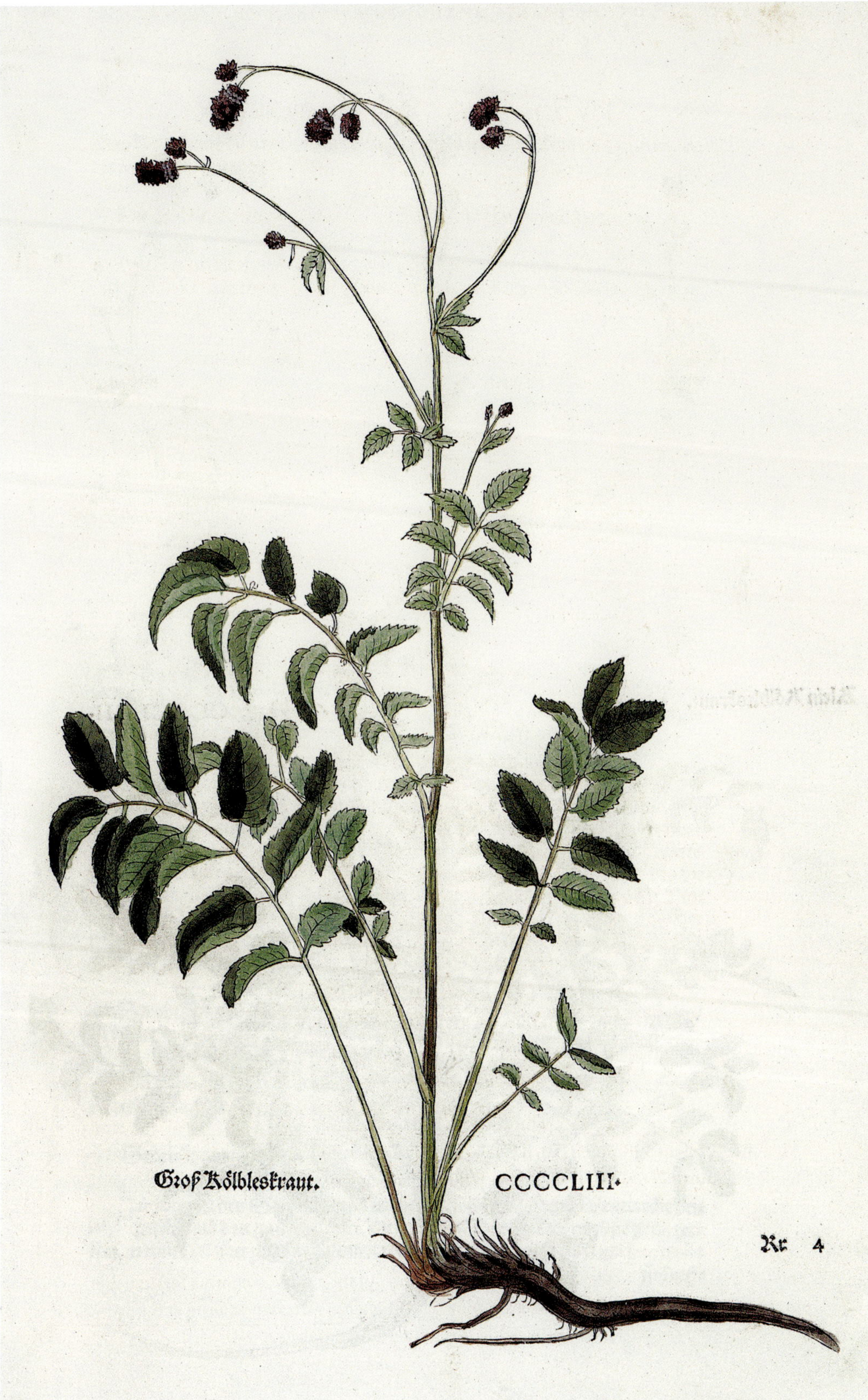
Groß Kölbleskraut.
CCCCLIII.
Kr 4

GLOBE ARTICHOKE

Even today, GLOBE ARTICHOKE (CCCVIII) is treasured both as a gourmet delicacy and as amedicinal plant. Now, however, the ARTICHOKE is no longer used externally, but only internally to aid the digestion of fat.

ARTISCHOCKE

Noch heute ist die ARTISCHOCKE (Cap. CCCVIII) als Heilpflanze ebenso begehrt wie als delikates Nahrungsmittel; medizinisch wird sie jedoch lediglich noch zur Unterstützung der Fettverdauung eingesetzt und nicht mehr äußerlich angewendet.

GRAND ARTICHAUT

Le GRAND ARTICHAUT (CCCVIII) est toujours autant apprécié comme légume que comme plante médicinale. En médecine moderne, il n'a plus d'usage externe et est prescrit pour la digestion des lipides alimentaires.

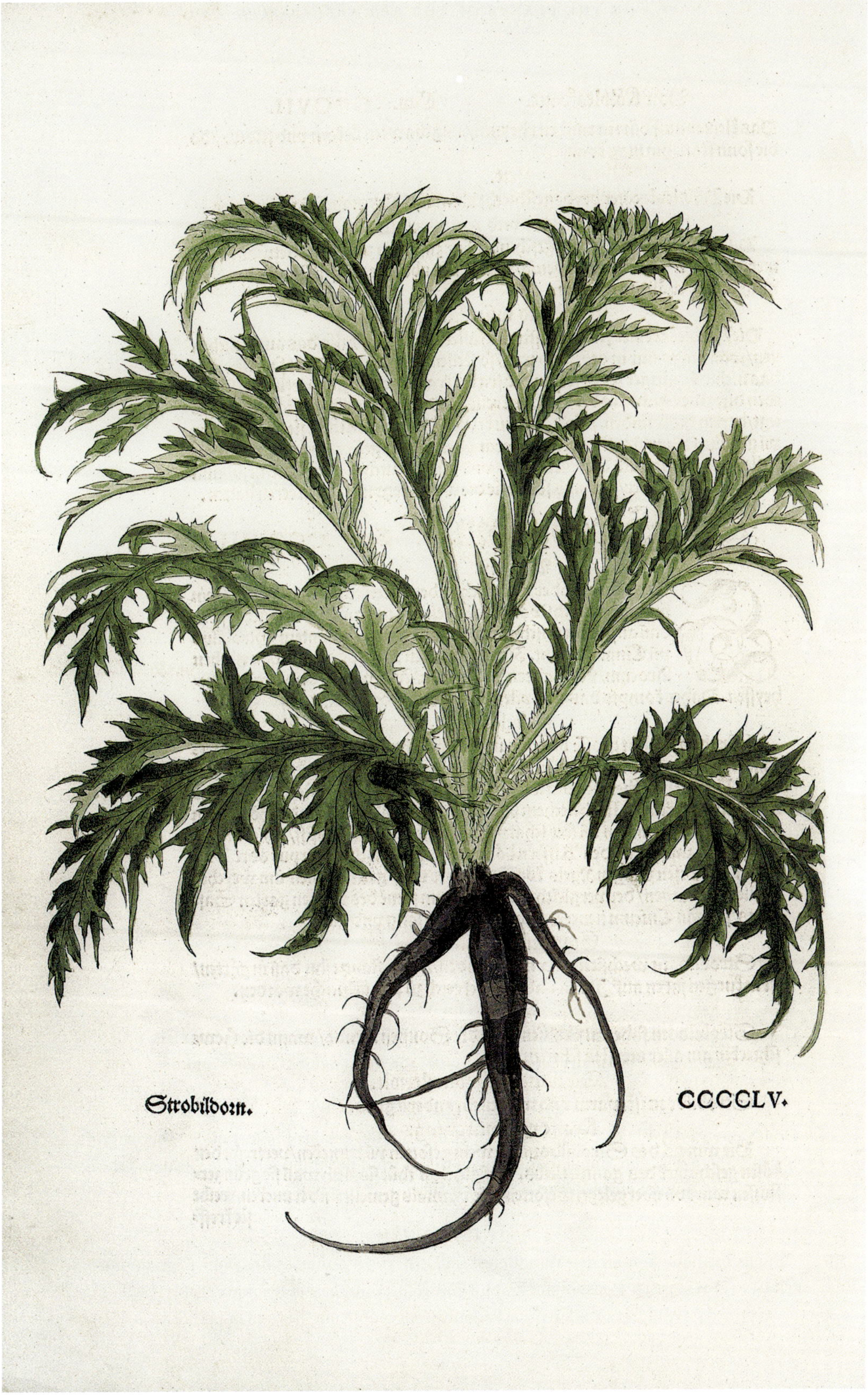
Strobildorn.
CCCCLV.

STINKING IRIS

The unpleasant odour of STINKING IRIS (CCCIX), also known as Gladdon iris, probably acted as a "signature" for the action of the plant against insects and lice.

„WANDTLEUSSKRAUT"

Den Namen „WANDTLEUSSKRAUT" (Cap. CCCIX) erklärt Fuchs mit der Verwendung der Pflanze gegen Wanzen und Läuse, wobei wohl der unangenehme Geruch der Stink-Schwertlilie die Signatur hierfür abgegeben haben dürfte.

IRIS FÉTIDE

Fuchs explique le nom de «Wandtleußkraut» (herbe à punaises des murs), qui désigne l'IRIS FÉTIDE (CCCIX), par son emploi contre les punaises et les poux. Toutefois, le nom s'expliquerait mieux par l'odeur désagréable que dégage la plante.

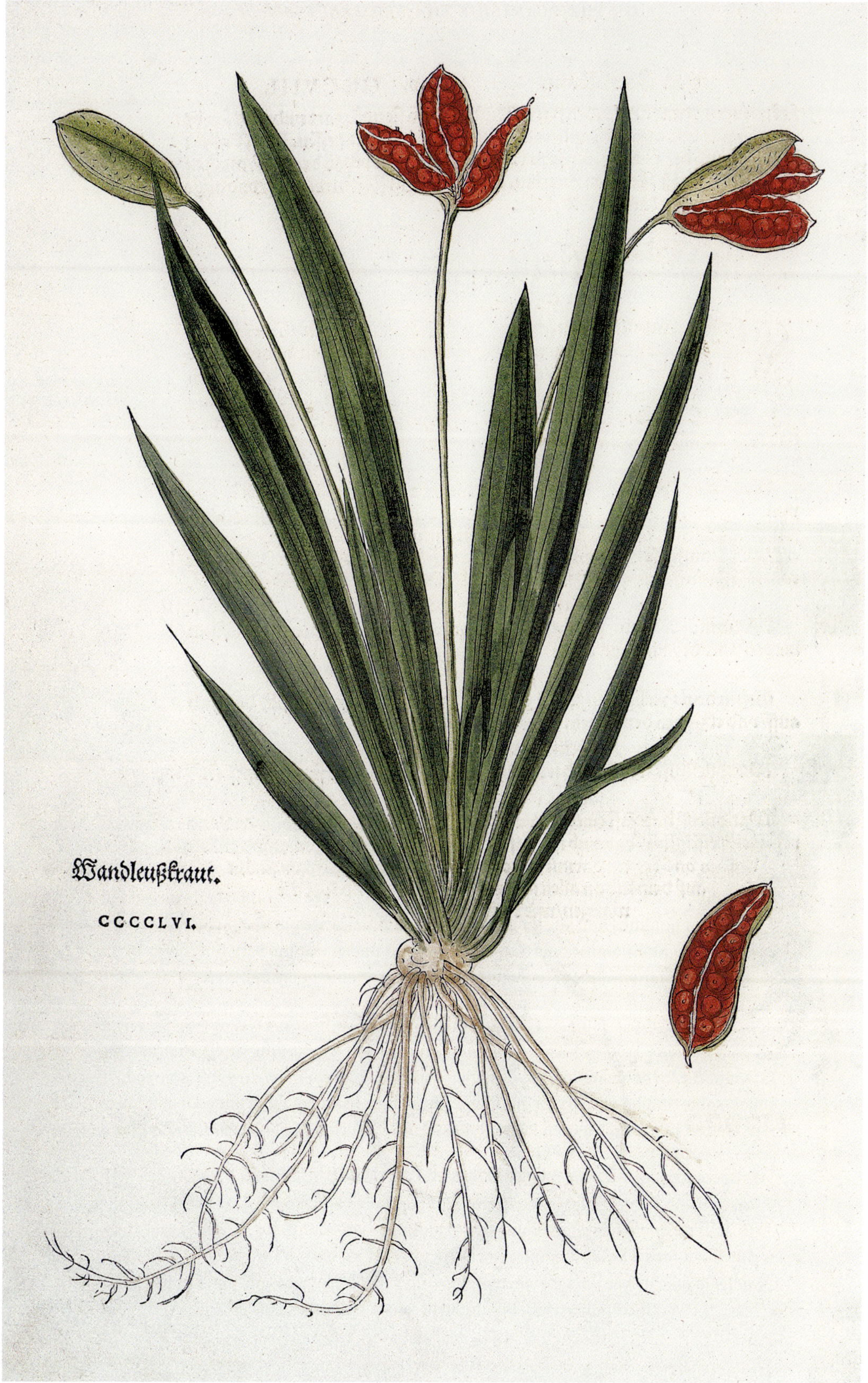
Wandleußkraut.
CCCCLVI.

SPLEENWORT

The public had great faith in SPLEENWORT (CCCX), which supposedly possessed magical qualities and was helpful against all illnesses, even death itself. Fuchs describes the plant more soberly: among other applications, the very fine stems of the plant traditionally justified its use as a remedy for hair loss.

„WIDERTODT“

Das Volk hatte größtes Vertrauen in den „WIDERTODT“ (Cap. CCCX), der auch zauberisch verwendet wurde und gegen alle Krankheiten, eben wider den Tod, helfen sollte. Fuchs beschreibt die Pflanze nüchterner, wobei nach alter Ansicht unter anderem die haarfeinen Stängel den Einsatz bei Haarausfall rechtfertigten.

CAPILLAIRE ROUGE

Les gens du peuple faisaient entièrement confiance à la CAPILLAIRE ROUGE (CCCX) puisqu'ils l'avaient baptisée «Widertodt», ou «contre la mort». Plante aux vertus magiques, elle était employée contre tous les maux – contre la mort justement. Fuchs la décrit avec plus d'objectivité, même s'il voit par exemple dans sa tige très fine l'indice d'effets salutaires sur la chute des cheveux.

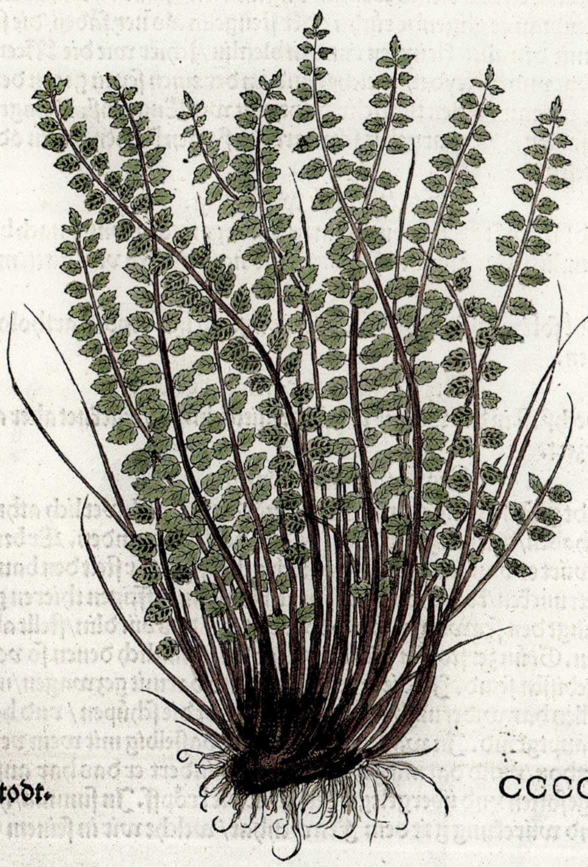

Widertodt. CCCCLVII.

Ss

GREEK CLOVER

According to long tradition, FENUGREEK, or GREEK CLOVER (CCCXI) was applied as a moist, warm poultice to soften boils. The unusual aromatic taste of the seeds also made FENUGREEK useful as a spice.

„FENUGRECK“

Lange Zeit wurden die Samen des „FENUGRECK“ (Cap. CCCXI), des Griechischen Bockshornklees, zur Erweichung bei Furunkeln als Bähung, also als feucht-warme Umschlagpackung, gebraucht, aber auch als Gewürz fand der eigenartig aromatisch schmeckende Same Verwendung.

FENUGREC

Les grains contenus dans les gousses du FENUGREC (CCCXI) ont été employés pendant longtemps sous forme d’emplâtres chauds et humides pour soigner les furoncles, mais également comme condiment à cause de leur arôme particulier.

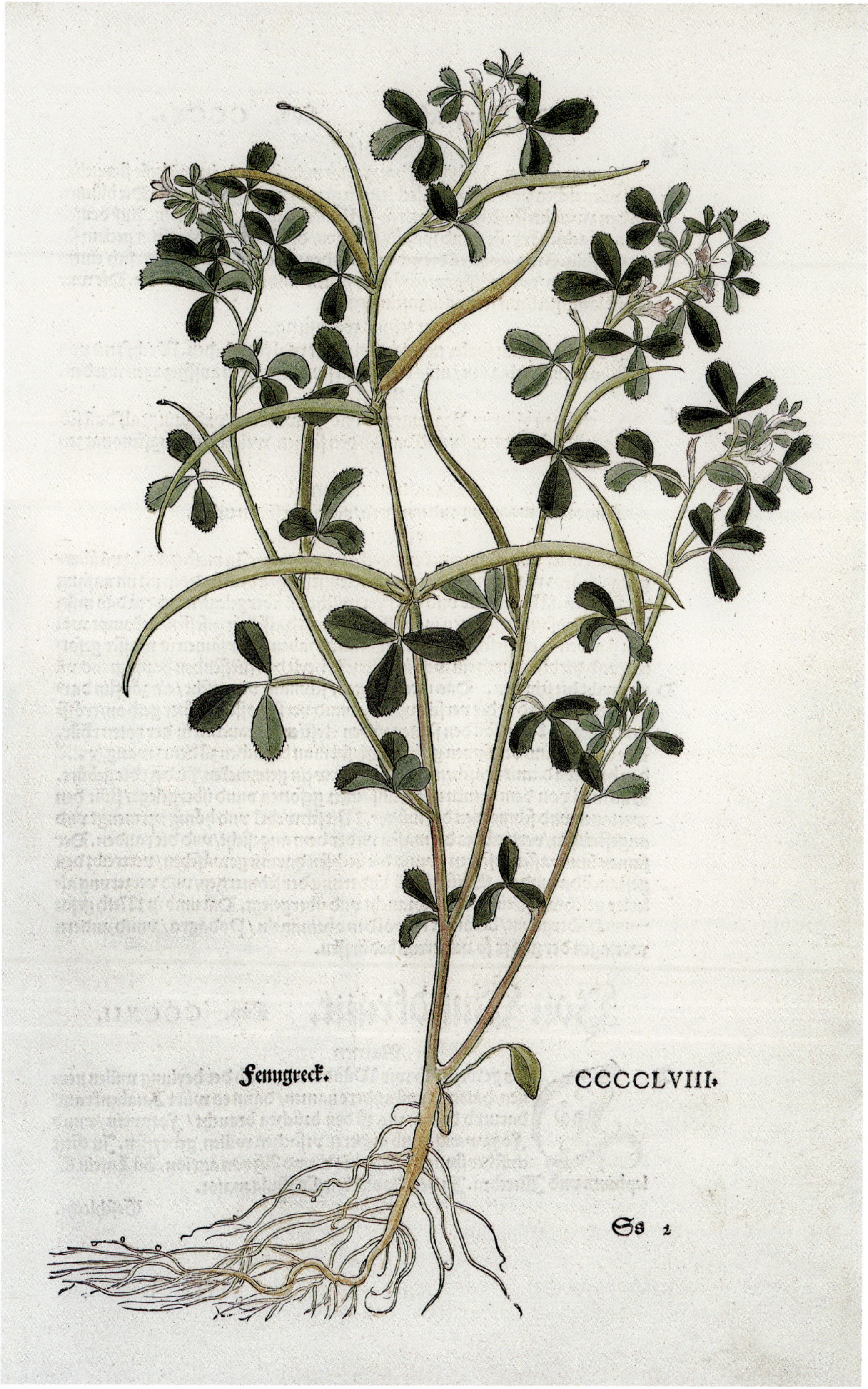
Fenugreck.
CCCCLVIII.
Ss 2

ORPINE

ORPINE, also known as LIVELONG (CCCXII) represents yet another vulnerary. It supposedly possessed strongly astringent qualities that helped not only in staunching blood and healing wounds but – as Fuchs discreetly expresses it – in healing "what is broken on the private end" – a reference to the use many women made of the plant.

„WUNDKRAUT"

Ein weiteres „WUNDKRAUT" (Cap. CCCXII) erscheint mit der Purpur-Fetthenne, der man stark zusammenziehende Wirkung zusprach, die zur Blutstillung und Wundheilung ebenso dienlich war wie zu dem, „was gebrochen ist an heimlichen enden", womit Fuchs dezent auf den Gebrauch anspielt, den manche Frauen vom Saft der Pflanze machten.

GRAND ORPIN

C'est une autre «herbe à plaies» («Wundtkraut») que nous découvrons ici : le GRAND ORPIN (CCCXII), ou herbe à la coupure. On lui prêtait des vertus hémostatiques et cicatrisantes. Les femmes auraient même fait usage de son suc pour soigner «ce qui est brisé aux extrémités secrètes», ainsi que l'écrit Fuchs pudiquement.

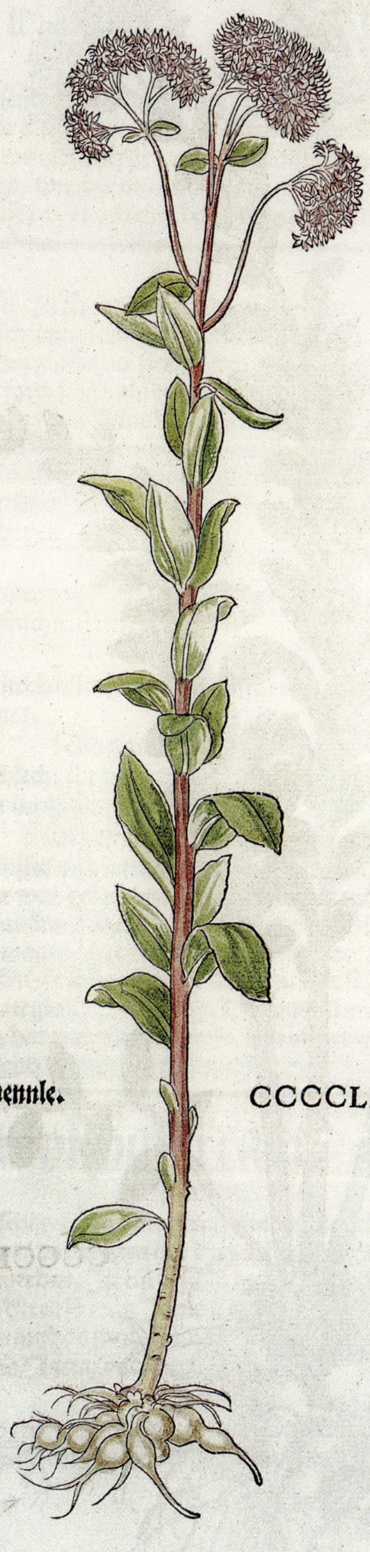

Wundkrautmennle.

CCCCLIX.

Ss 3

FIELD PANSY

Today, wild or FIELD PANSY (CCCXIII) is largely taken internally for skin ailments and "cleansing" the blood. Occasionally it maintains its traditional use as an expectorant to loosen the phlegm in coughing.

„FREYSCHAMKRAUT" (FELDSTIEFMÜTTERCHEN)

Das Feldstiefmütterchen, „FREYSCHAMKRAUT" (Cap. CCCXIII) genannt, wird heute vor allem innerlich bei Hautkrankheiten zur „Blutreinigung" verwendet, manchmal auch noch so wie früher bei verschleimtem Husten.

PENSÉE TRICOLORE

La PENSÉE TRICOLORE (CCCXIII), appelée «Freyschamkraut» (approximativement, herbe contre le danger), continue à être utilisée en médecine, surtout pour purifier le sang dans les maladies cutanées et comme expectorant.

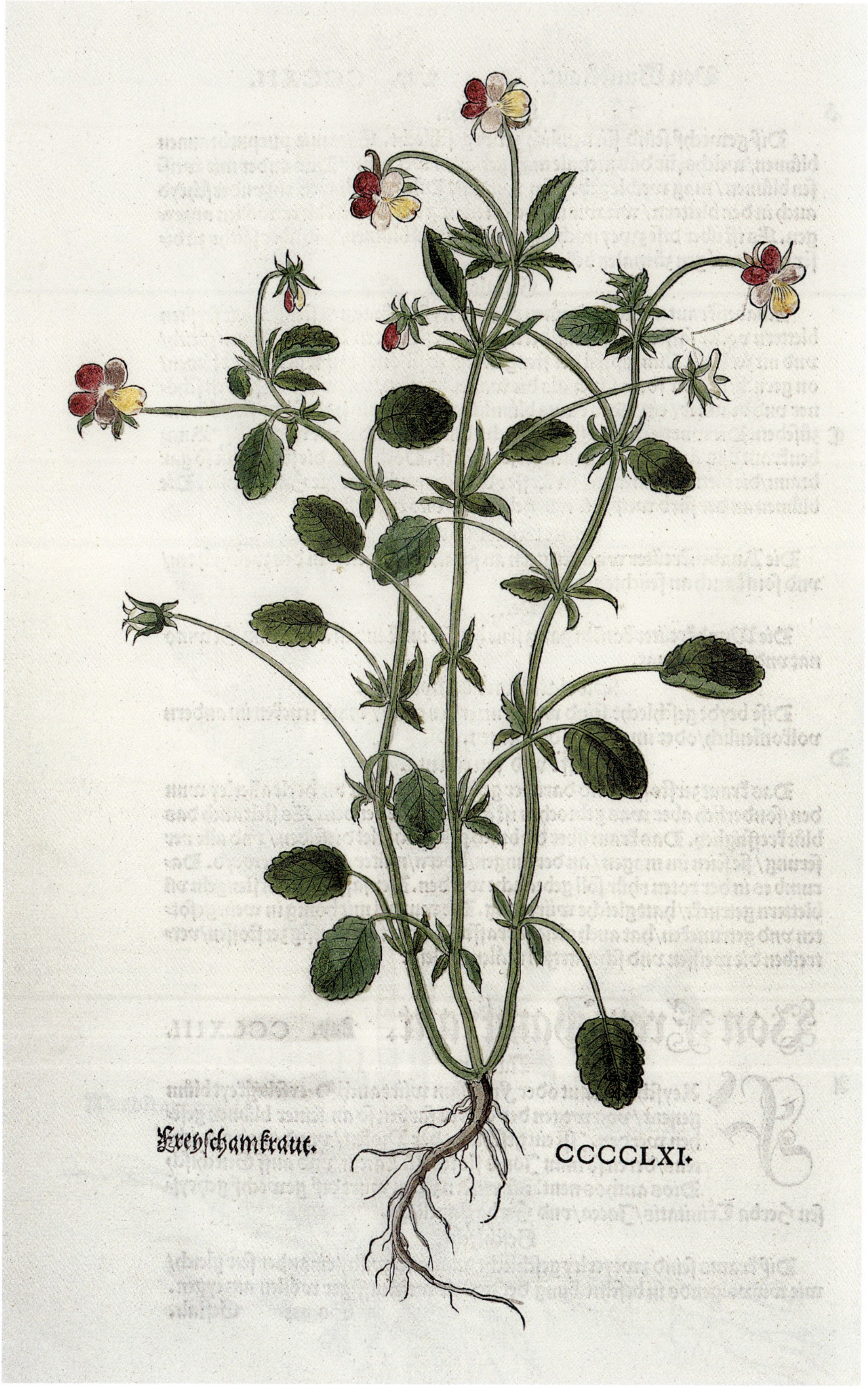
Freyschamkraut.
CCCCLXI.

SPINACH BEET

SPINACH BEET (CCCXIIII) still appears on the table as a vegetable delicacy, but it no longer has any medicinal application.

„MANGOLT“ (MANGOLD)

Als delikates Gemüse kommt auch heute noch der Mangold, bei Fuchs „MANGOLT“ (Cap. CCCXIIII), auf den Tisch, als Arznei wird er dagegen nicht mehr verwendet.

POIRÉE À COUPER

La POIRÉE À COUPER (CCCXIIII), plus connue sous son nom de bette, est un légume encore apprécié de nos jours, mais il n'a plus d'usage en pharmacopée.

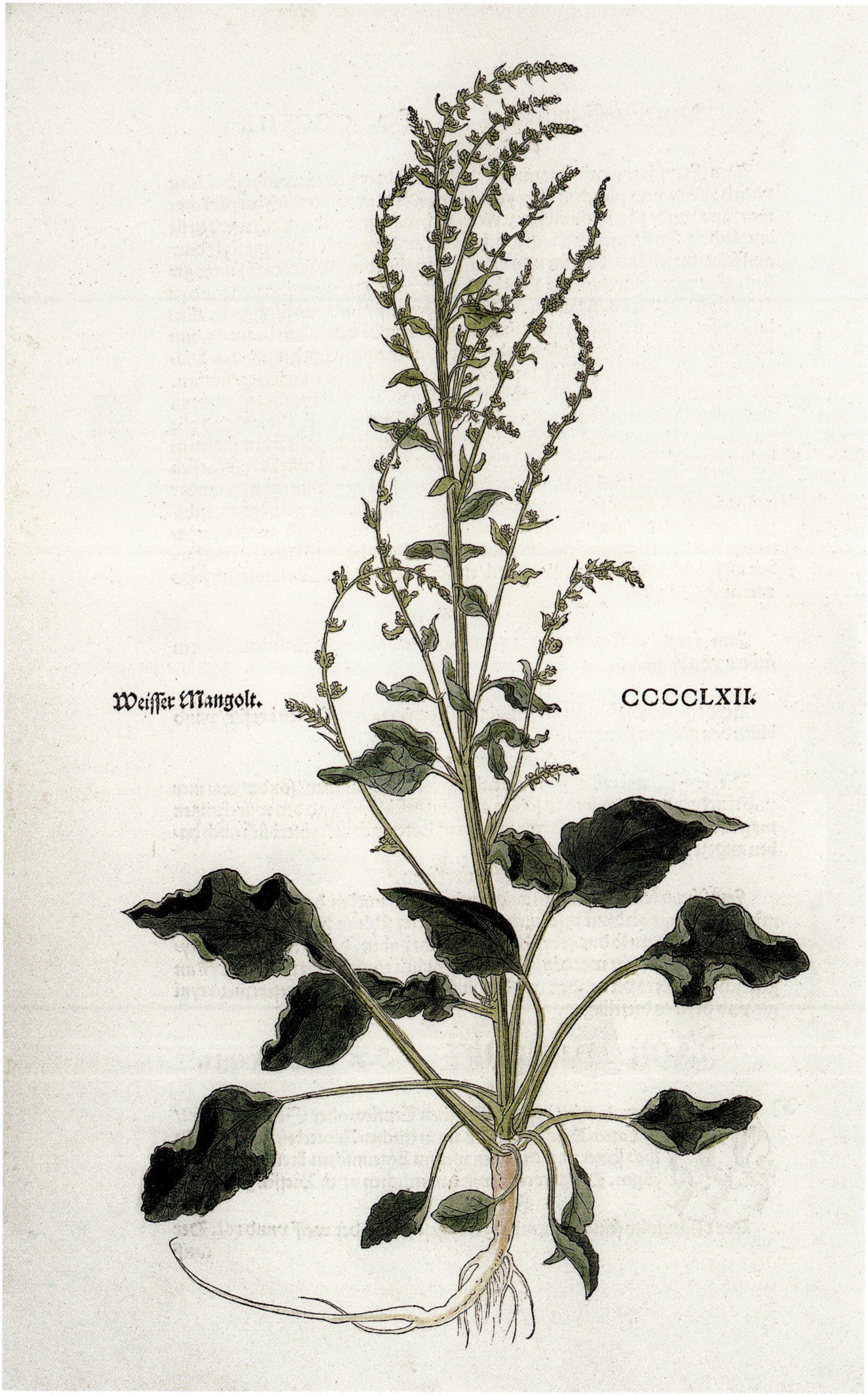
Weisser Mangolt.
CCCCLXII.

DYER'S BROOM

As it name implies, the yellow flowers of DYER'S BROOM or DYER'S GREENWEED (CCCXV) were once used as a colouring agent. Medicinally, its effects purportedly resembled those of Broom.

„FERBBLUMEN“ (FÄRBER-GINSTER)

In der Bezeichnung „FERBBLUMEN“ (Cap. CCCXV) kommt ebenso wie im modernen Namen Färber-Ginster der frühere Gebrauch als gelb färbende Pflanze zum Ausdruck. In der Medizin sollte seine Wirkung der des Ginsters entsprechen.

GENÊT DES TEINTURIERS

Son nom, GENÊT DES TEINTURIERS (CCCXV), en dit long sur l'usage qu'on en faisait : son pigment jaune servait en effet à teindre la laine. Ses propriétés thérapeutiques seraient équivalentes à celles du genêt.

PAGE 578

SPURGE

Fuchs, well aware of the toxicity of SPURGE (CCCXVI), expressly attempts to limit the application of the plant to external use, even though the juice may at times severely irritate the skin.

„WOLFFSMILCH“

Die Giftigkeit der „WOLFFSMILCH“ (Cap. CCCXVI) war Fuchs wohl bekannt, weshalb er ihre Anwendung ausdrücklich auf die äußerliche beschränken will, die mit teilweise starken Hautreizungen durch den Saft einhergehen kann.

EUPHORBE

Fuchs connaît la toxicité de l'EUPHORBE (CCCXVI). Aussi n'en conseille-t-il que l'usage externe, sans oublier de signaler que le suc peut provoquer de fortes irritations cutanées.

PAGE 579

CLOVER

Fuchs combines three plants under "CLOVER" (CCCXVII), even though they were not used by the apothecaries of the time and even Fuchs can offer only scant medicinal information about them.

„WISENKLEE“

Drei Kleearten erscheinen unter „WISENKLEE“ (Cap. CCCXVII) zusammengefasst, obwohl sie in den Apotheken damals ungebräuchlich waren und Fuchs auch nur wenige Angaben zur medizinischen Anwendung machen kann.

TRÈFLE

Trois espèces de TRÈFLE (CCCXVII) font leur apparition sous le nom de « Wisenklee » (trèfle des prés), alors qu'elles sont inusitées en pharmacopée et que Fuchs ne peut guère donner d'indications sur leurs propriétés médicinales.

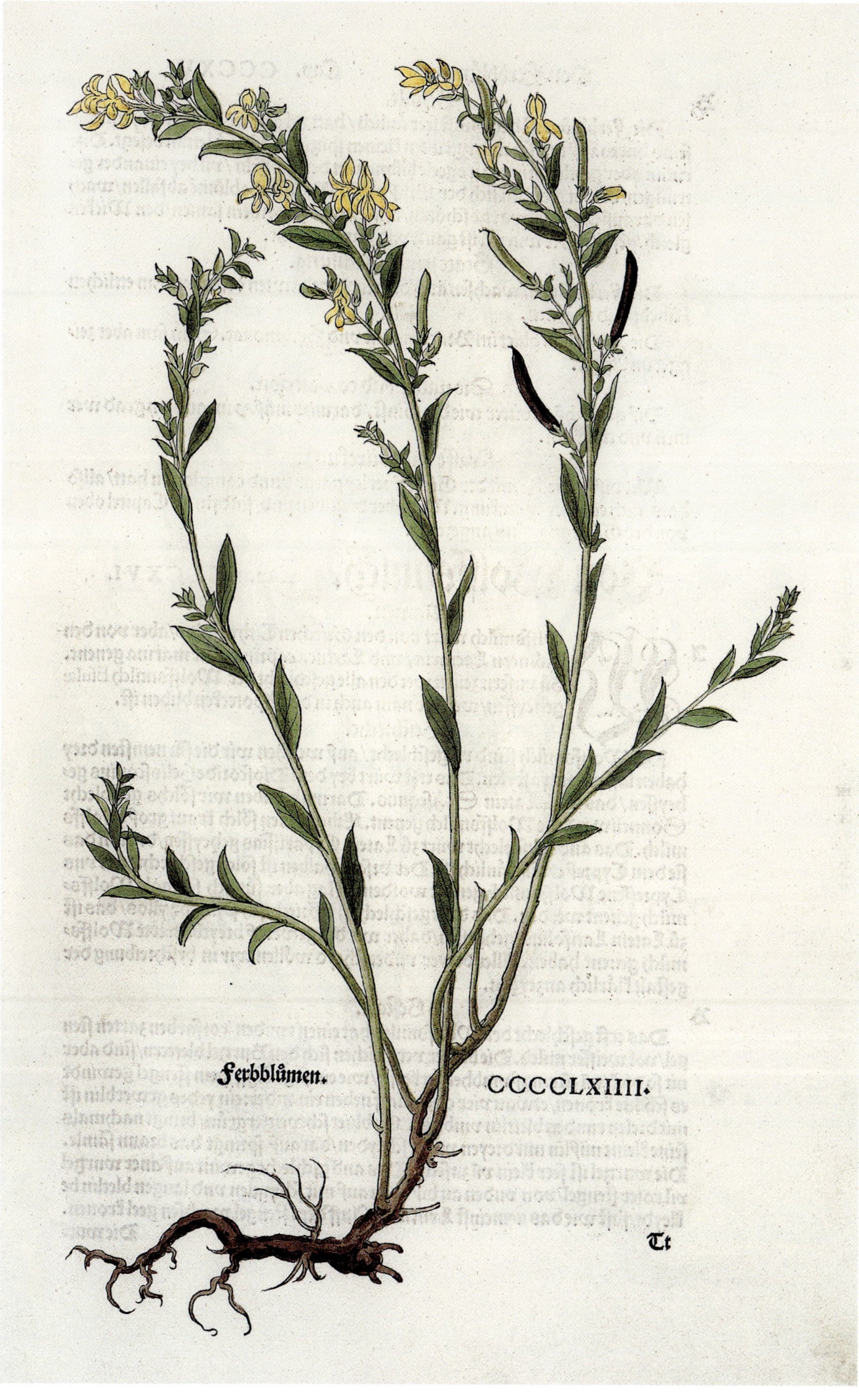
Ferbblůmen.
CCCCLXIIII.
Tt

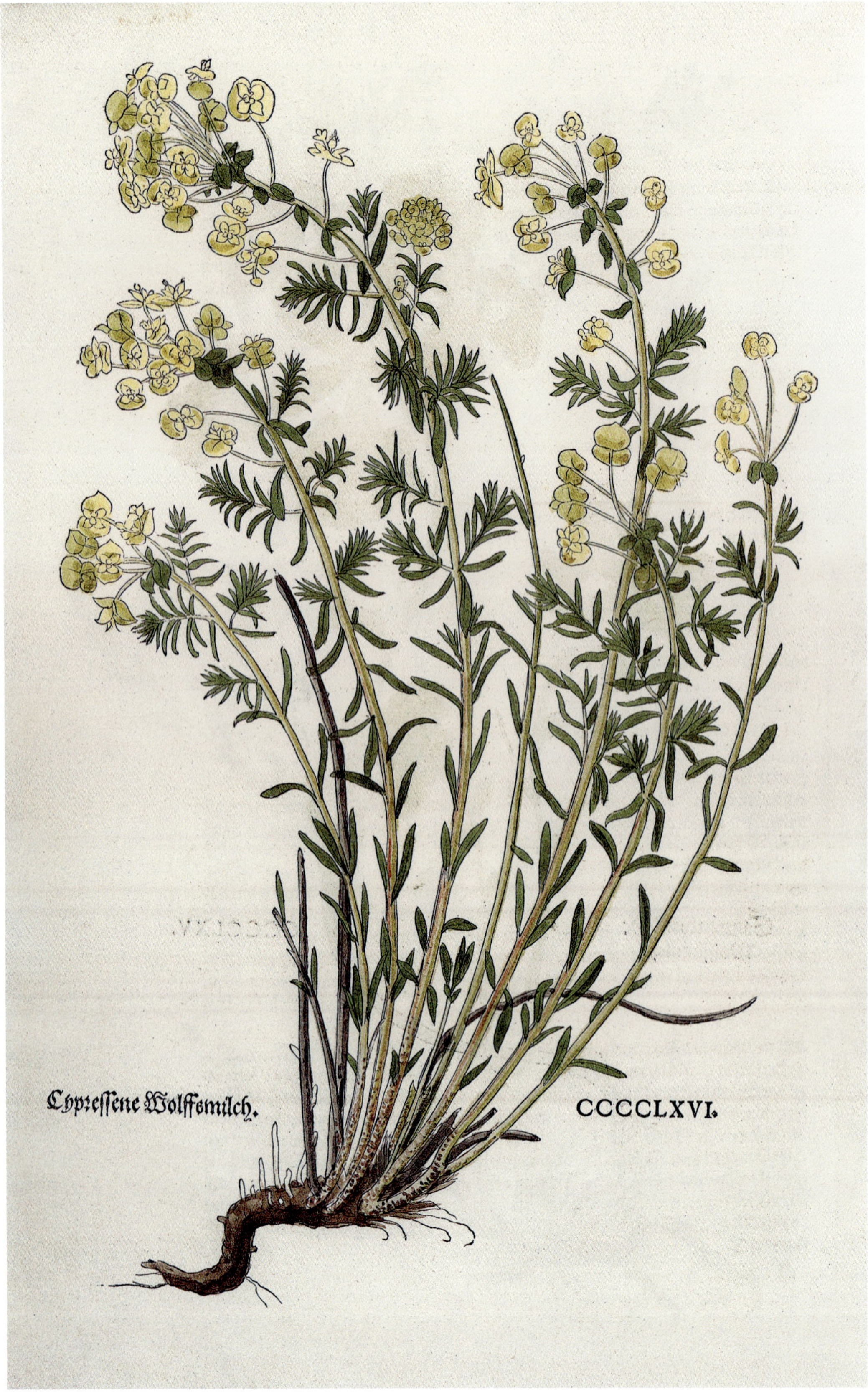
Cypreſſene Wolffsmilch.
CCCCLXVI.

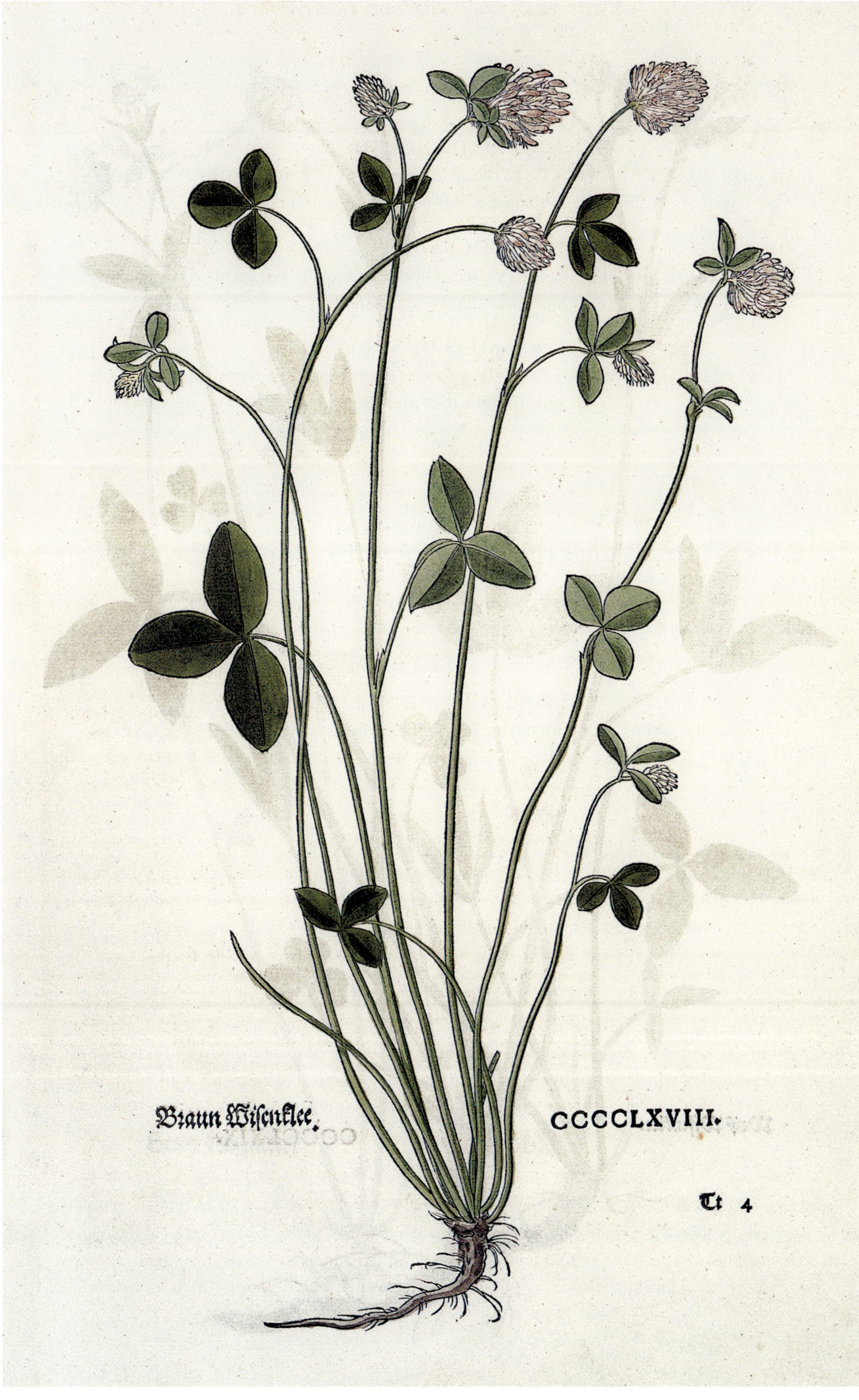
Braun Wisenklee.
CCCCLXVIII.
Tt 4

GOAT'S BEARD

Although GOAT'S BEARD (CCCXVIII), also known as JACK-GO-TO-BED-AT-NOON, is still widespread today, it is no longer used in medicine.

BOCKSBART

Der BOCKSBART (Cap. CCCXVIII) ist heute zwar noch weit verbreitet, in der Medizin jedoch ungebräuchlich.

SALSIFIS DES PRÉS

Le SALSIFIS DES PRÉS (CCCXVIII) est encore très répandu aujourd'hui, mais il n'a plus d'application en médecine.

PAGE 582

COMMON CAT'S TAIL

COMMON CAT'S TAIL, or GREAT REEDMACE (CCCXIX), played no medically significant role.

NARZENKOLBEN

NARZENKOLBEN (Cap. CCCXIX) war der wenig schmeichelhafte Name für den Rohrkolben, der als Medikament keine nennenswerte Rolle spielte.

MASETTE À LARGES FEUILLES

«Narrenkolben» (épi aux bouffons) est le nom peu flatteur de la MASETTE À LARGES FEUILLES (CCCXIX), dite aussi jonc d'eau. La plante ne jouait aucun rôle notable en médecine.

PAGE 583

MAIZE

MAIZE, or INDIAN CORN (CCCXX), originated in America, but reached Europe only after a detour through Turkey. Although Fuchs praised cornmeal ground from what he called "Turkish grain," he nonetheless stressed the difficulties in digesting bread made from the corn, which was used, even in Turkey, only when other meal became too expensive.

„TÜRCKISCHES KORN" (MAIS)

Der Name „TÜRCKISCHES KORN" (Cap. CCCXX) für den Mais täuscht, denn die Pflanze stammt ursprünglich aus Amerika. Da sie in Europa jedoch erst nach einem Umweg über die Türkei verbreitet wurde, wird dieser Name verständlich. Fuchs lobt zwar das Maismehl, betont aber die schlechte Bekömmlichkeit des daraus gebackenen Brotes, das auch in der Türkei nur zu Zeiten von Teuerungen genossen werde.

MAÏS

Fuchs qualifie le MAÏS (CCCXX) de «graine turque» («Türckisches Korn»). Le nom est trompeur car c'est une plante originaire d'Amérique, mais il s'explique par le fait qu'elle a été introduite en Europe via la Turquie. Certes, Fuchs loue les qualités de la farine, mais il souligne en même temps que le pain fabriqué avec elle est difficile à digérer. Ce pain ne serait d'ailleurs consommé en Turquie que lors des hausses de prix.

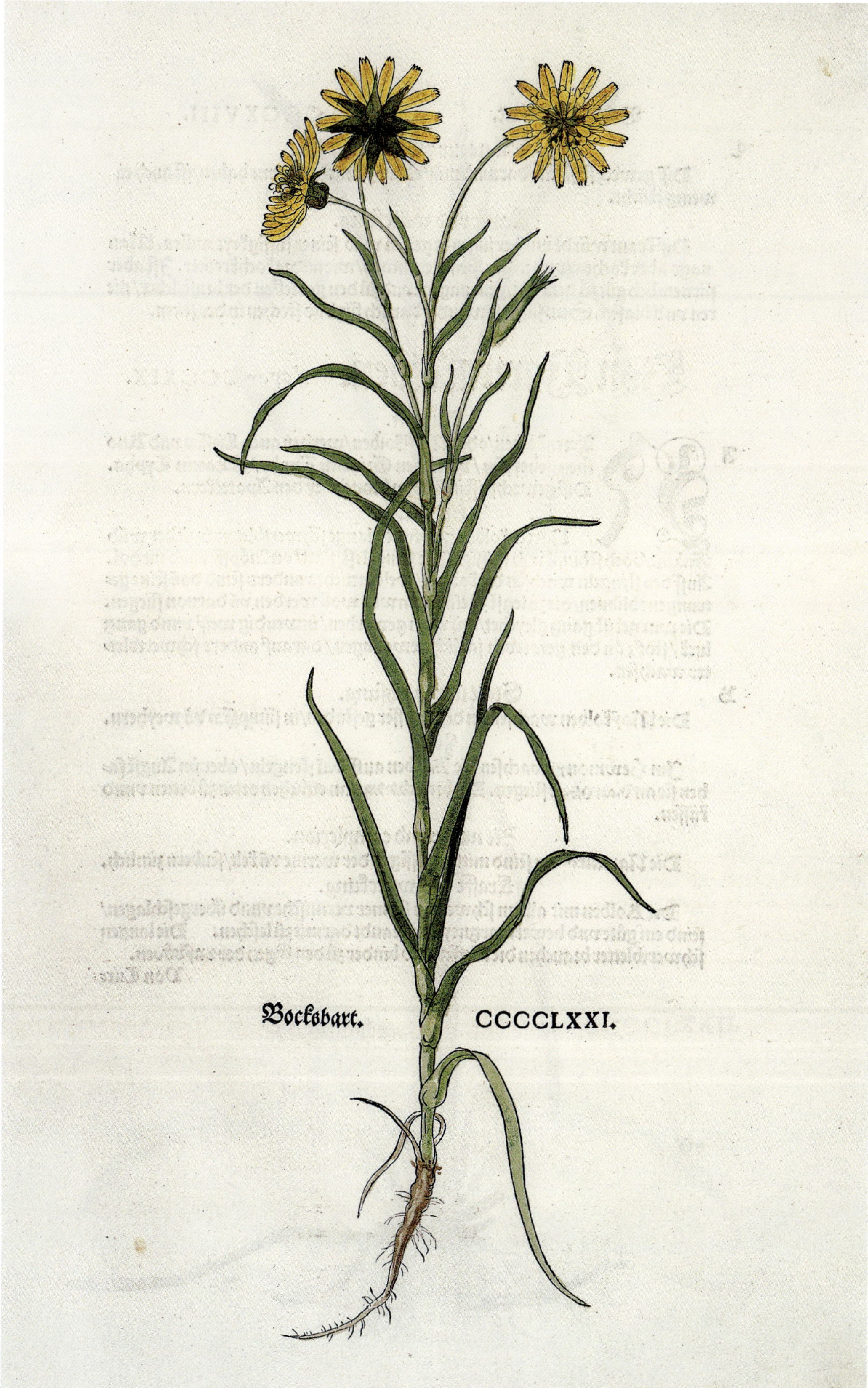
Bocksbart.
CCCCLXXI.

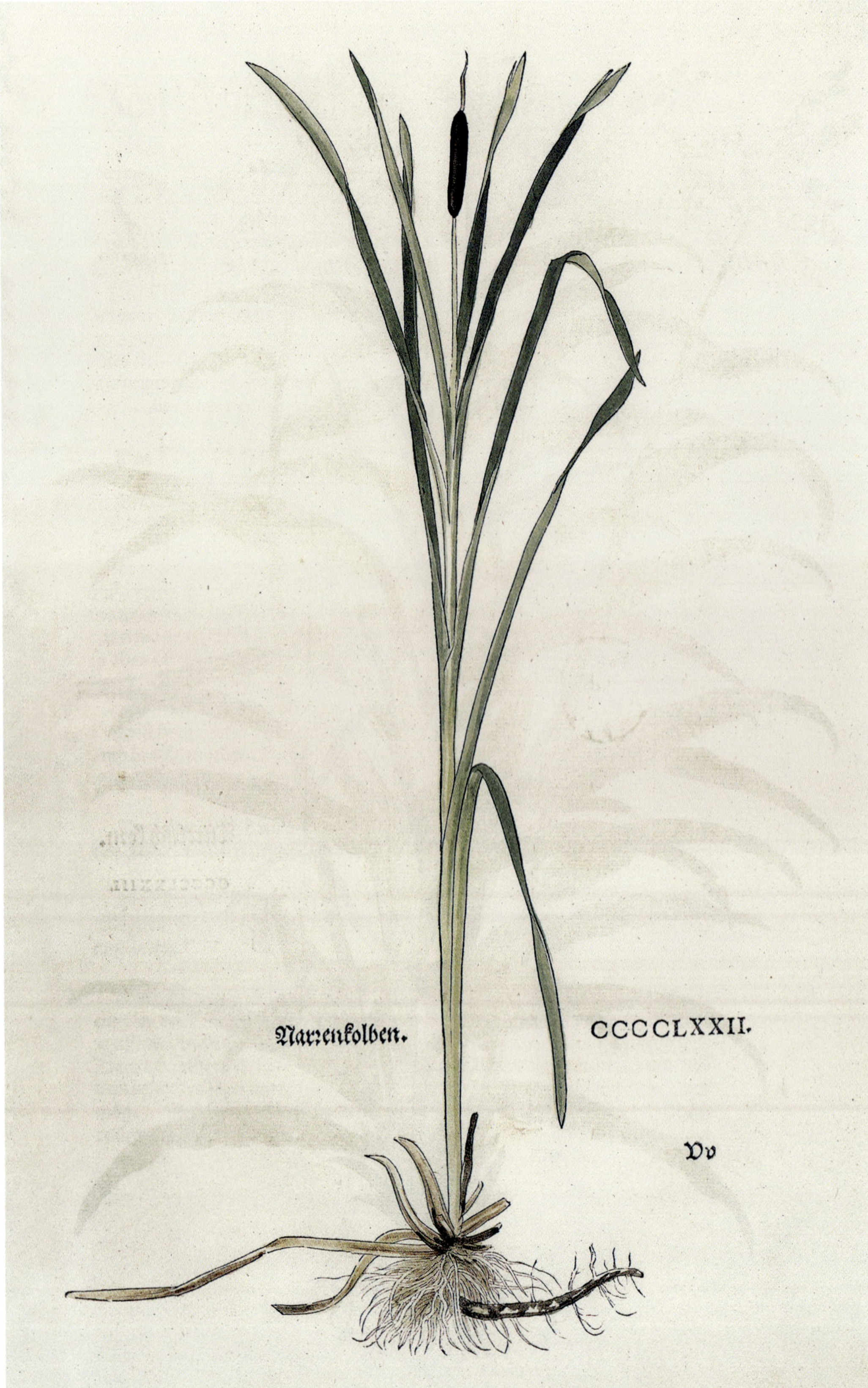
Narzenkolben.
CCCCLXXII.
Vv

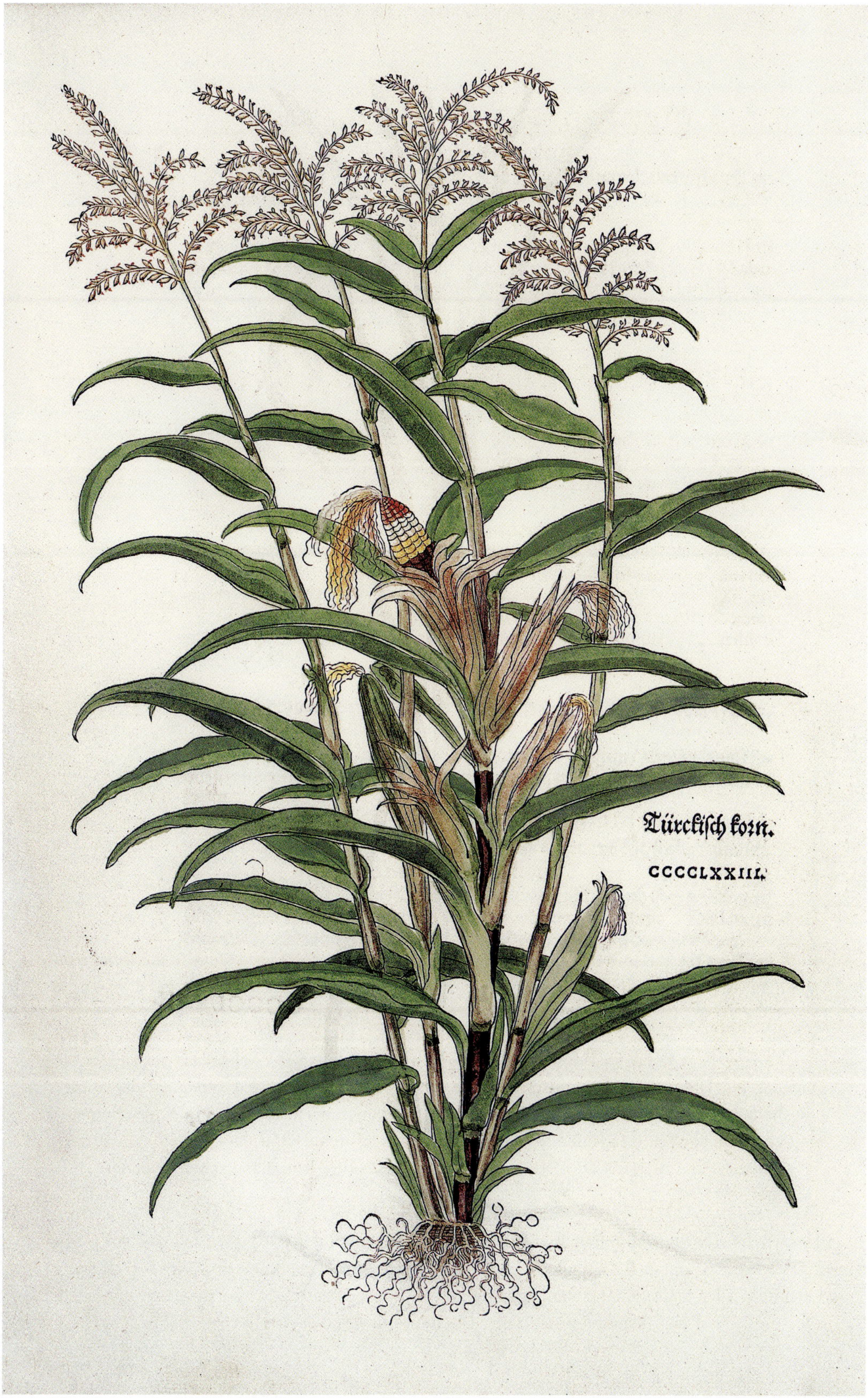
Türckisch korn.
CCCCLXXIII.

WILD THYME

Both WILD THYME and COMMON THYME (CCCXXI) are still used today in the treatment of coughs as well as stomach and bowel problems. Since COMMON THYME is not domestic to Europe, Fuchs termed it "foreign."

„WELSCHER QUENDEL" (ECHTER THYMIAN)

Quendel und Thymian sind botanisch und von ihren Wirkstoffen sehr eng verwandt und werden deshalb heute wie früher gleichartig bei Husten, aber auch bei Magen- und Darmproblemen eingesetzt. Da der echte Thymian in Mitteleuropa nicht einheimisch ist, nennt Fuchs ihn also zu Recht „WELSCHEN QUENDEL" (Cap. CCCXXI), d. h. fremdländischen Quendel.

THYM VRAI

Le serpolet et le thym sont très proches tant sur le plan botanique que par leurs principes actifs. Pour cette raison, on les a toujours utilisés comme antitussif et tonique des voies digestives. Le THYM VRAI (CCCXXI) n'étant pas originaire d'Europe centrale, c'est à juste titre que Fuchs le nomme « Welscher Quendel » ou serpolet étranger.

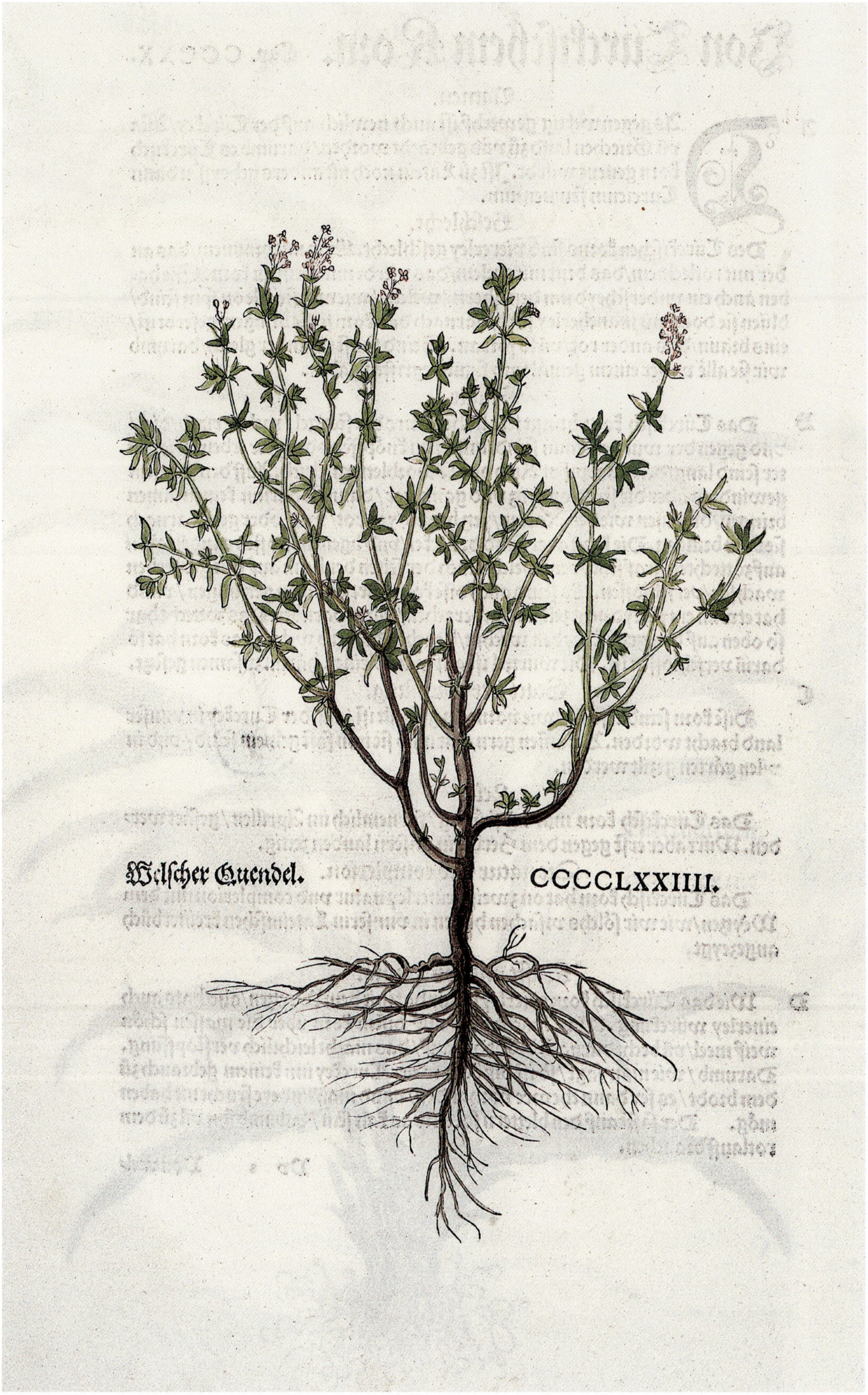

WILD THYME | „WELSCHER QUENDEL“ | THYM VRAI

YELLOW GERMANDER

The larger form of YELLOW GERMANDER (CCCXXII) and the smaller, which is treated later (CCCXXXV), are closely related from a botanical point of view. However, the plants are no longer put to the uses for which they were once valued.

„BATHENGEL“

Zwischen dem Großen „BATHENGEL“ (Cap. CCCXXII) und seiner kleinen Form, die im Kapitel CCCXXXV abgehandelt werden wird, besteht tatsächlich eine sehr enge botanische Verwandtschaft. Die angebliche Heilwirkung wird allerdings heute nicht mehr genutzt.

GRANDE GERMANDRÉE

Entre la GRANDE GERMANDRÉE (CCCXXII) et sa forme plus petite, qui sera présentée au chapitre CCCXXXV, il existe effectivement une proche parenté, mais leurs prétendues propriétés thérapeutiques ne sont plus reconnues aujourd'hui.

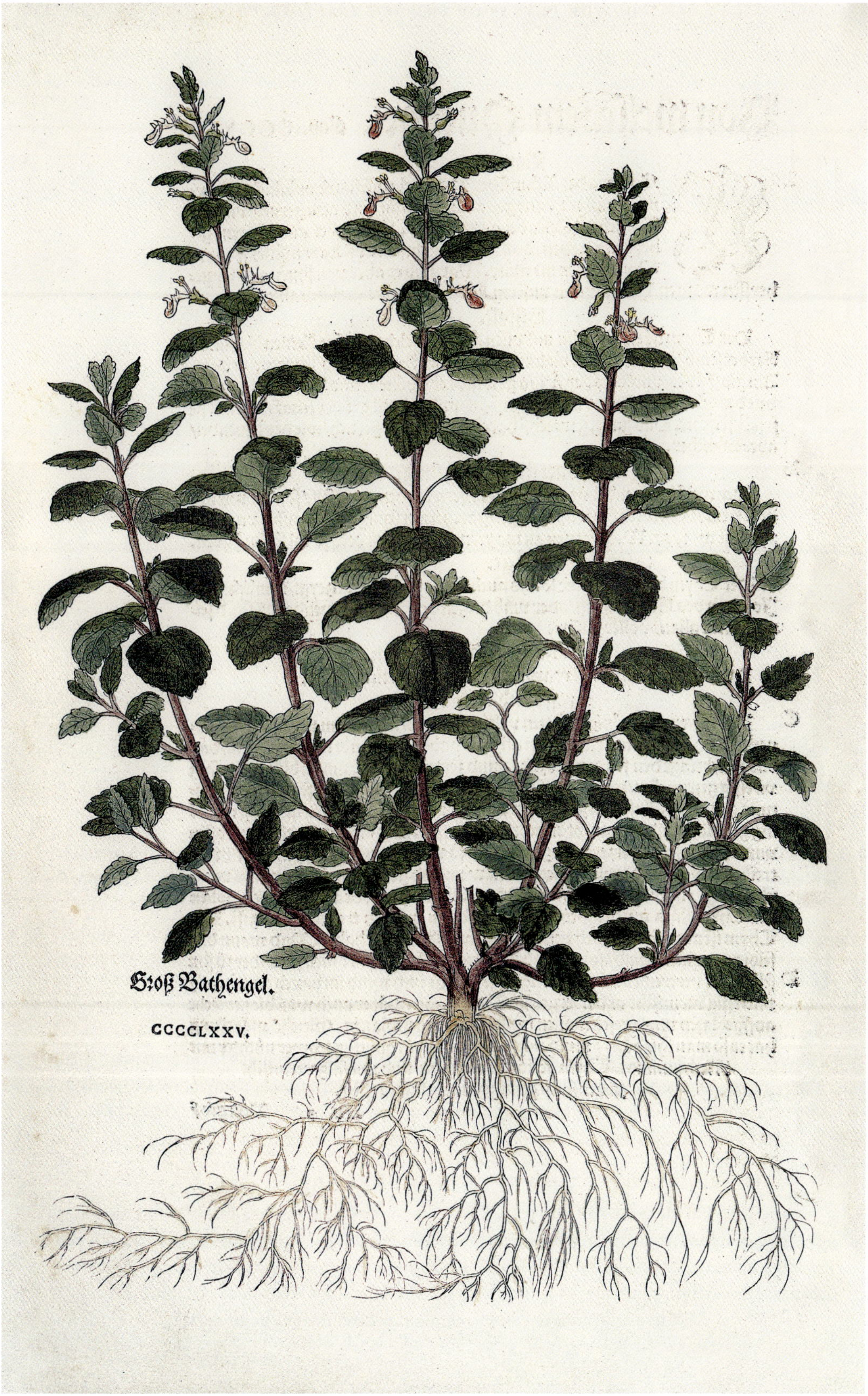
Groß Bathengel.
CCCCLXXV.

COMMON ST. JOHN'S WORT

COMMON ST. JOHN'S WORT (CCCXXIII) is certainly one of the best-known medicinal plants. When held up to the light, the transparent oil receptacles in its leaves make them appear as if they are pierced with fine needles – a characteristic that recommended the plant as a vulnerary. Today, the red oil of the plant is used in skin care, and the extract from the complete plant finds use as an antidepressant sedative.

„SANT JOHANSKRAUT" (JOHANNISKRAUT)

Zu den bekanntesten Heilpflanzen gehört zweifelsohne das „SANT JOHANSKRAUT" (Cap. CCCXXIII), heute Johanniskraut genannt. Die Blätter, die, gegen das Licht gehalten, wegen der durchscheinenden Ölbehälter wie von feinen Nadeln durchstochen aussehen, empfahlen seine Verwendung als Wundheilmittel. Heute wird das rote Öl zur Hautpflege, der Extrakt aus der ganzen Pflanze als stimmungsaufhellendes Beruhigungsmittel eingesetzt.

MILLEPERTUIS PERFORÉ

Le MILLEPERTUIS PERFORÉ (CCCXXIII), ou herbe de Saint-Jean, est sans conteste l'une des plus connues parmi les plantes médicinales. Ses feuilles parsemées de glandes translucides semblent percées d'une multitude de petits trous, aussi la recommandait-on pour cicatriser les plaies. Aujourd'hui, son huile rouge sombre est utilisée pour les soins de la peau, et l'extrait tiré de la plante entière comme calmant contre les états dépressifs.

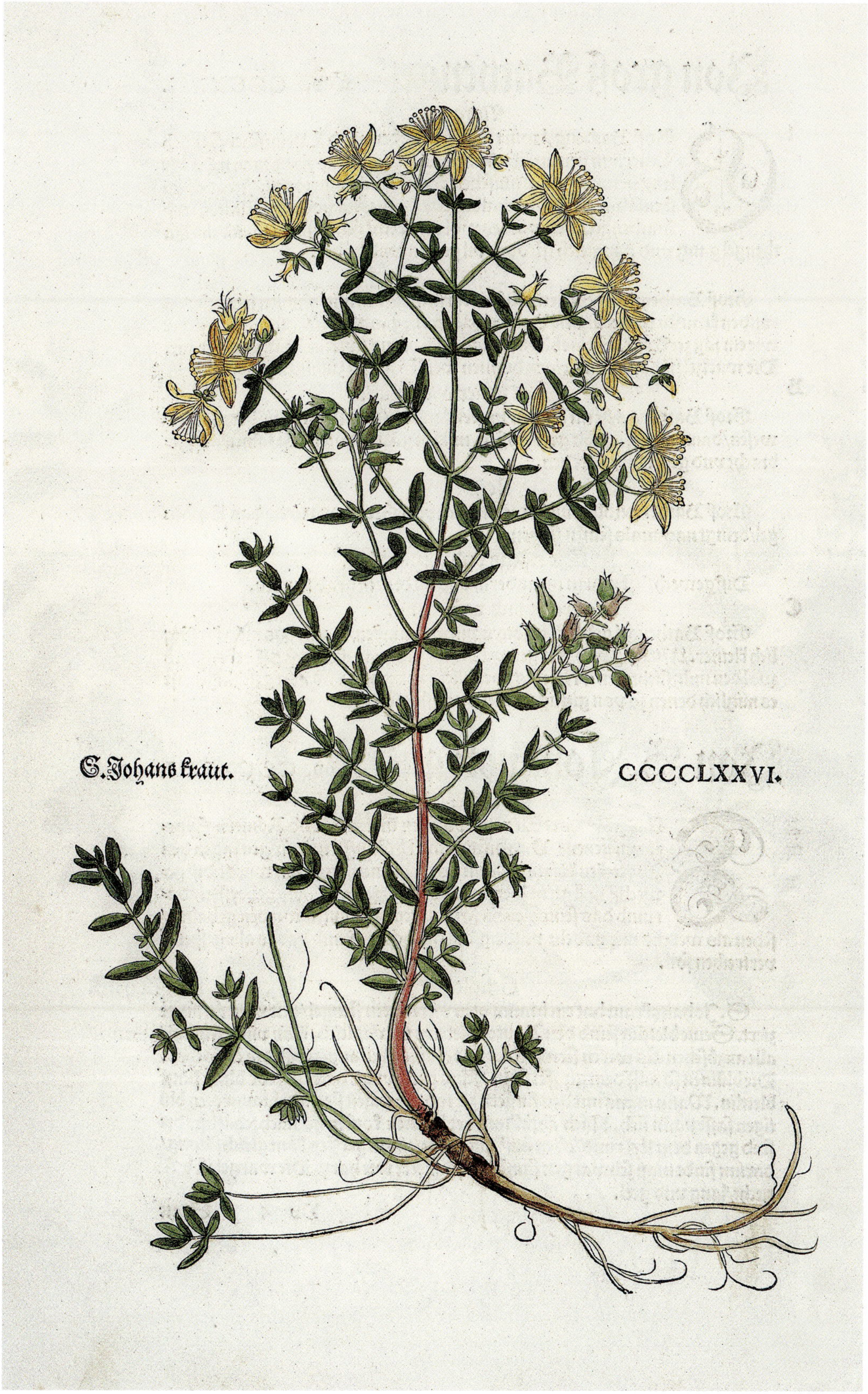
S.Johans kraut.
CCCCLXXVI.

HENBANE

Almost more than any other poisonous plant, HENBANE (CCCXXIIII) has collected a long train of legends. With careful application, a physician could use the plant to relieve pain, but there were also stories of poisonous snakes or even witches who used the plant to prepare their salves before attending their witches' sabbaths.

BILSENKRAUT

Das BILSENKRAUT (Cap. CCCXXIIII) gehört zu den sagenumwobensten Giftpflanzen überhaupt. Sorgfältig eingesetzt, konnte der Arzt damit Schmerzen lindern, aber man erzählte sich auch von Giftanschlägen damit oder gar von Hexen, die die Pflanze zur Zubereitung ihrer Salben benötigten, wenn sie zum Hexensabbat fliegen wollten.

JUSQUIAME NOIRE

La JUSQUIAME NOIRE (CCCXXIIII) fait partie des plantes vénéneuses légendaires. Prescrite avec circonspection, elle pouvait cependant soulager les douleurs. Mais on se racontait aussi des histoires d'empoisonnements à la jusquiame ou même d'onguents que les sorcières auraient confectionnés pour leurs chevauchées infernales.

PAGE 592

TASSEL

Much less dangerous are the TASSEL and GRAPE HYACINTHS and the ALPINE SQUILL (CCCXXV), which no longer play a role in today's pharmaceutics, but remain popular as garden plants.

„MERTZENBLUMEN"

Sehr viel weniger gefährlich sind die als „MERTZENBLUMEN" (Cap. CCCXXV) bezeichneten Traubenhyazinthen und Blausterne, die heute allerdings in der Pharmazie keine Rolle mehr spielen, nach wie vor aber gesuchte Zierpflanzen sind.

SCILLES À DEUX FEUILLES

Les muscaris et les SCILLES À DEUX FEUILLES (CCCXXV), figurant ici sous le nom de «Mertzenblumen» ou fleurs de mars, sont beaucoup moins dangereux. Si ces fleurs ne sont plus usitées en pharmacopée, elles restent néanmoins des plantes ornementales très recherchées.

PAGE 593

HYSSOP

HYSSOP (CCCXXVI) is rarely used in medicine today.

„ISPEN"

Nur noch sehr selten findet sich heute der „ISPEN" (Cap. CCCXXVI), den wir inzwischen Ysop nennen, in der Medizin.

HYSOPE OFFICINALE

L'utilisation de l'HYSOPE OFFICINALE (CCCXXVI) est devenue extrêmement rare en médecine.

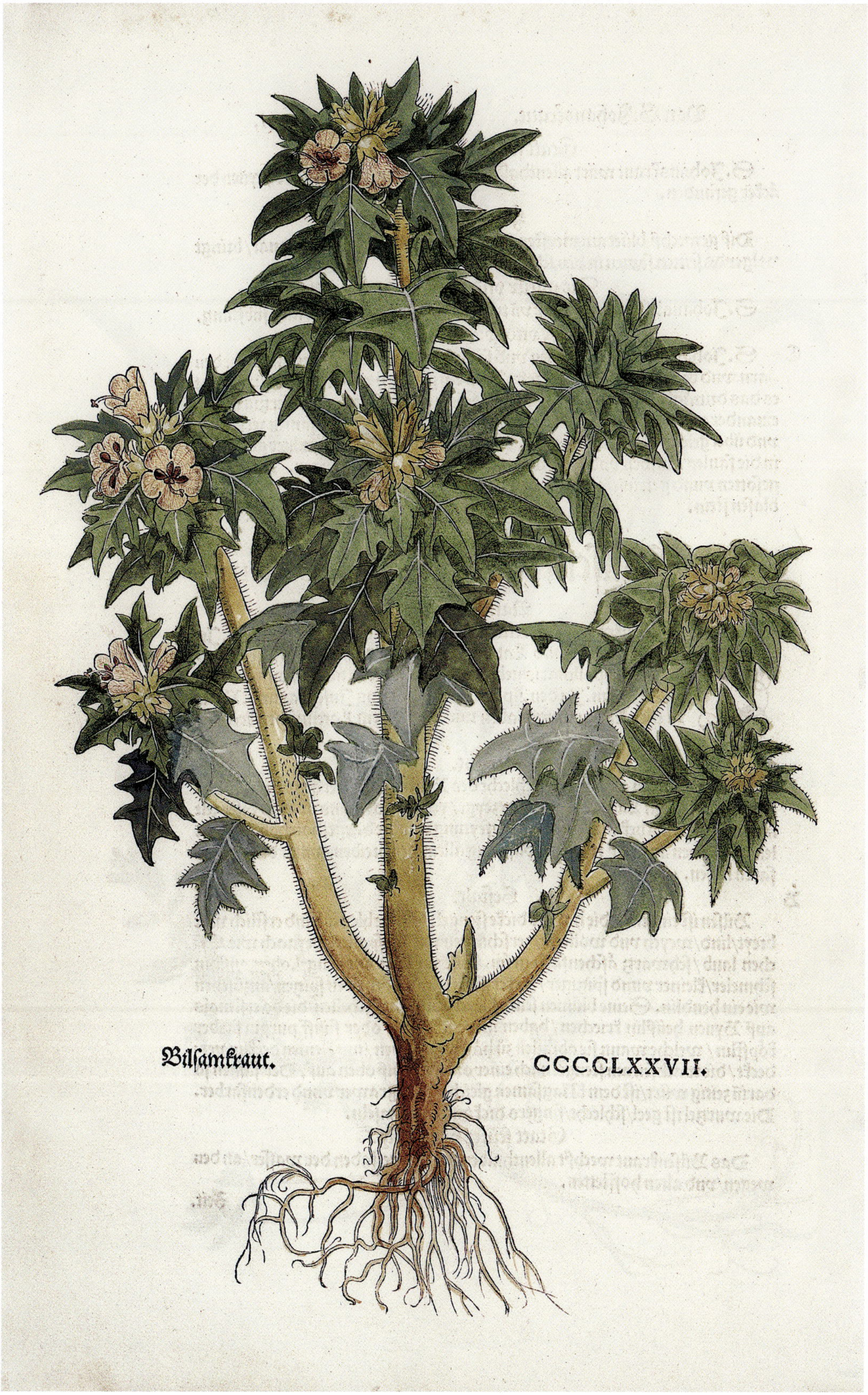

HENBANE | BILSENKRAUT | JUSQUIAME NOIRE

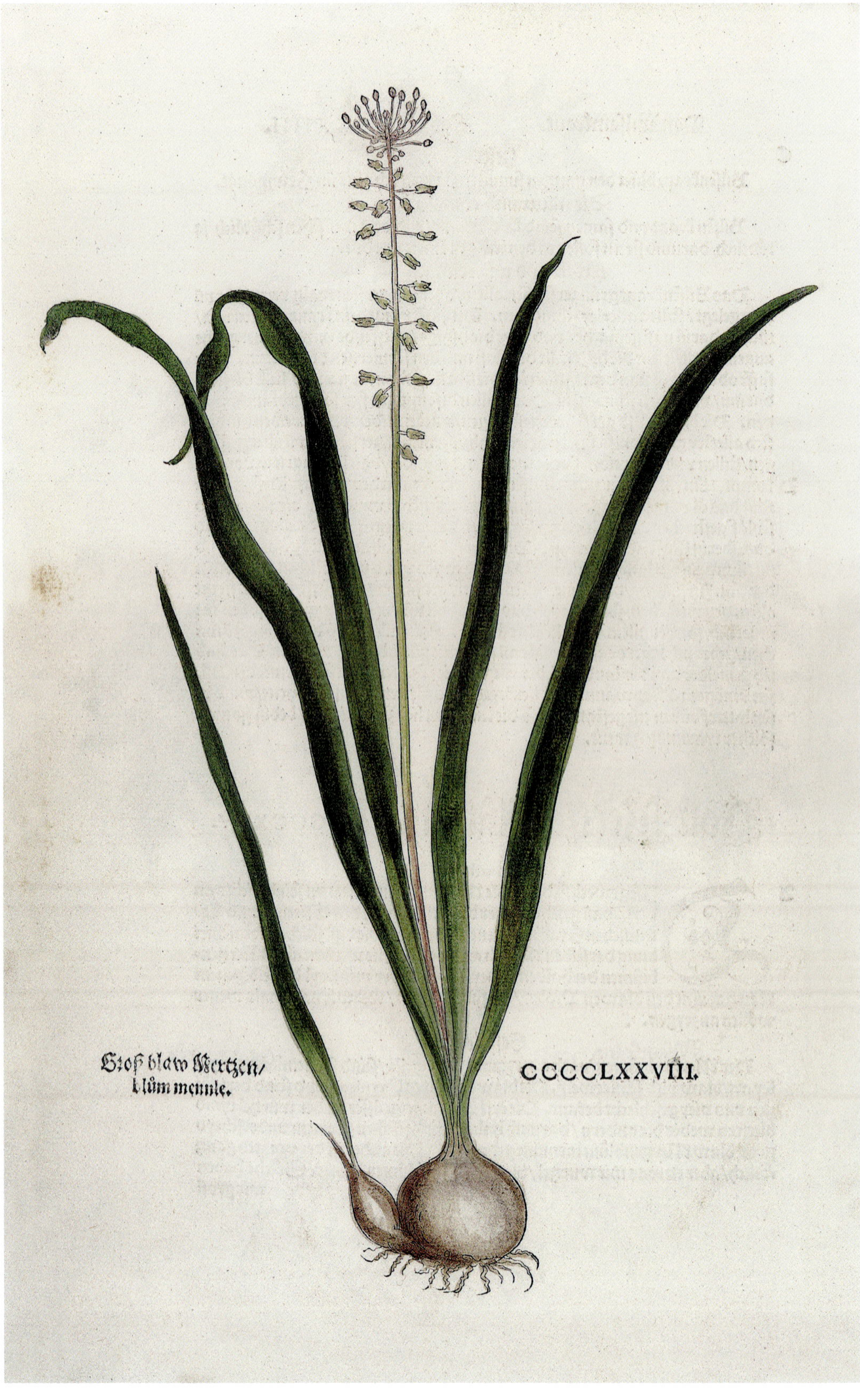
Groß blaw Mertzen/
blům mennle.
CCCCLXXVIII.

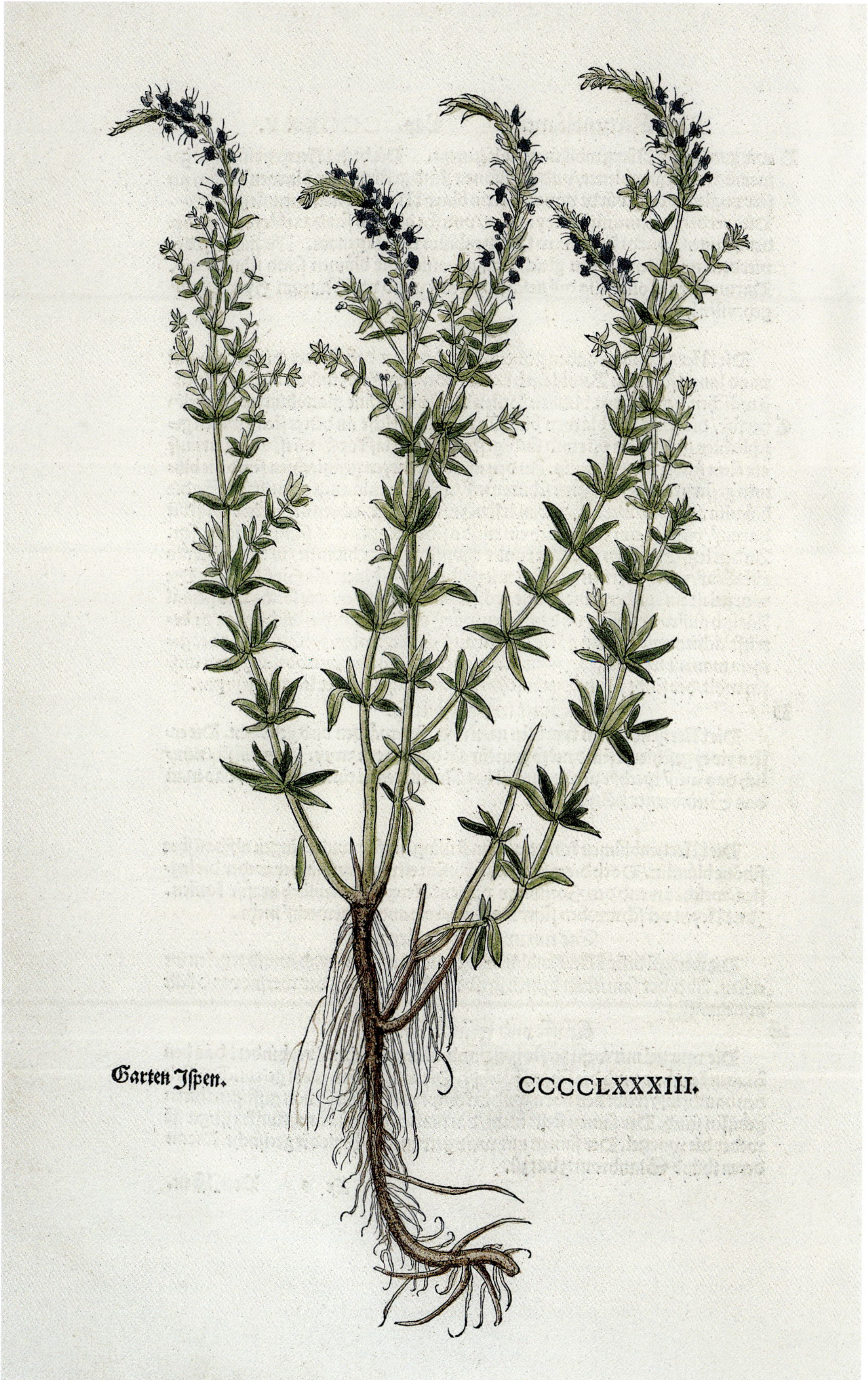
Garten Jspen.
CCCCLXXXIII.

WATER PEPPER

With its hot taste, WATER PEPPER (CCCXXVII) was not only accredited with a stimulating effect on the circulation, but was also used as a spice.

WASSERPFEFFER

Der scharf schmeckende WASSERPFEFFER (Cap. CCCXXVII) fand neben seiner durchblutungsanregenden Wirkung auch als Gewürz Verwendung.

POIVRE D'EAU

La renouée POIVRE D'EAU (CCCXXVII), à la saveur forte, s'utilisait comme tonique de la circulation sanguine et comme condiment.

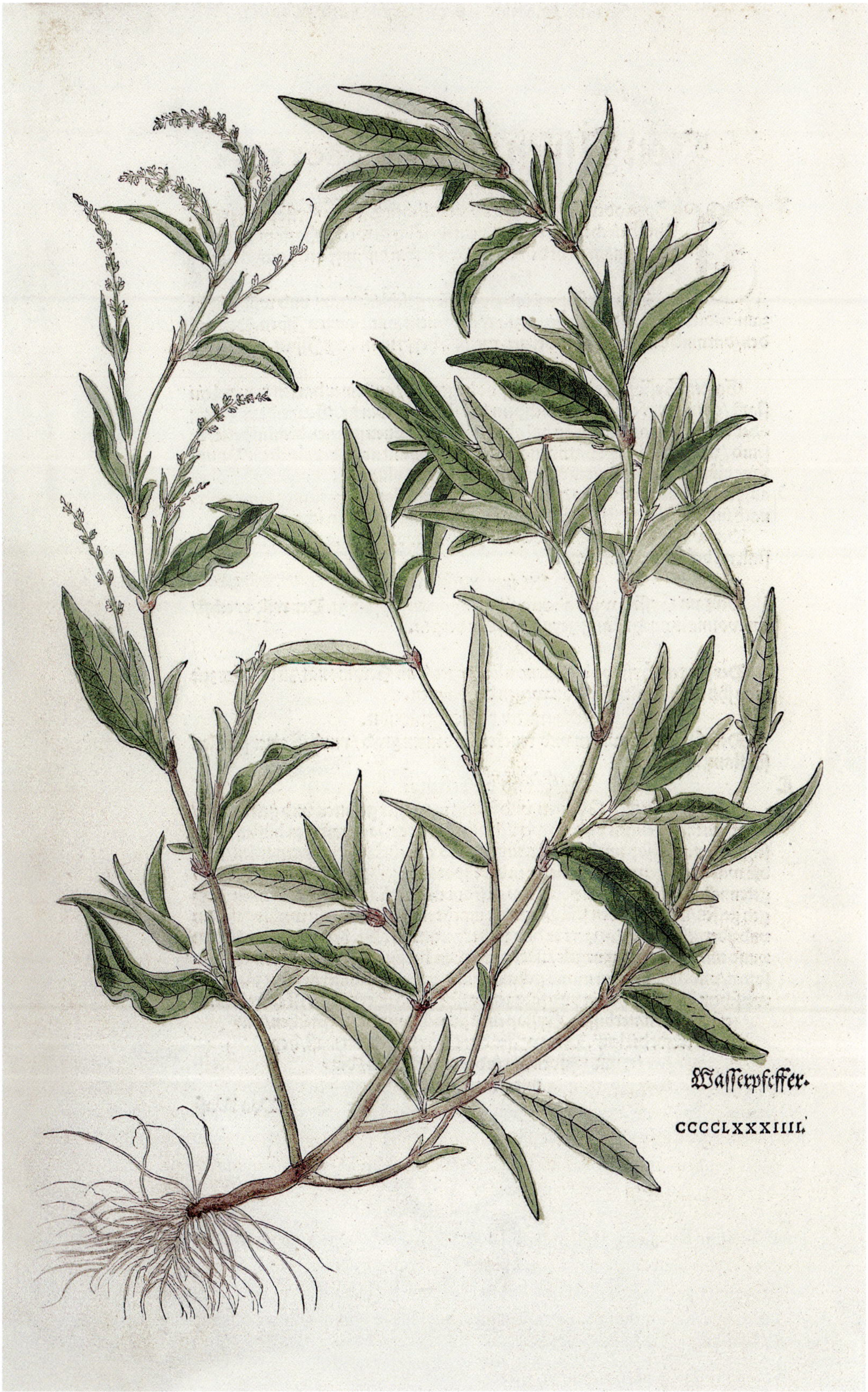
Wasserpfeffer.
CCCCLXXXIIII.

MULLEIN

Surprisingly, four kinds of MULLEIN, with their fine woolly hairs, appear here together with COWSLIP and OXLIP (CCCXXVIII). However, despite its many traditional applications, mullein is now only used as a remedy for bronchial problems.

„WULLKRAUT" (KÖNIGSKERZE)

Als „WULLKRAUT" (Cap. CCCXXVIII) findet sich zu Recht die wegen ihrer wolligen Behaarung noch heute „Wollblume" genannte Königskerze mit vier verschiedenen Arten, aber überraschenderweise auch die Schlüsselblume. Von den zahlreichen Anwendungsgebieten ist bis heute allerdings nur der Einsatz bei Bronchialerkrankungen übrig geblieben.

MOLÈNES

Fuchs qualifie les quatre MOLÈNES (CCCXXVIII) de « Wollblumen » (fleurs laineuses), nom qu'elles portent bien car la partie inférieure des feuilles est couverte d'un duvet laineux. Ce qui est surprenant par contre, c'est que Fuchs leur ajoute la primevère. Très usitées dans la passé, les molènes n'entrent plus aujourd'hui que dans la composition de tisanes pectorales.

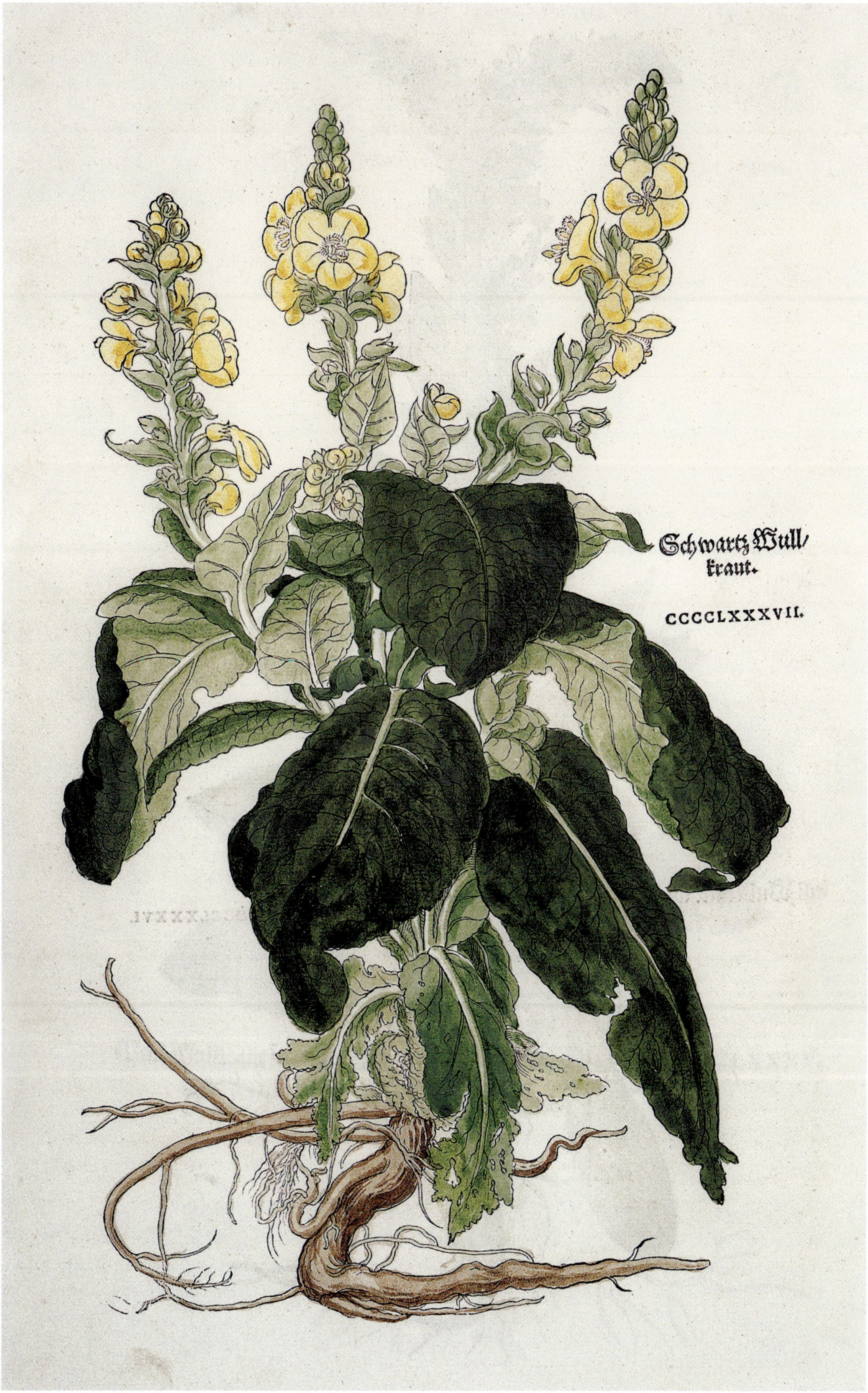
Schwartz Wull/
kraut.
CCCCLXXXVII.

STRAWBERRY

Physicians were not interested in the tasty fruits of STRAWBERRY (CCCXXIX), but rather in the complete herbage and the juice of the leaves, which are still today used in herbal teas.

„ERDTBEERKRAUT“

Beim „ERDTBEERKRAUT“ (Cap. CCCXXIX) richtete sich das Interesse der Ärzte nicht auf die wohlschmeckenden Früchte, sondern auf das ganze Kraut und den Saft der Blätter, die heute noch gerne in Haustees verwendet werden.

FRAISIER

En présentant le FRAISIER (CCCXXIX), Fuchs s'intéresse moins à ses fruits délicieux qu'à la plante entière et au suc de ses feuilles, avec lesquels on prépare des infusions encore appréciées dans la médecine domestique.

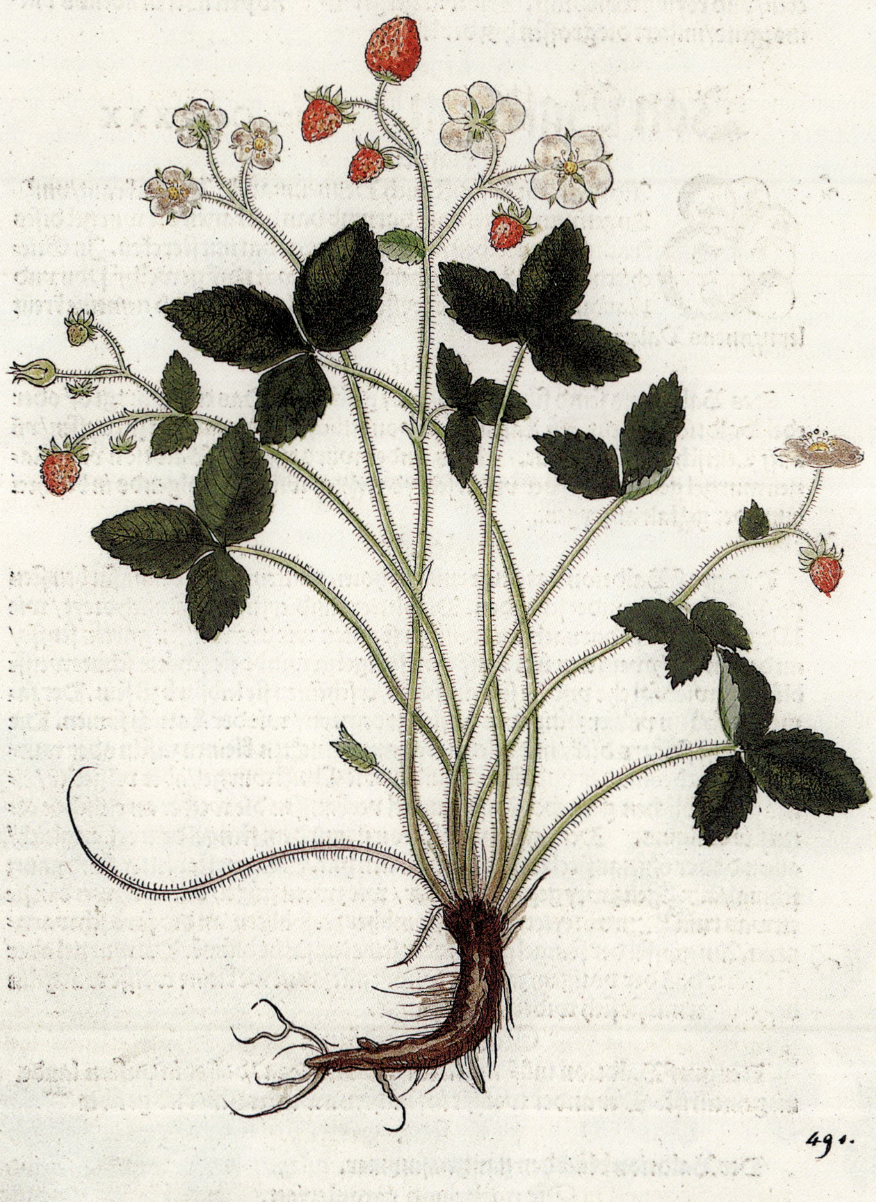

49 1.

Erdtbeer. CCCCXCI.

Ry 4

STRAWBERRY | „ERDTBEERKRAUT“ | FRAISIER

VALERIAN

The indications offered in this chapter (CCCXXX) hardly lead one to think of the well-known VALERIAN, which is today the most commonly used herbal sedative. In the 16th century the plant was valued for its diuretic and anti-toxic effects, as well as its ability to strengthen eyesight.

„BALDRION“ (BALDRIAN)

Liest man die Indikationen des „BALDRION“ (Cap. CCCXXX), meint man nicht, dass damit der wohlbekannte Baldrian gemeint ist, der heute als meistverwendetes pflanzliches Beruhigungsmittel aus der Therapie nicht wegzudenken ist. Im 16. Jahrhundert schätzte man dagegen nicht nur seine harntreibende und giftwidrige Wirkung, sondern auch die vermeintliche Stärkung der Sehkraft.

VALÉRIANE

Lorsqu'on lit les indications thérapeutiques de la plante suivante, on peut difficilement imaginer qu'il s'agit de notre VALÉRIANE (CCCXXX). Calmant le plus couramment employé aujourd'hui, elle était très prisée au XVIe siècle comme diurétique et topique contre les morsures de serpents venimeux et les plantes vénéneuses. On lui prêtait en outre le pouvoir de fortifier la vue.

PAGE 602

LENTIL

With LENTIL (CCCXXXI), the form of preparation played a great role in the effect of the plant both as a vegetable and as an astringent medicine.

LINSEN

Bei den LINSEN (Cap. CCCXXXI) spielte die Art der Zubereitung für die Wirkung sowohl als Gemüse als auch als adstringierendes Arzneimittel eine große Rolle.

LENTILLES

Pour ce qui est des LENTILLES (CCCXXXI), la manière de les préparer est déterminante pour leurs effets tant comme légume que remède astringent.

PAGE 603

LIME TREE

The LIME TREE (CCCXXXII), whose flowers are prepared today as a tea for colds, earlier provided a number of medicines that have since been forgotten.

LINDENBAUM

Der LINDENBAUM (Cap. CCCXXXII), dessen Blüten heute bei Erkältungen als Tee zubereitet werden, lieferte früher eine Vielzahl von Arzneien, die längst vergessen sind.

TILLEUL

Le tilleul (CCCXXXII), dont les feuilles sont aujourd'hui utilisées en tisanes contre les refroidissements, fournissait autrefois de nombreux remèdes, oubliés depuis longtemps.

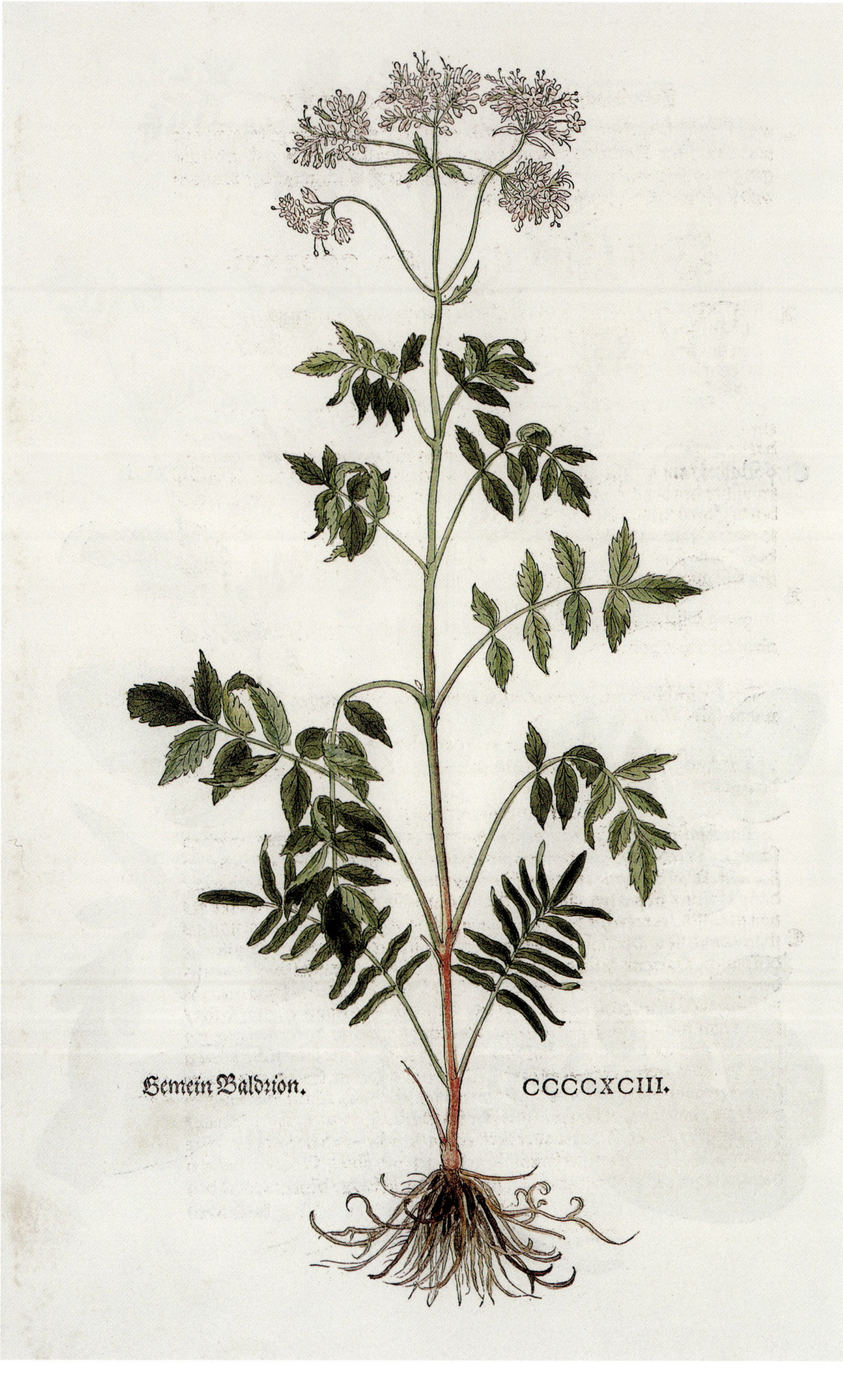
Gemein Baldrion.
CCCCXCIII.

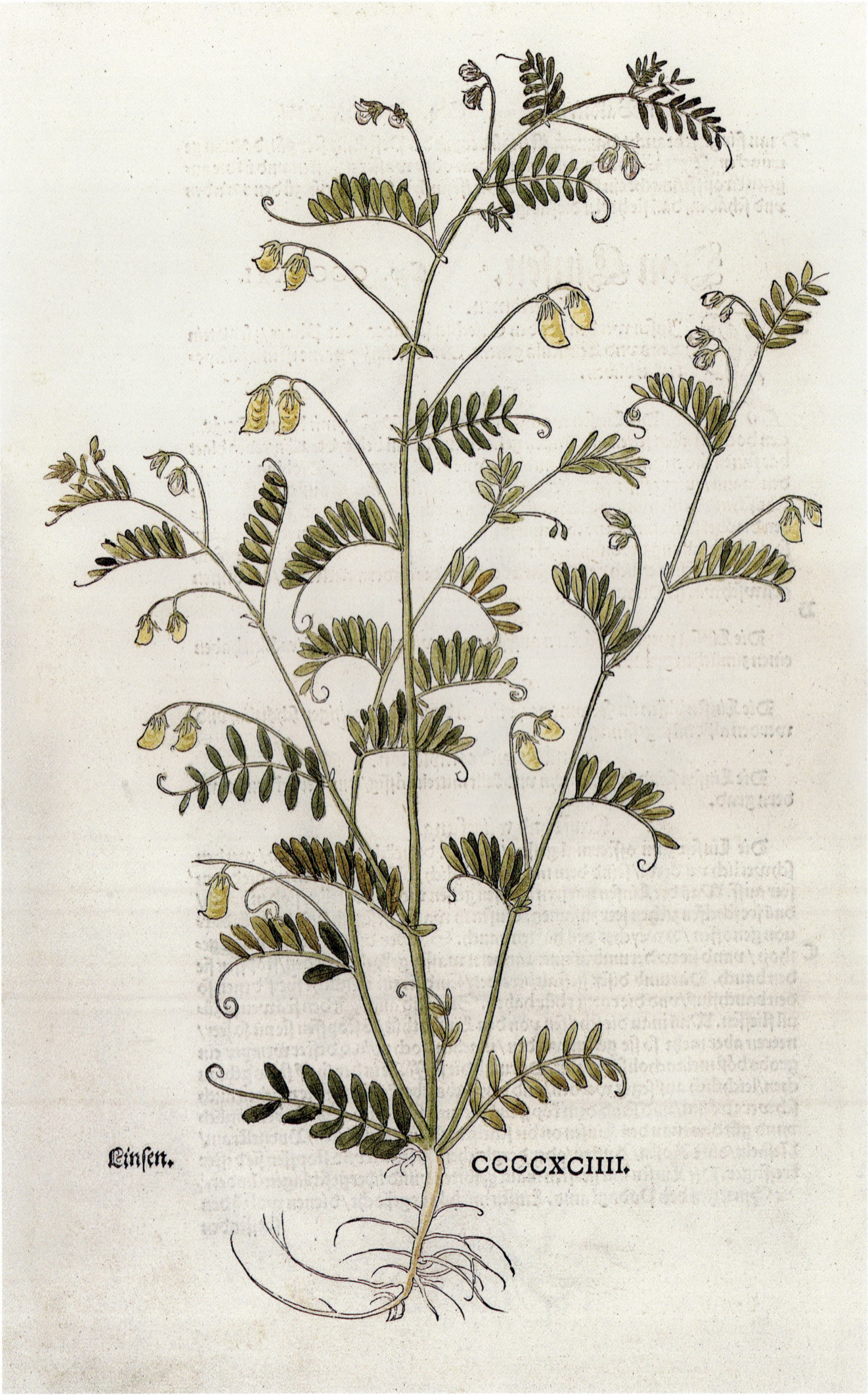
Linsen.
CCCCXCIIII.

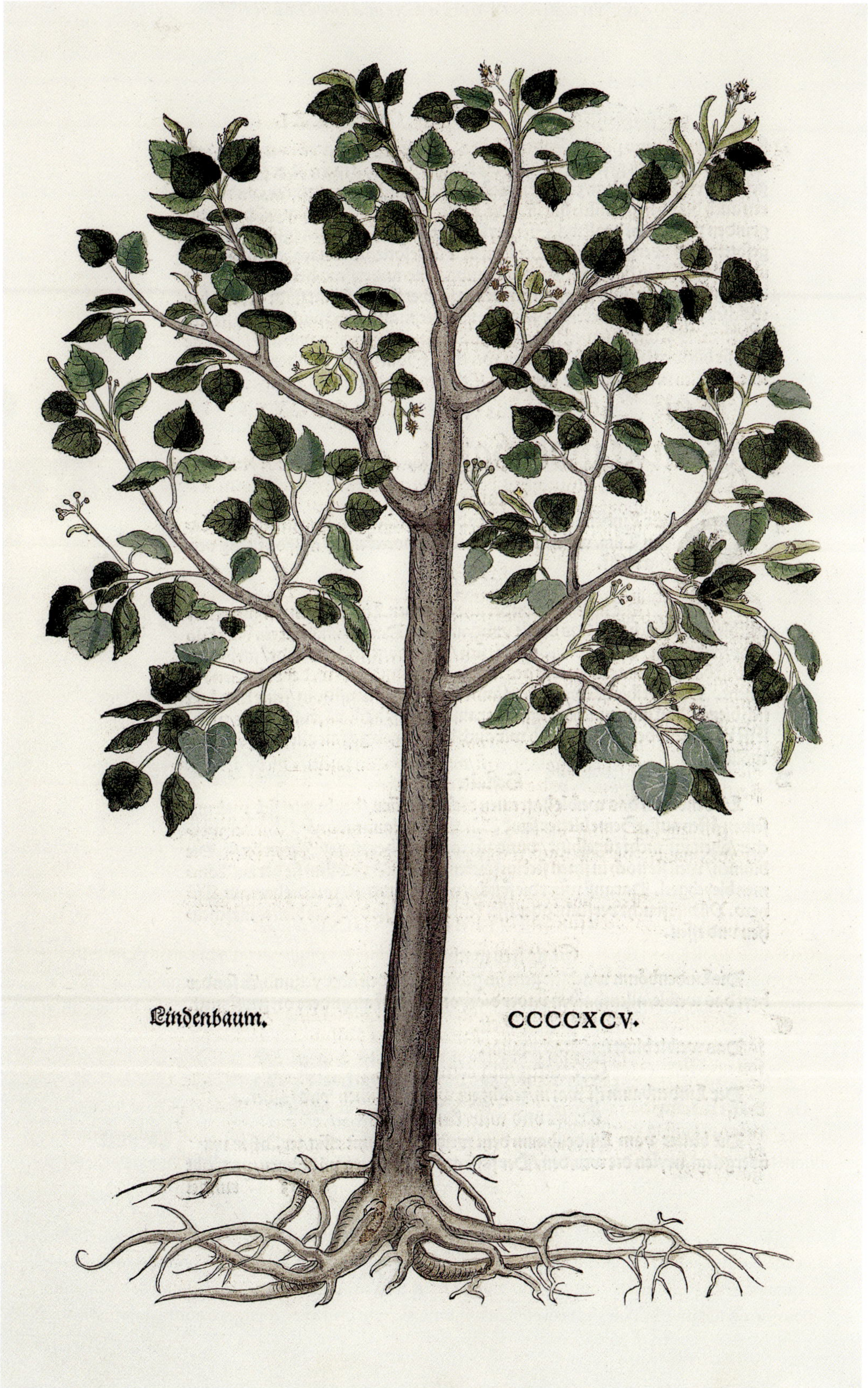
Lindenbaum.
CCCCXCV.

GREATER CELANDINE

GREATER CELANDINE (CCCXXXIII) evoked the interest of physicians because of its milky yellow sap, which was taken to indicate – this time correctly – an effective remedy for the bladder. In contrast, the claim that the plant strengthens the eyes is false, even if the belief still remains alive in folk medicine.

„SCHÖLKRAUT“ (SCHÖLLKRAUT)

Das „SCHÖLKRAUT“ (Cap. CCCXXXIII), als Schöllkraut auch heute noch bekannt, erregte wegen seines gelben Milchsaftes das Interesse der Ärzte, die daraus seine Gallenwirksamkeit ableiteten und damit tatsächlich Recht hatten. Dagegen ist die Behauptung einer augenstärkenden Wirkung falsch, auch wenn sie sich in der Volksmedizin bis heute findet.

GRANDE ÉCLAIRE

Les médecins avaient remarqué la GRANDE ÉCLAIRE (CCCXXXIII) pour son latex jaune que, par analogie de couleur, ils supposaient cholagogue. S'ils avaient raison sur ce point, son prétendu pouvoir de fortifier la vue s'est révélé faux, même si cette croyance a encore cours aujourd'hui.

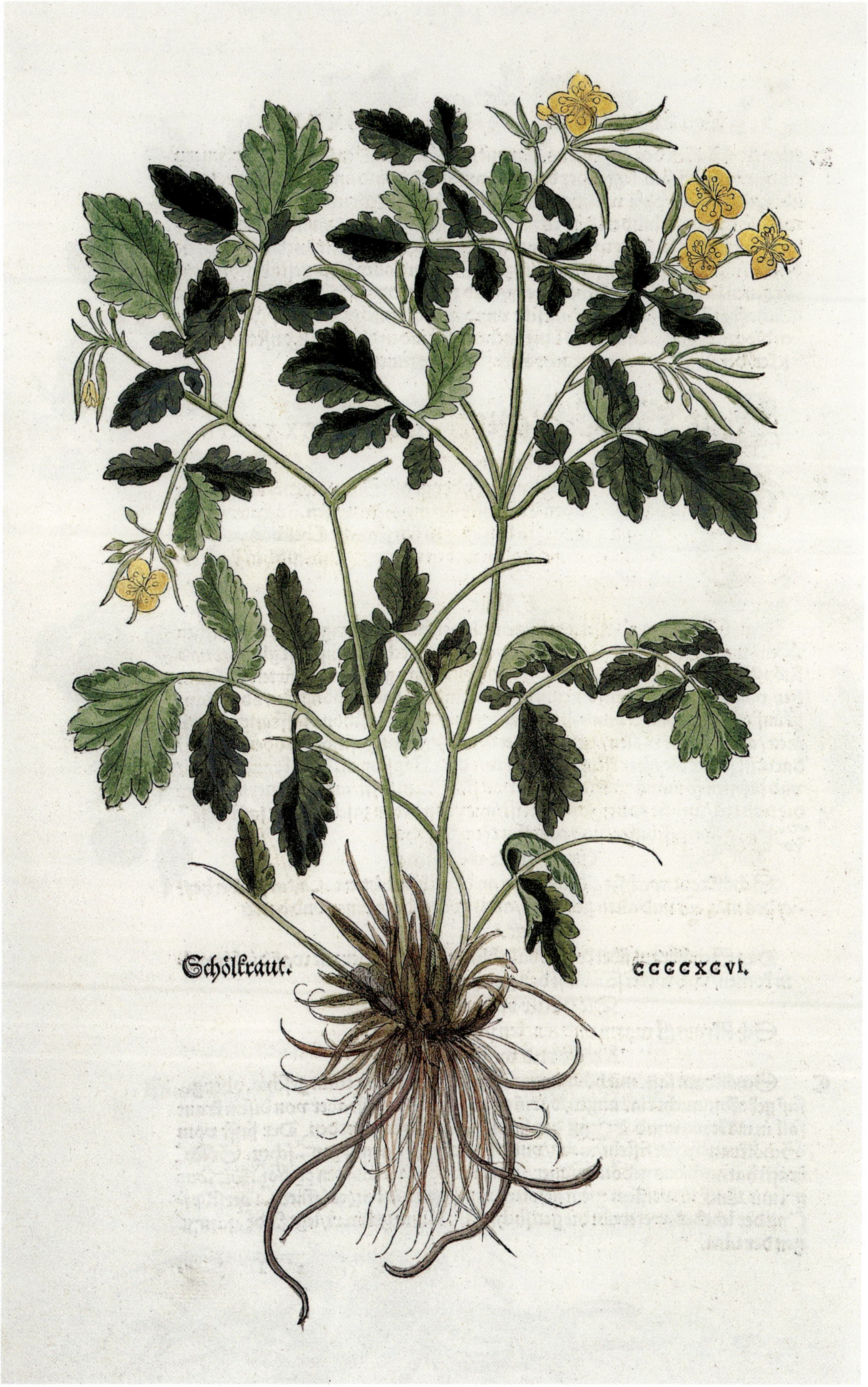
Schölkraut.
CCCCXCVI.

LESSER CELANDINE

LESSER CELANDINE, also known as PILEWORT (CCCXXXIIII), whose leaves are rich in vitamin C, was earlier eaten as a salad to guard against scurvy, a disease caused by a vitamin C deficiency.

„FEIGWARTZENKRAUT“ (SCHARBOCKSKRAUT)

Das „FEIGWARTZENKRAUT“ (Cap. CCCXXXIIII) ist heute als Scharbockskraut bekannt und weist mit diesem Namen darauf hin, dass seine Vitamin-C-reichen Blätter früher als Salat gegen den Scharbock, die Vitamin-C-Mangelkrankheit Skorbut, gegessen wurden.

RENONCULE FICAIRE

Sous le qualificatif de «Feigwartzenkraut» (herbe à condylomes) figure ici la RENONCULE FICAIRE (CCCXXXIIII). Son autre nom allemand, «Scharbockskraut» ou herbe à scorbut, indique ses propriétés anti-scorbutiques, car les feuilles, qu’on mangeait en salade, sont riches en vitamine C.

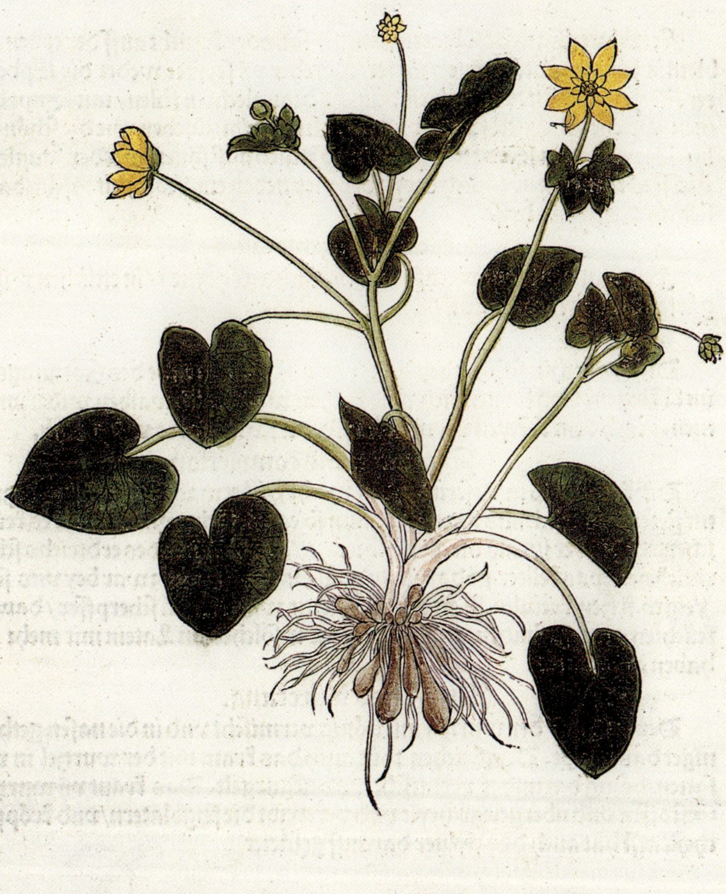

Feigwartzenkraut. CCCCXCVII.

Zz 3

LESSER CELANDINE | „FEIGWARTZENKRAUT“ | RENONCULE FICAIRE

GERMANDER

The reputation of the GERMANDER and SPEEDWELL group of plants (CCCXXXV), once highly valued for their medicinal effect, has not survived into modern times. The German word Germander still survives in three of the four illustrated plants.

„CHAMANDER“ (GAMANDER)

Die Bezeichnung „CHAMANDER“ (Cap. CCCXXXV), die Fuchs verwendet, hat sich als Gamander im Namen von drei der vier abgebildeten Pflanzen bis heute erhalten, die einst hochgeschätzte medizinische Verwendung allerdings konnte nicht in gleicher Weise überdauern.

GERMANDRÉE

Le nom de «CHAMANDER» (CCCXXXV) qui a perduré jusqu'à nos jours sous la forme «Gamander» ou GERMANDRÉE, s'applique effectivement à trois des quatre plantes représentées. Par contre, leur grande réputation n'a pas survécu en médecine.

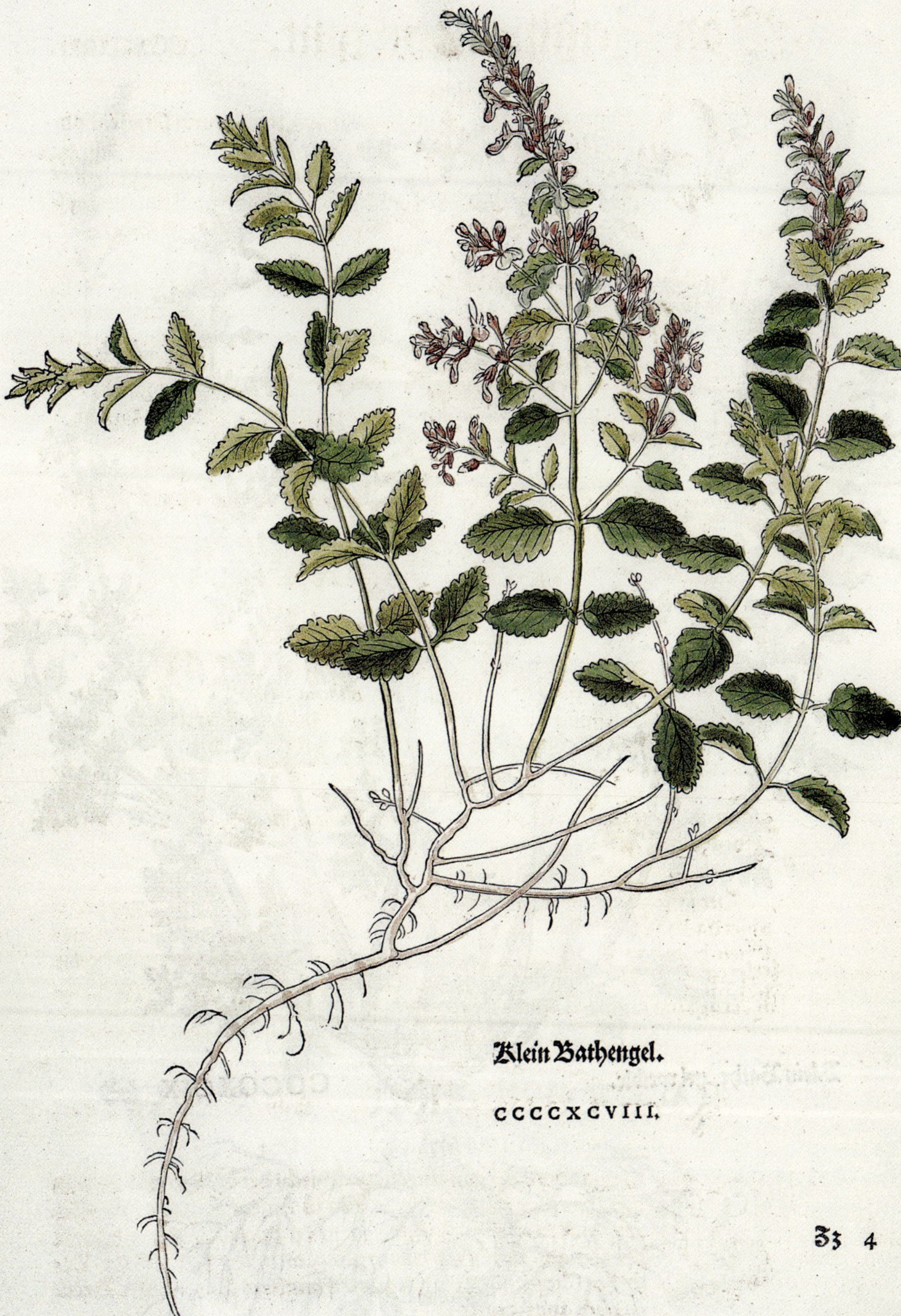

Klein Bathengel.

CCCCXCVIII.

Zz 4

SANTOLINA

SANTOLINA, also known as LAVENDER COTTON or GROUND CYPRESS (CCCXXXVI), whose Latin name *Santolina* suggests "holy," was used as a vulnerary with a dispersive and drying effect; later its chief medicinal use was as a vermifuge.

„CYPRESSEN"

Die „CYPRESSEN" (Cap. CCCXXXVI), wegen ihres lateinischen Namens *Santolina* auch Heiligenkraut genannt, werden als zerteilendes Wundkraut mit austrocknender Wirkung beschrieben, später arzneilich jedoch in erster Linie als Wurmmittel verwendet.

SANTOLINES

Les SANTOLINES (CCCXXXVI) figurent sous le nom de «Cypressen» ou cyprès. Décrites par Fuchs comme cicatrisantes et dessicatives, les santolines seront surtout utilisées comme vermifuge par la suite.

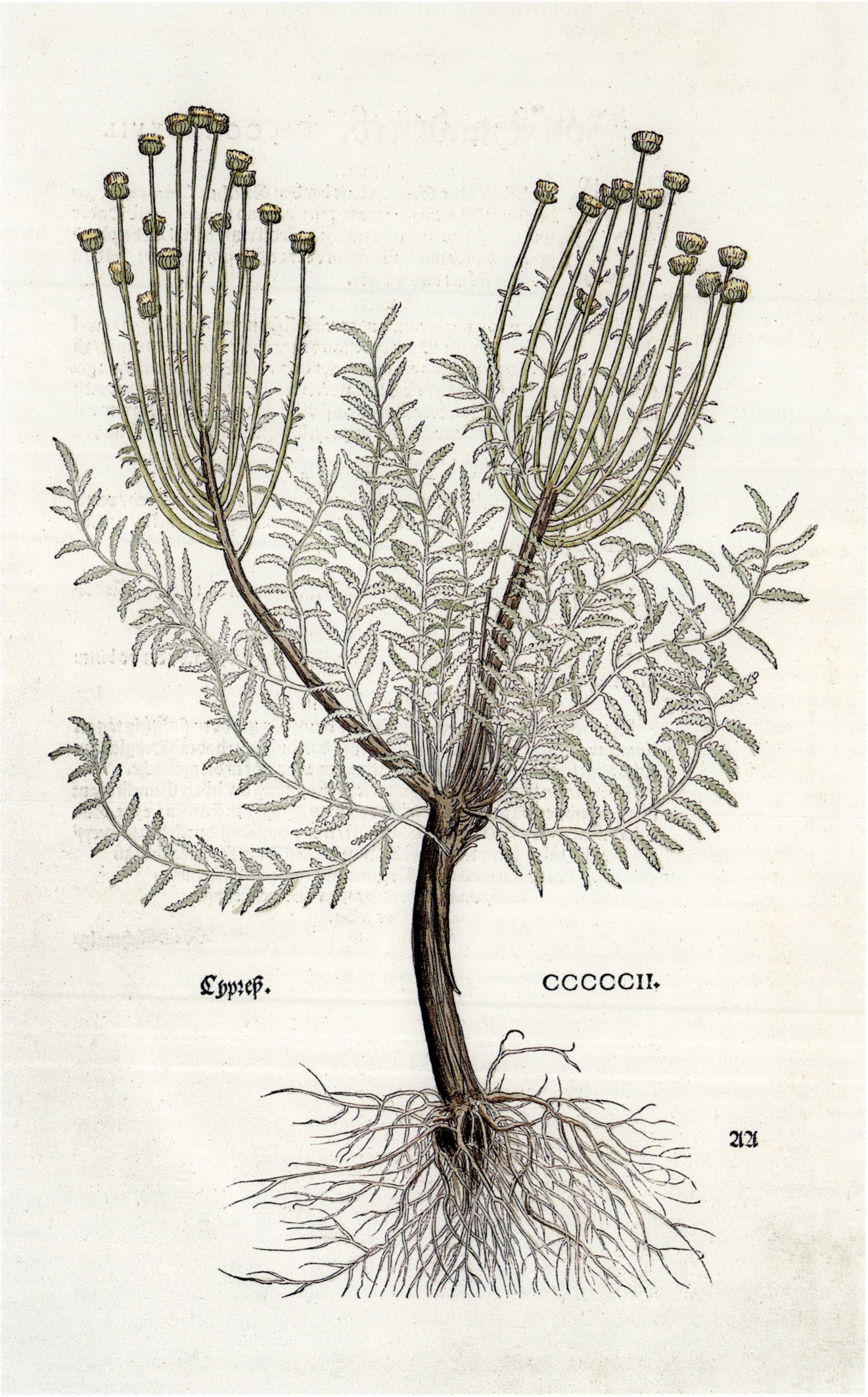
Cypreß.
CCCCCII.
Aa

GROUND IVY

One can still find GROUND IVY (CCCXXXVII), or Alehoof, growing wild today and it is still recognized in medicine; nonetheless, it is only rarely used for diarrhoea or as a diuretic.

GUNDELREBE

Die GUNDELREBE (Cap. CCCXXXVII) findet sich wildwachsend heute noch häufig, ist in der Medizin zwar noch bekannt, wird jedoch nur noch sehr selten bei Durchfall oder als harntreibendes Mittel eingesetzt.

LIERRE TERRESTRE

Le LIERRE TERRESTRE (CCCXXXVII) est encore très répandu dans la nature. Bien qu'il soit connu en médecine, son usage est très rare aujourd'hui, se limitant aux diarrhées et aux traitements diurétiques.

PAGE 614

CREEPING BUTTERCUP

For Fuchs, the gleaming yellow flowers of CREEPING BUTTERCUP (CCCXXXVIII) signified that the plant could well be applied for jaundice.

„SCHMALTZBLUMEN"

Die leuchtend gelben Blüten der bekannten „SCHMALTZBLUMEN" (Cap. CCCXXXVIII) ließen ihre Verwendung bei Gelbsucht sinnvoll erscheinen.

RENONCULE RAMPANTE

Le jaune éclatant de la RENONCULE RAMPANTE (CCCXXXVIII) paraissait l'indice d'effets salutaires sur la jaunisse.

PAGE 615

CARLINE THISTLE

The preferred habitat of stemless CARLINE THISTLE (CCCXXXIX) is the mountains. Earlier, it was a treasured medicinal plant for both people and animals, especially during the plague.

„EBERWURTZ" (SILBERDISTEL)

Als Silberdistel findet sich die „EBERWURTZ" (Cap. CCCXXXIX) bevorzugt im Gebirge und war früher eine begehrte Heilpflanze für Mensch und Tier, insbesondere auch zu Pestzeiten.

CARLINE SANS TIGE

La CARLINE SANS TIGE (CCCXXXIX) croît de préférence dans les montagnes. C'était autrefois une plante médicinale importante pour l'homme et le bétail, particulièrement en temps de peste.

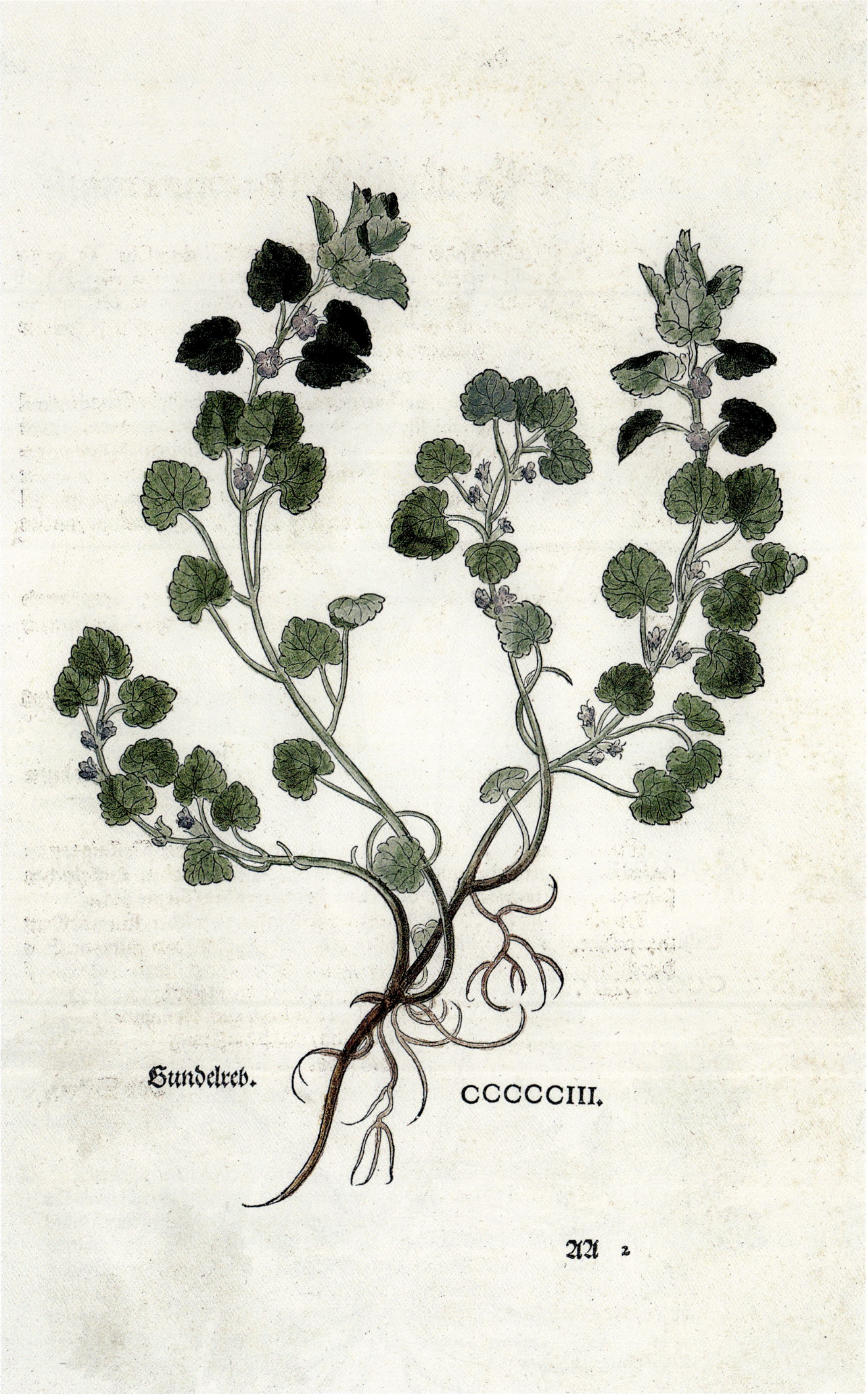

GROUND IVY | GUNDELREBE | LIERRE TERRESTRE

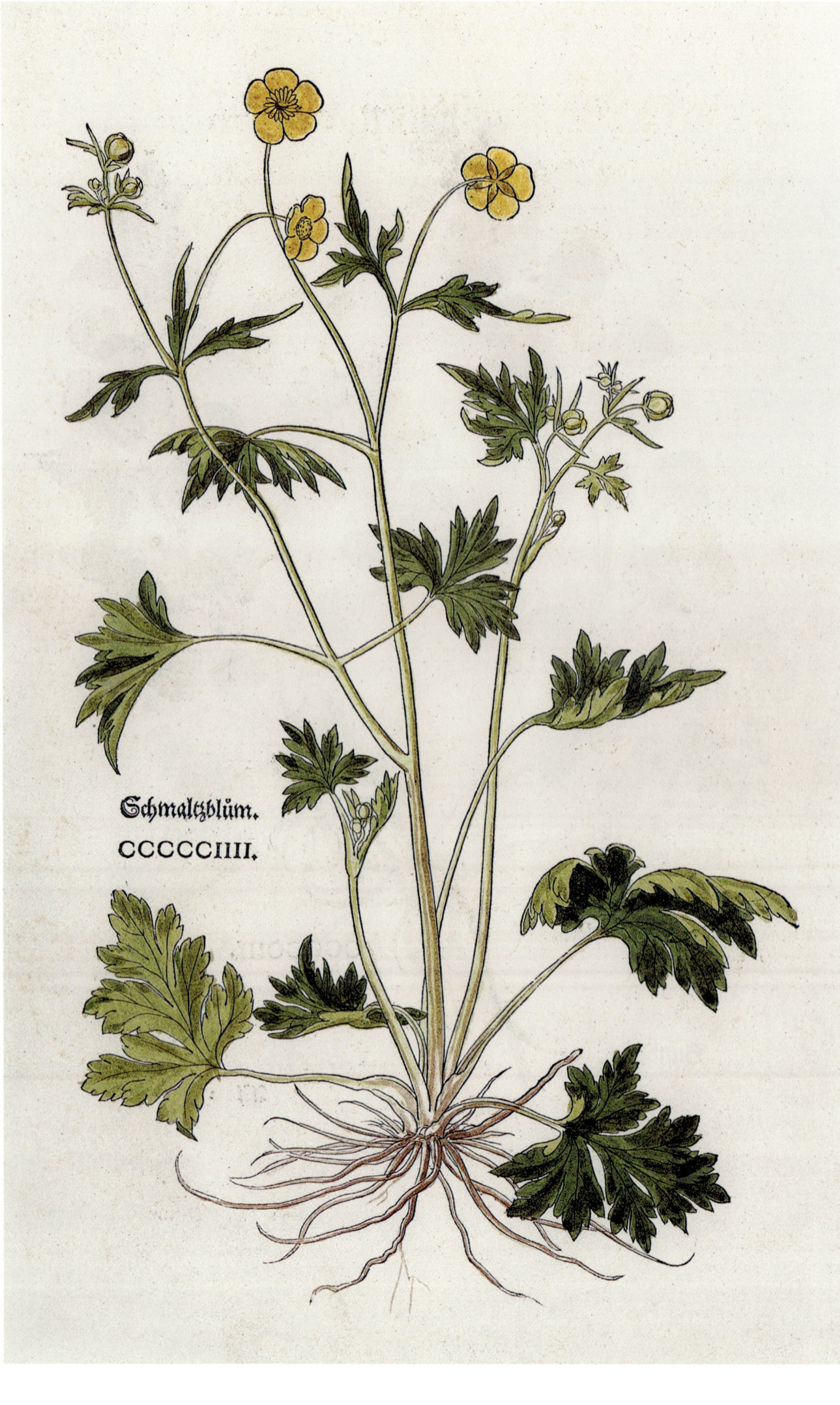
Schmaltzblům.
CCCCCIIII.

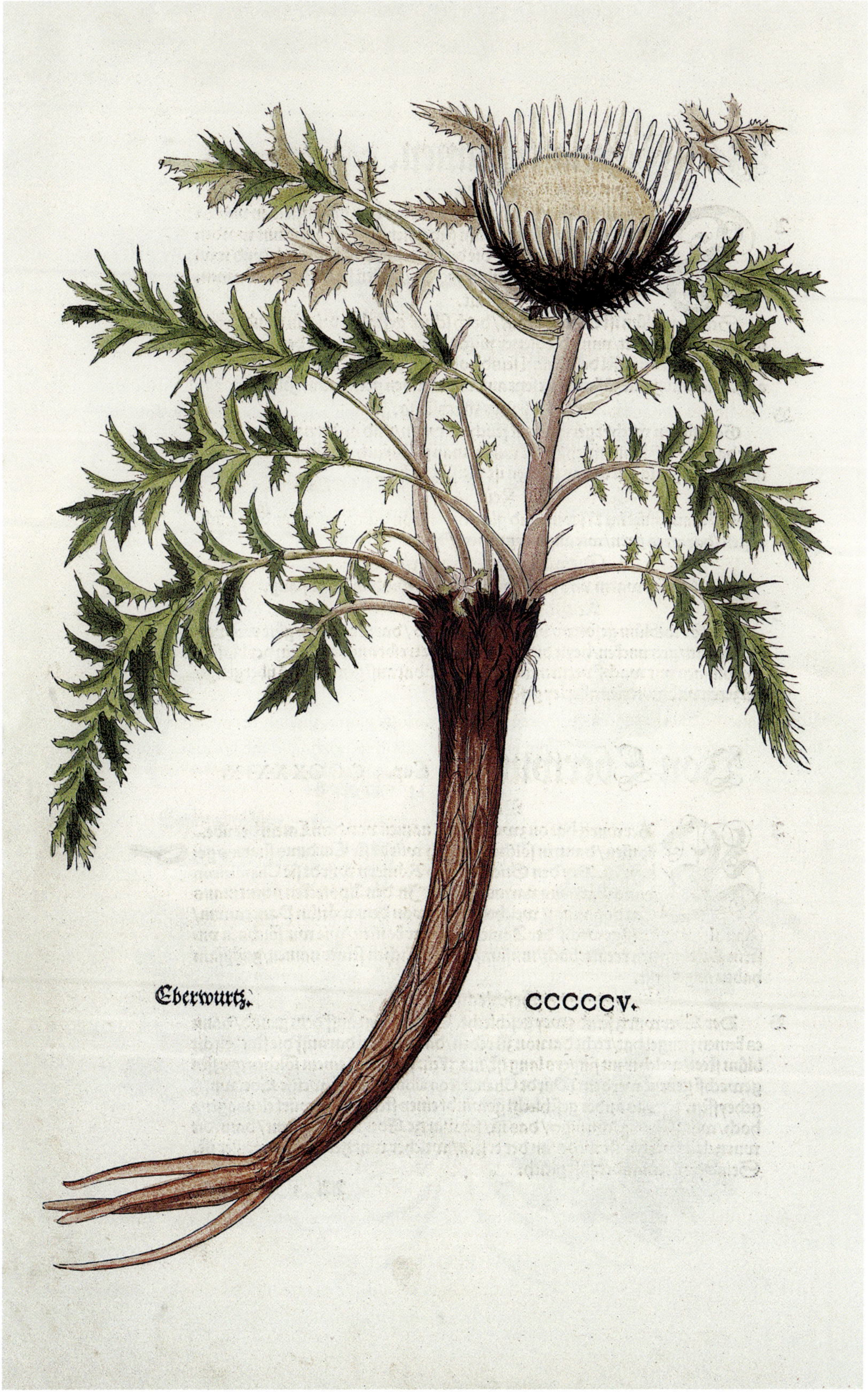
Eberwurtz.
CCCCCV.

PALE GLOBE THISTLE

Fuchs had illustrations made of the GREAT or PALE GLOBE THISTLE (CCCXL), whose name derives from the shape of the inflorescence, "on account of its beauty," even though its use as a medicament was uncommon.

„WELSCH DISTEL" (KUGELDISTEL)

Die „WELSCH DISTEL" (Cap. CCCXL), heute nach der Form ihrer Blütenstände Kugeldistel genannt, ließ Fuchs „umb seiner schönheit willen" abbilden, obwohl die medizinische Verwendung noch nicht üblich war.

ÉCHINOPS À TÊTE RONDE

Quoique son usage ne soit pas encore courant en médecine, Fuchs a représenté l'ÉCHINOPS À TÊTE RONDE (CCCXL), appelé dans le texte «Welsch Distel» (chardon étranger), «pour sa beauté».

PAGE 618

BUGLE

In this chapter (CCCXLI), Fuchs gathered together various plants, including two kinds of BUGLE. For these he describes a surprisingly large area of application in relation to the normal usage of the day.

„JE LÄNGER JE LIEBER"

„JE LÄNGER JE LIEBER" (Cap. CCCXLI) werden verschiedene Pflanzen genannt; Fuchs versteht darunter zwei Günsel-Arten mit einem überraschend breiten Wirkspektrum nach damaliger Ansicht.

BUGLE

Sous la singulière dénomination de «je länger je lieber» (approximativement, «plus longtemps, mieux ça vaut») figurent trois plantes différentes, dont deux variétés de BUGLE (CCCXLI), auxquelles Fuchs attribue un vaste champ d'application, surprenant en ce temps-là.

PAGE 619

FLEAWORT

FLEAWORT (CCCXLII), also known as African Plantain or Black Psyllium, is still used medicinally as a laxative, but its earlier applications have been forgotten.

„PSILIENKRAUT" (FLOH-WEGERICH)

Der Floh-Wegerich, bei Fuchs „PSILIENKRAUT" (Cap. CCCXLII), ist zwar heute noch als Abführmittel in medizinischem Gebrauch, die einstigen Anwendungen sind jedoch vergessen.

HERBE AUX PUCES

L'HERBE AUX PUCES (CCCXLII) s'utilise encore comme laxatif, mais ses autres indications sont oubliées depuis longtemps.

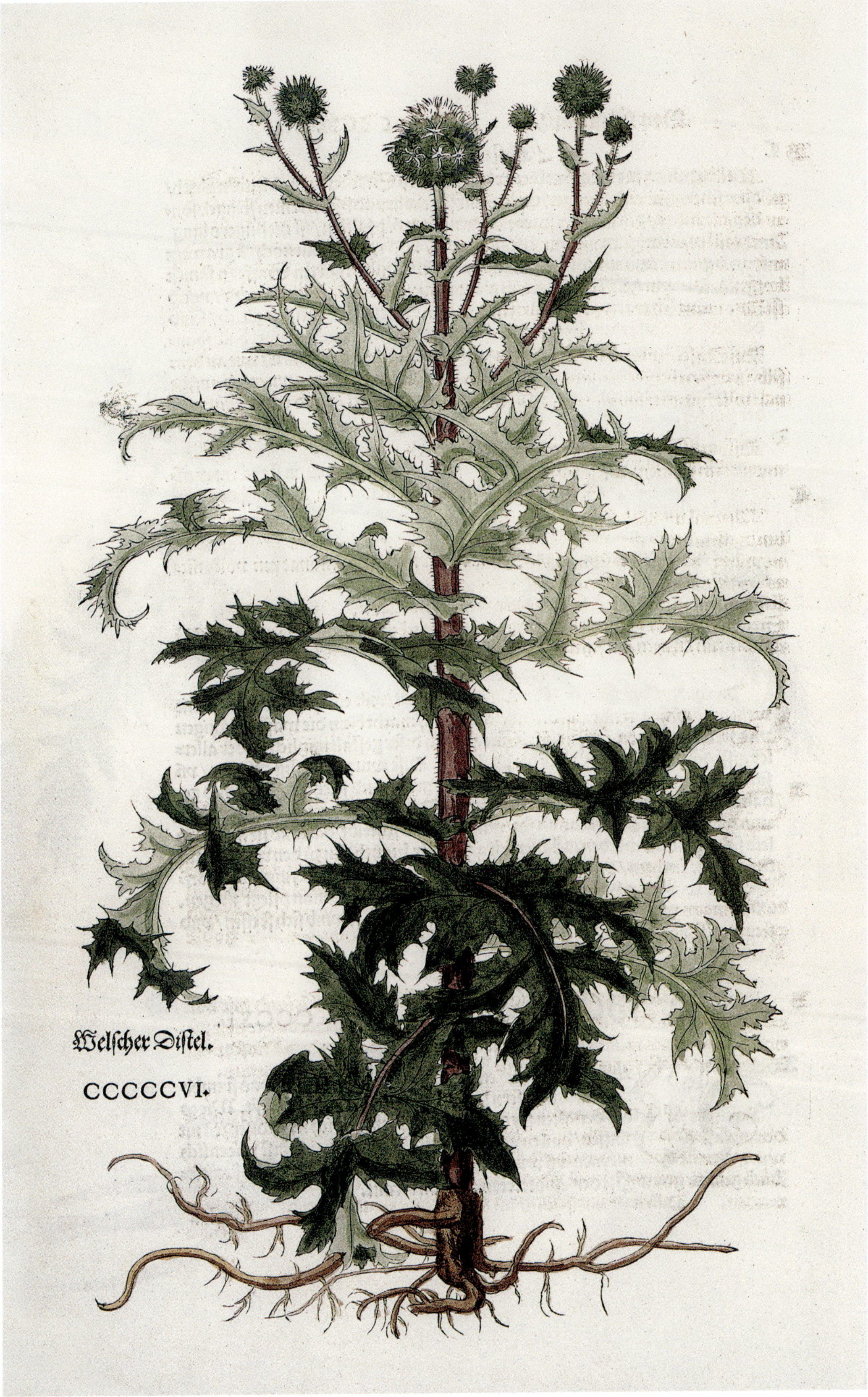
Welscher Distel.
CCCCCVI.

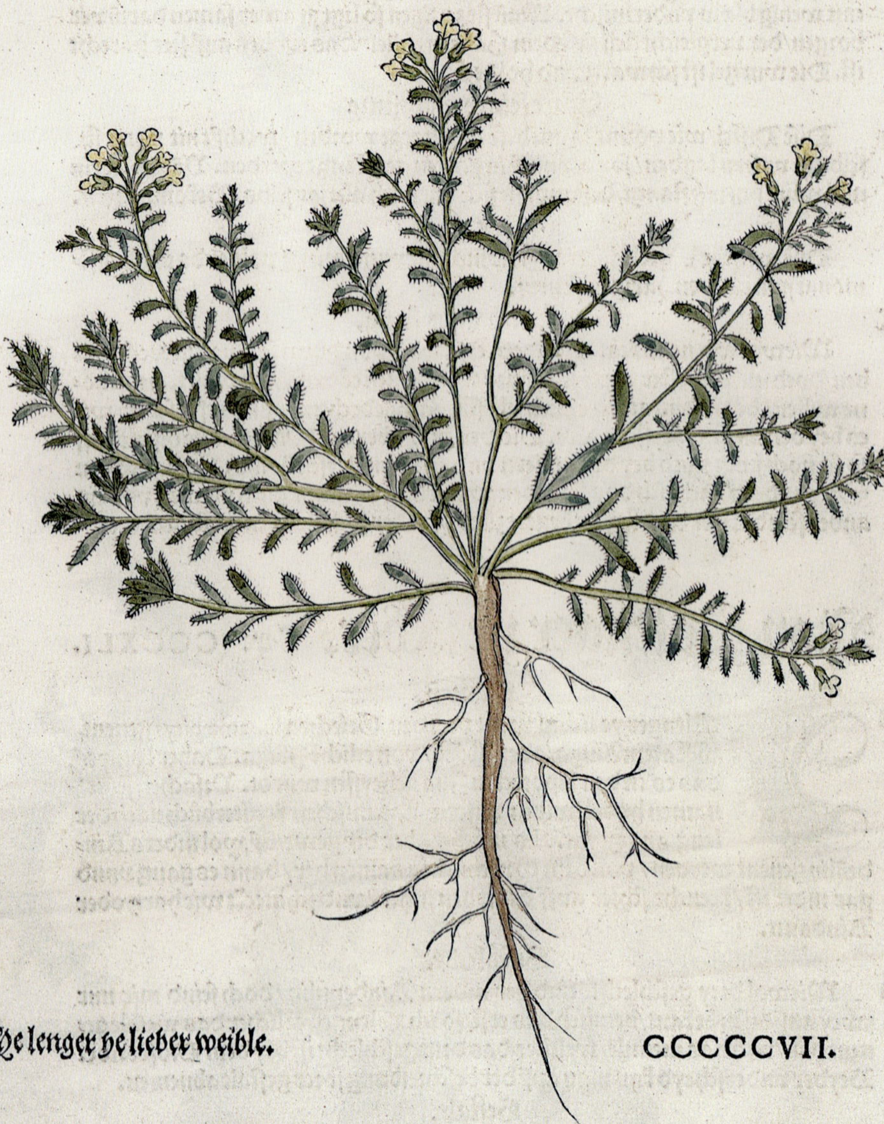

Ye lenger ye lieber weible. CCCCCVII.

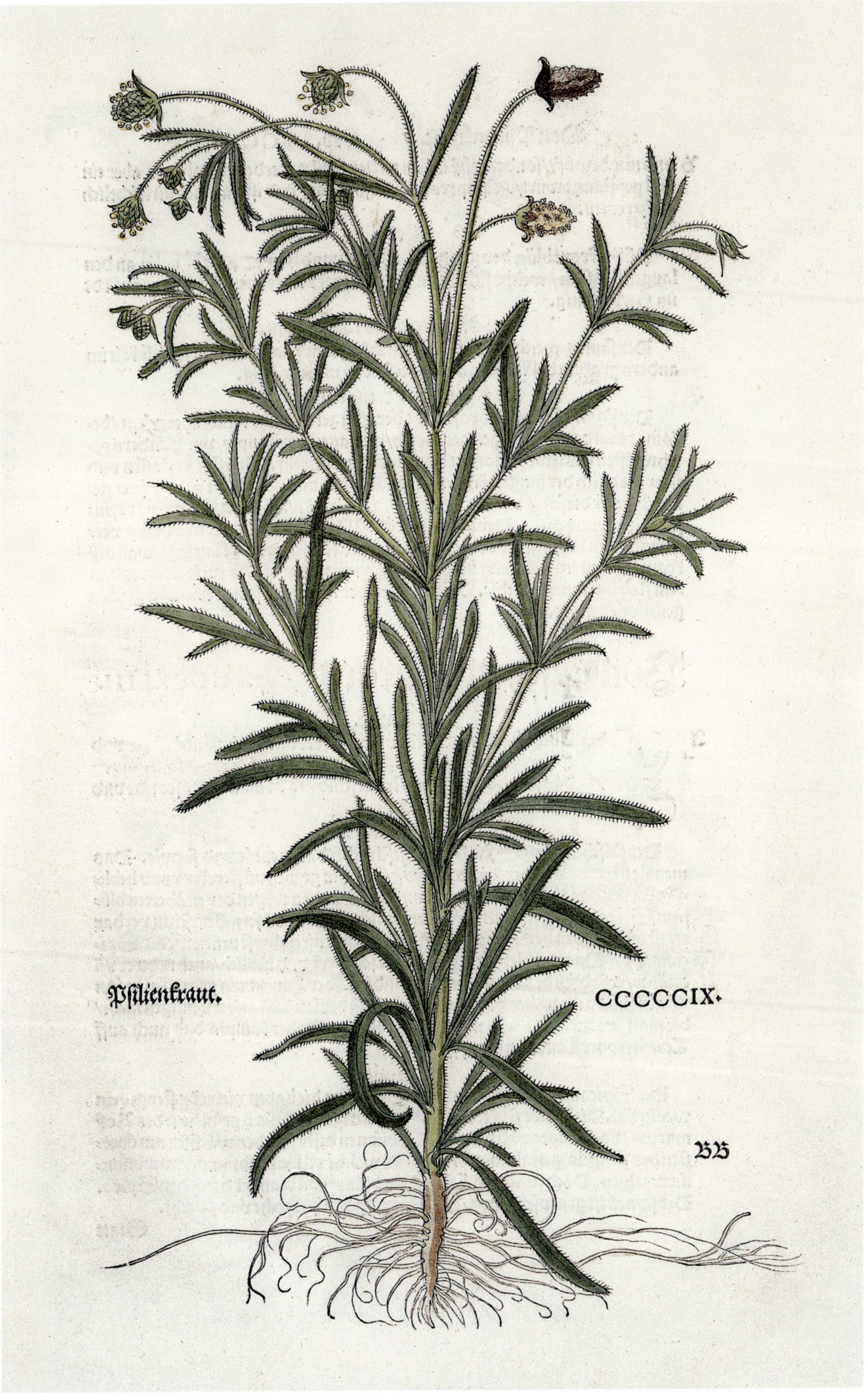
Psilienkraut.
CCCCCIX.
BB

FRAGRANT LAVENDERS

Ancient writings already spoke of the FRAGRANT LAVENDERS (CCCXLIII), although great problems arose with their identification. Nonetheless, both English, or common, lavender and spike, or broad-leaved, lavender found internal and external application in medicine.

„FALSCHE NARDEN"

Die wohlriechende Narde findet sich schon im antiken Schrifttum häufig genannt, doch bereitete ihre Identifizierung große Schwierigkeiten. Der Echte Lavendel und der Speik werden wegen ihres Wohlgeruchs hier als „FALSCHE NARDEN" (Cap. CCCXLIII) aufgeführt und innerlich wie äußerlich als Arznei gebraucht.

LAVANDE AROMATIQUE

Même si elle est déjà évoquée dans les traités médicaux de l'Antiquité, la LAVANDE AROMATIQUE (CCCXLIII) a toujours été difficile à identifier. La lavande vraie et la lavande aspic, présentées ici comme de faux nards («Narden», dans le texte) à cause de leur odeur agréable, s'emploient aussi bien en usage interne qu'externe.

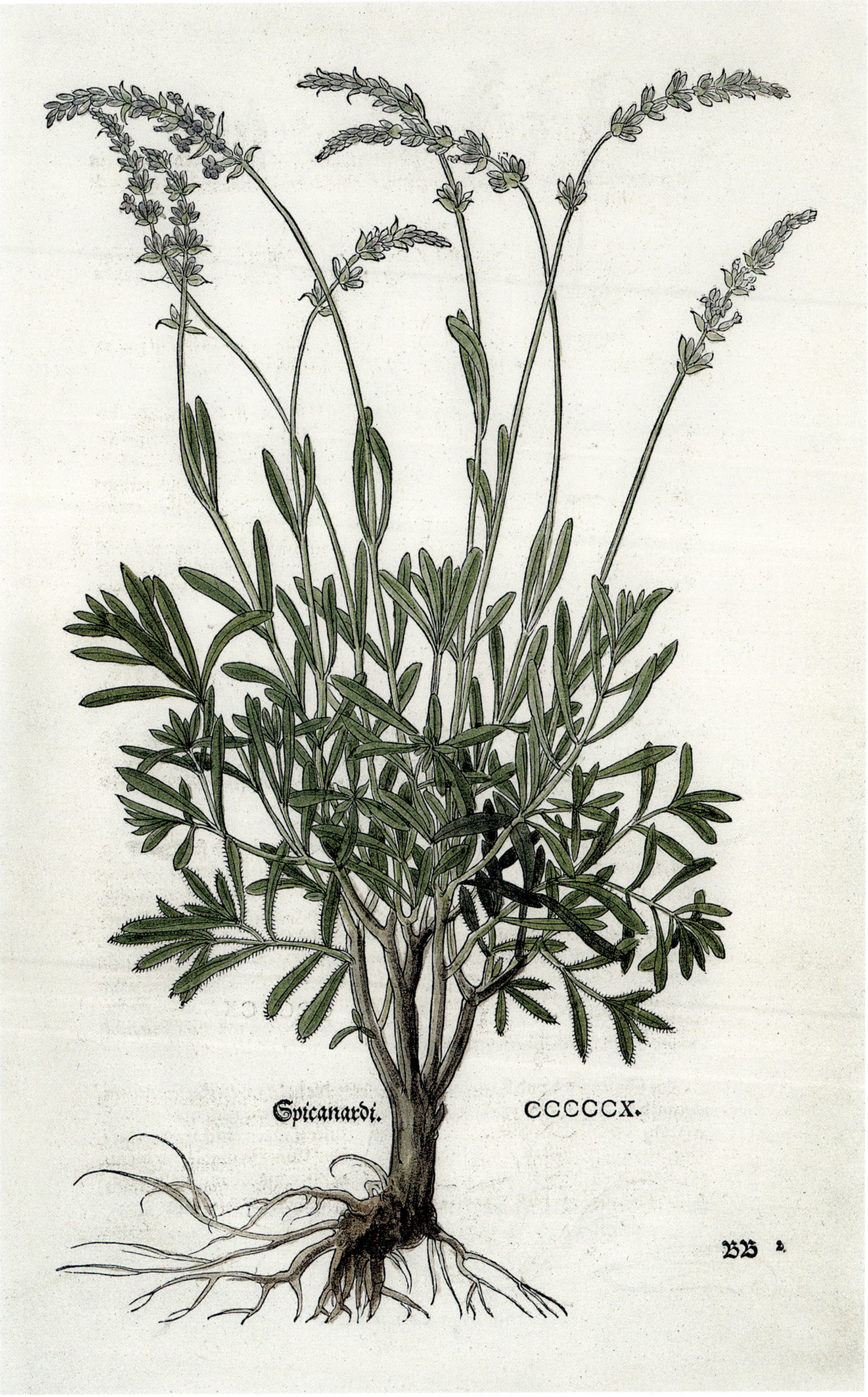
Spicanardi.
CCCCCX.
BB 2

PASQUE FLOWER

The beauty of PASQUE FLOWER (CCCXLIIII) should not distract from its toxicity. Externally, it causes severe skin irritation; internally, an overdose can strongly irritate the kidney and bile ducts. In the past, the plant was used as an abortifacient.

„KUCHENSCHELL"

Die Schönheit der „KUCHENSCHELL" (Cap. CCCXLIIII) darf nicht über ihre Giftigkeit hinwegtäuschen. Äußerlich tritt eine starke Hautreizung auf, bei Überdosierung der Einnahme kann es zu starken Reizungen der Niere und der Harnwege kommen. Die Pflanze wurde früher auch als Abtreibungsmittel verwendet.

PULSATILLE VULGAIRE

La beauté de la PULSATILLE VULGAIRE (CCCXLIIII) ne doit pas faire oublier sa toxicité. En usage externe, elle provoque des réactions cutanées très violentes, et peut même, en cas de surdosage par voie interne, entraîner de graves troubles rénaux et urinaires. On l'employait autrefois abusivement comme abortif.

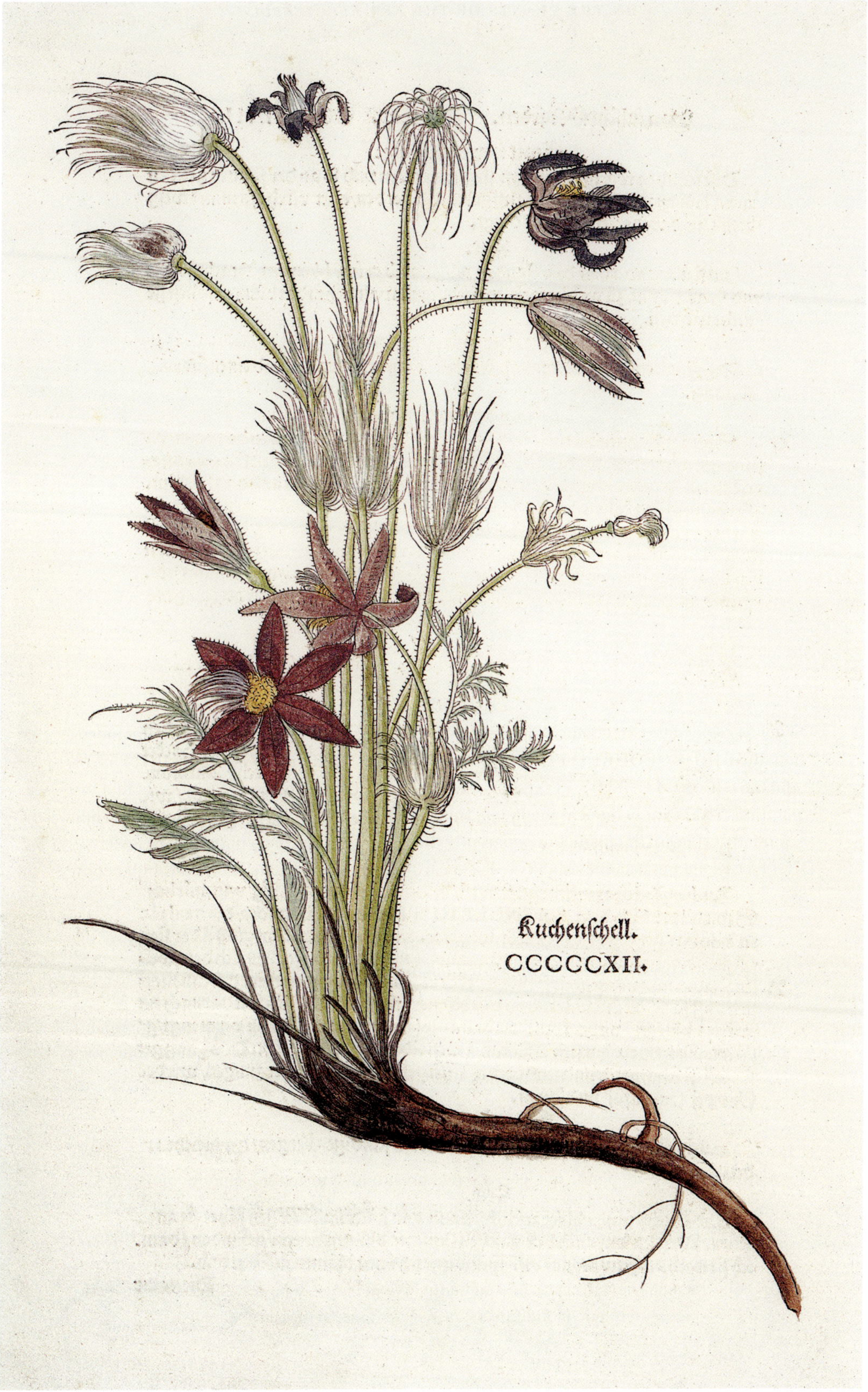
Kuchenschell.
CCCCCXII.

FOXGLOVE

Fuchs provided the first botanical illustration of the FOXGLOVE (CCCXLV). He included both the RED-COLOURED FOXGLOVE (plate CCCCCXIII), also known as DIGITALIS, and the GREAT YELLOW FOXGLOVE (plate CCCCCXIIII), correctly surmising that the plant was unknown to ancient medicine. He was also correct in identifying the diuretic and purgative effect of the plant, but apparently did not yet recognize its high level of toxicity. DIGITALIS did not become established as a cardiac remedy until the end of the 18th century.

FINGERHUTKRAUT

Mit dem ROTEN (Taf. CCCCCXIII) und dem GROSSBLÜTIGEN FINGERHUT (Taf. CCCCCXIIII) liefert Fuchs die ersten botanischen Abbildungen des FINGERHUT-KRAUTS (Cap. CCCXLV), das der antiken Medizin unbekannt war, wie er zu Recht vermutet. Er nennt richtig die diuretische und ausführende Wirkung, hat aber offenbar die hohe Giftigkeit noch nicht erkannt. Als Herzmittel kommt *Digitalis* erst am Ende des 18. Jahrhunderts in den Arzneischatz, wo es sich bis heute erhalten hat.

DIGITALE

Les planches suivantes sont consacrées à la DIGITALE (CCCXLV). Fuchs est le premier à avoir illustré cette plante qui, comme il le présumait à juste titre, était inconnue des médecins naturalistes de l'Antiquité. Il la présente sous deux formes : la DIGITALE POURPRE (pl. CCCCCXIII), ou gant de Notre-Dame, et la DIGITALE À GRANDES FLEURS (pl. CCCCCXIIII), de couleur jaune. Si Fuchs mentionne ses effets diurétiques et purgatifs, il n'a pas décelé cependant sa haute toxicité. C'est depuis la fin du XVIIIe siècle seulement que la digitale est utilisée comme remède cardiaque.

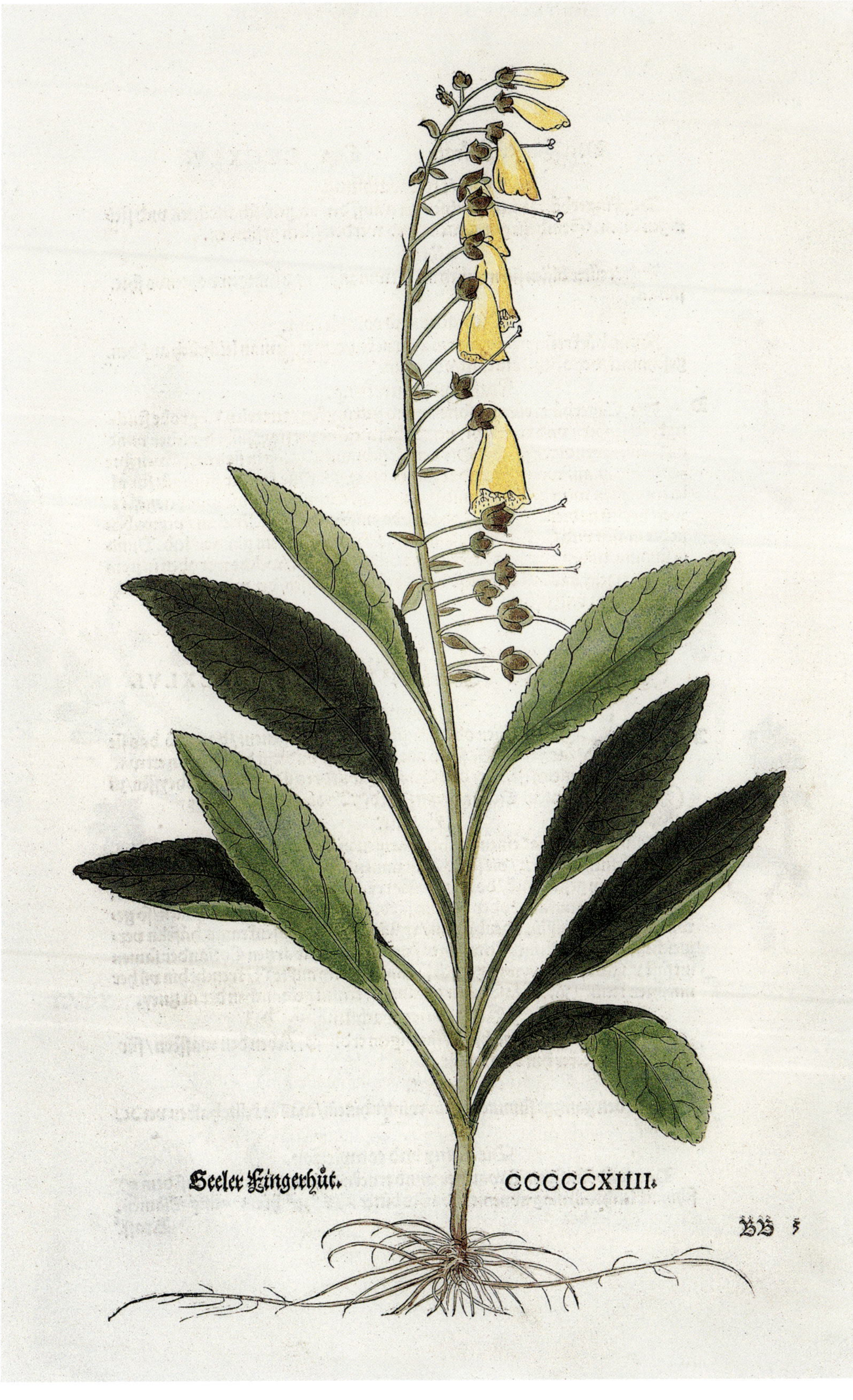
Geeler Fingerhůt.
CCCCCXIIII.
BB 5

BASIL-THYME

With BASIL-THYME, or MOTHER-OF-THYME (CCCXLVI) Fuchs once more presents a plant that was unknown to the apothecaries of the age, but was thought to be useful against poisons.

„WILD BASILIEN"

Mit dem „WILDEN BASILIEN" (Cap. CCCXLVI) führt Fuchs nochmals eine Pflanze auf, die den Apothekern seiner Zeit noch unbekannt war und besonders gegen Gifte helfen sollte.

ARRIETTE ACINOS

Pour finir, Fuchs nous présente une autre plante inconnue à l'époque en pharmacopée : la SARRIETTE ACINOS (CCCXLVI), qui serait en particulier très efficace contre les poisons.

PAGE 628

LEONHART FUCHS, *New Kreüterbuch*, 1543

CXI (111) *Gentiana lutea* (L.) – Great Yellow Gentian, Yellow Gentian / Gelber Enzian / Gentiane jaune, Grande gentiane

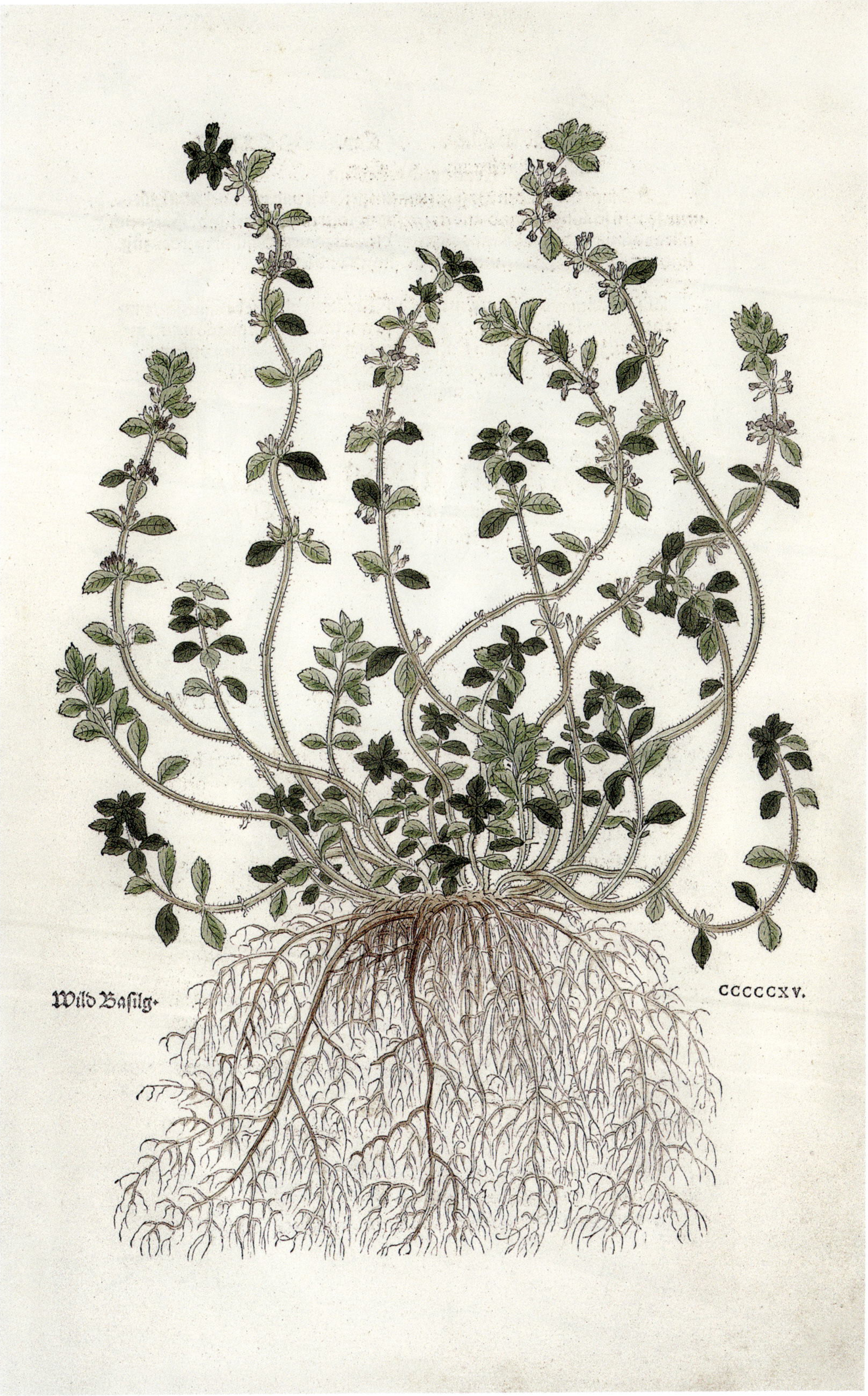
Wild Basilg.
CCCCCXV.

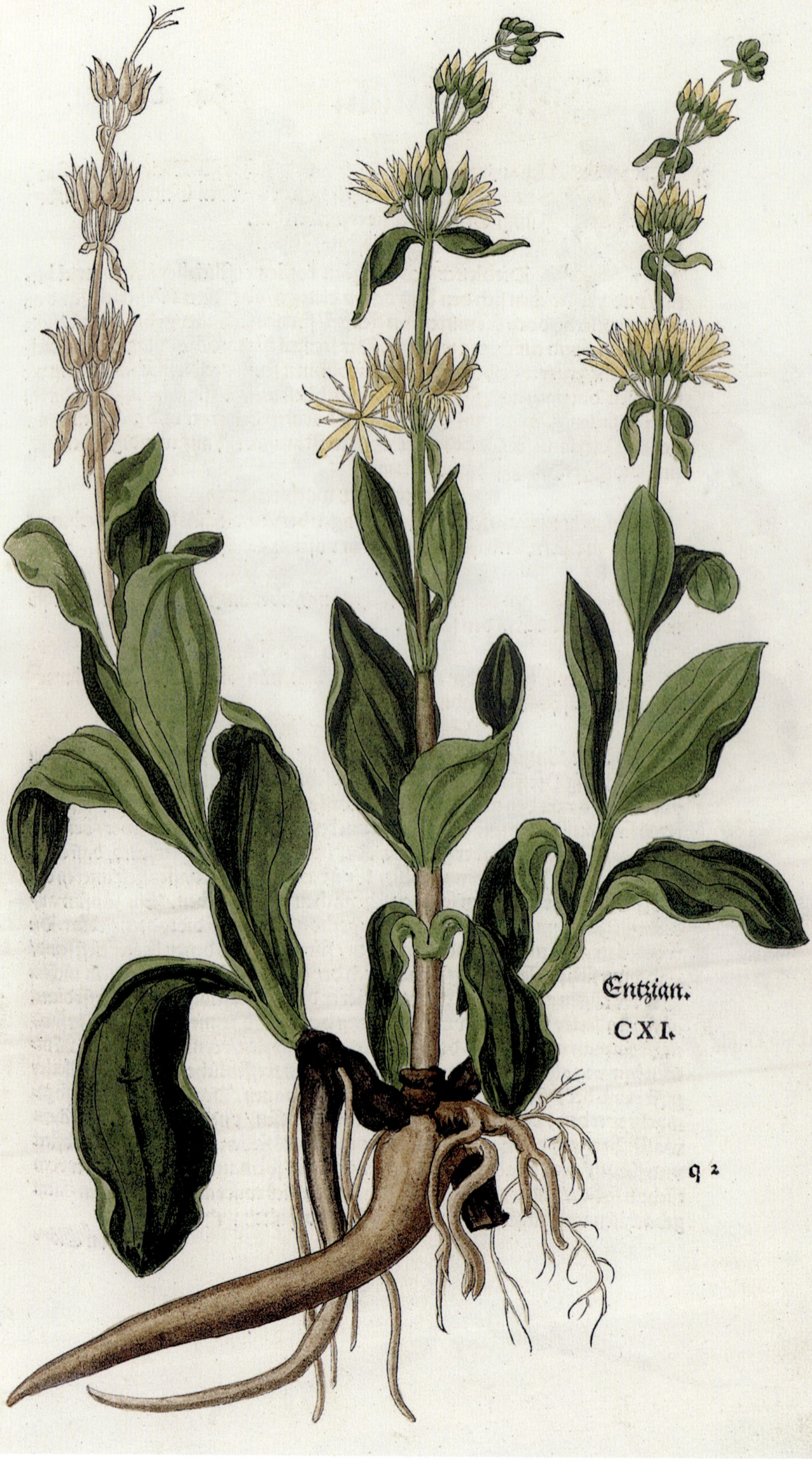

Entzian.
CXI.

WERNER DRESSENDÖRFER

The Medicinal Plants by Fuchs
in Modern Herbal Medicine

It will be perfectly clear to anyone carefully reading even a single section on "Power and Effect" in Leonhart Fuchs's herbal that if the doctor's assertions can provide any kind of basis for the modern and effective use of medicinal plants, it is only to a limited extent – and even then, treatment must be accompanied by factual knowledge and proceed with great care. The problem is not only that the text ascribes identical, and at times stereotyped, attributes to completely different plants, but also that the basis of the medicinal effects described by Fuchs derives largely from the assumptions of the theory of humours. These problems, together with the fact that a wide variety of applications are recommended for one and the same plant (the "indications lyric"), demonstrate clearly that standards of evaluation and judgement have changed profoundly in the course of the last 450 years. Therefore, an uncritical attempt to extract "traditional" or "tried-and-true" knowledge from the text out of a sense of romantic nostalgia would be quite erroneous. After all, people would not submit today to an operation conducted according to late medieval standards, for the immense progress that has been made in medical science is palpable in everyday life. In the same way, the knowledge and evaluation of medicinal plants have also developed, and methods have greatly changed in the process. Modern phytopharmacology, or plant medicine, no longer uncritically accepts the actual or supposed experience underlying the traditional handling of medicinal herbs, but instead is concerned with determining a scientific basis from which a reliable understanding of the plants, their ingredients, and their effects can be obtained. Thus it may be interesting to peruse the following short list concerned with the modern applications of a number of the important medicinal plants recommended by Leonhart Fuchs more than 450 years ago in his herbal. The Roman numerals following the plant names correspond to Fuchs's illustrations. The first item in the entry states the part of the plant that is used or the preparation derived from it; the second part of the entry gives the common application of the plant today. External use is clearly indicated as such. Today, the applications using extracts are usually based on ready-made medical preparations. In some cases, the entries point out serious side effects – it would however be false to conclude that the use of herbal remedies is completely unproblematic for the remaining cases! When in doubt, a physician or pharmacist should be consulted.

Die Heilpflanzen von Fuchs
in der modernen Phytotherapie

Liest man die jeweiligen Abschnitte zu „krafft und würckung" im Fuchs'schen Kräuterbuch aufmerksam durch, wird deutlich, dass diese Aussagen als Grundlage einer sinnvollen Heilpflanzenanwendung heute, wenn überhaupt, nur äußerst beschränkt und mit großer Vorsicht und Sachkenntnis herangezogen werden können. Die teilweise stereotypen Wiederholungen bei völlig unterschiedlichen Pflanzen, die zum großen Teil auf Mutmaßungen und Theorien der Säftelehre basieren, und ebenso die extreme Breite der unterschiedlichsten Anwendungsempfehlungen für ein und dieselbe Pflanze („Indikationslyrik"), machen deutlich, dass sich die Bewertungs- und Beurteilungsmaßstäbe im Lauf der letzten 450 Jahre grundlegend geändert haben. Es wäre also falsch, aus einem romantischen Gefühl heraus das vermeintlich „Altüberkommene" und „Altbewährte" kritiklos beizubehalten. Niemand wird sich heute nach dem Standard des ausgehenden Mittelalters operieren lassen, denn der ungeheuere Fortschritt der medizinischen Kenntnisse ist für ihn alltäglich erfahrbar. Genauso hat sich das Wissen um die Heilpflanzen und deren Beurteilung sehr weiterentwickelt und dabei stark verändert. Die moderne Phytotherapie vertraut deshalb nicht kritiklos der tatsächlichen oder vermeintlichen Erfahrung zum überlieferten Umgang mit Heilpflanzen. Sie ist vielmehr bestrebt, wissenschaftlich bestätigte Grundlagen für eine abgesicherte Kenntnis der Heilpflanzen, ihrer Inhaltsstoffe und ihrer Wirkungen zu schaffen. Nicht zuletzt deshalb mag es interessant sein, in der folgenden kurzen Aufzählung stichwortartig etwas über die heutige Anwendung jener wichtigen Heilpflanzen zu erfahren, die bereits Leonhart Fuchs vor mehr als 450 Jahren in seinem Kräuterbuch empfahl. Dabei entsprechen die römischen Zahlenangaben hinter dem Pflanzennamen den Nummern der Abbildungen bei Fuchs. Danach wird der verwendete Pflanzenteil oder die Zubereitung vermerkt, dann die heute gebräuchliche Anwendung. Äußerliche Anwendung wird ausdrücklich als solche bezeichnet. Die Verwendung von Extrakten erfolgt meist in Form moderner Fertigarzneimittel. Auf gravierende Nebenwirkungen wird in einigen Fällen hingewiesen, daraus kann jedoch nicht gefolgert werden, dass in allen anderen Fällen die Anwendung pflanzlicher Mittel problemlos möglich ist. Im Zweifelsfall sollten vor der Verwendung Arzt oder Apotheker befragt werden.

Les plantes médicinales de Fuchs
dans la phytothérapie moderne

En lisant avec attention le chapitre «Puissance et effet», dans lequel Fuchs énumère les vertus de chaque plante, on se rend parfaitement compte que les indications thérapeutiques mentionnées ne peuvent plus servir de base aujourd'hui à une médication raisonnable et sont à prendre avec la plus grande circonspection et des connaissances approfondies. Le fait même que ces indications, souvent stéréotypées et s'appuyant largement sur des suppositions et des principes de la théorie des humeurs, se répètent pour des plantes fort différentes et qu'une même espèce se voit attribuer un champ d'application extrêmement vaste («Lyrisme des motifs thérapeutiques») montre combien les critères d'appréciation et d'évaluation ont évolué au cours des 450 dernières années. Il serait par conséquent erroné de vouloir conserver par quelque romantisme ce qui est présumé «traditionnel» et «ayant fait ses preuves», sans rester critique. Personne ne serait prêt, de nos jours, à se faire opérer selon les pratiques chirurgicales de la fin du Moyen Âge, car l'homme moderne vit au quotidien les immenses progrès de la médecine. De même, les connaissances sur les plantes et herbes officinales, et leur évaluation, se sont considérablement enrichies, donc transformées. Aussi la phytothérapie moderne ne croit-elle plus sans discernement à l'expérience réelle ou supposée dans la pratique traditionnelle des plantes médicinales. Bien au contraire, elle s'emploie à poser les bases, corroborées par l'expérimentation scientifique, d'une connaissance avérée des plantes, de leurs composants et de leurs effets. Pour cette raison, il est intéressant de faire un tour d'horizon des indications actuelles de ces plantes majeures que Leonhart Fuchs conseillait déjà il y a plus de 450 ans. Ainsi les chiffres romains qui suivent le nom de plantes correspondent aux numéros des illustrations de Fuchs. Viennent ensuite la partie de la plante utilisée ou la préparation, enfin l'indication actuelle. L'usage externe est clairement spécifié. Les extraits s'emploient généralement sous forme de produits pharmaceutiques. Dans quelques cas sont mentionnés les effets secondaires graves, ce qui ne signifie pas que l'usage des autres plantes peut se faire sans problèmes. En cas de doute, il est bon de consulter un médecin ou un pharmacien avant utilisation.

COMMON ALOE (LXXV*)

Dried and purified cellular sap from the leaves. ❧ Laxative; side effects with long-term use. Active ingredient of Swedish bitters.

ALOE (LXXV*)

Eingetrockneter und gereinigter Zellsaft aus den Blättern. ❧ Abführmittel. Bei Langzeitanwendung ist mit Nebenwirkungen zu rechnen. Geschmacks- und wirkungsbestimmender Bestandteil des Schwedenbitters.

ALOÈS (LXXV*)

Suc cellulaire des feuilles, déshydraté et épuré. ❧ Laxatif. Effets secondaires en cas d'administration prolongée. Agent actif et amérisant de l'élixir du Suédois.

PAGE 634

COMMON ANISE (XXXV)

Fruits, essential oil. ❧ Carminative, spasmolytic; used for indigestion, coughs.

ANIS (XXXV)

Früchte, ätherisches Öl. ❧ Blähungstreibend, krampflösend, bei Verdauungsbeschwerden, Husten.

ANIS (XXXV)

Fruits, éther, huile. ❧ Antispasmodique ; contre l'aérophagie, les douleurs digestives et la toux.

PAGE 635

GLOBE ARTICHOKE (CCCCLV)

Extract, pressed juice. ❧ For indigestion, liver and gall disorders; lowers blood cholesterol (standardized extract).

ARTISCHOCKE (CCCCLV)

Extrakt, Presssaft. ❧ Bei Verdauungsstörungen, Leber- und Gallenerkrankungen, Blutcholesterin senkend (standardisierter Extrakt!).

ARTICHAUT (CCCCLV)

Extrait, suc pressé. ❧ Troubles digestifs, maladies du foie et de la vésicule biliaire, baisse le taux de cholestérol (extrait titré !).

* Roman numerals denote the plate. / Die römischen Ziffern beziehen sich auf die Tafeln. Les chiffres romains désignent les numéros d'illustrations.

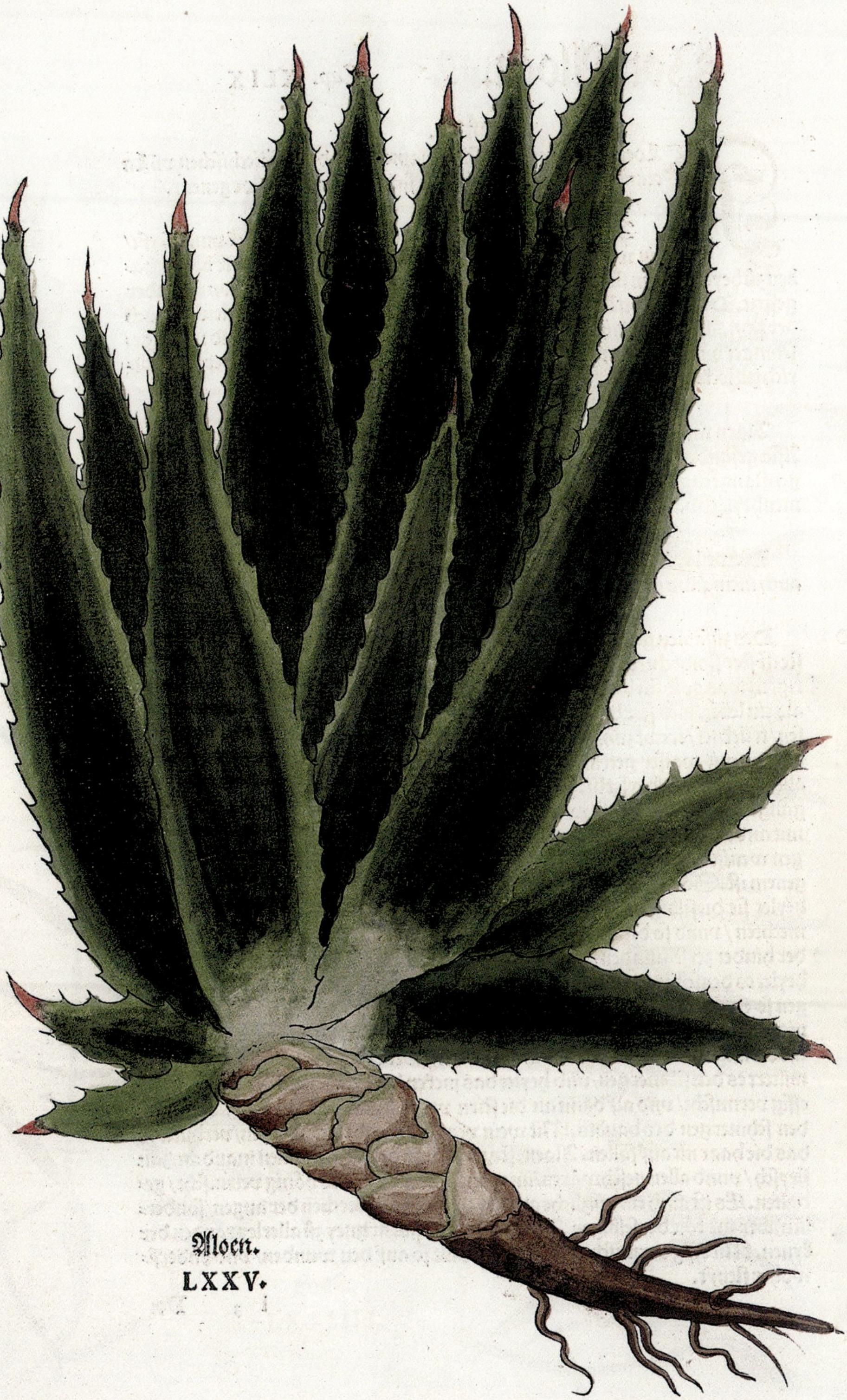

Aloen.
LXXV.

COMMON ALOE | ALOE | ALOÈS

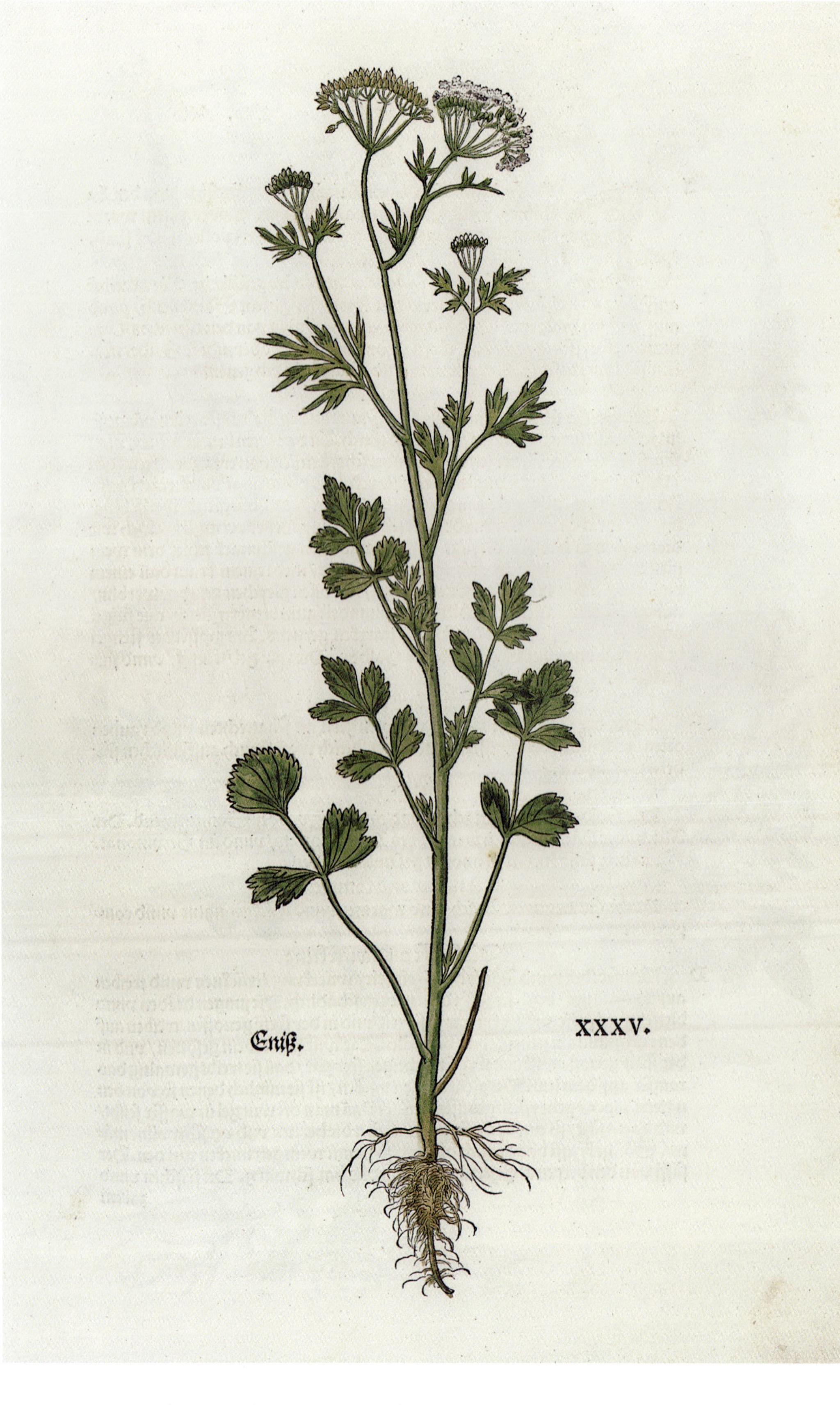
Eniß.
XXXV.

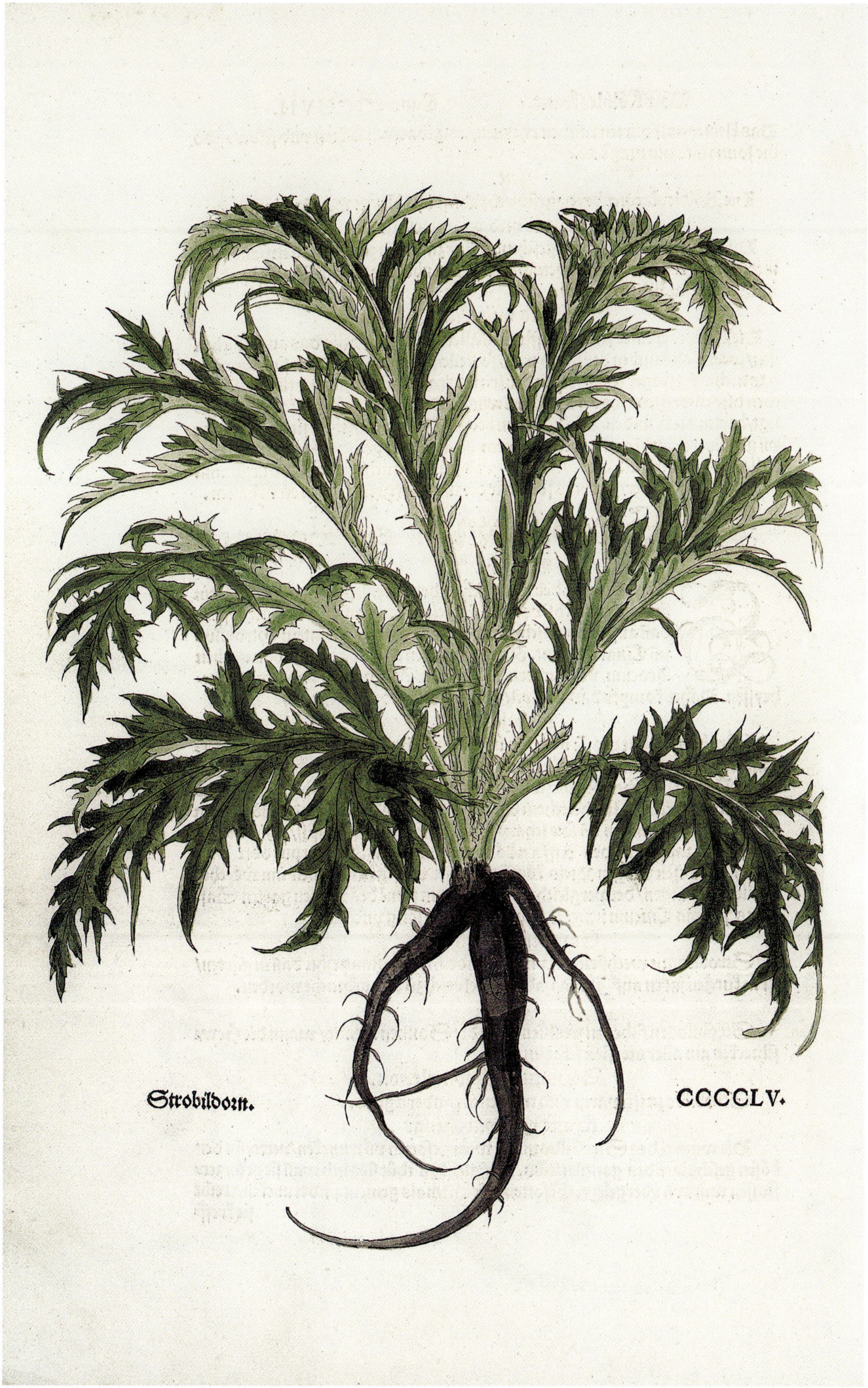
Strobildorn.
CCCCLV.

EYEBRIGHT (CXXXVI)

Herbage. ❧ Traditionally used as a rinse for inflammations of eyelids and conjunctiva; preventive eye care.

AUGENTROST (CXXXVI)

Kraut. ❧ Traditionell zur Spülung bei Entzündungen der Augenlider und der Bindehaut, zur vorbeugenden Augenpflege.

CASSE-LUNETTES (CXXXVI)

Partie verte. ❧ Employée traditionnellement contre les inflammations des paupières et de la conjonctive, soins prophylactiques des yeux.

PAGE 638

VALERIAN (CCCCXCIII)

Root. ❧ Sedative, calming, soporific effect.

BALDRIAN (CCCCXCIII)

Wurzel. ❧ Beruhigend, ausgleichend, einschlaffördernd.

VALÉRIANE (CCCCXCIII)

Racines. ❧ Effet bénéfique sur la nervosité, l'humeur et l'insomnie.

PAGE 639

BEAR'S GARLIC (CCCCXXIIII)

Herbage, bulb. ❧ Used like garlic in folk medicine.

BÄRLAUCH (CCCCXXIIII)

Kraut, Zwiebel. ❧ In der Volksmedizin Verwendung wie Knoblauch.

AIL DES OURS (CCCCXXIIII)

Partie verte, bulbe. ❧ Substitut de l'ail dans la pratique populaire.

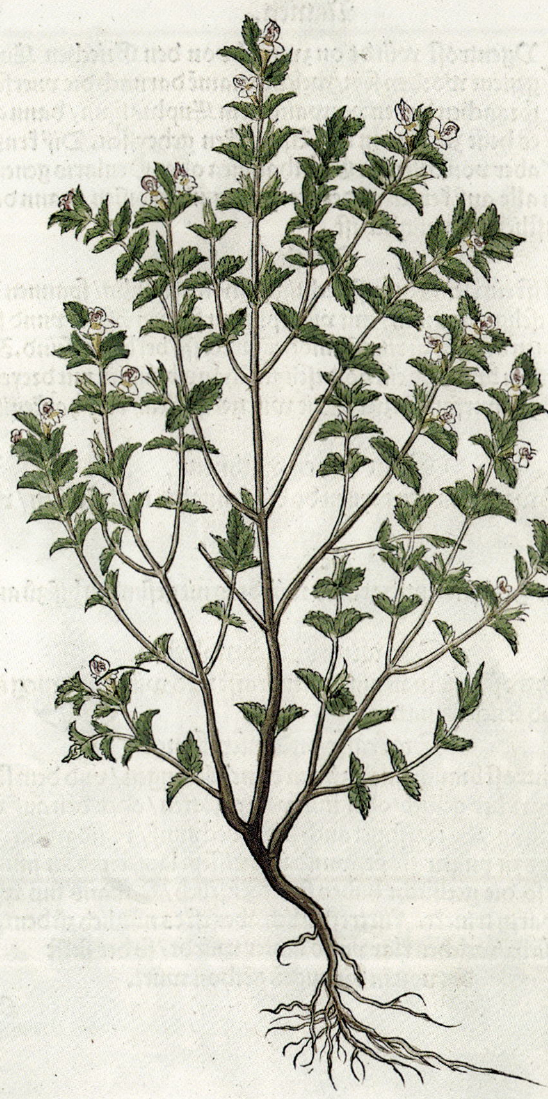

Augentrost. CXXXVI.

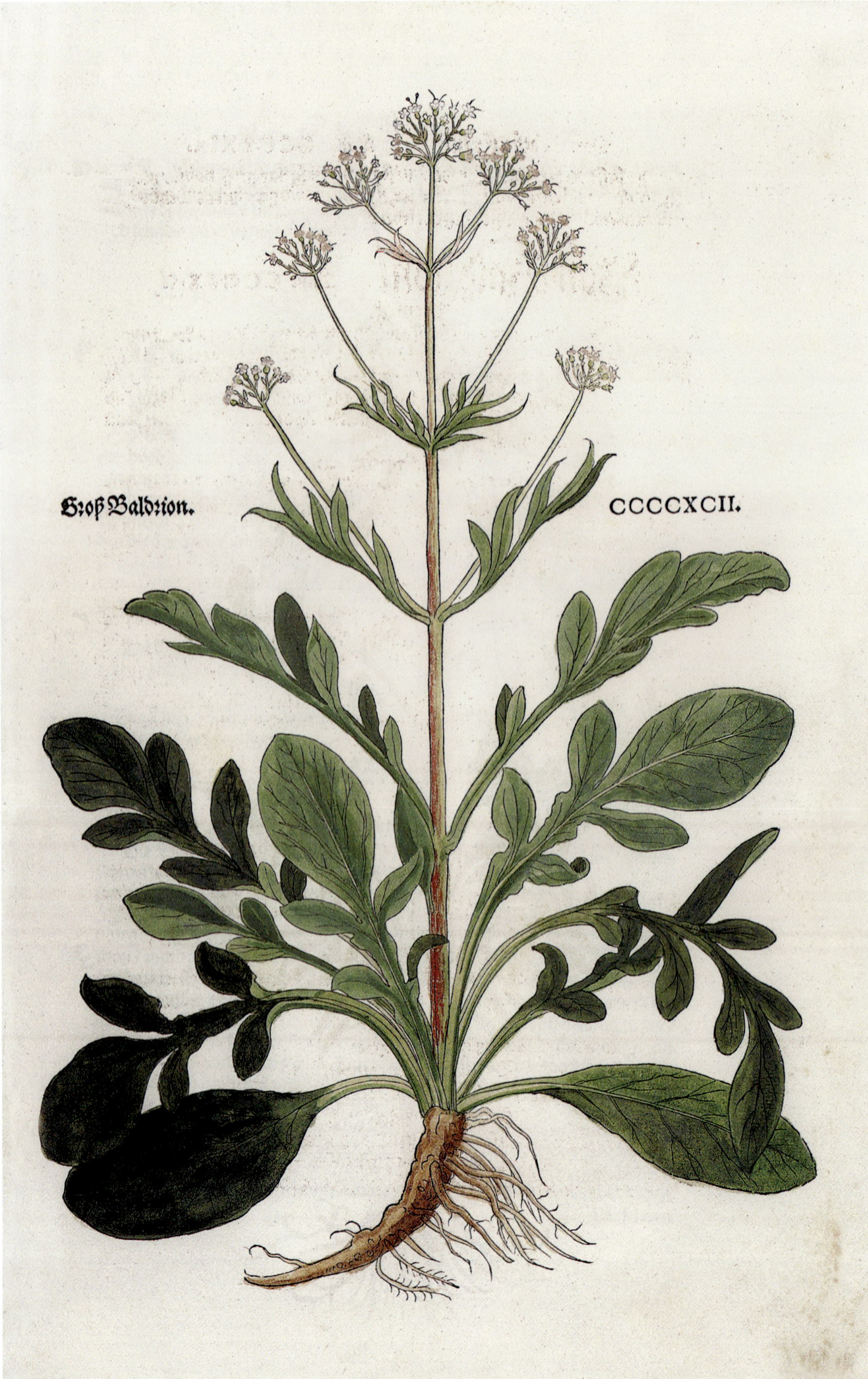
Groß Baldrion.
CCCCXCII.

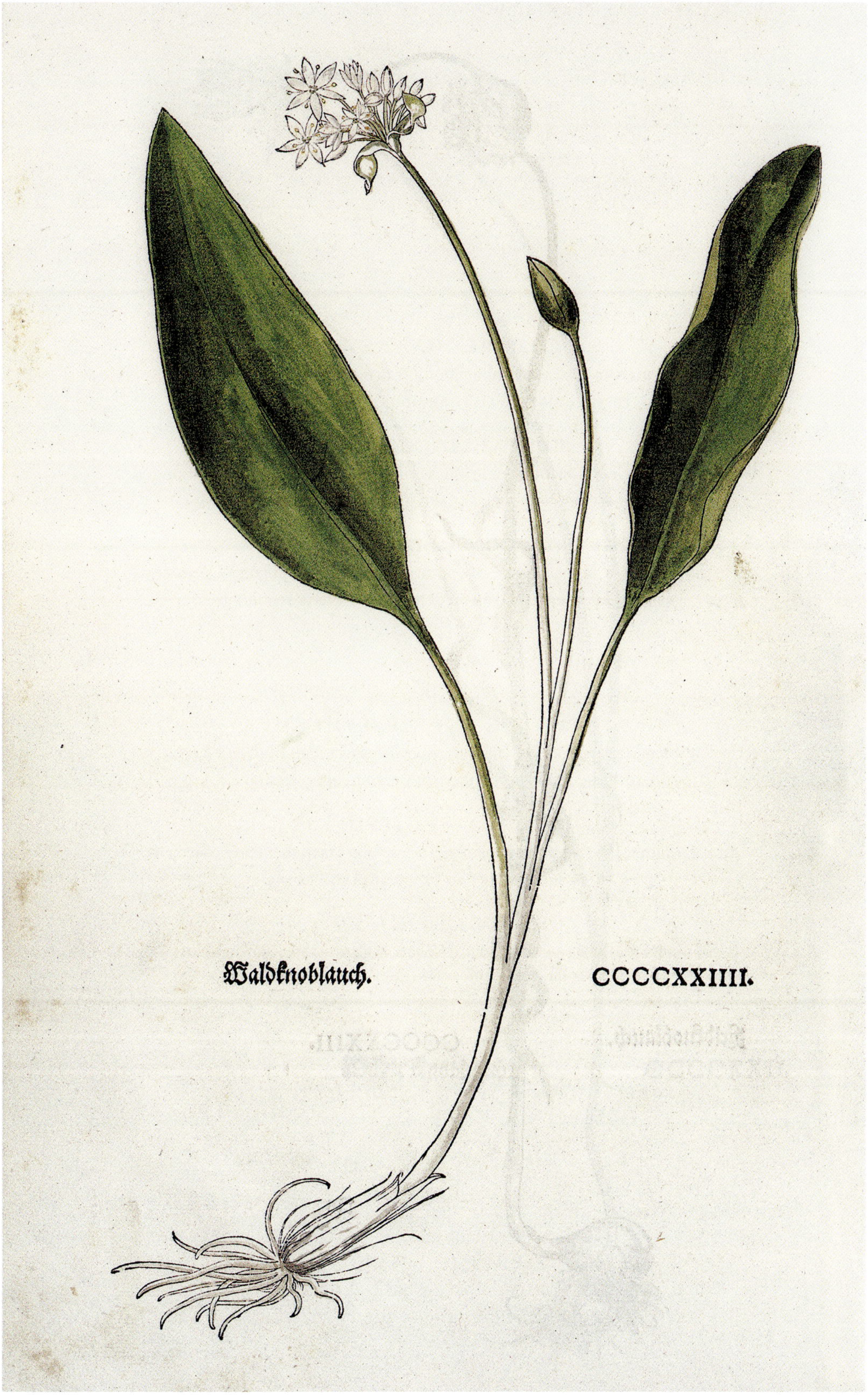
Waldknoblauch.
CCCCXXIIII.

COMFREY (CCCXCVII)

Root, leaves. ❧ External application for bruises, strains and sprains.
Possible side effects contraindicate internal use!

BEINWELL (CCCXCVII)

Wurzel, Blätter. ❧ Äußerlich bei Prellungen, Zerrungen und Verstauchungen.
Wegen möglicher Nebenwirkungen keine innerliche Anwendung.

GRANDE CONSOUDE (CCCXCVII)

Racines, feuilles. ❧ Usage externe pour contusions, claquages et entorses.
Pas d'usage interne en raison de possibles effets secondaires.

PAGE 642

STINGING NETTLE (LVIII F.)

Herbage, leaves, root. ❧ Diuretic, increases evacuation of uric acid;
root used for non-cancerous prostate enlargement.

BRENNNESSEL (LVIII F.)

Kraut, Blätter, Wurzel. ❧ Harntreibend, scheidet vermehrt Harnsäure aus.
Wurzel bei gutartiger Prostatavergrößerung.

GRANDE ORTIE (LVIII)

Partie verte, feuilles, racines. ❧ Diurétique, diminue l'excès d'acide urique.
Racines utilisées pour l'hypertrophie prostatique bénigne.

PAGE 643

IVY (CCXXXVII)

Leaf extract. ❧ Expectorant, spasmolytic, relieves coughs;
use should be restricted to standardized extracts.

EFEU (CCXXXVII)

Extrakt der Blätter. ❧ Auswurffördernd, hustenlindernd, krampflösend.
Verwendung sollten nur standardisierte Extrakte finden.

LIERRE (CCXXXVII)

Extrait des feuilles. ❧ Expectorant, sédatif de la toux, antispasmodique.
Utiliser uniquement les extraits titrés.

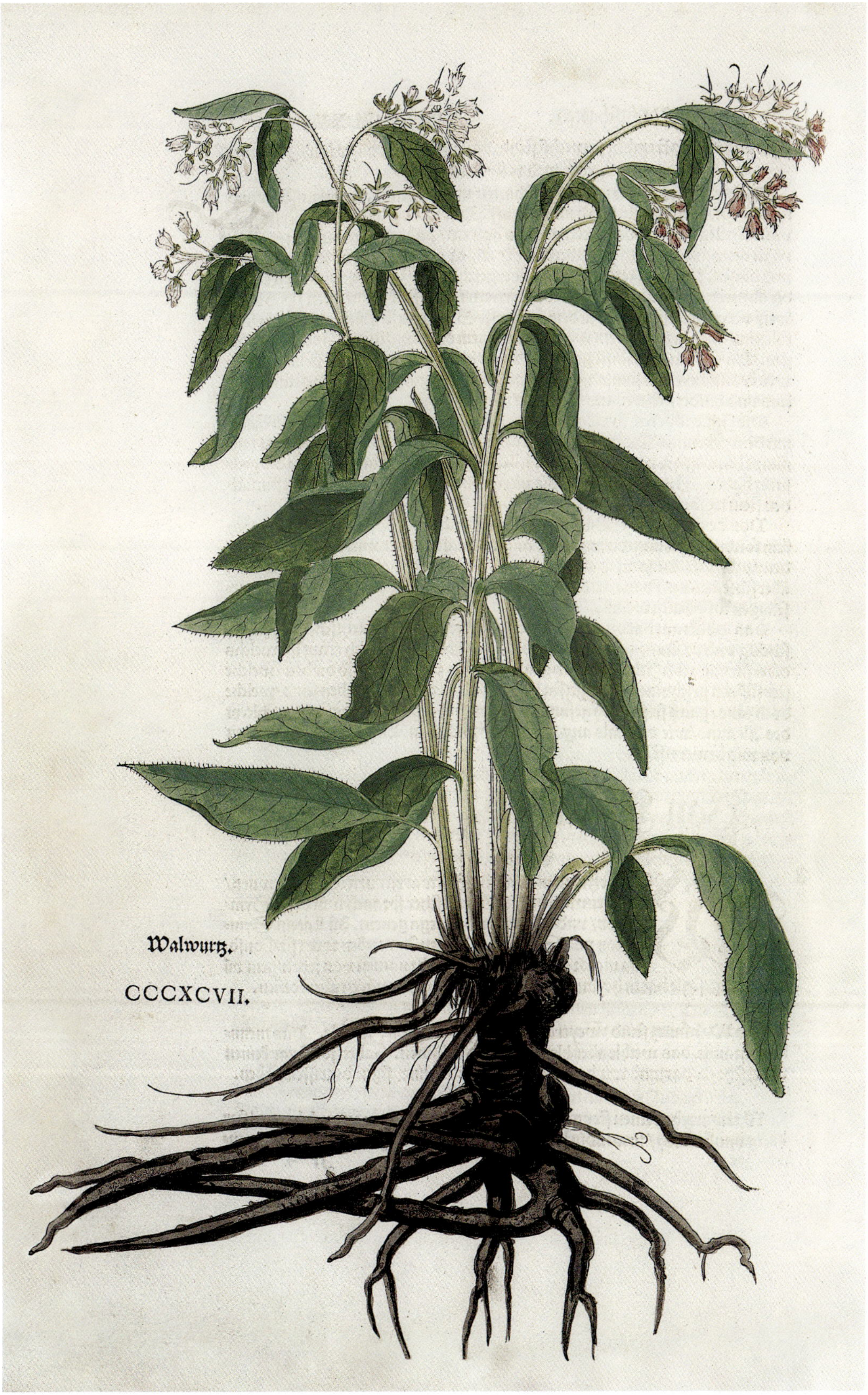
Walwurtz.
CCCXCVII.

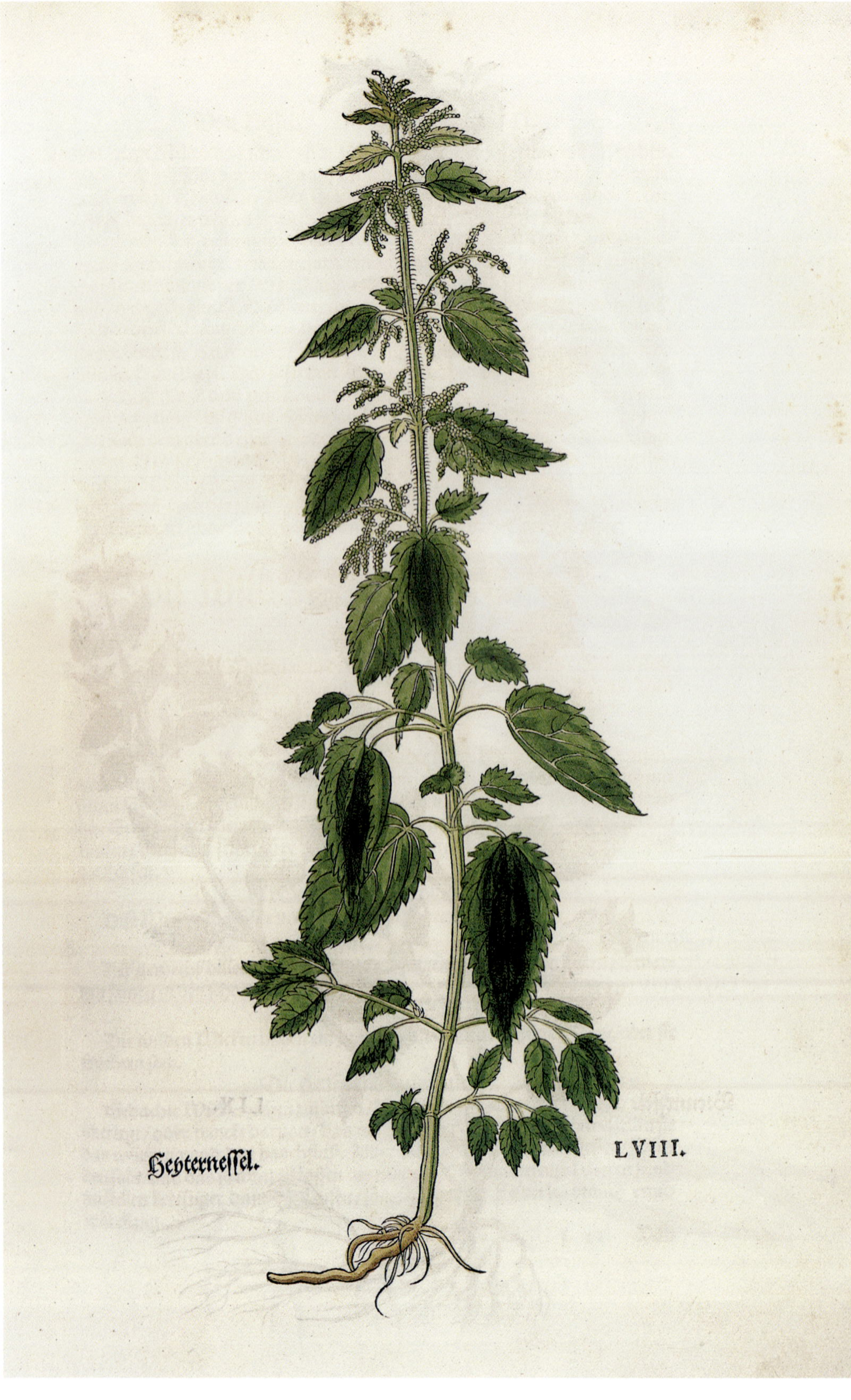
Heyternessel.
LVIII.

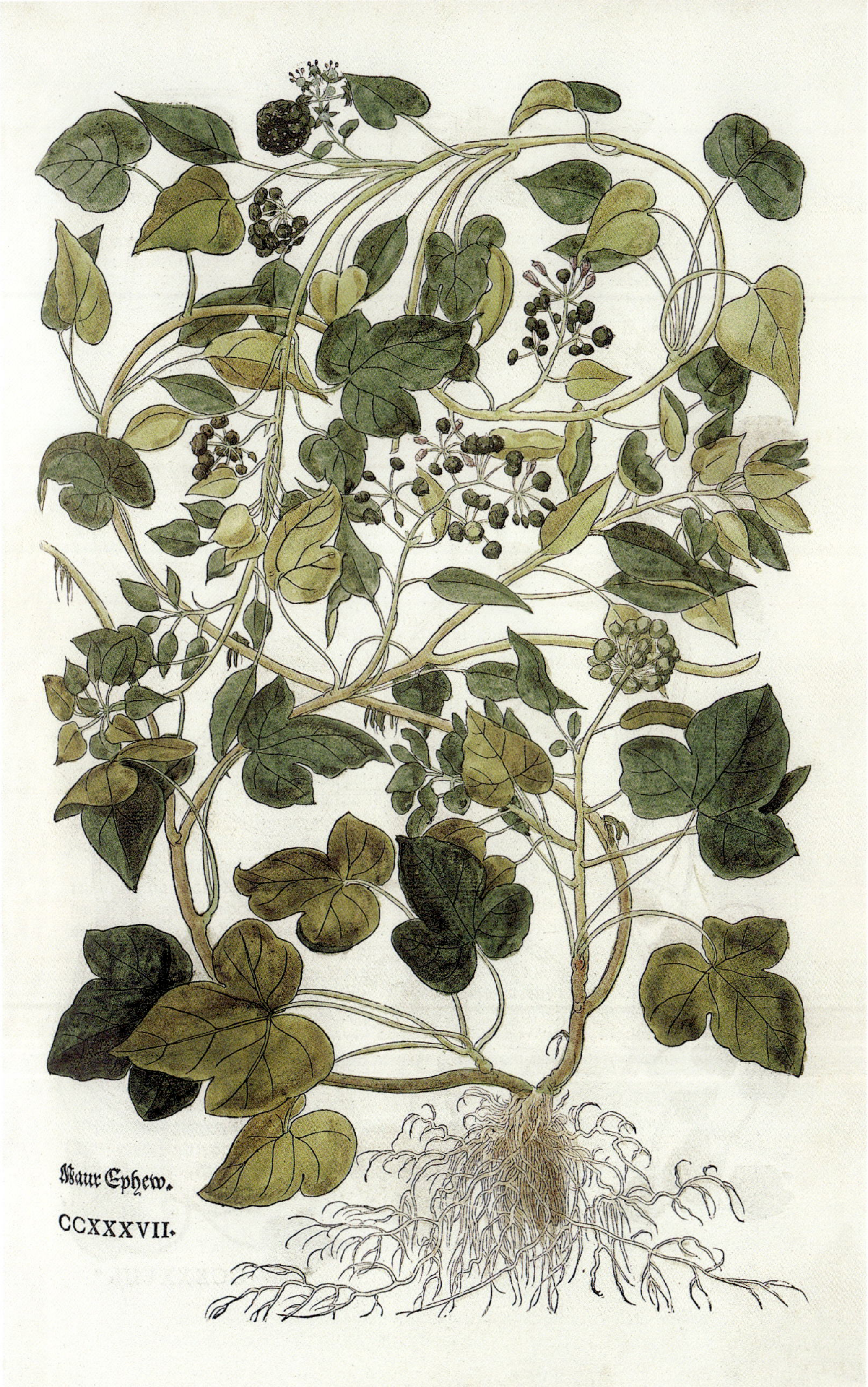

IVY | EFEU | LIERRE

MARSH MALLOW (VII)

Root, leaves. ❧ Irritated throat and coughs; because of high starch content, water-based extracts are prepared without heat.

EIBISCH (VII)

Wurzel, Blätter. ❧ Bei Rachenreizungen, Reizhusten. Wegen des hohen Stärkegehalts müssen wässrige Auszüge kalt angesetzt werden.

GUIMAUVE OFFICINALE (VII)

Racines, feuilles. ❧ Émollient dans les irritations de la gorge et la toux sèche. En raison de son taux d'amidon, utiliser des extraits aqueux à froid.

PAGE 646

OAK (CXXIX)

Bark of twigs. ❧ Externally for skin inflammations, sweaty feet, eczema.

EICHE (CXXIX)

Zweigrinde. ❧ Äußerlich bei entzündlichen Hauterkrankungen, Fußschweiß, Ekzemen.

CHÊNE (CXXIX)

Écorce des rameaux. ❧ Maladies inflammatoires de la peau, transpiration des pieds, eczéma.

PAGE 647

ANGELICA (LXVIII)

Root, essential oil. ❧ Loss of appetite, indigestion, flatulence.

ENGELWURZ (LXVIII)

Wurzel, ätherisches Öl. ❧ Appetitlosigkeit, Verdauungsbeschwerden, Blähungen.

ANGÉLIQUE (LXVIII)

Racines, éther, huile. ❧ Inappétence, troubles digestifs, météorisme.

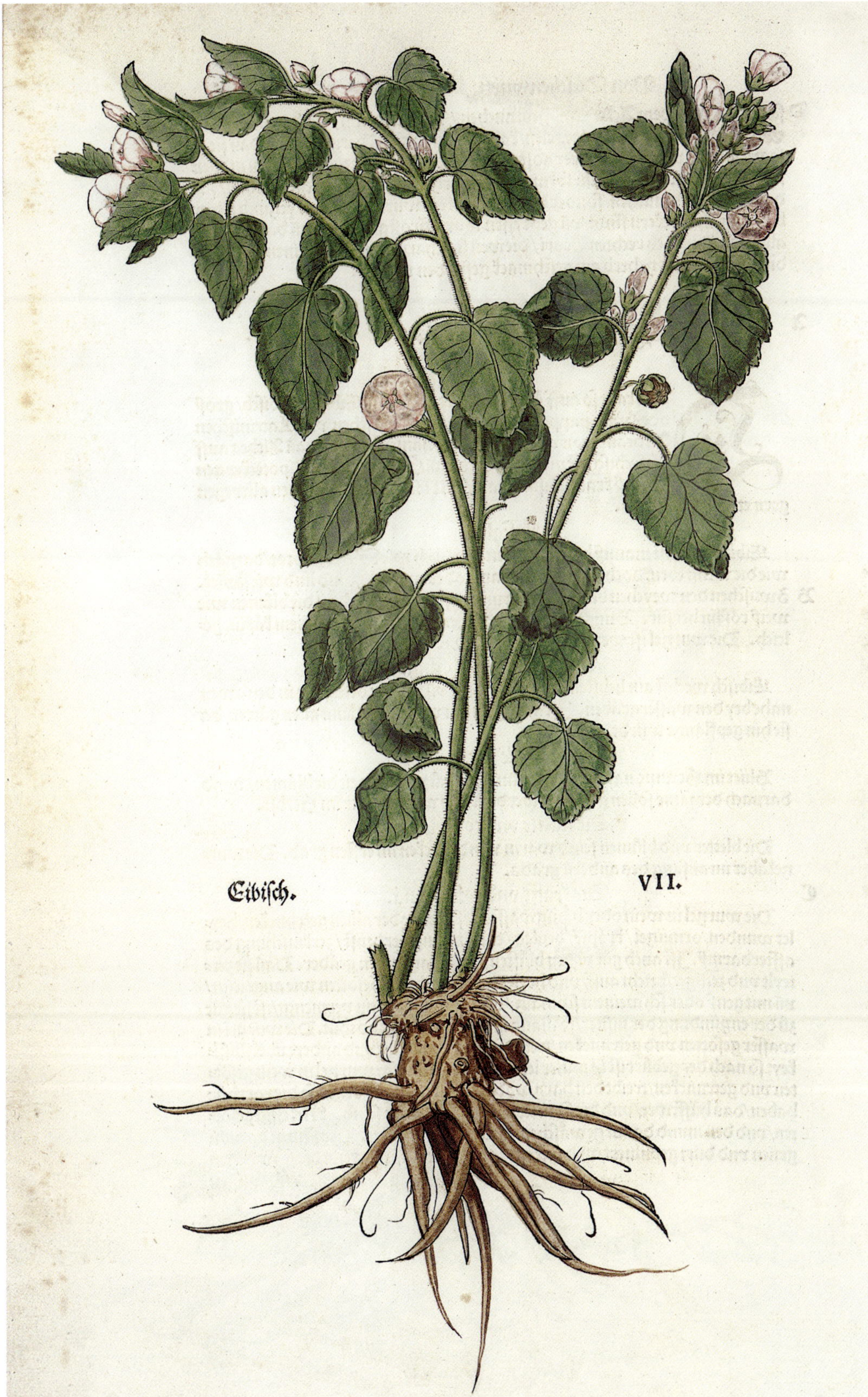
Eibisch.
VII.

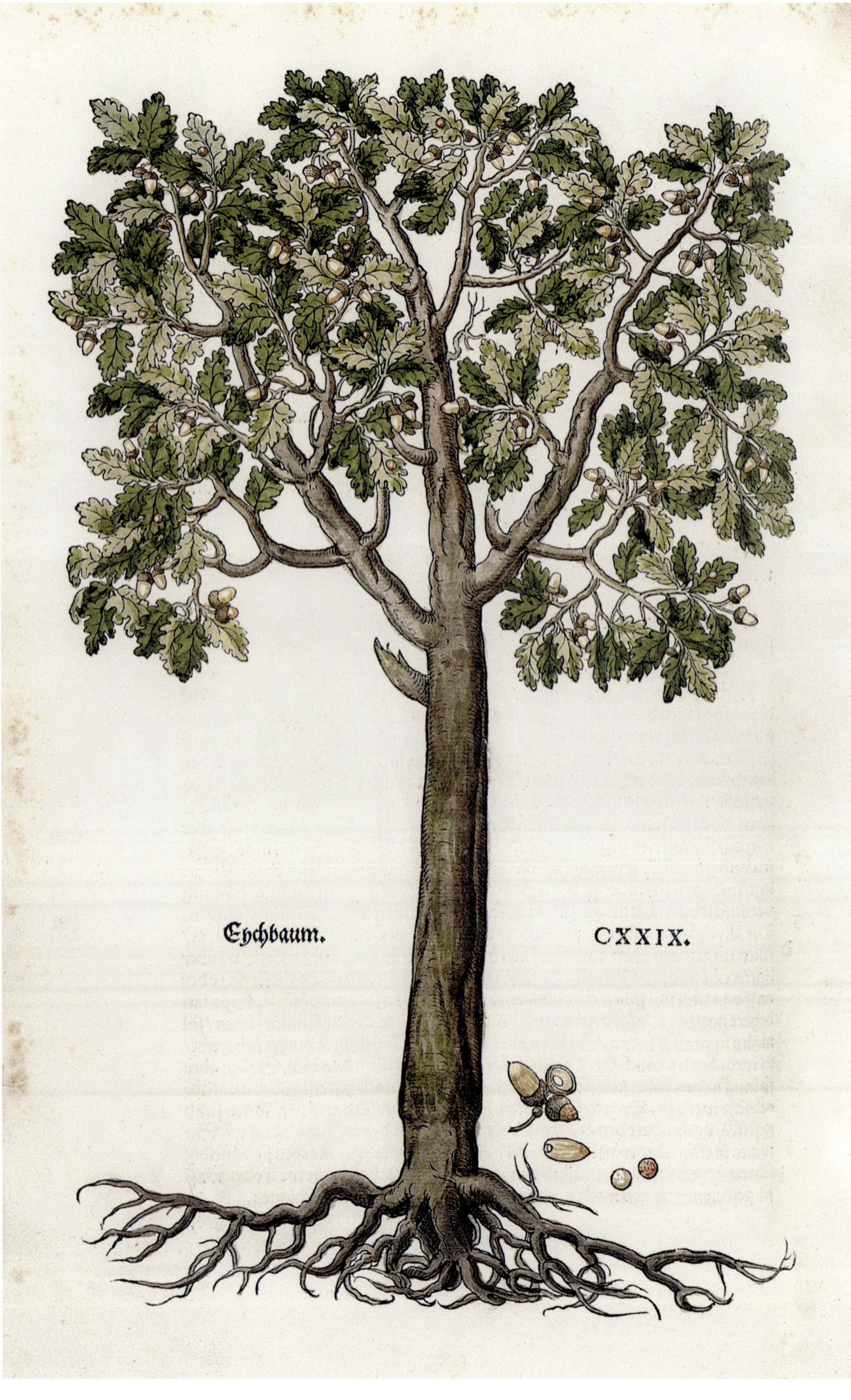
Eychbaum.
CXXIX.

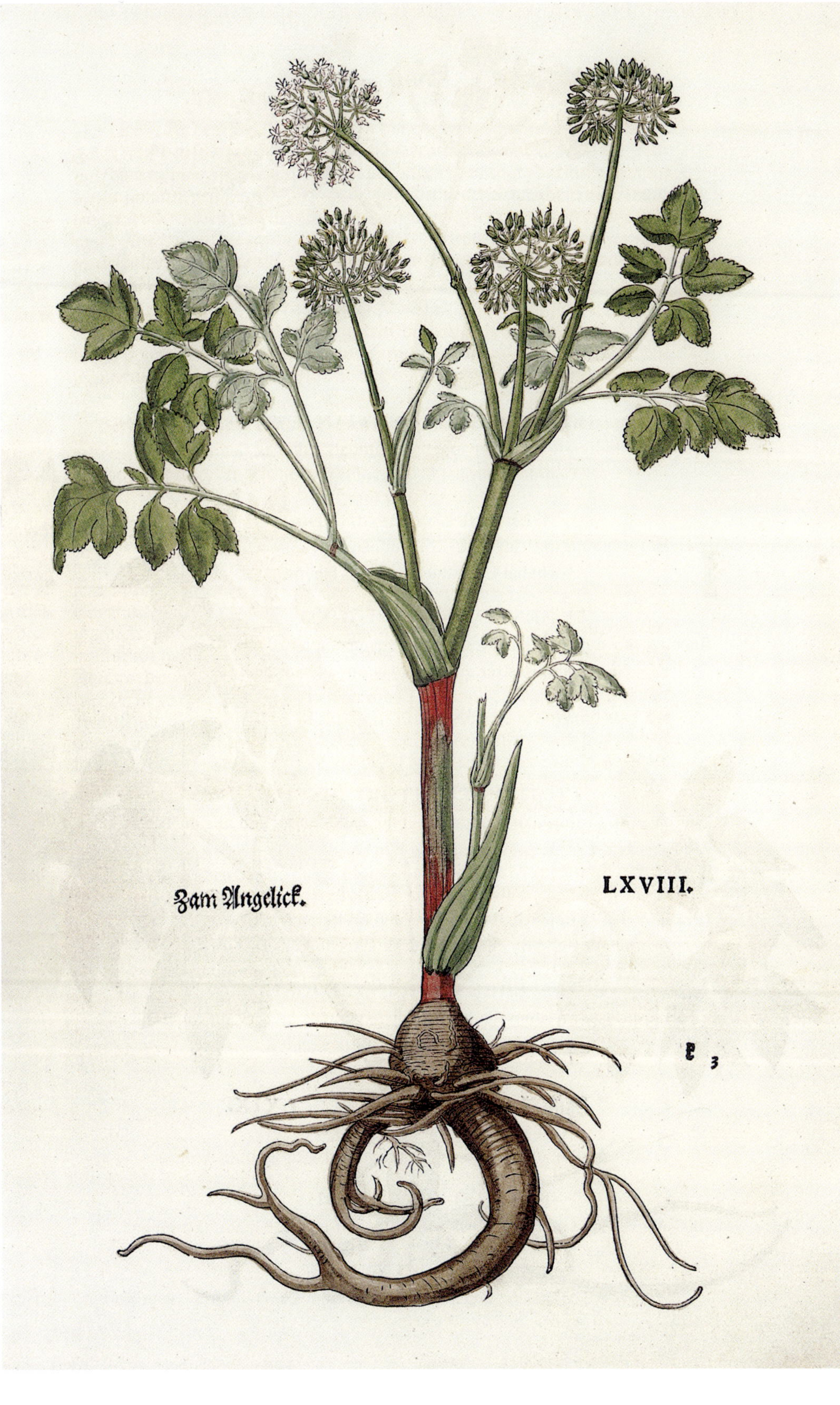
Zam Angelick.
LXVIII.

GREAT YELLOW GENTIAN (CXI)

Root. ❧ Indigestion, loss of appetite, feeling of fullness, flatulence. Counterindicated by an acid stomach.

GELBER ENZIAN (CXI)

Wurzel. ❧ Verdauungsbeschwerden, Appetitlosigkeit, Völlegefühl, Blähungen. Nicht bei Übersäuerung des Magens.

GENTIANE JAUNE (CXI)

Racines. ❧ Douleurs digestives, manque d'appétit, lourdeurs d'estomac. Ne pas administrer en cas d'hyperacidité gastrique.

PAGE 650

COMMON FUMITORY (CXCI)

Herbage. ❧ Cramp-like complaints of the gall bladder and bile ducts, stomach and bowels.

ERDRAUCH (CXCI)

Kraut. ❧ Bei krampfartigen Beschwerden im Bereich der Gallenblase und der Gallenwege sowie des Magens und des Darms.

FUMETERRE OFFICINALE (CXCI)

Partie verte. ❧ Spasmes douloureux de la vésicule biliaire, du canal cholédoque, des voies gastro-intestinales.

PAGE 651

FENNEL (CCLXXXIII)

Fruit, essential oil. ❧ Expectorant, spasmolytic, carminative.

FENCHEL (CCLXXXIII)

Früchte, ätherisches Öl. ❧ Auswurffördernd, entkrampfend, blähungstreibend.

FENOUIL (CCLXXXIII)

Fruits, éther, huile. ❧ Affections des voies digestives (coliques, météorisme), expectorant.

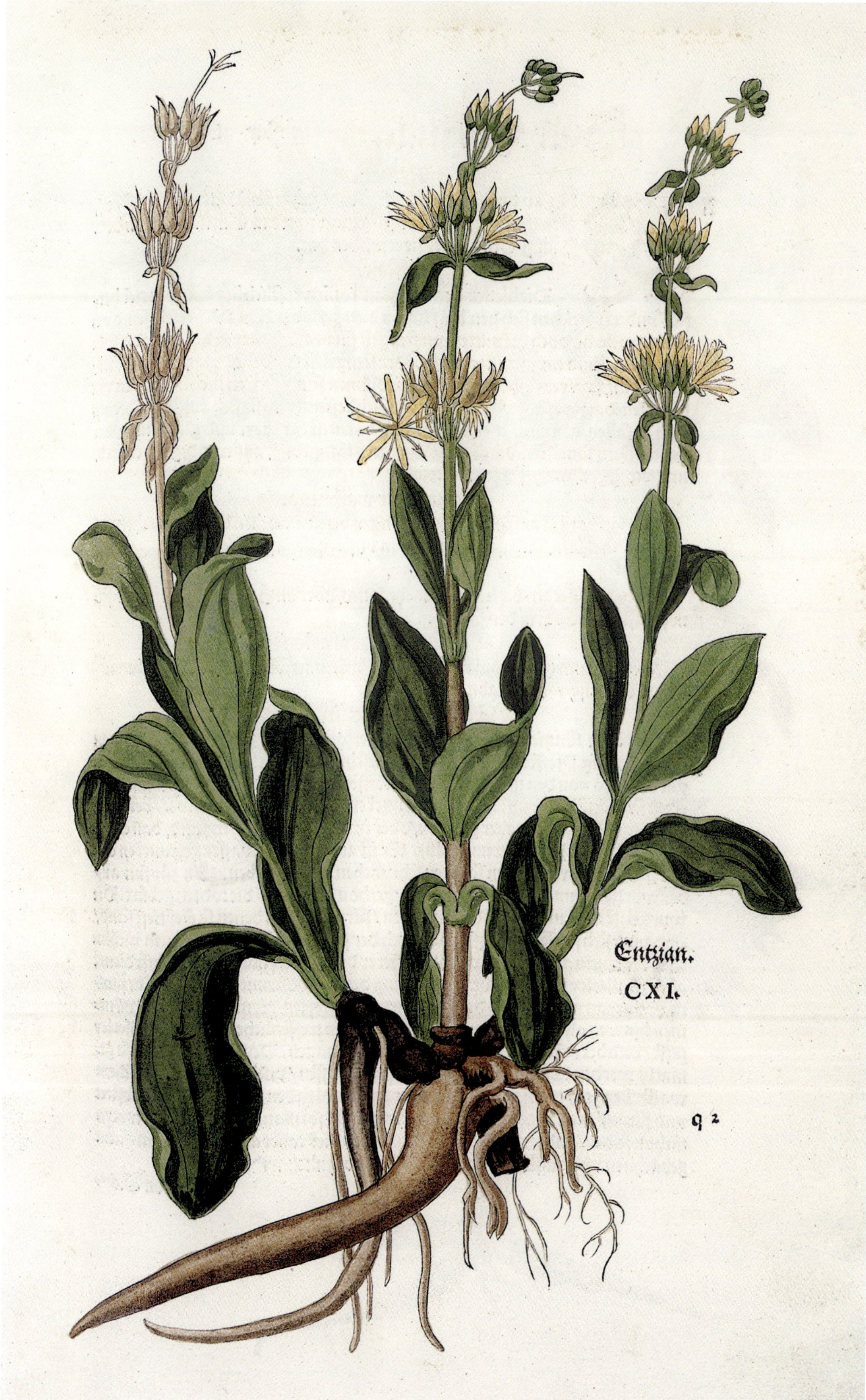
Entzian.
CXI.
q 2

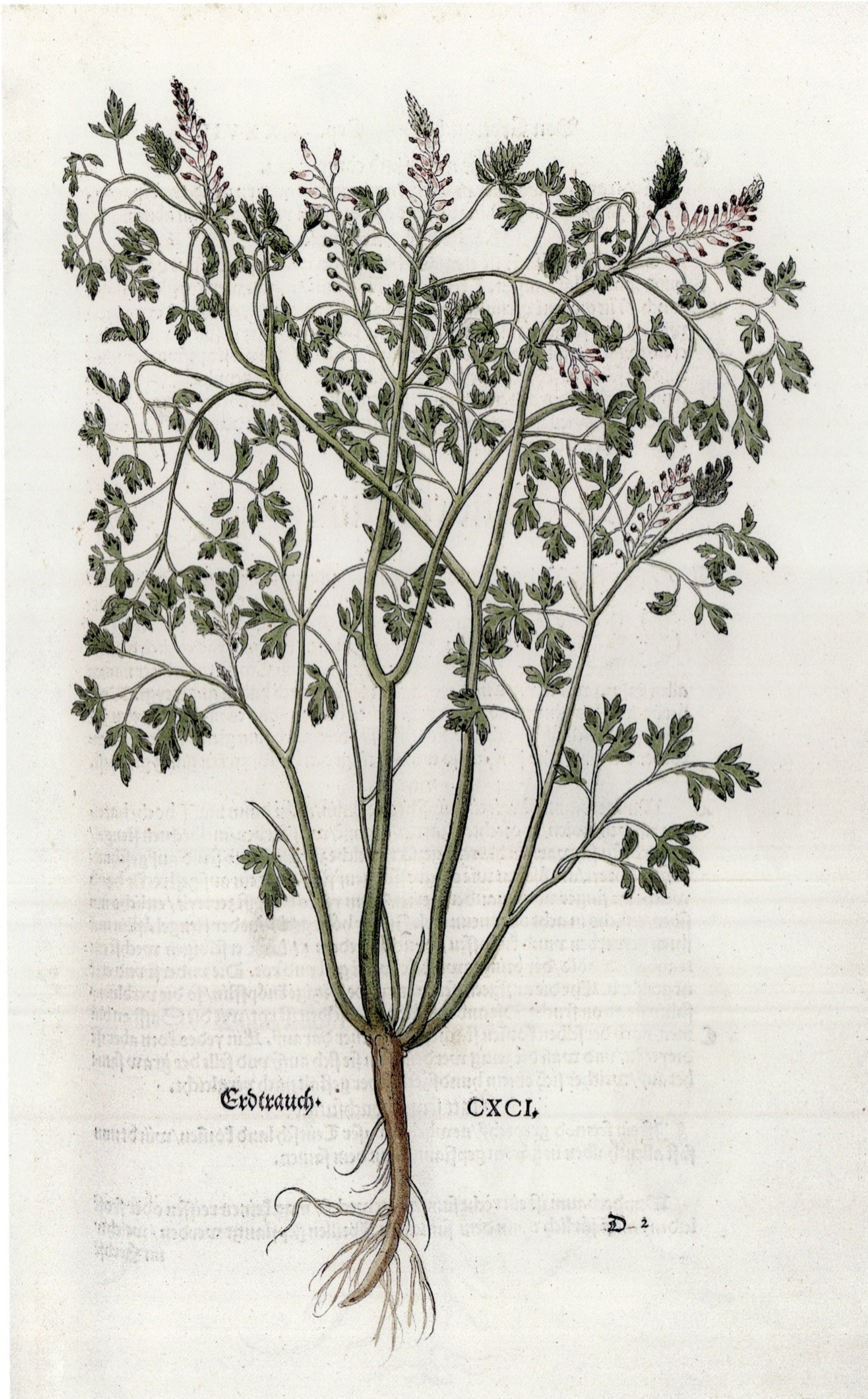
Erdtrauch.
CXCI.
D 2

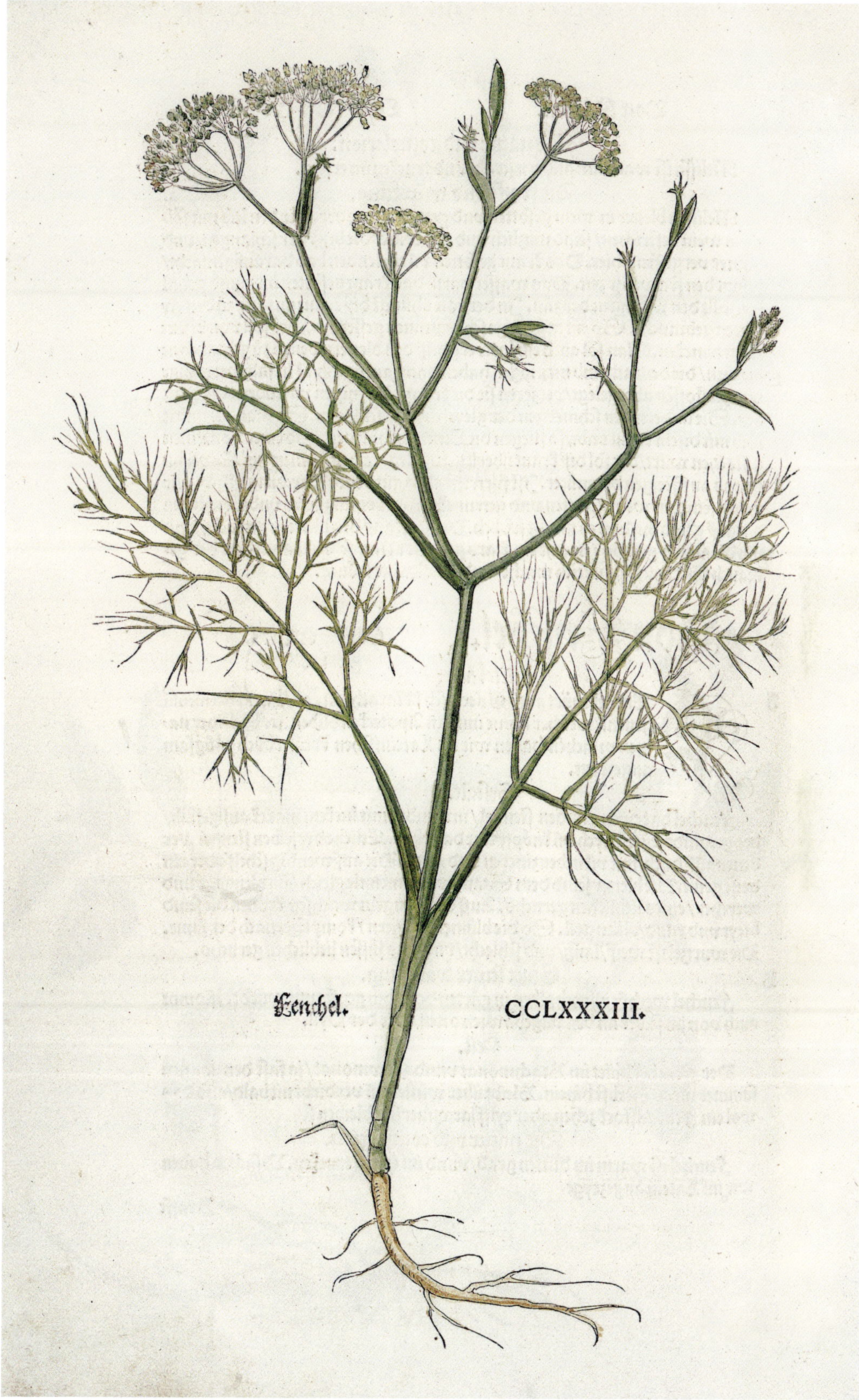
Fenchel.
CCLXXXIII.

FOXGLOVE (CCCCCXIII)

Isolated and, in part, chemically altered substances. ❧ For heart disease only by prescription and under supervision of a physician. Plant is highly toxic!

FINGERHUT (CCCCCXIII)

Isolierte und teilweise chemisch abgewandelte Inhaltsstoffe. ❧ Bei Herzerkrankungen nur nach Anweisung und unter Aufsicht des Arztes anzuwenden. Pflanze ist hochgiftig!

DIGITALE (CCCCCXIII)

Composants isolés, en partie transformés chimiquement. ❧ Maladies cardiaques – à n'administrer que selon les prescriptions du médecin et sous sa surveillance.

PAGE 654

FLEAWORT (CCCCCIX)

Seeds. ❧ Ballast-based laxative for constipation or irritated bowels. Simultaneous intake of liquid essential!

FLOHSAMEN (CCCCCIX)

Samen. ❧ Abführmittel auf Ballaststoffbasis bei Verstopfung oder Reizdarm. Gleichzeitige Flüssigkeitsaufnahme wichtig!

HERBE-AUX-PUCES (CCCCCIX)

Graines. ❧ Laxatif sur base fibreuse en cas de constipation ou d'irritation intestinale. Boire beaucoup d'eau en même temps !

PAGE 655

LADY'S MANTLE (CCCXLVIII)

Herbage. ❧ Light diarrhoea; traditionally for female disorders.

FRAUENMANTEL (CCCXLVIII)

Kraut. ❧ Bei leichtem Durchfall, traditionell bei Frauenkrankheiten.

ALCHÉMILLE (CCCXLVIII)

Partie verte. ❧ Diarrhées bénignes et usage traditionnel dans les maladies particulières à la femme.

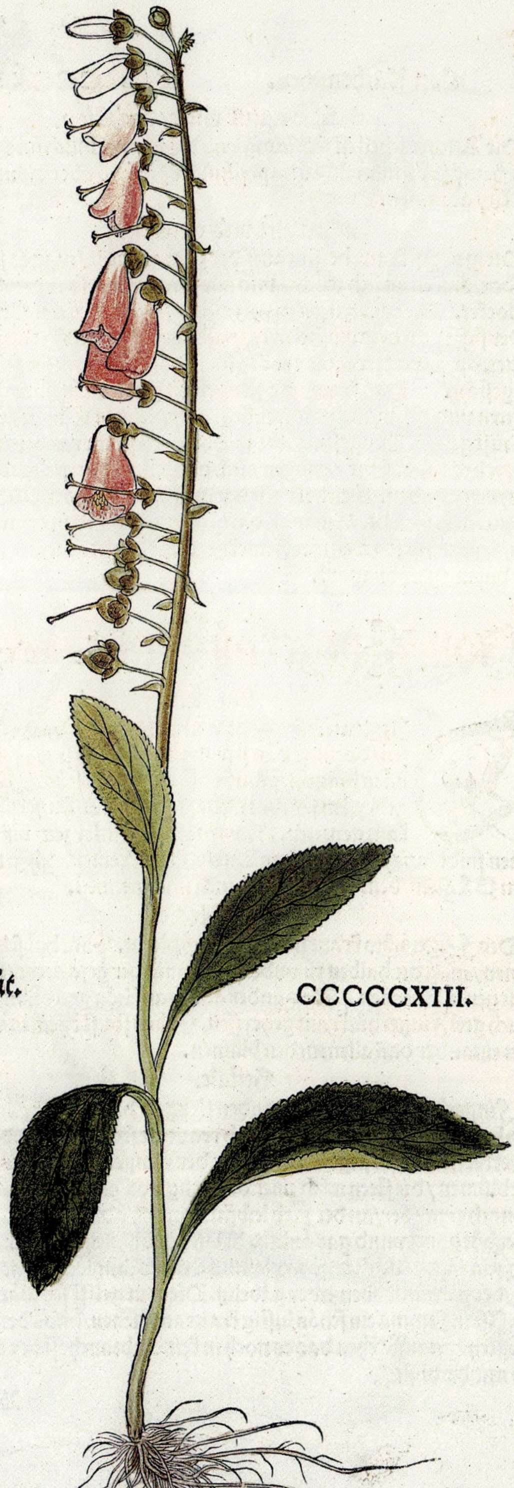

Brauner Fingerhůt. CCCCCXIII.

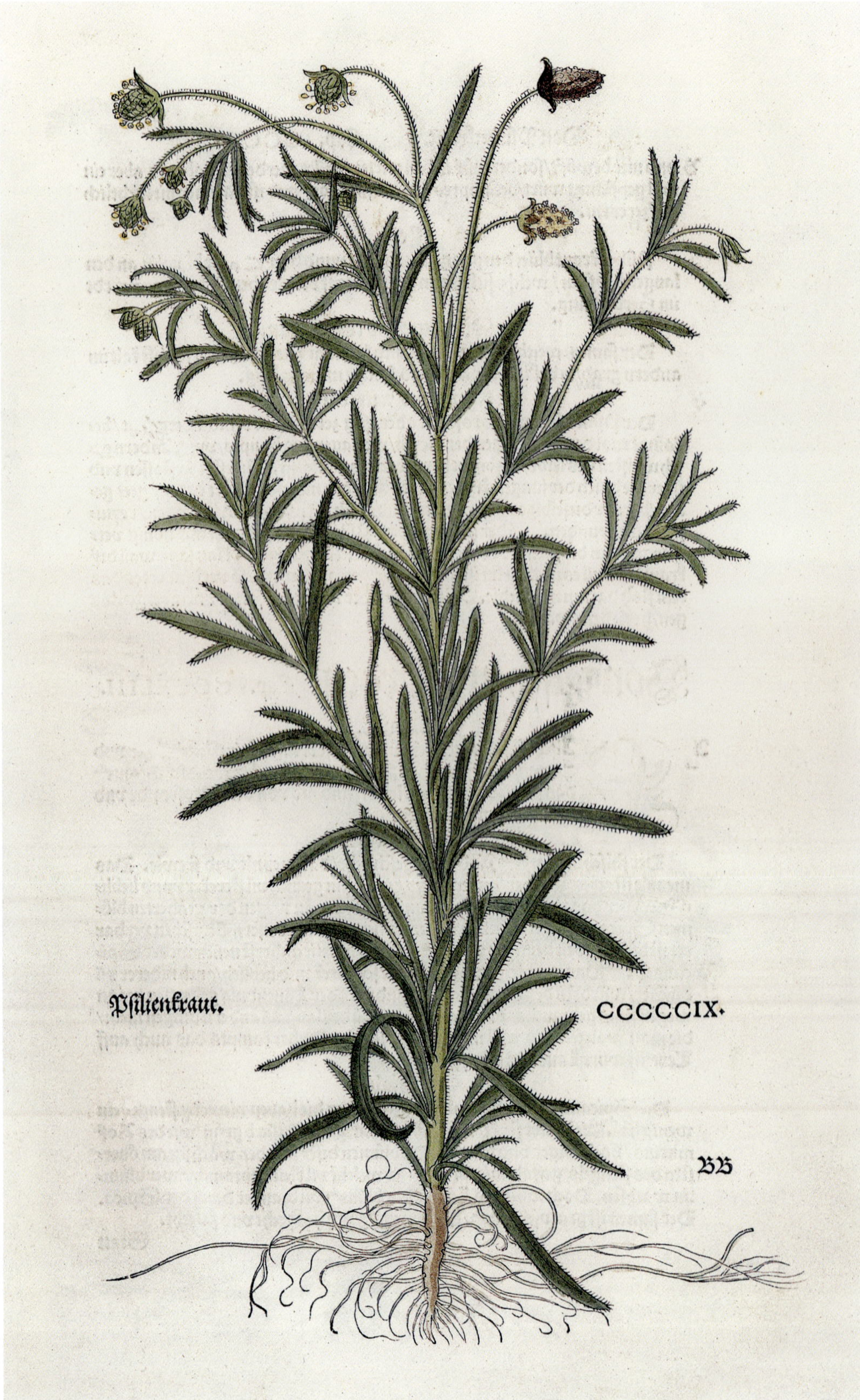
Psilienkraut.
CCCCCIX.
BB

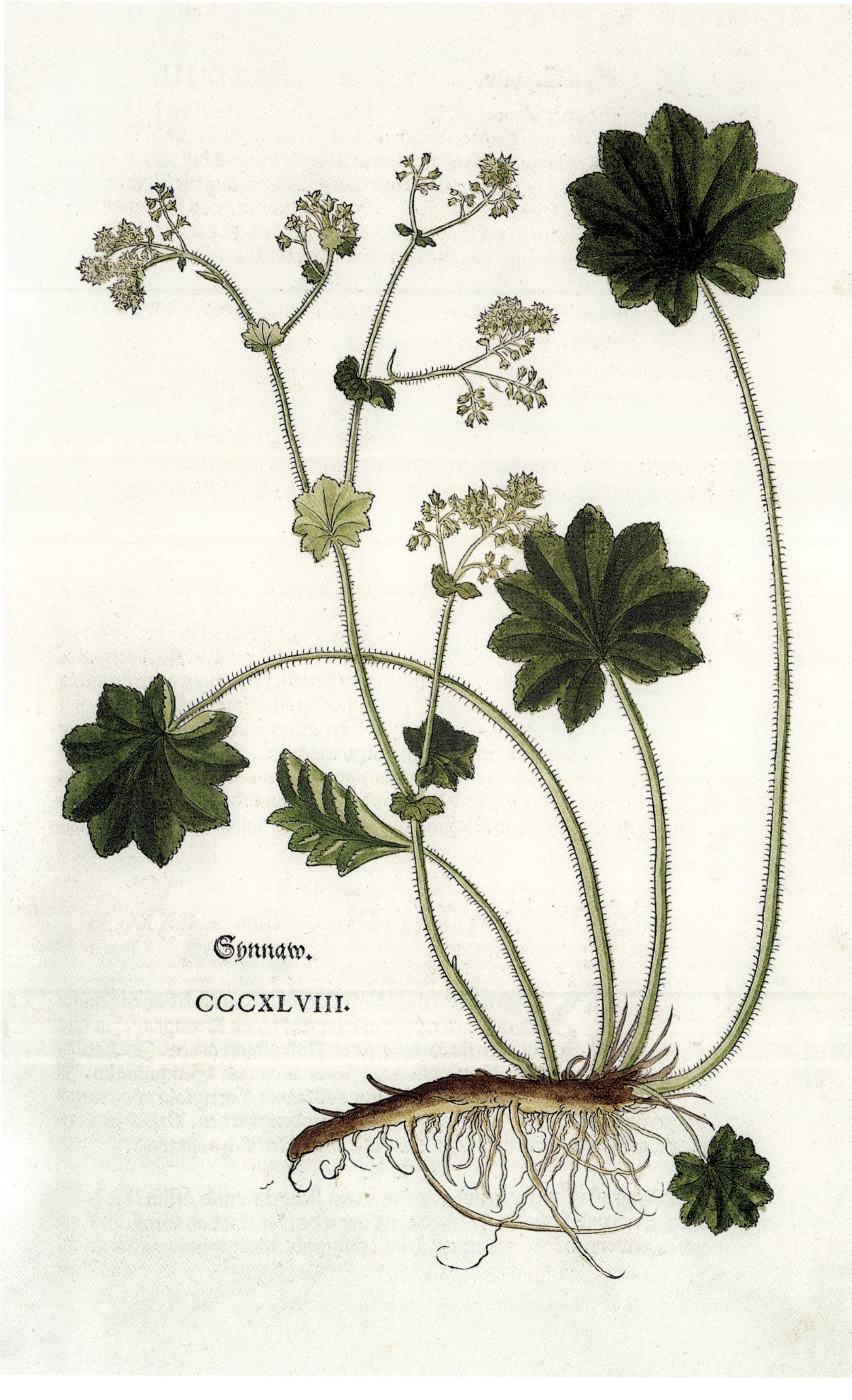
Synnaw.
CCCXLVIII.

SPINY RESTHARROW (XXXIIII)

Root. ❧ Diuretic, for flushing bladder infections and prevention of kidney stones. Although decreasing effectiveness limits application to only a few days, treatment may be resumed after a pause.

HAUHECHEL (XXXIIII)

Wurzel. ❧ Harntreibend, zur Durchspülung bei Blasenentzündungen und zur Vorbeugung von Nierensteinen. Anwendung nur wenige Tage wegen nachlassender Wirksamkeit. Nach Pause kann die Anwendung fortgesetzt werden.

BUGRANE ÉPINEUSE (XXXIIII)

Racines. ❧ Diurétique, lavements pour les infections urinaires et la prévention des calculs rénaux. Épuisement de l'effet au bout de quelques jours. Reprendre le traitement après interruption.

PAGE 658

MEADOW SAFFRON (CCI)

Isolated substances. ❧ Acute attacks of gout. Owing to high toxicity, only with doctor's prescription!

HERBSTZEITLOSE (CCI)

Isolierte Inhaltsstoffe. ❧ Zur Behandlung des akuten Gichtanfalls. Wegen der hohen Giftigkeit nur auf Verordnung des Arztes.

COLCHIQUE D'AUTOMNE (CCI)

Composants isolés. ❧ Crise de goutte aiguë. Uniquement sur ordonnance médicale en raison de sa haute toxicité.

PAGE 659

SHEPHERD'S PURSE (CCCXLVII)

Herbage. ❧ Blood coagulant for nosebleeds and excessive menstrual flow.

HIRTENTÄSCHEL (CCCXLVII)

Kraut. ❧ Blutungsstillend bei Nasenbluten und übermäßiger Monatsblutung.

CAPSELLE BOURSE-À-PASTEUR (CCCXLVII)

Partie verte. ❧ Hémostatique dans les hémorragies nasales et la ménorragie.

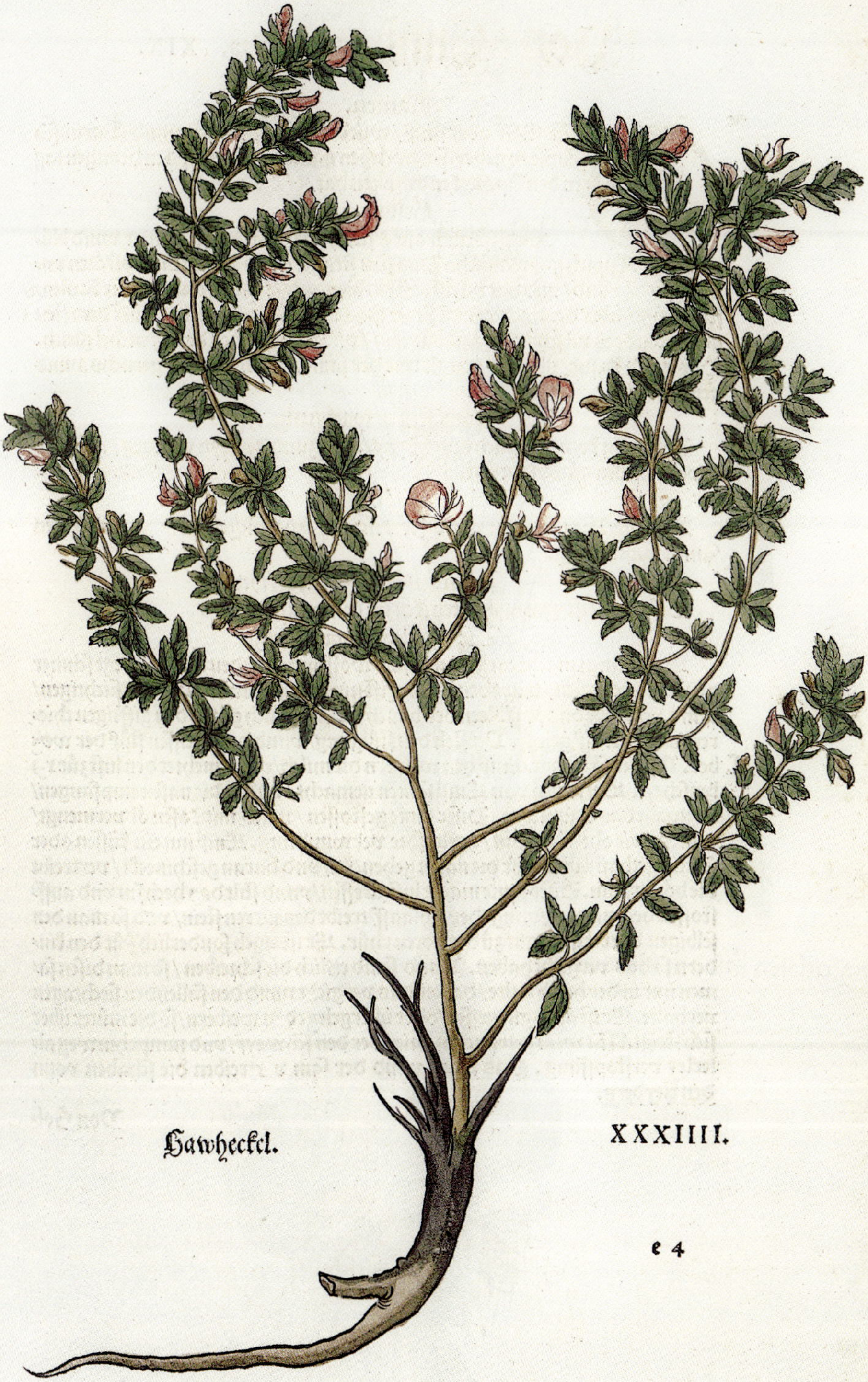

Hawheckel.

XXXIIII.

e 4

SPINY RESTHARROW | HAUHECHEL | BUGRANE ÉPINEUSE

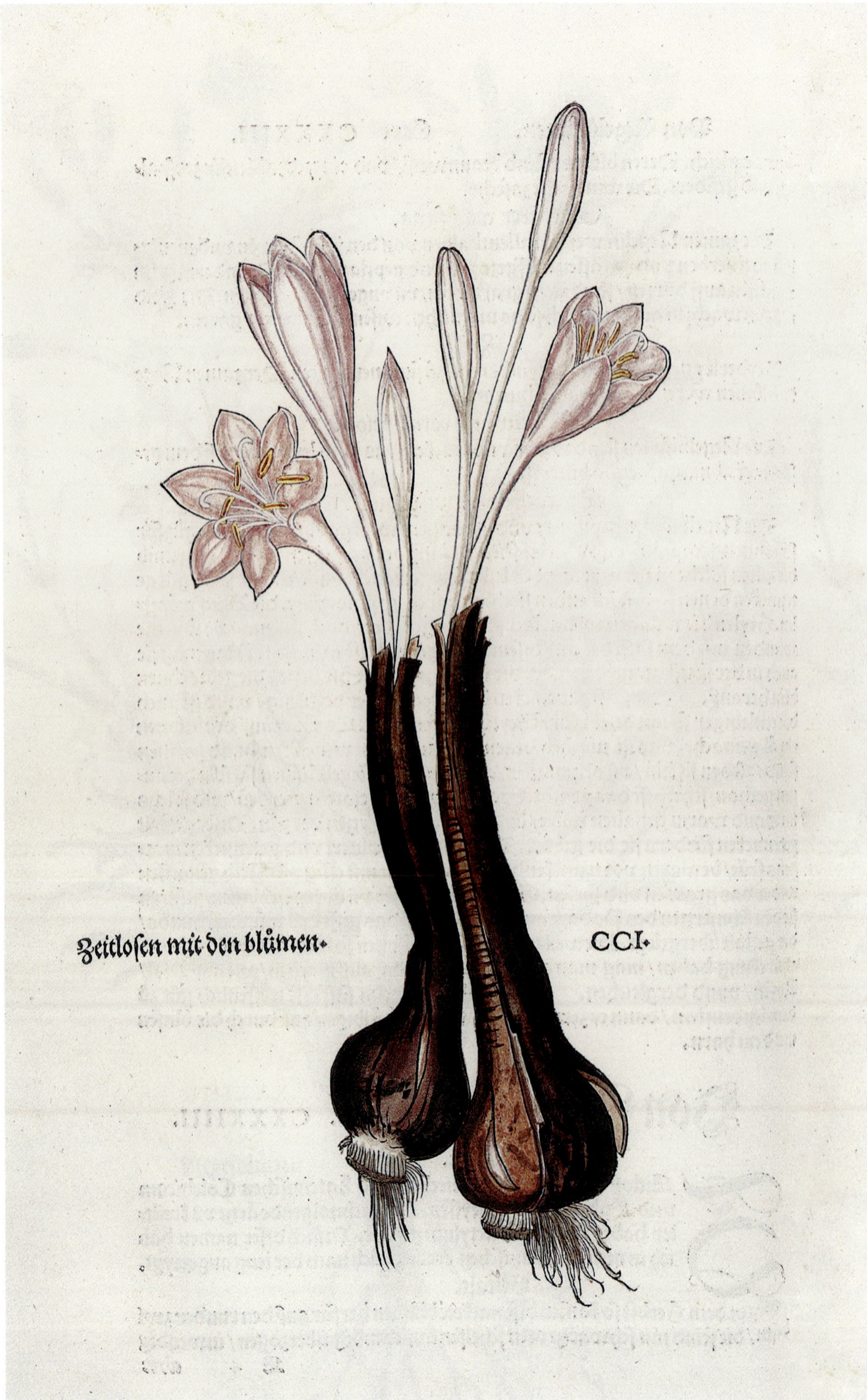
Zeitlosen mit den blůmen.
CCI.

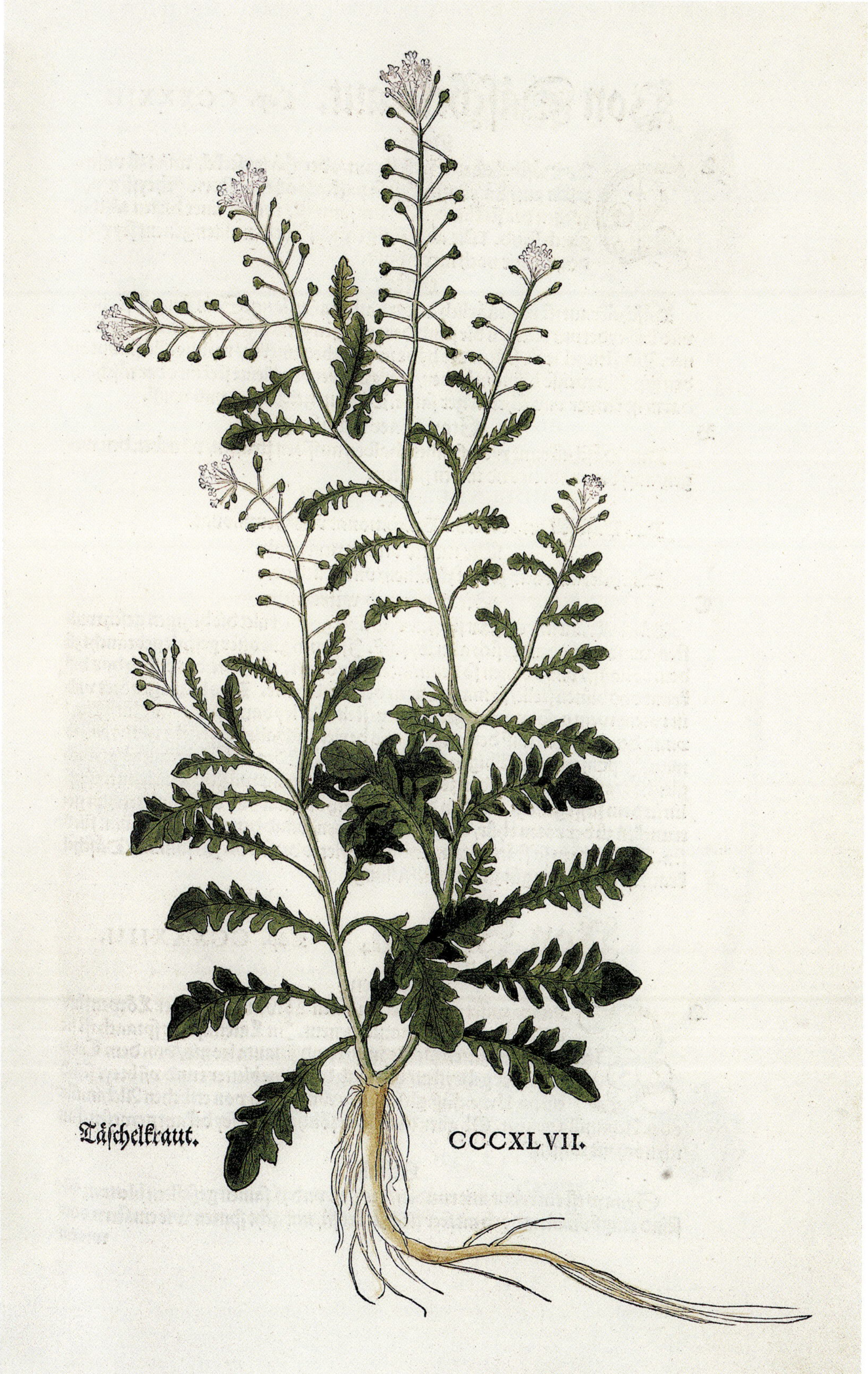
Täschelkraut.
CCCXLVII.

BLACK ELDER (XXXVI)

Flowers. ❧ Sudorific, used for colds.

HOLUNDER (XXXVI)

Blüten. ❧ Bei Erkältungskrankheiten, schweißtreibend.

SUREAU NOIR (XXXVI)

Fleurs. ❧ Contre les refroidissements, sudorifique.

PAGE 662

COMMON HOP (XCII)

Cones and cone scales, extract. ❧ Used as tea to stimulate appetite (bitter constituents!), as extract to sedate and regulate sleeping disorders.

HOPFEN (XCII)

Hopfenzapfen, Drüsenschuppen, Extrakt. ❧ Tee zur Appetitanregung (Bitterstoffe!), Extrakte zur Beruhigung und bei Schlafstörungen.

HOUBLON (XCII)

Cônes, glandes des écailles, extraits. ❧ Infusion pour l'inappétence (substances amères !), extraits comme calmant et somnifère.

PAGE 663

COLTSFOOT (LXXVI)

Leaves. ❧ Bronchial disorders, coughs, hoarseness, inflamed throat. Often confused with Butterbur (see below). Not to be used for an extended period!

HUFLATTICH (LXXVI)

Blätter. ❧ Bronchialerkrankungen, Husten, Heiserkeit, Rachenentzündungen. Oftmals mit Pestwurz (s. d.) verwechselt. Keine Langzeitanwendung.

PAS-D'ÂNE (LXXVI)

Feuilles. ❧ Affections des bronches, toux, enrouement, pharyngite. Souvent confondu avec le chapeau du diable (voir précédemment). Pas d'utilisation prolongée.

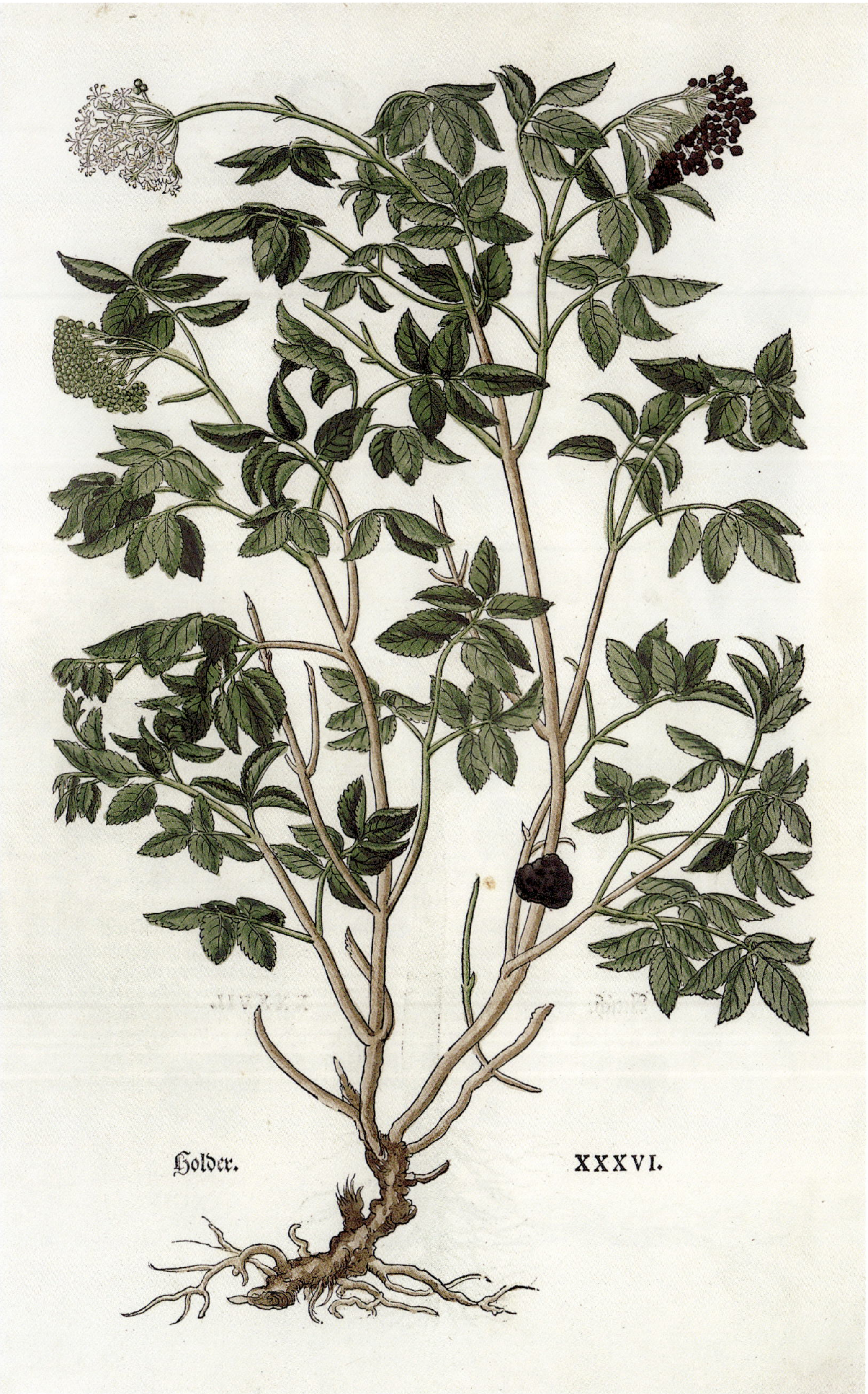
Holder.
XXXVI.

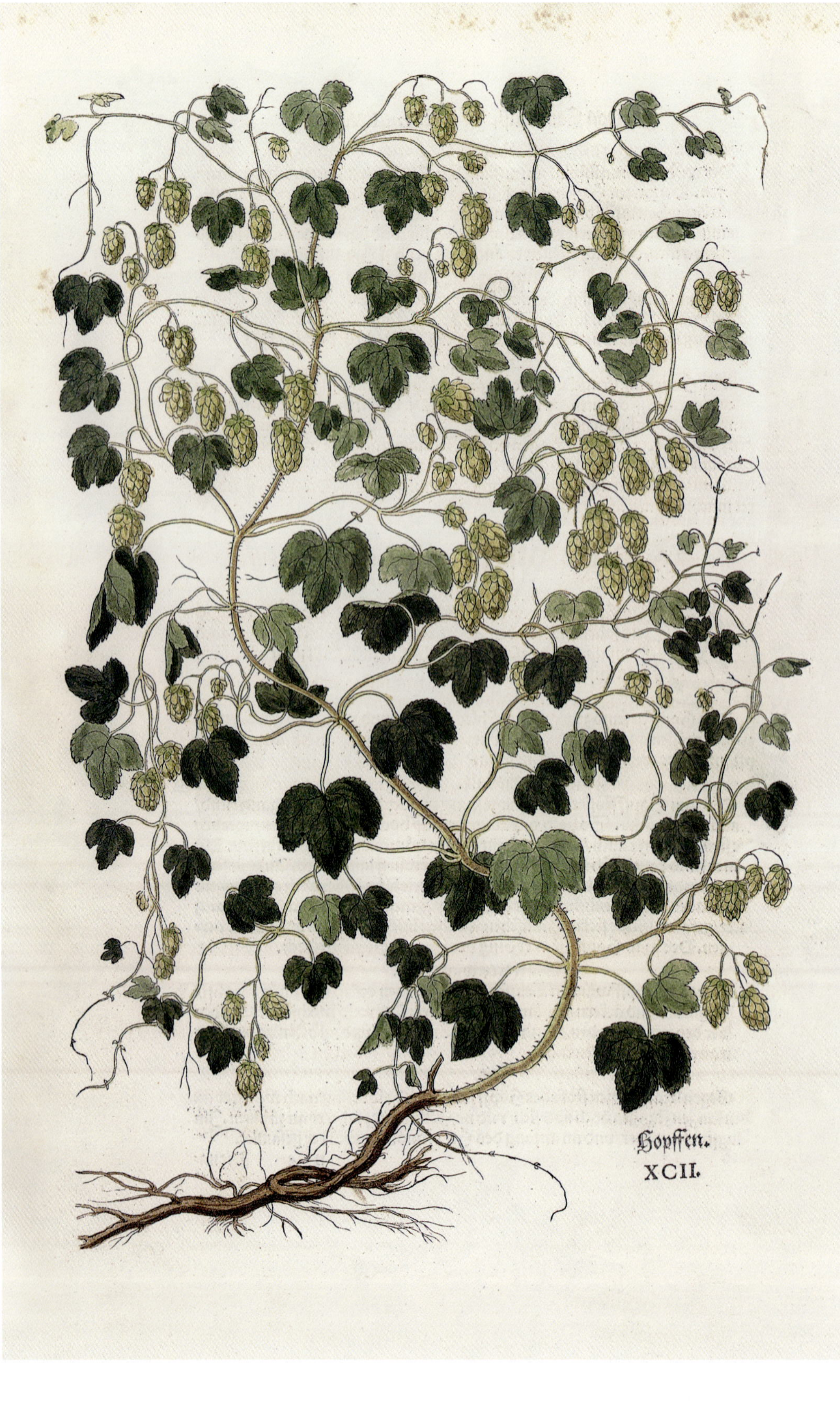
Hopffen.
XCII.

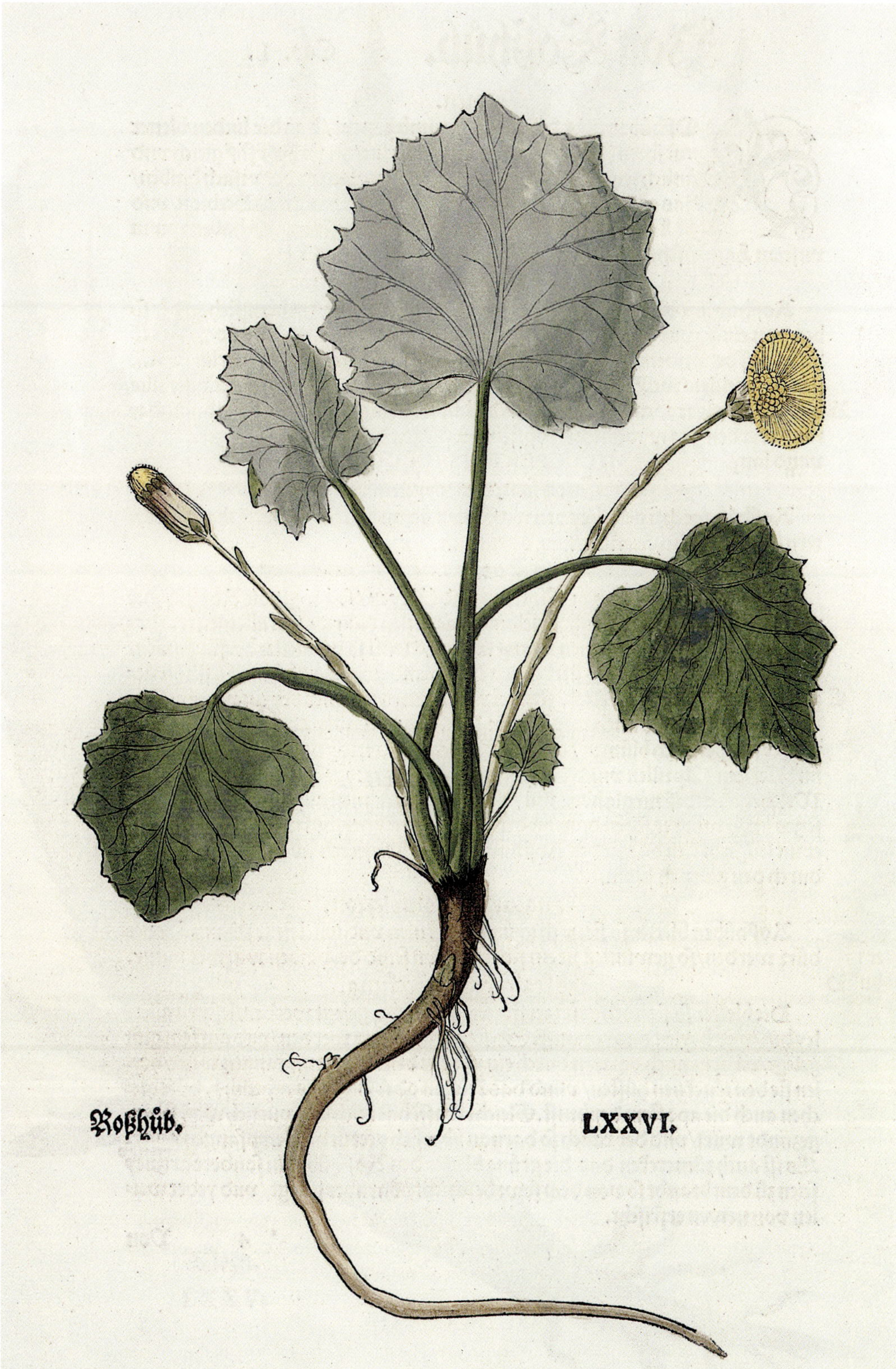
Roßhüb.
LXXVI.

ST. JOHN'S WORT (CCCCLXXVI)

Herbage, extract, oil-based extract. ❧ For depression, anxiety, nervousness (long-term treatment!). Oil applied externally for wounds, burns and skin care.

JOHANNISKRAUT (CCCCLXXVI)

Kraut, Extrakt, öliger Auszug. ❧ Depressive Verstimmung, Angst, nervöse Unruhe (Langzeitanwendung!). Öl äußerlich zur Nachbehandlung von Verletzungen und Verbrennungen, Hautpflege.

MILLEPERTUIS (CCCCLXXVI)

Partie verte, extrait, huile. ❧ États dépressifs, peur, nervosité (emploi prolongé !). L'huile est utilisée comme vulnéraire dans le traitement consécutif des blessures, brûlures et soins de la peau.

PAGE 666

CHAMOMILE (XIII)

Blossoms, extract. ❧ As herbal bath, rinses, inhalations for infections of the mucous membranes; promotes healing of wounds. Internally used as a weak spasmolytic for stomach and bowels, or irritations and inflammations of the stomach lining.

KAMILLE (XIII)

Blüten, Extrakt. ❧ In Form von Bädern, Spülungen, Inhalationen bei Schleimhautentzündungen, zur Wundheilung. Innerlich leicht krampflösend im Magen-Darm-Bereich sowie bei Reizungen und Entzündungen der Magenschleimhaut.

CAMOMILLE (XIII)

Fleurs, extrait. ❧ Sous forme de bains, de lavements, d'inhalations contre les inflammations des muqueuses, et de compresses sur les plaies. Par voie interne, légèrement antispasmodique dans la région gastro-intestinale ainsi que dans les irritations et les inflammations des muqueuses stomacales.

PAGE 667

GARLIC (CCCCXXI)

Bulb, extract. ❧ Reduces high fat content in blood, prevents hardening of arteries (arteriosclerosis); carminative, for intestinal fermentation processes. Sufficient dosage is important!

KNOBLAUCH (CCCCXXI)

Zwiebeln, Extrakt. ❧ Bei erhöhten Blutfettwerten, zur Vorbeugung von Gefäßveränderungen („Arteriosklerose"), blähungstreibend, bei Gärungsprozessen im Darm. Auf ausreichende Dosierung ist zu achten.

AIL (CCCCXXI)

Caïeux, extrait. ❧ Prévention de l'artériosclérose, excès de cholestérol, ballonnements et fermentations intestinales. Veiller à une posologie suffisante.

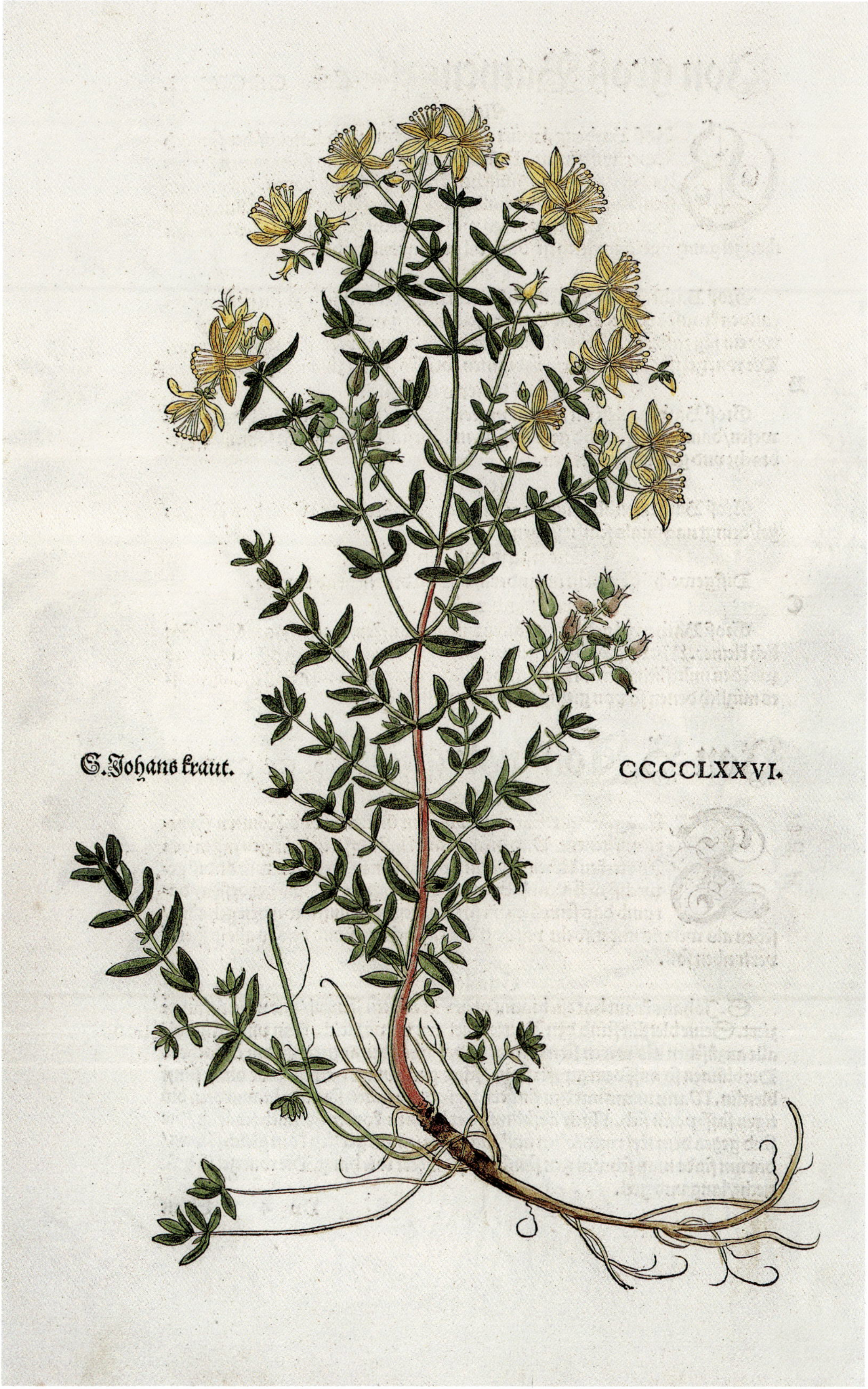
S. Johans kraut.
CCCCLXXVI.

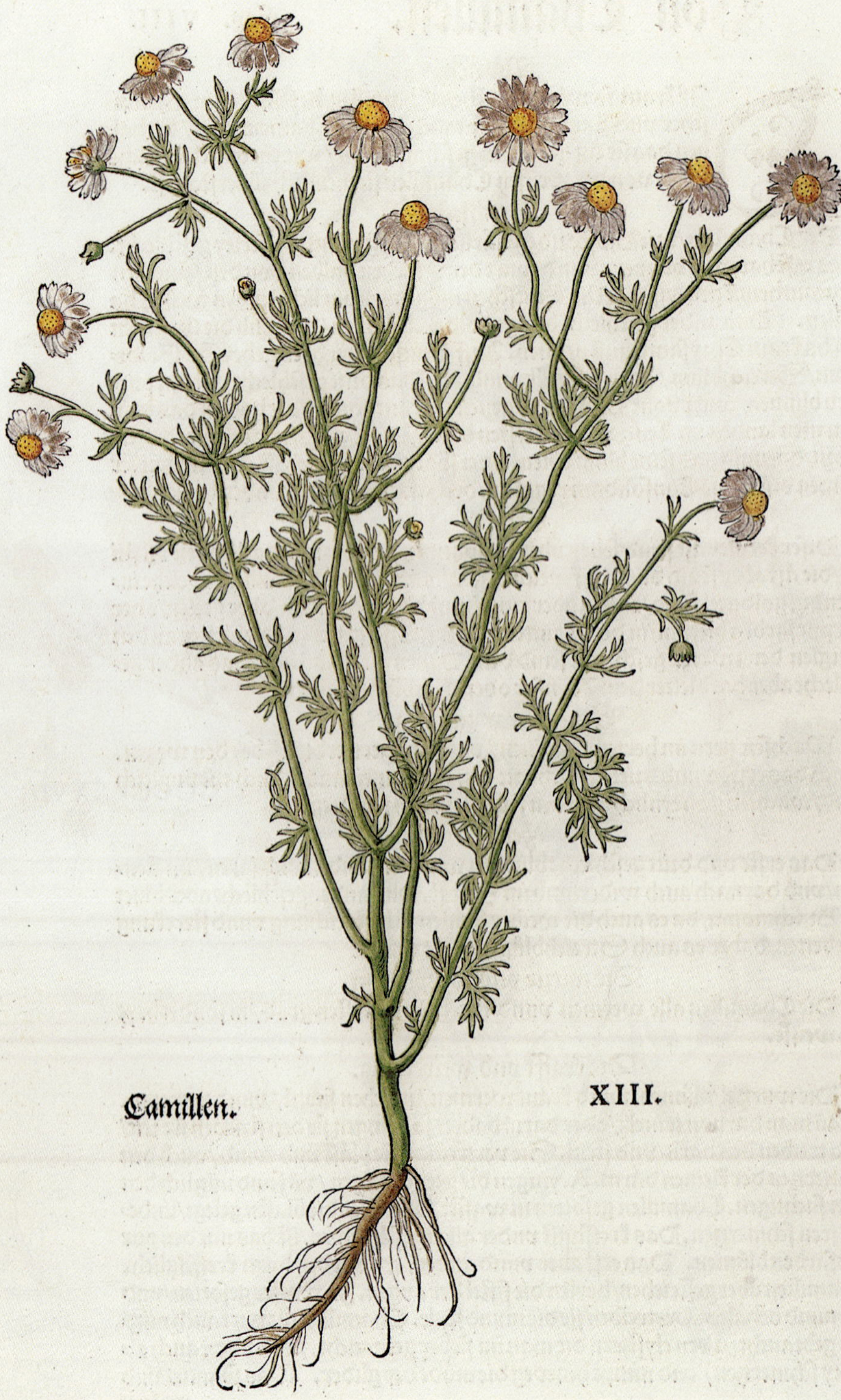
Camillen.
XIII.

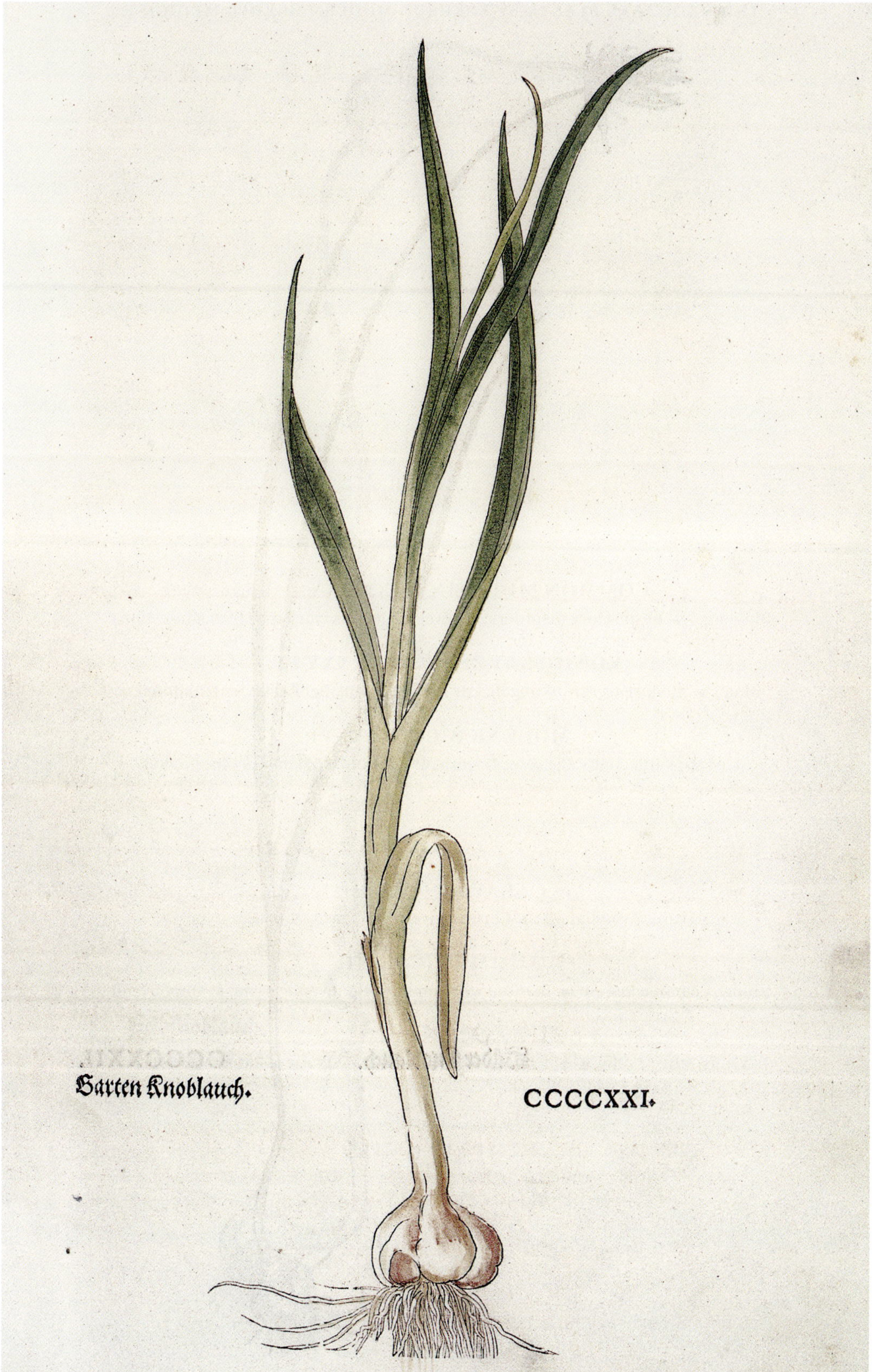
Garten Knoblauch.
CCCCXXI.

COMMON MULLEIN (CCCCLXXXV FF.)

Blossoms. ❧ Respiratory disorders; relieves irritations caused by throat infections.

KÖNIGSKERZE (CCCCLXXXV FF.)

Blüte. ❧ Atemwegserkrankungen, zur Reizlinderung bei Rachenentzündungen.

MOLÈNE (CCCCLXXXV)

Fleurs. ❧ Infections des voies respiratoires, antitussif dans les pharyngites.

PAGE 670

CARAWAY (CCXXII)

Fruits, essential oil. ❧ Carminative, aids digestion, spasmolytic.

KÜMMEL (CCXXII)

Früchte, ätherisches Öl. ❧ Blähungstreibend, verdauungsfördernd, krampflösend.

CUMIN (CCXXII)

Fruits, éther, huile. ❧ Antispasmodique, tonique de la digestion, météorisme.

PAGE 671

PUMPKIN (CCVII)

Seeds, extract. ❧ Irritated bladder, prostate problems.

KÜRBIS (CCVII)

Samen, Extrakt. ❧ Reizblase, Prostatabeschwerden.

COURGE (CCVII)

Graines, extrait. ❧ Inflammation de la vessie et de la prostate.

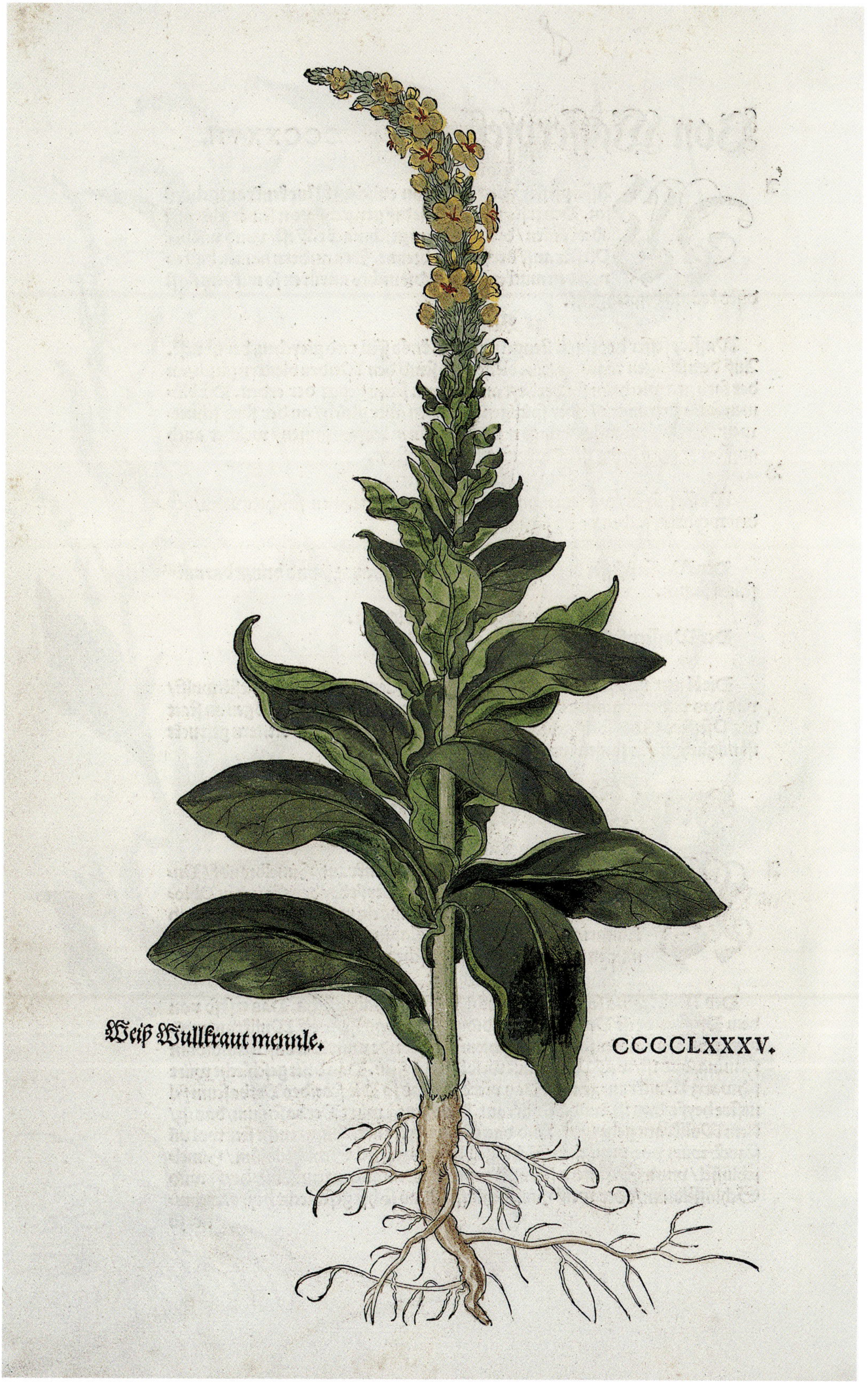
Weiß Wullkraut mennle.
CCCCLXXXV.

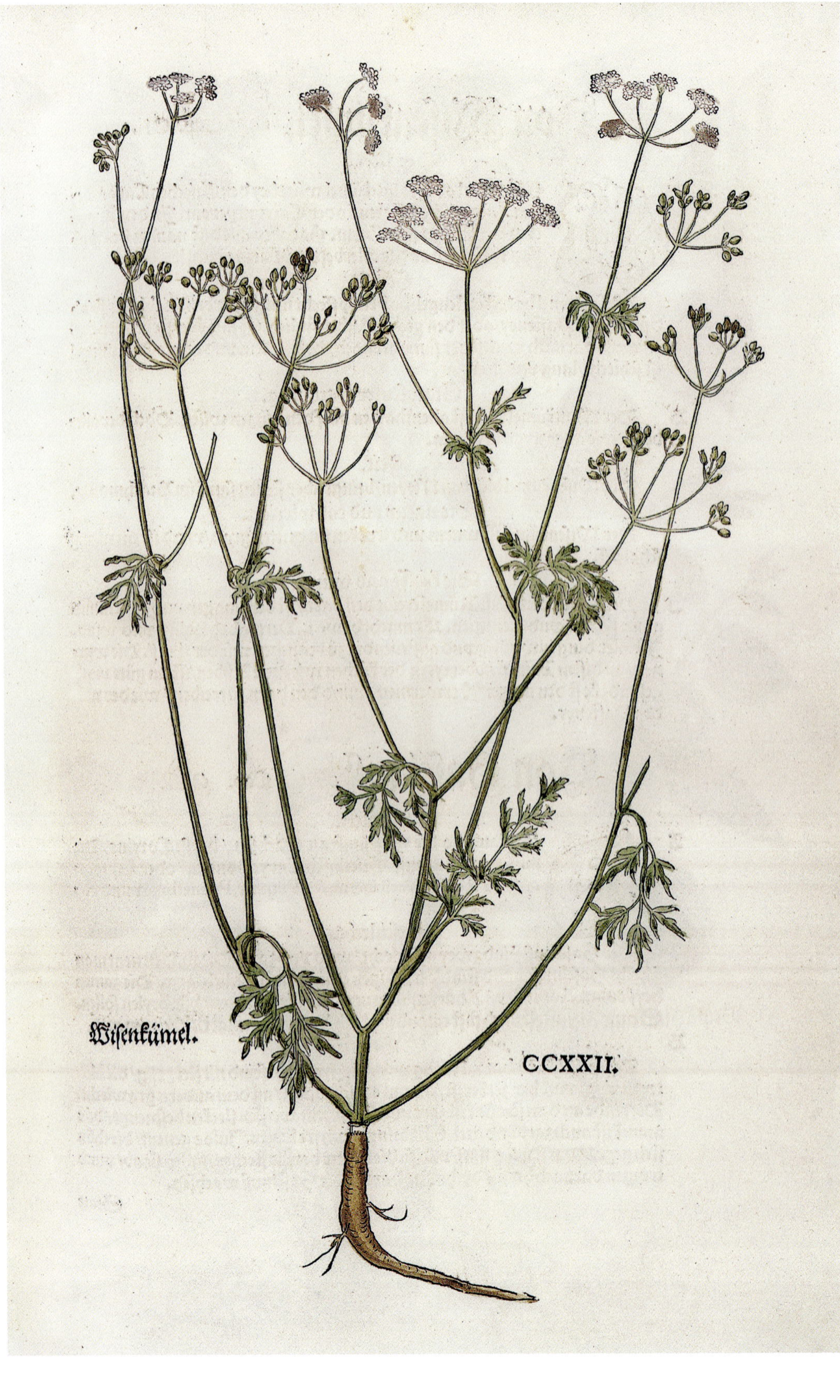
Wisenkümel.
CCXXII.

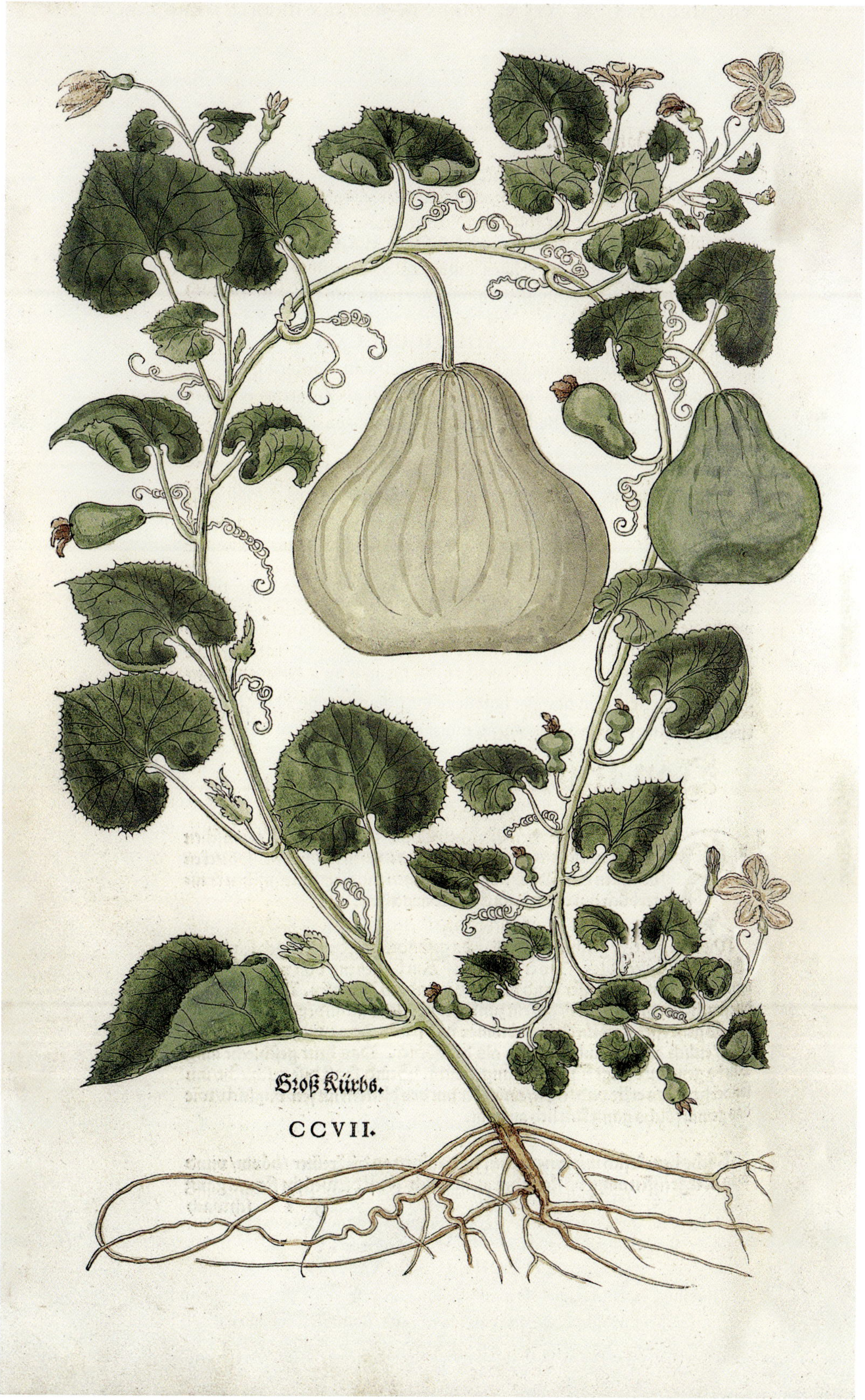
Groß Kürbs.
CCVII.

ENGLISH LAVENDER (CCCCCXI)

Flowers, essential oil. ❧ Sedates, induces sleep; nervous digestive problems; carminative. Oil as additive in relaxing baths and for reducing odours.

LAVENDEL (CCCCCXI)

Blüten, ätherisches Öl. ❧ Beruhigend, schlaffördernd, nervöse Verdauungsbeschwerden, blähungstreibend. Öl als Zusatz zu entspannenden Bädern und Geruchskorrigens.

LAVANDE (CCCCCXI)

Fleurs, éther, huile. ❧ Sédatif nerveux ; douleurs digestives d'origine nerveuse et flatulences. Huile utilisée dans les bains relaxants et agent de sapidité.

PAGE 674

FLAX (CCLXV)

Flax. ❧ Crushed or shredded seeds to be taken with a great deal of liquid for constipation, irritated bowels; mucilage for inflammation of the stomach lining. Externally used as warm, moist compress for local infections.

LEIN (CCLXV)

Samen. ❧ Der gequetschte oder geschrotete Samen mit viel Flüssigkeit bei Verstopfung, Reizdarm. Der Schleim bei Magenschleimhautentzündung. Äußerlich als warm-feuchte Packung bei lokalen Entzündungen.

LIN (CCLXV)

Graines. ❧ Graines concassées ou broyées, ingérées avec beaucoup d'eau, contre la constipation ou l'irritation de l'intestin ; mucilage dissous dans l'eau contre l'inflammation des muqueuses stomacales ; farine de lin comme cataplasmes.

PAGE 675

LOVAGE (CCCCXXXVI)

Root. ❧ Diuretic, as a flush for bladder infections, prevention of kidney stones; for digestive problems.

LIEBSTÖCKEL (CCCCXXXVI)

Wurzel. ❧ Harntreibend, zur Durchspülung bei Blasenentzündungen und zur Vorbeugung von Nierensteinen, Verdauungsbeschwerden.

LIVÈCHE (CCCCXXXVI)

Racines. ❧ Diurétique, lavements pour les infections des voies urinaires et prophylaxie des calculs rénaux, douleurs digestives.

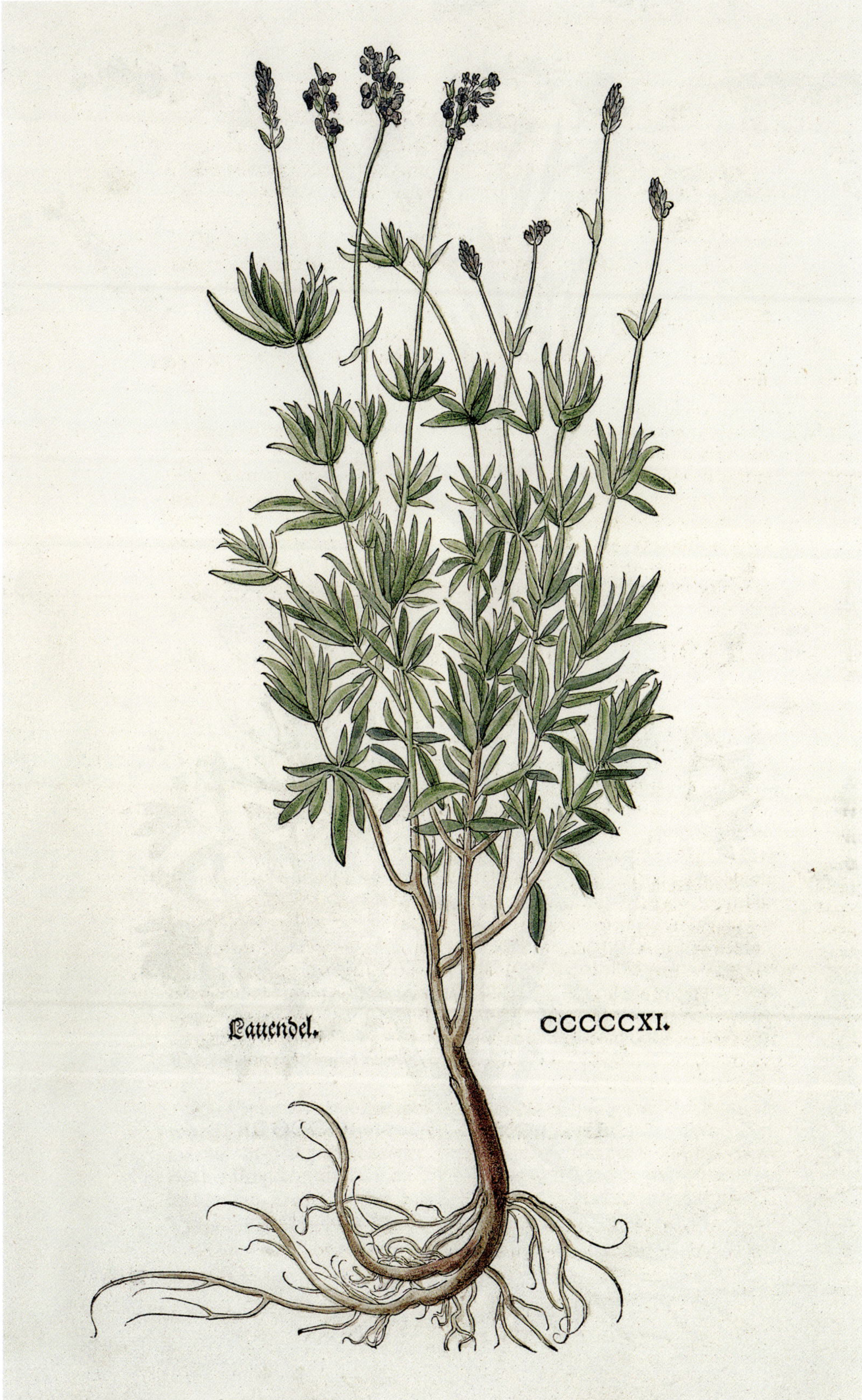
Lauendel.
CCCCCXI.

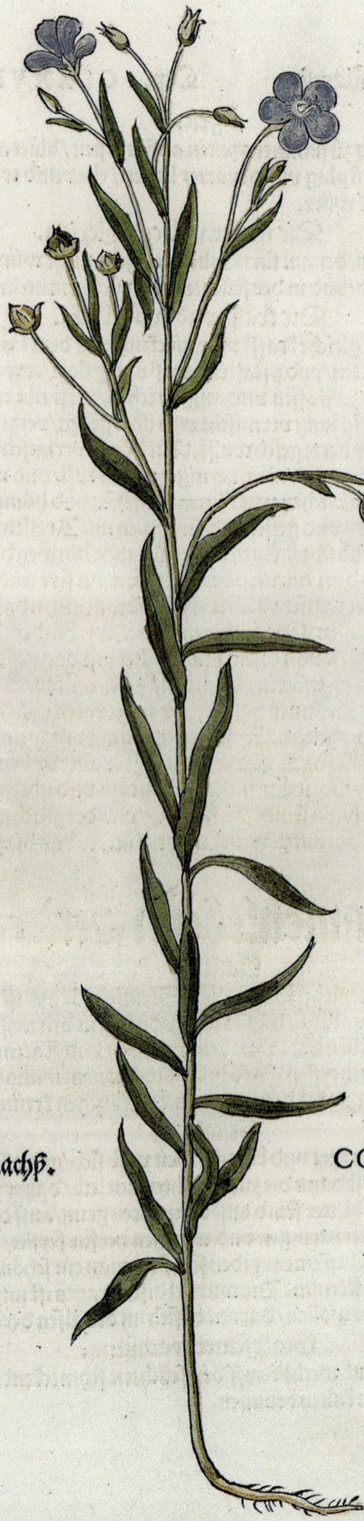

Flachß. CCLXV.

O 4

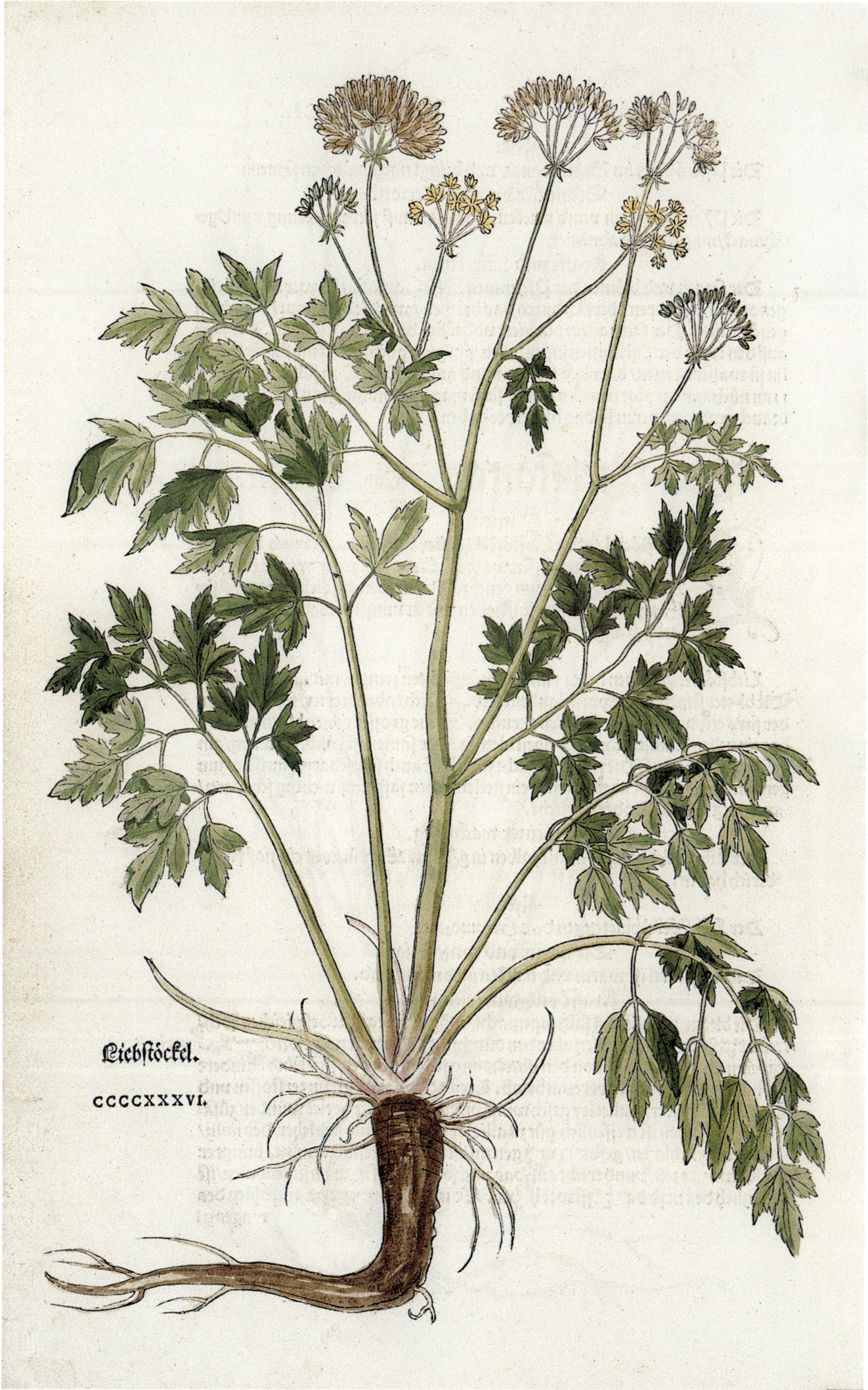
Liebstöckel.
CCCCXXXVI.

LIME TREE (CCCCXCV)

Inflorescence with basal rosette. ❧ Sudorific for colds.

LINDE (CCCCXCV)

Blütenstände mit Hochblatt. ❧ Schweißtreibend bei Erkältungskrankheiten.

TILLEUL (CCCCXCV)

Fleurs avec bractées. ❧ Sudorifique dans les refroi-dissements.

PAGE 678

COMMON DANDELION (CCCLXXXVIII)

Herbage, root. ❧ Stimulates flow of gall, for indigestion; diuretic.

LÖWENZAHN (CCCLXXXVIII)

Kraut, Wurzel ❧ Fördert Gallenfluss, bei Verdauungsbeschwerden, harntreibend.

PISSENLIT (CCCLXXXVIII)

Partie verte, racines. ❧ Diurétique, accroît le volume de bile excrétée et calme les douleurs digestives.

PAGE 679

LILY-OF-THE-VALLEY (CXXXIII)

Extract. ❧ Ingredient in heart meicines. Should be prescribed by a physician.

MAIGLÖCKCHEN (CXXXIII)

Extrakt. ❧ Bestandteil herzwirksamer Medikamente, die vom Arzt verordnet werden sollten.

MUGUET (CXXXIII)

Extrait. ❧ Tonicardiaque : composant de remèdes pour le cœur, que seul le médecin devrait prescrire.

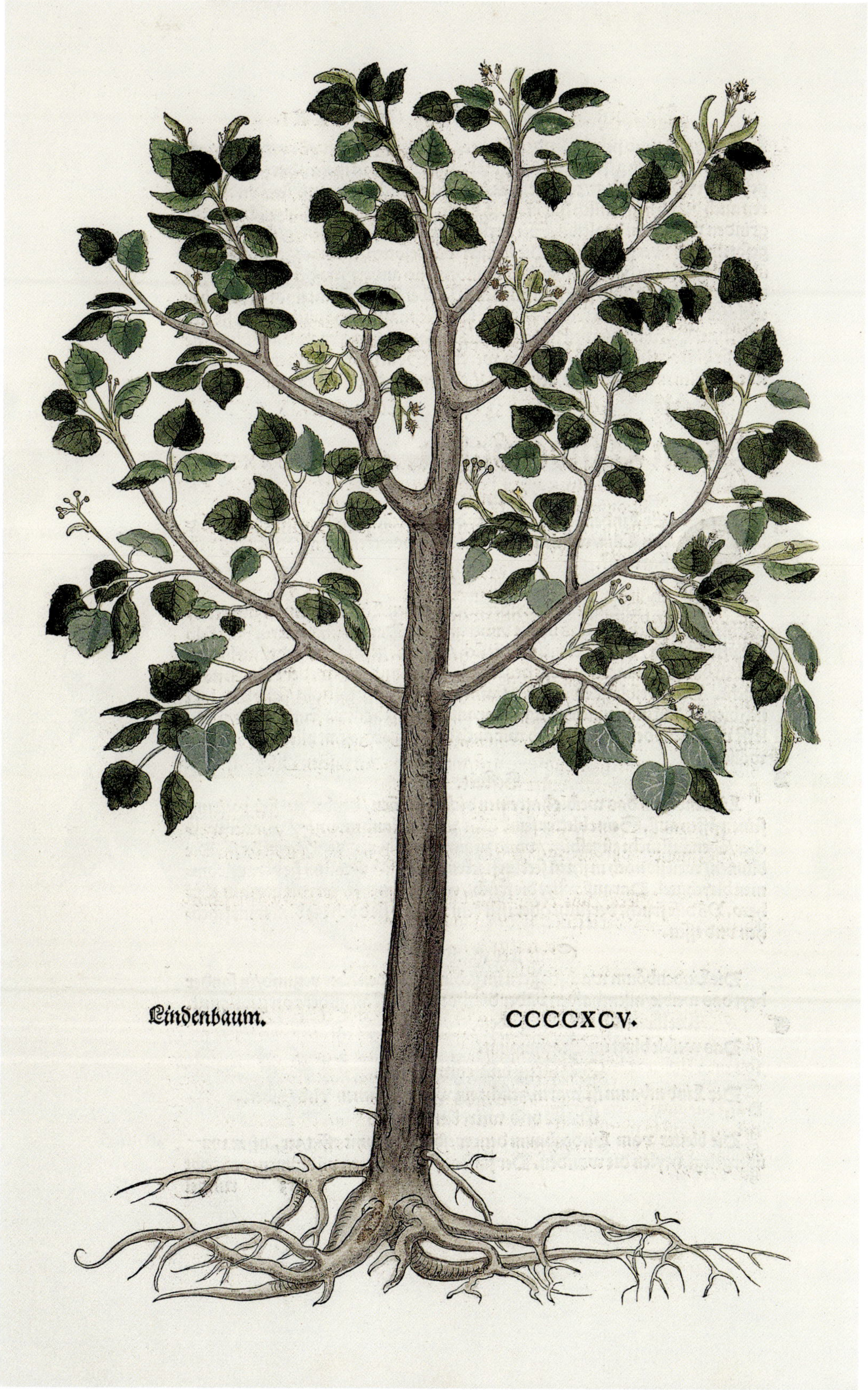
Lindenbaum.
CCCCXCV.

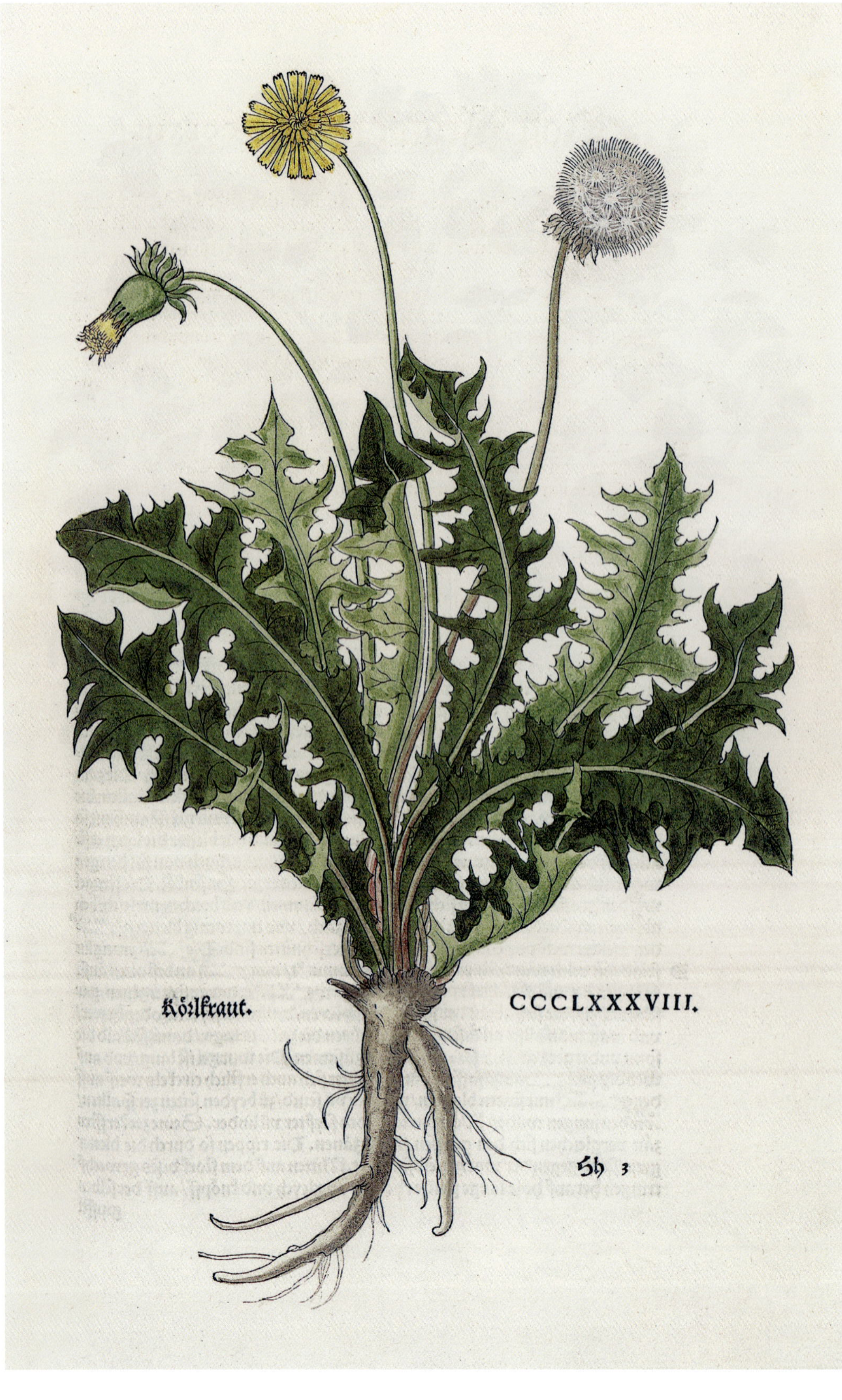
Rörlkraut.
CCCLXXXVIII.
Hh 3

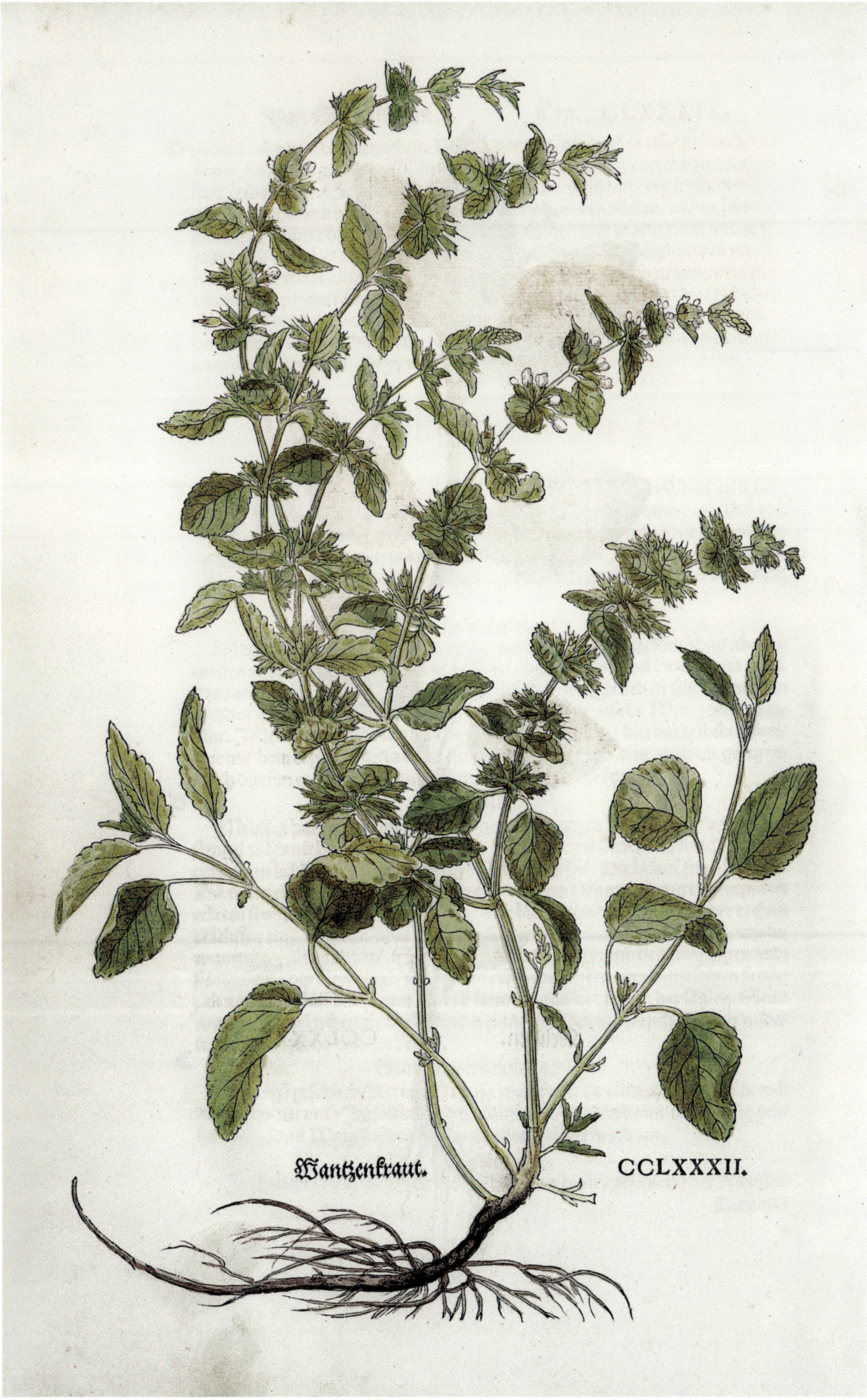
Wantzenkraut.
CCLXXXII.

MISTLETOE (CLXXXV)

Leaves, twigs. ❧ For prevention of arteriosclerosis; for high blood pressure (not proved). Special extract for degenerative joint diseases and as cancer therapy.

MISTEL (CLXXXV)

Blätter, Zweige. ❧ Zur Vorbeugung gegen Arteriosklerose, bei Bluthochdruck (nicht belegt). Spezialextrakte bei degenerativen Gelenkerkrankungen und zur Krebstherapie.

GUI BLANC (CLXXXV)

Feuilles, rameaux. ❧ Prophylaxie de l'artériosclérose, antihypertensif (non prouvé). Extraits spéciaux dans les affections dégénératives des articulations et le traitement du cancer.

PAGE 686

BUTTERBUR (CCCLXVII)

Herbage, leaves, flowers. ❧ Bronchial asthma, whooping cough. Unsuitable for long-term use. Often used similarly to coltsfoot.

PESTWURZ (CCCLXVII)

Kraut, Blätter, Blüten. ❧ Bronchialasthma, Keuchhusten. Keine Langzeitanwendung. Häufig ähnlich wie Huflattich verwendet.

CHAPEAU-DU-DIABLE (CCCLXVII)

Partie verte, feuilles, fleurs. ❧ Propriétés antitussives (asthme bronchique, coqueluche). Pas d'administration prolongée. Fréquent substitut du pas-d'âne (voir ci-après).

PAGE 687

WILD THYME (CXXXIX)

Herbage. ❧ Application similar to that of thyme.

QUENDEL (CXXXIX)

Kraut. ❧ Anwendung wie Thymian.

SERPOLET (CXXXIX)

Partie verte. ❧ Substitut du thym.

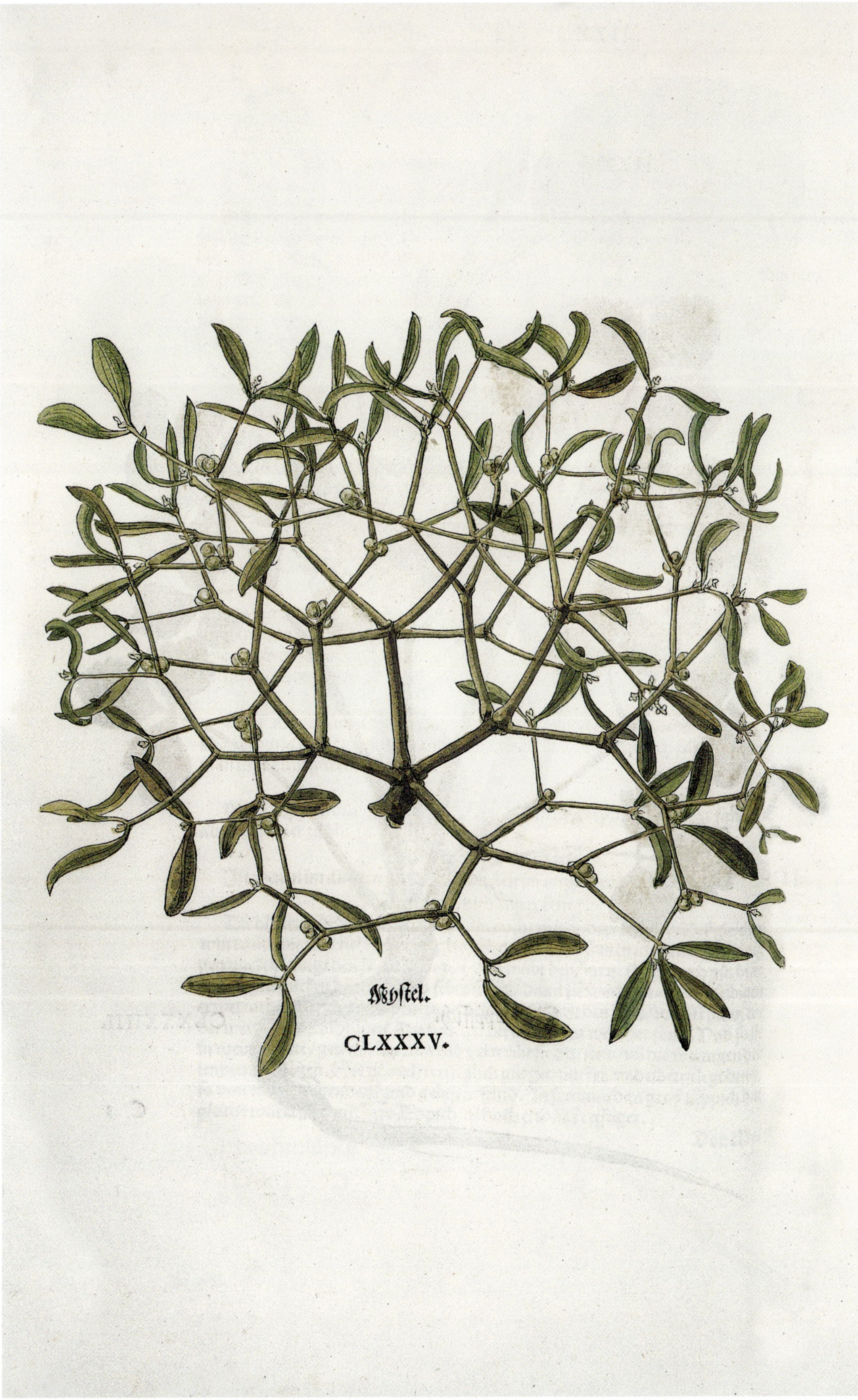
Myſtel.
CLXXXV.

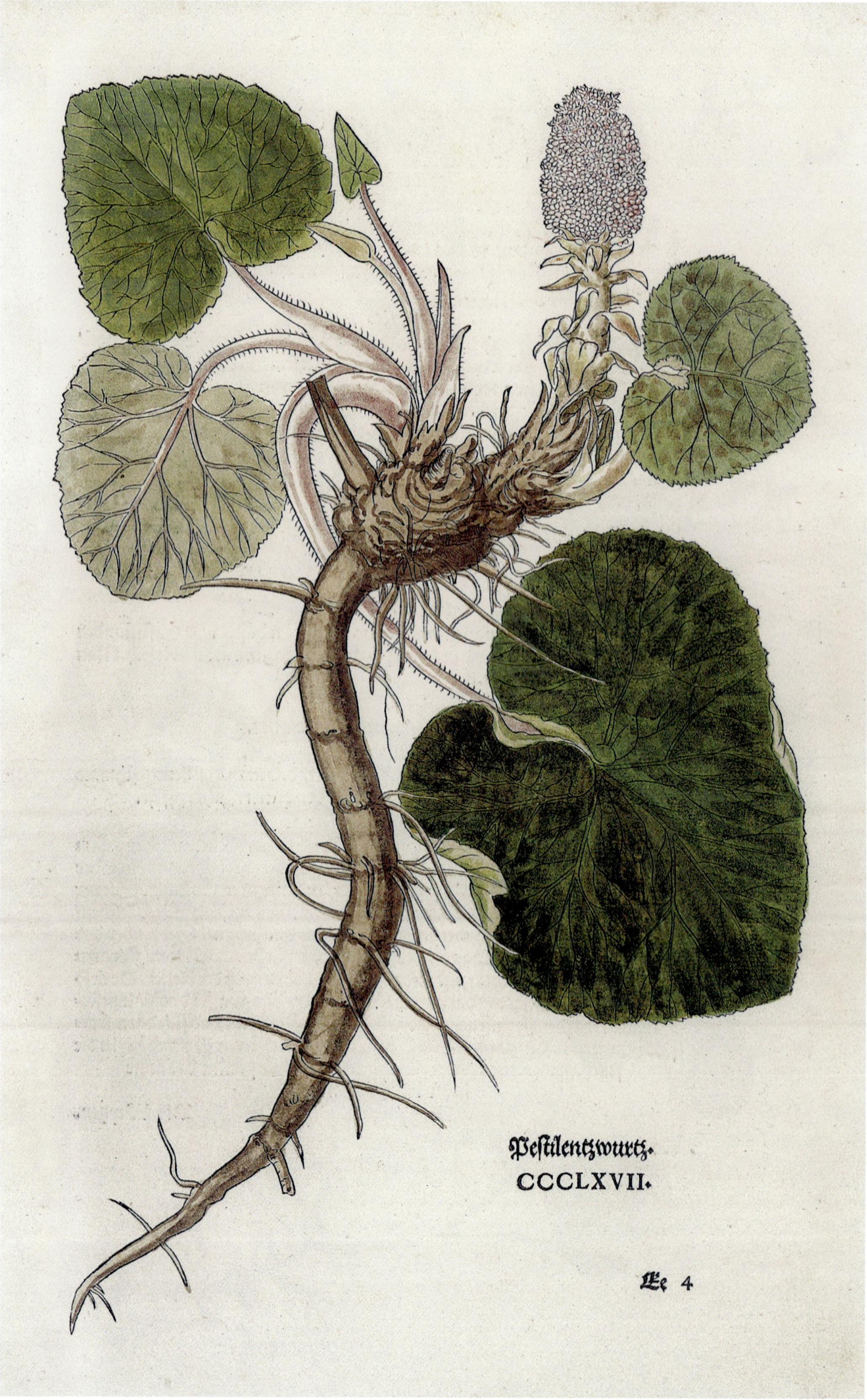
Pestilentzwurtz.
CCCLXVII.
Ee 4

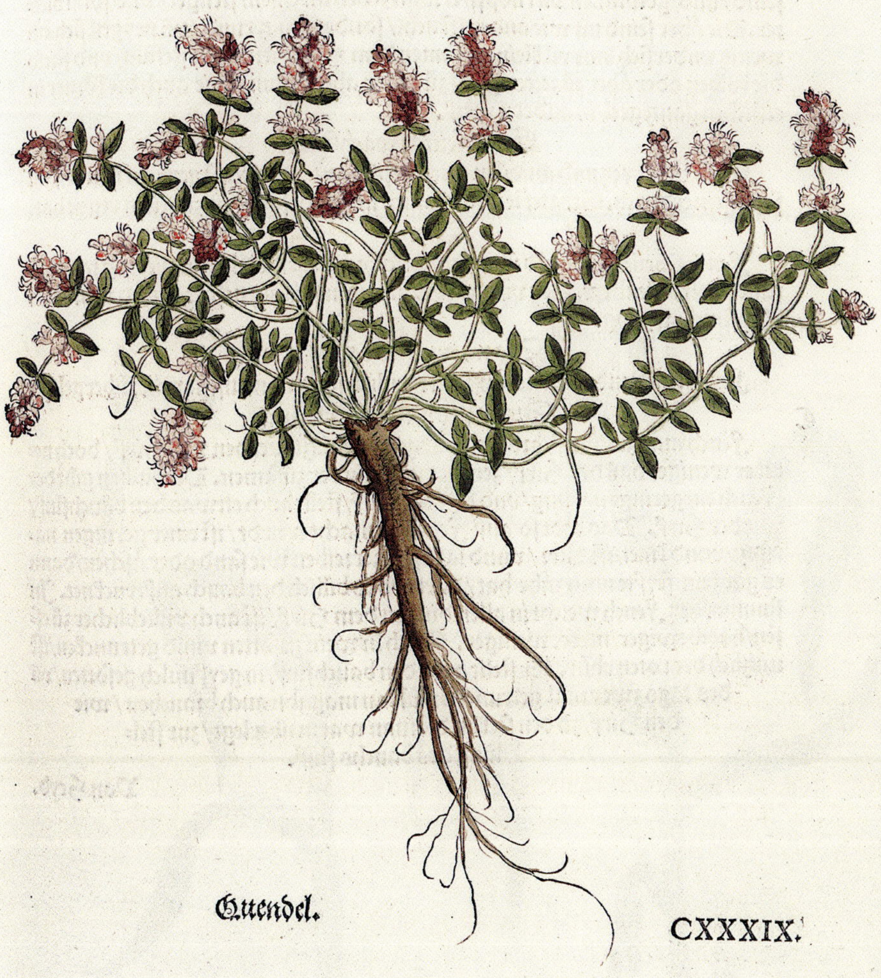

Quendel. CXXXIX.

U 2

CALENDULA (CCXIIII)

Flowers. ❧ Infections of mouth and throat; external application on slow-healing wounds.

RINGELBLUME (CCXIIII)

Blüten. ❧ Entzündungen im Mund-Rachen-Raum. Äußerlich bei schlecht heilenden Wunden.

SOUCI (CCXIIII)

Fleurs. ❧ Inflammations de la bouche et de la gorge. En usage externe, cicatrise les plaies rebelles.

PAGE 690

CASTOR OIL PLANT (CXCII)

Fatty oil. ❧ Laxative. Only the fixed oil is used medicinally; seeds are highly poisonous!

RIZINUS (CXCII)

Fettes Öl. ❧ Abführmittel. Medizinische Verwendung findet nur das fette Öl. Die Samen sind hochgiftig!

RICIN (CXCII)

Huile. ❧ Laxatif. Seule l'huile est utilisée en médecine. Les graines sont extrêmement toxiques !

PAGE 691

ROSEMARY (CCLXIX)

Leaves, essential oil. ❧ Indigestion; external application for rheumatic disorders, stimulates circulation.

ROSMARIN (CCLXIX)

Blätter, ätherisches Öl. ❧ Verdauungsbeschwerden. Äußerlich bei rheumatischen Erkrankungen, durchblutungsfördernd.

ROMARIN (CCLXIX)

Feuilles, éther, huile. ❧ Douleurs digestives ; usage externe pour les affections rhumatismales, tonique de la circulation sanguine.

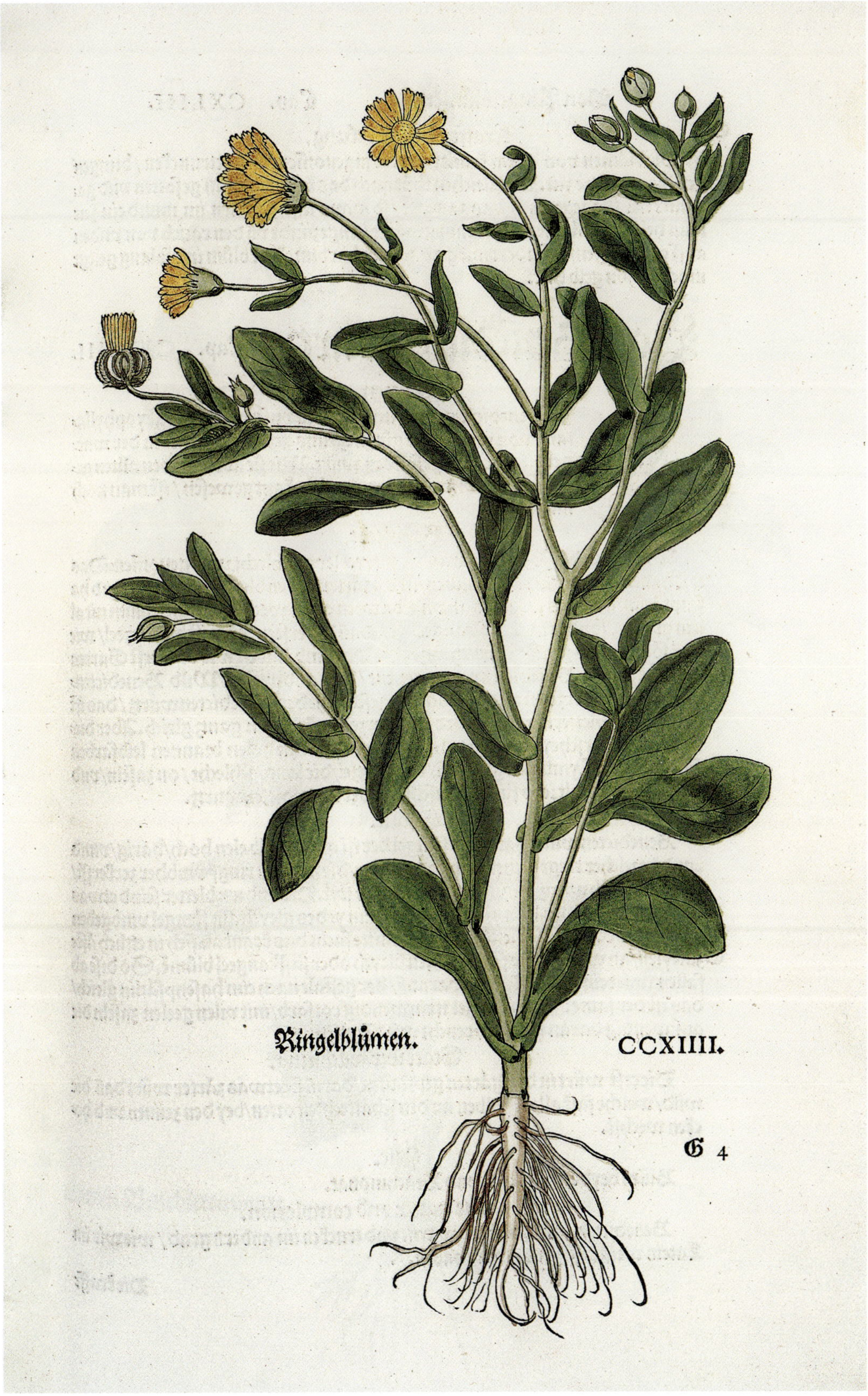
Ringelblůmen.
CCXIIII.
G 4

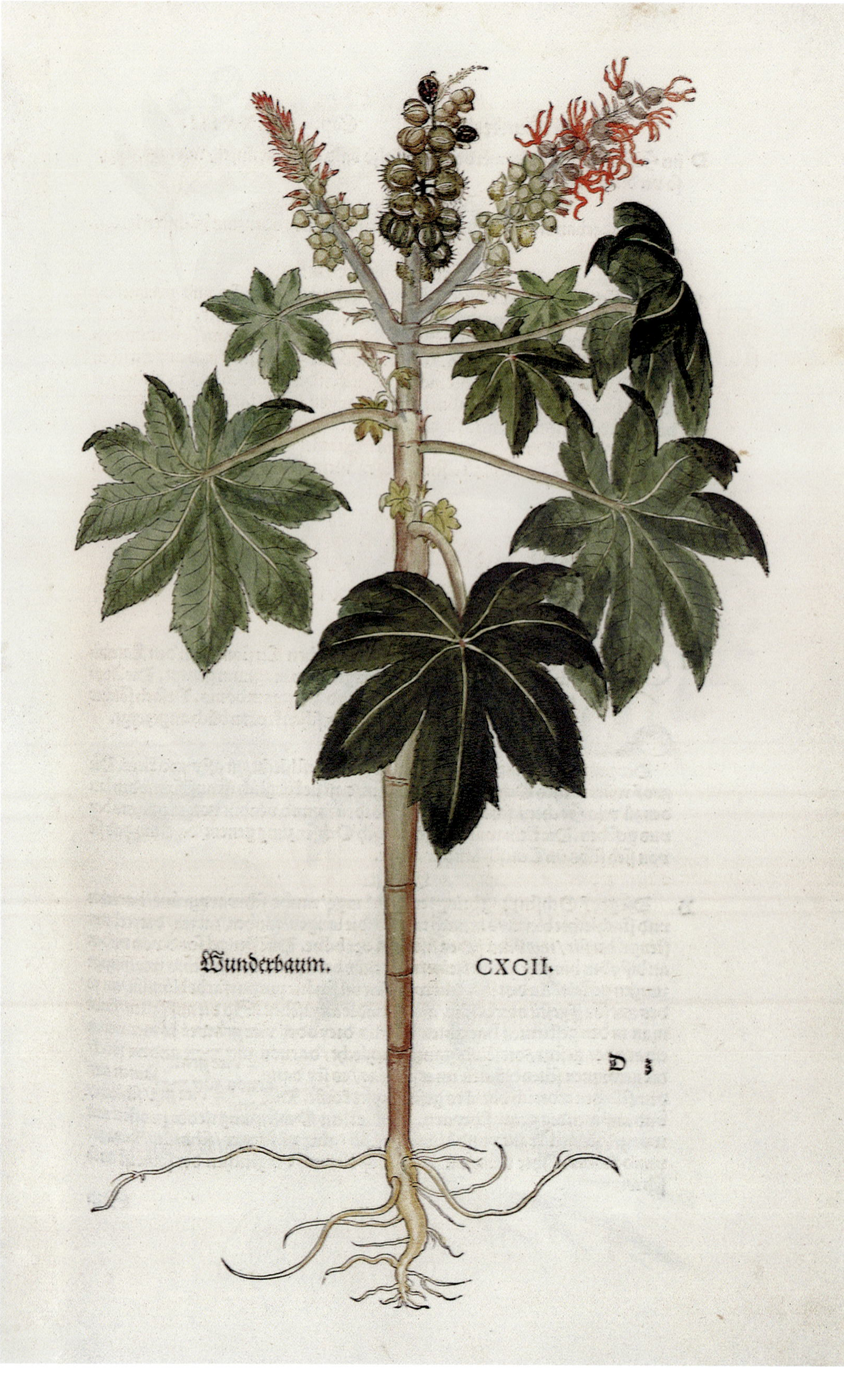
Wunderbaum.
CXCII.
D 3

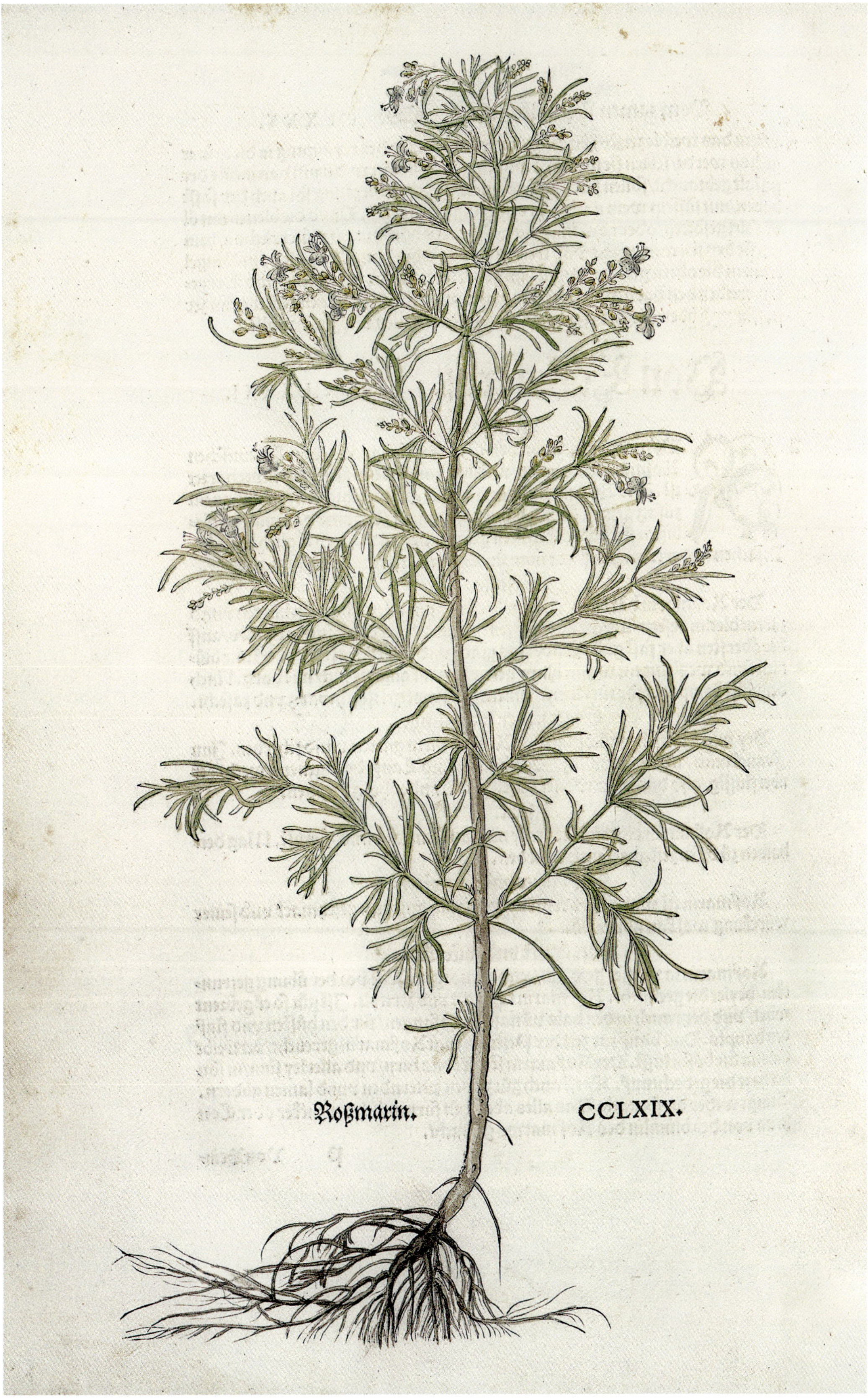

ROSEMARY | ROSMARIN | ROMARIN

COMMON SAGE (CXXXVII)

Leaves. ❧ Indigestion; reduces excessive perspiration. As a gargle for mouth and throat infections.

SALBEI (CXXXVII)

Blätter. ❧ Verdauungsbeschwerden, bei zu starkem Schwitzen. Zum Gurgeln bei Mund- und Rachenentzündungen.

SAUGE (CXXXVII)

Feuilles. ❧ Douleurs digestives, transpiration excessive. En gargarismes contre les inflammations buccales et de la gorge.

PAGE 694

COMMON HORSETAIL (CLXXXII)

Stem of the shoot. ❧ Diuretic, for oedema. External application aids healing of wounds. Care required when gathering owing to possible confusion with poisonous species!

SCHACHTELHALM (CLXXXII)

Sprossstängel. ❧ Harntreibend, bei Ödemen. Äußerlich zur Unterstützung der Wundheilung. Vorsicht beim Selbstsammeln, da Verwechslung mit giftigen Arten möglich!

PRÊLE DES CHAMPS (CLXXXII)

Tige de la pousse. ❧ Diurétique, agit sur les œdèmes. En usage externe, cicatrisante et aseptisante. Confusion possible avec d'autres espèces toxiques – attention en les cueillant !

PAGE 695

COMMON YARROW (CCCCXV)

Herbage, flower. ❧ Appetite stimulant; for indigestion accompanied by slight cramps in stomach and bowel area.

SCHAFGARBE (CCCCXV)

Kraut, Blüte. ❧ Appetitanregend; leichte krampfartige Verdauungsbeschwerden im Magen-Darm-Bereich.

ACHILLÉE MILLEFEUILLE (CCCCXV)

Partie verte, fleur. ❧ Stimule l'appétit, calme les légers spasmes digestifs dans la région gastro-intestinale.

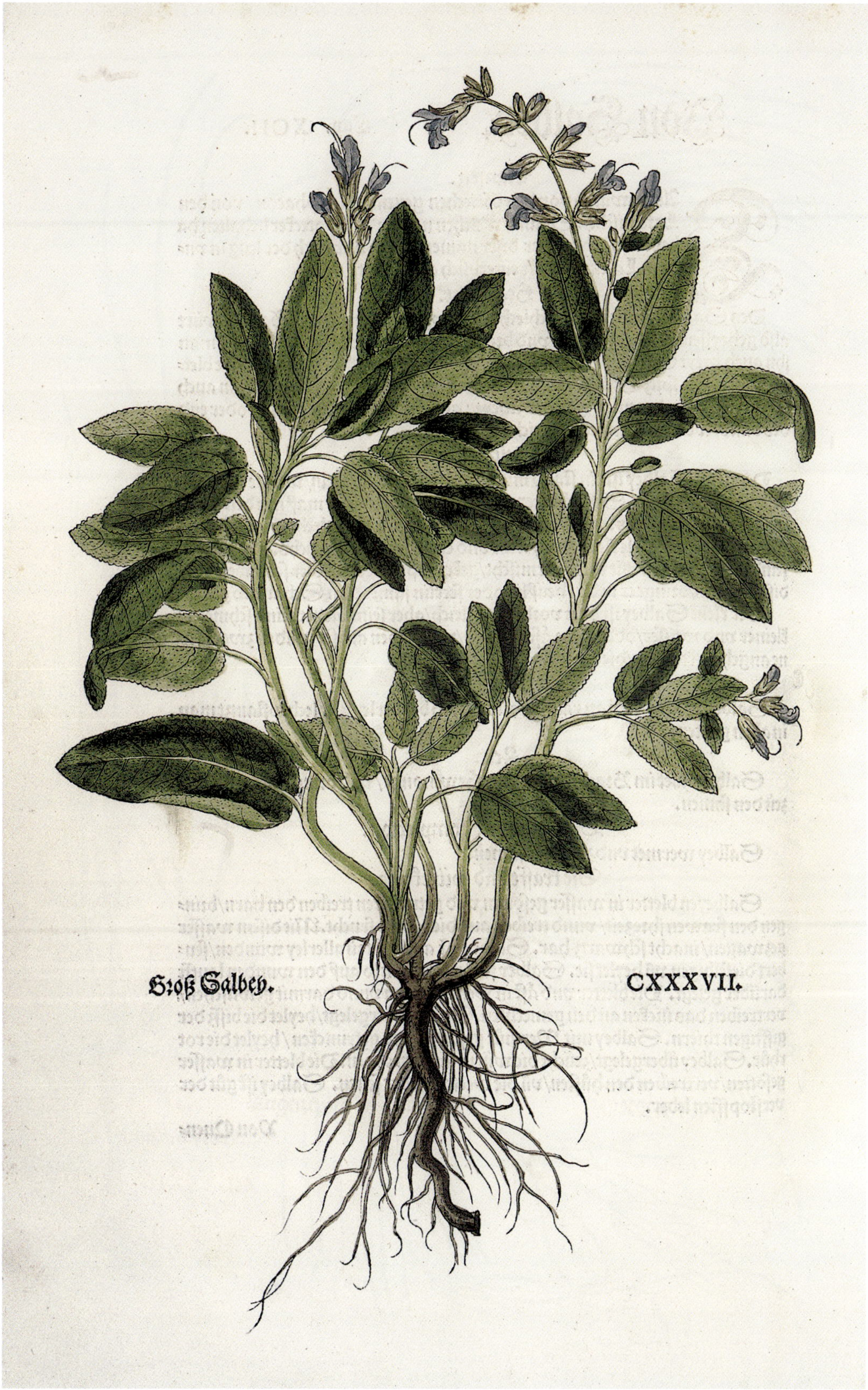
Groß Salbey.
CXXXVII.

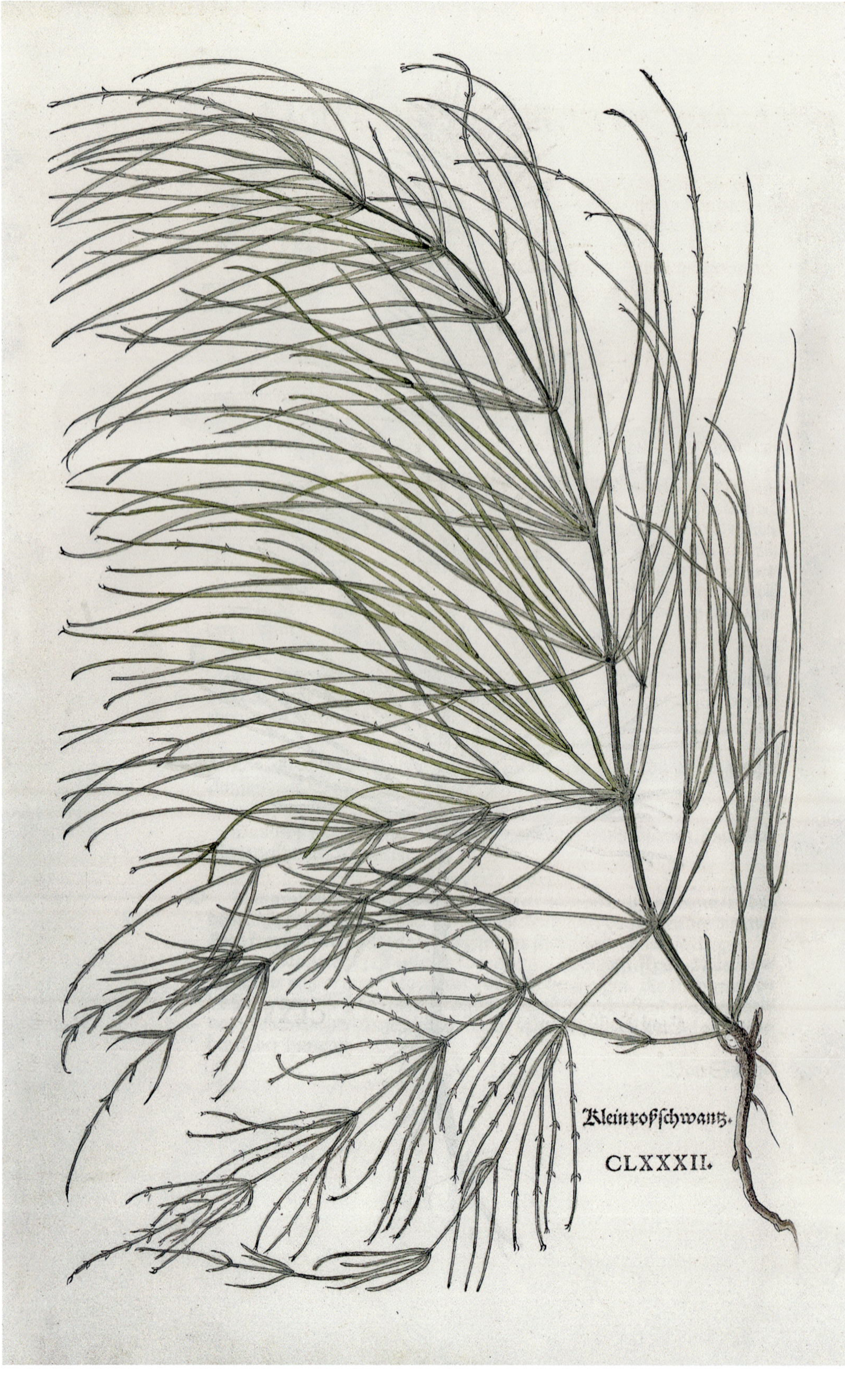
Kleinroßschwantz.
CLXXXII.

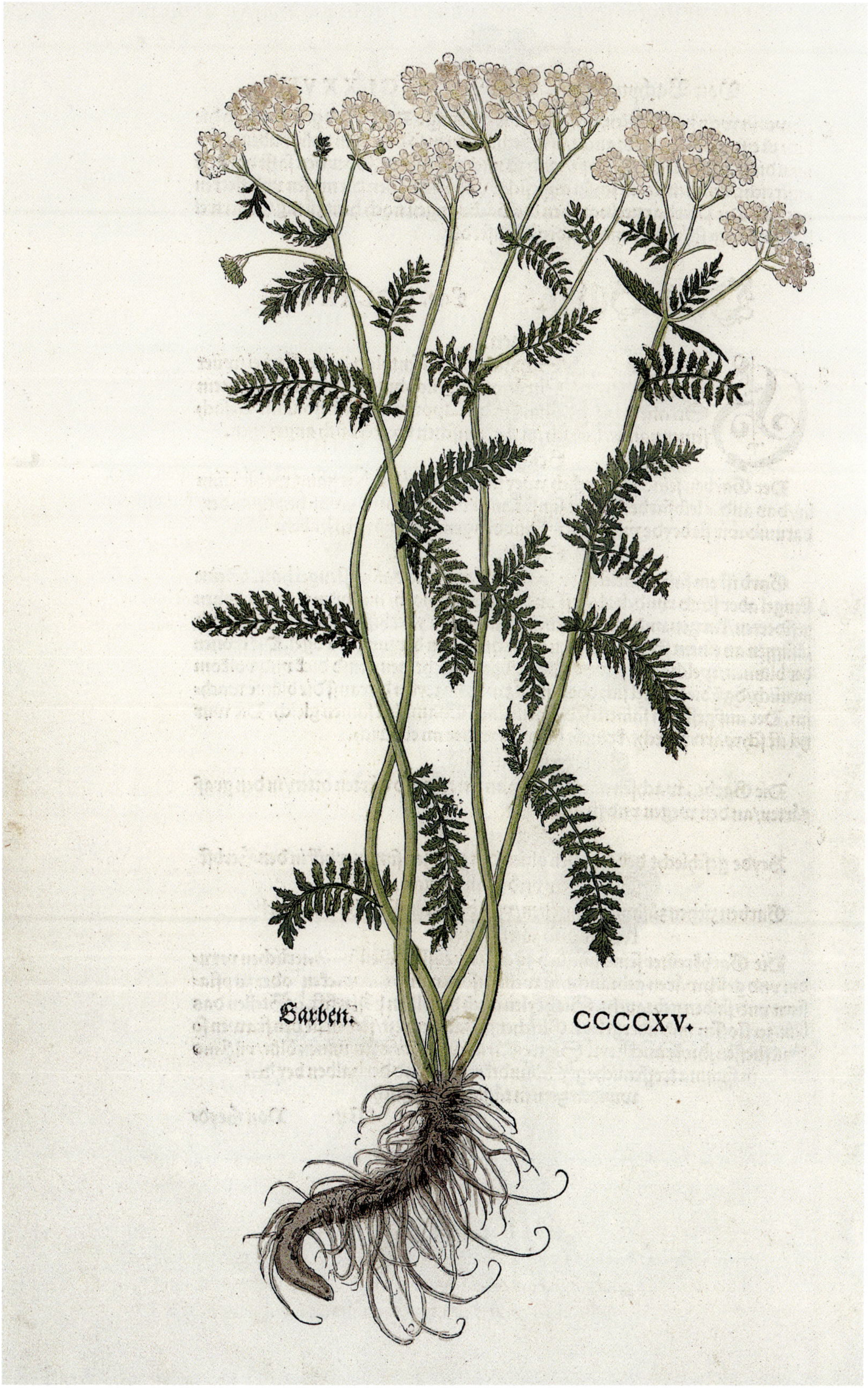

COMMON YARROW | SCHAFGARBE | ACHILLÉE MILLEFEUILLE

GIANT POPPY (CCXCIII)

Isolated substances of opium (morphine, codeine, etc.) are used only with a doctor's prescription because of the high danger of addiction. ❧ Pain-relieving, cough suppressant, for diarrhoea.

SCHLAFMOHN (CCXCIII)

Verwendung finden die isolierten Inhaltsstoffe des Opiums (Morphin, Codein usw.), die wegen ihres teilweise hohen Suchtpotenzials vom Arzt verordnet werden müssen. ❧ Schmerzstillung, hustendämpfend, bei Durchfall.

PAVOT (CCXCIII)

Les dérivés de l'opium (morphine, codéine etc.) sont utilisés en pharmacologie, mais ne peuvent être prescrits que par un médecin en raison des risques partiels d'accoutumance. ❧ Analgésique, antitussif et antidiarrhéique.

PAGE 698

COWSLIP (CCCCLXXXIX)

Root. ❧ Expectorant, diuretic.

SCHLÜSSELBLUME (CCCCLXXXIX)

Wurzel. ❧ Auswurffördernd, harntreibend.

PRIMEVÈRE OFFICINALE (CCCCLXXXIX)

Racines. ❧ Expectorant, diurétique.

PAGE 699

GREATER CELANDINE (CCCCXCVI)

Herbage. ❧ Stimulates gall production, spasmolytic; milky sap traditionally used for warts. As eye treatment not scientifically substantiated.

SCHÖLLKRAUT (CCCCXCVI)

Kraut. ❧ Zur Anregung der Galleproduktion, krampf-lösend. Der frische Milchsaft traditionell gegen Warzen. Die Anwendung am Auge ist wissenschaftlich nicht belegt.

CHÉLIDOINE (CCCCXCVI)

Partie verte. ❧ Accroît le volume de bile excrétée, antispasmodique. Le latex frais est un remède traditionnel contre les verrues. Son efficacité comme onguent pour les yeux n'est pas prouvée scientifiquement.

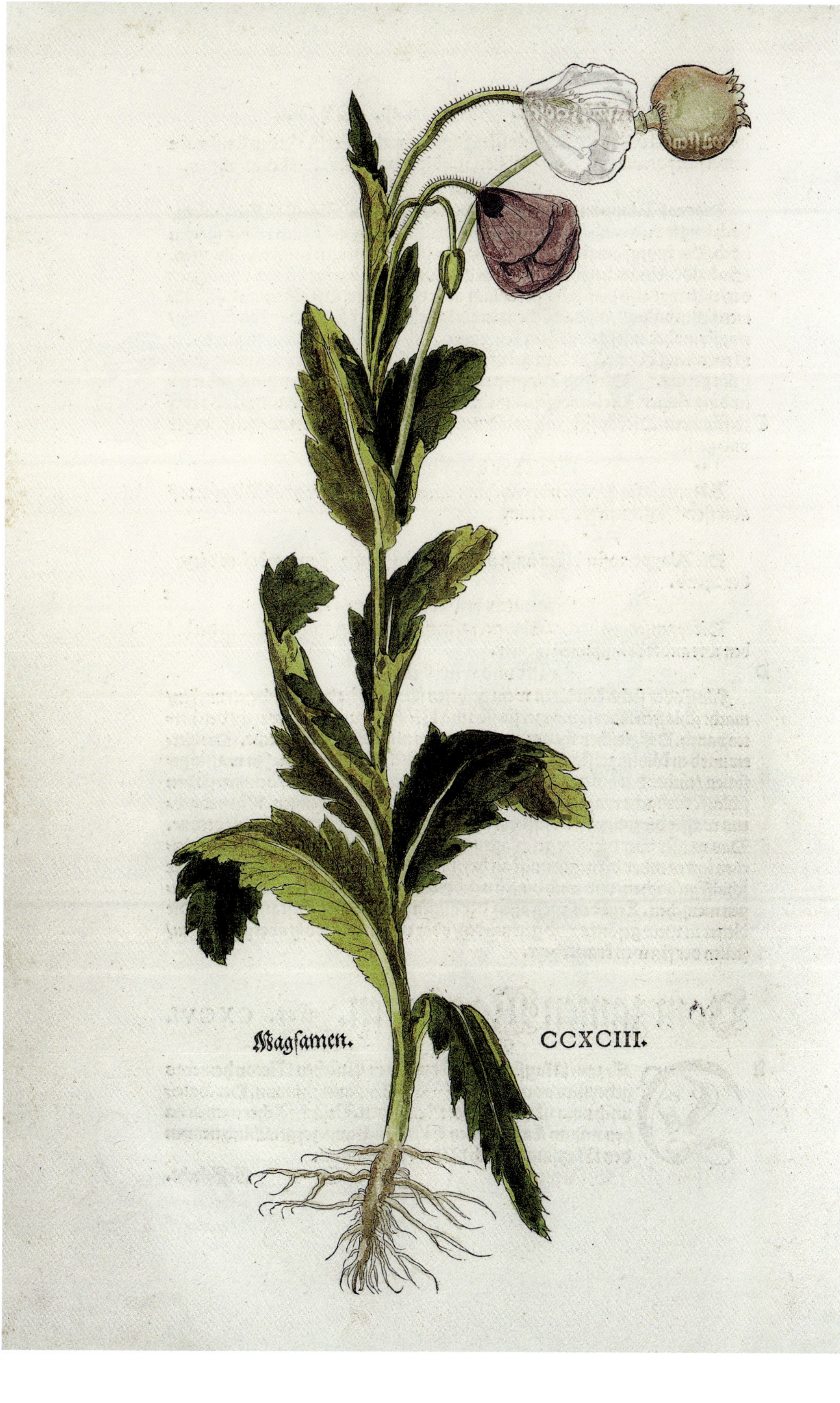

GIANT POPPY | SCHLAFMOHN | PAVOT

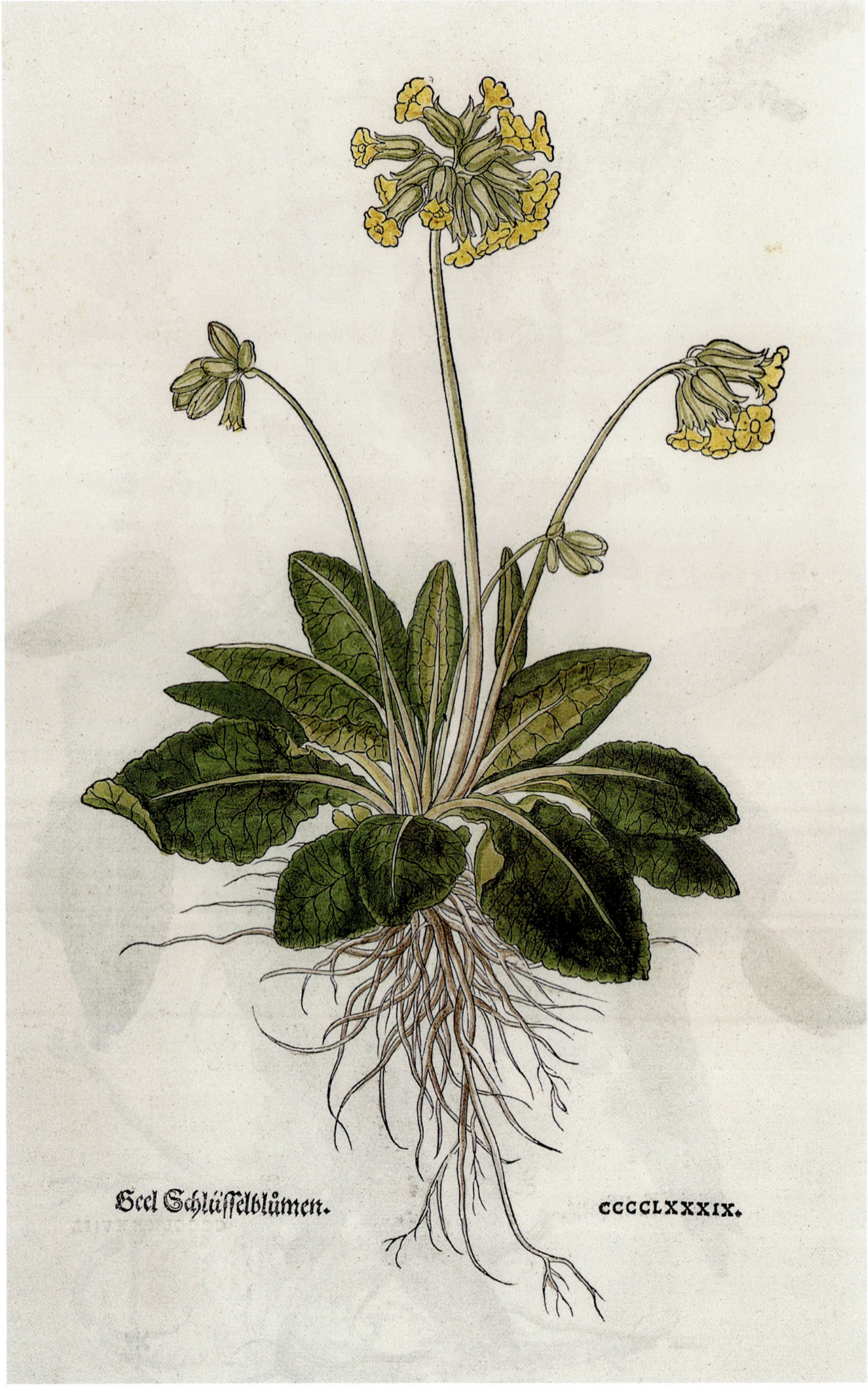
Seel Schlüsselblůmen.
CCCCLXXXIX.

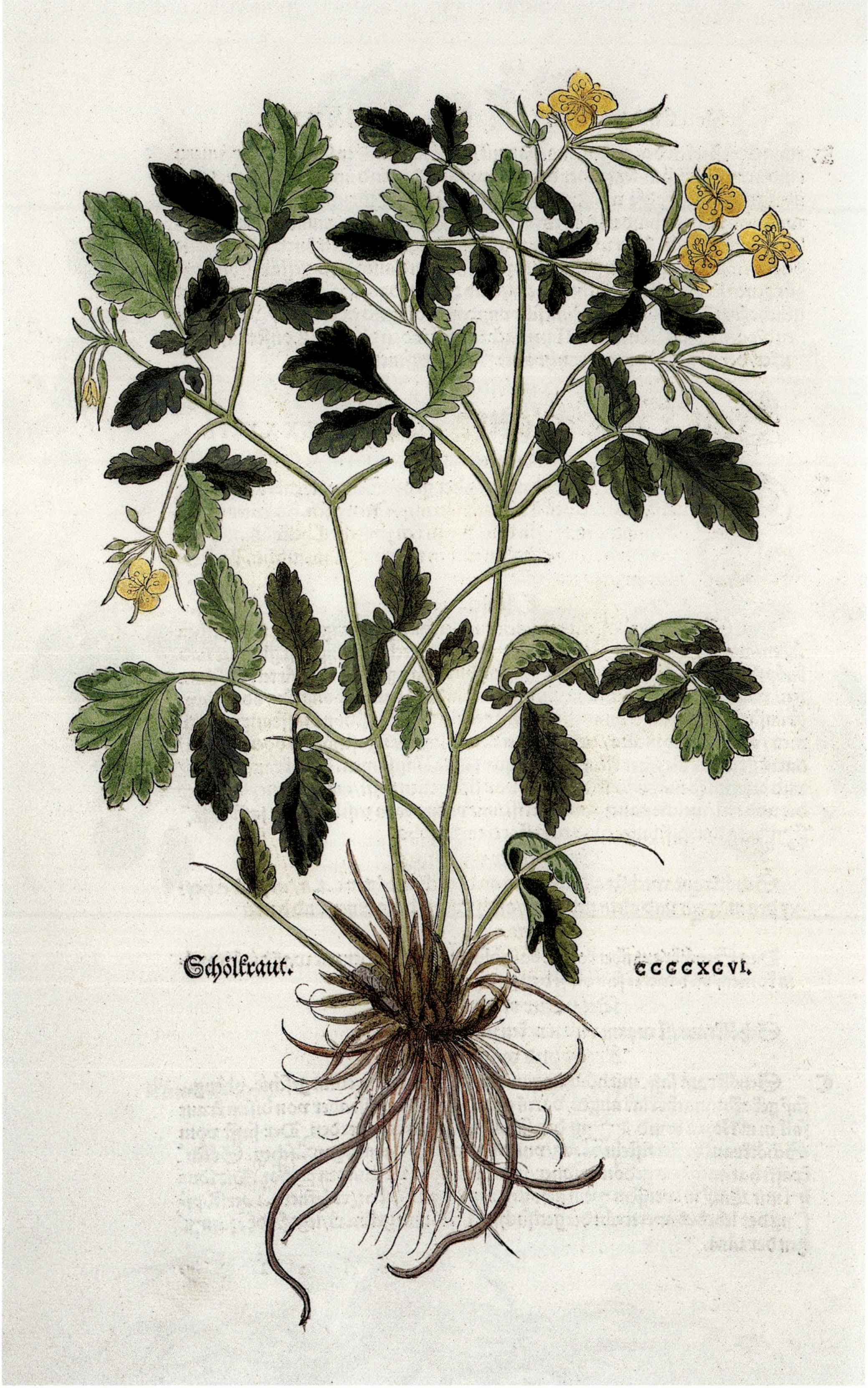
Schölkraut.
CCCCXCVI.

COMMON ASPARAGUS (XXXIII)
Root. ❧ Diuretic.

SPARGEL (XXXIII)
Wurzel. ❧ Entwässernd.

ASPERGE (XXXIII)
Racines. ❧ Provoque l'élimination d'eau.

PAGE 702

ENGLISH PLANTAIN (XXII)
Herbage. ❧ Bronchial disorders, infections of mouth and throat; externally for skin inflammations.

SPITZWEGERICH (XXII)
Kraut. ❧ Bronchialerkrankungen, Entzündungen im Mund- und Rachenbereich. Äußerlich bei Entzündungen der Haut.

PLANTAIN (XXII)
Partie verte. ❧ Affections bronchiques, inflammations de la bouche et de la gorge. Usage externe dans les dermatoses.

PAGE 703

LICORICE (CVII)
Root. ❧ Expectorant; irritations and infections of the mucous membranes of bronchial tubes, stomach and bowels. High dosage not to be taken over an extended period! Counterindicated by high blood pressure and reduced heart and liver function.

SÜSSHOLZ (CVII)
Wurzel. ❧ Auswurffördernd, Reizungen und Entzündungen der Schleimhäute von Bronchien, Magen und Darm. Die Einnahme höherer Dosen soll nicht über längere Zeit erfolgen! Nicht anwenden bei Bluthochdruck und eingeschränkter Herz- und Nierenfunktion.

RÉGLISSE (CVII)
Racines. ❧ Expectorant, émollient dans les irritations et inflammations du mucus bronchique ou gastro-intestinal.

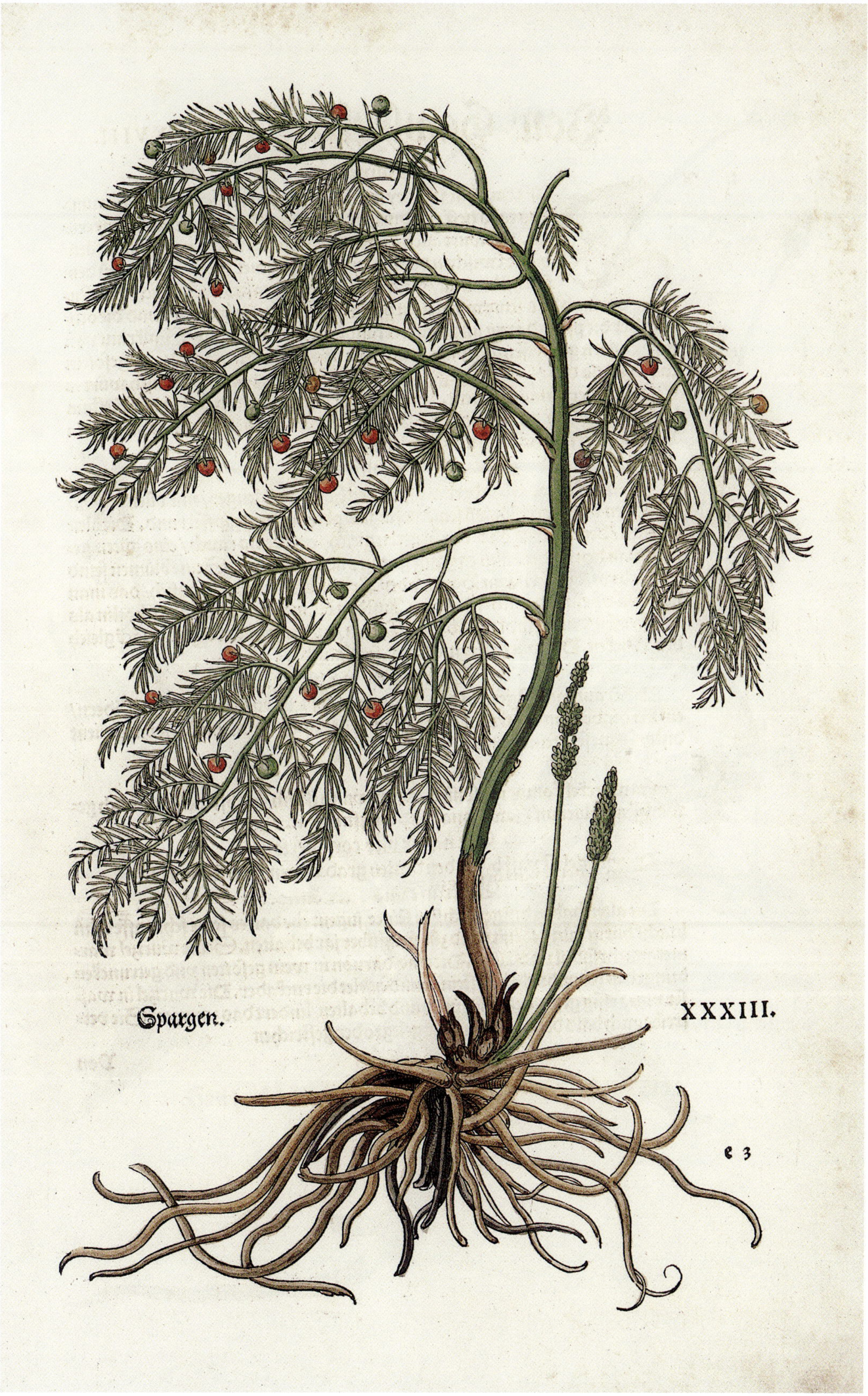
Spargen.
XXXIII.
e 3

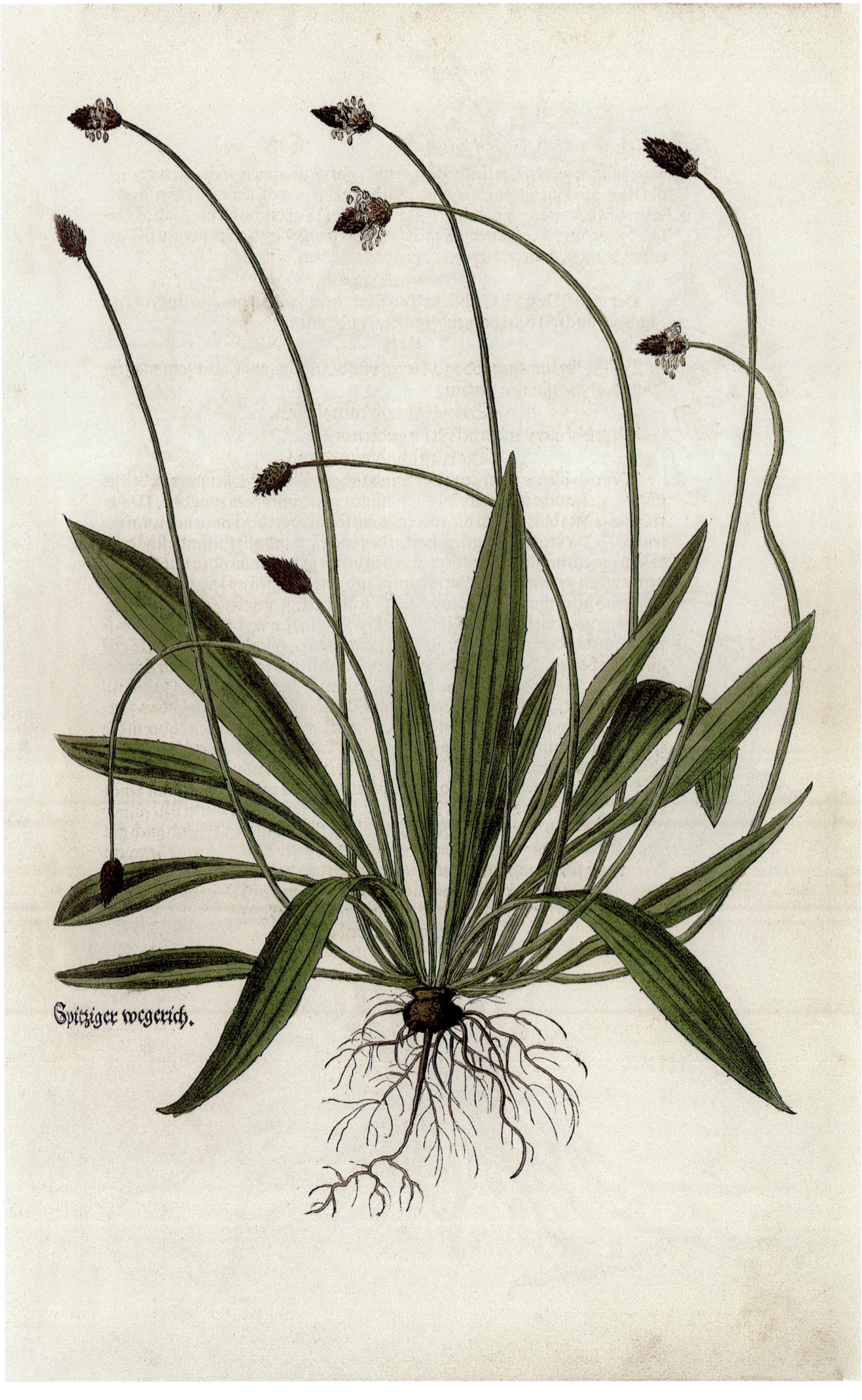
Spitziger wegerich.

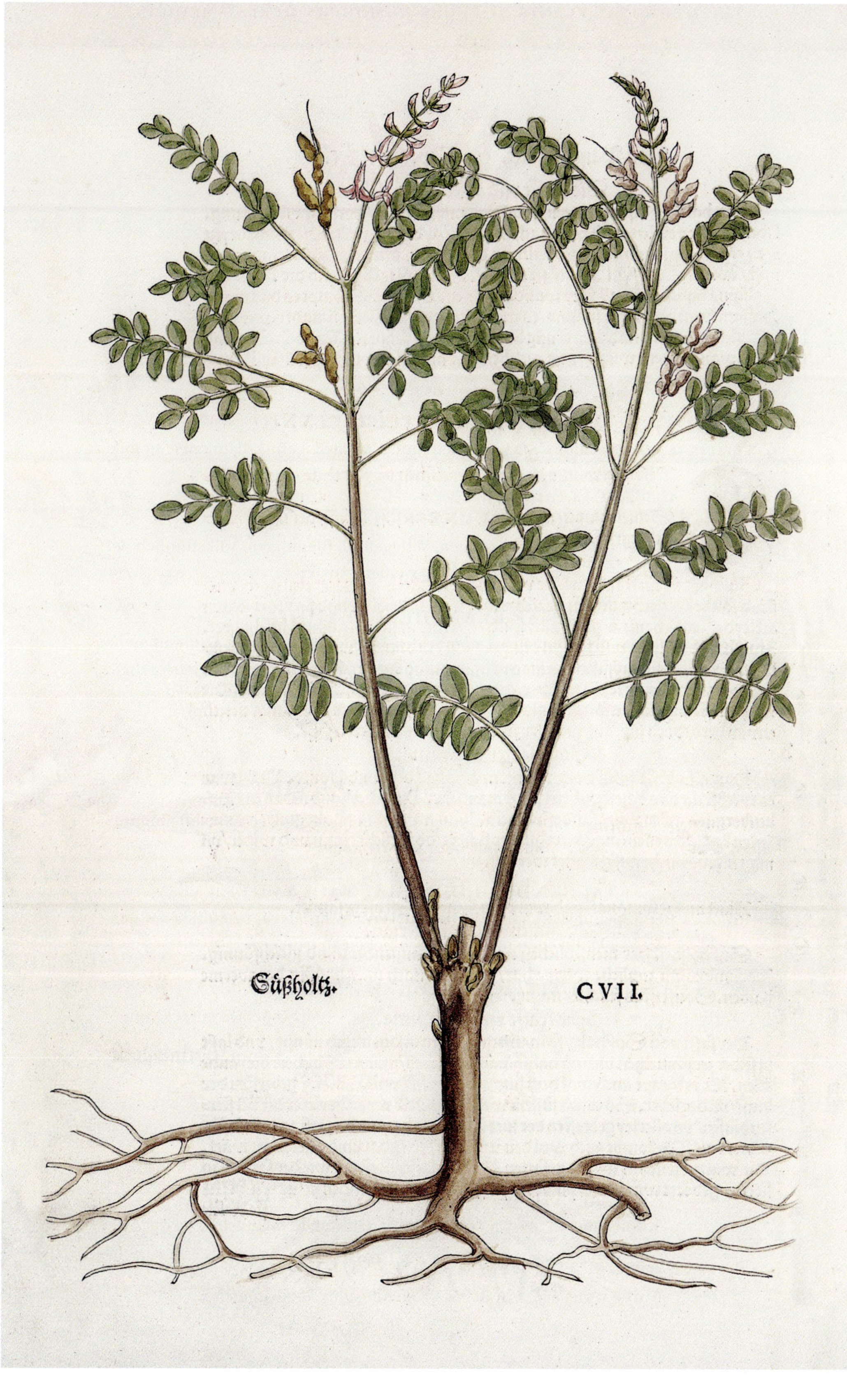
Süßholtz.
CVII.

WHITE DEADNETTLE (CCLXIIII)

Flowers. ❧ Inflammation of the stomach lining, bloated feeling, flatulence. In folk medicine, for female disorders, white discharge.

WEISSE TAUBNESSEL (CCLXIIII)

Blüten. ❧ Magenschleimhautreizungen, Völlegefühl, Blähungen. Volkstümlich bei Frauenkrankheiten, weißem Ausfluss.

ORTIE BLANCHE (CCLXIIII)

Fleurs. ❧ Irritation des muqueuses stomacales, lourdeurs d'estomac, ballonnements. Dans la pharmacopée populaire, maladies particulières à la femme et leucorrhée.

PAGE 706

COMMON CENTAURY (CCXVII)

Herbage. ❧ For loss of appetite and indigestion, to be swallowed in small amounts app. Half-hour before meals.

TAUSENDGÜLDENKRAUT (CCXVII)

Kraut. ❧ Bei Appetitlosigkeit und Verdauungsbeschwerden ca. 1/2 Stunde vor den Mahlzeiten in kleinen Schlucken zu trinken.

PETITE CENTAURÉE (CCXVII)

Partie verte. ❧ Inappétence et douleurs digestives – boire à petites gorgées une demi-heure avant les repas.

PAGE 707

COMMON THYME (CCCCLXXIIII)

Herbage, essential oil. ❧ Bronchitis, coughs, whooping cough.

THYMIAN (CCCCLXXIIII)

Kraut, ätherisches Öl. ❧ Bronchitis, Husten, Keuchhusten.

THYM (CCCCLXXIIII)

Partie verte, éther, huile. ❧ Bronchite, toux et coqueluche.

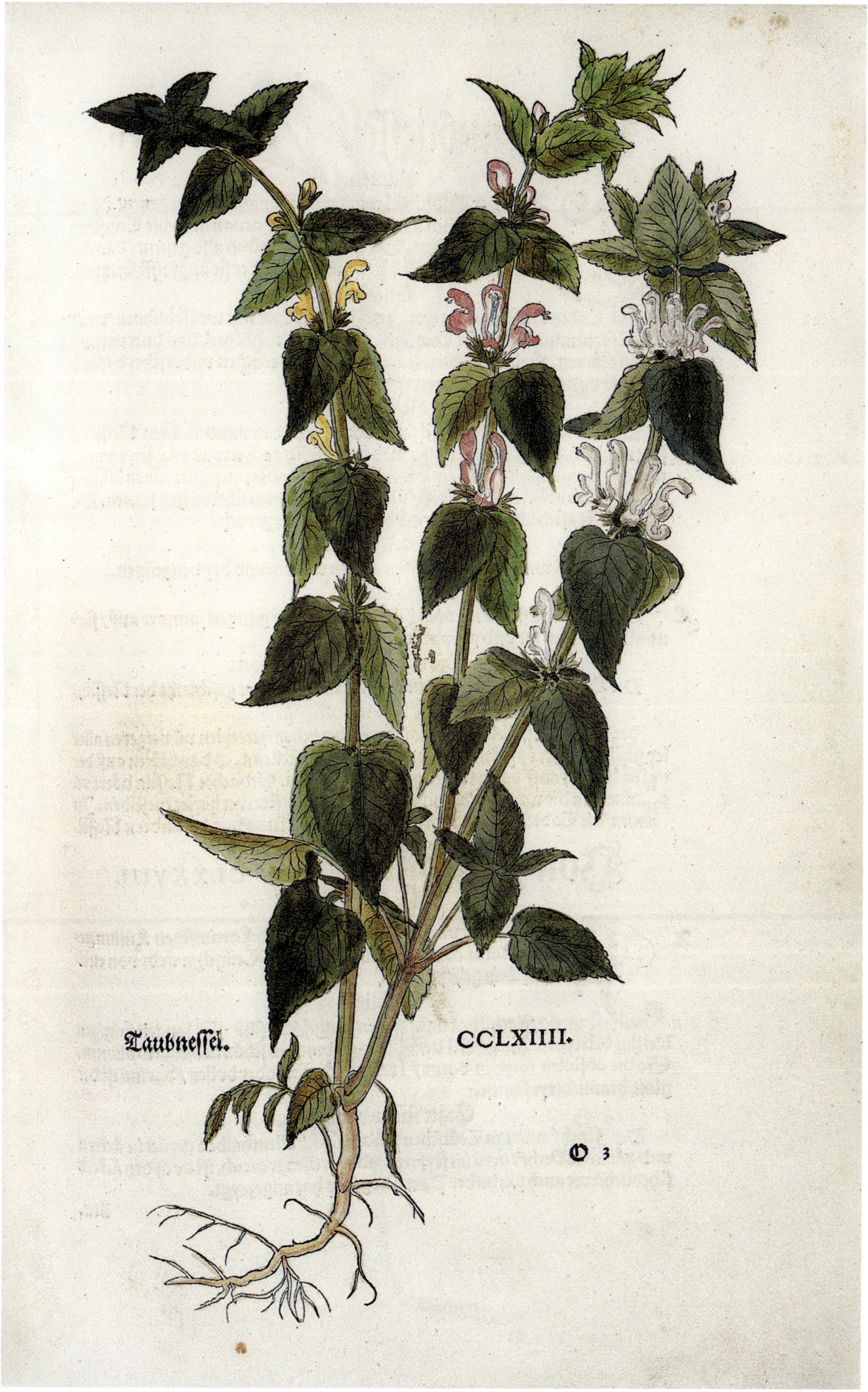
Taubnessel.
CCLXIIII.
O 3

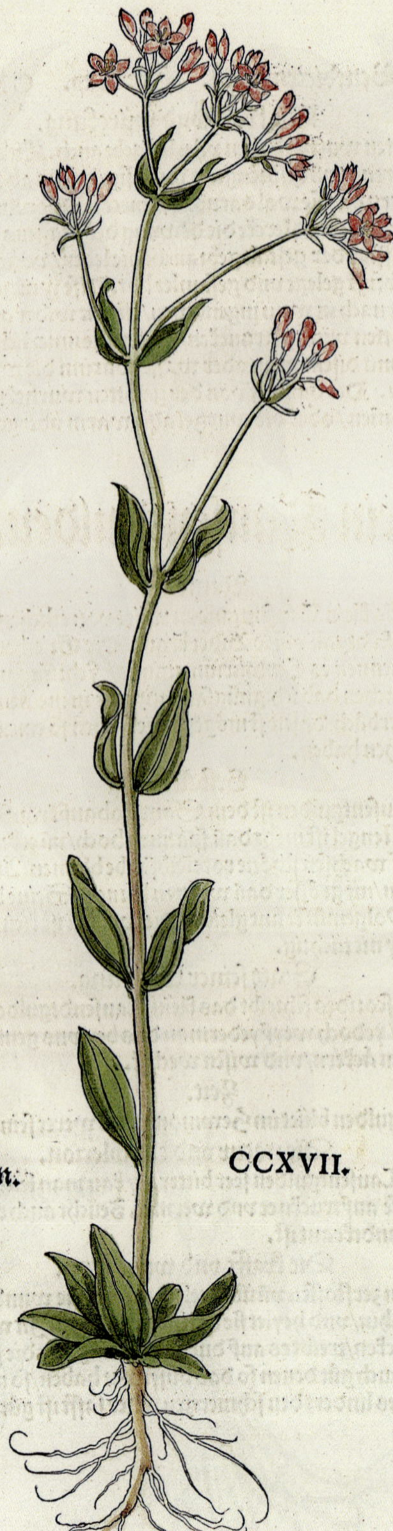

Klein Tausendtgulden. CCXVII.

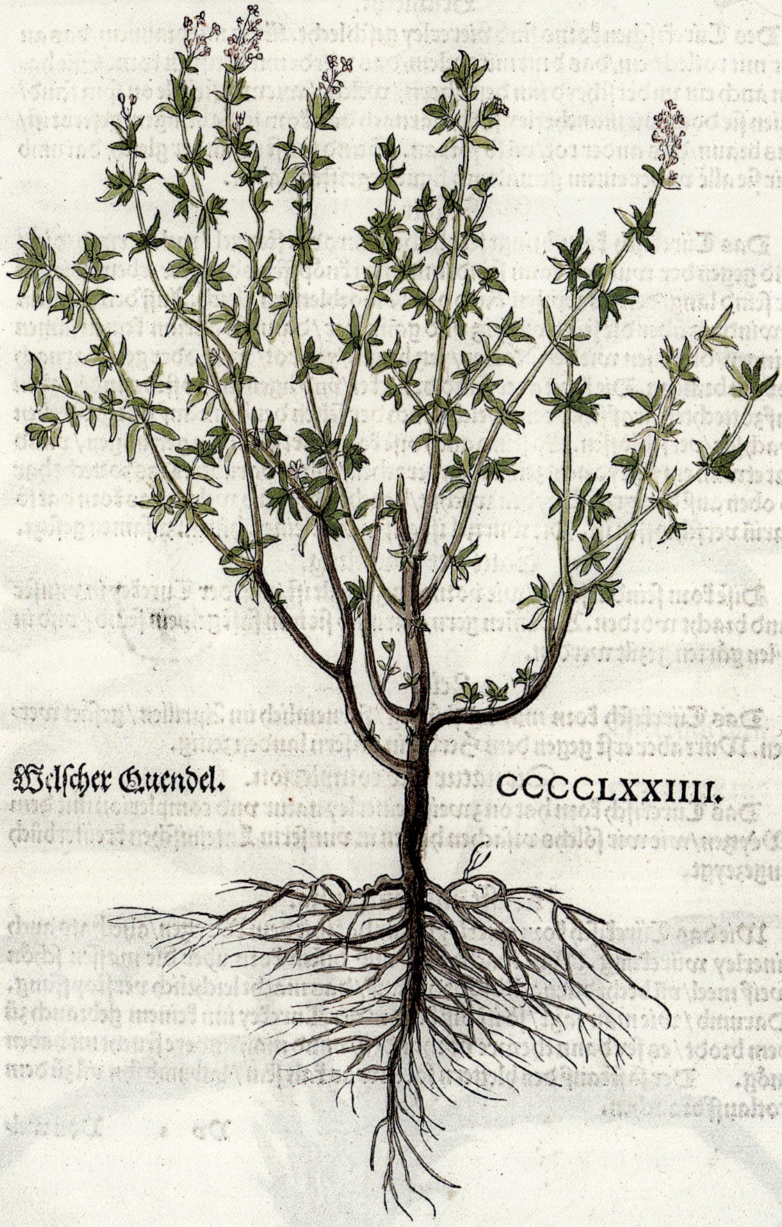

Welscher Quendel. CCCCLXXIIII.

COMMON THYME | THYMIAN | THYM

DEADLY NIGHTSHADE (CCCXCV)

Isolated alkaloid atropine and derivatives. ❧ Spasmolytic, pupil relaxant, antidote to poisons. Only with doctor's prescription owing to high toxicity!

TOLLKIRSCHE (CCCXCV)

Isoliertes Alkaloid Atropin und abgewandelte Formen. ❧ Krampflösend, pupillenerweiternd, Gegenmittel bei Vergiftungen. Wegen der hohen Giftigkeit dem Arzt vorbehalten.

BELLADONE (CCCXCV)

Alcaloïde – l'atropine – et dérivés. ❧ Antispasmodique, dilatateur de la pupille, antidote aux empoisonnements. En raison de sa haute toxicité, maniement réservé au médecin.

PAGE 710

COMMON JUNIPER (XLIII)

Cones with berries, essential oil. ❧ Diuretic, for indigestion; external application to stimulate blood circulation in rheumatism. Internal use counterindicated by kidney disease or pregnancy.

WACHOLDER (XLIII)

Beerenzapfen, ätherisches Öl. ❧ Harntreibend, bei Verdauungsbeschwerden. Äußerlich durchblutungs-fördernd bei Rheuma. Innerliche Anwendung nicht bei Nierenerkrankungen und während der Schwan-gerschaft.

GENÉVRIER (XLIII)

Baies, éther, huile. ❧ Diurétique, douleurs digestives. En usage externe, tonique de la circulation sanguine dans les rhumatismes. Contre-indiqué en usage interne dans les affections rénales et durant la grossesse.

PAGE 711

ENGLISH WALNUT (CCXIII)

Leaves. ❧ External application for light skin inflammations and excessive sweating; in folk medicine, dried green fruit casings traditionally used for skin disorders, eczema and scaly patches.

WALNUSS (CCXIII)

Blätter. ❧ Äußerlich bei leichten Entzündungen der Haut und übermäßigem Schwitzen. Die getrocknete grüne Fruchtschale volkstümlich bei Hauterkrankungen, Ekzemen, Schuppenflechte.

NOYER (CCXIII)

Feuilles. ❧ Usage externe pour les inflammations cutanées et la transpiration excessive. Dans la médecine populaire, brou vert séché contre les dermatoses, eczémas, psoriasis.

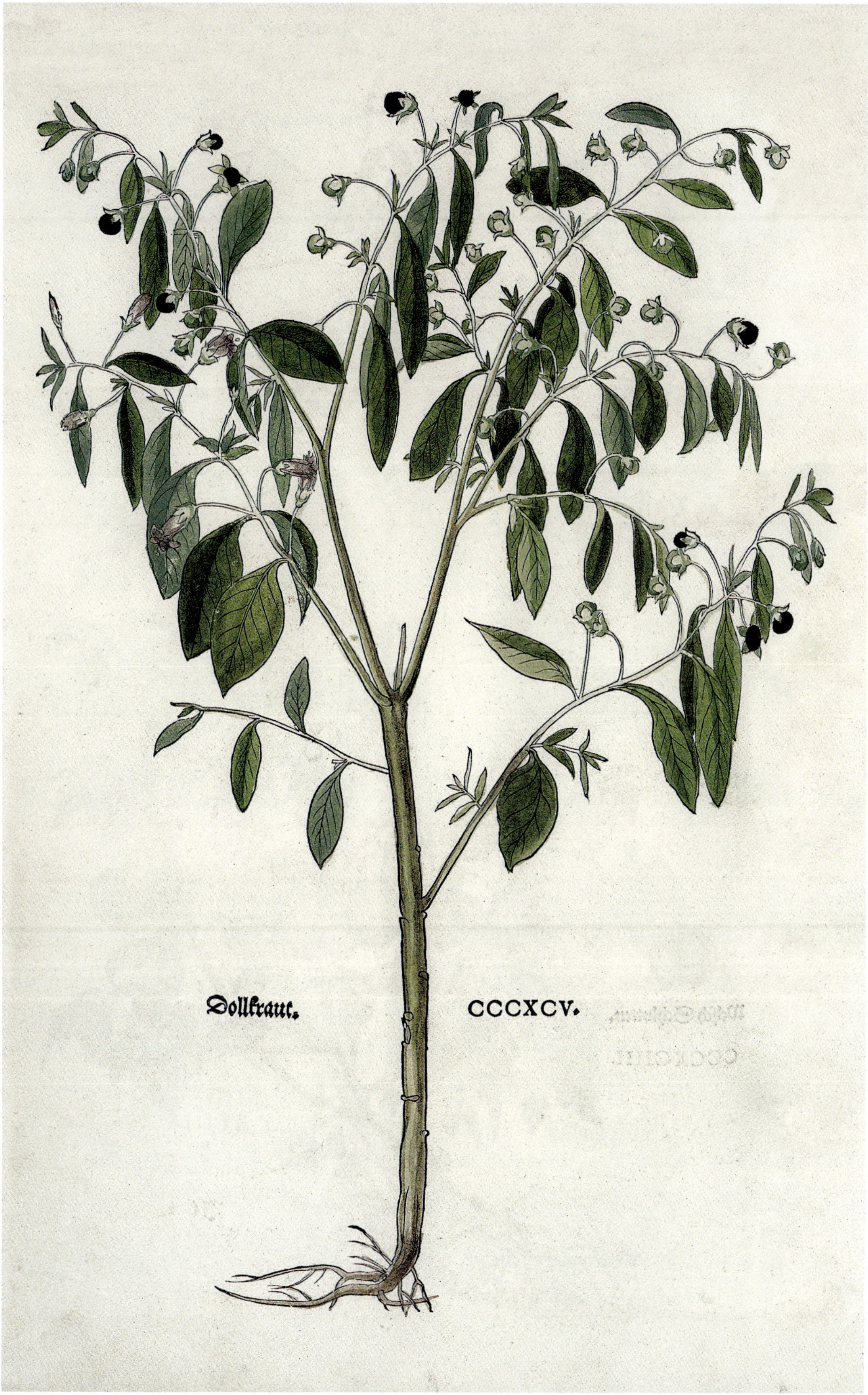
Dollkraut.
CCCXCV.

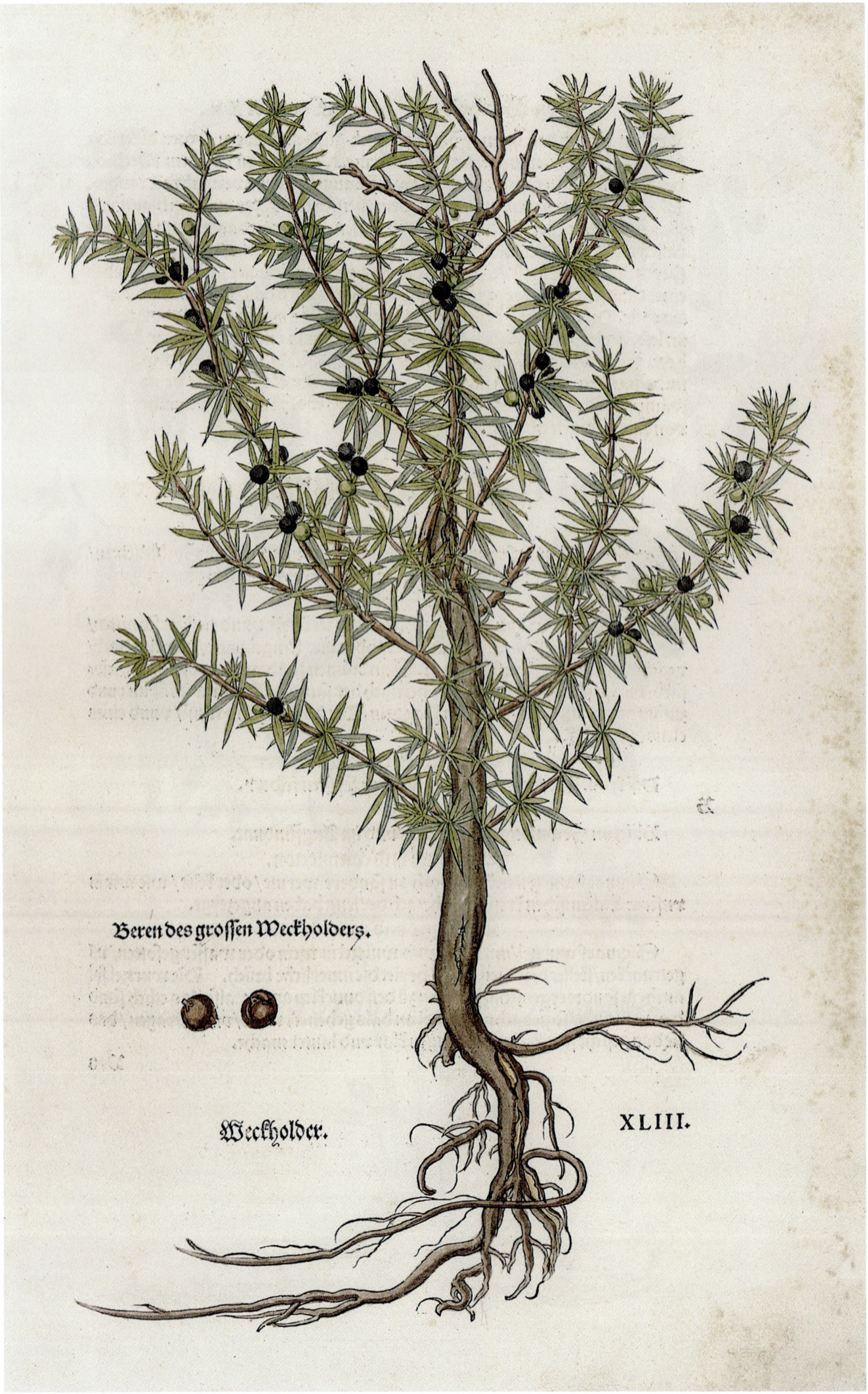
Beren des grossen Weckholders.
Weckholder.
XLIII.

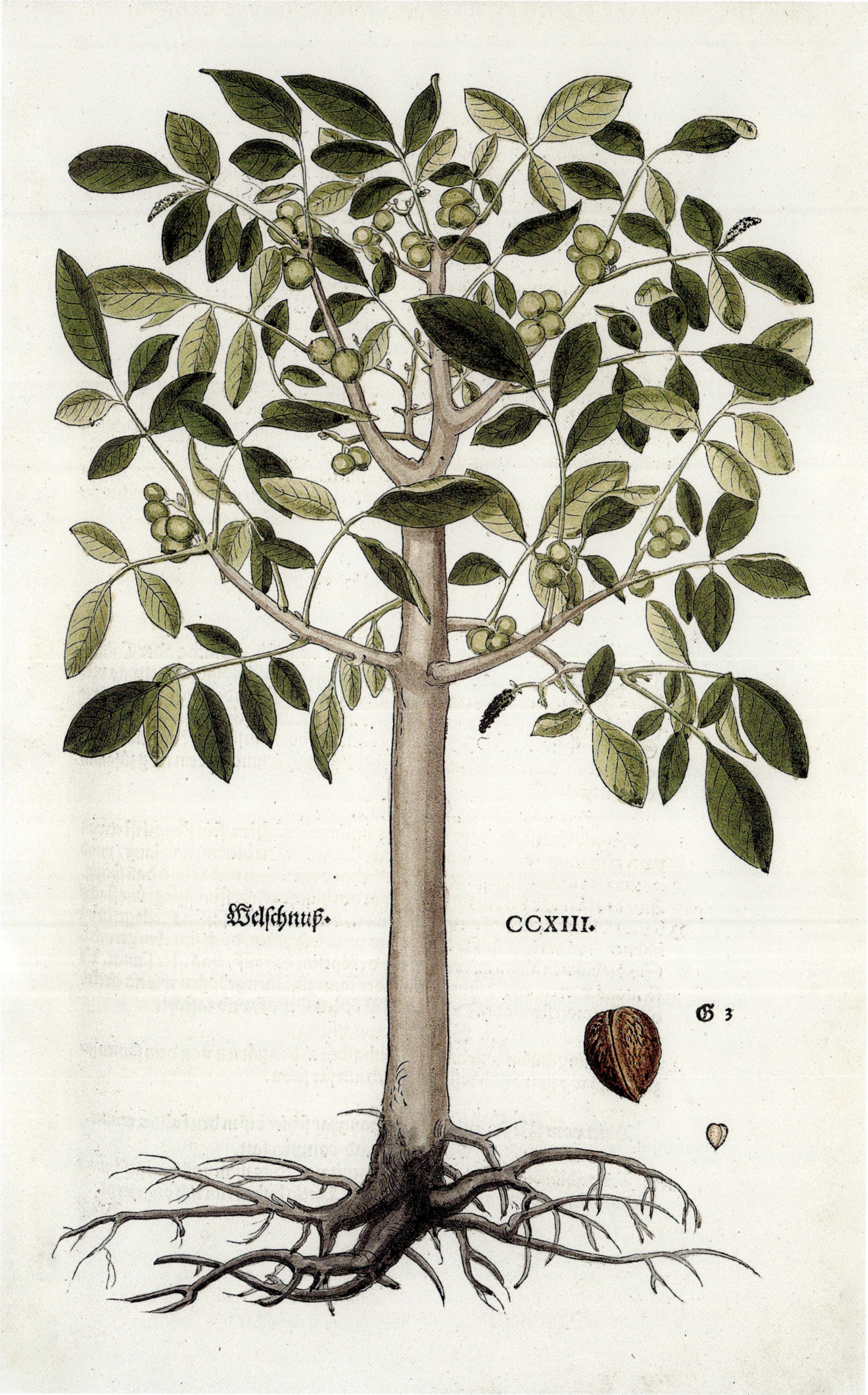
Welschnuß.
CCXIII.
G 3

WORMWOOD (I)

Herb (top). ☙ Stimulates appetite, used for indigestion, ailments of the gall bladder.

WERMUT (I)

Oberer Teil des Krautes. ☙ Appetitanregend, bei Verdauungsbeschwerden, Gallenerkrankungen.

ABSINTHE (I)

Sommités. ☙ Inappétence, douleurs digestives et maladies biliaires.

PAGE 714

LEONHART FUCHS, *New Kreüterbuch*, 1543

CVI (106) *Impatiens balsamina* (L.) – Garden Balsam, Common Balsam, Jewelweed / Garten-Balsamine, Garten-Springkraut / Balsamine, Balsamine des jardins

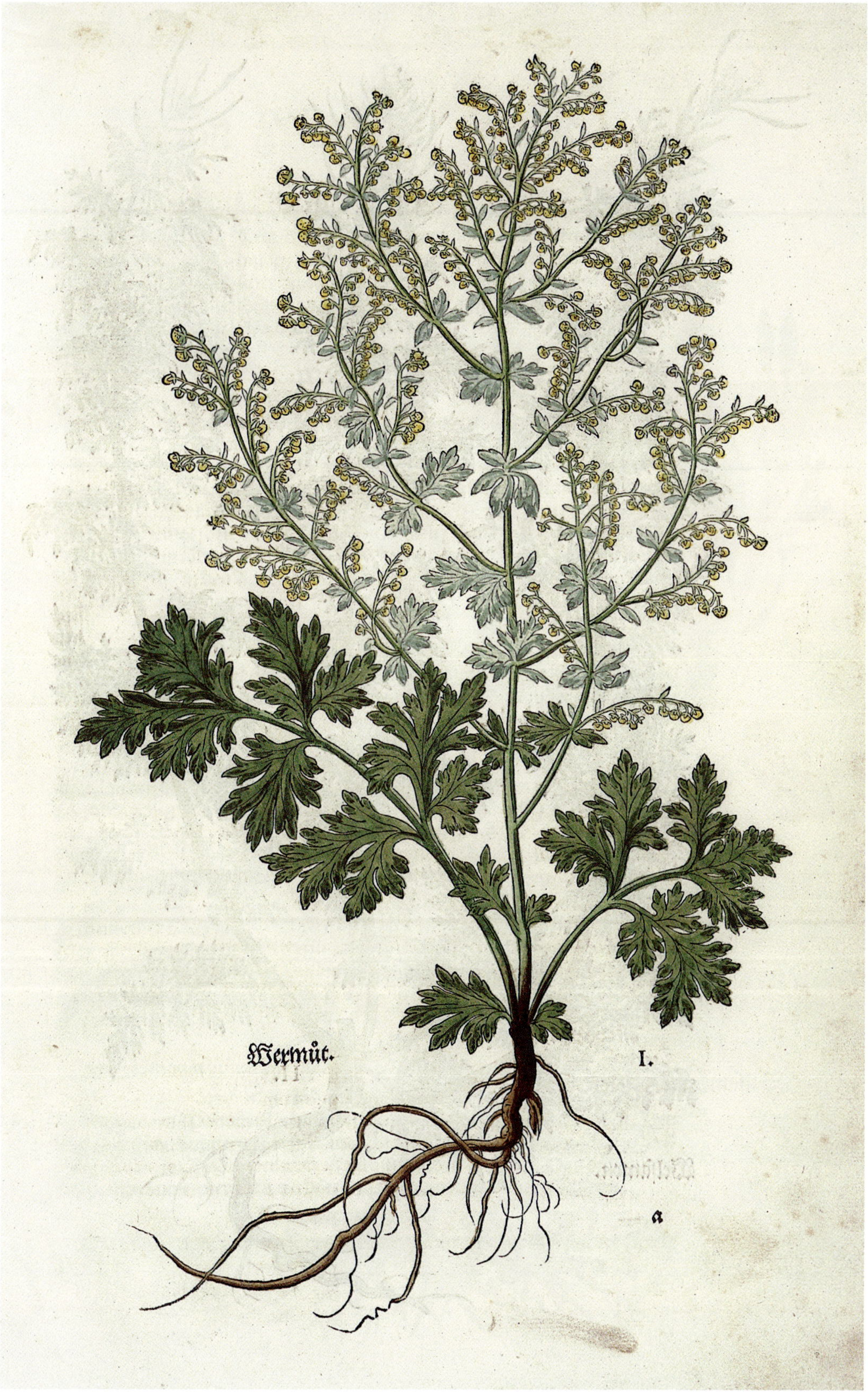
Wermůt.
I.
a

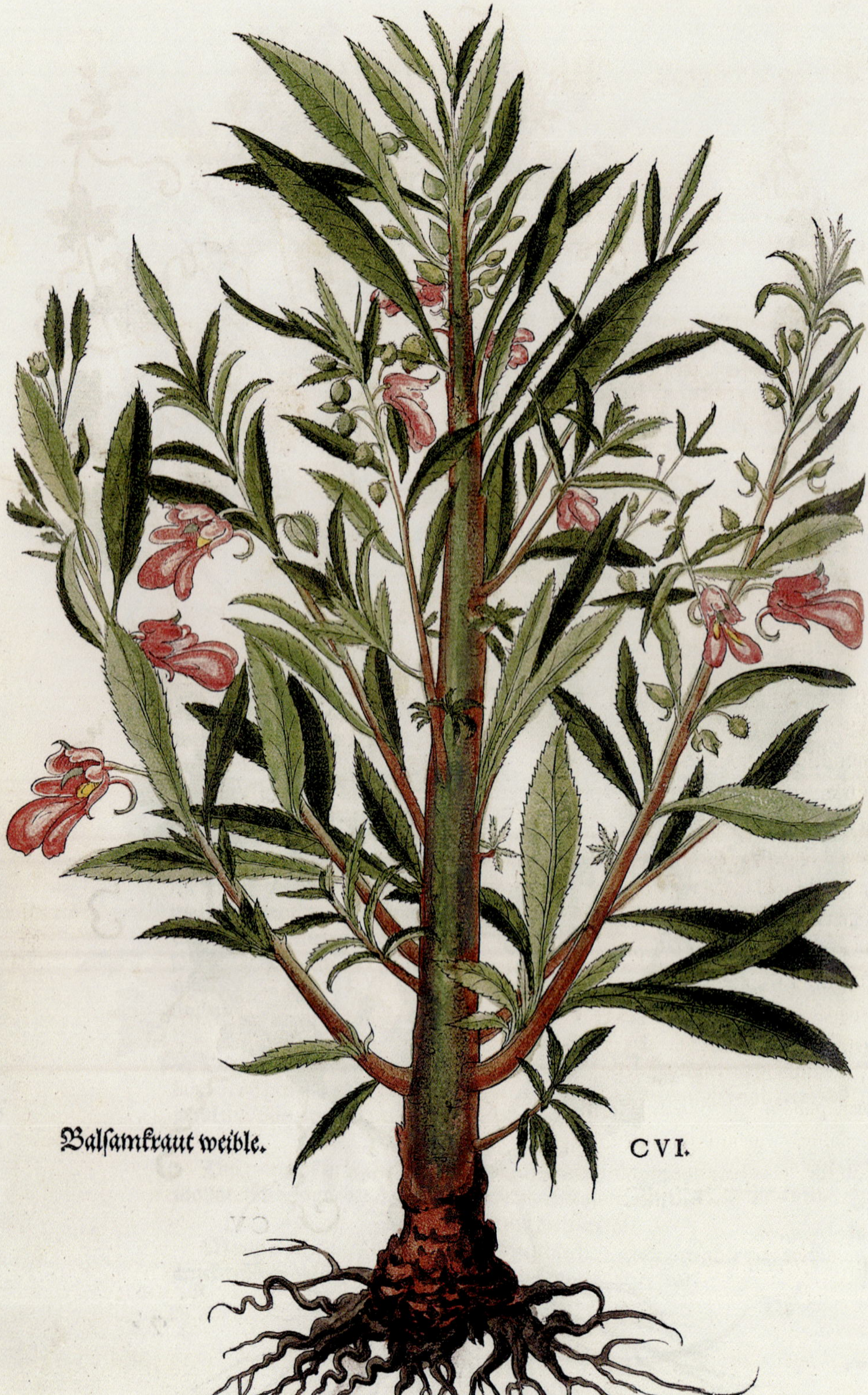

Balſamkraut weible. CVI.

KLAUS DOBAT

Index of Plants Depicted in the *New Kreüterbuch*

1. Index to the Latin and English Plant Names Arranged According to the Order of Appearance of the Woodcuts

All the plants illustrated in *New Kreüterbuch* (complete coloured edition of 1543; cf. TASCHEN, 2022) are listed here according to the consecutive numbering of the woodcuts, including those not shown in this edition. Since not every reader will be familiar with the Roman numerals, the corresponding Arabic figures have been added. The two woodcuts lacking a number in the original appear in both cases after the preceding illustrations (Ivy-leaved Speedwell, *Veronica hederifolia* L.: XII f. [12 f.]; English Plantain, *Plantago lanceolata* L.: XXII f. [22 f.]). Thus the work comprises a total of 517 plant illustrations. The "forgotten" plate C (100): "Sticky Goosefoot" (*Chenopodium botrys* L.), which in the original appeared at the end of the book after plate CCCCCXV (515), has been restored to its rightful place, along with the two plates that were originally switched, CCLXXIX (279): "Hare's Foot" (*Trifolium arvense* L.) and CCLXXX (280): "European Larch" (*Larix decidua* MILL.). Similarly, both instances of double numeration CXL/CXLI (140/141) and CCCCXLV/CCCCXLVI (445/446) have been corrected. The author has attempted to ensure that the Latin name accompanying every plate number corresponds to the valid contemporary scientific designation of the plant; occasional variant plant identifications found in botanical literature have been noted along with the "combinations" undertaken by Fuchs and his artist colleagues.

Abbreviations:
MR = MEYER et al. 1999; MZ = MARZELL 1938; S&N = SPRAGUE & NELMES 1931; agg. = aggregate: species aggregate, species; auct. = auctorum: of the authors; emend. = emendation: amendment, correction; fo. = forma: form; sp. = species: species; ssp. = subspecies: subspecies; subvar.= subvarietas: subvariety; var. = varietas: variety

Register der im *New Kreüterbuch* abgebildeten Pflanzen

I.

Register der lateinischen und deutschen Pflanzennamen in der Reihenfolge der Holzschnitte

Aufgeführt sind alle im *New Kreüterbuch* abgebildeten Pflanzen (vollständig kolorierte Ausgabe von 1543; vgl. TASCHEN, 2022), geordnet nach der fortlaufenden Nummerierung der Holzschnitte, einschließlich der in dieser Ausgabe nicht gezeigten Tafeln. Den römischen Ziffern, mit denen nicht jeder Leser vertraut sein dürfte, wurden die entsprechenden arabischen Zahlen hinzugefügt. Die zwei Holzschnitte ohne Nummer wurden der jeweils voranstehenden Abbildung zugeordnet [„Huenerbiß“, *Veronica hederifolia* L., Efeublättriger Ehrenpreis: XII f. (12 f.); „Spitziger wegerich“, *Plantago lanceolata* L., Spitzwegerich: XXII f. (22 f.)]. Insgesamt umfasst das Werk somit 517 Pflanzenabbildungen. Die „vergessene“ Bildtafel C (100): „Traubenkraut“ (*Chenopodium botrys* L., Drüsiger Gänsefuß), die am Schluss des Buches nach der Abbildung CCCCCXV (515) zu finden ist, wurde ebenso an den richtigen Platz gestellt wie die vertauschten Bilder CCLXXIX (279): „Katzenklee“ (*Trifolium arvense* L., Acker-Klee) und CCLXXX (280): „Lörchenbaum“ (*Larix decidua* MILL., Europäische Lärche). Auch die beiden Doppelzählungen CXL/CXLI (140/141) sowie CCCCXLV/CCCCXLVI (445/446) sind korrigiert. Der jeder Bildnummer folgende lateinische Pflanzenname entspricht nach Ansicht des Verfassers der heute gültigen wissenschaftlichen Bezeichnung. Auf die in der Literatur gelegentlich voneinander abweichenden Identifikationen wird hingewiesen, ebenfalls auf die von Fuchs und seinen künstlerischen Mitarbeitern vorgenommenen „Kombinationen“.

Abkürzungen:
MR = MEYER et al. 1999; MZ = MARZELL 1938; S&N = SPRAGUE & NELMES 1931; agg. = Aggregat: Artengruppe, Kollektiv- oder Sammelart; auct. = auctorum: der Autoren; emend. = Emendation: Berichtigung; fo. = forma: Form; sp. = species: Art; ssp. = subspecies: Unterart; subvar. = subvarietas: Subvarietät; var. = varietas: Varietät.

Index des plantes illustrées dans le *New Kreüterbuch*

1.

Quelques précisions sur l'index des noms botaniques et des noms français

La liste des plantes présentées dans le *New Kreüterbuch* (édition complète et coloriée de 1543 ; cf. TASCHEN, 2022) suit la numérotation consécutive des planches, y compris celles qui ne sont pas reproduites dans cette édition. Les chiffres romains ont été complétés par leurs équivalents arabes. Les deux planches non numérotées à l'origine ont été paginées en fonction des planches qui les précèdent [« Huenerbiß », *Veronica hederifolia* L., véronique à feuilles de lierre : XII f. (12 f.) ; « Spitziger wegerich », *Plantago lanceolata* L. , plantain lancéolé : XXII f. (22 f.)]. Le nombre total de plantes illustrées se monte ainsi à 517. La planche C (100) correspondant au chénopode botryde (*Chenopodium botrys* L., « Traubenkraut »), « oubliée » à l'impression et répertoriée en fin d'ouvrage après l'illustration CCCCCXV (515), a été remise à la bonne place. Il en est de même pour CCLXXIX (279) : « Katzenklee » (*Trifolium arvense* L., trèfle des champs) et CCLXXX (280) : « Lörchenbaum » (*Larix decidua* MILL., mélèze), deux planches interverties à l'origine. Les numérotations doubles CXL/CXLI (140/141) et CCCCXLC/CCCCXLVI (445/446) ont été également corrigées. Le nom latin qui suit chaque numéro d'illustration est conforme, de l'avis de l'auteur, à la dénomination scientifique moderne. Lorsque l'identification de certaines espèces diverge de la nomenclature scientifique ou que Fuchs et ses collaborateurs artistiques « combinent » des plantes différentes, nous en avons fait mention. Enfin, nous remercions infiniment madame Marion Hardegen, biologiste au Conservatoire botanique national de Brest, pour son fastidieux travail de vérification et de complémentation des noms français.

Abréviations :
MR = MEYER et al. 1999 ; MZ =MARZELL 1938 ; S&N = SPRAGUE & NELMES 1931 ;
agg. = agrégat : espèce collective ; auct. = auctorum : des auteurs ; emend. = émendation : correction, modification ; fo. = forma ; forme ; sp. = species : espèce ; ssp. = subspecies : sous-espèce ; subvar. = subvarietas : sous-variété ; var. = varietas : variété.

I (1) *Artemisia absinthium* L. – Wormwood / Wermut, Absinth / Absinthe, Armoise absinthe

II (2) *Descurainia sophia* (L.) WEBB ex PRANTL [*Sisymbrium sophia* L.] – Flixweed, Herb Sophia, Tansy-mustard / Besenrauke, Sophienkraut / Sagesse des chirurgiens, Sisymbre sagesse, Descurainie sagesse

III (3) *Artemisia abrotanum* L. – Southernwood, Old Man / Eberraute, Zitronenkraut / Armoise citronnelle, Aurone mâle

IIII (4) *Artemisia pontica* L. – Roman Wormwood / Pontischer Wermut, Pontischer Beifuß, Römischer Wermut / Armoise pontique, Petite absinthe

V (5) *Asarum europaeum* L. – Asarabacca, Hazelwort / Europäische Haselwurz, Haselwurz / Asaret d'Europe, Cabaret

VI (6) *Iris pseudacorus* L. – Yellow Flag, Water Iris, Jacob's Sword / Gelbe Schwertlilie, Sumpf-Schwertlilie, Wasser-Schwertlilie / Iris des marais, Iris jaune

VII (7) *Althaea officinalis* L. Marsh Mallow / Echter Eibisch, Heilwurz / Guimauve officinale

VIII (8) *Anagallis arvensis* L. – Scarlet Pimpernel / Acker-Gauchheil / Mouron rouge, Mouron des champs

IX (9) *Anagallis foemina* MILL. – Blue Pimpernel / Blauer Gauchheil / Mouron bleu, Mouron femelle

X (10) *Stellaria media* (L.) VILL. – Chickweed / Vogelmiere, Vogel-Sternmiere / Mouron des oiseaux, Stellaire intermédiaire

XI (11) *Veronica agrestis* L. – Field Speedwell, Germander Chickweed / Acker-Ehrenpreis / Véronique agreste, Véronique des campagnes

XII (12) *Arenaria serpyllifolia* L. – Sandwort, Thyme-leaved Sandwort / Quendel-Sandkraut / Sabline à feuilles de serpolet

XII f. (12 f.) *Veronica hederifolia* L. (without plate no.) – Ivy-leaved Speedwell, Ivy Speedwell / Efeublättriger Ehrenpreis / Véronique à feuilles de lierre

XIII (13) *Matricaria recutita* L. [*M. chamomilla* L., *Chamomilla recutita* (L.) RAUSCH.] Chamomile, Wild Chamomile / Echte Kamille / Petite camomille, Camomille vraie, Matricaire camomille

XIIII (14) *Anthemis tinctoria* L. – Yellow Chamomile, Dyer's Chamomile / Färber-Hundskamille, Färberkamille / Anthémis des teinturiers

XV (15) *Consolida regalis* GRAY [*Delphinium consolida* L.] – Field Larkspur, Forking Larkspur, Lark's Heel / Acker-Rittersporn, Feld-Rittersporn / Dauphinelle consoude, Pied-d'alouette

XVI (16) *Anethum graveolens* L. – Dill / Dill, Gewöhnlicher Dill / Aneth odorant, Fenouil bâtard

XVII (17) *Sempervivum tectorum* L. – Houseleek (Welcome home husband, however drunk you be) / Dach-Hauswurz, Echte Hauswurz / Joubarbe des toits, Herbe du tonnerre

XVIII (18) *Sedum reflexum* L. [*S. rupestre* L.] Rock Stonecrop / Felsen-Mauerpfeffer, Tripmadam / Orpin des rochers, Orpin réfléchi

XIX (19) *Sedum album* L. – White Stonecrop / Weißer Mauerpfeffer / Orpin blanc

XX (20) *Sedum acre* L. – Wallpepper, Common Stonecrop / Scharfer Mauerpfeffer / Poivre de muraille, Orpin âcre

XXI (21) *Plantago major* L. – Great Plantain, Common Plantain, Waybread / Breitwegerich, Großer Wegerich / Grand plantain, Plantain majeur, Plantain à larges feuilles

XXII (22) *Plantago*-combination: Leaves of *Plantago lanceolata* L., English Plantain, Ribwort / Spitzwegerich / Plantain lancéolé; inflorescences of *Plantago media* L., Hoary Plantain / Mittlerer Wegerich / Plantain moyen (see S&N, p. 575) [MZ, p. 23: *P. media* L.; MR, p. 308: perhaps variant of *P. media* L. with narrow leaves]

XXII f. (22 f.) *Plantago lanceolata* L. (without plate no.) English Plantain, Ribwort / Spitzwegerich / Plantain lancéolé

XXIII (23) *Alisma plantago-aquatica* L. Water Plantain / Gewöhnlicher Froschlöffel / Flûteau commun, Plantain d'eau

XXIIII (24) *Artemisia vulgaris* L. – Common Mugwort / Gewöhnlicher Beifuß / Armoise vulgaire, Armoise commune

XXV (25) *Tanacetum parthenium* (L.) SCH. BIP. [*Chrysanthemum parthenium* (L.) BERNH.] Feverfew, Flirtwort / Mutterkraut / Tanaisie parthénium, Grande camomille

XXVI (26) *Tanacetum vulgare* L. – Common Tansy / Rainfarn / Tanaisie vulgaire, Barbotine

XXVII (27) *Tagetes patula* L. – French Marigold / Studentenblume, Sammetblume, Stinkende Hoffart / Œillet d'Inde

XXVIII (28) *Galium aparine* L. – Bedstraw, Cleavers, Goosegrass / Kletten-Labkraut, Kleb-Labkraut, Klebkraut / Gaillet gratteron, Gratteron

XXIX (29) *Acanthus mollis* L. – Bear's-breech (see S&N, p. 576; MZ, p. 24) [MR, p. 312: *Acanthus spinosus* L., Prickly Bear's-breech / Echter Bärenklau, Weicher Bärenklau / Acanthe à feuilles molles] (vgL. – S&N, S. 576; MZ, S. 24) [MR, S. 312: *Acanthus spinosus* L., Prickly Bear's-breech / Stacheliger Bärenklau / Acanthe épineuse, Branc-ursine piquante]

XXX (30) *Heracleum sphondylium* L. agg. Cow Parsnip, Hogweed / Wiesen-Bärenklau / Berce commune, Berce des prés, Patte-d'ours

XXXI (31) *Silybum marianum* (L.) GAERTN. Milk Thistle, Holy Thistle / Mariendistel / Chardon Marie, Silybe de Marie

XXXII (32) *Onopordum acanthium* L. – Giant Thistle, Scotch Thistle / Gewöhnliche Eselsdistel / Onoporde acanthe

XXXIII (33) *Asparagus officinalis* L. Common Asparagus, Sparrowgrass / Spargel, Gemüse-Spargel / Asperge officinale, Asperge

XXXIIII (34) *Ononis spinosa* L. – Spiny Restharrow / Dornige Hauhechel, Dorn-Hauhechel / Bugrane épineuse

XXXV (35) *Pimpinella anisum* L. – Common Anise / Anis / Anis

XXXVI (36) *Sambucus nigra* L. – Black Elder, Common Elder / Schwarzer Holunder, Holder / Sureau noir, Grand sureau

XXXVII (37) *Sambucus ebulus* L. Danewort, Dwarf Elder / Zwerg-Holunder, Attich / Sureau yèble, Petit sureau, Yèble

XXXVIII (38) *Ammi majus* L. – False Bishop's Weed / Große Knorpelmöhre / Ammi élevé, Grand ammi

XXXIX (39) *Arum maculatum* L. – Cuckoo Pint, Wake Robin, Starchwort / Aronstab, Gefleckter Aronstab / Arum tacheté, Gouet tacheté, Gouet maculé, Pied-de-veau

XL (40) *Arctium lappa* L. [*Lappa officinalis* ALL.] – Great Burdock / Große Klette / Bardane commune, Grande bardane

XLI (41) *Hypericum hirsutum* L. – Hairy St. John's Wort / Behaartes Johanniskraut, Rauhhaariges Johanniskraut, Raues Hartheu / Millepertuis hérissé, Millepertuis velu

XLII (42) *Hypericum montanum* L. – Mountain St. John's Wort / Berg-Johanniskraut, Berg-Hartheu / Millepertuis des montagnes

XLIII (43) *Juniperus communis* L. Common Juniper / Gewöhnlicher Wacholder / Genévrier commun

XLIIII (44) *Malva alcea* L. – Cut-leaved Mallow, Hollyhock Mallow, Vervain Mallow / Rosen-Malve, Rosen-Pappel, Sigmarswurz / Mauve alcée

XLV (45) *Adiantum capillus-veneris* L. Maidenhair Fern, Southern Maidenhair, Venus Maidenhair / Frauenhaar, Frauenhaar-Farn, Venushaar / Cheveux de Vénus, Capillaire de Montpellier

XLVI (46) *Vitis vinifera* L. – Common Grape Vine, Grape, Vine / Echter Weinstock, Weinrebe / Vigne

XLVII (47) *Paris quadrifolia* L. – Herb Paris / Einbeere, Vierblättrige Einbeere / Parisette à quatre feuilles

XLVIII (48) *Aconitum vulparia* RCHB. [*A. lycoctonum* L. ssp. *vulparia* (RCHB.) NYMAN] – Monkshood, Yellow Wolfsbane / Gelber Eisenhut, Wolfs-Eisenhut, Fuchs-Eisenhut / Aconit tue-loup

XLIX (49) *Aristolochia clematitis* L. – Birthwort / Gewöhnliche Osterluzei / Aristoloche clématite, Pipe, Sarrazine

L (50) *Corydalis*-combination: Figure on left: *Corydalis cava* (L.) SCHWEIGG. et KOERTE [*C. bulbosa* (L.) auct. ssp. *bulbosa*], Holewort, Hollow-root / Hohler Lerchensporn / Corydale à tubercule creux. Figure on right: *Corydalis solida* (L.) SW. [*C. bulbosa* (L.) DC. ssp. *marschalliana* (PALL.) CHATER], Solid-rooted Fumewort / Fester Lerchensporn, Gefingerter Lerchensporn / Corydale à tubercule plein, Corydale solide

LI (51) *Bryonia cretica* L. ssp. *dioica* (JACQ.) TUTIN [*B. dioica* JACQ.] – Red Bryony / Rotfrüchtige Zaunrübe, Zweihäusige Zaunrübe / Bryone dioïque [S&N, p. 579: erroneously *B. alba* L., White Bryony / Weiße Zaunrübe, Schwarzfruchtige Zaunrübe / Bryone blanche]

LII (52) *Clematis vitalba* L. – Old Man's Beard, Traveller's Joy / Gewöhnliche Waldrebe / Clématite blanche, Herbe aux gueux, Clématite des haies

LIII (53) *Helichrysum arenarium* (L.) MOENCH [*Gnaphalium arenarium* L.] Live-ever, Yellow Everlasting Daisy, Yellow Chaste Weed / Sand-Strohblume / Gnaphale des sables, Immortelle des sables

LIIII (54) *Gomphrena globosa* L. – Globe Amaranth / Gewöhnlicher Kugelamarant/ Amarantoide (see MZ, p. 27) [S&N, p. 579; MR, p. 327: *Celosia argentea* L. var. *cristata* (L.) KUNTZE, – Wool Flower, Gentle Purple Flower / Silber-Brandschopf, Hahnenkamm / Amarante célosie, Célosie crête de coq]

LV (55) *Aquilegia vulgaris* L. – Colombine, Granny's Bonnet / Gewöhnliche Akelei / Ancolie vulgaire, Ancolie commune

LVI (56) *Alliaria petiolata* (M. BIEB.) CAV. et GRANDE [*A. officinalis* ANDR. ex M. BIEB.] Hedge Garlic, Garlic Mustard / Knoblauchsrauke, Lauchhederich / Alliaire pétiolée, Alliaire officinale

LVII (57) *Urtica pilulifera* L. – Roman Nettle / Pillen-Brennnessel / Ortie à pilules

LVIII (58) *Urtica dioica* L. – Nettle, Stinging Nettle / Große Brennnessel / Grande ortie, Ortie dioïque

LIX (59) *Urtica urens* L. – Small Nettle, Dog Nettle / Kleine Brennnessel / Petite ortie, Ortie brûlante

LX (60) *Vicia sepium* L. – Bush Vetch / Zaun-Wicke / Vesce des haies

LXI (61) *Portulaca oleracea* L. ssp. *sativa* (HAW.) SCHUEBL. et MARTENS Garden Purslane / Garten-Portulak, Gemüse-Portulak / Pourpier cultivé

LXII (62) *Portulaca oleracea* L. ssp. *oleracea* [*P. o.* var. *sylvestris* DC.] – Wild Purslane / Wilder Portulak / Pourpier commun, Pourpier potager

LXIII (63) *Lilium martagon* L. – Martagon Lily / Türkenbund, Türkenbund-Lilie / Lis martagon

LXIIII (64) *Atriplex hortensis* L. – Orache, Garden Orache / Garten-Melde / Arroche des jardins, Bonne-dame

LXV (65) *Chenopodium album* L. – Fat Hen, Pigweed, Lamb's-quarters / Weißer Gänsefuß / Chénopode blanc

LXVI (66) *Carlina vulgaris* L. – Carline Thistle / Gewöhnliche Eberwurz, Golddistel, Kleine Wetterdistel / Carline vulgaire, Carline commune

LXVII (67) *Cnicus benedictus* L. – Blessed Thistle / Echtes Benediktenkraut, Benediktendistel / Chardon béni

LXVIII (68) *Angelica archangelica* L. [*Archangelica officinalis* HOFFM.] – Angelica, Garden Angelica / Arznei-Engelwurz, Echte Engelwurz / Angélique

LXIX (69) *Angelica sylvestris* L. – Wild Angelica / Angelika, Gewöhnliche Engelwurz, Brustwurzel / Angélique des bois

LXX (70) *Agrostemma githago* L. – Corn Cockle / Korurade / Nielle des blés

LXXI (71) *Vincetoxicum hirundinaria* MED. [*V. officinale* MOENCH] – Swallow-wort, Common Vincetoxicum / Gewöhnliche Schwalbenwurz, Weiße Schwalbenwurz / Dompte-venin officinal, Dompte-venin

LXXII (72) *Lathyrus tuberosus* L. – Tuberous Pea, Earth-nut Pea, Earth-chestnut / Knollen-Platterbse, Erd-Eichel, Ackernuss / Gesse tubéreuse, Gland de terre

XCVII (97) *Chenopodium polyspermum* L. All-seed / Vielsamiger Gänsefuß / Chénopode polysperme, Ansérine graineuse

XCVIII (98) *Brassica rapa* L. ssp. *rapa* subvar. *communis* SCHUEBL. et MARTENS fo. *oblonga* (MILL.) SCHUEBL. et MARTENS Turnip / Lange Weiße Rübe / Rave longue

XCIX (99) *Brassica rapa* L. ssp. *rapa* subvar. *communis* SCHUEBL. et MARTENS fo. *depressa* (DC.) SCHUEBL. et MARTENS Turneps / Kurze Weiße Rübe, Tellerrübe / Navet rond, Navet plat

C (100) *Chenopodium botrys* L. – Illustr. is missing [= CCCCCXV f. (515 f.)] Sticky Goosefoot, Jerusalem Oak / Drüsiger Gänsefuß, Klebriger Gänsefuß / Chénopode botryde

CI (101) *Aruncus dioicus* (WALT.) FERN. [*A. sylvestris* KOSTEL.] – Goat's-beard / Wald-Geißbart, Großer Geißbart / Aronce dioïque, Barbe-de-bouc, Reine des bois

CII (102) *Verbascum blattaria* L. – Moth Mullein / Schabenkraut-Königskerze / Molène blattaire, Herbe aux mites

CIII (103) *Avena sativa* L. – Common Oat, Oats / Hafer, Saat-Hafer / Avoine

CIIII (104) *Ribes uva-crispa* L. – [*R. grossularia* L.] – Gooseberry / Stachelbeere / Groseillier épineux

CV (105) *Momordica balsamina* L. – Balsam Apple / Balsamapfel / Pomme de merveille

CVI (106) *Impatiens balsamina* L. – Garden Balsam, Common Balsam, Jewelweed / Garten-Balsamine, Garten-Springkraut / Balsamine, Balsamine des jardins

CVII (107) *Glycyrrhiza glabra* L. – Licorice, Liquorice, Sweet Root / Süßholz, Spanisches Süßholz / Réglisse

CVIII (108) *Scrophularia auriculata* L. [*S. aquatica* auct., non L.] – Water Betony, Water Figwort / Wasser-Braunwurz / Scrophulaire auriculée

CIX (109) *Galium verum* L. – Lady's Bedstraw, Yellow Bedstraw / Echtes Labkraut / Gaillet jaune, Caille-lait jaune

CX (110) *Mentha pulegium* L. – Pennyroyal, Pudding Grass / Polei-Minze, Polei, Flöhkraut / Menthe pouliot, Herbe de Saint Laurent

CXI (111) *Gentiana lutea* L. – Great Yellow Gentian, Yellow Gentian / Gelber Enzian / Gentiane jaune, Grande gentiane

CXII (112) *Paeonia officinalis* L. ssp. *officinalis* [*P. foeminea* MILL.] – Common Peony, Cottage Peony / Echte Pfingstrose / Pivoine des jardins, Pivoine officinale

CXIII (113) *Erodium cicutarium* (L.) L'HER. – Common Storksbill, Heron's Bill / Gewöhnlicher Reiherschnabel / Bec-de-grue commun, Bec-de-cigogne commun, Erodium à feuilles de ciguë

CXIIII (114) *Geranium rotundifolium* L. Round-leaved Cranesbill / Rundblättriger Storchschnabel / Géranium à feuilles rondes

CXV (115) *Geranium robertianum* L. – Herb Robert / Ruprechtskraut, Stinkender Storchschnabel / Géranium herbe-à-Robert

CXVI (116) *Geranium dissectum* L. Cut-leaved Cranesbill, Alum Root / Schlitzblättriger Storchschnabel / Géranium découpé

CXVII (117) *Geranium sanguineum* L. Blood Cranesbill / Blut-Storchschnabel / Géranium sanguin

CXVIII (118) *Geranium pratense* L. – Meadow Cranesbill / Wiesen-Storchschnabel / Géranium des prés

CXIX (119) *Brassica napus* L. var. *napobrassica* (L.) RCHB. [*B. napus* L. ssp. *rapifera* METZG.] – Rutabaga, Swede, Swedish Turnip / Kohlrübe, Steckrübe, Wruke / Rutabaga, Chou-navet, Navet de Suède

CXX (120) *Beta vulgaris* L. var. *rapa* DUM. fo. *rubra* DC. – Red Beet, Beet, Gardenbeet / Rote Rübe, Rote Bete / Betterave rouge, Betterave potagère

CXXI (121) *Campanula rapunculus* L. – Bellflower, Rampion / Rapunzel-Glockenblume / Campanule raiponce

CXXII (122) *Anthriscus cerefolium* (L.) HOFFM. – Chervil / Echter Kerbel, Garten-Kerbel / Cerfeuil

CXXIII (123) *Cytisus scoparius* (L.) LINK [*Sarothamnus scoparius* (L.) KOCH]

Common Broom; Scotch Broom / Besenginster / Genêt à balais, Cytise à balais

CXXIIII (124) *Genista germanica* L. German Broom / Deutscher Ginster / Genêt d'Allemagne

CXXV (125) *Filago vulgaris* LAM. [*F. germanica* L.] – Common Cudweed, Cotton-rose, Cuddleweed / Gewöhnliches Filzkraut, Deutsches Filzkraut, Deutsches Schimmelkraut / Cotonnière vulgare, Cotonnière allemande (the different shoot on the extreme right: perhaps *Gnaphalium uliginosum* L. [*Filaginella uliginosa* (L.) OPIZ, – Marsh Cudweed / Sumpf-Ruhrkraut/ Gnaphale des marais])

CXXVI (126) *Dipsacus sativus* (L.) HONCK. [*D. fullonum* L. var. *sativus* L.] – Fuller's Teasel / Weber-Karde/ Cardère cultivée

CXXVII (127) *Dipsacus fullonum* L. [*D. sylvestris* HUDS.] – Common Teasel, Wild Teasel / Wilde Karde, Wald-Karde, Schutt-Karde / Cardère sauvage, Chardon à foulon

CXXVIII (128) *Daphne mezereum* L. Mezereon, February Daphne, Paradise Plant / Gewöhnlicher Seidelbast, Kellerhals / Bois-gentil, Bois-joli, Daphné mézéréon

CXXIX (129) *Quercus robur* L. [*Q. pedunculata* EHRH.] – Pedunculate Oak, English Oak / Stiel-Eiche, Sommer-Eiche / Chêne pédonculé

CXXX (130) *Dracunculus vulgaris* SCHOTT Dragonwort, Dragon Plant / Drachenwurz / Serpentaire commune, Govet serpentaire

CXXXI (131) *Calla palustris* L. – Water Arum, Wild Dragon, Marsh Calla / Sumpf-Calla, Schlangenwurz / Calla des marais

CXXXII (132) *Ruscus hypoglossum* L. – Double Tongue, Alexander's Laurel, Butcher's Broom / Hadernblatt, Zungenblatt / Fragon hypoglosse

CXXXIII (133) *Convallaria majalis* L. – Lily-of-the-Valley / Maiglöckchen / Lis des vallées, Muguet de mai, Muguet

CXXXIIII (134) *Inula helenium* L. – Elecampane, Scabwort / Echter Alant / Grande aunée, Inula hélénie, Inule aunée

CXXXV (135) *Agrimonia eupatoria* L. Common Agrimony, Cocklebur, Liverwort / Kleiner Odermennig / Aigremoine eupatoire

CXXXVI (136) *Euphrasia rostkoviana* HAYNE [*E. officinalis* L. ssp. *rostkoviana* (HAYNE) TOWNS.] – Eyebright / Gewöhnlicher Augentrost, Gebräuchlicher Augentrost, Echter Augentrost / Casse-lunettes, Euphraise de Rostcov

CXXXVII (137) *Salvia officinalis* L. – Common Sage / Echter Salbei, Garten-Salbei / Sauge officinale

CXXXVIII (138) *Salvia fruticosa* MILL. [*S. triloba* L. f.; *S. officinalis* L. var. *aurita* SPRENG.] – Three-lobe Sage, Greek Sage / Kreuz-Salbei, Griechischer Salbei / Sauge à trois lobes

CXXXIX (139) *Thymus pulegioides* L. ssp. *chamaedrys* (FRIES) GUSULEAC – Larger Wild Thyme / Gemeiner Thymian, Arznei-Thymian / Thym serpolet [S&N, p. 589; MZ, p. 34; MR, p. 375: *Thymus serpyllum* L.]

CXL (140) *Setaria italica* (L.) P. BEAUV. – Plate incorrectly numbered [CXLI (141)] Italian Millet, Foxtail, Bristle Grass / Kolbenhirse, Italienische Borstenhirse / Sétaire d'Italie, Millet des oiseaux

CXLI (141) *Calluna vulgaris* (L.) HULL Heather, Ling / Besenheide, Heidekraut / Fausse bruyère, Callune vulgaire, Callune

CXLII (142) *Sinapis arvensis* L. – Field Mustard, Field Charlock, Wild Mustard / Ackersenf / Moutarde des champs, Ravenelle

CXLIII (143) *Convolvulus arvensis* L. – Cornbine, Field Bindweed / Acker-Winde / Liseron des champs

CXLIIII (144) *Potentilla erecta* (L.) RAEUSCH. [*P. tormentilla* NECK.; *Tormentilla erecta* L.] Common Tormentill, Bloodroot / Aufrechtes Fingerkraut, Blutwurz, Tormentill / Potentille dressée, Tormentille

CXLV (145) *Diplotaxis tenuifolia* (L.) DC. Perennial Wall Rocket / Schmalblättriger Doppelsame, Stinkrauke, Stink-Rampe / Diplotaxis à feuilles ténues, Diplotaxis vulgaire

CXLVI (146) *Rorippa sylvestris* (L.) BESS. Creeping Yellow-cress, Water Rocket / Wildkresse, Wilde Sumpfkresse / Cresson des forêts, Rorippe des champs

CXLVII (147) *Eupatorium cannabinum* L. Hemp Agrimony / Wasserdost, Kunigundenkraut / Eupatoire chanvrine

CXLVIII (148) *Cicer arietinum* L. – Chick Pea, Garbanzo / Kichererbse / Cicer tête de bélier, Pois chiche

CXLIX (149) *Anchusa arvensis* (L.) M. BIEB. [*Lycopsis arvensis* L.] – Field Bugloss, Wild Bugloss, Alkanet Bugloss / Acker-Krummhals, Acker-Ochsenzunge / Buglosse des champs, Lycopside

CL (150) *Berula erecta* (HUDS.) COV. [*Sium angustifolium* L.] – Narrow-leaved Water-parsnip / Aufrechte Bachberle, Schmalblättriger Merk / Berle dressée

CLI (151) *Veratrum album* L. – White Helleborine / Weißer Germer / Vérâtre blanc, Hellébore blanc

CLII (152) *Helleborus viridis* L. – Green Hellebore, Bear's Foot / Grüne Nieswurz / Ellébore vert, Hellébore vert

CLIII (153) *Helleborus foetidus* L. Stinking Hellebore, Setterwort / Stinkende Nieswurz / Ellébore fétide, Hellébore fétide

CLIIII (154) *Parietaria officinalis* L. Pellitory-of-the-Wall / Aufrechtes Glaskraut, Schutt-Glaskraut / Pariétaire officinale

CLV (155) *Rubia tinctoria* L. – Dyer's Madder / Echte Färberröte, Krapp / Garance des teinturiers

CLVI (156) *Galium mollugo* L. – Great Hedge Bedstraw / Wiesen-Labkraut / Gaillet mollugine, Gaillet blanc, Caille-lait blanc

CLVII (157) *Triticum spelta* L. [*T. aestivum* L. ssp. *spelta* (L.) THELL.] – Spelt, Dinkel Wheat / Dinkel, Spelz / Épeautre

CLVIII (158) *Triticum monococcum* L. One-grained Wheat / Einkorn / Petit épeautre, Engrain

CLIX (159) *Senecio vulgaris* L. – Common Groundsel / Gewöhnliches Greiskraut, Gewöhnliches Kreuzkraut / Séneçon vulgaire, Séneçon commun

CLX (160) *Mentha x gracilis* SOLE [*M. gentilis* auct., *M. sativa* L.] – Garden Mint, Ginger Mint / Edel-Minze, Saat-Minze / Menthe noble, Menthe des jardins

CLXI (161) *Mentha* x *villosa* HUDS. [*M. spicata* L. x *M. suaveolens* EHRH.] – Bowles Mint / Bach-Minze, Hain-Minze / Menthe bâtarde [S&N, p. 592: *M.* x *rotundifolia* (L.) HUDS., Round-leaved Mint / Apfel-Minze, Bastard-Rossminze / Menthe à feuilles rondes]

CLXII (162) *Mentha spicata* L. [*M. viridis* (L.) L.] – Spearmint / Ähren-Minze, Grüne Minze, Krauseminze / Menthe verte, Menthe en grappe

CLXIII (163) See CLX (160)

CLXIIII (164) *Mentha longifolia* (L.) HUDS. [*M. sylvestris* L.] – Biblical Mint, Horse Mint / Langblättrige Minze, Ross-Minze / Menthe à longues feuilles

CLXV (165) *Phyllitis scolopendrium* (L.) NEWM. [*Asplenium scolopendrium* L.] Hart's Tongue, Hart's-tongue Fern / Hirschzunge, Hirschzungenfarn / Langue-de-cerf, Scolopendre

CLXVI (166) *Eryngium campestre* L. Field Eryngo / Feld-Mannstreu / Panicaut champêtre

CLXVII (167) *Lactuca sativa* L. var. *crispa* L. – Curly Lettuce, Curled Lettuce, Leaf Lettuce / Römischer Salat, Pflück-Salat, Schnitt-Salat / Laitue frisée

CLXVIII (168) *Lactuca sativa* L. var. *capitata* L. – Cabbage Lettuce, Head Lettuce / Kopf-Salat, Garten-Lattich / Laitue pommée

CLXIX (169) *Lactuca serriola* L. [*L. scariola* L.] – Wild Lettuce, Prickly Lettuce / Wilder Lattich, Kompass-Lattich, Stachel-Lattich

CLXX (170) *Satureja hortensis* L. – Summer Savory / Echtes Bohnenkraut, Sommer-Bohnenkraut / Sarriette commune, Sarriette des jardins

CLXXI (171) *Lepidium campestre* (L.) R. BR. Pepperwort, Cow-cress / Feld-Kresse / Passerage des champs

CLXXII (172) *Lepidium ruderale* L. – Narrow-leaved Pepperwort / Schutt-Kresse, Stink-Kresse / Passerage des décombres

CLXXIII (173) *Lupinus albus* L. – White Lupine / Weiße Lupine / Lupin blanc

CLXXIIII (174) *Viola odorata* L. – Sweet Violet / März-Veilchen, Wohlriechendes Veilchen / Violette odorante

CLXXV (175) *Matthiola incana* (L.) R. BR. – Stock, Dame's Violet (cultivated form with white flowers) / Garten-Levkoje, Winter-Levkoje (weiß blühende Gartenform) / Giroflée des jardins (forme horticole à fleurs blanches)

CLXXVI (176) See CLXXV (175) Stock, Dame's Violet (cultivated form with red flowers) / Garten-Levkoje, Winter-Levkoje (rot blühende Gartenform) / Giroflée des jardins (forme horticole à fleurs rouges)

CLXXVII (177) See CLXXV (175) Stock, Dame's Violet (cultivated form with purple flowers) / Garten-Levkoje, Winter-Levkoje (purpurviolett blühende Gartenform) / Giroflée des jardins (forme horticole à fleurs pourpres)

CLXXVIII (178) *Iris germanica* L. – German Iris, Common Iris / Deutsche Schwertlilie / Iris d'Allemagne, Flambe, Iris bleu d'Allemagne

CLXXIX (179) *Sonchus arvensis* L. – Sow-Thistle, Field Milk-Thistle / Acker-Gänsedistel / Laiteron des champs

CLXXX (180) *Crepis biennis* L. – Rough Hawk's-beard / Wiesen-Pippau / Crépide bisannuelle, Crépis des prés, Chicorée jaune (see FUCHS, Cap. CXX (120)) [S&N, p. 594; MZ, p. 38; MR, p. 396: *Crepis tectorum* L., Smooth Hawk's-beard / Dach-Pippau, Mauer-Pippau / Crépide des toits]

CLXXXI (181) *Equisetum palustre* L. Marsh Horsetail / Sumpf-Schachtelhalm, Duwock / Prêle des marais

CLXXXII (182) *Equisetum arvense* L. Common Horsetail / Acker-Schachtelhalm / Prêle des champs

CLXXXIII (183) *Cardamine pratensis* L. Cuckoo Flower, Lady's Smock / Wiesen-Schaumkraut / Cardamine des prés

CLXXXIIII (184) *Smyrnium olusatrum* L. Alexanders, Black Lovage / Smyrnenkraut, Pferde-Eppich / Maceron

CLXXXV (185) *Viscum album* L. Mistletoe / Mistel / Gui

CLXXXVI (186) *Isatis tinctoria* L. var. *sativa* DC. – Domesticated Woad, Dyer's Woad (cultivated form) / Färber-Waid (kultivierte Form) / Pastel (forme cultivée)

CLXXXVII (187) *Isatis tinctoria* L. var. *vulgaris* KOCH – Wild Woad, Common Dyer's Weed (wild form) / Färber-Waid (verwilderte Form) / Pastel (forme sauvage)

CLXXXVIII (188) *Salix purpurea* L. – Purple Osier or Purple Willow / Purpur-Weide / Osier rouge, Saule pourpre (see S&N, p. 595; MZ, p. 39) [MR, p. 400: *Salix alba* L., White Willow, including a lower branch with aments of / Silber-Weide, mit hinzugefügtem Blütenzweig von / Saule blanc avec branche fleurie de *S. purpurea* L.]

CLXXXIX (189) *Salix alba* L. ssp. *vitel* (189) *lina* (L.) ARCANG. [*S. vitellina* L., *S. alba* L. var. *vitellina* (L.) STOKES] – Yellow Willow / Dotter-Weide, Bunt-Weide / Osier jaune (see S&N, p. 595; MZ, p. 39) [MR, p. 401: *Salix alba* L., White Willow, including a lower branch with aments of / Silber-Weide, mit hinzugefügtem Blütenzweig von / Saule blanc avec branche fleurie de *S. purpurea* L.]

CXC (190) *Salix repens* L. ssp. *rosmarinifolia* (L.) CELAK. [*S. repens* L. var. *rosmarinifolia* (L.) WIMM. et GRAB.] – Rosemary Willow / Rosmarin-Weide / Saule à feuilles de romarin (see S&N, p. 595; MZ, p. 39) [MR, p. 401: *Salix viminalis* L., Common Osier, including a lower branch with aments of / Korb-Weide oder Hanf-Weide, mit hinzugefügtem Blütenzweig von / Saule des vanniers avec branche fleurie de *S. purpurea* L.]

CXCI (191) *Fumaria officinalis* L. – Common Fumitory / Gewöhnlicher Erdrauch,

Gebräuchlicher Erdrauch / Fumeterre officinale

CXCII (192) *Ricinus communis* L. – Castor Oil Plant, Castor Bean / Echter Wunderbaum, Christuspalme, Läusebaum / Ricin

CXCIII (193) *Anchusa officinalis* L. – German Bugloss, Alkanet / Echte Ochsenzunge, Gewöhnliche Ochsenzunge / Buglosse officinale

CXCIIII (194) *Anchusa azurea* MILL. [*A. italica* RETZ.] – Italian Bugloss, Italian Alkanet, Large Blue Alkanet / Italienische Ochsenzunge / Buglosse d'Italie

CXCV (195) *Coriandrum sativum* L. Coriander / Garten-Koriander / Coriandre cultivée, Coriandre, Persil arabe

CXCVI (196) *Cuscuta epilinum* WEIHE – Flax Dodder / Flachs-Seide, Lein-Seide / Cuscute du lin

CXCVII (197) *Betonica officinalis* L. [*Stachys officinalis* (L.) TREVIS.] – Betony, Purple Betony, Bishop's Wort / Echter Ziest, Heil-Ziest, Echte Betonie / Bétoine, Epiaire officinale

CXCVIII (198) *Dianthus carthusianorum* L. Carthusian Pink, Thyme-leaved Sandwort / Karthäuser-Nelke / Œillet des Chartreux

CXCIX (199) *Dianthus superbus* L. – Fringed Pink, Superb Pink / Pracht-Nelke / Œillet superbe

CC (200) *Dianthus caryophyllus* L. – Clove Pink, Carnation / Garten-Nelke / Œillet-giroflée, Œillet des fleuristes

CCI (201) *Colchicum autumnale* L. – Meadow Saffron, Autumn Crocus, Naked Ladies / Herbstzeitlose / Colchique d'automne

CCII (202) See CCI (201)

CCIII (203) *Vinca minor* L. – Common Periwinkle, Lesser Periwinkle, Trailing Myrtle / Kleines Immergrün / Petite pervenche

CCIIII (204) *Lepidium sativum* L. – Garden Cress / Garten-Kresse / Cresson alénois, Passerage cultivée

CCV (205) *Lilium candidum* L. – White Lily, Madonna Lily / Weiße Lilie, Madonnen-Lilie / Lis blanc, Lis de la Madone

CCVI (206) *Lilium bulbiferum* L. – Fire Lily, Orange Lily / Feuer-Lilie/ Lis safrané [S&N, p. 597: L. *bulbiferum* L. var. *croceum* (CHAIX) PERS. [L. croceum CHAIX]], Orangerote Feuer-Lilie

CCVII (207) *Lagenaria siceraria* (MOL.) STANDL. [L. *vulgaris* SER.] ssp. *asiatica* (KOBIAK.) HEIS. – Bottle Gourd, Calabash Gourd / Flaschenkürbis / Gourde trompette, Calebasse

CCVIII (208) *Lagenaria siceraria* (MOL.) STANDL. [L. *vulgaris* SER.] ssp. *siceraria* – Bottle Gourd, Calabash Gourd / Flaschenkürbis / Gourde trompette, Calebasse

CCIX (209) See CCVII (207)

CCX (210) *Citrullus colocynthis* (L.) SCHRAD. – Colocynth, Bitter Apple, Sodom's Apple / Koloquinthe / Coloquinte commune

CCXI (211) *Cydonia oblonga* MILL. Common Quince, Quince / Echte Quitte, Quitte / Cognassier

CCXII (212) *Castanea sativa* MILL. – European Chestnut, Spanish Chestnut, Sweet Chestnut / Edelkastanie, Esskastanie, Marone / Châtaignier

CCXIII (213) *Juglans regia* L. – Persian Walnut, English Walnut / Echte Walnuss, Walnuss / Noyer royal

CCXIIII (214) *Calendula officinalis* L. Calendula, Pot Marigold / Garten-Ringelblume / Souci des jardins

CCXV (215) *Geum urbanum* L. – Wood Avens, Herb Bennet / Echte Nelkenwurz / Benoîte commune

CCXVI (216) *Geum* x *intermedium* EHRH. [*G. rivale* L. x G. *urbanum* L.] – Hybrid: Water Avens x Wood Avens / Bastard-Nelkenwurz: Bach-Nelkenwurz x Echte Nelkenwurz / Benoîte bâtarde : Benoîte des ruisseaux x Benoîte commune

CCXVII (217) *Centaurium erythraea* RAFN [*C. umbellatum* GILIB.] – Common Centaury / Echtes Tausendgüldenkraut /

Petite centaurée commune, Érythrée petite centaurée

CCXVIII (218) *Vicia faba* L. – Fava Bean, Broad Bean, Horse Bean / Acker-Bohne, Sau-Bohne, Pferde-Bohne / Fève

CCXIX (219) *Ajuga reptans* L. – Common Bugle / Kriechender Günsel / Bugle rampante

CCXX (220) *Cannabis sativa* L. – Hemp (composite figure: staminate flowers terminal, pistillate flowers below. The plant is normally dioecious) / Hanf (kombinierte Darstellung: im oberen Teil männliche, im unteren Teil weibliche Blüten. Die Pflanze ist normalerweise zweihäusig [diözisch]) / Chanvre (composition : partie supérieure fleurs mâles, partie inférieure fleurs femelles. La plante est normalement dioïque)

CCXXI (221) *Leonurus cardiaca* L. – Motherwort / Echtes Herzgespann, Echter Löwenschwanz / Agripaume cardiaque

CCXXII (222) *Carum carvi* L. – Caraway / Wiesen-Kümmel / Cumin des prés

CCXXIII (223) *Corylus avellana* L. – Hazelnut, Hazel, Cob-nut / Haselnuss, Gewöhnliche Hasel / Coudrier, Noisetier

CCXXIIII (224) *Corylus maxima* MILL. Filbert / Lambertsnuss, Große Hasel / Aveline, Noisetier tubuleux

CCXXV (225) *Lysimachia nummularia* L. Moneywort, Creeping Jenny / Pfennigkraut, Pfennig-Gilbweiderich / Nummulaire, Lysimaque nummulaire, Herbe aux écus

CCXXVI (226) *Prunus domestica* L. Plum / Pflaume, Zwetschge, Zwetsche / Prunier

CCXXVII (227) *Prunus spinosa* L. – Sloe, Blackthorn / Gewöhnliche Schlehe, Schlehe, Schwarzdorn / Prunellier, Épine noire

CCXXVIII (228) *Conium maculatum* L. Poison Hemlock, Hemlock / Gefleckter Schierling / Grande ciguë, Ciguë tachée

CCXXIX (229) *Echium vulgare* L. – Viper's Bugloss / Gewöhnlicher Natternkopf, Natternkopf, Stolzer Heinrich / Vipérine commune

CCXXX (230) *Carthamus tinctorius* L. Safflower, Dyer's Saffron, False Saffron / Färber-Distel, Färber-Saflor / Carthame des teinturiers, Safran bâtard

CCXXXI (231) *Panicum miliaceum* L. Common Millet / Echte Hirse, Gewöhnliche Rispenhirse / Panic millet, Millet cultivé, Millet commun, Mil

CCXXXII (232) *Brassica oleracea* L. var. *acephala* DC. subvar. *viridis* (L.) SCHULZ [B. *oleracea* L. var. *viridis* L.] – Collards, Cow Cabbage, Tall Kale, Tree Kale / Grüner Blattkohl, Blätterkohl, Kuhkohl, Futterkohl / Chou cavalier, Chou commun, Chou vert

CCXXXIII (233) *Brassica oleracea* L. var. *acephala* DC. subvar. *sabellica* (L.) SCHULZ [B. *oleracea* L. var. *sabellica* L.] – Curly Kale, Borecole, Feather Kale, Curled German Greens, Scotch Kale / Krauskohl, Federkohl, Grünkohl, Braunkohl / Chou d'aigrette, Chou frangé, Chou frisé, Chou lacinié

CCXXXIIII (234) *Brassica napus* L. var. *oleifera* DC. – Rape, Colza, Winter Rape, Summer Rape / Raps, Winterraps, Sommerraps, Kohlraps, Ölraps / Colza, Colza de printemps, Colza d'hiver [MZ, p. 43: B. *oleracea* L. var. *acephala* DC.]

CCXXXV (235) *Brassica oleracea* L. var. *capitata* L. – Cabbage / Kopfkohl / Chou cabus, Chou pommé blanc

CCXXXVI (236) *Gentiana cruciata* L. Cross Gentian / Kreuz-Enzian / Gentiane croisette

CCXXXVII (237) *Hedera helix* L. – Ivy / Gewöhnlicher Efeu, Efeu / Lierre

CCXXXVIII (238) See CCXXXVII (237)

CCXXXIX (239) *Prunus*-combination: 1. *Prunus cerasus* L. var. *caproniana* L., Amarelle group / Amarelle, Glaskirsche / Cerisier amarelle ; 2. *P. cerasus* L. var. *austera* L., Morelle group / Morele, Süßweichsel / Cerisier morello ; 3. *Prunus avium* L., Bird Cherry, Sweet Cherry / Vogelkirsche, Süßkirsche / Merisier des oiseaux, Merisier vrai

CCXL (240) *Centaurea cyanus* L. – Cornflower, Blue Bottle / Kornblume / Bleuet des champs

CCXLI (241) *Allium cepa* L. – Common Onion, Onion / Echte Zwiebel, Küchen-Zwiebel / Oignon

CCXLII (242) *Campanula trachelium* L. Bats-in-the-Belfry / Nesselblättrige Glockenblume / Campanule gantelée

CCXLIII (243) *Nepeta cataria* L. – Cat-mint, Catnip, Catnep / Echte Katzenminze, Gewöhnliche Katzenminze / Népéta chataire, Herbe-aux-chats

CCXLIIII (244) *Mentha arvensis* L. – Corn Mint / Acker-Minze, Korn-Minze / Menthe des champs

CCXLV (245) *Pulicaria dysenterica* (L.) BERNH. – Greater Fleabane, Fleabane / Großes Flohkraut, Ruhr-Flohkraut / Pulicaire dysentérique

CCXLVI (246) *Hordeum vulgare* L. [*H. polystichon* HALL. f., *H. tetrastichum* KOERN.] – Barley / Mehrzeilige Gerste, Saat-Gerste, Winter-Gerste / Orge carrée, Orge à quatre rangs

CCXLVII (247) *Hordeum distichon* L. Two-rowed Barley / Zweizeilige Gerste / Orge à deux rangs, Orge d'été, Orge plate

CCXLVIII (248) *Crocus sativus* L. Saffron / Safran-Krokus, Echter Safran / Safran, Crocus cultivé

CCXLIX (249) *Mercurialis perennis* L. – Dog's Mercury (pistillate plant) / Wald-Bingelkraut, Ausdauerndes Bingelkraut (weibliche Pflanze) / Mercuriale vivace (plante femelle)

CCL (250) *Colutea arborescens* L. – Bladder Senna / Gewöhnlicher Blasenstrauch / Baguenaudier commun, Arbre à vessies

CCLI (251) *Cassia italica* (MILL.) LAM. ex STEUD. [*C. obovata* COLL., *Senna italica* MILL.] – Aleppo Senna, Italian Senna, Senegal Senna / Aleppo-Senna, Italienische Senna, Sennesstrauch / Cassia séné, Séné

CCLII (252) *Plantago coronopus* L. – Buck's-horn Plantain / Krähenfuß-Wegerich, Schlitz-Wegerich / Plantain corne-de-cerf

CCLIII (253) *Cyclamen purpurascens* MILL. [*C. europaeum* L.] – Common Cyclamen, Sowbread / Gewöhnliches Alpenveilchen, Gewöhnliche Erdscheibe / Cyclamen pourpre

CCLIIII (254) *Cyperus longus* L. Galingale / Langes Zypergras, Wilder Galgant / Souchet long, Souchet odorant

CCLV (255) *Euphorbia lathyris* L. – Caper Spurge / Kreuzblättrige Wolfsmilch, Spring-Wolfsmilch / Euphorbe épurge, Épurge

CCLVI (256) *Erysimum cheiri* (L.) CRANTZ [*Cheiranthus cheiri* L.] – Wallflower / Goldlack, Gelbveigel, Levkoje / Giroflée, Violier

CCLVII (257) *Hesperis matronalis* L. – Dame's Violet, Vesper Flower (cultivated form with white flowers) / Nachtviole, Matronenblume (*H. matronalis* L. 'Alba': Weiße Nachtviole) / Julienne des dames (forme horticole à fleurs blanches)

CCLVIII (258) *Hesperis matronalis* L. – Dame's Violet, Vesper Flower (cultivated form with purple/red flowers) / Nachtviole, Matronenblume (*H. matronalis* L. 'Purpurea': Rote Nachtviole) / Julienne des dames (forme horticole à fleurs pourpres)

CCLIX (259) *Rumex obtusifolius* L.? Broad-leaved Dock? / Stumpfblättriger Ampfer? / Rumex à feuilles obtuses, Patience sauvage ? (see S&N, p. 603; MZ, p. 45) [MR, p. 441: *Polygonum lapathifolium* L., Pale Persicaria / Ampfer-Knöterich / Renouée à feuilles de patience]

CCLX (260) *Rumex patientia* L. – Patience, Dock / Englischer Spinat, Mönchs-rhabarber, Garten-Ampfer, Ewiger Spinat / Rumex patience, Épinard oseille, Patience (see MZ, p. 45) [S&N, p. 603: *Rumex alpinus* L.?, MR, p. 441: *R. alpinus* L., Alpine Dock, Monk's Rhubarb / Alpen-Ampfer / Rumex des Alpes, Rhubarbe des moines]

CCLXI (261) *Chenopodium bonus-henricus* L. – Good King Henry, All-good, Mercury / Guter Heinrich / Chénopode Bon-Henri, Ansérine Bon-Henri, Épinard sauvage

CCLXII (262) *Rumex acetosa* L. – Sorrel, Sorrel Dock, Sour Dock / Großer Sauerampfer, Wiesen-Sauerampfer / Rumex oseille, Surette, Oseille commune, Oseille des prés

CCLXIII (263) *Pyrola rotundifolia* L. – Round-leaved Wintergreen,

Larger Wintergreen / Rundblättriges Wintergrün / Pyrole à feuilles rondes

CCLXIIII (264) *Lamium*-combination: 1. (left branch): *Lamium galeobdolon* (L.) L. [*Galeobdolon luteum* HUDS.], Yellow Archangel / Goldnessel, Gelbe Taubnessel / Lamier jaune, Lamier galéobdolon, Ortie jaune ; 2. (middle branch): *L. maculatum* L., Spotted Deadnettle / Gefleckte Taubnessel / Lamier maculé, Lamier tacheté, Ortie morte, Ortie rouge ; 3. (right branch): *L. album* L., White Deadnettle / Weiße Taubnessel / Lamier blanc, Ortie blanche

CCLXV (265) *Linum usitatissimum* L. Cultivated Flax, Flax / Lein, Saat-Lein, Flachs / Lin cultivé

CCLXVI (266) *Marchantia polymorpha* L. Common Liverwort / Brunnen-Lebermoos / Hépatique des fontaines

CCLXVII (267) *Mercurialis annua* L. Annual Mercury (pistillate plant) / Einjähriges Bingelkraut (weibliche Pflanze!) / Mercuriale annuelle (plante femelle)

CCLXVIII (268) *Mercurialis annua* L. Annual Mercury (staminate plant) / Einjähriges Bingelkraut (männliche Pflanze!) / Mercuriale annuelle (plante mâle)

CCLXIX (269) *Rosmarinus officinalis* L. Rosemary / Rosmarin / Romarin officinal, Romarin

CCLXX (270) *Ligustrum vulgare* L. – Common Privet / Gewöhnlicher Liguster, Rainweide / Troène vulgaire, Troène

CCLXXI (271) *Botrychium lunaria* (L.) SW. Moonwort / Echte Mondraute / Botryche lunaire

CCLXXII (272) *Lepidium latifolium* L. Broad-leaved Pepperwort, Dittander / Breitblättrige Kresse, Pfefferkraut / Passerage à larges feuilles

CCLXXIII (273) *Leucojum-Galanthus*-combination: 1. (left flower): *Leucojum vernum* L., Spring Snowflake / Frühlings-Knotenblume, Märzenbeche / Nivéole du printemps ; 2. (right flower): probable *Galanthus nivalis* L., Common Snowdrop / Schneeglöckchen / Perce-neige

CCLXXIIII (274) *Leucojum vernum* L. Spring Snowflake / Frühlings-Knotenblume, Märzenbecher / Nivéole du printemps

CCLXXV (275) *Lithospermum officinale* L. Gromwell, Common Alkanet / Echter Steinsame / Grémil officinal, Herbe aux perles

CCLXXVI (276) *Lithospermum arvense* L. [*Buglossoides arvensis* (L.) JOHNST.] Corn Gromwell, Bastard Alkanet / Acker-Steinsame / Grémil des champs

CCLXXVII (277) *Epilobium hirsutum* L. Great Hairy Willow-herb, Codlins and Cream / Zottiges Weidenröschen, Rauhhaariges Weidenröschen / Épilobe hérissé, Épilobe hirsute

CCLXXVIII (278) *Lysimachia vulgaris* L. Yellow Loosestrife / Gewöhnlicher Gilbweiderich, Gold-Felberich / Lysimaque vulgaire, Lysimaque commune

CCLXXIX (279) *Trifolium arvense* L. – Hare's-foot, Trefoil Clover, White Clover / Acker-Klee, Hasen-Klee / Trèfle-des-champs, Pied-de-lièvre

CCLXXX (280) *Larix decidua* MILL. European Larch / Europäische Lärche / Mélèze

CCLXXXI (281) *Melittis melissophyllum* L. Bastard Balm / Immenblatt, Bienensaug / Mélitte à feuilles de mélisse

CCLXXXII (282) *Melissa officinalis* L. Balm, Lemon Balm / Melisse, Zitronenmelisse / Mélisse officinale, Piment des abeilles, Citronnelle

CCLXXXIII (283) *Foeniculum vulgare* MILL. – Fennel / Gewöhnlicher Fenchel, Fenchel / Fenouil commun, Fenouil

CCLXXXIIII (284) *Nigella sativa* L. Roman Coriander, Fennel Flower / Echter Schwarzkümmel / Nigelle de Crète, Nigelle aromatique, Nigelle cultivée, Toute-épice

CCLXXXV (285) *Nigella damascena* L. Garden Coriander, Love-in-a-Mist / Damaszener Schwarzkümmel, Gretel im Busch, Jungfer im Grünen / Nigelle de Damas

CCLXXXVI (286) *Nigella arvensis* L. – Wild Coriander / Acker-Schwarzkümmel / Nigelle des champs

CCLXXXVII (287) *Alcea rosea* L. – [*Althaea rosea* (L.) CAV.] Hollyhock, Garden Mallow / Gewöhnliche Stockrose, Chinesische Stockrose, Rosenpappel / Rose trémière

CCLXXXVIII (288) *Malva neglecta* WALLR. [*M. rotundifolia* auct., non L.] Dwarf Mallow / Übersehene Malve, Weg-Malve, Gänse-Malve, Kleine Käsepappel / Mauve négligée, Petite mauve (see MZ, p. 47) [S&N, p. 606; MR, p. 456: erroneously *M. pusilla* SM. [*M. rotundifolia* L.], Small-flowered Mallow / Kleinblütige Malve / Mauve à feuilles rondes]

CCLXXXIX (289) *Malva sylvestris* L. Common Mallow, High Mallow / Rosspappel, Wilde Malve, Große Käsepappel / Mauve sylvestre, Grande mauve

CCXC (290) *Myricaria germanica* (L.) DESV. – German Tamarisk, Shrub Tamarisk / Deutsche Tamariske, Deutscher Rispelstrauch / Tamarin d'Allemagne, Myricaire d'Allemagne

CCXCI (291) *Papaver rhoeas* L. – Corn Poppy, Field Poppy / Klatschmohn / Coquelicot

CCXCII (292) *Papaver rhoeas* L.? Corn Poppy, Field Poppy? / Klatschmohn? / Coquelicot ? (Determination uncertain, see S&N, p. 607; MZ, p. 48)

CCXCIII (293) *Papaver somniferum* L. – Giant Poppy, Opium Poppy / Schlafmohn, Gartenmohn / Pavot somnifère, Pavot à opium

CCXCIIII (294) *Glaucium flavum* CRANTZ – Yellow Horned-poppy / Gelber Hornmohn / Glaucière jaune, Pavot cornu

CCXCV (295) *Morus nigra* L. – Black Mulberry / Schwarzer Maulbeerbaum / Mûrier noir

CCXCVI (296) *Anthriscus sylvestris* (L.) HOFFM. Cow Parsley, Cow Parsnip / Wiesen-Kerbel / Cerfeuil des prés, Cerfeuil sauvage, Anthrisque sauvage

CCXCVII (297) *Lotus corniculatus* L. – Birdsfoot trefoil, Bacon and Eggs / Gewöhnlicher Hornklee / Lotier corniculé, Lotier commun, Pied-de-poule

CCXCVIII (298) *Trigonella corniculata* (L.) L. – [*Melilotus corniculata* L.] Sickle-fruited Fenugreek / Italienischer Bockshornklee, Traubiger Bockshornklee / Trigonelle à petites cornes, Lotier cornu

CCXCIX (299) *Mandragora officinarum* L. – Mandrake / Alraune, Alraunwurzel / Mandragore officinale

CCC (300) *Solanum melongena* L. – Aubergine, Eggplant / Aubergine, Eierpflanze, Eierfrucht / Aubergine, Mélongène

CCCI (301) *Nymphaea alba* L. – White Water-lily / Weiße Seerose / Nénuphar blanc

CCCII (302) *Nuphar lutea* (L.) SIBTH. et SM. – Yellow Water-lily / Gelbe Teichrose, Große Mummel / Nénuphar jaune, Nuphar jaune

CCCIII (303) *Sinapis alba* L. – White Mustard / Weißer Senf, Gelber Senf / Moutarde blanche

CCCIIII (304) *Eruca sativa* MILL. – [*E. vesicaria* (L.) CAV. ssp. *sativa* (MILL.) THELL.] Garden Rocket, Salad Rocket / Senf-Rauke, Öl-Rauke, Saat-Ölrauke, Ruke / Roquette cultivée

CCCV (305) *Nerium oleander* L. – Oleander / Oleander / Laurier-rose, Oléandre

CCCVI (306) *Berberis vulgaris* L. – Common Barberry, Barberry / Gewöhnliche Berberitze, Sauerdorn / Épine-vinette

CCCVII (307) *Linaria vulgaris* MILL. Toadflax, Butter and Eggs / Gewöhnliches Leinkraut, Frauenflachs / Linaire commune, Linaire vulgaire

CCCVIII (308) *Ocimum basilicum* L. [var. *minimum* (L.) ALEF.] – Basil / Basilikum / Basilic

CCCIX (309) *Ocimum basilicum* L. – [var. *vulgare* ALEF.] – Basil / Basilikum / Basilic

CCCX (310) *Ocimum basilicum* L. – [var. *major* BENTH. in DC.] Basil / Basilikum / Basilic

CCCXI (311) *Origanum vulgare* L. Majoram / Gewöhnlicher Dost, Wilder Majoran / Origan, Origan vulgaire, Marjolaine sauvage

CCCXII (312) *Orchis militaris* L. – Soldier Orchid, Military Orchid / Helm-Knabenkraut / Orchis militaire, Orchis guerrier

CCCXIII (313) *Orchis-combination*: Leaves and root / Blätter und Wurzel / Feuilles et racine : *Orchis mascula* L., Early Purple

Orchid / Männliches Knabenkraut / Orchis mâle ; Inflorescence: *Orchis morio* L., Green-winged Orchid / Kleines Knabenkraut, Salep-Knabenkraut / Orchis bouffon (see KÜNKELE 1987, p. 229–230) [S&N, p. 609; MR, p. 472–473: lower half *O. mascula* L., upper half *O. sambucina* L. – [*Dactylorhiza sambucina* (L.) SOO], Elder-flowered Orchid / Holunder-Knabenkraut / Orchis à odeur de sureau]

CCCXIIII (314) *Anacamptis pyramidalis* (L.) RICH. Pyramidal Orchid / Pyramiden-Hundswurz, Pyramiden-Spitzorchis / Orchis pyramidal

CCCXV (315) *Orchis ustulata* L. – Dark-winged Orchid, Burnt Orchid / Brand-Knabenkraut, Brandorchis / Orchis brûlé, Orchis mignon

CCCXVI (316) *Orchis morio* L. – Green-winged Orchid / Kleines Knabenkraut, Salep-Knabenkraut / Orchis bouffon (see KÜNKELE 1987, p. 230–231) [S&N, p. 609: *Orchis sambucina* L.?; MZ, p. 50: *O. purpurea* HUDS.?, Lady Orchid / Purpur-Knabenkraut / Orchis pourpré ; MR, p. 473–474: *Dactylorhiza sambucina* (L.) SOO, Elder-flowered Orchid / Holunder-Knabenkraut / Orchis à odeur de sureau]

CCCXVII (317) *Orchis morio* L. – Green-winged Orchid / Kleines Knabenkraut, Salep-Knabenkraut / Orchis bouffon

CCCXVIII (318) *Ophrys holosericea* (BURM. f.) GREUT. Late Spider Orchid / Hummel-Ragwurz / Ophrys bourdon, Ophrys frelon (see SEYBOLD 1986, p. 116; KÜNKELE 1987, p. 231; MR, pp. 474–475) [S&N, p. 610; MZ, p. 50: *Ophrys apifera* HUDS., Bee Orchid / Bienen-Ragwurz /Ophrys abeille]

CCCXIX (319) *Filipendula vulgaris* MOENCH [*F. hexapetala* GILIB.] Dropwort / Knolliges Mädesüß, Knollige Spierstaude, Kleiner Geißbart / Filipendule vulgaire, Filipendule à six pétales

CCCXX (320) *Oxalis acetosella* L. Wood-sorrel / Wald-Sauerklee / Oxalis petite oseille, Surelle, Pain-de-coucou

CCCXXI (321) *Listera ovata* (L.) R. BR. Twayblade, Common Twayblade / Großes Zweiblatt / Listère ovale, Listère à feuilles ovales, Grande Listère, Double-feuille

CCCXXII (322) *Salvia sclarea* L. – Clary Sage, Clary / Muskateller-Salbei, Scharlachkraut / Sauge sclarée

CCCXXIII (323) *Salvia pratensis* L. – Meadow Sage, Meadow Clary / Wiesen-Salbei / Sauge des prés

CCCXXIIII (324) *Lathyrus sativus* L. – Grass Peavine, Grass-pea, Chickling Pea / Saat-Platterbse / Gesse cultivée

CCCXXV (325) *Lathyrus sylvestris* L. Narrow-leaved Everlasting Pea / Wald-Platterbse / Gesse des bois

CCCXXVI (326) *Petroselinum crispum* (MILL.) NYM. ex HILL [*P. sativum* HOFFM.] – Parsley / Garten-Petersilie / Persil cultivé, Persil

CCCXXVII (327) *Sorbus domestica* L. – Sorb Apple, Service Tree / Speierling, Sperberbaum / Sorbier domestique, Cormier

CCCXXVIII (328) *Ophioglossum vulgatum* L. – Adder's Tongue / Gewöhnliche Natterzunge / Ophioglosse vulgaire, Langue-de-serpent

CCCXXIX (329) *Xanthium strumarium* L. Cocklebur / Gewöhnliche Spitzklette / Lampourde ordinaire, Lampourde glouteron

CCCXXX (330) *Gossypium herbaceum* L. Common Cotton, Levant Cotton / Krautige Baumwolle, Strauchige Baumwolle / Cotonnier, Coton de la Caroline, Coton des hautes terres

CCCXXXI (331) *Anthemis cotula* L. – Stinking Mayweed, Stinking Camomile, Mugwort / Stinkende Hundskamille, Stink-Kamille / Anthémis fétide, Camomille puante, Camomille des chiens

CCCXXXII (332) *Polygonatum multiflo rum* (L.) ALL. – Solomon's Seal / Vielblütige Weißwurz, Vielblütiges Salomonssiegel / Sceau-de-Salomon commun, Sceau-de-Salomon multiflore, Polygonate multiflore

CCCXXXIII (333) *Polygonatum verticillatum* (L.) ALL. – Whorled Solomon's Seal / Quirlblättrige Weißwurz, Quirlblättriges Salomonssiegel / Sceau-de-Salomon à feuilles verticillées, Sceau-de-Salomon verticillé, Polygonate verticillé

CCCXXXIIII (334) *Polypodium vulgare* L. Common Polypody / Gewöhnlicher Tüpfelfarn, Engelsüß / Polypode vulgaire, Réglisse des bois

CCCXXXV (335) *Marrubium vulgare* L. – White Horehound / Gewöhnlicher Andorn / Marrube commun, Marrube blanc

CCCXXXVI (336) *Sisymbrium officinale* (L.) SCOP. Common Hedge Mustard / Weg-Rauke / Sisymbre officinal, Vélar

CCCXXXVII (337) *Verbena officinalis* L. Vervain, Herb-of-grace / Echtes Eisenkraut, Gewöhnliches Eisenkraut / Verveine officinale

CCCXXXVIII (338) *Dryopteris filix-mas* (L.) SCHOTT [*Aspidium filix-mas* (L.) SW.] – Male Fern, Shield Fern / Gewöhnlicher Wurmfar / Fougère mâle

CCCXXXIX (339) *Pteridium aquilinum* (L.) KUHN – Bracken / Gewöhnlicher Adlerfarn / Fougère aigle, Fougère impériale

CCCXL (340) *Peucedanum officinale* L. – Hog's Fennel, Sulphur-weed / Echter Haarstrang, Arznei-Haarstrang / Peucédan officinal, Fenouil de porc

CCCXLI (341) *Prunus persica* (L.) BATSCH Peach / Pfirsichbaum, Pfirsich / Pêcher commun, Pêcher, Brugnonier

CCCXLII (342) *Euphorbia peplus* L. – Petty Spurge / Garten-Wolfsmilch / Euphorbe péplus, Euphorbe omblette, Omblette

CCCXLIII (343) *Hieracium pilosella* L. Mouse-ear Hawkweed / Kleines Habichtskraut, Mausohr-Habichtskraut, Langhaariges Habichtskraut / Épervière piloselle

CCCXLIIII (344) *Antennaria dioica* (L.) GAERTN. [*Gnaphalium dioicum* L.] Cat's-foot, Mountain Everlasting (pistillate plant) / Gewöhnliches Katzenpfötchen (weibliche Pflanze) / Pied-de-chat dioïque, Pied-de-chat (plante femelle)

CCCXLV (345) *Pimpinella major* (L.) HUDS. Greater Burnet Saxifrage / Große Bibernelle / Grand boucage

CCCXLVI (346) *Pimpinella saxifraga* L.? – Burnet Saxifrage, Lesser Burnet Saxifrage? / Kleine Bibernelle? / Boucage saxifrage ? (see MZ, p. 52) [S&N, p. 613; MR, p. 490-491: *Angelica sylvestris* L., Wild Angelica / Angelika, Gewöhnliche Engelwurz, Brustwurzel / Angélique sauvage]

CCCXLVII (347) *Capsella bursa-pastoris* (L.) MED. – Shepherd's Purse / Gewöhnliches Hirtentäschel, Hirten-Täschelkraut / Capselle bourse-à-pasteur

CCCXLVIII (348) *Alchemilla xanthochlora* ROTHM. [*A. vulgaris* auct.] – Lady's Mantle, Lion's-foot / Gelbgrüner Frauenmantel, Gewöhnlicher Frauenmantel / Alchémille vert jaunâtre, Alchémille vulgaire

CCCXLIX (349) *Polygonum aviculare* L. agg. Knotgrass, Knotweed / Vogel-Knöterich, Acker-Vogelknöterich / Renouée des oiseaux, Traînasse

CCCL (350) *Ruta graveolens* L. – Common Rue / Wein-Raute, Raute / Rue fétide, Rue des jardins

CCCLI (351) *Potentilla anserina* L. – Silverweed, Wild Agrimony / Gänse-Fingerkraut / Potentille ansérine, Ansérine, Potentille des oies

CCCLII (352) *Prunella vulgaris* L. – Self-heal, Heal-all / Gewöhnliche Braunelle, Kleine Braunelle, Gemeine Braunelle / Brunelle commune, Brunelle vulgaire

CCCLIII (353) *Potentilla alba* L. – White Cinquefoil / Weißes Fingerkraut / Potentille blanche

CCCLIIII (354) *Potentilla reptans* L. Creeping Cinquefoil / Kriechendes Fingerkraut / Potentille rampante, Quintefeuille

CCCLV (355) *Potentilla neumanniana* RCHB. [*P. tabernaemontani* ASCH., *P. verna* auct., non L.] – Spring Cinquefoil / Frühlings-Fingerkraut / Potentille du printemps, Potentille printanière

CCCLVI (356) *Pisum sativum* L. ssp. *sativum* Garden Pea, Field Pea / Garten-Erbse, Gemüse-Erbse, Erbse / Pois cultivé

CCCLVII (357) *Polytrichum formosum* HEDW. [*P. attenuatum* MENZ. ex BRID.] – Bank Haircap Moss / Schönes Frauenhaarmoos, Schönes Widertonmoos / Polytrich élégant,

Polytric élégant (det. Dr. M. NEBEL/Dr. K. DOBAT) [S&N, p. 614; MZ, p. 53; MR, p. 497: *Polytrichum commune* HEDW., Common Haircap Moss / Gemeines Widertonmoos, Goldenes Frauenhaar / Polytrich commun, Polytric commun]

CCCLVIII (358) *Bryum capillare* HEDW.? Capillary Thread-moss? / Haarblättriges Birnmoos? / Bryum capillaire ? (det. Dr. M. NEBEL/ Dr. K. DOBAT; see MZ, p. 53: *Bryum* sp.?) [S&N, p. 614; MR, p. 497-498: *Funaria hygrometrica* HEDW., Common Cord-moss, Cord Moss / Wetteranzeigendes Drehmoos / Funaire hygrométrique]

CCCLIX (359) *Polygonum lapathifolium* L.? [*Persicaria lapathifolia* (L.) DEL.] – Pale Persicaria? / Ampfer-Knöterich? / Renouée à feuilles de patience ? (see S&N, p. 614; MZ, p. 54) [MR, p. 498: *Polygonum persicaria* L. [*Persicaria maculosa* GRAY], Red Shank, Willow Weed, Persicaria / Floh-Knöterich, Pfirsichblättriger Flohknöterich / Renouée persicaire, Pied-rouge]

CCCLX (360) *Bupleurum rotundifolium* L. Hare's-ear, Thorow-wax / Rundblättriges Hasenohr, Rundes Hasenohr / Buplèvre à feuilles rondes

CCCLXI (361) *Allium porrum* L. – Leek / Lauch, Winter-Lauch, Porree / Poireau

CCCLXII (362) *Allium schoenoprasum* L. Chives / Schnittlauch / Ciboulette, Civette

CCCLXIII (363) *Lobaria pulmonaria* (L.) HOFFM. – Lungwort, Oak Lungs / Lungenflechte / Lichens poumons

CCCLXIIII (364) *Achillea ptarmica* L. Sneezewort / Sumpf-Schafgarbe, Sumpf-Garbe / Achillée ptarmique, Herbe à éternuer

CCCLXV (365) *Anacyclus pyrethrum* (L.) LINK – Roman Pellitory, Pellitory of Spain / Römischer Bertram, Zahnwurz / Pyrèthre, Pyrèthre d'Afrique

CCCLXVI (366) *Buxus sempervirens* L. – Box, Common Box, Boxwood / Immergrüner Buchs, Gewöhnlicher Buchsbaum / Buis

CCCLXVII (367) *Petasites hybridus* (L.) P. GAERTN., B. MEY. et SCHERB. – Butterbur (staminate plant) / Gewöhnliche Pestwurz, Rote Pestwurz (männliche Pflanze) / Pétasite hybride, Pétasite officinal, Chapeau-du-diable (plante mâle)

CCCLXVIII (368) *Lonicera periclymenum* L. Woodbine, Honeysuckle / Wald-Geißblatt / Chèvrefeuille des bois, Chèvrefeuille

CCCLXIX (369) *Triticum aestivum* L. ssp. *vulgare* (VILL.) MACKEY [*T. vulgare* VILL.] Common Wheat, Wheat / Saat-Weizen, Weizen / Froment, Blé

CCCLXX (370) *Triticum turgidum* L. Cone Wheat, Rivet Wheat / Rauh-Weizen, Englischer Weizen / Gros blé, Blé barbu

CCCLXXI (371) *Potamogeton natans* L. Broad-leaved Pondweed / Schwimmendes Laichkraut / Potamot nageant

CCCLXXII (372) *Chenopodium rubrum* L. Red Goosefoot, Goose Herb / Roter Gänsefuß / Chénopode rouge

CCCLXXIII (373) *Sison amomum* L. – Stone Parsley, Macedonian Parsley / Gewürzdolde, Würzsilge / Sison aromatique, Sison

CCCLXXIIII (374) *Rosa*-combination: 1. (left half): *Rosa canina* L., Dog Rose / Hunds-Rose / Rosier des chiens, Églantier commun ; 2. (right half): *Rosa gallica* L., French Rose / Essig-Rose / Rosier de France

CCCLXXV (375) *Raphanus sativus* L. – Garden Radish / Rettich, Garten-Rettich / Radis cultivé

CCCLXXVI (376) *Armoracia rusticana* P. GAERTN., B. MEY. et SCHERB. [*A. lapathifolia* GILIB., *Cochlearia armoracia* L.] Horseradish / Meerrettich, Gewöhnlicher Meerrettich / Raifort

CCCLXXVII (377) *Ribes rubrum* L. – Redcurrant / Rote Johannisbeere / Groseillier rouge

CCCLXXVIII (378) *Rhodiola rosea* L. [*Sedum roseum* (L.) SCOP.] – Rose-root, Midsummer-men, King's-crown / Rosenwurz / Orpin rose, Rhodiole rose

CCCLXXIX (379) *Origanum majorana* L. [*Majorana hortensis* MOENCH] – Sweet Majoram / Majoran / Marjolaine des jardins

CCCLXXX(380) *Sanicula europaea* L. Sanicle, Poolroot / Wald-Sanikel, Sanikel / Sanicle d'Europe

CCCLXXXI (381) *Astrantia major* L. – Mountain Sanicle, Great Masterwort / Große Sterndolde / Grande astrance

CCCLXXXII (382) *Spinacia oleracea* L. – Spinach / Spinat / Épinard

CCCLXXXIII (383) *Sonchus asper* (L.) HILL – Spiny Milk-Thistle, Prickly Sow-Thistle / Dornige, Gänsedistel, Raue Gänsedistel / Laiteron rude

CCCLXXXIIII (384) *Sonchus oleraceus* L. – Milk-Thistle, Sow-Thistle, Common Sow- Thistle / Kohl-Gänsedistel, Gemeine Gänsedistel / Laiteron maraîcher

CCCLXXXV (385) *Cichorium endivia* L. var. *latifolium* LAM. – Broad-leaved Endive / Breitblättrige Endivie, Winter-Endivie, Eskariol-Endivie, Eskariol / Chicorée scariole, Scariole, Endive à feuilles larges

CCCLXXXVI (386) *Cichorium endivia* L. (386) var. *endivia* [*C. endivia* L. var. *angustifolium* LAM.] – Narrow-leaved Endive / Schmalblättrige Endivie, Schnittendivie / Chicorée blanche, Petite endive

CCCLXXXVII (387) *Cichorium intybus* L. – Wild Chicory, Wild Succory / Gemeine Wegwarte, Wilde Zichorie / Chicorée sauvage, Witloof

CCCLXXXVIII (388) *Taraxacum officinale* F. H.WIGG. agg. – Common Dandelion / Löwenzahn, Kuhblume / Pissenlit

CCCLXXXIX (389) *Daucus carota* L. ssp. *sativus* (HOFFM.) ARCANG. [*D. sativus* HOFFM.] – Garden Carrot (red form) / Garten-Möhre, Mohrrübe (rote Form) / Carotte cultivée (forme rouge)

CCCXC (390) *Daucus carota* L. ssp. *sativus* (HOFFM.) ARCANG. [*D. sativus* HOFFM.] – Garden Carrot (yellow form) / Garten-Möhre, Mohrrübe, Gelbe Rübe (gelbe Form) / Carotte cultivée (forme jaune)

CCCXCI (391) *Daucus carota* L. – Wild Carrot / Wilde Möhre, Wilde Mohrrübe / Carotte sauvage

CCCXCII (392) *Solanum nigrum* L. – Black Nightshade / Schwarzer Nachtschatten / Morelle noire

CCCXCIII (393) *Physalis alkekengi* L. – Chinese Lantern, Japanese Lantern, Winter Cherry / Gewöhnliche Judenkirsche, Lampionblume, Blasenkirsche / Coqueret, Alkékenge

CCCXCIIII (394) *Cardiospermum halicacabum* L. – Balloonvine, Heart-pea / Herzsame / Pois de cœur, Cœur-des-Indes

CCCXCV (395) *Atropa belladonna* L. – Deadly Nightshade / Gewöhnliche Tollkirsche / Belladonne

CCCXCVI (396) *Datura metel* L. – Downy Thorn-apple, Hindu Datura / Weichhaariger Stechapfel, Metel-Stechapfel / Métel, Stramoine métel, Stramoine pubescente

CCCXCVII (397) *Symphytum officinale* L. – Comfrey, Boneset / Gewöhnlicher Beinwell, Arznei-Beinwell, Echte Wallwurz / Consoude officinale

CCCXCVIII (398) *Cucumis sativus* L. – Cucumber / Gurke / Concombre, Cornichon

CCCXCIX (399) *Cucurbita pepo* L. (var. *oblonga* DC.) – Pumpkin (Long Pumpkin) / Garten-Kürbis / Citrouille, Courgette

CCCC (400) *Cucurbita pepo* L. (var. *rotunda* DC.) – Pumpkin (Round Pumpkin) / Garten-Kürbis / Citrouille, Courgette

CCCCI (401) *Citrullus lanatus* (THUNB.) MATSUM. et NAKAI [*C. vulgaris* SCHRAD.] – Watermelon / Wasser-Melone, Angurie / Melon d'eau, Pastèque

CCCCII (402) *Cucumis melo* L. (con var. *cantalupa* (PANG.) GREB.) [*C. melo* L. ssp. *melo* var. *cantalupensis* NAUD.] – Cantaloupe / Zucker-Melone, Kantalupe / Melon, Melon cantaloup

CCCCIII (403) *Ecballium elaterium* (L.) RICH. – Squirting Cucumber / Spritzgurke / Concombre d'âne, Concombre sauvage, Momordique des champs

CCCCIIII (404) *Phaseolus vulgaris* L. – Garden Bean, French Bean, Kidney Bean / Garten-Bohne, Gemüse-Bohne, Bohne / Haricot commun, Haricot vert

CCCCV (405) *Platanthera bifolia* (L.) RICH. – Lesser Butterfly Orchid / Weiße

Waldhyazinthe, Zweiblättrige Waldhyazinthe / Plathanthère à fleurs blanches

CCCCVI (406) *Gymnadenia conopsea* (L.) R. BR. – Fragrant Orchid / Mücken-Händelwurz, Große Händelwurz / Orchis moucheron

CCCCVII (407) *Dactylorhiza maculata* (L.) SOO [*D. fuchsii* (DRUCE) SOO, *Orchis fuchsii* DRUCE, *O. maculata* L.] – Common Spotted Orchid / Geflecktes Knabenkraut, Fuchs-Knabenkraut / Orchis tacheté

CCCCVIII (408) *Succisa pratensis* MOENCH Devil's-bit Scabious / Gewöhnlicher Teufelsabbiss, Abbisskraut / Succise des prés

CCCCIX (409) *Knautia arvensis* (L.) COULT. Field Scabious / Acker-Witwenblume, Acker-Skabiose / Knautie des champs

CCCCX (410) *Smilax aspera* L. – Rough Bindweed / Raue Stechwinde / Liseron épineux, Salsepareille d'Europe

CCCCXI (411) *Calystegia sepium* (L.) R. BR. [*Convolvulus sepium* L.] – Hedge Bindweed, Larger Bindweed / Echte Zaunwinde / Liseron des haies

CCCCXII (412) *Mentha aquatica* L. – Water Mint / Wasser-Minze / Menthe aquatique

CCCCXIII (413) *Nasturtium officinale* R. BR. [*Rorippa nasturtium-aquaticum* (L.) HAYEK] Watercress / Echte Brunnenkresse / Cresson de fontaine

CCCCXIIII (414) *Veronica beccabunga* L. Brooklime / Bachbunge, Wasser-Ehrenpreis, Bachbungen-Ehrenpreis / Cresson de cheval

CCCCXV (415) *Achillea millefolium* L. agg. Common Yarrow, Milfoil / Gewöhnliche Schafgarbe / Achillée millefeuille

CCCCXVI (416) *Senecio ovatus* (P. GAERTN., B. MEY. et SCHERB.) WILLD. [*S. nemorensis* L. ssp. *fuchsii* (C. C. GMEL.) CELAK., S. *fuchsii* C. C. GMEL.] – Fuchs's Ragwort, Fuchs's Groundsel / Fuchs-Greiskraut, Fuchssches Kreuzkraut / Séneçon ovale, Séneçon de Fuchs

CCCCXVII (417) *Asplenium ruta-muraria* L. – Wall Rue / Mauerraute, Mauer-Streifenfarn / Rue des murailles

CCCCXVIII (418) *Capsicum annuum* L. Green Pepper, Red Pepper, Sweet Pepper, Capsicum Pepper, Chili Pepper etc. / Paprika, Gemüse-Paprika, Spanischer Pfeffer, Cayennepfeffer etc. / Piment annuel, Piment commun, Poivre d'Espagne, Poivre d'Inde, Poivre de Cayenne, Poivron doux etc.

CCCCXIX (419) *Capsicum annuum* L. [*C. longum* DC.]

CCCCXX (420) *Capsicum annuum* L. [*C. cordiforme* MILL.] CCCCXVIII (418)

CCCCXXI (421) *Allium sativum* L. Garlic / Knoblauch / Ail cultivé, Ail

CCCCXXII (422) *Allium vineale* L. – Crow Garlic, Field Garlic, False Garlic / Weinberg-Lauch / Ail des vignes

CCCCXXIII (423) *Allium oleraceum* L. Wild Garlic / Gemüse-Lauch, Kohl-Lauch / Ail des champs (see S&N, p. 622; MZ, p. 59) [MR, p. 535: *Allium vineale* L.]

CCCCXXIIII (424) *Allium ursinum* L. Ramsons, Bear's Garlic / Bärlauch, Bären-Lauch / Ail des ours

CCCCXXV (425) *Senecio jacobaea* L. St. Jacob's Herb, Common Ragwort / Jakobs-Greiskraut, Jakobs-Kreuzkraut / Séneçon jacobée, Herbe de Saint-Jacques

CCCCXXVI (426) *Apium graveolens* L. – Celery / Echter Sellerie / Céleri, Ache odorante

CCCCXXVII (427) *Barbarea vulgaris* R. BR. Common Winter Cress, Yellow Rocket / Echtes Barbarakraut, Barbenkraut, Echte Winterkresse / Barbarée vulgaire, Barbarée commune, Herbe de Sainte-Barbe

CCCCXXVIII (428) *Saxifraga granulata* L. Meadow Saxifrage / Knöllchen-Steinbrech, Körner-Steinbrech / Saxifrage granulée

CCCCXXIX (429) *Trigonella caerulea* (L.) SER. [*Melilotus caerulea* (L.) DESR.] Blue Fenugreek, Sweet Trefoil / Schabzigerklee / Trigonelle bleue

CCCCXXX (430) *Melilotus officinalis* (L.) LAM.? – Common Melilot? / Echter Steinklee, Gebräuchlicher Steinklee? / Mélilot officinal ? (see MZ, p. 60) [S&N, p. 623: *M. dentatus* (WALDST. et KIT.) PERS.; MR, p. 539: *Melilotus* sp.]

CCCCXXXI (431) *Pastinaca sativa* L. ssp. *sativa* [*P. sativa* L. var. *edulis* DC.] – Garden Parsnip / Garten-Pastinak / Panais cultivé

CCCCXXXII (432) *Sium sisarum* L. – Water Parsnip, Skirret / Zucker-Merk, Zuckerwurz / Chervis, Chirovis

CCCCXXXIII (433) *Pastinaca sativa* L. ssp. *sylvestris* (MILL.) ROUY et CAMUS Wild Parsnip (wild form) / Gewöhnlicher Pastinak (wildwachsende Form) / Panais sauvage (forme sauvage)

CCCCXXXIIII (434) *Ficus carica* L. – Common Fig / Feige, Feigenbaum / Figuier

CCCCXXXV (435) *Spartium junceum* L.?? (very unclear "combination"!) – Spanish Broom?? / Pfriemen-ginster, Spanischer Ginster?? / Genêt d'Espagne ?? (see S&N, p. 623; MZ, p. 60; MÄGDEFRAU 1992, p. 30) [MR, p. 542: indeterminable]

CCCCXXXVI (436) *Levisticum officinale* KOCH – Lovage / Gewöhnlicher Liebstöckel, Maggikraut / Livèche officinale, Herbe à Maggi, Céleri perpétuel

CCCCXXXVII (437) *Peucedanum ostruthium* (L.) KOCH – Masterwort / Meisterwurz / Peucedán ostruthium, Impératoire

CCCCXXXVIII (438) *Stachys germanica* L. Downy Woundwort, German Stachys / Deutscher Ziest, Filziger Ziest, Deutscher Wollziest / Épiaire de l'Allemagne, Sauge molle

CCCCXXXIX (439) *Secale cereale* L. Rye / Roggen / Seigle

CCCCXL (440) *Stachys recta* L. – Upright Hedge-nettle, Perennial Yellow Woundwort / Aufrechter Ziest / Epiaire droite, Épiaire dressée

CCCCXLI (441) *Sorghum bicolor* (L.) MOENCH [*S. vulgare* PERS.] – Sorghum, Kaffir Corn, Guinea Corn / Gewöhnliche Sorghumhirse, Sorghum-Hirse, Durra / Sorgho commun

CCCCXLII (442) *Polygonum bistorta* L. [*Bistorta officinalis* DEL.] – Bistort, Snakeroot, Easter-ledges / Wiesen-Knöterich, Schlangen-Knöterich, Schlangen-Wiesenknöterich / Renouée bistorte, Bistorte, Serpentaire

CCCCXLIII (443) See CCCCXLII (442)

CCCCXLIIII (444) *Teucrium scordium* L. Water Germander / Lauch-Gamander, Knoblauch-Gamander / Germandrée d'eau

CCCCXLV (445) *Saponaria officinalis* L. Plate incorrectly numbered CCCCXLVI (446) Soapwort, Bouncing Bett / Echtes Seifenkraut / Saponaire officinale

CCCCXLVI (446) *Lavandula stoechas* L. French Lavender / Schopf-Lavendel / Lavande à toupet, Lavande papillon, Stoechas arabique

CCCCXLVII (447) *Urginea maritima* (L.) BAK. [*Scilla maritima* L., *Drimia maritima* (L.) STEARN] – Sea Onion, Sea Squill, Red Squill / Meerzwiebel / Scille maritime

CCCCXLVIII (448) *Delphinium staphisagria* L. – Stavesacre, Licebane / Läuse-Rittersporn / Dauphinelle staphy-saigre, Staphisaigre

CCCCXLIX (449) *Laserpitium latifolium* L. Bastard Lovage / Breitblättriges Laserkraut / Laser à larges feuilles, Laser blanc

CCCCL (450) *Peucedanum cervaria* (L.) LAPEYR. Hog Fennel, Milk Parsley / Hirschwurz, Hirsch-Haarstrang / Peucédan cervaire, Herbe-aux-cerfs

CCCCLI (451) *Meum athamanticum* JACQ. Spignel, Meu, Baldmoney / Gewöhnliche Bärwurz / Fenouil des Alpes

CCCCLII (452) *Ammi visnaga* (L.) LAM. Bisnaga, Lesser Bishop's-weed, Toothpick Ammi, Pick Tooth / Echter Ammei, Zahnstocher-Ammei, Zahnstocherkraut / Herbe aux cure-dents, Petit ammi

CCCCLIII (453) *Sanguisorba officinalis* (453) L. – Great Burnet, Burnet Bloodwort / Großer Wiesenknopf / Grande pimprenelle, Pimprenelle officinale, Sanguisorbe

CCCCLIIII (454) *Sanguisorba minor* SCOP. [*Poterium sanguisorba* L.] – Small Burnett, Garden Burnett, Salad Burnett / Kleiner Wiesenknopf / Petite pimprenelle

CCCCLV (455) *Cynara scolymus* L. [*C. cardunculus* L. ssp. *scolymus* (L.) BEGER, *C. cardunculus* L. ssp. *cardunculus*] – Globe

Artichoke, Cardoon / Echte Artischocke, Gemüse-Artischocke / Artichaut commun, Cardon d'Espagne

CCCCLVI (456) *Iris foetidissima* L. – Stinking Iris, Gladdon Iris / Übelriechende Schwertlilie, Stink-Schwertlilie / Iris fétide

CCCCLVII (457) *Asplenium trichomanes* L. – Maidenhair Spleenwort / Braunstieliger Streifenfarn, Brauner Streifenfarn / Capillaire rouge [S&N, p. 626; MR, p. 555: *A. viride* HUDS., Green Spleenwort / Grünstieliger Streifenfarn, Grüner Streifenfarn / Asplénium à pétiole vert]

CCCCLVIII (458) *Trigonella foenum-graecum* L. – Fenugreek, Greek-clover / Griechischer Bockshornklee / Fenugrec

CCCCLIX (459) *Sedum telephium* L. agg. Orpine, Livelong / Purpur-Fetthenne, Purpurroter Mauerpfeffer, Großes Fettkraut / Grand orpin

CCCCLX (460) See CCCCLIX (459)

CCCCLXI (461) *Viola tricolor* L. – Wild Pansy, Field Pansy / Wildes Stiefmütterchen / Pensée tricolore /

CCCCLXII (462) *Beta vulgaris* L. var. *cicla* (L.) ALEF. – Spinach Beet (with light green leaves) / Mangold (mit hellgrünen Blättern) / Poirée à couper, Poirée ordinaire (à feuilles vertes claires)

CCCCLXIII (463) *Beta vulgaris* L. var. *cicla* (L.) ALEF. – Spinach Beet (with purplish leaves) / Mangold (mit rötlichen Blättern) / Poirée à couper, Poirée ordinaire (à feuilles rougeâtres)

CCCCLXIIII (464) *Genista tinctoria* L. – Dyer's Broom, Dyer's Greenweed / Färber-Ginster / Genêt des teinturiers

CCCCLXV (465) *Euphorbia helioscopia* L. Sun Spurge / Sonnenwend-Wolfsmilch / Euphorbe réveille-matin

CCCCLXVI (466) *Euphorbia cyparissias* L. – Cypress Spurge / Zypressen-Wolfsmilch / Euphorbe faux cyprès

CCCCLXVII (467) *Euphorbia platyphyllos* L. – Broad Spurge / Breitblättrige Wolfsmilch / Euphorbe à larges feuilles

CCCCLXVIII (468) *Trifolium pratense* L. Red Clover, Meadow Trifoil / Wiesen-Klee, Rot-Klee / Trèfle des prés

CCCCLXIX (469) *Trifolium montanum* L. Mountain Clover / Berg-Klee / Trèfle des montagnes

CCCCLXX (470) *Medicago lupulina* L. Black Medick / Hopfen-Klee, Hopfen-Schneckenklee / Luzerne lupuline, Minette

CCCCLXXI (471) *Tragopogon pratensis* L. Goat's Beard, Jack-go-to-bed-at-noon / Wiesen-Bocksbart / Salsifis des prés

CCCCLXXII (472) *Typha latifolia* L. Common Cat's-tail, Great Reedmace / Breitblättriger Rohrkolben, Breiter Rohrkolben / Masette à larges feuilles

CCCCLXXIII (473) *Zea mays* L. – Maize, Indian Corn / Mais / Maïs

CCCCLXXIIII (474) *Thymus vulgaris* L. – Common Thyme / Echter Thymian, Garten-Thymian / Thym vulgaire

CCCCLXXV (475) *Teucrium flavum* L. Yellow Germander / Gelber Gamander / Germandrée jaune

CCCCLXXVI (476) *Hypericum perforatum* L. – Common St. John's Wort / Echtes Johanniskraut, Tüpfel-Hartheu / Millepertuis perforé, Herbe à mille trous

CCCCLXXVII (477) *Hyoscyamus niger* L. Henbane / Schwarzes Bilsenkraut / Jusquiame noire

CCCCLXXVIII (478) *Muscari comosum* (L.) MILL. [*Leopoldia comosa* (L.) PARL.] – Tassel Hyacinth, Feather Hyacinth / Schopfige Traubenhyazinthe, Schopfige Bisamhyazinthe / Muscari à houppe

CCCCLXXIX (479) *Muscari botryoides* (L.) MILL. – Grape Hyacinth / Kleine Traubenhyazinthe, Hellblaue Bisamhyazinthe / Muscari botryoïde

CCCCLXXX (480) *Scilla bifolia* L. – Alpine Squill / Zweiblättriger Blaustern / Scille à deux feuilles

CCCCLXXXI (481) See CCCCLXXX (480)

CCCCLXXXII (482) See CCCCLXXX (480)

CCCCLXXXIII (483) *Hyssopus officinalis* L. Hyssop / Ysop / Hysope officinale

CCCCLXXXIIII (484) *Polygonum hydropiper* L. [*Persicaria hydropiper* (L.) DEL.] – Water Pepper / Wasserpfeffer-Knöterich, Pfeffer-Knöterich / Renouée poivre d'eau

CCCCLXXXV (485) *Verbascum thapsus* L. Common Mullein, Great Mullein, Aaron's Rod / Kleinblütige Königskerze, Echte Königskerze / Molène thapsus, Bouillon-blanc

CCCCLXXXVI (486) *Verbascum lychnitis* L. White Mullein / Mehlige-Königskerze, Helle Königskerze, Lampen-Königskerze / Molène lychnite

CCCCLXXXVII (487) *Verbascum phlomoides* L. – Woolly Mullein / Windblumen-Königskerze, Filzige Königskerze / Molène faux phlomis

CCCCLXXXVIII (488) *Verbascum nigrum* L. – Dark Mullein / Schwarze Königskerze, Dunkle Königskerze / Molène noire

CCCCLXXXIX (489) *Primula veris* L. [*P. officinalis* (L.) HILL] – Cowslip / Echte Schüsselblume, Arznei-Schlüsselblume, Wiesen-Schlüsselblume / Primevère officinale, Primevère du printemps

CCCCXC (490) *Primula elatior* (L.) HILL Oxlip / Hohe Schlüsselblume / Primevère élevée

CCCCXCI (491) *Fragaria*-combination: 1. (centre with larger flowers and fruits): *Fragaria moschata* DUCH. [*F. elatior* EHRH.], – Hautbois Strawberry / Zimt-Erdbeere/ Fraisier musqué ; 2. (on the left with smaller flowers and fruits): *F. vesca* L., Wild Strawberry / Wald-Erdbeere / Fraisier des bois (see S&N, p. 630) [MZ, p. 65: complete figure *F. vesca* L.; MR, p. 576: composite drawing of both the cultivated and wild forms of *F. vesca* L.]

CCCCXCII (492) *Valeriana phu* L. – Greek Valerian, Garden Valerian / Garten-Baldrian, Theriakkraut, Zehrkraut / Grande valériane

CCCCXCIII (493) *Valeriana officinalis* L. Valerian, Common Valerian, Garden Heliotrope / Echter Baldrian, Arznei-Baldrian / Valériane officinale, Valériane commune, Herbe-aux-chats

CCCCXCIIII (494) *Lens culinaris* MED. Lentil / Linse / Lentille comestible, Lentillon

CCCCXCV (495) *Tilia* sp. – Lime Tree / Linde / Tilleul (no clear identification possible, see MR, p. 579) [S&N, p. 631; MZ, p. 66: *Tilia cordata* MILL., Small-leaved Lime / Winter-Linde / Tilleul à petites feuilles or *T. platyphyllos* SCOP., Large-leaved Lime / Sommer-Linde / Tilleul à larges feuilles]

CCCCXCVI (496) *Chelidonium majus* L. Greater Celandine / Großes Schöllkraut / Chélidoine, Éclaire, Herbe aux verrues

CCCCXCVII (497) *Ranunculus ficaria* L. [*Ficaria verna* HUDS.] – Lesser Celandine, Pilewort / Scharbockskraut, Feigwurz / Renoncule ficaire

CCCCXCVIII (498) *Teucrium chamaedrys* L. – Common Germander, Wall Germander / Echter Gamander, Edel-Gamander / Germandrée petit-chêne

CCCCXCIX (499) *Teucrium botrys* L. Cut-leaved Germander / Trauben-Gamander / Germandrée botryde

CCCCC (500) *Veronica teucrium* L. [*V. austriaca* L. ssp. *teucrium* (L.) WEBB] – Large Speedwell, Heavenly Blue Speedwell / Großer Ehrenpreis, Breiter Ehrenpreis / Véronique germandrée

CCCCCI (501) *Veronica chamaedrys* L. Germander Speedwell, Bird's Eye / Gamander-Ehrenpreis / Véronique petit-chêne

CCCCCII (502) *Santolina chamaecyparissus* L. – Santolina, Lavender Cotton, Ground Cypress / Graue Heiligenblume, Heiligenkraut, Zypressenkraut / Santoline petit-cyprès, Petit-cyprès

CCCCCIII (503) *Glechoma hederacea* L. Ground Ivy, Alehoof / Efeublättriger Gundermann, Efeublättrige Gundelrebe / Lierre terrestre

CCCCCIIII (504) *Ranunculus repens* L. Creeping Buttercup / Kriechender Hahnenfuß / Renoncule rampante

CCCCCV (505) *Carlina acaulis* L. – Stemless Carline Thistle / Silberdistel, Stängellose

2.

Alphabetical Index of the Latin Plant Names with the Corresponding Plate Number

Acanthus mollis L. – XXIX (29)
Achillea millefolium L. agg. – CCCCXV (415)
Achillea ptarmica L. – CCCLXIIII (364)
Acinos arvensis (LAM.) DANDY CCCCCXV (515)
Aconitum lycoctonum L. ssp. *vulparia* (RCHB.) NYMAN see *Aconitum vulparia*
Aconitum vulparia RCHB. – XLVIII (48)
Adiantum capillus-veneris L. – XLV (45)
Agrimonia eupatoria L. – CXXXV (135)
Agrostemma githago L. – LXX (70)
Ajuga chamaepitys (L.) SCHREB. CCCCCVIII (508)
Ajuga reptans L. – CCXIX (219)
Ajuga sp.? – CCCCCVII (507)
Alcea rosea L. – CCLXXXVII (287)
Alchemilla vulgaris auct. see *Alchemilla xanthochlora*
Alchemilla xanthochlora ROTHM. CCCXLVIII (348)
Alisma plantago-aquatica L. – XXIII (23)
Alliaria officinalis ANDR. ex M. BIEB. see *Alliaria petiolata*
Alliaria petiolata (M. BIEB.) CAV. et GRANDE LVI (56)
Allium cepa L. – CCXLI (241)
Allium oleraceum L. – CCCCXXIII (423)
Allium porrum L. – CCCLXI (361)
Allium sativum L. – CCCCXXI (421)
Allium schoenoprasum L. – CCCLXII (362)
Allium ursinum L. – CCCCXXIIII (424)
Allium vineale L. – CCCCXXII (422)
Aloe vera (L.) BURM. f. – LXXV (75)
Althaea officinalis L. – VII (7)
Althaea rosea (L.) CAV. see *Alcea rosea*
Ammi majus L. – XXXVIII (38)
Ammi visnaga (L.) LAM. – CCCCLII (452)
Anacamptis pyramidalis (L.) RICH. CCCXIIII (314)
Anacyclus pyrethrum (L.) LINK – CCCLXV (365)
Anagallis arvensis L. – VIII (8)
Anagallis foemina MILL. – IX (9)
Anchusa arvensis (L.) M. BIEB. – CXLIX (149)
Anchusa azurea MILL. – CXCIIII (194)
Anchusa italica RETZ. see *Anchusa azurea*
Anchusa officinalis L. – CXCIII (193)
Anemone nemorosa L. – XC (90)
Anemone pulsatilla L. see *Pulsatilla vulgaris*
Anemone ranunculoides L. – XCI (91)
Anethum graveolens L. – XVI (16)
Angelica archangelica L. – LXVIII (68)
Angelica sylvestris L. – LXIX (69)
Antennaria dioica (L.) GAERTN. CCCXLIIII (344)
Anthemis cotula L. – CCCXXXI (331)
Anthemis tinctoria L. – XIIII (14)
Anthriscus cerefolium (L.) HOFFM. – CXXII (122)
Anthriscus sylvestris (L.) HOFFM. – CCXCVI (296)
Apium graveolens L. – CCCCXXVI (426)
Aquilegia vulgaris L. – LV (55)
Archangelica officinalis HOFFM. see *Angelica archangelica*
Arctium lappa L. – XL (40)
Arenaria serpyllifolia L. – XII (12)
Aristolochia clematitis L. – XLIX (49)
Armoracia lapathifolia GILIB. see *Armoracia rusticana*
Armoracia rusticana P. GAERTN., B. MEY. et SCHERB. – CCCLXXVI (376)
Artemisia abrotanum L. – III (3)
Artemisia absinthium L. – I (1)
Artemisia pontica L. – IIII (4)
Artemisia vulgaris L. – XXIIII (24)
Arum maculatum L. – XXXIX (39)
Aruncus dioicus (WALT.) FERN. – CI (101)
Aruncus sylvestris KOSTEL. see *Aruncus dioicu*

Bibliography

Baumann, B., H. Baumann & S. Baumann-Schleihauf, *Die Kräuterbuch-Handschrift des Leonhart Fuchs*. Stuttgart 2001

Berger, F., *Handbuch der Drogenkunde*. Vol. 1–7, Vienna 1949–1967

Bertsch, K. & F., *Geschichte unserer Kulturpflanzen*. Stuttgart 1947

Besler, B., *The Garden at Eichstätt. The Book of Plants by Basilius Besler*. With an introduction by Klaus Walter Littger and botanical annotations by Werner Dressendörfer. Cologne 2000

Clapham, A. R., T. G. Tutin & E. F. Warburg, *Flora of the British Isles*. Cambridge 1962

Clapham, A. R., T. G. Tutin & E. F. Warburg, *Excursion Flora of the British Isles*. Cambridge 1968

Decker-Hauff, H. & W. Setzler (eds.), *Die Universität Tübingen von 1477 bis 1977 in Bildern und Dokumenten*, Tübingen 1977

Dobat, K., Tübinger Kräuterbuchtafeln des Leonhart Fuchs (1501–1566), in: *Botanisch-Historische Raritäten der Eberhard-Karls-Universität Tübingen*, supplementary leaflet, 1–23, Tübingen 1983

Dobat, K., Kalender 2001 der Eberhard Karls Universität Tübingen zum 500. Geburtsjubiläum von Leonhart Fuchs (1501–1566). Tübingen 2000 (a)

Dobat, K., Ein Leben für die Wissenschaft: Leonhart Fuchs (1501–1566), in: *Tübinger Blätter*, vol. 87 (2000/2001), 4–15. Tübingen 2000 (b)

Dobat, K. & K. Mägdefrau, Vom Heilpflanzenbeet zum Neuen Botanischen Garten. Zur Geschichte der Tübinger Botanischen Gärten, in: *Attempto*, leaflet 55/56, 8–31. Tübingen 1975

Dörfler, M., *Deutsches Krankheitsnamen-Buch*. Hildesheim 1970

Erhardt, W., E. Götz, N. Bödeker & S. Seybold (ed.), *Zander. Handwörterbuch der Pflanzennamen*. 16th ed. Stuttgart 2000

Fahrig, D., *Zum Kräuterbuch von Adam Lonitzer aus den Jahren 1569, 1587, 1630 und 1679. Aspekte der Interpretation*. Doctoral dissertation. Frankfurt am Main 1992

Fichtner, G., Die Paradoxa des Leonhart Fuchs, in: *Welt am Oberrhein* 7, leaflet 4, 1–6. Karlsruhe 1967

Fichtner, G., Neues zu Leben und Werk von Leonhart Fuchs aus seinen Briefen an Joachim Camerarius I. und II. in der Trew-Sammlung, in: *Gesnerus* 25, leaflet 1/2, 65–82. Aarau 1968

Fintelmann, V., *Phytotherapie-Manual. Pharmazeutischer, pharmakologischer und therapeutischer Standard*. Stuttgart 1993

Franke, W. *Nutzpflanzenkunde. Nutzbare Gewächse der gemäßigten Breiten, Subtropen und Tropen*. Stuttgart & New York 1989

Froriep, A., Vorwort zur Geschichte der anatomischen Anstalt zu Tübingen, in: Häcker, R., *Katalog der anthropologischen Sammlung in der anatomischen Anstalt der Universität Tübingen...*, V–XIV. Brunswick 1902

Froriep, L. F. von, *Ueber die anatomischen Anstalten zu Tübingen, von Errichtung der Universität bis auf gegenwärtige Zeit*. Weimar 1811

Ganzinger, K., Ein Kräuterbuchmanuskript des Leonhart Fuchs in der Wiener Nationalbibliothek, in: *Sudhoffs Archiv für Geschichte der Medizin und der Naturwissenschaften*, vol. 43, 213–224. Wiesbaden 1959

Ganzinger, K., Rauwolf und Fuchs. Ein Beitrag zur Geschichte der Botanik im

16. Jahrhundert, in: *Veröffentlichungen der Int. Gesellschaft für Geschichte der Pharmazie* e. V., N. F., vol. 22, 23–33. Stuttgart 1963

Genaust, H., *Etymologisches Wörterbuch der botanischen Pflanzennamen.* Basel et al. 1996

Gerth van Wijk, H. L., *A Dictionary of Plant-Names*, vol. 1. Vaals-Amsterdam 1971

Habrich, C., Zur Geschichte des medizinischen Gartens und des botanischen Unterrichts in Ingolstadt, in: *Jahrbuch des Deutschen Medizinhistorischen Museums* 1/1973–1975, 75–96. Ingolstadt 1975

Hänsel, R., *Pharmakognosie – Phytopharmazie.* Berlin 1999

Hager ROM 2001. *Hagers Handbuch der Drogen und Arzneistoffe.* CD-ROM. Heidelberg 2001

Hagers Handbuch der Pharmazeutischen Praxis. Drogen. vol. 4–6, vol. 2 et. 3. Berlin 1992 f.

Haller, J., *Die Anfänge der Universität Tübingen 1477–1537*, vol. 1. Stuttgart 1927

Hoppe, B., *Das Kräuterbuch des Hieronymus Bock. Wissenschaftshistorische Untersuchung. Mit einem Verzeichnis sämtlicher Pflanzen des Werkes, der literarischen Quellen der Heilanzeigen und der Anwendung der Pflanzen.* Stuttgart 1969

Hunnius Pharmazeutisches Wörterbuch. Edited by Artur Burger and Helmut Wachter. Berlin 1998

Kahr, P. H., Zum 450jährigen Jubiläum des "New Kreüterbuch" von Leonhart Fuchs, in: *Pharmazeutische Zeitung* 138 (1993), 2497–2502

Kahr, P. H., New Kreüterbuch (series of articles), in: *Pharmazeutische Zeitung* 138 (1993) 2742, 3264 f., 3842 f., 4254 f.; 139 (1994), 1276 f., 2608–2610, 4256 f., 3368–3370; 141 (1996), 2866 f.

Körber-Grohne, U., *Nutzpflanzen in Deutschland. Kulturgeschichte und Biologie.* Stuttgart 1987

Krafft, F., Fuchs (Fuchsius, Füchsel), Leonhart, in: Boehm, L. et al. (eds.), *Biographisches Lexikon der Ludwig-Maximilians-Universität München.* Part 1, Ingolstadt-Landshut 1472–1826, 135–142. Berlin 1998

Krausch, H.-D., *Alte Nutz- und Zierpflanzen in der Niederlausitz. Verhandlungen des Botanischen Vereins von Berlin und Brandenburg*, supplementary leaflet 2. Berlin 1992

Künkele, S., Beiträge zur Geschichte der europäischen Orchideen. – I. Leonhart Fuchs, der Vater der Väter der Botanik, in: *Mitteilungsblatt Arbeitskreis Heimische Orchideen Baden-Württemberg*, vol. 19 (2), 197–383. Stuttgart 1987

Lauber, K. & G. Wagner, *Flora Helvetica.* Bern, Stuttgart & Vienna 1998

Mägdefrau, K., *Geschichte der Botanik. Leben und Leistung großer Forscher.* Stuttgart & New York 1992

Mansfeld, R., *Verzeichnis landwirtschaftlicher und gärtnerischer Kulturpflanzen (ohne Zierpflanzen).* Vol. 1–4, Berlin, Heidelberg, New York & Tokyo 1986

Marzell, H., Leonhart Fuchs und sein New Kreüterbuch (1543), in: *Fuchs, Leonhart, New Kreüterbuch* [Facsimile of the Basel ed., 1543]. Leipzig 1938

Marzell, H., *Wörterbuch der deutschen Pflanzennamen.* 5 vols., Leipzig 1943–1958

Meyer, F. G., E. E. Trueblood & J. L. Heller, *The Great Herbal of Leonhart Fuchs. De historia stirpium commentarii insignes, 1542.* Vol. 1, Commentary; vol. 2, Facsimile. Stanford 1999

Moll, A., Leonhard Fuchs. Ein ärztliches Bild aus der Vergangenheit Würtembergs, in: *Medicinisches Corresp.-Blatt des Würtembergischen Ärztlichen Vereins*, vol. XXII, no. 44, 349–354; no. 45, 357–361. Stuttgart 1852

Pahlow, M., *Das große Buch der Heilpflanzen.* Munich 1993

Prantl, C., *Geschichte der Ludwig-Maximilians-Universität in Ingolstadt, Landshut, München.* Vol. 1, Munich 1872

Rath, U. von, Botanik und Pharmakologie in der Renaissance, in: *Veröffentlichungen der Stadtbibliothek Lübeck.* 3rd series, vol. 1, 1–188. Lübeck 1998

rororo Pflanzenlexikon. 5 vols., Reinbek 1969

Roth, F. W. E., Leonhard Fuchs, ein deutscher Botaniker, 1501–1566, in: *Botanisches Centralblatt*, vol. 8, supplementary leaflet 3, 161–191. Kassel 1898

Roth, L., M. Daunderer u. K. Kormann, *Giftpflanzen – Pflanzengifte*. Landsberg/Lech 1994

Roth, R. von (ed.), *Urkunden zur Geschichte der Universität Tübingen aus den Jahren 1476 bis 1550*. Tübingen 1877

Rytz, W., Das Herbarium Felix Platters. Ein Beitrag zur Geschichte der Botanik des XVI. Jahrhunderts, in: *Verhandlungen der Naturforschenden Gesellschaft in Basel*, vols. XLIV, 1st part, 1–222. Basel 1933

Schneider, W., *Lexikon zur Arzneimittelgeschichte*. 7 vols., Frankfurt am Main, 1968–1975

Schubert, Rudolf (ed.), *Exkursionsflora von Deutschland*. Vol. 3, *Atlas der Gefäßpflanzen*. Berlin 1991

Sebald, O., S. Seybold & G. Philippi (eds.), *Die Farn- und Blütenpflanzen Baden-Württembergs*. Vol. 3, 1992a; vol. 4, 1992b; vol. 1, 2nd ed. 1993a; vol. 2, 2nd ed. 1993b. Stuttgart

Sebald, O., S. Seybold, G. Philippi & A. Wörz (eds.), *Die Farn- und Blütenpflanzen Baden-Württembergs*. Vol. 5, 1996a; vol. 6, 1996b; vol. 7, 1998a; vol. 8, 1998b. Stuttgart

Seybold, S., Orchideenfundangaben aus dem sechzehnten Jahrhundert. Der Beginn der Floristik in Baden-Württemberg, in: *Mitteilungsblatt Arbeitskreis Heimische Orchideen Baden-Württembergs*, volume 15 (4), 479–502. Stuttgart 1983

Seybold, S., *Die Orchideen des Leonhart Fuchs*. Tübingen 1986

Seybold, S., Luca Ghini, Leonhard Rauwolff und Leonhart Fuchs. Über die Herkunft der Aquarelle im Wiener Kräuterbuchmanuskript von Fuchs, in: *Jahreshefte der Gesellschaft für Naturkunde in Württemberg* 145, 239–264. Stuttgart 1990

Seybold, S., Die ältesten Pflanzenangaben von Baden-Württemberg aus der Literatur, in: *Stuttgarter Beiträge zur Naturkunde*, Ser. A, no. 514, 1–8. Stuttgart 1994

Sprague, T. A. & E. Nelmes, The herbal of Leonhart Fuchs, in: *Journal of the Linnean Society of London (Botany)* 48, 545–642. London 1931

Sprengel, K., *Versuch einer pragmatischen Geschichte der Arzneykunde*, 3rd ed., 3rd part. Halle 1827

Stübler, E., Leonhart Fuchs, Leben und Werk, in: *Münchener Beiträge zur Geschichte und Literatur der Naturwissenschaften und Medizin*, leaflet 13/14, 158–299. Munich 1928

Teedrogen und Phytopharmaka. Ein Handbuch für die Praxis auf wissenschaftlicher Grundlage. Edited by Max Wichtl. Stuttgart 1997

Tschirch, A., *Handbuch der Pharmakognosie*. Leipzig 1909–1927

Urania Pflanzenreich. 5 vols., Leipzig, Jena & Berlin 1995

Vogellehner, D., Tübinger Floristik in fünf Jahrhunderten, in: *Der Spitzberg bei Tübingen. Die Natur- und Landschaftsschutzgebiete Baden-Württembergs*, vol. 3, 156–173. Ludwigsburg 1966

Voigt, J., *Briefwechsel der berühmtesten Gelehrten des Zeitalters der Reformation mit Herzog Albrecht von Preussen*. Königsberg 1841

Wagner, H., *Arzneidrogen und ihre Inhaltsstoffe*. Stuttgart 1999

Wiersema, J. H. & B. Léon, *World Economic Plants. A Standard Reference*. London, New York & Washington, D. C. 1999

Acknowledgements / Imprint

This volume is based on Leonhart Fuchs's personal hand-coloured copy, now owned by the Stadtbibliothek Ulm. We would like to thank Jürgen Lange, former library director, and Dr. Gerd Brinkhus of the Manuscript Department at the University of Tübingen Library for their helpful support. Our thanks also goes to Alexander Rosenstock, deputy director of the Stadtbibliothek Ulm and his colleague Dorothea Schoch for the new images.

We would like to thank the following museums, libraries and institutions for their kind support in the publication of this book:

Bayerische Staatsbibliothek, Munich: pp. 25, 32. bpk/Landesmuseum Württemberg/Hendrik Zwietasch: p. 6. / bpk/Kupferstichkabinett, SMB/ Volker-H. Schneider: p. 10. / Historisches Museum Frankfurt: pp. 8/9. / Courtesy of Hunt Institute for Botanical Documentation, Carnegie Mellon University, Pittsburgh, PA: p. 41. / Ketterer Kunst, Munich: pp. 38, 39. / Niedersächsische Staats- und Universitätsbibliothek Göttingen: p. 11 r. / Österreichische Nationalbibliothek, Vienna: pp. 12, 17, 20, 23, 43, 46–47, 50, 53, 57, 62, 66, 70, 74–75. / Universitätsbibliothek Tübingen, Handschriftenabteilung: pp. 11 l., 35.

EACH AND EVERY TASCHEN BOOK PLANTS A SEED!
Each year, we offset our annual carbon emissions with carbon credits at the Instituto Terra, a reforestation program in Minas Gerais, Brazil, founded by Lélia and Sebastião Salgado. To find out more about this ecological partnership, please check: *www.taschen.com/institutoterra.*
Inspiration: unlimited.
Carbon footprint: (almost) zero.

Want to see more? Visit *taschen.com* to view our current publications, browse our latest magazine, and subscribe to our newsletter.

Hohenzollernring 53, D–50672 Köln
www.taschen.com

Project management: Petra Lamers-Schütze, Cologne
Translation: Annie Berthold, Düsseldorf (French), Sally Schreiber, Cologne (English)
Design: Andy Disl, Los Angeles; Claudia Frey, Cologne

Printed in Bosnia-Herzegovina
ISBN 978-3-7544-0215-3

FRONT COVER: *Cyclamen purpurascens* MILL. – Common Cyclamen / Gewöhnliches Alpenveilchen / Cyclamen pourpre

BACK COVER: *Anthemis tinctoria* L. – Yellow Chamomile / Färber-Hundskamille / Anthémis des teinturiers

PAGE 1: *Citrullus colocynthis* (L.) SCHRAD. – Colocynth / Koloquinthe / Coloquinte commune

PAGE 2: Leonhart Fuchs at the age of 42 / im Alter von 42 Jahren / à l'age de 42 ans, from: *New Kreüterbuch*, Tübingen, 1543

PAGE 4: Title page from / Titelblatt von / Page de titre de: *New Kreüterbuch*, Tübingen, 1543

PAGE 752: *Cichorium intybus* L. – Wild Chicory / Gemeine Wegwarte / Chicorée sauvage

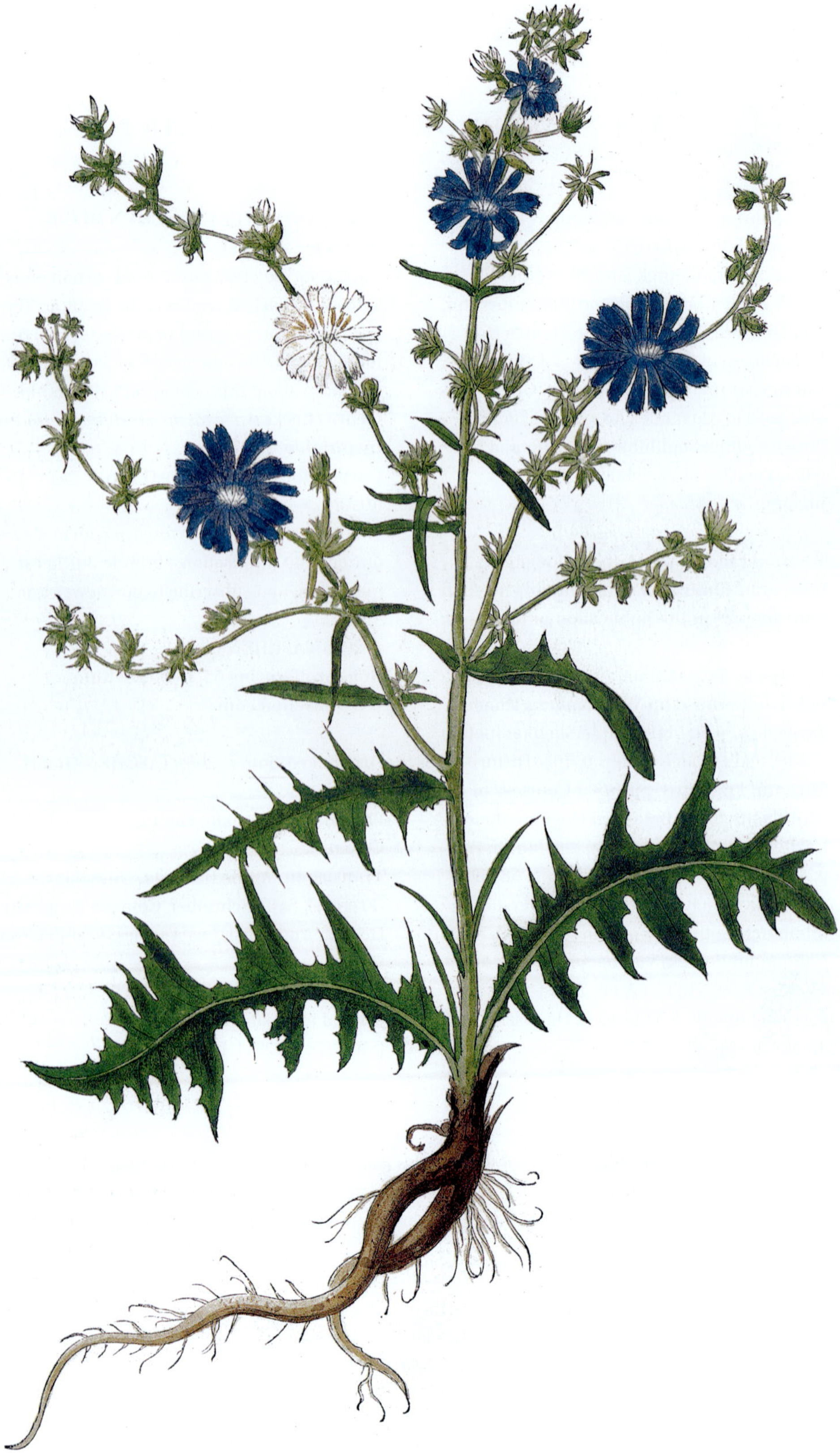